Encyclopedia of
Modern Asia

Editorial Board

Encyclopedia of Modern Asia

Volume 5
Possession to Turkey

A Berkshire Reference Work
David Levinson · Karen Christensen, Editors

CHARLES SCRIBNER'S SONS®

THOMSON
★
GALE™

New York • Detroit • San Diego • San Francisco • Cleveland • New Haven, Conn. • Waterville, Maine • London • Munich

THOMSON

GALE

™

Encyclopedia of Modern Asia

David Levinson and Karen Christensen, Editors

Copyright © 2002 Berkshire Publishing Group

Charles Scribner's Sons
An imprint of The Gale Group
300 Park Avenue South
New York, NY 10010

Gale and Design™ and Thomson Learning™ are trademark s used herein under license.

For more information, contact
The Gale Group, Inc.
27500 Drake Rd.
Farmington Hills, MI 48331–3535
Or you can visit our Internet site at
http://www.gale.com

LIBRARY OF CONGRESS CATALOGING-IN-PUBLICATION DATA

Levinson, David, 1947-
  Encyclopedia of modern Asia : / David Levinson, Karen Christensen,
    p. cm.
Includes bibliographical references and index.
  ISBN 0-684-80617-7 (set hardcover : alk. paper)
  1. Asia—Encyclopedias. I. Christensen, Karen, 1957- II. Title.
DS4 .L48 2002
950'.03—dc21

2002008712

Printed in United States of America
1 3 5 7 9 11 13 15 17 19 20 18 16 14 12 10 8 6 4 2

Contents

List of Maps

Survey of Asia's Regions and Nations

The *Encyclopedia of Modern Asia* covers thirty-three nations in depth and also the Caucasus and Siberia. We have divided Asia into five major subregions and assigned the thirty-three nations to each.

West and Southwest Asia

The West Asian nations covered in detail here are Turkey, Iran, and Iraq. Afghanistan and Pakistan form Southwest Asia, although in some classifications they are placed in Central and South Asia, respectively. Afghanistan, on the crossroads of civilizations for thousands of years, is especially difficult to classify and displays features typical of Central, West, and South Asia.

Despite diversity in language (Persian in Iran, Arabic in Iraq, Turkish in Turkey) form of government (theocracy in Iran, dictatorship in Iraq, and unstable democracy in Turkey) and international ties (Iran to the Islamic world, Iraq to the Arab Middle East, Turkey to the West), there are several sources of unity across West Asia. Perhaps the oldest is geographical location as the site of transportation routes between Europe and Central, East, and South Asia. Since ancient times, people, goods, wealth, and ideas have flowed across the region. In 2002 the flow of oil was most important, from the wells of Iran and Iraq through the pipelines of Turkey. Another source of unity is Sunni Islam, a major feature of life since the seventh century, although Iran is mainly the minority Shi'a tradition and there have long been Zoroastrian, Jewish, Christian, and Baha'i minorities in the region. Diversity is also evident in the fact that Turkey is a "secular" state while Iran is a theocracy, and in the conflict between fundamentalist and mainstream Islam in all the nations.

Another important common thread is the shared historical experience of being part of the Ottoman Empire and having to cope with British and Russian designs on their territory and, more recently, American influence. And, in the twentieth century, all three nations have sought to deal with the Kurdish minority and its demands for a Kurdish state to be established on land taken from all three nations.

Unity across Afghanistan and Pakistan is created by adherence to Sunni Islam (although there is a Shi'ite minority in Afghanistan) and the prominence of the Pashtun ethnic group in each nation. Both nations also experienced British colonialism, although the long-term British influence is more notable in Pakistan, which had been tied to India under British rule. West Asia is the only region in the world never colonized by Britain, although some experts argue that it did experience significant British cultural influence. In all nations resistance to external control—British, Russian, or United States—is another common historical experience.

Across the region (although less so in Afghanistan) is the stark contrast between the traditional culture and the modernity of liberation from imperial rule, still not complete across the region. This contrast is apparent in clothing styles, manners, architecture, recreation, marriage practices, and many elements of daily life.

In 2002 all the nations faced a water crisis of both too little water and water pollution. They all also faced issues of economic and social development, including reducing external debt, controlling inflation, reducing unemployment, improving education and health care, and continually reacting to the ongoing Arab-Israeli conflict, which exacerbates many of these problems. The governments also faced the difficult task of solving these problems while resisting Americanization and also while controlling internal political unrest. Political unrest is often tied to efforts at creating democratic governments and the persistence of elite collaboration with tyrannical governments.

Central Asia

Central Asia is known by many names, including Eurasia, Middle Asia, and Inner Asia. At its core, the region is composed of five states that became independent nations following the collapse of the Soviet Union in 1991: Kazakhstan, Kyrgyzstan, Tajikistan, Turkmenistan, and Uzbekistan. Scholars sometimes include Afghanistan, Mongolia and the Xinjiang province of China within the label Central Asia. For this project, Central Asia is restricted to the five former Soviet countries, while Afghanistan is classified in Southwest Asia, and Mongolia and Xinjiang as part of East Asia. These states have a shared landmass of 1.5 million square miles, about one-half the size of the United States.

The region's unity comes from a shared history and religion. Central Asia saw two cultural and economic traditions blossom and intermix along the famed Silk Road: nomadic and sedentary. Nomadic herdsmen, organized into kinship groupings of clans, lived beside sedentary farmers and oasis city dwellers. Four of the countries share Turkic roots, while the Tajiks are of Indo-European descent, linguistically related to the Iranians. While still recognizable today, this shared heritage has developed into distinct ethnic communities.

The peoples of Central Asia have seen centuries of invasion, notably the legendary Mongol leader Genghis Khan in the thirteenth century, the Russians in the nineteenth and the Soviets in the twentieth century. For better or worse, each invader left behind markers of their presence: the Arabs introduced Islam in the seventh century. Today Islam is the predominant religion in the region, and most Central Asians are Sunni Muslims. The Russians brought the mixed legacy of modernism, including an educated populace, alarming infant mortality rates, strong economic and political participation by women, high agricultural development, and environmental disasters such as the shrinking of the Aral Sea. It was under Russian colonialism that distinct ethno-national boundaries were created to divide the people of the region. These divisions largely shape the contemporary Central Asian landscape.

Today the five Central Asian nations face similar challenges: building robust economies, developing stable, democratic governments, and integrating themselves into the regional and international communities as independent states. They come to these challenges with varied resources: Kazakhstan and Turkmenistan have rich oil reserves; several countries have extensive mineral deposits; and the Fergana Valley is but one example of the region's rich agricultural regions.

Finally, the tragic events of September 11, 2001, cast world attention on Afghanistan's neighbors in Central Asia. The "war on terrorism" forged new alliances and offered a mix of political pressure and economic support for the nations' leaders to suppress their countries' internal fundamentalist Muslim movements.

Southeast Asia

Southeast Asia is conventionally defined as that subregion of Asia consisting of the eleven nation-states of Brunei, Cambodia, East Timor, Indonesia, Laos, Malaysia, Myanmar, Philippines, Singapore, Thailand, and Vietnam. Myanmar is sometimes alternatively classified as part of South Asia and Vietnam as in East Asia. The region may be subdivided into Mainland Southeast Asia (Cambodia, Laos, Myanmar, Thailand, and Vietnam) and Insular Southeast Asia (Brunei, East Timor, Indonesia, Philippines, and Singapore). Malaysia is the one nation in the region that is located both on the mainland and islands, though ethnically it is more linked to the island nations of Indonesia, Brunei, and the Philippines.

Perhaps the key defining features for the region and those that are most widespread are the tropical monsoon climate, rich natural resources, and a way of life in rural areas based on cooperative wet-rice agriculture that goes back several thousand years. In the past unity was also created in various places by major civilizations, including those of Funan, Angkor, Pagan, Sukhothai, Majapahit, Srivijaya, Champa, Ayutthaya, and Melaka. Monarchies continue to be significant in several nation—Brunei, Cambodia, Malaysia, and Thailand—today. Subregional unity has also been created since ancient times by the continued use of written languages, including Vietnamese, Thai, Lao, Khmer and the rich literary traditions associated with those languages.

The region can also be defined as being located between China and India and has been influenced by both, with Indian influence generally broader, deeper, and longer lasting, especially on the mainland, except for Vietnam and Singapore, where influences from China have been more important. Islamic influence is also present in all eleven of the Southeast Asian nations. Culturally, Southeast Asia is notable for the central importance of the family, religion (mainly Buddhism and Islam), and aesthetics in daily life and national consciousness.

In the post–World War II Cold War era, there was a lack of regional unity. Some nations, such as Indonesia under Sukarno, were leaders of the nonaligned nations. Countries such as Thailand and the Philippines joined the U.S. side in the Cold War by being part of the Southeast Asia Treaty Organization (SEATO). A move toward greater unity was achieved with the establishment of the Association of Southeast Asian Nations (ASEAN) in 1967, with the founding members being Indonesia, Malaysia, the Philippines, Singapore, and Thailand. Subsequently other Southeast Asian nations joined ASEAN (Brunei, 1984; Laos, Myanmar, and Vietnam 1997; Cambodia 1999). As of 2002, communism was still the system in Laos and Vietnam and capitalism in Brunei, Cambodia, East Timor, the Philippines Thailand, Indonesia, Malaysia and Singapore. Political, economic, and cultural cooperation is fostered by the Association of Southeast Asian Nations (ASEAN), with headquarters in Jakarta, Indonesia. Economically, all the nations have attempted to move, although at different speeds and with different results, from a reliance on agriculture to an industrial or service-based economy. All nations also suffered in the Asian economic crisis beginning in July 1997.

Alongside these sources of similarity or unity that allow us to speak of Southeast Asia as a region is also considerable diversity. In the past religion, ethnicity, and diverse colonial experience (British, Dutch, French, American) were major sources of diversity. Today, the three major sources of diversity are religion, form of government, and level of economic development. Three nations (Indonesia, Malaysia,

Brunei) are predominately Islamic, five are mainly Buddhist (Vietnam, Laos, Cambodia, Thailand, Myanmar), two are mainly Christian (Philippines and East Timor), and Singapore is religiously heterogeneous. In addition, there is religious diversity within nations, as all these nations have sizeable and visible religious minorities and indigenous religions, in both traditional and syncretic forms, also remain important.

In terms of government, there is considerable variation: communism in Vietnam and Laos; state socialism in Myanmar; absolute monarchy in Brunei; evolving democracy in the Philippines, Thailand, Cambodia, and Indonesia; and authoritarian democracy in Malaysia and Singapore. The economic variation that exists among the nations and also across regions within nations is reflected in different levels of urbanization and economic development, with Singapore and Malaysia at one end of the spectrum and Laos and Cambodia at the other. Myanmar is economically underdeveloped, although it is urbanized, while Brunei is one of the wealthiest nations in the world but not very urbanized.

In 2002, Southeast Asia faced major environmental, political, economic, and health issues. All Southeast Asian nations suffer from serious environmental degradation, including water pollution, soil erosion, air pollution in and around cities, traffic congestion, and species extinctions. To a significant extent all these problems are the result of rapid industrial expansion and overexploitation of natural resources for international trade. The economic crisis has hampered efforts to address these issues and has threatened the economies of some nations, making them more dependent on international loans and assistance from nations such as Japan, Australia, and China. The persisting economic disparities between the rich and the poor are actually exacerbated by rapid economic growth. Related to poverty is the AIDS epidemic, which is especially serious in Cambodia, Myanmar, and Thailand and becoming more serious in Vietnam; in all these nations it associated with the commercial sex industry.

Politically, many Southeast Asian nations faced one or more threats to their stability. Political corruption, lack of transparency, and weak civic institutions are a problem to varying degrees in all the nations but are most severe in Indonesia, which faces threats to its sovereignty. Cambodia and Thailand face problems involving monarch succession, and several nations have had difficulty finding effective leaders. Myanmar's authoritarian rulers face a continual threat from the political opposition and from ethnic and religious separatists.

In addition, several nations faced continuing religious or ethnic-based conflicts that disrupt political stability and economic growth in some provinces. The major conflicts involve Muslim separatists in the southern Philippines, Muslims and Christians in some Indonesian islands and Aceh separatists in northern Sumatra, and Muslims and the Karen and other ethnic groups against the Burman government in Myanmar. Since the economic crisis of 1997, ethnic and religion-based conflict has intensified, as wealthier ethnic or religious minorities have increasingly been attacked by members of the dominant ethnic group. A related issue is the cultural and political future of indigenous peoples, including the so-called hill tribes of the mainland and horticulturalists and former hunter-gatherers of the islands.

In looking to the future, among the region's positive features are the following. First, there is Southeast Asia's strategic location between India and China, between Japan and Europe, and between Europe and Oceania. It stands in close proximity to the world's two most populous countries, China and India. Singapore, the centrally located port in Southeast Asia, is one of two major gateways to the dynamic Pacific Basin (the other is the Panama Canal). Second, there is the region's huge population and related economic market, with a total population approaching that of one half of China's. Indonesia is the world's fourth most populous nation. Third, there is enormous tourist potential in sites and recreational locales such as Angkor Wat, Bali, Borobudur, Phuket, and Ha Long Bay. Fourth, there is the region's notable eclecticism in borrowing from the outside and resiliency in transcending tragedies such as experienced by Cambodia and Vietnam. Fifth, there is the region's significant economic potential: Southeast Asia may well have the world's highest-quality labor force relative to cost. And, sixth, there is the region's openness to new technologies and ideas, an important feature in the modern global community.

South Asia

South Asia is the easiest region to demarcate, as it is bounded by the Hindu Kush and Himalayan ranges to the north and the Bay of Bengal and Arabian Sea to the south. It contains the nation-states of Bangladesh, Bhutan, India, Nepal, and Sri Lanka and the more distant island nations of the Maldives and Mauritius. Myanmar and Pakistan, which are considered part of South Asia in some schemes, are here classified in Southeast Asia and Southwest Asia, respectively.

While the region is diverse economically, culturally, linguistically, and religiously, there is unity that, in some form, has existed for several thousand years. One source of unity is the historical influence of two major civilizations (Indus and Dravidian) and three major religions (Hinduism, Buddhism, and Islam). Regionally, Sikhism and Jainism have been of great importance. There is also considerable economic unity, as the majority of people continue to live by farming, with rice and especially wet-rice the primary crop. In addition, three-quarters of the people continue to live in rural, agricultural villages, although this has now become an important source of diversity, with clear distinctions between urban and rural life. A third source of unity is the caste system, which continues to define life for most people in the three mainland nations. Another source of unity is the nature and structure of society, which was heavily influenced by the several centuries of British rule. A final source of political unity in the twentieth century—although sometimes weakened by ethnic and religious differences—has been nationalism in each nation.

South Asia is diverse linguistically, ethnically, religiously, and economically. This diversity is most obvious in India, but exists in various forms in other nations, except for the isolated Maldives, which is the home of one ethnic group, the Divehi, who are Muslims and who have an economy based largely on tourism and fishing.

The dozens of languages of South Asia fall into four major families: Indo-European, Austroasiatic, Dravidian, and Tibeto-Burman and several cannot be classified at all. Because of its linguistic diversity, India is divided into "linguistic" states with Hindi and English serving as the national languages.

Hinduism is the dominant religion in South Asia, but India is the home also to Buddhism, Jainism, and Sikhism. India also has over 120 million Muslims and the world's largest Zoroastrian population (known in India as Parsis) and Bangladesh is a predominately Muslim nation. India also has about twenty-five million Christians and until recently India had several small but thriving Jewish communities. Nepal is mainly Hindu with a Buddhist minority, and Bhutan the reverse. Sri Lanka is mainly Theravada Buddhist with Hindu, Muslim, and Christian minorities. Mauritius, which has no indigenous population, is about 50 percent Hindu, with a large Christian and smaller Muslim and Buddhist minorities.

Linguistic and religious diversity is more than matched by social diversity. One classification suggests that the sociocultural groups of South Asia can be divided into four general and several subcategories: (1) castes (Hindu and Muslim); (2) modern urban classes (including laborers, non-Hindus, and the Westernized elite); (3) hill tribes of at least six types; and (4) peripatetics.

Economically, there are major distinctions between the rural poor and the urban middle class and elite, and also between the urban poor and urban middle class and elite. There are also significant wealth distinctions based on caste and gender, and a sizeable and wealthy Indian diaspora. There is political diversity as well, with India and Sri Lanka being democracies, Bangladesh shifting back and forth between Islamic democracy and military rule, the Maldives being an Islamic state, and Nepal and Bhutan being constitutional monarchies.

In 2002, South Asia faced several categories of issues. Among the most serious are the ongoing ethnic and religious conflicts between Muslims and Hindus in India, the conflict between the nations of Pakistan and India; the ethnic conflict between the Sinhalese and Sri Lankan Tamils in Sri Lanka; and the conflict between the Nepalese and Bhutanese in both nations. There are also various ethnic separatists movements in the region, as involving some Sikhs in India. The most threatening to order in the region and beyond is the conflict between India and Pakistan over the Kashmir region, as both have nuclear weapons and armies gathered at their respective borders.

A second serious issue is the host of related environmental problems, including pollution; limited water resources; overexploitation of natural resources; destruction and death caused by typhoons, flooding, and earthquakes; famine (less of a problem today), and epidemics of tropical and other diseases. The Maldives faces the unique problem of disappearing into the sea as global warming melts glaciers and raises the sea level. Coastal regions of Bangladesh could also suffer from this.

There are pressing social, economic, and political issues as well. Socially, there are wide and growing gaps between the rich and middle classes and the poor, who are disproportionately women and children and rural. Tribal peoples and untouchables still do not enjoy full civil rights, and women are often discriminated against, although India, Sri Lanka, and Bangladesh have all had women prime ministers. Economically, all the nations continue to wrestle with the issues involved in transforming themselves from mainly rural, agricultural nations to ones with strong industrial and service sectors. Politically, all still also struggle with the task of establishing strong, central governments that can control ethnic, religious, and region variation and provide services to the entire population. Despite these difficulties, there are also positive developments. India continues to benefit from the inflow of wealth earned by Indians outside India and is emerging as a major technological center. And, in Sri Lanka, an early 2002 cease-fire has led to the prospect of a series of peace negotiations in the near future..

East Asia

East Asia is defined here as the nations of Japan, South Korea, North Korea, China, Taiwan, and Mongolia. It should be noted that Taiwan is part of China although the People's Republic of China and the Republic of China (Taiwan) differ over whether it is a province or not. The inclusion of China in East Asia is not entirely geographically and culturally valid, as parts of southern China could be classified as Southeast Asian from a geographical and cultural standpoint, while western China could be classified as Central Asian. However, there is a long tradition of classifying China as part of East Asia, and that is the approach taken here. Likewise, Mongolia is sometimes classified in Central Asia. As noted above, Siberia can be considered as forming North and Northeast Asia.

Economic, political, ideological, and social similarity across China, Korea (North and South), and Japan is the result of several thousand years of Chinese influence (at times strong, at other times weak), which has created considerable similarity on a base of pre-existing Japanese and Korean cultures and civilizations. China's influence was greatest before the modern period and Chinese culture thus in some ways forms the core of East Asian culture and society. At the same time, it must be stressed that Chinese cultural elements merged with existing and new Korean and Japanese ones in ways that produced the unique Japanese and Korean cultures and civilizations, which deserve consideration in their own right.

Among the major cultural elements brought from China were Buddhism and Confucianism, the written language, government bureaucracy, various techniques of rice agriculture, and a patrilineal kinship system based on male dominance and male control of family resources. All of these were shaped over the centuries to fit with existing or developing forms in Korea and Japan. For example, Buddhism coexists with Shinto in Japan. In Korea, it coexists with the indigenous shamanistic religion. In China and Korea traditional folk religion remains strong, while Japan has been the home to dozens of new indigenous religions over the past 150 years.

Diversity in the region has been largely a product of continuing efforts by the Japanese and Koreans to resist Chinese influence and develop and stress Japanese and Korean culture and civilization. In the twentieth century diversity was mainly political and economic. Japanese invasions and conquests of parts of China and all of Korea beginning in the late nineteenth century led to hostile relations that had not been completely overcome in 2002.

In the post–World War II era and after, Taiwan, Japan, and South Korea have been closely allied with the United States and the West; they have all developed powerful industrial and postindustrial economies. During the same period, China became a Communist state; significant ties to the West and economic development did not begin until the late 1980s. North Korea is also a Communist state; it lags behind the other nations in economic development and in recent years has not been able to produce enough food to feed its population. In 2002 China was the emerging economic power in the region, while Taiwan and South Korea hold on and Japan shows signs of serious and long-term economic decline, although it remains the second-largest (after the United States) economy in the world. Mongolia, freed from Soviet rule, is attempting to build its economy following a capitalist model.

Politically, China remains a Communist state despite significant moves toward market capitalism, North Korea is a Communist dictatorship, Japan a democracy, and South Korea and Taiwan in 1990s seem to have become relatively stable democracies following periods of authoritarian rule. Significant contact among the nations is mainly economic, as efforts at forging closer political ties remain stalled over past grievances. For example, in 2001, people in China and South Korea protested publicly about a new Japanese high school history textbook that they believed did not fully describe Japanese atrocities committed toward Chinese and Koreans before and during World War II. Japan has refused to revise the textbook. Similarly, tension remains between Mongolia and China over Mongolian fears about Chinese designs on Mongolian territory. Inner Mongolia is a province of China.

Major issues with regional and broader implications are the reunification of Taiwan and China and North and South Korea, and threat of war should reunification efforts go awry. Other major regional issues include environmental pollution, including air pollution from China that spreads east, and pollution of the Yellow Sea, Taiwan Strait, and South China Sea. A third issue is economic development and stability, and the role of each nation, and the region as a unit, in the growing global economy. A final major issue is the emergence of China as a major world political, economic, and military power at the expense of Taiwan, South Korea, and Japan, and the consequences for regional political relations and stability.

Overview

As the above survey indicates, Asia is a varied and dynamic construct. To some extent the notion of Asia, as well as regions within Asia, are artificial constructs imposed by outside observers to provide some structure to a place and subject matter that might otherwise be incomprehensible. The nations of Asia have rich and deep pasts that continue to inform and shape the present—and that play a significant role in relations with other nations and regions. The nations of Asia also face considerable issues—some unique to the region, others shared by nations around the world—as well as enormous potential for future growth and development. We expect that the next edition of this encyclopedia will portray a very different Asia than does this one, but still an Asia that is in many ways in harmony with its pasts.

David Levinson (with contributions from Virginia Aksan, Edward Beauchamp, Anthony and Rebecca Bichel, Linsun Cheng, Gerald Fry, Bruce Fulton, and Paul Hockings)

Regional Maps

CENTRAL ASIA

CHINA AND
EAST ASIA

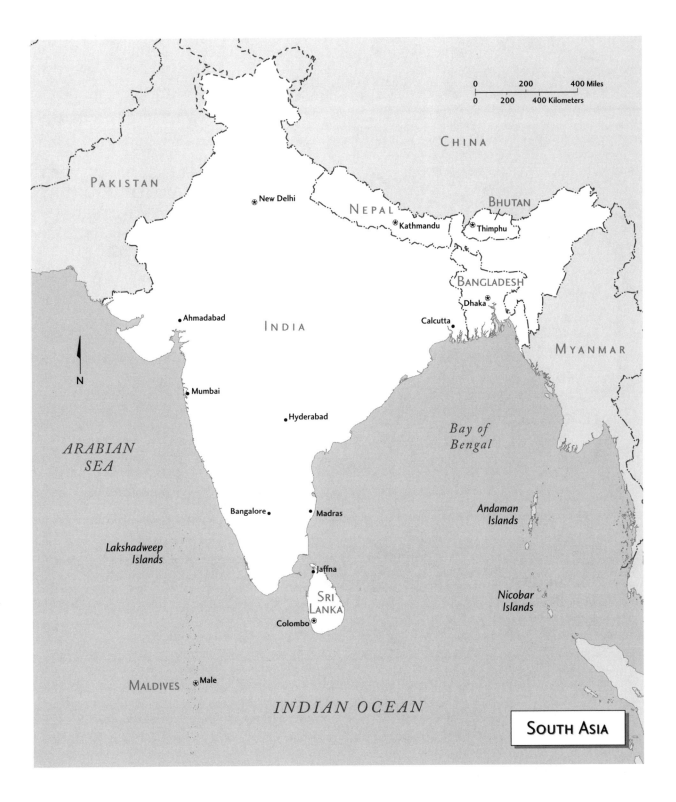

CHINA

PAKISTAN

⊛ New Delhi

NEPAL

BHUTAN

⊛ Kathmandu   ⊛ Thimphu

BANGLADESH

• Ahmadabad

INDIA

Dhaka ⊛

Calcutta •

MYANMAR

N

• Mumbai

ARABIAN
SEA

• Hyderabad

Bay of
Bengal

Bangalore •   • Madras

Andaman
Islands

Lakshadweep
Islands

• Jaffna

SRI
LANKA

Nicobar
Islands

Colombo ⊛

MALDIVES   ⊛ Male

INDIAN OCEAN

0   200   400 Miles
0   200   400 Kilometers

SOUTH ASIA

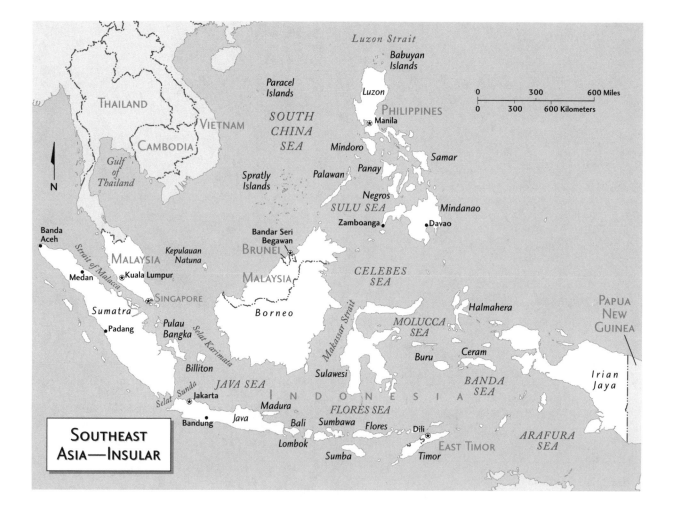

SOUTHEAST ASIA—INSULAR

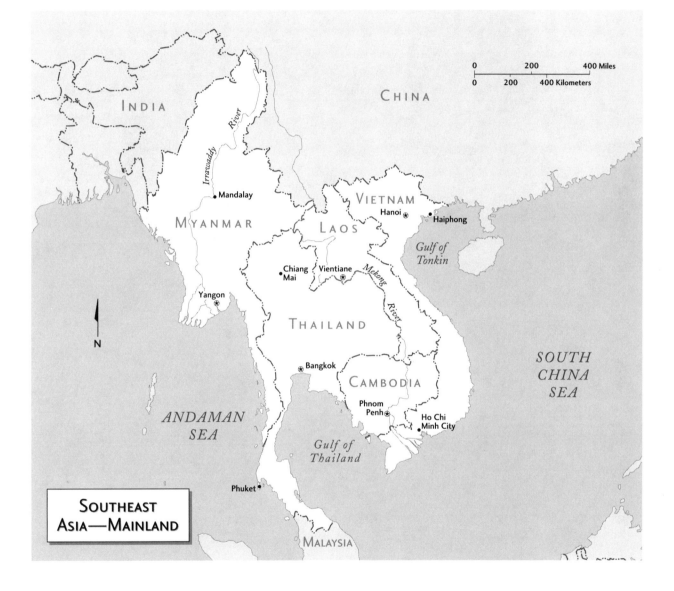

SOUTHEAST
ASIA—MAINLAND

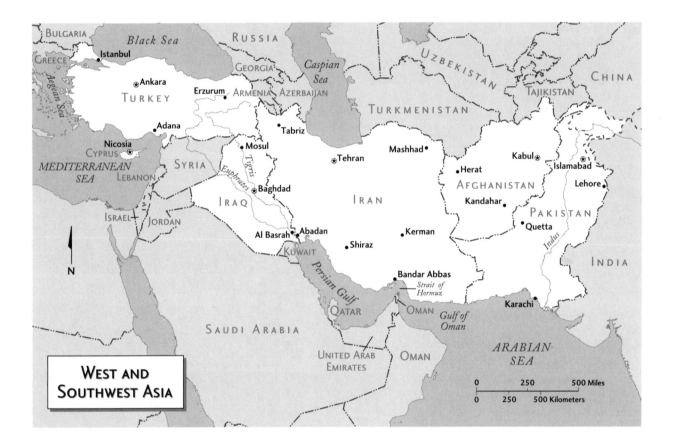

BULGARIA

Black Sea

RUSSIA

GREECE

•Istanbul

⊛Ankara

TURKEY

GEORGIA

Aegean Sea

Erzurum•

ARMENIA AZERBAIJAN

Caspian Sea

UZBEKISTAN

CHINA

TURKMENISTAN

TAJIKISTAN

Tabriz•

Nicosia

CYPRUS ⊛

MEDITERRANEAN SEA

SYRIA

LEBANON

•Mosul

Euphrates

Tigris

⊛Tehran

Mashhad•

Kabul⊛

Islamabad⊛

⊛Baghdad

Herat•

AFGHANISTAN

Lehore•

ISRAEL

JORDAN

IRAQ

IRAN

Kandahar•

PAKISTAN

•Quetta

Indus

Al Basrah•

•Abadan

Kerman•

INDIA

N

•Shiraz

KUWAIT

Bandar Abbas•

Strait of Hormuz

Persian Gulf

QATAR

OMAN

Gulf of Oman

•Karachi

SAUDI ARABIA

UNITED ARAB EMIRATES

OMAN

ARABIAN SEA

0   250   500 Miles

0   250   500 Kilometers

WEST AND SOUTHWEST ASIA

Reader's Guide

ASIA

Arts, Literature, and Recreation

Asian Games
Board Games
Chinese New Year
Jade
Kabaddi
Kites and Kite Flying
Mountaineering
Olympics
Storytelling

Economics, Commerce, and Transportation

Asian Development Bank
Asian Economic Crisis of 1997
Asia-Pacific Economic Cooperation Forum
Automobile Industry
Bogor Declaration
Drug Trade
Export-Led Development
Golden Crescent
High-Technology Industry
Information Technology Industry
Intellectual Property
Islamic Banking
Manila Action Plan
Measurement Systems
Osaka Action Plan
Shanghai Cooperation Organization
Silk Road
Spice Trade
Sustainability
Tin Industry
Tourism
World Bank in Asia

Geography and the Natural World

Air Pollution
Bamboo
Buffalo, Water
Camel, Bactrian
Caspian Sea
Chicken
Cormorant
Deforestation
Duck and Goose, Domesticated
Earthquakes
Endangered Species
Goat
Mangroves
Monsoons
Opium
Pacific Ocean
Pacific Rim
Pig
Rhinocerous, Asiatic
Rice and Rice Agriculture
Soil Loss
South China Sea
Surkhob River
Tiger
Toxic-Waste Disposal
Typhoons
Volcanoes
Water Issues

Government, Politics, and Law

Corruption

International Relations

Africa-Asia Relations
Australia-Asia Relations

Economic Planning Agency
Economic Stabilization Program
Electronics Industry—Japan
Farmer's Movement
Financial Crisis of 1927
Fishing Industry—Japan
Furukawa Ichibei
Japan—Economic System
Japan—Money
Japanese Firms Abroad
Japanese Foreign Investments
Japanese International Cooperation Agency
Kawasaki
Nikkyoso
Overseas Economic Cooperation Fund
Quality Circles
Ringi System
Settai
Shibusawa Eiichi
Shunto
Whaling—Japan
  Koreas
Chaebol
Fishing Industry—Korea
Food Crisis—North Korea
North and South Korean Economic Ventures
North Korea—Economic System
South Korea—Economic System
Steel Industry—Korea
  Mongolia
Cashmere Industry
Forest Industry—Mongolia
Mongolia—Economic System
Trans-Mongolian Railway

Education
  China
Academia Sinica
China—Education System
Hu Shi
National Taiwan University
Peking University
Taiwan—Education System
  Japan
Asiatic Society of Japan
Cram Schools
Daigaku
Ebina Danjo
Gakureki Shakai
Ienaga Saburo
Imperial Rescript on Education
Japan—Education System
Kyoiku Mama
Nitobe Inazo
Shiga Shigetaka

  Koreas
Korea Institute of Science and Technology
North Korea—Education System
Seoul National University
South Korea—Education System
  Mongolia
Mongolia—Education System

Geography and the Natural World
Siberia
Yellow Sea
  China
Bramaputra River
Cathaya Tree
Chang River
East China Sea
Emei, Mount
Famine—China
Greater Xing'an Range
Hengduan Ranges
Huang River
Huang Shan
Huanglongsi
Jiuzhaigou
Kunlun Mountains
Lu, Mount
Panda
Qinling Range
Tai Shan
Taiwan Strait
Taklimakan Desert
Tarim Basin
Tian Shan
Wudang Shan
Wulingyuan
Wuyi, Mount
Yak
  Japan
Amami Islands
Chrysanthemum
Chubu
Chugoku
Etorofu Island
Fuji, Mount
Hokkaido
Honshu
Iriomotejima Island
Kansai Region
Kanto Region
Kinki Region
Kunashiro Island
Kyushu
Sado Island
Setouchi Region
Shikoku

Indian Ocean
Indian Subcontinent
Indo-Gangetic Plain
Jhelum River
Jute
K2, Mount
Kangchenjunga, Mount
Kaveri River
Kistna River
Mongoose
Punjab
Reunion Island
Sundarbhans
Tarai
   India
Abu, Mount
Andaman and Nicobar Islands
Bhopal
Chenab River
Dekkan
Eastern Ghats
Ganges River
Godavari River
Hindu Kush
Jumna River
Lion, Asiatic
Mahanadi River
Narmada Dam Controversy
Narmada River
Rann of Kachchh
Satpura Range
Sutlej River
Thar Desert
Tungabhadra River
Vindhya Mountains
Western Ghats
Zebu
   Nepal
Everest, Mount
Kathmandu Valley

Government, Politics, and Law
Bahadur Shah
Birla Family
Colombo Plan
Hastings, Warren
Humayun
Ibn al-Qasim, Muhammad
Jahangir
Marxism—South Asia
Poros
Raziya
Roy, Rammohan
Shah Jahan
Singh, Jai

Tata Family
Tipu Sultan
   Bangladesh
Awami League
Bangladesh—Political System
Bangladesh Nationalist Party
Chittagong
Dhaka
Ershad, H.M.
Hasina Wajid, Sheikh
Jatiya Party
Rahman, Mujibur
Rahman, Ziaur
Zia, Khaleda
   Bhutan
Thimphu
Wangchuck, King Jigme Singye
   India
Afzal Khan
Agartala
Agra
Ahmadabad
Ajanta
Ajodhya
Akbar
Ali Janhar, Mohamed
Allahabad
Ambedkar, B.R.
Amritsar
Andhra Pradesh
Arunachal Pradesh
Asoka
Assam
Aurangabad
Aurangzeb
Awadh
Azad, Abu'l-Kalam
Babur
Bangalore
Bengal, West
Bentinck, William Cavendish
Bhosle, Shivaji
Bhubaneshwar
Bihar
Bodh Gaya
Bose, Subhas Chandra
Calcutta
Calicut
Canning, Charles John
Chandigarh
Chhattisgarh
Coimbatore
Constitution—India

Romusha
Weld, Frederick
Brunei
Azahari, A.M.
Bandar Seri Begawan
Brooke, James
Hassanal Bolkaih
Parti Rakyat Brunei
Cambodia
Buddhist Liberal Democratic Party—Cambodia
Cambodia—Civil War of 1970-1975
Cambodia—Political System
Cambodian People's Party
Fa Ngoum
FUNCINPEC
Heng Samrin
Hun Sen
Jayavarman II
Jayavarman VII
Khieu Samphan
Khmer Rouge
Killing Fields
Lon Nol
Phnom Penh
Phnom Penh Evacuation
Pol Pot
Ranariddh, Norodom
Sam Rainsy
Sihanouk, Norodom
East Timor
Belo, Bishop Carlos
Dili
Dili Massacre
Fretilin
Gusmao, Xanana
Ramos-Horta, José
Indonesia
Airlangga
Amboina Massacre
Bandung
Batavia
Bosch, Johannes van den
Budi Utomo
Coen, Jan Pieterszoon
Cukong
Daendels, Herman
Darul Islam
Ethnic Colonial Policy—Indonesia
Gajah Mada
Gerindo
Gestapu Affair
Golkar
Habibie, B.J.
Hamengku Buwono IX, Sri Sultan

Hatta, Mohammad
Hizbullah
Indonesia—Political Parties
Indonesia—Political System
Indonesian Democratic Party
Indonesian Revolution
Irian Jaya
Jakarta
Jakarta Riots of May 1998
Java
Kalimantan
Malik, Adam
Medan
Megawati Sukarnoputri
Military, Indonesia
Moerdani, Leonardus Benjamin
New Order
Old Order
Pancasila
Partai Kebangkitan Bangsa
Partai Persatuan Pembangunan
Rais, Muhammad Amien
Sarekat Islam
Solo
Speelman, Cornelius
Suharto
Sukarno
Sulawesi
Sumatra
Surabaya
Taman Siswa
Treaty of Giyanti
Umar, Teuku
Wahid, Abdurrahman
Yogyakarta
Laos
Bokeo
Chao Anou
Civil War of 1956–1975—Laos
Kaysone Phomvihan
Lao People's Revolutionary Party
Laos—Political System
Louangnamtha
Pathet Lao
Setthathirat
Souphanuvong, Prince
Souvanna Phouma, Prince
Vientiane
Xayabury
Malaysia
Abdul Razak
Abu Bakar
Anwar, Ibrahim
Badawi, Abdullah Ahmed

l

Encyclopedia of
Modern Asia

POSSESSION   Possession refers to some of the fierce dances still practiced today in India, mainly in the Kerala region, called Thirai Attam and Teyyam. The spirit supposedly possessing the dancer is that of a hero, not a demon, and the term "devil dancing" used by Western anthropologists conveys a false image. In popular imagination this hero has been accorded a kind of godhood through local worship, and through the performance his blessings are sought as a means of receiving personal cures and for general well-being.

The word *teyyam* is derived from the Sanskrit *devam* (god), which indicates that the spirit being placated is not evil. The confusion may have arisen because the dancer is dressed in a horrifying costume. The actor *(kolam)* wears a huge headdress, sometimes with two skulls as ear covers; he is bare chested, his arms are loaded with bangles, and he wears many necklaces and a wide skirt with painted snakes. A cobra is painted on his chest, a huge halo from the head to the hips emphasizes his figure, and he wields a scimitar with consummate skill. There are some three hundred Teyyams, each telling a different story about a hero.

In Kerala the custom of raising stones in honor of great warriors was practiced as early as the second century CE. Later in makeshift temples *(sthanams)* for these heroes, the sword or other weapon was kept on a wooden stool. No daily ceremony is performed in these temples, which still exist today, but an annual Teyyam dance funded by the community is held for the hero.

The performance sometimes begins with preliminary dances and often, but not always, the sacrifice of a cock. After putting on his costume, the performer invokes the spirit *(bhootam)* of the hero and is slowly possessed by it. Finally he dances in great frenzy for hours. When the divine force subsides and he is calm, he is considered to be the holy embodiment of divinity. He goes into the temple, brings out some turmeric with rice, and distributes it to the participating audience and devotees, personally giving blessings to each of them.

The Teyyams are still popular in Kerala, where they are patronized not only by the rural population but also by urban and educated people.

Bharat Gupt

Further Reading

Banerji, Projesh. (1959) *The Folk Dances of India.* Allahabad, India: Kitabistan.
Gautam, M. R. (1980) *The Musical Heritage of India.* Delhi: Abhinav Publications.
Kurup, K. K. N. (1973) *The Cult of Teyyam and Hero Worship in Kerala.* Calcutta, India: Indian Publishers.
Roy Chaudhury, H. C. (1962) *Materials for the Study of the Early History of the Vaisnava Sect.* Calcutta, India: n.p.

POTALA PALACE   A huge structure that dominates the Tibetan capital of Lhasa, Potala Palace has been the home of Tibet's Dalai Lamas since 1642, when the unfinished building was consecrated. It was built by the great fifth Dalai Lama, Ngawang Lozang Gyamtsho (1617–1682), to represent the cosmic mountain abode of the bodhisattva of compassion, Chenrezi, who is believed to dwell on Potala Mountain in south India and to be embodied in the Dalai Lamas. The Red Hill, 130 meters above Lhasa and already sacred to Chenrezi, was chosen as the site. The

POTALA PALACE—WORLD HERITAGE SITE

The winter palace of the Dalai Lama since the seventh century, Potala Palace in Lhasa was designated a UNESCO World Heritage Site in 1994, 2000, and 2001. The palace complex stands as a symbol of Tibetan Buddhism.

Potala was also built as a fortress, thus expressing its dual religious and political function. So important was this palace that the death of the Dalai Lama was kept secret for twelve years so that it could be finished without political interference. The Dalai Lamas are interred in sepulchers in the palace.

The Potala consists of a huge central keep painted maroon, the religious color, surrounded by a white palace, representing the secular. This creates an effect of wings, so that the whole edifice, with its golden roofs, seems to soar. There are two thousand rooms, numerous temples and shrines, and the private rooms of the Dalai Lamas, now open to tourists. UNESCO has declared Potala a World Heritage Site. China claims it has spent some $6.7 million between 1989 and 1994 on extensive renovation work on the palace.

Michael Kowalewski

Further Reading
Batchelor, Stephen. (1987) *The Tibet Guide.* London: Wisdom.
Dorje, Gyurme. (1996) *Tibet Handbook.* Bath, U.K.: Trade & Travels Handbooks.
Dowman, Keith. (1988) *Power Places of Central Tibet.* London: Routledge & Kegan Paul.
Karmay, Samten G. (1994) *Secret Visions of the Fifth Dalai Lama.* London: Serindia.
Richardson, Hugh. (1994) *Ceremonies of the Lhasa Year.* London: Serindia.

PPP. See **Partai Persatuan Pembangunan.**

PRABANG The Prabang is a Buddha image revered by the Lao nation. The Prabang is 76.2 centimeters (30 inches) tall and is an image of Buddha standing in the "no fear" stance. Legend states that the Prabang originated in Sri Lanka and was taken to the Khmer kingdom Angkor. King Fa Ngoum (1316–1374), the founder of the Kingdom of Lan Xang, used the Prabang to legitimize his rule as a righteous Buddhist monarch by taking the image to Vientiane in the 1350s. Vixun (reigned 1501–1520), a great patron of Buddhism, moved the Prabang from Vientiane to Xiang Dong Xiang Thong (Luang Prabang) and began the royal cult of worshiping the image. The image presided over religious and political ceremonies conducted by Lao monarchs. When King Setthathirat (1534–1571) moved the capital of the Kingdom of Lan Xang from Xiang Dong Xiang Thong to Vientiane, he left the Prabang image and renamed the city Luang Prabang in honor of the icon and ordered the construction of Vat Xieng Thong to house the Prabang. During the Siamese invasion of 1778–1779, the Siamese took the Prabang and Emerald Buddha images to Bangkok to symbolize the Lao kingdom's loss of independence and power. During the reign of the Siamese king Mongkut, the Prabang was returned to King Chantarat in 1867. The Prabang presently resides in the Royal Palace Museum of Luang Prabang.

Linda S. McIntosh

Further Reading
Stuart-Fox, Martin. (1996) *The Lao Kingdom of Lan Xang: Rise and Decline.* Bangkok, Thailand: White Lotus.

PRAKARANA *Prakarana* drama is one of the ten dramatic genres of classical Indian theater; indeed, it was one of the two main types, the other being *nataka* drama. Nataka dramas took their plots from the great epics (the *Ramayana* and the *Mahabharata*); their principle characters were gods or kings. *Prakarana* drama, on the other hand, has been called social drama; its plots came from tales, and its protagonists were not royalty, but—though this was not explicitly said—members of the sophisticated urban elite: merchants and learned brahmans.

Differences between Nataka and Prakarana Drama

Unlike *nataka* drama, *prakarana* drama had a large number of characters. In addition to the protagonist, minor characters such as servants, pimps, small traders, courtesans, and servant women were given important roles. The episodes of the play centered on a household and the city; unlike in *nataka* drama, there was no travel to heaven or the underworld, or even to other regions of India.

Modesty and restraint were uncompromisingly demanded from the performers by ancient law-makers.

The *prakarana* was supposed to be the ideal family show, revealing life in all its aspects, but viewed decorously.

As with the *nataka*, this dramatic form took love stories for its plots, but unlike the *nataka*, *prakarana* often had a courtesan as the heroine. It must be remembered that in ancient India prostitution was not only a legitimate part of the social order, the fulfillment of sexual desire outside the marital bond with women of pleasure was coveted for personal well-being and prized as a mark of social status. It could be justly considered as a part of one of the four aims (*purusharthas*) of life, namely, the fulfillment of desires (*kama*). Ideally, to elevate it from the purely physical level, sexuality was to be embellished with fine arts like dancing, music, poetry and painting in which all the courtesans of the higher ranks were adept. As a social norm, it was obligatory for the courtesans and their visitors to patronize and support the arts. Given those facts, wherever there was genuine affection between the customer and the courtesan (which was not uncommon), the result was a near tragic situation, as it was neither easy nor practical to convert the bond into a respectable marriage. Given this historical background, the *prakarana* should be seen as a natural representation of mainstream ancient urban life rather than as a fanciful dramatic set-up.

The Little Clay Cart

Mrichchakatika (The Little Clay Cart), attributed to Shudraka, a king who lived sometime between the third and tenth centuries, is the most famous *prakarana* drama. It demonstrates the conventions of the form.

Vasantasena, the richest courtensan of the city Ujjaiyani, is fascinated by the personal accomplishments and the great magnanimity of Charudatta, a famous merchant whose charity has reduced him to bankcruptcy. As the play opens, she is seen running in the dark night to escape the clutches of Sansthanaka, the cruel brother-in-law of the king. She accidentally enters the house of Charudatta, in whose custody she leaves her jewelry before being escorted home. The jewels are stolen at night by Sharvilaka, who needs money to free his beloved Madanika, a slave of Vasantasena. While receiving the jewels as slave price, Vasantasena recognizes them as her own and realizes that Charudatta has been robbed. She frees Madanika and marries her to Sharvilaka but the couple are separated immediately as Sharvilaka is callled upon to free his friend Aryaka from the prison of the unjust king.

On learning of the theft, to save her husband's honor, Charudatta's wife Dhuta sends Vasantasena her own necklace to replace what has been stolen. Charudatta sends along a letter in which he claims that he had lost Vasantasena's jewelry in a gambling bout and as compensation is sending this necklace. An overwhelmed Vasantasena visits Charudatta at home and tells him about the theft. The lovers enjoy the cooling summer rain and Vasantasena, accepted by the whole household, spends the night there. In the morning she sends back the necklace of Dhuta, but Dhuta does not accept it, saying that her husband is her best jewel. In the meantime, Vasantasena sees Dhuta's little son crying because he must play with a clay cart while the neighbor child plays with a golden cart. Moved by Charudatta's fall in the fortunes, Vasantasena gives the child the necklace so that he can get a golden cart.

The lovers plan to spend a day together, but by a mistake Vasantasena boards the wrong carriage and is accosted by Sansthanaka. When Vasantasena rebuffs him, Sansthanaka becomes enraged and strangles her. He then accuses Charudatta of murdering Vasantasena for jewelry. Charudatta is tried, and as jewels are found on his friend, he is condemned to death. A shattered Dhuta decides to immolate herself. Meanwhile Vasantasena is revived by a Buddhist monk and taken to the magistrates. Charudatta is saved at the last moment and united with both Dhuta and Vasantasena. Sansthanaka is caught but saved from execution by a forgiving Charudatta. A new ruler, who has just deposed the old king, confers the status of a lawful wife on Vasantasena and the play ends with a benediction.

This *prakarana* emphasizes that good action and purity of heart can reverse all ill fortune. Vasantasena is the opposite of the average courtesans, who love for money, and Charudatta is the opposite of the common merchants, who hide wealth. They both bring about a change of heart in many who come in contact with them, and the power of their selflessness even brings about a change in government.

Prakarana Drama in Context

The *prakarana*, like *nataka*, was done with plenty of dance, music, and elaborate gestures reflecting a full range of subtle emotions with postures, movements, and facial expressions. It was meant to be a fine combination of speech, gesture, dance, music, stage conventions, and symbols used in a highly embellished manner. *Prakarana* drama had five to ten acts, and used many different languages. Ancient Indian drama, so often wrongly called Sanskrit drama, was actually a multilingual theater; Sanskrit was spoken only by educated and rich male characters and did not account for more than 30 percent of its total speech text. Most of the songs, not written by the dramatist but added by the producer, were in vernacular tongues. The *prakarana* specialized even more than the *nataka* in multilingual expression as it had a larger caste. It was the best mirror of ancient society.

By the end of the eleventh century, when ancient theater disintegrated, *prakarana* had become extinct, as the ancient life and ideals it portrayed was either disrupted or transformed. The advent of Islamic rule meant the end of prostitution as a social institution managed by the state, and the patronage of painting, dance, and music as combined with public sexuality was unthinkable. The new theater, which centered around religious devotion, was too otherworldly an environment for *prakarana*.

Bharat Gupt

Further Reading
Byrski, Christopher. (1974) *Concept of Ancient Indian Theatre.* Delhi: Munshiram Manoharlal.

Gupt, Bharat. (1994) *Dramatic Concepts: Greek and Indian. A Study of Poetics and the Natyasastra.* Delhi: D. K. Printworld.

Marasinghe, E. W. (1989) *The Sanskrit Theatre and Stagecraft.* Delhi: Sri Satguru Publications.

Raghavan, V. (1952) *The Social Play in Sanskrit.* Bangalore, India: IIC.

Shekhar, Indu. (1960) *Sanskrit Drama, Its Origin and Decline.* Lieden, Netherlands: E. J. Brill.

Ryder, Arthur William, trans. (1905) *The Little Clay Cart (Mrchchakatika): A Hindu Drama Attributed to King Shudraka.* Harvard Oriental Series, no. 9. Cambridge, MA: Harvard University Press.

PRAMBANAN HINDU

Prambanan is a village near Yogyakarta, Java that has lent its name to the largest Hindu temple complex in Indonesia, built in the ninth and tenth centuries CE. An inscription from the site dates to 856 CE, mentioning a royal funeral in which the deceased shivaitic king of Central Java was united with Siva. The largest temple (47 meters high), probably the tomb of the king, has four inner chambers containing statues of Siva Mahadeva, Siva Mahaguru, Ganesha, and Durga. The reliefs on the inner side of the temple's balustrade depict episodes from the *Ramayana*. Its story is continued in the reliefs on the balustrade of the smaller Brahma temple, south of the Siva temple. The Brahma temple has only one chamber with a statue showing Brahma as a manifestation of Siva. The Vishnu temple north of the Siva temple is encircled by a relief depicting episodes from the Krishnayana. The statue in this temple represents Vishnu also as an aspect of Siva. The three opposite temples originally housed the statues of the deities' vehicles. Today, only that of Siva can still be seen. The restoration of the main temples was completed between 1951 and the mid-1990s.

Martin Ramstedt

Further Reading
Bernet Kempers, A. J. (1959) *Ancient Indonesian Art.* Cambridge, MA: Harvard University Press.

Dumarçay, Jacques. (1987) *The Temples of Java.* Singapore: Oxford University Press.

Stutterheim, Willem. (1989) *Rama-Legends and Rama-Reliefs in Indonesia.* New Delhi: Indira Gandhi National Centre for the Arts.

PRAMOEDYA ANANTA TOER

(b. 1925), Indonesian novelist. Born in Blora, Central Java, on 6 February 1925, Pramoedya first built a reputation as a writer during the struggle for Indonesian independence (1945–1949), writing *Perburuan* (*The Fugitive*) while imprisoned by the Dutch (1947–1949). In the 1950s he was active in teaching, writing, and journalism, and was connected to the Communist-linked Lekra (Institute of People's Culture), though not a member of the Party itself. After the anti-Communist purge in 1965, Pramoedya was incarcerated in the Buru Island prison camp. There he began telling stories to fellow inmates, stories that formed the basis of the tetralogy of novels: *Bumi Manusia* (*This Earth of Mankind*), *Anak Semua Bangsa* (*Child of All Nations*), *Jejak Langkah* (*Footsteps*), and *Rumah Kaca* (*House of Glass*). The first two were published on Pramoedya's release in 1980, briefly becoming best-sellers before being banned for promoting Communism. During the 1980s and 1990s he lived mainly under house arrest in Jakarta, being released only after Suharto's fall. Pramoedya's novels combine deep knowledge of Indonesia's history and culture with passionate concern for its people.

Tim Byard-Jones

Further Reading
Pramoedya Ananta Toer. (1950) *Perburuan* (*The Fugitive*). Trans. by Willem Samuels. New York: William Morrow.

———. (1980) *Anak Semua Bangsa* (*Child of All Nations*). Trans. by Max Lane. New York: William Morrow.

———. (1980) *Bumi Manusia* (*This Earth of Mankind*). Trans. by Max Lane. New York: William Morrow.

———. (1985) *Jejak Langkah* (*Footsteps*). Trans. by Max Lane. New York: William Morrow.

———. (1988) *Rumah Kaca* (*House of Glass*). Trans. by Max Lane. New York: William Morrow.

PREMCHAND (1880–1936), Hindi and Urdu writer. Premchand is the pen name of Dhanpat Rai Srivastana, who was born on 31 July 1880 in the village of Lamahi near Varanasi (Benares), India. Rai Srivastana was not good at his studies and could not pass the matriculation examination. After the death of his father, he became a schoolteacher in 1899 with a salary of eighteen rupees per month. He began his literary career and wrote under the pen name Premchand. In 1907, he published short stories in Urdu but switched to Hindi eight years afterward. In 1916, he published his first short story in Hindi, *Panch Parameswar* (Five Gods).

During the period between 1917 and 1936, Premchand dominated the Hindi literary scene with his stories and novels. His works reflected contemporary social and political realities in India at the time. Sympathizing with the downtrodden, he wrote powerful and gripping stories and novels about social inequality, poverty of the peasants, and exploitation of women. He was influenced by Gandhian ideals and even joined the noncooperation movement. The novel *Godan* (Gift of a Cow) is a vivid account of a helpless peasant, exploitation by landlords, and problems of untouchability. *Gaban* (Misappropriation) is about the destruction of a family caused by the materialism of a female member. He wrote 250 short stories and eleven novels. Some of his important novels are *Premashrama* (Hermitage of Love, 1918), *Rangabhumi* (Theater, 1925), and *Karmabhumi* (Workplace, 1932). He died on 8 October 1936.

Patit Paban Mishra

Further Reading
Jidal, K. B. (1993) *A History of Hindi Literature*. New Delhi: Munshiram.
Rai, Alok. (1993) *Premchand*. Reprint ed. New Delhi: National Book Trust.

PRIBUMI *Pribumi* (literally "offspring of the soil") is an Indonesian term referring to people considered as natives of the country, belonging to various ethnic groups in the archipelago. As a sociodemographic category, it refers to the Dutch colonial policy of differentiating three classes of people—Europeans, Asian migrants (primarily ethnic Chinese), and *pribumi (inlander* in Dutch).

Pribumi and the Malaysian term *bumiputra* have equivalent meaning. However, in Malaysia, the *bumiputra* make up only just over half of the country's population, whereas the *pribumi* are around 95 percent of Indonesia's 220 million inhabitants; only about 5

percent of the population are considered as non-*pribumi*, mainly people of Chinese descent.

Also unlike Malaysia, where the *bumiputra* are largely Malay Muslims (as well as several ethnic minorities indigenous to the states of Sabah and Sarawak on Borneo island, many of whom are non-Muslims), in Indonesia the *pribumi* are not associated with any specific ethnic group or religion. Indonesia is the largest Muslim country in the world, and close to 90 percent of its population profess Islam as their religion. Yet there are regions and ethnic groups, mostly in the eastern part of the archipelago, in which people of other faiths are in the majority. For instance, the areas of southern Maluku and Irian Jaya (the western half of New Guinea island) are predominantly Protestant; the province of East Nusa Tenggara is predominantly Catholic; and Bali is home to Indonesian Hindus. Despite the differences in religious beliefs compared with the Muslim majority, they are also considered *pribumi*.

Similar to the *bumiputra* in Malaysia, the *pribumi* are mainly a socioeconomic category, especially in terms of true economic disparity. Although only a small percentage of the total population of Indonesia, the non-*pribumi*, especially the ethnic Chinese, control much of the country's economic activities, primarily in the manufacturing, financial, and trading sectors. As a result, the non-*pribumi* are perceived as an affluent class, while the *pribumi* are economically disadvantaged.

On the other hand, the Indonesian state has an unofficial discriminatory policy toward non-*pribumi*. Hurdles discourage them from entering public civil or military services and state universities. In the past, many of them were even persuaded to change their names from mainly Chinese to *pribumi* ones, so that they might be more readily assimilated with the *pribumi*.

There have been efforts to ameliorate the tense *pribumi*–non-*pribumi* relationship in Indonesia. On the economic front, to bridge the gap between the poorer *pribumi* and the more affluent non-*pribumi*, some have suggested the idea of developing a people's economy, more or less inspired by the perceived success of Malaysia's New Economic Policy. This economy would direct state resources toward helping small and medium enterprises as well as cooperatives owned overwhelmingly by *pribumi* entrepreneurs.

On the social side, people have suggested allowing the non-*pribumi* access to public services, including political posts. This proposed policy would aim at offsetting the non-*pribumi* preoccupation with economic-related activities while fostering greater social integration.

Irman G. Lanti

Further Reading

Center for Information and Development Studies. (1998) *Pribumi dan Non-Pribumi dalam Perspektif Pemerataan Ekonomi dan Integrasi Sosial* (Pribumi and Non-Pribumi in the Perspective of Economic Redistribution and Social Integration). Jakarta, Indonesia: Center for Information and Development Studies

Suryadinata, Leo. (1992) *Pribumi Indonesians, the Chinese Minority, and China.* Singapore: Heinemann Asia.

Wahono, Riyanto D., et al., eds. (1997) *70 Tahun Junus Jahja: Pribumi Kuat Kunci Pembauran* (70 Years Junus Jahja: Strong Pribumi Key to Assimilation). Jakarta, Indonesia: Bina Rena Pariwara.

PRIDI BANOMYONG (1900–1983), Thai political and intellectual figure. Pridi Banomyong (Luang Pradit Manutham) is one of Thailand's most prominent and influential political and intellectual figures of the twentieth century. While studying on a king's scholarship in France, in February 1927 he and six colleagues founded the People's Party with the objective of overthrowing Siam's absolute monarchy. Following the revolution of 24 June 1932, which transformed Siam into a constitutional monarchy, he became one of Siam's leading political figures.

Among his many diverse roles were minister of the interior (1934), minister of foreign affairs (1937), regent (1941–1945), secret leader of the resistance movement against the Japanese occupation (1941–1945), senior statesman (1945), and prime minister (1946). His intellectual influences included the founding of Thammasat University (1934) and extensive publications dealing primarily with political economy and including a novel and film, *The King of the White Elephant.*

Over time, considerable controversy arose concerning Pridi and his vision for the future of Thailand. He was falsely accused of being a communist and wanting to transform Thailand into a republic. The mysterious death of King Rama VIII in June 1946, while Pridi was prime minister, led to never-substantiated accusations against him. Eventually he was forced into lifelong exile in China (1949–1970) and France (1970–1983). In Pridi's honor a statute was built at Thammasat University (1984) and a Pridi Banomyong Foundation (1983) and a Pridi Banomyong Institute (1995) were created.

Pridi was included in UNESCO's list of Great Personalities and Historic Events for the year 2000, and this year was declared by UNESCO as the centennial of Pridi. Also, the Université Paris (1 Panthéon-Sorbonne) in 2000 celebrated the centenary of Pridi and honored him as "one of the great constitutionalists of the twentieth century," comparing him to such figures as Rousseau, Montesquieu, and de Tocqueville.

Gerald W. Fry

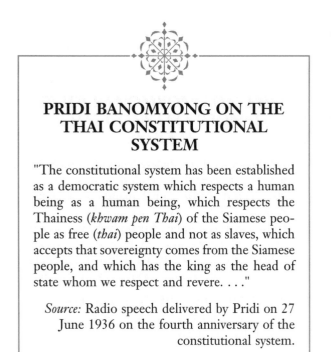

PRIDI BANOMYONG ON THE THAI CONSTITUTIONAL SYSTEM

"The constitutional system has been established as a democratic system which respects a human being as a human being, which respects the Thainess (*khwam pen Thai*) of the Siamese people as free (*thai*) people and not as slaves, which accepts that sovereignty comes from the Siamese people, and which has the king as the head of state whom we respect and revere. . . ."

Source: Radio speech delivered by Pridi on 27 June 1936 on the fourth anniversary of the constitutional system.

Further Reading

Baker, Chris, and Pasuk Phongpaichit. (2000) *Pridi by Pridi: Selected Writings on Life, Politics, and Economy.* Chiang Mai, Thailand: Silkworm Books.

Narong Petchprasoet, ed. (1999) *Pridi Phanomyong.* Bangkok, Thailand: Political Economy Centre and Pridi Banomyong Institute.

Pridi Banomyong. (1974) *Ma vie mouvementée et mes 21 ans d'exil en Chine populaire.* Paris: Imprimerie Varap.

———. (1990) *The King of the White Elephant.* Bangkok, Thailand: Song Sayam.

Sulak Sivaraksa. (1999) *Powers That Be: Pridi Banomyong through the Rise and Fall of Thai Democracy.* Bangkok, Thailand: Committee on the Centennial Anniversary of Pridi Banomyong.

Vichitvongna Pombhejara. (1982) *Pridi Banomyong and the Making of Thailand's Modern History.* Bangkok, Thailand: Siriyod Printing.

PRINTING AND PAPERMAKING Printing and papermaking were two key Chinese inventions that created two different communications revolutions in the premodern world, one in Asia and the other in Europe, by permitting the rapid transmission of information and ideas.

The Invention of Paper

The invention of paper is attributed to a court official of the Han dynasty. In 105 CE, the eunuch Cai Lun (d. 121) presented the Han emperor with a new writing material. With the rise of the first Chinese empire (the Qin dynasty, 221–206 BCE) came a rise in the imperial bureaucracy and an increasingly urgent need for new writing materials and methods of record keeping. The earliest Chinese records (sixteenth–eleventh centuries BCE) were etched on tortoise shells and animal bones. Later, these cumbersome materials were gradually replaced with wooden tablets and strips of bamboo. Though less costly, imperial record keeping generated hundreds of pounds of records on these materials. Though the inventor of paper remains anonymous, Chinese archaeologists in 1957 dated the earliest known sample of paper found in China to 49 BCE, over 150 years before Cai Lun's presentation.

This early sample of paper shares basic features of manufacture with today's machine-made paper. Early papermakers macerated old rope ends, rags, and fishing nets in water to free the component vegetable fibers, then sifted the solution with a screen to form thin sheets of matted fibers. They could leave the wet sheets to dry on the screen or place them on another drying surface. What distinguishes paper formed this way from the papyrus of the ancient Egyptians is this process of separating and reforming vegetable fibers into a single sheet (papyrus, by comparison, is simply pithed and flattened to create a writing surface). Once dry, the fibers in paper form chemical bonds and create a strong but light writing surface.

By the fourth century, paper had replaced wood and bamboo strips as the writing material of choice, and by the sixth century, Chinese papermakers had learned how to extract vegetable fiber from the bark of the mulberry tree, one of the best sources of paper fiber. Mulberry bark is still favored by fine papermakers in China, Korea, and Japan today because of its strength and beauty.

In papermaking, the longer the length of the fibers, the stronger the paper. As a result, much of the subsequent history of papermaking in Asia has been the development of techniques that preserve fiber length. To ensure the even distribution of the paper fibers, papermakers learned to add a starch solution to the pulp to suspend the fibers.

Stamps and Rubbings

Having produced an inexpensive, light medium on which to write, the Chinese next searched for a way to mass-produce text and images, primarily for religious reasons. In the eighth century, devout Buddhists sought to spread their religion by producing thousands of copies of the Buddha's word and image. One early technique was to produce a stamp with an image carved in relief on its surface. Once inked with a combination of black soot and oil, the stamp could be pressed onto a sheet of paper, sparing the patron the cost of reproducing the image by hand. This technique was fine for relatively small images but larger and more complex images and texts were much more difficult.

Another technique frequently used by government artisans was making rubbings from stone stele. Though not as fast as stamping, rubbings could be taken from large surfaces with complex engravings. To make a rubbing, the artisan would take a moist sheet of fine paper and place it onto the surface of the text- or image-bearing stone stele or tablet. When the paper adhered to the surface of the stele, the artisan carefully pressed some of the moist paper into the crevices of the stele or tablet with a pad. Then the artisan would take another pad, this time inked with water and black soot, and pad the ink onto the surface paper. The pad would not touch the paper the artisan had pressed into the engraving. When the paper was dry, the artisan would peel the inked sheet off the stone, revealing a copy of the engraving in white on a black background. The rubbing technique is still valued for its precision and aesthetic quality, and it is used to duplicate images of fine calligraphy for Chinese art collectors.

By the eighth century, all the prerequisites for printing were in place. With stamps and rubbings, artisans knew how to take prints from both relief and engraved images. Stamps could replicate small images quickly, and rubbings could reproduce large, detailed images, albeit slowly. Neither method could satisfy the increasing demand in Chinese society for more books. Buddhists, Taoists, and Confucians all sought to produce more copies of their canonical texts for a increasingly literate public. Sometime in the eighth century, an artisan thought of combining the advantages of stamps and rubbings by making woodblock prints.

Woodblock Printing

Xylography, or woodblock printing, is both a simple and sophisticated technique for printing, unrivaled until the advent of machine printing presses in the nineteenth century. Three skilled artisans are needed to prepare a page of text for xylographic printing. First, a calligrapher writes the text to be printed on a thin sheet of paper, using black ink. Next, a woodcarver takes the sheet of paper and turns it over, pasting the face of the sheet onto a foot-long block of fruit wood. Once the sheet has dried onto the block, the carver can see the characters in reverse through the back of the paper. The carver then carefully cuts into the wood and removes white background, leaving the characters in relief. Once the remaining paper is rubbed off, the block is ready for printing. A printmaker inks the block with an ink pad, inking only the raised characters, then lays a thin sheet of paper on top. The printmaker presses the sheet of paper onto the characters to take an impression. A skilled printmaker can make two or three impressions a minute this way. This technique was used to make the world's earliest extant printed book, the Buddhist Diamond Sutra, which is dated 868 CE.

The printing press was not invented in China because the xylographic process has no use for it. The critical technical requirement for Chinese printing is strong, thin paper, already perfected with the development of strong mulberry papers in the sixth century. By the twelfth century, Europeans learned to make paper from the Arabs, who had captured some Chinese papermakers in a battle at Samarqand five centuries earlier. European papers however, are much thicker, especially papers made from macerated cotton rags. European printmakers needed a great deal more pressure to take a relief impression with these thick papers and required massive presses. Another important difference between European and Chinese printmaking is the composition of the printing surface. In Asia, a single woodblock was the preferred medium because the aesthetics and complexity of Chinese characters can be easily captured by a skilled calligrapher. Some Chinese printers experimented with movable type—tiny relief blocks of each character—but the capital investment required to produce and maintain the thousands of tiny blocks of type needed for Chinese printing was greater than the cost of a few skilled calligraphers and woodblock engravers who could set up shop anywhere and begin producing printed books on demand.

The World's First Print Culture

The nature of the communications revolution brought on by the development of inexpensive book production is still debated. In China, wide access to a large number of texts whose cost was less than one tenth that of books a few centuries earlier reinforced the education and examination system as a vehicle for recruiting talent from a much wider portion of the population than had been previously possible. This correlation between printing and the examination system is supported by the fact that those areas in China that produced 84 percent of the successful examination candidates also produced 90 percent of China's printed books.

While there was a dramatic reduction in the cost of books in China, there was also an explosion of printing for profit. By the eleventh century, xylographic printing was already a mature technology, and had created the world's first print culture in China. New literary genres emerged, such as storybooks, aimed at a popular as well as an elite audience. Popular *shanshu*, or "morality books," were also aimed at the newly created mass audience. The sheer volume and variety of publications for popular consumption prompted the Chinese government to censor, prohibit, or monopolize the printing of various materials, especially those works, like the dynastic histories, which could be a source of intelligence if exported. However, the fact that these prohibitions were repeatedly issued indicates that the government had very little real impact on the commercial trade. Printing technology was well established even among the seminomadic empires to the north. The Chinese government found it necessary to establish strict prohibitions on the import of books from these rival states.

The expansion of critical scholarship based on the easy circulation of the printed word is another important feature of print culture. Not only were more people reading books in the eleventh century, the social elites who were already literate were reading more books and comparing a greater diversity of ideas. While we might expect the Chinese imperial library to have a large collection, by the twelfth century government holdings were rivaled by private libraries sometimes containing more than a million volumes.

Easy access to books allowed writers and scholars to compare ideas and generate new ones with greater facility. When writing new books, Chinese writers could draw upon a wider variety of books and challenge old ideas. In his memoirs, the eleventh-century Song scholar-scientist Shen Gua, made over 250 citations to a wide variety of works that were available to him, sometimes using those works to support his conclusions, at other times challenging his sources. When he finished his memoirs in the 1080s, they were printed and sold to his peers and other aspiring members of Song society. This highlights another important aspect of print culture: Not only could people now compare and challenge older ideas, their own ideas could be easily published and disseminated, adding to the intensity of public debate and discussion. The creation of a larger and more critical reading public outside the auspices of government agencies was a key Chinese development of the eleventh century.

Paul Forage

Further Reading

Ho Peng Yoke. (1985) *Li, Qi, and Shu: An Introduction to Science and Civilization in China.* Seattle: University of Washington Press.

Temple, Robert. (1986) *The Genius of China: 3,000 Years of Science, Discovery, and Invention.* New York: Simon & Schuster.

PRIVATIZATION—CHINA China has a long and rich history of private enterprise during the time of the dynasties. By the early part of the twentieth century, however, Chinese private industry had become foreign dominated. Most firms were small, with less than five hundred employees, and produced consumer goods, such as textiles, cigarettes, and flour, owing to the exclusive concessions on manufactured and processed goods ceded to the Western powers under military coercion. In short, the lion's share of the financial benefit of Chinese private industry did not accrue to the Chinese themselves.

As for private agriculture, most peasants subsisted on tiny tracts of land (in the 1930s, 73 percent of peasants owned one hectare of land or less), and a relatively very small number of people owned large pieces of land (in the 1930s, 0.015 percent of rural residents owned 66 hectares or more), which were parceled up and leased to the landless. Here again, the Chinese experience of private ownership was not one of general prosperity.

After the Chinese Communist victory in 1949, the new rulers did not immediately forsake private ownership. Agricultural land was not organized into communes but rather redistributed (in 1950 71.74 percent of peasants owned more than one hectare). State-owned enterprises were quickly formed, accounting for 34.7 percent of gross value of industrial output (GVIO) in 1949, but private firms continued to function, accounting for 55.8 percent of GVIO in 1949. Therefore, in retrospect the outbreak of the Korean War in 1950 and the involvement of the United States and China as the two principal combatants was extremely detrimental to Chinese economic development. China had just emerged from a century of civil war and internecine conflict (prolonged by repeated interventions by the Western powers), not to mention resisting the Japanese invasion during World War II. Any lingering goodwill toward the West and tolerance of or interest in the Western economic perspective completely dissipated.

Convinced that a larger future armed conflict with the United States was imminent, private enterprises were eliminated, foreign commercial banks were expelled from the country, and agriculture was communized to produce the massive volumes of grain judged necessary to see the country through the coming struggle. The country converted completely to a Soviet-style planned economy, which made it terribly vulnerable to mismanagement at the top. Mao Zedong initiated the Great Leap Forward in 1958 to catch up to first the United Kingdom and eventually the United States in steel production, and over the ensuing few years this manic pursuit combined with unfavorable dry weather led to a plunge in grain production and disruption in grain distribution. An estimated 20 to 35 million Chinese starved to death. For this debacle, Mao was isolated within the central leadership. Mao's countermove against his rivals took the form of the Cultural Revolution, which caused economic and technological stagnation from 1966 to 1976.

The Reform Era

The death of Mao and the demise of the surviving radical leftists within the central leadership in the late 1970s finally provided an opportunity for positive change. In 1978, the least productive households of a commune in Anhui Province were given responsibility by local authorities for their own incomes in the hope that they would at least attain self-sufficiency. The dramatic gains in productivity prompted expansion of the experiment to the entire commune. To avoid accountability, the central leadership officially banned the leasing of land for private use, but in practical terms it did nothing to curb the experiment. The greater diffusion of the model to other communes progressed rapidly, spreading largely spontaneously to encompass the entire country and to nearly totally dismantle the commune system within five years.

While short of privatization, a nationwide system was established in which peasants enjoyed the right to long-term, renewable lease agreements with the state for the use of their land. Moreover, peasant families could pass land tenure rights down to their children. The liberalization of prices and crop determination progressed haltingly throughout the next two decades. Nevertheless, the foundations of the privatization of agricultural production had been laid. The reform of industry proved a much more difficult proposition.

Early Efforts to Reform
State-Owned Enterprises

Privatization in the contemporary sense of transition economics refers to the legal transfer of ownership within state-owned enterprises (SOEs) to private entities. In the Chinese context, privatization refers mainly to the partial transfer of SOE ownership to private entities and the separation of management, even while still affiliated with the state, from state agencies. It also refers to the growth "from scratch" of the sector of entirely private firms.

The latter has been slow. Openly and officially private or "individual" firms in China tend to be small in size. Their numbers reached nearly 8 million in 1993 but declined to around 6 million after 1995 due to various factors including the paucity of credit accessible to private firms and the Asian financial crisis of 1997. Within the sector of township and village enterprises (TVEs), there are an unknown number of discreetly or secretly private firms.

The crux of privatization in China lies within the sector of the SOEs, which dominate heavy industry and have long been renowned for extreme inefficiency. By the early 1990s, enterprise money losses and nonperforming bank loans were threatening the continued stable development of nearly every province. A finance-department survey conducted in Liaoning Province indicated that 70 percent of the province's firms had hidden losses, which were on average 1.4 times greater than profits. By 2001, official publicized estimates of unpaid SOE debt reached $218 billion or 27 percent of total bank lending. Most Western analysts pegged the actual figures at double these values or more. Ernst & Young estimated a total of $480 billion in unpaid SOE debts for 2001 or 44 percent of the national economy's $1.08 trillion output of that year. Not surprisingly, therefore, the Chinese central leadership started trying to reform SOEs almost from the outset of economic liberalization in 1978. At the same time, the government's long-standing political and philosophical aversion to private ownership of property affected the nature of reform efforts and arguably limited their impact.

The first four mainstream reform programs (1987–1993) were completely divorced from the factor of ownership. Instead, they focused on such issues as worker wage reform, managerial autonomy, and enterprise taxation. The naïveté of these schemes invariably resulted in questionable efficiency gains, if not

losses. For example, at the inception of the reform era the "floating wages" system made workers' total compensation variable and heavily dependent upon bonuses linked to output. But the bonus policy also fostered counterproductive tendencies, as vividly illustrated by the 1980 case of a chemical fertilizer plant that increased its output—but at the price of higher production costs and a loss of profits.

The Emergence of Shareholding Systems

With very limited access to credit from state-owned banks and encouraged by official decrees supporting peasant investment in enterprises, rural TVEs started selling shares to workers and local residents in the early 1980s. This development proved fortuitous for the state sector, mired as it was in ineffectual reform efforts. By 1986, Premier Zhao Ziyang (b. 1919) was ordering an expansion of stock capitalization, and by 1988, there were about 3,880 shareholding enterprises (SHEs) in both the rural and urban sectors. Stocks issued by most reform enterprises entitled holders to interest, dividends, a share of profits, or a combination of these. Shares could be traded within the firm, but their principal value never changed. In a modest number of cases (sixty firms in 1988), shares could be publicly traded at prices determined by the market.

The demise of Zhao in the wake of the Tiananmen insurrection (1989) resulted in a temporary contraction of the experiment he had championed, but by this point the concept had gripped the public's imagination. Between December 1990 and July 1991, stock exchanges opened in Shanghai and Shenzhen (servicing a combined total of eighty-nine firms), and the number of SHEs rapidly mushroomed to nearly 11,500 in 1993 and 50,000 in 1995.

What had in the 1980s been a more or less spontaneous movement came under official guidance in the 1990s. The issuance of publicly traded stock was limited to firms in the vicinities of Shanghai and Shenzhen. The China Securities Regulatory Commission was established in 1992 to oversee public trading, and legislation was passed in 1994 to standardize all the country's SHEs. As with the peasant land reforms, central edicts were not enforced to allow for what were essentially a variety of different experimental models for reform and privatization.

When in that same year the state initiated its fifth round of enterprise reform, it did so by corporatizing one hundred major SOEs. Most of these experimental firms became limited-liability companies (LLCs), which were still fully held by state-owned investment entities, but a few became SHEs, which were required to be no more than 35 percent state held. Due to the predominance of LLCs, which mainly granted firms a right to a greater share of profits retained after taxes (as in earlier reforms), employees concentrated on maximizing sales and income distribution, with far less regard for costs since firms were not yet made accountable for unpaid debts.

Perhaps due in part to this setback, Zhu Rongji (b. 1928), the central leadership's preeminent economic reformer and then-vice-premier (current premier), announced in 1997 that loss-making SOEs could be bought out by publicly listed firms, signaling the ascendance of the shareholding system over corporatization. This move paved the way for the Fifteenth Chinese Communist Party Congress in September 1998, during which the shareholding system was officially endorsed as the country's main strategy for SOE reform. Moreover, the Congress vowed that, while state control was to be maintained over large SOEs, small and medium firms might travel truly independent trajectories.

Between 1990 and 1999, China's SOEs and collective firms lost thirty-five jobs while her private sector gained 60 million jobs. By 2001, 35 percent of firms were private in designation, 25 percent were still state owned, and 40 percent were of a hybrid, collective nature. Encouraging initial results from privatization have motivated the central leadership to move in previously unthinkable directions. In 2001, the state contracted with a consortium led by Morgan Stanley to recover what it could of the bad loans of 254 debt-stricken firms with a face value of $1.3 billion. The state also announced that it would reduce by 10 percent its holdings in firms listed on China's stock markets, and in July 2001, on the eightieth anniversary of the Chinese Communist Party, its chairman and the country's president, Jiang Zemin, called on the Party to allow business executives and entrepreneurs to join the ranks of the party, which would presumably make it easier for private firms to compete for loans, contracts, and licenses. Bankruptcies, accounted for under law but hitherto very rare, have been allowed to take place. In 2001, 1,504 bankruptcies and mergers were officially approved. Finally, in 2002 twenty-eight cities held auctions to sell off the assets of failed SOEs.

Greater China refers to China proper along with China's special economic region, comprising Hong Kong, Taiwan, and Singapore. It is ironic that while the smaller economic "tigers" of Greater China have had recent problems stemming from the Confucian social order—strict social hierarchy and cronyism—it may be mainland China, with the shattering experi-

ences of the Cultural Revolution and the Great Leap Forward, that ultimately proves to have the social impetus to undertake profound change.

Be that as it may, reform is not without its perils. It has been estimated that in the first decade of the twenty-first century, 10 million jobs will be eliminated annually while only 7 million will be created to replace them every year. The current official urban jobless rate is 3.6 percent, but economists estimate a rate of 15 percent nationally and 25 percent in the industrial cities of the northeast. Not surprisingly, labor unrest has been on the rise over recent years. In July 1997, 4,000 silk workers in Mianyang, Sichuan, demonstrated when their plants were shut down. In August 2000, workers fearful of losing their jobs in a Tianjin foreign joint venture took three expatriate managers, including one American, hostage for several days. In March 2002, tens of thousands of workers in Daqing, Fushun, and Liaoyang in the northeast protested layoffs and unpaid unemployment benefits. In its quest for long-term change, China may have to weather short-term political instability.

Freedom for Smaller Firms

Originally, only firms with 75 percent state ownership were allowed to be listed on either of China's stock exchanges, but in seeming recognition of the growing private stake in numerous firms throughout the country, this requirement was relaxed to 51 percent. Similarly, for large SOEs (those with more than $61 million in sales and assets) in general, the state settled the aforementioned 35 percent stake, provided it was the largest shareholder. Needless to say, many investors, especially foreign ones, still found this arrangement unsatisfactory, since potential managerial interference by the state remained an issue.

As for the small firms, the sell-off has been impressive. According to the State Economic and Trade Commission, ultraconservative Liaoning Province had by November 1998 already sold 60 percent of its small and medium SOEs, while coastal and southern provinces had sold nearly all of theirs. Local officials became so frantic to sell assets that at least $12 billion in bad enterprise loans had been written off by summer 1998, prompting the central government to issue orders demanding a curtailment.

Firms have found buyers in other companies, private individuals, and foreign investors. In many areas, firms seem mostly to be going to their own managers and workers. For example, in Zhucheng, Shandong Province, all of the city's 248 SOEs were 100 percent bought out by employees. In Leshan, Sichuan

Province, about 320 of its 400 small SOEs were sold, with 80 percent of these going to employees.

In stark contrast to a few years ago when potential foreign investors found plants and equipment with asking prices far in excess of market value, recent buyers have often discovered exceptional bargains. Interestingly, foreign investors are currently tending to look elsewhere in Asia, such as Thailand and Korea, where assets are similarly cheap, past buyouts have already proved profitable, the culture is more Westernized, and the legal system more mature and therefore reliable.

Fully privatized SOEs often if not usually face the same stark problem long encountered by the millions of small private shops and restaurants throughout China, namely, limited access to investment funds from state-owned banks and credit institutions. This situation may correct itself as bank reform proceeds and truly commercial banks, including branches of foreign ones, expand to meet the growing private demand for credit.

Township and Village Enterprises

Township and village enterprises (TVEs), which are officially collective enterprises with various types and degrees of community affiliation but in actuality also include some fully private firms, had been the virtual engine of China's economic miracle. Between 1978 and 1994, the nonstate sector's share of industrial output increased from 22 to 66 percent, with TVEs and other collective-type enterprises accounting for 62 percent of this output (calculations based on values given in *China Statistical Yearbook 1995*). By 1995, TVEs enjoyed $76 billion in exports, or 50 percent of the national total (calculations based on values given in *China Statistical Yearbook 1999* and *China Agricultural Yearbook 1996*).

Since the mid 1990s, however, ever-increasing domestic competition for all market niches and a slight slackening in the growth rate of domestic household consumption have combined to dampen TVE expansion. In 1997 and 1998, for example, collective sector growth attained only 10.2 and 9.1 percent, respectively, down from 20.9 percent in 1996 and a high of 35 percent in 1993 (values from *China Statistical Yearbook 1999*). Consequently, more and more TVEs are being sold to individuals and wholly private entities

Also, TVEs in general have vigorously pursued the stock capitalization that they initiated almost two decades earlier. In 1991, the Chinese rural sector had a negligible number of stock cooperatives; two years

later, there were 1.3 million. In many if not most joint-stock TVEs, 70 to 80 percent of shares seem to be retained by the firms or local governments, while the rest of the shares are distributed or sold to employees, community residents, and other shareholding entities.

A rapid decrease in the total number of TVEs from 22 million firms engaging 128.6 million employees in 1995 to 9 million firms with 91.6 million employees in 1997 reflects a decline in business (due in part to the shrinking market for regional exports during the outset of the Asian financial crisis) as well as substantial conversion to pure private ownership (values from *China Statistical Yearbook 1999*). The number of rural unemployed reached 130 million in 1997, and the tide of peasant laborers flooding urban labor markets in search of livelihood is rising. Hence, the success or failure of rural privatization and TVE shareholding-system reform may help determine the continued political stability of the nation into the inaugural decade of the new century.

George Tseo

Further Reading

China Agricultural Yearbook 1996. (1996) Beijing: Agricultural Publishing House.

China Statistical Yearbook 1995. (1995) Compiled by the State Statistical Bureau of the People's Republic of China. Beijing: China Statistical Information and Consultancy Service and International Center for the Advancement of Science and Technology.

China Statistical Yearbook 1999. (1999) Compiled by the State Statistical Bureau of the People's Republic of China. Beijing: China Statistical Information and Consultancy Service and International Center for the Advancement of Science and Technology.

Clegg, Jenny. (1996) "China's Rural Shareholding Cooperatives as a Form of Multi-Shareholder Cooperation." *Journal of Rural Cooperation* 24, 2: 119–142.

Oi, Jean C., and Andrew G. Walder. (1999) *Property Rights and Economic Reform in China*. Stanford, CA: Stanford University Press.

Shu Y Ma. (1998) "The Chinese Route to Privatization: The Evolution of the Shareholding System Option." *Asian Survey* 38, 4: 379–397.

Tung, Ricky. (1994) "The Development of Rural Shareholding Cooperative Enterprises in Mainland China." *Issues & Studies* 30, 5: 1–30.

Walder, Andrew G. (1987) "Wage Reform and the Web of Factory Interests." *China Quarterly* 109: 22–41.

Weitzman, Martin L., and Chenggang Xu. (1994) "Chinese Township-Village Enterprises as Vaguely Defined Cooperatives." *Journal of Comparative Economics* 18: 121–145.

Wilhelm, K., and Handan. (1999) "Out of Business: Restructuring the State Sector, Part 1." *Far Eastern Economic Review* 162, 7 (18 February): 10–12.

Yatsko, Pamela. (1997) "Cracks in the Ceiling: China Struggles to Wean Workers Off Free Housing." *Far Eastern Economic Review* 160, 43 (23 October): 85–86.
———. (1998) "Chinese Fire Sale: It's Getting Cheaper for Foreigners to Buy State Firms." *Far Eastern Economic Review* 161, 21 (21 May): 15.
———. (1998) "New Owners: Privatization Comes to China's Township Enterprises." *Far Eastern Economic Review* 161, 5 (5 February): 52–53.
Zhang, Joe. (1998) "Saving China's Private Firms." *Far Eastern Economic Review* 161, 47 (19 November): 33.

PRIYAYI *Priyayi* refers to members of the Javanese aristocracy whom the Dutch employed as salaried colonial administrators in their Indonesian provinces. Following an anticolonial rebellion led by the *priyayi* from 1825 to 1830, the Dutch abandoned their antifeudal policies, intended to strip the *priyayi* of their power, and used the native elite as colonial administrators in the countryside. The relationship between Dutch colonial officials and the *priyayi* was symbiotic. On the one hand, the status-obsessed aristocrats were humiliated by their inability to prevent the Dutch conquest of Java, but on the other hand, their colonial masters gave them high status and special legal rights, including the right not to appear before native law courts, in return for their role in administering the colony.

The Dutch left daily governmental affairs in the hands of the *priyayi*, who were responsible for tax collection, policing, justice, and public works. The Dutch also tried to consolidate responsibility for local religious affairs under the *priyayi* and tended to see nationalist challenges to their control in the form of Islamic movements that attacked the official Islam controlled by the *priyayi*. The *priyayi* did not see themselves as collaborators with the Dutch or as traitors to their compatriots, but rather as defenders of the traditional order, respectful of the hierarchical Javanese culture, religion, and power structure. There were many levels of *priyayi*, from *pangreh pradja*, who served as local administrators, to the highest level, the *bupati*, appointed by the Dutch to administer an entire region.

Priyayi gained financially from their positions until the late nineteenth century, when the government began to promote large-scale economic enterprises and state-owned monopolies. As the *priyayi* lost their traditional base of support, the wealthy landowners, they had to rely more on official Dutch largesse. Attempts to professionalize the civil service were made between 1900 and 1910, when a series of reforms to train the *pangreh pradja* were implemented. These reforms included educational requirements to reduce hereditary aspects of the position. The reforms, however, were implemented slowly so as to not antagonize the *priyayi*, especially as nationalist sentiments were beginning to increase.

The Dutch were afraid of antagonizing the *priyayi* for fear that they could use their traditional status to lead or give weight to an anticolonial nationalist movement. Yet as a result of the reforms, by 1910–1915, the *priyayi* had lost nearly all of their special legal and social status and had become mere civil servants, part of a large centralized bureaucracy. Culturally conservative and insular, the *priyayi* were unable to modernize and become a force in the nationalist struggle.

Zachary Abuza

Further Reading

Steinberg, Joel, ed. (1987) *In Search of Southeast Asia*. Honolulu, HI: University of Hawaii Press.

PROTESTANT FUNDAMENTALISM— SOUTHEAST ASIA The greatest religious influences in Southeast Asia (except for the Philippines) are Buddhism, Hinduism, and Islam. Religious fundamentalism in Southeast Asia is generally associated with these three faiths, and even in the Philippines— the only Christian nation in Asia—religious fundamentalism is usually ascribed to Islamic zealots in the archipelago's southern region. However, a Protestant fundamentalist dynamism is spreading throughout Southeast Asia.

The origins of Protestant fundamentalism are rooted in Western religious movements of the nineteenth century. During that era, some Christian leaders created a theology that emphasized human potential and the use of reason to decipher every portion of the Bible. They created this theology in response to the rise of liberal theology, Darwinism, and the premium placed on science. Fundamentalists concluded that the world was on the precipice of God's wrath but that Christians would be taken out of the world (an event called the rapture) prior to a great tribulation. Three implications of this theology are a literal interpretation of the Bible, the short-term goal of gaining converts before the end of the world, and a conscious withdrawal from popular society and culture. This withdrawal from the world distinguished these fundamentalists, and by the beginning of the twentieth century, mainstream Protestant denominations distanced themselves from them. Protestant fundamentalism reached full development by the 1920s, and it has remained a religious force since that time.

Protestant Fundamentalism and Missionary Activity

Missionary activity is central to fundamentalists for two reasons. First, they teach that individuals are converted by saying a prayer in which the individuals acknowledge that they believe in Jesus Christ as their personal savior. The key, therefore, is to give all people an opportunity to choose whether they want to be saved (that is, to embrace the fundamentalists' brand of Christianity) or not. Second, fundamentalists emphasize missionary activity because they assume that these are the last days, that the great tribulation—when God's grace is removed from the earth—is imminent. Desperate times call for desperate measures, and so their missionary programs are pragmatic, with an eye on the clock.

Protestant fundamentalism's influence in pre–World War II Southeast Asia was minimal. In fact, during the first half of the twentieth century fundamentalists retreated into what Professor George Marsden, the Francis A. McAnaney professor of history at the University of Notre Dame, terms a subculture. Their social atrophy during the Great Depression was in response to the increased prejudice against the "nonrational" arguments that conservative Christians were making against antibiblical scientific conclusions. In those crisis years, it was difficult for the fundamentalists to expend resources on missionary endeavors.

Although the preponderance of Protestant fundamentalist activity in Asia took place after 1945, a few fundamentalist missionaries sought to spread their message throughout Southeast Asia prior to World War II. The work of Adoniram Judson (1788–1850) in Myanmar (at that time Burma) is a case in point. Since World War II, however, thousands of fundamentalist missionaries and indigenous pastors have established congregations, mission agencies, and Bible training centers in Southeast Asia. Whether one travels to the most remote regions of the Philippines or the northern section of Thailand, the landscape is dotted with Baptist Bible Church buildings. During the 1990s, fundamentalist churches were established in Cambodia, Vietnam, and Laos—nations that were once closed to Christian missionary activity.

Fundamentalists' intense proselytizing in Southeast Asia is attributable to historical realities. Western influence in Southeast Asia, whether superficial or entrenched, is tied to the colonial era. Western imperial powers incorporated all of Southeast Asia, except for Thailand, into their growing empires. Catholic and Protestant missionaries propagated their faith throughout the region. Although this initial Christian evangelization did not have a fundamentalist theology, it did prepare Southeast Asia for a more radical Christianity. Indeed, many independent Baptists now gather converts from the Catholic Church and from liberal Protestant denominations.

A Policy of Separatism

A major tenet of fundamentalist theology is the belief that true Christians must not become entangled in popular society and culture. In Southeast Asia this means that fundamentalists do not participate in animism-based rituals, non-Christian religious celebrations, or any social gathering that does not have conservative Christian overtones. In Thailand, Myanmar, Vietnam, Laos, and Cambodia—where Buddhism is the state religion—the implication of Christian fundamentalist separatism affects every area of social interaction. In the predominately Islamic nations of Brunei, Malaysia, and Indonesia, conservative Christians are a subculture and societal pariahs who gladly accept the persecution that is promised to all who truly follow the teachings of Jesus. Even in the Christian Philippines, a distinction is made between fundamentalists and Catholic or other Protestant citizens. The separation between these groups is based on the fundamentalists' claim that anyone who follows religious tradition rather than the Bible is not a Christian. Consequently, Filipino fundamentalists refuse to participate in celebrations such as a town's annual fiesta celebrating the town's patron saint.

Southeast Asian communities are noted for their intense kinship loyalty and the emphasis placed on communal behavior. Yet, fundamentalism stresses the primacy of individual spirituality. Some observers, then, might be astonished to see that there are thousands of fundamentalist congregations throughout Southeast Asia. What would possess individuals to make such a radical step and depart from tradition and culture? The answer to this question is multifaceted, rooted in three aspects of fundamentalist doctrine: the explanation for current suffering, the guarantee of a glorious future, and the personal aspect of this conservative community.

As an anti-intellectual movement, fundamentalism in Southeast Asia does not attract the professional elite. Demographically, the economic lower class fills the conservative Christian congregations. A dominant theme in the preaching to these believers, then, is that their poverty and persecution in this life are due to the wickedness of this world and the rule of the devil. The focus of the fundamentalist message is on the brevity of this life and the imminent return of Christ, so adherents are encouraged to hold on for just a while; soon their suffering will be turned to joy.

Fundamentalist Motivation

Another motivation for conversion is the biblical promise that in the end, the last will be first and the first will be last. Fundamentalists proudly hold to the literal translation of the Bible; therefore, they promise that all believers will receive a mansion and walk on streets of gold when they get to heaven. It takes only a prayer to secure eternal riches. Pastors and missionaries tell their followers that although every true believer must wear the badge of an antisocial religious fanatic, this brief humiliation will result in eternal rewards.

Finally, in a region where monks, priests, nuns, and imams must minister to millions of people, religious relations can feel impersonal. Many Southeast Asians claim that their spiritual needs are not met because of the volume of people that their spiritual leaders must minister to. Fundamentalists, on the other hand, emphasize the duty of pastors to visit all their church members and to create a community in which accountability, emotional and financial support, and a close-knit subculture are nurtured. So long as poverty and alienation from mainstream religious traditions remain the experience of many Southeast Asians, the Protestant fundamentalist denominations will continue to win converts.

L. Shelton Woods

Further Reading

Anderson, Gerald H., ed. (1969) *Studies in Philippine Church History*. Ithaca, NY: Cornell University Press.

Caplan, Lionel. (1987) *Class and Culture in Urban India: Fundamentalism in a Christian Community*. New York: Clarendon Press.

Chopra, V. D., ed. (1994) *Religious Fundamentalism in Asia*. New Delhi: Gyan Publishing House.

Clymer, Kenton J. (1986) *Protestant Missionaries in the Philippines, 1898–1916: An Inquiry into the American Colonial Mentality*. Chicago: University of Illinois Press.

Cooley, Frank L. (1982) *The Growing Seed: The Christian Church in Indonesia*. New York: Division of Overseas Ministries.

Frank, Douglas W. (1986) *Less Than Conquerors: How Evangelicals Entered the Twentieth Century*. Grand Rapids, MI: William B. Erdman's Publishing.

Hutchinson, William R. (1987) *Errand to the World: American Protestant Thought and Foreign Missions*. Chicago: University of Chicago Press.

Tarling, Nicholas, ed. (1992) *The Cambridge History of Southeast Asia*. 2 vols. Cambridge, U.K.: Cambridge University Press.

PUISI While the term puisi can mean any poetry in traditional Indonesian forms, such as the Malay *pantun*, the term commonly refers to modern Indonesian poetry, especially since the 1928 Youth Conference, which declared Indonesian to be the national language. Poets from the 1930s onward—most particularly after independence—intended to create a new form of poetic expression to form part of the national culture of the new state. They rejected traditional poetic forms, such as *pantun* and metrical Javanese verse forms, and adopted a much freer approach to verse structure. Traditional Indonesian, Buddhist, Hindu, Islamic, and Western literature influenced other aspects of the work of this new school of poets. Major themes in modern Indonesian poetry include Indonesia's place in the world, Indonesians' reactions to other cultures, and the place of tradition in modern culture; leading poets have often commented on politics in their works. Chairil Anwar (1922–1949) was dominant early on, while notable later poets include W. S. Rendra (b. 1936) and Sitor Situmorang (1948–1993).

Tim Byard-Jones

See also: **Rendra, W. S.**

Further Reading

Raffel, Burton. (1967) *The Development of Modern Indonesian Poetry*. Albany, NY: State University of New York Press.

PUNE (2001 pop. 2.5 million). The eighth-ranking industrial metropolis of India, Pune is located at the confluence of the Mutha and Mula rivers in the state of Maharashtra. Between the seventeenth and nineteenth centuries, Pune (or Poona) served as the capital and headquarters of the mighty Maratha empire under the Peshwas. The British defeated the Maratha Confederacy in 1818 and incorporated it within their empire. The rest of the nineteenth century witnessed a few minor uprisings in and around Pune, but the city was an important military station, and the British retained their supremacy until the transfer of power in 1947.

Pune today is a modern city, one of the fastest-growing industrial and business areas of India, with a number of well-known corporate houses. It is the cultural capital of Maharashtra state and is famed as an educational center as well. Under British rule, many colleges were established in Pune—Deccan College, the College of Engineering, and Ferguson College. Today there is a university and a number of educational institutions. The Film and Television Institute

ENJOYING THE PUNE SEASON

"It was not till June that it was really fashionable to be in Poona. . . . This was the Poona Season. Everyone in Bombay who was anyone came up to Poona for week-ends during the Season, or, in the case of wealthy merchants, rented bungalows for the Season and installed their wives there to avoid the tiresome climate of Bombay during the monsoon. . . . The correspondents of Bombay newspapers kept their reader informed about the trend of fashion in the ballroom or on the croquet-lawn. New-comers to the Poona Season were warned not to "do too much", and above all not to eat too many mangoes, which in the first half of the June are most luscious and enticing. Too many mangoes gave one diarrhea, or a it was carefully called "Poonaitis". . . . While the ladies drove to the Gymkhana soon after tea, the gentleman drove there straight from office so as to be able to put in a full hour or two hours at tennis or croquet. Many of the ladies played croquet too, but others preferred to sit on basket chairs in the veranda and sew. . . . They would visit the Club Library, but would be unlikely to find any books there. . . . No one under the rank of a Collector's wife had a hope of securing one except by luck. So they would content themselves with gossip about the last ball at Government House, the delinquencies of their servants and the health of their children. And indeed what else should they talk about? There were no theatres or cinemas and only an occasional concert. . . Their children rolled and crawled and played on the lawn that was of almost English thickness and was bordered by the banks of many-coloured cannas for which Poona was justly famous and by the blue-grey shrubs of sensitive plants. . . . There were a few English and Eurasian nurses and these kept rigidly to themselves sewing like their mistresses and nodding together over the events at the Sergeants' Dance on Saturday night—those dances at [which] the girl's reputation was gone if she were not returned to her parents by her partner as soon as each dance was over."

Source: Charles Kincaid. (1938) *British Social Life in India (1608–1937)*. London: Routledge.

of India, which offers training in all branches of the film industry, is located in Pune. The headquarters of the Southern Command of the Indian Army and an air base of the Indian Air Force are also located here.

Sanjukta Das Gupta

Further Reading
Davies, Philip. (1989) "Pune (Poona)." In *The Penguin Guide to the Monuments of India*, edited by Philip Davies. Vol. 2. New York: Viking, 492–496.

PUNJAB Literally the land of the "five rivers" from the Persian words *panj* (five) and *ab* (water), the name "Panjab" (Punjab in English) identifies a large alluvial plain in the northwestern part of the Indian subcontinent, defined by the basin of the Indus River. All the five rivers of its name—the Beas, Chinab, Jhelum, Rawi, and Satlej—are tributaries of the Indus. Historically, the region of Punjab overran its geographic borders including, before the Partition of 1947, areas such as the district of Dera Ghazi Khan, portions of the Sirhind, and the Sind-Sagar Doab.

Most of the region is characterized by a flat plain sloping gradually from northeast toward the southwest, following the direction of the rivers. Due to its subtropical inland position, its climate is continental and semiarid, with marked variations of temperature between winter and the hot season.

At present divided between the rival states of Pakistan and India, this fertile region (once called the "granary of the Raj") has always been of crucial importance in the history of the Indian subcontinent because of its richness and its location and because Punjab has been the cradle of several civilizations.

From Ancient Periods to the Creation of the Mughal Empire

During the third millennium BCE, the Indus Valley became the cradle of an advanced urban civilization, generally called the Indus civilization or Harappan empire, from the name of an ancient city in Punjab, largely excavated since 1920, together with its "twin city" of Mohenjo Daro in Sind. From about 2500 to 1600 BCE, this civilization built up a large empire stretching from Punjab and Sind to Baluchistan and Rajasthan, having strong commercial ties with both East and West. Recent archaeological and historical research has largely undermined the old theory that held that the Harappa and Mohenjo Daro civilization was brought to an end by Aryan invasions (c. 1700–1500 BCE). More probably, natural catastrophes and changes in the course of the Indus were the major reasons for its decline. However, the Aryan peoples effectively settled in the region around the midway point of the first millennium BCE, imposing their own civilization on the area.

In historic times (c. 518 BCE), Punjab became part of the Achaemenid empire (559–330 BCE), when the Persian Emperor Darius I conquered the region of Gandhara, whose capital was Taxila, near Islamabad, the present capital of Pakistan. In 326, Alexander of Macedon (356–323 BCE) marched through Punjab in his attempt to conquer India, when the mutiny of his troops obliged him to withdraw. King Candragupta I (d. 297 BCE), the founder of the Maurya dynasty, soon afterward incorporated the Punjab into his empire. After some centuries the region became part of the territories under the control of the Gupta dynasty (320–c. 550 CE).

In 713 CE, the Arab commander Muhammad ibn Qasim captured Sind and the rich city of Multan, the main urban center of southwest Punjab, while east Punjab remained subjected to Hindu kingdoms. Only at the beginning of the eleventh century was the region completely subjected to Muslim power, represented by the Turk dynasty of the Ghaznavids (977–1186), who moved from the Afghan region. In 1186 CE, Muhammad Ghuri (d. 1206) conquered Punjab, which became on his death a province of the sultanate of Delhi until the rising of Mughal power during the sixteenth century.

From the Mughals to the British Empire

In 1526, the Afghan dynasty of the Lodis was defeated at Panipat by Zahir-ud-din Muhammad (Babur, 1483–1530), a commander of Turkish-Mongol origins, and the founder of the great Mughal dynasty (1526–1858). Within a few years, Babur was able to create a large empire over the northern territories of the Indian subcontinent, Punjab included. During the reign of Akbar the Great (1542–1605), the territories of Punjab were divided among the *suba*s (provinces) of Delhi, Multan, and Lahore, considered the prominent city of the region. Under Mughal power, the region enjoyed a long period of economic prosperity, artistic and architectural enrichment, and political stability.

However, during the first half of the eighteenth century, the declining Mughal power was unable to defend northwest India from the raids and attacks coming from Afghanistan. In 1747, Lahore itself fell under control of Ahmad Shah Durrani (1722–1773), the first emir of Afghanistan. His ephemeral empire over Punjab was challenged by the growing power of the Sikhs, a militant religious sect. Although disastrously defeated by Ahmad Shah in 1762, the Sikhs rapidly recovered their military force, challenging the power of both the Hindu confederation of the Marathas in north central India and the Afghans to the west.

When the former were crushed by the rising British power and the latter weakened by their intertribal feuds, the Sikhs emerged as the main political and military power in Punjab, especially under Ranjit Singh (1781–1839), the so-called Lion of Punjab. His army of 100,000 men—called *khalsa* (the army of the pure)—represented a powerful challenge even for the British, who entered into treaty relations with Singh in 1809. After his death, however, internal rivalries among the numerous heirs and antagonists for the throne shattered Sikh unity and worsened relations with the British. Two bloody wars broke out in 1845–1846 and in 1848–1849; British victories over the Sikhs led to their annexation of Punjab in 1849.

Under British rule, Punjab rapidly became the main recruitment center for the India Army. The British supported the expansion of irrigated agriculture as a means of social and political stability, since this policy favored landlords and rural traditional authorities. With the gradual introduction of some sort of representation through assemblies and councils (for example, the Provincial Assembly created in 1937), the British colonial administration left the urban, more politicized communities almost deprived of power and political representation, allocating to the rural elite an exaggerated level of political visibility.

Until World War II, the main political party was therefore the Unionist Party, strongly linked with Muslim and Hindu landowners. With the outbreak of the conflict and the signals of an end to British rule over India, however, the Muslim League of Mohammed Ali Jinnah (1876–1948)—who championed the idea of a separate state, named Pakistan, for the Muslims of the Indian subcontinent—became the main party. Similarly to the rest of the country, the end of the British period saw the outbreak of ethnic and religious violence among the different local communities of Muslims, Hindus, and Sikhs—the latter suffered (in percentage terms) the highest casualties.

On 15 August 1947, the Partition of the Indian subcontinent created two states: India and Pakistan. Punjab was divided between them.

The Contemporary Period

According to the so-called 3 June plan for the partition of the Indian territories, Punjab was divided between Pakistan and India, with a boundary line that crossed the region between the cities of Amritsar (in India) and Lahore (in Pakistan). Dominant cultural-religious communities present at that time in Punjab were the Muslims and the Hindus; there was a small Christian Punjabi community, too. But the real peculiarity of the region was the presence of the Sikhs, a syncretistic sect founded at the beginning of the sixteenth century. During the eighteenth century they became a military power, conquering Kashmir and Punjab. Defeated by the British (1845–1849), the Sikhs remained an important minority, separated by both the Muslims and the Hindus. The only possibility for them was to migrate from the territories given to Pakistan toward the new Indian state of Punjab (in 1981 they represented more than 60 percent of the total population).

In Pakistan, Punjab represents the second-largest province (about 205,000 square kilometers), but it is the most densely populated, with more than 50 percent of the total population and also the more industrialized, though agriculture is still the first source of income. At present, the population is almost completely Muslim. The Punjabi are the political, administrative, and military elite of the country, a predominance that has negatively affected their relations with the other Pakistani ethnic groups (Sindhi, Baluchi, Pashtun/Pathans, Bengali until 1971) during these decades.

Inside the Indian Union, the region of Punjab (about 100,000 square kilometers) has seen several administrative reorganizations, which have attempted to divide it according to cultural and linguistic differences. Besides the state of Punjab (where the majority of the Sikhs are settled), the states of Haryana (Hindi-speaking) and mountainous Himachal Pradesh have been created within the region.

Riccardo Redaelli

See also: **Sikhism; Sind; Sindhi**

Further Reading

Ali, Imran. (1988) *The Punjab under Imperialism 1885–1947.* Princeton, NJ: Princeton University Press.

Fox, Richard Gabriel. (1985) *Lions of the Punjab: Culture in the Making.* Berkeley and Los Angeles: University of California Press.

Gilmartin, David. (1989) *Empire and Islam: Punjab and the Making of Pakistan.* Berkeley and Los Angeles: University of California Press.

Kapur, Rajiv. (1986) *Sikh Separatism: The Politics of Faith.* London: Allen & Unwin.

Spear, Percival. (1961) *India: A Modern History.* Ann Arbor, MI: University of Michigan Press.

Talbot, Ian. (1988) *Punjab and the Raj, 1849–1947.* New Delhi: Manohar.

Wolpert, Stanley. (1977) *A New History of India.* Oxford: Oxford University Press

PUNJABI. See **Panjabi.**

PUPPETRY, WATER Vietnamese water puppets, in Vietnamese *mua roi nuoc* (puppets that dance on water), have a long and unique history. The earliest reference to the water puppets is on a stele commemorating King Ly Nan Thong found in Nam Ha province (1121 CE). Both north and central Vietnam were centers for water puppetry, in villages as well as in the courts. The art of water puppetry reached its apex in the eighteenth century. Troupes were composed of families who passed down special techniques from father to son, and most troupes had strong clan alliances. Until recently, women were not taught the manipulation of the puppets.

The puppet shows are performed by a group of puppeteers who stand waist high in water behind a bamboo screen. The water is the stage floor. The puppets range in height from 60 to 90 centimeters and are attached to floats on long bamboo poles from 3.6 to 4.6 meters in length manipulated by the puppeteers. The floats have rudders to change direction and long lines used to activate the puppets' bodies. Several people may manipulate one puppet.

The puppets are made of polychromatic fig wood, which is lightweight and easily carved. The theater consists of the manipulation area in which the puppeteers operate; the stage, or water surface on which the dramas unfold; and the seating for the audience. The stage setting is a traditional Vietnamese house with a red curved roof. Ripples, waves, tidal waves, and reflections on the water are incorporated into the dramas. The puppets may also dive in and out of the water and, in the case of dragons, often spout smoke and breath fire.

Musical accompaniment traditionally consisted of drums, cymbals, and gongs, with the drumbeats augmenting the mood of the drama. Modern troupes include stringed instruments, flutes, and bowed instruments. Singers behind the bamboo stage curtain produce the voices of the puppets. The performances include traditional folktales, historical drama, supernatural stories, and amusing genre scenes of daily life. A comic character, Chu Teu, announces the program and opens the performance. The folk scenes include water-buffalo fights and peasants fishing, in which the fish is often the victor. Water-puppet theater went into a decline until the mid-twentieth century, when government funding revived it. Currently the Hoan Kiem lake is the main center for Hanoi's water puppets, and several troupes tour internationally, including the renowned Thang Long troupe.

Noelle O'Connor

Further Reading
Taylor, David. "Vietnamese Water Puppets." Retrieved 4 March 2002, from: http:sagecraft.com/puppetry/traditions/Vietnamese.html.

PURI (2001 pop. 1.3 million). One of the four holiest cities in India, Puri lies on the east coast of the state of Orissa and is the abode of the Hindu God Jagannath, the Lord of the Universe. Puri is also known as Sri Purusottama Dham or Martya Vaikuntha, "the abode of Lord Vishnu on Earth," and Purusottama Kshetra, "the abode of the supreme being." This seaside town revolves around the Jagannath Temple, where Lord Jagannath is enshrined with his sister Subhadra and his brother Balabhadra.

The Jagannath Temple was built in the twelfth century by King Choda Ganga Deva (reigned 1077–1146) of the Ganga dynasty (1028–1434/1435) to commemorate the shifting of his capital from south to central Orissa. More than six thousand men are employed by the temple to perform its functions and rituals. The

Ratha Yatra, or the Chariot Festival, commemorating the journey of Lord Krishna from Gokul to Mathura, takes place every June or July. The images of Lord Jagannath and his siblings are taken out in immense chariots (or *rath*s), each supported by sixteen wheels and drawn by thousands of devotees, to the Gundicha Mandir, or Garden House. There, the images reside for a week and are brought back to the temple after ritual purification. Puri is also the administrative headquarters of the Puri district and a bustling holiday resort; its fine beach attracts a large number of tourists.

Sanjukta Das Gupta

Further Reading
Khuntia, Somanath. (1998) *Puri, Heritage of an Ancient Land.* Delhi: Bhaktivedanta Book Trust.
Michell, George. (1989) "Puri." In *The Penguin Guide to the Monuments of India.* Vol. 1. New York: Viking, 249–251.

PUSAN (2002 pop. 4.1 million). Located at the southeastern corner of the Korean Peninsula, Pusan is the second-largest city in South Korea (after Seoul) and is South Korea's major international seaport. Like Seoul, it is a "special" (partly autonomous) city.

Due to its location and its deep harbor, Pusan has long been the main port of trade between Japan and Korea and has been a focal point of Korean-Japanese tensions. Pusan was opened to Japanese merchants in 1443 when King T'aejong (1397–1450) confirmed a trade treaty with Japan. In the sixteenth century, the Japanese established a small enclave in Pusan. In 1592 and again in 1596, Admiral Hideyoshi (1537–1598) used Pusan as the embarking point for the Japanese invasion of the Korean Peninsula. In 1876, Pusan was a point of conflict between Japan and Korea when Japanese marines battled with local Korean troops.

Pusan was officially opened to foreigners as a treaty port under the Kanghwa Treaty of 1883, and by the end of the nineteenth century, Japan had begun to build a railway to link Seoul with Pusan. During the Korean War, Pusan gained fame as where American and South Korean troops held the "Pusan Perimeter," a line 80 kilometers wide and 160 kilometers deep on the southeastern tip of the Korean Peninsula against the advancing North Korean Army. Today, Pusan is a leading industrial and manufacturing center and is best known for its ironworks, railway yards, and shipping industries. For three decades it enjoyed a reputation as a boomtown, which attracted many wealthy and educated young people. The economic downturn of the late 1990s slowed but did not halt the city's growth.

Keith Leitich

Further Reading

Eckert, Carter. (1990) *Korea Old and New: A History.* Seoul: Ilchokak Publishers.

Pusan History Compilation Committee. (1993) *The History and Culture of Pusan.* Pusan, South Korea: City of Pusan.

PUTONGHUA. See **Mandarin**.

PYONGYANG (1999 pop. 3 million).

Pyongyang is the capital city of the Democratic People's Republic of Korea (North Korea). It is situated south of South P'yongan Province in an alluvial plain on the lower reaches of the Taedong River. Pyongyang consists of sixteen administrative districts. The city was completely destroyed during the Korean War (1950–1953) and has been rebuilt into a modern city with large avenues and parks and a two-line subway.

Pyongyang became the last capital of the Koguryo kingdom (37 BCE–668 CE) in 427 CE. Several tombs and monuments from this period still dot the vicinity of the city. It was the western capital of the Koryo kingdom (918–1392). Several private Western-style schools were founded in Pyongyang before the demise of the Choson dynasty (1392–1910), among them the Sungsil School (1897) and the Sungui Girls' School (1903).

The city features many monuments, such as the Grand Monument on Mansu Hill and the Tower of the Juche Idea. Among its historical sites are the Eastern and Western Gates of the old walled city, the Ryongwang Pavilion, and the Sungnyong (1429) and Sungin (1325) temples. Major educational establishments include Kim Il-Sung University, the People's Palace of Culture, and the Grand People's Study House. The city is also an important center for the textile, food, chemical, and heavy equipment industries.

Adriane Perrin

QADIRIYA Qadiriya refers to a Sufi *tariqa* (mystic way or order) named after 'Abd al-Qadir ibn Abi Salih Jangidost al-Jilani (1077–1166), born in the province of Jilan in Persia, a stronghold of Hanbalism (the Sunni school of law attributed to Ahmad ibn Hanbal [d. 855] and known for its conservative orientation) in the eleventh century. At first 'Abd al-Qadir's education in Baghdad, where he arrived in 1095, was fairly conventional; he was trained to be a lawyer *(faqih)* in the Hanbali school and appears to have showed no inclination for mysticism. 'Abd al-Qadir then received training from the Sufi master Abu 'l-Khayr Hammad al-Dabbas (d. 1131), as a consequence of which he adopted an austere lifestyle, practiced night vigils, and is said to have wandered off in the deserts of Iraq without provisions.

Yet in his lifetime 'Abd al-Qadir achieved renown not as a Sufi master but rather as a gifted Hanbali preacher. Although he became the principal of a Hanbali *madrasah* (religious school) and its attached *ribat* (Sufi hospice) in Baghdad around 1133, he seems not to have developed a Sufi following, as no Sufi appears to have claimed to be 'Abd al-Qadir's follower.

After his death, however, in 1166, his *khirqa* (the mystic's patched cloak) was, according to one biographer, bestowed on someone, which signified the official transfer of his authority. The Qadiriya order then began to spread, due to the efforts of two of his sons, 'Abd al-Razzaq (d. 1206) and Abd al-'Aziz (d. 1205), who promoted their father's *tariqa* or way. Little evidence, however, suggests that 'Abd al-Qadir himself had bequeathed a complete system of Sufi thought and practice or that the Qadiri *tariqa* had become widespread before the fifteenth century. In Baghdad, 'Abd al-Qadir's mausoleum became the site of a local Qadiri order; there were other Qadiri centers in Iraq and Syria by the beginning of the fourteenth century.

Through time, a system of beliefs and practices identifiable as that of the Qadiriya emerged; the first Qadiri *zawiya* (conventicle) in Damascus was established in the early fifteenth century. 'Abd al-Qadir's fame as a mystic grew in this period, although the *tariqa* itself never became as popular the Naqshbandiyya and the Suhrawardiyya Sufi orders in general. The spread of the Qadiriya was limited in India, Egypt, and the Hejaz (western Saudi Arabia). In the first half of the seventeenth century, the Qadiri order was introduced into Istanbul by Isma'il Rumi (d. 1631 or 1643), who founded a *khanaqah* (Sufi center) there and established over forty Sufi lodges *(tekke*s). In North Africa, the form of Qadiriya known as Jilaliyya is centered on cultic reverence for the *tariqa's* founder.

Asma Afsaruddin

Further Reading
Knysh, Alexander D. (2000) *Islamic Mysticism: A Short History*. Leiden, Netherlands: Brill.
Margoliouth, D. S. (1960–) "Kadiriyya." *The Encyclopaedia of Islam*, edited by H. A. R. Gibb et al. New ed. Leiden, Netherlands: Brill, 4:380–383.
Trimingham, J. Spencer. (1971) *The Sufi Orders in Islam*. Oxford: Clarendon Press.

QAJAR DYNASTY The Qajar dynasty in Persia (present-day Iran) spanned 130 years, beginning with Agha Mohammad Qajar in 1795 and ending with Ahmad Shah in 1925. It was a period in Persian history that saw substantial British and Russian regional influences that eventually created a backlash over time in the form of the Constitutional Revolution.

The Qajar Dynasty Comes to Power

Before the establishment of the Qajar dynasty, Persia was in a state of chaos following the demise of the Safavid empire (1501–1722/1736) as power struggles intensified among several tribes (Qajars, Zands, Afshers, and others). In 1794, Agha Mohammad Qajar (1742–1797) was able to eventually defeat the last Zand ruler and proclaim himself shah (king) of the country. However, his reign did not last long, as he was murdered just a year later during a second trip to Georgia. He was succeeded by his nephew Fath Ali Shah.

Fath Ali Shah ruled for thirty-seven years and was able to bring certain measures of stability to the country. Nonetheless, this was the era when Britain and Russia began to encroach on the regional political scene. Persia lost two wars to Russia, resulting in two treaties (the Treaty of Gulistan in 1812 and the Treaty of Turkmanchai in 1828) that relinquished substantial territory in the Caucausus to Russia. Furthermore, Britain kept Persia from exercising its authority in Afghanistan. Finally, both Russia and Britain were able to obtain favorable trading agreements. In fact, their influence was so great that they were able to name Fath's successor in 1834. Fath's grandson Mohammad Ali took the reins and governed for fourteen years until he died in 1848. As his grandfather had done, he emphasized the supremacy of the monarch's respect for the divine Islamic order and continued the consolidation of power.

Consequences of European Influence

Naser al-Din Shah succeeded Mohammad Ali in 1848 and reigned for forty-eight years. He faced growing European influence, which was difficult to combat due to the weakness of the Persian government. Government revenues were so low that they could not cover the lavish expenditures of the royal court, a situation that led the ruling class to accept bribes from outside power sources in exchange for favors that were contrary to national interests. The prime minister, Mirza Taqi Khan Amir Kabir, tried to correct this situation by taking measures to centralize power. He also created new offices, reformed the tax system, and established a chain of command within the bureaucracy and provinces. Unfortunately, his efforts were halted due to jealousy and fear of his growing popularity and power. He was fired and ultimately assassinated in 1851.

Closer association with European powers also had another impact. It led to the emergence of reformists

Ahmad Shah, the last ruler of the Qajar dynasty, in c. 1909. (HULTON-DEUTSCH COLLECTION/CORBIS)

such as Malkam Khan, who advocated that Persia could be strengthened politically and economically if it emulated and mastered the European methods. This line of thinking led to the creation of a cabinet modeled after those found in Europe.

Meanwhile, financial difficulties compelled Naser al-Din Shah to give lucrative concessions to both Britain and Russia. In 1890, the monarch gave Britain a monopoly on the tobacco trade in the country, and this turned out to be the straw that broke the camel's back. Upset with the constant submission to outside interests, the entire nation boycotted tobacco, which forced the shah to revoke the monopoly concession. However, this was not enough to appease the people, who continued to oppose the monarch's policies. Finally, he was assassinated in 1896 at the alleged urging of the well-known Islamic leader Jama al-Din al-

Afghani. Soon, Naser al-Din Shah's son Muzaffar al-Din was proclaimed king.

The Constitution of 1906

Muzaffar al-Din Shah was often physically ill and was politically unable to reverse the tide of political and economic turmoil that had begun during his father's reign. On the contrary, he exacerbated the situation by his extravagant expenditures. He received two major loans from Russia, which he promptly spent on luxury items, including a trip to Europe. Meanwhile, masses of Persians were suffering from inflation and mounting poverty. This caused the populace to question, criticize, and finally revolt against the monarchy. Strikes took place all over, and religious services were withheld in protest. The monarch was unable to receive assistance from Russia, which was dealing with its own internal strife. Therefore, he had no choice but to promise the people a constitution. Soon they formed an assembly, composed of Qajar princes, merchants, religious leaders, artists, and landowners, to write a constitution, which was completed in the fall of 1906. Muzaffar al-Din Shah signed it on 30 December and died just days later. This constitution limited the powers of the royal family and supplanted it with the Majlis (Parliament) and a cabinet whose members had to be approved by the Majlis.

This constitution, however, faced challenges before it became a reality. After Muzaffar al-Din Shah's death, his successor, Mohammad Ali Shah, was able to garner Russian support and close down the Majlis. This started a prolonged struggle between the monarch and supporters of the constitution. Eventually, the supporters of the constitution were able to raise armies to march on Tehran and overthrow the new king, who was exiled to Russia. His eleven-year-old son, Ahmad Shah, was chosen as the shah, and the Majlis was repaired of the damages incurred in the military struggle. The country was in a vulnerable position, which the deposed king tried unsuccessfully to exploit in 1911.

The new constitutional system did not survive. Under the 1907 Anglo-Russian Agreement, Britain and Russia split the country into spheres of influence: Russia took the northern part of Persia, while Britain took the south and east. Faced with financial ruin, the Majlis had hired Morgan Shuster, an American administrator, to help put their finances in order. Both the Persian elite and the Russians criticized his hiring. The latter did not appreciate tax collectors approaching them in their sphere of influence. In fact, Russia demanded Shuster be fired. When the Majlis refused, Russian troops shut it down and with this action destroyed any hope for a constitutionally based system.

World War I and Its Aftermath

Ahmad Shah was powerless against the British and Russian influence. In 1914, World War I started, and the Qajar monarch had no choice but to remain neutral. This, however, was not enough to keep Persia secure. British, Ottoman, and Russian armies fought on Persian soil and brought death and destruction to innocent Persian civilians; the war also gave the local population the opportunity to rise up against the Qajar monarch. At the end of World War I, Russia had its own revolution to contend with and was unable to maintain its influence in Persia. This provided the British with an opportunity to bring an order in their own favor. They supported Reza Khan (Reza Shah Pahlavi, 1878–1944) in a coup against Ahmad Shah. Reza Khan became the defense minister first, then prime minister, and ultimately the first shah of the Pahlavi dynasty, which formally ended Qajar rule.

Houman A. Sadri

Further Reading

Amanat, Abbas. (1997) *Pivot of the Universe: Nasir al-Din Shah Qajar and the Iranian Monarchy, 1831–1896*. Berkeley and Los Angeles: University of California Press.
Bosworth, Clifford Edmond, and Carole Hillenbrand, eds. (1983) *Qajar Iran, 1800–1925: Political, Social, and Cultural Change*. Edinburgh, U.K.: Edinburgh University Press.
Cleveland, William L. (1994) *A History of the Modern Middle East*. Boulder, CO: Westview Press.
Wright, Denis. (1977) *The English amongst the Persians during the Qajar Period 1787–1921*. London: Heinemann.

QI BAISHI (1864–1957), Chinese painter. Qi Baishi (original name Qi Huang; numerous art names), the most famous painter of China's Republican period (1912–1949), developed an expressive style of brushwork that captured the essential qualities of a wide range of subjects. Born in Hunan Province to a peasant family, Qi Baishi continually sought self-betterment in a class-conscious society. Despite having little education, he rose from lowly carpenter's apprentice to acceptance by the elite. He learned the art of woodcarving and improved his designs by studying the famous *Mustard Seed Garden Painting Manual*. He then began artisan painting. Various scholars recognized his talents and taught him, successively, the traditional *gongbi* (meticulous) style of brushwork for portraiture, flowers and birds, and landscape. He also learned seal carving, calligraphy, and poetry, skills that granted him entry to the literati class and for which he later became famous.

In 1902 Qi Baishi began traveling outside Hunan and in 1917, fleeing civil disorder at home, he made

Beijing his residence. There he mastered the literati mode of *xieyi* (expressive) brushwork and developed a personal style. His closely observed, ordinary subjects were limned in vigorous lines and bright hues, the latter an innovation in literati painting. After 1949 the Chinese government granted him numerous honorary titles, including First Peoples Artist and chairman of the Chinese Artists' Association.

Iris Wachs

Further Reading

Hejzlar, Josef. (1980) *Chinese Watercolors*. Trans. by Till Gottheinerova. London: Octopus Books.
Tsao, Jung Ying. (1993) *The Paintings of Xugu and Qi Baishi*. San Francisco: Far East Fine Arts.

QIBILAI QAN. See **Khubilai Khan.**

QIGONG *Qigong* refers to Chinese mental and physical exercises that cultivate *qi (ch'i)*. Daoist in origin and often associated with healing, longevity, and enlightenment, these practices increase suppleness, develop relaxation, and improve circulation while expanding awareness of body, mind, and environment. A *qigong* exercise involves controlled breathing, relaxation, and calm and careful focus of attention.

Qigong is a combination of two Chinese characters. The second, the "gong," refers to work or merit. The "qi," however, is more difficult. *Qi* is understood to be ever changing and ever flowing, a force at work in nature and society as well as in the human body. Tangible expressions of *qi* in the body include respiration, circulation of the blood, and sexual energy. Less obvious manifestations include the circulation of *qi* itself along channels independent of the circulatory and nervous systems, called meridians.

While the exercises known today as *qigong* are ancient, traceable at least to texts found in Han period tombs from 2,000 years ago, the term itself is relatively recent, not seen before the Ming period (1368–1644). Furthermore, before 1900, knowledge and dissemination of such exercises extended to a relative few, who received training through traditional lineage holders. (In educational contexts that emphasize the personal transmission of knowledge from master to disciple, a lineage holder is someone who has received transmission from a recognized master and is sanctioned by that master to impart instruction.) Only in the 1980s was *qigong* popularized to become the widespread form of exercise it is today.

Qigong is generally practiced to increase martial ability and to improve health. It can be divided between *qigong* for oneself and for others. Practiced for oneself, *qigong* can be done at rest or while moving. *Taijiquan*, a martial art and health exercise, is a dynamic *qigong* exercise done for oneself. Laying on of hands, massage, and acupuncture are forms of *qigong* practiced for others.

Qigong stands at the nexus between science and religion in modern societies. Questions about its uses, effects, and reality persist. As the number of *qigong* practitioners increases worldwide and its principles are incorporated in new contexts, it remains to be seen whether the claims for its salutary effects will be balanced by a body of evidence accepted by a wider scientific community.

Warren Frerichs

Further Reading

Kohn, Livia, ed. (1989) *Taoist Meditation and Longevity Techniques*. Ann Arbor, MI: University of Michigan, Center for Chinese Studies Publications, 61.
———. (1993) *The Taoist Experience: An Anthology*. Albany, NY: State University of New York Press.
Maspero, Henri. (1981) *Taoism and Chinese Religion*. Trans. by Frank A. Kierman Jr. Amherst, MA: University of Massachusetts Press.
Robinet, Isabelle. (1993) *Taoist Meditation: The Mao-shan Tradition of Great Purity*. Trans. by Julian F. Pas and Norman J. Girardot. Albany, NY: State University of New York Press.
Schipper, Kristofer. (1993) *The Taoist Body*. Trans. by Karen C. Duval. Berkeley and Los Angeles: University of California Press.

QIN DYNASTY Although lasting for only fifteen years, the Qin dynasty (221–206 BCE) brought centralized administration to China and introduced a model of government that Chinese emperors followed until the abdication of the emperor of China's final dynasty, the Qing, in 1912. The very name of China was probably derived from the name "Qin" (pronounced "chin"). Unfortunately, the accomplishments of the Qin rulers were achieved by harsh, ruthless, totalitarian acts that hastened the dynasty's untimely demise.

The Rise to Power of the Qin Dynasty

Living in the present-day province of Shaanxi among various nomadic tribes in the far west of ancient China, the people of the Qin dynasty had long proved to be fierce warriors. Their weapons industry was aided by a wealth of iron ore found in their region. After the collapse of the Western Zhou dynasty

(1045–771 BCE), the state of Qin emerged as one of many small states that sprang up in the absence of a strong ruling house. The Qin began to rise to prominence during the Warring States period (475–221 BCE), when Shang Yang (d. 338 BCE), a scholar and politician, set about reforming the Qin state. He moved the Qin capital to Xianyang (located near the modern city of Xian), abolished feudalism, gave land to the peasants, taxed them, and introduced a law code that favored no one class. To replace the feudal aristocracy that he had abolished, he set up a central government to administer the country. In the bureaucracy, official positions were designated according to a reward system, rather than being inherited as earlier. *Fajia* (Legalism), a philosophy that emphasized that rulers should have absolute power and that they should govern with the help of a strict law code, pervaded Shang Yang's ideas about government.

The Rise and Fall of the Qin Dynasty

Although because they had absorbed various Central Asian invaders into their state the Qin were viewed as too barbaric to pose a serious threat to the other states, from 230 to 221 BCE, the Qin successively conquered these states of the Eastern Zhou (770–221 BCE) confederacy. By 221 BCE, with a final military victory over the Zhou, the Qin had unified all the states of the feudal Zhou rule. Zheng, the Qin king (c. 259–210 BCE) proclaimed himself Shi Huangdi ("first sovereign emperor") and assumed control over the empire.

Upon his death in 210 BCE, court intrigues, primarily involving a eunuch, Zhao Gao, and an adviser, Li Si, tricked the heir apparent into committing suicide, and the title of emperor was conferred on a younger son, then known as the Second Emperor (reigned 210–207 BCE), who ended his own turbulent reign by also taking his life. Rule then passed to a young boy, known only as the child-emperor. Although the boy surrendered to the usurping Han dynasty (206 BCE–220 CE) leaders at Xianyang, he was killed and his capital destroyed, bringing the rule of the Qin to an end in 206 BCE, fifteen years after its inception.

Changes Introduced by Zheng

Once in power, Zheng initiated sweeping changes, following the philosophical tenets of Legalism as modeled by Shang Yang, to consolidate and support Qin authority. (Some aspects of Confucianism, such as the importance of filial duty and ancestor worship, were still emphasized during the Qin dynasty.) Zheng divided the land into units administered by a highly centralized bureaucracy, applied a rigorous penal code,

CHINA—HISTORICAL PERIODS

Xia dynasty (2100–1766 BCE)
Shang dynasty (1766–1045 BCE)
Zhou dynasty (1045–256 BCE)
    Western Zhou (1045–771 BCE)
    Eastern Zhou (770–221 BCE)
Spring and Autumn period (770–476 BCE)
Warring States period (475–221 BCE)
Qin dynasty (221–206 BCE)
Han dynasty (206 BCE–220 CE)
Three Kingdoms period (220–265 CE)
North and South dynasties (220–589 CE)
Sui dyansty (581–618 CE)
Tang dynasty (618–907 CE)
Five Dynasties period (907–960 CE)
Song dynasty (960–1279)
    Northern Song (960–1126)
    Southern Song (1127–1279)
Jurchen Jin dynasty (1125–1234)
Yuan dynasty (1279–1368)
Ming dynasty (1368–1644)
Qing dynasty (1644–1912)
Republican China (1912–1927)
People's Republic of China (1949–present)
Republic of China (1949–present)
Cultural Revolution (1966–1976)

and relocated the Zhou aristocratic families to the capital of Xianyang, where they could be closely watched in grand mansions built for the purpose.

Zheng also standardized weights, currency, and measures; set cart-wheel measurements, had a national system of highways and a canal system built; constructed monumental palaces; and reformed the writing system, which had gradually become more regional, by creating a new script called *xiao zhuan ti* ("small seal script") to be used throughout his empire. To form a defense against troublesome nomads from Central Asia such as the Xiongnu, vast numbers of peasant laborers were conscripted to construct a walled fortification; subsequent emperors added to this construction, which eventually become known the Great Wall.

To ensure his life after death, Zheng provided himself with a huge tomb complex; that complex has not yet been explored. In 1974, however, archaeologists did unearth a remarkable army of thousands of life-size terra-cotta figures, the army who would protect him in the next life. Each figure was represented wearing the costume and carrying the weapons that were appropriate for his branch of service, be it infantry, cavalry, or chariot driver, and each figure's face was individually modeled as if copying a real person. Armed crossbows were set within the chambers to guard against invaders.

Oppression during Zheng's Rule

The reign of Zheng lasted for eleven of the fifteen years of this dynasty, and most of the achievements, and crimes, of the Qin refer to acts perpetuated by the First Emperor. The massive undertakings credited to him were achieved in only a few years' time, at the cost of harsh, repressive laws regulating his subjects. Overworked peasants not only served as agricultural workers, but also doubled as soldiers and as builders of the immense projects undertaken by the Qin ruler. Prison sentences and maiming punishments were commonly handed out to dissenters or to those unlucky enough to gain the emperor's disapproval. Zheng reportedly executed officials who were late to their assigned tasks, even if their tardiness resulted from weather conditions that made traveling impossible. He also created enemies among the aristocrats who in the new meritocracy were no longer entitled to inherited court office.

Fearing the power of intellectual debate, in 213 BCE Zheng ordered that all texts, except for those on the subjects of divination, medicine, forestry, and agriculture, be burned, aside from a single copy of each, which was held in the imperial library (itself burned to the ground by the invading Han forces in 206 BCE). To end dissension in his court, he ordered the execution of 460 scholars (Han writers claimed he had them buried alive, but this is supported by no other extant evidence). Fearing a popular uprising because the people were well armed, having fought for centuries against neighboring states and nomadic invaders, the First Emperor confiscated weapons, melting them down to supply bronze for ritual vessels and musical bells.

Obsessed with attaining eternal life, Zheng sent thousands of youths to search for the islands of immortality, called Peng Lai, rumored to exist in the mythical Eastern Sea. Some believe that this expedition resulted in the settling of Japan by the youths, who never returned to their homeland. He claimed as one of his ancestors Huang Di ("Yellow Emperor"), the semimythic founder of the ancient Chinese people, who reputedly never died but instead rose to *tian* (heaven) in a chariot drawn by dragons.

Within his palace, the emperor employed alchemists to seek the secret to eternal life. An extensive network of tunnels connecting his palaces was constructed on the advice of one of these shamans, and the emperor was said to have moved throughout the network, sleeping in different places each evening as a further deterrent to harm; his occupancy was kept secret, with death as the punishment for anyone who revealed his whereabouts. He undertook long journeys to the mountains, where he practiced sacrificial rituals for the same purpose of gaining immortality. Traveling to Mount Tai, he staged the sacrifices known as *feng* and *shan* also in hopes of warding off death. Ironically, Zheng died when returning from one of these immortality-seeking expeditions. Not surprisingly, after he died, civil unrest led to an uprising that the ineffectual Second Emperor and subsequent Child-Emperor were helpless to abate.

Nevertheless, the Qin rulers created the nation of central authority that the Han dynasty inherited. While adjusting its boundaries according to ever-changing political and social factors, this nation has continued until today as the land and population now called China, giving its centrally unified regions the claim of being the longest-lasting nation on Earth.

Dallas L. McCurley

Further Reading

Bodde, Derk. (1938) *China's First Unifier: A Study of the Ch'in Dynasty as Seen in the Life of Li Ssu.* Leiden, Netherlands: E. J. Brill.

Kern, Martin. (2000) *The Stele Inscriptions of Ch'in Shihhuang: Text and Ritual in Early Chinese Imperial Representation.* New Haven, CT: American Oriental Society.

Li Xueqin. (1985) *Eastern Zhou and Qin Civilizations.* Trans. by Chang Kwangshih. New Haven, CT: Yale University Press.

Sima, Qian. (1994) *Shiji: The Grand Scribe's Records,* edited by William H. Nienhauser Jr.; translated by Caifa Cheng and Chan Chiuming. Bloomington, IN: Indiana University Press.

QIN TOMB The mausoleum of the "First Qin Emperor" Ying Zheng , also known as Qin Shi Huang (259–210 BCE), was built over a period of thirty-seven years with as many as 720,000 workers involved. Situated at the foot of Mount Lishan, 35 kilometers east of Xi'an, the mausoleum consists of an inner city that was 1,355 meters long and 580 meters wide and an outer city that was 2,165 meters long and 940 meters wide.

Excavation of the central tomb has not yet begun, but since 1974 archaeologists have been unearthing a subterranean army of thousands of life-size terra-cotta warriors and horses, guarding access to the main tomb. Each figure is a faithful representation of a distinctive individual. The mausoleum continues to turn up surprising discoveries as archaeologists work patiently on the site. An excavation in 2000 unearthed what probably represented the Supreme Court in the Qin dynasty (221–206 BCE), adding a civilian dimension to the burial that had been regarded as all military.

The magnificent mausoleum bespeaks the power and achievements of the First Qin Emperor, who unified China for the first time in its history, standardized weights and measurements, the monetary system, and the written language, and linked sections of the existing walls to form what is known as the Great Wall. The mausoleum came onto the UNESCO World Heritage List in 1987.

Jian-Zhong Lin

Further Reading

Cotterell, Arthur. (1989) *The First Emperor of China*. Harmondsworth, U.K.: Penguin.
Wu, Xiaocong. (2000) *Valiant Imperial Warriors 2200 Years Ago—Terra-cotta Armored Warriors and Horses of Qin Shi Huang Mausoleum*. Xi'an, China: Xi'an World Publishing Corporation.

QING DYNASTY Founded by the Manchus in 1644, the Qing was the last imperial dynasty to rule China. It built the largest consolidated empire in China's history and witnessed tremendous achievements in governmental administration, economic expansion, regional integration, and intellectual exploration. The dynasty lasted 268 years until it was overthrown by the Republican revolution of 1911; the last emperor abdicated in 1912.

Political Changes

The Manchu were descendants of the Jurchen tribes who controlled north China as the Jin dynasty (1125–1234). Unified under their leader Nurhachi (1559–1626), the Jurchen tribes were organized into large feudal and military units called banners. In 1616, using the Chinese political term *tianming* (Mandate of Heaven) as his reign title, Nurhachi established a dynasty that he called the Hou (Later) Jin. While continuing to imitate Chinese institutions, Nurhachi's successor Hongtaiji (or Abahai; 1592–1643) changed the name of his people from Jurchen to Manchu in 1635 and the dynastic name from Hou Jin to Qing the next year.

Under the new emperor Shunzhi (1638–1661, reigned 1644–1661), who was guided by his uncle, the imperial regent Dorgon (1612–1650), the Manchu entered Beijing in 1644 and crushed the rebellion that

CHINA—HISTORICAL PERIODS

Xia dynasty (2100–1766 BCE)
Shang dynasty (1766–1045 BCE)
Zhou dynasty (1045–256 BCE)
 Western Zhou (1045–771 BCE)
 Eastern Zhou (770–221 BCE)
Spring and Autumn period (770–476 BCE)
Warring States period (475–221 BCE)
Qin dynasty (221–206 BCE)
Han dynasty (206 BCE–220 CE)
Three Kingdoms period (220–265 CE)
North and South dynasties (220–589 CE)
Sui dyansty (581–618 CE)
Tang dynasty (618–907 CE)
Five Dynasties period (907–960 CE)
Song dynasty (960–1279)
 Northern Song (960–1126)
 Southern Song (1127–1279)
Jurchen Jin dynasty (1125–1234)
Yuan dynasty (1279–1368)
Ming dynasty (1368–1644)
Qing dynasty (1644–1912)
Republican China (1912–1927)
People's Republic of China (1949–present)
Republic of China (1949–present)
Cultural Revolution (1966–1976)

had already overthrown the Ming dynasty (1368–1644). During the course of their conquest, the Qing crushed the Southern Ming resistance and recruited the Chinese elite into the Manchu regime. While they tried to repress antiforeign sentiment among the Han Chinese, the Qing established an empire on the Chinese model, which included Confucianism as the state orthodoxy, governmental institutions such as the Grand Secretariat and six ministries, and the Ming taxation system. The Qing government was essentially a Manchu-Chinese dyarchy, in which offices were held by equal numbers of Manchu and Chinese who worked side by side.

During the reigns of emperors Kangxi (1654–1722, reigned 1662–1722), Yongzheng (1678–1735, reigned 1723–1735), and Qianlong (1711–1799, reigned 1735–1795), the Qing reached its apogee of power and prosperity and established the most extensive empire of the world. In addition to China proper, it subjugated Taiwan (1683), Outer Mongolia (1690s), Tibet (1720), and Xinjiang (1759). Beyond the Chinese empire, the Qing strengthened the tributary relationship with neighboring countries, including today's Myanmar

(Burma), Annam (in present-day Vietnam), and Korea. In governing the country, these emperors worked hard to be exemplary Confucian rulers. Meanwhile, imperial authority was more and more concentrated through institutions such as the Grand Council (1729), which enabled the emperor to direct and deal with all important government matters efficiently. The minority regions were brought into the provincial administrative system, making them more closely controlled by the central government. In foreign trade, the emperor Qianlong inherited the Chinese tradition of restricting foreign contacts, and in 1760 he established the "Canton system," which confined foreign commerce to Guangdong (Canton).

After the first Opium War (1839–1842), a treaty port system was established in the coastal cities; it gave foreign imperialist powers political, economic, and legal privileges in Chinese ports. During the 1850s, the Qing also had to deal with large-scale popular uprisings, including the Nian Rebellion (1853–1868) in the east, the Muslim rebellion (1855–1873) in Yunnan, and the Taiping rebellion (1851–1864) across the empire. Although these rebellions did not destroy the Qing dynasty, they led to the shift of power from the Manchu central government to members of the provincial Chinese elite, such as Zeng Guofan (1811–1872), who rallied their own regional armies to defeat the peasant rebels.

In order to revive the dynasty, the Qing instituted a series of modernization programs, the *yangwu yundong* ("self-strengthening movement"), during the reigns of Tongzhi (1856–1875, reigned 1862–1874) and Guangxu (1871–1908, reigned 1875–1908), who were both directed by Tongzhi's mother, Ci Xi (1835–1898), behind a silk screen at court. Under the principle of *zhongxue weiti, xixue weiyong* (Chinese learning as the essence and Western learning as practical use), modern industrial development, led by the high-ranking officer Li Hongzhang (1823–1901), included building arsenals, machine factories, schools, railways, shipyards, telegraph lines, postal services, and a modern army, navy, and press.

While the self-strengthening movement made some progress in modernizing the nation, it did not make the dynasty strong enough to fight off imperialist encroachments. In the Sino-French War of 1884–1885, China lost Vietnam. In 1887, China officially ceded Macao to Portugal. During the Sino-Japanese War of 1894–1895, Japan defeated China and forced it to recognize Korean independence and to cede Taiwan to Japan. Consequently foreign powers started scrambling for concessions (areas of land that were leased in perpetuity by foreign governments) in China.

Responding to the danger of partition, Chinese from various social strata launched new social movements. In 1898, during the so-called Hundred Days of Reform, a group of intellectuals persuaded Emperor Guangxu to call for changes in education, political administration, industry and commerce, and foreign relations. The reform movement, however, produced no practical results because it was opposed by the powerful and conservative Empress Dowager Ci Xi.

Meanwhile, the foreign advances in north China aroused a furious antiforeign uprising, the Boxer Rebellion (1900). In the late 1890s, a secret society called the Boxers United in Righteousness directed its wrath against Christian converts and foreign establishments such as churches, railways, and mines, which the society blamed for the miserable changes in people's lives. In 1900, when the Qing court began to support them, the Boxers attacked the foreign legations in Beijing. This popular movement was put down by a military alliance of eight countries, which forced the Qing to pay a huge indemnity and to accept the establishment of foreign military guards in Beijing. In order to preserve its commercial interests in China, the United States announced the Open Door policy and requested that all countries agree not to deny others access to their spheres of influence. China's territorial integration was maintained due to mutual restraint among the powers.

Foreign aggressions and the Qing's failure to deal with the crises stimulated Han-Chinese nationalism. Zou Rong's *Geming jun* (The Revolutionary Army, 1903) called on the Chinese to reject the Manchu yoke and seize their own destiny. The nationalists led by Sun Yat-sen (1866–1925), a Chinese commoner who had received a Western education in Hawaii and Hong Kong, looked to political revolution to solve China's problems. Under his "Three Principles of the People"—nationalism, democracy, and people's livelihood—Sun undertook the mobilization of various groups, such as secret-society members and overseas students. In 1905, he combined his revolutionary organization with other radical groups and founded the *Tongmeng hui* (Revolutionary Alliance) in Japan, which guided the revolutionary activities in China.

During the first decade of the twentieth century, the Qing court engaged in more radical reforms in order to save the dynasty. In 1905, the age-old civil-service examination system was abolished. Thousands of Chinese students were sent to study abroad. The government was structured and legal institutions were modified along modern lines. In 1908, the court issued the *Xianfa dagang* (Outline of Constitution), which for the first time introduced constitutional monarchy to China and defined the "rights and responsibilities" of

OPENING CHINA TO THE WEST

Following the Opium War, China's ports were opened to western nations. This extract is from the 1844 Treaty of Peace, Amity, and Commerce, which opened ports to the United States.

The United States of America and the Ta Tsing Empire, desiring to establish firm, lasting, and sincere friendship between the two nations, have resolved to fix, in a manner clear and positive, by means of a treaty or general convention of peace, amity, and commerce, the rules which shall in the future be mutually observed in the intercourse of their respective countries:

For which most desirable object the President of the United States has conferred full powers on their Commissioner, Caleb Cushing, Envoy Extraordinary and Minister Plenipotentiary of the United States to China; and the August Sovereign of the Ta Tsing Empire on his Minister and Commissioner Extraordinary Tsiyeng, of the Imperial House, a Vice Guardian of the Heir Apparent, Governor General of the Two Kwangs, and Superintendent General of the Trade and foreign intercourse of the five ports.

And the said Commissioners, after having exchanged their said full powers, and duly considered the premises, having agreed to the following articles:

Article I. There shall be a perfect, permanent, and universal peace and a sincere and cordial amity, between the United States of America on the one part, and the Ta Tsing Empire on the other part, and between their people respectively, without exception of persons or places.

Article II. Citizens of the United States resorting to China for the purposes of commerce will pay the duties of import and export prescribed in the tariff, which is fixed by and made a part of this treaty. They shall, in no case, be subject to other or higher duties than are or shall be required of the people of any nation whatever. Fees and charges of every sort are wholly abolished, and officers of the revenue, who may be guilty of exaction, shall be punished according to the laws of China. If the Chinese Government desire to modify, in any respect, the said tariff, such modification shall be made only in consultation with Consuls or other functionaries thereto duly authorized in behalf of the United States, and with consent thereof. And if additional advantages or privileges, of whatever description, be conceded hereafter by China to any other nation, the United States, and the citizens thereof, shall be entitled thereupon to a complete, equal and impartial participation in the same.

Article III. The citizens of the United States are permitted to frequent the five ports of Kwang-chow, Amoy, Fuchow, Ningpo and Shanghai, and reside with their families, and trade there, and to proceed at pleasure with their vessels and merchandise to and from any foreign port and either of the said five ports to any other of them. But said vessels shall not lawfully enter the other ports of China, nor carry on a clandestine or fraudulent trade along the coasts thereof. And any vessel belonging to a citizen of the United States which violates the provision, shall, with her cargo, be subject to confiscation by the Chinese Government.

Source: Treaties and Conventions Concluded between the United States of America and Other Powers since July 4, 1776. (1899) Washington, DC: Government Printing Office.

---

the people. The Qing court also opened provincial assemblies in 1909 and a consultative national assembly in 1910. But the eleventh-hour reform efforts did not satisfy the revolutionaries. The 1911 Revolution resulted in the founding of a new government—the Republic of China. The last emperor of the Qing, Xuantong (1906–1967, reigned 1909–1912), formally abdicated on 12 February 1912. The imperial system officially came to a close in China.

Socioeconomic Changes

By creating a multiethnic empire, the Qing brought significant changes to the Chinese social landscape. In the vast Inner Asian regions of Mongolia, Xinjiang, and Tibet, a number of different peoples were incorporated into the Chinese territory, but they enjoyed considerable political and cultural autonomy. In particular, the Qing sought to preserve their ethnic identity as Manchu. Manchu were urged to retain the skills in archery and horsemanship; the Chinese practice of foot binding was prohibited among Manchu women; intermarriage between Manchu and Chinese was banned; Manchuria was maintained as a homeland base to which the Han Chinese were forbidden from migrating; the native Manchu civil-military units, the banners, were kept intact and stationed separately from the Chinese at garrisons across the empire; members of the ruling elite were encouraged to receive Manchu-style education, particularly mastery of the Manchu language; and Manchu were granted preferential political, legal, and social treatment. In addition, all Han Chinese males were forced to shave the front of their hair and wear a braid in the back, a Manchu style that signified political loyalty. Meanwhile, to build a "Confucian" empire, the Manchu conquerors, deliberately or unconsciously, undertook a systematic policy of sinicization, adopting Chinese values, institutions, cultural practices, and social customs. The Qing witnessed an intensive cultural integration of different peoples.

Despite macroregional diversity, the traditional economy thrived under the Qing. By the late eighteenth century, agricultural production was increased because of the spread of better seeds and fertilizers, enlarged land areas, improved techniques, and cultivation of new crops native to the Americas. Government tax policy facilitated agricultural development. In 1713, the emperor Kangxi froze the number of taxpaying adults, permanently exempting the increased population from taxation; Yongzhen instituted a fiscal reform in which taxes were based on land and collected in silver; this benefited poor peasant farmers. The industries that flourished included textiles, porcelain, paper, sugar, mining, and metalworking. Commercialization continued its course. Efficient transport networks and marketing mechanisms such as a banking system promoted domestic trade and developed an empirewide market. China traded with Japan, Southeast Asia, Europe, and the Americas, and foreign trade expanded rapidly in China's favor. China's explosion in population, which grew from 150 million at the beginning of the dynasty to 360 million in the early 1800s, in part reflected the prosperity of the most dynamic economy in the preindustrial world (though that same population explosion also caused tremendous social stresses).

The foreign encroachments following the Opium War changed the Qing economic and social structures, especially in the coastal areas. Enormous war indemnities drained the resources of the dynasty. Foreigners held the post of inspector-general of the Maritime Customs Service and served as commissioners of customs across the empire. Powerful foreign factories, railways, and banks dominated the Qing's incipient modern industry and commerce. Foreign concessions in the treaty ports built up independent foreign communities within Qing society. Yet, along with the introduction of foreign values and technology, the late Qing started China's own modern enterprises, operated by either the government or private entrepreneurs. Despite tremendous difficulties, progress was made in armaments, shipping, textiles, communications, mining, machinery, and banking. While industrialization started to transform business patterns along the coast, the traditional sector retained its dominance in the interior.

Along with the emergence of a modern economy, the late-Qing social order changed dramatically. Cosmopolitan cities developed. Shanghai grew into the largest city in China and an economic center in East Asia. In the treaty ports, Chinese commercial bourgeoisie—either entrepreneurs or compradores (merchants working for foreign firms)—became influenced by foreigners, embracing Western modes of life and ideas. Western-style education, both at home and abroad, trained a new class of people who confronted the old educated elite. Laborers who migrated overseas built up foreign economic and social connections. The first group of Chinese proletariat appeared in mines, railways, docks, and factories of the industrial centers. A new type of army, equipped and trained along Western lines, began to play an important role in Qing political life. Some "new women," as represented by the revolutionary Qiu Jin (1875–1907), unbound their feet, joined sisterhoods, and obtained education—by 1909, there were thirteen thousand girls attending schools in China and several hundred studying overseas. These new social elements, joined by the dispossessed peasants from the countryside, became more and more alienated from the old order and finally toppled the Qing regime.

Cultural and Intellectual Changes

The Qing was a period of cultural flowering and intellectual searching. In the early Qing, when the Manchu endeavored to reconstruct the world order, they declared Neo-Confucianism the state orthodoxy. In order to control intellectuals and the spread of knowledge, the state sponsored enormous literary projects, including the *Gujin tushu jicheng* (Synthesis of Books and Illustrations Past and Present, 1726–1728) and *Siku quanshu* (Complete Library of the Four Treasuries, 1772–1782). Partly due to the government's repressive policy, a great many scholars devoted themselves to the laborious literary work known as the "evidential research movement," which contributed immensely to critical studies of Chinese history, philosophy, and philology. Beyond government control, nonofficial thinkers, such as Huang Zongxi (1610–1695), Gu Yanwu (1613–1682), and Wang Fuzhi (1619–1692), searched for new meanings of life. Literary works such as *Liaozhai zhiyi* (Strange Tales from a Chinese Studio) by Pu Songling (1640–1715), *Rulin waishi* (The Scholars) by Wu Jingzi (1701–1754), and *Honglou meng (Dream of the Red Chamber)* by Cao Xueqin (1715–1763) incisively and vividly exposed social problems with outstanding artistry.

European missionaries continued to work at the imperial court and in the provinces. During Kangxi's reign, the Jesuits' accommodating interpretation of Confucianism was attacked by such European orders as the Dominicans and the Franciscans. In a struggle known as the Chinese Rites Controversy, Catholic authorities in Rome rejected the Jesuit approach in 1704; Kangxi, enraged by European interference, expelled a number of missionaries who were intolerant of Chinese culture. During the nineteenth century, Protestant missionaries brought Western values, science, technology, medicine, and education to China. By the end of the century, there were about 750 Catholic and 1,300 Protestant missionaries in China, who converted about 200,000 Chinese. The missionary efforts from time to time encountered native antiforeign sentiment, as demonstrated in the Tianjin Massacre of 1870 and the Boxer Rebellion, which hindered the missionaries from making greater achievements.

Foreign aggression after the Opium War forced the Chinese political and intellectual elite to turn to the West for plans to enrich the country and strengthen the military. Wei Yuan (1794–1856), in his famous *Haiguo tuzhi* (Illustrated Treatise on Overseas Countries), suggested using the foreigners' own techniques to overcome them. The Qing self-strengthening movement brought in Western values as well as modern science and technology. Yan Fu (1853–1921), a Qing student who studied naval science in England, translated influential works by Darwin, Huxley, Spencer, and Adam Smith. Modern nationalism as promoted by Sun Yat-sen and his revolutionary followers became a powerful weapon that eventually destroyed the old imperial order.

The Qing dynasty holds a significant position in China's history. Despite difficulties and disasters, the Qing left distinctive territorial, political, demographic, economic, and intellectual legacies for present-day China.

Jiang Yonglin

Further Reading
Elman, Benjamin. (1984) *From Philosophy to Philology: Intellectual and Social Aspects of Change in Late Imperial China.* Cambridge, MA: Harvard University Press.
Fairbank, John K., ed. (1978) *The Cambridge History of China.* Vol. 10, *Late Ch'ing, 1800–1911, Part I.* New York: Cambridge University Press.
Hao, Yen-p'ing. (1986) *The Commercial Revolution in Nineteenth-Century China: The Rise of Sino-Western Mercantile Capitalism.* Berkeley and Los Angeles: University of California Press.
Mann, Susan. (1997) *Precious Records: Women in China's Long Eighteenth Century.* Stanford, CA: Stanford University Press.
Wakeman, Frederick, Jr. (1985) *The Great Enterprise: The Manchu Reconstruction of Imperial Order in Seventeenth-Century China.* 2 vols. Berkeley and Los Angeles: University of California Press.

QINGHAI (2002 pop. 5.3 million). A remote province in western China, Qinghai (Blue Sea) has a population that includes Han Chinese and Tibetans, as well as Mongols and Kazakh, Hui, Salar, and Tu minorities. The capital Xining (Western Peace) has a population of 1 million. Qinghai is the fourth-largest official province in China, having six autonomous prefectures, thirty counties, and seven autonomous counties spread across 721,000 square kilometers.

Bordering Sichuan (northeast), Tibet (southwest), Xinjiang (northwest), and Gansu (northeast), Qinghai encompasses part of the Qinghai-Tibetan plateau averaging over 4,000 meters above sea level, the world's largest and highest plateau. From Qinghai arise three of Asia's major rivers, the Chang (Yangtze), Huanghe, and Mekong. Qinghai Lake (Koko Nor in Mongolian) is China's largest inland lake. Over 105 kilometers long, the turquoise lake is 3,205 meters above sea level. Its brackish waters host Niao Dao (Bird Island) sanctuary, where thousands of waterfowl congregate, including the rare black-necked crane. The Tsaidam (Mongolian for salt marsh) Basin of central Qinghai has an area of 240,926 square kilometers. Part salt marsh, part desert and rich in minerals, coal, and oil, the area is of increasing interest for the exploitation of natural resources. Native fauna include wild yak, Przewalski's horse, blue sheep, wolf, and a wide variety of birds. The saltwater-drinking camel, newly discovered in 2001, also inhabits part of Qinghai.

Qinghai's harsh climate has an average winter temperature of –15° C and an annual rainfall of 25 to 51 centimeters. The east produces spring wheat, highland barley, peas, potatoes, and rapeseed. The vast grasslands of the west are suitable for herding yaks, horses, sheep, and goats. Other products include wool, animal skins, oil, natural gas, common salt, and minerals. Per capita income is small. China's main nuclear facility and waste site are in Haiyan, by Qinghai Lake. Qinghai is known as "China's Siberia" due to the huge population of prisoners sent there from the rest of the nation to work in the prison factories.

Once part of Tibet (Amdo), Qinghai came under Mongol rule during the Yuan dynasty (1279–1368), becoming part of Gansu Province. About 20 kilometers southwest of Xining at Huangcheng is the famous Taer monastery, home of the reformer of Tibetan Buddhism Tsong-kha-pa (fifteenth century). After 1724, the Qing dynasty (1644–1912) continued to rule Qinghai, then called Koko Nor. In 1928, Qinghai became an official province of China, including autonomous districts for Tibetans, Chinese Muslims, and Kazakh and Mongol minorities.

Noelle O'Connor

Further Reading

Haw, Stephen G. (2001) *A Traveller's History of China*. 3d ed. Northampton, MA: Interlink Books.

Shaughnessy, Edward L., ed. (2000) *China: Empire and Civilization*. New York: Oxford University Press.

QINGKE Having a multiplicity of meanings in Chinese culture, the term *qingke* (guest hospitality) refers both to an overt strategy employed in *guanxi* (interpersonal relationships) management and, more generally, to the entertainment of guests. The former sense denotes a mundane social phenomenon, while the latter has positive connotations that evoke the notions of pride, group identity and superior warm feelings, personal flavor, and hospitality that the Chinese associate with their culture.

Invitations

Literally, *qingke* signifies either an invitation or a polite overture of goodwill. An offer to *qingke* can be an expression of the acceptance of the responsibilities associated with the role of host ("I will entertain you") or can simply be a gesture employed to maintain harmonious social relations ("We should get together sometime"). Although occasionally there is difficulty in assessing whether such statements are genuine in-

vitations, contextual cues such as specific times and locations inform listeners. As a genuine invitation, *qingke* is a display of hospitality, warmheartedness, and a desire to deepen the bonds of the relationship.

Entertainment of Guests

Among the multitude of occasions associated with *qingke* are tea dates, trips to the movies, holidays, festivals, weddings, birthdays, promotions, seeing someone off or welcoming someone back from a journey, requesting assistance, conducting social transactions, and maintaining *guanxi*. The nature of *qingke* activities is dictated by the closeness of the relationships among participants, with a major distinction being made between in-groups and out-groups. Frequently occurring in private, in-group events tend to be more relaxed, are often held because something good has happened to the host, and are focused on the exchange of feelings. The more formal out-group occasions take place in public settings, are characterized by stricter adherence to codes of etiquette, involve large amounts of resources, and are frequently motivated by personal gain.

Tradition of Proper Etiquette

As early as the Zhou dynasty (1045–256 BCE), the *Book of Rites* recorded in extensive detail that social activity among virtuous men was governed by strict codes of protocol and that without an understanding of ritual and etiquette, one could not become a functional member of society. Culturally defined norms of etiquette have since delineated an intricate web of social roles, spelled out responsibilities associated with those roles, and shaped public behavior and hospitality in China.

As China moves into the twenty-first century and social relationships continue to deepen in complexity, acknowledging hierarchy, knowing one's place in the social dynamic, reciprocating, exchanging *ganqing* (feelings), and maintaining social harmony are still behaviors recognized and maintained through the Chinese system of etiquette. These behaviors constitute a large part of the repertoire of skills that socially competent Chinese draw on to manage interpersonal relationships and are, therefore, an integral part of hospitality.

Regional Variations

Due to its vast size and enormous population, contemporary China is characterized by tremendous cultural variation and regional diversity. The degree to which traditional protocol in the entertainment of guests is adhered to in developed urban centers such as Beijing and Shanghai varies drastically from that found in conservative rural areas such as Shandong and much of inland China. Moreover, China is made up of numerous ethnic and cultural subgroups that often maintain distinct social practices. Although notions of what is involved in hospitality differ across region and subculture, most Chinese share an intense pride in their complex systems of etiquette and hospitality. This pride is reflected in the use of such phrases as *liyizhibang* (nation of ritual and etiquette) to refer to China.

Private Contexts

Invitations to attend private homes signify the trust and closeness assigned to a relationship. Hosts expend tremendous time and energy cleaning, cooking, and preparing food and spirits before the arrival of guests. However, these *qingke* events are relatively relaxed because they occur in the private setting of the home and involve small numbers of intimate friends and family. As a result, private events are normally focused on strengthening existing bonds.

After greeting guests, primary hosts, often men, begin with a period of *hanxuan* (small talk) that may take place on a couch in a sitting room. While one host, usually the lady of the house, prepares the meal, a second host offers tea, cigarettes, fruit, and candy between assisting in the preparation of the food. Although more relaxed than public banquets, private meals proceed in a similarly prescribed manner. After the meal is completed, hosts escort guests from the eating area to a more comfortable setting to relax, chat, smoke, eat fruit, or sing karaoke. *Qingke* events end with hosts seeing guests off while urging them to stay longer and to visit again.

Public Contexts

In the public arena, *qingke* may be realized as an invitation to attend a movie with a friend on the least formal level or as an invitation to a banquet that takes place in a large hotel or restaurant on the most formal level. Informal *qingke* events are viewed simply as opportunities for friends to spend time together chatting, eating, or doing something interesting.

Formal banquets, on the other hand, are large-scale cultural performances involving vast quantities of food and drink, which serve as the primary venue for both social interaction and *guanxi* maintenance. Banquets, a microcosm of Chinese society, are conducted with particular emphasis placed on conforming to the proper norms of etiquette, with themes of modesty, sincerity, and mutual respect framing behavior. Because many Chinese organizations exhausted signifi-

cant amounts of public resources to finance extravagant banquets during the 1980s and 1990s, banquets and the notion of *qingke* are sometimes associated with waste and corruption.

Hosting

During formal *qingke* occasions, hosts are subdivided into primary hosts, assistant hosts, and escorts, while guests are hierarchically differentiated as main and secondary guests. Participants must conduct the ritual behaviors and fulfill the responsibilities associated with the roles they are assigned. The standard rule that underlies all hospitality events is *ke sui zhu bian* ("guests follow the host's wishes").

Thus, hosting involves a significant burden of responsibility and affords enormous interactional power. Hosts are responsible for arranging a suitable location, sufficient food and spirits, an interesting and harmonious group of guests, transportation, seating assignments, and entertainment. Hosts also have the duty to maintain the hierarchy of the event, create a festive atmosphere, lead conversation, maintain harmony, facilitate the exchange of feelings, and ensure a pleasant experience for every guest.

Hosts often feel obligated to spend prodigious amounts of time planning the event, preparing the site, and learning guests' tastes before the event. In addition to bearing all costs, hosts arrange everything and accompany guests at all times, a practice many Western visitors to China find stifling. They arrive early, welcome guests, lead toasts, order dishes, issue self-deprecating remarks, serve food, pour drinks, and control every aspect of the interaction. Hosts often make offers with particular vigor, because the default assumption is that guests will politely decline offers of hospitality even if they plan to accept.

Centrality of *Qingke*

In Chinese culture, where strict norms of etiquette dictate public interaction, human relationships are emphasized, and a balanced social ledger is the ideal, *qingke* events hold special significance. Entertaining guests is a skill that plays a vital role in social, political, and economic life. With varying degrees of frequency and formality, *qingke* is used as a tactic in the flow of social capital, a mechanism in the exchange of feelings, a means of displaying status, a key to accessing the group, a strategy for managing social relationships, an instrument of reciprocity, and a method for balancing social harmony.

Eric Todd Shepherd

Further Reading

Bond, Michael Harris. (1991) *Beyond the Chinese Face: Insights from Psychology.* Hong Kong: Oxford University Press.

Hamilton, Gary, and Wang Zheng. (1992) *From the Soil: The Foundations of Chinese Society.* Berkeley and Los Angeles: University of California Press.

Seligman, Scott. (1999) *Chinese Business Etiquette: A Guide to Protocol, Manners, and Culture in the People's Republic of China.* New York: Warner Books.

Yang, Mayfair Mei-hui. (1994) *Gifts, Favors, and Banquets: The Art of Social Relationships in China.* Ithaca, NY: Cornell University Press.

QINGMING   Qingming is the second-most-important seasonal festival, after the Lunar New Year, involving ancestral veneration in China. The term literally means clear and transparent, or brightness, implying the arrival of spring, after the dark and cold winter.

Traditional Chinese earth tombs were built above ground and were shaped like round mounds (in southern China) or triangular pyramids (in northern China). Rainfall often washed away part of the soil and defaced the desired smooth surface. Wild grass and small trees also sometimes grew on the tombs. On Qingming day, 5 or 6 April in the Western calendar, offspring of the departed ancestor gather around the tomb in the morning to trim the outgrown vegetation and repair its cracks. They lay sacrifices in front of the tomb, including half-cooked food in dishes (such as a whole chicken, a slice of pork, and fried fish, rice cakes, and fruits) and alcoholic drinks in glasses. Firecrackers are lit to ward off evil spirits, and incense is burned to invite the ancestor's spirit to return for the meal.

The offspring take turns to pray (from the most senior ones to the least senior in terms of generation) by kowtowing in front of the tombs. Then they burn square-shaped ritual paper money for the departed ancestor. After that, they place another kind of ritual paper money, in elongated rectangular shape, either white or yellow in color, above the tomb.

Even though Qingming was recorded as a major seasonal node (one of twenty-four in the traditional Chinese calendar) before the Han dynasty (206 BCE–220 CE), there was no indication of tomb-sweeping rituals in that period. Scholars suggest that this was probably an incorporation of two distinct customs. The first one was a Yao tribal custom of spring worship in southern and southwestern China. This Yao festival worships dead females along the riverside on the third day of the third month of the lunar year, which falls approximately a half month after the spring equinox. The second custom was borrowed from nomadic Turks from Central Asia, who celebrated the beginning of the spring season with field outings and picnics. Confucian scholars incorporated these two festivals into an ancestral rite to commemorate the dead on the day of Qingming.

Huang Shu-min

Further Reading

Eberhard, Wolfram. (1958) *Chinese Festivals.* New York: Abelard-Schuman.

———. (1968) *The Local Cultures of South and East China.* Leiden, Netherlands: E. J. Brill.

QINLING RANGE   The Qinling mountain range runs 1,500 kilometers from the borders of Gansu and Qinghai provinces in the west to the middle of Henan Province in the east. In China the term particularly refers to the section located in Shaanxi Province in central China. The peaks reach 2,000–3,000 meters, the highest being Mount Taibai (3,767 meters), located about 100 kilometers west of Xi'an. The steep northern slopes of the range overlook the Wei River valley and separate the southern part of the province from the rest. The range also constitutes a natural border between north and south China, featuring dry temperate climate in the north and humid subtropic climate in the south. There are only four passes crossing the range, so the mountains have also served as a natural defense against nomadic invasions from the north. In 1998 the construction of a double-track railway tunnel through the mountains was begun. The Qinling Mountains cover more than 50,000 square kilometers and are home to a great variety of wildlife and endangered species. Some 200 giant pandas, about one-fifth of the total population, live in nature reserves in the mountains, and more than 3,000 rare plants have been observed. The region is sparsely populated, and the main sources of income are forestry and some coal mining.

Bent Nielsen

Further Reading

Rost, Karl Tilman. (1992) *Geomorphologische Höhenstufen im Qinling Shan (VR China) unter besonderer Berückischtigung der jungpleistzänen Vergletscherungen.* Göttingen, Germany: Göttinger geographische Abhandlungen.

Schlütz, Frank. (1999) *Palynologische Untersuchungen über die holozäne Vegetations-, Klima- und Siedlungsgeschichte in Hochasien (Nanga Parbat, Karakorum, Nianbaoyeze, Lhasa) und das Pleistozän in China (Qinling-Gebirge, Gaxun Nur).* Berlin: J. Cramer.

QIU JIN   (1875–1907), Chinese revolutionary and advocate of women's rights. Qiu Jin (Ch'iu Chin) was born into a well-to-do family in China's Shaoxing, Zhejiang Province. She received a good education, but at the age of twenty-one she was forced into a marriage arranged by her parents. Qiu Jin had two children before she left her family behind in 1904 and went to Japan, where she studied and was influenced by Western ideas. Having returned to Zhejiang in 1906, she founded *Zhongguo Nubao* (Chinese Women's Journal) in Shanghai. In the articles she wrote for the magazine, she condemned such practices as arranged marriages and foot binding and called for equal rights and modern education for women. In her outward appearance and activities, such as martial arts and horse riding, she was often at odds with her community. She joined Sun Yat-sen's (1866–1925) revolutionary organization and supported anti-Manchu movements, and together with a male cousin, Xu Xilin, she coordinated several secret societies and planned a rebellion. In July 1907 both Xu and Qiu Jin were arrested and executed before the plans were carried out. Qiu Jin became a martyr and a symbol of a true heroine in the fight against the Manchu government.

Bent Nielsen

Further Reading

Gipoulon, Catherine. (1976) *Qiu Jin: Pierres de l'oiseau Jingwei. Femme et révolutionnaire en Chine au XIXe siècle.* Paris: Éditions des femmes.

QOM (2001 pop. 873,000). Approximately 130 kilometers south of Tehran, Qom is situated in a semiarid interior basin of central Iran along the Qom River, which flows down from the Zagros Mountains, through Qom, and into the large Darya-e Namak salt marsh to the city's east. Qom is bordered to the east by the western edge of the Dasht-e-Kavir (Great Salt Desert). The city depends on both ground and subterranean water sources, the latter derived from channels known as *qanat*s; its history has included significant incidents of water shortage and drought.

The vicinity of present-day Qom has been settled since early antiquity, and it is cited by many authorities as among the oldest sites of inhabitance in Iran. The city's earliest manifestation was reportedly razed amid Alexander of Macedon's fourth century BCE advance, and it was not truly restored until the late fifth century CE during the Sasanid dynasty (224–228–651 CE). It was a regional center of Zoroastrianism prior to its incorporation into the Islamic world. Thereafter, Qom emerged as a center of Iranian Shi'ism in the seventh century and continues as such into the pre-

Minarets surround the golden-tiled dome of a mosque in Qom. (CORBIS)

sent. In 816, Fatima, the sister of Reza the Eighth Imam, died and was buried in Qom; a shrine was erected, and the city began to develop as a major Shi'ite pilgrimage site. Qom remained a religious center even when the wider region was subjugated by invading Turkic and other armies, although some destruction did occur. Its prominence as a theological center inspired the gradual development of a holy precinct in Qom through the construction of additional mosques, shrines, *madrasah*s (religious schools), and other religious infrastructure usually endowed by notables over the following centuries; most notable is the golden-domed shrine that covers Fatima's tomb.

While Mashhad is regarded as the holiest of cities in historic Persia and contemporary Iran, Qom has been the principal seat of both the country's *ulama* (religious leadership) and Islamic education for centuries, albeit with some marginal periods of relative inactivity. As such, it is not only noted for its mosques, *madrasah*s (in fact, the largest *madrasah* in Iran is located in Qom), and libraries, but Qom also stands out as a historic political rival of Tehran and its secular rulers. This was particularly true during the Qajar (1794–1925) and Pahlavi (1925–1979) dynasties, and it was in this context in Qom that Ayatollah Ruhollah Khomeini was educated and came to prominence in Iran. Qom was the location of prominent anti-Pahlavi riots during the revolution. Since the formation of the Islamic Republic of Iran, it has retained its theological significance, and many clerical politicians commute regularly between Qom and Tehran.

Levels of food production in the vicinity of Qom have historically been marginal. However, the city has been able to thrive—although fitfully at times—due to industries other than just those oriented around religion and pilgrimage, including food and cotton processing, the production of ceramics, glasses, and tiles, the weaving of textiles—especially carpets—and facilities ancillary to the production of petroleum and chemicals. Although there have been discoveries of both of oil and natural gas in the immediate vicinity, issues of quality and accessibility have largely prevented subsequent development on a significant scale. Qom's recent development has been associated with its location in a dynamic transportation corridor including highways, railways, and pipelines from Tehran in the north, through Qom, toward other cities in the south. The related expansion in infrastructure and linkages with other areas have led to dramatic increases in the city's population over the past decades, from 637,700 in 1985 to 873,300 in 2001.

Kyle T. Evered

Further Reading

Lambton, Ann K. S. (1948) "An Account of the Tarikhi Qomm." *Bulletin of the School of Oriental and African Studies* 12: 586–596.
———. (1990) "Qom: The Evolution of a Medieval City." *Journal of the Royal Asiatic Society of Great Britain and Ireland* 2: 322–339.

QUALITY CIRCLES The term quality circles refers to small groups of line employees (usually ten or fewer) who meet periodically outside of regular work hours to discuss ways to improve the quality of products they produce and the efficiency and effectiveness of the production processes they oversee. Although nominally voluntary, supervisors typically initiate quality circles, and attendance is considered by employees as a required part of their jobs. Proponents consider quality circles an effective way to foster a sense of involvement and to effectively harness the knowledge and expertise of lower-ranking workers. According to a 1994 Japanese Ministry of Labor report, 70 percent of Japanese firms with over five thousand workers and 61 percent of firms with one to five thousand employees have established groups of this kind.

The inspiration for the development of quality circles is attributed to American advisers W. Edwards Deming and Joseph Juran, who were brought to Japan under U.S. sponsorship in the early 1950s to help Japanese industry address rampant quality problems. The American statistical quality control techniques that were introduced at this time were then adapted to the Japanese context during the late 1950s and early 1960s as part of the Total Quality Control (TQC) movement promoted throughout Japanese industry by the Union of Japanese Scientists and Engineers (JUSE) with government backing. What was distinctive about the JUSE's effort was its emphasis on moving responsibility for quality control out of the exclusive ken of specialized staff employees to include rank-and-file line workers. Quality circles first emerged in the early 1960s as study groups devoted to discussing JUSE publications. The JUSE subsequently established regional quality circle promotion offices and held quality circle conventions and other gatherings. A primary motivation on the part of Japanese managers in encouraging quality circles was the fear that Japanese manufacturers would lose out to foreign competition as Japanese trade rules were liberalized. There was also a concern about radicalism and alienation among younger workers.

Quality circles were considered one of the secrets of Japanese industrial success during the 1980s boom in foreign interest in Japanese management techniques. Japanese firms introduced quality circles in their overseas subsidiaries, and they have been an important component in the Japanese government's international technical cooperation programs. The Singaporean government has gone so far as to establish an award for the country's most outstanding quality circles.

Lonny E. Carlile

Further Reading

Cole, Robert E. (1992) "Some Cultural and Social Bases of Japanese Innovation: Small-Group Activities in Comparative Perspective." In *The Political Economy of Japan*, vol. 3: *Cultural and Social Dynamics*, edited by Shumpei Kumon and Henry Rosovsky. Stanford, CA: Stanford University Press, 292–318.
Tsutsui, William M. (1998) *Manufacturing Ideology: Scientific Management in Twentieth-Century Japan*. Princeton, NJ: Princeton University Press.

QUAN TANGSHI The *Quan Tangshi* (Complete Tang Poems) is the most complete collection of Tang dynasty (618–907 CE) and Five Dynasties (907–960 CE) verse. It consists of 900 fascicles, with 48,900 works by more than 2,200 writers.

The compilation of the *Quan Tangshi* was ordered by Emperor Kangxi (reigned 1661–1722) of the Qing dynasty (1644–1912). Pang Dingqiu was appointed editor-in-chief, and Cao Yin (1658–1712) was in charge of organizing and publishing the project, which began in the spring of 1705 and was completed in the autumn of 1706. The relative completeness of the *Quan Tangshi* was the result of its incorporation of the efforts of a long lineage of previous collectors. Its basic framework was drawn from a compilation by Ji Zhenyi (b. 1630) under the same title; this, in turn, was based on a collection by Qian Qianyi (1582–1664), who himself had drawn heavily from Wu Guan's (c. 1571) *Tangshi ji* (Records of Tang Poetry), itself an expanded version of Ji Yougong's (flourished 1121–1161) *Tangshi jishi* (Events of Tang Poetry). Furthermore, the *Quan Tangshi* absorbed all 1,033 fascicles of poems in Hu Zhenheng's (1569–1644/45) *Tangyin tongqian* (Comprehensive Booktags of Tang Sounds). The works appearing in the *Quan Tangshi* are divided according to a fourfold periodization of Tang poetry into "Early," "High," "Mid," and "Late" periods, a schema first suggested by Yan Yu (c. 1230) in his *Canglang shihua* (Canglang Remarks on Poetry), which, though problematic, has long been followed in anthologies and in scholarship on the subject. Writers are arranged according to year of birth or, if that is unknown, the year in which they passed the *jinshi* (presented scholar) examination. Short biographical sketches appear at the head of each writer's collected poems.

The *Quan Tangshi* has been criticized for certain shortcomings. First, it is, in fact, far from complete. Tang poems discovered in the Dunhuang caves at the turn of the twentieth century were, of course, unknown to its editors; certain poems and fragments quoted in other sources were overlooked as well. Another recurrent problem arises from the abundance of incorrect or overlapping attributions, and other works are out of sequence. Finally, no source references are given.

In the pursuit of a truly complete collection of Tang poetry, studies on commentary, supplements, collation, and other critical issues concerning the *Quan Tangshi* have been published. These works will eventually contribute to the updated version of the *Quan Tangshi* now being compiled.

Timothy Wai Keung Chan

Further Reading

Kroll, Paul W. (1986) "Ch'uan T'ang-shih." In *The Indiana Companion to Traditional Chinese Literature*, edited by William H. Nienhauser. Bloomington, IN: Indiana University Press, 364–365.

Spence, Jonathan. (1966) *Ts'ao Yin and the K'ang-hsi Emperor: Bondservant and Master*. New Haven, CT: Yale University Press, 157–165.

Yu Dagang. (1937) "Ji *Tangyin tongqian*." *Bulletin of the Institute of History and Philology* 7, 3: 355–384.

QUEMOY AND MATSU (1990 est. pop. 43,000). The islands of Quemoy and Matsu are part of a group of fifteen islands that are located in the Min River estuary about twelve kilometers off the coast of Fujian Province in China. The two islands, which were occupied by the Chinese Nationalist Party (Guomindang) forces during the Nationalist evacuation of the mainland in 1949, belong to Taiwan. The larger island is Quemoy (also known as Kinmen, Chin-men, or Jinmen), which covers an area of 132 square kilometers, while the smaller island of Matsu (also known as Ma-tsu or Mazu) covers only 12 square kilometers. The heavily fortified islands became the focus of political crises between the People's Republic of China (PRC), which controls the remaining thirteen islands in the group, and the Republic of China on Taiwan, 210 kilometers to the east. Today, agriculture is the main occupation on Quemoy, and the islands have a population of about 43,000 (1990).

Historically, the islands have served as refuges for people fleeing wars on the mainland or as shelter for pirates. The famous pirate Cheng Cheng-kung (Koxinga) fought the Manchus and the Dutch from his stronghold on Quemoy. Following the outbreak of the Korean War in 1950, the United States's Seventh Fleet was placed in the Taiwan Straits to prevent the Nationalists and the Communists from attacking each other. Having just been elected U.S. president, Dwight D. Eisenhower withdrew the fleet in February 1953, and in August 1954 the Nationalist government in Taiwan moved 58,000 soldiers to Quemoy and 15,000 to Matsu. In September the two islands came under heavy bombardment from mainland forces, and the fighting spread to other islands in the East China Sea. In the early months of 1955, the fighting further escalated and involved coastal ports on the mainland. In the United States, nuclear strikes against the PRC were considered, but this was opposed by leading European members of NATO. In April 1955 the PRC offered to negotiate a ceasefire, and the bombardment of the islands stopped on 1 May 1955.

In 1958 the crisis flared up again, and the islands were shelled once more. This time the United States extended its mutual security pact with Taiwan to include Quemoy and Matsu and once again deployed the Seventh Fleet to the area. It has been proposed that the reason large numbers of native Taiwanese soldiers were sent to the two islands was to prevent them from staging an armed rebellion in Taiwan. The island of Quemoy has now been opened to tourism.

Bent Nielsen

QUIT INDIA MOVEMENT

QUIT INDIA MOVEMENT The Quit India movement was the most militant of the mass movements led by the Indian National Congress (INC) against British rule, 1942–1943. The defeat of the European powers in Southeast Asia during World War II destroyed British prestige and revealed the hollowness of British military superiority. The pressure placed on the Indian economy by the war created great hardships for the population, leading to food shortages and directly to the terrible Bengal famine (1943). Repeated British attempts at formulating a constitutional settlement between the Congress and the Muslim League had been unsuccessful, most recently with the failure of the Cripps Mission (1942). In the summer of 1942, Mohandas K. Gandhi had urged the British to leave India to God or anarchy, and the Quit India resolution was passed by the Congress in Mumbai (Bombay) on 8 August 1942, with the leaders calling upon all Indians to protest against British rule on nonviolent lines.

The British, faced with the strains of the war and the prospect of a Japanese invasion through Myanmar (Burma), responded with immediate and sustained suppression, including mass arrests, brutal punishments, machine gun fire from the air, and preemptive attacks against suspected rebels. The INC leaders were arrested almost immediately in the early morning of 9 August. However, this was followed by a largely spontaneous popular outbreak that far exceeded the expectations of even the Congress.

Three broad phases can be distinguished. The first was predominantly urban and violent, consisting of strikes and clashes with police, and was quickly suppressed. From mid-August the center of protest moved to the rural areas with peasant rebellions being fanned by militant student leadership. From the end of September 1942 there was an outbreak of terrorism led by educated youths against imperial signs of oppression, such as police stations and communications. This was the longest phase, which continued into 1943.

There was considerable regional variation. Punjab, North West Frontier Province, Madras, and Kerala remained relatively quiet, whereas Bihar, Maharashtra, Karnataka, Eastern United Provinces, Manipur, and Orissa witnessed "really formidable mass rebellion" (Sarkar 1983: 399). Among the princely states only Mysore was affected to any significant extent. Muslims as a whole remained indifferent, and there were no major communal incidents. There was also relatively little social and class conflict. The main social groups involved included labor in the early phase. Middle-class student protest played a prominent role, and in particular mass rebellion among the peasantry was important.

Chandrika Kaul

Further Reading

Gandhi, Mohandas Karamchand. (1942) *Quit India.* Mumbai, India: Padma Publications.

Hutchins, L. (1971) *Spontaneous Revolution.* Delhi: Manohar Book Service.

Low, D. A., ed. (1977) *Congress and the Raj.* London: Heinemann.

Moon, Penderel, ed. (1973) *The Viceroy's Journal.* London: Oxford University Press.

Moore, R. J. (1979) *Churchill, Cripps and India.* Oxford: Oxford University Press.

Panigrahi, D. N. (1984) *Quit India and the Struggle for Freedom.* New Delhi: Vikas Publishing House.

Sarkar, Sumit. (1983) *Modern India 1885–1947* New Delhi: Macmillan.

QUQON, KHANATE OF

QUQON, KHANATE OF The khanate of Quqon (Kokand) was a state centered in the Fergana Valley from the early eighteenth century until its absorption into the Russian empire in 1876. The Fergana Valley had been an economically important part of Central Asia for generations, but had never been the center of its own state until the foundation of the khanate of Quqon.

The khanate of Quqon was founded by Shahrukh biy, the chief of the Ming Uzbeks, when he carved a small independent principality (c. 1700) from the lands of the emirate of Bukhara. He chose the village of Quqon as his capital and built a citadel there.

Quqon remained a small principality confined to the western and central Fergana Valley until sometime around 1798. Alim biy (reigned 1800–1809), the eighth ruler of Quqon, formed a mercenary army and subjugated the rest of the Fergana Valley. Upon his consolidation of power, Alim took the title Khan.

Quqon expanded swiftly over the next forty years. Alim, his brother Omar (reigned 1809–1822), and Omar's successor Madali (reigned 1822–1840) added the cities of Khojend (present-day Khudzhand), Tashkent, Karategin, Darvaz, Kulob, and Alai to the khanate.

The reigns of Omar and Madali coincided with a time of rapid expansion of the economy that saw the Fergana Valley become the center of Central Asia's cotton and silk industries. Unfortunately Madali antagonized his people with his cruelty and corruption. Quqon's neighbor Bukhara took advantage of the unrest and invaded in 1842.

A popular uprising drove the Bukharans out quickly. In the aftermath of the invasion Ququn was torn by internal conflicts between sedentary Turkic and Iranian peoples and the nomadic Kipchak Turks. Kazakh rebellions, dynastic conflicts, and continuing conflicts with Bukhara also plagued Ququn.

Ququn's fate was sealed by Russia's interest in Central Asia. Russia began moving into the area around 1850 and in 1864 captured Tashkent. Soon after, Russia captured the important city of Khojend. In 1868 Khudoyar Khan signed a commercial convention with Russia that granted them a number of concessions. The Khan's seeming favor towards Russia antagonized many elements in Ququnian society and an anti-Russian uprising broke out that deposed the khan. The Russians moved in and put down the rebellion. Unrest continued and Russia invaded in 1876 and absorbed Ququn into the Russian empire as the Fergana Oblast in February 1876.

Andrew Sharp

QURGHONTEPPA (2002 est. pop. 62,000).

Qurghonteppa is the fourth-largest city in the republic of Tajikistan in Central Asia and the administrative center of Khalton Province. The city is situated in the southwestern part of the country, in the Vakhsh River valley, 100 kilometers south of the capital city, Dushanbe. Founded in the seventeenth century as a trading post, Qurghonteppa was part of the Bukhara khanate (1583–1740) and the Bukhara emirate (1747–1920). The city was the administrative center of Kurgan-Tyube Province of the Tajik Soviet Socialist Republic (established in 1929) and, after the collapse of the Soviet Union in 1991, was renamed Qurghonteppa in 1993. The city became the administrative center of Khalton Province as a result of the merger of the former Kurgan-Tyube and Kulob Provinces. Qurghonteppa and Kulob were the hardest-hit regions during the civil war in Tajikistan (1992–1997).

The city is the center of Tajikistan's main farming area and has food- and cotton-processing plants. Ajina-tepe, the remains of an ancient Buddhist temple and monastery of the seventh to eighth centuries CE, is 12 kilometers northeast of Gurghonteppa.

Natalya Yu. Khan

Further Reading
Roy, Oliver. (2000) *The New Central Asia: The Creation of Nations.* New York: New York University Press.

RADIOACTIVE WASTE AND CONTAMINATION—CENTRAL ASIA

Various aspects of nuclear energy research, nuclear fuel processing, and weapons production took place in every republic of the former Soviet Union. In the Central Asian republics, areas of radioactive contamination are widespread.

By far the worst situation exists at the former nuclear-weapons test site west of Semey (formerly Semipalatinsk), in Kazakhstan. At this test site 1.8 million hectares in area, 456 nuclear explosions, including many atmospheric ones, were conducted between 1949 and 1989. The new Kazakhstan government closed this test site in 1991.

As a result of some of the atmospheric tests, fallout traveled far beyond the test site. Tests revealed that 14 percent of the region's inhabitants received elevated radiation doses from the explosions. Farther downwind, measurable fallout from tests was detected in the adjacent Altay Kray (Altay Territory) on twenty-two different occasions. During the 1960s, about 38,000 curies of radioactive strontium and 50,000 curies of cesium entered the Irtysh River in Kazakhstan.

An estimated one million people inhabit areas contaminated by this testing. International Atomic Energy Agency specialists examined the area in 1994 and concluded that while most of the test site presented no health risk to local populations, portions should remain off limits to human occupancy. Bradley (1997: 512) stated that 72,000 hectares are too contaminated for human use.

Many other potential sources of radioactive contamination exist in Central Asia, though none as serious as the Semipalatinsk test site. Four of the five republics (excepting Turkmenistan) either produced or processed uranium ore, collectively providing the majority of the Soviet Union's output. Several of these mines and milling plants were shut down following independence in 1991. A major fuel-processing facility also existed at Oskemen (formerly Ust'-Kamenogorsk). Radioactive waste storage sites occur in Kazakhstan, Kyrgyzstan, and Uzbekistan.

The USSR's first commercial breeder reactor (which can process plutonium) was completed in 1972 at Aqtau (formerly Shevchenko) on Kazakhstan's Caspian Sea coast. It provides electricity and desalinizes saltwater for local use and is the only commercial nuclear reactor in Central Asia. It is under the control of Kazakhstan's Atomic Energy Agency.

The first "peaceful atom" subsurface nuclear detonation in the USSR occurred in Kazakhstan in 1965, creating a large crater called Lake Chagan. Contamination levels here required the site to be closed to the public. Numerous other underground tests were conducted in Kazakhstan and a few in Turkmenistan and Uzbekistan. Varying amounts of low-level radiation were released by these tests.

During the Cold War, a number of intercontinental-ballistic-missile complexes were constructed in Kazakhstan; all have now been deactivated and the warheads sent to Russia for disassembly.

Philip R. Pryde

Further Reading
Bradley, Don J. (1997) *Behind the Nuclear Curtain: Radioactive Waste Management in the Former Soviet Union*, edited by D. R. Payson. Columbus, OH: Battelle Press.

Potter, William. (1993) *Nuclear Profiles of the Soviet Successor States.* Monterey, CA: Monterey Institute of International Studies.

Pryde, Philip. R., and Don J. Bradley. (1994) "The Geography of Radioactive Contamination in the Former USSR." *Post-Soviet Geography* 35, 10: 557–593.

Shkolnik, Vladimir. (1995) "Nuclear Safety and the Regulatory Process in the Republic of Kazakhstan." *CIS Environmental Watch* 7: 29–36.

RAFFLES, THOMAS STAMFORD

RAFFLES, THOMAS STAMFORD (1781–1826), British colonial official in Malaya. Thomas Stamford Raffles, the son of an English sea captain, was born in Jamaica in 1781. In 1795 he went to work for the British East India Company. In 1805 he went to Penang (part of present-day Malaysia); he was made lieutenant-governor of Java in 1811 after the British defeated the Dutch and French there. He published a *History of Java* in 1817, the same year he was knighted and became lieutenant-governor of Benkulen (present-day Bengkulu, on the southwest coast of Sumatra).

Although he viewed Malay society as corrupt and backward, he also appreciated much of the culture and his career was marked by major reforms in colonial administration. He ended slavery, established schools, tried to distribute some wealth to the Malays, and sought to weaken the power of Malay rulers. He also did much to strengthen English and weaken Dutch influence in the region. He is credited with making British policy in its Asian colonies more humanitarian, but was criticized for often acting with-

RAFFLES' TREATY

On 6 February 1819 Sir Thomas Stamford Raffles acquired the island of Singapore for Great Britain. The basic parties to the agreement and conditions are set forth in the first two articles of the treaty provided below.

Treaty of Friendship and Alliance concluded between the Honourable Sir Thomas Stamford Raffles, Lieutenant-Governor of Fort Marlborough and its dependencies, Agent to the Most Noble Francis, Marquis of Hastings, Governor-General of India, &c, &c, &c., for the Honourable English East India Company, on the one part, and their Highness Sultain Hussain Mahummed Shah, Sultan of Johore, and Datoo Tumungong Sri Maharajah Abdul-Rahman, Chief of Singapore and its dependencies, on the other part.

ARTICLE 1. The preliminary Articles of Agreement entered into on the 30th of January 1819, by the Honourable Sir Stamford Raffles, on the part of the English East India Company and by Datoo Tumungong Sri Maharajah Abdul-Rahman, Chief of Singapore and its dependencies for himself and for Sultan Hussain Mahummed Shah, Sultan of Johore, are hereby entirely approved, ratified and confirmed by His Highness, the aforesaid Sultan Mahummed Shah.

ARTICLE 2. In furtherance of the objects contemplated in the said Preliminary Agreement, and in compensation of any and all the advantages which may be foregone now or hereafter by High Highness Sultan Hussain Mahummed Shah, Sultan of Johore, in consequence of the stipulations of this Treaty, the Honourable English East India Company agree and engage to pay to his aforesaid Highness the sum of Spanish Dollars five thousand annually, for, and during the time that the said Company may, by virtue of this Treaty, maintain a factory or factories on any part of His Highness' hereditary dominions, and the said Company further agree to afford their protection to His Highness aforesaid as long as he may continue to reside in the immediate vicinity of the places subject to their authority. It is however clearly explained to and understood by His Highness, that the English Government, in entering into this Alliance, and in thus engaging to afford protection to His Highness, is to be considered in no way bound to interfere with the internal politics of his States, or engaged to assert or maintain the authority of His Highness by force of arms.

Source: William George Maxwell and W. S. Gibson, eds. (1924) *Treaties and Engagements Affecting the Malay States and Borneo.* London: Truscott, 19.

out official approval. He is perhaps best known for founding Singapore (1819), one of the acts he took without receiving permission from superiors. Always interested in zoology, Raffles also founded the London Zoo in 1826.

Further Reading

Barley, Nigel. (1992) *The Duke of Puddle Dock: Travels in the Footsteps of Stamford Raffles.* New York: Henry Holt.

Hahn, Emily. ([1946] 1968) *Raffles of Singapore, a Biography.* Reprint ed. Kuala Lumpur, Malaysia: University of Malaysia Press.

RAGA The raga is the basic ingredient of Indian classical music. In simplest terms, it can be defined as a combination of notes in an octave, expressing a distinct "melody type." Different ragas consist of different note combinations. In southern India, the raga is characterized by the *mela* system—the 72-scale system in which each scale consists of seven notes in ascent and descent—and hence has stayed relatively stable over time. In northern India, influenced by Persian music, the tradition of performance more than Sanskrit musical theory has served to shape the raga.

The performance of Indian classical music consists of an exploration of the raga. The larger objective of the music is to generate an emotional response in the audience. In premodern texts of musical theory the intended emotional effects of ragas tended to be precisely indicated. The *ragamala* group of paintings provides visual icons of these conventional moods. In modern rendition, musicians frequently break with these conventions and interpret ragas differently.

The major Sanskrit treatises on Indian musical theory and performance include the *Natya Sastra* (Theory of Dance) of Bharata, of indeterminate date, *Sangita-ratnakara* (The Essence of Music) of Sarangadeva, about the thirteenth century, and a series of works between the seventeenth and the nineteenth centuries that built upon Sarangadeva's work, but developed the raga repertoire. The distinction between south and north Indian music became gradually articulated in these works.

The inspiration for ragas has come not only from classical musical theory but also from folk songs and ballads, court poetry, and devotional songs. In more recent times, with technology bringing different musical traditions into closer proximity, there has been an exchange of ideas between southern and northern Indian music and between Indian and Western music.

Tirthankar Roy

Further Reading

Danielou, Alain. (1954) *Northern Indian Music.* 2 vols. London: United Nations Educational, Scientific and Cultural Organization.

RAHMAN, A. R. (b. 1966), Indian film-music composer. Allah Rakha Rahman is considered to be the most innovative Indian film-music composer of his generation. He was born A. S. Dileep Kumar in Madras, India, to a musically talented family. Rahman's music lessons began at the age of four. When his father died, Rahman, at the age of eleven, dropped out of school and joined a musical troupe as a keyboard player to support his family. In 1988 Rahman converted to Islam under the spiritual influence of Sheik Abdul Quadir Jeelani, a *pir* (holy man), who was thought to have cured Rahman's sister of a mysterious illness.

Rahman's talent earned him a scholarship to the Trinity College of Music at Oxford University. In 1987 Rahman started composing jingles for commercials, which brought him to the attention of Maniratnam, a radical young filmmaker from Tamil Nadu, who signed Rahman for his next film *Roja*, the score for which won every conceivable award in India in 1992. Rahman continued to compose innumerable musical scores for Indian blockbuster films and to generate astounding record sales. He received the prestigious Padma Shri Award, the highest honor for an Indian civilian, in 2000.

Mehrin Masud-Elias

RAHMAN, MUJIBUR (1920–1975), founding father of Bangladesh. Sheikh Mujibur Rahman is considered the founding father of Bangladesh. When Pakistan achieved its independence from Great Britain in 1947, it was composed of two distinct geographical regions, East Pakistan and West Pakistan. The economic and political powers distributed between the two regions were unequal; West Pakistan clearly wielded more power. Consequently, Sheikh Mujibur Rahman, a Bengali leader, formed an opposition party called the Awami League to resolve this power imbalance. In 1970, the Awami League won the majority of seats in the Pakistani general elections. Instead of awarding Sheikh Mujibur Rahman an appropriate leadership position such as premier, however, the West Pakistan political elite had him imprisoned. On 26 March 1971, the Awami League proclaimed the independence of East Pakistan, which was renamed Bangladesh. This move initiated a nine-month civil war between East and West Pakistan that led to the independence of

Cleveland, William L. (1994) *A History of the Modern Middle East.* Boulder, CO: Westview Press.

Cole, Juan R. I., ed. (1992) *Comparing Muslim Societies: Knowledge and the State in a World Civilization.* Ann Arbor, MI: University of Michigan Press.

Haynes, Jeff, ed. (1999) *Religion, Globalization, and Political Culture in the Third World.* New York: St. Martin's Press.

Sheikh Rahman waves on his return to Bangladesh on 10 January 1972. (BETTMANN/CORBIS)

Bangladesh on 17 December 1971, with the military support of India.

In January 1972, Sheikh Mujibur Rahman was released from prison and became the first prime minister of Bangladesh. During his rule, Bangladesh was besieged by famine, natural disasters, and political unrest. In early 1975, the Constitution was modified to confer all executive powers to the president. Therefore, Sheikh Mujibur Rahman resigned as prime minister and became president. In this position, he proclaimed Bangladesh a one-party state and dismissed all other political parties. In August 1975, Sheikh Mujibur Rahman was killed during a military coup, which also resulted in the death of fifteen of his family members.

Houman A. Sadri

Further Reading
Binder, Leonard, ed. (1999) *Ethnic Conflict and International Politics in the Middle East.* Gainesville, FL: University Press of Florida.

RAHMAN, ZIAUR   (1935–1981), president of Bangladesh. Ziaur Rahman was commissioned in the Pakistan army in 1953 and was a major in Chittagong when Bangladesh's war of independence began in 1971. He led a force against Pakistan and continued in the Bangladesh army, becoming chief of staff in 1975 after the assassination of Mujibur Rahman (1920–1975; first prime minister of Bangladesh). Rahman's career had not prospered under Mujibur Rahman, presumably as the result of the latter's annoyance with Ziaur Rahman's proclamation of independence on 27 March 1971, which did not mention Mujibur Rahman.

Ziaur Rahman became deputy chief martial law administrator in November 1975, chief martial law administrator in November 1976, and in April 1977 he assumed the presidency. In his steps to restore democracy, he was elected president in 1978, ended martial law in 1979, and conducted parliamentary elections in the same year. In these elections, a party formed to support him, which became the Bangladesh Nationalist Party (BNP), won the majority of the seats. Rahman was assassinated in a failed coup attempt on 30 May 1981.

Rahman's nineteen-point program had been aimed at economic development and was well on the road to success at his death. He had taken the lead in forming the South Asia Association for Regional Cooperation. After his death, following another period of military-dominated rule under H. M. Ershad, parliamentary elections in 1991 returned the BNP to power under the prime minister Begum Khaleda Zia (b. 1945), Ziaur Rahman's widow.

Craig Baxter

RAHMAT ALI, CHAUDURI   (1897–1951), one of the founders of Pakistan. An Indian Muslim, Chauduri Rahmat Ali worked for the creation of Pakistan ("Land of the Pure") a word he coined to refer to the northwestern Muslim majority provinces of British India, i.e., Punjab, Afghan (North-West Frontier Province), Kashmir, Sind, and Baluchistan.

Rahmat Ali graduated from Islamia College, University of the Punjab, Lahore (1918), and Cambridge

University (1941). While studying at Cambridge in the 1930s, Rahmat Ali befriended members of the Khyber Union, a London debating society and sociopolitical group of Pathan and other Indian Muslim students in England. His ideas of Muslim separatism were stimulated by his association with the Khyber Union, and in 1933 he wrote a historic pamphlet, *Now or Never*, that justified the creation of a separate country to save the Muslim minority from Hindu majority rule in India. His other pamphlets on Muslims' rights and their need for Pakistan were: *What Does the Pakistan National Movement Stand For?* (1933); *The Millat of Islam and the Menace of Indianism* (1941); and *Pakistan: The Fatherland of the Pak Nation* (1947). But soon after the establishment of Pakistan on 14 August 1947, Rahmat Ali developed differences with the country's new leaders and left Pakistan for Cambridge, England, where he died in February 1951.

Abdul Karim Khan

Further Reading
Aziz, Khursheed Kamal. (1987) *Rahmat Ali: A Biography*. Lahore, Pakistan: Vanguard.
Wasti, Jamil. (1982) *My Reminiscences*. Karachi, Pakistan: Royal Books.

RAIPUR

(2002 est. pop. 617,000). Raipur is the capital of the new state of Chhattisgarh, created in 2000 from territory formerly in the state of Madhya Pradesh. The city, which is also the headquarters of the Raipur district, was founded in the fourteenth century by the by Rai Brahma Deo, ruler of the Ratunpur dynasty. The city is situated on a plateau some 300 meters in elevation, not far from the Mahanadi River, and some 290 kilometers east of the city of Nagpur. Much of the surrounding forested countryside is occupied by the Gond and Halba tribes. The town is home to ruins of an immense fort built by Bhubaneswar Singh (a local king) in 1460, with old Hindu temples and many rather more recent manmade ponds, some of them very scenic.

The modern town of Raipur was laid out by the British in 1830; it featured a wide central street flanked by houses with balconies and elaborately carved pillars. There is a fine collection of eighth- to ninth-century Indian sculptures in the Mahant Ghasidas Memorial Museum. The 1968 Nobel Laureate geneticist Har Gobind Khorana (b. 1922) was born in Raipur. The local university was established in 1963. Iron ore is common in the region, and the principal local crop is rice.

Paul Hockings

Further Reading
Babb, Lawrence A. (1975) *The Divine Hierarchy: Popular Hinduism in Central India*. New York and London: Columbia University Press.

RAIS, MOHAMMAD AMIEN

(b. 1944), Indonesian political figure. Mohammad Amien Rais was a prominent politician and one of the leading figures in the 1998 movement that toppled Indonesian President Suharto on 21 May 1998. He was born in Solo, Central Java, on 26 April 1944. He came from a modernist Muslim (Muhammadiyah) background and was educated in Islamic schools before attending Indonesian and overseas universities. After finishing his master's degree at Notre Dame University, Indiana, and his Ph.D. in political science at the University of Chicago, Rais established a reputation as a dedicated lecturer and a preacher in Friday prayer services while present at the Gadjah Mada University, Yogyakarta. He became politically active after joining the Indonesian Muslim Intellectual Organization (Ikatan Cendikiawan Muslim Indonesia or ICMI) and soon became a vocal critic of Suharto. Rais was elected as the chairman of the social-religious organization Muhammadiyah from 1994 to 1998. Muhammadiyah is the second largest Muslim organization in Indonesia after the traditional Muslim organization Nahdlatul Ulama (NU).

As an academic turned politician, Rais was notable for his tough critiques against his political opponents. He espoused eradicating corruption, collusion, and nepotism, rampant during the Suharto government. These open criticisms gained significant support from young and urban Indonesians, and became the rallying point in undermining Suharto's government. After the fall of Suharto, Rais left Muhammadiyah to lead his newly formed party, the National Mandate Party (Partai Amanah Nasional or PAN) in 1988. His party contested the June 1999 general election and he also was nominated as a presidential candidate. He was disappointed, however, when his party gained only 7 percent of the national vote. He nevertheless was chosen as the speaker of MPR (Upper House) in October 1999 and through political maneuvering forged a "middle axis" of Muslim parties into a coalition to choose Abdurrahman Wahid as the fourth Indonesian president on 21 October 1999. Rais grew disappointed with Wahid's performance as president and was a leading figure in Wahid's impeachment during the MPR special session on 21–23 July 2001.

Abubakar E. Hara

Further Reading

Najib, Muhammad, and Kuat Sukardiyono. (1998) *Amien Rais, Sang Demokrat* (Amien Rais, A Democrat). Jakarta, Indonesia: Gema Insani Press.

RAJAGOPALACHARI, CHAKRAVARTI

(1870–1972), Indian political leader. Known to the Indian people as "Rajaji," Chakravarti Rajagopalachari was a prominent freedom fighter and leading politician from 1919 to the late 1960s. He was born a Brahman in Salem, Tamil Nadu, in 1870 and later practiced law there. He first met Mohandas K. Gandhi (1869–1948) in Madras in 1919 and then joined his noncooperation campaign in 1920. Later on, Gandhi's son Devdas married Rajaji's daughter. The bond between Rajaji and Gandhi always remained strong, even when they differed on certain political issues. Rajaji was twice chief minister of the erstwhile Madras Presidency: 1937–1939 and 1952–1954. After independence, he had first been governor of West Bengal (1947–1950) and then the first Indian governor-general (1950–1952) of independent India. He was critical of Jawaharlal Nehru's (1889–1964) policies, particularly after the Congress Party adopted a more radical leftist program in 1955.

Rajagopalachari in c. 1948. (BETTMANN/CORBIS)

Rajaji then became a cofounder of the Swatantra Party in 1959, which scored good results in the elections of 1962 and thus forced Nehru to desist from this program. Once Nehru's Congress Party gave up its leftist agenda, the Swatantra Party was made superfluous and faded away before Rajaji's death in 1972.

Dietmar Rothermund

Further Reading

Felton, Monica. (1962) *I Met Rajaji.* London: Macmillan.

RAJASTHAN (2002 est. pop. 57.6 million). Home of the inhospitable Thar Desert and with an overall arid climate, site of nuclear tests, and defender of a politically sensitive border with Pakistan, Rajasthan is nonetheless regarded as the major tourist destination in India. India's second-largest state, Rajasthan ("abode of the rajas") is an amalgam of nineteen princely states and three chiefdoms in an area with evidence of continuous human habitation for 100,000 years. Exotic palaces, forts, and temples; the holy lake and camel fair at Pushkar; the golden city of Jaisalmer; the glorious palaces of Udaipur; the pink city of Jaipur, capital of Rajasthan; and the blue city of Jodhpur all hold historic and contemporary appeal, reflecting heroic battles and artistic deeds.

The Rajput rulers appeared in the ninth century, reputed descendants of fifth- and sixth-century Huns, and by the eleventh century had carved out numerous principalities. The Mughal emperor Akbar (1542–1605) subjugated the Rajasthan rulers beginning in 1562; in the eighteenth century, the Mughals lost control and the Rajput chieftains consolidated their kingdoms, retaining elegance and ceremony in vital centers of art.

From 1817 to 1823, the rulers accepted British suzerainty in return for internal control of their states, and Rajputana, as it was known under the British, became the center for princely India, the two-fifths of the subcontinent left in the hands of Indian rulers. Following India's independence in 1947, the Rajputs gradually accepted uniform administration, education, and representative government.

Two trade routes gave Rajasthan great importance in Indian history. One led from Agra through Marwar (Jodhpur) to the port of Surat in Mumbai (Bombay). The other led across the Thar Desert to Jaisalmer and thence to the Indus River. Southeast of the Aravallis mountain range, the soil is fertile. Since the 1950s, irrigation has increased the production of millet, maize, wheat, barley, rice, and cotton. Leading industries and resources are textiles, chemicals, precision instruments, lead and zinc, emeralds, garnets, and silver.

Nationwide religious events, local folk heroes, and village deities provide frequent occasions for festivals featuring dazzling costumes and ornaments and vigorous dancing and singing to the music of pipes, drums, and stringed instruments. Dances include the *geer*, *gloomar*, and *panihari* for women, and the *kacchi ghori*, in which males ride dummy horses. Hindus and Muslims join in one another's festivals. The state boasts a rich literary tradition, famous pilgrim centers, and universities at Jaipur, Udaipur, Jodhpur, Ajmer, and Kota.

C. Roger Davis

Further Reading

Gahlot, Sukhvir Singh, and Banshi Dhar. (1989) *Castes and Tribes of Rajasthan.* Jodhpur, India: Jain Brothers.

Ganguli, Kalyan Kumar. (1983) *Cultural History of Rajasthan.* Delhi: Sundeep.

Kathuria, Ramdev P. (1987) *Life in the Courts of Rajasthan during the Eighteenth Century.* New Delhi: S. Chand.

Matheson, Sylvia A., and Roloff Beny. (1984) *Rajasthan, Land of Kings.* London: Frederick Muller; New York: Vendome Press.

Rudolph, Suzanne Hoeber, and Lloyd I. Rudolph. (1984) *Essays on Rajputana: Reflections on History, Culture, and Administration.* New Delhi: Concept.

Sankalia, Hasmukhlal Dhirajlal. (1988) *Archaeology in Rajasthan.* Udaipur, India: Sahitya Sansthan, Rajasthan Vidyapeeth.

Sharma, G. N. (1968) *Social Life in Medieval Rajasthan, 1500–1800 A.D.* Agra, India: Lakshmi Narain Agarwal.

Singh, Raghubir. (1981) *Rajasthan: India's Enchanted Land.* London and New York: Thames & Hudson.

RAJKOT (2001 est. pop. 654,000). Rajkot is a city in Gujarat state, India. It was once the capital of the princely state of Rajkot, and is now the headquarters of Rajkot District. It is located in the middle of the peninsula of Kathiawar, some 70 kilometers from the Gulf of Kachchh. The town is bisected by the Aji River. Its most notable institution is Rajkumar College, which was founded in 1870 for the education of the sons of local chiefs and princes, and was modeled by its founder, Col. R. H. Keatinge, on Eton College. Mahatma Gandhi was educated in Rajkot at the Alfred High School (founded in 1875).

Paul Hockings

RAJPUT Rajput is a category of Indian warrior castes that is widespread across northwestern India, some neighboring Himalayan valleys, the Ganges plains, and Madhya Pradesh. Following India's independence in 1947, twenty-three small Rajput states that had formed Rajputana were consolidated into the state of Rajasthan. The great majority of Rajputs are Hindus who assign themselves to the Kshatriya caste (an upper caste assigned to governing and military occupations), but well over a million are Muslims. Their Kshatriya status was acknowledged by all Indians because they formed most of the fighting, landowning, and ruling caste categories, including among their number many lesser kings and princes. In the early 2000s, landowning is their major occupation.

Traditional Rajput society was characterized by its many hierarchically ranked clans and lineages: 103 clans were well known. There were other rankings based on regional location, the degree of centralized political control, and the practice of hypergamy (marriage into a higher caste or social group). In modern times, formerly dependent castes have sought political and economic independence from their Rajput overlords or landlords, and the power of the latter has correspondingly declined. Even so, the glorious military past of the Rajputs is not forgotten, and many men still find a place for themselves in the Indian army.

Rajput royal courts were centers of literate culture, where the visual arts as well as Sanskrit and Hindi literature and drama flourished for centuries. The princes were great builders of forts, palaces, and shrines, most of which are still standing.

Paul Hockings

Further Reading

Minturn, Leigh, and John Hitchcock. (1966) *The Rajputs of Khalapur, India.* New York: John Wiley & Sons.

Russell, R. V., and Hira Lal. (1969) "Rajput." In *The Tribes and Castes of the Central Provinces of India,* edited by R. V. Russell and Hira Lal. Oosterhout, Netherlands: Anthropological Publications.

RAKHINE STATE (2002 est. pop. 3.0 million). Rakhine (formerly Arakan) State is located in western Myanmar (Burma), bounded by Bangladesh to the northwest; Chin State to the north; the Irrawaddy, Magwe, and Pegu Divisions to the east; and the Bay of Bengal to the west and the south. Rakhine State has an area of 36,778 square kilometers (14,200 square miles). The capital and chief port is Sittwe (formerly known as Akyab), located at the mouth of the Kaladan River. Rakhine's other chief towns include Kyaukpyu and Sandoway. Rakhine's main rivers include the Kaladan, the Mayu, and the Lemro. Rakhine State's economy chiefly depends on wet-rice agriculture.

Generally, the residents of Rakhine State speak Burmese, although many also speak Bengali or other languages. The population consists mainly of the Arakanese and the Rohingyas, although the current anti-Muslim policies of the regime make it difficult to ascertain the exact percentage of their overall representation in the population. Smaller ethnic groups include the Burmans and the Chins. The majority of Arakanese are Buddhists, while the Rohingyas are mostly Muslims.

The Arakan Yoma mountain range has kept the Burmese-speaking peoples of Rakhine and the Irrawaddy Valley politically and sometimes culturally divided. The existence of a low population base and extensive reserves of fertile land has had two effects on the history of Rakhine State. First, the former Arakanese kingdoms were raiding states; that is, they depended for their prosperity on captive labor groups drawn from Bengal in the north and hill tribes and Burmese from the east. In order to do so, the Arakanese kings built powerful fleets and armies, strengthened by hired mercenaries from India and, in the sixteenth and seventeenth centuries, Portugal. Second, when the British acquired Arakan from the Burmese after the First Anglo-Burmese War (1824–1826), attempts to develop a colonial export economy focused here on rice and led to the opening of settlements by thousands of Muslim Bengali agriculturalists, highlighting an Islamization of Rakhine that has led to communal opposition by some Arakanese Buddhists.

Despite Arakan's early economic promise—for a brief period in the 1840s and 1850s Sittwe (Akyab), Arakan's capital, was the world's largest rice-exporting port—the British acquisition of Lower Burma and the port of Rangoon (Yangon) as a result of the Second Anglo-Burmese War (1852) led to Arakan's economic stagnation in the shadow of prosperous Lower Burma.

The Arakanese have indicated desires for autonomy from the Burmese government from the beginning of the independence period (from 1948 to the present). Under the military government, however, anti-Muslim repression has encouraged feelings of solidarity between Rakhine's Buddhist majority and the staunchly Buddhist military regime, confusing the lines of political and religious communal loyalties.

Michael W. Charney

Further Reading

Charney, Michael W. (2000) "A Reinvestigation of Konbaung-era Burman Historiography on the Relationship between Arakan and Ava (Upper Burma)." *Journal of Asian History* 34, 1: 53–68.
Harvey, G. E. ([1925] 1967) *History of Burma: From the Earliest Times to 10 March 1824. The Beginning of the English Conquest*. Reprint ed. London: Frank Cass.
Socialist Republic of the Union of Burma. (1987) *Rakhine: 1983 Population Census*. Rangoon, Burma: Government of Burma, Immigration and Manpower Department.

RAKHMONOV, IMOMALI (b. 1952), president of the Republic of Tajikistan. Imomali Rakhmonov was born on 5 October 1952 in the village of Dangara, in the Kulyab region of Tajikistan. He received a degree in economics from Tajik State University and worked in various technical jobs throughout much of his career. He also rose through the ranks of the Communist Party of the Soviet Union (CPSU) apparatus. After Tajikistan's independence in 1991, he became the chair of the Kulyab Region Supreme Soviet. As a result of a political crisis in 1992, which saw the resignation of President Rakhmon Nabiyev in September of that year, Rakhmonov assumed the position of chair of the Tajik Supreme Assembly (Supreme Soviet) on 19 November 1992. He won his first presidential election on 6 November 1994 and was reelected on 6 November 1999. Rakhmonov received 58 percent of the vote in the 1994 contest (against Abdumalik Abdullajonov's 42 percent) and received a resounding 96 percent in the second. His opponent, Davlat Usmonov, won only 4 percent of the vote. Rakhmonov is currently serving a seven-year term and will not face another election until 2006.

Rakhmonov has remained in office by successfully controlling the various factions within the government, by agreeing to a limited power-sharing agreement with the United Tajik Opposition, and by appealing to a popular sentiment that a strong leader is needed in this time of transition. His call to recognize the historic legacy of the Samanid and Sogdian dynasties for the modern Tajik state has also struck a positive chord in the country. However, he still must contend with internal factions, threats of assassination (including a 1997 attempt on his life), and concerns about foreign incursions, especially from Afghanistan.

Roger D. Kangas

Further Reading

Akiner, Shirin. (2002) *Tajikistan: Disintegration or Reconciliation?* London: Royal Institute of International Affairs.
Cummings, Sally, ed. (2002) *Power and Change in Central Asia*. London: Routledge.

RAMA V. See **Chulalongkorn, King.**

RAMA KHAMHENG (1239–1298), Thai monarch. Rama Khamheng or Rama the Great was one of the greatest Siamese monarchs. The third son of Indraditya of Sukhothai ascended the throne in 1275 and at the time of his death left a vast empire. His domain in the north extended up to Luang Prabang and Nakhorn Sri Thammarat in the south. He subjugated substantial parts of the lower Me Nam, the upper Mekong, and the lower Salween valleys. His friendly relations with China assured the stability of his kingdom. In 1317, he visited Beijing and brought Chinese potters back with him, establishing a ceramic industry that was economically important for long time.

Many important facets of Siamese culture developed under Rama Khamheng's reign. The Mons, Khmers, Indians, and Sri Lankans had close cultural contact with Sukhothai. The Sri Lankan variety of Buddhism (Theravada Buddhism, also known as Lankavong) became predominant in Thailand. In continuity with the indigenous Siamese tradition of worshiping spirits, Rama Khamheng continued to make offerings to Phra Khaphung, the spirit deity located on a hill south of Sukhothai, even after adopting Theravada Buddhism, thus merging the two religious traditions.

Rama Khamheng was the originator of Thai script. His famous inscription dated 1292 and written in the new script bears testimony to the prosperous kingdom of Sukhothai. The reign of Rama Khamheng, the warrior and benevolent monarch, is aptly recalled as the golden age in Thai history.

Patit Paban Mishra

Further Reading
Hall, D. G. E. (1968) *A History of South-East Asia*. London: Macmillan.
Chu, Valentin. (1968) *Thailand Today*. New York: Thomas Y. Crowell.

RAMA TIBODI I (1312–1369), founder of Ayutthaya. In 1350 CE Rama Tibodi I (U Thong) founded the kingdom of Ayutthaya in central Siam (present-day Thailand), which dominated Siamese power and culture for four centuries. The adventurous Rama Tibodi, who had matrimonial alliances with royalty in the Siamese cities of Lop Buri and Suphan Buri, occupied Mon Lavo, subjugated the Sukhothai kingdom, and established a new city. He named it Ayutthaya after the capital of Rama, the hero of the *Ramayana*, one of two ancient South Asian epics (the *Mahabharata* being the other) influencing Theravada Buddhism and culture in Southeast Asia for ages. In 1350, he was crowned as Rama Tibodi.

From a modest settlement of teakwood houses, Ayutthaya became the center of imperial grandeur.

Rama Tibodi extended his domain to the lower Chao Phraya River, the Gulf of Martaban, and the Malay Peninsula. He exerted pressure against the kingdom of Angkor and subdued it in 1369. He had to suppress frequent rebellions in Chiang Mai and Sukhothai. Comprised of self-governing principalities, the kingdom had to be held together by the monarch's sagacity and vigilance. Rama Tibodi had to buttress his authority and legitimize his claims by following the practice of Indian kings, who declared themselves to be the *devaraja* or divine king.

The laws promulgated by Rama Tibodi continued in principle for six centuries. A combination of indigenous practices and Indian legal concepts, this legal system exhibits characteristics of the society of that time. Rama Tibodi embraced Theravada Buddhism as the state religion in 1360 and is known as the first king of Thailand.

Patit Paban Mishra

Further Reading
Marr, David G., and A. C. Milner, eds. (1986) *Southeast Asia in the 9th to 14th Centuries*. Singapore: Australian National University.
Tarling, Nicholas, ed. (1992) *The Cambridge History of Southeast Asia*. Vol. 1. Cambridge, England: Cambridge University Press.

RAMACHANDRAN, MARUDUR GOPALAMENON (c. 1912–1987), Tamil film star and politician. Marudur Gopalamenon Ramachandran was a superstar in Tamil films from about 1950 to 1978. After that he moved into state politics to become the chief minister of Tamil Nadu state in southeast India for three terms. MGR, as he is popularly known, was born in Kandy, Sri Lanka, possibly in 1912. Supposedly, his father died as he was born, and so the poor family moved to Tamil Nadu at that time. He joined a theatrical group in Madurai at the age of six. His first film was *Sati Leelavathi* (1936). From then on he starred in dozens of other movies, usually playing the underdog oppressed by upper-caste or wealthy villains. Repeatedly, he is seen dispensing justice and well-merited violence, winning access to young women and to education. He also directed three films.

When C. N. Annadurai, the founder of the Dravida Munnetra Kazhagam (DMK) Party, died in 1969, MGR set up a rival political party, renamed in 1977 the All-India Anna Dravida Munnetra Kazhagam

(AIA-DMK), which then won state elections in alliance with the national Congress Party of Indira Gandhi (1917–1984). AIA-DMK never became a force outside Tamil Nadu. While serving as chief minister, MGR died in office. His funeral procession was attended by two million people and was broadcast live on television. Almost immediately, his mistress, Jayaram Jayalalitha (b. 1948), was appointed the chief minister. (She was elected to another term in 1991.) A temple was built in the city of Madras in Tamil Nadu state in which MGR's image was enshrined as the deity.

Paul Hockings

Further Reading
Pandian, M. S. S. (1992) *The Image Trap: M.G. Ramachandran in Film and Politics.* New Delhi: Sage Publications.
Mohandas, K. (1992) *MGR, The Man and the Myth.* Bangalore, India: Panther Publishers.

RAMAKIEN The *Ramakien* is the Thai version of the Indian literary epic the *Ramayana*. Essentially, the story portrays the abduction of Rama's wife, Sida, to Langka by the demon king Thotsakan and her subsequent rescue by Rama and a monkey army led by Hanuman. The Thai version has been adapted to a Thai setting and differs from the Indian original in a number of episodes.

The only complete version of the story is one sponsored by King Rama I (1737–1809) written in *klon*—a four-line verse form—as an accompanying narration for *khon*, masked drama performances. It is an enormously long work, running to nearly three thousand pages in a recent printed edition, although only certain scenes are ever performed. Other versions include a shorter one written by Rama II (1768–1824), a version based on the Sanskrit original by Rama VI (1881–1925), and episodes attributed to Rama IV (1804–1868).

The *Ramakien* is much more than a literary classic, and its influence is evident in many facets of everyday life in Thailand. Apart from the dramatic arts, it provides an important source of inspiration in the visual arts, ranging from the famous series of bas reliefs recounting the story at Wat Phra Chetuphon (Wat Po) temple in Bangkok to the representation of characters in advertisements, tattoos, textbook covers, and tourist souvenirs. The designation of monarchs of the Bangkok dynasty by the title *rama*, thereby linking the king with the victorious hero, is a further example of the way the epic has filtered into everyday consciousness.

David Smyth

Further Reading
Cadet, J. M. (1975) *The Ramakien: The Stone Rubbings of the Thai Epic.* New York: Kodansha International.
Mechai Tongthep. (1993) *Ramakien: The Thai Ramayana.* Bangkok, Thailand: Naga Books.

RAMAKRISHNA (1836–1886), Hindu religious leader. Ramakrishna, or more fully Swami Ramakrishna Paramahamsa, was from Dakshineswar in Bengal, eastern India. A year after his early death a dozen of his disciples, led by Swami Vivekananda, formed a monastic order and mission in his name. They took monastic vows and pledged to spread the philosophy of Ramakrishna, who had found "divinity in humanity," and, consequently, in service to it. Ramakrishna maintained that all religions equally point the way to God and sanctioned the worship of images, viewing them all as different forms of one God. Conceptually he thus was a monotheist as well as a Vedantist (following the Vedanta system of Hindu philosophy). His mission idealized Hinduism and opposed Western materialism. Ramakrishna's bequest was a curious mix of modern and traditional ideas. His mission approved of polytheism and idol worship, yet it attracted a number of young Bengali revolutionaries, including B. C. Pal and Sister Nivedita. Inspired by Vivekananda's call for patriotism, they engaged in anarchic activities.

Ramakrishna contributed much to the development of a Hindu national consciousness. By the later twentieth century the mission had more than one hundred branches, operating not only in India but in the United States, Britain, Fiji, Mauritius, Sri Lanka, Bangladesh, Singapore, France, Switzerland, and Argentina.

Paul Hockings

Further Reading
Gambhirananda, Swami. (1957) *History of the Ramakrishna Myth and Mission.* Calcutta, India: Advaita Ashrama.

RAMANUJA (1017–1137), Bhakti saint and philosopher. Ramanujacharya tried to bring about a rapprochement between the Vedanta philosophy based on metaphysics and the tradition of bhakti (devotion). He was born in India near Chennai at Perumbudur in 1017 CE. His parents were Kesava Somayaji and Kantimathi. Well versed in the Vedic texts, Ramanuja began to interpret them, much to the consternation of his teacher, Yadavaprakasha, a proponent of Advaitya philosophy. The activities of Ramanuja centered around Vaishnavite temples at Srirangam. Tanjama, his wife, had left him by this time.

Ramanuja renounced the world, and he was referred to as "Prince of Ascetics."

Ramanuja established a *math* (monastery) near the temple of Srirangam. People belonging to all social levels came to him. According to tradition, he lived to the age of 120. Striking a balance between bhakti and Hindu metaphysics, Ramanuja believed in salvation through devotion. The God of Ramanuja was full of devotion and love. His philosophy of Visistadvaita (qualified nondualism) advocated spiritual experience of God through intuition. *Shribhasya* (Commentary on the *Brahma Sutra*), *Vedanta Sara* (essence of Vedanta), *Vedanta Sangraha* (Résumé of Vedanta), and *Vedanta Deepa* (Light of Vedanta) were some of his important works. His ideas were carried to centers of learning in India, and latter-day bhakti saints were greatly influenced by him.

Patit Paban Mishra

Further Reading
Bhattacharya, Haridas. (1983) *The Cultural Heritage of India*, Vol. 3. Calcutta, India: Ramakrishna Mission.
Parthasarathy, R. (1969) *Ramanujachary*. New Delhi: NBT.
Radhakrishnan, S. (1998) *Indian Philosophy*, Vol. 2. 4th ed. Delhi: Oxford University Press.
Sharma, C. (1987) *A Critical Survey of Indian Philosophy*. Delhi: Motilal Banarasidass.

RAMAYANA The great Sanskrit epic poem, the *Ramayana*, attributed to the legendary poet-sage Valmiki, appears to have been largely composed during the first half of the first millennium BCE. Since that time, it has firmly established itself as one of the most enduring, widely diffused, and popular narratives in all of human history. In innumerable folk, literary, dramatic, painted, sculpted, cinematic, and video representations in virtually all of the regions of South and Southeast Asia, it has made a profound impact on the aesthetic, social, political, and religious lives of many hundreds of millions of people.

The Framing Story
The narrative of the tragic and heroic life of Rama, a legendary prince and later king of the ancient north Indian country of Kosala is significantly framed in the *Valmiki Ramayana* by the tale of the poem's composition. The legendary sage Valmiki—who is said to have created the world's first true poetry in a spontaneous utterance motivated by his compassion for the mate of a bird struck down by a hunter—is commissioned by the creator divinity Brahma to compose the world's first poem about the career of the righteous King

Rama. The poet does so, and teaches the poem to Lava and Kusa, disciples of his who, unbeknownst to their father, are the twin sons of Rama by his banished wife Sita who has borne them in the sage's hermitage. Thus, the *Ramayana* has attained the reputation as the first example of—and, in fact, the inspiration for—poetry in the Indian tradition.

Rama and His Brothers
In the opening chapters of the poem, we learn that Rama is no ordinary prince but in fact an earthly manifestation of the supreme divinity Vishnu Narayana. The god, as the story makes clear, has—in response to an appeal by the lesser divinities—agreed to take on human form in order to rid the world of an otherwise invincible and tyrannical demon, the mighty *rakshasa* (demon) lord Ravana, who is invulnerable to all supernatural beings. The god infuses his divine essence into a food, which is to be shared among the three wives of the great but childless king Dasaratha of Kosala. When this is accomplished, the eldest queen, Kausalya, gives birth to a splendid son, Rama; the king's middle wife, Kaikeyi, bears the prince Bharata; and the youngest wife, Sumitra, delivers the heroic twins Laksmana and Satrughna.

Rama is outstanding among the four brothers for his beauty, courage, intelligence, and righteousness. In his youth, he goes on a journey with a powerful sage in order to protect the latter's sacrifices from the depredations of the demons. During this journey, he participates in a contest of strength for the hand of the beautiful princess Sita of the neighboring kingdom of Mithila, a woman who as an infant had emerged from the bosom of the earth goddess herself. Unique in his

PRAMBANAN TEMPLE COMPOUNDS—WORLD HERITAGE SITE

Designated a UNESCO World Heritage Site in 1991, Prambanan's massive Siva complex in Indonesia consists of three sets of temples. One set graphically illustrates the epic *Ramayana*; another is dedicated to the Hindu divinities (Siva, Vishnu, and Rama); and the third represents the animals that serve them.

power to wield a mighty divine bow, Rama wins Sita and the two fall deeply in love.

Rama's Banishment and Sita's Abduction

The happy couple settles in to life in the Kosalan capital of Ayodhya and the aged king decides to consecrate Rama as prince regent and retire to a life of contemplation. On the eve of his consecration, however, a serving woman of Dasaratha's middle and most deeply beloved queen, Kaikeyi, persuades her mistress that the succession of Rama, which Kaikeyi had at first welcomed, will have disastrous consequences for her and her son Bharata. She also reminds the queen that the king had promised long ago to grant the queen some boons (requests or favors) and tells her that she can now have them granted to her political advantage. Using her boons and exploiting the king's unwavering adherence to his given word, Kaikeyi succeeds in banishing Rama to the wilderness for a period of fourteen years. Bharata is consecrated as prince regent in Rama's place. Rama receives the stunning news of his reversal of fortune with extraordinary equanimity an he sets out uncomplainingly for the forest accompanied only by his beloved wife Sita and his devoted younger brother Laksmana. Bharata, who had been away from the capital during these events, returns to find his brother banished and his father dead from grief. He rejects his mother's scheme and sets out to persuade Rama to return and rule. Rama refuses to violate his father's command and Bharata returns to Ayodhya, governing as a kind of steward in anticipation of his brother's return from exile.

The idyllic life of Rama and Sita in the forest is disastrously interrupted when the former arouses the wrath of the demon king and the latter his desire. Using his shape-shifting power, Ravana manages to abduct Sita in the absence of Rama and Laksmana and carry her off to his island fortress of Lanka. There she is held prisoner and given a year in which to choose either marriage to the demon or death at his hands.

At first despondent over the loss of Sita, Rama recovers his resolve and sets out to recover her. He forms a pact with the banished king of the monkeys, Sugriva, and the monkey armies scour the world for the lost princess. Eventually the heroic monkey Hanuman locates her and reassures her, showing her Rama's signet ring.

The Rescue of Sita and Thereafter

Rama and the monkeys build a bridge across the ocean and lay siege to Ravana's citadel. After a protracted war, Rama slays Ravana on the battlefield and recovers Sita. The long-suffering princess must pass through a fire ordeal to publicly prove her chastity before she is reunited with Rama, and the two return to Ayodhya, where Rama is at long last consecrated as king. At length, after hearing of rumors concerning Sita's fidelity when in captivity, Rama resolves to banish her, although she is pregnant. She is sheltered in the hermitage of the sage Valmiki, the author of the poem, where she bears Rama's twins, the epic bards Lava and Kusa. After the twins perform the poem for the king, Valmiki brings Sita back to Rama and attests to her virtue. Rama agrees to take her back, but she calls on her mother the earth to take her if she has been true to her husband. She disappears into the earth, leaving Rama desolate. He continues to rule righteously until he is reminded that the purpose for which he incarnated has been accomplished. Rama then enters the Sarayu River at Ayodhya, followed by all the inhabitants of the city, and ascends to heaven to resume his place in heaven as the great lord Vishnu.

The Enduring *Ramayana*

In the nearly three thousand years since its composition, the poem has undergone a truly extraordinary number of reworkings in every major language and every significant indigenous religious tradition of the vast, rich, and diverse cultural domains of South and Southeast Asia. In one form or another, the text has been widely available and continually in use by countless hundreds of millions of people for as long or longer than virtually any non-Indian text still known and read by a mass audience.

Robert P. Goldman

Further Reading

Brockington, J. L. (1984) *Righteous Rama*. New York: Oxford University Press.

———. (1998) *The Sanskrit Epics*. Leiden, Netherlands: Brill.

Goldman, Robert P., et al. (1984) *The Ramayana of Valmiki: An Epic of Ancient India*. Princeton, NJ: Princeton University Press.

Richman, Paula. (1991) *Many Ramayanas: The Diversity of a Narrative Tradition in South Asia*. Berkeley and Los Angeles: University of California Press.

RAMOS, FIDEL (b. 1928), president of the Republic of the Philippines. Born on 18 March 1928, the son of the Philippine minister of foreign affairs, Fidel Ramos was a career military officer. He graduated from U.S. Military Academy at West Point, New York, in 1950, earned a master's degree in civil engineering from the University of Illinois in 1951, and proposed amending the constitution to allow a second term but met with considerable opposition; his vice president, Joseph Estrada, succeeded him. Ramos played a major role both in persuading the military to withdraw their support for Estrada following his impeachment trial and corruption scandal and in installing of Gloria Macapagal Arroyo as president in February 2001. As of 2002, Ramos held the post of chairman of the Ramos Peace and Development Foundation, an influential think tank in Manila, and was serving on many corporate and foundation boards.

Zachary Abuza

RAMOS-HORTA, JOSÉ (b. 1946), East Timorese political activist. José Ramos-Horta became known as the internationally recognized spokesperson for an independent East Timor and as the recipient of the 1996 Nobel peace prize. He was born on 26 December 1946 in Dili, the capital of East Timor, the son of a Timorese mother and Portuguese father, and was educated in a local Catholic mission school.

At the age of twenty-four, Ramos-Horta became active in the Timorese Social Democratic Association (ASDT), the predecessor of the Revolutionary Front for an Independent East Timor (Fretelin). Working as a radio and television journalist, he was appointed secretary for external affairs and information for the pro-independence parties. After Fretelin had unilaterally declared the independence of East Timor in 1975, Ramos-Horta was elected to represent East Timor overseas and left the island just three days before Indonesian troops invaded.

Ramos-Horta became the permanent representative of Fretelin to the United Nations from 1976 until 1989, and since then he has been a tireless advocate for a free and independent East Timor. He studied international law at The Hague Academy of International Law and completed a master's degree in Peace Studies at Antioch University in 1984. His dedication to the defense of human rights led him to set up the Diplomacy Training Programme at the University of New South Wales in Sydney for the purpose of training indigenous peoples, minorities, and activists from the Asia Pacific Region.

In 1994, as part of an ongoing dialogue under the auspices of the U.N., Ramos-Horta met with Indonesian Foreign Minister Ali Alatas, the first public meeting between an Indonesian government official and leaders of East Timor since Indonesia's invasion of the territory. He was elected vice president of the National Council of the Timorese Resistance (CNRT) in 1998

Former president Fidel Ramos at a news conference in Manila in January 2002. (AFP/CORBIS)

served in the Korean and Vietnam Wars. A cousin of Ferdinand Marcos, Ramos served as chief of the Philippine Constabulary, director-general of the civilian Integrated National Police, and deputy chief of staff of the Armed Forces of the Philippines throughout the martial law era. He became chief of staff and a four-star general in 1986.

Despite his close ties to Marcos, Ramos joined the opposition and was instrumental in forcing Marcos from power on 25 February 1986. President Corazon Aquino had some misgivings about Ramos, who had previously ordered the arrest of her husband Benigno Aquino, yet she immediately appointed Ramos chief of the armed forces of the Philippines. Acquino increasingly came to rely on Ramos, who proved his loyalty by putting down several coup attempts. In 1988, Aquino appointed Ramos secretary of national defense, replacing a Marcos cabinet holdover, Juan Ponce Enrile. Ramos used his position to launch a successful presidential bid, running as a candidate for the Lakas-National Union of Christian Democrats (Lakas-NUCD) party. In 1992, Ramos was elected as the twelfth president of the Republic of the Philippines.

The Ramos presidency was a period of political and economic stability. He negotiated peace in 1995 with the largest Muslim separatist group, defeated the communist insurgency, successfully liberalized the economy, and attracted much foreign investment. Ramos and functioned as the personal representative of Xanana Gusmão, the president of the CNRT, during the time the latter was imprisoned by the Indonesian government.

For his work on behalf of the people of East Timor, José Ramos-Horta was awarded, together with his countryman Bishop Carlos Filipe Ximenes Belo, the 1996 Nobel peace prize. The Oslo committee in its laudation considered him the leading international spokesman for East Timor since 1975. After the U.N. consultation on the future of East Timor in 1999, Ramos-Horta continued in his role as an international mediator to promote the development of East Timor.

Frank Feulner

Further Reading
Ramos-Horta, José. (1997) *Funu: The Unfinished Saga of East Timor.* Lawrenceville, NJ: Red Sea Press.
Taylor, John G. (1999) *East Timor: The Price of Freedom.* London: Zed Books.

RANA The Ranas were a powerful family that became the effective rulers of the Himalayan kingdom of Nepal from 1846 to 1951. They rose to prominence in the nineteenth century under Jang Bahadur Kunwar (1817–1877), who ruthlessly eliminated his rivals to put an end to decades of bitter factional strife within the kingdom's ruling elite. In 1846 Jang Bahadur assumed the office of prime minister to become the most powerful man in Nepal. Jang also added the name Rana to his family name, claiming descent from the Ranas of Chittor, one of the most prominent warrior aristocracies of north India. From this time onward, until their downfall in 1951 and despite rifts within their ranks, the Ranas occupied the highest military and administrative offices in Nepal, which included hereditary succession to the office of the prime minister. The Ranas were careful not to overthrow the Shah kings of Nepal, whom they reduced to the status of mere figureheads.

Rana rule was notable for a number of reasons. By concentrating power in their hands, they restored political stability to a kingdom whose ruling elite had long been deeply divided. Other notable achievements included an increase in the area under cultivation, expansion of the country's administrative machinery, the introduction of a uniform law code, and the abolition of social practices such as slavery and sati (widow burning). In foreign affairs, they followed a policy of loyal but cautious friendship with the British, who were then emerging as the preeminent colonial power in South Asia. Thus, while they willingly provided trained soldiers and military recruits to assist Britain's imperial designs, they denied the British free access to Nepal. This policy not only preserved Nepal's independence in South Asia, but also led to the restoration of territories that were earlier lost to the British after the Anglo-Nepal War of 1814–1816. The British, through the Anglo-Nepal Treaty of 1923, officially recognized Nepal's special status as an independent kingdom in South Asia.

Despite these achievements, Rana rule was on the whole extremely conservative and self-serving in character. Rana families accumulated huge personal fortunes, filled the military and administration with their own supporters, and tolerated no dissent. At the same time, they made every effort to preserve the status quo. The privileges enjoyed by traditional rural elites were never encroached upon. Even the uniform legal code introduced in 1854 sanctioned social inequality as it was based on an elaborate scheme of caste discrimination. Under Rana rule, no efforts were made to develop basic infrastructure such as hospitals, educational institutions, electricity, and all-weather roads. Trade, production, and industrial development also remained depressed.

The Ranas were toppled from power in 1951 by a popular Nepali nationalist movement that restored the authority of the Shah kings. Rana rule left behind a mixed legacy. While the Ranas succeeded in preserving Nepal's independence from foreign rule, their failure to modernize their country has left it in a severely disadvantaged position in the modern world.

Bernardo A. Michael

Further Reading
Adhikari, Krishna Kant. (1984) *Nepal under Jang Bahadur, 1846–1877.* Kathmandu, Nepal: Sahayogi Press.
Manandhar, Tri Ratna. (1983) *Some Aspects of Rana Rule in Nepal.* Kathmandu, Nepal: Purna Devi Manandhar.
Regmi, Mahesh C. (1988) *An Economic History of Nepal, 1846–1901.* Varanasi, India: Nath Publishing House.
Sever, Adrian. (1993) *Nepal under the Ranas.* Delhi: Oxford and IBH Publishing Company.

RANARIDDH, PRINCE NORODOM (b. 1944), president of the National Assembly of Cambodia. Prince Norodom Ranariddh, a son of King Sihanouk, was born in Phnom Penh in January 1944. After completing secondary school in Cambodia, he received a law degree in France and later taught university courses in law and political sociology. Ranariddh rose to political prominence in Cambodia in 1989 as secretary-general of the National United

Front for an Independent, Neutral, Peaceful and Co-operative Cambodia, known by its French acronym as FUNCINPEC, which at the time was one of two non-Communist armed groups allied with the Khmer Rouge against the Vietnamese-backed People's Republic of Kampuchea (PRK). He retained leadership in 1992 when FUNCINPEC became a political party.

During the United Nations–sponsored election of 1993, Ranariddh, as president of FUNCINPEC, advocated the return of Sihanouk, negotiating peace with the Khmer Rouge, ending illegal Vietnamese immigration, and replacing corruption with political openness and economic prosperity. FUNCINPEC won a plurality of the votes, 45 percent compared to 38.6 percent for the CPP (Cambodian People's Party). The CPP refused to acknowledge the results and threatened to secede with the eastern provinces and renew civil war. Sihanouk then brokered a power-sharing agreement whereby Ranariddh became first prime minister and Hun Sen became second prime minister.

Under this arrangement, parallel systems existed throughout all levels of government. FUNCINPEC and CPP were not so much political parties as factions, with Ranariddh and Hun Sen each controlling their own army and police. The CPP, however, retained control of the infrastructure.

The coalition came to an end with the political instability of 5–6 July 1997, which included two days of street fighting in Phnom Penh. An estimated one hundred people were killed, including top FUNCINPEC military advisers. Ranariddh was forced into exile and was replaced as first prime minister by Foreign Minister Ung Huot of FUNCINPEC.

Ranariddh returned to Cambodia in the spring of 1998 under protection of the United Nations. In the election of July 1998, FUNCINPEC received 30 percent of the vote, but the CPP did not receive enough votes to form a government without a coalition. Both FUNCINPEC and the Sam Rainsy Party contested the election results, and demonstrators filled the streets of Phnom Penh in the month after the election. In November, after meetings with the King Sihanouk, FUNCINPEC agreed to join a coalition with the CPP, and a new government was formed. Prince Ranariddh has been president of the National Assembly since that time.

Jeanne Morel

Further Reading
Frieson, Kate. (1996) "The Politics of Getting the Vote in Cambodia." In *Propaganda, Politics, and Violence in Cambodia: Democratic Transition under United Nations Peace-keeping,* edited by Steven Heder and Judy Legerwood. New York: M. E. Sharpe.
Metha, Harish C. (2001) *Warrior Prince: Norodom Ranariddh, Son of King Sihanouk of Cambodia.* Singapore: Graham Brash.

RANDAI *Randai* is a form of traditional theater originating in what is now West Sumatra, Indonesia, home of the Minangkabau people. *Randai* consists of a number of actors who act their roles in full costume in the center of a ring of chorus members. The chorus squats during each scene, but rises to sing and dance when the actors leave the ring between scenes. The dance of the chorus members derives from the traditional martial arts of the Minangkabau and presents stylized versions of offensive and defensive moves. The costumes of the chorus are similar to those traditionally worn in the martial arts. The music for *randai,* which is played on drums, bamboo flutes, and other instruments, employs traditional melodies that may be characteristic of specific regions, but the lyrics of which are frequently variable. Many *randai* stories come from the *kaba*—the traditional cycle of semi-historical legends of the Minangkabau—but modern stories are sometimes presented as well. While men traditionally acted all roles, some *randai* groups now include women.

Rebecca Fanany

Further Reading
Nor, Mad. (1986) *Randai Dance of Minangkabau, Sumatra.* Kuala Lumpur, Malaysia: Universiti Malaya.
Pauka, K. (1998) *Theater and Martial Arts in West Sumatra: Randai and Silek of Minangkabau.* Athens, OH: Ohio University Center for International Studies.

RANGOON. See **Yangon.**

RANN OF KACHCHH The Rann of Kachchh (Cutch, or Kutch) is the name of a great low-lying salt marsh on the coast of the western Indian state of Gujarat, lying between the Gulf of Kachchh and the India/Pakistan border. Flanked by the Arabian Sea on the west, the higher part of the District of Kachchh on the south, and merging imperceptibly with the Thar Desert to the north and east, the Rann has long served as a corridor between Gujarat and Sind (now in Pakistan). It covers an area of about 20,700 square kilometers, stretching over 400 kilometers from east to west, and perhaps 200 kilometers from north to south. From May to October it is flooded with salt water that enters from both the Gulf of Kachchh and the Gulf of Cambay (or Khambhat), the two gulfs actually uniting during the monsoon, when the Rann becomes nearly impassable except perhaps on foot. In July the temperature averages over 30° C. By December the Rann becomes quite dry, and the ground hard. To the southeast of the Rann, and immediately east of the Kachchh District, is a smaller area called the Little Rann, also a salt marsh. Because of its peculiar geography the Rann is quite unsuited to agriculture but is an important source of salt. Aside from camel trains that may often be seen here, the distinctive local animal is the wild ass, found only in this part of India (*Equus hemionus khur*; there is a Wild Ass Sanctuary in the Little Rann). The chief town of the district, Bhuj, which lies just to the south of the Rann, was largely destroyed by a devastating earthquake in 2001. Previous earthquakes, for example in 1819, have altered the geography of the Rann significantly.

Paul Hockings

Further Reading

Spate, O. H. K. (1972) *India and Pakistan: A General and Regional Geography.* 3d ed. New York: E. P. Dutton & Co.

RAO, RAJA

(b. 1909), Indian novelist. Raja Rao was born in Hassan, a provincial town of Karnataka, India. He graduated from the University of Madras and continued his studies at Montpellier and the Sorbonne. His remarkable literary reputation is based mainly on three novels, though he did write some short stories, too. He has lived for much of his life in the West, and has been married to two Western women. His long novel, *The Serpent and the Rope* (1960), about an Indian student married to a Frenchwoman, shows his deep understanding of French history and medieval Christian philosophy. His first novel, *Kanthapura* (1938), on the other hand, is set in his home state of Mysore and is a fine depiction of an Indian village and the impact of Gandhian teaching on its people. In l988 Raja Rao became the tenth recipient of the prestigious Neustadt International Prize for Literature. In the late twentieth century he taught philosophy in several American and French universities.

Paul Hockings

Further Reading

Narasimhaiah, C. D. (1987) *Raja Rao.* London: Lucas Publications.

RASA

Rasa, the final outcome of the various constituents of an artistic or theatrical performance, has been a central concept in Indian art and aesthetics from ancient times. It is enshrined in the Indian theory of aesthetic pleasure the same way that the "pleasure proper to art" *(oikia hedone)* and catharsis of Aristotle are in the Greek and European tradition.

From Vedic literature (1200 BCE or earlier) to classical Sanskrit usage (500 BCE to 1000 CE), *rasa* has had two primary meanings. Literally it means sap, juice, or fluid. The secondary meaning is extract. In the terminology of Ayurveda, the ancient Indian medicine, *rasa* was used to denote the vital juice that the digestive system extracts from food to be converted into blood, flesh, bones, marrow, fat, and sperm. The *Natya Sastra* of Bharata (second century CE), the primary text of the theory of performing and plastic arts, also uses the word in the sense of extract.

Classifying Emotions

To understand *rasa*, it is important to look at the theory of aesthetic expression as formulated in ancient India. It was postulated that while thoughts, or intellectual concepts, may vary or differ with time, emotional states are an unchanging part of human nature. Emotions, or *bhava*s, freshly felt in new situations and ideas, remain the same in terms of emotional content. They can thus be classified as permanent categories. Bharata divides them into three groups: *sthayi* (dominant), *vyabhicari* (transient), and *satvika* (psychosomatic). Certain emotions by their very nature are more deeply seated in the human heart. Therefore, they can be expanded upon for a longer time in dramatic action or poetic imagination. These dominant (*sthayi*) ones are categorized as eight in number: *rati*, or intense pleasure (sexual or otherwise); *hasya*, or humor; *shoka*, or grief; *krodha*, or anger; *utsaha*, or confidence; *bhaya*, or fear; *jugupsa*, or revulsion; and finally *vismaya*, or wonder.

There are thirty-six transient, or *vyabhicari*, emotional states, including *nirveda* (dejection), *glani* (guilt), *asuya* (envy), *mada* (intoxication), *shrama* (fatigue), *lasya* (indolence), *dainya* (obsequiousness), *cinta* (worry), *moha* (fondness), and so on. *Satvika* or psychosomatic states include the face turning pale with fear and the choking of the voice with fear and excitement.

The Communication of Emotion

The other part of this theory is that the emotions are communicated through certain channels to the audience or the receivers. The actors and stage decor (or words and musical notes) are the instruments of carrying and are called *vibhava*s; gestures indicative of emotional states are named *anubhava*s. The communication of emotion takes place through the *vibhava*s and *anubhava*s. The presumption here is that art is essentially a transfer of emotional message between two human or anthropomorphic agencies. It is not between formless Nature, Divinity, or Universe on one side and humanity on the other. Also all art is presumed to be narrative and praxic, not merely an emotional experience of the artist. A special combination of the actions, gestures, and feelings on the stage (or their description in words or song) results in *rasa*. To translate the famous text:

> By a union of *vibhava*, *anubhava*, and *vyabhcari* there is emergence of *rasa*. Is there any example? It is thus. Just as in (eating) a mixture of various foods, spices and herbs, there is the emergence of *rasa*, similarly, in (watching) a union of various *bhava*s, there is emergence of *rasa*. Just as by mixing sugar and such edibles with foods, spices, and herbs, the six *rasa*s (sweet, sour, bitter, pungent, salt, and astringent) are tasted, similarly, by combining with different *bhava*s, the *sthayi bhava*s are transformed into the state of *rasa*. What thing is this *rasa*? That which is capable of being tasted is *rasa*. How is *rasa* tasted? When appreciative gourmets eat foods laced with seasonings and taste *rasa* (the six *rasa*s, sweet, bitter, etc.) they experience joy; in the same way appreciative spectators taste *sthayi bhava*s laced with verbal, gestural, and *satvika* enactments of various emotions and thus experience joy.

(Bharata Muni, *Natyasastra*, Chapter 6)

The dominant emotions, such as sexual passion, fear, anger, disgust, and humor are transformed into *rasa* when they are mixed with transitory emotions like dejection, guilt, doubt, and intoxication. This occurs when they are communicated through verbal and physical acting. On this primary enunciation of Bharata, there have been innumerable commentaries over the ages. They all attempt to make a close analysis of what exactly is the cause of *rasa* emergence. There are some basic questions that have occupied the analysts. Who experiences *rasa*? The poet, the actor, the spectator, or all of them together? Is the experience of all these people the same, or does each have his own distinctive experience? How long does *rasa* last? Does it change the inner psyche of the spectator? And so on.

Not only in the areas of performing art but in music, painting, sculpture, and poetry, the *rasa* concept has remained central through the ages. Even after the advent of modern art forms like the novel and realistic theater, creation of emotional arousal through art and the consequent experience of *rasa* has been greatly valued. Throughout the ages, *rasa* has also been thought to complement and promote other pleasures or life whether secular or spiritual. It has thus reconciled art with commerce, sensuality, ethics, and renunciation.

Bharat Gupt

Further Reading

Bharatakosa. (1951) *A Dictionary of Technical Terms with Definitions Collected from the Works on Music and Dramaturgy by Bharata and Others*. Compiled by M. Ramakrishna Kavi. Tirupati, India: Tirupati Devasthanam.

Bharata Muni. (1956–1964) *Natyasastram Abhinahavabhi Sametam* (*Natyasastram* with *Abhinahavabhi*). Edited by Ramakrishna Kavi. 4 vols. Gaekwad's Oriental Series. Vadodara, India: Oriental Institute.

———. (1971–1981) *Natyasastram*. With *Abhinavabharati* and *Madhusandani* by Madhu-sudana Sastri. 3 vols. Varanasi, India: Benares Hindu University.

Byrski, Christopher. (1974) *Concept of Ancient Indian Theatre*. Delhi: Munshiram Manoharlal.

Gupt, Bharat. (1986–1987) "The Date of the *Natyasastra*." *Journal of Oriental Institute* 36.1–4: 69–86.

———. (1994) *Dramatic Concepts: Greek and Indian. A Study of Poetics and the Natyasastra*. Delhi: D. K. Printworld.

———. (1994) *Natyasastra, Chapter 28: Ancient Scales of Indian Music*. With *Sanjivanam* commentary by Acarya Brihaspati. Delhi: Brahaspati Publications.

Panchal, Govardhan. (1996) *The Theatres of Bharata and Some Aspects of Sanskrit Play Production*. Delhi: Munshiram Manoharlal.

Raghavan, V. (1940) *The Number of Rasas*. Adyar, India: The Adyar Library.

Shekhar, Indu. (1960) *Sanskrit Drama: Its Origin and Decline*. Leiden, Netherlands: E. J. Brill.

Tarlekar, G. H. (1975) *Studies in Natyasastra*. Delhi: Motilal Banarsidas.

RASHIDOV, SHAROF RASHIDOVICH

(1917–1983), Uzbek politician and writer. Sharof Rashidovich Rashidov led the Uzbekistan Soviet Socialist Republic from 1959 until 1983 as the first secretary of the Communist Party. He was a member of the Soviet Politburo, the highest policy-making institution in the Soviet Union (USSR). Born in Dzizak (then a small town in central Uzbekistan) in 1917, he spent most of his career in the Communist Party apparatus. From 1947 to 1950 he worked as editor of the leading national newspaper, *Kizil Uzbekiston*, and from 1950 to 1959 was chairman of the Supreme Soviet (the parliament of Uzbekistan), before being appointed as the first secretary of the ruling party in 1959. As one of the most influential politicians in the USSR, he played an important role in managing the modernization of Uzbekistan.

As a member of the Soviet Politburo, Rashidov influenced major decisions concerning Soviet Central

Asia, measuring modernization purely in terms of state-led industrialization and social construction of the Soviet identity (as reflected in his writing). His political legacy is controversial. On the one hand, he managed to attract huge investments into Uzbekistan's industrial and agricultural sector, while resisting a policy of Russification and attempting instead to consolidate Uzbek national awareness. On the other hand, patronage and corruption flourished under his leadership, and excessive exploitation of the arable land and natural resources led to ecological disasters in many areas of the republic.

After his unexpected death in October 1983, the Soviet government launched a major investigation of economic mismanagement and funds embezzlement, purging thousands of Rashidov's supporters. (This was also known as the "Uzbek affair," or the "cotton affair.") After Uzbekistan gained independence in 1991, the Uzbek leadership rehabilitated Rashidov's reputation, making him a national hero and a symbol of national pride, alongside medieval heroes such as Tamerlane (1336–1405) and Babur (1483–1530), in an attempt to consolidate the Uzbek people's sense of national identity.

Rafis Abazov

Further Reading

Allworth, Edward. (1990) *The Modern Uzbeks: From the Fourteenth Century to the Present: A Cultural History*. Stanford, CA: Hoover Institution Press, Stanford University.
Rashidov, Sharof. (1969) *The Banner of Friendship*. Moscow: Progress Publishers.
———. (1980) *Sobranie sochinenii* (Collected Writings). 5 vols. Moscow: Khudozhestvenaia Literatura.
Rizaev, Saidakbar. (1992). *Sharaf Rashidov: shtrikhi k portretu* (Sharaf Rashidov: A Detailed Portrait). Tashkent, Uzbekistan: Ezuvchi.

RAVI RIVER The Ravi River is one of five rivers in the northwestern region of India that give the Punjab ("five rivers") province its name. It rises in the southeast of the Pir Panjal Range in the Himalayas and to the south of Srinagar in the state of Himachal Pradesh. After flowing southwest along the India-Pakistan border, it enters Pakistan just to the northeast of Lahore and then proceeds past that city in a southwesterly direction, midway between and parallel to the Sutlej and the Chenab Rivers. After a course of some 765 kilometers, it falls into the Chenab River 53 kilometers north-northeast of the Pakistani city of Multan. Some 60 kilometers southwest of Lahore is the Baloki Barrage, part of an extensive irrigation system on the Punjabi plain, which drains away much of the Ravi's water.

Paul Hockings

RAY, SATYAJIT (1921–1992), Indian filmmaker. One of the most prominent figures in the history of cultural production in India, Satyajit Ray is best known in international circles for his films. A cursory glance at his oeuvre, however, shows that he was not only a filmmaker but also a designer, illustrator, music composer, and creative writer. Born on 2 May 1921 in Calcutta, Ray was raised in a distinguished family of artists and intellectuals. In 1955, he gained worldwide acclaim for his debut film, *Pather Panchali* (The Song of the Little Road). Soon after, he made a sequel, *Aparajito* (The Unvanquished, 1957), and, in 1959, he produced *Apur Sansar* (The World of Apu), completing the Apu trilogy. Ray sought to carve a new space for cinema in India, one that was attentive to the specificity of film as an artistic medium, and one that eschewed the song-and-dance routines and formulaic stories found in the dominant commercial cinema. Ray, with his peers Ritwik Ghatak and Mrinal Sen, is credited with the development of "art cinema" in India. In 1992, Ray received both the Bharat-Ratna, the highest honor given by the Indian state, and an Academy Award for lifetime achievement in filmmaking. He died on 23 April 1992.

Monika Mehta

Further Reading

Banerjee, Surabhi. (1986) *Satyajit Ray: Beyond the Frame*. New Delhi: Allied Publishers.

RAZIYYA (d. 1240), Delhi sultanate ruler. Daughter of Shams-ud-din Iltutmish, who ruled Delhi for a quarter of a century, Sultana Raziyya was the third major ruler of the Delhi sultanate (1192–1526). After the brief and ineffectual rule of her brother, whom she toppled, Raziyya ascended to the throne in 1236. In doing so, she inherited the most powerful state in northern India. During her four-year reign, a period of relative peace, she dispensed with the veil and thus provoked the ire of Muslim orthodoxy. Perhaps more controversial was her decision to appoint Jamal-ud-din Yakut, an "Abyssinian" who was probably once an African slave, as her "personal attendant." In 1240, while she was dashing across the Punjab to quell a revolt in Bhatinda, Raziyya was captured and deposed by a Turkish junta, the Mamluks, or "the Forty," as they were also called. While in their custody, she managed to win the backing of one of her captors, whom she subsequently married and with whose help she marched on Delhi. Their army was soundly defeated, and Raziyya was killed in October 1240. Thus ended the reign of the only Muslim woman ever to rule on Indian soil.

Vivek Bhandari

Further Reading
Jackson, Peter. (1999) *The Delhi Sultanate: A Political and Military History.* New York: Cambridge University Press.

RECRUIT SCANDAL The Recruit scandal lifted the lid on the shockingly pervasive corruption in Japanese politics and caused a profound loss of public confidence in Liberal Democratic Party (LDP) rule. It came to light when a local newspaper reported that some of Japan's leading politicians and bureaucrats had received gifts of stock in a company called Recruit Cosmos in return for eased regulatory supervision of this firm's parent company.

In the 1980s, the Recruit Company was a relatively new firm that specialized in selling employment information to young job seekers through magazines. When the Labor Ministry threatened closer supervision of its business, Recruit president Ezoe Hiromasa took the countermeasure of bribing seventeen elected officials, using shares of pre-issue stock in Recruit Cosmos, a subsidiary involved in real estate. The value of this stock multiplied when it was subsequently listed on the stock exchange in 1986. Ezoe also was a generous contributor to the fund-raising efforts of political leaders, distributing about $10 million to nearly fifty Diet members. Virtually all the leading members of the LDP, including former prime minister Nakasone Yasuhiro, then–prime minister Takeshita Noboru, then–finance minister Miyazawa Kiichi, and LDP secretary-general Abe Shintaro received secret gifts from Ezoe.

Even more shocking to the Japanese public was the revelation that the system of corruption under LDP rule had spread to include top bureaucrats and opposition party members who previously were thought to be relatively honest and untainted. The administrative vice-ministers of the Labor Ministry and the Education Ministry were both arrested, as was the former chairman of Nippon Telephone and Telegraph (NTT). In addition, the leaders of the Democratic Socialist Party of Japan (DSP) and the Clean Government Party (Komeito) were forced to resign in

disgrace. In all, some twenty individuals were arrested in this scandal, and after the suicide of his secretary, Prime Minister Takeshita along with four of his cabinet members were forced to resign.

The Recruit scandal, combined with an unpopular 3 percent consumption tax introduced by Takeshita and a sex scandal involving his successor as prime minister, Uno Sosuke, caused the LDP to lose its majority in the upper house in the 1989 election. It also upset the internal factional dynamics of the LDP, leading to its loss of power in 1993. The scandal provoked widespread demands for new leadership, political reform, and higher ethical standards in government that would set the agenda for Japanese politics in the 1990s and beyond.

David Arase

See also: **Liberal Democratic Party—Japan**

Further Reading
Hirose, Michisada. (1993) *Seiji to kane* (Politics and Money). Tokyo: Iwanami.
Mitchell, Richard J. (1996) *Political Bribery in Japan.* Honolulu, HI: University of Hawaii Press.

RED GUARD ORGANIZATIONS An important factor in the Cultural Revolution, particularly from 1966 to 1968, the Red Guards were groups formed from junior and senior high school students and university students, who made it their cause to be the personal guards of Mao Zedong (1893–1976) and of the socialist revolution. First formed on 29 May 1966 at the Quinhua University Middle School in Beijing as a reaction to the criticism of Mao in the play *Hai Rui* (Dismissed from Office) by the historian Wu Han, the group used slogans and demonstrations to express disapproval of its schools and faculty. Using the organization as a powerful tool in his political struggle with his rivals in the Communist Party and the government, Mao gave his blessing to the Red Guards by sending them a personal letter praising their activities and by reviewing almost 10 million Red Guards in six gigantic rallies in Beijing during late 1966. Encouraged by Mao, the Red Guards organizations quickly spread to other schools and universities in Beijing and then to the rest of the country.

The activities of the Red Guards, which centered on a personal glorification of Mao and an aggressive push against foreign or traditional culture, were focused by Mao's campaign to destroy the "Four Olds": old thought, old culture, old customs, and old prac-

READ RIVER AND DELTA

Red Guards carrying a portrait of Mao and red flags march through the streets of Beijing in 1967. (BETTMANN/CORBIS)

tices. The campaign began in late 1966, and the activities were largely those of the Red Guards. Mao's campaign was a personal attack on the "Four Olds," and the Red Guards implemented certain physical measures based on Mao's philosophies. These took the form of renaming streets, attacking foreign fashions and hairstyles, and attempting to redirect traffic after determining that the color red should signify "go." Such tactics turned violent, as Red Guards began torturing and killing people with "bad class backgrounds," destroying stores selling luxury goods, burning theater and opera props, smashing Confucian tombstones, and ransacking cultural treasures such as the Ming portion of the Great Wall, Han dynasty archaeological sites, and religious sites like mosques and Buddhist monasteries. Only direct action by the Central Committee prevented the Red Guards from storming the Imperial City.

By 1967, the Red Guards had splintered into factions violently contesting one another's loyalty and commitment, while continuing to arrest, torture, and harass those they saw as threats to the revolution, including translators, scholars, and military officials. The Red Guards confiscated jewelry, gold, and valuable real estate, while destroying art collections and priceless records. Faced with the horde of Red Guards, the government took the first step in halting their activities in March 1967 by ordering them to cease national networking and travel. In 1968, the army was sent into schools and universities to restore order and to control the Red Guards.

Although deeply committed to Mao and the revolution, the Red Guards built nothing new, while they terrorized China for more than two years, in the name of tearing down the old. Too dangerous to be allowed

to continue, the Red Guard organizations, which mobilized hundreds of thousands of Chinese students, had to be stopped with official force and ceased to be an important part of the Cultural Revolution.

Margaret Sankey

Further Reading
Chan, Anita. (1985) *Children of Mao.* Seattle, WA: University of Washington Press.
Jiaqi, Yan, and Gao Gao. (1996) *Turbulent Decade: A History of the Cultural Revolution.* Translated and edited by D. W. Y. Kwok. Honolulu, HI: University of Hawaii Press.
Lin, Jing. (1991) *The Red Guards' Path to Violence: Political, Educational, and Psychological Factors.* Westport, CT: Praeger.

RED RIVER AND DELTA The Red River (Song Hong), beginning in China's Yunnan province and flowing through northern Vietnam, runs about 1,200 kilometers to where it empties into the Gulf of Tonkin and the South China Sea. The river system is composed of two main tributaries, the Song Lo (Lo River, or Clear River) and the Song Da (Da River, or Black River), and has a large delta. The Red River delta is a triangular region of 3,000 square kilometers. The Red River has a high water volume of 500 million cubic meters per second and may increase as much as sixty times that amount at the peak of the rainy season. The river area and delta are subject to frequent flooding because the delta is no more than three meters above sea level. Flood control has been a part of the delta's history for centuries. The Viet-

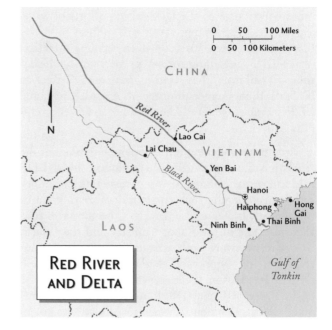

namese have built, with much success, numerous dikes and a system of canals in order to attempt to contain the river and to irrigate the agriculturally rich delta region. The successful dike and canal system has enabled the Vietnamese to produce rice in mass quantities, making Vietnam one of the world's leading rice exporters. The delta was once an inlet of the Gulf of Tonkin, but, over millennia, it has been filled in by the large alluvial deposits of the rivers that make up the system and advances one hundred meters into the gulf annually.

For centuries the Red River and its delta have provided a means of transportation for the many people living nearby and have significantly aided commerce in the region. In fact, though smaller than the Mekong Delta to the south, the Red River delta is more intensely developed and populated. The delta region is the ancestral home of the ethnic Vietnamese and accounted for nearly 80 percent of the industry and 70 percent of the agriculture of North Vietnam before 1975. Today, the Red River and its delta remain Vietnam's most densely settled region, accounting for at least 80 percent of the population of northern Vietnam. The capital of Vietnam, Hanoi, and the industrial port city Haiphong are the two major population centers located on the Red River.

Richard B. Verrone

Further Reading

Admiralty, Naval Intelligence Division, Great Britain. (1943). *Indo-China*. London: HMSO Geographical Handbook Series.

Cima, Ronald J., ed. (1989) *Vietnam: A Country Study*. Washington, DC: U.S. Government Printing Office.

REFAH AND FAZILET PARTIES

During the 1990s Refah was the fastest-growing political party in Turkey; when it was closed down in 1998, the Fazilet party took its place. In 1983 the Refah (Welfare) party was founded and headed by the leader of political Islam in Turkey, Necmettin Erbakan (b. 1926). It replaced the National Salvation party, which, after serving in different coalition governments during the 1970s, was closed down in 1980 by the military regime that suspended parliamentary politics. Starting with a 4.4 percent vote in 1984, Refah steadily increased its showing and multiplied its vote nearly five times in twelve years. Refah alarmed the secular establishment of Turkey by achieving a big leap of popularity, first in the municipal elections of 1994, with 19 percent of all votes nationwide and the mayors' seats in both Istanbul and Ankara (the two largest cities in the country), and then in the general elections of 1995, when it won a plurality with 21.4 percent of the national vote.

Refah briefly led a coalition government (June 1996–July 1997) with the right-wing True Path party before military pressure forced it out of power. In early 1998 the Constitutional Court closed down Refah for violating the principle of secularism and banned its leader, Erbakan, from politics for five years. Refah was immediately replaced by the Fazilet (Virtue) party, which inherited Refah's political cadres and parliamentary seats but was more circumspect and eager to distance itself from Refah's legacy. Fazilet, too, was closed down by the Constitutional Court in June 2001, leading to the split of the movement into two separate political parties.

Refah owed its ascendance to the crisis of mainstream politics in Turkey, and the party reflected the decline of the state ideology, Kemalism, which had directed the Turkish project of Westernization. Challenging the basic pro-Western orientation of this ideology and radically opposing the status quo, Refah's Islamist themes appealed to a wide range of disaffected social segments. Refah confounded the left-right division by leading a multiclass political movement that sought changes in lifestyle, culture, and ideology. The party cut through class divisions by uniting, around a common Islamic identity, elements from all classes who were marginalized in relation to the politics and ideology of the Kemalist state. Party members found in Refah an alternative identity around which to build networks of solidarity.

Turkish Islamism's social base was traditionally among the small-scale, provincial businesspeople. Refah expanded this base to win the support of both the impoverished working-class population in big cities, left unprotected by the now-defunct welfare state, and of upwardly mobile people seeking opportunities and acceptance. The latter included new and currently marginal, but rapidly growing, export-oriented sectors of the capitalist class and some ideologically marginal but highly vocal members of the young professional middle class, including students. Refah's political Islam, then, was not a traditionalist relic and did not originate from a backward-looking position.

Refah's closure caused political Islam to recast itself in Turkey. Fazilet, Refah's immediate successor, shed the radical elements of Refah's political ideology and claimed to be the champion of human rights and democracy. Yet both Refah and Fazilet shared the same exclusionary approach to political rights that were demanded for members and supporters but denied to the opposition and detractors. Neither Refah nor Fazilet were capable of developing an inclusive politics or a language for expanding political freedoms; instead both parties focused on capturing the institutions of state power through political ploys.

Haldun Gulalp

Further Reading

Gülalp, Haldun. (1999) "The Poverty of Democracy in Turkey: The Refah Party Episode." *New Perspectives on Turkey* 21: 35–59.
———. (2001) "Globalization and Political Islam: The Social Bases of Turkey's Welfare Party." *International Journal of Middle East Studies* 33, 3: 433–448.

REFUGEES—SOUTH ASIA The South Asian subcontinent is ringed by four countries with such poor civil-rights records—Afghanistan, Tibet, Myanmar (Burma), and Sri Lanka—that during the 1990s refugees poured from these countries into neighboring nations. At the end of 2000 the U.N. High Commission on Refugees estimated that 3,573,682 Afghans had fled Taliban rule, the Islamic fundamentalist organization that seized full control in 1998 and barred women from work or education outside the home. Afghans sought refuge beyond Afghan borders—1,482,000 to Iran, 2,000,000 to Pakistan, with small numbers going to India, Kazakhstan, Tajikistan, and Saudi Arabia.

After China overran Tibet in 1959, imposing martial law and forcing Tibet's spiritual leader the Dalai Lama into exile in India, many Tibetans fled the country—some to Canada and the United States, others to Nepal and India. (The Dalai Lama now resides in Dharmsala in northern India.) By the late 1990s, it was estimated that more than 120,000 Tibetans were in exile.

When the military regime known as the State Law and Order Restoration Council (SLORC) replaced the constitutional government in Myanmar (Burma), violently quelling student protests and placing Nobel Prize winner and nationalist Aung San Suu Kyi under house arrest, this prompted a sizable Burmese exodus to northeast India and Bangladesh, with still other refuges going to Thailand.

Sri Lanka has virtually no foreign refugees, but many Sri Lankan Tamilians currently live in south India, mainly in the state of Tamil Nadu, where because of increasing tensions between Muslim Tamils and the Sinhalese Buddhist majority, a civil war has erupted with Tamil militants fighting the central government, endeavoring to create their own state. As a result, some thousands of Tamils have fled the country and now live in Europe.

In addition to political strife, climatic conditions may cause people to leave their homelands. For example, if global warming continues to raise sea levels in the future, all the inhabitants of the Maldive Republic, with its many low-lying islands, will be forced to flee, probably to neighboring Sri Lanka.

At the end of 1998 sub-Himalayan areas also held numerous refugees: As the result of Bhutan engaging in "ethnic purification," Bhutanese refugees (generally of Nepali ethnicity) numbered 100,000 in Nepal and 15,000 in India. During the 1973 Bangladesh war of independence many Bihari Muslims were displaced and sought to reestablish themselves in Pakistan.

Indians, Pakistanis, and Sri Lankans number several millions in the present-day populations of Canada, Australia, the United States, Germany, South Africa, and Britain, but in these cases they were "economic migrants" rather than refugees. This diaspora continues, as criminals smuggle in desperate South Asian men, whose families will pay large sums to get a relative working in the West.

Paul Hockings

Further Reading

UNHCR: The U.N. Refugee Agency. Retrieved 5 March 2001, from: http://www.unhcr.ch/cgi-bin/texis/vtx/home.

REFUGEES—SOUTHEAST ASIA In the mid-1970s, Southeast Asia was a major source of refugee movement in the world, arising from armed conflict and political and social upheavals following the Communist victories in Cambodia, Vietnam, and Laos. Over the next two decades, more than 3 million people in this region fled from their homes. The Cold War climate encouraged flight from Communist countries and supported a policy of permanent resettlement in non-Communist countries. Cold War politics saw the conventional definition of the refugee, as enshrined in the 1951 United Nations Convention Relating to the Status of Refugees, focus on fundamental individual political and civil rights that Western governments held were violated in Communist countries. The 1951 Refugee Convention and its 1967 Protocol define a refugee as a person who has physically crossed into a neighboring country because of a fear of persecution on the basis of race, religion, nationality, or membership in a certain group.

The Southeast Asian refugee crisis led to the single largest resettlement program including those Asian countries of first asylum, which provided temporary protection, and the industrialized states that offered permanent new homes to more than 2.5 million refugees. To date, it remains one of the most comprehensive and costly refugee programs ever organized by the United Nations High Commissioner for Refugees (UNHCR).

History

The first wave of Vietnamese refugees in Southeast Asia was between 1946 and 1948. During this period, some fifty thousand Vietnamese, primarily from the north, along with a few thousand who had been long-term residents of Laos or Cambodia, fled to Thailand (then Siam) to escape the fighting between the French and the Vietnamese nationalists in the First Indochina War. After the French withdrawal in 1954, internal conflict erupted in the newly independent states of Cambodia, Vietnam, and Laos. The Geneva Accords of 1954 temporarily partitioned Vietnam at the seventeenth parallel pending a nationwide election to decide on one government to reunify the country. This political division saw over 1 million refugees move from northern to southern areas. The U.S. war in Vietnam (1954–1975) resulted in more refugees.

The Cambodian civil war (1970–1975) between the U.S.-backed Khmer Republic and the Vietnamese- and Chinese-supported Khmer Rouge regime, and the related massive U.S. bombing of the Cambodian countryside, left 500,000 dead and uprooted 2 million people. Political developments from 1975 caused even greater flows of refugees, which posed enormous humanitarian and security problems for the countries in the region. In 1975, the Khmer Rouge victory on 17 April saw several thousand Cambodians escape to Thailand; almost all foreigners were expelled from the country, including 170,000–270,000 ethnic Vietnamese. Cambodian refugees significantly increased in number after Vietnam's intervention in Cambodia at the end of 1978, and after the Khmer Rouge regime was subsequently overthrown, as approximately 140,000 refugees crossed into Thailand.

In Vietnam, North Vietnamese and Viet Cong troops seized control in Saigon and reunified the country on 30 April 1975. After the collapse of the Saigon government, only a relatively small number of people, mainly ethnic Chinese, fled Vietnam between 1975 and 1978. In 1978 when the first cases of Vietnamese boat people began arriving in Southeast Asia, the flow of Vietnamese refugees increased.

Refugee movements also continued following the Communist victory in Laos in 1975. The vast majority of the 54,000 Lao refugees to flee to Thailand were members of the Hmong (Mong), a highland-dwelling ethnic minority. The Hmong had reason to fear persecution as they had assisted U.S. attempts to stop the North Vietnamese troops from using the Ho Chi Minh Trail during the Vietnam War. From 1975 to 1995, some 360,000 refugees had arrived in Thai camps.

International Response

Fearing that the boat people would pose economic, social, and political problems, countries in the region that were not signatory to the 1951 Refugee Convention and its 1967 Protocol began pushing refugees and their boats back to sea. International concern over the plight of the boat people led to the convening of the first International Conference on Indochinese Refugees in 1979. This saw the Vietnamese government agree to allow people to leave the country to seek asylum under the Orderly Departure Program (ODP), and the regional countries agreed to provide temporary protection on the basis that the West was committed to resettling the refugees.

The presence of refugee camps in Thailand, Malaysia, and Indonesia, and the continuing outflow of large numbers of refugees from Vietnam and Laos a decade later despite political stabilization, decreased regional and international support for the program. Asylum nations claimed that many boat people were no longer escaping persecution; instead they were escaping poverty. The second International Conference on Indochinese Refugees in 1989, recognizing the need for a new solution, adopted a Comprehensive Plan of Action (CPA). The objective of the CPA was twofold: to reduce the flow of economic migrants and to assist in the return to their country of origin of those found not to be refugees.

The CPA represented a turning point in the attitudes of states toward resettlement as a solution to the refugee crisis. With the end of the Cold War, the West was no longer prepared to support a policy of group recognition of refugees or their blanket resettlement. The CPA determined that those arriving in refugee camps in most countries after 14 March 1989 should be screened to determine their status. The CPA has successfully stopped the Southeast Asian refugee flow and has repatriated 109,000 of those who remained in UNHCR refugee camps throughout Southeast Asia. In late 1998, the UNHCR considerably reduced its activities in the region.

Contemporary Movements

More than half a century after the adoption of the 1951 Convention Relating to the Status of Refugees, refugee protection is under threat. Traditional asylum states have become more concerned about controlling migration movements than with providing protection to persecuted people. At the same time, it is becoming increasingly difficult to distinguish among the reasons that motivate people to migrate and flee from their homes.

The UNHCR estimates that there are currently close to 22 million refugees and other persons of concern in the world, more than 8 million of whom are in Asia. While refugee numbers have substantially declined, developments within Southeast Asia have continued to generate refugee flows. In 1999, an estimated 250,000 East Timorese fled or were forcibly moved to West Timor during the violence that ensued after the pro-independence referendum. By September 2001, about 80,000 remained in West Timor.

Since February 2001, the Vietnamese government's alleged repression of the indigenous Hmong people from the country's central highlands, following protests for land-tenure rights, religious freedom, and independence, has seen more than 1,500 Hmong flee to Cambodia. The Cambodian government initially granted more than 900 refugees temporary asylum but in March 2002 announced its intention to cease protecting and providing temporary asylum for newly arriving Hmong. In a more positive move, the Cambodian government has given authorization for Hmong refugees to be processed for resettlement to the United States. In another development, the Thai government, which has traditionally been generous with refugees from Cambodia, Laos, and Myanmar (Burma), has forcibly repatriated a number of ethnic Burmese refugees.

More than two decades since the Southeast Asian exodus, the refugee problem has shifted to elsewhere in the region. According to the *Human Rights Watch World Report 2002*, there are currently 850,000 to 1 million internally displaced persons (IDPs) in Indonesia, 600,000 to 1 million IDPs in Myanmar, 200,000 Burmese refugees in Thailand, and 120,000 in Bangladesh.

In the current post–Cold War political climate, government and public attitudes have hardened toward potential asylum seekers. Increased flows of refugees in the world due to continuing civil and ethnic conflicts and human-rights abuses are perceived as threats to the security, identity, and social cohesion of states. This attitude has resulted in many traditional asylum states abrogating their obligations under the Refugee Convention, as refugees and their resettlement are increasingly seen as an unwanted burden on limited resources. It has also led to the redefinition of who qualifies for legitimate refugee status, as well as legitimate means of flight and entry.

Thuy Do

Further Reading

Hitchcox, L. (1990) *Vietnamese Refugees in Southeast Asian Camps*. New York: St Martin's Press.

Human Rights Watch. (2002) *Human Rights Watch World Report 2002: Asia Overview*. Retrieved 1 May 2002, from: http://www.hrw.org/wr2k2/print.cgi?asia.html

Loescher, G. (2001) *The UNHCR and World Politics: A Perilous Path*. Oxford: Oxford University Press.

Ogata, S. (1993) "Refugees: Lessons from the Past." Richard Storry Memorial Lecture 6, Saint Anthony's College, Oxford, 5 May.

Osborne, M. (1980) "The Indochinese Refugees: Cause and Effects." *International Affairs* 56, 1 (January): 37–53.

Reynell, Josephine. (1989) *Political Pawns: Refugees on the Thai-Kampuchean Border*. Oxford: Refugees Studies Program.

Robinson, W. Courtland. (1998) *Terms of Refuge: The Indochinese Exodus and the International Response*. London: Zed Books.

Rogge, J. R., ed. (1987) *Refugees: A Third World Dilemma*. Lanham, MD: Rowman & Littlefield.

United Nations High Commissioner for Refugees. (2000) *The State of the World's Refugees: Fifty Years of Humanitarian Action*. Geneva: UNHCR.

———. (2001) *Refugees by Numbers*, 2001 ed. Geneva: UNHCR.

RELIGION, FOLK—CHINA In China, major religions such as Taoism, Buddhism, and state religion, or Confucianism, were never powerful or popular enough to displace the communal religion of the people. They have had to be satisfied with sharing the spiritual loyalties of the people with community and family-based religious observances. There is no question that they have been successful in infusing the communal religion with certain of their doctrines and traditions. The Buddhist vision of Hell and the afterlife, for example, became the commonly accepted vision among all Chinese. Confucian morality became the morality of the common people. The Taoist pantheon fused with the pantheon of communal religion, and Taoist priests were able to establish themselves as the ritual specialists of choice for both the common people and the state. But the masses of the Chinese people, the vast majority of whom lived in small rural villages, always remained faithful to their local gods. Only under the most dire circumstances, when famine, military unrest, or natural disaster destroyed their villages and livelihoods, did they voluntarily throw their support be-

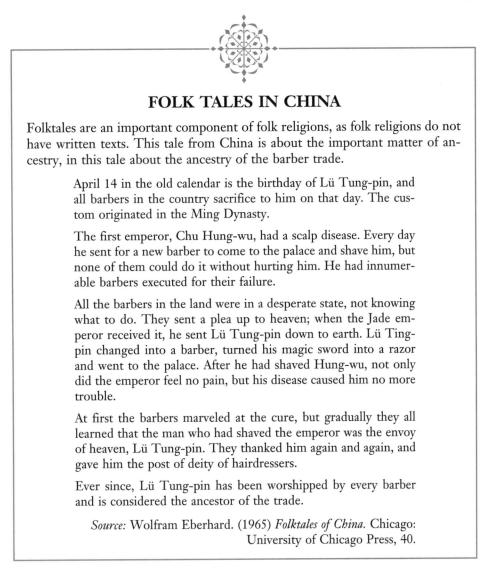

FOLK TALES IN CHINA

Folktales are an important component of folk religions, as folk religions do not have written texts. This tale from China is about the important matter of ancestry, in this tale about the ancestry of the barber trade.

April 14 in the old calendar is the birthday of Lü Tung-pin, and all barbers in the country sacrifice to him on that day. The custom originated in the Ming Dynasty.

The first emperor, Chu Hung-wu, had a scalp disease. Every day he sent for a new barber to come to the palace and shave him, but none of them could do it without hurting him. He had innumerable barbers executed for their failure.

All the barbers in the land were in a desperate state, not knowing what to do. They sent a plea up to heaven; when the Jade emperor received it, he sent Lü Tung-pin down to earth. Lü Ting-pin changed into a barber, turned his magic sword into a razor and went to the palace. After he had shaved Hung-wu, not only did the emperor feel no pain, but his disease caused him no more trouble.

At first the barbers marveled at the cure, but gradually they all learned that the man who had shaved the emperor was the envoy of heaven, Lü Tung-pin. They thanked him again and again, and gave him the post of deity of hairdressers.

Ever since, Lü Tung-pin has been worshipped by every barber and is considered the ancestor of the trade.

Source: Wolfram Eberhard. (1965) *Folktales of China.* Chicago: University of Chicago Press, 40.

hind charismatic religious leaders who promised to lead them out of their misery and into some divine utopia.

Because China is such a vast country with many regional variations, it is extremely difficult to give an accurate account of the general characteristics of the communal religion. Only the fact that Chinese culture was remarkably integrated despite regional differences makes it reasonable to even attempt to do so. Ironically, the fact that the major religious traditions worked hard to infiltrate the religion of the people also means that many unifying features exist from one region to another.

Characteristics of Popular Religion

To the common people of traditional China, as for those in most premodern societies, the natural world was animated by a great number of unseen forces and beings. The focus of popular religion was always on seeking the assistance of those forces in protecting the social and economic interests of the local community. Certain divinities were identified as being primarily responsible for maintaining order in the unseen world just as certain authority figures were charged with ensuring the smooth functioning of the material world. One of the most striking features of the Chinese vision of the realm of the gods is the manner in which the gods were believed to operate through a centralized bureaucratic government, which was undeniably patterned after the imperial government of traditional China. The means of communicating with the gods also replicated the means of dealing with officials of the imperial government. Requests were made via formally worded memorials, and sacrifices were conceived of as being similar to official banquets at which local people entertained visiting government representatives.

A curious but significant aspect of the relationship between humans and gods in China was the fact that the gods were assumed to be subject to human authority, or at least that they existed in a relationship of mutual obligation with humans. Not only priests of various affiliations, but also government officials could issue orders to the officials of the unseen world. They could promote or demote those holding position in the divine bureaucracy. They could also order punishment for spirits who had not fulfilled their correct roles. The official titles carried by certain prominent gods were often determined by the imperial government in recognition of service to humans. The idea that gods could be given orders by humans is something quite foreign to the Judeo-Christian tradition, which assumes an all-powerful god who controls all aspects of human endeavor. To a certain extent it also explains why religious institutions in China never achieved the same power as they did in the West.

In any village or city of medieval China it would have been possible to find many temples, large and small, which housed gods who were believed to possess special powers. They might be thought to protect against natural disaster, cure illnesses, assist women in childbirth, or save sailors at sea. Sometimes there were legends to explain how a god had acquired his or her powers, sometimes there were not. The temples of these gods were maintained by the surrounding community and for the most part there would have been no full-time priest in residence. When the occasion called for it, certain members of the community would preside over ceremonies. For the more important rituals, Taoist priests with specialized knowledge of ritual procedure would be invited. In other cases, the local magistrate would be the master of ceremonies. The state had since very early times maintained a religious presence in the local communities by charging their local representatives with the duty of conducting sacrifices and rituals of various sorts, especially those directed toward the control of the forces of nature. Sacrifices begging for rain or seeking to end pestilence were commonly carried out by government officials.

One of the most characteristic tendencies of Chinese folk religion was the deification of real historical personalities. This usually occurred on a local level, but in some cases the popularity of such a figure might spread to other areas, or even become a national phenomenon. Very often those deified were cultural heroes, people who had distinguished themselves for their moral strength or military prowess. The process of deification was very much like the canonization of saints by the Catholic church. The major difference was that in China no central authority had control over who should and should not be deified. The imperial government in theory held that authority, and con-

stantly tried to enshrine those whom it felt embodied values it wished to promote. In the vast majority of cases, however, it was the general acceptance of the people themselves that determined the survival and popularity of a given cult. If the people did not feel that the god was effective in helping them, his or her temple fell into disrepair in a relatively short time.

The God of the Soil

One of the most widely dispersed and oldest divinities in China is the God of the Soil (Tudi gong). Virtually every village and urban neighborhood in traditional China recognized a god of the soil. He was the protector of not only the people of the community, but also of their livelihoods. In very ancient China there were also gods who specifically protected the crops that the people grew, but as Chinese social structure changed, these gods were usually displaced by the more versatile God of the Soil. Generally speaking, worship of the God of the Soil was done by the community as a whole, and not by individuals. Worship was carried out in times of crisis, but also on special days, such as the god's birthday. On these latter occasions lavish offerings of food and drink, as well as music and dance, were made and a generally festive atmosphere prevailed. Such occasions were a natural opportunity for the members of the community to mix with each other informally, lifting the spirits of all those involved.

The City God

Another god found in many Chinese communities is the City God (Chenghuang). City God temples are still found in Chinese cities where traditional religion is still practiced. Often one city will have several city gods who are distributed among its different wards. Cults of the City God are not as old as those of the God of the Soil. They begin to appear more and more widely in the Tang dynasty (618–907 CE) and Song dynasty (960–1279). It is natural to assume that their popularity was related to the increased urbanization of those periods, but the cult is quite probably of Indian origin. City gods have a somewhat different role to play in the community than do gods of the soil. While they too have an important function in protecting the area under their control from disaster, and in bolstering its prosperity, they are more concerned with the souls of the departed and other ghostly presences. Another point of dissimilarity is in the fact that city gods are considered to be appointed to their positions. If they did not carry out their duties properly, they could be relieved of their posts and replaced. City gods are generally housed in impressive urban temples that can serve as community centers as well as religious institutions, very much as the plazas in front of certain European cathedrals served as meeting places for the citizens of the city.

Family-Based Religion

The Chinese family had been a center of ritual activity since ancient times. However, the nature of family religion changed significantly over time as Confucianism seeped slowly down through the social scale from the nobility to the common people. Confucianism brought normative, or universal, values to the common people of all regions of China, providing them with standard rituals and standard ethics. This was particularly so in the case of the cult of the ancestors. Although ancestor worship appears very early on in China, formal and ideological aspects of such things as funerals, weddings, and posthumous rites became steadily more imbued with Confucianism. With the triumph of Neo-Confucianism among the literati of the Song dynasty and the Ming dynasty (1368–1644), this process was accelerated. Yet even today we can observe that there remains considerable regional diversity in such rites.

The Chinese traditionally held the belief that human destiny was not determined by effort alone. It was necessary to enlist the help of superhuman agencies to assist in protecting and bringing prosperity. The closest, most obvious place to look for such assistance was among one's ancestors. The ancestors were very much considered part of the family as a whole. They had moved on to a different level of existence and had special needs, but they were dealt with as if their interest in family affairs remained as strong as when they had lived.

Rituals for the ancestors were aimed at making their afterlife as comfortable as possible. Some were also intended to assist their passage through otherworldly purgatories in which their past conduct was judged by divine authorities. It was believed that only if the ancestors were free from the clutches of hellish officials and materially well-attended to would they give their protection and help to living members of the family. This meant that altars were maintained in every household. Tablets with the names of the ancestors were placed there, along with offerings of food and drink. On special occasions more elaborate rites were enacted before those altars, at the graveside, or at a temple. On such occasions more lavish offerings were also provided. Paper money was burned in the belief that it would be transformed and conveyed to those in the afterlife. Anyone who visits a country where traditional Chinese religion is still practiced will note small metal containers filled with ashes on the sidewalks in front

TOMBS OF THE MING AND QING DYNASTIES— WORLD HERITAGE SITE

Aside from their immense historical value, the Ming and Qing dynasty imperial tombs are the very embodiments of the design principles of the Chinese art of geomancy (feng shui). The tombs were designated as UNESCO World Heritage Sites in 2000.

of people's houses and businesses. These are for the sole purpose of burning money for the ancestors of the family. Paper money is burned on a number of occasions during the year, especially at New Year's, the grave-sweeping festival (Qingming), and on death anniversaries.

The ancestors were not the only spiritual presence in the Chinese household. Gods and spirits were believed to inhabit strategic locations inside and out. The most important of these was no doubt the God of the Stove (Zaoshen). His dominion over the fire and the food-preparation area of the home guaranteed his prestige. The God of the Stove was responsible for watching over the activities of the family and for reporting those activities to the gods in the heavens. His yearly ascent to make his report was believed to take place shortly before New Year's. The family prepared a feast to send him off and tried to ensure that he would make only favorable comments about them.

Most houses would also have an altar to the God of the Soil placed close to the ground. He would be charged with protecting the family against evil spiritual influences. Door gods, whose images were painted on or beside entrance ways, protected against the entry of undesirable spirits and ghosts. Statues of the God of Wealth, the Buddhist Goddess of Mercy (Guanyin), and other popular divinities became common in the late imperial age. The help and protection of these gods was considered essential to the preservation and prosperity of the family.

Shamanism in Chinese Religion

Shamanism is a form of religion that focuses on direct means of contacting the world of spirits. It is the main religious and cultural tradition in many preliterate cultures. The shaman is a person, either male or female, who has undergone a radical initiation into the means of communicating with the spirits. The shaman is known primarily as one who can gain temporary release from their physical body and travel to the realms of the spirits. There he (or she, since in many cultures the shaman is a woman) can speak with the spirits and request their assistance in human affairs. Alternatively, shamans can vacate their bodies and allow spirits to make use of their voices to speak with humans. One of the most important roles of the shaman is to cure illness. Both spiritual and medical means are employed to this end. Often it is necessary to exorcise evil influences, and the shaman is an expert at this task. In preliterate cultures the shaman is also the person who learns and teaches the history of the tribe in which he or she serves. He or she is the storyteller and historian who allows people to learn from their past.

In China, although purely shamanic religion has not been practiced since prehistoric times, shamanic elements have always been a central in religious practice. The kings of the Xia (2100–1766 BCE) and Shang (1766–1045 BCE) periods relied on the services of priests capable of contacting the spirits to plan their every move. Among the people, mediums who could enter a trance and allow spirits to speak through their mouths, or write with their hands have been a basic part of village religion right up the present day. Despite the fact that spirit mediumship played a major role in the government of early China, representatives of later governments, as well as of the major religions, were always suspicious of the practice and sought to suppress it. This was because a medium capable of receiving information from the highest level of heavenly government could potentially challenge the legitimacy of earthly government, or religious authority—a dangerous thing in the eyes of those authorities. Despite official disapproval, however, techniques of shamanic trance and mediumship have always been a basic part Chinese folk religion.

Ledgers of Merit and Demerit

The role of religion is not primarily to provide moral and ethical guidance. However, moral behavior is often seen as a prerequisite to the achievement of spiritual goals. As societies become more sophisticated they require better explanations of the existence of evil. People want to believe that there are mechanisms or agencies that provide ultimate recompense to those who have been wronged, and punishment for those who have wronged. In Chinese religion it is believed that there are gods whose main activity is keeping track of the deeds of humans. At death, the deceased individual is brought before a tribunal of spirit-officials for judgment. Since the Chinese adopted the Buddhist concept of rebirth, it is often a case of determining not

only which punishments or rewards to mete out, but also how long these will last before rebirth occurs. Living descendants can modify the sentence by undertaking certain ritual activities, such as reciting scriptures and employing priests to intercede on behalf of the departed souls.

In China, beginning in the third century CE, if not before, another variation on this theme of morality and retribution came into play. This was the practice of maintaining one's own personal record of good and evil deeds. The fourth century Taoist text *Baopu zi* by Ge Hong (c. 280–343) details how it was necessary to do a specific number of good deeds in order to proceed with the quest of immortality. Evil deeds were marked off against the total of good deeds at a high rate. Divine authorities ultimately verify the correctness and validity of these records. This belief continued to gain popularity, until by the late Song dynasty we find scriptures that give detailed information on which sorts of deeds count for how many points, and how many points are required to achieve a given reward.

By the Ming dynasty the practice of recording one's own merits and demerits had become even more widespread and formalized. Registers for keeping track of merit and demerit points were being published commercially and by religious establishments. Belief in the validity of the practice had also spread from Taoism and popular religion to Buddhism and Confucianism. Well-known Confucian officials and Buddhist priests were actively keeping their own records, and writing about the subject. One would expect that the understanding of what constituted good and evil could vary depending on the main affinity of the writer. In fact, by the late Ming, moral principles from all sources had become thoroughly mixed and universalized. This mixing and unifying of moral values is once again symptomatic of the strong forces of integration at work in the realm of religion and philosophy in late imperial China.

Terence C. Russell

See also: **Buddhism—China; Confucianism—China; Taoism**

Further Reading

Ebrey, Patricia Buckley, and Peter N. Gregory, eds. (1993) *Religion and Society in T'ang and Sung China*. Honolulu, HI: University of Hawaii Press.

Granet, Marcel. (1975) *The Religion of the Chinese People*. Translated and edited by Maurice Freedman. New York: Harper and Row.

Hansen, Valerie. (1990) *Changing Gods in Medieval China, 1127–1276*. Princeton, NJ: Princeton University Press.

Jochim, Christian. (1986) *Chinese Religion.* Englewood Cliffs, NJ: Prentice-Hall.

Lopez, Donald S., Jr (1996) *Religions of China in Practice.* Princeton, NJ: Princeton University Press.

Yang, C. K. (1961) *Religion in Chinese Society.* Berkeley and Los Angeles: University of California Press.

RELIGION, FOLK—JAPAN

Minkan shinko, literally "popular beliefs," refers to the vast array of folk beliefs, customs, and rituals that make up what can be called Japanese folk religion and that play an important role in Japanese daily life. Indeed, especially in rural areas of the country, such the Tohoku, or northern Honshu, Sado Island, and the mountainous regions that border the Sea of Japan, these beliefs and practices still manifest themselves in a wide variety of contexts, from planting and harvesting rice to building boats and houses, caring for sick people, getting married, celebrating the New Year, and coping with earthquakes, typhoons, volcanic eruptions, and other disasters. And even in modern, high-tech urban Japan, folk religious beliefs remain important, as evidenced by the continuing popularity of *uranai,* or folk divination.

It is impossible to separate many concrete manifestations of Japanese folk religious practices from those related to the two major established religions, Buddhism and Shinto, but unlike these religions, folk religious practices have no clear-cut doctrine, written texts, or priesthood; they rely heavily on oral transmission. They are also highly variable, and each region of the country has a wealth of unique traditions.

Seasonal Rituals

Many *minkan shinko* rituals are connected with the seasonal cycle. The most important of these occurs during *oshogatsu matsuri,* or the New Year festival, which, since 1872 has taken place during the first three days of January. Traditionally, a house will be thoroughly cleaned to rid it of the previous year's impurities. Great care is taken to adorn the home with a variety of sacred objects signifying purity, renewal, and good fortune. A straw rope (*shimenawa*) indicating that the house has been purified is tied above the main entrance, and pine cones are placed on either side of the gate, symbolizing the new life that will shortly appear. The first visitor, the first food eaten, even the first dream of the new year all have ritual significance.

One of the most ubiquitous customs associated with the new year is the pounding of rice into *mochi,* or rice cakes, which are placed on small household altars and topped by a *mikan,* or mandarin orange, symbolizing the rebirth of the sun. The occasion is also marked by

A man dressed as a samurai warrior hits a kagami-michi rice cake with a mallet at the 2000 Kagami Biraki festival in Tokyo. It is a traditional New Year's celebration to mark the cleaning and purification of weapons and armor, a practice that dates to the fifteenth century. (REUTERS NEWMEDIA INC./CORBIS)

the consumption of special foods, including a special soup made from pounded rice and vegetables called *ozoni,* and a form of sake, or rice wine, drunk only during the New Year's festival. While all of these customs have links to both Shinto and Buddhism, they vary considerably from region to region and have no canonical forms.

Other important folk-religious holidays include *Setsubun* (3 February), in which beans are thrown into the four corners of a room to insure good luck while chanting *Oni wa soto, fuku wa uchi!* ("Out with the demons, good luck to the house!"); *Hina matsuri,* or the Doll Festival (5 February), when young girls set up displays of traditional dolls arranged in the form of the imperial court; Children's Day (5 May; formerly called Boys' Day), when paper carp, or *koi nobori,* are flown to symbolize the presence of young males in a household; and *Obon* (from mid-August to early September), when every neighborhood or village honors the souls of the dead by cleaning graves and many perform a special dance known as the *Bon odori* or *Obon odori. Obon* is basically a Buddhist celebration, but it is so encrusted with local beliefs and practices that it can legitimately be conceived of as a folk holiday.

Rites of Passage

Life-cycle rituals, or rites of passage, also play an important role in Japanese folk religion, marking major points of transition from the cradle to the grave. Many of these rituals relate to the two main religions, but they also contain a great many folk-ritual features. *Miyamairi*, or the first visit of a baby to a nearby Shinto shrine, occurs thirty and thirty-three days after birth for boys and girls, respectively, and includes offerings of sake and beans to the local *kami* (spirit or god). *Shichi-go-san*, or the "Seven-Five-Three" ceremony (15 November), is for children who have recently turned three, five, and seven. They visit the local shine with their parents, are purified, and later receive a bag of sweets and a toy or two. Coming of age, at twenty, is celebrated on 15 January. A public official addresses the new young adults at the shrine, usually with remarks about their new rights and duties; the girls present are usually dressed in fancy long-sleeved kimonos. Finally, *kanreki* celebrates having reached one's sixty-first birthday. The person so honored dons red garments symbolic of childhood; indeed, the symbolism of the *kanreki* is expressed in the name of the celebration, which can be translated "return of the calendar" (i.e., the traditional sixty-year Chinese cycle).

Another extremely important rite of passage, of course, is marriage. It would be impossible here to describe all the folk elements in Japanese marriage, which is almost always celebrated in a Shinto context, though rarely at a shrine. Today, the vast majority of Japanese marriages are celebrated in hotels or special "wedding palaces." The central element of the ritual is an exchange of sake between the bride and groom. But almost every item of clothing worn by the bride has an important symbolism. The most striking of these is the *tsunokakushi*, or "horn-hider," which forms part of her headdress and serves to hide the so-called horns of jealousy and other potentially "demonic" characteristics which might impede her obedience to her husband.

Uranai

An additional feature of Japanese folk religion that deserves mention is *uranai*, or folk divination. In early fall, tiny tables illuminated by small lanterns dot the streets of Tokyo and other big cities, manned by fortune-tellers practicing one or another variety of divination. Japanese *uranai* includes a great many specific techniques, most of which are rooted in the ancient Chinese *Yi jing* (Classic of Changes), and based on its eight well-known trigrams. *Ekikyo*, as the *Yi jing* is called in Japanese, is generally performed by professional diviners who employ the traditional Chinese method, which includes the use of yarrow stalks.

In recent years almost every conceivable basis for foretelling the future has been drawn upon, including blood types. That is, types A, B, O, or AB, as well as Rh+ and Rh−, are believed by some diviners to have specific implications for a person's fortune. Although this form of *uranai* is still in its infancy, it underscores the extent to which Japanese folk religion has been able to absorb beliefs and practices from a wide variety of sources, from ancient China to modern biological science.

C. Scott Littleton

See also: **Buddhism—Japan; Shinto**

Further Reading

Ashkenazi, Michael. (1993) *Matsuri: Festivals of a Japanese Town*. Honolulu, HI: University of Hawaii Press.

Bestor, Theodore C. (1988) *Neighborhood Tokyo*. Stanford, CA: Stanford University Press.

Blacker, Carmen. (1975) *The Catalpa Bow: A Study of Shamanistic Practices in Japan*. London: Allen & Unwin.

Earhart, H. Byron. (1983) "Folk Religion." In *Kodansha Japan Encyclopedia*, vol. 2. Tokyo: Kodansha, 298–300.

———. (1982) *Japanese Religion: Unity and Diversity*. 3d ed. Belmont, CA: Wadsworth.

Edwards, Walter. (1989) *Modern Japan through Its Weddings*. Stanford, CA: Stanford University Press.

Hendry, Joy. (1981) *Marriage in Changing Japan*. New York: St. Martin's Press.

Littleton, C. Scott. (2000) "Japanese Religions." In *Religion and Culture: An Anthropological Focus*, edited by Raymond Scupin. Upper Saddle River, NJ: Prentice-Hall, 294–321.

Nelson, John K. (1996) *A Year in the Life of a Shinto Shrine*. Seattle, WA: University of Washington Press.

Reader, Ian. (1991) *Religion in Contemporary Japan*. Honolulu, HI: University of Hawaii Press.

Reischauer, Edwin O., and Marius O. Jansen. (1995) *The Japanese Today: Change and Continuity*. Cambridge, MA: Harvard University Press.

RELIGIONS, NEW—JAPAN The term "new religions" refers to religions that have been founded within approximately the last two centuries and are considered to be outside the mainstream formally organized religions, specifically Buddhism and Shinto. The Japanese term *shin shukyo* ("new religion"), and the less common *shinko shukyo* ("newly-arisen religion"), came into use in the 1950s.

Classifications and Common Characteristics

Scholars often categorize these religious groups according to the period in which they emerged or expanded and the predominant religious traditions they reflect. The first group was founded in the nineteenth century, the second from the late nineteenth century to World War I, and the third from the end of World War I to the present. Some scholars suggest a fourth designation of "new New Religions" (*shin shin shukyo*) for those founded after World War II, especially during the 1970s and 1980s. It is important to point out, however, that the majority of these movements are not fundamentally or radically new. Regarding the latest "wave" of new religions, Reader (1991: 195), for example, comments, "[T]hey appear, in the midst of a rapidly technologising, modernising and internationalising society, to express anti-modern and Japanocentric sentiments, focusing on miracles, spirit possession and a view of causation that is rooted very firmly in the Japanese folk tradition." One factor differentiating them from the mainstream of religious thought and activity is their independence from government, state, and social norms.

A second common characteristic is that rather than taking a radical departure in content, their newness comes from their innovative approach, interpretation, and methodology. For example, they may claim to have discovered a new truth in the old tradition, one that has not been recognized before, and to have found a way to make that truth available for the benefit of all who believe. In most cases, this involves spiritual healing following the discoveries made by a charismatic founder.

A third element in many new religions is the binding together of solutions to *byoki naoshi* (physical healing), *kokoro naoshi* (spiritual healing) and the goal of *yo naoshi* (world renewal). Most claim that such problems as illness and misfortune have spiritual causes, and that through their newly discovered methods, individuals can identify and eventually eradicate the source of their suffering. They offer the hope that each person can overcome his or her problems, and thereafter help solve the problems of the world at large. To a large extent this in done through participation in some form of small group in which members share, discuss, and suggest solutions to other members' problems.

Japanese tradition includes the formal religions (*kisei shukyo*) Shinto and Buddhism and influential but rarely organized Confucianism and Taoism. In addition, there is a broad, unsystematized body of beliefs and practices that can be called popular religion or even folk religion. Those movements which Earhart (1989) views as evolving from the general background of Japanese religion may include the worship of nature and holy persons (whether they be deities or respected religious leaders), devotion to family and country, stress on sincerity and self-reflection, self-cultivation and dedication to hard work.

In many cases, new religions in this last category incorporate elements from Buddhism, Shinto, and popular religion. Gedatsu-kai (founded in 1929 by Eizo Okano), for example, combines all of these elements by encouraging worship before the Buddhist-style altar, worship before the Shinto-style altar, veneration of deities and ancestors, family values, the ethical value of self-reflection, patriotic spirit, and appreciation of the benefits of nature. The beliefs and practices are traditional, but the modification and reconstruction make them into a new whole, and this is typical of most new religions.

Although Shinto, Buddhism, and popular religion account for the clear majority of influences, certain Christianity-related movements also belong among the New Religions. Groups such as Mukyokai (the Non-Church movement, founded 1901 by Uchimura Kanzo) claim only that they are Japanese expressions of Christianity, but others, like Iesu no Mitama Kyokai (Spirit of Jesus Church, founded by Murai Jun in 1941), make exclusivistic claims to having discovered the truth of Christianity prior to distortion by Hellinistic influences and Western church history.

Membership

It is often suggested that new religions flourish during times of social crisis and unrest, such as the transition from Tokugawa rule to the restoration of imperial rule in the Meiji Restoration (1868), the poverty and economic depression of the late 1920s, and the traumatic period following the devastations of World War II. In his 1989 study of Gedatsu-kai, H. Byron Earhart cogently argues that attributing such growth entirely to the social milieu is inadequate and that one ought to interpret the formation of such new religions through a more balanced view of social conditions, religious history, and personal innovation. Social disruption and personal anxiety may well be important factors, but Earhart refers to them as "precipitating" factors (236), essential for triggering the timing of a movement's appearance and growth, but not sufficient for beginning the movement or establishing its primary teachings. The influence of religious history, in the same way, is insufficient to stimulate the formation of a new religion. The weakening of established religious traditions and practices may well leave a void to be filled, but on the other hand these preexisting elements are vital to the constitution of new movements through the innovations of the founder. In sum, the social climate helps precipitate, religious factors help enable, and the founder helps innovate—all three factors must be taken into account.

Reflecting the establishment view of the newcomers, until recently the media and academics tended to view the new religions as peddling false ideas and superstitions to a gullible, undereducated, alienated underclass. More balanced contemporary research, however, indicates that those who join these various new movements today are slightly better educated than the average Japanese, to a large degree have white-collar jobs, and are somewhat conservative politically.

Shinto-Related Religions

Largest of the Shinto-related new religions is Tenri-kyo (Religion of Heavenly Origin), which in 1990 had a membership of 1.8 million. (All movement membership figures herein are taken from Mullins, Shimazono, and Swanson's 1993 *Religion and Society in Modern Japan: Selected Readings*). Tenri-kyo was founded in 1838 by Nakayama Miki (1798–1887), a farmer's wife who began to have revelatory experiences. During a shamanistic rite, she received healing gifts and revelatory scriptures while possessed by the deity Tenri-O-no-mikoto (Lord of Heavenly Reason). Originally classified as an actual Shinto sect, in 1970 it was reclassified by the government among "Other Religions" because it had come to see itself as having a mission that extended beyond Japan.

Now emphasizing "The Path to the Joyous Life," members seek to rid themselves of evil thoughts and purify themselves in order to lead a balanced, harmonious life, hence approaching the perfect divine kingdom when humanity will live in union with the deity.

Other Shinto-related movements, and their founding dates include Kurozumi-kyo (1814, named after its founder, Kurozumi Munetada), Konko-kyo (1859), Omoto (1899), and Honmichi (1913).

Buddhist-Related Religions

Buddhist-related new religions notably focus on Nichiren (a Japanese Buddhist sect dating to the mid-thirteenth century and focused exclusively on the Lotus Sutra), the Lotus Sutra, and ancestors. They focus less on *kami* (deities of Shinto tradition) and more on the divinities of Buddhist tradition. A typical example of how newer movements have drawn on traditional Buddhism is the memorial rituals that Reiyukai (Society of Friends of the Spirits, 3.2 million members in 1990) holds for the dead. Founder Kubo Kakutaro

(1892–1944) saw veneration of the ancestors as essential to social harmony and national salvation.

Soka Gakkai (Value Creation Society) was founded in 1930 by Makiguchi Tsunesaburo (1871–1944), an educator who wrote about "value-creating education," and his follower Toda Josei (1900–1958) and is closely associated with Nichiren Buddhism. Makiguchi was imprisoned during World War II for encouraging his followers not to purchase Shinto amulets; he died while incarcerated. Toda was also imprisoned, and following release at the end of the war, he began to build a highly organized movement. The group's agressiveness and its declared aim of uniting religion and politics led to much criticism, but it succeeded in creating the political party Komeito (Clean Government Party) in 1964.

The movement is currently under the leadership of Ikeda Daisaku (b. 1928), and under his leadership it has become less militant, severed official ties with Komeito, and separated entirely from the organized priesthood of Nichiren Shoshu (the official name for the Nichiren sect). Soka Gakkai's two central aims are to realize personal happiness through lay practice of Nichiren Buddhism and achieve a peaceful world through the application of Buddhism to culture and education. As is typical of many of the larger movements, the group operates schools, publishes several weekly and monthly magazines, and, beginning in the mid-1960s, established branches in many nations overseas. In 1990, the group had a membership of 17.7 million.

Other Buddhist-related movements (with founding date and membership in 1990) include Rissho Kosei-kai (Society for Establishing Righteousness and Friendly Relations, founded 1938; 6.3 million members), Perfect Liberty Kyodan (founded 1925; 1.3 million members), Seicho-no-ie (House of Growth, founded 1930; 838,496 members), Sekai Kyusei-kyo (World Salvation Religion, founded 1935; 835,756 members), Byakko Shinko-kai (White Light Association, founded 1951; 500,000 members), and Kofuku-no-Kagaku (Institute for Research in Human Happiness, founded 1986; 13,300 members).

Several additional movements are worth a brief mention for different reasons. Agon-shu (membership of 206,606 in 1990), was founded in 1954 by Kiriyama Seiyu (b. 1921), who suffered a childhood of poverty and a series of business failures that eventually landed him in prison for tax offenses. In despair, he attempted to hang himself, only to find on the overhead beam a copy of a Buddhist text elucidating the compassion of the Buddha Kannon. Believing that Kannon had directly interceded to save him, he studied the work diligently and came to the conclusion that his earlier misfortunes were the result of karmic pollution, some of which he had inherited from his ancestors.

Meditation and esoteric practices, he claimed, could transform the suffering of the spirits of the dead and allow them to become Buddhas. The movement is now well-known for an elaborate, well-attended Star Festival, during which pyres of sticks, upon which are written prayers for the ancestors and personal prayers, are burned in a rite of purification.

Shukyo Mahikari (Religion of True Light), currently divided into two splinter groups with a combined membership of about 600,000 in 1990, was founded by Okada Yoshikazu in 1959. This movement is centered on a purification ritual that is held to heal both physically and mentally, through the transmission of the True Light (Mahikari) through the palm of the hand of an initiate. Mahikari is based on a syncretism of Shinto, Buddhism, and Shamanistic elements, with stress on the first in its emphasis on purity. "The Light can be used to purify not only people, but also food, rivers, animals, trees, cities, houses, etc. It may serve to prevent calamities as well as recover from them." (Clarke and Somers 1994: 92). The Buddhist influence appears in Mahikari's emphasis on karma carried over from previous lives and from one's ancestors, which is seen as the root of all disease and misfortune. The shamanistic factor is the contention that the majority of all diseases and misfortunes result from spirit possession by an ancestor who must be suitably pacified. There is another important influence from Christianity, from which Mahikari has borrowed themes, teachings, and the figure of Jesus Christ. According to Mahikari's teachings, Jesus traveled through India and China to Japan, practiced with mountain ascetics there, returned to Judea to teach, was sentenced to death, but was voluntarily replaced on the cross by his brother. Jesus then traveled to Europe, Asia, and the Americas before returning to Japan, where he lived until his death at the age of over one hundred.

Aum Shinri-kyo was founded by Matsumoto Chizuo (b. 1955; later known as Asahara Shoko), who was born almost totally blind. Matsumoto was sent to a boarding school for the blind, where he lived until moving to Tokyo to work as an acupuncturist while waiting to take the examinations to enter Tokyo University. Failing in the exam, in despondence about his role in the world, he began to study the teachings of Agon-shu. Eventually turning away from Agon-shu, he founded what later became Aum Shinri-kyo (Aum Supreme Truth Sect) in 1984, proclaiming himself a messianic leader appointed by the Hindu deity Siva to create a perfect society that would be composed of all

those who followed his teachings, methods, and example. Gradually his ideas about overcoming the physical barriers to immortality evolved into a justification of using destruction and violence as means of salvation. The result of this was widely reported. Beyond the public's revulsion as a result of the group's sarin gas attack on the Tokyo subways in March 1995, several murders, abductions, and a long list of other crimes, these incidents generated considerable fear and suspicion of other new religions. Believers in other movements became quick to distance themselves from the mindless fanaticism and violent methods of the Aum cultists.

New Religions Abroad

While some movements have restricted their activities to Japan, others have established missionary activities abroad, primarily to the Americas. Peter Clarke notes that there are over thirty such religions in Brazil alone, where there are an estimated 1.3 million people of Japanese descent. Mahikari has established itself on the Caribbean islands of Martinique and Guadeloupe and adapted to local conditions to the degree that its Japanese character is considerably obscured. Movements are also active in other nations of South, Central, and North America as well as South and Southeast Asia and Africa. Soka Gakkai is the largest of the group in Europe, followed by Mahikari.

Success outside of Japan has reflected a willingness to adapt to local customs and traditional views. Tenrikyo, for example, was established in Brazil, Hawaii, and the mainland United States in the 1930s but failed to make significant inroads, especially outside the community of Japanese immigrants and their descendents. Yet in Korea, where it has local leadership and liturgy in Korean, it has been highly successful.

Overview

The new religious movements are clearly manifestations of a religious feeling, whether motivated by a quest for the irrational, a distrust of science, or a need for spirituality that goes beyond the monotony of everyday life. The fact that they continue to appear and that some experience considerable growth is indicative of the fact that traditional religious paths have not addressed all the spiritual needs of the Japanese people. The new movements do this with vigor and enthusiasm that often seems lacking in the more restrained established religions. The new movements have to a considerable extent built on the traditional religiosity of Japan—including Buddhist, Shintoist, Taoist, Confucianist, and folk religious elements—adopting what is appealing and infusing the new composites with new interpretations, rituals, approaches and promises. Among the traditional elements, almost all groups emphasize the importance of one's ancestors. When neglected, these ancestors may become potential causes of misfortune, but when properly venerated they become sources of benevolence.

Most groups seek to provide members with the benefits of this world, including success, peace of mind, and happiness. They tend to feature deep personal experience that may be linked to a miraculous cure of a physical illness or sudden awareness of how to cope with a debilitating personal problem.

While it may be said that some of these movements are quasi-religious and make claims that are beyond the bounds of probability, one should not lump them all together, nor should one dismiss the valuable lessons taught by certain groups merely because some of their occult practices may seem dubious at best. Whatever the appeal, an estimated 10 to 20 percent of the Japanese people belong to such movements.

James M. Vardaman, Jr.

Further Reading

Clarke, Peter B., ed. (1999) *Bibliography of Japanese New Religions*. Richmond, U.K.: Japan Library/Curzon Press Ltd.

——, and Jeffrey Somers. (1994) *Japanese New Religions in the West*. Sandgate, U.K.: Japan Library/Curzon Press Ltd.

Earhart, H. Byron. (1989) *Gedatsu-kai and Religion in Contemporary Japan*. Bloomington: Indiana University Press.

Kisala, Robert. (1999) *Prophets of Peace: Pacifism and Cultural Identity in Japan's New Religions*. Honolulu: University of Hawaii Press.

McFarland, H. Neill. (1967) *The Rush Hour of the Gods: A Study of New Religious Movements in Japan*. New York and London: The Macmillan Company.

McVeigh, Brian J. (1997) *Spirits, Selves and Subjectivity in a Japanese New Religion*. Lewiston, NY: The Edwin Mellen Press, Ltd.

Mullins, Mark R., Shimazono Susumu, and Paul L. Swanson, eds. (1993) *Religion and Society in Modern Japan: Selected Readings*. Berkeley, CA: Asian Humanities Press.

Reader, Ian (1991) *Religion in Contemporary Japan*. London: Macmillan Press Ltd.

Shukyo Nenkan (1991). Tokyo: Gyosei.

RELIGIONS, NEW—KOREA The first indigenous organized religion in Korea originated on 5 April 1860, when Ch'oe Che-u (1824–1864) began having visions in which the Lord of Heaven told him that he had been selected to save humanity. Ch'oe Che-u's Tonghak (Eastern Learning) religion, now known as Ch'ondogyo (Religion of the Heavenly Way), was but the first of dozens of religions that have been generated by the inroads of Christianity, the trauma of Japanese colonial rule, and the rapid urbanization and industrialization that dramatically transformed Korea in the second half of the twentieth century.

These new religions can be classified into five categories. The first category includes Ch'ondogyo and those religions derived from it that worship the deity with whom Ch'oe Che-u is said to have spoken and that ground their doctrines and practices in a twenty-one-syllable incantation that Ch'oe Che-u revealed. The second category includes Chongsan'gyo and the dozens of related religions such as Chungsando (The Chungsan Way) and Taesun Chillihoe (The Society for the Truth of Kang Chungsan), which view Ch'oe as a prophet who prepared the way for the advent of Kang Chung-san (1871–1909). Members of the Chongsan family of religions believe that Kang is the Lord on High and that he descended to earth and took human form in order to establish the Rites of Cosmic Renewal, which will assist humanity in the transition from the current age of discord and injustice to the coming age of cosmic harmony.

The third category of new religions in Korea worships Tan'gun, the legendary first ancestor of the Korean people. Taejonggyo (The Religion of the Grand Progenitor), founded in 1909, is the most prominent example of this category of religions, which urges Koreans to reject foreign gods in favor of one of the most illustrious of their own ancestors, who, they believe, established a powerful Korean kingdom five thousand years ago. Worshippers of Tan'gun believe that he is part of the Divine Trinity of three persons (Creator, Teacher, and Ruler) in one God.

In addition to new religions with indigenous roots, there are two other categories of new religions: modifications of Buddhism and modifications of Christianity. Won Buddhism is the best-known Buddhist new religion in Korea. Founded in 1916, it represents a modernized urban approach to Buddhism. The Unification Church, based on the belief of its founder, Sun Myong Moon (b. 1920), that he is the messiah sent to complete the mission that Jesus began, is the best-known new Korean religion with Christian origins.

Don Baker

See also: **Ch'ondogyo; Taejonggyo; Tonghak; Unification Church**

Further Reading

Ministry of Culture and Sports, Republic of Korea, ed. (1996) *Religious Culture in Korea.* Elizabeth, NJ: Hollym International.

Royal Asiatic Society. (1967) "The New Religions of Korea." Special issue of *Transactions of the Royal Asiatic Society* 43.

RELIGIOUS   SELF-MORTIFICATION

Avoidance of pain is assumed to be an instinctive human drive, yet religious self-mortification involves deliberate self-infliction of physical pain during a culturally sanctioned, often annual, ritual or festival. In South and Southeast Asia in particular, self-mortification has undergone a dramatic revival. Usually, rituals involve either self-administered beatings and intentional bloodletting (Muslim and Christian self-flagellation) or piercing the face and body (Hindu and Buddhist rites). To an observer, self-mortification appears to be painful and injurious. To a ritual participant, the primary objective is to achieve analgesia or absence of pain: not simply to control or even conquer pain, but to feel its absence as a transcendent spiritual experience.

Origins and History

Religious self-mortification is a complex phenomenon that has been differently understood and enacted across time and space. In Mesoamerica, the ancient Maya performed elaborate bloodletting rituals during the late preclassic period (200 BCE onward). In India, sadhus, holy men outside the Hindu caste system, cultivated acts of self-mortification, such as fasting, staring at the sun, and burial alive, as part of an ascetic lifestyle for millennia. Native American Indians hung from hooks (inserted in the chest or back) during Sun Dances to expedite a vision quest, while Shi'ite Muslims in Iran and Pakistan have long commemorated the assassination of Husayn, the grandson of Muhammad, with acts of *matam*, ritual mortification, especially scourging, as mourning or condolence.

No single definition of religious self-mortification can encompass the contested and contingent meanings underlying each historical and cultural performance. The English term "mortification," for example, has Christian origins and exegesis: "mortificare" derives from ecclesiastical Latin, "to put to death," a reference to the crucifixion of Jesus of Nazareth. In early Christianity, mortification of the flesh involved subjugation of the penitential body by discipline or denial as a vicarious imitation of the Passion of Christ. Yet religious self-mortification had been practiced in different parts of the world prior to the birth of Jesus and evolved in a variety of manifestations independent of Christianity. Past and present, each of these theological traditions has approached self-mortification differently: the purpose of the act and its myriad meanings, the role of pain and bloodshed during performance, as well as the type of religious body (subjugated, empowered, or invulnerable) that must be physically and symbolically prepared in order to receive divine blessing.

Decline and Revival

The revival of religious self-mortification in Asia represents a new chapter in the history of human ideas about pain. Prior to the Asian renaissance, self-mortification had suffered a serious decline, almost to the point of extinction in the West. This was not a natural atrophy, but derived from a conscious intent to suppress and eradicate the custom. During the Enlightenment, emerging ideas about rationality, civilization, and what it means to be human transformed the ways Europeans imagined pain, especially self-inflicted pain. Pain was no longer considered useful or transformational. Consequently, the eighteenth and nineteenth centuries marked the decline of religious self-mortification throughout the West and its colonies. Christian self-flagellation was not only banned in Europe, but also in the Hispanic Philippines and Mexico. British colonial authorities in India prohibited hook-swinging festivals, while government officials in the United States forbade self-mortification at Sun Dances. Despite the fact that pain was voluntarily self-inflicted in a religious context by actors who insisted that performance was not painful, ritual mortification was condemned as irrational, barbaric, and inhuman. Pain embodied negativity, and religious "self-torture" was perceived as morally unjustifiable.

However, not only did religious self-mortification survive Western disapprobation, in postcolonial Asia the practice has undergone a striking revival, especially in and around maritime Southeast Asia. This revival took place synchronously throughout the mid- to late twentieth century in both capital cities and rural provinces. It transcended cultural and religious boundaries, embracing localized and syncretic versions of Hinduism, Buddhism, Christianity, and Islam, as well as Chinese popular religion. While it is impossible to estimate the number of (predominantly male) ritual actors, the visible resurgence of participants, the vast audiences, the rapacious international media attention, the promotion of religious self-mortification festivals by state departments of tourism, the declaration of public holidays, the new ritual regulations, even the sponsorship of multinational corporations—all testify to the magnitude of the revival, as well as its ongoing commercialization and appropriation as a spectacle of cultural exoticism.

South and Southeast Asia

In South and Southeast Asia alone, a host of countries have been involved in the revival. In the Philippines, Catholic rituals of self-flagellation and crucifixion (by nailing) are performed during Holy Week. In India, Malaysia, and Singapore, the Tamil Hindu festival of Thaipusam involves *kavadi* (wooden arch) carrying and body piercing. In Thailand, Chinese Thai Buddhists perform increasingly ostentatious corporeal piercing at the Vegetarian Festival. In Taiwan and Singapore, Chinese spirit-mediums also practice ritual piercing. In Indonesia, certain Sufi Muslim rituals require self-stabbing and piercing. In Sri Lanka, the Kataragama festival now attracts Sinhalese Buddhists and Tamil Hindus, who perform various types of self-mortification, including hook-hanging.

Rationale

Why is religious self-mortification undergoing a revival? Why in Asia? Why at this moment in history? The withdrawal of colonial powers from Southeast Asia created a space for indigenous renegotiation and reaffirmation of cultural and ethnic identity. Significantly, Thailand, which was not colonized, joined the revival later (in the 1980s), influenced partly by ritual events in Malaysia. However, the colonized countries of mainland Southeast Asia have not participated, nor have East Asian countries such as Korea and China, or Japan, despite a tradition of asceticism.

To what extent has ritual participation been truly voluntary? Almost always it has been the poorer members of society who sought alternative ways to make suffering sufferable and to symbolically contest and mitigate status hierarchy. By achieving analgesia during ritual performance, sometimes via altered states of consciousness, evidence of divine contact is demonstrated and rewarded with assurances of guidance, protection, and blessing. This ritual empowerment of the powerless is often contracted under vow as a repeated act of supplication or thanksgiving for a sick family member. (The rituals are not penitential, even in the Catholic Philippines.) Indigenous healers, who are often at the heart of the revival, have also sought to access sacred powers released via divine communion. For these healers, ritual self-mortification represented a new medium to acquire, test, and replenish esoteric potency, a traditional foundation for political leadership in Southeast Asia.

At the dawn of the twenty-first century in Asia, the revival of religious self-mortification is far from over.

When ritually self-inflicted, physical pain has a sacred, if not transformational purpose.

Nicholas H. Barker

Further Reading

Asad, Talal. (1997) "On Torture, or Cruel, Inhuman, and Degrading Treatment." In *Social Suffering*, edited by Arthur Kleinman, Veena Das, and Margaret Lock. Berkeley and Los Angeles: University of California Press, 285–308.

Barker, Nicholas H. (1998) *The Revival of Religious Self-Flagellation and the Birth of Crucifixion in Lowland Christian Philippines*. Discussion Paper no. 63. Nagoya, Japan: Graduate School of International Development, Nagoya University.

Cohen, Erik. (2001) *The Chinese Vegetarian Festival in Phuket: Religion, Ethnicity, and Tourism on a Southern Thai Island*. Bangkok, Thailand: White Lotus.

Collins, Elizabeth Fuller. (1997) *Pierced by Murugan's Lance: Ritual, Power, and Moral Redemption among Malaysian Hindus*. Dekalb, IL: Northern Illinois University Press.

Crapanzano, Vincent. (1973) *The Hamadsha: A Study in Moroccan Ethnopsychiatry*. Berkeley and Los Angeles: University of California Press.

Glucklich, Ariel. (2001) *Sacred Pain: Hurting the Body for the Sake of the Soul*. Oxford and New York: Oxford University Press.

Gross, Robert Lewis. (1992) *The Sadhus of India: A Study of Hindu Asceticism*. Jaipur and New Delhi, India: Rawat.

Obeyesekere, Gananath. (1981) *Medusa's Hair: An Essay on Personal Symbols and Religious Experience*. Chicago: University of Chicago Press.

Oddie, Geoffrey A. (1995) *Popular Religion, Elites, and Reform: Hook-Swinging and Its Prohibition in Colonial India, 1800–1894*. New Delhi: Manohar.

Pinault, David. (1992) *The Shiites: Ritual and Popular Piety in a Muslim Community*. New York: St. Martin's.

Sabbatucci, Dario. (1987) "Mortification." In *The Encyclopedia of Religion*, vol 10, edited by Mircea Eliade. New York: Macmillan, 113–115.

Singer, André. (1974) "The Dervishes of Kurdistan." *Asian Affairs* 61, 2: 179–182.

Sutton, Donald S. (1990) "Rituals of Self-Mortification: Taiwanese Spirit-Mediums in Comparative Perspective." *Journal of Ritual Studies* 4, 1: 99–125.

REMITTANCES   In the field of international labor migration, a distinction usually is made between two types of financial flow from emigrants to the country of origin. Unrequited transfers, whether for consumption or for investment, are termed "remittances," while repatriated deposits are seen as "capital inflows." This article treats both types of inflows as remittances. Compared to the size of the Indian national economy, these remittances are small, but as a source of foreign exchange, they are significant for the national exchequer. The Reserve Bank of India manipulates the interest rate for its Non-Resident Indian (NRI) bank deposits to encourage the flow of foreign currency into India.

The indentured emigrants of the nineteenth century who went to far-flung British colonies earned meager wages and could not afford regular contact with India. However, the Punjabis who went as sojourners to North America in the early twentieth century did remit much of their wages back to India. Throughout the years the emigrants who serve the overseas Indian populations as merchants and traders have contributed to India's economy through the import and export of their goods and services.

Postindependence emigrants who sent remittances to India tended to be of two kinds, those who were highly skilled and settled permanently in the more industrialized countries like the United Kingdom, the United States, Canada, and Australia; and those who were unskilled or semiskilled and traveled on a temporary basis to the countries of the Middle East. Remittances to India from the Middle East experienced a spectacular rise in the 1970s, fueled by the oil boom. Subsequently remittances stabilized at an average of US$2–2.5 billion per annum. Indians who succeeded abroad invested their earnings in a variety of industrial ventures in the Indian market, especially following the economic liberalization of the 1990s. Indians also invested in real estate. Entire colonies in Indian metropolitan areas were developed for NRI retirement.

In addition Indians abroad transfer technology back to India; finance charitable institutions, such as schools and hospitals; and volunteer their expertise in the fields of science and medicine. The information technology revolution of the 1990s especially benefited Indians abroad and made Indian Americans in Silicon Valley millionaires. These "software barons," driven by a sense of gratitude and obligation to India and its educational institutions that made it possible for them to attain such professional and financial pinnacles, donate millions of dollars to Indian engineering and scientific institutions. Social causes, such as raising AIDS awareness, helping women in distress, and promoting sustainable development in rural sectors, find favor with Indians abroad. At times of crisis, such as war or famine, or when natural disasters, such as earthquakes and cyclones, strike, Indians abroad rally to the aid of India.

Their motives range from assuaging guilt for leaving the motherland to sheer joy and satisfaction in sharing newfound wealth with the less fortunate. Whatever their reasons, Indians have maintained economic ties with their homeland throughout centuries and generations of living abroad.

Padma Rangaswamy

Further Reading

Nayyar, Deepak. (1994) *Migration, Remittances, and Capital Flows: The Indian Experience.* Delhi: Oxford University Press.

Rangaswamy, Padma. (2000) *Namasté America: Indian Immigrants in an American Metropolis.* University Park, PA: Pennsylvania State University Press.

Tinker, Hugh. (1974) *A New System of Slavery: The Export of Indian Labour Overseas: 1830–1920.* Oxford: Oxford University Press.

RENDRA, W. S. (b. 1936), Indonesian poet, playwright, actor, director. Born in Solo, Central Java, in 1936, Rendra was influenced by naturalism, the movement of realism in art and literature, as is evident in plays such as *Bunga Semerah Darah* (A Blood-Red Flower). He was also a director. In the 1960s he spent time in the United States where he was influenced by avant-garde experimental theater. Returning to Indonesia in 1967, Rendra founded Bengkel Teater Yogya (Yogyakarta Theater Workshop). This group pioneered a style of experimental theater known as *Teater Mini Kata* (Minimal Word Theater), in which monotonous sounds, rhythmic movement, and choreography were prominent. In the 1970s he became more political in works such as *Perjuangan Suku Naga* (The Struggle of the Naga Tribe) and *Mastodon dan Burung Condor* (Mastodon and Condor), and in translations of ancient Greek plays such as Sophocles' *Antigone*. These works were also presented by the Yogyakarta Theater Workshop. Rendra is commanding and charismatic as an actor or in poetry readings and was among the more outspoken supporters of reform at the time of President Suharto's fall in 1998. His work is often underpinned by a powerful sense of social justice and a desire to use theater as a force for change.

Tim Byard-Jones

RENOVATION POLICY. See **Doi Moi.**

REPELITA Repelita—an acronym from Rencana Pembangunan Lima Tahun (Five Year Development Plan), and a pun on *pelita* (lamp, or light)—was the planning unit adopted by New Order Indonesia to coordinate the country's "accelerated modernization."

Indonesia's planned economy declined seriously under President Sukarno's Guided Democracy, and recovery became a central aim of General Suharto's New Order government from 1967 on. Although the New Order partly deregulated the economy, creating opportunities for foreign investment, economic policymakers in the National Planning Board (BAPPENAS) remained committed to planning, making strategic direct public-sector investments and channeling private-sector investment.

Repelita I (1969–1974) focused on meeting basic needs and providing a framework for growth by stressing agricultural and infrastructure development. It was 66 percent financed by foreign aid, mainly through the Inter-Governmental Group on Indonesia (IGGI). Repelita II (1974–1979) continued emphasizing agriculture and infrastructure, but sought also to stimulate development outside the densely populated islands of Java, Bali, and Madura. Funded 35 percent by foreign aid, it heavily subsidized transmigration from these islands to other regions. Repelita III (1979–1984) emphasized industrialization, especially the development of labor-intensive, export-oriented manufactures, as well as agricultural and forest products and non-oil-gas minerals. Repelita IV (1984–1989) continued stressing these new exports and emphasized the creation of employment and the introduction of advanced industrial technology industry. In 1987, the value of oil and gas exports was first surpassed by the value of other exports. Repelita V (1989–1994) again emphasized infrastructure—especially transport, communications, and electric power—as well as education, but paid the greatest attention to manufacturing, which in 1991 surpassed agriculture as the largest economic sector.

These five plans constituted Indonesia's First 25-Year Long-Term Development Period, and their results were impressive: the plans achieved annual growth rates of 8.6 percent, 7.7 percent, 5.7 percent, 5.2 percent, and 8.3 percent respectively. Thanks to revenues from oil, gas, timber, and other products there was steady reduction in the proportion of expenditure provided by foreign aid (25 percent in Repelita V). Indonesia achieved self-sufficiency in rice production and was widely seen as a future economic giant.

Repelita VI (1994–1999) also emphasized manufacturing and initially appeared to be continuing the success of earlier plans, achieving 7.8 percent average annual growth in its first three years. The plan ceased to be relevant with the onset of the Asian economic crisis in 1997.

Robert Cribb

Further Reading
Hill, Hal. (1996) *The Indonesian Economy since 1966: Southeast Asia's Emerging Giant.* Cambridge, U.K.: Cambridge University Press.

REPUBLICAN CHINA   During a few brief weeks in the fall of 1911, the hollow shell of the Qing dynasty (1644–1912) disintegrated. Shortly afterward, on 1 January 1912, Sun Yat-sen (1866–1925) and his fellow revolutionaries proclaimed the founding of the Republic of China. China's last emperor had no choice but to abdicate the throne. Thus, in a matter of weeks, two millennia of dynastic rule ended and the Republican era began.

Early Republic and Warlordism, 1912–1928
The revolution of 1911 began on 10 October with an accidental explosion in the revolutionary headquarters at Hankou. Hankou soon fell to supporters of the republicans, starting a revolutionary wave that quickly spread throughout the country. On 29 December 1911, Sun Yat-sen—the "father of the revolution"—was elected provisional president of the new republic. Despite this auspicious beginning, the young republic soon encountered troubles. While Sun enjoyed respect and admiration, he lacked military might. To remedy this problem, he sought the support of a former Qing general, Yuan Shikai (1859–1916). Yuan accepted Sun's offer of the presidency in exchange for his military assistance. Known for his opportunism, Yuan quickly betrayed the revolution by disbanding the parliament and calling for a new constitution. Additionally, he declared Sun's revolutionary party illegal, forcing Sun to flee into exile. In 1915 Yuan brazenly assembled a special "representative assembly," which voted unanimously to make Yuan emperor. China's various provincial assemblies denounced the action. Yuan's "reign" was cut short less than three months later, when a rebellion against this monarchic scheme in the southern provinces broke out, and Yuan died in the summer of 1916. Yuan's death did not bring about the reconstitution of the republican government because Sun still lacked the military force necessary to control national affairs. Regional military commanders exploited this weakness, choosing to expand their own local power at the expense of national solidarity. For the next decade, China fell into a state of perpetual chaos, as various warlords attempted to take control of the capital city of Beijing.

During this period of chaos and instability, Sun retreated to his home province and reorganized his political party, the Guomindang (Kuomintang, or Nationalists). He also established a military academy to train loyal troops. The head of this academy, a young soldier named Chiang Kai-shek (1887–1975), quickly rose in power and influence. Concurrent with his political and military reorganization, Sun turned to the Soviet Union and the fledgling Chinese Communist

Party for support. Forming a "united front" in 1923, the Guomindang and the Communists vowed to rid China of warlords and to establish a stable government.

Following the death of Sun in 1925, Chiang became the preeminent leader of the Guomindang. In 1926 he launched the Northern Expedition, a military campaign to unite the entire country under Guomindang rule. At roughly the same time, he denounced continued cooperation with the Communists. After brutally suppressing Shanghai's labor movement, Chiang sought to destroy all traces of the Chinese Communist Party. Some Communists went underground, while others, led by Mao Zedong (1893–1976), retreated into the mountainous countryside to establish the Jiangxi Soviet. By 1928 Chiang had succeeded in either eliminating or undermining both the warlords and the Communists.

Republican Decade, 1928–1937

Having established control, Chiang and his associates were finally able to implement the republican ideas of Sun. Following Sun's plans, the country entered a period of "party tutelage." Accordingly, the party created democratic organizations but suspended popular elections. Historians refer to this decade of tutelage, between 1928 and 1937, as the Republican Decade. From their capital in Nanjing, Guomindang leaders set out to strengthen China both domestically and internationally. The government took control of four national banks and introduced monetary reform to modernize China's financial system and promote modern industrial development. Simultaneously, the Ministry of Education created or reorganized twenty-two universities, while the Ministry of Transportation extended railways, opened new highways, and created domestic airline routes. To complement these domestic achievements, Chiang's ministers attempted to improve China's position within the international community. By 1931 they had regained China's tariff autonomy and had revoked many foreign concessions. As such, the government brought closure to a century of humiliation at the hands of Western powers.

Despite the improvements in education, finance, and communications, most individuals saw very little change in their daily lives. Land reform and rent reduction would have greatly benefited the peasantry, which comprised 80 percent of the population, but the Guomindang neglected these tasks, choosing instead to focus on the needs of the urban middle class. Consequently, many peasants looked instead to the Communists for relief. In the early 1930s, Chiang continued his campaign against the Chinese Communist Party, forcing it to abandon its Jiangxi Soviet in 1934. After

CHINA—HISTORICAL PERIODS

Xia dynasty (2100–1766 BCE)
Shang dynasty (1766–1045 BCE)
Zhou dynasty (1045–256 BCE)
    Western Zhou (1045–771 BCE)
    Eastern Zhou (770–221 BCE)
Spring and Autumn period (770–476 BCE)
Warring States period (475–221 BCE)
Qin dynasty (221–206 BCE)
Han dynasty (206 BCE–220 CE)
Three Kingdoms period (220–265 CE)
North and South dynasties (220–589 CE)
Sui dyansty (581–618 CE)
Tang dynasty (618–907 CE)
Five Dynasties period (907–960 CE)
Song dynasty (960–1279)
    Northern Song (960–1126)
    Southern Song (1126–1279)
Jurchen Jin dynasty (1126–1234)
Yuan dynasty (1279–1368)
Ming dynasty (1368–1644)
Qing dynasty (1644–1912)
Republican China (1912–1927)
People's Republic of China (1949–present)
Republic of China (1949–present)
Cultural Revolution (1966–1976)

its famous Long March, the Communist Party established a new soviet in the northwest city of Yan'an, where Mao and his followers continued to push forward their program of rural reform.

Guomindang relations with Japan also deteriorated throughout the Republican decade. Following a questionable railroad explosion in 1931, the Japanese military invaded the northeast region of Manchuria. Though the League of Nations condemned the invasion, Tokyo refused to surrender control of the region, creating a puppet regime instead. While many individuals hoped the Guomindang would check Japanese aggression, Chiang chose to ignore Japan and concentrate his military forces against the Yan'an Communists.

War with Japan and the Communists, 1937–1949

By 1937, war with Japan appeared inevitable. When Chiang reluctantly agreed to cooperate with the Communist Party and confront Japanese troops, Japan launched a complete invasion of the Chinese heartland.

Though Japan succeeded in gaining control over much of the coast and the major cities, it could not force Chiang to surrender. Instead, the Guomindang continued its westward retreat, establishing a new capital in the remote city of Chongqing. Those cities that fell to Japan experienced incredible destruction and loss of life. In Nanjing, Japanese troops murdered, raped, and tortured the civilian population, killing as many as 300,000 people (though the Japanese government and military dispute this figure). For the Guomindang, the war was disastrous. Continual fighting destroyed Chiang's best military troops and bankrupted his government. Government ministers responded by printing more money, but the resulting inflation devastated China's middle class and eroded Chiang's primary base of support. By the war's end, many Chinese had lost faith in the Guomindang regime. Furthermore, the surviving troops were demoralized, discouraged, and ripe for rebellion.

With their common enemy gone, the Guomindang and Communists were able to devote their full energies to fighting each other. Although Chiang's troops greatly outnumbered Mao's, the war quickly turned in the Communists' favor. In 1949 Chiang retreated to the island province of Taiwan, taking with him two million of his faithful supporters. Mao's Communists, lacking the military equipment to invade Taiwan, chose instead to wait for a more fortuitous opportunity to wrap up the campaign and eliminate the remaining Guomindang forces. On 1 October 1949, the Communist Party leaders stood atop the last emperor's palace and declared the founding of the People's Republic of China. For his part, Chiang established the government of the Republic of China in exile, hoping to one day retake the mainland.

Republic of China on Taiwan

Since 1949 the Republic of China has continued to exist on Taiwan. Under Guomindang control, Taiwan has grown to become a major economic force in Asia and the world. Relations between Taiwan and the mainland remain tense, with the mainland government insisting on the eventual reunification of the two entities. In Taiwan, pro-independence forces have grown in strength, challenging the very existence of the Republic of China. Whatever Taiwan's future holds, the republican ideals of the Guomindang have left an indelible mark on twentieth-century China.

David L. Kenley

See also: **Chinese Communist Party; Guomindang; Northern Expedition; Sino-Japanese Conflict, Second.**

Further Reading

Chan, F. Gilbert, and Thomas H. Etzold, eds. (1976) *China in the 1920s: Nationalism and Revolution.* New York: New Viewpoints.

Eastman, Lloyd, ed. (1991) *The Nationalist Era in China, 1927–1949.* New York: Cambridge University Press.

Eto, Shinkichi, and Harold Schiffrin, eds. (1994) *China's Republican Revolution.* Tokyo: University of Tokyo Press.

Fitzgerald, John. (1996) *Awakening China: Politics, Culture, and Class in the Nationalist Revolution.* Stanford, CA: Stanford University Press.

Rankin, Mary. (1997) "State and Society in Early Republican Politics." *The China Quarterly* 150 (June): 260–81.

Wakeman, Frederic, Jr. (1997) "A Revisionist View of the Nanjing Decade: Confucian Fascism." *The China Quarterly* 150 (June): 395–432.

Yeh, Wen-hsin. (1997) "Shanghai Modernity: Commerce and Culture in a Republican City." *The China Quarterly* 150 (June): 375–94.

REPUBLICAN PEOPLE'S PARTY—TURKEY

Founded in 1922 by Mustafa Kemal Ataturk (1881–1938), the Republican People's Party (RPP) was the ruling party of the Turkish Republic from 1923 to 1950 and held power in coalition governments in the 1960s and 1970s. After the military coup of 1980, all political parties were banned, but the Republican People's Party was reestablished in 1992.

During the Turkish War of Independence (1919–1923) the Grand National Assembly in Ankara opposed the Allied occupation and the Ottoman government, and this opposition united former members of the Committee of Union and Progress, which held power in the Ottoman government from 1912 to 1918, and the nationalist landowning and religious elites. Hoping to gain more support and to bring more discipline to the Assembly, Ataturk, the leader of the nationalist forces, organized his supporters into the Republican People's Party. With the exception of the Progressive Republican Party (1924–1925) and the Free Party (1930), the RPP was Turkey's sole party until 1945, when a multiparty system came into being.

In 1931 an RPP congress enunciated a program of reform with six points: nationalism, republicanism, secularism, populism, reformism, and statism. These became known as the six arrows of Kemalism, an ideological justification for legal, political, economic, and social reforms aimed at modernizing and Westernizing the Turkish state and society. Party leaders, including Ataturk, the prime minister Ismet Inonu (1884–1973), and the general secretary Recep Peker (1888–1950), saw the role of the RPP as one of educating the new Turkish Republic and envisioned a prolonged period of single-party rule.

Following Ataturk's death in November 1938, a special RPP congress named Ataturk "eternal chief" of the party and resolved that his reforms would forever be the party's guiding principle. Ismet Inonu was named permanent leader of the RPP. In 1945 responding to demands for change, Inonu called for the creation of a multiparty system. In the 1950 election the RPP lost by a landslide to the Democrat Party, which had been formed by Celal Bayar (1884–1987) and other former members of the RPP in 1946.

Out of power throughout the 1950s, the RPP regained power after the military coup in 1960, joining a series of coalition governments. In 1972 Bulent Ecevit launched a successful challenge to the leadership of Inonu and then led the RPP in a series of coalition governments during the 1970s.

After the military took power in 1980, all parties were shut down, and all active politicians were banned from politics. Three new center-left parties, the People's Party, the Social Democratic Party, and the Democratic Left Party, put forth programs similar to that of the RPP. In 1992 the old parties were allowed to be reestablished, and the RPP reemerged, led by Deniz Baykal. Throughout the 1990s the RPP won around 20 percent of the popular vote and joined coalitions with other center-left parties.

John M. VanderLippe

Further Reading

Berkes, Niyazi. (1964) *The Development of Secularism in Turkey*. Montreal, Canada: McGill University Press.
Heper, Metin, and Jacob Landau, eds. (1991) *Political Parties and Democracy in Turkey*. London: I. B. Tauris.

REPUBLICAN REVOLUTION OF 1911

By the end of the nineteenth century, nearly every political and intellectual leader in China saw the need for change. Some, such as Sun Yat-sen (1866–1925), felt that rather than reforming the imperial system, China needed a thoroughgoing revolution. Consequently he called for the formation of a new republic based on his "Three Principles of the People," namely nationalism, democracy, and socialism (often translated as "people's livelihood").

During the late nineteenth and early twentieth centuries, Sun and his fellow revolutionaries (organized as the Tongmeng Hui, or Revolutionary Alliance) traveled throughout the country promoting their republican form of government. Sun's actions led to his political exile, yet his followers succeeded in infiltrating the military and spreading Sun's revolutionary ideals. On 9 October 1911 an accidental explosion rocked the revolutionaries' secret headquarters in Hankou. Police raided the building, discovering a stash of weapons and membership rolls. Knowing the rolls had revealed their identity, those soldiers loyal to Sun quickly mutinied. By the afternoon of 10 October, they had captured the entire city. Over the next several weeks, province after province declared its independence from Beijing. Sun, who had been in the United States at the time of the initial explosion, returned to China and on 29 December 1911 was elected provisional president of the Republic of China. The court was helpless as events spiraled out of its control. As a result, the Qing dynasty (1644–1912) unceremoniously abdicated the throne, bringing to an end more than two millennia of imperial rule.

The early years of the Republic were fraught with confusion and civil war, leading many historians to question the leadership abilities of Sun and the conclusiveness of his revolution. Though the leaders of 1911 failed immediately to create a stable and lasting government system, they did succeed in toppling the imperial system and establishing Asia's first republic. For this reason, 10 October was celebrated as National Day (Double Tenth) in China until 1949 and continues to be celebrated on Taiwan today. With the perspective of a century, the events of 1911 appear quite revolutionary.

David L. Kenley

Further Reading

Eto, Shinkichi, and Harold Schiffrin, eds. (1994) *China's Republican Revolution*. Tokyo: University of Tokyo Press.
Wei, Julie Lee, Romon Myers, and Donald Gillin, eds. (1994) *Prescriptions for Saving China: Selected Writings of Sun Yat-sen*. Stanford, CA: Hoover Institution Press.
Wright, Mary, ed. (1968) *China in Revolution, The First Phase, 1900–1913*. New Haven, CT: Yale University Press.

RESIDENT SYSTEM

The British introduced the Resident System in Malaya through the Pangkor Engagement, a treaty between the British and local sultans under which the British appointed a resident to assist each local sultan. The first state to get a resident was Perak (1874), followed by Selangor (1874), Negeri Sembilan (1874), and Pahang (1888). These four states were later called the Federated Malay States (FMS).

According to the Pangkor Engagement, each resident was to advise the sultan on all administrative matters except those pertaining to Malayan religion and custom, but in practice the resident ruled.

The resident system had weaknesses. First, there weren't enough British officers to administer it, and few of these officers could converse in the native language. Second, there was already a hierarchy in the states. Third, religious matters could be separated from politics, but custom was strong. Revenues collected were the personal income of the sultan and his chiefs. To implement a new taxation system was a violation of custom. Indeed, J. W. W Birch, the first British resident (1874–1875), was murdered as he tried to interfere with custom in Perak. His lack of respect and understanding of Malayan custom, language, and religion caused his administration to fail.

The resident system, however, was administered well in Selangor and Negeri Sembilan by Sir Hugh Low and Martin Lister, respectively. They did not attempt to interfere with Malayan custom. The economy developed as railroads were built, making the production of tin easier, and as state councils were set up to discuss policy matters in order to gain the confidence of the Malayan people through their chiefs. Underdeveloped Pahang, too, benefited from the revenue brought in by the system, although it did not receive a resident until 1888.

By the 1880s the British ruled all the states in the Malay Peninsula. The states that the British obtained from Siamese rule—Kedah, Perlis, Kelantan, and Trengganu—were called the Unfederated Malay States (UMS), and an adviser was placed in each of these states. Thus, the British used the Resident System to spread their influence across the Malay Peninsula.

Mala Selvaraju

Further Reading

Kennedy, J. (1964) *A History of Malaya* A.D. *1400–1959*. Kuala Lumpur, Malaysia: Macmillan.

Khong, Kim Hong. (1984) *Merdeka: British Rule and the Struggle for Independence in Malaya, 1945–1957*. Kuala Lumpur, Malaysia: Institute for Social Analysis.

Ryan, N. J. (1974) *The Making of Modern Malaysia & Singapore: A History from Earliest Times to 1966*. Singapore: Oxford University Press.

RÉUNION ISLAND (1999 est. pop. 706,000). Réunion Island, in the Indian Ocean, was known as Bourbon during the nineteenth century. Elliptic in shape, it is 2,512 square kilometers in area. It is a French Overseas Territory, and its president is, consequently, the president of France. The capital is St. Denis (est. pop. 125,000). The status of Réunion was changed in 1946 from a colony to a department of France. It is administered by the prefect of St. Denis.

There is a locally elected general council and four district councils covering twenty-four communes. The educational curriculum is the same as in France.

The island was first colonized by the Compagnie des Indes in the seventeenth century. The major industry is sugar growing; minor products include coffee, potatoes, maize, and cocoa. One fifth of the population is descended from indentured laborers—Malabars—brought in from South India in the nineteenth century to work on the plantations. The rest of the population is Chinese, Indian, and European.

The island has 2,709 kilometers of roads but no railroads. There is an anthropology institute, and a university (with 3,340 students in 1989). There are a number of sugar factories and rum distilleries.

Paul Hockings

Further Reading

Benoist, Jean. (1978) "La Réunion." In *Ethnologie régionale*, edited by Jean Poirier. Paris: Gallimard (Encyclopédie de la Pléiade), 2: 1882–1899.

Government of France. (1983) *Réunion, the Perfume Island*. New York: Ambassade de France.

REVOLT OF THE SHORT HAIR The Revolt of the Short Hair was a part of the modernization movement that was advocated by a group of Vietnamese Confucian scholars. In 1907 they founded a private school called the Dong Kinh Nghia Thuc (Tonkin Free School) on the model of the Japanese Keio Gijuku Daigaku. This school aimed at fostering the study of Western sciences, because its founders felt that the French-established educational system neglected such studies in favor of the humanities. Surprisingly enough, for those Confucian scholars, modernization meant first Westernization and then rejection of Confucianism and, by extension, of anything Chinese. They wanted to emulate France in order to fight against French colonialism. Students attending the Dong Kinh Nghia Thuc were urged to wear their hair short so that they could look like Frenchmen, and to cut off their long hair, because it had been the Chinese invaders who forced Vietnamese men to wear their hair long and tied in a bun. Thus, the proponents of the movement aimed at severing Vietnam from any cultural values, including Confucian ones, that the Chinese had inculcated in the Vietnamese.

It was indeed a revolutionary suggestion. For the traditional Vietnamese, hair has the same significance as the head, and the head corresponds to a symbolic altar where the ancestors are worshiped. To cut one's hair is, therefore, a sacrilegious act, equivalent to a repudiation of everything worth living for. Some early opponents of the French invasion went as far as asking: What is the meaning of life when you have to share their wine and nibble their bread? What is the meaning of life when you must cut your hair and shave your beard? Yet the movement that promoted the cutting of hair was a successful one, and in the large body of literature created by the Dong Kinh Nghia Thuc, a dozen short and easy-to-memorize popular songs are found. However, the cutting off of hair may not have represented such a trauma after all, because the Vietnamese must have been quite familiar with Buddhist monks and nuns who had to shave off their hair before entering the monastery. However, the Dong Kinh Nghia Thuc was short lived: the French colonial authorities closed down all their schools less than a year after their establishment. The Revolt of the Short Hair, however, survived, and, in the late 1920s, those from both town and city were amused whenever they encountered a man who wore his hair in a chignon at the back of his head.

Truong Buu Lam

Further Reading
Jamieson, Neil L. (1995) *Understanding Vietnam*. Berkeley and Los Angeles: University of California Press.
Truong Buu Lam, ed. (2000) *Colonialism Experienced: Vietnamese Anti-Colonial Writings: 1900–1931*. Ann Arbor, MI: University of Michigan Press.

REVOLUTIONARY YOUTH LEAGUE OF VIETNAM
In 1925, Vietnamese revolutionary leader Ho Chi Minh (1890–1969) formed the Revolutionary Youth League (Viet Nam Thanh Nien Cach Menh Dong Chi Hoi) as an organization that would begin the process of concentrating the Vietnamese people on the goal of overthrowing the colonial government of the French. Within the Youth League, Ho formed an inner communist group, the Communist Youth League (Thanh Nien Cong San Doan), which served to introduce communist theory to the Vietnamese independence movement, mainly through the secretly distributed journal *Thanh Nien*. In February 1930 the Revolutionary Youth League became Vietnam's communist party after the founding conference of the first Indochinese Communist Party (ICP), held in 1929 in Hanoi. In 1941, the Revolutionary Youth League, the ICP, factions of the Vietnam Nationalist Party, and the New Vietnam Party were formed into a united front organization called the Viet Nam Doc Lap Dong Minh Hoi, the League for the Independence of Vietnam, better known more by its more common name, the Viet Minh.

Richard B. Verrone

Further Reading
Buttinger, Joseph. (1968) *Vietnam: A Political History*. New York: Praeger.
Cima, Ronald J., ed. (1989) *Vietnam: A Country Study*. Washington, DC: U.S. Government Printing Office.
Duiker, William J. (2000) *Ho Chi Minh*. New York: Hyperion.
———. (1976) *The Rise of Nationalism in Vietnam, 1900–1941*. Ithaca, NY: Cornell University Press.
Marr, David (1971) *Vietnamese Anti-Colonialism, 1885–1925*. Berkeley and Los Angeles: University of California Press.

RHEE, SYNGMAN
(1875–1965), first president of South Korea. Syngman Rhee (Yi Sung-man) was the first president of South Korea from 1948 until 1960. Rhee was born on 26 April 1875 in Hwangwae Province to an aristocratic family. Rhee was educated in both the Confucian classics as well as at a Methodist missionary school. By the time Rhee had reached his teens, he was an ardent nationalist advocating Korean independence. Rhee was arrested for his membership in the Independence Club and was jailed for six years. Upon his release, Rhee left for the United States, where he studied at Harvard and at Princeton, where he earned a doctorate in 1910.

While in the United States, Rhee was elected president of the Korean Provisional Government (in exile in Shanghai) and served as its representative in Washington, DC. He returned to Korea on 16 October 1945, following the cessation of fighting, and called

President Syngman Rhee displays the Korean flag at his headquarters in July 1950. (BETTMANN/CORBIS)

for immediate independence. Rhee held elections in the south and was elected president of the Republic of Korea (ROK).

On 25 June 1950 North Korea launched an attack over the thirty-eighth parallel, forcing Rhee and his government to retreat to Pusan. For the duration of the Korean War, Rhee tried to sabotage armistice negotiations, hoping to reunify the Korean peninsula by force under his rule. To this end, Rhee threatened to withdraw South Korean troops from United Nations command. Rhee then ordered the release of 25,000 prisoners of war not scheduled for repatriation and summarily conscripted them into South Korean army. His relationship with the United States can be characterized as difficult, as he sought to reunify Korea by military means, while the United States preferred a negotiated settlement. Domestically, Rhee intimidated political oppenents and threatened to disband the National Assembly.

Rhee remained president following the Korean War, but in 1960 student-led demonstrations forced his resignation. For all Rhee had done, he failed to meet the peoples' expectations for modernization and economic development. The highlights of Rhee's career include the U.S.-ROK mutual security treaty, which secured long-term economic aid to Korea as well as rebuilding the South Korean military.

Keith Leitich

Further Reading
Allen, Richard C. (1960) *Korea's Syngman Rhee: An Unauthorized Portrait.* Rutland, VT: Charles E. Tuttle.
Cumings, Bruce. (1997) *Korea's Place in the Sun: A Modern History.* New York: W. W. Norton.
Oliver, Robert. (1978) *Syngman Rhee and American Involvement in Korea, 1942–1960: A Personal Narrative.* Seoul: Panmun Books.

RHINOCEROS, ASIATIC   Three distinct species of rhinoceros, large herbivorous mammals with a horn or horns on the snout, live in Asia. The great Indian one-horned rhinoceros *(Rhinoceros unicornis)* is the only one still living in the Indian states of Assam and West Bengal and in the Himalayan kingdom of Nepal (today numbering perhaps 1,500 animals). This species was illustrated on seals discovered from the Indus Valley culture that flourished four millennia ago; the animal was known as far west as Peshawar in today's Pakistan in the sixteenth century, and as far east as Myanmar (Burma) in the nineteenth century.

The smaller one-horned, or Javan, rhinoceros *(R. sondiacus)* once lived from Bengal eastward through Myanmar and Malaysia as far as Java, Sumatra, and Borneo, and in China during the Shang dynasty (1766–1045 BCE). The Asiatic two-horned rhinoceros *(Didermocerus sumatrensis)*, the smallest of the three species, once inhabited the same range, except for Java.

About 1.6 million to ten thousand years ago, a now-extinct genus of rhinoceros lived in regions of Europe, Asia, and North Africa—the woolly rhinoceros, a massive creature with two large horns and a thick coat of hair. About 5 million years ago, there were several other Indian species, known today only from their fossils, such as *R. sivalensis* and *R. paleoindicus*. Still earlier, from 30 to 16.6 million years ago, the areas of today's Pakistan and Mongolia were home to the largest land mammal ever to live, the Indricotherium, a genus related to the rhinoceros. It was almost six meters high at the shoulder, eight meters long, and weighed about thirty tons, more than four times the weight of an elephant.

The largest of the modern Asian species, the Indian rhinoceros, can be as tall as 186 centimeters at the shoulders in the male; the average height is 170 centimeters. Males weigh up to 2,070 kilograms, and females about 1,600 kilograms. The skin is thick, folded, and gray in color. The distinctive horn or horns are made of keratinized skin, a matted hairlike material with no bony substructure, which grows back if cut off. The magical properties of these horns have long made these animals the object of hunting, and a creature that

CHITWAN NATIONAL PARK— WORLD HERITAGE SITE

One of the last homes of the exceedingly rare Asiatic rhinocerous, the royal Chitwan National Park was designated a UNESCO World Heritage Site in 1984. Probably the last unpopulated tract of the Terai region, Chitwan is also home to the Bengal tiger.

once roamed from present-day England and France through India to China is now in danger of extinction.

The rhinoceros lives in swampy, forested areas and has never been domesticated. It feeds on shrubs and tree leaves. It is either solitary or lives in pairs; the female produces only one young at each pregnancy. Although its eyesight is poor, it has a keen sense of smell. The Asiatic rhinoceros does not use the horn to attack, but fights with its sharp lower tusks. The rhinoceros can live for half a century; but the Javan and Sumatran species are in peril of extinction from hunters and the Chinese market in aphrodisiacs.

Paul Hockings

RIANTIARNO, NANO (b. 1949), Indonesian playwright, actor, stage director. One of Indonesia's leading playwrights and cultural figures, Nano Riantiarno was born in 1949. He began as a dramatist in the realist tradition, writing plays such as *Pelangi* (Rainbow) and *Cermin* (Mirror), which deal with domestic problems. He was influenced by the German playwright Bertolt Brecht, whose *Threepenny Opera* he adapted as *Opera Ikan Asin*. Riantiarno's most celebrated plays are *Bom Waktu* (Time Bomb) and *Opera Kecoa* (Cockroach Opera). These works are infused with a strong sense of social justice and deal with Jakarta's underclass of prostitutes, beggars, and thieves. Riantiarno is also the director of one of Indonesia's leading theater companies, *Teater Koma*, which he founded in 1977 with his wife, Ratna.

Tim Byard-Jones

Further Reading
Riantiarno, Nano. (1992): *Time Bomb & Cockroach Opera: Two Plays. Time Bomb* trans. by Barbara Hatley; *Cockroach Opera* trans. by John H. McGlynn. Jakarta, Indonesia: Lontar Foundation.

RICCI, MATTEO (1522–1610), Jesuit missionary to China. Matteo Ricci, known to the Chinese as Li Madou, was born in Italy and entered the Jesuit order in 1571, at the age of nineteen. After studying at Jesuit seminaries in Florence and Rome, he traveled to Lisbon to take up the study of Portuguese, presumably with the intention of joining the Portuguese mission in Asia. In 1578 Ricci departed Lisbon for Goa where he taught for four years. He finally arrived in Macao in 1582.

Ricci was an impressive figure of a man, both visually and intellectually. He was tall, and strong with curly black hair and blue eyes. He was well-versed in such sciences as mathematics and astronomy and had a talent for learning languages. He put this latter ability to work in Macao as he began his study of both modern and classical Chinese. He studied the Confucian classics in order to understand the intellectual background of his future social contacts. Ricci moved onto Chinese soil in 1583, establishing a mission in a small city in Guangzhou (Canton) Province. He and his fellow priests tried to engage the local gentry by sharing with them some of the latest scientific and technological information from Europe. The Chinese were especially interested in mathematics, astronomy and geography. Devices such as prisms, clocks, and astronomical instruments were also popular. Having piqued the curiosity of the gentry, the priests would attempt to discuss philosophy and religion.

Reaction to the Jesuits was mixed, but through hard work Ricci managed to develop a network of contacts among powerful officials and eventually gained entry to the imperial court in Beijing. In 1601 he made a present of two clocks and a clavichord to the emperor. He was rewarded with a scholar's stipend. Some later Jesuits were given actual positions at the courts. However, those positions, and Ricci's own success, were almost entirely based on their mastery of scientific and technological skills. Ricci collaborated with a Chinese convert to translate several classical works on geometry by Euclid. His treatise on geography was also very popular. He also wrote several treatises on religious topics, but these were considerably less successful.

In the end Matteo Ricci and the Jesuits did experience some modest progress in finding Chinese converts for the Christian church. Their mission was not more successful primarily because the Chinese already possessed a strong socioreligious tradition that had taken shape over the course of thousands of years. Ricci went so far as to lead a Jesuit campaign to have the Roman Catholic church declare native Chinese rituals to be fundamentally nonreligious, and symbolic in nature. This would have allowed for the conversion of Chinese without requiring them to give up their own religious practices. In the end, the Vatican rejected the arguments of the Jesuits in favor of a less compromising position. This effectively spelled the end of this era of Christian missionary work in China. Ricci died in 1610 and was buried outside of Beijing. His grave was restored in 1980.

Terence Russell

Further Reading
Gernet, Jacques. (1985) *China and the Christian Impact: A Conflict of Cultures.* Translated by Janet Lloyd. Cambridge, U.K.: Cambridge University Press.
Neill, Stephen. (1986) *A History of Christian Missions.* 2d edition. London: Penguin Books.

RICE AND RICE AGRICULTURE

Rice is Asia's most important food crop, and Asian rice production and consumption account for over 90 percent of the world total. About two-thirds of Asian caloric consumption comes from cereals: about 40 percent of that comes from rice, while 15 percent more is from wheat. Rice and wheat are also the major prestige grains. In areas where rice is the dominant crop, it is almost always symbolic of food and well-being in general. In Japan, the word *gohan* means both rice and meal; major deities are associated with rice, and national festivals mark the times of planting, transplanting, and harvest. In southern and eastern India, no meal would be considered complete without rice, even if it also included bread made of some other grain. All over India, a paste of crushed cooked rice and turmeric is the quintessential material for marking a *tilak*—the mark made on one's forehead in ceremonies seeking a good beginning, such as weddings.

Rice itself is, however, generally not deified, just as bread is not in the West. Although local deities associated with rice or rice fields are widely reported, the ceremonies associated with them are better understood as ways to take recognized oaths regarding farming arrangements than worship as such.

Rice yield has commonly been used to assess land, and taxes have been levied in rice. Maintaining stable rice prices has been a major concern of government policy for virtually all of recorded history. In recent decades, the improvement of rice production has been a major focus of international development agencies and governments throughout Asia.

Origins and Ecology

Rice is unique among the major cereal crops in its ability to grow in standing water. It is therefore uniquely

THE RICE MEASURE

"The measure is generally made from willow wood and is a simple square; it has many symbolic uses."

"The peck measure holds ten catties of rice; is a symbol of full measure of justice, mercy and virtue, which should be the right of all, irrespective of station."

"The Chinese say that rice is the staff of life, therefore the rice measure is the measure of life."

Source: T. Harry. (1942) *Chinese Symbols and Superstitions.* South Pasadena, CA: P. D. and Ione Perkins, 56

adapted to the periodic heavy flooding that often accompanies Asian monsoons.

Worldwide, there are two domesticated species—*Oryza sativa* and *O. glabberima*—and about twenty-six wild species. *O. sativa* evolved in Asia and is divided into two subspecies: *indica*, which is more prominent in South Asia, and *japonica*, which dominates in East Asia. Both subspecies are now distributed worldwide. *O. glabberima* is indigenous to West Africa and is still localized there. Both domestic species appear to have the same wild ancestor, commonly thought to be *O. rufipogon*, an inhabitant of ponds and flooded ditches.

The main differences between the *indica* and *japonica* subspecies is that the former has a taller growth habit and produces long, thin grains that are separate when cooked. With *japonica*, the grains are shorter and wider, tending to be stickier when cooked, and the plants are shorter stemmed. There is, however, much variation within both groups. The differences involve taste and texture, yield, whether the rice is "floating" or not, the length of time to maturity, and whether the growth cycle is photoperiod-sensitive or not. "Floating" means that the stems tend to lengthen as water depth increases, preventing the plant from drowning in deep water (some floating rice varieties can grow to heights of several meters). Photoperiod sensitivity is the tendency for the time of maturation to be controlled by the length of the day.

It is most likely that *O. sativa* was domesticated from its wild ancestor at several places and at several times. The most likely zone of domestication extends from the upper Ganges and Brahmaputra valleys, across

86

northern Burma and Thailand, and across southern China. It seems probable that *indica-japonica* differentiation occurred in different niches in the eastern Himalayas and into mountainous Southeast Asia, with *japonica* varieties emerging in lowlands and *indica* in uplands. Such differentiation is found in the area today, and the indigenous *aus* and *aman* varieties that are commonly grown as a first and following crop in Bangladesh appear in many characteristics to be midway between the two subspecies.

The earliest evidence of domestication appears to be from China, where carbonized *japonica* grains dating from about 7000 BCE have been found mixed with *O. rufipogon* in the Hemedu site in the lower Chang (Yangze) river valley. In South Asia, the earliest evidence is from Lothal and Rangpur in Gujarat, dating from 4300 and 4000 BCE, respectively. From Southeast Asia, the oldest evidence comes from Nok Tha in Thailand, dating from 5500 BCE. From its origin points, rice has steadily spread north and south through the wetter areas of monsoon Asia, mainly replacing taro-based cultivation systems, such as survive in Papua New Guinea.

Rice and wheat are complementary rather than competitive. Wheat does better in cooler weather, and some wheats have a chilling or freezing requirement before they will form grain, while frost inhibits or kills rice. Rice is, therefore, generally a tropical- and temperate-climate crop, while wheat is a temperate- and cold-climate crop. In areas where both can grow, rice is consistently a summer crop and wheat a winter crop.

Rice is grown in four major ways: in shifting swiddens, on rain-fed dryland like other cereals, in rain-fed flooded fields, and in irrigated flooded fields. Since archaeological evidence of rice consists mainly of carbonized grains or grain-impressions on pottery, it is not known whether rice was originally domesticated as a dryland or wetland crop. While rice yields well without flooding, providing the soil remains moist, under such conditions it is less resistant to weeds than other cereals. Flooding controls weeds and provides an environment in which certain waterweeds (notably Azolla), blue-green algae, and bacteria supply necessary nitrogen on a sustained basis. Over recent history, flooded cultivation has been consistently more important, and this importance continues to increase.

Different modes of cultivation dominate in different regions. In South Asia, rice cultivation depends entirely on irrigation in Pakistan and from a third to a half on irrigation in India. Although India still has a few pockets of shifting cultivation and some dryland farming along the edges of the mountains, most rice

farming is in flooded fields in the high rainfall zones along the western Ghats, in the lower Ganges and Brahmaputra valleys, and in the Himalayas to their north. Rice land in Nepal is about 21 percent irrigated, the rest being rain fed, with spectacular terraced fields on the steep Himalayan slopes. In Bangladesh, the crop is watered by the annual floods of the summer monsoon season, and floating rices of comparatively low yield are often grown. The winter is nearly rainless, but in recent years extensive cultivation of a winter rice crop has been introduced by using high-yielding varieties irrigated with pumped water or planted in areas that remain wet because they are at sea level. Sri Lanka is geographically divided into wet and dry zones. The former is the mountainous two-thirds of the island, which receives heavy rain in the summer monsoon; here rice is generally grown in the lower parts of mountain valleys, in terraced fields watered by direct rain and small rain-fed streams. The dry zone is an area of ancient large-scale reservoir and canal systems, abandoned in the thirteenth century, which have recently been largely restored. Rice fields in this area are

Terraced rice paddies in Tampaksiring, Bali, Indonesia, in 1996. (STEPHEN G. DONALDSON PHOTOGRAPHY)

THE COMPLEXITIES OF RICE

While people in the Western world usually think of rice as either white or brown or long- or short-grained, the matter of classifying types of rice is much more complicated for people who grow rice and consume it everyday. The following text details how Malay farmers classify the varieties of rice they grow and eat.

Pegasi farmers use a number of easily recognizable characters to distinguish between cultivators . . . Special importance is given to the hardness or texture of the grain, since this determines its use. There are 23 cultivators in the common category of *gangsa* or *padi biasa* ("common rice"), which have hard starchy grains that are dry and "fluffy" when cooked. These are frequently referred to as "vitreous" in English because the uncooked grain is translucent; or as "common" because these are the most widely cultivated on a worldwide basis. Rice varieties of the vitreous type are the major food grown, eaten and, when necessary, purchased by Pegasi households (the per capita consumption for adults being about 278 pounds per year).

There are 18 cultivars in the category called *pulut* ("sticky"), having soft grains that become sticky and clump together when cooked. In the past, these were only required in small quantities for consumption during special ceremonies, for making rice starch cosmetic and medicinal preparations, and for making the traditional snack foods and cakes. In recent years *pulut* rices have commanded a premium price in local market towns, since they symbolize high status and are desired by urbanized Malaysians. While Pegasi growers formerly considered *pulut* only a minor, locally consumed crop, they are increasingly aware of the cash crop capabilities of these varieties.

The final eight cultivars are called *lembut* ("soft"), described by informants as so soft and almost gelatinous when cooked that the label "viscous" is perhaps appropriate. *Pulut* and *lembut* have not been distinguished as separate categories by western rice specialists. The *lembut* cultivars are pounded into flour and used for making a special class of cakes and pastries, though unlike the cakes that require *pulut* rice flour, informants say that in most cases imported wheat flour is an acceptable and cheap substitute for *lembut* flour. In 1976 there was little local interest in the *lembut* group, as evidenced by the fact that only a couple of households planted small plots to three types.

Color is another important character, and while almost any part of the rice plant can be pigmented, it is specifically the color of the husk and the pericarp or outer layers of the kernel that merit significant cultural attention. Colors noted are *puteh* ("white"), *kuning* ("yellow to light brown"), *meraah* ("dark brown to red"). A color term is often part of the cultivar name, and it serves to distinguish closely related cultivars, such as *mele kuning* and *mele merah*. Some have fanciful names which are indicative of color, such as the *ganga* with red-brown husks called *darah belut* ("swamp-eel blood") and the *gangsa* with black husks called *ekar musang* ("civit cat tail").

Other terms are descriptive of husk color patterns, such as *choring* which describes splotches and stripes of red and white on a *serendah*, and *bunga machang* ("machang flower") glutinous rice which to the local eye resembles the striking red and white flower of the *machang* variety of mango.

While vitreous rice may have husks of any color, the pericarps are always white. This is probably a local cultural preference, since colored vitreous rices are common elsewhere (e.g., in Sarawak and the Philippines from personal observation). When buying "food" rice, Pahang people demand white polished rice types, and they boast about the whiteness of the rices they grow themselves.

The attitude towards color in glutinous rices is quite different, with the full range of colors being in demand. Each type and color of the glutinous rice has specific ritual uses, or is required when making special confections and cakes.

Growers frequently distinguish cultivars according to their size and shape of the grain.

CONTINUED ON NEXT PAGE

CONTINUED FROM PREVIOUS PAGE

Terms describing size and shape include: *panjang* ("long"), *pendik* ("short"), *gemuk* ("fat") and *bulat* ("round").

Source: Donald H. Lambert (1985) *Swamp Rice Farming: The Indigenous Pahang Malay Agricultural System.* Boulder, CO, and London: Westview Press, 55–58.

irrigated by a combination of large government canals and village-level, rain-fed storage tanks closely akin to those in southern India.

Southeast Asian countries—mainly Burma, Thailand, and Vietnam—are traditional rice exporters. Like Bangladesh, they have large areas of rice irrigated by rainfall and by inundation as the monsoon-fed rivers rise out of their banks. Unlike Bangladesh, their production has historically been relatively high and their costs relatively low. The Philippines has a combination of large river plains now watered by a combination of canals, flooding, and rainfall, and mountain systems like those of Sri Lanka. Indonesia is similar, with ancient, extensive, and extremely well-managed indigenous systems, on Bali, in particular, watered by locally managed channels from rain-fed mountain-top reservoirs.

In East Asia, rice cultivation is mostly irrigated. In China and Korea, it is more than 91 percent irrigated, while in Japan it is entirely irrigated, although this is mainly in river valleys that have always been naturally wet and subject to flooding. Rice cultivation is commonly combined with fish- or shrimp-raising. Chinese, Korean, and Japanese irrigation systems are recognized as very efficiently managed.

Farm-Level Management

Rice production requires complex social discipline. Throughout Asia, this has consistently involved social systems with strong independent family units operating in the context of close interfamily cooperation at several higher levels. Rice has been essentially a crop of family farmers with small, intensively cultivated holdings that have not lent themselves to mechanization or economies of scale. Most Asian rice farms are three hectares or less, and a very large part of their output is either consumed on the farm or paid out in local wages.

As a rule, family farmers everywhere try to organize their cropping so as to avoid sharp peaks in labor demand that require the heavy use of hired labor. Usually this done by planting several crops each season with different planting, weeding, and harvest times. The ecology of rice militates against this. It precludes other crops, because very few can grow in the conditions rice requires, and a common system of water management requires rice fields to be located side by side over large areas so that water can flow through them. Consequently, a given block of farmers often plants the same rice varieties at substantially the same times. This necessarily means that the labor requirements all tend to peak at about the same time, creating intense local labor shortages. The result is that in rice-growing areas an extremely large portion of the population is made up of non-landowning agricultural laborers; they are, however, exceptionally well organized, and their wages are usually relatively high. Alternatively, in East Asia, particularly in Japan where rural labor has become extremely scarce, it is common to replace wage labor with agreements for cooperative labor exchange among landowners, who work in teams on one another's fields.

The high labor demand is mainly for four sets of operations: weeding if the fields are not flooded, transplanting of seedlings if fields are flooded, harvest, and threshing and milling. Transplanting must be done in a short period, because if seedlings are too young they are unlikely to survive, and if they are too mature yields will decline. It is most commonly done by teams of women. Harvesting is most commonly done by hired labor of both sexes, since this is the period of greatest labor scarcity. Payment to the team may be anywhere from a tenth to a sixth of the crop.

Threshing and milling are more difficult with rice, as the husks cling to the individual rice grains more tightly than do other grains. The husks must be removed in a further operation after the grain is separated from the stalk, leaving brown rice. Brown rice is superior in nutrient content to white (milled) rice, but the bran layer that gives it its color contains oils that decompose within a few weeks, spoiling the grain. For long-term storage, unless it is possible to dry the paddy to about 14 percent moisture content, this layer must be removed by milling. In some areas, the rice is also parboiled. Milling was formerly done by pounding the unhusked rice in wooden mortars, usually by the women of a household. Now it is often mechanized. Rice husks are commonly used for fuel and as an abrasive. The bran is a high-quality livestock feed, while the straw is used for fodder, fuel, basketry, and thatch.

Social Implications

In general, interhousehold cooperative arrangements involved in rice production have two major functions: securing resources as needed and managing infrastructure. There are two main patterns.

In areas where rice land makes up only part of total village lands, there is commonly a village reservoir or other water source. The rice lands are those below the reservoir, while higher ground is used for complementary crops. In this case, cooperative arrangements include provisions for maintaining the irrigation infrastructure and distributing the water and also very often for reducing rice plantings in years of low water in such a way as to assure that all those with a right to the water get the use of a proportional section of the land.

In areas where large irrigation systems completely surround whole villages, especially where water flows from one farmer's fields to another's, there must be complex agreements on cropping and water flows below the outlets, as well as on taking turns accessing water from the channels. In East Asia, these arrangements are mainly under farmer control. In South Asia, the larger channels are always controlled by national or provincial officials; farmer responsibility begins at the level of the minor watercourse only, and coordination between the two levels is often poor. In the Philippines, systems were initially built and run as in South Asia. In 1976, however, the National Irrigation Authority nearly went bankrupt. Since then, it has reorganized in such a way as to allow local-level officials to make binding arrangements for construction and management with farmers, which allows the farmers to control what is done and how it is to be paid for, and this system has been a great success.

The Future

Asian rice production has so far kept pace with increases in population. This is mainly because of the expansion of irrigation and national and international research programs that have introduced new varieties with higher yields, faster maturation, and greater responsiveness to fertilizer inputs. Expanded irrigation and faster maturation allow farmers to go from one crop per year to two or even three. Until recently, intensification and greater areas planted in rice have been the major sources of increased production. Further gains, however, will have to come more from increased yields.

In the twentieth century, total Asian rice production increased from about 49.38 million metric tons in 1911 to over 322 million metric tons in 1980 and about 540 million metric tons in 1999. Average yields increased from 1.78 metric tons per hectare in 1930 to 2.55 tons in 1980 and over 3.9 tons in 1999. Yet much more is needed: malnutrition is still endemic, poverty is an important constraint on food intake, and population is still increasing. Hope lies in the fact that rice yields, along with yields of other grains, can rise well above present levels. This has often been demonstrated experimentally, but more important it is also evident in the great variations in productivity within and between countries, ranging from 1.7 tons/hectare in Cambodia through 2.92 in India to 6.3 in China and 6.8 in the Republic of Korea. While some of these differences may reflect natural conditions, the more likely explanation lies in farmers' differing access to resources, and this can readily be improved.

Murray J. Leaf

Further Reading

Barker, Randolph, Robert W. Herdt, and Beth Rose. (1985). *The Rice Economy of Asia*. Washington, DC: Resources for the Future.

Food and Agricultural Organization of the United Nations (FAO). (2000). "FAOStat Database Gateway." Retrieved 27 June 2000, from: http://apps.fao.org/lim500/nph-wrap.pl?Production.Crops.Primary&Domain=SUA&servlet=1.

Lansing, J. Stephen. (1991) *Priests and Programmers: Technologies of Power in the Engineered Landscape of Bali*. Princeton, NJ: Princeton University Press.

Leaf, Murray J. (1998) *Pragmatism and Development: The Prospect for Pluralist Transformation in the Third World*. New York: Bergin and Garvey.

Randhawa, M. S. (1980–1986) *A History of Agriculture in India*. 4 vols. New Delhi: Indian Council of Agricultural Research.

RINGI SYSTEM The *ringi* system is a collective process of decision making by circular letter (*ringisho*) that is known to be specific to large bureaucratic organizations and companies in Japan. The *ringi* system of sharing authority is a practice that dates back to the Tokugawa shogunate during the Edo period (1600/1603–1868). A proposal is initiated at the middle or lower level of management. It then takes the form of a written proposal that is circulated among the interested parties through the organizational hierarchies, as well as at the divisional and corporate levels for consultation, comment, and approval. After each individual involved has signified agreement by stamping a personal seal (*hanko*) on the document, it is returned to the original person in charge for implementation. From this process, a final decision emerges that will be enacted by the authority of the organization or company. This process is called *ringiseido* (request for decision system), which emphasizes the importance the Japanese place on group decisions. In negotiations, it means that the confidence of the entire group will have to be reached. In the end, the decision can be implemented quickly and with full cooperation because it already has unanimous support.

This practice of sharing the responsibility for decision making that emphasizes group consensus is time consuming and explains why the negotiating process takes so long. The reason is that a great deal of informal discussion will have taken place before the *ringisho* is even drawn up. This informal decision-making stage in a Japanese organization is called *nemawashi* (prior consultation). When used together, the *nemawashi* and *ringi* systems ensure that corporate management at both horizontal and verticals level are kept completely informed.

A basic condition for implementing the *ringi* system effectively is the necessity for each individual involved to have shared understanding and values. The *ringi* system, however, has been criticized. Consensus-based decision making does not clarify with whom the responsibility rests. Accountability for actions and decisions is diffused, which protects an individual from being criticized for proposals that are ill-advised. In situations where a quick decision is desirable, Western-style decision making involving top-level management has been adopted. More and more, in order to accelerate the speed of the *ringi* process and to eliminate bureaucracy, some companies are simplifying the procedure by the use of in-house communication networks, including intranets.

Nathalie Cavasin

See also: **Quality Circles**

Further Reading
Taplin, Ruth. (1995) *Decision-Making and Japan: A Study of Corporate Japanese Decision-Making and its Relevance to Western Companies.* Folkestone, Kent, U.K.: Japan Library.

RIZAL, JOSÉ (1861–1896), Filipino physician, writer, patriot. José Rizal was born in Calamba, Laguna Province, Philippines, on 19 June 1861, to a well-to-do landowner and sugar planter family. Rizal obtained a bachelor of arts degree in 1877 at the Jesuit Ateneo Municipal school in Manila and in 1882 left for Spain to enter the Central University of Madrid, where he studied medicine and philosophy.

In Spain, he committed himself to the reform of Spanish rule in the Philippines. Rizal insisted that it was the religious institutions, specifically the Franciscan, Augustinian, and Dominican friars, that had a stranglehold on the politics and economy of the Philippines. He continued his graduate studies in Paris and Heidelberg and in 1886 published his novel *Noli Me Tangere* (Touch Me Not), which reflected the suffering that his fellow citizens had had to endure under the years of Spanish domination. His book was

Monument dedicated to the execution of José Rizal in José Rizal Park, Manila, in 1996. (STEPHEN G. DONALDSON PHOTOGRAPHY)

JOSÉ RIZAL'S FINAL MESSAGE

Philippine patriot José Rizal was executed by the Spanish on 30 December 1896. On the night before his execution he smuggled the following poem—a classic statement in Philippine history—in a small alcohol lamp from his prison cell to his sister.

Farewell, dear fatherland, clime of the sun caress'd,
Pearl of the Orient seas, our Eden lost!
Gladly now I give to thee this faded life's best,
And were it brighter, fresh, or more blest,
Still would I give it thee, nor count the cost.
On the field of battle, 'mid the frenzy of fight
Others have given their lives, without doubt or heed;
The place matters not—cypress or laurel or lily white,
Scaffold or open plain, combat or martyrdom's plight,
'Tis ever the same, to serve our home and country's
    need.
I die just when I see the dawn break,
Through the gloom of night, to herald the day;
And if color is lacking my blood thou shalt take,
Pour'd out at need for thy dear sake,
To dye with its crimson the waking ray.
My dreams, when life first opened to me,
My dreams, when the hope of youth beat high,
Were to see thy lov'd face, O gem of the Orient sea,
From gloom and grief, from care and sorrow free;
No blush on thy brow, no tear in thine eye.
Dream of my life, my living and burning desire;
All hail; cries the soul that is now to take flight;
All hail! And sweet it is for thee to expire;
To die for thy sake, that thou mays't aspire;
And sleep in thy bosom eternity's long night.
If over my grave some day thou seest grow,
In the grassy sod, a humbled flower,
Draw it to thy lips and kiss my soul so,
While I feel on my brow in the cold tomb below,
The touch of thy tenderness, thy breath's warm
    power.
Let the moon beam over me soft and serene,
Let the dawn shed over me its radiant flashes,
Let the wind with sad lament over me keen;
And if on my cross a bird should be seen,

Let it trill there its hymn of peace to my ashes.
Let the sun draw vapors up the sky,
And heavenward in purity bear my tardy protest;
Let some kind soul o'er my untimely fate sigh,
And in the still evening a prayer be lifted on high
From thee, O my country, that in God I may rest . . .
Pray for all those that hapless have died,
For all who have suffered the unmeasur'd plain;
For our mothers that bitterly their woes have cried;
For widows and orphans, for captives by torture tried;
And then for thyself that redemption thou mays't gain.
And when the dark night wraps the graveyard around,
With only the dead in their vigil to see;
Break not my repose or the mystery profound,
And perchance thou mays't hear a sad hymn resound;
'Tis I, O my country, raising a song unto thee.
When even my grave is remembered no more,
Unmark'd by never a cross nor a stone;
Let the plow sweep through it, the spade turn it o'er,
That my ashes may carpet thy earthly floor,
Before into nothingness at last they are blown.
Then will oblivion bring me no care,
As over thy vales and plains I sweep,
Throbbing and cleansed in thy space and air,
With color and light, with song and lament I fare,
Ever repeating the faith that I keep.
My Fatherland adored, that sadness to my sorrow lends,
Beloved Filipinas, hear now my last good bye!
I give thee all, parents and kindred and friends;
For I go where no slave before the oppressor bends,
Where faith can never kill, and God reigns e'er on
    high!
Farewell to you all, from my soul torn away,
Friends of my childhood in the home dispossessed!
Give thanks that I rest from the wearisome day!
Farewell to thee, too, sweet friend that lightened my
    way;
Beloved creatures all, farewell! In death there is rest!

Source: Jaime C. DeVeyra. (1946) *El Ultimo Adios de Rizal.* Manila, Philippines: Bureau of Printing. Translated into English by Charles Derbyshire.

banned in the Philippines. He went on to become a leading spokesman for the Philippine reform movement, writing articles for the Filipino propaganda newspaper *La Solidaridad* in Barcelona. Key among Rizal's political goals were that the Philippines become a province of Spain, that Spanish friars be replaced by Filipino priests, and that both Filipinos and Spaniards be given equal rights and freedoms in the Philippines.

In 1887, Rizal returned to the Philippines but quickly returned to Europe because he believed his prolonged presence would serve only to endanger his family and relatives. In 1891, he wrote another book, *El Filibusterismo* (The Subversive), which centered on the abuses of the friars in his nation, especially the way they dealt with the landowners, of which Rizal's family was one. Among other things, this book predicted the outbreak of a mass peasant revolution in the Philippines.

After practicing medicine for a short time in Hong Kong, Rizal, against the advice of his parents and friends, returned to the Philippines in 1892 and founded a nonviolent reform society, La Liga Filipina (Philippine League), in Manila and was arrested and deported to Dapitan, Mindanao, in July 1892. For four years he remained in exile, practicing medicine, building a school, planning town improvements, and continuing his writing. In 1896, the Katipunan, a nationalist secret society, launched a revolt against Spain. Although Rizal was in no way affiliated with the society, he was arrested, returned to Manila, falsely tried for treason and complicity with the revolution, and found guilty. On the eve of his execution, confined to Fort Santiago, Rizal wrote *Mi Ultimo Adios* (My Last Farewell). On 30 December 1896, José Rizal was publicly executed by a firing squad in Manila. To this day, José Rizal is celebrated as a national hero in the Philippines. His death inspired Filipino revolutionaries to continue their struggle for independence from Spain.

Craig Loomis

Further Reading

Santos, Alfonso P. (1974) *Rizal in Life and Legends.* Quezon City, Philippines: National Book Store.

Zaide, Gregorio F. (1984) *Jose Rizal: Life, Works and Writings of a Genius, Writer, Scientist and National Hero.* Manila, Philippines: National Book Store.

RIZE (2002 pop. 82,000). Rize, the largest Turkish town east of Trabzon on the Black Sea coast, is the capital of Rize Province (2002 pop. 363,300) and the center of Turkish tea cultivation. Its ancient name was Rhizaion; a fortress east of the modern town was built by the Byzantine emperor Justinian along the frontier with Persia. This fortress was rebuilt and expanded by the Grand Comneni of Trebizond.

Rize has been the home of Persian Armenians, Georgians, Pontic Greeks, and settlers from the European lands of the Ottoman empire, such as Rumeli, Bosnia, and Morea, who were granted lands by Mehmet the Conqueror. In the sixteenth century the majority of the population was Christian, with many villages having Greek names. Rize follows the traditional Black Sea non-nucleated settlement pattern of villages and neighborhoods spread out over a large area outside the city center.

Local production, aside from tea, includes citrus and other fruits, nuts, corn, small-scale boats, and a local specialty textile called *peshtemal*, a kind of striped linen, which has been in constant production since the Comnenian period and was exported to Baghdad and Egypt during Ottoman times. Tea was introduced in the 1920s, and Rize tea is the main Turkish domestic tea.

Sylvia Wing Önder

Further Reading

Freely, John. (1991) *Classical Turkey.* London: Penguin Books.

Hann, C. M. (1990) *Tea and the Domestication of the Turkish State.* School of Oriental and African Studies Modern Turkish Studies Programme, Occasional Papers 1. Huntingdon, U.K.: Eothen Press.

ROH TAE WOO (b. 1932), president of South Korea. Roh Tae Woo was president of South Korea from 1988 to 1993. Roh was born in Talsong, near Taegu, in North Kyongsang Province, the son of a minor local official. He joined the South Korean Army in 1951 and soon after attended the Korean Military Academy. While there, Roh met fellow classmate Chun Doo Hwan. He graduated in 1955, whereupon he received his commission in the South Korean Army as a second lieutenant.

During his career in the military Roh attended the U.S. Special Warfare School at Fort Bragg, North Carolina, and graduated from the South Korean War College in 1968. Roh served with South Korean forces in Vietnam during the Vietnam War (1954–1975). He was eventually promoted to the rank of brigadier general. Roh helped engineer the coup d'etat that brought Chun Doo Hwan to power in December 1979 and succeeded Chun as commander of the Defense Security Command. Roh retired from the army to become minister of state for political and security affairs. He held various governmental posts and as minister of sport was instrumental in bringing the Olympics to Seoul in 1988.

Roh succeeded Chun Doo Hwan as president in the first peaceful transfer of power in South Korean history. Roh was elected president in 1988 and served until 1993, when he did not stand for reelection. He instituted political and economic reforms, including more local autonomy, more freedom of the press, and more influence for labor unions, and in 1991 saw that South Korea was accepted into the United Nations.

In 1995–1996, Roh and Chun were found guilty of treason, mutiny, and corruption in what was treated in South Korea as the trial of the century. The trial stemmed from charges that the men had stashed enormous slush funds while in office and from their roles in the Kwangju massacre by the military in 1980. Roh and Chun claimed that the trial was politically motivated. Roh was sentenced to 22.5 years in prison and fined $350 million. In 2002, an appeals court reduced the sentence to seventeen years.

Keith Leitich

Further Reading

Cotton, James, ed. (1993) *Korea under Roh Tae-Woo: Democratization, Northern Policy and Inter-Korean Relations.* Sydney: Allen & Unwin.

Oberdorfer, Don. (1997) *The Two Koreas: A Contemporary History.* Reading, MA: Addison-Wesley Longman.

Sigor, Christopher J., ed. (1992) *Democracy in Korea: The Roh Tae Woo Years.* New York: Carnegie Council on Ethics and International Affairs.

ROHINGYA   The Rohingyas are the Muslim minority of the Rakhine (formerly Arakan) State of Myanmar (Burma); although they number in the hundreds of thousands, available statistics are unreliable. Traditions hold that the Rohingyas have been settled in Rakhine since the seventh century, although strong evidence of their presence in Rakhine exists only from the fifteenth century. The Rohingyas are the descendants of Muslim traders from Persia and India, Muslim refugees from the Middle East and Bengal, and indigenous Arakanese converts to Islam.

Generally, tensions between the Rohingyas and the Buddhist Arakanese date from the nineteenth century, under colonial rule, when colonial efforts to define these communities and to identify shared religious sites on an either-or basis and a land crisis brought these two communities into conflict. The emergence of Rohingya and Buddhist Arakanese communalism

led to bloody confrontations in the twentieth century. Under Burma's military regime, efforts by the government to suppress the Muslim community, including denial of citizenship, forcible seizure of land, and violent intimidation forced hundreds of thousands of Rohingyas to seek refuge in neighboring (and Muslim) Bangladesh. Unable to shoulder the burden of so many refugees, poverty-stricken Bangladesh has, through agreements made with Myanmar, encouraged and often forced the majority of Rohingya refugees to return to Rakhine. Many other Rohingya refugees remain, however, scattered throughout the Middle East, Malaysia, and the United States. In order to reduce Muslim claims to heritage in Rakhine, some Buddhist Arakanese have made efforts to eradicate evidence of the antiquity of Rohingya settlement in Rakhine.

Michael W. Charney

Further Reading

Yegar, Moshe. (1972) *The Muslims of Burma: A Study of a Minority Group.* Wiesbaden, Germany: O. Harrassowitz.

ROHTAS FORT   Built as a strategic northwestern outpost and named after a similar stronghold in Bihar, India, Rohtas Fort is located about 100 kilometers south of Islamabad, the capital of modern Pakistan, off the Grand Trunk Road. Sher Shah Suri (reigned 1539–1545), an Indian-born Pashtun whose rule marked an interregnum in the Mughal control of India, ordered the construction of both the fort and the road. The site was strategic in that it was located at the northwestern frontier of the empire, and was meant as a stronghold against local tribesmen as well as against the armies of the recently defeated Mughal

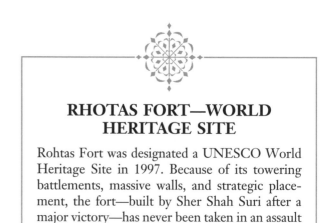

RHOTAS FORT—WORLD HERITAGE SITE

Rohtas Fort was designated a UNESCO World Heritage Site in 1997. Because of its towering battlements, massive walls, and strategic placement, the fort—built by Sher Shah Suri after a major victory—has never been taken in an assault and has survived centuries of war unscathed.

king. Work on Rohtas Fort began around 1540 and continued for ten years, so that the fort was not completed until after the death of Sher Shah.

Rohtas Fort has a perimeter of 5 kilometers; ten gates punctuate the wall. The fort is built of gray ashlar masonry, and the exterior wall is in places 10 to 13 meters thick and 10 to 16 meters high. The ceremonial main entrance is through the majestic Sohal Gate. In addition the fort contains large, arcaded wells with underground chambers. The primary citadel area, located on high ground in the northwest quadrant of the fortress, consists of an imperial mosque as well as the residential palace of the Mughal governor, Raja Man Singh. Rohtas Fort is an important example of sixteenth-century fortress building in the Indian subcontinent.

Kishwar Rizvi

Further Reading

Mumtaz, Kamil Khan. (1985) *Architecture in Pakistan*. Singapore: Concept Media.
Schimmel, Annemarie. (1980) *Islam in the Indian Subcontinent*. Leiden, Netherlands: Brill.

ROMANIZATION SYSTEMS, CHINESE

Because the Chinese do not use the Roman (Latin) alphabet to record their language, if it is to be written in the Roman alphabet it must be transliterated, or romanized. This is true whenever one wants to represent in the Roman alphabet a language that uses another script, whether the other script uses an alphabet (as do Arabic and Russian), a syllabary (as does Japanese), or ideographic characters, such as Chinese.

Chinese Characters

The Chinese developed *hanzi* (Chinese characters) to represent words, concepts, or ideas. The earliest attested Chinese characters, found on bones used for divination that date to the second millennium BCE, imitated the objects they represented (that is, the character for "eye" would look something like an eye). More complicated characters were formed by joining two or more visual shapes, by using certain shapes to symbolize concepts, and by the development of standard elements that could indicate pronunciation or some aspect of meaning (for example, the element meaning "tree" will occur in the characters for any number of specific types of tree, such as pine or plum).

Chinese characters have allowed people speaking widely varying Chinese dialects (so different, in fact, as to be more like separate languages) to communicate with each other. Because Chinese is a language with many homophones (words with different meanings but the same pronunciation), it is useful to have a system of writing that distinguishes between homophones visually, as Chinese characters do. This is especially true when the way in which words are pronounced differs so markedly from region to region.

Wade-Giles and Pinyin

Therefore it is perhaps no surprise that it was the foreign missionaries, diplomats, and merchants who first attempted to use alphabets to represent Chinese sounds. Jesuit missionaries, active in China in the sixteenth and early seventeenth centuries, introduced phonetic scripts based on the Roman alphabet. In 1867, British diplomat Thomas F. Wade (1818–1895) devised a phonetic script system based on Mandarin, one of the major Chinese dialects. Forty-five years later, in 1912, the Wade system was modified by H. A. Giles (1845–1935), an English scholar of Chinese. This modification was called the Wade-Giles system, and it has been in use for almost a century.

In 1918, the Chinese themselves developed a phonetic alphabet, called *zhuyin zimu* ("national phonetic alphabet"), using portions of characters to represent sounds. Realizing the importance of using the Roman alphabet, in 1828 the Chinese government promulgated a second form of phonetic script, *guoyu lomazi* ("national romanized writing"), which used the Roman alphabet along with special markers to indicate tones. However, neither the *zhuyin zimu* nor the *guoyu lomazi* succeeded in replacing Chinese characters. The *Zhuyin zimu* failed to become popular among foreigners, and the latter failed partially due to its clumsy tone symbols.

In the meantime, influenced by the Soviet approach to the problem of illiteracy, a group of Chinese residing in the Soviet Union (with help from Moscow), started the "Latinization of Chinese" movement. The features of pinyin romanization that make it most mysterious to English speakers (its use of *q* for the *ch* sound in the English word *church*, or its use of *x* for the palatal spirant represented in Wade-Giles by *hs*) came about because the system was based on Russian methods of romanizing Cyrillic—and those were the letters the Russians used for the equivalent sounds in Russian.

One of the most prominent early leaders of the movement was Qu Qiubai (1899–1935), who published a pamphlet entitled "Chinese Latinized Alphabet" in 1930. The final version of Qu's system used only those letters appearing on regular typewriters. It grouped syllables together as words and omitted sym-

CHINESE ROMANIZATION SYSTEMS

Depending on when a Chinese place became well known, the romanization of its name that seems most familiar may vary. Old historical cities such as Canton and Nanking may seem unfamiliar, especially to older readers, when they are romanized Guangzhou or Nanjing. China's capital is one exception: once universally known to English speakers as Peking, it is now equally or better known as Beijing. On the other hand, a modern industrial powerhouses such as Shenzhen would be unfamiliar if it were romanized Shen-chen. Below is a table of some well-known Chinese place names under three different systems of romanization.

Pinyin	Wade-Giles	Chinese Post Office System
Beijing	Pei-ching	Peking
Guangzhou	Kuang-chou	Canton
Nanjing	Nan-ching	Nanking
Shanghai	Shang-hai	Shanghai
Sichuan	Szechuan	Szechwan
Suzhou	Su-chou	Soochow
Tianjin	T'ien-chin	Tientsin
Xi'an	Hsi-an	Sian
Xinjiang	Hsin-chiang	Sinkiang

bols representing tones. This system covered Mandarin only; Qu suggested that different systems for other dialects or minority languages be developed.

Qu's system was introduced to China in 1931, with a notion that eventually the Chinese characters would be replaced by this romanization system. But advocates of *guoyu lomazi* criticized the new system, especially for its lack of tone marks. Many left-wing writers, including Lu Xun, Guo Moruo, Mao Dun, and Ba Jin, favored the new system, although Soviet support for this movement disappeared from 1939, when the Soviet Union abandoned the Roman alphabet in favor of Cyrillic script.

The new system was called *xin wenzi* (new script) or *ladinghua xin wenzi* (latinized new script). During the period of the Second World War (1939–1945), petitions were made by advocates of *xin wenzi*, but these were not given much attention either by the Nationalists or by the Chinese Communists. In 1958 the *xin wenzi* was replaced by pinyin (*pinyin* in Chinese means "to spell phonetically"), a modification of Qu's system. Pinyin was adopted by the United Nations in 1977. It has gradually increased in popularity outside China,

where it allows a standardization in romanizing Chinese (previously German, French, and English transliteration systems all romanized Chinese in accordance with how the Roman alphabet is pronounced in those languages—which made them differ from one another).

Pinyin, like Wade-Giles, is based on Mandarin. Characteristic of Mandarin is that the distinction between *b* and *p*, *d* and *t*, and *g* and *k* is one of aspiration versus non-aspiration, not voiced versus voiceless pronunciation. Wade-Giles represents the distinction with a mark indicating aspiration: the *b* sound is represented with a *p*, while the *p* sound is represented with a *p'*. In pinyin, by contrast, the *b* sound is represented with a *b* and the *p* with a *p*. Similarly, in Wade-Giles the *d* sound is represented with a *t*, while the *t* sound is represented with a *t'*. In pinyin, the *d* sound is represented with a *d* and the *t* with a *t*.

Both pinyin and Wade-Giles are limited in that they were not designed to represent the speech of some of the other Chinese languages and dialects. Also, neither system represents tones. There are only four tones in Mandarin, but there are nine in Yue, another dialect. In the future, it is possible that different spelling systems for other Chinese languages and dialects will be developed and that symbols for tones and other linguistic features may also be developed.

Other Romanization Systems

Other methods of romanizing Chinese include the early-twentieth-century Chinese Post Office System, which gave the world the romanizations Peking and Nanking for the cities known in pinyin as Beijing and Nanjing (in Wade-Giles they would be Pei-ching and Nan-ching, respectively). *Tongyong* pinyin is a romanization system based on Wade-Giles that used in Taiwan, where, nevertheless, there is growing use of *Hanyu* pinyin, the pinyin used in the rest of China. (In 1999, the government of Taiwan announced that street signs would be romanized in *Hanyu* pinyin). The Yale system, created in 1948, was used in the United States as a teaching tool. *Gwoyeu romatzyh* (National Romanization) was created in 1928. It indicates differences in tone with different spellings and has also been popular as a teaching tool in the United States. It also enjoys some use on Taiwan, where a simplified version was promulgated in the 1980s.

John Young and the editorial staff of
Berkshire Publishing Group

Further Reading

DeFrancis, John. (1950) *Nationalism and Language Reform in China*. Princeton, NJ: Princeton University Press.
Karlgren, Bernhard. (1928) *The Romanization of Chinese*. London: China Society.
Ramsey, S. Robert. (1987) *The Languages of China*. Princeton, NJ: Princeton University Press.
Seybolt, Peter J., and Gregory Kuei-ke Chiang, eds. (1979). *Language Reform in China*. White Plains, NY: M. E. Sharpe.
Zhao Yuanren. (1922) "A System in Romanization of the National Language." *The Chinese Students' Monthly* 17, 3.

ROMANIZATION SYSTEMS, KOREAN

The two main romanization systems (that is, systems for writing Korean using the roman alphabet) for the Korean language are the McCune-Reischauer (MR) system and the Ministry of Education (ME) system.

McCune-Reischauer System

The McCune-Reischauer system is the most widely used romanization system for the Korean language. (See Tables 1 and 2.) Designed in 1939 by George S. McCune (1908–1948), an American missionary and principal of the P'yŏngyang Sungsil School, and Edwin O. Reischauer (1910–1990), then a graduate student of Japanese history at Harvard University, the MR

TABLE 1

McCune-Reischauer Consonants

Korean spelling	ㄱ	ㄷ	ㅂ	ㅈ	ㅅ
MR system	k, g (ng)	t, d (n)	p, b (m)	ch, j (t, n)	s, sh (t, n)
Korean spelling	ㅋ	ㅌ	ㅍ	ㅊ	ㅎ
MR system	k' (k, ng)	t' (t, n)	p' (p, m)	ch' (t, n)	h (n)
Korean spelling	ㄲ	ㄸ	ㅃ	ㅉ	
MR system	kk (k, ng)	tt (t, n)	pp (p, m)	tch, (t, n)	ss (t, n)
Korean spelling	ㄴ	ㅁ	ㅇ	ㄹ	
MR system	n (l)	m	zero, ng	l, r (n)	

Notes for consonants:
1. *G, d, b,* and *j* are used for ㄱ, ㄷ, ㅂ, and ㅈ, respectively, between two voiced sounds as pronounced.
2. The apostrophe (') indicates aspiration (extra puff of air coming out of the mouth).
3. Double consonants (*kk, tt, pp, tch,* and *ss*) are glottalized sounds. For the doubling of *ch, tch* is used instead of *chch*.
4. The symbols in parentheses are not specified in the system but would be used in some contexts due to pronunciation variation in Korean words.
5. Actual pronunciation of some symbols: *ng* [ŋ]as in the English word *sing, ch* [ts] as in church, *sh* [ʃ] as in *she,* and *r* [r] as t in *water.*
6. *Sh* is used when the following vowel is *wi,* that is, *shwi;* otherwise, *s* is used.
7. ㅇ in Korean has a sound value [ŋ] only in syllable-final position. Therefore, no symbol is used for ㅇ in syllable-initial position.
8. As for ㄹ, r is used between two vowels as well as at the beginning of a word.

romanization system is used in nearly all the references to Korean words in international society, including, maps, documents, and scholarly writings on Korea.

Sometimes the MR system uses different alphabet letters for the same Korean consonant spelling because it

TABLE 2

McCune-Reischauer Vowels

Korean spelling	ㅏ	ㅐ	ㅑ	ㅒ	
MR system	a	ae	ya	yae	
Korean spelling	ㅓ	ㅔ	ㅕ	ㅖ	
MR system	ŏ	e	yŏ	ye	
Korean spelling	ㅗ	ㅘ	ㅙ	ㅚ	ㅛ
MR system	o	wa	wae	oe	yo
Korean spelling	ㅜ	ㅝ	ㅞ	ㅟ	ㅠ
MR system	u	wŏ	we	wi	yu
Korean spelling	ㅡ	ㅣ	ㅢ		
MR system	ŭ	i	ŭi		

Notes for vowels:
1. A breve (˘)indicates a lip spreading of the pronunciation of the corresponding alphabet without it.
2. Actual pronunciation of some symbols: *ae* is pronounced [æ] as in the English word *at* and *oe* as [ø]or[œ],as in the French words *bleu* or *oef.*

aims to transcribe the actual pronunciation of Korean words, not the standard Korean spelling. For example, *hanguk* ("Korea") contains two syllables, the second of which means "nation." The same syllable would be transcribed differently for the word *kukpo* ("national treasure"). The variation is due to a sound variation rule in Korean by which stop consonants (*p, t, k,* and *ts*) become voiced between two voiced sounds; that is, *b, d, g,* and *j,* respectively. For another example, the first syllable of the name Silla (57 BCE–935 CE), one of the three ancient kingdoms that existed on the Korean peninsula, means "new" and would be romanized as *sin* in other contexts, such as in the name Sinchon (a district in Seoul), because *n* is pronounced as *l* before another *l*.

Ministry of Education System

In 1984, the Ministry of Education (ME) Romanization system was promulgated in order to unify all the different romanization systems that had been used to represent the Korean language using the Roman alphabet. The 1984 ME system was the official romanization system of the Korean government until 30 June 2000. A newly revised romanization system was promulgated 1 July 2000 by the Ministry of Culture and Tourism (MCT) as the official romanization system of the Korean government. To allow for complete transition, the complete replacement of the 1984 ME system with the newly revised MCT system is set for 31 December 2005.

The 1984 ME system is almost identical to the McCune-Reischauer system except that *wŏ* in the McCune-Reischauer system is transcribed in the 1984 ME system as *wo*, without the diacritic marker. The diacritic marker is unnecessary because there is no sequence of *w* and *o* in Korean. Therefore, Wŏnju (a city name) in the McCune-Reischauer system would be transcribed Wonju in the 1984 ME system.

Another difference between the McCune-Reischauer system and the 1984 ME system is the way in which the two systems use *sh*. In the 1984 ME system, *sh* is used only before *wi*, but not before *i*. Therefore, Silla in the McCune-Reischauer system is transcribed as Shilla in the 1984 ME system. Like the McCune-Reischauer system, the 1984 ME system transcribes the actual pronunciation of Korean words, not standard Korean spellings.

The new MCT romanization system, promulgated in 2000, is drastically different from the 1984 ME system. (See Tables 3 and 4 for comparison.)

There are some notable differences between the 1984 ME system and the new system:

1. To facilitate computerization, the proposed system uses no diacritic devices (e.g., breve ˘ and

TABLE 3

Consonants in Ministry of Education (ME) System and in the New (MCT) System

Korean spelling	ㄱ	ㄷ	ㅂ	ㅈ	ㅅ
1984 ME system	k, g (ng)	t, d (n)	p, b (m)	ch, j (t, n)	s, sh (n)
2000 MCT system	g, k (ng)	d, t (n)	b, p (m)	j (t, n)	s (n)
Korean spelling	ㅋ	ㅌ	ㅍ	ㅊ	ㅎ
1984 ME system	k', (k, ng)	t' (t, n)	p' (p, m)	ch' (t, n)	h (n)
2000 MCT system	k (ng)	t (n)	p (m)	ch (t, n)	h (n)
Korean spelling	ㄲ	ㄸ	ㅃ	ㅉ	ㅆ
1984 ME system	kk (k, ng)	tt (t, n)	pp (p, m)	tch (t, n)	ss (t, n)
2000 MCT system	gg(k, ng)	dd (t, n)	bb (p, m)	jj (t, n)	ss (t, n)
Korean spelling	ㄴ	ㅁ	ㅇ	ㄹ	
1984 ME system	n (l)	m	zero, ng	l, r (n)	
2000 MCT system	n (l)	m	zero, ng	l, r (n)	

Notes for consonants are the same as for Table 1, except that the double consonants for the new system are *gg, dd, bb, jj,* and *ss*.

apostrophe '). Therefore, the vowels ŏ (ㅓ) and ŭ (ㅡ) in the 1984 ME system are transcribed as *eo* and *eu*, respectively, in the new system, except for the vowel ㅢ, which is transcribed as *ui*, not *eui*, in the new system. For consonants, aspirated stops would be represented with plain *k, t, p,* and *ch*. For example, Ch'unch'ŏn (a city name) in the ME system is transcribed Chuncheon in the new system.

2. In the 1984 ME system, ㄱ, ㄷ, ㅂ, and ㅈ are represented with letters for voiceless sounds *k, t, p,* and *ch*, and symbols for the voiced sounds *g, d, g,* and *j* are used only between two voiced sounds. In the new system, those Korean letters are represented with *g, d, g,* and *j*, under the assumption that voiced letters would bring about pronunciation closer to Korean pronunciation to Korean people's ears, and *k, t,* and *p* are used only before another consonant or at the and of a word. For example, Pusan and Kwangju (both city names) in the 1984 ME system are transcribed as Busan and Gwangju in the new system. The glottalized consonants *kk, tt, pp,* and *tch* in 1984 ME system are represented with *gg, dd, bb,* and *jj* in the new system.

3. For ㅅ, the new system uses only *s*, ignoring the variation between *s* and *sh* regardless of the following vowel.

Hyo Sang Lee

TABLE 4

Vowels in the 1984 Ministry of Education and in the New (MCT) system

Korean spelling	ㅏ	ㅐ	ㅑ	ㅒ	
1984 ME system	a	ae	ya	yae	
2000 MCT system	a	ae	ya	yae	
Korean spelling	ㅓ	ㅔ	ㅕ	ㅖ	
1984 ME system	ŏ	e	yŏ	ye	
2000 MCT system	eo	e	yeo	ye	
Korean spelling	ㅗ	ㅘ	ㅙ	ㅚ	ㅛ
1984 ME system	o	wa	wae	oe	yo
2000 MCT system	o	wa	wae	oe	yo
Korean spelling	ㅜ	ㅝ	ㅞ	ㅟ	ㅠ
1984 ME system	u	wo	we	wi	yu
2000 MCT system	u	weo	we	wi	yu
Korean spelling	ㅡ	ㅣ	ㅢ		
1984 ME system	ŭ	i	ŭi		
2000 MCT system	eu	i	ui		

Notes for vowels are the same as for Table 2.

ROMULO, CARLOS PEÑA

(1899–1985), Philippine author, educator, soldier, diplomat. Born 14 January 1899 in Manila, Carlos Peña Romulo was educated at the University of the Philippines and Columbia University in New York. He went on to become publisher and editor of the *Philippines Herald* (1933–1941) and in 1941 was awarded the Pulitzer Prize for a series of articles on the political and military situation in the Far East. With the outbreak of World War II, Romulo joined General Douglas MacArthur's staff as a press relations officer; by war's end he held the rank of brigadier general. After the war, he acted as a Philippine delegate to the U.N. organization conference in San Francisco. From 1946–1954 he was the Philippine ambassador to the U.N.; in 1949 he became the first Asian president of the U.N. General Assembly. Romulo was secretary of foreign affairs for the Philippines (1950–1951) and went on to become ambassador to the United States (1952–1953). After serving as president of the University of the Philippines and secretary of education between 1963 and 1968, he again served as secretary of foreign affairs, this time under President Ferdinand Marcos (1969–1984).

Aside from Romulo's many governmental duties, he continued to write. Some of his well-known works are *I Saw the Fall of the Philippines* (1942), *Mother America* (1943), *My Brother Americans* (1945), *I See the Philippines Rise* (1946), *The Magsaysay Story* (1956), *I Walked with Heroes* (1961), and *Identity and Change* (1965).

Craig Loomis

Further Reading

Smith, Robert A. (1958) *Philippine Freedom, 1946–1958*. New York: Columbia University Press.
Spencer, Cornelia. (1953) *Romulo: Voice of Freedom*. New York: John Day.

ROMUSHA

The term *romusha*, literally a person (*sha*) on labor (*ro*) duty (*mu*), was widely used in Southeast Asia by Japanese occupying forces during World War II. Avoiding the pejorative term "coolie," Japanese authorities embarked on an intensive scheme of labor recruitment under the *romu* banner. Conceptions of local autarky and the requirements of the war effort heightened the need for labor, which was mobilized by the offer of wages, deception, and force.

At present, the term *romusha* is generally used to refer to forced labor in Indonesia, because of the exceptional intensity of Japanese labor mobilization there. In all areas of the Indonesian archipelago, but most intensively on Java, men were conscripted for labor on plantations, docks, and mines, and for the construction of defense works, railroads, and airstrips. Treatment was without exception harsh, and many died of exhaustion, inadequate medical treatment, and starvation. Most laborers were employed in areas close to their home villages, but about 225,000 Javanese *romusha* were shipped to other parts of the archipelago, and 69,000 elsewhere in Southeast Asia.

All countries of Southeast Asia under Japanese rule had their share of forced-labor conscription, with similar patterns of recruitment and employment at military constructions sites. One infamous site was the Burma-Thailand Railway, which was constructed by Allied prisoners of war and Asian *romusha* between November 1942 and October 1943. About 75,000 laborers were recruited in Malaya, from among Indian (Tamil) plantation laborers, but also from Malay villages. On the Burma side, some 85,000 Burmese laborers were employed, while laborers were also recruited in Thailand. The death rate of Asian laborers on the railroad was more than 35 percent.

Remco Raben

ROY, RAMMOHAN

ROY, RAMMOHAN (1772–1833), Indian religious and social reformer. Rammohan Roy was among the foremost religious and social reformers of modern India. Born in an orthodox Hindu family of Calcutta, Roy's education and early travels exposed him to a wide variety of cultural and religious experiences. Between 1786 and 1803, Roy received intensive training in Arabic and Persian from scholars based in the north Indian city of Patna, traveled with a group of Tibetan monks, learned English, and studied Hindu philosophy in Varanasi (Benares). That exposure to the world, his love for books, and his reflections on Hinduism led him as a young man to question the orthodoxy in his own background. It seemed to him that the spirit of the Vedas and the Upanishads—freedom of thought and respect for human dignity—was lost in the mire of rituals that later typified Hinduism. This was to be a central tenet in his beliefs and one that he earnestly wrote on in later life. Religious decadence and social repression thus became connected in his ideas.

While briefly in service of the East India Company (1809–1814), he studied European history and culture and was deeply influenced by the pursuit of freedom and equality in postrevolutionary Europe. After 1814, he devoted himself to popularizing his ideas and putting them in practice, often attracting fierce resistance from influential contemporaries, such as Radhakanta Deb, a powerful landlord and leader of a group of orthodox Hindus. Among his best-remembered contributions are his critical support for laws prohibiting the burning of widows (1829); advocacy of liberal ideals of education; foundation of the Brahma Samaj (1828), a religious order based on Vedic faith; support for Indian participation in the colonial bureaucracy; and popularization of the written version of his own language, Bengali. Roy died during a trip to England and Wales to plead a case of the Mughal emperor. Bristol, where he died, has a memorial and a statue of Roy.

Tirthankar Roy

Further Reading
Robertson, Bruce C. (1995) *Raja Rammohan Ray: The Father of Modern India*. Delhi: Oxford University Press.

ROYAL UNIVERSITY OF PHNOM PENH

The Royal University of Phnom Penh (UPP) was first established in 1960 as a result of the efforts of Prince Sihanouk (now King Sihanouk) to modernize Cambodia and focus on education. Built with money largely donated by the French, the Royal University was one of Cambodia's first institutions of higher education and played a significant role in educating Cambodia's urban population before the atrocities of the Khmer Rouge period (1975–1979). The university was closed during this turbulent time and remained vacant until the early 1990s, when efforts were made to reestablish the institution. The university was officially reopened in 1998.

The current university consists of faculties of letters and human sciences and of science. Majors include Khmer literature, geography, psychology, philosophy, sociology, and history. In addition, students may major in mathematics, physics, chemistry, biology, or computer science. There also is a master's program in education.

The total enrollment of approximately four thousand includes both Cambodians and a small number of international students, with more than 250 faculty and staff members. In 1997 the university opened the Hun Sen Library, the first modern library of its kind to be opened in Cambodia for over seven decades.

John D'Amicantonio

Further Reading
Ayres, David M. (2000) *Anatomy of a Crisis: Education, Development, and the State in Cambodia, 1953–1998*. Honolulu, HI: University of Hawaii Press.
Bywater, Margaret A. (1998) "Libraries in Cambodia: Rebuilding a Past and a Future." *IFLA Journal* 24, 4 (July): 223.
Osborne, Milton. (1994) *Sihanouk: Prince of Light, Prince of Darkness*. Honolulu, HI: University of Hawaii Press.
Pit, C. (2000) "Willing Hands and Hearts: The Rebuilding of the Royal University of Phnom Penh." *International Higher Education* (Spring). Retrieved 21 August 2001, from: http://www.bc.edu/bc_org/avp/soe/cihe/newsletter/News19/text10.html.
Wheeler, David L. (1999) "After 30 Years of War and Neglect, Cambodia's Royal U. Begins to Revive." *The Chronicle of Higher Education* 45, 45 (18 June): A47.

RUBAB

RUBAB *Rubab*, an Arabic term, is widely used throughout the Islamic world to denote a bowed lute. It is usually played on the knees with the bow held from underneath. *Rubab*s are of two main types: fiddles with wooden, pear-shaped bodies and spike fiddles, in which a single spike, or neck, holding the string or strings and piercing the resounding chamber, emerges from the other end. The first type is found in North Africa and is popular in Morocco. In Turkey instruments carved from a single piece of wood with a sound table of skin were called *rubab* in the seventeenth century. They are now known as *kamance*. The Indian *sarod* is also related to it. It usually has more strings than the African instruments.

Some spike fiddles, such as the quadrangular *rubab* of Egypt, Syria, and Iraq appear to have evolved from frame drums. Its body is a wooden frame with a belly and back of skin. Originally plucked, it later became a bowed instrument. A second type of spike fiddle has a hemispherical body of carved wood, usually gourd or coconut, covered with a skin belly. It is widely found over a large area from North Africa to Southeast Asia and the Far East. In Java it is known as the *rebab*, which has an important melodic role in the gamelan orchestra.

Sanjukta Das Gupta

Further Reading
Jenkins, Jean, and Poul Rovsing Olsen. (1976) *Music and Musical Instruments in the World of Islam.* London: Horniman Museum.
Marcuse, Sibyl. (1975) *A Survey of Musical Instruments.* New York: Harper & Row.

RUBBER INDUSTRY

The rubber industry in Asia today consists primarily of the cultivation of *Hevea brasiliensis* in various countries, primarily Indonesia and Malaysia, and the export of raw rubber and manufactured rubber products throughout the world. The industry owes its existence to Western imperialism, which developed rubber cultivation in subject territories until rubber became a prime reason for continued European political dominance in the Far East. In the process, the industry helped to change radically the economic and social dynamics of indigenous rubber-producing societies and even their ethnic composition. The rubber industry was, as well, at least partially responsible for embroiling the peoples who cultivated the source plants in the catastrophic Japanese invasions of their native lands during World War II.

Rubber is a manufactured product, the raw material for which has traditionally consisted of fluids obtained from various tropical plants. (Much modern "rubber" is, in fact, chemically synthesized and independent of Asian sources and so not relevant here.) Europeans first encountered rubberlike products during the fifteenth century when Iberian explorers came into contact with indigenous peoples in today's Latin America who used gum to fashion various domestic items. A simple process of slashing certain trees and shrubs and collecting the resulting fluid gathered the gum itself. This gum, in turn, when diluted with water and strained will congeal at room temperature into a soft, malleable lump. This remains the basic method to this day.

Rubber was something of an oddity in European culture until it began to be used early in the nineteenth

Women processing rubber in a rubber factory in Malaya in about 1950. (HORACE BRISTOL/CORBIS)

century to waterproof fabric. Demand soared when, at midcentury, various processes—vulcanization, most especially—were discovered that overcame its cold-weather brittleness and allowed it to be conveniently worked. Rubber quickly became a constituent part of the industrial world with the bulk of it supplied from the regions around the Amazon River in South America.

The development of the automobile created an insatiable demand for rubber. Tires were the prime use for the substance, but it was utilized widely throughout industry and quickly became, along with such raw materials as oil and tin, one of the key strategic needs of any developed economy. In wartime, it was absolutely essential.

The Amazon basin, Brazil primarily, was unable to satisfy the world's increased demand for rubber. As inhabitants of an independent country (as opposed to a colony), the population of Brazil could not simply be commanded to produce the product. Innumerable individual entrepreneurs, acting on the most primitive level, tapped the forest trees and brought raw rubber to market. This scattered production system, combined with geographical barriers, restrained the industry's growth despite booming demand. All of this set the stage for Asia's emergence as a prime source.

Asia's Emergence as a Rubber-Producing Area

The climate of various Asian colonies, particularly the Dutch East Indies (present-day Indonesia) and the

THE RUBBER INDUSTRY— PROFITABLE FOR WHOM?

The rubber industry is closely associated with the colonial exploitation of natural resources in Southeast Asia. As this report about Malay agriculture makes clear, rubber exploitation was not necessarily a profitable activity for the Malays.

While Pegasi informants report that most households began planting rubber just after the 1925 flood, it was many years before rubber sales became a major means of earning cash. Pegasi villagers, attracted by the high rubber price of 1910 (see Appendix G), saw this as a new and easy way to make money. However the lack of suitable land, scarcity of planting materials, and limited knowledge slowed adoption of the new crop. Moreover, the first harvests in the Pegasi occurred at a time when rubber prices continued low for almost 10 years. Informants say that their first sales in 1932 brought only three dollars per *pikul* with total earnings each month at only two or three dollars per household. By 1934 the price paid to Pegasi village was five to eight dollars per *pikul*; and the few households with plantings of an acre or more earned five to ten dollars each month. However, it was not until 1939, when rubber sold at $20 per *pikul*, that prices reached a level high enough for rubber gardening to become a major means of supporting a household.

Source: Donald H. Lambert (1985) *Swamp Rice Farming: The Indigenous Pahang Malay Agricultural System.* Boulder, CO, and London: Westview Press, 23.

Malay States (present-day Malaysia), was ideal for growing *Hevea brasiliensis.* There was a large indigenous settled population that could be recruited to cultivate the labor-intensive plant in orderly plantation style. The political control exerted by colonial occupiers over the local population almost guaranteed a reliable and servile workforce.

Rubber production in Asia grew at an astonishing rate during the first decades of the twentieth century. In 1936, researchers wrote: "Malaya and its neighboring islands today dominate a production stretched to so vast a figure that little more than two decades ago it would have been regarded as a fantasy" (Wolf and Wolf 1936: 152). In the mid-1930s, rubber production reached 1,019,000 tons annually, with 467,000 tons extracted from the Malay States and 380,000 from the Dutch East Indies. French Indochina (present-day Vietnam, Laos, and Cambodia) and India contributed small shares as well, whereas Brazil's production was by now almost insignificant.

Consequences of the Growth of the Rubber Industry

Western-supervised rubber cultivation profoundly changed the indigenous Asian cultures. This was especially true in Malaya, where the very ethnic composition changed—with cultural complications and animosities that continue to this day. The British colonizers, used to dealing with docile, English-speaking Indian labor, imported huge numbers of workers from the Indian subcontinent until these constituted nearly 10 percent of the local population. Native Malays, who regarded them as so many cat's-paws of the colonizers, resented the imported workers.

The rubber trade changed local societies in other ways. In Borneo, for example, the local, essentially mercantilist, economy in various luxury goods, such as native gold products, fine woods, or exotic animals, was increasingly supplanted by a "peripheral" economy oriented away from local demand and toward far-off Europe, with its appetite for rubber. This disrupted, and even destroyed, local native industries, such as gold working and wood carving, along with the social infrastructure these had created. Similar social disruption accompanied the introduction of the plantation system into other regions.

The native populations were exploited wherever the rubber culture spread. Rubber production is labor intensive, as are all plantation economies, and requires countless individuals to tend the plants, tap them one by one for their gum, and then bring the raw material to a collection point. In some colonies, a state of virtual peonage was created to ensure a steady supply of cheap, tractable labor. Throughout Asia, labor contracts were drawn up in such a way that the locals were kept in a state of virtually continuous debt and so tied to the land. Such time-honored techniques as the "company store" kept local populations in enforced servitude. With near-total political control, European colonial masters were able to squelch labor unrest.

Some semblance of the rule of law existed in the British colonies. But in the Dutch and French possessions, the political situation of the labor force was little better than submission to tyranny. Contract labor was moved in bulk and kept in draconian conditions. Medical care and child care was virtually nonexistent. Among the Vietnamese laborers a popular song ran: "What a mistake to enter the rubber lands/Like life imprisonment without a jail" (Tran 1985: 28).

Independence and After

Imperial Japan was attracted especially by the easily accessible Malayan rubber culture. The brilliant Japanese campaign over the winter of 1941–1942 temporarily expelled the British from their Malayan colony. The Dutch were likewise quickly expelled from the East Indies. The Japanese proved every bit as ruthless in exploiting the local populations in order to secure strategically vital rubber, with economic and social results similar to that of European exploitation.

The European colonial empires in Asia survived the Japanese surrender in 1945 for only a few years, and by 1955 the prime rubber-producing Asian countries—Malaya, Indonesia, the Indochinese nations, and India—were independent. Overseas investment in the area continued to be of prime importance, especially from Great Britain, but during the second half of the twentieth century these Asian economies matured, albeit at varying rates, and control passed increasingly into local hands. Domestic manufacturing rose in importance, and the Far Eastern countries increasingly participated in a global economy.

Today, rubber remains a prime Asian resource but has declined in relative importance. Increasingly, rubber is shipped from Asia in the form of tires, latex gloves, gaskets, and other rubber-based finished products that require advanced technology. The plantation system remains an economical mode of production but without the peonage system of colonial times.

Robert K. Whalen

Further Reading

Babcock, Glen. (1966) *History of the United States Rubber Company.* Bloomington, IN: Indiana University Press.
Cleary, M. C. (1996) "Indigenous Trade and European Economic Intervention in North-West Borneo c. 1860–1930." *Modern Asian Studies* 30: 301–324.
Drabble, John H. (1991) *Malayan Rubber.* New York: Macmillan.
Lief, Alfred. (1951) *The Firestone Story: A History of the Firestone Tire & Rubber Company.* New York: Whittlesy House.
Murray, Herbert. (1999) "Tin Cans and Tyres: Soaring Demand for Tin and Rubber in the West during the Early 20th Century Radically Altered the Ethnic Landscape of Asia." *Far Eastern Economic Review* 162: 62.
Tran, Bu Binh. (1985) *The Red Earth: A Vietnamese Memoir of Life on a Colonial Rubber Plantation.* Trans. by John Spargens Jr. Athens, OH: Ohio University Press.
Wolf, Howard, and Ralph Wolf. (1936) *Rubber: A Story of Glory and Greed.* New York: Convici, Friede.

RUBBER INDUSTRY—MALAYSIA
Rubber (*Hevea brasiliensis* species) as a commercial crop had contributed immensely to the Malaysian economy since the late 1890s and remained the predominant export crop until the early 1980s. Peninsular Malaysia is particularly ideal for rubber owing to the soil, terrain, and climatic conditions.

While rubber prices steadily appreciated in the 1890s, coffee prices had tumbled due to Brazilian overproduction. Disease almost crippled the coffee industry of peninsular Malaysia and coffee planters were in need of substitutes to cut losses. Rubber came upon the scene and within a decade became the chief export crop.

Breakthrough discoveries and inventions were important early boosts to the industry. But the phenomenal upswing in world rubber prices during the first decade of the twentieth century spurred by the automobile industry of the United States was the greatest motivation for the rapid growth and spectacular expansion of the rubber industry of peninsular Malaysia. A rubber "fever" spread throughout peninsular Malaysia where estates and smallholdings covered the western coast from Perak to Johor, southern Kedah and central Pahang, and the western coast of Sabah.

In Sarawak Chinese smallholdings predominate in the Lower Rejang. Within a decade (1897–1907), the area under rubber in peninsular Malaysia jumped from 140 hectares to over 51,000 hectares.

European agency houses (commercial firms) of Singapore and Penang were instrumental in convincing British capital to finance large-scale plantation enterprise by floating public companies in Britain. A cheap and plentiful supply of labor came from South India. By 1930 the European-dominated plantation sector accounted for 60 percent and the remainder by Malay and Chinese smallholdings.

By 1919 peninsular Malaysia accounted for half of the total world rubber supply. Overproduction created a slump in prices in the 1920s. Prices drastically plummeted during the world depression (1929–1931). Restriction schemes were implemented to control production in order to maintain high prices, but the schemes favored the large estates and discriminated against smallholdings in terms of under assessment and inability to benefit from replanting.

The Japanese occupation (1941–1945) witnessed the cutting down of millions of rubber trees for food crop production that was the priority of the Japanese military authorities. After World War II the Malaysian rubber industry faced competition from synthetic rubber that was developed in the United States during the war years. Nonetheless the postwar years witnessed a dramatic rise in rubber prices due to stockpiling by the United States and the Korean War (1950–1953).

Following independence in 1957, the Malaysian rubber industry focused on three objectives: maintaining Malaysia's leading position as the largest producer and exporter of natural rubber, restructuring the industry to allow greater local participation in estate ownership and production, and ensuring fairer treatment of the smallholding sector. Numerous government agencies were set up to realize these objectives, for example Rubber Research Institute of Malaysia (RRIM), and Rubber Industry Smallholders' Development Authority (RISDA).

Ooi Keat Gin

Further Reading
Allen, G. C., and Audrey G. Donnithorne. (1954) *Western Enterprise in Indonesia and Malaya: A Study in Economic Development*. London: Allen & Unwin.

Amarjit, Kaur. (1998) *Economic Change in East Malaysia: Sabah and Sarawak since 1850*. Basingstoke, U.K., and London: Macmillan; New York: St. Martin's Press.

Drabble, J. H. (1973) *Rubber in Malaya 1876–1922. The Genesis of the Industry*. Kuala Lumpur, Malaysia: Oxford University Press.

Jackson, James C. (1968) *Planters and Speculators: Chinese and European Agricultural Enterprise in Malaya, 1786–1921*. Kuala Lumpur, Malaysia: University of Malaya Press.

Lim, Teck Ghee. (1977) *Peasants and their Agricultural Economy in Colonial Malaya 1874–1941*. Kuala Lumpur, Malaysia: Oxford University Press.

Ooi, Keat Gin. (1997) *Of Free Trade and Native Interests: The Brookes and the Economic Development of Sarawak, 1841–1941*. Kuala Lumpur, Malaysia: Oxford University Press.

RUDAKI (c. 859–940/941), first of the great classical Persian poets. The talents of Abu ʿAbdollah Jaʿfar ibn Mohammad, known as Rudaki, were not limited to poetry; he was also a gifted singer and musician. E. G. Browne (1811–1926), in his *Literary History of Persia*, called him "peerless among the Arabs and the Persians" and the "Sultan of poets." Rudaki was extremely prolific: He supposedly composed about 100,000 couplets, although because most of his *divan* (collection of poems) are lost, only about 1,000 are known today. As court poet of Nasr ibn Ahmad (914–943), he seems to have followed the Ismaiʿili Shiʿi faith of his Samanid patron. Rudaki was famed for his mastery of the *qasida* (an elegaic ode of between 60 and 100 lines) and the *ghazal* (a shorter lyrical love poem). He also composed *Kalilah wa Dimnah*, based on the well-known Indian Bidpai tales. Rudaki's writings marked the emerging genre of Persian poetry, which other figures such as Anvari, Firdawsi, Attar, Saʿdi, Rumi, Nizami, and Jami continued for centuries. While Persian poetry later became suffused with mystical themes, in Rudaki's time the dominant theme was the praising of rulers.

Omid Safi

Further Reading
Browne, E. G. ([1902] 1997) *A Literary History of Persia*. Vol. 1. Reprint ed. Oxford: Oxford University Press.

RUIZ, SAINT LORENZO (c. 1600–1637), Filipino martyr. Lorenzo Ruiz was born in the district of Binondo in Manila, Philippines, around 1600 to a Christian Chinese father and a Filipina native mother. He grew up around the church and served as an acolyte during mass. He was married, had three children, and was a member of the Confraternity of the Holy Rosary.

In 1636, authorities sought Ruiz for his alleged involvement in a murder. Fearing he would be given a death sentence and believing he did not commit the crime, Ruiz decided, with the help of his priest friends, to join a missionary group leaving for Japan. In 1636, he secretly left the Philippines with the missionaries, and he served as a lay worker, assisting the missionaries as they spread the word of God covertly because Christianity was banned in Japan at the time. Ruiz and his companions were eventually arrested in Okinawa and imprisoned in Kyushu. In prison they endured torture intended to force them to renounce their faith. In 1637, Ruiz was put before a tribunal and given one last chance to renounce his faith under penalty of death. He sealed his fate by saying, "I'll never recant because I am a Christian and I shall die for God. If I were to live a thousand lives, I would give them all up" (Villaroel 1987: 108). On 27 September 1637, Ruiz and his companions were taken to a hill near Nagasaki and were hung upside down in a pit for three days. He died of suffocation and was burned along with the others; their ashes were scattered at sea. In 1981 Pope John Paul II beatified Ruiz and fifteen of his companion martyrs in a ceremony in Manila, and in 1989 Ruiz was canonized along with his companion martyrs at St. Peter's Basilica in Rome, making him the first Filipino saint.

Aaron Ronquillo

Further Reading

Valiente, Ethel. (1989) *Lorenzo Ruiz: Ang Unang Martir ng Pilipinas* (Lorenzo Ruiz: The First Filipino Martyr). Manila, Philippines: San Lorenzo Ruiz Society, Inc.

Villaroel, Fidel. (1987) *Lorenzo de Manila: The Protomartyr of the Philippines and His Companions*. Manila, Philippines: USP Press.

RUKUNEGARA The Rukunegara (Nationhood) is the national pledge of Malaysia. Introduced in 1971 as a result of the riots of 13 May 1969 caused by ethnic tensions, the Rukunegara consists of five principles, which act as the pillars of the national philosophy. The Rukunegara was formulated in an attempt to base national unity on certain concepts that are acceptable to all citizens, regardless of ethnic or religious differences. The Rukunegara is usually pledged in school assemblies, at formal gatherings, and on nationally celebrated occasions.

The Rukunegara is formulated as follows:

Our Nation, Malaysia, is dedicated to achieving a greater unity for all her peoples; to maintaining a democratic way of life; to creating a just society in which the wealth of the nation shall be equitably distributed; to ensuring a liberal approach to her rich and diverse cultural traditions; and to building a progressive society which shall be oriented to modern science and technology.

We, her peoples, pledge our united efforts to attain these ends guided by these principles: belief in God, loyalty to king and country, upholding the constitution, rule of law; good behavior and morality.

In the first principle the word "God" is used instead of "Allah"; since the majority of Malaysians are Muslim, this implies a respect for other religious beliefs. The second principle expresses the respect due the king as the country's ruler. The third principle expresses the respect due the constitution as Malaysia's highest law. The fourth principle emphasizes the supremacy of the rule of law. The fifth principle recognizes Malaysia's multiethnic society and expresses the idea that mutual respect between ethnic groups is necessary in order to achieve national unity.

The Rukunegara was also formulated to unite the citizens of Malaysia, who had previously been divided under the British "divide and rule" policy. Under colonial administration, the three main races (Malays, Chinese, and Indians) had been segregated and oppressed, a strategy the British hoped would avoid any interaction that might undermine their rule. The Rukunegara is also intended to accelerate the national development into a more progressive society.

Mala Selvaraju

RURAL WORKERS, SURPLUS—CHINA

Surplus labor refers to the existence of human resources that are potentially capable of productive effort but are unused or underused. This condition often results in underemployment or disguised unemployment. A large supply of labor in rural areas, in excess of the quantity demanded, is a problem shared by many developing countries. Estimates of surplus rural workers in China were in the range of 100 to 200 million, or up to one-sixth of the nation's population, in the mid-1990s.

The sheer size of surplus rural workers in China is rooted in age-old traditions of family-centered agriculture and high fertility. Traditional agriculture in China is intensive and relies heavily on family labor, motivating for thousands of years rural households to desire many children. This pronatalist philosophy was sustained during the Communist collective period (1953–1978), when the burden of provision in the countryside was shifted from the family to the commune. High population growth further worsened the already low ratio of cultivable land to person, which decreased from about one-half an acre in the late 1940s to one-fourth of an acre in the late 1970s. Prohibited from leaving the countryside, the rural surplus labor was hidden as redundant and underemployed workers in communes.

Meanwhile, agricultural productivity increased steadily and especially since the economic reforms that began in 1978. More extensive use of mechanization and inputs that improve yield, such as chemical fertilizers and pesticides, as well as the implementation of the "household responsibility system" that induces rural households to maximize output, further aggravated the surplus in rural labor. The government was compelled to invent ways to absorb the surplus, which became a major force of social and economic change in China during the past two decades and more.

Absorption of surplus rural workers has been experienced both in situ and via migration. The *litu bu lixiang* (leaving the land but not the village) strategy involves shifting surplus labor from agriculture to rural industrial enterprises, commonly known as township-village enterprises (TVEs), near the home village. At the same time, relaxation of migration control by the government unleashed millions of rural workers to migrate to work in towns and cities, a strategy known as *litu you lixiang* (leaving the land and the village). These migrants constitute the "floating population" that flood cities and towns and have become a timely supply of labor for China's industrial and services development. But their large numbers and willingness to work for low wages and in poor conditions have subjected them to exploitation that is especially rampant in foreign-invested enterprises.

C. Cindy Fan

Further Reading

Lee, Ching Kwan. (1998) *Gender and the South China Miracle: Two Worlds of Factory Women.* Berkeley and Los Angeles: University of California Press.

Solinger, Dorothy J. (1999) *Contesting Citizenship in Urban China: Peasant Migrants, the State, and the Logic of the Market.* Berkeley and Los Angeles: University of California Press.

RUSSIANS IN CENTRAL ASIA The Russian empire conquered Central Asia between 1865 and 1876. For the next forty years most Russians who lived in Turkestan (as it was called until 1924) were soldiers, merchants, or government officials and their families. The first large wave of Russian settlers came only after the Trans-Siberian and related railways were built in the 1890s; by 1916 over one million Russian and Ukrainian farmers had arrived, concentrated in the northeastern steppe lands.

The Soviet Period

After the Bolshevik Revolution of October 1917 Turkestan experienced several years of war and famine, but Russian rule continued. The new Communist government sent hundreds of Russian workers to Central Asia to construct a revolutionary Soviet society. In principle these Russian Communists were supposed to learn Central Asian languages; in reality most refused and lived separately from Central Asians. Russians dominated the most technically skilled jobs, running factories and collective farms, and held final political authority.

By the 1930s the Russian language had become the language of government and higher education throughout the U.S.S.R., and Russians felt no need to learn native languages. Russians were concentrated in the capital cities of the five republics (Uzbekistan, Turkmenistan, Tajikistan, Kyrgyzstan, and Kazakhstan), with access to Russian newspapers and television, while the majority of the native population lived in rural areas. In 1959 Russians made up an average of 18.5 percent of the population in the southern republics and 43 percent of the population in Kazakhstan, living much the same way as did Russians in Moscow.

The Russians' position in Central Asia began to crumble in the late 1980s, under Mikhail Gorbachev's policy of glasnost (openness). Central Asian writers and political dissidents felt free to express their discontent with Russian cultural and political dominance, to the dismay of the Russian population. Ordinary Central Asians became increasingly rude or occasionally violent in daily dealings with Russians. Russians had begun migrating from Central Asia in the 1970s; the trend accelerated in the 1980s. (See Table 1.)

After the Soviet Collapse

When the Soviet Union dissolved in December 1991, leaders of the newly independent republics made it clear to Russians that they and their skills were welcome to

TABLE 1

Russians as a Percentage of the Central Asian Population			
Republic	1959 %	1992 %	2000 %
Kazakhstan	43	36	34.7
Uzbekistan	14	8	5.5
Turkmenistan	17	10	6.7
Kyrgyzstan	30	21	18
Tajikistan	13	8	3.5

SOURCE: Derived from Haghayeghi (1995: 202–206) and CIA *World Factbook 2000.*

stay. However, civil war in Tajikistan drove most Russians to emigrate. In Uzbekistan and Turkmenistan the restoration of native languages and increasing national chauvinism made life uncomfortable for Russians. These two regimes also banned Russian-language television and most Russian newspapers in the mid-1990s, on the grounds that these media were too politically liberal. Kyrgyzstan and Kazakhstan had more open and democratic governments until the late 1990s; Kazakhstan also retained Russian as an official language. For these reasons the latter republics have seen the least outmigration. However, it appears likely that the Russian population in Central Asia will continue to dwindle.

Shoshana Keller

Further Reading
Allworth, Edward, ed. (1994) *Central Asia: 130 Years of Russian Rule.* Durham, NC: Duke University Press.

CIA *World Factbook 2000.* Retrieved 1 June 2001, from: http://www.cia.gov/cia/publications/factbook/docs/concopy.html.

Haghayeghi, Mehrdad. (1995) *Islam and Politics in Central Asia.* New York: St. Martin's Press.

Keller, Shoshana. (2001) *To Moscow, Not Mecca: The Soviet Campaign against Islam in Central Asia, 1917–1941.* Westport, CT: Praeger Publishers.

Kolstoe, Paul. (1995) *Russians in the Former Soviet Republics.* Bloomington, IN: Indiana University Press.

Soucek, Svat. (2000) *A History of Inner Asia.* Cambridge, U.K.: Cambridge University Press.

RUSSIANS IN MONGOLIA

A Russian presence in Mongolia dates to the appearance of Russians in those portions of Siberia adjacent to territories occupied by Mongols in the seventeenth and eighteenth centuries. At that time Mongolia was coming under the control of the Manchu Qing dynasty (1644–1911), and Russia was attempting to forestall a Manchu presence anywhere near its frontiers and protect its long-range economic interests in an area increasingly penetrated by Russian trappers and traders. Ultimately a series of treaties was signed, the first treaties ever drawn up between China and a foreign power with both parties on an equal footing. The treaties set more or less the present frontiers between China and Russia except for what was formerly Tannu-Tuva (now Tuva), which remained part of Mongolia for the time being.

Despite these treaties, Russian penetration of Mongolia continued, and the Mongolian peoples themselves became bones of contention between the two Asian powers. For example, western Mongolian Junggars, then the dominant steppe group, moved back and forth across the loosely guarded frontier to resist military pressure from one side or the other. Later, Russian Old Believers settled in Mongolia to escape religious persecution by Czar Peter and his successors who sought to modernize Russian Orthodoxy at the expense of this primitivist religious minority. The descendents of these refugees have remained in Mongolia down to the present day.

With the weakening of Qing power in the nineteenth century, Russian pressures on Mongolia increased. These pressures came from the Russians themselves, primarily traders and also explorers, and from Russian surrogates including the Siberian Buryats, a Mongolian people living on both sides of Lake Baikal who were highly Russified. By this time, Russia had become the first country in Europe to develop a large-scale Mongolian studies program and in the 1840s had produced the first multilingual Mongolian dictionary. This program gave Russia an enormous advantage in dealing with Mongolia and the Mongols.

During the Mongol autonomous period (1911–1921), Russia was not only well represented in Mongolia through its merchants, diplomats, explorers, and agitators but also increasingly in a position to serve as an alternative to Chinese influence. Mongolia proved unable to resist direct foreign intervention, at first by Chinese, then by White Russians, and the new Soviet regime was quick to offer its services.

Between 1920 and 1921, Mongolian forces organized by the Soviets were finally able to defeat the White Russian general Ungern-Sternberg (shot 1921) and drove out the occupying Chinese as well. A People's Republic was established in 1924.

The period of paramount Russian influence in Mongolia, not only in politics, but also in language and manners, sometimes enforced by Red Army bayonets, lasted until 1991 and the Soviet collapse. Since then, Russian influence has fast receded, and American (and other) influence has taken its place. Mongolia's native Russians, of course, still remain, and relations with the Buryats in the Russian Republic continue to be strong. Nowadays the Buryats are also rediscovering their Mongolness.

Paul Buell

Further Reading
Bawden, C. R. (1989) *The Modern History of Mongolia.* London: Kegan Paul International.

Shirendev, Bazaryn. (1997) *Through the Ocean Waves: The Autobiography of Bazaryn Shirendev.* Trans. by Temujin Onon. Bellingham, WA: Western Washington University Center for East Asian Studies.

RUSSIFICATION AND SOVIETIZA-TION—CENTRAL ASIA

After capturing Kazan in 1552, the Russians, under Czar Ivan IV (1530–1584), took several hundred years to assimilate the Muslim lands of Central Asia. Before the nineteenth century, Central Asia was partly ruled by the Muslim khanates of Bukhara, Khiva, and Quqon (Kokand) and partly by uncontrolled and warring nomad tribes: Turkic- and Persian-speaking ethnic groups such as the Uzbeks, Kazakhs, Kyrgyz, Turkmen, and Tajiks. Between 1730 and 1855, Russian troops had gradually moved south, conquering northern Central Asia and part of the Kazakh-occupied steppe. This conquest was consolidated with the surrender of Shymkent in present-day Kazakhstan to the east of the Syr Dar'ya River in 1855 under Czar Alexander II (1818–1881) and his son Czar Alexander III (1845–1894) and came to an end with the subjugation of the Pamir Mountains region north of present-day Afghanistan in 1896 as the result of a Russo-British agreement. In 1865, under Alexander II, the Russian province of Turkistan was established, and the earlier system of independent khanates was gradually demolished: Bukhara in 1868, Khiva in 1873, and Quqon in 1875–1876. Following the battle of Geok-Tepe in present-day Turkmenistan in 1881, the Russians, under Alexander III, also annexed the lands of the Turkmen tribes to the czarist empire.

During the final stages of Russian expansion into Central Asia, diplomatic and economic domination dramatically increased, but interethnic conflicts and political rivalries in the region were so deeply rooted that the full implications of the Russian incursion were overlooked by those involved in local power struggles. To consolidate their military domination, the Russians employed various means, ranging from genocide, colonial protection, linguistic assimilation, and territorial incorporation.

Genocide was committed against the Turkmen in 1881 in the course of Russian efforts to annex the Transcaspian region. Colonial protection was imposed on the khanate of Bukhara in 1868 according to the terms of a peace treaty resulting from the khanate's defeat by the Russian commander General Kaufman. Linguistic assimilation was initiated in Tashkent in the last decades of the nineteenth century through mass Russian immigration to the region. The Pamirs were enclosed in 1896.

The Expansion of the Russian Empire

Following the czarist annexation of Central Asia, the area east of the Caspian Sea was divided into the Ural, Turgai, and Transcaspian governments-general of the steppe provinces, the government-general of Turkistan, the emirate of Bukhara, and the khanate of Khiva. To avoid a possible military confrontation with the British, the Russians decided to leave Bukhara as a protectorate enjoying autonomy in its internal affairs.

The Russians' economic penetration in the region, which eventually fashioned Central Asia into a monocultural economy producing solely cotton, had far-reaching social implications. A new propertied middle class of local people benefited directly from the economic transformations, and a new salaried middle class came into existence to function as the local office-holders of non-key positions in the local administration. The new colonial administration weakened local ethnic groups by encouraging ethnic animosity among them. Russian was introduced as the official language, and educational institutions were founded to educate the local elites, whose aspirations and values were directly influenced by the Russian style of life.

The Aftermath of the Russian Revolution

When the turmoil of the Russian Revolution of 1917 reached Central Asia, most Muslims were separated not only from the recently arrived Russians but also from their own fellow coreligionists in Central Asia. Only a few circles of intellectuals in big cities, which transcended ancestral tribal loyalties and linguistic divergences, were interested in a greater Muslim community.

The Bolsheviks' first task in Central Asia in October 1917 was to secure the territories inherited from the czarist empire. While calling for national self-determination, the Bolsheviks embarked on a military campaign to crush any resistance to the Sovietization of the region. Launching an air raid on Bukhara in 1920, the Bolsheviks inaugurated a decade-long war against the local resistance, mainly the Basmachis, a movement of Central Asians opposed to the Bolsheviks. Meanwhile to enforce total authority on the southern frontiers, the new regime annulled all earlier territorial entities and redrew the map of Central Asia according to its long-term strategic needs.

In April 1924, the Central Asian Bureau (Sredazburo) of the Central Committee of the Russian Communist Party voted to partition the czarist administrative province of Turkistan. Subsequently, a process of administrative realignment of Central Asia began, which was finally completed in 1936. According to the new legislation, all of Central Asia was administratively divided into three organizational categories: autonomous republics (separate national states within Soviet socialist republics), autonomous regions (autonomous regional administrations formed in a national territory or autonomous republic because of its national composition or ethnic way of life), and national territories (the fifteen constituent Soviet socialist republics). By adopting a policy of governmental administration based on ethnicity, the Bolsheviks initially divided Central Asia into three national-territorial entities for Uzbeks, Kazakhs, and Turkmen.

However, to avoid any revival of the former territorial solidarity, the Soviets offered the heartland of former Turkistan to the Uzbeks, extending from Osh at the eastern edge of the Fergana Valley to Khiva and Khwarizm in the west, and from Tashkent in the north to Zarafshan and Termiz near the northern border of Afghanistan, including the three former khanates of Bukhara, Ququn, and Khiva. The new demarcation, however, left the other major ethnic groups like the Tajiks and the Kyrgyz with a strong sense of betrayal. Fearful of the escalation of national sentiment among the Tajiks, who spoke Persian, the language of neighboring Iran and Afghanistan, the Soviets recognized the Tajiks and the Kyrgyz as the other two major ethnic groups in the region. They thus concluded their territorial realignment by allocating administrative territory to these ethnic groups.

The Creation of the Central Asian Republics

Subsequently, five republics were formed in the Central Asian region; each supposedly accommodated a titular (dominant) ethnic group after whom the republic was named. These groups were the Kazakhs, the Kyrgyz, the Tajiks, the Uzbeks, and the Turkmen. However, in the new partition, efforts were made to ensure that none of the new republics was politically or economically capable of seceding from the rest of the union. For example, in Uzbekistan and Tajikistan, the road linking the capital cities and some provinces passed through the neighboring republics.

Following this engineered partition, a new project for the homogenization of each Central Asian republic was initiated. To enhance this project, a process of nativization began, whereby the dominant ethnic group gained access to high positions in the local administration. Although it was possible for the so-called recognized ethnic minorities to enjoy cultural freedom, it soon became clear that if one wished to advance one's career it was necessary to adopt the ways of the dominant ethnic group. Ethnic cultural distinctiveness was gradually constructed and Sovietized, and members of the titular *nomenklatura* (elite) were encouraged to advance the particular interests of their republic. Likewise, the Soviet policy of registering nationality at the republic level, in people's internal passports, tended to encourage members of nontitular ethnic groups to declare themselves as members of the titular group in official documents, for the sake of advancement in the government apparatus.

In the centralized government of the U.S.S.R., the party-state system monopolized the key command positions throughout the Soviet Union and denied access to these positions to almost all non-Russians. High-ranking administrators formed the privileged core of a transethnic population not belonging to any particular local ethnic group. Even at the republic level, native Russians without exception filled the positions of deputy or first secretary of the Communist Party.

The Soviet Person (*Sovetskii Chelovek* in Russian) was the ideological embodiment of this transethnic party system. The Soviet Person's identity was grounded in a sense of loyalty to the Soviet Union; absolute loyalty to Moscow predominated over loyalty to any constituent republic.

However, in the republics, a concealed ethnic nationalism gradually developed, not only among each dominant group, but also among ethnic minorities. Ethnic nationalism among minority ethnic groups fostered interests different from those of the dominant ethnic group. This ethnic nationalism in the Central Asian republics was the direct outcome of the Soviet Union having created the republics along ethnic lines. When the Soviets attempted to link each ethnic group to its own state, in the drive to achieve social homogeneity and political cohesion, they denied the smaller ethnic groups in each republic equal rights. By constructing constituent republics along ethnic lines but then applying elitist and centralizing policies and ideals (such as the ideal of the Soviet Person and Soviet state patriotism), in the end the government unwittingly stimulated ethnic nationalism as a form of resistance.

Complicating the matter was the fact that the imposed territorial borders never adequately corresponded to the cultural groupings. While the titular nationalities in each republic enjoyed preferential treatment and tended to make up the local administrative hierarchy, the ethnic minorities strove to consolidate their presence in particular sectors of the administration, especially those more strictly controlled by the Russians, by practicing nepotism.

Linguistic Sovietization

In an additional attempt to make a clear break with the past and to stifle any call for unity among people who shared a common language and culture and yet lived under different national flags, the Soviet authorities in the early days of their rule launched a widespread linguistic refashioning project in Central Asia. The Sovietization of the languages in Central Asia was initiated under the authority of Russian Orientalists working at institutions inherited from the Russian empire, such as the Academy of Sciences in Leningrad (St. Petersburg) and Moscow. The chief aim of this project was to form national languages based on spoken dialects and to introduce these languages as the written as well as literary languages. Accordingly, each republic would have a national language different from the languages spoken or written by members of the same ethnic or linguistic group who lived outside the Soviet Union. Moreover, the Russian language was disseminated as the only lingua franca welding the entire Soviet Union together.

The first attempt to create a national language occurred in 1923, when a new language called the Uzbek language was developed; this was close to Kipchak, a Turkic tongue. However, the Soviet social linguists soon became alarmed that the new language might bring Turkic people together, and thus another version of the Uzbek language was introduced in 1929. This version was based on the Tashkent dialect. In October 1924, the Uzbekistan Soviet Socialist Republic was formally established, with Uzbek as its national language. Consequently, Uzbek cultural institutions launched a new campaign to foster national homogeneity based on the introduction of the new language throughout Uzbekistan. In bilingual or multilingual regions of Uzbekistan, although the inhabitants had the right to use their own languages for teaching in elementary schools, ethnic minorities were denied a fair share of the republic's financial revenues.

At the same time, the eastern provinces of the old khanate of Bukhara were renamed the Autonomous Region of Tajikistan, with Tajik as the national language, a new name for the Persian language spoken in present-day Iran and Afghanistan. Based on different local dialects and some grammatical modifications, the Tajik language was invented by Soviet social linguists as a written literary language for Tajikistan. In 1929, Tajikistan's status was elevated from an autonomous region attached to Uzbekistan to a Soviet Socialist Republic. The village of Dushanbe, with a population of forty-seven families, was honored as the capital of the new republic, while Samarqand and Bukhara, with their significant Persian-speaking populations, were left in the Soviet Socialist Republic of Uzbekistan.

The invention of national languages led to the creation of modern Kyrgyz and Turkmen in 1924 and Karakalpak in 1925. To break all links with the past, the Arabic alphabet used for all national languages was changed in 1929 to Latin and in 1940 to Cyrillic. By then, the Soviet territorial state building in Central Asia was finally concluded, with the five Soviet Socialist Republics of Kazakhstan, Kyrgyzstan, Uzbekistan, Tajikistan, and Turkmenistan being established, along with the Autonomous Republic of Karakalpakstan in Uzbekistan and the Autonomous Province of Gorno-Badakhshan in Tajikistan.

Other Sovietization Projects in Central Asia

Along with territorial state building and language policies, the Soviet regime implemented a wide range of projects for social engineering in Central Asia. In the 1930s, the Bolsheviks instigated a policy of forced sedentarization of nomadic people and mass collectivization of agricultural lands into the collective farming units known in Russian as *kolkhoz* (collective farm) and *sovkhoz* (soviet farm). Forced migration and population dislocation were the result of this project, which was nevertheless expected to build a more homogeneous Soviet society.

Because the Bolsheviks' ultimate aspiration was to create a universal, common working-class culture, they considered the promotion of national cultures as a transitional trend, guiding the Soviet society toward the final phase of communism. To observe this transformation, egalitarian ideology was conceived as an indisputable part of all national cultures. Folk music and literature were revised, and national histories were rewritten accordingly. Moreover, to propagate the new (Soviet) culture throughout the society—especially in rural areas—along with local Communist Party groups, various mass-pressure groups, such as the Communist Youth, or Komsomol, were founded. These organizations were charged to eliminate all the old institutions and beliefs that obstructed the new revolutionary tasks. Nonetheless, religious faith soon became an obstacle to Sovietization.

Soviet Attitudes to Islam in Central Asia

Following the fall of Bukhara in 1920, the Bolsheviks accelerated their anti-Islamic campaign in Central Asia. In its earliest stage, this campaign was coupled with the crusade against the Basmachis. Later, in harmony with the anti-Christian indoctrination occurring throughout the rest of the Soviet Union, the Bolsheviks launched a massive assault against Islam. Besides prohibiting Islamic institutions' interference in the country's education and judicial life, a widespread cultural offensive against the practice of Islam was initiated by the government. In this new campaign, traditional Islamic customs, such as pilgrimages to shrines, praying at mosques, polygamy, and veiling, were the first targets. Within a few years, almost all holy shrines in Central Asia were closed down, and the number of mosques dropped dramatically. For instance, in the city of Khudzhand (former Khojend) in northern Tajikistan, the total number of mosques was drastically reduced from 451 to 1.

The campaign for abandoning the veil in Muslim areas of the Soviet Union, which began in 1927, had a twofold purpose. It was designed not only to jeopardize an old Islamic custom but also to destroy the traditional Islamic family by dragging women into the labor market. Judicial changes in 1927 facilitated this process. First the system of law courts was changed, and a year later the penal code was modified. Meanwhile, all remaining religious courts were abolished, and the old, official Islam was gradually manipulated and transformed into a new, legal, Soviet Islam. This was a private form of Islam, devoid of social aspects. Finally, the only remnants of traditional Islam for the newborn Soviet Person to identify himself or herself with were circumcision, not eating pork, religious marriage, and religious burial. Therefore, for the majority of Soviet Central Asians, the conventional boundary between private and public spaces was refigured. Marxist mentality prevailed over every aspect of public life in the Soviet Union; however, it failed to penetrate into the realm of a contemporary Muslim's private life.

Touraj Atabaki

Further Reading

Allworth, Edward. (1967) *Central Asia: A Century of Russian Rule*. New York: Columbia University Press.

Bennigsen, Alexander. (1983) *The Islamic Threat to the Soviet State*. New York: St. Martin's Press.

Brower, Daniel R., and Edward J. Lazzerini, eds. (1997) *Russia's Orient: Imperial Borderlands and Peoples, 1700–1917*. Bloomington, IN: Indiana University Press.

Caroe, Olaf. (1953) *Soviet Empire: The Turks of Central Asia and Stalinism*. London: Macmillan.

Carrere d'Encausse, Hélène. (1992) *The Great Challenge: Nationalities and the Bolshvik State, 1917–1930*. New York: Holmes & Meier.

———. (1988) *Islam and the Russian Empire: Reform and Revolution in Central Asia*. London: Tauris.

Khanikov, A. (1845) *Bokhara: Its Amir and Its People*. London: Madden.

Rohrlich, A. A. (1995) *The Volga Tatars*. Stanford, CA: Hoover Institution Press.

Roy, Olivier. (2000) *The New Central Asia: The Creation of Nations*. London: Tauris.

Smith, Jeremy. (1999) *The Bolsheviks and the National Question, 1917–1923*. London: Macmillan.

Vambéry, Arminius. (1873) *Voyages d'un Faux Derviche dans l'Asie Centrale*. Paris: Hachette.

RUSSO-JAPANESE WAR (1904–1905).

Japan's use of Western-style military organization and armaments to triumph over Russia in 1905 was a turning point in relations between Asia and the West, in part because it was seen by many as a race war or a clash of civilizations. This allegation was denied by Japanese leaders, including Prime Minister General Katsura Taro, who admitted at the war's outset that Japan could never conquer Russia or force it to pay an indemnity for Japan's war expenses. They also knew that Japan's economic future was dependent on Western markets and the vast loans needed to fight the war could be obtained only in London and New York. Japan's military successes, however, were celebrated by anticolonial leaders from Asia to Africa; even Christian nationalist statesman Yun Chiho in Korea, who knew that a Japanese victory would endanger his country, still welcomed the humbling of Western arrogance. This revolution in Asian confidence made Japan feared in North America and Australasia; new defense policies were created in both these regioins against the perceived threat of Japanese invasion. By 1907, there was already talk of a coming war between Japan and the United States. As Japan became the target of Western suspicion, its own nationalist ideology increasingly stressed the Russo-Japanese war as a triumph of a uniquely Japanese spirit. In this way, Japan also ended up viewing the war in racial terms.

The direct regional significance of the war was that Japan became a continental power in Asia, at the expense of China and Korea. In the peace treaty of September 1905, negotiated at Portsmouth, New Hampshire, Russia conceded Japan's special interest in Korea and also transferred to Japan its territorial concessions, which included rail and mines in southern Manchuria (northeast China). To protect these rights, Japan stationed troops in Manchuria that were to be the vanguard of further military expansion in the 1930s. In November 1905, Japan also intimidated the Korean government into signing a protectorate treaty whereby a Japanese resident-general in Seoul took charge of Korea's foreign relations and increasingly of its domestic politics. In 1910 Japan annexed Korea outright; it remained part of Japan's empire until the end of World War II.

Hostilities

The cause of the Russo-Japanese War was Japan's sense of insecurity. Japanese leaders feared that Korea could be used as a platform from which to attack Japan, as in the thirteenth-century Mongol invasion. Russian expansion in Manchuria in the 1890s, and its ongoing construction of the Trans-Siberian Railway, were viewed in Tokyo as a threat to Korea. Japan attempted negotiations through 1903, with a view to trading spheres of influence (Russia to dominate Manchuria, Japan to dominate Korea). When negotiations failed, Japan attacked Russian vessels in the region in February 1904 without first declaring war. Japan was to do the same thing at Pearl Harbor in 1941, but in 1904, this covert action was applauded by its British ally. Initial land battles in Korea were easily won by the Japanese as Russian forces retreated to consolidate. The major conflicts were at Port Arthur (Lushun), where the Japanese forces under General Nogi Maresuke were held for five months and suffered enormous casualties. At the battle of Mukden in March 1905, approximately half a million Russian and Japanese troops fought in the biggest land battle before 1914. Shortly thereafter, the Japanese navy under Admiral Togo Heihachiro destroyed the exhausted Russian Baltic fleet at the battle of Tsushima. Although Japan appeared to have won every engagement, it had been forced to mobilize over one million men and had lost 81,000 (over six times the total figure for its 1894–1895 war with China), along with 381,000 sick and wounded. The losses in men and money actually crippled Japan and the government hurriedly accepted the peace treaty of September 1905, despite anger among the Japanese public at its terms.

Wartime Japan

The common wisdom has long been that the Japanese public demanded war with Russia (in revenge for Russia's diplomatic obstruction of Japan in its earlier war with China) and unhesitatingly supported the war effort. More recent scholarship, however, has revised this impression. There was broad wartime resentment in Japan at the rising number of mass funerals, the higher wartime taxes, and the length of the war. This was Japan's first war to be seen in moving pictures, yet audiences varied in their responses: some war movies and newsreels were very popular; others, especially those with fraudulent advertising, were scorned. Many people did respond to the recurring campaigns for war donations, often conducted by patriotic women's groups, but there was also a backlash as the demands continued. In this sense, there was a divergence between the public (propaganda) face of Japan accepted by the West, and the actuality of a Japanese public in-

creasingly tired of the war. Public support of the military in Japan was always conditional, based on a balance between costs and rewards. One result of this was a growing fear among army commanders after 1905 of socialism among new conscripts. At the time, however, the socialist movement in Japan remained largely intellectual and peripheral. The major public protest at the war's end, the Hibiya riots in central Tokyo, are usually regarded as an ultranationalist demonstration insisting the war be reopened so that Japan might improve its meager rewards. These riots had no lasting impact on Japanese military or diplomatic policies or on the domestic polity; the changeover of cabinets from General Katsura to the head of the largest political party, the Seiyukai, had been agreed long before the war's end. Where the war did influence post-1905 politics was in civil-military relations. The huge debt burden of the war prevented the army from obtaining the extra forces some of its leaders felt essential to defend Japan's new position in Asia, and it was to clash with an alliance of the navy and the Seiyukai in the constitutional crisis of 1912–1913. This clash was to influence attitudes between politicians and the army until 1945.

Stewart Lone

See also: **Sino-Japanese War**

Further Reading

Connaughton, R. M. (1988) *The War of the Rising Sun and the Tumbling Bear: A Military History of the Russo-Japanese War 1904–1905.* New York: Routledge.

Iguchi Kazuki, ed. (1994) *Nis-Shin Nichi-Ro Senso* (The Sino-Japanese and Russo-Japanese Wars). Tokyo: Yoshikawa Kobunkan.

Lone, Stewart. (2000) *Army, Empire, and Politics in Meiji Japan.* New York: St. Martin's Press.

Sakurai Tadayoshi. (1908) *Human Bullets: a Soldier's Story of Port Arthur.* London: Constable.

Warner, Denis, and Peggy Warner. (1975) *The Tide at Sunrise: a History of the Russo-Japanese War 1904–1905.* London: Angus and Robertson.

Wells, David, and Sandra Wilson, eds. (1999) *The Russo-Japanese War in Cultural Perspective, 1904–1905.* New York: St. Martin's Press.

RYUKYU ISLANDS.   See **Okinawa.**

SABAH (2000 est. pop. 2.4 million). Sabah is a Malaysian state on the northern part of the island of Borneo, bordered by Indonesia in the south, Sarawak in the west, and the Philippines in the east. Its coastline includes the South China Sea, the Sulu Sea, and the Celebes (Sulawesi) Sea. Once known as British North Borneo, Sabah has a land area of 73,619 square kilometers (28,400 square miles) and is the second-largest state of the Federation of Malaysia, with almost 22 percent of its territory and 12 percent of its population. Sabah's capital city, Kota Kinabalu (formerly Jesselton), is located in the northwest of the state. The capital's population was 354,100 in 2000, up from 209,200 in 1991.

According to historical records, the area of what is now Sabah was under control of the sultans of Brunei before the fifteenth and sixteenth centuries. In the early eighteenth century some of its coastal areas were ruled by the sultans of Sulu. In the seventeenth and eighteenth centuries the power of the Brunei sultanate was weakened by internal political instability and rivalry between traditional rulers. In 1877 Baron Von Overbeck and Alfred Dent leased 28,000 square miles of territory from the sultans of Brunei and Sulu. In 1882 the British North Borneo Chartered Company was established, and in 1884 it named Sandakan city the capital of British North Borneo, which became a British protectorate in 1888. However, from 1942 to 1945 most of Sabah was occupied by the Japanese Imperial Army. In 1946 Sabah became a British crown colony. In 1963 it gained independence from Britain and joined Malaysia.

Agriculture, forestry, tourism, and mining are the main sectors of the Sabah economy. Traditionally, Sabah exported rubber, copra, and timber, but since the 1980s crude oil has become one of the most important export items. In the 1990s the state attempted to diversify its economy, attracting manufacturing and services, especially tourism. Due to ecological concerns, the export of timber was banned by the state government in 1994, but the tropical rain forest is still under heavy exploitation for domestic needs. Oil palm was introduced in the 1960s and has become an important crop.

Rafis Abazov

Further Reading

Kaur, Amarjit. (1998) *Economic Change in East Malaysia: Sabah and Sarawak since 1850.* New York: St. Martin's Press.

Leong, Cecilia. (1982) *Sabah, The First 100 Years.* Kuala Lumpur, Malaysia: Pecetakan Nan Yang Muda.

Roff, Margaret Clark. (1974) *The Politics of Belonging: Political Change in Sabah and Sarawak.* New York: Oxford University Press.

SABAH DISPUTE The Sabah Dispute was a twenty-five-year territorial wrangle between the Republic of the Philippines and the Federation of Malaysia over territory in the northern part of the island of Borneo. The Philippines' claim was based on a historical family linkage between the sultan of Brunei, who in the seventeenth century ceded Sabah to his relative the sultan of Sulu, which is now part of the Philippines. In 1798 the territory was leased to the British North Borneo Company and brought under direct British control in 1946. Malaysia contends that the territory was purchased by the British North Borneo Company.

The dispute over Sabah was directly linked to the formation of the Malaysian state. On 31 August 1957 the Federation of Malaya was established on the Malay Peninsula, while Britain kept Singapore, Sarawak, Brunei, and British North Borneo (Sabah) outside the federation. On 12 May 1961 the Malay prime minister Tunku Abdul Rahman proposed the founding of the Federation of Malaysia—the political union of Malaya, Singapore, Sarawak, and Sabah. The proposal was well received in peninsular Malaya and Singapore but was less popular in the three Borneo territories. For Malaya, union with Singapore alone was unacceptable because it would make the Chinese the majority ethnic group; including the Borneo territories would keep ethnic Chinese in the minority. Following a September 1962 referendum, an Anglo-Malay commission reported that a majority of the population was in favor of integration.

The proposal infuriated the Philippines, which formally laid claim to Sabah in June 1962 and tacitly allied itself with Indonesia, whose president Sukarno began a low-intensity conflict with Malaya known as Konfrontasi in January 1963. Philippine president Diosdado Macapagal proposed the establishment of a Greater Malay Confederation that would include Indonesia, Malaysia, and the Philippines in the place of the Federation of Malaysia, but the proposal was quickly rejected.

Although Brunei opted to remain outside the Union, on 16 September 1963 Sabah, Sarawak, and Singapore were constitutionally added to peninsular Malaya to create the Federation of Malaysia. As a result, the Philippines severed diplomatic relations with Malaysia in 1963. They were not reestablished until June 1966, after Ferdinand Marcos was elected president. Ties with Indonesia were also restored after Sukarno was ousted in a military coup led by General Suharto, who wanted to mend relations with his neighbors. In August 1967 the Association of Southeast Asian Nations (ASEAN) was established. Yet in September 1968, the Philippine Congress published maps showing Sabah as part of the Philippines, causing Malaysia to sever ties until December 1969.

Tensions flared again in the early 1970s when the largest Muslim separatist group in the Philippines, the Moro National Liberation Front, began to receive material support from the Sabah chief minister, Tun Mustapha. Only after his electoral defeat in 1976 did Malaysian aid to the Philippine rebels cease and bilateral relations begin to improve.

Philippine president Marcos indicated at the second ASEAN summit in Kuala Lumpur in August 1977 that the Philippines would take steps to waive the claim to Sabah, though no formal action was taken. His successor, President Corazon Aquino, submitted legislation to the Philippine congress in November 1987 to formally withdraw the territorial claim, though the congress did not act on the legislation. The 1987 constitution, however, does not include Sabah in its definition of Philippine territory.

Zachary Abuza

See also: **Konfrontasi**

Further Reading
Steinberg, Joel, ed. (1987) *In Search of Southeast Asia*. Honolulu, HI: University of Hawaii Press.
Tarling, Nicholas, ed. (1999) *The Cambridge History of Southeast Asia*. New York: Cambridge University Press.

SABRI BROTHERS   The Sabri Brothers are a Pakistani *qawwali* (Sufi devotional music) group founded by brothers Haji Ghulam Farid Sabri (1930–1994) and Haji Maqbool Ahmed Sabri (b. 1945). Descended from a line of *qawwali* singers in northern India, the Sabri family moved to Karachi, Pakistan, at the time of partition in 1947. Ghulam Farid Sabri and Maqbool Sabri began recording together in the late 1950s. In the 1980s the ensemble gained international recognition as one of the greatest exponents of modern *qawwali* originality and innovation. Praised by *qawwali* practitioners throughout the subcontinent, their recordings have received wide recognition for their artful composition and arrangement, varied patterns of linguistic incorporation, and expansive modes of instrumentation. The song "Tajdar-e-Haram," for example, includes refrain phrases in Urdu and verses that incorporate Hindi and Farsi, while "O Mustafa" features Middle Eastern drumbeats that enhance its Arabian quality. The Sabri Brothers also offer a distinctive musical delivery: Ghulam Farid Sabri's deep and powerful voice complements the lighter, more melodious tones of Maqbool Sabri. Although the personnel has changed over the years, the Sabri Brothers have offered a consistently high standard of performance. Since the death of Ghulam Farid Sabri, Maqbool Sabri has continued to perform and record with other members of the Sabri family.

Haley Duschinski

Further Reading
Babb, Lawrence, and Susan Wadley, eds. (1995) *Media and the Transformation of Religion in South Asia*. Philadelphia: University of Pennsylvania Press.

Querishi, Regula. (1986) *Sufi Music of India and Pakistan: Sound, Context, and Meaning in Qawwali.* Cambridge, U.K.: Cambridge University Press.

SADAEJUUI Literally translatable as "serving the great-ism" (or in some sources, "toadyism"), the term *sadaejuui* has a decisively pejorative meaning to modern Koreans, north and south. It has served throughout the twentieth century as a wake-up call to national energies, and has figured as one of the central "terms of engagement" in the ideological and propaganda wars between North and South Korea, and within South Korea itself, since national division in 1948.

The term *sadaejuui* is one born of the twentieth century, but it has its roots in the much older concept of *sadae*, "to serve the great" (*juui* being a modern addition, translatable as "ism"). In the traditional moral and political worldview of East Asia the concept of *sadae* was in no way pejorative. It described the natural relationship between the lesser and the greater, based upon Confucian teachings, that kept the universe in moral and political working order. It was perhaps most clearly articulated by the fourth century BCE Confucian sage Mencius, who said that only by serving the greater state could the lesser both preserve itself and keep the way of heaven. In traditional times, this meant for Korea a symbolic deference to China as its moral superior, and its emperor as the bestower of the mandate to rule. This symbolic relationship of deference, best manifested in the biannual tribute missions Korea sent to China, was in many ways just that—symbolic. Korea continued to preserve its internal sovereignty. This deference to China, however, was also clearly seen in the cultural realm, with the Korean aristocracy emulating Chinese arts and literature as well as Neo-Confucian thought, particularly during the Choson period (1392–1910).

With the troubled path Korea has tread since opening to the outside world in 1876, and the concomitant rise of Korean nationalism, this tradition of *sadae* came to be seen as highly deleterious to the independent development of Korean institutions, culture, and character. This became a particular critique of such nationalist historians as Sin Ch'ae-ho (1880–1936) and Ch'oe Nam-son (1890–1957). It was viewed as a primary cause for what some saw as a Korean predilection for emulating and relying upon the powerful, and a corresponding lack of originality or independent spirit. This in turn was seen as a central contributor to Korea's eventual domination by foreign powers in the last quarter of the nineteenth century and its colonization by Japan from 1905 to 1945. North Korea continues to accuse South Korea of *sadaejuui* in what it sees as that state's overreliance upon the United States. The political reality of national division, coupled with a historical legacy of colonization, has assured a particular potency to the term *sadaejuui* in all aspects of Korean society.

Daniel C. Kane

Further Reading
Robinson, Michael. (1984) "National Identity and the Thought of Sin Ch'ae-ho: Sadaejuûi and Chuch'e in History and Politics." *Journal of Korean Studies* 5: 121–142.
———. (1988) *Cultural Nationalism in Colonial Korea, 1920–1925.* Seattle, WA: University of Washington Press.

SADEQUAIN (1930–1987), Pakistani artist. Sadequain's paintings, in media ranging from oils to felt markers, are evidence of his skillful draftsmanship and imaginative visual vocabulary. Sadequain was born in Amroha, India, to a family of Qu'ran scribes, and moved to Karachi, Pakistan, in the early 1950s.

The civic activism that was a hallmark of Sadequain's art arose during his early experience of painting nationalistic, anti-British slogans in Delhi on the eve of the Indian partition. His politically charged canvases found a responsive audience among 1960s intelligentsia, both in Pakistan and abroad.

Sadequain's personal iconography was a complex merging of Hindu and Muslim ideology, using Eastern and Western artistic traditions, such as figurative art and calligraphy. His human figures, often self-portraits, are rendered abstractly as thorny cacti. Sadequain also wrote poetry and illustrated poems of reformist Pakistani thinkers like Faiz Ahmad Faiz (1911–1984).

His large-scale murals are in a socialist vein, such as the *Saga of Labor* (1967), installed at the Mangla Dam power plant, which depicts human struggle. His last, incomplete project was a series of murals inside Frere Hall in Karachi, where he died.

Kishwar Rizvi

Further Reading
Sirhandi, Marcella Nesom. (1992) *Contemporary Painting in Pakistan.* Lahore, Pakistan: Ferozsons.

SADO ISLAND (2001 pop. 73,000). Japan's fifth-largest island, Sado (Sadogashima), is located in the Sea of Japan, 35 kilometers from the city of Niigata in Honshu. The island is 853 square kilometers. Beginning in the Nara period (710–794), Sado was an independent province. From the mid-twelfth to the sixteenth century, it was a site of exile for political prisoners. During the Edo period (1600/1603–1868), Sado became a prison colony and came under direct control of the shogunate, which started gold and silver mines there. Today, it is administratively a part of Niigaṭa Prefecture.

Sado, a mountainous island, is formed of three regions. In the northwest the Osada Mountains have the highest peak, Mount Kinpoku (1,172 meters). The southern part is formed by the Kosado Mountains, which average between 500 and 640 meters in height. The Kuninaka Plain, which runs from the northeast to the southwest, has 80 percent of the island's population, mostly in the cities of Ryotsu, Kanai, Sawata, Hatano, Itano, and Mano. The climate is mild, with an annual average temperature of 13° C. Japanese plum trees and mandarin orange trees grow on the island. The main products include rice, squid, oysters, and seaweed. The island is home to the Toki, the Japanese crested ibis (*Nipponia nippon*), an endangered species.

Nathalie Cavasin

Further Reading
Sugata Masaaki. (1995) *Nihon no shima jiten* (Dictionary of Japanese Islands). Tokyo: Mikosha.
Waycott, Angus. (1996) *Sado: Japan's Island in Exile*. Berkeley, CA: Stone Bridge Press.

SAEK   Saek is a member of the Tai family of languages, which are spoken across a wide area of northern Southeast Asia, from northern Vietnam and Southern China in the east to Assam in the west. The family includes Thai and Lao, the national languages of Thailand and Laos, as well as dozens of languages with speakers varying in numbers from a few thousand to several million.

The Saek people are believed to have originated in Vietnam and to have migrated into Laos and Thailand at least two hundred years ago. Today, Saek is spoken in Muang, Na Wa, and Si Songkhram districts of Nakhon Phanom Province in northeast Thailand near the border with Laos, and also on the opposite side of the Mekong River in Laos itself. There are no reliable statistics about the size of the Saek-speaking population, but one estimate puts it at thousands rather than tens of thousands. Schliesinger reports an estimated total population of Saek to be about 25,000 including both those in Laos and Thailand. The 1995 official Lao census placed the number of Saek at 2,745.

In culture, Saek people are indistinguishable from other Thai and Lao people in northeast Thailand and adjacent Laos. Most Saek speakers in Thailand speak not only their own language but also the local northeastern Thai dialect and standard central Thai. The future of the language is precarious. Thirty years ago it was noted that children understood the Saek spoken by their parents and grandparents yet usually answered in Isan (Thailand) or Lao (Laos) when spoken to. Since then, increasing migration to urban areas in search of a better life, and marriage outside the Saek-speaking community, have taken a further toll.

Saek is of particular interest to scholars interested in the history of the Thai language, because its differences from other Tai languages in Thailand set it apart. This is because it belongs to the northern branch of Tai languages, spoken mainly in southern China, unlike the majority of Tai languages in Thailand and Laos, which belong to the southwestern branch of the family.

Although Saek does not differ from Thai in syntax, the languages are not mutually intelligible. Saek has six tones and a vowel system similar to Thai, but a number of initial consonant clusters that are so strange to average Standard Thai speakers' ears that, on hearing Saek spoken, they will often assume that the language must be Cambodian.

For linguists perhaps the most curious feature of the Saek sound system is the final *l*, which is not found in any other Tai language. Possible theories are that it is evidence of contact with Mon-Khmer languages, such as Cambodian, which do have final *l*, that it is preserving an otherwise lost feature of Proto-Tai, the parent language of all present-day Tai languages, or that it reflects some wider affiliation between the Tai and Malayo-Polynesian languages. This, and the more general question of how and why Saek came to be separated from other northern Tai languages, still remain to be answered.

David Smyth

Further Reading
Chamberlain, James R. (1998) "The Origin of the Saek: Implications for Tai and Vietnamese History." *Journal of the Siam Society* 86, 1 and 2: 27–48.
Chazee, Laurent. (1999) *The People of Laos: Rural and Ethnic Diversities*. Bangkok, Thailand: White Lotus Press.
Gedney, William J. (1970) "The Saek Language of Nakorn Pathom Province." *Journal of the Siam Society* 58, 1: 67–87.
Schliesinger, Joachim. "Saek." In *Tai Groups of Thailand: Profile of the Existing Groups*. Bangkok, Thailand: White Lotus Press, 2: 96–102.

Smalley, William A. (1994) *Linguistic Diversity and National Unity: Language Ecology in Thailand.* Chicago: University of Chicago Press.

SAGA (2002 est. pop. 878,000). Saga Prefecture is situated in the northwest of Japan's island of Kyushu, where it occupies an area of 2,440 square kilometers. Saga's primary geographical features are the Sefuri Mountains and the southern Saga Plain. Saga is bordered by the Genkai and Ariake Seas, and by Fukuoka and Nagasaki prefectures. Once known as Hizen Province, it assumed its present name and borders in 1883.

The original province was ruled by a series of warlords until Nabeshima Naoshige (1538–1618) was granted sovereignty. Nabeshima participated in the invasions of Korea that Japan's paramount warlord, Toyotomi Hideyoshi (1535–1596), launched in 1592 and 1597, and returned to his province with captive Korean potters. The discovery of kaolin clay near Arita fueled Japan's porcelain industry, and the Korean potters began to make export wares to replace those from Ming dynasty China. The Nabeshima family continued its rule through the Edo period (1600/1603–1868).

The prefecture's capital is Saga city. Originating as an Edo period castle town, in the early 2000s, it is a market and distribution center for local agricultural goods such as rice, vegetables, mandarin oranges, and dairy products. It also is the site of industrial facilities for brewing, foodstuff processing, textiles, and paper manufacture. The prefecture's other important cities are Karatsu, Arita, Imari, and Tosu.

In recent times, Saga was a productive coal mining region, though many of the mines now are closed. Its waters are the site of prolific fisheries, pearl beds, and of *nori* (edible seaweed) production in the Ariake Sea. Karatsu, once a thriving port for trade with China, has long been noted for its elegant pottery, made since the pre-Korean pottery era. Other attractions include the scenic Genkai Sea shoreline with its nearby coastal pine forest, the nation's foremost sylvan preserve.

E. L. S. Weber

Further Reading
"Saga Prefecture." (1993) *Japan: An Illustrated Encyclopedia.* Tokyo: Kodansha.

SAGAING DIVISION (2002 pop. est. 5.6 million). The Sagaing Division is the largest of the modern political divisions in Myanmar (Burma). It has an area of 94,622 square kilometers, and is situated between the Indian border to the north, Chin State to the west, Kachin and Shan states to the east and northeast, and Magwe and Mandalay divisions to the south.

It is a territory of geographic and ethnic diversity. The population consists mainly of ethnic Burmans, but there also are substantial communities of Shans, Chins, Nagas, and Kachins, especially in the northern hills. The Academy for the Development of National Groups, established by the Burma Socialist Program Party in 1965 to promote national unity, is located at Ywathitkyi within the division.

The main economy of the territory, which consists of thirty-eight townships and nearly two thousand wards and village-tracts, is agriculture. The division is the main producer of wheat, pulses, and sunflowers in Myanmar. Other important crops include paddy rice, groundnuts, cotton, and tobacco, and timber, including teak, is the most valuable natural resource. There also are substantial copper deposits in Salingyi township, west of the Chindwin (Chindwinn) River.

After Burma's independence in 1948, the development of the division was held back by armed conflict. The capital is the former royal capital of Sagaing, 24 kilometers downstream from Mandalay on the Irrawaddy River. It remains a major center for Buddhist pilgrimage. Another former capital was located at Shwebo farther north. In contrast, the other major town in the division, Monywa, was little more than a village until the twentieth century. At the beginning of the twenty-first century, it was the main commercial gateway to the Chindwin valley.

Under the State Law and Order Restoration Council (1988–1997) and successor State Peace and Development Council, Monywa and the western region of the division were scheduled for economic expansion. Major resettlement and road-building programs were to link up through the Kale-Kabaw valley to the Indian border at Tamu. Similar plans were mooted for the Khamti region and the historic Ledo Road in the far north.

Government authority, however, continued to be challenged in the latter decades of the twentieth century by ethnic Naga, Kachin, and Chin opposition groups in several frontier regions. The creation of a Naga "self-administered zone" was considered for inclusion in Myanmar's future constitution and a ceasefire agreed with the Kachin Independence Organization in 1994, but substantive reforms were not yet completed by the end of the twentieth century.

The division contains several areas of rare natural biodiversity. These include the Naga Hills of the

Paktai Range and the Htamanthi reserve, which lies between the Uru and Chindwin rivers. This was designated as a wildlife sanctuary in 1974.

Martin Smith

Further Reading
Bunge, Frederica M, ed. (1983) *Burma: A Country Study*. Washington, DC: American University Foreign Area Studies, U.S. Government Printing Office.
Images Asia, Karen Human Rights Group, and the Open Society Institute's Burma Project. (1998) *All Quiet on the Western Front?: The Situation in Chin State and Sagaing Division, Burma*. Chiang Mai, Thailand: Images Asia.
Minority Rights Group. (1980) *India, the Nagas, and the North-East*. London: Minority Rights Group.
Smith, Martin. (1994) *Ethnic Groups in Burma: Development, Democracy, and Human Rights*. London: Anti-Slavery International.
Tinker, Hugh. (1967) *The Union of Burma: A Study of the First Years of Independence*. Oxford: Oxford University Press.

SAI BABA, SATYA (b. 1926), Indian spiritual leader. Sai Baba is a twentieth-century Indian spiritual leader whose mission is to bring peace to India and the world. He was born at sunrise on 23 November 1926 in Puttaparthi, a village near Hyderabad, Andhra Pradesh, South India. Sai Baba is the third child of Pedda Venkappa Raju and Easwaramma. He was given the name Sathyanarayan (*sathya*, "truth"; *Narayan*, "God residing in our hearts") and began performing miracles at the age of eight. He is considered to be the reincarnation of Shirdi Sai Baba, saint and mystic, who died in 1918 and foretold of Sai Baba's birth. On 23 May 1940, at the age of fourteen, he renounced his familial ties and proclaimed his mission to restore truth, love, harmony, and righteousness in a discordant world. He is considered a *purna* (full) avatar (God in human form, after the Indian doctrine of divine incarnation). He claims both divine and human consciousness. Sai Baba has said that he will live until the age of 95, in 2021.

His name evokes his mission: Satya (unchanging truth), Sai (true mother or the female aspect of the universe), Baba (true father or the male aspect of the universe), and he is Anandaswarupa (the nature of bliss, unconditional love). Advocating a life of frugality and emphasizing the sanctity of work, he does not aim to convert, proclaiming that all religions are his. Sai Baba says that there is only one caste—of humanity; only one language—of the heart; only one religion—of love; and only one God—who is omnipresent. His followers come from all over the world and number more than 50 million in sixty countries. He has initiated large-scale social and educational programs based on spiritual lines, including more than 10,000 *bal vikas* (kindergartens) and *seva dals* (volunteers trained to serve). His main ashram (retreat, hermitage) is located in Puttaparthi and is called Prashanti Nilayam (Abode of Great Peace). Other institutions include an ashram on the grounds of his residence in Brindavan, his college at Whitefield near Bangalore, and more than 3,500 Sai centers in India and elsewhere.

Chandrika Kaul

Further Reading
Mason, Peggy, and Ron Laing. (1987) *Satya Sai Baba: The Embodiment of Love*. 2d ed. Norwich, U.K.: Pilgrim.
Sandweiss, Samuel. (1975) *Sai Baba: The Holy Man and the Psychiatrist*. San Diego, CA: Birth Day Publishing.

SAICHO (767–822 CE), Japanese Buddhist monk. Born Mitsu no Obito Hirono in Japan's Omi Province, east of Mount Hiei, Saicho was the son of a devout Buddhist. After following the normal path to ordination as a priest, Saicho took to a small hermitage on Mount Hiei outside Heiankyo (Kyoto), where he meditated on the impermanence of existence and the Tiantai Buddhist doctrines of China, especially the notion that all beings have the potential for Buddhahood.

When the emperor moved the capital to Heiankyo in 794, Saicho was appointed to serve at court. In 804, Saicho set forth on one of the four diplomatic ships sailing to China. There he studied under two of the leading dharma heirs of the Tiantai sect. After spending eight months studying and copying sutras, he received dharma transmission and returned to Japan with 230 Buddhist texts.

In 806, Saicho founded the Tendai school of Buddhism, the Japanese branch of the Chinese Tiantai sect. At the monastery of Enryakuji on Mount Hiei, Saicho commenced lectures concerning such works as the *Lotus Sutra*. Out of these discussions of Buddhist teachings came a comprehensive school of Buddhist studies. Saicho sought out the younger Kukai and requested instruction in the esoteric texts Kukai had copied while in China. Among other reforms, Saicho advocated an end to government control over ordination, an autonomy that was not granted until after his death.

James M. Vardaman, Jr.

Further Reading
Kashiwahara Yusen and Koyu Sonoda, eds. (1994) *Shapers of Japanese Buddhism*. Trans. by Gaynor Sekimori. Tokyo: Kosei Publishing.

Tsunoda, Ryusaku, et al. (1958) *Sources of Japanese Tradition*. Vol 1. New York: Columbia University Press.

SAILENDRA   A powerful ancient dynasty in maritime Southeast Asia, especially in Java and Sumatra, Sailendra dominated Java from about 760 to 860 CE. This dynasty was credited with building a large Buddhist stupa, Borobudur, in the Kedu plain of present-day Central Java. Unlike later predominantly Hindu and then Muslim Javanese dynasties, Sailendra was Mahayana Buddhist.

In the mid-ninth century, Sailendra rule in Java was challenged by an expanding Hindu dynasty that later established the Mataram kingdom. The Sailendra were forced to leave Java for Sumatra, where they had good relations with the powerful Srivijaya kingdom. Sharing the same religion, Srivijaya's ruler accorded the Sailendra the utmost respect, and efforts were made to unite the courts through intermarriage.

The Sailendra found good fortune in Sumatra. They not only received refuge from Srivijaya, but the courts effectively merged into the Sailendra identity, perpetuating this heritage until the kingdom's eleventh-century demise.

Irman G. Lanti

Further Reading
Hall, Kenneth R. (1999) "Economic History of Early Southeast Asia." In *The Cambridge History of Southeast Asia*, vol. 1, part 1, edited by Nicholas Tarling. Cambridge, U.K.: Cambridge University Press.
Taylor, Keith W. (1999) "The Early Kingdoms." In *The Cambridge History of Southeast Asia*, vol. 1, part 1, edited by Nicholas Tarling. Cambridge, U.K.: Cambridge University Press.

SAINT PAUL   (d. c. 62–68 CE), early Christian saint, apostle to Gentiles. Saint Paul converted the Jews and Christians of the Roman empire to Christianity from about 40 to 64 CE. He undertook three missionary journeys in Asia Minor and Greece and traveled to Rome to appeal his death sentence. His efforts resulted in the expansion of the Church to include Gentile converts based in southern Asia Minor, Greece, and Rome, thus changing the nature of the Church members from the original congregants of Jewish Christians. He probably died for his beliefs in Rome. His conversion and mission are described in the Bible in both the Acts of the Apostles (written by Luke) and Paul's own letters to the churches.

Paul (or Saul) was born in Tarsus, in today's Turkey, and was trained as a rabbi and a tent maker. Educated in Jerusalem as a strict Pharisee, he purged heresy from the Jewish faith by persecuting the followers of Jesus. Later he had a mystical experience, a vision of Jesus on the road to Damascus, which completely recast his beliefs. He became a leading member of the Church in Antioch, the second Christian community after Jerusalem.

As a church official, Paul, with Barnabas, made the first journey to Cyprus, Antalya, Perge, Antioch in Pisidia, Iconium (now Konya), Lystra, and Derbe, founding churches along the way, and returning by the same route. The message that Jesus was the Messiah promised by God to the prophets was adapted for Gentile consumption to proclaim Jesus as son of a self-evident supreme deity who provided eternal life for his believers. Paul's Christianity diverged from Jesus' message of righteous behavior within Jewish law. On his return, Paul and Peter (then primate of Antioch) obtained permission from the Church in Jerusalem to admit uncircumcised Gentiles to the Church, which thus lost its Jewish links.

Paul revisited his congregations in Asia Minor and continued to Troas, Philippi, Thessalonica, Athens, and Corinth. Returning, he paused at Ephesus and Caesarea en route to Antioch. On the third journey, a reprise of the second, he spent three years in Ephesus, where the most important letters were written and funds were collected to support Jewish Christians in Jerusalem. His preaching provoked an attack from worshipers of Artemis, one of several attacks on his person.

Back in Jerusalem, Paul was attacked by "Jews of Asia," imprisoned for two years, and tried by successive Roman governors of Caesarea; appealing (as a Roman citizen) to the emperor, he spent two years in Rome under house arrest. According to the Palestinian historian Eusebius (c. 260–c. 339), Paul was beheaded during Nero's persecutions of 64 CE.

Paul was the best known and hardest working of the Christian fathers; Christianity in Jerusalem almost perished in the Jewish revolt of 70 CE and was kept alive largely by Paul's beleaguered communities of Gentile converts.

Kate Clow

SAIONJI KINMOCHI   (1849–1940), Japanese leader. Descended from the most influential imperial court family, the Fujiwara, Saionji is known as the "last genro" for his behind-the-scenes leadership as Japan's last active surviving elder statesman after the death of Prince Yamagata Aritomo in 1922. A native of Kyoto, Saionji, at age eighteen, served as imperial representative in battles waged by the new government against northern enemies after the fall of the Tokugawa shogunate in 1867. He helped found Meiji Law School in 1880 (later Meiji University) and was president of the liberal newspaper *Toyo jiyu shinbun* (Oriental Free Press) in 1881. Saionji's political appointments included minister of education (1894–1896; 1898), acting minister of foreign affairs (1895–1896), vice president of the House of Peers (1893–1894), president of the Privy Council (1900–1903), president of the Seiyukai political party (1903–1914), and prime minister (1906–1908; 1911–1912).

Saionji studied law in France (1871–1880), was a member of Ito Hirobumi's entourage investigating European constitutions (1882), Japan's minister to Austria (1885–1887) and Germany (1887–1891), and Japanese plenipotentiary to the Versailles Peace Conference (1919). As principal power broker in Tokyo (1922–1936), his efforts on behalf of representative government and cooperative relations with Britain and the United States were exceeded only by his passion for protecting the throne.

Frederick R. Dickinson

Further Reading

Connors, Lesley. (1987) *The Emperor's Adviser: Saionji Kinmochi and Pre-War Japanese Politics*. London: Croom Helm.

Oka Yoshitake. (1986) *Five Political Leaders of Modern Japan: Ito Hirobumi, Okuma Shigenobu, Hara Takashi, Inukai Tsuyoshi, and Saionji Kimmochi*. Trans. by Andrew Fraser and Patricia Murray. Tokyo: University of Tokyo Press.

SAITAMA

(2002 est. pop. 7.2 million). Saitama Prefecture is situated in the central region of Japan's island of Honshu. One of the nation's leading agricultural areas, it occupies an area of 3,799 square kilometers. Saitama's primary geographical features are the fertile Kanto Plain and several Kanto Mountain peaks in the west. The main rivers are the Tonegawa and the Arakawa. Saitama is bordered by Gumma, Tochigi, Ibaraki, Chiba, Tokyo, Yamanashi, and Nagano prefectures. Once part of Musashi Province, it assumed its present name and borders in 1876.

Many archaeological excavations from the Jomon (10,000 BCE–300 BCE) and Yayoi (300 BCE–300 CE) cultures indicate early agriculture in the region. Musashi Province was ruled from the twelfth century on by the Minamoto, Hojo, Uesugi, and Later Hogo warlord families. During the Edo period (1600/1603–1868), the Tokugawa shogunate administered the area directly.

The prefecture's capital city is Urawa. In the early 2000s, it is a residential suburb of Tokyo with numerous apartment complexes and factories for the processing of foodstuffs and metals, and for the production of machinery. During the Edo period, Urawa was a post station town. The prefecture's other important cities are Kawaguchi, Omiya, Kawagoe, and Tokorozawa.

Saitama Prefecture continues to grow food (mainly rice and vegetables) and raises livestock for the Tokyo market. Recent decades have seen the rapid growth of industries related to chemicals and metals processing. A historic attraction is Kawagoe, a one-time castle town known as "little Edo" for its traditional merchant quarter. Visitors also are drawn to Chichibu-Tama National Park.

E. L. S. Weber

Further Reading

"Saitama Prefecture." (1993) *Japan: An Illustrated Encyclopedia*. Tokyo: Kodansha.

SALOTH SAR. See Pol Pot.

SALT TAX

Salt is exuded in perspiration and other body excretions and must be replaced; therefore salt is absolutely necessary for human beings. Salt is also useful for preserving and flavoring food, but it is not evenly distributed throughout the world. For these reasons, most governments have seen salt as a suitable commodity to tax. Since salt in excess is unpleasant, consumption by the rich does not much exceed that of the poor, and thus a tax on salt is fundamentally a poll tax.

China

China has a long history of taxing salt. The large volumes of fresh water discharged by the major rivers make salt extraction from the diluted sea difficult. Over two millennia ago, salt was pumped from subterranean brine pools and then evaporated. These wells became controlled by the Chinese Board of Revenue. By 900 CE the salt tax became the most important item of government revenue. This situation continued until China's administrative collapse in the seventeenth century and was revived in the early twentieth century, under foreign pressure, to repay foreign loans. In general, although burdensome to poor people, the Chinese salt taxes were not high. Typically it took two days of a peasant's wages to meet the family's salt needs for a year.

India

India also has a long history of salt taxation. Chandra Gupta, who ruled much of India from 324 to 301 BCE, imposed a salt tax. The Mughals taxed salt from the sixteenth century until they were usurped by the British. Generally the tax was relatively low.

In 1765 severe taxation of salt in India was initiated by Robert Clive, governor of Bengal, as a private monopoly. In 1780 Warren Hastings, governor-general, brought the tax under government control. Thereafter successive administrators consolidated tax collection and expanded the tax base as the British spread across India.

Before the level of salt taxation was almost equalized across British India in 1879, it was much higher in the Bengal presidency than in Madras or Mumbai (Bombay). At the beginning it cost a peasant about two months' wages to provide yearly salt for his family; by 1879 it was nearer one month's wages. To stop untaxed salt coming in from the princely states, Bengal was enclosed by a customs line 4,030 kilometers (2,500 miles) long, much of it formed by an impenetrable thorn hedge.

After 1879 until the end of British rule, wage inflation gradually eroded the severity of the salt tax. Nevertheless in 1930 Mahatma Gandhi protested against the unjust tax. He and his followers marched to the sea to illegally gather salt. This and their subsequent imprisonment were key episodes in the fight for independence, when the salt tax was abolished.

Roy Moxham

Further Reading

Moxham, Roy. (2001) *The Great Hedge of India*. London: Constable.
Multhauf, Robert P. (1978) *Neptune's Gift*. Baltimore: Johns Hopkins University Press.

SALWEEN RIVER

The Salween (Thanlwin) River is one of the major waterways of Myanmar (Burma). Entering northeastern Myanmar from China's Yunnan Province, it flows southward through the mountain valleys of Shan, Kayah, and Karen (Kayin) States before reaching the Gulf of Martaban in Mon State. Although it is locally navigable, it is too hazardous in many areas, with deep ravines and plunging rapids, to allow navigation for any extended length. The only exception is the lower reaches in Karen and Mon States, where timber and other goods are transported.

In these lowland areas, the state capitals of Moulmein (Mawlamyine) and Paan (Hpa-an) are located along its banks, but there are few other settlements of any size along the rest of its 1,600-kilometer course. There are bridges across the Salween near Paan as well as at Takaw and Kunlong in Shan State. Other bridges were planned during the 1990s, but most crossings of the river are only by local ferries.

There have also been plans in recent decades for hydroelectric dams at various locations along the river, but many of these areas have been affected by insurgencies. In the late 1990s, there were reports of detailed discussions, involving various international interests, about building a dam in southern Shan State, but this project continued to be criticized by opposition groups.

Martin Smith

Further Reading

Tinker, Hugh. (1967) *The Union of Burma: A Study of the First Years of Independence*. Oxford: Oxford University Press.
Woodman, Dorothy. (1962) *The Making of Burma*. London: Cresset Press.

SAM RAINSY

(b. 1949), Cambodian opposition leader. Sam Rainsy was born in Phnom Penh, the son of Sam Sary, deputy prime minister in Prince Sihanouk's government. He moved to France in 1965, where he received degrees in business, accounting, economics, and political science. He returned to Cambodia in 1992 and worked for the Cambodian political party known as FUNCINPEC in the U.N.-sponsored election of 1993.

In 1993 Sam Rainsy was named minister of finance for FUNCINPEC. He was an outspoken critic of government corruption, the two prime ministers, and his own party's policies. He was removed from office in October 1994, expelled from FUNCINPEC in May 1995, and forced out of Parliament the following month. He filed a complaint in a Phnom Penh court, but the court declined to take the case. His dismissal was interpreted by some not only as a means to silence him, but also as an act of political intimidation against future challengers.

From that time, he became a force for the opposition. Sam Rainsy has been successful in tailoring his image to the international community. He travels widely, speaks English and French, and uses the language of anticorruption and democracy. In his appeals to Cambodian people, however, he often uses anti-Vietnamese rhetoric.

In 1996 Sam Rainsy and the Khmer Nation Party were instrumental in the formation of the first labor union under the new government, the Free Trade Union of Khmer Workers (FTUKW). The FTUKW supported garment workers in and around Phnom Penh. They organized work stoppages and demonstrations, often with Sam Rainsy playing a prominent role.

On 30 March 1997 a grenade attack on a peaceful demonstration outside the National Assembly killed thirty people. Sam Rainsy was at the demonstration but was not injured. It is commonly believed that he was the intended target. No charges were ever filed.

He founded the Sam Rainsy Party in 1995 and became its president. In the election of July 1998, the party won 14 percent of the vote. Initially both the Sam Rainsy Party and FUNCINPEC contested the vote, but in November 1998, FUNCINPEC and the CPP agreed to form a coalition government. The Sam Rainsy Party became the sole opposition in the National Assembly. As a member of Parliament, Sam Rainsy remains an outspoken critic of the government.

Jeanne Morel

Further Reading

Brown, Frederick Z., and David G. Timberman. (1998) *Cambodia and the International Community: The Quest for Peace, Development, and Democracy.* New York: Asia Society.

Sorpong Peou. (2000) *Intervention and Change in Cambodia.* Singapore: Institute of Southeast Asian Studies.

SAMARQAND (2002 pop. 373,000). Samarqand in Uzbekistan is one of the world's oldest extant cities, and is Central Asia's most senior urban setting. Narrow streets wind through the old quarter of Samarqand. The historic heart of Samarqand is the Registan, an open square dominated by three great *madrasah*s, or Islamic colleges. Visitors can see the mausoleum of the Turkic conqueror Timur (1336–1405), an octagonal structure with a fluted dome, azure in color, with sixty-four separate ribs. Other important buildings include the Bibi Khanum Mosque, with its turquoise cupola, erected by Timur to the memory of his favorite wife, Saray Mulk Khanum. The city also houses other magnificent mosques, mausoleums, and the ruins of the observatory of Ulug Beg (d. 1449).

SAMARQAND—WORLD HERITAGE SITE

Samarqand was designated a UNESCO World Heritage site in 2001 because of its importance in the development of Islamic architecture and its role in the development of urban life in Central Asia.

Built on the site of Afrosiab, which dated from the third or fourth millennium BCE, Samarqand was first known to the ancient Greeks as Maracanda. Today visitors can see ruins of the old settlement north of the present city. The chief city of Sogdiana, on the ancient trade route between the Middle East and China, Samarqand was conquered in 329 BCE by Alexander of Macedon. Based on its location, it became a meeting point of Western and Chinese culture.

The Arabs took Samarqand in the eighth century, and it flourished as a trade center on the route between Baghdad and China. In the ninth and tenth centuries, as capital of the Abbasid dynasty in Central Asia, Samarqand emerged as a center of Islamic civilization. Samarqand continued to prosper under the Samanid dynasty of Khorasan (874–999) and under the subsequent rule of the Seljuks and of the shahs of Khwarizm.

In 1220, Genghis Khan captured and devastated the city. Timur revived the city in the fourteenth century, naming it capital of his empire and raising it to its greatest heights with his architectural achievements. Samarqand eventually became part of the emirate of Bukhara and fell to Russian troops in 1868. In 1925,

The marketplace is a standard element of life in many Central Asian cities. Here, a baker sells loaves of bread at the Bibi Bazaar market in Samarqand. (DAVID SAMUEL ROBBINS/CORBIS)

Samarqand became the capital of the Uzbek SSR, but in 1930 it was replaced by the more modern Tashkent.

In the twenty-first century Samarqand remains an industrial city with tea, wine, textiles, fertilizer, and motor-vehicle parts its primary products. It is also a major tourist attraction, with points of interest being the Registan, Bibi Khanum Mosque, Shahr-i-Zindah (street of tombs), Guri Amir Mausoleum (the tomb of Timur and his sons and grandsons), Ulug Beg's observatory, and the streets of the old city.

Rebecca M. Bichel

SAMSUN

SAMSUN (2002 est. pop. 377,000). Samsun is the capital of Turkey's Samsun Province and is located on the Black Sea coast between the Kizel Irmak and Yesil Irmak Rivers. Originally called Amisus, it was ruled by the Greeks in the seventh century BCE and later came under Roman and Byzantine influence. The Seljuks gained control of the city in the eleventh century CE. Under Seljuk rule, the Genoese enjoyed trading privileges that continued until Samsun fell to the Ottoman sultan Bayezid I (1389–1402) in 1393. In protest, the Genoese chose to burn down the city rather than leave it to the Ottomans. This fire, as well as subsequent fires, account for the lack of surviving ancient monuments. According to the famous Turkish traveler Katip Celebi, in the seventeenth century there were four mosques, a few shop-lined streets, and a bathhouse in the town. Celebi does not mention any commercial activity. By the early nineteenth century, Samsun became an important trade center, and by the mid-nineteenth century, there was a covered market and a khan (rest house). The population in 1860, a combination of Turk, Armenian, and Greek inhabitants, was recorded at six thousand and grew to sixteen thousand by 1890.

After the end of World War I, the area saw tension between the Greeks and the Turks. On 19 May 1919 Mustafa Kemal Ataturk (1881–1938), the founder of the Turkish Republic, landed at Samsun. He immediately began organizing the national resistance army (which he was originally sent to disband) that would eventually overthrow the sultanate and lead to the foundation of the republic in 1923. After the declaration of the Turkish Republic, 19 May was proclaimed a national holiday in honor of sports and the nation's youth.

The Samsun region was known for tobacco and hemp growing in Ottoman times (hemp was used to make rope for the army), and these continue to be its chief exports. The port of Samsun continues to be used, as it was in its early trading days, for agricultural imports and exports; tourism is not a major industry.

T. Isikozlu–E.F. Isikozlu

Further Reading
Faroqhi, Suraiya. (1960) "Samsun." In *The Encyclopedia of Islam.* 2d ed. Leiden, Netherlands: E. J. Brill, 1052–1054.
(1999). *Statistical Yearbook of Turkey, 1998.* Ankara, Turkey: Devlet Istatistik Enstitusu.

SAN FRANCISCO PEACE TREATY

SAN FRANCISCO PEACE TREATY The San Francisco Peace Treaty, officially known as the Treaty of Peace with Japan, was signed on 8 September 1951 at the Opera House in San Francisco and brought an end to the state of war between Japan and forty-eight of the fifty-one nations in attendance at the conference. Symbolic of the Cold War divisions at the time, the Soviet Union, Poland, and Czechoslovakia did not sign, and neither the Republic of China nor the People's Republic of China was invited (although Japan later agreed to establish a separate treaty with the Republic of China to ensure ratification by the U.S. Senate). The United States took the initiative in the peace settlement, and as a result, the peace treaty, comprised of eighteen sections and thirty articles, was relatively generous and nonpunitive in nature. The treaty itself was drafted by U.S. special emissary John Foster Dulles and his State Department assistants, who consulted with each of the Allied countries and Japan on its contents. The treaty went into effect on 28 April 1952, at which time the U.S.-led Allied Occupation of Japan (which officially began on 2 September 1945 with Japan's signing of the Instrument of Surrender) ended.

Robert D. Eldridge

Further Reading
Dunn, Frederick S. (1963) *Peace-Making and the Settlement with Japan.* Princeton, NJ: Princeton University Press.

SANA'I

SANA'I (d. 1131), Persian poet. Sana'i (Abu al-Majd Majdud ibn Adam) flourished in the region encompassing present-day Iran, Afghanistan, and Central Asia. His early work was probably panegyric poetry in praise of secular rulers. Legendary accounts depicting his conversion from a courtly life to a pious one, while doubtful, contributed to the notion of Sana'i as a mystical poet, earning him the later honorific *hakim* (sage). His most influential poem, the *Hadiqat al-haqiqa* (Garden of Spiritual Reality), was the first major mystical Persian work using rhyming couplets, *masnavi*. The *masnavi* pattern influenced later mystical Muslim (Sufi) poets, especially the thirteenth-century masters Attar and Rumi. Less widely read, but perhaps of higher literary quality, is Sana'i's *Divan.*

Omid Safi

Further Reading
Browne, E. G. ([1902] 1997) *A Literary History of Persia.* Vol. 2. Reprint ed. Oxford: Oxford University Press.
De Bruijn, J. T. P. (1983) *Of Piety and Poetry: The Interaction of Religion and Literature in the Life and Works of Hakim Sana'i of Ghazna.* Leiden, Netherlands: Brill.
Pendlebury, D. L. (1974) *Hakim Sana'i: The Walled Garden of Truth.* London: Octagon Press.

SANDIWARA *Sandiwara* refers to a variety of regional popular forms of theater in Indonesia. *Sandiwara* is based on older forms of *tonil* (theater) from the Dutch colonial period; its name was changed during the Japanese occupation because of official Japanese linguistic policy prohibiting the use of the Dutch language. Among the Sundanese ethnic group of West Java, *sandiwara* refers to an urban popular theater in which costumed actors dramatize stories through Sundanese language, singing, and dance. In its heyday (1940s–1970s), performances took place in permanent theater buildings where audiences paid a small admission fee. The proscenium stage was fitted with curtains and painted backdrops depicting different scenes (for example, inner palace, outer palace, village, forest, and so on). Electric lighting illuminated the stage in the darkened auditorium.

The form is similar to *bangsawan* (Malaysia) and *kethoprak* (central Java). Using a scenario, actors improvise dialogue, elaborating stories and jokes relevant to the social issues of the day. Plays (*lakon*) are based on local histories and tales from the *wayang* theater, as well as romances and modern life. In contrast to stylized *wayang* theater, *sandiwara* emphasizes more realistic vocal inflections, movements, and acting. Comic sketches play an important role. Gamelan accompanies Sundanese dances as well as interlude songs featuring female singers interspersed throughout a performance. In the Sundanese region, *sandiwara* is rarely performed nowadays, although a few troupes still exist. Audiences in the Cirebon cultural area of coastal West Java still enjoy this form of theater. In addition to being commercial theater, *sandiwara* was also a popular form of radio broadcast. The radio version of *sandiwara*, however, is not generically related to the theatrical form of the same name.

Andrew Weintraub

Further Reading
Brandon, James. (1974) *Theatre in Southeast Asia.* Cambridge, MA: Harvard University Press.
Cohen, Matthew. (1998) "Hybrid Tradition: Cirebonese *Sandiwara* and the Popular Theatre Movement in South and Southeast Asia." In *Proceedings of the International Symposium on the Humanities V, in Honor of the Retirement of Professor Dr. Umar Kayam and Professor Dr. Djoko Soekiman, 8–9 December 1998.* Yogyakarta, Indonesia: Faculty of Letters, Gadjah Mada University, 100–116.

SANKARA (c. 788–820 CE), Brahman philosopher. Sankara (commonly called Sankaracarya) was born in Kaladi, Kerala, southern India, in about 788 CE. The most important of this philosopher's many works is the *Brahmasutra Bhasya*, a masterpiece of logical analysis and graceful Sanskritic style. It has acquired many commentaries by later authors. Sankara himself wrote commentaries on the principal Upanishads and on the Brahma Sutra and *Bhagavad Gita*. It was in these that he developed his doctrine of monism (*advaita*), his lasting contribution to Indian philosophies. He traveled all over India explaining the idea of monism, a metaphysical view that there is only one form of reality, called Brahman (not the same word as the Brahman, which denotes a member of the priestly castes). The apparent plurality of things and persons in the observable world is the result of cosmic ignorance (Maya), which hides the underlying unity of Brahman. All selves are basically identical, since in essence they are one with Brahman.

Although he died fairly young, the fruit of Sankara's missionary travels demonstrated that he was a great organizer, who established famous monasteries in India at Sringeri in Karnataka, Puri in Orissa, Dwaraka in Gujarat, and Badrinath in the Himalayan foothills. The influence of these religious centers has been immeasurable, and they are still flourishing. In the twentieth century, the Advaita School was revived as Vedantic Hinduism and developed a worldwide following.

Paul Hockings

Further Reading
Bhattacharya, Surendranath. (c. 1947) "The Philosophy of Sankara." In *The Cultural Heritage of India.* Sri Ramakrishna Centenary Memorial. Vol. 1. Calcutta, India: Sri Ramakrishna Centenary Committee, 549–575.

SANKARACHARYA. See **Sankara.**

SANSKRIT The earliest traces of Sanskrit, an Indo-Aryan language that is part of the larger family of Indo-European languages, occur in the hymns of the Rig Veda (the earliest Hindu sacred writings), which may have been composed as early as the second millennium BCE. By the second century BCE, Sanskrit had become the medium of many religious and philosophical texts on the Indian subcontinent and in Sri Lanka. From the fourth to thirteenth centuries CE, the role of Sanskrit as a language appropriate for the expression of sacred material greatly expanded not only throughout the Indian subcontinent, but also to large parts of mainland and insular Southeast Asia. It thus became the language of scholars across a region that connected a wide spectrum of cultures, a phenomenon that has recently been termed the Sanskrit cosmopolis.

Sanskrit grammar was reputedly first codified by Panini, an Indian grammarian who flourished around 400 BCE. Nouns and pronouns are declined in the nominative, vocative, accusative, instrumental, dative, ablative, genitive, and locative cases. Along with singular and plural forms, Sanskrit also recognizes a dual. The verb forms distinguish seven moods: present, imperfect, aorist (indefinite), imperative, perfect, future, and conditional. A marked phenomenon in Sanskrit is sandhi: many vowels or consonants slurring together to form different phonemes.

Sanskrit was the medium in which many Indian religious, philosophical, and literary texts were transmitted. Written in Sanskrit, the great Indian epics of the *Mahabharata* and *Ramayana* became known in many Southeast Asian courts where they were recited and performed, inspiring local artists with their narratives, rich imagery, and symbolism. Also, the cosmology of the Puranas (religious texts of the Hindus, dating from the third century CE, with eternal cycles of 4,320,000,000 years) was transmitted to Southeast Asia in Sanskrit. Until Theravada Buddhism, with its use of the Pali language, gained the upper hand during the eleventh and twelfth centuries CE, many Mahayana Buddhist texts also were transmitted in Sanskrit.

From the seventh century onward, religious and political texts appeared in both Sanskrit and vernacular languages, and gradually the role of Sanskrit diminished in favor of local forms of speech. On the Indian subcontinent, Sanskrit continues to be used as a sacred language. In the early twenty-first century, Sanskrit has gained new support as an aspect of Indian nationalism.

B. J. Terwiel

Further Reading

Houben, Jan E. M., ed. (1996) *Ideology and Status of Sanskrit, Contributions to the History of the Sanskrit Language.* Leiden, Netherlands: E. J. Brill.
Pollock, Sheldon. (1996) "The Sanskrit Cosmopolis, 300–1300: Transculturation, Vernacularization." In *Ideology and Status of Sanskrit, Contributions to the History of the Sanskrit Language*, edited by Jan E. M. Houben. Leiden, Netherlands: E. J. Brill, 197–249.

SANSKRITIZATION The Indian sociologist M. N. Srinivas coined the term "Sanskritization" to identify a dominant strand of Indian society and culture, characterized by "the process by which a low caste or tribe or other group takes over the customs, ritual, beliefs, ideology, and style of life of a high and in particular a twice-born (*dwija*) caste" (1989: 56). Sanskritization has been widely interpreted as representing a form of social mobility. By pointing out that Sanskritization legitimizes upward social mobility, Srinivas questioned the widespread view of Indian society as a rigid hierarchy preventing social mobility. Noting that the concept has more than mere structural relevance, Srinivas regarded Sanskritization as the thread connecting local cults, values and beliefs, sectarian deities, and deities specific to a particular caste or region with the values, beliefs, rituals, gods, and mythologies of Sanskritic Hinduism. He associated the ideology underlying *varnashramadharma* (the scheme of division of society into ranked *varnas* and the scheme of different stages in the life of a human being) and ideas such as dharma (morality and moral order), karma (the idea that one's actions in this existence have consequences in one's next life), samsara (the cycle of birth and death), *moksha* (release from the cycle of birth and death), bhakti (devotion), *papa* (sin), and *punya* (religious merit acquired through good action) with Sanskritic Hinduism.

Sanskritization as a Structural Process

Sociologists studying Indian society have commented extensively on the concept of Sanskritization, especially as it refers to an important aspect of social structural. Viewed in the social context, Sanskritization provides a culturally specific instance of the model of reference-group behavior, which Robert Merton expounded. Merton's model holds that those who want to enhance their social status seek to emulate the lifestyles of groups called reference groups, those who enjoy a superior social status.

In India any of the *dwija* castes may be reference groups for members of castes lower in the hierarchy. A "second birth" is conferred on male members of *dwija* castes in an *upanayana* (initiatory) ceremony, which allows participants the right to don the sacred thread (worn on the shoulder) and perform rituals of *sandhya vandana* at sunrise and sunset every day. Because of their ritual entitlement, *dwija* castes are considered pure, but there is a rank order of purity among these castes, legitimized by the *purusha sukta* hymn of the Hindu *Dharma Shastra* (Law Book). This myth sanctifies the four-tiered *varna* scheme that provides the model of caste division.

According to myth, the Brahman emerges from the mouth of Purusha, the primordial being, and hence embodies maximum purity. The Brahman is associated with learning and knowledge and enjoys highest ritual status. The Kshatriya, who emerges from the shoulders of Purusha, is ranked after the Brahman. The Kshatriya *varna* is associated with the exercise of power and the use of arms to protect a person's subjects and to conquer enemies. The Vaisya, who emerges from the thighs of the Purusha, is ranked below the Kshatriya and is associated with trade and commerce. The Brahman, Kshatriya, and Vaisya form the *dwija* category of castes and are ranked above the Sudra, who emerges from the legs of Purusha. The Sudra is considered impure, and so he is required to serve others.

The *Dharma Shastra* delineates the hierarchy in caste society and ensures its immutability by prescribing severe punishments for breach of codes resulting in mixing of castes. Thus, if a Brahman woman marries a man of a lower *varna*, the couple is banished to the social fringes to lives as Chandalas in crematoriums and burial grounds. Chandala is among the lowest untouchable castes. Because Chandalas deal with dead bodies, which are associated with extreme pollution in Hinduism, they are suffer the social disability of untouchability in caste society.

Because knowledge of the Vedas or sacred texts is the exclusive preserve of Brahmans, scriptures prescribe pouring molten lead into the ears of a Sudra who as much as hears the recitation of these holy texts. No wonder Indologists have regarded the caste system as a rigid, closed scheme of stratification.

There is no scope for Sanskritization in Hindu society if it works according to the prescriptions and sanctions of the *Dharma Shastra*. By identifying the process of Sanskritization, Srinivas not only noted the disjuncture between the theory of caste and its practice but also indirectly showed the hold that the values and beliefs propagated by the scriptures exercised on Hindu society. He pointed out that in practice the caste system is more open than the texts suggest. The *varna* scheme provides only a reference framework for intercaste relationships and relevant rules of conduct.

In practice, castes appear as *jati*s. A *jati* is an endogamous group confined to a geographic region, speaking the local dialect or language, and sharing many local beliefs, customs, and practices. There are more than five thousand *jati* groups in Indian society, in contrast to the four *varna*s of the scriptures. Localized *jati*s link themselves to the *varna* scheme by claiming to belong to one or another *varna* and by appropriating its ritual status. Many *jati*s may fuse into a megacaste, spread across several regions of India; in other cases a *jati* may break up into smaller groups. Thus, the caste system has considerable fluidity.

Models of Sanskritization

The *jati* system makes caste hierarchy fuzzy. Disputes about ranking are especially intense when closely ranked *jati*s live together in one locality. Local interpretations, interpolations, and amendments of scriptures and local caste Puranas (sacred writings), and genealogies of various *jati*s add to the fuzziness. Thus, contests over ranking are endemic to the caste system, and here Sanskritization makes a crucial difference.

Usually the established Brahman caste in a locality or a locally dominant caste claiming *dwija* status provides a model for other local castes. The Brahmanical model of Sanskritization emphasizes vegetarianism and avoidance of items of non-*satvic* (impure) diet such as onions and garlic and of alcoholic beverages; it also emphasizes the observance of festivals and rituals associated with this caste. Adoption of Vedic rituals in the worship of local deities, construction of mythologies to establish a relationship between local deities and gods of the Hindu pantheon, adoption of local Brahmanical codes for the treatment of married and unmarried women and widows—these are prominent features of this model of Sanskritization.

If the locally dominant caste claims Kshatriya status, the local lifestyle offers a model that may allow eating meat and even drinking alcoholic beverages. This model emphasizes power and patronage; a patron must be wise and generous to clients to command their loyalty and respect. Honor and prestige of family, lineage, clan, or caste become overriding considerations, and men belonging to these castes have impressive mustaches, wear elaborate turbans, clothing, and jewelry, and speak in a loud voice to command attention. A popular strategy in claiming Kshatriya status is to trace ancestry to mythological heroes of the *Mahabharata* and *Ramayana*. Because women symbolize the family and *jati*'s status and prestige, they are subject to severe restrictions. As *jati* members acquire economic or political prosperity and want to enhance their caste ranking, they withdraw their women from extramural labor. They may also impose on women the custom of purdah, which requires women to cover their heads, especially before elders and strangers. Even in their homes, women's movements are restricted.

Srinivas thought that the Kshatriya model of Sanskritization is prominent in north India, whereas the Brahmanical model is common in the south. He believed it possible to identify a Vaisya model of Sanskritization as well, especially where merchant castes were prosperous and enjoyed great prestige, as in Rajasthan, Gujarat, and Punjab.

Among Vaisya castes, the Bania lifestyle is marked by piety and pragmatism. Banias are vegetarians and teetotalers; they are frugal and keep meticulous accounts even within the family. This latter characteristic has added to the caste's prosperity. In emergencies Banias are assured of help from their kin network. In Rajasthan, Gujarat, and Punjab, Banias are bulwarks of Hinduism; they donate generously to the construction of temples, hospitals, and hospices for humans as well as animals. More than the Brahmans, Banias have been leaders in protecting the cow, a sacred animal among the Hindus. Some Banias may adopt the Kshatriya model to gain social prestige. In the past, Banias occasionally convinced rulers to give them the title of rajas and the associated political privileges. Srinivas noted that upward mobility through Sanskritization was dominant in both British and pre-British India. He also thought that pre-British India enjoyed favorable human-to-land ratios, allowing castes to move from a region, resettle in a virgin area, and claim superior caste status. Through Sanskritization, ethnic groups on the fringes of caste society may acquire caste characteristics, so that Sanskritization played a cohesive role by allowing ethnic groups to be drawn in the fold of the caste system.

Cultural Aspects of Sanskritization

Srinivas pointed out the role of Sanskritization in India's struggle for freedom. Political leaders could mobilize support by invoking Hindu notions and images, whereby the nation was seen as *Bharat Mata* (Mother India), chained by the British regime. Gandhi contributed a unique interpretation of the Hindu idea of bhakti (devotion), ahimsa (nonviolence), karma, and dharma, to mobilize the masses.

Criticisms of Srinivas's Theories

Critics have pointed out that Sanskritization also expressed protest against and defiance of upper-caste norms. If caste members who were prohibited from wearing the sacred thread now deliberately flaunt it, they are debunking Brahmanical norms rather than conceding superiority to the Brahmans. If members of formerly untouchable castes wear leather sandals and prominent mustaches, they are openly defying caste codes.

The growth of the Dalit movement in the last several decades has also led to a critique of Sanskritization. The Dalits (the oppressed)—a term that now generally refers to former untouchables—have claimed that Sanskritization perpetuates upper-caste, if not Brahmanical, hegemony. If the Dalits are seen as merely aping upper-caste lifestyles, Sanskritization denies the cultural autonomy of Dalits and other Sudra castes.

Kanch Illiah has sharply differentiated the culture of the Dalits and that of upper-caste Hindus. According to him, notions of purity and impurity so strong among upper castes are not critical for Dalits. Illiah viewed Dalit culture as community centered, unlike the individualistic upper-caste culture. Dalit culture emphasizes sharing resources and communal festivities. Dalit women enjoy greater freedom than upper-caste women; they can easily divorce and remarry, even if they are widows. Dalit religious attitudes are worldly and pragmatic, unlike the ritualistic and otherworldly orientation of upper-caste religion. Dalits have no professional priests, and they value manual labor and productive work, unlike members of upper castes, who consider working with their hands defiling and degrading.

Illiah's criticism of Sanskritization extends to its tacit support of the movement to make the culture and ideology of Sanskritic Hinduism dominant in India. He saw Sanskritization as an intellectual attempt to appropriate indigenous non-Sanskritic cultures and to present them as inferior to Sanskritic Hinduism.

Changing Forms of Sanskritization

Despite these criticisms, Sanskritization seems not to have weakened in contemporary India. New strains have emerged to assert the identities of low-ranking castes. Even now members of prosperous and powerful low-ranking castes build temples for Hindu gods. Although the radical anticaste ideology of B. R. Ambedkar, a Dalit leader and intellectual, has spread rapidly among the Dalits, Sanskritization also continues among them. For example, when the Dalits opposed the participation of their women in the nude worship of the goddess Renuka in north Karnataka, they invoked upper-caste ideas of women's respectability. Despite their commitment to the Ambedkar legacy, upwardly mobile Dalits observe many upper-caste customs, such as the practice of dowry, which has replaced the Dalit tradition of bride price.

A militant and virulent form of Sanskritization is evident in India today. The Bharatiya Janata Party's movement professing *Hindutva* ideology (an ideology maintaining and promoting Hindu traditions and heritage) is another example. *Hindu Rashtra* (Hindu nation), a movement supported by militant organizations, aimed to build a temple for Rama by "liberating" his sacred birthplace from the Muslim Babri mosque that was built above it. In 1992, a massive demonstration in Ayodhya, the city of Rama, went out of control as rampaging mobs scaled the mosque's walls and destroyed it. A severe Muslim backlash and widespread Hindu-Muslim riots followed.

Many participants in this movement belong to upwardly mobile "backward castes," a term referring to castes in the hazy zone between ritually polluting and pure castes. This movement also shows that *dwija* castes are no longer role models. Now people who belong to backward castes want to emulate Sadhus and Sanyasins (renouncers), gurus, godmen, and godwomen. Leaders of this movement are propagators of militant Hinduism. They reject Brahmanical hegemony and the "tolerant" model of Hinduism, which they see as acquiescing to anti-Hindu forces. This militancy seeks to rectify perceived injustices that Muslims and Christians perpetrated on Hindus, and to mold India into a strong Hindu Rashtra (Hindu nation).

Politicized Sanskritization no longer brings about positional changes in the caste hierarchy in an accommodative fashion. Instead it amplifies antagonisms based on religion. Far from playing a cohesive role, the new Sanskritizations act as a divisive force threatening to rupture the secular social fabric of India.

M. N. Panini

See also: **Hindu Nationalism**

Further Reading

Illiah, Kanch. (1996) *Why I Am Not a Hindu: A Sudra Critique of Hindutva Political Economy, Culture, and Philosophy.* Calcutta, India: Samya.

Singer, Milton. (1972) *When a Great Tradition Modernizes.* New York: Prager.

Srinivas, M. N. (1969) *Social Change in Modern India.* Berkeley and Los Angeles: University of California Press.

———. (1986) *The Cohesive Role of Sanskritization and Other Essays.* New Delhi: Oxford University Press.

SANTAL The Santal (Santhal, Saonta, Saonthal, Saunta) are the largest tribal population in South Asia. They are found in Assam, northeastern Bangladesh, the Terai region of Nepal, and Bihar, West Bengal, and Orissa states in India. "Santal" is their common name; however, traditionally they refer to themselves as *Hor hopon ko* (human children) and *Hor ko* (men). A census in 1995 counted approximately 5.1 million speakers of Santal (an Austroasiatic language of the Munda family) in India, where the Santal are the largest tribal group. They are also the largest ethnic minority in Bangladesh, second in number only to the Bengali majority. Norwegian missionaries introduced writing in the late nineteenth century, so Santali literature uses Roman characters. More recently, the Santal use the Devanagari alphabet.

Santal villages typically number from four hundred to one thousand inhabitants. In larger urban areas, Santal prefer to live in the tribal or low-caste quarters. Houses are sturdy mud structures, often decorated with floral designs. Inside, there are at least two rooms: one for the ancestors and a granary protected by them. Located at the center of the house is a post (*khunti*) to which sacrifices are made upon building the house. It stands as a ritual center. Household units include the nuclear family and the sons and their wives. Adulthood is attained when boys are initiated at age eight or ten, when a maternal uncle brands their forearms with the five tribal marks. Muslim or Hindu specialists tattoo the girls at age fourteen, following the first menstruation ceremony. Grandparents are important in the cultural education of children. Modern education is not readily available to Santal children in outlying areas.

The Santal grow several varieties of wet rice in terraced fields or in irrigated fields. Leguminous vegetables, fruit, mustard, groundnuts, cotton, and tobacco are also important crops. As well, the Santal keep domesticated animals for products and food. Most of these activities are subsistence based; however, the Santal will barter or sell these goods at tribal markets in times of surplus. The marketing of agricultural and craft (basketwork, weaving, and leafwork) products is dominated by women, whereas men tend to handle the goats and cattle. Many Santal work as migrant workers on plantations and in mines and industries. Women commonly work as seasonal migrant workers in construction or mining. A small number of the educated elite serve as lawyers, doctors, politicians, and, for women, nurses, among other white-collar careers.

Santal are divided into 12 clans and 164 subclans, which are trace descent through the father and do not intermarry. There are considerable differences in the wealth and status of the clans and subclans. Senior members of local clans, religious specialists and, more recently, political leaders are sources of authority and have great status. At the village level, the headless village assembly is the most important political institution. At the intervillage level, the *pargana* (like a petty king) presides over the tribal court.

Many Santal are Hindu; some practice a tribal religion that features a supreme deity as well as lesser spirits that are generally benevolent. Some have also converted to Christianity. Village priests and their wives represent the original Santal couple and oversee festivals and annual ceremonies; they also perform religious duties within the village. The Santal healer and diviner (*ojha*) is responsible for folk and spiritual medical practices, although modern medicine is used as a backup on occasion.

Stephanie L. Ware

Further Reading
Archer, William G. (1974) *The Hill of Flutes: Life, Love and Poetry in Tribal India; A Portrait of the Santals.* London: Allen & Unwin.
Bodding, P. O. (1932–1936) *A Santal Dictionary.* Vols. 1–4. Oslo, Norway: Det Norske Videnskaps Akademi.
Duyker, Edward. (1987) *Tribal Guerrillas: The Santals of West Bengal and the Naxalite Movement.* Oxford: Oxford University Press.

SANTRI *Santri* (Malay from Tamil, "trainee religious scholar") is a term popularized by the anthropologist Clifford Geertz to describe orthodox Javanese Muslims in contrast with the heterodox *abangan*. The distinguishing feature of *santri* was their adherence to the Five Pillars of Islam—the confession of faith, regular daily prayer and attendance at the mosque on Friday, fasting during Ramadan (Puasa), pilgrimage to Mecca if possible, and payment of *zakat*, a religious tax on behalf of the poor. As *abangan* means "red," *santri* are sometimes described as *putihan* (white).

Islam penetrated Java gradually over several centuries, and many Javanese considered themselves Muslim while maintaining some beliefs from earlier religions. Sufi practice was especially tolerant of mystical elements from Hinduism and Buddhism and there emerged a complex continuum from entirely non-Islamic belief through beliefs influenced by Islam and thinly Islamic beliefs to various degrees of orthodoxy.

This continuum split into increasingly opposing camps in the early twentieth century with the emergence of modern political and religious associations in Indonesia. The Sarekat Islam (founded in 1909), the Muhammadiyah (1912), and the Nahdlatul Ulama (1926) were all formed partly to promote particular

views within orthodox Islam, but their existence tended to crystallize Islamic orthodoxy as a distinct stream (*aliran*) within Javanese political and social life. The *abangan*, by contrast, were represented by a series of explicitly secular parties, notable the prewar and postwar Partai Nasional Indonesia (PNI) and, from the late 1950s, the Partai Komunis Indonesia (PKI). Antagonism between *santri* and *abangan* was partly doctrinal (*santri* saw *abangan* as impious), partly cultural (*santri* saw *abangan* as dangerous practitioners of witchcraft), and partly class-based (large landholders and moneylenders in villages were often *santri*). Many *santri* therefore took part in the massacre of Indonesian Communists in 1965–1966.

The term *santri* is sometimes applied to orthodox Muslims from any part of Indonesia. There is a growing tendency, however, to use it only for the so-called traditionalist Muslims of Java. Traditionalists differ from modernists in placing much greater emphasis on the authority of local teachers (*kiai*) and scholars (*ulama*), generally based in *pesantren* (Islamic residential schools, especially in East Java), and proportionately less emphasis on global Islamic solidarity or on direct Qur'anic exegesis. Many such *santri* include in their beliefs *abangan* elements such as the *slametan* (ritual communal feast) and an awareness of spirits and magic.

Robert Cribb

Further Reading
Geertz, Clifford. (1960) *The Religion of Java.* Glencoe, NY: Free Press.

SAPPORO (2002 est. pop. 1.8 million). Sapporo is the capital city of Hokkaido, Japan's northernmost island. It is situated in the southwestern Ishikari Plain, which is one of the island's most productive agricultural areas. Sapporo's site originally was that of an Ainu village. The Ainu, most of whom live in Hokkaido, are an ethnically distinct indigenous people related to the ancient peoples of Siberia. The Meiji government established the Hokkaido Colonization Office in 1869, after changing the island's name from Ezo to Hokkaido. Charged with the island's administration and development, the office stripped the Ainu of their land and fishing and hunting rights.

The office brought in foreign advisers and founded Sapporo Agricultural College, which later became Hokkaido University. Some of these Westerners assisted with laying out the new capital of Sapporo on a grid system, with wide avenues and parks. Here the colonization office promoted the resettlement of unemployed samurai and others from the southern islands.

The office was closed in 1882 after a political scandal over the sale of its assets. In the same year, Hokkaido was divided into the three prefectures of Sapporo, Hakodate, and Namuro. Four years later these were done away with, and Hokkaido was reorganized as a single entity with a prefectural form of government in Sapporo, its administrative center.

After World War II, Sapporo developed into an important commercial and industrial city. The Tohoya mines of its western region produce zinc and lead. Its construction and machinery repair industries are supplemented by printing and food-processing plants, including those brewing Sapporo's noted beer. In February 1972, Sapporo hosted the eleventh Winter Olympic Games, the first to take place at an Asian site.

Visitors are drawn to the Hokkaido University campus and botanical gardens, Nakajima Park, Maruyama Zoological Gardens, and the Jozankei hot spring resort in scenic Hohei Gorge.

E. L. S. Weber

Further Reading

"Sapporo." (1993) *Japan: An Illustrated Encyclopedia*. Tokyo: Kodansha.

SARANGI

The *sarangi* is a bowed string instrument used to play Hindustani classical music of north India. The name *"sarangi"* goes back to the eleventh century, but the *sarangi* in use today developed at a later date. Initially used to accompany singers and dancers, the *sarangi* also became a solo instrument by the eighteenth and nineteenth centuries. The main instrumental repertoire is based on song-tunes. The very expressive, heartfelt sound of the *sarangi* might be compared with the human voice. Most *sarangi* players are often singers themselves.

The *sarangi* is manufactured from one piece of wood, with an obvious three-part construction: an almost rectangular sound box with concave sides covered in skin; a comparatively small, hollowed, thick neck, open at the back; and a peg box (containing movable pegs used for tuning) with a small decorative opening just above the nut (a fret on the upper neck). There are three gut melodic strings (c', g, c); a fourth, made of brass and with alternative tuning, is often added. These strings are fastened at the top to the pegs and at the bottom to the inferior string holder. Eleven to thirty metal sympathetic strings are attached to side pegs located on the neck. Melodic strings are stopped by placing one's fingernails at the side of the strings, often by touching the strings with the soft skin above the nails. This unique technique is akin to that of playing the Kazakh bowed string instrument the *qobyz*, as well as the Cretan *lyra* and the Bulgarian *gadulka*. Bows are made of rosewood or ebony, and the bowstring is of horsehair.

Less elaborate *sarangi*, often without sympathetic strings, are found in northern and northwestern India, Pakistan, and Afghanistan. The term *"sarangi"* is also used for a number of folk fiddles of South Asia and is sometimes applied to another kind of folk fiddle, for instance, the *sarinda*.

Aygul Malkeyeva

Further Reading

Bor, Joep. (1987) "The Voice of the *Sarangi*: An Illustrated History of Bowing in India." *Quarterly Journal, National Center for the Performing Arts* 15, 3–4; 16, 1.

Kothari, Komal S. (1968) *Indian Folk Musical Instruments*. New Delhi: Sangeet Natak Akademi.

———. (1977) *Folk Musical Instruments of Rajastan: A Folio*. Borunda, India: Rajastan Institute of Folklore.

SARAWAK

(2000 pop. 2 million). Situated in the northwest coast of the island of Borneo, Sarawak is the largest state in Malaysia and has a land area of 124,449 square kilometers. Its population is divided among thirty distinct ethnic groups. Most of these peoples, the

SARAWAK

GUNUNG MULU NATIONAL PARK—WORLD HERITAGE SITE

Gunung Mulu National Park on the Malaysian side of Borneo (the state of Sarawak) was designated a World Heritage Site in 2000. The park contains many natural wonders including the world's most cavernous mountain (some of which remains unexplored), millions of bats and swiftlets, and an abundance of different plant and animal species.

ancestors of whom emerged about 2000 BCE, are collectively referred to as Dayaks, and include the Ibans, Bidayuh, Kenyah, Kayan, Punan, Kelabit, Penan, and others. Malays and, later, Chinese, who arrived from about the mid-eighteenth century, constitute a large percentage of the coastal and urban population.

Sarawak, which formed a province of the Brunei Sultanate, began its history as an independent entity when the English adventurer James Brooke was granted the cession of territory between Tanjung Datu at the western tip of the state and the Samarahan River in the east of the Samaharan Division in 1841 in return for his services in helping Raja Muda Hassim of Brunei put down a riot in the province. Sarawak's colonial status came to an end with the proposal to form Malaysia in 1961, which the state joined on 16 September 1963. Sarawak's major sectors of economy are mining, agriculture, and forestry. Although its economy is expanding, Sarawak remains the least urbanized state in Malaysia. Sarawak is popularly known as "the land of the hornbill" in tribute to the majestic bird found there.

Shanthi Thambiah

Further Reading
Chater, W. J. (1969) *Sarawak Long Ago.* Kuching, Borneo: Borneo Literature Bureau.
Jackson, James C. (1968) *Sarawak: A Geographical Survey of a Developing State.* London: University of London Press.
Pringle, Robert. (1970) *Rajahs and Rebels: The Ibans of Sarawak under Brooke Rule, 1841–1941.* London: Macmillan.

SARDIS Sardis, once the terminus of the Persian royal road from Susa (in modern Iran), was an ancient city in today's Turkey, famed as the capital of the kingdom of Lydia. The city is situated on the Sart River (the ancient Pactolus), 90 kilometers inland along the road from Izmir. Hittite records show that King Tudhaliyas IV campaigned against the Assuwa in this area in the late second millennium BCE; pottery remains indicate that the Greeks captured Sardis at the time of the siege of Troy (c. 1200 BCE); the first ruling dynasty of the region claimed descent from Herakles.

Gyges (c. 680–652 BCE), of a Lydian tribe called the Mermnadae, murdered his predecessor and married the queen of the region of Sardis; the oracle at Delphi supported the usurper but predicted that the descendants of Herakles would be revenged. Gyges and his successor kings of Lydia minted the world's first coins, of gold stamped with a lion's head, exploiting the gold washed down by the Pactolus River. Commanding the road system and thus trade, Lydia expanded by capturing Ionian cities on the coast.

King Croesus (reigned 560–546 BCE) made peace with the Ionians and defeated the Cimmerians, nomads from the north, to reach a common frontier with Persia on the Halys River. Lydia blossomed under Croesus, and when the oracle at Delphi ambiguously advised the king that if he attacked the Persians he would destroy a great empire, Croesus invaded Persia. His invasion was quickly routed, and Cyrus, the Persian ruler, besieged and captured Sardis; Croesus's own empire, not that of the Persians, had been destroyed.

The Persian satrap of Lydia was unable to prevent Sardis from being burned during the Ionian revolt (499–494 BCE), but the kingdom was peacefully ceded to Alexander of Macedon after the battle of Granicus (334 BCE). After Alexander's death Sardis fell to the Seleucids.

In 189 BCE the battle of Magnesia was fought nearby, and the Pergamene kings ended Seleucid rule in Asia Minor. From 133 BCE Sardis fell under Roman rule; trade prospered; the population grew to 100,000, with a high Jewish and Christian element guaranteed by Imperial decree; and the city became the seat of one of the seven churches of Asia Minor, persisting in importance during the Byzantine era. Timur (Tamerlane) finally destroyed Sardis in 1402 CE.

The most striking feature of the extensive site is the steep acropolis with the ruins of the palace of Croesus, but most ruins are on low ground near the river. In 1910–1914, a Princeton University archaeological expedition excavated the huge temple of Artemis; work continued in the 1950s, and parts of the temple have been reerected. Other excavations have revealed the riverside site of the gold refinery with a shrine to

Cybele. A huge Roman civic center, currently under reconstruction, was erected after an earthquake in 17 CE and includes a gymnasium with baths surrounding a marble court. Rows of shops and a synagogue line a main street due north of a residential area.

Tumuli, or burial mounds, heaped above the tombs of the Lydian kings have been identified three kilometers east of the site in an area known as Bin Tepe (1,000 hills); the largest is the tomb of King Alyattes. The grave goods in the huge tumuli were raided long ago.

Kate Clow

Further Reading
Akurgal, Ekrem. (1969) *Ancient Civilizations and Ruins of Turkey.* Ankara, Turkey: Haslet Kitabevi.
Darke, Diana. (1989) *Discovery Guide to Aegean and Mediterranean Turkey.* London: Michael Haag.

SAREKAT ISLAM
The Sarekat Islam ("Islamic Association"), the first political party with Indonesian-nationalist leanings in the Netherlands' Indies, evolved out of an Islamic trade association, Sarekat Dagang Islam, which was founded in 1905 with the goal of advancing the interests of Muslim merchants over those of their Chinese competitors. In 1912 it was reorganized as Sarekat Islam (SI) by Omar Said Tjokroaminoto (1882–1935), with the much broader goal of improving the general welfare and religious life of its members. Aligning itself with the international socialist movement, SI began to demand self-government for the Dutch colony in 1916. Infiltration by Communists into SI led to a power struggle with its religious leaders, and the party split in 1921. The left wing formed the "red SI," which later became the Sarekat Rakjat ("People's Association"), an organ of the Indonesian Communist Party. Although considerably weakened by the split, SI, which now called itself Partai Sarekat Islam Indonesia, survived until 1973, when it was coercively incorporated into the Partai Persatuan Pembangunan by the Suharto regime. After the fall of Suharto in May 1998, the ensuing democratization of Indonesia brought about the reemergence of many political parties. The Sarekat Islam reemerged as two distinct political parties, Partai Syarikat Islam Indonesia and Partai Syarikat Islam Indonesia 1905.

Martin Ramstedt

Further Reading
Dahm, Bernhard. (1969) *Sukarno and the Struggle for Indonesian Independence.* Ithaca, NY, and London: Cornell University Press.

Kahin, George McTurnan. (1952) *Nationalism and Revolution in Indonesia.* Ithaca, NY: Cornell University Press.
Pompe, Sebastiaan. (1999) *De Indonesische Algemene Verkiezingen 1999.* Leiden, Netherlands: KITLV (Royal Institute of Linguistics and Anthropology) Uitgeverij.
Vlekke, Bernard H. M. (1959) *Nusantara: A History of Indonesia.* The Hague, Netherlands, and Bandung, Indonesia: W. van Hoeve.

SAREZ LAKE
Sarez Lake in the southeastern Pamir Mountains of Tajikistan is the largest natural sediment reservoir in Central Asia. Located east of the Pamir crest in the semiautonomous Gorno-Badakshan region, the lake formed when a 1911 tremor shook loose 6 billion metric tons of debris, damming the Murgab River. The Usoi Dam—named after the village it buried—is the highest dam, natural or manmade, on Earth. The water level rose 240 meters (787 feet) in three years and inundated 60 kilometers (37 miles) before filtration through a subterranean outlet reestablished the river. The current estimated lake area is 2 square kilometers (.7 square miles), with a maximum height above the original valley floor of 500–700 meters (1,640–2,300 feet). The lake level currently rises up to 20 centimeters (8 inches) annually.

Failure of the Usoi Dam is a potential cataclysmic disaster that would alter the economy and sociopolitical environment of Tajikistan. In a worst-case scenario that assumes collapse of the dam, a catastrophic outburst flood from Sarez Lake would destroy the villages and infrastructure in the Amu Dar'ya basin between the lake and the Aral Sea. The size and complexity of this problem will also almost certainly require financial and technical assistance from the international community. Close monitoring and an early warning system appear the most likely precautionary measures because increasing the stability of the dam is too costly. At stake are many lives, national pride, future economic development, and significant freshwater resources.

Stephen F. Cunha

Further Reading
Alford, Donald, Stephen F. Cunha, and Jack D. Ives. (2000) "Lake Sarez, Pamir Mountains, Tajikistan: Mountain Hazards and Development Assistance." *Mountain Research and Development* 20, 1 (February).
Cunha, Stephen F. (1994) "Summits, Snow Leopards, Farmers, and Fighters: Will Politics Prevent a National Park in the High Pamirs of Tajikistan?" *Focus* 44, 1.

SARIT THANARAT
(1909–1963), Thai prime minister. Sarit Thanarat graduated from the military

Sarit Thanarat with Robert F. Kennedy in Bangkok in February 1962. (BETTMANN/CORBIS)

academy of Chula Chom Klao in 1929. He was an efficient and ambitious army officer. Commander of the First Division stationed in Bangkok, Sarit supported military dictator Pibul Songgram (ruled 1948–1957). Sarit served as defense minister and commander in chief from 1947 to 1957. He engineered a nonviolent coup that deposed the government of Pibul in 1957. Following a year of the caretaker government, in October 1958 Sarit declared himself the prime minister of Thailand. Sarit proceeded to rule the country with an iron hand, banning opposition parties and newspapers and suspending constitutional amendments, while simultaneously seeking to stamp out Thailand's opium trade, end police corruption, and battle organized crime.

Sarit tried to build up traditional Thai values. Promotion of Buddhism and cultivation of the monarchy were the main features of his policies. Sarit cleverly utilized the monarchy both to enhance his own legitimacy and to strengthen the institution of the monarchy itself. Sarit collaborated closely with the United States to contain communism in Southeast Asia. Bilateral relations between Thailand and the United States were further strengthened by the Rusk-Thanat Agreement of 1962, which represented an American guarantee of Thai security. Sarit supported the right-

ists in Laos in their fight against the Communist-oriented leftist organization Pathet Lao. His economic policies resulted in U.S. and Japanese investment, rise of a new wealthy class due to land speculation, and sustained economic growth of 5 percent per year. The legacy of Sarit after his death in 1963 was Thai involvement in the Vietnam War and the establishment of development-oriented technocratic agencies.

Patit Paban Mishra

Further Reading

Chaloemtiarana, Thak. (1979) *Thailand: The Politics of Despotic Paternalism*. Bangkok, Thailand: The Social Science Assocation of Thailand.

Fineman, Daniel. (1997) *A Special Relationship: The United States and Military Government in Thailand, 1947–1958*. Honolulu, HI: University of Hawaii Press.

Tarling, Nicholas, ed. (1992) *The Cambridge History of Southeast Asia*. Vol. 2. Cambridge, U.K.: Cambridge University Press.

Wyatt, David K. (1986) *Thailand: A Short History*. New Haven, CT: Yale University Press.

SARNATH   Sarnath, 10 kilometers north of Varanasi (Benares) in Uttar Pradesh State, India, is the site of the deer park (still extant) where Siddartha Gautama the Buddha (c. 566–486 BCE) preached his first sermon nearly 2,500 years ago. The message he revealed there formed the basis for the entire future development of Buddhism, hence its and Sarnath's tremendous importance. In Sarnath, Buddha also established the order of monks, the Sangha, which is today the world's oldest still-functioning association. Dhamekh Stupa, a Buddhist shrine constructed in the fifth and sixth centuries CE, marks the spot where this sermon was supposed to have been given. Other important monuments are five monasteries; a column erected by the Emperor Asoka (reigned c. 273–232 BCE), with an inscription threatening dissident monks; the main shrine (third century BCE and fifth century CE) and the Dharmarajika Stupa (attributed to Asoka, but enlarged until the twelfth century). A modern addition is the superb Archaeological Museum nearby. It contains the famed lion capital, which has become a symbol of modern India.

Paul Hockings

Further Reading

Agrawala, V. S. (1984) *Sarnath*. Delhi: Archaeological Survey of India.

Michell, George. (1989) "Sarnath." In *The Penguin Guide to the Monuments of India*. New York: Viking, 186–189.

SAROD A stringed instrument from northern India that is three to three and a half feet long. The instrument has a round head, with a resonating chamber made of teak wood and a parchment or skin belly soundboard that is attached to a triangular neck and fingerboard. The fingerboard has a thin polished metal sheet covering and is fretless, allowing the player to execute *meend*s, or sliding of the pitch. The modern sarod has twenty to twenty-five metal strings; fifteen *tarab* (sympathetic) strings; four main strings; three *chikari* (*jhala*), raised strings that provide a rhythmic drone; and three *thaat* strings that are tuned to the raga that is being played. The instrument is played with a plectrum, fashioned from coconut shell, in the right hand, while the left hand is used on the upper neck of the instrument. The sarod has its origins in Indian and Afghan lutes, and, more particularly, the *rebab* of the Middle East. It also was developed from the *sursringar* and *veena* stringed instruments. The present form of the sarod developed in the nineteenth century. The word sarod is linked to the Sankrit *shorode* (good noise), the Persian *sarrod* (melody), and Arabic *sahrood* (music) as well as to the word *swarode* (music) from Bengal.

Stacey Fox

Further Reading
Krishmaswamy, S. (1967) *Musical Instruments of India*. New Delhi: Publications Division, Government of India.

SARYSHAGAN Saryshagan, a town in eastern Kazakhstan, was chosen as the site of a ballistic missile test range during the Cold War. It is located on the southwestern shore of Lake Balkhash, in the province of Qaraghandy, one thousand miles downrange from the launching site of Kapustin Yar and remote yet accessible from the Trans-Siberian Railway. Saryshagan has been a testing range and research facility since the mid-1950s; the United States learned of it only in 1958. During a series of atmospheric nuclear tests in the years 1961–1962, several nuclear weapons were detonated directly above Saryshagan. Since the collapse of the Soviet Union in 1991, Russia has maintained control of the facility, conducting missile tests as late as 1999. However, negotiations are ongoing to turn control of the Saryshagan range over to the government of Kazakhstan.

Andrew Sharp

Further Reading
Yost, David. (1988) *Soviet Ballistic Missile Defense and the Western Alliance*. Cambridge, MA: Harvard University Press.

SASAGAWA RYOICHI (1899–1995), Japanese right-wing leader and postwar businessman. In 1931, Sasagawa took leadership of the Kokusui Taishuto (National Essence Mass Party). In 1933, with other party members, he secretly carried out a plan to assassinate the politician Wakatsuki Reijiro (1866–1949). During the national *kokutai* ("polity") clarification campaign (1935–1936), this same group was engaged in a campaign of terror against the scholar Minobe Tatsukichi (1873–1948). After Japan's surrender to the Allied Forces, Sasagawa reorganized his National Essence Party into a new right-wing organization; both the old and the new party were outlawed. In 1945, he was arrested as a Class A war criminal and spent three years in Sugamo Prison. After his release, Sasagawa became an adviser to Zen-Nippon Aikokusha Dantai Kaigi (National Council of Patriotic Societies). Beginning in 1951, he was engaged in the motorboat racing business. He established the Japan Motorboat Racing Association and, in 1962, became chairman of the newly created Japan Shipbuilding Industry Foundation. In 1986, he established the Sasagawa Peace Foundation, the funding for which comes from motorboat racing revenues. He was twice decorated by the Showa emperor (1926–1989), first with the First Order of the Sacred Treasure in 1978, and then with the First Order of Merit with the Grand Cordon on the Rising Sun in 1987.

Nathalie Cavasin

Further Reading
Dubro, Alec, and David E. Kaplan. (1986) *Yakuza*. London: Futura.

SATI Sati (suttee) is the practice of a wife burning herself to death on the funeral pyre of her husband. The custom is linked to Hindu India but throughout history has also been reported elsewhere, from ancient Egypt and Greece to pre-Christian northern Europe. Within Hinduism, sati is not a required act; it is considered to be voluntary. Despite considerable popular interest outside India, sati has always been quite rare and generally confined to northern India and especially Rajasthan. Prior to its being banned by India's British colonial rulers in 1829, only several hundred cases were reported each year. Since then, few cases have been reported, although several drew media attention in the 1990s.

The origins and reasons for sati are unclear and subject to dispute among scholars. Evidently, it is a product of Hinduism, as the practice is mentioned and tales of sati are set forth in early Hindu sources. The first documented case occurred in 908 CE. The custom was noted by several early travelers to India including the Portuguese trader Barbosa in 1510 and the Italian Pietro Della Valle in 1623. While sati was never required of widows, such behavior was considered prestigious, and a woman who committed sati was seen as brave and self-sacrificing. Furthermore, the act was thought to bring salvation to her deceased husband and to release herself and her family from the cycle of death and rebirth.

Sati was most common among the Rajput warrior caste in northern India. About forty cases have been reported since 1947, and twenty-eight of them have been in Rajasthan. The reasons for the association of sati with the Rajputs is unclear, although some experts believe that is reflects the value they place on bravery and self-sacrifice. It is also true that the frequency of sati has varied over time in India, with more cases reported during times of social unrest. From the viewpoint of feminist scholars, it represents the traditional repression of women in Hindu India as well as the difficult lives often facing widows.

Sati was banned by the British in 1829, with the support of the anti-Hindu Brahmo Samaj movement. However, it was not until after independence in 1947 that the practice almost completely disappeared. Since then, there have been a few reported cases, with perhaps the sati of Roop Kanwar in Rajasthan in 1987 drawing the most attention. She was an educated eighteen year old married to her husband for only a few months when he died. There were charges that she was coerced or forced to commit sati by Hindu traditionalists in the village, and the incident was cited by some as evidence of the continuing repression of women in India. In 1996 the Indian Court acquitted those accused of assisting her and ruled that sati was a Hindu social tradition.

Further Reading

Dalrymple, William (1997) "The Survival of Suttee" *World Press Review* 44, 7: 16–17.

Hawley, John S. (1994) *Sati, The Blessing and the Curse: The Burning of Wives in India.* New York: Oxford University Press.

SATO EISAKU (1901–1975), prime minister of Japan. Sato Eisaku was prime minister of Japan from November 1964—following Ikeda Hayato's sudden resignation for health reasons—until July 1972, making him the longest-serving premier in the country's history. During his tenure, Sato realized the normalization of relations with South Korea in 1965 and the return

Prime Minister Sato in San Francisco in November 1969 following talks with U.S. President Richard Nixon. (BETTMANN/ CORBIS)

of Ogasawara in 1968 and Okinawa in 1972, issues that had been pending since the 1952 peace treaty. In 1967 he announced Japan's three non-nuclear principles, for which he received the Nobel Peace Prize in 1974. Domestically, however, Sato was unpopular due to problems of pollution and overcrowding, as well as his support of America's involvement in the Vietnam War.

The younger brother of Kishi Nobusuke, Sato was born in Yamaguchi Prefecture in 1901, making him the first postwar prime minister born in the twentieth century. After graduating from Tokyo Imperial University in 1924, Sato joined the ministry of railways, rising to vice minister. In 1948 he was made cabinet secretary in the second Yoshida cabinet, and in 1949 successfully ran for the Diet.

In early 1954, his career was tainted when he was reported to have taken bribes in the Shipbuilding Scandal, but he was saved by the intervention of the prime minister and later served in several cabinets.

Sato was known for his skilled management of people, balancing of factions, and his "wait and see" style of politics.

Robert Eldridge

SATPURA RANGE   The Satpura Range is a mountain range running east-west across the southwestern part of Madhya Pradesh State of India, but reaching westward through southern Gujarat almost to Broach and the Gulf of Khambhat, and eastward into the new state of Chhattisgarh. It takes its name from the small town of Satpura. The range is at most 150 kilometers wide and approximately 1,000 kilometers in length, but not very high: The eastern peak of Amarkantak, in Bilaspur District, reaches 1,092 meters. It has Hindu temples and waterfalls, and one basin near a temple is considered to be the source of the Narmada River. East of this point there are a few higher peaks, the highest being Dhokgarh, and the Satpuras merge into the Maikala and Hazaribagh Ranges.

The westerly part of the range forms the divide between the valleys of the Tapti and Narmada Rivers. In this area is a small hill station, Pachchmarhi, at about 1,150 meters. East of Khandwa, an important junction town, the Satpuras are here called the Mahadeo Hills, and further east they open up to form a broader plateau, the Chhindwara Plateau, which lies between Nagpur and Jabalpur cities. Though most of the Satpura Range falls within Madhya Pradesh, it effectively forms the border between that state and northwestern Maharashtra. Geologically, in the west the Satpuras are a steep-sided Deccan lava block. More easterly stretches are a great window of Archaean and Middle Gondwana rocks, plateaus formed from thick masses of red sandstone.

Paul Hockings

SATYAGRAHA   Mohandas K. Gandhi (1869–1948) devised a system of civil disobedience called satyagraha (from the Sanskrit *satya*, meaning "truth," and *agraha*, meaning "persistence") in 1894, during his stay in South Africa. At that time, Indian residents and indentured laborers suffered many indignities at the hands of the white authorities there, and Gandhi, a lawyer, sought to improve conditions for Indians. Satyagraha involved the application of soul-force, which was based on truth and nonviolence, to remove these grievances.

After he returned to India, Gandhi led his distinctive, nonviolent protests against the excesses of British rule in India, beginning in 1920. In its initial stages, satyagraha involved noncooperation, but later it took on tones of civil disobedience. This style of passive resistance was ultimately successful, because it put the use of force by the police and others in authority against these resisters in such a bad light. Satyagraha was thus a major factor in the march toward Indian independence in 1947. Later the method was adopted by Martin Luther King (1929–1968) for the civil-rights movement in the United States

Paul Hockings

Further Reading
Gandhi, Mohandas K. (1970) *An Autobiography: The Story of My Experiments with Truth*. Boston: Beacon Press.

SAYYID AHMAD KHAN   (1817–1898), Indian Muslim educator. Often given the honorific title of Sir Sayyid, Ahmad Khan is probably the most famous Indian Muslim educator. Since the seventeenth century, his family had been closely connected with the Mughal emperors, holding important positions in the Indian Muslim administration. However, in 1838, on the death of his father, who received an allowance from the Mughal court, Ahmad Khan's family faced financial difficulties, which forced him to enter the service of the East India Company. Starting as a simple clerk in the Delhi court of justice, within a few years he attained the rank of *munsif* ("subjudge").

While he held this position, Ahmad Khan studied education, religion, history, archaeology, and politics. In 1847, he published the famous *Athar al-sanadid* (Monuments of the Great). Between 1858 and 1861, he wrote two pamphlets about the so-called Great Mutiny, the 1857 insurrection against British rule in India, during which he had remained loyal to the East India Company. In these pamphlets—which influenced the subsequent policy of the colonial British government—he analyzed the reasons for the insurrection, blaming both Indians and British.

Ahmad Khan's most significant achievements were in the field of education. During the 1850s and 1860s, he established schools and a scientific society to diffuse the Urdu and English languages. After a visit to England in 1869–1870, in 1878 he established Muhammadan Anglo-Oriental College, modeled after the colleges of Oxford and Cambridge. Established in Aligarh, it was elevated to university rank in 1920 and became the most famous and innovative Muslim educational institution of the Indian subcontinent. In the meantime, he had launched an influential journal,

Tahdhib al-Akhlaq (Social Reform), and established the All-India Muhammadan Educational Conference to diffuse modern sciences and knowledge and to reform traditional Muslim religious ideas, harmonizing them with Western thought.

His attempts to demonstrate the conformity of modern sciences and doctrine with the principles of Islamic faith provoked harsh reactions from the traditional *ulama* and *faqih* (experts of religious law); their reactions were particularly violent against his demythologizing approach to the Qur'an and his "rationalistic" approach toward religion.

Loyal to his view of peaceful coexistence of Hindus, Indian Muslims, and the British, Ahmad Khan opposed the Indian National Congress and its political ideas. He argued that for Muslims of the Indian subcontinent, education was more important and effective than politics.

Riccardo Redaelli

Further Reading
Ikram, Sheikh Mohammad. (1950) *Makers of Pakistan and Modern Muslim India.* Lahore, Pakistan: M. Ashraf.
Baljon, Johannes Marinus Simon. (1949) *The Reforms and Religious Ideas of Sayyid Ahmad Khan.* Leiden, Netherlands: E. J. Brill.
Troll, W. Christian. (1978) *Sir Sayyid Ahmad Khan: A Reinterpretation of Muslim Theology.* New Delhi: Vikas.

SCIENCE. See **Abacus; Gunpowder and Rocketry; High-Technology Industry—Asia; Intellectual Property—Asia; Korea Institute of Science and Technology; Magnetism; Science Towns—Korea; Science, Traditional—China.**

SCIENCE TOWNS—KOREA *Yeongu danji* are South Korean science towns, also known as science parks. Such parks can be either private undertakings, as in Silicon Valley in the United States, or public undertakings and generally have four major sets of political and economic objectives: (1) forge links among universities, private industrial enterprises' research, and industrial production operations, and state-run research and development facilities to gain synergistic effects through frequent contact; (2) promote knowledge-based businesses in high technology and new ("sunrise") industries; (3) facilitate the transfer of technology from research and development to production operations and encourage corporate start-ups, spin-off companies, new corporate divisions, and "incubator" companies where researchers gain experience before launching their own

enterprises; and (4) pursue a grab bag of state policy goals, such as promoting export industries and boosting economic development in laggard regions.

South Korea's Taedok Science Town (TST) was established in Taejon by the Ministry of Science and Technology in 1973 to concentrate state-run laboratories and to provide a conducive site for corporate research and development. Due to the energy crisis and budgetary problems late in the Fourth Republic (1972–1980), major construction was delayed until the 1980s. TST was not formally dedicated until 1992, and major corporate research did not begin until 1994. The Korean Advanced Institute of Science and Technology, Korea's premier technical institute, has its main campus in TST. The LG Group's biotechnology research since the mid-1990s has been centered at TST. During the 1980s, the government decided to establish a science town in each of the major regions of Korea, but currently only the small Kwangju Science Town in South Cholla Province has been opened.

Joel R. Campbell

Further Reading
Choi, Hyung Sup. (1986) "Science and Technology Policies for Industrialization of Developing Countries." *Technological Forecasting and Social Change* 29: 225–239.
———. (1986) *Technology Development in Developing Countries.* Tokyo: Asian Productivity Organization.
Lee, Chong-ouk. (1991) "Stages of Economic Development and Technology Policy: The Experience of Korea." *Science and Public Policy* 18, 4: 219–224.
Taedok Science Town Administration Office. (1996) *Taedok Science Town.* Taejon, South Korea: Ministry of Science and Technology.

SCIENCE, TRADITIONAL—CHINA As elsewhere in the premodern world, scientific thought in China emerged with early attempts to think about the natural world systematically and abstractly. One of the earliest approaches to organize the natural and phenomenological world is found in the ancient divination text known today as the *Book of Changes (Yi jing).* Although popular writers today find antecedents for many modern scientific ideas in this ancient text, to early Chinese science and many other areas of Chinese philosophy, the *Book of Changes* offered a way of organizing and classifying natural phenomena—the first step in any scientific tradition. As many of the terms used in this system of classification came from ancient mystical traditions of shamanism and divination, assigning them strict definitions is particularly for Western students of Chinese science and life. The terms "yin and yang," *wu xing*, and *qi* have been the subject of a great deal of debate in the vain quest for precise Western equivalents. The fact that these terms are still used in schools of traditional medicine in China today, however, testifies to their usefulness in Chinese science.

From these beginnings, four kinds of organizing principles emerged to form the basis of all premodern Chinese scientific thought: Heaven and Man, yin-yang duality, the *wu xing* or Five Phases, and *qi*.

Heaven and Man

The relationship between Heaven and Man is central in Chinese scientific thought and is expressed in several different ways. In Chinese astronomy and astrology, man is not only part of the natural world, but heaven above also reflects and responds to the human world below. The second-century BCE *fenshu* (field allocation theory maps) divided the heavens first into political regions in the human world and then into specific agencies within the imperial government. Particular constellations corresponded to specific government ministries, and the unpredicted appearance of an object in a ministry's constellation was seen as an ominous sign.

Chinese medicine interprets the relationship between nature and man in terms of microcosm and macrocosm. The human body could be interpreted as both a natural world in miniature and an integral part of a larger natural world. As a result, ailments and disease are diagnosed as either dysfunctional imbalances within the microcosm of the human body itself or imbalances between the body and the external world.

Yin and Yang

"Yin" and "yang" are early terms used in Chinese thought used to express the basic duality of all phenomena. The earliest examples can be found in the *Book of Changes*, and some writers maintain that conscious expression of the notion of polar dualities can be found in the art of the Shang dynasty. The terms "yin" and "yang" are used to express the observation that many things have a dual nature: there is both dark and light, cold and hot, female and male. The Chinese characters for yin and yang literally describe the shaded and illuminated sides of a hill. In medicine the terms are most frequently used as adjectives, qualifying things based on their observed qualities, such as yang *qi* or yin *qi*.

The Five Phases

The Five Phases (*wu xing*) are used in Chinese science to further describe and classify phenomena, especially processes. An emphasis on process and interaction is one of the distinguishing characteristics of Chinese science and medicine. While much of early Western medicine stressed the mechanical relationships of body parts and organs, Chinese medicine looked at how the many characteristics of the body and nature interacted and sought ways to describe and classify these interactions and processes. Often confused with the Aristotelian "elements," the Five Phases in China are the metal phase, wood phase, water phase, fire phase, and earth phase. The word *xing*, translated here as "phase," means "to do or act, action, activity." These five phases or activities of *qi* are often used to explain cyclical transformations found in medicine and elsewhere.

Qi and the Five Phases

Qi is the most important term in Chinese science and one of the most difficult to translate. Most scholars today choose not to translate or interpret the term, but some of the better Western equivalents for the term *qi* include "matter–energy" or "vital energy or substance." Nathan Sivin explains that *qi* is simultaneously "what makes things happen in stuff" and "stuff in which things happen." *Qi* can either take form and become visible and substantial or be an agent that activates processes and influences their development. As a result, the concept of *qi* is central in Chinese medicine. *Qi* circulates throughout the body as a kind of vital energy, but unlike blood it has no substance. Instead *qi* activates and influences how the blood and organs function. Often *qi* is beneficial, but sometimes *qi*, particularly from some outside source, can upset the balance within the body to create some from of ailment. The responsibility of the Chinese doctor is to diagnose this imbalance and take corrective measures.

The Five Phases describe five aspects of *qi* and their cyclical relationship. The wood phase does not describe the texture of *qi*, but *qi* that is growing and developing a certain potential. When it moves on to the next phase, fire, it realizes this potential and becomes active. The fundamental sequence of the Five Phases is sometimes called the cycle of mutual production. The order of cycle is based on early empirical observations, but in practice its use is much more theoretical. When wood is burned it produces fire; fire produces ash (earth); ores from the earth become metal; water condenses on cold metal; and wood can grow with water. The logic behind this sequence is more mnemonic than practical. What was important for the Chinese scientist or doctor was the relationship between the different aspects of *qi*.

All these basic concepts, yin and yang, the Five Phases, and *qi* can be combined to build a complex theoretical structure for the patterns and relationships Chinese scientists and doctors found in nature. One important point to note is that even though Chinese thinkers confronted the same physical universe—human bodies in China differ in only superficial ways from bodies elsewhere in the world—Chinese science and medicine developed a unique theoretical structure for understanding the phenomena found in the universe, a system of understanding that Chinese scientists employed and refined for almost two thousand years.

Paul Forage

Further Reading

Ho Peng Yoke. (1985) *Li, Qi, and Shu: An Introduction to Science and Civilization in China.* Seattle, WA: University of Washington Press.

Nakayama Shigeru and Nathan Sivin, eds. (1973) *Chinese Science: Explorations of an Ancient Tradition.* Cambridge, MA: MIT Press.

Needham, Joseph. (1969) *The Grand Titration: Science and Society in East and West.* Toronto: University of Toronto Press.

———, Wang Ling, and Derek de Solla Price. (1986) *Heavenly Clockwork: The Great Astronomical Clocks of Medieval China.* 2d ed. Cambridge, U.K.: Cambridge University Press.

Sivin, Nathan, ed. (1977) *Science and Technology in East Asia.* New York: Science History.

Temple, Robert. (1986) *The Genius of China: 3,000 Years of Science, Discovery, and Invention.* New York: Simon and Schuster.

SCULPTURE—SOUTH ASIA

The beginnings of South Asian sculpture may be found in the early Indus-Sarasvati civilization of the second millennium BCE. The mature phase of this civilization (2500–1700 BCE) carries evidence of a high level of technical knowledge and skill but, curiously, a lack of large structures, such as temples or palaces, or monumental sculpture. From its ruins, small figurines in stone or cast bronze or copper have been recovered, as have terra-cotta animals and female figures, the last presumed to be cultic objects. A large number of steatite (soapstone) seals with impressions of bovine unicorns, buffaloes, bulls, tigers, rhinoceroses, and composite animal figures and some enigmatic human forms, surmised to have commercial or ritual uses, have been recovered.

Little material evidence has been found from the period intervening between the Indus Valley civilization and the Maurya empire of the third century BCE. The reasons for this absence are unclear, but the use of perishable materials of construction and strictures on representation are possible explanations. Vedic rit-

A stone relief of footprints on a pillar at the Great Stupa of Asoka in Sanchi, India. (ADAM WOOLFITT/CORBIS)

ual culture is presumed to have been established around 1500 BCE, followed by the contemplative esotericism of the Upanishads (Vedic speculative texts) around 800 BCE and the birth of Buddhism and Jainism in the sixth century BCE.

Stone Monuments

In 326 BCE, Alexander of Macedon's incursion into the northwest border of the South Asian subcontinent, part of his conquest of the extensive Achaemenid Persian empire of Darius III, created a political vacuum that was swiftly filled by the first Mauryan king, Candragupta (reigned c. 322–c. 298 BCE). Candragupta Maurya's imperial ambitions were styled after those of Darius and Alexander, and to his successor Asoka is attributed the Persian practice of building stone monuments and the incorporation of Achaemenid and Hellenistic motifs and devices in his structures. In 265 BCE Asoka (reigned c. 273–232 BCE) embraced Buddhism and proceeded to mark numerous prominent pilgrimage routes and Buddhist centers throughout his vast

A sculpture from the eleventh century in India showing Siva appearing out of the linga. (GIAN BERTO VANNI/CORBIS)

empire with tall polished stone pillars inscribed with edicts expounding the Buddhist law of righteousness. Though this practice and the literary style of the inscribed proclamations are reminiscent of an Achaemenid device for establishing the law of the emperor, the custom also extends an ancient indigenous Vedic tradition of the cosmic pillar, Skambha.

Asoka's pillars are topped by a capital with an inverted lotus base, which supports a circular abacus carved with four royal animals and four wheels, on which stands a quartet of stylized addorsed (back-to-back) lions, supporting on their heads an enormous wheel representing the Buddhist law (*dharmachakra*). The stylized lions are again derived from Achaemenid sources. Achaemenid and Hellenistic decorative motifs, such as rosettes, palmettes, spirals, and reel-and-bead patterns, also appear in other structural remains from Asoka's time, attesting to the cosmopolitan nature of his court and its culture.

Other monuments attributed to Asoka's patronage include Buddhist stupas, or relic-mounds, and rock-

cut caves, serving as shelters for itinerant renunciants, both of which remained important settings for sculpture for a thousand or more years. Asoka's monuments were created in sandstone and finished to a high polish, a technique that was lost to South Asia after Mauryan times.

A number of massive frontal stone sculptures depicting male and female figures (*yaksha*s and *yakshini*s, respectively) also remain from Mauryan times. These are representations of supernatural elementals that had been in popular propitiatory worship for protection, fertility, or wealth. These beings, as well as gods of the Vedic pantheon, became assimilated into early Buddhism and soon reappeared iconically as Buddhist threshold deities, protectors of devotees, bestowers of auspiciousness, and servants of the Buddha.

Monastic Monuments

The Mauryan dynasty lasted barely fifty years after the death of Asoka and was followed by the Brahmanical Shunga dynasty (c. 185–73 BCE) in northern South Asia. Buddhist lay patronage, however, had developed a strong foundation, and monastic monuments continued to flourish during the second century BCE. Typical examples of the sculpture of this period are found among the remains of the stupa of Bharhut. The circular stone railing *(vedika)* enclosing the stupa has carved roundels on its horizontal and vertical elements, often elaborated into ornate lotuses. Some of these contain carvings of human heads or animals at their center, and some are filled in with narrative scenes from the life of the Buddha or episodes from tales of his past lives as told in the *jataka* texts. At this stage, Buddha's figure is never depicted and is represented by symbols such as the Bodhi tree, the Wheel of the Law, or a stupa, according to narrative context. The relief carving is shallow and frontal and harks back to a tradition of carving in wood. On the vertical entrance posts of the *vedika* are chiseled large figures of *yaksha*s and *yakshini*s, standing on animal or dwarf mounts. The *yaksha*s are shown with their hands folded *(anjali mudra)* in a gesture of self-offering, while the *yakshini*s pose angularly with one leg bent outward and a hand raised to hold a fruiting bough. Such *yakshini*s are known as *shalabhanjika*s, fertility figures believed to cause trees to blossom at their touch, now emblems of creativity and auspiciousness at the service of the Buddha and the Buddhist community.

This post-Mauryan Buddhist relief tradition reaches its full maturity around the first century BCE, as evidenced in the gateways *(torana)* of the Mayastupa (Great Stupa) at Sanchi. This stupa, at the center of a monastic complex, was established by Asoka and fur-

Sculptured gate of the Great Stupa in Sanchi, India. (ARCHIVO ICONOGRAFIC, S.A./CORBIS)

ther enlarged during Shunga times. Around 100 BCE, four great gateways were provided at the cardinal entrances to this stupa. The horizontal and vertical elements of these gateways carry carvings thematically similar to those at Bharhut. However, these carvings demonstrate much greater assurance: The narrative arrangements, particularly on the extended horizontal architraves, show a refined clarity of form, a varied mobility of posture, and a judicious use of devices to enhance the sense of depth where necessary. Large and powerful figures of elephants, lions, or dwarfs are deeply carved out on the vertical pillars and seem to support the upper portions. But perhaps the most perfect realizations on these gates are the *shalabhanjika*s, now almost disengaged from the stone, the rhythmic swing of their voluptuous forms naturalistically posed against the fruiting branches. The perfect combination of ecstatic sensuousness and contemplative repose in these figures becomes one of the aesthetic ideals of South Asian sculpture, seeking fulfillment in different forms through history.

Figurative Depictions

Around the beginning of the Christian era, the Kushan dynasty (78–200 CE), originating in the borderlands of Central Asia and China, established itself as the imperial power in northern South Asia. The most famous king of this dynasty was Kanishka (c. 120–160 CE). It is around this time that the first figural depictions of the Buddha make their appearance, almost simultaneously in the northwest province of Gandhara and the Gangetic metropolis of Mathura. Reasons for this iconic appearance are unknown but may be related to doctrinal shifts in Buddhism from the more austere Theravada toward the devotionalism of Mahayana, with its emphasis on worship and its expanded pantheon of bodhisattvas. A consistent iconography finds expression in both the Gandhara and Mathura Buddha images, though they are stylistically divergent. The Gandhara Buddha is modeled after a Greco-Roman Apollonian prototype, while the Mathura figure derives from indigenous *yaksha* traditions. In both cases, the Buddha is draped in monastic robes *(sanghati)*, has a halo behind his head, and is shown with a cranial protuberance *(ushnisha)* symbolizing transcendental knowledge, and with a whorl of hair between the eyebrows *(urna)*. He is seated in meditation or standing erect with his right hand raised in a gesture of bestowing fearlessness *(abhaya mudra)*.

But whereas a predominant naturalism marks the features and costuming of the Gandhara figure, the Mathura image is characterized by its simplified

A statue of the river goddess Ganga in Kathmandu, Nepal. (MICHAEL FREEMAN/CORBIS)

reign, patronage, and courtly culture are credited with the development of the classical style in South Asian art. This was the Gupta dynasty (c. 320–c. 500 CE), whose most famous king was Candra Gupta II (c. 375–415 CE). During this period, the major center for the production of Buddha images in the east shifted from Mathura to Sarnath, and the Kushana Buddhas were replaced stylistically by a type characterized by its idealized soft modeling and the self-absorbed tranquillity of its features. A standardization and compaction of iconic elements and a vocabulary of distinctive hand gestures (mudras) marking special occasions accompany these images. Bodhisattvas, *yakshas*, *nagas* (mythical snake deities), and their consorts all undergo a similar elaboration and stylistic change, the Buddha and several bodhisattvas also appearing in bronze casting.

A proliferation of Hindu deities, organized spatially in integrated contexts of ritual worship, was produced in this period. Initially, the sites for these reliefs were niches in cave-temples, but the stand-alone Hindu temple in stone also evolved at this time and henceforth became the setting for sculpture. The Guptas being followers of Vishnu, images of this deity and his incarnations (avatars), particularly the boar *(varaha)*, lion-man *(narasimha)*, and dwarf *(vamana)*, find frequent representation. An increased emphasis on goddesses and other female images also occurred at this time. Apart from Durga, the Seven Mothers (Saptamatrika) were often depicted, as were the river goddesses Ganga and Jamuna. By the sixth century, Buddhism also witnessed the apotheosis of feminine power, in the form of Tara, the consort of the bodhisattva Avalokiteshvara.

A developed Saivite iconography, depicting mythical episodes connected with Siva and his consort Parvati, also found expression in sites of worship by cults such as the Pashupatas. Images of Ganesha, Skanda, Parvati, and Ganga were given prominence here along with Siva's bull mount, Nandi, his dwarf-retinue of the *gana*s, and several other gods and goddesses. Saivite cultic placement consigned the abstract phallic icon of Siva to the sanctum, faced from the entrance of the temple by Nandi, and surrounded along a clockwise circumambulatory path *(pradakshinapath)* by niches sheltering other gods and goddesses and scenes showing the pastimes of Siva. An image of Ganesha invariably initiated this procession, and Skanda or Durga often concluded it.

Stylistically, all these figures evolved an aesthetic by the end of the fifth century that shared the monumental repose of the Gupta Buddha but integrated this

rounded features—its see-through draping and its monumentality and physical tension projecting power. Bodhisattva figures in the characteristic styles of Gandhara and Mathura also appear at this time, wearing regal accouterments and carrying their distinctive attributes—Maitreya with his water pot, Vajrapani with the thunderbolt, Padmapani with his lotus and the seated Buddha in his headdress.

The Kushan period also yields the earliest Brahmanical images in stone, representing the three major cults of Hindu worship—Siva in the form of the phallus, or lingam, symbolizing infinite creative potential; Vishnu as the deity of universal protection, related to the Vedic solar godhead; and the Mother Goddess, particularly in her form as Durga, the destroyer of evil. Other prominent Brahmanical deities represented include Surya and Skanda.

Emergence of Classical Style

During the fourth century, a new Hindu imperial dynasty established itself in northern South Asia. Its with a power of massiveness and restrained ecstatic delight. Contemporaneously, in the Deccan, a related but more voluptuous aesthetic developed in Buddhist and Hindu figural expression, under the patronage of the powerful Vakatakas, related by marriage to the Guptas. Examples of the full fruition of the Vakataka Buddhist style are evident at the cave excavations at Ajanta, while the early excavations at nearby Ellora or at the island of Elephanta, datable to the early sixth century, show examples of Deccan Saivite sculpture of this period at its ripeness.

Temple Imagery: A New Fluidity

Though the stand-alone Hindu stone temple first appeared in South Asia under the Guptas, it evolved into maturity in the sixth century under the Western Chalukyans in the southern Deccan and through the seventh century in southern India under the Pallavas. Sculpture during this period continued to develop local variants of the Gupta iconography and style, but there was also a marked tendency in these southern centers toward an infusion of greater plastic dynamism into the figures. A fine example of this may be observed in a seventh-century panel depicting Durga battling the buffalo demon Pallava Mamallapuram. The iconic stillness and massiveness of Gupta deities is here replaced by dramatic interest and a capture of power in motion. Subsequent sculpture in South India continued to develop in fluidity, reaching perhaps the zenith of its integration of stillness and movement in the tenth-century image of the dancing Siva, Nataraja, developed in south India under Chola (c. 850–1200) patronage.

From the tenth to the twelfth centuries, South Asian sculptors evolved such consummate skill and facility in carving that sculpture during this period

Reclining Buddha in the Ajanta Caves, Maharashtra, India. (LINDSAY HEBBERD/CORBIS)

spills out of the measured enclosure of niches and dominates the temple surface. Khajuraho under the Chandella kings, Orissa under the Gangas, and the Hoysala kingdom of the southern Deccan bear witness to this trend, where temple architecture adapted itself to accommodate a prolific presentation of imagery. The temple, as an integral whole, projects the impression of the mighty immobile cosmic Mount Meru, which contains the multitudinous, varied activity of the world at its base. The sculpted forms of deities and celestial denizens stand or interact in various fluid postures, expressing the ecstatic repose of transcendental action. In the case of Orissa and Khajuraho, a strong erotic element also finds expression, indicating the prominent presence of Tantric cults. This high achievement of the successful marriage of static soaring temple forms and teeming mobile surfaces marks the final creative outburst of the South Asian tradition in sculpture.

Buddhism withdrew from India by the thirteenth century, and gradual Islamic dominance of northern South Asia from the twelfth century inhibited the production of large-scale Hindu temple environments. The Vijayanagara kingdom of the south and other pockets that offered resistance to Muslim conquest managed to continue the tradition until the sixteenth and seventeenth centuries, but with a progressive diminution of ideational creativity.

Debashish Banerji

Further Reading
Bajpai, K. D. (1997) *Five Phases of Indian Art*. Jodhpur, India: Rajasthan Vidya Prakashan.

Coomaraswamy, Ananda K. ([1927] 1972) *History of Indian and Indonesian Art*. Reprint. New York: Dover Publications.

Craven, Roy C., Jr. (1997) *Indian Art*. Rev. ed. London: Thames and Hudson.

Harle, J. C. ([1974] 1996) *Gupta Sculpture*. Reprint ed. Oxford: Oxford University Press.

Huntington, Susan L. ([1985] 1999) *The Art of Ancient India: Buddhist, Hindu, Jain*. Reprint. New York and Tokyo: Weatherhill.

Kramrisch, Stella. ([1946] 1996) *Indian Sculpture*. Reprint ed. New Delhi: Motilal Banarsidass.

Rowland, Benjamin, Jr. ([1953] 1970) *The Art and Architecture of India—Buddhist, Hindu, Jain*. Reprint ed. London: Pelican Books.

———. ([1963] 1968) *Evolution of the Buddha Image*. Reprint. New York: Penguin Books.

Saraswati, S. K. ([1957] 1975) *A Survey of Indian Sculpture*. Reprint ed. Calcutta, India: Coronet Books.

Williams, Joanna G. (1982) *The Art of Gupta India: Empire and Province*. Princeton, NJ: Princeton University Press.

SEHWAN (2002 pop. 38,000). The city of Sehwan, Pakistan, is located in the lower Indus valley, 135 kilometers from the city of Hyderabad. Sehwan is one of the oldest settlements in the region and was once protected by a large fort whose remains exist to the north of the city. La'l Shahbaz Qalandar, a Sufi mystic who emigrated from Sistan in Iran in the mid-thirteenth century, is buried here. His 'urs (wedding) ceremony is celebrated from the eighteenth through the twentieth day of the month of Shaban. The shrine is famous for the *dhammal* (ritual dancing) that takes place every evening and involves the beating of vast drums.

The shrine of La'l Shahbaz Qalandar, which is on the site of an old Shiva sanctuary, was originally built in 1356 by the Indian monarch Feroz Shah Tughlaq (reigned 1351–1388) and has since been renovated many times. In the 1970s the prime minister of Pakistan, Zulfiqar Ali Bhutto (1928–1979), built a new entrance to the south, which is marked by a pair of gold doors presented by Muhammad Reza Shah Pahlavi (1919–1980), the shah of Iran. The main entrance is through a monumental portal that is covered in blue and white tiles and has corner minarets. The arcaded courtyard leads into a domed enclosure under which the saint is buried.

Kishwar Rizvi

Further Reading
Schimmel, Annemarie. (1980) *Islam in the Indian Subcontinent.* Leiden, Netherlands: E. J. Brill.

SEIFULLIN, SADUAKAS (1894–1938), Kazakh writer, poet, editor, dramatist. Saduakas Seifullin was born to a poor nomadic family in Karaganda. Initially educated in his native village, in 1908 he was sent by his parents to study at the Russian-Kazakh school in Akmolinsk. Between 1913 and 1916 he attended school at the Omsk Teachers' Seminary, where he helped create the youth groups Birlik (Unity) and Zhas Kazak (Young Kazakh). Following the February Revolution, he participated in numerous revolutionary activities, joining the Bolsheviks in February 1918. In June 1918 he was arrested by political opponents but avoided execution and eventually escaped. He was elected to the Kazakh Party central committee, and from 1925 to 1937 he was the editor of the party's newspaper, *Engbekshi Kazak* (Kazakh Worker). In addition, he taught for many years at the Kazakh State Pedagogic Institute in Almaty and helped edit the literary journal *Adebiet maidany* (Literary Front). He published numerous poems and prose during these years, including the collection of poems *Asau tulpar* (Irritable Steed), considered by many scholars to be the first work to employ Soviet-style realism and motifs in the Kazakh language. He is best known, however, for his 1926 semiautobiographical novel *Ternistyi put'* (The Difficult Path, published in Kazakh as *Tar zhol taighaq keshu* [Narrow Road, Unsteady to Cross]), based on his exploits during the revolutionary years. It describes his arrest, imprisonment on the "death train," escape, and subsequent political activities during the Russian civil war. Despite being honored by the Soviet government with the Order of Workers of the Red Banner, in 1938 he was arrested at the height of the Stalinist purges and executed. On 23 March 1957 he was rehabilitated.

Steven Sabol

Further Reading
Kakishev, Tursynbek. (1967) *Saken Seifullin.* Almaty, Kazakhstan: Rauan.
Seifullin, Saken [Saduakas]. (1984) *Izbrannoe (Stikhotvoreniia I Poemy).* Almaty, Kazakhstan: Zhazushy.
———. (1977) *Tar zhol taighaq keshu: Tarikhi-memuarlyq roman* (Narrow Road, Unsteady to Cross). Almaty, Kazakhstan: Zhazushy.
———. (1964) *Ternisty Put'* (The Difficult Path). Almaty, Kazakhstan: Kazakskoe Gos. Izdatel'stvo.

SEJONG, KING (1397–1450), Choson dynasty ruler. King Sejong was the fourth king of the Choson dynasty (1392–1910) of Korea. He is remembered for his contributions to Korean culture, such as establishing the Hall of Worthies (Chiphyonjon), a group of scholars in the king's employment. King Sejong assigned these scholars the task of inventing a native writing system to replace literary Chinese as the official writing system and may have personally participated in this effort. This new script was promulgated in 1446 as *Hunmin chongum* (Proper Sounds to Instruct the People) and developed into the modern Korean alphabet/syllabary known as hangul. King Sejong had hoped to enable the masses to become literate and toward that end also commissioned many classics and Buddhist texts to be translated into the native script. But because literati shunned the new writing system, it was used mostly by upper-class women and commoners of both sexes.

King Sejong's other cultural accomplishments included the commissioning of numerous histories such as *Koryo sa* (History of Koryo), annals, geographies, and manuals. He was also a patron of the arts and sciences, promoting advances in agriculture, astronomy, meteorology, medicine, movable type, and military technology. King Sejong also reformed government and defended Choson against Japanese pirate raids. Because of these varied accomplishments, he is considered one of Korea's most important kings.

Jennifer Jung-Kim

Further Reading
Saccone, Richard. (1993) *Koreans to Remember: 50 Famous People Who Helped Shape Korea*. Elizabeth, NJ: Hollym.
Eckert, Carter J., Ki-baik Lee, Young Ick Lew, Michael Robinson, and Edward W. Wagner. (1990) *Korea Old and New: A History*. Seoul: Ilchogak.

SELF-CENSORSHIP   Self-censorship (also called autocensorship or internal censorship) is the conscious suppression of one's ability, right, or freedom to express oneself. Individuals, groups, organizations, or institutions may deliberately withhold or suppress their ideas, emotions, opinions, values, information, or intentions, which they consider to be in conflict with their own interests or those of others.

While self-censorship is usually deliberate, it is often not voluntary. In Asia, for instance, state dictatorship imposes considerable self-policing on individuals and institutions. By contrast, in Western democracies, the market and its profit-making imperatives play a prominent role in both censorship and the self-regulation of expression. Even when freedom of expression is guaranteed in constitutions and laws of a country (e.g., Japan after the end of the Allied Occupation in 1952), there are codes that protect morality and censor obscenity and, by doing so, impose self-censorship.

Many proverbs in Asian languages warn people of the dangers of unrestrained expression; for instance, "The red tongue lets the green head be chopped off" (Persian); "He who speaks truth is kicked out of nine towns" (Turkish); "Mouths are to eat with, not to speak with" (Japanese). In spite of these warnings, there is considerable resistance against self-censorship. Figurative language, humor, jokes, cartoons, rumors, and gossip are some of the vehicles the public and the mass media use to express ideas that may otherwise be violently repressed.

Amir Hassanpour

Further Reading
Gomez, James. (2000) *Self-Censorship: Singapore's Shame*. Singapore: Think Centre.

DEATH BY A THOUSAND CUTS

"The censorship process [in Indonesia] begins with the first script, most of whose contents are scratched out and amended. Then the script is returned. And so it goes on, back and forth, until the final product becomes celluloid—and then it's censored again so it can be distributed. In my own case, I sometimes wondered whether the final product was really my own film. . . . Producers and script writers know that films that reflect social realities are going to be cut so they practise a lot of self-censorship. Over the years that pressure builds up, with the result that many of our directors—including me—have lost their creativity."

Source: Sophan Sophiaan. (1997) "Death by a Thousand Cuts." *Index on Censorship*. Vol. 26, no. 2: 73.

SELF-STRENGTHENING MOVEMENT (1861–c. 1895). The self-strengthening movement, which began in 1861, was an effort by the Qing dynasty (1644–1912) of China to restore power to resist Western encroachments, especially after the Second Opium War, which resulted in the burning and looting of the Summer Palace in Beijing by British and French forces.

The goal of the movement was to employ Western technology while retaining traditional Chinese values to meet the new imperialist threat. It was assumed that China could adopt technology and not the values and philosophies that produced that technology. Thus, from 1861 until 1895, the Qing government and various provincial officials launched a series of projects, including creating Zongli Yamen (a foreign affairs office), establishing the Jiangnan Arsenal, the Fuzhou Dockyard, the Nanjing Arsenal, and the Tianjin Machine Factory, sending Chinese students to the United States, and constructing the Beiyang Fleet. The series of projects clearly centered on a program of military modernization initially and subsequently on an effort at economic self-strengthening, all designed to improve the nation's position vis-à-vis the imperialist powers.

The time period of the movement roughly approximates that of the Meiji Restoration in Japan, and it is instructive to note differences. Japanese leaders were more willing to throw off the past, change the structure of government and the structure of society because of the powerful desire to resist imperialist encroachments. By contrast, Chinese leaders were unwilling to change dramatically the system of government or the social hierarchy and thus truly struggled at the margins. China's defeat by Japan in the Sino-Japanese War (1894–1895) exposed the weaknesses of the nearly four-decades-long self-strengthening movement.

Charles Dobbs

Further Reading

Feuerwerker, Albert. (1975) *Rebellion in Nineteenth-Century China*. Ann Arbor, MI: University of Michigan Press.

Wright, Mary C. (1966) *The Last Stand of Chinese Conservatism: The T'ung-chih Restoration, 1862–1874*. New York: Atheneum.

SEMIPALATINSK MOVEMENT The Semipalatinsk movement, officially known as the Nevada-Semipalatinsk-Mururoa International Movement to Halt Nuclear Weapons Testing, was the first Soviet antinuclear movement organized in 1989. It is credited with closing the Semipalatinsk nuclear test site in the former Soviet Union. Created in the then Soviet Republic of Kazakhstan and named after the main nuclear test sites in the United States of America (Nevada), the Soviet Union (Semipalatinsk, Kazakhstan), and French Polynesia (Mururoa Atoll), the movement galvanized large public support, halting eleven of eighteen planned Soviet nuclear tests in 1989 and eventually forcing the closure of the Semipalatinsk site in August 1991.

The movement's leader, Olzhas Suleimenov, a Kazakh poet and politician, was motivated by the devastating environmental and health damage caused by the 1986 Chernobyl nuclear disaster in Ukraine and Belarus and the potentially similar harm being caused by nuclear tests in Kazakhstan. Despite the dangerous effects of nuclear testing, little information was available to the general public within the closed political system of the Soviet Union. However, as the system gradually began to open in the 1980s under then party secretary-general Mikhail Gorbachev, information became more available, prompting protests.

The origins of the movement lay in a televised speech made by Suleimenov in February 1989, during which he jettisoned a scripted poetry reading in favor of releasing information on the detrimental effects of nuclear testing and asked for an immediate public demonstration in Almaty, Kazakhstan. After the success of the first demonstration, further street protests were organized in cities across the USSR, including Moscow, demanding an end to nuclear testing. The movement quickly gathered mass support, claiming membership of several hundred thousand members.

While the movement's main objective was a closure of the test site in Kazakhstan, it also pressed for a parallel closure of the Nevada test site in the United States. Other goals included protection of human rights, protection and regeneration of the environment, and the prohibition of production and storage of nuclear weapons, radioactive and poisonous waste, and other weapons of mass destruction. There were cooperative projects between Nevada-Semipalatinsk and several other organizations around the world, and international branches of the movement itself were founded in the United States, Germany, Turkey, and Mongolia.

The movement's main activities ceased soon after the August 1991 decision to halt nuclear tests conducted at Semipalatinsk. A total of 498 nuclear tests were conducted on the site between 1949 and 1991. The movement subsequently turned its attention toward both the end of world nuclear tests and aid to the citizens of Kazakhstan affected by the four decades of nuclear testing. The former leader, Suleimenov, is an ambassador for the now-independent Republic of Kazakhstan.

Carter Johnson

Further Reading

Chastnikov, I. Y. (1996) *Echo of Nuclear Tests*. Almaty, Kazakhstan: Almaty Press.

U.S. Center for Soviet-American Relations. (1991) "Nevada-Semipalatinsk—The Soviet Union's Anti-Nuclear Movement: An Interview with Amlaz Estekov." In *Cleaning Up the Environment in the Soviet Union and Eastern Europe* 1, 4. Washington, D.C.: Center for American-Eurasian Studies and Relations.

Zholamanova, Lira. (2000) "Environmental Impact of Semipalatinsk Nuclear Complex." *Central Asian Journal of Economics, Management, and Social Research* 1, 1.

SENDAI (2000 est. pop. 1 million). Sendai is the capital of Miyagi Prefecture and the largest city in northeast Japan. The city extends from the Pacific coast on the east to the mountainous border of Yamagata Prefecture on the west. Founded as a castle town in 1601, it lies at the foot of Aoba Castle, constructed by Date Masamune (1567–1636), a feudal lord who gained sway over most of the Tohoku region.

Quickly becoming the administrative, economic, educational, and cultural center of the region, Sendai is the major metropolis of the northern five prefectures of Honshu. The center of the city was completely destroyed during World War II, although the Osaki Hachiman Shrine and Toshogu Shrine survived. While retaining the original attractiveness of its tree-lined boulevards and the natural environment of the Hirose River, Sendai is convenient and modern. Connected domestically by air and Shinkansen (superexpress train) and internally by a new subway system, the city ranks high nationally in terms of quality of life. The site of the prestigious national Tohoku University and a large number of private colleges and universities, Sendai is referred to as an "academic city." Regional offices of major government agencies and banking and trading companies are located here. Commercial activities center on petrochemicals and marine and agricultural products. Sendai draws tourists especially for the elaborate decorations of the Tanabata Festival, 6 to 8 August.

James M. Vardaman, Jr.

Further Reading
Vardaman, James M. (2001) *In and around Sendai*. Sendai, Japan: Keyaki no Machi Co.

SEOUL (1999 pop. 10.3 million). Seoul, the capital of South Korea (Republic of Korea), has an area of 605 square kilometers and is one of the most densely populated cities in the world. Archaeological remains indicate that people inhabited the Seoul region at least as far back as the Neolithic period, although it is likely that prehistoric settlement dates back to Paleolithic times. Throughout history, the region has had numerous names. It was known as Hansong, the capital of the Paekche kingdom (18 BCE–663 CE); Hanyang during the Unified Shilla period (668–935 CE); and Yangju and Hanyang during the Koryo period (918–1392). With the establishment of the Choson dynasty (1392–1910), King T'aejo moved the capital from Kaegyong (present-day Kaesong) to Hanyang in 1394. The region was also called Hansong, and to ensure auspiciousness and longevity for the new Choson kingdom, the city was carefully planned according to geomantic principles, which dictate the proper placement of man-made structures among natural surroundings. An 18-kilometer wall was built to surround the new capital, but the city was ravaged by the Hideyoshi and Manchu invasions of the late sixteenth and early seventeenth centuries and gradually rebuilt by the eighteenth century. The capital grew rapidly

Seoul is a city that many people compare to New York City, a view supported by this 1990 photo of large, modern buildings in downtown Seoul. (BOHEMIAN NOMAD PICTUREMAKERS/ CORBIS)

from the late nineteenth century with the introduction of modern transportation and communication systems.

Under Japanese occupation (1910–1945), the city was called Kyongsong and downgraded from capital status because of the loss of Korean national sovereignty. In 1945, the city's capital status was restored and the city was renamed Seoul, meaning "nation's capital." Seoul twice fell to North Korean forces during the Korean War (1950–1953). The capital has undergone rapid urbanization in the postwar decades, especially with the industrialization of the 1970s and infrastructural improvements of the 1980s in anticipation of the 1988 Seoul Olympics.

The city has grown vastly beyond its original walls and today has 25 autonomous districts (*ku*) and 522 wards (*dong*). The Han River divides the city into nearly equal northern and southern sections. The city also has eight mountains, the most visible being Mount

Nam in the center of the city. In 1949, Seoul was designated as a "special city" and became administratively independent from surrounding Kyonggi Province. Kyonggi Province and Seoul's satellite cities make the Seoul metropolitan area the nation's center of politics, economy, and culture.

Jennifer Jung-Kim

Further Reading
Korean Overseas Information Service. (1993) *A Handbook of Korea*. Seoul: Korean Overseas Information Service.
Nilsen, Robert. (1997) *South Korea Handbook*. Chico, CA: Moon Publications.
Storey, Robert, and Alex English. (2001) *Korea*. 5th ed. Berkeley, CA: Lonely Planet Publications.

SEOUL NATIONAL UNIVERSITY Seoul National University (SNU) is a major institute of higher education in South Korea, recruiting the best high school graduates in the nation. Various ranking indexes have placed the university first among universities in Korea and fortieth in the world for 2001.

SNU was established as the first national government-funded university in modern Korea in 1946. As of 2000, the total student enrollment is 12,882: 20,470 at the undergraduate level and 9,412 at the graduate level. Women students constitute 41 percent of the total number. The faculty numbers 1,891. In recent years, SNU has made efforts to internationalize its programs to attract foreign students. Currently about six hundred foreign students from fifty-two countries enroll in various academic programs.

For the bachelor's degree, a four-year residence is required. Medical and dental students are required to spend two additional years for premedical and pre-dental education, respectively. Both master's and doctoral programs have a two-year residence requirement. The academic year starting March 1 consists of two semesters: spring semester from March through mid-June and fall semester from September through mid-December. Admission is given only for the spring semester.

SNU offers programs for bachelor's, master's, and doctorate degrees at sixteen colleges as well as four graduate schools covering almost every academic and professional area, including public health, environmental studies, and international area studies. Especially strong fields are law, business administration, medicine, and engineering, which has expanded tremendously since 1980. SNU also includes the International Vaccine Institute, a United Nations–related

research center established in 1999. SNU graduates play leading roles in various fields in Korean society, especially in government, large enterprises, and law.

Like most universities in Korea, restructuring has been underway at SNU since the early 1990s. Matters in dispute are the reorganization of academic structure and evaluation of faculty members.

Kim Shinil

Further Reading
Seoul National University. (2001) *Bulletin, 2001–2002*. Seoul: Seoul National University.
Seoul National University. (2001) *General Information for International Students*. Seoul: Seoul National University.

SEPAK TAKRAW Sepak takraw is the official, international name for the Southeast Asian sport in which teams compete by moving a small ball back and forth over a net without using their hands or arms. The name is derived from *sepak* which means "kick" in Indonesia, Malaysia, and Singapore and *takraw* which means "ball" or "woven ball" in Thailand. The sport is the modern, competitive version of an ancient Southeast Asian game in which participants stand in a circle and keep the ball in the air, using only their feet, legs, and bodies. It is popular in Thailand, Malaysia, Indonesia, Singapore, Myanmar, Vietnam, the Philippines, southern China, and more recently, in the West. The game is called *sepak, takraw, sepak takraw, sepak raga, sipa, ching long, kator*, and *tago*, depending on the nation. The sport of sepak takraw was first included in the Asian Games in 1990 as a men's sport; a women's event was added in 1998. The governing body for the sport, the International Sepak Takraw Federation, is working to have it accepted as an Olympic sport.

The origin of the game is unclear. A similar game was played in Japan and south-central China over a thousand years ago, but it is likely that the games played in Southeast Asia developed indigenously, and likely in more than one place, anywhere from five hundred to a thousand years ago. The game emerged as a village recreational activity in which boys or men stood in a circle and kicked a woven rattan ball to one another while attempting to keep it from touching the ground. Other varieties of the game include kicking the ball into a hoop, racing while keeping the ball in the air, and keeping as many balls in the air as possible at one time. The modern game is similar to volleyball, with a rectangular court and net, teams of three players each, formal rules, three hits per side, 15-point

Thai and Brunei players compete in takraw at the Southeast Asian Games in Brunei in August 1999. (REUTERS NEWMEDIA INC./CORBIS)

games, and a two-out-of-three set format. Modern balls are made out of plastic rather than the traditional rattan, to maintain uniformity in size, shape, and weight.

Supporters believe it only a matter of time before sepak takraw is accepted as an international sport beyond Southeast Asia. It is a source of considerable pride in Southeast Asia, and debates continue—especially between Malaysia and Thailand—over which nation can claim ownership of the sport.

David Levinson

Further Reading

Trevithick, Alan. (1996) "Takraw." In *Encyclopedia of World Sport: From Ancient Times to the Present*, edited by David Levinson and Karen Christensen. Santa Barbara, CA: ABC-Clio, 1010–1014.

SERALIN, MUKHAMMEDZHAN (1872–1929), Kazakh educator, poet, writer, publisher, social activist.

Mukhammedzhan Seralin was born in 1872 in Kustanay uezd (Kustanay region), Turgai oblast. His father, Seraly, was a well-known *aqyn*, or poet-bard, who died at the age of forty, when Seralin was only three years old. His father left the family in financial debt but with a rich legacy of music and poetry. Seralin's mother was related to a wealthy Tatar merchant, Mollakhmet Iaushev, who provided her family some financial and material support. When Seralin was eight years old, he was enrolled in the local *madrasah* (Muslim school) in Troitsk, considered the best school for Kazakhs in the oblast. He studied there from 1880 until 1887.

Seralin was influenced by the writings of many Tatar reformers, in particular Shihabeddin Merjani (1815–1889), a nineteenth-century intellectual who urged his fellow Tatars to take pride in their national heritage. Seralin was deeply influenced by the Muslim reform movement Jadidism (*usul-u-jadid*, new method), devoted to secular education among the Muslims of czarist Russia. In 1891 he undertook his own "to the people" mission and traveled to a small *aul* (small nomadic unit) situated on the shore of the Aral Sea, teaching there for several years. While there he completed his first collection of poems, *Top zharghan* (often translated as "Worthless Horse"). It was initially rejected by the government's censor but was allowed to appear in print in 1903. Also in 1903 he published his second work, *Gulkashima*, a collection of poetry based upon traditional themes. While *Top zharghan* dealt with a historical topic, his second collection of poems focused on a contemporary issue that concerned many Muslims throughout the Russian empire: the question of *qalyng* (bride price). Written in 1901, it depicts a cruel system that forced young girls to marry against their will. Seralin believed it was a harmful custom that must cease.

In 1905 Seralin was involved in various undertakings related to the revolution, helping to form the Kustanai branch of the Russian Social Democratic Revolutionary Party. In 1911 he realized his long-held dream to publish a Kazakh-language periodical, *Ai qap*, which was one of the most influential prerevolutionary Kazakh periodicals. The journal published domestic and foreign news, editorials and readers' letters, scholarly articles, book reviews, feuilleton, and poetry. It ceased publication in 1915. Following the 1917 Russian Revolution, Seralin became active in the Bolshevik Party. In 1919 he was made a member of the Bolsheviks' Kazakh Revolutionary Committee and selected to the editorial board of the Bolsheviks' new newspaper in the steppe, *Ushqyn* (The Spark). In the 1920s Seralin served in many capacities in the Soviet government, in particular as the editor of a regional newspaper, *Aul*, and on educational committees. He was so active that by 1924 there were thirty villages in Kazakhstan named for Seralin. In 1925 poor health made him retire from active service, and he returned to his birthplace. He died in 1929.

Steven Sabol

Further Reading
Elenov, Zhumash. (1947) *Burynghy* Ai qap *zhurnalynyng redaktory Mukhametzhan Seralinning omir baiany* (A Biography of the Former Journal *Ai qap* Editor Mukhammedzhan Seralin). Almaty, Kazakhstan: Akademiia Nauka.

Seralin, Mukhametzhan. (1985) *Topzharghan: shygharmalary* (The Nag: Collected Works). Almaty, Kazakhstan: Zhazushy.

Zimanov, Salyk, and Kabdesh Idrisov. (1989) *Obshchestvenno-politicheskie vzgliady Mukhamedzhana Seralina* (The Sociopolitical Views of Mukhammedzhan Seralin). Almaty, Kazakhstan: Akademiia Nauka.

SERICULTURE—CHINA

Although its exact origins are unknown, experts agree that sericulture (the production of raw silk from silkworms) began in China about 2500 BCE. Chinese mythology supports this view. In one popular myth, the empress of one of the legendary emperors is credited with the intensification of mulberry tree cultivation, the breeding and raising of silkworms, and the invention of the loom in 2640 BCE. This myth is important because it gives public recognition to the major role women played in silk production and processing.

Silk production was an important part of the rural economy, and over the centuries many technical advances speeded up the production of silk thread, though weaving remained time-consuming and difficult until the advent of mechanized looms in the twentieth century. Though silk was primarily produced in rural areas, it was usually woven in urban centers for the imperial court or wealthy city dwellers, and a great deal of raw silk cloth was paid as taxes to the central government.

Silk production spread from China to India in about 140 BCE and a few centuries later to Japan. It spread to Europe in about 550 CE, when two Persian monks were asked by the Byzantine emperor Justinian I to smuggle silkworms from China. Silk was such an important product in ancient times that the major trade route between East Asia, West Asia, and Europe was called the Silk Road. The Chinese traded silk for wool, gold, and silver. At the beginning of the twenty-first century, China remains the world's major producer of silk, producing about 80 percent of the world's silk each year. However, the development of synthetic fibers such as rayon (which went into production in 1910) and nylon (which went into production at the end of the 1930s) has diminished the demand for silk clothing. Silk continues to be, as it was in ancient times, a luxury item, and it is no longer a major export for China.

The Silkworm

Silk production is largely determined by the life cycle of the silkworm (*Bombyx mori*). Silkworm caterpillars hatch from eggs and require large quantities of mulberry leaves for food to reach full growth. This growth period lasts thirty-four or thirty-five days and is interrupted by several dormant periods. At the end of this stage of their cycle, the caterpillars spin cocoons of a single strand of silk thread that can be from six hundred to nine hundred meters long.

Under natural conditions, uncontrolled by human beings, the adult moths would then emerge from the cocoons and reproduce. In terms of silk production, however, the emergence of the moth from the cocoon is a disaster: the emerging moth breaks the silk strand and renders it virtually useless for cloth production. Most moths are killed while still in the cocoon, with only a few allowed to reach maturity for breeding purposes.

The Mulberry Tree

Most phases of the silkworm's life cycle can be controlled by the careful regulation of mulberry leaves (the silkworm's sole food) and temperature. From an early period, mulberry trees were planted in orchards and new varieties were developed. By the twelfth century, the most crucial development had occurred, with the perfection of a technique for grafting a particularly leafy variety of tree onto the hardier trunk of a separate variety. Agricultural treatises of the twelfth century describe the technique and recommend that silk producers everywhere adopt it. The use of these grafts permitted two crops of leaves a year in the central region of China and three in the southern regions.

Controlling the Process

Providing the worms with leaves was always of great importance, and in the fifth century a technique was devised to regulate the hatching time of the eggs to coincide with maximum leaf production. The eggs were bathed in cold water to lower their temperature and delay hatching, often for as long as twenty-one days. The addition of periods of warming and cooling in the thirteenth century improved the technique, with

SERICULTURE IN BURMA

Although sericulture is most closely associated with China, it was and is found in neighboring nations as well. The following firsthand account describes traditional silk breeding as it was carried out in Burma (now Myanmar) in the late 1800s.

Neither the worm nor the mulberry are indigenous to the province but were, most probably, imported from China by the valley of the Irrawaddy and not across the hills from India. The Burmese mulberry, which has not been identified by any competent botanist but which has been pronounced not to be the *Morus Indica*, is a thin, lanky shrub throwing out several vertical shoots from near the ground and growing to a height of eight or ten feet. It will not flower and is therefore propagated by cuttings. After about three years a plantation ceases to bear good and succulent leaves and is then abandoned or the plants are uprooted. . . . Should the mulberry leaves fail the larvae are fed the *Brousonettia papyrifera*, but then the silk produced is comparatively worthless. The silk is of a very rough and inferior description but well suited for the silks made on the ordinary loom of the country.

All the processes of breeding the worm and winding the silk are carried on in the ordinary smoke-begrimed and dirty bamboo houses of the people. . . . When the moths have laid their eggs, which takes about a day, they are wrapped up and left to themselves. In about eight days the larvae appear and the cloth being opened are swept with a feather on to a tray. The produce of one circular cartoon will, when the worms are full-grown, more than fill a large tray two or three feet in diameter. About twelve hours after they are hatched the worms are fed with finely-chopped pieces of the tenderest mulberry leaves and are so fed for four or five days, when they shed their skins. After this change they require plenty of strong leaves and beyond being supplied with food, they receive little or no care. . . . After thirty days the larvae, which have then molted four times, are ready to spin their cocoons. The ripe ones are picked out by hand and thrown in heaps into a small tray called a "cocooning tray." This is three or four feet in diameter and within it is a ribbon of plaited bamboo, a couple of inches wide, wound round and round in a spiral with its edge on the tray. The larvae are taken in handfuls and scattered [on] the tray with as little care as if they were so many grains of corn. They attach their cocoons, which are completed in 24 hours, to the spiral. The cocoons are torn off the plaited bamboo ribbon and thrown into baskets and two or three days later are placed in a pot to simmer in water over a slow fire. Above the pot are placed a pair of cross-sticks from which a bamboo reel is suspended and beside the pot is a wooden cylinder turning on a pivot. Some filaments of silk are caught and drawn out of the pot, run over the bamboo reel and fastened to the cylinder. The reeler with an iron fork in one hand and handle of the cylinder in the other keeps catching up the filaments in the pot with the fork and reeling them on to the cylinder. The thread produced is coarse and dirty and mixed with bits of pupae and other refuse all of which go with the silk on to the cylinder. When the silk is exhausted from the pot the larvae are taken out and fried in oil for the dinner of the household.

Source: *Gazetteer of Burma*. (1893) New Delhi: Cultural Publishing House, 412–414.

the added advantage that eggs containing weak or malformed worms could not survive the temperature changes. Once the eggs hatched, it was best to have the worms grow as quickly as possible, so various methods of warming the growing sheds were devised. In the sixth century fires of manure were generally used, though they sometimes produced unwanted smoke. By the twelfth century small portable stoves had been developed that warmed the shed without producing smoke; these could be moved out if necessary. Large-scale operations often had large fire pits in the growing sheds; fires would be lit five to seven days before the eggs hatched and left to warm the sheds during the growth phase of the worms. With the use of these methods, the growth phase of the worms could be reduced to twenty-nine to thirty days.

A woman in Chengdu, China, separates larvae from the silk cocoons, an early step in the process that produces silk. (TOM NEBBIA/CORBIS)

Silk Thread

Reeling the silk fibers into thread was preferable while the moths were still alive in the cocoons, since it produced a higher quality of silk, but this was impracticable because it was such a labor-intensive process. Since most silk thread was produced by small rural operations without large workforces, the moths were killed before they damaged the cocoons. Three techniques in common use were leaving the cocoons out in the sun, salting them, and steaming them in ovens. By the nineteenth and twentieth centuries, when mass production was introduced, steaming became the most common method for killing the moths.

The reeling procedure involves unraveling the cocoons and twisting several fibers together to form a thread, then winding the thread onto a reel. This can be done by hand, but by the late eleventh century, a treadle-operated reeling frame had been invented that allowed one person to reel large quantities of yarn relatively quickly. The design of the frame incorporated detailed knowledge of the qualities of silk. The cocoons were placed in a basin of heated water because water loosened the fiber in the cocoons, the heat caused the fibers to move and twist of their own accord, and the motion of the water caused the threads to be more rounded. Despite this technical advance, silk reeling required constant labor once it was begun and was difficult and time-consuming.

Weaving

Weaving was less amenable to improvements. The reeled yarn had to be made into the warp and weft by a spindle wheel, and preparation could often take days. Weaving even plain silk required two people to operate the loom, and if elaborate patterns or designs were to be added, the production of even small amounts of cloth could take days or weeks. Early silk weaving operations were controlled by weaving families who worked from their own homes, and many of the practices involved were passed down for thousands of years with relatively little change. Technological innovation in silk production reached its height during the Song dynasty (960–1279), but it was not until the founding of the first modern silk-weaving factory in 1905, in Hangzhou, that the silk industry was further transformed.

After the silk cloth was woven, it could be left raw or it could be "finished" by being boiled in a solution of ash, steeped overnight in soap, and rinsed to make it softer. Many peasants produced silk to pay taxes and so left the cloth raw.

Silk in Chinese Society

Although there was much rural production of silk, complicated designs were usually woven in urban workshops or imperial factories, which produced elaborate luxury goods for the imperial court, aristocrats, or wealthy city dwellers. Silk was a prestigious commodity, and it was jealously guarded by the imperial court, which often stockpiled bolts of silk in preference to precious metals. During the Song period, when the imperial government was threatened by foreign invasion, silk was an important diplomatic tool, with millions of bolts paid in tribute throughout the eleventh and twelfth centuries. Silk was also used by the rulers to reward outstanding acts, to give relief to victims of disasters, and to pay government officials.

Use of silk in everyday dress was sharply regulated by sumptuary law. Laws were also enacted against the use of gold thread, garments of certain colors, "foreign" styles of dress, and silk embellished, with certain patterns reserved for the court. Though penalties such as jail sentences and caning were prescribed, these laws seem to have been generally ignored by anyone wealthy enough to afford luxury items. Enemies of the Chinese were also familiar with the prestige attached to clothing, because they often requested certain grades of silk cloth with decorations reserved for the imperial family as tribute.

Paul Forage

Further Reading

Nakayama, Shigeru, and Nathan Sivin, eds. (1973) *Chinese Science: Explorations of an Ancient Tradition.* Cambridge, MA: MIT Press.
Temple, Robert. (1986) *The Genius of China: 3,000 Years of Science, Discovery, and Invention.* New York: Simon and Schuster.

Yoke, Ho Peng, (1985) *Li, Qi and Shu: An Introduction to Science and Civilization in China.* Seattle, WA: University of Washington Press.

SESHI CUSTOMS
The most important of Korea's annual *(seshi)* customs have origins that date back millennia and are observed according to the oriental lunar calendar. They have traditionally combined ancestral homage, family gatherings, and entertainment.

The lunar calendar begins with Sol, lunar New Year's Day, and its ancestral rites, ceremonial bows, and traditional foods. This follows immediately after Sottal, the last lunar month of the year, in which preparations for an auspicious new year are made. Traditionally, Sol is only the beginning of the New Year's festivities, which stretch from the new moon on Sol to the full moon of Taeborum, fifteen days later. During this interval, farmers' bands play door-to-door, kites are flown, and the stubbles of rice paddies are set ablaze to ensure an auspicious new year. On the evening of Taeborum, children twirl tin cans of bright coal, representing full moon circles. In the past, village stone and torch fights were also engaged in by young men, with a year of good fortune secured by the winning village.

On the full moon of the eighth lunar month, the Harvest Moon Festival, Ch'usok, is celebrated. This day is equal in importance to Sol for observing ancestral rites and family reunions. Observances at ancestral tombs are made on Hanshik, 105 days after the winter solstice. The late spring celebration of Tano, the fifth day of the fifth lunar month, traditionally included important ancestral veneration rites but today is filled with gaiety and entertainment.

Buddha's birthday is celebrated in Korea on the eighth day of the fourth lunar month (usually in May) and is known as the Feast of the Lanterns. Long rows of lanterns line the way to Buddhist temples, where elaborate and solemn rituals are held; temple courtyards are filled with hanging lanterns, each accompanied by an individual supplication. The day also includes the ceremonial release of fish into streams and dancing around stone pagodas on temple grounds.

Sambok is collectively the three hottest days of summer, Ch'obok, Chungbok, and Malbok, designated as the first, middle, and last day of summer heat and occurring ten to twenty days apart. On these days it has long been the tradition to have chicken or dog soup to restore health and fight off the effects of the overbearing summer heat.

Ch'ilsok, the seventh day of the seventh lunar month, falls in late summer. On this day summer clothes were traditionally washed and dried in the sun and maidens looked to the stars to pray for improved weaving skills. Ch'ilsok is closely associated with a folk tale of a herd boy and his love, a weaving girl, who were banished to opposite ends of the heavens by her father and only allowed to meet on this day. It is said that on this day no magpies or crows can be seen, as they have left to form a bird-bridge over the Milky Way for the two lovers. Rain on Ch'ilsok is said to be the tears of joy shed by the two on the occasion of their annual meeting.

The winter solstice, Tongji, was traditionally a day to drive off evil spirits with porridge. The porridge, made of red beans *(p'at)*, was first offered to the ancestors and then sprinkled on the house and courtyard to dispel evil spirits, who were thought to fear the color red. The red porridge was then eaten, as it still often is today.

David E. Shaffer

Further Reading
Adams, Edward B. (1995) *Korea Guide.* Seoul: Seoul International Publishing House.
Choe, Sang-su. (1983) *Annual Customs of Korea.* Seoul: Seomun-dang Publishing Co.
Koo, John H., and Andrew C. Nahm, eds. (1997) *An Introduction to Korean Culture.* Elizabeth, NJ: Hollym International.

SETOUCHI REGION
The Setouchi Region encompasses the coasts of the Inland Sea (Seto Naikai) in the southern part of the Chugoku Region and the northern part of the Shikoku Region in Japan. The Inland Sea includes between 700 and 800 islands, the largest being Awajima, scattered over an area of 9,500 square kilometers. Numerous islands have been designated as Inland Sea National Park. The climate is mild all year and favors the production of mandarin oranges. From the Edo period (1600–1603–1868), the fishing industry has been important. The cultivation of red algae, oysters, yellowtails, sea bream, and prawns is economically vibrant.

Since the end of World War II, with rapid industrialization and population growth, the Setouchi Region has become one of Japan's major industrial areas with petrochemicals, steel, shipbuilding, and automobile manufacturing. The recently constructed multiple bridges connecting Honshu and Shikoku have facilitated access and regional change. In the 1990s, this area produced over 8 percent of Japan's industrial output. The Inland Sea is now suffering pollution by industrial and urban wastes. Many efforts are oriented toward the conservation of the marine environment.

Nathalie Cavasin

Further Reading
Yagasaki Noritaka, ed. (1997) *Japan: Geographical Perspectives on an Island Nation.* Tokyo: Teikoku-Shoin.

SETTAI *Settai* (or *tsukiai*), business entertainment, refers to outings initiated by a company or business for the purpose of bringing workers together in a setting different from formal work. Work-related outings are a common practice in Japan and occur across the spectrum of blue-collar to white-collar labor. *Settai* is institutionalized in larger, corporate enterprises (pharmaceutical companies and investment banks) where higher-ranked, white-collar workers (particularly male) are expected to entertain and be entertained on a regular basis. Such outings can take place at an array of places—golf courses, restaurants, hostess clubs, bars—and are intended to bond workers both to one another and to the company itself. The relations served by *settai* can be either intracompany (employees from one department and their boss) or intercompany (one company entertaining a client to either solicit or acknowledge their business). The agenda of *settai* is to play (*asobi*). In addition, there is the expectation that to remain a good and loyal worker one should routinely go out with one's coworkers. Under the influence of alcohol or sharing recreation like karaoke or golf, it is thought that people get to know and trust one another. It is widely believed that such *ningenkankei* ("interpersonal relations") fuel and sustain the workplace.

Anne Allison

Further Reading
Allison, Anne. (1994) *Nightwork: Sexuality, Pleasure, and Corporate Masculinity in a Tokyo Hostess Club.* Chicago: University of Chicago Press.

SETTHATHIRAT (1534–1571), Lao monarch. Setthathirat (Xetthathirat) ruled the Lao kingdom of Lan Xang from 1548 to 1571. He was born in Xieng Dong Xieng Thong (Luang Prabang). His father, Phothisarat, placed him on the throne of the Lanna kingdom in 1546. Accompanied by the image of the Emerald Buddha, a Buddha image originally from Sri Lanka and the symbolic spiritual protector of the Lanna kingdom, Setthathirat returned to Lan Xang in 1547 to rule both that kingdom and Lanna after Pho-

thisarat's accidental death. He formed an alliance with the Ayutthaya kingdom to fight the Burmese, after losing Chiang Mai, the capital of Lanna, to them in the 1550s. In 1560 he moved the capital from Xiang Dong Xiang Thong to Viang Chang (present-day Vientiane) to defend against Burmese invasion. When he abandoned his former capital for the more strategically located Viang Chang, Setthathirat left behind the Prabang image, the Buddha image the founder of Lan Xang Fa Ngoum used to legitimize his reign by using it as the spiritual protector of Lan Xang, but initiated the construction of Vat Xiang Thong temple complex to house it. He then renamed Xiang Dong Xiang Thong to Luang Prabang in honor of the sacred image. Setthathirat took the Emerald Buddha to Viang Chang, however, and undertook the construction of Vat Pha Keo to enshrine it. He also erected Phathat Luang stupa, or shrine, in Viang Chang on the grounds of a religious complex housing a relic of Buddha. Setthathirat repelled Burmese invasions of his kingdom in 1570. He died in 1571 after an unsuccessful attempt to invade Angkor, the Khmer kingdom of present-day Cambodia. He never returned to Viang Chang.

Linda McIntosh

Further Reading
Stuart-Fox, Martin. (1998) *The Lao Kingdom of Lan Xang: Rise and Decline.* Bangkok, Thailand: White Lotus.

SHAANXI (1996 est. pop. 34.6 million). The northern Chinese province of Shaanxi (Shensi, Shanxi) borders on Gansu and Ningxia in the west; on Inner Mongolia in the west; on Shanxi, Henan, and Hubei, following the course of the Huang (Yellow) River, in the east; and on Sichuan in the south. Covering an area of 205,000 square kilometers, Shaanxi is geographically divided into a large northern and a much smaller southern part by the Qinling mountain range. The northern region is high, eroded loess plateau about 1,000 meters above sea level. This is a fertile, but dry, steppe with temperate climate and an annual precipitation of 300–500 millimeters. South of the Qinling the climate is subtropical, with annual rainfall of 750–1,000 millimeters. All of Shaanxi has a continental climate, with monsoon rain from July to September. The capital is Xi'an (1996 pop. 3.03 million), which is situated in the valley between the Wei River and the Qinling range. Shaanxi is divided into eight regions and ninety-three counties.

The Wei River valley was inhabited by settled peasants before 5,000 BCE, and it was the homeland of the

Zhou people who overthrew the Shang dynasty (1766–1045 BCE) and founded the Zhou dynasty (1045–256 BCE). The capitals of the Qin (221–206 BCE), Han (206 BCE–220 CE), Tang (618–907), and some minor dynasties were located in the vicinity of modern Xi'an. Following the downfall of the Tang, the capitals of the succeeding dynasties were established in eastern China, and Shaanxi lost its importance as a political center and declined, becoming one of the most destitute areas in China.

Rebellions, famine, and civil war have caused havoc in the province well into the twentieth century. In 1935, following the Long March, the Chinese Communist Party established its headquarters in Yan'an on the northern plateau, from where they fought the Japanese occupying forces from 1937 to 1945.

The majority of the population lives in the valleys of the Wei and Han Rivers, and the most important agricultural products are wheat, millet, rice, and tubers, but rape, tobacco, and soybeans also account for a considerable part of the agricultural economy. Sheep breeding is important on the northern plateau, and south of the Qinling range corn, beans, fruits (especially apples), tea, and medical herbs are grown. Industry, which is concentrated along the Wei River, has a relatively high output of light industrial products such as cloth, sewing machines, TV sets, and watches, but heavy industry is also significant.

Bent Nielsen

Further Reading

Vermeer, Eduard B. (1930) *Economic Development in Provincial China: The Central Shaanxi since 1930.* Cambridge, U.K.: Cambridge University Press.

Liu, Xin. (2000) *In One's Own Shadow: An Ethnographic Account of the Condition of Post-reform Rural China.* Berkeley and Los Angeles: University of California Press.

Keating, Pauline B. (1997). *Two Revolutions: Village Reconstruction and the Cooperative Movement in Northern Shaanxi, 1934–1945.* Stanford, CA: Stanford University Press.

SHADOW PLAYS AND PUPPETRY

SHADOW PLAYS AND PUPPETRY Two classical accounts indicate that puppets, or at least animated figures, were used in China as early as the first half of the Han dynasty (206 BCE–220 CE). Documents record both wooden puppets, "mechanisms of motion" that were made to dance on top of a wall as a military strategy, and shadows staged by a shaman, which mimicked the form and movements of the emperor's favorite concubine to convince the emperor that she had returned from the dead.

By the Tang dynasty (618–907 CE), the budding institution of puppetry included a puppet character named Official Guo or Baldy Guo who was often employed as a comic master of ceremonies in theatrical skits. During the Song (960–1279), puppet theater (*kuileixi* or *mu'ou ju*) was popular both on the street and in the courts. Song dynasty puppet types included "stick-heads" (*zhangtou kuilei*), marionettes (*xuansi kuilei*), water puppets (*shui kuilei*), and a form of puppets activated by gunpowder (*yaofa kuilei*).

Chinese puppets have generally displayed the same song and dance skills as human performers, often sharing the same repertoire and being similarly accompanied by small musical ensembles. This similarity is likely due to the fact that the same governmental offices managed human and puppet troupes throughout their early development in the Tang and Song dynasties. A simpler form of presentation (*biandanxi*, "shoulder-pole theater") was also practiced by roving puppeteers who carried all the materials necessary for performances in round bags attached to shoulder poles.

Continuing as a popular folk form in later dynasties, puppets have secured a place in both religious and entertainment activities. In addition to marionette and shadow puppets, glove puppetry (*budaixi* or *zhangzhongxi*, "palm theater") also flourished as an amusement in the southern regions of the Chinese mainland and in Taiwan. Today, in primarily rural southern areas of mainland China, and especially in Hong Kong, Taiwan, and Singapore, where they are featured during celebrations such as the Hungry Ghost Festival, puppets are still essential elements of religious events.

Shadow theater (*yingxi* or *piyingxi*, "skin-shadow theater") flowered during the Song dynasty, when shadow shows were commonly presented as part of holiday events. *Yingxi* became a frequent attraction in the quarters of the Mongol troops occupying northern China during the Yuan (1279–1368 CE); these conquering armies then carried it throughout the empire and into Central Asia. Shadow plays continued to increase in popularity so that during the Ming dynasty (1368–1644 CE) more than forty troupes of *yingxi* players existed in Beijing alone. During the eighteenth century, shadow theater spread to Europe via missionaries who returned to France and publicized the *ombres chinoises.*

Materials for the traditional puppets vary by region; northwest China companies use puppet figures made from colored strips of buffalo hide, while donkey hide is used in the Hebei shadow puppets. Additionally, some forms now feature paper or hand shadow plays. In each case, the puppeteer (usually alone) narrates and sings while manipulating the foot-high figurines attached to sticks. A small musical ensemble customarily accompanies the action. Torches or electric lights are used to project the silhouettes onto a white screen. Unfortunately, various forms of *yingxi*, such as the renowned lantern shadow theater (*dengyingxi*) of Chengdu, are now on the verge of extinction.

Dallas L. McCurley

Further Reading
Hsu, Tao-Ching. (1985) *The Chinese Conception of the Theatre*. Seattle, WA: University of Washington Press.
Ma, Niansheng. (1993) "Zhangzhou Puppets—The Wonderful Art of Puppet-Making." *China Tourism* (June): 72.
Stalberg, Roberta Helmer. (1984) *China's Puppets*. San Francisco: China Books.

SHAH JAHAN (1592–1666), Mughal emperor. The third son of Jahangir, Shah Jahan ascended the throne of the Mughal empire in February 1628 following bloody battles with his brothers, and remained throughout his reign a ruthless monarch. The *Padshahnama*, written by Abdul Hamid Lahawri, chronicles his reign of thirty-one years.

Shah Jahan's reign saw the empire reach new heights of magnificence. He amassed bullion, which financed his architectural projects in Delhi and Agra, including the Taj Mahal, a marble mausoleum commemorating his beloved wife Mumtaz Mahal. The empire was simultaneously being torn apart by political infighting and internecine quarrels. The economic foundations of the country were undermined by heavy taxation, which contributed to the outbreak of appalling famines, such as that in Gujarat (1630–1631). He persecuted the Jesuits, and in 1632 ordered the destruction of all recently built Hindu temples. His move into the Deccan after 1630 saw early (albeit temporary) successes in the conquest of Bijapur, Golconda, and Ahmednagar. He also moved against the Portuguese, destroying their settlement in Hugli (1631). Shah Jahan spent the last eight years of his life in Agra Fort, where he was imprisoned by his son Aurangzeb, and it was there that he died in 1666 at the age of seventy-five.

Chaudrika Kaul

Further Reading
Alam, M., et al., eds. (1998) *The Mughal State, 1529–1750*. Vol. 1. New Delhi: Oxford University Press Manoharlal.
Beach, Milo Cleveland, and Ebba Koch. (1997) *The Padshahnama*. London and New York: Sackler Gallery and Thames and Hudson.

Lal, Muni. (c. 1986) *Shah Jahan*. New Delhi: Vikas Publishing House.
Marshall, D. N. (1993) *The Mughal Empire*. Cambridge, U.K.: Cambridge University Press.

SHAH, LALON (1774–1890), Baul singer of Bengal. A wandering ascetic who infused his songs with a strong mixture of Sufi and Hindu mystical thought, Fakir Lalon Shah is considered the greatest Baul singer in Bengal, a former Indian province now divided between India and Bangladesh. Bauls are a sect of wandering mystics who do not adhere to any organized religion, and as such they can be either Hindu or Muslim.

The Baul tradition, a blend of Sufism and Hinduism, is centuries old in Bengal. Bauls are itinerant beggars who sing of humans' desire for union with the divine. They often play a simple one-stringed instrument to accompany their singing. The Bauls' message is iconoclastic, in that they deny all traditional religious authority and strongly condemn rituals, caste, and priests.

Lalon Shah's name as well blends the typically Hindu—Lalon—with the typically Muslim—Shah. His title "Fakir" designates a wandering Muslim ascetic. Typical of Baul thought, Lalon Shah's songs glorify human beings, wherein the divine is said to dwell. Therefore, it is pointless to look for God in places of worship, or in rituals, or in holy books. God, for the Bauls, is immediate and immanent; he is as close as the human heart. Lalon Shah sings of innate human goodness. For him, practices, cultures, outlooks, attitudes, prejudices, religions, beliefs that divide humanity are an evil to be expunged. In Lalon Shah's vision, as expressed in his songs, people should love their fellow human beings regardless of race, color, creed, or sect. His shrine is at Chheuria, in Kushtia Province in Bangladesh. It is visited by both Hindus and Muslims.

Nirmal Dass

Further Reading
Bandhyopadhyay, Pranab. (1989) *Bauls of Bengal*. Calcutta, India: Firma KLM.
Capwell, Charles. (1986) *The Music of the Bauls of Bengal*. Kent, OH: Kent State University Press.

SHAH, MIHR ALI (1859–1937), Sufi saint. An important Sufi (Islamic mystic) saint who advocated a strong personal relationship with God, Mihr Ali Shah believed that the divine was immediately knowable through praise and righteous living. He was a distant descendant of Abdul Qadir Jilani (d. c. 1166), the Persian Sufi master, whose shrine is in Baghdad.

Mihr Ali Shah was born in Rawalpindi, in the Punjab, now in Pakistan. He traveled extensively, spreading the word of Islam among various people, preaching through his songs, which are written in an immediately accessible idiom; he composed both in Persian and Punjabi. His message is one of humility, openheartedness, and rejection of pride and worldly love. For Mihr Ali Shah, God is not known by way of distinction, but by universality. In this way, he criticized the pervading caste prejudices that affected much of society in India in his day. He also suggested that God could not be known through rituals and religious practices, but only through utter devotion. It was in his lifetime that he was given the title *pir*, religious master.

After his death, he was buried in the village of Golra Sharif, located a few miles from Islamabad, Pakistan. Only in recent years was a mausoleum constructed over his grave, and the village of Golra Sharif acquired greater prominence.

Nirmal Dass

Further Reading
Rizvi, Athar Abbas. (1978–1983) *A History of Sufism in India*. New Delhi: Munshiram Manoharlal.

SHAH, WARIS
(c. 1710–1780), Punjabi literary figure. Renowned for his contributions to Punjabi literature, Waris Shah created a version of the tale of Hir and Ranjha that is popular to this day and considered by many the Punjab's greatest literary epic. Little concrete evidence is available about Waris Shah's life. He was probably born in Jandiala Sher Khan, a village in Punjab's Sheikhupura district, today in Pakistan. Waris Shah belonged to a respected family that claimed descent from the prophet Muhammad. After early education at a local mosque, he went to Kasur, Pakistan, a contemporary center of learning near Lahore, and then to Pakpattan, Pakistan, an important site in Sufi Islam. Shah died in his natal village where his tomb is located and where an annual festival is held in his name.

Hir Waris Shah, completed in 1767, is Shah's only literary composition. It is a story of carnal love, which many interpret as an allegory of love for the divine. Shah's text also includes much description of customs and practices in the Punjab, leading some literary critics to call his *Hir* an encyclopedia of contemporary life in the Punjab.

Farina Mir

Further Reading
Sekhon, Sant Singh. (1996) *A History of Panjabi Literature*. Vol. 2. Patiala, India: Punjabi University, 2: 56–73, 87–95.
Singh, Gurcharan. (1988) *Warris Shah*. New Delhi: Sahitya Akademi.

SHAHBAZ QALANDAR LAL
(1177–1274), patron saint of Sind. Shahbaz Lal is the honorific title of Sheikh Osman Marvandi, the patron saint of Sind province in Pakistan. He was born in Marwand, Afghanistan, and was initiated into mystic Sufi thought by his father, who was a wandering dervish (member of a Muslim religious order who practices exercises that lead to a trance state). At the age of twenty, Shahbaz Lal was initiated into the Qalandar order of Sufis, who believe in the ecstatic expression of love for God and who are known for their whirling dances to the heady beat of drums, which often cause them to go into a trance.

It is said that he wandered across Western Asia and eventually came to Sind province, settling in the town of Sehwan. Here he received the title "Shahbaz Lal," where "Shahbaz" (falcon) signified the holy man's free spirit, and "Lal" (red) described the color of his robes. In Indian culture, red is the color that brides wear, and Shahbaz thereby signaled his "marriage" to God. He was also known as the intoxicated mendicant, forever drunk with knowledge of the divine.

By the time he died, his fame had spread throughout the Sind as well as the Punjab. Many of his poems still survive and are sung at his shrine, which was built around his grave in 1354. To this day, his shrine is visited by thousands of pilgrims, both Muslim and Hindu, during the annual three-day religious festival that marks the anniversary of his death.

Nirmal Dass

Further Reading
Bari, Moin. (1994) *Saints of Sindh*. Lahore, Pakistan: Jang.
Jotwani, Motilal Wadhumal. (1986) *Sufis of Sindh*. New Delhi: Publications Division, Ministry of Information and Broadcasting, Government of India.

SHAHNAMEH EPIC
The *Shahnameh*, or *Book of Kings*, by the Persian poet Abu al-Qasim Firdawsi, is Iran's national epic and one of the great epics of

world literature. Abu al-Qasim (who used the pen name Firdawsi) was born around 920 CE near Tus in northeastern Iran into a family of small landowners. He died about 1020 or 1025.

With more than 50,000 couplets, Firdawsi's epic is of monumental size. It treats the mostly legendary history of Iran from the creation of the world and the reign of mythical kings to the end of the Sassanian dynasty and the Arab conquest of Iran in the first half of the seventh century.

The *Shahnameh* is based both on written records, among them an unfinished epic by the poet Daqiqi, and on oral tradition. The best-known episode of the epic is the tragic fight between Rustam, one of the epic's major legendary heroes, and his son Sohrab. After Ferdawsi completed the revised version around 1010, he presented his work to his ruler, Mahmud of Ghazna. But the latter remunerated the poet in such a miserly way that Firdawsi wrote bitter satires against the sultan.

Karl Reichl

Further Reading
Davidson, Olga M. (1994) *Poet and Hero in the Persian Book of Kings*. Ithaca, NY: Cornell University Press.

Ferdowsi, Abu al-Qasim. (1967) *The Epic of the Kings: Shah-Nama the National Epic of Persia by Ferdowsi*. Trans. by Reuben Levy, rev. by Amin Banani. Persian Heritage Series 2. London: Routledge & Kegan Paul.

———. (1987) *The Tragedy of Sohrab and Rostam: From the Persian National Epic, the Shahname of Abol-Qasem Ferdowsi*. Trans. by Jerome W. Clinton. Seattle, WA: University of Washington Press.

SHAKUHACHI
The shakuhachi is a Japanese vertical bamboo flute with a notched mouthpiece, four finger holes in front, and one hole in back. Traditionally, the flute is made from a stalk of mandrake bamboo severed at the root, which becomes the bell of the instrument. The bamboo is hollowed, the holes bored, the instrument divided into two parts for easy storage and transport, and the inside lacquered.

The word "shakuhachi" comes from the standard size of the instrument, which is one *shaku* and eight (*hachi*) *sun* long (about 54 centimeters), but shakuhachi also come in other sizes, each of which is tuned to a different key. Performers use various techniques, including half-holing, cross-holing, glissandos, flutter tonguing, and chin and neck movements, to produce a wide range of pitches and timbres.

In the seventh century, the ancestor of the shakuhachi, a slender, Chinese six-holed flute, was intro-

duced into Japan, but it was several centuries later that the instrument evolved into its present form. In the seventeenth century, the Fuke sect of Zen Buddhism began to use shakuhachi performance as a form of meditation, thus associating the instrument with Zen philosophy and the itinerant Fuke monks called *komuso* ("monks of emptiness and nothingness"). Recent centuries have seen the development of various schools of shakuhachi performance, including the widespread Kinko and Tozan schools.

The shakuhachi has a large repertoire, including *honkyoku* (solo pieces), *min'yo* (folk music), and *sankyoku* (chamber music performed with koto and *shamisen*). Recently, the shakuhachi has also been used for contemporary and jazz compositions.

Jeffrey Angles

Further Reading
Blasdel, Christopher Yohmei, and Yuko Kamisango. (1988) *The Shakuhachi: A Manual for Learning*. Tokyo: Ongaku no Tomo Sha.

Taniguchi, Yoshinobu. (1985) *How to Play the Shakuhachi: A Guide to the Japanese Bamboo Flute*. Willits, CA: Tai Hei Shakuhachi.

———, and Michael Gould. (1996) *How to Play Classical Shakuhachi*. Willits, CA: Tai Hei Shakuhachi.

Tanimura Ko, and Kitahara Kozo, eds. (1990) *The Shakuhachi: The Encyclopedia of Musical Instruments*. Tokyo: Ongaku Sha.

SHAMANISM
Shamanism is a vocation, social role, and ritual cosmos recognizable over a vast geographical range from the Arctic and boreal forests, to the Central Asian steppes, East Asia, the Himalayas, South Asia, and the tropical rainforest cultures of Southeast Asia.

North Asia is the locus classicus of shamanism (the word "shaman" is derived from the Siberian Evenk word *"saman"*). Although shamanism is not considered by most scholars to be a religion per se, it plays a central role in small hunting and reindeer herding cultures such as those of the Selkups, Khanti, Evens, and Evenks of Siberia. For the western Siberian Buryat, shamanism is intimately tied to the welfare of the clan, whereas for the Buryat east of Lake Baikal, shamanism plays an inferior role to Buddhism. In northern Nepal, Gurung shamanism stands opposed to neighboring Tibetan Buddhist morality, whereas in Tuva, shamans and Buddhist lamas are often seen as complementary ritual specialists. Farther west, in Uzbekistan, shamanism also plays a complementary role within Islamic cultures. In Malaysia, shamanism is the central religious activity of many Orang Asli (Aboriginal) cultures such as that of the Temoq. The relation between shamanism and other religions is highly variable, but in almost all cases, shamanism is under the hegemonic pressure of polities that subscribe to universal religions or globalizing economic ideologies.

Principal Features

Shamanism, despite some controversy, can be identified by the following features.

1. The shaman's mode of supernatural action, such as magical flight to upper or lower spirit realms, is integral to the ideational and moral order of the world within which people live their daily lives.

2. The shaman is a person who acts as an intermediary between the supernatural and the community and who may take on one or more roles of healer, hunting magician, diviner, psychopomp, and sacrificer.

3. The shaman is inspired by his or her spirits, who provide protection and guidance and who often play a significant part in the shaman's arduous initiation.

4. The shaman enters into ecstatic trance states to establish relations with supernatural powers.

The Evenk Shaman's Séance

The Evenks inhabit the Siberian taiga. The shaman specializes in rites such as the *kamlanye* for healing and the *shingkelevun*, in which the shaman travels to his clan's spirit-mistress of the taiga in the upper world and petitions her to release greater numbers of game animals.

The *kamlanye* healing rite takes place, in severe cases of illness, in a specially constructed tent called a *shevenchedek*. The tent symbolizes the middle earth *(dulyu)* between the upper world *(ugu)* and lower world *(khergu)*, and also stands for an island in the mythical clan-river running from the upper to the lower world. The tent contains wooden carvings of ancestors, and guardian spirits such as loons, ducks, geese, and elk. There are also carvings of watchman-spirits who guard against agents sent by hostile shamans in other communities.

A larch tree *(turu)*, symbolizing the world tree, is placed in the center of the tent with its top protruding through the smoke hole. The *turu* is the shaman's ladder for ascending into the upper world.

A couple of days before the performance, and while the special tent is being constructed, the shaman, while

A Yenesei Ostyak shaman in traditional dress in northern Siberia. (BETTMANN/CORBIS)

fasting and excessively smoking, sends his *khargi* (animal double soul) to the underworld to consult with his shaman ancestors about the upcoming rite.

On the eve of the *kamlanye* rite the shaman makes a loon's cry, signaling his kinsmen to assemble inside the tent. When the shaman is seated, the entrance is sealed by spirit-watchman figurines, and the shaman's assistant passes him his ritual coat, gloves, and drum. The drum is not only a musical instrument, but also the shaman's vehicle, imaged as a boat or deer. The shaman then begins drumming and singing, calling on his spirit-helpers to fight the disease-spirit afflicting the patient. With loud and fast drumming, and singing replete with animal sounds, the shaman sends his *khargi* to the lower world to discover the cause of the illness. Reaching a crescendo, the shaman, foaming at the mouth, collapses on the mat and lies silent while his *khargi* travels the lower world. Gradually the shaman begins to sing, at first in quiet muffled tones, and then more loudly as he returns with knowledge of the affliction.

Moving through a series of therapeutic strategies, the shaman finally tries to induce the disease-spirit to

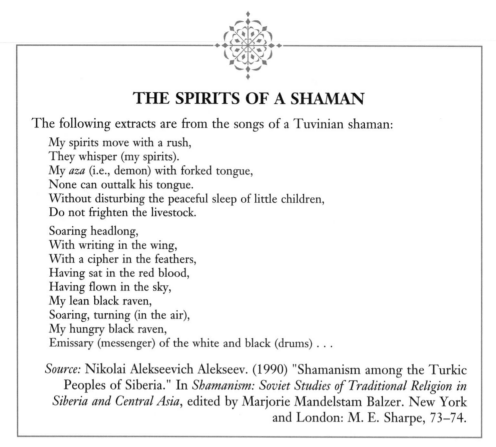

THE SPIRITS OF A SHAMAN

The following extracts are from the songs of a Tuvinian shaman:

My spirits move with a rush,
They whisper (my spirits).
My *aza* (i.e., demon) with forked tongue,
None can outtalk his tongue.
Without disturbing the peaceful sleep of little children,
Do not frighten the livestock.

Soaring headlong,
With writing in the wing,
With a cipher in the feathers,
Having sat in the red blood,
Having flown in the sky,
My lean black raven,
Soaring, turning (in the air),
My hungry black raven,
Emissary (messenger) of the white and black (drums) . . .

Source: Nikolai Alekseevich Alekseev. (1990) "Shamanism among the Turkic Peoples of Siberia." In *Shamanism: Soviet Studies of Traditional Religion in Siberia and Central Asia*, edited by Marjorie Mandelstam Balzer. New York and London: M. E. Sharpe, 73–74.

enter the body of a reindeer, which is then quickly sacrificed to entrap it. The strategy fails in this performance, so heavy pressure is applied through invective and ridicule. Finally, the shaman is able to extract the disease-spirit, and with the help of a familiar spirit, cast it into the abyss of the world of the dead.

At the end of the rite the shaman takes the patient's soul and climbs the *turu* to the upper world and gives the soul to a higher deity for safekeeping. He finishes the rite with divinatory services to individual kinsmen using his rattle and scapulamancy, the latter being the art of foretelling events by the examination of cracks in a burned reindeer shoulder blade.

Temoq Shaman's Séance

The Temoq are Aslian-speaking hunters, gatherers, horticulturalists, and forest-product collectors living in lowland tropical rain forest in Pahang, Malaysia. At the beginning of the Mountain Journey (Teng Bnum) séance, the shaman *(puiyang)* calls his familiar and guardian spirits to assemble and lead the entourage into the night sky. Clambering up the World Cloud-Mountain, the shaman takes on the garb of his familiar and guardian spirits to cross dangerous chasms

and safely navigate obstacles. For long journeys, carved bees' nests and models of bearded pigs and tigers are ensouled and accompany the shaman to the earth's farthest reaches.

The shaman's entourage of Tiger Cat, Wreathed Hornbills, and Malayan Sun Bear is led by beautifully warbling White-Rumped Shama birds and swarms of droning bees. The shaman may visit more than one hundred celestial regions associated with natural species, meteorological phenomena, and ancestors, over several consecutive nights. Normally, the shaman focuses on six or seven regions during a night's performance, which ends with the bathing and purifying of the patient's soul in the cool, misty, pandanus-fringed waters of the celestial pool where resides the shaman's tutelary spirit Puteri Bungsu.

To the accompaniment of intense drumming and singing, the shaman moves back and forth between the inner recesses of the patient's body and the far outer reaches of the stone-vaulted, snake-encircled cosmos. Overwhelmed by the visionary earth, the shaman drifts into deep ecstasy, his voice becoming blurred and soft, and he must periodically struggle back, signified by sudden bursts of loud singing, to achieve the healing purpose of the rite. The shaman's séance is invariably a communal event; male drummers facilitate the shaman's journey, and female assistants fashion the shaman's costume and whisk, and tend the censer.

Meanwhile, the ritual house, imaged as a microcosm with incense cloud-mountains, beautiful music, and sonorous singing, lulls the disease-spirit into a state of ecstasy. The shaman beguiles it into leaving the patient's body, and he lustrates the patient with cooling decoctions to neutralize the disease-spirit's toxins. After extraction the weakened disease-spirit is sent back to its source in the black scudding clouds.

Sometimes colorful spirit houses, rafts, and canoes lit by candles are used to entice disease-spirits out of patients with the promise of an exquisite abode. After launching on a stream or placement in the forest, the spirit abodes rapidly deteriorate and fall apart.

Shamanism Today

Shamanism is typically the religious and spiritual focus of peoples occupying the periphery of dominant cultural and political systems. In Malaysia, for example, the incursion of universal religions, supported by the government in the case of Islam, has had little impact on Orang Asli shamanism and religion. In contrast, the height of Soviet repression saw intense persecution, imprisonment, and the deaths of numerous shamans who were seen as reactionary obstacles to Sovietization and state hegemony.

Today, shamanism is ascendant in the Commonwealth of Independent States (CIS). The empowering fusion of shamanism and ethnicity in such newly emerged republics as Tuva and Khakassia and the transformation of shamanic rites and themes into theatrical genres performed at folk festivals throughout the world, bode well for an ancient spirituality that speaks directly to critical issues facing the world.

Evenk and Temoq shamans, like shamans everywhere, play an important role in the health and welfare of individuals and their communities. Increasingly, shamanism is also playing a key role in the reemergent ethnicities shaping the cultural and political landscape of Asia.

Peter Frederick Laird

Further Reading

Balzer, Marjorie Mandelstam, ed. (1990) *Shamanism: Soviet Studies of Traditional Religion in Siberia and Central Asia*. New York: M. E. Sharpe

Dioszegi, Vilmos, and Mihaly Hoppal. (1996) *Shamanism in Siberia*. Vol 2. Budapest, Hungary: Akademiai Kiado.

Eliade, Mircea. (1964) *Shamanism: Archaic Techniques of Ecstasy*. Bollingen Series, no. 76. Princeton, NJ: Princeton University Press.

Grim, John A. (1983) *The Shaman: Patterns of Siberian and Ojibway Healing*. Norman, OK: University of Oklahoma Press.

Hoppal, Mihaly, and Juha Pentikainen, eds. (1992) *Northern Religions and Shamanism*. Budapest, Hungary: Akademiai Kiado.

Michael, Henry N., ed. (1963) *Studies in Siberian Shamanism*. Toronto: University of Toronto Press.

Nowak, Margaret, and Stephen Durrant. (1977) *The Tale of the Nisan Shamaness: A Manchu Folk Epic*. Seattle, WA: University of Washington Press.

Mumford, Stan Royal. (1989) *Himalayan Dialogue: Tibetan Lamas and Gurung Shamans in Nepal*. Madison, WI: University of Wisconsin Press.

Thomas, Nicholas, and Caroline Humphrey, eds. (1996) *Shamanism, History, and the State*. Ann Arbor, MI: University of Michigan Press.

Waley, Arthur. (1973) *The Nine Songs: A Study of Shamanism in Ancient China*. San Francisco: City Lights Books.

SHAMANISM—MONGOLIA
Prior to the mass conversion to Buddhism in the sixteenth century, the Mongols were primarily shamanistic. Although Nestorian Christianity (a sect of Christianity that spread through Asia in the first millennium CE) could be found throughout Mongolia, the converts were mainly among the elites, not among the common people. Furthermore, Nestorian Christianity died out in Mongolia in the fifteenth century. The vast majority of people in Mongolia, however, subscribed to the amorphous belief system known as shamanism.

The Spirit World

Mongolian shamanism posited an afterlife that was identical to the present. Upon death, one was usually buried with one's possessions, including animals, in order to have them in the afterlife. Just as in this world, the transcendent world (afterlife) possessed a hierarchy. Thus if one was a khan or prince in the human world, this status would be retained in the afterlife.

The spirit world could interact with the human world and were generally viewed as neither good nor evil. There was also a supreme being, the *Koke Mongke Tengri*, or Eternal Blue Sky. *Tengri* translates from Mongolian as heaven, sky, or god. There were other *tengri*s and powerful spirit beings, but the *Koke Mongke Tengri* presided as the chief spiritual being. An earth goddess also existed, known as *Etuken*, but she played a less significant role than *Koke Mongke Tengri*. The shamanistic Mongols did not possess a single concept for the soul; for them, the soul appeared in three basic forms. The first was the "bone" *hunehun*, which, as

A shaman shrine erected in the desert of Inner Mongolia. (Keren Su/Corbis)

the name suggests, resided in the bone. The second soul was the "flesh" *hunehun,* which resided in the flesh or blood. The final soul was the *sulde* or shadow/ghost, a flesh soul that continued to exist after the death of the person to which it was attached. In an ordinary person, the flesh soul passed away with the decomposition of the body. In the case of a powerful person such as Genghis Khan, however, the flesh soul could continue on as a *sulde.* The bone *hunehun* could live on as it died only when the pelvic bone, in which it resided, was shattered. The bone *hunehun* could become vengeful and give nightmares to disrespectful people. The bone *hunehun* remained in the area of the body.

While a person was alive, the flesh soul could vacate the body by flying out of the nose during sleep. In this case, the person became sick, suffered from bizarre nightmares, and lost energy. The bone soul could escape if a person suffered a broken bone. The flesh soul could also be captured, and magicians existed who could capture souls.

Although the spirit world was, as a rule, neutral toward the living, if one transgressed against a spirit the spirit would seek retribution. Therefore, an intermediary was needed to communicate with and propitiate the spirits. This individual was the shaman *(boge)* or shamaness *(idughan).* In addition to their roles as intermediaries with the spirit world, shamans also acted as doctors for both physical and spiritual ailments and played important roles in communal gatherings.

Healing Ceremonies

Because illness was caused by the soul wandering away from the body, the only way to cure the afflicted individual was to retrieve the soul. If the soul had not wandered far, it could be retrieved with the *sasalga* or sprinkling rite. The shaman sprinkled wine, koumiss (fermented mare's milk), or vodka toward the smoke hole of the tent while ringing a bell or cracking a whip. Then the patient would drink a bowl of the same substance. The ceremony ended and the soul would have been restored. The elders then took food and distributed it among the people.

If the soul had traveled a great distance, then the shaman had to retrieve it. Occasionally, the soul even reached *Erlik Khan* or the God of Death. The shaman would first have the sick person's tent made attractive to the soul by placing in the open personal possessions of the patient and gathering the patient's friends. The patient also dressed in his or her best clothes and lights were placed so the soul could find its way back. The shaman then requested the assistance of the *zayan* and *ezen.*

The *zayan* were a special set of spirits who had suffered a terrible death; they included suicides, those who had died as children, and those who had suffered emotional deaths, dying while frightened, under extreme stress, or violent deaths, dying from torture but not in battle or from illness. These spirits could be very cruel, as they were filled with suffering and frustration. However, if the shaman could control them, they could help locate the lost soul. The *ezen* were lords in the spiritual world, possessed great power, and commonly received requests for assistance. The *udkha* or helping spirit also assisted the shaman. The *udkha* was the spirit of the shaman's family. Soul retrieval was a difficult process. The shaman, through ecstatic techniques consisting of chanting and drumming, entered a trance. During the trance, the shaman or *boge* sprinkled koumiss or vodka toward the smoke hole of the *ger* (tent), while he rang a bell or cracked a whip. The "patient" also drank from a bowl. Through this the *boge* ventured into the spirit world and searched for the lost soul. If successful in finding the soul, the shaman would retrieve it, heal the person, and awaken from the trance. Every time the shaman encountered a spirit or being who assisted him or her, the shaman would have to pay that spirit or being. Naturally, this could become expensive. The patient and family supplied the shaman with the appropriate funds, either as paper money or bronze coins.

A more serious rite was the *khyryk* rite, which was performed if the spirit was no longer in this world. Essentially the *khyryk* was an exorcism. The sick person was placed outside the yurt or tent by a bonfire. The shaman burned the scapula bone of a sheep and read the cracks in the bone in order to find the guilty spirit. The shaman then drank wine, koumiss, or vodka while chanting. The shaman often swayed, and approached and retreated from the fire as if he were driving something out of it. Eventually the shaman collapsed in an ecstatic trance. Once the shaman regained consciousness, a sheep was cooked. While the sheep was being cooked, the shaman drank koumiss for the spirits and shared the alcohol with the patient and then the elders. Once the mutton was ready, part of the meat was thrown into the fire as a sacrifice. All participants in the rite ate the remainder while the bones were burned in the bonfire.

Specialists

In addition to the shaman, there were several other spirit-world specialists. The *dallachi* or *dallalga* was a scapulamancer, or one who could tell the future by examining the cracks in burned sheep scapula bones. Another diviner was the *togelechi*, who worked with a variety of objects, including coins and arrows.

Among healers, there was the *domchi*, who was thought to be a sorcerer or healer, perhaps even a traditional shaman. Another healer or doctor was the *emchi*. A final specialist who appears frequently in medieval sources was the *yadchi*, who possessed the ability to summon rain- or hailstorms through the use of special stones.

Although mass conversions to Buddhism took place in the sixteenth century, shamanism never completely disappeared. Instead, Buddhism in Mongolia took on some aspects of shamanism. Even today, one may find a *boge* in Mongolia.

Timothy M. May

Further Reading

Banzarov, Dorji. (1981) "The Black Faith, or Shamanism among the Mongols." Trans. by Jan Nattier and John R. Krueger. *Mongolian Studies* 7: 53–91.

Heissig, Walther. (1980) *The Religions of Mongolia*. Trans. by Geoffrey Samuel. Berkeley and Los Angeles: University of California Press.

Lattimore, Owen. (1941) *Mongol Journeys*. London: Doubleday.

SHAMISEN The *shamisen* (in English, samisen) is a three-stringed, fretless, lute instrument from Japan played by using a plectrum *(bachi)* to strike the strings. The overall shape is like the banjo; the neck and frame are made from red sandalwood or mulberry and the sides of the body are covered by calfskin. The pegs can be ebony, ivory, or plastic, with twisted silk or synthetic tetron material for the strings. The instrument was imported from China through Okinawa and into Japan in the sixteenth century and was firmly established by the Edo period (1600/1603–1868).

The word *shamisen* is from the Chinese *sanxian* (three strings). The instrument has a distinct sound called *sawari*, caused by the resonation of the bass string against a metal plate that is adjusted using the *azuma-zawari*, a screw on the back of the neck. The three standard types of tuning are the *hon-choshi* (original, a third and fifth), *niagari* (raise the second, a fifth and fourth), and the *sansagari* (lower the third, two fourths). Originally used by folk musicians and professional geishas, the instrument made its way into the concert hall during the nineteenth century. The *shamisen* is used to accompany Kabuki, *nagauta* (epics songs), *min'yo* (folk songs), and Bunraku plays.

Stacey Fox

Further Reading

De Ferranti, Hugh. (2000) *Japanese Musical Instruments*. New York: Oxford University Press.

Malm, William P. (2001) *Traditional Japanese Music and Musical Instruments*. Tokyo: Kodansha International.

SHAN The Shan are an ethnic group in Southeast Asia belonging to the Tai-Kadai language family. "Shan" is probably a Chinese designation for this ethnic Tai group. They call themselves Tai, Tai Luang ("luang" meaning "greater" or "main"), or Tai Mao [Luang] (according to their ancient capital Muang Mao). They were generally called Tai Yai by the Siamese ("yai" also meaning "greater"). The Shan live mainly in the Shan states of Myanmar (Burma), where they have a population of 3.2 million. Other Shan live in southern China and as political refugees in Thailand, Europe, and the United States.

Culturally, the Shan are closely related to the Lao, the Lue, and the Khon Muang (or Yuan). Like these ethnic groups, the Shan profess Theravada Buddhism as well as traditional ancestor and spirit cults. Traditionally, the main economic product was rice, but also important were vegetables and fruits, animal breeding (cattle, buffalo, pigs, chickens, elephants), silk, and cotton and handicrafts such as weaving, silverwork, woodcarving, and *Hsa* paper production. The region of the Shan states also ranks among the world's highest in opium production. After the military coup of 1962, when the Union of Burma was brought under a military regime, the sociopolitical and economic structures of the Shan changed radically.

History

The Shan, who migrated to the southwest from southern China (Nanchao) probably before the tenth or twelfth century, founded the Mao Luang kingdom in the early thirteenth century as the result of a forced unification of numerous small Shan states (*muang* or *mong*). The Mao Luang kingdom maintained considerable power until it was challenged by the Burmese in 1604 after the kingdom had been weakened during a long series of wars with China. However, only some of the many Shan principalities came under Burmese control; others continued to exist as independent or semi-independent Shan states (*mong Tai*).

During the colonial period, the Shan aristocracy negotiated protectorate agreements with the British and in 1922 founded the Federated Shan States. During World War II, the Shan states came under Japanese occupation. In 1947, the Shan rulers signed the Panglong Agreement, by which the Shan states officially became part of the Union of Burma for a trial period of ten years. The Panglong Agreement was the cornerstone of the Union of Burma, and the Shan prince Chao Shwe Thaike became provisional president. After that period, according to the agreement, they should have been free to secede, but they were hindered when the military under the Burman General Ne Win took power in 1958. With the military coup in 1962, a great part of the leading Shan aristocracy was arrested or assassinated, and the Shan states finally came under full control of the

military government, which to date is being opposed by a Shan armed resistance.

Oliver Raendchen

Further Reading

Adams, Nel. (2000) "Remembering the Tai of the Shan States." *Tai Culture—International Review on Tai Cultural Studies* 5, 1: 143–162.

Mangrai, Sao Saimong. (1965) *The Shan States and the British Annexation.* Cornell Data Papers, no. 57. Ithaca, NY: Southeast Asia Program, Cornell University.

Milne, Leslie. (1910) *Shans at Home: With Two Chapters on Shan History and Literature.* London: J. Murray.

Shan Human Rights Foundation, ed. (1994) *The Shan Case: Rooting Out the Myth of the Golden Triangle.* Rev. ed. Maehongson, Thailand: Shan Human Rights Foundation.

Tannenbaum, Nicola Beth. (1995) *Who Can Compete against the World? Power-Protection and Buddhism in Shan Worldview.* Ann Arbor, MI: Association for Asian Studies.

Yawnghwe, Chao Tzang. (1987) *The Shan of Burma: Memoirs of a Shan Exile.* Singapore: ISEAS.

SHAN STATE (1990 est. pop. 4.25 million). The Shan State in northeastern Burma is the country's largest ethnic minority state. A highland plateau covering 156,000 square kilometers, it is home to a diversity of peoples with strong traditions of local independence. This is reflected in the state's turbulent history.

No accurate ethnic census has ever been taken, but in the 1990s the population was estimated by the government at 4.25 million, of whom 1.64 million were majority Shans (Tais), 450,000 Paos, 400,000 Palaungs and Was, 170,000 Lahus, 100,000 Kachins, and 100,000 Akhas. Other substantial populations include Burman, Kokang, Danu, Intha, Lisu, and Kayan.

In precolonial history, the state consisted of a loose political system of over forty substates ruled by local *sawbwa*s (princes), who were recognized by the British in the process of annexation in the late nineteenth century. Some of these valley kingdoms had histories dating back to at least the fourteenth century CE, when Shan rulers had vied with Burmans and Mons for control over central Burma. In contrast, in mountain areas many of the minority peoples, such as the Wa and Lahu, continued lives that were little touched by the outside world until well into the twentieth century.

At Burma's independence in 1948, the Federated Shan States (established in 1922), which had been under British administration, were reconstituted as a single state with the right of secession after a ten-year period. However, armed conflicts broke out within two years of the British departure, and these have continued through the long years since.

A major factor in this destabilization was the late-1949 invasion by Guomindang remnants from China. Insurgency then escalated from the early 1960s when General Ne Win seized power to prevent Shan and other ethnic minority leaders from attempting to renegotiate nationality rights. Up to a dozen minority armies operated in the state, and descentded into full-scale civil war in 1968 when the Communist Party of Burma (CPB) invaded the eastern borderlands with the military backing of China. Only after the CPB's collapse in 1989 did peace return to a number of war-afflicted regions under the cease-fire policy of the State Law and Order Restoration Council government. The situation, however, remained complex and unstable in many areas.

Decades of conflict have taken a serious toll on human lives and development. Agriculture is the main economy, with crops such as paddy rice, wheat, cotton, pulses, tobacco, and groundnuts all being grown. Varieties of fruit, vegetables, and tea are also produced in the mountain climate. However, it is opium and heroin production for which the state is internationally notorious. During the early 1990s, Shan State was reputedly the world's largest illicit producer.

The state also contains valuable natural resources, including silver, lead, zinc, copper, antinomy, and precious stones. The Namtu-Bawdwin mines are the largest mineral enterprise. There is also potential for power generation along the Salween (Thanlwin) River as well as tourism in the Inle Lake region. However infrastructural links remain poor, and road journeys between the state capital Taunggyi and other key towns, such as Kengtung and Lashio, are long and often interrupted.

Only during the 1990s were efforts begun by both the government and cease-fire groups to upgrade the local economy. Trade links to central Burma, as well as neighboring China and Thailand, were the major priority. But the people of the state continued to face a daunting array of social problems, and the spread of HIV/AIDS has been another cause of concern.

Martin Smith

Further Reading

Amnesty International. (2000) *Myanmar: Exodus from Shan State*. London: Amnesty International.

Lintner, Bertil. (1984) "The Shans and the Shan States of Burma." *Contemporary Southeast Asia* 5, 4: 403–450.

———. (1998) "Drugs and Economic Growth: Ethnicity and Exports." In *Burma: Prospects for a Democratic Future*, edited by Robert Rotberg. Washington, DC: Brookings Institution Press, 165–183.

Saimong Mangrai, Sao. (1965) *The Shan States and the British Annexation*. Ithaca, NY: Cornell University Southeast Asia Program, Data Paper 57.

Scott, James George, and J. P. Hardiman. (1900) *Gazetteer of Upper Burma and the Shan States*. Rangoon, Burma: Superintendent, Government Printing.

Tzang Yawnghwe, Chao. (1987) *The Shan of Burma: Memoirs of a Shan Exile*. Singapore: Institute of Southeast Asian Studies.

SHAN STATE ARMY The Shan State Army (SSA) is historically the most influential of the various armed movements promoting the Shan (Tai) cause of greater autonomy and political rights for the Shan State in Myanmar (Burma). It was formed in 1964 by the alliance of three existing ethnic Shan nationalist forces. Popular with students and intellectuals, the SSA was quickly able to establish base areas from north to south across the state under such youthful leaders as Khun Kya Nu, Sai Myint Aung, and Chao Tzang Yawnghwe. In 1971 the SSA was further strengthened by the establishment of a political wing, the Shan State Progress Party.

The SSA, however, faced considerable obstacles in maintaining its authority. Frequent Burmese army offensives as well as rivalries with other insurgent groups all undermined its position. Several of its opponents were involved in narcotics trafficking, and in the 1970s this led the SSA to coordinate an unsuccessful attempt to gain control of the opium trade for preemptive sale to international antinarcotics agencies.

Subsequently, the party was weakened by the loss of key leaders and a damaging split that saw its northern forces ally with the Communist Party of Burma (CPB), while the southern SSA worked with the ethnic minority National Democratic Front. In 1989 the northern SSA followed the CPB mutineers in signing a cease-fire with Myanmar's military State Law and Order Restoration Council. This faction then began a development program in its territory designated as Shan State Special Region 3. In the south meanwhile, following the 1996 surrender of Khun Sa's Mong Tai Army, SSA remnants joined together with other Shan nationalists, headed by Yord Serk, to form a new force known as the SSA (South), which in the year 2002 was still fighting against Myanmar's military government.

Martin Smith

Further Reading

Aye Saung. (1989) *Burman in the Back-Row: Autobiography of a Burmese Rebel*. Hong Kong: Asia 2000; Bangkok, Thailand: White Lotus.

Boucaud, Andre, and Louis Boucaud. (1988) *Burma's Golden Triangle: On the Trail of the Opium Warlords*. Hong Kong: Asia 2000; Bangkok, Thailand: Pacific Rim.

McCoy, Alfred. (1972) *The Politics of Heroin in Southeast Asia*. New York: Harper Torchbooks.

Shan Human Rights Foundation. (1994) *The Shan Case: Rooting Out the Myth of the Golden Triangle*. Mae Hong Son, Thailand: Shan Human Rights Foundation.

Smith, Martin. (1999) *Burma: Insurgency and the Politics of Ethnicity*. 2d ed. London: Zed Books.

Tzang Yawnghwe, Chao. (1987) *The Shan of Burma: Memoirs of a Shan Exile*. Singapore: Institute of Southeast Asian Studies.

SHANDONG (2000 est. pop. 90.79 million). Shandong is a large, densely populated Chinese northern coast province on the Shandong Peninsula, which separates the Bohai Gulf from the Yellow Sea. Bordered on the northwest by Hebei Province, on the southwest by Henan Province, and on the south by Anhui and Jiangsu Provinces, Shandong Province is about the size of Mexico both in terms of land area and population. It covers about 153,300 square kilometers, and its population density of 579.5 persons per square kilometer makes it second only to its neighboring province of Henan in Chinese provincial population. In the nineteenth and twentieth centuries, emigrants from the crowded province became a major source of the present population of China's northeast (Manchuria).

Historically, the Grand Canal traversed the province, bearing grain and other trade to Beijing from the lower Changjiang (Yangtze River) valley, but today this commercial route is of no importance. Shandong's dominant geographic feature is the Huang (Yellow) River that now crosses the North China Plain to empty into the Bohai Gulf near the large Shengli (Victory) oil field. Before 1950, the Huang River floods caused great suffering, but these have posed no threat in the past half century, because flood control projects and water diversions have shrunk the river's flow.

Shandong was home to several Neolithic cultures that made up parts of ancient Chinese culture. In the Zhou period (1045–256 BCE), modern Shandong encompassed several important states, including the powerful state of Qi and the smaller state of Lu, closely associated with the Zhou ruling house and its traditions. The ancient philosophers Confucius (551–479 BCE) and Mencius (371–289 BCE) both lived in what is now southern Shandong. Mount Tai in the central mountains has been a major north China religious site from prehistoric times down to the present. The Boxer Rebellion (1899–1901) began in Shandong as attacks on Chinese Christians and foreign missionaries, but in 1900 it shifted its center northward to the Beijing-Tianjin area. German imperialism created the port of Qingdao and Shandong's first railroad after 1898; Japan took over German interests in 1915 during World War I and remained the dominant foreign presence there until 1945.

Agriculturally, Shandong produces wheat, cotton, and sorghum. Its richest land and largest cities run from Jinan, the provincial capital, eastward through Weifang to Qingdao. Shandong's peninsula has good ports at Qingdao, Yantai, and Weihai. These have grown rapidly since 1978, when Communist leader Deng Xiaoping (1904–1997) started China's reform era. In the decade before the 1997 Asian economic crisis, South Korean interests invested heavily in Shandong.

David D. Buck

Further Reading

Buck, David D. (1978) *Urban Change in China: Politics and Development in Tsinan, Shantung, 1890–1949*. Madison, WI: University of Wisconsin Press.

Cohen, Paul. (1997) *History in Three Keys: The Boxers as Event, Experience and Myth*. New York: Columbia University Press.

Goodman, Paul. (1989) *China's Regional Development*. London: Routledge.

Pomeranz, Kenneth. (1993) *Making of a Hinterland: State, Society and Economy in North China, 1853–1937*. Berkeley and Los Angeles: University of California Press.

Naquin, Susan, and Chun-fa Yu, eds. (1992) *Pilgrims and Sacred Sites in China*. Berkeley and Los Angeles: University of California Press.

SHANG DYNASTY The Shang (1766–1045 BCE) is the earliest Chinese dynasty for which any significant archaeological documentation exists, placing it at the historical forefront of the Chinese cultural sphere. It is true that evidence of a prior dynasty, known in legend as the Xia (2100–1766 BCE), may soon be confirmed by ongoing archaeological studies of the settlement at Erlitou (which presently is considered to be either pre- or early Shang), or through new discoveries at other sites. Traditional Chinese historiography suggests that thirty kings ascended to the Shang throne through the rather complicated system of determining social status through ancestral connections. The first of these was said to have been named Cheng Tang (Tang the Successful; reigned 1766–1754?).

Writing

Extant written records dating from the Shang itself cover only the reigns of the last nine kings (Wu Ding, said to have reigned 1198–1189 BCE, through to Di Xin, who died around 1045 BCE), and it is of this later period that one can speak with some authority. The oldest form of writing from this period exists as brief inscriptions on bronze ritual vessels *(jin wen)* or as oracle-bone inscriptions *(jia gu wen)*, which were either the shells of turtles or scapulas of oxen on which questions concerning divinatory or ceremonial matters were "answered" in the cracks appearing when the materials were heated. The language of the inscriptions is an early form of written Chinese.

State and Religious Ritual

One of the most important characteristics of the Shang, as it appears from the surviving traces of their civilization, is that the basis of the empire's governance was a comprehensive combination of religious ceremony and state ritual. At least by the end of the dynasty, the king, as the sole interpreter of the oracle-bone messages, acted as head shaman. The importance of the king's religious obligations may account for the many moves that appear to have been made in the location of the capital city. The king was said to have regularly marked and claimed his empire by performing ceremonial acts at sacred mountains located at the four cardinal directions on the boundaries of his realm. It is likely that he moved the center of government as he traveled. In addition, the political authority of the ruler was reaffirmed in the state worship of the royal ancestral line. The Shang ancestors, in return, were believed to have used their otherworldly positions to ensure an orderly and beneficial influence on the state. The interrelationship between political governance and ancestor worship served to perpetuate Shang rule. Rulers acquired legitimacy from their genealogical charter, and the Shang was ratified as a ruling house.

The pervasiveness of ritual in court life is well documented in the area of Anyang in northern Henan Province, settled during the reign of Wu Ding and therefore considered the final stage in Shang development. Especially at the royal residence, enormous tombs evidence the practice of human and animal sacrifice, the ritual burial of chariots, and the ceremonial use of vessels and oracle bones. To assist in providing ceremonial materials, the central court assumed control of natural resources. Mining became a particularly important industry; Chinese casting techniques, unmatched in the rest of the world, made possible the production of large and complex items. A bronze foundry used to cast ritual items and covering 10,000 square meters was discovered at the Miaopubei site, south of Anyang.

Urban and Rural Development

Palaces and temples have also been tentatively identified (on the basis of size) near Anyang at the Xiao-

CHINA—HISTORICAL PERIODS

Xia dynasty (2100–1766 BCE)
Shang dynasty (1766–1045 BCE)
Zhou dynasty (1045–256 BCE)
    Western Zhou (1045–771 BCE)
    Eastern Zhou (770–221 BCE)
Spring and Autumn period (770–476 BCE)
Warring States period (475–221 BCE)
Qin dynasty (221–206 BCE)
Han dynasty (206 BCE–220 CE)
Three Kingdoms period (220–265 CE)
North and South dynasties (220–589 CE)
Sui dyansty (581–618 CE)
Tang dynasty (618–907 CE)
Five Dynasties period (907–960 CE)
Song dynasty (960–1279)
    Northern Song (960–1126)
    Southern Song (1127–1279)
Jurchen Jin dynasty (1125–1234)
Yuan dynasty (1279–1368)
Ming dynasty (1368–1644)
Qing dynasty (1644–1912)
Republican China (1912–1927)
People's Republic of China (1949–present)
Republic of China (1949–present)
Cultural Revolution (1966–1976)

tun compound. Another settlement yielding archaeological finds of primary importance is that of Zhengzhou, situated directly beneath the modern city of the same name in central Henan Province. Artifacts from Zhengzhou predate those from Anyang, and therefore the Zhengzhou developments are felt to represent a middle period of Shang development. Urban populations would have been engaged for the most part in the concerns of the state, including enterprises such as metallurgy, as well as in running or providing support services for the offices of the court. The rural populations, primarily engaged in the farming of millet, also served the Shang state. Often the agricultural lands are referred to as the "king's land" or the "Shang's land," indicating that a significant portion of the crops was intended for collection by the state.

The extent of Shang influence is astounding. Over five hundred sites that were culturally (although not necessarily politically) Shang have been found in Henan, Hebei, Shanxi, Shaanxi, Anhui, Shandong, Jiangsu, Zhejiang, Hubei, Jiangxi, Hunan, Sichuan, Inner Mongolia, and Liaoning Provinces (an area covering much of present day China). Remnants of Shang culture have even been discovered among the artifacts of cultures that were distinctively non-Shang.

Geographic and Historical Influences

The Shang means of ruling the many scattered cultures under its influence was essentially that of an aristocratically configured feudalism based on clan birthright, perpetuated in the cult worship of royal Shang ancestors. Advanced techniques of metallurgy also aided Shang control, because military might allowed the Shang to maintain authority and prevail in the frequent wars against neighboring tribes, and especially against members of the Qiang tribal clan, who were often the victims of Shang sacrificial practices. Alliances between the Shang core authority and other clans were in a constant state of flux, and the true area through which the king and his retinue could travel safely was limited to the heartland of the Shang state in northern and eastern Henan and western Shandong. The population of the Shang is, as of yet, inestimable.

The fall of the Shang at the hands of a neighboring clan-state, the Zhou (1045–256 BCE) did not cut short the dynasty's influence on subsequent mainstream Chinese development. The Zhou, and to an extent successive dynasties, perpetuated the legacy of the Shang through continuing practices of ancestor worship, a patrimonial system of inheriting political status, an elaborate burial ritual, divination as a primary means of state advisement, and writing.

Dallas L. McCurley

See also: **Zhou Dynasty**

Further Reading

Allan, Sarah. (1991) *The Shape of the Turtle: Myth, Art, and Cosmos in Early China.* Albany, NY: State University of New York Press.

Chang, Kwang-chih. (1980) *Shang Civilization.* New Haven, CT: Yale University Press.

Keightley, David, ed. (1983) *The Origins of Chinese Civilization.* Berkeley and Los Angeles: University of California Press.

Loewe, Michael, and Edward L. Shaughnessy, eds. (1999) *The Cambridge History of Ancient China: From the Origins of Civilization to 221 B.C.* Cambridge, U.K.: Cambridge University Press.

SHANGHAI (2002 est. pop. 9 million). China's leading port city since the late nineteenth century, Shanghai is located in Jiangsu Province on the Huangpu tributary near the mouth of the Chang (Yangtze) River in central China. Along with the important role that it plays in the national transportation network, Shanghai is a major financial and industrial city, with hundreds of modern factories situated in its Pudong region—a·special economic zone that has been developed since the opening of China in the 1980s.

Shanghai has long been a major commercial and transportation center in China since the Song (960–1279) and Yuan (1279–1368) dynasties and during the Ming (1368–1644) and Qing (1644–1912) dynasties emerged as an important location in China's cotton industry. During the seventeenth century, a hundred years before the arrival of the Europeans, Shanghai was already one of the Qing dynasty's largest cities and an important port for both domestic and coastal trade.

Shanghai as a Western Trade Port

Under the conditions of the 1842 Treaty of Nanjing (Nanking) that concluded the First Opium War, Shanghai was opened, along with four other Chinese ports, to foreign trade and residence. The foreign presence in Shanghai grew throughout the latter half of the nineteenth century as British, American, French, Japanese, and other Western traders and adventurers moved to the city to engage in commerce. The foreign community in Shanghai resided in two settlements, the French Concession and the larger International Settlement, both of which were set apart from the Chinese city. Under the terms of the unequal treaties that were imposed on China in the nineteenth century, the foreign population was self-governed by a Municipal Council and a Mixed Court. The city's famous Bund along the Huangpu River was dominated by examples of European colonial architecture that housed foreign banks, trading houses, and consulates. The foreign community in Shanghai also constructed a horse-racing track, cricket field, and other facilities for its recreation during this period. During the late nineteenth and early twentieth centuries, Shanghai was the center of foreign culture and commerce in China.

Shanghai under the Nationalists

As a bustling port and industrial city, Shanghai had a large working-class population during the early twentieth century, and this class played an important role in the development of both trade unions and political ideologies in modern China. The city's foreign concessions unwittingly provided sanctuary to many early socialist and communist leaders. During this period, resentment against foreign imperialism in China grew and boiled over on 30 May 1925, when tens of thousands of students and workers held a major protest in the city's International Settlement. Dissatisfaction with the state of the nation continued to grow among

Shanghai's population, and in March 1927, the city's General Labor Union, under the direction of the Chinese Communist Party, launched a general strike that was brutally suppressed by the army of Chiang Kaishek (1887–1975) on its return from the Northern Expedition, a campaign against warlords in the north.

As the city emerged as China's leading port, a new class of Chinese entrepreneurs developed, a group often referred to as the comprador class. These merchants acted as both middle persons in the trade between China and foreigners and as an emerging native community of entrepreneurs and business people. The Chinese merchant community in Shanghai was extremely powerful and dominated local politics in the city's chambers of commerce and native place associations. Shanghai's Chinese bankers and industrialists were an important source of revenue for Chiang Kaishek's Guomindang (Nationalist) government during the 1920s and 1930s. During the Nanjing Decade (1927–1937), Shanghai's businesses were heavily taxed by the new national government. In the early twentieth century, another group also wielded influence in the city—the triads, or criminal gangs. The triads profited by controlling Shanghai's lucrative drug and prostitution trades and by blackmailing local Chinese business leaders.

Shanghai was captured by the Japanese army after a bloody battle in the fall of 1937 and was occupied until Japan's defeat in August 1945. After the Communist victory in 1949, many of the city's bourgeoisie, however, fled the port and relocated to Hong Kong and Taiwan, helping to spur the economic development of both locations. During the first few decades of Communist rule, Shanghai was viewed with distrust by the new regime because the city was seen as not only a former center of foreign imperialism, but also home to middle-class values. Despite being tainted by its capitalist past, Shanghai continued to serve as a major source of tax revenue for the new Communist government and as a key industrial city in central China.

Shanghai since 1980

In the 1980s, with the opening of China, Shanghai was reborn and quickly resumed its role as the nation's premier port and point of contact with the outside world. Shanghai's industrial quarter attracted foreign investors who developed modern factories in the city. Chinese entrepreneurs helped to revitalize Shanghai's economy, making it one of the success stories of the post-Mao era and home to bustling financial and commercial enterprises. An important component of Shanghai's growth since the early 1990s has been the development of the Pudong New Area—a 100-square kilometer development zone that is home to a new international airport, deep-water harbor, and modern industrial and high-technology parks. In 1990, Pudong's local gross domestic product (GDP) was 6 billion renminbi (RMB), a figure that was dwarfed by the 2000 GDP figure of 92 billion RMB. Since the 1980s, Shanghai's industrial base has been diversified from the emphasis on heavy industries (steel and petrochemical) that dominated during the Communist era, to new, "cleaner" industries that emphasize light manufacturing, including textiles and electronic goods. Shanghai remains China's leading banking and financial center and an important site of foreign investment.

Robert John Perrins

Further Reading

Cooke Johnson, Linda. (1995) *Shanghai: From Market Town to Treaty Port, 1074–1858.* Stanford, CA: Stanford University Press.

Fu, Poshek. (1993) *Passivity, Resistance, and Collaboration: Intellectual Choices in Occupied Shanghai, 1937–1945.* Stanford, CA: Stanford University Press.

Goodman, Bryna. (1995) *Native Place, City, and Nation: Regional Networks and Identities in Shanghai, 1853–1937.* Berkeley and Los Angeles: University of California Press.

Henriot, Christian. (1993) *Shanghai, 1927–1937: Municipal Power, Locality, and Modernization.* Trans. by Noel Castelino. Berkeley and Los Angeles: University of California Press.

Murphey, Rhoads. (1953) *Shanghai: Key to Modern China.* Cambridge, U.K.: Cambridge University Press.

Perry, Elizabeth J. (1993) *Shanghai on Strike: The Politics of Chinese Labor.* Stanford, CA: Stanford University Press.

Sergeant, Harriet. (1990) *Shanghai, Collision Point of Cultures, 1918–1939.* New York: Crown Publishers.

Wakeman, Federic, and Wen-hsin Yeh, eds. (1992) *Shanghai Sojourners.* Berkeley, CA: Institute of East Asian Studies, University of California, Center for Chinese Studies.

SHANGHAI COOPERATION ORGANIZATION

The Shanghai Cooperation Organization (also known as the Shanghai Forum or the Shanghai Five) was established by five nations, China, Kazakhstan, Kyrgyzstan, Russia, and Tajikistan, during the gathering of the heads of state in Shanghai in April 1996. It was the first large-scale cooperation initiative since the China-Soviet split in the 1960s. The main purpose was the resolution of disputed territorial issues, demilitarization of the borders, and removing the last vestiges of the Cold War–era confrontation. Additionally, the members sought to boost economic cooperation, the movement of investment between these neighboring countries, and encourage trade, especially border trade.

During their first meetings in 1996 and 1997, the Shanghai Five members signed agreements on borders and on demilitarization. These fundamentally important documents endorsed resolution of the long-standing disputes that existed between the USSR (and later the Confederation of Independent States, or CIS) on one hand and the People's Republic of China on the other, which had led to several military conflicts in the past.

After the delimitation of the borders and resolving the disputed territorial issues, the Shanghai Five turned to other problems of mutual importance such as terrorism, the growing militancy of opposition groups, and separatism. During the meeting in Almaty in July 1998, the members decided to initiate annual summits. In August 1999 during the summit in Bishkek, Kyrgyzstan, the Shanghai Five members issued the so-called Bishkek Statement, expressing their desire to tackle "international terrorism, illegal dealing in drugs and narcotics trafficking, arms smuggling, illegal immigration and other forms of cross-border crimes," setting up a joint consultative group and launching military cooperation. Another outcome was the establishment of an Anti-Terrorist Center in Bishkek.

In June 2001 the Shanghai Five decided to relaunch the organization as the Shanghai Cooperation Organization (SCO) in response to the increasing marginalization of Russia in the international arena and China's worries about the prospects of the United States–dominated unilateral world order. The SCO members emphasized military cooperation against terrorism, and promotion of economic development and trade. In addition, China and Russia stressed their support for a "multipolar world," and a new world order based on "democratic, fair, and rational" principles. The SCO members also agreed to extend the cooperation into new fields, such as cultural issues, ecological problems, and disaster relief. They also declared the organization open to new members. During the 2001 summit, Uzbekistan officially joined as the sixth full member.

Rafis Abazov

Further Reading

Allison, Roy, and Lena Jonson, eds. (2001) *Central Asian Security: The New International Context.* Washington, DC: Brookings Institution.

"Bishkek Statement." (1999) *Beijing Review* (13 September).

"Combating the Three Evil Forces." (2001) *Beijing Review* (5 July).

Marcus, Ustina, ed. (2002) *Eurasian and East Europe Security Yearbook.* Washington, DC: Brassey's Press.

"Shanghai Statement." (1996) *Beijing Review* (13 May).

SHANGHAI PUDONG NEW AREA A stroll along the famous stretch of river called the Bund in Shanghai, China, is a stroll between two different periods of time. On the Shanghai side of the Huangpu River are the grand Western-style buildings built mostly in the 1910s and 1920s. Across the river, in what used to be rural marsh, farmland, shabby housing, and run-down factories, is the 350-square-kilometer Special Economic Zone called the Pudong New Area.

A ten-year building boom in the 1990s shaped the Pudong skyline with nearly 300 financial and commercial towers, hotels, and apartments. Some of these many buildings can be seen from the Bund. The first to catch the eye is the gigantic and visually challenging 468-meter Oriental Pearl TV Tower. It includes eleven spheres of various sizes, located at different points along the tower. In the distance, the Jinmao Building rises to 88 floors, the top part of which, not apparent to the viewer, is a five-star hotel. Situated in the foreground on the riverfront is a long, low-level building with a huge dome on each side. This is the Shanghai International Convention Center.

In the 1990s Pudong was the fastest growing urban area in the world. It is likely that the overall pace of development will continue until at least 2010. Construction in Pudong continues to involve massive infrastructure and housing development and the provision of production, office, and warehousing space on an unprecedented scale. Shanghai planners have long considered the development prospects of Pudong, recognizing that the Huangpu River represents a formidable transportation barrier. The construction of several major bridges, tunnels, and a subway system in the 1990s supplemented earlier cross-river tunnel and ferry connections. This has considerably improved accessibility, though congestion is still severe at peak periods. A subway will eventually connect the huge new international airport in Pudong to the financial and cultural centers of Shanghai.

A Special Economic Zone

The Pudong New Area was designated an "open" area in 1990 by the Chinese government. This initiative stimulated Shanghai's economic restructuring after years of neglect. It also reaffirmed the central government's commitment to economic reform and foreign investment. The leasing and ownership of buildings, restricted elsewhere in China at the time, would largely be market based. In addition, foreign investment would be allowed in financial services, retailing, and infrastructure development, notably roads, subways, and airports.

Pudong is divided into four functional development zones: Lujiazui finance and trade zone, Zhangjiang high-tech development park, Jinqiao export processing area, and Waigaoqiao free-trade zone. The financial center is home to the Shanghai Stock Exchange, domestic and international banking, investment houses, other businesses, and major accounting and consulting firms. High technology in particular is encouraged. The high-tech development park is to become the Silicon Valley of China. It will be the site for education, research, development and high-tech incubation. Export processing is facilitated in the Waigaoqiao free-trade zone by a shipping port and bonded storage. Manufacturing enterprises from all over the world are represented in the Pudong area.

In setting up offices ahead of China's entry into the World Trade Organization, many foreign firms have made considerable investments in Pudong. They have also had to weather the real estate bubble of the mid-1990s and its subsequent collapse, compounded in part by the Asian financial crisis of 1997. Rents that peaked in 1995 declined 75 percent by 1999. As a consequence, Pudong was left with tremendous overcapacity in commercial rental space. Vacancy rates varied from 40 to 70 percent of capacity between 1996 and 2000. This made the rental market for foreign businesses difficult in that period. Low rents are attractive because they reduce overhead costs. However, the prospect of locating in a building with few or no tenants raised questions about the real market for commercial space and the viability of business operations in this location. Efforts to control the building boom in the late 1990s may reduce the excess capacity and increase investor confidence.

Environment and Development

Known as the "dragon's head," the Pudong New Area is not just a financial center for Shanghai. It also is one of several developments in the Chang (Yangtze) River Basin (population 400 million) designed to integrate China into the global economy in the twenty-first century. The pressures to create economic wealth from this region have profound social and environmental implications. The challenge in many respects will be to avoid the worst excesses of urban and industrial development, particularly unsustainable transportation, energy, and manufacturing production processes.

Control over development and integration of the two regional areas, the older Shanghai Puxi area of 12.7 million people and the new Pudong area of 1.5 million people, is gradually shifting from the central government to the Shanghai municipal government. The matter of policy and administrative control may become increasingly important as Shanghai struggles with economic, social, and environmental pressures brought on by economic reforms.

Among the many environmental problems are air and water pollution. Smoggy days are a consequence of coal-fired power plants and emissions from automobiles. Water pollution has typically been the result of inadequate controls, addressed in part with new water treatment plants in Pudong. A longer-term issue, one that will be important to the next generation, is the rise in sea level. Climate change models suggest that the level of the East China Sea could rise by 50 to 70 centimeters by 2050, exposing Shanghai, and especially Pudong, to flooding.

Regarding social issues, city planners may have to deal with the problems caused by growing income disparity, a result of economic reform. China is facing problems such as unemployment that did not exist under central planning. The new Shanghai will increasingly have disparities in wage income between urban and rural residents and even among urban residents. A key focus of city planners is job creation in the financial-services and high-technology industries. There is every reason to believe that the new Shanghai will rival Hong Kong and Taiwan as a leading financial and commercial center by 2010.

Robert Gale

Further Reading

Han, Sun Sheng. (2000) "Shanghai between State and Market in Urban Transformation." *Urban Studies* 37: 2091–2113.

Wu, Fulong. (2000) "The Global and Local Dimensions of Place-Making: Remaking Shanghai as a World City." *Urban Studies* 37: 1359–1378.

SHANXI (1997 est. pop. 31.4 million). The northern China province of Shanxi borders on Shaanxi Province on the west, Nei Monggol Autonomous Region (Inner Mongolia) on the north, Hebei Province on the east, and Henan Province on the south. Shanxi covers an area of 156,300 square kilometers of highly eroded plateau at an altitude of about 1,000 meters above sea level. On the western, northern, and eastern fringe, mountains rise from 500 to 2,000 meters above the plateau. The Huang (Yellow) River constitutes parts of the border to Hebei and Henan. Sheltered from winds from the ocean by the eastern mountains, Shanxi has a typical continental climate, with cold winters and dry summers, and an annual precipitation of 400 to 650 millimeters, which makes irrigation necessary. The capital of Taiyuan (estimated population of 1.9 million as of 1997) is situated in the center of the Shanxi, which is divided into six regions and one hundred counties.

Shanxi was inhabited by farmers as early as 5000 BCE, and during the Western Zhou dynasty (1045–771 BCE), the state of Jin was established in the area. After the unification of China in 221 BCE, Shanxi often came into play as a crucial part in the Chinese empire's defense against nomad invasions. Both the Northern Wei (386–534 CE) and the Tang (618–907 CE) dynasties were established from Shanxi, but when succeeding dynasties set up their capitals in eastern China, the area declined into a poverty-stricken region ruled by warlords or nomad chiefs. Shanxi was occupied by Japanese forces from 1937 to 1945.

The province is sparsely populated in the northwestern mountainous parts where sheep, cattle, and other livestock are raised. In the agricultural areas, relatively little wheat and rice is grown, the major products being millet, soybeans, and potatoes. Other main crops are cotton, sugar beets, tobacco, fruit, and vegetables. Shanxi has the largest known deposits of coal in China, accounting for one-third of the total. The coal is of high quality and the fields cover an area of 57,100 square kilometers and are easily mined near the surface. Other natural resources in significant amounts include iron ore, copper, and gypsum. The industry is concentrated around Taiyuan and Datong in the north. The coal industry is, of course, by far the most important, but important industrial products also include locomotives, automobiles, and tractors. The light industry produces consumer goods such as watches, television sets, and washing and sewing machines. Shanxi is home for the famous Yungang grottoes from the Northern Wei dynasty, containing fifty-three caves with about 51,000 statues of various Buddhist deities.

Bent Nielsen

Further Reading
Goodman, David S. G. (1989) *China's Regional Development*. London: Routledge.
Schran, Peter. (1976) *Guerrilla Economy: The Development of the Shensi-Kansu-Ninghsia Border Region, 1937–1945*. Albany, NY: State University of New York Press.
Tong, Ya-ming. (1991). *Poverty Issues and Policies in China: The Case of Luliang District in Shanxi Province*. Canberra, Australia: National Centre for Development Studies, The Australian National University.

SHARI'A Many pious Muslims believe that one of the most remarkable and valuable features of their religion is the comprehensive and dynamic nature of its legal system. Islamic religious law is an elaborate and vigorous system that has been evolving from the time of the Prophet Muhammad (c. 570–632), the founder of Islam, until the present, and continues to be taken very seriously by a large number of Muslims, who use its rules and values as guiding principles in their lives. This system of law is called *shari'a*, a word that literally means "path to water." This meaning shows how Muslims see *shari'a* not only as something that is essential to life but also as a very obvious path, because in a desert nothing is more obvious to the residents than the path to a reliable source of water.

Qur'anic Law

Muslims believe Islamic law to be the collected prescriptions dictated by God for the running of the universe. This law is revealed by God in the Qur'an, which provides some very clear rules on issues as diverse as how to perform acts of worship, what not to eat, and how to distribute inheritance property. However, the Qur'an does not provide clear rules for all of the innumerable situations encountered in the course of human life. During Muhammad's lifetime, that level of detail was not thought necessary, because the Islamic community had the living example of the Prophet to follow.

The generations immediately after the death of Muhammad also did not see any problem with the fact that the Qur'an did not provide a comprehensive list of laws, because the memory of Muhammad was very much alive in the community, and people felt they had a good idea of what Muhammad would have done in any given situation. However, as generations passed and the Islamic community spread to new cultures and was faced with new situations, it became more and more difficult to use the practices of Muhammad as they were remembered by the community to guide all aspects of life. It therefore became necessary to develop a system by which laws could be developed to deal with new situations. This system is called *fiqh*, and is believed to have four principles called *usul al-fiqh* (principles of jurisprudence).

Principles of Jurisprudence

The primary source of Islamic law is the Qur'an. Rules and precepts that are clearly stated in the Qur'an are not open to debate and must be accepted as is. This is the first principle of jurisprudence. For example, since the Qur'an explicity forbids the eating of pork, Muslims who are observant of *shari'a* need look no further for rules concerning whether or not they should eat pork.

If the Qur'an does not provide clear rules concerning a question of law, then one looks to the example of the Prophet, otherwise referred to as his sunna (the second rule of jurisprudence). Sunna, often translated as "tradition," is the way Muhammad lived his life. This is preserved as living sunna in the practices of a virtuous Islamic community, and as recorded sunna in the anecdotes concerning Muhammad's actions, which are known as hadith. The concept of sunna is complicated and open to interpretation, since the vast number of individual hadith accounts sometimes contradict each other; furthermore, the concept of living tradition can cause conflict because not everyone agrees on which traditions of a society are in keeping with what Muhammad would have done and which of them are innovations.

From the ninth century onward, Muslim jurists have attempted to balance Qur'an and sunna and have tried to derive laws from these sources that can then be applied to new situations. This normally involves reasoning by analogy (the third principle of jurisprudence) and consensus of the community (the fourth).

Islamic Legal Schools

Sunni Muslim jurists belong to four schools, which differ in whether or not they trust more in the textual sources of Qur'an and hadith or in the human ability to reason by analogy. These schools are called the Maliki, Hanbali, Hanafi, and Shafi'i. The Maliki school is traditionally strongest in North Africa and considers the living sunna of the community to be more reliable than human reason. The Hanbali school is strongest in Saudi Arabia; it has historically given a great deal of weight to the literal interpretation of written texts, so much so that some Hanbali scholars insisted that an unreliable hadith should be preferred over a strong example of reasoning by analogy. The Shafi'i school resembled the Hanbali school in relying on hadith in preference to the living sunna, although Shafi'i scholars accept analogical reasoning when there is no clear guidance from the Qur'an or hadith. The Hanafi school is notable for accepting personal opinion in matters of law if there is no precedent on which to rely.

The Shafi'i and Hanafi schools together account for the majority of Sunni Muslims and have a wide distribution, the Shafi'i school being more popular among the Arabs of the Middle East and in Indonesia, and the Hanafi school being more accepted in South and Central Asia and in Turkey. The Hanafi school has had a wider distribution since the sixteenth century, but before that the Shafi'i school was the most influential legal tradition in the Islamic world. Among Shi'ite Muslims, one important legal school was the

Narinder Bhatia of Faridabad, India, holds up what may be the world's smallest Qur'an. Owned by his father, the book measures 15x20x10 mm and contains 572 pages. (AFP/CORBIS)

Ja'fari school. It was established by Nadir Shah (1688–1747), the Iranian conqueror, in an attempt to heal the schism between Shi'ite and Sunni Islam. However, the positions adopted by the new school proved unacceptable to Shi'ites and Sunnis alike, and it failed.

Because the Hanafi and Shafi'i schools use the principle of reasoning by analogy to a much greater degree than do the Hanbali and Maliki schools, many people see these schools as being better able to adapt to new circumstances. The process of using reasoning by analogy to come up with new laws for new circumstances is called *ijtihad*, and someone who is qualified to engage in this form of independent reasoning is called a Mujtahid. Mujtahid is not normally a formal title given by a ruler or government, but is bestowed by the local Islamic community in recognition of a religious scholar's reputation for learning and good character.

Muftis and *Fatwas*

A mufti is a highly respected legal authority who obtains his title by virtue of achieving a reputation among the local populace as a good, reliable scholar. The mufti's legal opinion is called a *fatwa*. In theory, the mufti's opinion is binding on the person who poses the legal question to the mufti. In practice, people frequently ignore the mufti's opinion if it displeases them, largely because there is no institution that enforces the decision of the mufti.

Jamal Elias

Further Reading

Bakhtiar, Laleh, and Kevin Reinhart. (1996) *Encyclopedia of Islamic Law: A Compendium of the Major Schools.* Chicago: Kazi Publications.

Rauf, Feisal Abdul. (1999) *Islam, A Sacred Law: What Every Muslim Should Know about the Shariah.* Aptos, CA: Threshold Books.

Siddiqui, M. S. (1972) *Islamic Sharia and the Muslims.* Chicago: Kazi Publications.

SHARIATI, ALI (1933–1977), Iranian Islamic intellectual. Ali Shariati was an Iranian Islamic intellectual whose writings and teachings contributed to the growth of revolutionary Islam in Iran. He was born in the village of Mazinan. Soon after, he moved with his family to Mashhad. His father was Mohammad Taqi Shariati, a reformist Muslim cleric. After high school, Ali Shariati studied at a teachers training college and later began teaching in elementary schools in the area. During the oil nationalization movement, Shariati supported Prime Minister Muhammad Musaddeq; he was arrested and held in jail. After his release Shariati studied Arabic and French at Mashhad University while continuing his teaching duties. In 1959 he was awarded a scholarship to study sociology and Islamic studies at the University of Paris. It was in France that he came into contact with the scholars and intellectuals who shaped his thinking on sociology, religion, revolution, and imperialism. He earned a doctorate in sociology and theology in 1964. Upon his return to Iran he was arrested and jailed on suspicion of being a subversive. He was released six months later and went back to teaching at village schools. Soon after, Shariati began teaching at Mashhad University. He was eventually fired and moved to Tehran, where he began lecturing at Husseini Ershad, a socioreligious educational association organized by the liberation movement. He spoke in favor of mass political participation and against the regime of Muhammad Reza Shah Pahlavi. The government shut down Husseini Ershad in the early 1970s. Shariati was arrested, and his writings banned. Three years later he was released to house arrest. In 1977 he received government permission to travel to Britain, where he died in Southampton on 19 June 1977

of an apparent heart attack; there was suspicion that the Iranian secret police was involved in his death. He was buried in Damascus.

Shariati further developed the lines of thinking on Islam by presenting the religion as modernizing and revolutionary rather than conservative and fatalistic. Furthermore, he explained the ideological position of Islam as a moderate one between socialism and capitalism. His lectures were very popular and were published in fifty volumes. One of Shariati's best-known works in the West is *On the Sociology of Islam*, translated into English by Hamid Algar. Although his writings and teachings provided the undercurrent for the Iranian Revolution in 1979, he has been denounced for his anticlerical message in the years since the revolution.

Houman A. Sadri

Further Reading

Boroujerdi, Mehrzad. (1996) *Iranian Intellectuals and the West: The Tormented Triumph of Nativism.* Syracuse, NY: Syracuse University Press.

Rahnama, Ali. (1998) *An Islamic Utopian: A Political Biography of Ali Shariati.* London, New York: I. B. Tauris.

Shariati, Ali. (1979) *On the Sociology of Islam.* Trans. by Hamid Algar. Berkeley and Los Angeles: University of California Press.

SHATT AL ARAB RIVER.   See **Karun River.**

SHEEP, KARAKUL   Karakul sheep, also known as Russian, Astrakhan, or Bukhara sheep, are medium-sized, fat-tailed, and one of the earliest domesticated sheep breeds of Central or West Asian origin. They are raised mainly for the lustrous black, curly pelt of very young lambs, called Persian lamb (once popular in expensive coats) and are also a source of milk, meat, tallow, and wool. Mature Karakul sheep have so-called carpet wool, a mixture of coarse and fine fibers fifteen to twenty-five centimeters long that produces a superior carpet yarn. This is the wool from which the art of felting evolved. Native flocks exhibit wide variations in type and color, with significant differences from other breeds of sheep. Their broad, fat tail is a fat storage organ, a source of nourishment, similar in function to the camel's hump.

Archaeologists have discovered Persian lambskin dating back to 1400 BCE, and carvings of a distinct Karakul type have been found on ancient Babylonian temples. The name originates from a village in the Amu Dar'ya River valley (now Uzbekistan). Native to this desert land, the Karakul sheep are adapted to harsh environment (shortage of vegetation and water, and extreme high and low temperatures). Large flocks are found in Central Asia and South Africa.

Victor Fet

Further Reading
American Karakul Sheep Registry. Retrieved 7 March 2002, from: http://www.karakulsheep.com.
Dmitriev, N. G., and L. K. Ernst. (1989) *Animal Genetic Resources of the USSR.* Animal Production and Health Paper. Rome: FAO.

SHEEP, MARCO POLO Marco Polo sheep (*vis poli*), the largest living wild sheep, are a subspecies of the once vast Argali (*Ovis ammon*) herds that ranged from Mongolia to Afghanistan. Today, these ungulates roam the Eastern Pamir Mountains and Pamir Plateau of Tajikistan, and in smaller numbers the neighboring Wakhan Corridor of Afghanistan, northern Pakistan (especially within Khunjerab National Park), and in China's eastern Xinjiang Province. Unlike most wild sheep, they favor open basins instead of rocky crags. They use their powerful bodies to outrun predatory snow leopards and wolves. The common name honors the legendary thirteenth-century Venetian traveler who noted the Central Asian practice of stacking sheep horns to demarcate travel routes across the Pamir Plateau.

Larger males measure 1.3 meters (4 feet) high at the shoulders, and weight 140 kilograms (300 pounds). The ram horns curl 1.8 meters (6 feet) or more in length and are prized by trophy hunters. Normally, a single lamb is born after a 150-day gestation and lives 6–7 years. Soviet-era travel restrictions protected this species in much of its range until the 1990s. Today foreign sport hunters, locals seeking meat, and poaching for body parts (used in Chinese potions) are depleting *Ovis poli* throughout its range.

Stephen F. Cunha

Further Reading
Geist, Valerius. (1974) *Mountain Sheep: A Study in Behavior and Habitat.* Chicago: University of Chicago Press.
Schaller, George B. (1983) *Mountain Monarchs: Wild Sheep and Goats of the Himalaya.* Chicago: University of Chicago Press.

SHEHNAI The *shehnai* is a North Indian wind instrument now familiar in the performance of classical music but originally associated with ceremonial occasions. It is a double-reed instrument with a wood body and brass bell and has six to eight holes. The *shehnai* is accompanied by a second *shehnai* that plays the first note of the octave. Percussion is provided by a small drum called a *tikara* and not ordinarily by the more standard tabla. The *shehnai* team used to be known as *raushanchauki* or *nahabat* in northern India. Like its southern counterpart, the *nadaswaram*, the *shehnai* was a feature of festivals, celebrations, temples, and royal courts. The contents of the music associated with such specific occasions came from Indian classical music but not in its most skilled or refined form. The traditional use of the *shehnai* has not completely disappeared, but its reputation greatly increased in the late twentieth century due to a few musician families, two of them hailing from Benares (Varanasi), who succeeded in establishing the *shehnai* in the concert hall. The greatest living exponent of classical *shehnai*, Bismillah Khan (b. 1908), belongs to one of the Benares families.

Tirthankar Roy

Further Reading
Krishnaswamy, S. (1965) *Musical Instruments of India.* Delhi: Publications Division, Government of India.

SHEN CONGWEN (1902–1988), twentieth-century Chinese writer. Born in Phoenix Town Village, Hunan Province, Shen briefly attended primary school and then went to a military training camp to carry on the family tradition of soldiering. Shen began writing after witnessing the horrors associated with military campaigns. At age twenty, he went to Peking, became coeditor of the journal *Modern Critic*, and gradually gained recognition for his literary talents. Shen worked in many genres including poetry, novels, and essays but was best known for short stories and novellas, including "Three Men and a Girl," "The Lovers," and "Gazing at Rainbows." Like his contemporaries, Shen was influenced by Western writers such as Maupassant, Chekhov, and Joyce. Later, he moved to Shanghai where he continued to write. Shen's main sources of inspiration were the Chinese countryside, military life, and the Miao minority ethnic group of Hunan. In 1949, Shen's productive streak ended after the Communists took power. The Chinese Communist party labeled Shen a conservative and banned his books. For several decades, Shen ceased to write fiction and instead studied porcelain making and the history of Chinese costume. In the 1980s, already an old man, Shen wrote again, enjoying a resurgence in popularity, until his death in 1988.

Elizabeth VanderVen

Further Reading
Nieh Hua-ling. (1972) *Shen Ts'ung-wen.* New York: Twayne.
Shen Congwen. ([1947] 1982) *The Chinese Earth: Stories by Shen Tseng-wen.* Trans. by Ching Ti and Robert Payne. New York: Columbia University Press.
———. (1995) *Imperfect Paradise.* Edited by Jeffrey Kinkley. Honolulu, HI: University of Hawaii Press.

SHENZHEN SPECIAL ECONOMIC ZONE

Shenzhen is a city in the south of China's Guangdong province. It borders Hong Kong and the Pearl River, with an area of 2020 square kilometers, 327.5 square kilometers of which have been designed as a special economic zone (SEZ) since 1979. Shenzhen was only one of four SEZs established to carry out experiments with greater economic freedom. But the transformation of the former rural community into a major export center is the showcase of economic reforms in post-Mao China and has attracted worldwide attention, especially from developing countries.

Historical Background and Foundation of Shenzhen SEZ

Since the 1960s, so-called export processing zones (EPZs) have been established in various parts of the world with the goal of attracting foreign direct investment (FDI) and promoting industrialization. While Latin America's experience with EPZs has been mixed, such East Asian countries as South Korea and Taiwan have made their EPZs centers of export-driven growth.

Until the end of the Maoist era (1976), the People's Republic of China followed a strategy of development that was diametrically opposed to that of EPZs. The open-treaty ports of the nineteenth century, which had to accept free trade as a result of unequal treaties with the Western powers and Japan, were symbols of national decay. Therefore, Communist China followed a policy of self-sufficiency and isolation. However, China's Great Leap Forward program in the 1950s and its Cultural Revolution in the 1960s resulted in economic and political catastrophe.

After the death of Mao Zedong and the arrest of the "Gang of Four," his hard-line supporters, in 1978, the new leadership under Deng Xiaoping (1904–1997) changed China's economic-development strategy. In July 1979, Guangdong and Fujian provinces were granted the right to carry out economic experiments, and four SEZs were set up: Shenzhen, Zhuhai, and Shantou of Guangdong province, and Xiamen of Fujian province. Later, in 1988, the island of Hainan became the fifth SEZ. All of these regions were coastal, rich in labor, and located close to the successful market economies of Hong Kong and Taiwan. The economic opening of these regions was intended to promote growth and exports, but the possibility of growing economic ties with Hong Kong and Taiwan was also seen as facilitating eventual reunification.

Development of Shenzhen SEZ

The newly established town of Shenzhen had originally been a county called Baoan, whose residents earned their living mainly from fishing. When Shenzhen city was established in 1979, it had 314,000 inhabitants. In 2000, it was a town of around 4 million inhabitants. The development of Shenzhen SEZ can be divided into four phases. The first phase, lasting from 1979 to 1984, saw the establishment of some legal preconditions for the existence of a special economic regime in the SEZ, but only slow changes in

Shenzhen was the first place in China designated as a special economic zone. The designation in 1980 turned what was once a town into a modern city. (JOSEPH SOHM; CHROMOSOHM INC./CORBIS)

economic activity. In 1984, Deng Ziaoping set up an economic framework for the SEZs as "windows to technology, management, knowledge, and foreign policies," opening a second phase in the institution of preconditions for growth. The inflow of foreign capital, mainly from Hong Kong, slowly accelerated from the mid-1980s, but production processes, contrary to expectations, were mostly characterized by low-technology intensity and were based on the comparative advantage of Shenzhen's low labor costs. Twice, in 1985 and after the events on Tiananmen Square in 1989, the SEZs were criticized by conservative Communist Party leaders.

In the early 1990s, the third phase of development began. During this takeoff period, foreign companies from all over the world rushed in, and by 1997, fifty-one of the world's top five hundred enterprises had taken root in Shenzhen. The export volume of Shenzhen increased to around one-seventh of China's total ($26 billion in 1998). Deng's much-publicized trip to Shenzhen in 1992 helped gain the trust of domestic and foreign investors. The technology intensity of production also increased, and in 1998 more than 35 percent of Shenzhen's production was in the high- and new-technology sectors.

The fourth phase of development began with the challenge of the Asian financial crisis in 1997 and China's preparation for entry in the World Trade Organization (WTO). This will bring a major redirection of economic activities in Shenzhen SEZ. While competition in the domestic market will be tougher due to market entry of new competitors and more domestic competition, the WTO accession in 2001 opens the world market even wider for Chinese exports.

Characteristics and Economic Effects of SEZs

When the EPZs were first established in various parts of the world, they were delineated as areas to provide procedural and operational ease for producers and to offer tax holidays, tax reductions, and duty-free import of capital goods and raw materials for export manufacture. This policy was designed to attract FDI, generate employment, earn foreign exchange, and eventually link the less-developed hinterland and facilitate technology transfer and transfer of modern-management practice. Infrastructure in the EPZs was limited to industrial estate development.

The Chinese SEZs, by contrast, additionally focused on the provision of supportive infrastructure such as housing, airports, roads, ports, telecommunications, electricity, and transportation. Also, the reform activities expanded to include agriculture,

commerce, development of the financial sector, including the opening of a stock exchange, tourism and the service sector, and increasingly since the mid-1990s, privatization of state-owned enterprises and housing. This expansion enabled Shenzhen SEZ to escape from the fate of many EPZs, which attracted only labor-intensive, low-technology production processes with few possibilities for economic development of the hinterland. Since a general liberalization of the Chinese economy was not possible because of political considerations, the SEZs served as a model for the reform of the rest of the economy in a politically closely controlled area. This indirect effect of the SEZs as models for the economy is as important as the direct effect of attraction of FDI and the transfer of technology and modern management practices.

Future of Shenzhen SEZ

Shenzhen SEZ not only became one of the centers of export, technology, and economic reform in China, but it was also gradually able to cope with such early problems as growing inequality, the fate of migrant workers, and environmental degradation. Shenzhen was awarded the first urban planning award in China by the International Architecture Association.

As China moves through the early years of the twenty-first century, however, the economic position of Shenzhen SEZ must be redirected. Labor costs are increasing, and firms are migrating to cheaper locations. The mushrooming of SEZs and the introduction of open ports and special zones for technological development as well as general economic reforms in China make competition for FDI harder. In the future, the upgrading of production and infrastructure, especially in areas such as education, will be crucial for Shenzhen SEZ.

Bernhard Seliger

Further Reading

Ge Wei. (1999) *Special Economic Zones and the Economic Transition in China.* Singapore: World Scientific.

Kundra, Ashok. (2000) *The Performances of India's Export Zones: A Comparison with the Chinese Approach.* New Delhi: Sage.

Lu Ding and Tang Zhimin. (1997) *State Intervention and Business in China.* Cheltenham, U.K.: Edward Elgar.

Park Jung-Dong. (1997) *The Special Economic Zones of China and Their Impact on Its Economic Development.* Westport, CT: Praeger.

Van Kemenade, Willem. (1997) *China, Hong Kong, Taiwan, Inc.: The Dynamics of a New Empire.* New York: Knopf.

Wu Weiping. (1999) *Pioneering Economic Reform in China's Special Economic Zones.* Aldershot, U.K.: Ashgate.

SHI The *shi* is China's classic lyric form. The early poetry anthology and Confucian classic *Shijing* (Classic of Poetry), compiled during the Zhou dynasty (1045–256 BCE), contained poems with four-character rhymed lines, the earliest sort of *shi*. Although composed on nonpolitical topics, the poems of the *Shijing* were believed to contain messages on good governance and the well-run state, and poetry from the Zhou dynasty forward was seen as, among other things, a vehicle for criticizing and reforming the state. Because a main characteristic of *shi* is indirection and allusion, meanings other than the readily apparent surface meaning were sought for and identified.

During the Han dynasty (206 BCE–220 CE) *shi* with either five- or seven-character lines developed. This style of *shi*, like the *shi* of the *Shijing*, featured grammatical parallelism and rhymed lines. Melancholy themes were popular; this tendency carried over into the Six Dynasties period (c. 222–589), when it became a conventionalized stance. The poetry of Tao Qian (365–427) stands out during this period; his poems on turning away from officialdom and embracing the joys of drink and the life of the gentleman farmer were models for later disaffected bureaucrats.

The *shi* form developed further in the Tang dynasty, with *lushi* ("regulated verse"—*shi* whose tonal pattern and rhyme scheme were closely dictated) and *jueju* ("broken-off lines"), an exceptionally short form of just four lines. In contradistinction, the older styles of *shi* came to be called *gushi* ("old-style verse"). The great poets of the Tang include Li Bo (701–772), who preferred *gushi*, and Du Fu (712–770), who wrote *lushi* and was admired by later generations for his realism and his choice of mundane subjects, which had earlier been thought inappropriate for poetry. The *shi* of Wang Wei (699–759), another great poet of the Tang, are informed by Buddhist sensibilities and a deep appreciation for landscape (Wang Wei was also a celebrated painter).

Shi continued as a major poetic form in subsequent eras and even into modern times, but with the compositions of the Tang, the form is considered to have reached its high point.

Francesca Forrest

Further Reading
Ayling, Alan and Donald Mackintosh. (1965) *A Collection of Chinese Lyrics*. Nashville, TN: Vanderbilt University Press.

Yoshikawa, Kojiro. (1989) *Five Hundred Years of Chinese Poetry, 1150–1650*. Princeton, NJ: Princeton University Press.

Owen, Stephen. (1981) *The Great Age of Chinese Poetry, The High T'ang*. New Haven, CT: Yale University Press.

Watson, Burton. (1971) *Chinese Lyricism: Shih Poetry from the Second to the Twelfth Century*. New York: Columbia University Press.

SHIBUSAWA EIICHI (1840–1931), father of modern Japanese business. Born in 1840 to the family of a textile merchant, Shibusawa Eiichi is considered a father of modern Japanese business. He was opposed to the Tokugawa family then in power, but his hopes of helping to bring down the Tokugawa regime (1600–1603–1868) were never realized. Shibusawa later accompanied a Tokugawa prince to Europe and nearly accompanied him into exile. As a person with experience abroad and training in Western ideas, Shibusawa became a member of the powerful Home Ministry under the Meiji government (1868–1912). In the Home Ministry he helped draft modern banking laws. Later Shibusawa resigned from the government to help found and run more than one hundred joint stock companies, including the first commercially successful cotton-spinning mill.

Shibusawa also made his mark in his efforts to apply Confucian ideas to business. Working both through schools he helped to found and through a society of followers, Ryumonsha (Dragon Gate Society), Shibusawa argued for a business ideology based on service to Japan which downplayed profit. Following his own philosophy, Shibusawa made a far smaller fortune from his many enterprises than one would expect. His efforts helped to create a banking system for Japan and an environment for business.

David W. Blaylock

Further Reading
Hirschmeier, Johannes. (1964) *The Origins of Entrepreneurship in Meiji Japan*. Cambridge, MA: Harvard University Press.

Obata Kyugoro. (1937) *An Interpretation of the Life of Viscount Shibusawa*. Tokyo: Tokyo Insatsu Kabushiki Kaisha.

Shibusawa, Eiichi. (1994) *The Autobiography Shibusawa Eiichi: From Peasant to Entrepreneur*. Trans. by Teruko Craig. Tokyo: University of Tokyo Press.

SHIGA (2002 est. pop. 1.4 million). Shiga Prefecture is situated in the central region of Japan's island of Honshu, where it occupies an area of 4,016 square kilometers. Shiga's primary geographical feature is the nation's largest freshwater body, Lake Biwa, located in a basin ringed by mountains. Biwa is divided into the deeper North Lake and the shallow South Lake.

Shiga is bordered by Kyoto, Mie, Gifu, and Fukui prefectures. Once known as Omi Province, it assumed its present name and borders in 1881.

The prefecture's capital city is Otsu, situated on Lake Biwa's southwest shore. Emperor Tenji established his palace and capital there in 667. After Tenji's death in 672, the capital was moved to Asuka. In later centuries Otsu flourished as a lake port and a highway post station during the Edo period (1600/1603–1868). In 1891, an assassination attempt was made on Russian Crown Prince Nicholas (later Czar Nicholas II) while he was visiting Otsu. In recent decades, Otsu has become the heart of the industrial zone south of Lake Biwa that abuts the Kyoto-Osaka metropolitan area. The prefecture's other important cities are Hikone, Nagahama, Kusatsu, and Omi Hachiman.

Ruled by a series of feudal warlords and often a strategic battlefield, the province came under the control of Oda Nobunaga (1534–1582), who in 1579 built a mountaintop castle in Azuchi to defend Kyoto. During the Edo period, most of the region was ruled by the Ii family from their castle town of Hikone.

Rice remains the prefecture's main agricultural product, while Lake Biwa is the source of various kinds of freshwater fish and also the site of pearl culture. Water from the lake is used for drinking, irrigation, and industry, both locally and in Kyoto, by way of the Biwako canal. Shiga's industries include textiles, electrical goods, chemicals, and transport machinery. Visitors are drawn to Lake Biwa, the Enryakuji Buddhist temple complex on Mount Hiei, Otsu's Hie Shrine and Buddhist temples, and the Edo-period merchant quarters in Omi Hachiman.

E. L. S. Weber

Further Reading
"Shiga Prefecture." (1993) *Japan: An Illustrated Encyclopedia.* Tokyo: Kodansha.

SHIGA SHIGETAKA

SHIGA SHIGETAKA (1863–1927), Japanese journalist and educator. A journalist and a professor of geography at Waseda University, Tokyo, Shiga was also a world traveler, and an advocate of emigration to Hawaii, California, and other destinations. In the late 1880s, schools of thought such as Shiga's Seikyosha (Society for Education and Politics) dominated the debates over the course Japan should take. Shiga advocated preservation of Japanese cultural identity (*kokusui shugi*) in the face of increasing internal and external pressures toward modernization. *Ni-*

honjin (Japanese), a fortnightly magazine, became a mouthpiece for the Seikyosha members. Shiga's major works are *Nan'yo jiji* (Current Affairs in the South Seas, 1887) and *Nihon fukeiron* (Japanese Landscape, 1894), best-sellers in the 1880s and 1890s, respectively, the latter still in print.

Shiga was also concerned about educating for a "new" Japan, especially following the promulgation of *Kyoiku chokugo* (The Imperial Rescript on Education, 1890), which called for people's obedience to the state. Shiga believed that education should be free from the state control and provide international perspectives for Japanese in Japan and overseas; it was vital to promote geography through journalism and educational institutions as a way of understanding the contemporary world.

Masako Gavin

Further Reading
Gavin, Masako. (2001) *Shiga Shigetaka: The Forgotten Enlightener.* London: Curzon Press.
Gluck, Carol. (1985) *Japan's Modern Myths: Ideology in the Late Meiji Period.* Princeton, NJ: Princeton University Press.

SHIJING

SHIJING *Shijing*, literally "classic of poetry," is the first collection of poetry in Chinese history and remains the most prestigious. The *Shijing*'s status as a classic is partly related to the legend attributing its compilation to Confucius (551–479 BCE), who was said to have selected its 305 poems from a base of 3,000. The reliability of this legend is rather uncertain; what the textual evidence does clearly show is that Confucius highly respected the *Shijing*, used it in his teaching, and commented on it.

The compilation of the *Shijing* has also been credited to officials dispatched by the central government to various regions to collect poems in order to observe local customs and people's lives and thereby improve the government. In the Western Han period (206 BCE–8 CE) when Emperor Wu (reigned 104–87 BCE) legitimized the school of Confucianism, the *Shi* became one of the Five Classics included in the curriculum of the national academy and was thereafter called *Shijing*.

The attribution and dating of the *Shijing* poems are uncertain. The works roughly date from the Early Western Zhou dynasty (eleventh century BCE) to the middle of the Spring and Autumn period (seventh century BCE). The traditional classification of the *Shijing* involves the Six Principles, which fall into two types. The first three principles denote three genres, namely, *feng, ya*, and *song*, or "air," "elegantia," and "hymn." *Feng*, also known as *guofeng* (airs of states), are folk songs from fifteen states. These songs, numbering 160 titles and making the major part of the *Shijing*, skillfully describe common people's lives. The 105 *ya* titles are divided into "greater *ya*" and "lesser *ya*." The former includes poems on court life, banquet scenes, harvest celebrations, and also epiclike verse on the Zhou ancestors. The lesser *ya* depict army life and the grievances of lower officials. Collected from three regions, Zhou, Lu, and Shang, the *song* include hymns sung at ceremonious occasions. The latter three principles refer to three rhetorical devices, namely *fu, bi,* and *xing*. The first means "elaboration," a plain narrative or descriptive mode of writing. *Bi* is "comparison," or analogy. *Xing,* referring to "arousing," is loosely understood as "metaphor."

A considerable number of the *Shijing* poems provide aesthetic pleasure and valuable information about the time. They profoundly influenced later Chinese literature. During the Han, most poems were given allegorical readings and were treated as political satires or ethical lessons. There were four major schools of such interpretation: Qi, Lu, Han, and Mao. The last one later assumed orthodoxy in the exegeses of the classic, and for this reason the *Shijing* is also called *Maoshi* (Poetry of the Mao School).

Timothy Wei Keung Chan

Further Reading

Karlgren, Bernhard. (1950) *The Book of Odes.* Stockholm, Sweden: Museum of Far Eastern Antiquities.

Waley, Arthur. (1996) *The Book of Songs.* Rev. ed. New York: Grove Press.

Zoeren, Stephen van. (1991) *Poetry and Personality: Reading, Exegesis, and Hermeneutics in Traditional China.* Stanford, CA.: Stanford University Press.

SHIKOKU (2001 pop. 4.2 million). Shikoku is located in the southwest part of the Japanese archipelago, facing the Seto Inland Sea between Honshu and Kyushu. It is the smallest of Japan's four main islands, with an area of 18,808 square kilometers. It is divided into four prefectures: Kagawa, Tokushima, Kochi, and Ehime. In the past, each prefecture's capital was built around a castle and therfore known as a "castle town" (*Joka-machi*). The cities of Matsuyama (2001 pop. 472,000) and Takamatsu (2001 pop. 333,000) are the largest on the island. The northern part of Shikoku has mild winters and long dry summers and is little affected by the wind. The southern part of the island, which is influenced by the Pacific Ocean, is warmer

and wetter. Here average temperature ranges from 14° C to 16° C. The island is mountainous including high peaks such as Mount Ishizuchi (1,982 meters) in Ehime and Mount Tsurugi (1,955 meters) in Tokushima. The Shikoku Karst, a limestone plateau with an elevation of 1,400 meters, runs along the borders of Ehime and Kochi Prefectures.

It is this range of elevation of Shikoku that has limited agricultural conditions, habitation, and communication. For a very long time, Shikoku was isolated from the rest of Japan, and it was last of the main islands to be linked by bridge to the main island Honshu. The 1988 completion of the Seto Ohashi Bridge, a high-speed transportation system, has contributed to the development of industry in the north of Shikoku. Seto Ohashi, a series of six bridges using five small islands, links Kojima in Okayama and Sakaide in Kagawa. At 12.6 kilometers in length, it represents the world's longest roadway and railway formed by a bridge. Other bridges connected to Honshu are the Naruto, Akashi, and Kanmon bridges. They are expected to attract further industrial development to Shikoku.

The main industries in the northern and western parts of Shikoku are metallurgy, machinery, pulp and paper, textiles, heavy chemicals, and oil refineries. Projects in Ehime and Kagawa Prefectures are currently focused on research and development in advanced technology industries and various development schemes are being implemented. Agricultural products include rice, vegetables, mandarin oranges, persimmons, and tea. Forestry is important, and the fishing industry includes cultured pearls. In recent years tourism has increased.

Nathalie Cavasin

Further Reading

Association of Japanese Geographers, eds. (1980) *Geography of Japan.* Tokyo: Teikoku Shoin.

Yagasaki Noritaka, ed. (1997) *Japan: Geographical Perspectives on an Island Nation.* Tokyo: Teikoku Shoin.

SHILLONG (2001 pop. 133,000). Capital of the state of Meghalaya ("abode of the clouds") in northeastern India, Shillong was the capital of Assam state from 1874 until 1972. Named for nearby Shillong Peak, the area of rolling hills and elegant pines veiled in clouds (altitude 1,520 meters) became known as the "Scotland of the East" under the British, who built it on the site of a thousand-year-old Khasi settlement. An earthquake destroyed the city in 1897. It was entirely rebuilt and became an important trade center for agricultural products, as well as a military base and appealing summer resort with championship golf course and polo ground.

Spread on hills covered with Victorian bungalows and churches, Shillong abounds in waterfalls. Crinoline Falls, Beadon Falls, Bishop Falls, Elephant Falls, Ward's Lake and gardens, Lady Hyari Park and mini zoo, and the Butterfly Museum are popular. Pineapple and betel plantations lie nearby. Research stations include dairy farms and fruit- and silkworm-growing institutions. The Police Bazaar deals in cane furniture, handicrafts, shawls, and textiles; the Bara Bazaar offers produce and provisions, with some jewelry and handicrafts. Migration has caused social unrest, with the native Khasi population reacting unfavorably to the arrival of Bengalis and others.

C. Roger Davis

Further Reading

Pakem, B. (1982) *Shillong, 1971–1981.* Calcutta, India: Research India Publications for North-East India Council for Social Science Research.

Goswami, B. B. (1979) *Cultural Profile of Shillong.* Calcutta, India: Anthropological Survey of India.

SHIMANE

(2002 est. pop. 753,000). Shimane Prefecture is situated in the western region of Japan's island of Honshu, it occupies an area of 6,629 square kilometers. Shimane's primary geographical features are a mountainous terrain, coastal plains, and the offshore Oki Islands. Shimane is bordered by the Sea of Japan, and by Tottori, Hiroshima, and Yamaguchi prefectures. Once divided into Izumo, Iwami, and Oki provinces, it assumed its present name and borders in 1881.

According to legend, Izumo Province once was an ancient religious and political center rivaling Nara. In feudal times the region was ruled successively by the Sasaki, Yamana, Kyogoku, and Amako warrior families, and later by the Matsudaira. The Oki Islands once were a refuge for elite political exiles such as Emperor Godaigo (1288–1339), who opposed the Kamakura shogunate.

The prefecture's capital city is Matsue, situated along Lake Shinji. In the Edo period (1600/1603–1868), Matsue was a castle town ruled by the Matsudaira family. In the early 2000s, it is part of Nakaumi New Industrial City, with factories producing machinery and textiles. The prefecture's other important cities are Hamada, Izumo, and Masuda.

The main economic activities are rice agriculture, fishing, and molybdenum mining, as well as wood-working and the production of farm tools. On the Oki Islands livestock and horses are raised. Pilgrims are drawn in great numbers to the venerable Izumo shrine, a focus of the Shinto creation story. The shrine rituals include the performance of the Izumo Kagura, a series of dances depicting Shinto myths. Other popular destinations are the Oki Islands and Daisen-Oki National Park on the Shimane Peninsula around Mount Sambe (Sambesan).

E. L. S. Weber

Further Reading

"Shimane Prefecture." (1993) *Japan: An Illustrated Encyclopedia.* Tokyo: Kodansha.

SHIMAZAKI TOSON

(1872–1943), poet and novelist. Shimazaki Toson is the pen name of Shimazaki Haruki. Born in Magome in Nagano Prefecture, Toson worked as a teacher before turning exclusively to writing. Early in his career, Toson wrote "new style poetry," a romantic strain of poetry longer and freer than traditional Japanese verse. Many literary historians consider his anthology *Wakanashu* (Collection of Young Leaves, 1897) one of the earliest works of modern poetry in Japan. Nonetheless, Toson is best remembered as the foremost novelist of Japanese Naturalism, a movement that aspired to depict the human condition with scientific precision. Toson's first novel, *Hakai* (The Broken Commandment, 1906) displays an unprecedented attention to psychological detail and represents a milestone in the development of the modern Japanese novel. It also is one of the first novels to depict the difficult lives of the *burakumin*, a caste of social outcasts relegated to the edge of Japanese society.

Toson drew upon his own experiences and those of his family in later work. *Haru* (Spring, 1908) was based upon his experiences as a young writer. In *Ie* (The Family, 1910–1911), Toson depicted the decline of two families, one much like his own. *Shinsei* (New Life, 1918–1919) describes the tortured emotions of a protagonist, who like Toson, had an affair with his niece, and *Yoake Mae* (Before the Dawn, 1929–1935) is a reworking of Toson's father's experiences in the tumultuous Meiji era. A 1981 Japanese edition of Toson's complete works contains twelve volumes.

Jeffrey Angles

Further Reading

McClellan, Edwin. (1969) *Two Japanese Novelists: Soseki and Toson.* Tokyo: Charles E. Tuttle.

Shimazaki Toson. ([1906] 1974) *The Broken Commandment.* Trans. by Kenneth Strong. Tokyo: University of Tokyo Press.

———. ([1929–1935] 1981) *Before the Dawn.* Trans. by William E. Naff. Honolulu, HI: University of Hawaii Press.

SHIN SAIMDANG (1504–1551), Korean painter and poet. Shin (pen name Saimdang) was from a *yangban* (aristocratic) family and her father was a high-ranking scholar-official in Kangwon Province. From a young age, she was taught literary Chinese and Confucian classics, rare even for aristocratic daughters. Shin was skilled at painting, calligraphy, poetry, and embroidery. She learned to paint by imitating the style of An Kyon, considered one of the three masters of Choson-period painting of the mid-fifteenth century. She eventually developed her own unique style of painting, readily recognized for its natural motifs such as flowers, grapes, and insects. Her paintings are noted for their simplicity and realistic depiction. Only two of her poems, both written in literary Chinese, are extant today. Both poems depict her longing for her aged mother and natal home.

Shin's husband was Yi Won-su, a government official. She provided her husband with much guidance in his professional dealings. Although Shin was praised as an exemplary daughter, wife, daughter-in-law, and mother, she is most famous for being the mother of Yi I (1536–1584, pen name Yulgok). Yulgok was one of the two most preeminent scholars of Korean neo-Confucianism.

Jennifer Jung-Kim

Further Reading
Saccone, Richard (1993) *Koreans to Remember: 50 Famous People Who Helped Shape Korea.* Elizabeth, NJ: Hollym.

Kim, Yung-Chung, ed. and trans. (1976) *Women of Korea: A History from Ancient Times to 1945.* Seoul: Ewha Womans University Press.

SHINRAN (1173–1262), Japanese Buddhist philosopher. Entering the monastic life as a child, Shinran served as a menial monk at the Enryakuji, a center of Tendai (in Chinese, Tiantai) Buddhist teaching near the summit of Mount Hiei, located northeast of Kyoto. Distressed by his inability to overcome desires and attachments, he was deeply moved by the teachings of Honen of the Jodo (Pure Land) sect and in 1201 became a disciple. When Honen was banished for his antiestablishment ideas, Shinran was also implicated and banished to the area that is now Japan's Niigata Prefecture.

Pardoned four years later, Shinran migrated to the Kanto area of eastern Japan and resumed preaching the absolute power of the Buddha Amida through the incantation of the *nembutsu*, the name of the Buddha Amida. Following the death of Honen, Shinran was forced to grapple with his doubts and problems on his own. In the monumental *Teaching, Practice, Faith, Attainment*, he describes the three stages of conversion and concludes that faith, bestowed by the grace of the Buddha Amida, is all that is necessary for attaining rebirth in the Pure Land.

Developing Honen's teachings, he founded Jodo Shinshu (True Pure Land Faith) as an offshoot of Jodo Buddhism. Whereas Jodo Buddhism had held that chanting Amida's name could bring salvation, in Jodo Shinshu a single recitation, if made with true faith, was enough for salvation. Shinran also defended the Buddhist clergy's abandonment of celibacy and the prohibition against eating meat.

James M. Vardaman, Jr.

Further Reading
Kashiwahara, Yusen, and Koyu Sonoda, eds. (1994) *Shapers of Japanese Buddhism.* Trans. by Gaynor Sekimori. Tokyo: Kosei Publishing.

Tsunoda, Ryusaku, William Theodore de Bary, and Donald Keene. (1958) *Sources of Japanese Tradition.* Vol 1. New York: Columbia University Press.

SHINTO Shinto is one of the two major religions of Japan, with adherents numbering between 40 and 85 percent of a population of 124 million. The disparity in numbers arises from two sources. Many Japanese adhere to both Shinto and Buddhism; and statistical studies are unable to identify clearly what is meant by "adherent" or "member." Shinto has often been defined as "the way of life of the Japanese people," and many of its ideas and practices (such as social hierarchies, feelings of cultural unity, the importance of the family, and ideas about pollution) persist as nonreligious elements of Japanese culture.

History

Indigenous beliefs focusing on purification and veneration of powerful natural phenomena—mountains, waterfalls, and spiritual beings—were current in all communities in pre-state Japan. The rulers of the Yamato state, which eventually subjugated all of the Japanese islands, worshiped a tutelary solar deity. As the Yamato state expanded, it had to accommodate the deities of other states it brought under its control. Thus a nascent pantheon emerged, probably by the fifth century CE, distinguishing between "heavenly" deities (essentially, the tutelary deities of the Yamato, such as Amaterasu Omikami) and "terrestrial" deities (essentially, deities such as Okuni-nushi, of formerly powerful subjugated regions).

With the arrival of Buddhism, the accommodationist policies of Yamato religion were further tested. Introduced in about 538 CE from Korea, Buddhism was strongly opposed by a coalition headed by the Mononobe military and the Nakatomi priestly families, who saw their privileges, partly or largely resting on their claims of descent from heavenly deities, challenged. The Mononobe were defeated in battle by the Soga, an offshoot of the ruling house, in 587. The Soga, presumably anxious to strengthen imperial dominance on the Chinese model at the expense of the Yamato noble houses, proceeded to promote the cause of Buddhism, which was more monolithic and potentially more nationalistic than native beliefs. Under this pressure, the native beliefs were systematized and gradually assumed the label of "Shinto" (Way of the Gods), in contrast to "Butsudo" (Way of the Buddha[s]).

Between the eighth and eighteenth centuries, Shinto and Buddhism merged at many levels, Shinto often playing a subordinate role in ritual and political importance. Exceptions were the strong role of some shrines associated with the imperial family, for example, Ise Jingu on the Kii Peninsula, and others, more independent, for example, Izumo Taisha, north of modern Kyoto, which had been the main shrine of the Izumo state before its subjugation by the Yamato.

In the eighteenth century, intellectual ferment in Japan led to skepticism and questioning of the Confucian bases of the shogunal government. An emerging ideological movement, Kokugaku (School of National Learning), laid the intellectual foundations for the separation of Shinto and Buddhism. Scholars such as Arai Hakuseki (1657–1725) and particularly Motoori Norinaga (1730–1801) argued that Japan's origins and the authority of government rested with the unique nature of its history and myths, as recorded in two books, the *Kojiki* (Record of Ancient Matters, compiled c. 712 CE) and the *Nihon Shoki* (Chronicles of Japan, compiled c. 720).

By 1873, after the Meiji Restoration of 1868, Shinto was seen by many in government as the pure essence of the Japanese people, particularly since it seemed to support Japanese nationalism and resistance to the encroachment of foreign ideas brought about by Japan's

ITSUKUSHIMA—WORLD HERITAGE SITE

The Japanese island of Itsukushima and its Shinto shrines were designated a UNESCO World Heritage Site in 1996. The Shinto have considered the island to be sacred since at least the sixth century CE.

opening to the world (1856) and the end of its political isolation. That year saw the *butsume haikshaku* ("Throwing out the Buddhas"), in which Shinto was forcefully separated by government edict from Buddhism, which was identified with foreign ideas. Clergy were obligated to declare themselves either Shinto or Buddhist, and Buddhist images and rituals were removed from the grounds of Shinto shrines. Those shrines came under the authority of the Department of Shinto Affairs and became an element in the creation of the Japanese uniqueness myth and of Japanese militarism. Shinto priests became government officials. Subsequently, the government attempted to "rationalize" Shinto practice. Priests were required to be licensed; shrines were formally ranked according to historical, political, and financial criteria; and many small hamlet and neighborhood shrines were (often forcibly) joined, particularly during the shrine-amalgamation period (1908–1912).

The last historical phase of Shinto occurred with the American Occupation (1945–1950). Following the Shinto Directive issued by the occupation authorities in December 1945, religion was detached from government, and the ordinances that supported and controlled Shinto shrines were removed. Shrines are currently supported mainly by *kifu* (donations and benefices). Most shrines are owned by public religious associations or neighborhood/hamlet associations, though ownership by individuals, families, or limited religious associations is not unknown.

Ritual and Beliefs

Shinto is a ritual-centered religion. With the exception of some central concepts, dogma plays a small part. Several early books—the *Kojiki* and *Nihon Shoki* are the most prominent—are important sources of ideas, but do not have the authority or stature of canonical texts such as the Bible in Christianity. Both of these works are of similar scope, providing cosmological and foundation myths, in slightly different versions. They detail the creation of the Earth, the birth and positions of the heavenly and earthly *kami* (deities), records of culture heroes, and brief annals of the first emperors.

The two main ideological elements in Shinto are *hare-ke* (purity-pollution) and *kami*, which may be translated as "deity" or "holy." In Shinto ideology, all beings share to varying degrees in purity and pollution, with the *kami* having the greatest purity. Certain actions are inherently polluting (for example, bloodshed), others inherently purifying (for example, lustration). Morality, in the form of sincerity, concern for the group and family, and avoidance of polluting actions, flows from these two major concepts.

Kami include humanlike divine beings of greater or lesser power, headed by Amaterasu Omikami, the clan deity of the imperial house, and first among equals in the Japanese pantheon. Other notable *kami* include Hachiman *(kami* of war and learning), Okuni-nushi *(kami* of the land), and Inari *(kami* of material wealth, prosperity, and grain). A large number of other *kami* are worshiped at one or more shrines. Nonhuman *kami* include dragons, snake-beings, mountains, and waterfalls. The Japanese often refer to "the eight million *kami*" as an indication of the very large number and dynamic nature of the pantheon. All of these *kami* fall into a number of categories, which include well-known and widely worshiped ones such as Inari, deified historical figures, syncretic Shinto-Buddhist deities, and also the *yaoyorozu-no-kami* (eight million deities), who are often unnamed, or barely known, and are worshiped only by specific individuals, families, or single shrines. The heavenly *kami* are noted as such in the *Kojiki* and *Nihon Shoki*. The earthly *kami* are noted in these works as well, and both make clear the subordination of the earthly *kami* to heavenly authority.

Though *kami* are generally well disposed toward humankind, they can be sources of calamities inflicted on the world, usually in response to violations of purity. Such *tatarigami* (malevolent *kami*) are often viewed as negative aspects of otherwise benign *kami*. An individual is free to worship any single deity or combination of deities; major deities such as Amaterasu Omikami are not necessarily worshiped by all people, but may even be included in the *yaoyorozu* category by an individual or a congregation.

Rituals are designed to purify as well as to solicit the positive inclination of the *kami* by prayer and offerings. Thus most Shinto rituals can be divided into four elements: *harai* (purification by the sprinkling of water and salt or by sparking flint and steel); *norito* (the recitation of praises of and invitation to the *kami*); *tamagushi hoten* (the offering of sanctified evergreen branches tied with flax and white paper, along with other pure gifts, to the *kami*); and *naorai* (entertainment for the visiting *kami* and feasting, in which participants share a meal in the presence of the *kami*). Any of these elements may be abbreviated, extended, or elaborated upon. The degree to which they differ from year to year, ritual to ritual, or one place to another depends on economic, social, and personal factors.

Most Shinto rituals take place either in the home or the *jinja* (shrine). Traditionally, homes in Japan would have a small replica of a shrine *(kamidana)* set up in a niche near the ceiling, beside the main pillar *(daikoku-bashira)* of the house. These *kamidana* were supposed to be cleaned daily, and offerings of water, wine, food, and salt placed before them. The miniature shrines held talismans from the shrines(s) that the household supported or had visited. The *kamidana* would be purified annually by the priest of the supported shrine. In modern Japan, few houses have the space for a *kamidana*, and the practice of maintaining one is declining.

Shrines may be of any size (from shoebox size to complexes with halls, courtyards, and several attached buildings), are preferably placed in wooded groves on hills, and are built according to one of several architectural conventions. They are marked by the presence of a square archway with a double crossbeam called a *torii*. *Torii* styles conventionally fit the design of the shrine, and certain designs are associated with particular *kami*. The main halls of shrines hold objects of veneration *(shintai)* associated with the *kami*, which may be stones, items of use (such as a writing brush), or a statue. Many of these are hidden in elaborate boxes and wrappings. Rituals and festive events take place inside a shrine hall, if large enough, or before the shrine. Many modern shrines in urban environments are placed at the top of multistoried buildings.

Most shrines will hold an annual main ritual, normally accompanied by a popular *matsuri* (festival). Rituals for minor festivals may take place at other times in the calendar. There are no nationally recognized calendrical festivals, though many shrines throughout Japan are open on New Year's Eve and New Year's Day, as well as for the children's festival *Shichi-go-san* (15 November). Major festivals at most shrines are composed of a ritual conducted by a priest in the presence of representatives of the community or owners and a parade during which some object representing the *kami*—a *mikoshi* (palanquin in the shape of a miniature shrine), a riderless horse, a straw figure, or even a rice bale—is paraded through the streets. These wholly ritual activities are usually embedded in a pop-

THE FUKKOO KYOODAN SECT OF SHINTO

Listed below are the basic principles of the Fukkoo Kyoodan (The Light of Happiness) Sect of Shinto:

1. To believe in a God, the creator of the universe and all living things, who is absolute and eternal and indestructible, and the guiding principle of the human spirit. To reject all false beliefs in superstition, spiritualism and prophecy.

2. To inflict no harm physical or spiritual, on oneself or on others; to reject revenge and to love one's neighbour.

3. Not to desire the possessions of others.

4. To eschew lewdness.

5. To avoid falsehood.

6. To reflect constantly on thought, word and deed, that they may always accord with the dictates of conscience.

As methods of carrying out these principles,

A. To take deep breaths every morning, and thus compose the body and spirit.

B. By contemplation to strive to realize the state of *sammai* (samadhi, trance), and to practice a transcendentally religious life.

Source: R. P. Dore. (1967) *City Life in Japan: A Study of a Tokyo Ward.* Berkeley and Los Angeles: University of California Press, 354.

---

ular, often raucous street festival and fair. Some *matsuri* have become international tourist attractions.

Shrines—with or without a priest in attendance—are often visited by passersby, who perform an abbreviated ritual of washing, announcing their presence by ringing a bell and clapping hands twice, praying, and offering a coin at an offertory box. At other times, groups of individuals may request a special ritual with one or more priests. Weddings, which used to be private functions, are now often performed in large shrines, some of which have made wedding ceremonies a mainstay of their finances. Shrines are supported by these ritual activities, as well as by donations in money, in kind, or in income-producing land.

Priests also conduct rituals either to ward off *tatarigami* (malevolent *kami)* or to ensure success, peace, health, and so on. Owners of particular enterprises (for example, buses) might request such a purification ritual, individually or collectively.

Organization

In traditional Japan, most communities worshiped one or more *kami* at a local shrine. *Ujiko* (family ritual associations) of several families would also worship *kami* at shrines constructed for the purpose. *Ko* (ritual associations) and occupational associations might erect a shrine for the worship of a particular deity. Since World War II, there has been somewhat of a resurgence in the construction of shrines. Many that were delegitimized during the shrine-consolidation period have been reestablished, and some new ones have been built. There has been a general movement away from ownership by family groups to ownership by neighborhood associations, community organizations, and even commercial firms.

Shrines are normally maintained by one or more groups that own or financially subscribe to the premises. These maintenance arrangements are often complex and differ widely from one shrine to another.

A Shinto priest and followers bathe in ice-cold water at Teppozu Shrine in Tokyo in January 1999 to cleanse their bodies and souls. (AFP/CORBIS)

Rituals are normally conducted by one or more *kannushi* (priests) who are ritual specialists (as in Protestantism and Islam), not consecrated prelates (as in Catholicism). A layperson who knows the proper ritual forms may conduct rituals if the "congregation" agrees. There are a small number of female priests. *Kannushi* of small shrines normally service a number of shrines in the same area. Large shrines are served by several priests who fulfill ritual and administrative duties and by *miko* (shrine maidens) who perform ritual dances and minor administrative duties. Ranks are denoted by the color of the split skirts worn by priests on a daily basis—purple for chief priests, pastel blue or green for ordinary priests, and red for *miko*—and by the elaboration of robes and different types of headgear worn while conducting rituals.

Larger shrines—usually those with an ancient recorded provenance—may be members of one or another of the shrine associations, the largest of which, Jinja Honcho, encompasses about 80 percent of the ten thousand or so shrines listed in the prewar government register. About an additional fifty thousand unlisted shrines throughout Japan are not registered. These shrine associations act as pressure and mobilization groups; they also train and certify priests. Jinja Honcho, for instance, is closely associated with Kokugakuin University, which trains Shinto priests. Smaller shrines may be associated in looser local support networks.

Kannushi often inherit their position. They are expected to serve a period of apprenticeship at some well-known shrine, after which they return to their home shrine or remain as qualified priests where they can find work. With the exception of those who serve at large and prosperous shrines, many priests have difficulty supporting themselves and often work at other jobs as well. Since the 1950s, Jinja Honcho and other shrine associations have made efforts to have all priests university trained or at least to have them participate in training seminars and courses.

Current Shinto

Many authors have divided Shinto into four broad classes: Kokka Shinto (National Shinto), the official dogma perpetuated by the government between the Meiji Restoration and the end of World War II; Jinja Shinto (Shrine Shinto), the practice of Shinto in "officially recognized" (by Jinja Honcho or some similar organization) shrines; Kyoha Shinto (Sect Shinto), the ritual practices, organizations, and shrines that elected not to enter the national system during the separation from Buddhism and the shrine-consolidation periods; and Minzoku Shinto (Folk Shinto), an ill-defined residual category embracing common national and local rituals and beliefs prevalent throughout the population, as well as rituals and practices at "unofficial" shrines not belonging to any of the other categories.

A fifth category, Imperial Shinto, refers to rituals prescribed for the emperor, including those performed at Ise Jingu.

This analytical separation clearly represents more the political stand of its presenters and authors than the reality of Shinto as a religion, in which all of these categories blend imperceptibly into one another. In practice, Shinto's rather loose dogma allows for multiple interpretations of ritual and belief, and these often coexist within the same community. Moreover, there is constant dynamic movement as rituals are renewed, learned, and transmitted between shrines and practitioners. Perhaps the only constant is that the richer and more famous a shrine is, the more it is likely to claim its orthodoxy and the ancient origins of its rituals and traditions.

Shinto has been tainted by its support of Japan's imperial and colonialist past during and before World War II. This is particularly notable in the controversy surrounding Yasukuni Jinja, the shrine dedicated to Japan's war dead. Visits to this shrine by government officials have been controversial because of an item in the constitution forbidding government support of religious bodies—a clause right-wing Japanese feel is an attack on Shinto, and left-wing Japanese feel is a protection against government interference in religious affairs.

Shinto has proved itself a dynamic, flexible religious system with the capacity to adapt to changing circumstances, including processes of modernity. A great many Japanese continue to deny that they are at all religious, while performing Shinto rituals at shrines or at home.

Michael Ashkenazi

See also: **Religion, Folk—Japan**

Further Reading

Ashkenazi, Michael. (1993) *Matsuri: The Festivals of a Japanese Town.* Honolulu, HI: University of Hawaii Press.

Aston, W. G. (1905) *Shinto: The Way of the Gods.* London: Longmans, Green.

Creemers, Willhelmus, H. M. (1968) *Shrine Shinto after WW II.* Leiden, Netherlands: E. J. Brill.

Hardacre, Helen. (1989) *Shinto and the State: 1868–1988.* Princeton, NJ: Princeton University Press.

Herbert, Jean. (1967) *Shinto: At the Fountainhead of Japan.* London: Allen & Unwin.

Jinja Honcho. (1985) *Basic Terms of Shinto.* Tokyo: Kokugakuin University and Institute for Japanese Culture and Classics.

Nelson, John K. (2000) *Enduring Identities: The Guise of Shinto in Contemporary Japan.* Honolulu, HI: University of Hawaii Press.

Ono, Sokyo. (1962) *Shinto: The Kami Way.* Tokyo: Tuttle.

Smyers, Karen. (1998) *The Fox and the Jewel: Shared and Private Meanings in Contemporary Japanese Inari Worship.* Honolulu, HI: University of Hawaii Press.

SHIPBUILDING SCANDAL   The Shipbuilding Scandal marked the end of post-Occupation Japanese politics dominated by Yoshida Shigeru and the beginning of serious efforts to consolidate conservative elements into a single hegemonic party. In 1953 leading Japanese shipbuilding firms collaborated to bribe the government into revising a law to increase government shipbuilding subsidies. The desired revision was enacted in August 1953 but the presidents of Japan's major shipbuilders, along with several Diet members and bureaucrats, were arrested on corruption charges the following spring. Further investigations implicated top officials, including key lieutenants of Premier Yoshida Shigeru such as Sato Eisaku, the Jiyuto (Liberal Party) secretary-general. In April, when the public prosecutor's office moved to arrest Sato, Justice Minister Inukai Takeru ordered the withdrawal of the indictment, an extraordinary move supposedly ordered by Premier Yoshida Shigeru. His attitude toward this scandal was revealed in his comment that "party government would come to an end if it abided by the Political Funds Control Law."

This scandal accelerated a general decline of support for Yoshida and affected members of his party. The result was a decision by the Diet's lower house audit committee to investigate Yoshida's role in the scandal. In September 1954, when he refused to obey a formal summons, the audit committee passed a motion of censure. At the same time, conservative nationalists led by Hatoyama Ichiro and Kishi Nobusuke banded together to form an anti-Yoshida party and force him into retirement. This group became known as the Japan Democratic Party (Nihon Minshuto) and was inaugurated in November. As the fratricidal conflict developed between pro- and anti-Yoshida conservatives, the Japanese business community, led by the Keidanren (The Federation of Economic Organizations), the voice of Japanese industry, began to call for conservative unity under new leadership, if necessary. In December, the day before a scheduled no-confidence vote in the Diet, Yoshida's cabinet members resigned. Hatoyama then took over as premier, and Yoshida retired from politics. Another result of the Shipbuilding Scandal was Japanese big business organizations' pledge to create large new legal political funding mechanisms. Big business hoped to persuade conservative politicians to merge and thereby secure a stable conservative majority in the Diet. The Nihon

Minshuto and the Jiyuto merged the following year to form the Liberal Democratic Party, which subsequently ruled Japan uninterruptedly until 1993.

David Arase

Further Reading
Dower, John. (1988) *Empire and Aftermath: Yoshida Shigeru and the Japanese Experience, 1878–1954.* Cambridge, MA: Council on East Asian Studies, Harvard University.
Junnosuke, Masumi. (1985) *Postwar Politics in Japan, 1945–1955.* Berkeley, CA: Institute of East Asian Studies, University of California Press.

SHIRAZ (2002 pop. 1.2 million). Located at the western edge of a sizable valley at the southern end of the Zagros Mountains in southwestern Iran, the city of Shiraz benefited historically as the ideal point between the Persian Gulf coast and cities located farther inland on the Iranian plateau. Except for rare but notable instances of flooding—especially in the seventeenth century—extreme aridity has made past and present settlement dependent upon underground aquifers accessed by *qanats* (channels) for water supplies. Nonetheless the area is distinguished agriculturally, both for its famed gardens and historic vineyards, which are noted for the famed Shiraz grape.

The area around Shiraz has been settled since at least the Achaemenian period (559–330 BCE). However, it only began to develop as a city under the Sasanians (224–651 CE), and only flourished with the late-seventh-century Arab-Islamic advance into Persia, when the city became the staging area for further conquests. Shiraz became the provincial capital of Fars in 693 CE and continues as such today. By the twelfth century the city was emerging as a major center for the arts, handicrafts, and commerce. The city avoided severe hardships amid invasions by Mongol and Turkic armies in the thirteenth and fourteenth centuries through the rapid surrender of the city by its leaders. During the brief Zand dynasty (1750–1794) Shiraz enjoyed the benefits of being the national capital.

Shiraz's greatest achievements are in the wider realm of the arts. Although famed for its traditions of building and landscape architecture, styles of painting (especially the Shiraz school of miniatures), ceramics, tiles, and textiles, Shiraz is most often regarded as the center of Persian language and literature. Much of this renown can be attributed to the literary achievements of two poets: Sa'di (1184–1292) and Hafez (c. 1320–1389), master of the *ghazal*, a lyric poetry written in Arabic and Persian. Closely related to its literary fame, the city is also highly regarded for its traditions in cal-

The mausoleum of the poet Hafez in Shiraz. (K. M. WESTERMANN/CORBIS)

ligraphy. Prior to a wider adoption of printing presses, Shiraz was a major center for the production of high quality manuscripts that circulated throughout the Islamic world as late as the seventeenth and even into the eigthteenth centuries.

Today, Shiraz's vitality is still based heavily on its artistic traditions. The mausoleums that enshrine the tombs of the poets Hafez and Sa'di continue to be major attractions, and the city's university is highly regarded in Iran and beyond. The production of handwoven carpets, miniature paintings, and works of inlaid wood are major handicraft industries. Key modern industries include food processing, tile and cement production, chemical and pharmaceutical factories, and textile mills. As with other Iranian cities, Shiraz has seen dynamic population growth over the past decades, from 416,408 in 1976 to 1,053,025 in 1996.

Kyle T. Evered

Further Reading
Arberry, Arthur J. (1960) *Shiraz: Persian City of Saints and Poets.* Norman, OK: University of Oklahoma Press.

Clarke, John I. (1963) *The Iranian City of Shiraz*. Research Papers Series No. 7. Durham, U.K.: University of Durham.

SHIZUOKA

SHIZUOKA (2002 est. pop. 3.8 million). Shizuoka Prefecture is situated in the central region of Japan's island of Honshu, where it occupies an area of 7,773 square kilometers. Part of Mount Fuji is located in Shizuoka, whose other primary geographical features are generally mountainous terrain and the Izu Peninsula. The main rivers are the Fujikawa, Abekawa, Oigawa, and Tenryugawa. The prefecture is bordered by the Pacific Ocean, and by Yamanashi, Nagano, and Kanagawa prefectures. Once divided into Suruga, Totomi, and Izu provinces, it assumed its present name in 1876 and its present borders in 1878.

The Toro archaeological excavation of late Yayoi culture (100–300 CE) artifacts indicates early habitation of the region. In feudal times, the provinces were ruled by a series of powerful warrior families, including the Hojo and the Tokugawa.

The prefecture's capital is Shizuoka city, situated on Suruga Bay. It came to prominence when Tokugawa Ieyasu (1542–1616), the founder of the Tokugawa shogunate, which ruled Japan during the Edo period (1600/1603–1868), retired there to Sumpu Castle, built in 1589. During the Edo period, it flourished as a Tokaido highway post station and as a regional market for textiles, looms, paper, wooden clogs, sewing boxes, and lacquerware. In the early 2000s, it is home to Shizuoka University. The prefecture's other important cities are Hamamatsu, Numazu, Shimizu, and Fuji.

Shizuoka Prefecture is noted for its green tea, mandarin oranges, strawberries, and Japanese horseradish (*wasabi*). Also productive are the forestry industry and fisheries. Lake Hamana is the site of the culture of eels, soft-shelled turtles, oysters, prawns, and edible seaweed. The former castle town of Hamamatsu today is headquarters of Yamaha, which makes quality musical instruments. The Yamaha Motor Company in Iwata produces motorcycles, car engines, air conditioners, and industrial robots. The main tourist attractions are Mount Fuji, Fuji-Hakone-Izu National Park, and the region's hot spring resorts.

E. L. S. Weber

Further Reading
"Shizuoka Prefecture." (1993) *Japan: An Illustrated Encyclopedia*. Tokyo: Kodansha.

SHOWA DENKO SCANDAL

SHOWA DENKO SCANDAL In June 1948, the president of the Showa Denko Company was arrested for passing bribes to government officials in an effort to gain government-financed loans. Later, the arrest of Deputy Prime Minister Suehiro Nishio, who was implicated in the scandal, caused the fall of the government led by Ashida Hitoshi (March–October 1948). Shortly thereafter Ashida himself was indicted and arrested. Of the sixty-four individuals arrested in this scandal, however, only two lesser figures were ever found guilty. Nevertheless, the event changed the course of postwar Japanese politics and foreign policy.

This scandal removed the Japan Socialist Party (JSP) from power and effectively changed the direction of its postwar development. In the first election held under the new postwar constitution, the JSP became the single largest party in the key lower house of the Diet. Control of the government then changed from the conservative Liberal Party (Jiyuto) led by Yoshida Shigeru to the JSP led by Katayama Tetsu and Nishio Suehiro in coalition with the conservative Democratic Party (Minshuto) led by Ashida. The Katayama government (May 1947–March 1948) was brought down by a legislative failure, but the JSP remained in power as a junior partner of the Minshuto in the next government under Ashida. In this period the JSP was willing to work with conservative parties due to the leadership of Katayama and Nishio. But the Showa Denko Scandal torpedoed the JSP-Minshuto coalition, tarnished the JSP's image, and discredited Katayama and Nishio's leadership. In the next general election both lost their Diet seats amid a resounding JSP electoral defeat. Thereafter the left-wing vision of the JSP as an opposition party valuing ideology above power gained ascendancy within the party.

This scandal also weakened the Jiyuto's main conservative rival, the Minshuto. Yoshida was then able to regain the premiership, which he held until 1954. In these years, Yoshida set a course for postwar Japan by negotiating the San Francisco Peace Treaty and the United States–Japan Security Treaty, and he created a cohort of political protégés that included future prime ministers such as Ikeda Hayato, Sato Eisaku, and Miyazawa Kiichi who would carry on his conservative internationalist vision of postwar Japan.

Finally, the Showa Denko scandal affected Occupation policy in Japan. The scandal broke as the so-called "reverse course" in U.S. Occupation policy was being deliberated. The government section (GS) of the Supreme Commander for the Allied Powers (SCAP) viewed Yoshida's disdain of democracy with concern, and it supported the JSP's participation in government as a healthy democratic development. In contrast, SCAP's intelligence section (G2) gave more weight to U.S. Cold War interests than to democratization. The G2 used allegations stemming from this scandal to investigate whether key members of GS had accepted bribes from Japanese sources. These allegations reduced GS influence over Occupation policy, and SCAP then firmly backed the conservative but pro–United States Yoshida.

David Arase

See also: **Japan Socialist Party**

Further Reading
Masumi Junnosuke. (1985) *Postwar Politics in Japan, 1945–1955*. Berkeley, CA: Institute of East Asian Studies, University of California.
Jiro Tanaka, Isao Sato, and Jiro Nomura, eds. (1980) *Sengo seiji saiban shiroku* (Record of Postwar Political Trials). Vol. 1. Tokyo: Daiichi Hoki.

SHOWA PERIOD   Showa is the name given to the reign of the Japanese emperor commonly known as Hirohito (1901–1989). Lasting sixty-three years (1926–1989), the Showa period was not only one of the longest imperial reigns in Japanese and world history but also one of the most dramatic. War and peace, devastation and prosperity, authoritarianism and democracy all fit into the puzzle of Showa. Showa still elicits mixed emotions, divided loyalties, and political controversy. To think about modern Japanese history is ultimately to confront the meaning of this period.

The years 1926 and 1989 do not mark obvious turning points. Hirohito became de facto emperor in 1920 as regent for his ailing father, the Taisho emperor (1879–1926, reigned 1912–1926). The grand ceremony for Hirohito's enthronement came in 1928, a year remembered more for persecution of Communists and other leftists. At the closing end, historians see 1991, a year of economic crisis, as the sharp break from the mood of the late Showa period. In between, Hirohito never provided charismatic leadership, despite the potent cult of emperor worship that rose up around him. His intervention in national events occurred infrequently, and for the last forty years, he was politically insignificant. The most important year of his reign was 1945, the year of Japan's surrender at the end of the Pacific phase of World War II (1937–1945). That year split Showa into two distinct eras.

Hirohito's importance as a symbol, by contrast, cannot be overstated. In early years, his subjects learned to view him as the supreme repository of all values, the transcendent object of national loyalty and devotion. In later years, his grandfatherly image mirrored Japan's role as a pacifist state. His presence provided a sense of continuity over a period of dramatic political, economic, and social change. Many historians argue that, despite the sense of two Showas, continuity in individuals, attitudes, social practices, and the system of imperial rule itself unites the period.

Democracy, Fascism, and War, 1925–1945
By the early 1920s, Japan emerged as a full-fledged member of the international community. Although its economy only ranked twelfth globally in per capita income, the foundations of a modern industrial economy had been laid in the preceding fifty years. Through treaties and wars, the country had acquired a level of prestige in international politics. In social and political affairs, Japan was changing rapidly as well. One event that symbolized the mood of the early Showa period was a 1925 law giving the right to vote to all males over the age of twenty-five. The law captured a democratic spirit borne of new prosperity in urban centers, expanding educational opportunities, rising literacy, and mass consumerism. These changes indicated that Japan was becoming more like other modern nations. At an international level, this mood was reflected by a spirit of cooperation between Japan and the other Western powers, especially in coping with the political instability of China.

There were definite limits on this democracy, however. Women had no right to vote. Their educational opportunities were far fewer than those for men, and many women lived as virtual slaves in factories and brothels. A pervasive ideology saw women as second-class subjects of the emperor. Their main purpose in life was seen as bearing children and raising them as his loyal soldiers. Women's lives, however, were changing too. New jobs as teachers, store clerks, and café waitresses created new opportunities for women. A vigorous publishing industry rose up to appeal to women who had acquired an independent income or control over household budgets. Women were becoming the principle consumers in an expanding consumer society.

Other limits on democracy loomed ominously over the early Showa period. Under the Meiji Constitution (1890–1945), the emperor was "sacred and inviolable." In his person, he embodied the sovereign authority of the government. In practice, political authority was divided among many governing bodies, only one of which, the lower house of the Diet (parliament), was a democratic institution. A hereditary aristocracy dominated the upper house of the Diet and held many influential posts in the government. The military asserted considerable influence in the political system and declared its autonomy from civilian authority.

This system of contending democratic, autocratic, and militarist elements could function effectively if a broad consensus over national goals existed. Although democratic forces were poised to claim ascendancy over others, society experienced political and economic challenges over which no consensus could be achieved easily. A bank panic in 1927, the global economic depression of 1929, and political revolution in China played into the hands of those who opposed the democratic trends, the system of international cooperation, and ultimately the transformation of Japan into a modern consumer society.

In 1931, a group of army officers stationed in southern Manchuria (northeast China) initiated a conspiracy to invade China and create a new Japanese colony. Civilian leaders opposed such actions as a violation of international treaties, but they were overruled by the military and a surge in the popularity of war. A reign of terror ensued at home during which right-wing organizations assassinated political leaders, menaced dissenting voices, and demanded ideological conformity. This war on democracy and internationalism culminated in the 26 February (1936) Incident. This coup sought to install Hirohito as a quasi religious dictator. Hirohito and leading generals opposed the coup, and it was suppressed. Nevertheless, the event propelled Japan toward further restrictions on democratic freedoms, greater authoritarian policies, harsher patriotic indoctrination, and further conflict with the United States and other Western powers.

After 1936, Japanese leaders struggled in vain to assert coherence over national goals and actions. Full-scale war broke out between Japan and China in July 1937. Branches of the military jockeyed among each other, seeking to define national priorities. Reform-minded bureaucrats promoted a reorganized economy and social order. Radical visionaries called for a new alliance among Asians against Western imperialism. This whirlwind would have overtaxed even a good leader. No supreme leader, including the emperor, emerged to unify the government in this time of self-made crisis. Instead, Japanese diplomacy operated without a clear aim, buffeted by events in Europe and eliciting strong opposition from Western states. The brutality of the war in China and Japan's alliances with Nazi Germany and Fascist Italy hardened Western resolve to oppose Japanese actions in the Pacific. In the end, Japanese leaders could only agree on the foolish decision to attack the United States, hoping with one blow to clarify political options, resolve economic contradictions of its war in China, and escape its diplo-

JAPAN—HISTORICAL PERIODS

Jomon period (14,500–300 BCE)
Yayoi culture (300 BCE–300 CE)
Yamato State (300–552 CE)
Kofun period (300–710 CE)
Nara period (710–794 CE)
Heian period (794–1185)
Kamakura period (Kamakura Shogunate) (1185–1333)
Muromachi period (1333–1573)
Momoyama period (1573–1600)
Tokugawa or Edo period (Tokugawa Shogunate) (1600/1603–1868)
Meiji period (1868–1912)
Taisho period (1912–1926)
Showa period (1926–1989)
Allied Occupation (1945–1952)
Heisei period (1989–present)

matic straightjacket. The fateful Japanese attack on Pearl Harbor (7 December 1941) did none of these things. The subsequent war with the United States and its allies (1941–1945) led to unspeakable suffering for many Asians, including Japanese. It destroyed the political and social systems Japan's leaders had fought to preserve, brought ruin to the economy, and cost the country its independence.

Occupation and the New Japan, 1945–1955

In 1945 Japan was a devastated and occupied country. A decade later it reemerged as an independent state within an U.S.-led order of capitalist states. This rapid transformation was the product of the unusual circumstances of the U.S. occupation and the global rivalry called the Cold War (1948–1989). The Allied Occupation began with the goals of democratization, decentralization, and demilitarization, enacted through firm, but rarely punitive, policies. Some military and civilian leaders were executed as war criminals, and leading figures throughout society were purged from public positions. The occupation not only refused to hold Hirohito accountable, but also rehabilitated him as the symbol of a new democratic state. This decision has been the subject of intense controversy ever since. The United States imposed a new constitution that vested sovereignty in the people, guaranteed civil rights, abolished the aristocracy, and stripped Japan of autonomy as a military power. The constitution's guarantee of the civil rights of women is more explicit than any found in the U.S. Constitution, and its famous Article 9, which abjures war as an instrument of national policy, is unique among the world's constitutions. The military lost its preeminent role in Japanese life. Other important steps in democratization included reform of rural landholdings and new freedoms for labor unions.

After 1947, a third goal of the occupation, reintegration, emerged. Some Japanese and Americans believed that the earliest years of the Showa period had demonstrated the potential for civilian rule in Japan. Moderate politicians, bureaucrats, intellectuals, and businesspeople would serve as pillars of democracy at home and peaceful partners in the world economy. The election of many women legislators in the first postwar elections committed them to the new peace state. Reintegration was not driven by solely altruistic motives, and many viewed it as a reversal of earlier policies. The specter of an ideological conflict between the United States and the Soviet Union shaped the course of the occupation and derailed some democratic reforms. This proved especially true after the Chinese Revolution of 1949 and the outbreak of the Korean War (1950–1953). Eager to ensure Japan's dependability as an anti-Communist ally in Asia, staunch anti-Communist leaders found favor with the occupation, while leftists and labor radicals were purged from the government. Japan became a base for U.S. operations in Korea, and the U.S. presence poured cash into the struggling Japanese economy. Eager for Japan to defend itself, the United States encouraged growth of a national defense force.

Reintegration was achieved in concrete terms through the Treaty of San Francisco (1951), which ended the Allied Occupation in 1952 and restored Japan's political independence. Japan's entry into the General Agreement on Trade and Tariffs (GATT) in 1955 realized the goal of integrating Japan into a U.S.-led system of free trade.

Growth in a Cold War World, 1955–1973

Postwar Japan was born as a coalescence of renewed commitments to democracy, a drive toward reintegration with the world community, and an East Asia fractured by U.S.-Soviet rivalry. The primary beneficiaries of this formula became Japan's export industries. Favorable currency exchange rates gave Japanese manufactures easy access to the large U.S. market. In these years, Japan's economy grew at a breathtaking double-digit pace. The incomes of Japan's consumers grew dramatically as well, with the refrigerator, the automatic clothes washer, and the color television becoming new measures of success in Japan. In the 1960s, few households owned a refrigerator or washer; the

color television was a new consumer item. By the early 1970s, nearly every Japanese household had all three.

These symbols of progress could not mask the concessions made to breakneck growth. The great successes of the steel and chemical industries brought pollution to the national stage. Public outcry eventually forced the government to confront the fouled waterways, concrete beaches, and poisonous air that had also become symbols of the new Japan. The problems of public accountability in government were felt in many areas. While the post-Allied Occupation years had seen the rise of diverse political movements, by 1955 moderate and conservative parties consolidated into one political party, the Liberal Democratic Party (LDP), which ruled for the remainder of the Showa period. Many LDP politicians had strong links to wartime politics, most notably Prime Minister Kishi Nobusuke, in office from 1986 to 1987, whom the Allied Occupation had deemed a "class A" war criminal. The LDP pursued closer relations with the United States, culminating in the 1960 U.S.-Japan Security Pact that effectively made the countries partners in regional defense. The prospects of the long-term hosting of U.S. military bases, continued growth of Japan's self-defense force, and undemocratic speed with which Kishi pushed such measures through the Diet elicited mass protests. Protesters wondered how such a military alliance could be seen as consistent with Article 9 and Japan's commitment to peace.

By the early 1970s, the United States proved no longer willing to support Japan's easy access to U.S. markets. New currency exchange rates provided an immediate shock to the economy. Conflict in the Middle East destabilized world oil prices, adding additional shocks to the economy. The period of high growth could not continue forever.

Japan as Number One, 1974–1991

Economic growth slowed in the aftermath of these shocks to a manageable 4 percent per year, but the accumulated gains pushed national wealth to dizzying heights. Per capita income was the highest among major industrial nations. No longer content with mere affluence, a large segment of the Japanese population enjoyed the opulence of luxury consumer goods and international travel in a global playground. Such wealth brought corresponding influence and responsibility. The last days of the Showa period displayed Japan's struggles to accommodate itself to its new life as "number one."

While many Japanese shared in this wealth, they did not all share equally. The strengthening of feminist and citizens' movements against inequality, social injustice, and pollution and the health and safety concerns of these elements exposed cracks in "number one" status. By contrast, the labor movement and opposition political parties declined. The LDP became ever more entrenched, purchasing the favor of rural voting districts through generous funding of new public-works projects. Disenchanted voters saw a party mired in scandal and machine politics, driven to preserve itself rather than serve a public interest.

No issue symbolized the struggle for international respectability more than questions over the legacy of Japan's aging emperor. Pride in postwar accomplishments encouraged Japanese to look favorably on the past and seek explanations for the nation's accomplishments in unique and innate qualities of its people. This surge of cultural nationalism seemed to many, especially in countries victimized by Japan's aggression in World War II, to be a resurgence of the nationalism of the early Showa period. The persistence of the emperor himself implied that no clean break from the past and no accounting of responsibility and war guilt had been properly undertaken. Such questions had been suppressed during the Cold War and Japan's phoenix-like rebirth. Critics pointed to the odious system of registration that reminded second- and third-generation Korean residents of their separate status. Many Koreans traced their families' appearances in Japan to prewar forced labor. This and other examples suggested that unquestioned faith in collective goals and national prosperity had concealed discrimination on the basis of minority status, gender, and race.

The Legacy of Showa

The death of the Showa emperor in 1989 intensified reflection on the long period bearing his reign name. Hundreds of books and articles on his legacy appeared in 1989 alone. A sharper sense of ending for the Showa period came in 1991. The booming Japanese economy slumped, victim of overspeculation in real estate and securities. The burst of the so-called Bubble Economy shook public confidence in government institutions, political leadership, major corporations, and ultimately pride in Showa-era accomplishments. The Showa period has been equally haunted by its past. After years of government denials of wartime sexual slavery run by the military (the women were euphemistically called "military comfort women"), former Korean sex slave Kim Haksun (1924–1997) broke fifty years of silence in 1991 by offering public testimony of these misdeeds. Scholars subsequently uncovered documentary evidence of the system, forcing a public admission from the gov-

ernment. The government has been unwilling, however, to pay compensation to former slaves.

The legacy of Showa Japan will remain contradictory. The emperor came to symbolize a postwar peace state, the remarkable advances in the material wealth of the country, and progress toward peace with its neighbors. In the early Showa period, by contrast, he was an object of mystical reverence, the justification for authoritarian thought control, social conformity, and horrific warfare that swept across Asia in his name. Whether the later Showa generation can bear responsibility for acts of that early generation persists as the enduring challenge for Showa.

Michael A. Schneider

See also: **Heisei Period; Hirohito; Taisho Period; Women in Japan; World War II**

Further Reading
Bernstein, Gail Lee, ed. (1991) *Recreating Japanese Women, 1600–1945.* Berkeley and Los Angeles: University of California Press.
Bix, Herbert. (2000) *Hirohito and the Making of Modern Japan.* New York: HarperCollins.
Dower, John. (1999) *Embracing Defeat: Japan in the Wake of World War II.* New York: W. W. Norton.
Gordon, Andrew. (1993) *Postwar Japan as History.* Berkeley and Los Angeles: University of California Press.
Imamura, Anne E. (1996) *Re-imaging Japanese Women.* Berkeley and Los Angeles: University of California Press.
Iriye, Akira. (1987) *The Origins of the Second World War in Asia and the Pacific.* New York: Longman.
Large, Stephen S. (1998) *Showa Japan: Political, Economic and Social History, 1926–1989.* New York: Routledge.
Nakamura Takafusa. (1998) *A History of Showa Japan, 1926–1989.* Tokyo: University of Tokyo Press.
Vogel, Ezra F. (1979) *Japan as Number One: Lessons for America.* Cambridge, MA: Harvard University Press.
Yoshimi Yoshiaki. (2000) *Comfort Women: Sexual Slavery in the Japanese Military during World War II.* New York: Columbia University Press.

SHUNTO *Shunto* (spring struggle) refers to the distinctive wage-bargaining practices that play a central role in determining Japanese wage levels. Under the *shunto* system, collective bargaining occurs annually during the spring (February through May) and is generally conducted between individual enterprise unions and their respective managements. Despite this formal independence, a high degree of coordination occurs at both the industrial and national levels. Settlements in one enterprise or industry are tabulated and help set the pattern for wage hikes in other enterprises and industries in a way that makes all bargaining in a given round part of a single inter-related system.

Shunto was originally conceived as a way to over-come some of the disadvantages of Japanese labor's enterprise-based organizational structure. Ota Kaoru of Sohyo, Japan's leading left-leaning national con-federation between 1950 and 1989, felt that by simul-taneously coordinating wage demands and bargaining (and striking) enterprise unions could prevent em-ployers from playing one union off against another and so could drive a harder bargain. From an initial foothold in eight industries in 1955, *shunto* expanded to the point where the national *shunto* coordinating committee represented nearly ten million unionists by the late 1970s.

The significance of *shunto* has changed over time. Politically, the first round in 1955 was intended to cir-cumvent Sohyo's divisive emphasis on politics in favor of more attractive economic gains. During *shunto's* first two decades, bargaining tended to be confrontational, and unions regularly used strikes to press their de-mands. This confrontational quality conspicuously dissipated in the wake of the first oil crisis as the la-bor-management–cooperation-oriented International Metalworkers Federation—Japan Council unions seized the initiative in the *shunto* rounds. Concerned about the macroeconomic consequences of wage hikes on their industry's international competitiveness, these unions exerted a moderating influence. Since 1975, *shunto* wage hikes have closely adhered to the level of increase in the productivity of the national economy as a whole. During the late 1990s, Rengo (the current national confederation) labeled its effort the Spring Struggle for a Better Life, with the implication that *shunto* involved various policy struggles aimed at bringing about government and corporate policies that would improve the lifestyle of Japanese workers.

There is considerable debate over the degree to which *shunto* has in fact raised Japanese wages. Critics argue that even during the height of *shunto* militancy, wage increases were in line with what one would ex-pect, given supply and demand in the labor market. Others argue that *shunto* encouraged a relative level-ing of wages within and across industries and, through annual bargaining, allowed Japanese industry to adjust quickly to economic changes.

Lonny Carlile

Further Reading

Sako, Mari. (1997) "Shunto: The Role of Employer and Union Coordination at the Industry and Inter-Sectoral Levels." In *Japanese Labor and Management in Transition: Diversity, Flexibility, and Participation*, edited by Mari Sako and Hiroki Sato. New York: Routledge, 236–264.

Takanashi Akira. (1996) *Shunto Wage Offensive*. Japanese Econ-omy and Labor, no. 1. Tokyo: Japan Institute of Labor.

Weathers, Charles. (1997) *Japan's Fading Labor Movement*. JPRI Working Paper, no. 35. Cardiff, CA: Japan Policy Research Institute.

SIBERIA Siberia is a vast region of Russia, cover-ing some 10- million-square kilometers from the Ural Mountains in the west to the Pacific Ocean in the east and from the Arctic Ocean in the north to the bor-ders of China, Mongolia, and Kazakhstan in the south. In 1992 it had an estimated population of 32.5 million (17 percent of the population of Russia), nearly all of whom were Russians or other peoples of European origin, save for about one million indigenous peoples.

Whether Siberia should be classified as part of Asia or Europe is the subject of debate. Geographically, Siberia forms the northeast region of Eurasia or north Asia. Culturally, it is mainly European as 98 percent of the population is Russian or of other European ances-try, Russian is the primary language, and Russian Or-thodoxy the primary religion. Politically, all or part of Siberia has been part of Russia since the Russian con-quest of western Siberia began in the sixteenth century.

Geography

Siberia is bordered by the Kara, Laptev, and East Siberian seas to the north; the Bering Sea and Sea of Okhotsk to the east; by China, Mongolia and Kazakh-stan to the south; and the Ural mountains to the west. Major geographical features include the New Siberian Islands, the Severnaya Zemlya Archipelago, Wrangel Island, and the Taymyr Peninsula in the north; Kam-chatka Peninsula and Sakhalin Island in the east; Lake Baikal (the deepest freshwater lake in the world) in south central Siberia, and the Yablonovyy, Stanovoy, Ver-khoyanski, Kolyma, and Cherskiy mountain ranges and the central uplands in eastern Siberia. From west to east, Siberia is divided by its three major south-to-north flowing river systems—the Ob', Yenisey, and Lena— and their tributaries. Rivers provide the primary north-south transportation routes, while the 12,800-kilome-ter Trans-Siberian Railroad provides east-west transportation. The highway system is not well devel-oped, especially beyond western Siberia, and air travel remains limited as well.

Located nearer to European Russia, southwest Siberia contains about 60% of the region's population, its largest city (Novosibirsk) and several other large cities (Omsk, Tomsk, Tobolsk, Barnaul, and Novokuz-

SIBERIA

netsk), and much of the regions industry. With a population of nearly 1.5 million, Novosibirsk is Russia's third largest city (after Moscow and St. Petersburg). It was established in 1893 and incorporated in 1903.

Eastern Siberia is sparsely populated and contains most of the region's indigenous peoples. Cold temperatures in the north and hot temperatures in the south during the summer make the climate difficult to live in and the rough terrain makes communication and transportation difficult. The major cities include Krasnoyarsk (1992 est. pop. 925,000), Irkutsk (1992 est. pop. 639,000), Yakutsk (1992 est. pop. 198,000), and Chita (1992 est. pop. 377,000).

History

The traditional view that Siberia was first inhabited about 30,000 years ago has been challenged by recent research, which suggests settlement as early as 300,000 years ago. Russian conquest began when a Cossack force captured the city of Sibir' (the capital of the Sibir' khanate in western Siberia) in 1581 and then the Tatar khanate in 1598. The Cossacks pushed east, establishing a series of forts until they were halted by the Chinese and ceded control over the Far East in the Treaty of Nerchinsk in 1689.

Early Russian administration focused on exploiting the region and indigenous peoples for furs, which were traded for and collected as tribute. Colonization expanded after the fur trade declined in the early eighteenth century. The fur trade was replaced by mining for silver, lead, copper, and later gold. Russians moved to the region to work as miners, which stimulated the growth of agriculture to support the new communities. In 1861 newly emancipated peasants were allowed to settle in Siberia, although the harsh conditions led to many deaths and many failed communities.

The construction of the Trans-Siberian Railroad from 1892 to 1904 stimulated settlement of the region

LAKE BAIKAL—WORLD HERITAGE SITE

Lake Baikal, the oldest and deepest of the world's lakes, was designated a UNESCO World Heritage Site in 1996. The ancient Siberian lake, which contains almost 20 percent of the world's unfrozen fresh water, has evolved a unique freshwater ecosystem.

and exploitation of its natural resources. From 1906 to 1911 many Russians were urged to migrate to Siberia to relieve the population stress to the west of the Urals. Siberia was the scene of considerable political activity during the Russian Civil War (1918–1920). Forces opposed to the Bolsheviks organized there and were aided by expeditionary forces from the United States, Great Britain, France, and Japan. In 1920, the government of Admiral Aleksandr Vasiliyevich Kolchak (1873–1920), an anti-Bolshevik who had held the Siberian city of Omsk against the Bolsheviks (1918–1919), disintegrated. Kolchak was executed, and Siberia came under Soviet rule.

The Soviets exploited the region for its mineral resources, developed industrial centers, and, in the south, agriculture. Russians and other Slavic peoples were forced or encouraged to move to Siberia, and the population expanded rapidly, with the indigenous peoples often displaced by the new settlers. Forced labor camps were established for political prisoners and many remained in use until the late 1980s. During World War II (1939–1945), industrial and scientific operations were moved to Siberia for protection from the Germans. At the same time, ethnic Germans and others accused of being disloyal to the Soviet state were forcibly relocated to the region.

After World War II, exploitation of the region accelerated with the building of new industrial centers, hydroelectric power plants, and massive agricultural development in the south. The long-term result has been massive environmental destruction.

Agitation for economic, political, and human rights began among some indigenous groups such as the Yakut in the 1980s and became more aggressive in the early 1990s following the collapse of the Soviet Union in 1991. In the post-Soviet era major issues include conflict over regional versus national political control, indigenous peoples' economic independence, the revival of shamanism and other elements of indigenous culture, and ending environmental degradation.

Political Organization

As a part of Russia, Siberia is divided into the Sakha (Yakutia), Bashkortostan, Buryat, Khakass, and Tuva republics and the Chukchi, Koryak, Taymyr, Magadan, Kamchatka, Evenki, Krasnoyarsk, Khabarovsk, Irkutsk, Tomsk, Omsk, Sakhalin, Amur, Chita, Novosibirsk, Kemerovo, Altay, Primorskiy, Ust-Ordyn-Buryat, Yevreyskaya, and Agin-Buryat administrative districts. In the post-Soviet era, there has been a movement among some regional and local political leaders for more control over regional affairs and economic resources. An indigenous-rights movement that predates the collapse of the Soviet Union remains active and campaigns for greater autonomy for indigenous peoples, religious freedom, and the control of environmental pollution.

Economy

Siberian territory is diverse and can be divided into three zones. The north is tundra, the middle zone is a mixed-forest taiga belt, and the south is the steppe zone.

A major motivation for the Russian conquest of Siberia was exploitation of the rich natural resources of the region. Russian traders were first interested in the furs trapped by the indigenous peoples and when they gave out, mining of mineral resources became the major target. Over time, all of Siberia's resources have been exploited. In the 1990s, Siberia produced over 50 percent of Russia's oil, timber, natural gas, coal, water, and hydroelectric power. It also contains vast reserves of copper, nickel, zinc, aluminum, precious metals, mica, fluorite, black lead, asbestos, mercury, salt, and limestone.

Western Siberia is a major industrial region where natural resources such as coal, gas, and timber are processed for use. Western Siberia is also a major agricultural region with the major products being wheat and other grains, potatoes, sugar beets, and butter.

Eastern Siberia surpasses even Western Siberia in the production of fossil fuel, forest, and mineral resources; it is Russia's leading producer of these resources. Exploitation of the region's hydroelectric potential began in the mid-1950s, and there are now four major hydroelectric stations on the Angara River.

Wheat is the major farm product in the warmer south, and animal husbandry is still the primary activity of some indigenous peoples. Recreational activ-

SOLOVETSKY—WORLD HERITAGE SITE

The six islands of Solovetsky on the western edge of the White Sea were designated as a World Heritage Site by UNESCO in 1992. The islands—where evidence of life dating back to 3000 BCE has been found, along with labyrinths and megalithic structures—are the site of several important Russian Orthodox monasteries.

ities centered on Lake Baikal and the Sayan Mountains represent a recent development initiative for southern Siberia. In the north, which is still remote and not suitable for agriculture, indigenous pursuits such as reindeer herding, fishing, sealing, hunting, and fur processing remain major activities.

The centuries of exploitation have taken a toll on the land, water, and air of the region. Almost all areas of heavy human exploitation or settlement suffer from air, water, and soil pollution, often from discarded toxic wastes at industrial complexes or mining sites. The cities of Angarsk, Bratsk, Kemerovo, Krasnoyarsk, and Noril'sk, are ranked as among the most polluted in the world. With the movement for greater regional control and the indigenous-rights movement, there is a possibility that pollution might lessen and some of its effects might be reversed in the next few decades.

Peoples and Cultures

The great majority of Siberia's population is made up of Russians and other peoples of European ancestry, including Ukrainians, Belorussians, Estonians, Lithuanians, Poles, and Germans. Many of the non-Russians arrived in the 1930s and 1940s, having been exiled. There are also distinct populations of Russian members of religious minorities who fled to Siberia to avoid persecution. There are also about 500,000 Siberian Tatars (Turkic Muslims), Koreans, and Dungans (from China).

A distinct subgroup within the Siberian population are the Siberaki, generally defined as people descended from Russians (and Belorussians and Ukrainians) who arrived before the Russian Revolution of 1917 and have especially strong allegiance to Siberia. They see themselves as distinct from people who arrived later and from Russians in European Russia. Traditional Siberaki communities were rural, and the economy was based on limited farming, hunting, and fishing.

Their religion is a mix of Russian Orthodoxy and Siberian shamanism. Those who moved to the cities or became involved in industry tended to assimilate into Russian culture, although the mid-1980s marked the beginning of a revival of Siberaki ethnic consciousness.

The indigenous peoples of Siberia consist of from thirty to sixty groups, depending on the criteria used to measure cultural distinctiveness. Linguistically, these peoples can be divided into ten groups, whose populations range from a few thousand to over 400,000. The traditional economies were based on hunting, fishing, trapping, and reindeer herding and the traditional religion was shamanistic. The traditional ways of all groups were adversely impacted by Russian and Soviet rule, which disrupted their subsistence economies, forced nomadic peoples to settle in collectives, and severely repressed shamanism. Since the 1980s there has been a revival of some of the traditional cultures and some large groups, such as the Yakut and the Buryats, have campaigned for political autonomy and greater control of economic resources in their territories. In 1990 an Association of Peoples of the North was formed, with the Yakut a leading member. In 1999 the capital cities of Yakutsk (capital of Sakha, or Yakutia) and Ulan-Ude (capital of the Buryat republic, or Buryatia) signed a treaty of economic and social cooperation.

David Levinson

Further Reading
Balzer, Marjorie Mandelstam. (1992) *Russian Traditional Culture.* Armonk, NY: M. E. Sharpe.
Derev'Anko, Anatoliy P., Demitri Boris Shimkin, and W. Roger Powers, eds. (1998) *The Paleolithic of Siberia: New Discoveries and Interpretations.* Urbana, IL: University of Illinois Press.
Forsyth, James. (1992) *A History of the Peoples of Siberia: Russia's North Asian Colony.* Cambridge, U.K.: Cambridge University Press.
Friedrich, Paul, and Norma Diamond, eds. (1994) *Russia and Eurasia/China.* Vol. 6 of *The Encyclopedia of World Cultures,* edited by David Levinson. New York: Macmillan/G. K. Hall.
Kaapcke, Gretchen. (1994) "Indigenous Identity Transition in Russia: An International Legal Perspective." *Cultural Survival Quarterly* (Summer/Fall): 62-68.
Levin, Maksim G., and Leonid P. Potapov, eds. ([1956] 1964) *The Peoples of Siberia.* Trans. by Stephen P. Dunn and Ethel Dunn. Chicago: University of Chicago Press.
Olson, James S., ed. (1994) *An Ethnohistorical Dictionary of the Russian and Soviet Empires.* Westport, CT: Greenwood Press.
Thubron, Colin. (2000) *In Siberia.* New York: HarperCollins.

SIBURAPHA (1904–1974), Thai writer. "Siburapha" is the pen name of Kulap Saipradit, who is regarded as one of the most important figures in the development of the novel in Thailand and a major figure in Thai intellectual history of the twentieth century. His literary reputation rests on his pioneering role as one of the first Thai novelists and, later, one of the most prominent writers of the socialist-influenced "literature for life" movement, which aimed to use fiction to highlight social injustice. His non-journalistic writings include translations from Gorky and Chekhov, and books on Marxism, Buddhism, his impressions of a yearlong study-trip to Australia, and the status of women.

After achieving fame in the late 1920s as a writer of popular romantic fiction, at a time when the Thai novel was still in its infancy, Siburapha soon moved into political journalism, where his views on social injustice and undemocratic practices frequently got him into trouble with newspaper owners and government alike. Nevertheless, his abilities were widely recognized and by the age of thirty he had edited several of Bangkok's major dailies. By the late 1940s he was one of a number of prominent writers to have absorbed Marxist literary ideas, and his fiction from this time on became primarily a means for highlighting social injustice and criticizing the government. In 1952 he was imprisoned in a government clampdown on those with left-wing sympathies, and in 1958, a year after his release, he went into exile in China rather than risk further imprisonment under the new military regime. He died in Beijing in 1974 without ever returning to his homeland. His later short stories and novels, with their uncompromising political message, were rediscovered, reprinted, and promoted during the mid-1970s by a progressive Thai youth movement and became a major influence on many young writers at the time. While radical fiction fell out of vogue with the increased political stability in the 1980s, Siburapha's reputation has continued to grow. There have been regular reprints of his earlier works and a steady stream of newspaper and magazine articles on his life; a Siburapha Foundation has been established, which awards an annual prestigious literary prize in his name; and there is now a Siburapha Road in Bangkok, the first road in Thailand to be named after a writer.

Siburapha's most famous novels are *Songkhram chiwit* (The War of Life, 1932), *Khang lang phap* (Behind the Painting, 1937), *Chon kwa rao cha phop kan ik* (Until We Meet Again, 1950) and *Lae pai khang na* (Look Forward, 1955–1957). Of these, *Behind the Painting* and *Until We Meet Again* have been translated into English.

David Smyth

Further Reading
Barmé, Scot. (1995) *Kulap in Oz: A Thai View of Australian Life and Society in the Late 1940s*. Clayton, Australia: Monash University.
Smyth, David (1990). *Siburapha: Behind the Painting and Other Stories*. Singapore: Oxford University Press.

SICHUAN (2002 est. pop. 87.4 million). Located on the upper reaches of the Chang (Yangtze) River, Sichuan (Szechwan), with a land area of 485,000 square kilometers, is one of China's most populous provinces. It has long played a key role in China's economy and relations with Tibet and other western regions. Currently, Sichuan is an important focus in the plan of the People's Republic of China (PRC) to develop the interior of the country.

Archeological discoveries at Sanxingdui in eastern Sichuan suggest that the area was inhabited as early as the eleventh century BCE by a technologically advanced people whose culture was distinct from that of the north China heartland. By 311 BCE, the kingdoms of Ba (in eastern Sichuan) and Shu (in western Sichuan) had fully developed. In that year, the armies of the Qin state from north China incorporated the territory of Ba and Shu into the Qin empire, although the two kingdoms' names are still used to refer to regions of Sichuan.

Qin engineers built the Dujiangyan waterworks on the Min River west of the provincial capital, Chengdu, which made the Chengdu Plain a productive agricultural center. However, Sichuan's geography—surrounded on all sides by mountain ranges and the Chang River gorges—kept it relatively isolated from the rest of China. The Qin built a highway from its capital near the Huang (Yellow) River southwest into Sichuan, carving ledges on the steep mountain slopes. Over the last thousand years, Sichuan has been a center of the tea and horse trade with Tibet. It also supplies rice, sugar, silk, and medicinal products to eastern China. Salt wells drilled up to 1,460 meters deep produced brine that was boiled down using local deposits of natural gas.

The name Sichuan ("four rivers") was given to the area during the Yuan dynasty (1279–1368). At the end of the Ming dynasty (1368–1644), the Sichuan population was devastated by a rebellion. The Qing dynasty (1644–1912) promoted resettlement of the province by immigrants from eastern China. After the fall of the Qing in 1912, Sichuan remained isolated from national politics until 1937, when it became the base of anti-Japanese resistance. In 1939 the Nationalist government created a new province, Xikang, out of parts of western Sichuan and eastern Tibet. In 1955 the PRC government dismantled Xikang and reassigned its territory to Sichuan, with the result that today the population of western Sichuan includes many Tibetans and other national minority groups.

Sichuan is home to the Xichang satellite launching center and many scientific research institutes. Large government investments in transportation and energy networks are intended to promote the economic development of the province. The new dam in the Chang River's Three Gorges area, for example, is meant to provide electricity for much of western China, as well as create a great reservoir extending west to the city of Chongqing. Sichuan and Chongqing (which, until a 1997 administrative reorganization, was a part of Sichuan) are the focal regions of a government campaign to "Develop the West." This campaign, launched in 2000, is intended both to tap the resources of western China and to reduce the economic and cultural disparities between the interior and coastal China.

Kristin Stapleton

Further Reading
Bramall, Chris. (1993) *In Praise of Maoist Economic Planning: Living Standards and Economic Development in Sichuan since 1931.* New York: Oxford University Press.

Endicott, Stephen Lyon. (1988) *Red Earth: Revolution in a Sichuan Village.* London: I. B. Tauris.

Kapp, Robert A. (1973) *Szechwan and the Chinese Republic: Provincial Militarism and Central Power, 1911–1938.* New Haven, CT: Yale University Press.

Lo, Winston Wan. (1982) *Szechwan in Sung China: A Case Study in the Political Integration of the Chinese Empire.* Taipei, Taiwan: University of Chinese Culture Press.

Ruf, Gregory. (1998) *Cadres and Kin: Making a Socialist Village in West China, 1921–1991.* Stanford, CA: Stanford University Press.

Sage, Steven F. (1992) *Ancient Sichuan and the Unification of China.* Albany, NY: State University of New York Press.

Smith, Paul. (1991) *Taxing Heaven's Storehouse: Horses, Bureaucrats, and the Destruction of the Sichuan Tea Industry, 1074–1224.* Cambridge, MA: Council on East Asian Studies, Harvard University.

Von Glahn, Richard. (1987) *The Country of Streams and Grottoes: Expansion, Settlement, and the Civilizing of the Sichuan Frontier in Song Times.* Cambridge, MA: Council on East Asian Studies, Harvard University.

SIDDHARTHA GAUTAMA (c. 566 BCE–486 BCE), founder of Buddhism. Siddhartha Gautama, known as the Buddha, was also titled Sakyasinha and later Sakyamuni, or Sage of the Sakyas. He was born into a princely Kshatriya-caste family in Kapilavastu, on the border between India and Nepal, in a garden

LUMBINI—WORLD HERITAGE SITE

The palatial birthplace of Siddhartha Buddha, the beauty of which led the young prince to seek a life of aesthetic suffering, can still be seen today, some 2,500 years after his birth in 623 BCE. The site has become one of the most important areas for Buddhist pilgrims, and in 1997 was designated a UNESCO World Heritage Site.

identified by archaeologists in the twentieth century. His mother, Maya, died giving birth to him. His father, Suddhodhana, was of the Gautama family. At the age of sixteen the Siddhartha married Yasodhara, and they lived in his father's luxurious palace for the next thirteen years.

Buddha statue at Wat Yai Chai Mongkol, Ayutthaya, Thailand, in 2001. (MACDUFF EVERTON/CORBIS)

A TOOTH-RELIC OF THE BUDDHA

"The relic of the left eye-tooth of Gautama Buddha, here said to be enshrined, has a curious history. Rescued from his funeral pile, B.C. 543, it was preserved for eight centuries at Dantapura in South India, and bought to Ceylon A.D. 310. The Malabars afterwards captured it, and took it back to India, but the great Prakrama recovered it. The Portuguese missionaries got possession of it in the sixteenth century, carried it away to Goa, and after refusing a large ransom offered for it by the Singalese, reduced it to powder and destroyed it at Goa in the presence of witnesses. The account of this destruction of the tooth is most circumstantial in the Portuguese records. Nevertheless, the Buddhist priests at Kandy produced another tooth, which they affirmed to be the real relic, that taken by the Portuguese being a counterfeit, and they conducted this to the shrine with great pomp and ceremonial. This is the relic now treasured with such care and reverence. It is probably not a human tooth at all, being, as those who have seen it affirm, much too large (two inches long) ever to have belonged to man. Then the British got possession of it in 1815, there was great excitement, the relic being regarded as a sort of national palladium. They allowed it, however, to be restored to its shrine amid great festivities. The sanctuary in which it reposes is a small chamber, without a ray of light, in which the air is stifling, hot and heavy with the perfume of flowers, situated in the inmost recesses of the temple. The massive silver table, three feet six inches high, stands before the bell-shaped shrine, jeweled and hung around with chains, and consisting of six cases, the largest five feet high, formed of silver gilt, inlaid with rubies, the others similarly wrought, but diminishing in size gradually, until, on removing the innermost one, about one foot in height, a golden lotus is disclosed, on which reposes the sacred relic. In front of the silver altar is a table upon which worshippers deposit their gifts."

Source: Rev. William Urwick. ([1891] 2001) *India Illustrated with Pen and Pencil*. Revised and enlarged by Prof. Edward P. Thwing. New Delhi, Asian Educational Services.

Then, when only twenty-nine years old, he renounced that life, leaving his wife and newborn son behind as he went out into the world to seek enlightenment. His search began with a year of studying Indian philosophy. He then sought salvation by practicing severe austerities for five years. It was on a day when he was sitting meditating under the famous Bo tree at what would later be called Bodh Gaya that enlightenment came to him, and he was thenceforth known as the Buddha, or Enlightened One.

Beginning now a lifetime of teaching, he preached his first sermon in the Deer Park at Sarnath, near Varanasi, where five disciples joined him. For the next forty-five years he wandered the region now comprising the Indian states of Uttar Pradesh and Bihar, preaching the truth as he saw it, and converting both prince and peasant to his view, regardless of their caste. He organized his disciples into the great Buddhist *sangha*, the oldest religious order that is still in existence. According to one tradition he passed from this world in 486 BCE at Kusinagara, at the age of eighty.

The Buddha left behind a collection of traditions and teachings, written down in Pali by his disciples, that became the Tripitaka. Later translated into Chinese, Japanese, and Tibetan, the Tripitika became the basic texts for hundreds of millions of Asian Buddhists.

The Buddha, whose historicity is definitely established, never made claims of divinity for himself. He only claimed to have attained a certain knowledge that others could also attain. He was the first religious figure to found a brotherhood of monks (the *sangha*), through which he promoted an organized, widespread, and peaceful evangelization of the peasant masses.

Paul Hockings

Further Reading
Thomas, Edward J. (1949) *The Life of Buddha as Legend and History*. 3d rev. ed. London: Routledge and Kegan Paul.

SIEMENS INCIDENT Allegations that high-ranking officers in Japan's Imperial Navy had received bribes from the German munitions firm Siemens Schuckert caused a political crisis that culminated in the resignation of the premier, Admiral Yamamoto Gonnohyoe (1852–1933) and his cabinet on 24 March 1914. The Siemens incident was indicative of the competition, which was especially bitter in 1905–1915, among rival factions associated with Japan's army and navy commanders as well as among rival party organizations. The subject of heated public discussion and official debate, the scandal also marked a step toward greater government accountability in the early history of parliamentary democracy in Japan.

On 23 January 1914 Japanese newspapers printed reports of the trial in Berlin of a former Siemens employee who was charged with stealing confidential company documents from files in the firm's Tokyo office. The defendant testified that he had sold the documents to a Reuters News Service reporter in order to expose a duplicitous deal between Japanese naval officers and the British firm Vickers, represented by a Japanese company, Mitsui Bussan. By accepting an offer from Vickers of regular secret "commissions" of 25 percent of the value of equipment procurement contracts placed with the firm, the naval officers contravened an agreement reached with Siemens earlier to place large orders for ammunition and communications equipment with the German firm in exchange for kickbacks of 15 percent of the value of the orders.

Admiral Yamamoto, premier since February 1913, had authorized a program of lavish expenditures on naval expansion. Critics of his generosity seized on the information released in Berlin to confirm suspicions of corruption in connection with naval spending. In a Diet session on 23 January 1914, Shimada Saburo, a leading member of the opposition Doshikai, opened a two-month period of public debate and political crisis by calling Yamamoto to account with a series of embarrassing questions about the navy's purchasing practices.

During February and March, Yamamoto succeeded in maintaining his position, partly by dismissing naval officers implicated in the allegations of corruption. But the admiral's position was irretrievably weakened by opposition within the upper house of the Diet, the army, and the public.

The Siemens incident contributed to greater instability in Japan's parliamentary politics by ousting the majority party, the Seiyukai, from the premiership and the cabinet. Yamamoto's government survived a no-confidence vote on 10 February, but failed to survive the loss of support in the upper house of the Diet, where the peers had slashed the naval expansion budget and refused to yield to the principle that only the lower house had authority over the budget. In an arrangement brokered by Yamagata Aritomo and other senior leaders, a new cabinet was installed in April 1914 with the veteran parliamentarian Okuma Shigenobu (1838–1922) as premier. Competition for budgetary appropriations between the navy and army continued to be a bone of contention within Japan's government, even at the time of the attack on Pearl Harbor in 1941. Corruption connected to public contracts with foreign firms continued as well, although it did not precipitate another political crisis until the Lockheed scandal of 1976.

Emily M. Hill

Further Reading
Najita, Tetsuo. (1967) *Hara Kei in the Politics of Compromise, 1905–1915*. Cambridge, MA: Harvard University Press.
Yanaga, Chitoshi. (1949) *Japan since Perry*. New York: McGraw-Hill.

SIERRA MADRE The Sierra Madre is the longest mountain range in the Philippines. It forms the backbone of the eastern coastline of the main island of Luzon, running from Cagayan Province up to Quezon Province. The range is approximately 500 kilometers long. The location of the Sierra Madre in the eastern part of Luzon protects the lowlands against strong typhoons during the rainy season in the middle of the year. The range is divided into the Northern Sierra Madre, which stretches from Cagayan to Isabela, and the Southern Sierra Madre, which stretches from Aurora Province to Quezon. There is a short gap dividing the two portions.

The mountains are wild and remote and not totally accessible; hence they cannot be fully developed. They are one of the remaining bastions of virgin forests and home to numerous flora and fauna, particularly the Philippine (monkey-eating) eagle. They are also rich in mineral resources yet to be tapped. The mountain range was formed in prehistoric times when tectonic plates moved inward, pushing up landmasses.

Aaron Ronquillo

Further Reading
Action Asia. (1999) *Adventure and Travel Guide to the Philippines.* Hong Kong: Action Asia.
Department of Tourism. (1994) *The Philippines: Spirit of Place.* Manila, Philippines: Department of Tourism.
Lancion, Conrado, Jr. (1995) *Fast Facts about Philippine Provinces.* Manila, Philippines: Tahanan.
Parkes, Carl. (1999) *Philippines Handbook.* Emeryville, CA: Moon Travel Handbooks.

SIHANOUK, NORODOM (b. 1922), king of Cambodia. King Norodom Sihanouk is the enduring figure of modern Cambodian politics. Born in Phnom Penh, Sihanouk was an unlikely candidate for the Cambodian throne, which he first ascended to in 1941. A student at the Lycée Chasseloup-Laubat in Saigon (Vietnam), he was selected by Cambodia's French colonial rulers to assume the throne after the death of his grandfather, Monivong. The French believed that Sihanouk would be a flexible and easily manipulated national leader. The passage of time has revealed the extent to which their judgment was wrong. Sihanouk quickly established himself as a shrewd and formidable politician, with his self-titled Royal Crusade for Independence providing the catalyst for the end of colonial rule in Cambodia.

Sihanouk's most surprising political move was his decision, in 1955, to fully immerse himself in popular politics by abdicating the Cambodian throne in favor of his father, Suramarit. He formed a political organization, the Sangkum Reastr Niyum (People's Socialist Community), which swept all before it in the 1955 national elections (and then again in 1958, 1962, and 1966). The National Assembly, whose members were all Sangkum politicians, became a rubber stamp for the prince and his policies. He tirelessly traveled throughout Cambodia, inaugurating new schools and hospitals and ingratiating himself among an adoring population.

By the late 1960s, as Cambodia became increasingly embroiled in the conflict in neighboring Vietnam, Sihanouk gradually lost his stranglehold over Cambodia's political system. In 1970, while the then prince was overseas, he was deposed by the National Assembly, which had become frustrated with the nepotism, corruption, and incompetence that characterized government in Cambodia. Sihanouk immediately aligned himself with his sworn enemies in the Khmer Rouge (Communist) movement. For the next five years, Cambodia was at war, with Sihanouk's Communist allies enjoying the ascendancy.

After the war was won, in April 1975, Sihanouk eventually returned to Phnom Penh. No longer of any use to the Communists, he was immediately placed under house arrest in the royal palace and would likely have been executed if it weren't for the support he had from China. When the Khmer Rouge regime was ousted by Vietnamese-supported defectors in 1979, Sihanouk fled to China. He eventually formed a non-Communist resistance movement along the Thai-Cambodian border and played a significant role in negotiations that led to peace agreements in 1991. After United Nations–sponsored elections in 1993, Sihanouk resumed his place on the Cambodian throne. Increasingly frail, he alternates between the royal palace in Cambodia, and China, where he receives ongoing medical treatment. He is also involved with film making and enjoys playing jazz.

David M. Ayres

Further Reading
Chandler, David. (1991) *The Tragedy of Cambodian History: Politics, War, and Revolution since 1945.* Bangkok, Thailand: Silkworm.
Martin, Marie. (1994) *Cambodia: A Shattered Society.* Berkeley and Los Angeles: University of California Press.
Osborne, Milton. (1973) *Politics and Power in Cambodia: The Sihanouk Years.* Camberwell, Australia: Longman.
Osborne, Milton. (1994) *Sihanouk: Prince of Light, Prince of Darkness.* Honolulu, HI: University of Hawaii Press.

SIKHISM Sikhism is a monotheistic religion of India founded by Guru Nanak (1469–1539) around 1500; it is marked by a rejection of idolatry and caste. It was an offshoot of the Bhakti (devotional) cult of vaishnava Hinduism, which first developed in Tamil Nadu in the eighth century and later spread throughout India in the fifteenth and sixteenth centuries. The Bhakti tradition taught that God is the one and only reality and that the rest is *maya*, or illusion. The best way to serve God is by absolute submission to God's will, which is revealed through the guidance of a guru, or spiritual mentor. The followers of Nanak came to be known as Sikhs, from the Sanskrit word *shishya*, "disciple."

Guru Nanak and His Message
Guru Nanak was born in Talwandi, a small village in what is now part of Pakistan. His father was a Khatri, a high caste among Punjabi Hindus. He grew up in a philosophically and culturally vibrant milieu, one

in which he freely met and conversed with Hindus, Muslims, Buddhists, and Jains. As a young man, Nanak went in search of his fortune to Sultanpur, where for about a decade he lived the life of an ordinary family man. However, he was constantly searching for something more valuable: the purpose of life.

During the first quarter of the sixteenth century, he undertook long journeys around the Indian subcontinent, visiting important centers of Hindu and Muslim pilgrimage. After the age of fifty-five, Nanak finally settled down at Kartarpur on the right bank of the Ravi River; there he delivered his message of salvation to all. A community of disciples grew up around him. The daily routine and moral ideals fostered in this first Sikh community constituted the core of Sikh life, whereby men and women shared equally in the Sikh institutions of *seva* (voluntary labor), *langar* (community kitchen), and *sangat* (congregation).

In the eyes of Guru Nanak, the contemporary social order had lost its legitimacy, and in his metaphors there is a direct denunciation of the Turko-Afghan rule of the time. The rulers were unjust; they discriminated against their non-Muslim subjects by levying a pilgrimage tax and *jizya* (a religious tax). The ruling class oppressed the cultivators and the ordinary people. A new religious ideology was therefore needed to form the basis of a new social order. Nanak exhorted people to turn to God, the true king. Service to God alone was true service; he who found a place with the true king did not have to look to an earthly potentate for succor. Nanak described God without reference to either Hindu or Muslim conceptions.

God, for Guru Nanak, was the eternally unchanging formless One. Nanak equated God with truth *(sachch)*. God's creation is real, but not everlasting. God alone is eternal. Nanak preached that people should lodge truth in their hearts and act accordingly. Nanak made the institution of guruship the pivot of his religious system. Without the guru as a guide, no one can attain *moksha*, or salvation, and one wanders through the cycle of death and rebirth in the darkness of ignorance. Nanak, however, insisted on the separation between God and the guru. The guru is to be consulted, respected, and cherished, but not worshiped. He is a teacher, a messiah, but not an incarnation of God.

Nanak denounced caste distinctions and social differentiations. He repudiated the Hindu deities and scriptures. The protagonists of such beliefs and practices, the pundits, the ulama, and the shaikhs (although not Islam itself) naturally came in for criticism as well. He disapproved of asceticism, of penance, and of tor-

A Sikh at the Golden Temple in Amritsar, India, in 1996. (STEPHEN G. DONALDSON PHOTOGRAPHY)

turing the flesh as a step toward enlightenment and instead propagated *grhastha dharma*, the religion of the householder. He refused to grant audiences to people unless they first broke bread in the community kitchen *(guru ka langar)*, where the Brahman and the untouchable, the Muslim and the Hindu sat alongside one another as equals. He was just as critical of the concepts of purity and impurity that had sprung up from notions of higher and lower categories of human beings.

This emphasis on simple living, the absence of incomprehensible ritual, and, most importantly, the concern with the reordering of society on egalitarian lines had a strong appeal, and he won large followings from a diverse group of people. There were many Khatris among his followers, but there also were petty traders, shopkeepers, agents of merchants, itinerant salespeople, artisans, and cultivators, mostly of the Jat peasant community. They came from both the towns and the countryside, and they all considered themselves equal. Many belonged to the lower castes. Nanak taught using the local language, capturing the imagination, and

SIKH SEPARATISM

Although a minority in India, the Sikhs are the dominant group in the Punjab region of northwestern India. They have for their entire history resisted outside rule, first by the Mughals (Muslims) and then the Hindus and at least some elements have agitated for an independent Sikh nation. The governments of modern India have steadfastly refused Sikh independence, a policy that predates Indian independence, as indicated by this statement issued by the Working Committee of the Indian national Congress political party in 1946.

The Sikhs and the Constituent Assembly

The Working Committee have learnt with regret of the decision of the Sikhs not to seek election to the Constituent Assembly. The Committee are aware that injustice has been done to the Sikhs and they have drawn the attention of the Cabinet Delegation to it. They are, however, strongly of opinion that the Sikhs would serve their cause and the cause of the country's freedom better by participation in the Constituent Assembly than by keeping out of it. The Committee, therefore, appeal to the Sikhs to reconsider their decision and express their willingness to take part in the Constituent Assembly. The Working Committee assure the Sikhs that the Congress will give them all possible support in removing their legitimate grievances and in securing adequate safeguards for the protection of their just interests in Punjab.

Source: Jagdish Saran Sharma. (1962) *India's Struggle for Freedom: Select Documents and Sources.* Vol. I. Delhi: S. Chand, 723.

---

echoing the aspirations of the lowest of the low as he laid stress on cleanliness, honesty, and earning one's living through honest labor (*kirat karma*).

Evolution of the Sikh Panth

Nanak was therefore a messenger of bhakti, advocating a personal relationship between God and humans. His religion, however, survived long after the other Bhakti cults had slowly lost their earlier significance in India. Before his death at Kartarpur, Guru Nanak chose his disciple Angad (1504–1552) as his successor, setting aside the claims of his own sons. This nomination was important, as it laid the basis of the guru *parampara* (tradition), whereby the entire organization of the Sikh community revolved around the guru. It also established the idea that the positions of the guru and the disciple were interchangeable and that there was no difference between the founder and the successor.

Guru Angad's pontificate was an extension of Guru Nanak's work but with significant shifts of emphasis.

He had a thorough grasp of the compositions of Guru Nanak, and to preserve them for posterity, he adopted a new script called the Gurumukhi. Gradually, however, from the Bhakti code of surrender to a personal God, Sikhism slowly moved toward a radical reform program as it came in conflict with the Mughal state. The number of Sikhs increased considerably in the Punjab during the pontificate of the third guru, Amar Das (1479–1574). During the time of the fifth guru, Arjun (1563–1606), Sikhs spread to Kashmir, Kabul, Delhi, and Agra. Indeed, Sikhs could be found in all provinces of the Mughal empire during the rule of Emperor Akbar (1542–1605).

Guru Arjun had to appoint a number of representatives, *masands*, authorized to look after the affairs of the local *sangat*s at various places. Once a year, authorized representatives brought to the guru at Ramdaspur (Amritsar) offerings that had been collected from the Sikhs under their supervision. The guru was at the center of the whole organization and was recognized as the Saccha Badshah, or the true king. He came to be seen not just as the temporal authority, but also as the human form of the true God *(niranjan)*. This assumption of parallel authority by the gurus naturally earned for the Sikh brotherhood, or the Panth, the hostility of the Mughal empire. Thus, by the beginning of the seventeenth century, the socioreligious community of Guru Nanak's followers showed the tendency to form "a state within a state."

Akbar's liberalism provided some protection to the guru and his followers, but with the removal of imperial protection, a cycle of violence was unleashed against the Sikhs. The interference of the Mughal emperors Jahangir (1605–1627), Shah Jahan (1627–1658), and Aurangzeb (1658–1707) in the affairs of the Sikh Panth was an important feature of the seventeenth century. Jahangir put Guru Arjun to death for placing the saffron mark on the forehead of the rebel Prince Khusrau as a token of his blessings. State interference encouraged dissent within the Panth and accelerated disunity within it. In such a situation, the successors of Guru Arjun shifted their base to the east of the River Sutlej, and places beyond the land of the five rivers became associated with Sikhism, namely Patna in Bihar, Anandpur and Muktsar in Punjab, and Nanded in Maharashtra.

The sixth guru, Hargobind (1595–1644), was in open conflict with the Mughal administrators in the province of Lahore during the reign of Shah Jahan. The Mughal army attacked Amritsar, and Hargobind took refuge in Kartarpur. The guru's dependence on his *masands* had increased, and some of them started appointing their own deputies or agents for collecting offerings and initiating others into the Sikh faith. In the face of the Mughal onslaught, the Sikhs were forced to retreat to fastnesses in the hills of East Punjab, where they came in contact with the cult of the Mother Goddess, or Shakti worship. This cult involves the worship of power, and hence the rituals associated with it are more violent than the Bhakti rituals. This contact may have indirectly encouraged the Sikh use of violence in dealing with enemies and inspired the transition from a peaceful sect to an increasingly militant one. The Sikhs then looked upon themselves as the instrument of God, using physical force in favor of the good.

Birth of the Khalsa

Gobind Singh (1666–1708) became the tenth guru in 1675. He was determined to eliminate external influence on the Panth through the use of physical force. For this, he had to set the Panth in order and deal with the internecine quarrels plaguing the brotherhood. In 1699, at a large gathering at Anandpur, Gobind Singh inaugurated the Khalsa, the Order of the

Pure. Henceforth all Sikhs, that is, those initiated into Sikhism by the guru himself and not through the *masands*, were to be his Khalsa. This implied that dissidents were not to be considered true Sikhs. The direct link of the Khalsa with the guru was symbolized by a new baptismal ceremony introduced by Gobind Singh. After initiation, both men and women had to wear the emblems of the Khalsa, the five *k*'s, namely, *kesha*, or uncut hair, denoting the way of nature; *kangha*, a comb tucked into the *kesha* to keep it tidy; *kara*, a steel bracelet worn on the right arm; *kaccha*, or short breeches; and *kirpin*, a sword symbolizing self-defense and the fight against injustice. Once initiated into the order, men were given the surname Singh (lion) and the women Kaur (princess). Their rebirth into the order represented the annihilation of family and caste lineage and the destruction of their confinement to hereditary occupations. The principles of unity and equality were therefore reintroduced into the Sikh Panth, and, with the birth of the Khalsa, the Sikhs were committed to resist oppression.

In the meantime, peasant dissatisfaction with the imperial rule increased, but in battles with the Mughals, the Sikhs were forced to retreat. Guru Gobind Singh wished to settle the issue with the Mughals but could not meet Emperor Aurangzeb, who died in 1707. Instead, he met the new emperor, Bahadur Shah (1643–1712), but there was no solution. Before his death in 1708, the tenth guru ended the line of personal gurus by passing the succession not to another person, but to the Adi Granth, the holy book of the Sikhs, which had been compiled by Guru Arjun and installed in the Harmandir, or Golden Temple, at Amritsar in 1604. Thus, leadership of the Panth came to be vested in the community. This was essential to forge the unity necessary to fight the Mughals.

The Sikh Empire

Resistance against the Mughals continued throughout the eighteenth century. Bahadur Shah successfully repressed the uprising led by Banda Bahadur (1670–1716), a follower of Guru Gobind Singh. But gradually the Mughal fortunes declined, and the later mughals faced a rapidly contracting empire. The struggle of the Sikhs against the Mughal government eventually became a people's war. Amritsar emerged as the rallying center of the Singhs (the title used by all male Sikhs, and a term interchangeable with "male Sikh"), and eventually they established their sway over Punjab. The doctrine of Guru Panth ("the guru's method" or "rule"), which provided the basis for concerted action, ensured the right of every Singh to fight, to conquer, and to rule and gave legitimacy to every individual Sikh chief. In the eighteenth century, the region between the Jamuna and Indus Rivers came to be divided among a number of Sikh principalities that were continually involved in internecine wars.

In 1799, a process of unification was started by Maharaja Ranjit Singh (1780–1839), who occupied Lahore and established a Sikh empire extending over a large portion of the Punjab. The British, who had in the meantime established their direct or indirect political control over the greater part of the subcontinent, recognized him as the sole sovereign ruler of the Punjab by the Treaty of Amritsar in 1809.

British Annexation

Within ten years of Ranjit Singh's death, his empire was taken over by the British. Rival claimants to power approached the British for assistance, and taking advantage of the internal turmoil, the British involved themselves in the internal politics of the Sikh empire. After two Anglo-Sikh wars in 1845–1846 and 1848–1849, Punjab was annexed to the British empire. Although the army of the Khalsa was disbanded after 1849, it rendered loyal service to the British in the Indian Mutiny of 1857. After being reinstated, they attained an honored position in the Indian army and fought in nearly all the major wars of the British.

Colonial rule saw a renaissance among the Sikhs. Popularly known as the Singh Sabha movement, it was initiated by the Sikh elite and was characterized by a serious interest in Western education and science. Later, it was appropriated by radicals, who, perceiving a threat from Christian missionaries and the Arya Samaj (a Hindu reform movement started by Swami Dayanand Saraswati in Punjab in 1875), pressed for religious reform. A search for a Sikh identity distinct from the Hindus, particularly the Arya Samaj, began in earnest. The radical Sikh reformists were committed to maintaining a separate Sikh identity and to introducing and preserving distinct Sikh rituals and customs in the *gurdwara*s (Sikh temples). This was opposed by the conservative section of the Sikhs. Ultimately, in 1925, the Shiromani Gurdwara Prabandhak Committee (SGPC) was formed as managing committee of all Sikh *gurdwara*s. The SGPC opposed the partition of India in 1947, because agriculturally fertile land in West Punjab would become part of Pakistan. It sided with the Indian National Congress on this issue, but after the Congress capitulation on the partition plan, the radicals raised the cry for Khalistan, a separate homeland for the Sikhs. The transfer of power and partition of the country in 1947 resulted in large-scale migration of the Sikhs from the West to East Punjab, Uttar Pradesh, and Delhi.

Post-Independence Developments

The government of independent India abolished the privileges previously extended by the British to religious minorities, including the Sikhs. Thus the proportion of Sikhs in the defense and civil services declined. The Sikh agricultural classes, who had been forced to abandon rich farmlands in Pakistan for smaller holdings in East Punjab, also nursed a sense of grievance. This gave rise to an agitation for a Punjabi-speaking province in India. The Indian government conceded, and the new state of Punjab was created in 1966 on the linguistic principle.

Increased wheat production during the 1970s brought unprecedented prosperity to Sikh farmers. This material improvement was accompanied by a growth in Sikh fundamentalism under the leadership of Jarnail Singh Bhindranwala (1947–1984). Tension between Hindus and Sikhs increased, as the predominant Sikh political party, the Shiromani Akali Dal (SAD), demanded further economic and political advantages for the Sikhs. By the early 1980s, the SAD had become more militant, and the Indian government responded by arresting and imprisoning thousands of Sikhs. Armed groups under Bhindranwala's direction spread terror throughout Punjab. Finally, in 1984, when Bhindranwala and his followers entrenched themselves in the Golden Temple, the Indian army launched an attack (code-named Operation Bluestar), killing several hundred Sikhs, including Bhindranwala, and damaging the temple building. Sikh outrage at the attack on the Golden Temple was manifested through the assassination of the prime minister, Indira Gandhi (1917–1984), by her Sikh bodyguards. The new prime minister, Rajiv Gandhi (1944–1991), signed an accord with the Sikh leaders in 1985, hoping to restore peace in Punjab. However, militancy continued in the 1980s. Ultimately a compromise was achieved in 1996 between the Sikh leaders and the Indian government, and affairs in Punjab have remained largely peaceful since then.

Sanjukta Das Gupta

Further Reading

Akbar, M. J. (1985) *India: The Siege Within.* Harmondsworth, U.K.: Penguin.

Banerjee, Indubhusan. (1962) *Evolution of the Khalsa.* Calcutta, India: A. Mukherjee.

Cunningham, Joseph Davey. (1849) *A History of the Sikhs.* London: John Murray.

Grewal, J. S. (1990) *The Sikhs of the Punjab:* Vol. 3 of *The New Cambridge History of India*, edited by Gordon Johnson, C. A. Bayly, and John F. Richards. Cambridge, U.K.: Cambridge University Press.

Kapur, Rajiv A. (1986) *Sikh Separatism: The Politics of Faith.* London: Allen & Unwin.

Loehling, C. H. (1971) *The Granth of Guru Gobind Singh and the Khalsa Brotherhood.* Lucknow, India: Lucknow Publishing House.

Macauliffe, Max Arthur. (1909) *The Sikh Religion.* Oxford: Clarendon.

Mcleod, W. H. (1975) *The Evolution of the Sikh Community.* Oxford: Oxford University Press.

———. (1968) *Guru Nanak and the Sikh Religion.* Oxford: Clarendon.

Ray, Nihar Ranjan. (1975) *The Sikh Gurus and Sikh Society: A Study in Social Analysis.* New Delhi: Munshiram Manoharlal.

Singh, Khushwant. (1977) *A History of the Sikhs.* Oxford: Oxford University Press.

SIKKIM (2001 est. pop. 540,000). Sikkim (in Tibetan, *Dejong,* the rice country) is a small state with a total area of 7,100 square kilometers in northeastern India, lying east of Nepal, south of the Tibetan border, immediately west of the state of Bhutan, and north of Bangladesh. Sikkim is located on the southern slopes of the Himalaya Range. On its western border lies Kanchenjunga (8,598 meters), the third-highest mountain in the world, which the Sikkimese regard as a deity; Mount Everest is also visible beyond Kanchenjunga. Several passes lead through the mountains from Sikkim into Tibet. The land rises from about 350 meters elevation in the south to 6,000 meters in the north. Sikkim has steep valleys separated by high ridges and open plateaus; about one-third of the country is forested.

The capital of Sikkim is Gangtok. The state is governed by a legislative assembly of thirty-two members. Most of the population is Nepalese (who are Hindu), with minorities of Lepcha (probably Sikkim's original inhabitants, whose religion is a combination of animism and Buddhism) and Bhutia (Buddhists who originally came from Tibet). English is the official language, but the languages of the various ethnic groups—Lepcha, Bhutia, Nepali, and Limbu—are also spoken. Crops cultivated include maize, rice, wheat, potatoes, cardamom, ginger, oranges, and tea. The country's exports are mainly fruits and small plastic, electrical, or leather goods. Some copper is produced.

The kingdom of Sikkim was established in the seventeenth century. Coming under British influence early in the nineteenth century, Sikkim became a British protectorate in 1886, but remained an independent territory ruled by its own *chogyal,* or hereditary ruler. Sikkim elected to join the Indian Union in 1952 and was created a state of India in 1975, at which time its hereditary monarchy came to an end. Palden Thondup Namgyal (1923–1982), the last *chogyal,* died in New York. He is survived by his second wife, Hope Cooke, an American writer.

Paul Hockings

Further Reading
Gorer, Geoffrey. (1967) *Himalayan Village: An Account of the Lepchas of Sikkim.* 2d ed. New York: Basic Books.

Lama, Mahendra P., ed. (1994) *Sikkim: Society, Polity, Economy, Environment.* London: Thames & Hudson.

SILK ROAD The ancient Silk Road began in the Chinese city of Changan (present-day Xi'an) and ran westward across deserts to oases and over mountain passes, through the great Central Asian trading cities of Samarqand and Bukhara in modern Uzbekistan and Merv (modern Mary) in Turkmenistan to Tyre on the Mediterranean Sea. Including all the twists and turns, it covered about 9,600 kilometers, or a quarter of the way around the globe. Scholars have considered the Silk Road one of the most significant links connecting various peoples and cultures. The term "Silk Road," which refers to the route along which silk traveled from China to the West, is modern and was coined as late as 1877 by the German geographer Ferdinand von Richtofen.

The earliest Chinese explorations of Central Asia began in the second century BCE, when a Chinese emperor sent an embassy northward to negotiate with hostile tribes on the border. The embassy was headed by Zhang Qian, who was promptly taken prisoner and who, after ten years' captivity, escaped and reported back to the emperor of the vast territories, high civilizations, and great wealth that lay beyond China.

Goods

When merchants began to travel, amber, furs, and honey came to China from northern Russia and the Baltic; pottery, coral and textiles, gold and silver, ivory, and precious stones came from Rome and elsewhere in the Mediterranean region, along with metalware from the foundries of Sidon and Tyre. In turn, China sent perfumes, silks, porcelain, tea, spices, mirrors, lacquerware, and via Samarqand the priceless gift of paper. From Central Asia came jade, cloth, and the horses of Fergana.

The Route

In reality there was no fixed road, but a series of tracks that ran through steppe and desert, branched, then converged on the many oases that offered sustenance to the traveler. The starting points in China

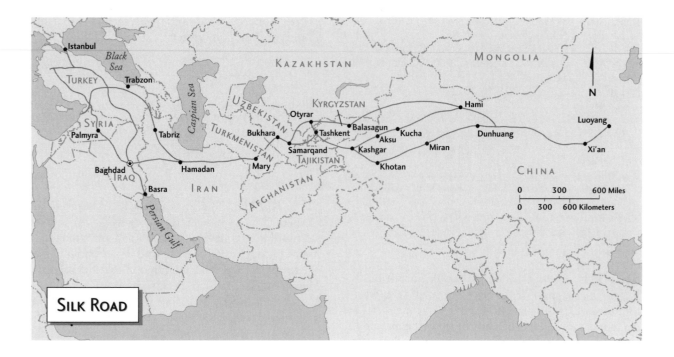

SILK ROAD

were the imperial capital cities of Luoyang and Changan (now Xi'an). From there the route turned northwest, splintering into three: *Bei lu*—the great North Road, leading across the Gobi Desert and passing through the oasis town of modern Turpan in western China, where Buddhist monks left their devotions in the form of painting and carvings on the walls of nearby caves; *Nan lu*—the South Road—passing through Hotan and Shache (Yarkant) in western China, skirting the dreaded Taklimakan Desert, whose name some translated as "You go in, you don't come out"; and a third road going due west, past the oasis town of Loulan. The three routes merged in western China at Kashgar, the last Chinese emporium between East and West. From here Chinese merchants set out on their journey to the lands of the barbarians across the Snowy Mountain, down the passes, to the fabled cities of Central Asia, to Persia (Iran), then to the cities of Antioch and Tyre on the Mediterranean coast, where their precious cargoes were shipped to Rome.

Regular caravans seldom traveled beyond the major trading centers, from which goods were transshipped by those coming from the other direction. Samarqand and Bukhara were the common endpoints for caravans arriving from Baghdad and Aleppo. Here they exchanged their cargoes with merchants from Kashgar and farther east. On the other hand, individual travelers—merchants and emissaries, pilgrims and missionaries—of necessity traversed the entire route.

The Silk Road cities supplied all the needs of travelers, commercial and otherwise: camels and provisions, brokers to draw up contracts and guarantee delivery, banking houses to supply credit and bills of exchange, and markets to buy and sell things of every description. Even so, the journey was not easy. Travelers' accounts record the corpses of people and animals seen along the way. The ever-present danger of bandits was as great a threat as the menacing forces of nature. There are vivid descriptions of sandstorms, the desert's withering heat, and the freezing winds in the high mountain passes. Away from the oases, the need for water was always pressing.

The Rise and Fall of Empires

At the heart of the Silk Road, Central Asia linked the sedentary civilizations on its periphery—Rome, Persia, the Kushans of northern India, and China—and the fierce nomadic hordes of the steppes. From the time of Zhang Qian in the second century BCE, Chinese fortunes ebbed and flowed, checked at times by the Huns, whose dominions (in the fourth century CE) reached from Korea to the Ural Mountains, and by other nomads of the Altay Mountains and the Gobi Desert.

In the eighth century, just as the Chinese seemed about to conquer all of Central Asia, another power appeared on the scene: the Arabs, newly converted to Islam. Gradually the armies of Allah had been moving eastward, dispatching decadent rulers and spreading the word of the Prophet. The two worlds collided in Central Asia. In 751, the Arabs, along with their Turkish and Tibetan allies, defeated the Chinese at the battle of Talas River, marking forever the limits of Chinese dominions.

In 1219, the Mongols burst out of northeastern Asia and came to rule an empire that stretched from Moscow to Beijing. Genghis Khan, a strong protector of trade and of the Silk Road between Europe and China, ensured that merchants could travel in security. Timur (Tamerlane), who presided over the last great Mongol empire, kept the route alive until the beginning of the fifteenth century.

The Demise of the Silk Road

As an increasing number of European merchants, missionaries, and adventurers traveled to the east, they returned with tales both factual and fabulous. Paradoxically, the stories of the East partly accounted for the demise of the Silk Road. Europeans who sought to gain access to the riches of the East and wanted to avoid the long and perilous land journey eventually found the sea route around the Cape of Good Hope and across the Indian Ocean. The importance of the Silk Road declined, and by the sixteenth century Central Asia began to fade from the horizon of history.

Significance of the Silk Road

Across the Silk Road East and West exchanged ideas and discoveries. The Zoroastrians of Persia may have bequeathed to the biblical religions their concept of the duality of good and evil. From the West came the early offshoots of Judaism and Christianity—the Manichaeans and Nestorians. From the east and south came Taoists and Confucians, Hindus and Buddhists, and from the north, the worldview of the shamans. And last, to overlay them all, came Islam. Today, in the ruins of long-vanished oasis settlements, Nestorian chapels stand side-by-side with Buddhist temples. Remains include wooden documents written in Kharosthi, an Indian alphabet dating back to the fifth century BCE and related to Aramaic, the language of Jesus. These artifacts are reminders that in the Silk Road oases merchants, missionaries, and other travelers exchanged their understandings of the world and shared reflections on the things beyond their understanding.

Steven Darian

Further Reading

Boulnois, L. (1966) *The Silk Road*. Trans. by Dennis Chamberlin. New York: Dutton.

Foltz, Richard. (1999) *The Religions of the Silk Road*. New York: St. Martin's.

Grousset, René. (1970) *The Empire of the Steppes*. New Brunswick, NJ: Rutgers University Press.

SIMLA (2002 est. pop. 145,000). Capital of Himachal Pradesh state in northern India since 1966, Simla (also known as Shimla) was the summer capital of the British government of India from 1865 to 1939. Simla is named after the Hindu goddess Shyamala, a manifestation of Kali. Situated on a ridge of the Himalayan foothills (altitude 7,200 feet), it was built by the British in 1819 on land they retained following the Gurkha War. Its cool climate and scenic setting soon made it a popular summer resort, and completion of the Kalka-Simla Railway in 1903 placed the town within a two-day ride from Delhi. Its population rose dramatically following Independence and its selection as state capital. In 1945 and 1946, Simla was the site of historic but futile efforts to resolve differences between what became India and Pakistan. It was the scene, as well, of the 1972 Simla Agreement between the two nations, which also failed to produce lasting peace.

C. Roger Davis

Further Reading

Barr, Pat, and Ray Desmond. (1978) *Simla: A Hill Station in British India*. London: Scholar Press.

SIN, JAIME (b. 1928), Roman Catholic Archbishop of Manila. Jaime Cardinal Sin is well known for his role in the ouster of president and dictator Ferdinand Marcos in 1986. When the minister of defense, Juan Ponce Enrile, and vice–chief of staff, Fidel Ramos (later president, 1992–1998), refused to support Marcos's attempt to manipulate the presidential election and staged a revolt, Cardinal Sin called on Filipinos throughout metropolitan Manila to support Enrile and Ramos. Thousands responded by swarming the two military camps along Epifanio de los Santos Boulevard (also known as EDSA) where Enrile and Ramos were holed up. Within days Marcos went into exile in Hawaii and Corazon Aquino was sworn in as president (1986–1992).

With the "EDSA Revolution," Sin emerged as a major moral force in Philippine politics. In 1997–1998, for example, he opposed constitutional amendments that would allow President Ramos a second term, and in 1999–2000 he supported the impeachment of President Joseph Estrada for taking millions in illegal gambling payoffs. An outspoken critic of graft and corruption in Philippine politics, Sin has worked to improve Philippine democracy and has repeatedly urged Filipinos to cast their vote based on the issues, not personalities.

Robert L. Youngblood

Further Reading

Bautista, Felix B. (1987) *Cardinal Sin and the Miracle of Asia.* Manila, Philippines: Vera-Reyes.

Cerbo, Nestor C., ed. (1999) *Along the Right Path.* Manila, Philippines: Archdiocesan Office for Research and Development.

Suerte Felipe, Virgilio T. J., ed. (1987) *Cardinal Sin and the February Revolution.* Manila, Philippines: TJ Publications.

SIND (2002 pop. 33 million). Sind (Sindh) is a province in southeastern Pakistan, extending over the lower Indus River valley, including the alluvial plain and river delta, between India and the Arabian Sea. Karachi is its capital and largest city. Sind is an arid region with some hilly and desert areas and depends largely on irrigation for agriculture. Its major crops are wheat, rice, millet, cotton, and sugarcane. Sheep, cattle, and poultry are raised, and fishing is important in the area along the Arabian Sea. The chief language is Sindhi, a member of the Indo-Aryan group related to Baluchi and Urdu. The province's land area is approximately 141,000 square kilometers.

Early History

Sind derives its name from the Indus River, which was traditionally called Sindhu. It was an early center of the Indus Valley civilization (c. 2500–1600 BCE); the ancient site of Mohenjo Daro is located in northwest Sind. The region was apparently settled by several waves of Indo-European–speaking peoples between 1500 and 1000 BCE (whether this settlement was peaceful is a matter of dispute among scholars). The Persians conquered Sind in the late sixth century BCE, and Alexander of Macedon invaded it in 325 BCE. Following the dissolution of Macedonian hegemony, Sind was fought over by numerous empires, including the Mauryan empire (c. 324—c. 200 BCE) of central India , the Greco-Bactrian kingdom, the Iranic Sakae and Kushans, and the Epethalites or White Huns. By the late 600s CE, Sind was composed of numerous states owing varying degrees of fealty to Sasanid (224/228–651) Persia. The majority of the inhabitants were Buddhist or Hindu.

Muslim Conquest and Rule

The Arab general Muhammad al-Thakafi invaded Sind in 711, and within three years Arab forces controlled the entire lower Indus. Sind was ruled by governors nominally loyal to the caliphs until the eleventh century, when it was partitioned between the Ghaznavids (977–1187) of Afghanistan in the north and a Rajput dynasty, the Sumeras, in the south. In the 1200s, all of Sind fell under the sway of the Ghurid

THATTA—WORLD HERITAGE SITE

Thatta, designated a UNESCO World Heritage Site in 1981, was the capital of the Sind before it was conquered by Mughal emperors and ruled from Delhi. The city and its mausoleums are a vivid reminder of the Sind civilization.

sultanate. It soon passed under the control of various local dynasties, and though the Mughals (1526–1857) briefly incorporated it into their empire in 1591, Sind remained largely independent. By the late eighteenth century, a Baluchi dynasty had established an emirate over all of Sind.

British Rule

The last emir of Sind was defeated by the British under Sir Charles Napier (1782–1853) in 1843. Under the British, Sind became part of the Bombay presidency. The area was relatively passive during the major Indian revolts against British rule, and it was made an autonomous province in 1937. When Pakistan became independent in 1947, Karachi became the national capital. Tens of thousands of Muslims displaced by the 1947 partition were resettled in Sind.

Current Issues

Ethnic violence broke out in the 1990s between Sindhi speakers and Urdu-speaking Mohajirs demanding a separate province, killing thousands. As a result, in 1998 the provincial governor was dismissed and federal rule imposed. Karachi is also a hotbed of Islamist activity and support for the al-Qaeda terrorist network is strong.

Brian M. Gottesman

Further Reading

Lari, Suhail Z. (1994) *History of Sindh.* Oxford: Oxford University Press, 7–210.

SINDHI Sindhi is the name of the community that occupies Sind (or Sindh) in Pakistan with an estimated population of 20 million people. Sind is located in the southern part of Pakistan. It shares a border with India on the east, while the province of Baluchistan is to its west and north and the Punjab is to the northeast. There are three particular geographic parts to Sind:

mountains, desert, and river. Most of the cities are situated along the Indus River. The word "Sindhi" as well as "Sind" come from another word "Sindhu," which is the old name of the Indus. The Sindhis speak a language named after themselves: Sindhi. The language is Indo-Aryan, but has elements of Persian and Arabic. Several dialects exist: Vicholi, Siraiki, Thareli, and Lari.

Most Sindhis are Muslims who belong to the Sunni sect. Their religious rituals follow those set out by the Qur'an. However, the Sindhis diverge from orthodox Islam by worshiping Muslim saints, a trait that probably developed due to the influence of Hinduism in Sindhi history. One particularly revered saint is Lal Shabhaz Qalander, who was a Sufi mystic in the thirteenth century. The anniversary of his death is a major holiday that is celebrated with a festival featuring singers, musicians, and dancers.

The Sindhis have a strong cultural heritage, with a folk literature and poetry that dates back to the fourteenth century if not earlier. One famous Sindhi poet is Shah Abdul Latik, whose best-known work is *Shah Jo Risalo*, widely recited throughout the area. There are several historical sites, including Mohenjo Daro, Amri, and Kot Diji, that show the cultural legacy left by the culturally advanced Harappan civilization that flourished in Punjab and Sind in the third millennium BCE. Although there are those who do not believe there is much connection between the Harappan culture and today's Sind culture, others have shown that certain items, such as a bullock cart or a musical instrument, have not changed significantly since the days of the Harappans.

Today, agriculture is the main source of income for the Sindhis. They grow wheat, millet, maize, rice, cotton, and oilseeds. They also grow bananas, mangoes, and dates. Because there is little rain in this area, the Sindhis rely heavily on irrigation for their water. The main source of water is the Indus River, which has three irrigation dams on it. Other economic activities include herding camels, goats, and sheep in the areas away from the Indus River, and fishing catfish, shad, pomfret, and shrimp in the Indus River and on the coast of the Arabian Sea.

Industrial activity takes place mostly in Karachi. Karachi is the provincial capital of Sind and also the largest city in Pakistan. It has a population of more than 9 million people. Because Karachi is the commercial and industrial center of Pakistan, it lends considerable status to Sind. Karachi has industrial plants that manufacture cotton, sugar, cement, steel, and cars. Unfortunately, Karachi has seen the development of squatter populations as people migrate from the rural areas, drawn by the lure of the city and the promise of the riches they believe it contains. This migration reduces the agricultural labor force, which has an adverse effect on the economy. The Sindhis suffer from the standard ills of an agricultural society within the developing countries: a low standard of living, overpopulation, and lack of education.

In addition to the economic problems the Sindhis face, they have to deal with ethnic and political concerns within Pakistan. The Sindhis perceive the Punjabis' power as threatening to their identity. Therefore, they have resisted efforts to supplant the Sindhi language with Urdu in schools. This ethnic divisiveness between Sindhis and the Urdu-speaking *muhajir*s (Muslims who fled their homeland in India and settled in the Sind following the partition of the subcontinent upon independence from Great Britain) has resulted in several violent clashes.

Houman A. Sadri

Further Reading

Cleveland, William L. (1994) *A History of the Modern Middle East.* Boulder, CO: Westview.

Norton, Augustus Richard, ed. (1996) *Civil Society in the Middle East.* Leiden, Netherlands, and New York: Brill.

SINDHIA FAMILY The Sindhia family, a prominent lineage of rulers in western India in the eighteenth century, played an important role in the ultimate transference of power to the British in much of the area that was to become the Bombay Presidency in the following century.

The founder of the dynasty, Nemaji Sindhia, invaded Malwa in central India in 1704. Ranoji Sindhia was an ordinary Maratha (inhabitant of south central India) warrior who served the *peshwa* (the prime minister of the Maratha) so well that he was endowed with a part of Malwa as its chieftain (1726–1745); he made Gwalior, his birthplace, into his headquarters.

An illegitimate son, Mahadaji Sindhia, succeeded Ranoji Sindhia after his death. Though wounded at the third battle of Panipat (1761), where other Sindhias died, he became the leader among the Maratha chiefs. His power and influence continued to grow, until in 1771 he reestablished the emperor Shah Alam II on the shaky Mughul throne and became his protector. He then mediated between the British and the Marathas to bring the First Anglo-Maratha War (1775–1782) to an end. With the help of some European officers, he remodeled the army to create a powerful force equipped with artillery. After defeating several Indian princes' armies (1790–1792), he gained the title of vice-regent of the empire. He died in 1794 after a short illness.

He was immediately succeeded by his grand-nephew, Daulat Rao Sindhia (1779–1827), who intrigued against the Maratha *peshwa*, Baji Rao II (d. 1852), at his court in Poona (Pune) in western India. Daulat Rao and Baji Rao II fought against Jaswant Rao Holkar, who rose in rebellion, in the battle of Poona (1802), but their forces were beaten. The *peshwa* then fled to Bassein on the west coast of India and concluded a treaty with the British, which was deeply resented by the Marathas and led to the Second Anglo-Maratha War (1803–1805). In this, Daulat Rao found himself pitted against Arthur Wellesley (later the Duke of Wellington; 1769–1852), who defeated him. Despite his involvement in the Third Anglo-Maratha War (1817–1819), Daulat Rao remained in control of his power base at Gwalior, though he was required to cede much of his territory.

Paul Hockings

Further Reading
Majumdar, R. C., ed. (1977) *The History and Culture of the Indian People*. Vol. 8: *The Maratha Supremacy*. Mumbai (Bombay), India: Bharatiya Vidya Bhavan.

SINGAPORE—PROFILE (2001 est. pop. 4.3 million). The republic of Singapore, at the southern tip of the Malay Peninsula, is strategically located at the convergence of the world's major sea-lanes. The Chinese-dominated multiethnic country is politically stable and is a world-class business center, but it still faces the task of allaying minority groups and coping with recurring economic crises.

Geography
Dominating the Straits of Malacca, the republic of Singapore consists of the island of Singapore and sixty adjacent islets, altogether having an area of about 648 square kilometers. The country lies between the Indian Ocean and the South China Sea, with the Singapore Strait separating it from Indonesia to the south and the Johore Strait separating it from Malaysia to the north. The terrain is mostly lowland; the highest point of elevation is 177 meters at Bukit Timah. Keppel Harbor is the port, and Singapore City the capital and chief port. Singapore has a tropical climate with a humidity of 80 percent and average temperatures of 26°C, with rainfall throughout the year. Because most of Singapore island is urbanized, there is no difference between the countryside and Singapore City. Except for some secondary rainforest and mangrove swamp, the island has little vegetation. Current environmental problems are caused by industrial pollution, forest fires in Indonesia, a scarcity of freshwater, and limited land resources.

People
Singapore, with about 5,855 people per square kilometer, is one of the most densely populated countries in the world. The Chinese constitute the largest ethnic group, with about 77 percent of the population; Malays represent around 14 percent, Indians 8 percent, and others 1 percent. The largest age group is that of people fifteen to sixty-four, who are 71 percent of the population, with those below fifteen years making up 22 percent. The population growth rate is around 3.5 percent according to 2001 estimates.

Free-trade opportunities meant an influx of immigrants into Singapore, and by the beginning of the twentieth century, Singapore had become a cosmopolitan country with Chinese, Peninsular Malays, Sumatrans, Javanese, Bugis, Boyanese, South Asians, Arabs, Jews, Eurasians, and Europeans. Transport and communication rapidly developed to cope with the increasing number of commercial enterprises. The well-organized Chinese immigration from the mid-nineteenth century resulted in this group's dominance in commercial life. The Malays and Indonesians from neighboring islands

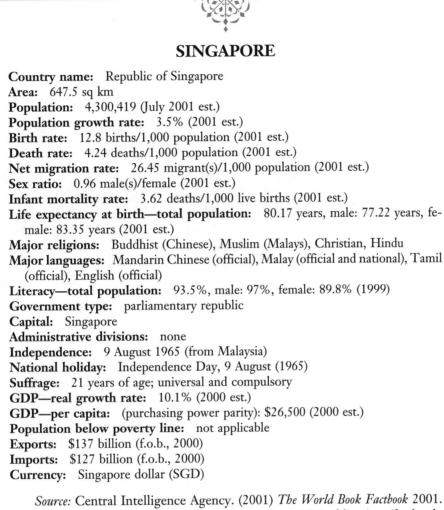

SINGAPORE

Country name: Republic of Singapore

Area: 647.5 sq km

Population: 4,300,419 (July 2001 est.)

Population growth rate: 3.5% (2001 est.)

Birth rate: 12.8 births/1,000 population (2001 est.)

Death rate: 4.24 deaths/1,000 population (2001 est.)

Net migration rate: 26.45 migrant(s)/1,000 population (2001 est.)

Sex ratio: 0.96 male(s)/female (2001 est.)

Infant mortality rate: 3.62 deaths/1,000 live births (2001 est.)

Life expectancy at birth—total population: 80.17 years, male: 77.22 years, female: 83.35 years (2001 est.)

Major religions: Buddhist (Chinese), Muslim (Malays), Christian, Hindu

Major languages: Mandarin Chinese (official), Malay (official and national), Tamil (official), English (official)

Literacy—total population: 93.5%, male: 97%, female: 89.8% (1999)

Government type: parliamentary republic

Capital: Singapore

Administrative divisions: none

Independence: 9 August 1965 (from Malaysia)

National holiday: Independence Day, 9 August (1965)

Suffrage: 21 years of age; universal and compulsory

GDP—real growth rate: 10.1% (2000 est.)

GDP—per capita: (purchasing power parity): $26,500 (2000 est.)

Population below poverty line: not applicable

Exports: $137 billion (f.o.b., 2000)

Imports: $127 billion (f.o.b., 2000)

Currency: Singapore dollar (SGD)

Source: Central Intelligence Agency. (2001) *The World Book Factbook* 2001. Retrieved 5 March 2002, from http://www.cia.gov/cia/publications/factbook.

were early immigrants who engaged in agriculture. South Indians constitute about 80 percent of the South Asian people in Singapore; others include descendants of the indentured laborers that the British brought from South Asia. Many European professionals, including the British, have also become citizens of Singapore, but the Portuguese form the bulk of Eurasians. Arabs, who came as traders, settled after marrying Malays. The arrival of foreign workers, professionals, and students in large numbers has resulted in an increasing growth rate for foreigners compared with citizens of Singapore.

Singapore's standard of living is the second highest in Asia after Japan; the per capita gross national product (GNP) is $26,500. With a developed free-market economy, a favorable business environment, and the fifth-highest per capita gross domestic product (GDP)

in the world, Singapore is economically stable in spite of the recurring global crises.

The country does not depend on agriculture and raw material production. Manufacturing accounts for 24 percent of real GDP. The workforce is employed mainly in financial-related services (38 percent), manufacturing (22 percent), commerce (21 percent), and construction (7 percent). In 1960 a slum-clearance program was instituted, and 86 percent of the population live in public apartments constructed by the Housing and Development Board. Living conditions are good, with a life expectancy of 77.2 years for males and 83.4 for females, an infant mortality rate of 3.6 per 1,000, and 13 doctors per 10,000 people. The crime rate is low, with 1,005 cases per 100,000 population. Family planning and a strict immigration policy are intended

Downtown Singapore as seen from Mount Faber in February 1996. (KEVIN R. MORRIS/CORBIS)

to reduce population growth. The Central Provident Fund, to which both employers and employees contribute, is the country's central welfare institution. Singapore also has one of the world's highest literacy rates (93.5 percent) and has four official languages: Mandarin Chinese, Malay (national), Tamil, and English.

Society and Culture

The pluralistic society of Singapore reflects a multifaceted culture, a meeting ground for diverse cultural influences, with both traditional and contemporary aspects. The government has emphasized the unique identity of being a Singaporean with Asian values and Asian heritage. Although the core national value system is Confucian, there are many other traditions. The major religions of the nation are Buddhism (54 percent), Islam (15 percent), Christianity (13 percent), and Hinduism (about 3 percent). The Chinese are predominantly Buddhists, generally Mahayana, and Taoists, who follow the teachings of Confucius and Lao Zi and practice ancestor worship. Some Chinese temples, such as Thian Hock Keng, Siong Lim, and Hong San See, are national monuments. The Malays are generally Muslims, and there is a sizable proportion of South Asian Muslims. The supreme Islamic religious body among Singapore's Muslims is the Majlis Ugama Islam Singapura (Islamic Religious Council of Singapore). Sri Mariamman Temple and Sri Srinivasa Perumal Temple, built in South Indian style, are famous Hindu monuments of Singapore. There are

thirty Catholic churches and seven Gurdwaras (Sikh temples) in Singapore. All the major festivals of all these religions are celebrated throughout the year. A national holiday is Independence Day, 9 August.

Chinese opera, Chinese dance, and Malay and Indian dances are popular. The Singapore Lyric Theater presents poplar music shows and operas. The Singapore Dance Theater, a professional ballet company, is noted for dance forms that fuse Eastern and Western styles. The Singapore Symphony Orchestra highlights European classical composers. The Singapore theater has been experimenting with new trends since 1988 and has produced plays of artistic excellence. The Chinese Theater Circle, Theater works, Teater Kami, and Agni Koothu are some of the major theater groups.

With features such as a disciplined workforce, high productivity, modern amenities, and strong foreign investment, Singapore's future looks bright. However, there are some discordant notes. The government's emphasis on the unique Singaporean identity and Confucian values creates suspicion and mistrust among non-Chinese groups. In addition to emphasizing the Chinese identity of Singapore, the government is bent on cementing its power through rigid control of society. As the nation moves toward a first-world economy, some experts on Singapore think that the emphasis instead should be on human development and political liberalization.

Patit Paban Mishra

Further Reading

Huff, W. G. (1994) *The Economic Growth of Singapore.* Cambridge, U.K.: Cambridge University Press.

Lee, Kuan Yew. (1998) *The Singapore Story.* Upper Saddle River, NJ: Prentice Hall.

Turnbull, Constance M. (1989) *A History of Singapore, 1819–1988.* Singapore: Oxford University Press.

SINGAPORE—ECONOMIC SYSTEM

As one of the Asian "tigers" (along with Hong Kong, Taiwan, and Korea), the resourceful but resourceless island city-state of Singapore, one of the most densely populated countries in the world, has achieved rapid economic development. Since its independence from Malaysia in 1965, it has roughly doubled its gross domestic product (GDP) every twelve years.

Singapore has succeeded in turning itself from a slum-ridden former British colony and commercial trading port centered on the Singapore River into a modern industrialized economy, producing and exporting electronic goods, chemicals, and business and financial services. It boasts the best airport in the world, the busiest seaport in terms of shipping tonnage, and a foreign exchange market with a daily turnover exceeded only by London, New York, and Tokyo.

The republic also has one of the highest standards of living in the world, according to international development agencies such as the World Bank (2001), measured in terms of access to good-quality housing and education and life expectancy at birth (seventy-five years for men and seventy-nine for women). Poverty has been virtually eliminated, the distribution of income is comparable to countries such as the United Kingdom and Australia, and Singapore probably has the world's highest proportion of shareholders.

Characteristics of the Economy

A dearth of natural resources and absence of an agricultural sector has meant that economic activity in Singapore is split into manufacturing (two-thirds) and services (one-third) and that the country is extremely reliant on international trade, with the value of exports and imports taken together accounting for more than twice its GDP. Almost all food and natural resources, including about half its water needs, are imported from abroad, and much of the value of its manufactured exports comes from processing imported components.

Foreigners also play a crucial role in the Singapore economy, both indirectly as a source of investment funds (particularly from the United States and Japan), and directly through production by multinational companies located in the republic. In 1999 about 14 percent of those residing in the country were non-Singaporean, with foreign workers being employed in occupations as diverse as stockbrokers, construction workers, and domestic maids. This has prompted the government to take the unusual step of publishing a measure of "indigenous" national income, which excludes the contribution of foreign workers or foreign-owned firms located in Singapore. Singapore's national income is about one-third smaller when this measure is used.

These characteristics make it difficult to compare Singapore with other economies. Indeed, in many ways, a better comparison might be with other cities, such as New York, Tokyo, or Shanghai. There even are thousands of daily commuters from beyond the city's borders, from neighboring Malaysia and Indonesia, just as in any large city. This partly explains why the Singapore authorities have, so far, resisted attempts by international organizations to reclassify Singapore as a fully developed country, while other countries at a similar stage of development, such as South Korea, have recently been "graduated."

Economic Policy

Economic policy in Singapore has focused primarily on mobilizing the nation's high levels of saving and investment, promoting manufactured exports, and developing Singapore as an international financial center. The resources of the Central Provident Fund, a compulsory retirement fund to which both employees and employers contribute, are used to build an efficient infrastructure, including roads and ready-made industrial estates, to build an education and housing system, and to establish a climate of good labor relations that is attractive to foreigners. Multinational corporations, in particular, are welcomed with open arms and given tax and other incentives to locate in the republic.

The Singapore economy has largely operated in a competitive global environment, with low levels of protection against foreign competition, although import taxes are high on foreign cars, alcohol, and tobacco. However, at the same time, economic policy has been subject to strong guidance from the public sector through planning agencies such as the Economic Development Board. The National Wages Council sets guidelines on pay increases. Government-linked companies, such as the Development Bank of Singapore and Singapore Airlines (the national airline), and statutory boards, including the Public Utilities Board and Port of Singapore Authority, also account for a significant proportion of output.

Budgetary policy has been characterized by prudence, and the country has enjoyed a long history of

FIVE LARGEST COMPANIES IN SINGAPORE

According to *Asia Week* the five largest companies in Singapore are as follows:

Company	Sector	Sales ($ in millions)	Rank in Asia
Caltex Trading	Oil Trading	27,703.5	32
Shell Eastern Trading	Oil Distributing	18,124.0	57
Felxtronics	Electronics	12,109.7	105
SK Energy Asia	Oil Trading	7,989.0	170
Hewlett-Packard	Computers	7,893.9	172

Source: "The Asia Week 1000." (2001) *Asia Week* (9 November): 115.

government budget surpluses. Those surpluses, together with a conservative monetary policy, kept the rate of consumer price inflation and unemployment during the last decades of the twentieth century low by international standards. The national currency, the Singapore dollar, has tended to increase in value over time against most foreign currencies. The balance of payments, a measure of Singapore's trading account with the rest of the world, has consistently been in overall surplus, resulting in a steady accumulation of national wealth in the form of foreign exchange reserves. Singapore has the highest per capita reserves in the world.

Challenges

A lack of indigenous resources, combined with dependence on foreigners, particularly in the manufacturing sector, has led to fears in Singapore that there might be a loss of markets in traditional manufactured goods to emerging Asian competitors, especially China. There have also been fears that foreign multinationals may choose to relocate their operations away from Singapore in countries with lower production costs.

Current policy initiatives are thus aimed at increasing the quality of the manufactured goods produced and at encouraging development in such fields as integrated circuits for computers and other electronic devices, biotechnology (including genetic engineering), and pharmaceuticals. To achieve this, educational facilities at the tertiary level are being upgraded and foreign talent is being actively recruited.

Singapore is also seeking to diversify the destination of exports away from regional markets in East and Southeast Asia and toward new markets in Europe and Latin America. It also hopes to entice tourists to stay more than the typical two to three days in transit, and to encourage homegrown companies to venture abroad to produce and sell their products. It is hoped that the flow of profits earned by such companies will in time provide an additional source of income, a "second wing" for the Singapore economy, to balance the outflow of profits from foreign companies and the current overreliance on the income earned by government agencies investing abroad.

Another key challenge is to establish Singapore as a premier international financial center with a wider range of activities than at present, including the management of a full range of financial assets such as shares, bonds, and unit trusts. To achieve this, local financial institutions, such as the banks, are being encouraged to compete more with foreign banks in the Singapore market. In addition, some government-linked companies, such as Singapore Telecom, have been privatized, and emphasis is shifting from reliance on government initiatives toward more private-sector innovation and self-regulation in the financial sector.

The government's vision is to transform Singapore into a global hub or "intelligent island," offering a base for company headquarters, conferencing, and exhibitions. To this end, it is busy constructing a multimedia Internet computing infrastructure to which all residents, educational institutions, and companies will eventually be wired. Already in widespread use are electronic payments at the point of sale, automatic teller machines at which you not only can withdraw money but also can buy shares and pay police fines, and stored-value cards for use on public transport. Singapore has even had a Miss Internet competition, in which the contestants are judged on intellectual as well as physical qualities.

Peter Wilson

Further Reading

Huff, W. G. (1994) *The Economic Growth of Singapore: Trade and Development in the Twentieth Century.* Cambridge, U.K.: Cambridge University Press.

Lim Chong Yah and Associates. (1988) *Policy Options for the Singapore Economy.* Singapore: McGraw-Hill.

Ministry of Education and Arts. (2000) *Singapore 2000.* Singapore: Ministry of Education and Arts.

Peebles, Gavin, and Peter Wilson. (1996) *The Singapore Economy.* Cheltenham, U.K.: Edward Elgar.

———. (2002) *Economic Growth and Development in Singapore: Past and Future.* Cheltenham, U.K.: Edward Elgar.

Tan Chwee Huat. (1999) *Financial Markets and Institutions in Singapore.* 10th ed. Singapore: Singapore University Press.

World Bank. (2001) *World Development Report 2000/2001.* Oxford: Oxford University Press for the World Bank.

SINGAPORE—EDUCATION SYSTEM

Singapore's strong education system, especially its vocational and tertiary education, contributed to the country's so-called economic miracle—its rapid economic growth from the 1970s through the 1990s. The British had established a modern education system in Singapore during the colonial era, and Singapore's strong government developed it further between the 1970s and 1990s.

During the colonial era, the British established a comprehensive primary and secondary education system in Singapore, focusing on preparing a workforce for service in colonial administration and commerce. The education was conducted in four major languages—English, Chinese, Malay, and Tamil. After gaining independence in 1965, the government of Singapore emphasized the development of bilingual education, encouraging education in English and in one of the local languages. By 1968, all primary school-age Singaporean children were enrolled in public or private schools, and the literacy rate rose rapidly. By the late 1990s, the adult literacy rate reached 89.1 percent: 95 percent among males and 83 percent among females.

The Ministry of Education of Singapore is responsible for the registration of all schools in the country and for establishing national standards. According to official statistics, the government spends around 3 percent of the gross domestic product on education.

Presently, children begin a three-year preschool education program at the age of three. Kindergartens in Singapore are usually run by the private sector, communities, or religious bodies, but they must register with the Ministry of Education. At the age of six, children begin a four-year foundation program with a common government-approved curriculum, which includes English, their mother tongue, mathematics, and other subjects. At the age of ten, children enroll in a two-year orientation-education program, which includes English, their mother tongue, mathematics, science, and other subjects. On completion of the orientation program, pupils must sit for the Primary School Leaving Examination (PSLE).

At the age of twelve, children enter four- or five-year secondary-education programs. On completion of secondary school, pupils sit for an exam for a Singapore-Cambridge General Certificate of Education (GCE). There are several compulsory subjects, including English, their mother tongue, mathematics, humanities, history, and geography.

According to official figures, in 2000 there were 197 primary schools with 12,287 teachers providing education for 306,000 pupils, and 159 secondary schools with 9,462 teachers providing education for approximately 176,100 students. The official statistics show that Singapore achieved nearly 95 percent enrolment of relevant age-group children at primary schools.

After completing secondary school, students may join a two-year pre-university program at a junior college or a three-year pre-university program at a centralized institute. After completing this program, students must sit for the Singapore-Cambridge General Certificate of Education "Advanced" (GCE "A") Level Examinations. Most education programs at the tertiary level are conducted in English, but some are in Chinese. Students may choose to study in Singapore, but a considerable number choose to study overseas, especially in Australia, Canada, the United States, the United Kingdom, and Japan.

After receiving a bachelor's degree, students may continue their education at a postgraduate level. A master's degree takes between two and four years of study. Upon completion of a master's degree, students may enter a three- or four-year doctorate program

Official figures for 2000 listed fifteen junior colleges with 1,781 teachers providing education for 23,900 pupils, and seven higher-education institutions attended by approximately 84,000 students. Traditionally, the prestige of tertiary education is high, and competition among students is keen.

Rafis Abazov

Further Reading

Gopinathan, Saravanan, Anee Pakir, Wah Kam Ho, and Vanithamani Saravan, eds. (1998) *Language, Society, and Education in Singapore: Issues and Trends.* Singapore: Federal Publications.

Mortimore, Peter, ed. (1999) *The Culture of Change: Case Studies of Improving Schools in Singapore and London.* London: University of London, Institute of Education.

Soh, C. (2002) *The Use of Information Technology for the Management of Education in Singapore.* Singapore: Commonwealth Publications.

Wong, Ting-Hong. (2002) *State Formation and Hegemony: Chinese School Politics in Postwar Singapore and Hong Kong.* Reference Books in International Education. Singapore: Routledge Falmer.

SINGAPORE—HISTORY

Singapore, a group of islands, is situated at the tip of the Malay Peninsula at the mouth of the Strait of Malacca and separated from the peninsula by the narrow Strait of Johore. Singapore is a tiny but politically stable and economically prosperous city-state. It is a key member of the Association of Southeast Asian Nations (ASEAN) as well as the Asia Pacific Economic Council (APEC). Singapore's position on the sea route between India and China makes it strategically important. Robust annual economic growth of about 9 percent during the last three decades made Singapore a model for other nations. However, one-party rule, draconian laws, and alleged human rights violations mar this positive picture. Nevertheless, Singapore remains an Asian miracle thanks largely to the efforts of its first prime minister, Lee Kuan Yew (b. 1923, served 1959–1990).

Ancient History

Local legend and foreign travel accounts provide only a murky picture of Singapore's ancient history. Third-century Chinese accounts mention an island at the end of the Malay Peninsula. There is evidence of Tamil (South Indian) and Persian trading with the island since the fifth century. Some sources suggest that Italian traveler Marco Polo visited Singapore. However, although he did visit nearby Sumatra, there is no evidence that he visited Singapore. A fourteenth-century Chinese traveler recorded that piracy was the main business on Singapore's islands.

Singapore once was an outpost of the Sumatran empire of Srivijaya (flourished seventh through thirteenth centuries), which was situated on the southern coast of Sumatra along the Palembang River. At its height, Srivijaya extended its control as far as Kedah and beyond in northern Malay Peninsula. Srivijaya controlled both the Malacca and Sunda Straits. The Chola rulers of southern India, who contested Srivijayan control of the straits, proved to be a serious challenge, especially during the eleventh century. Although a Chola invasion seriously damaged the Srivijayan empire, it continued until the end of the thirteenth century.

Meanwhile, elsewhere in Southeast Asia, Chinese intervention in the civil war in Java between 1292 and 1293 enabled Prince Vijaya, the legitimate heir to Senghasari Java, to become ruler of Java in 1293 and establish a new capital at Majapahit in eastern Java; his reign marked the start of the Majapahit empire. In 1360, when Tribhuvana became queen, she appointed Gajah Mada as her chief minister. He was the real ruler of the empire from 1330 to 1364. During his rule, Majapahit controlled Bali, Macassar, Singapore (called in Javanese accounts Temasek or Tumaskik), Sumatra, and western Java. The exact nature of this control is not known. Perhaps it was limited to extracting tribute from those territories. Soon after Gajah Mada's death in 1364, Singapore fell into the hands of the Siamese kingdom of Ayutthaya. The Siamese and the Majapahits continued to vie for control of Singapore during the fourteenth century. Paramesawar, a rebel exile from Majapahit, sought asylum in Singapore, and in about 1390 he established his throne there. Eventually, the Siamese ousted him, but he went on to establish himself at Melaka, where he later embraced Islam, became Iskandar Shah, and established the Melaka sultanate, which would last for several centuries.

Portuguese capture of Melaka in 1511 drove many well-to-do people to migrate to Singapore. The sultan of Melaka set up his headquarters at Bintan Island in the Riau Archipelago of the Singapore Channel. In 1526, he lost Bintan and moved to Johor. During the seventeenth century, with the expulsion of the Portuguese from Melaka, Singapore fell into Dutch hands. Singapore, however, was not highly sought after by the Europeans for a while, and the local chieftains ruled the islands.

The British Period

The modern history of Singapore began in the nineteenth century with the arrival of the British, especially the British governor of Java, Thomas Stamford Raffles (1781–1826). During the Napoleonic wars in Europe, France occupied Holland, and the Dutch colonies in Southeast Asia fell into British hands. After Napoleon's defeat, when Java returned to Dutch hands, Raffles was transferred to Bengkulu, a pepper port of Sumatra. In 1818, Melaka was also returned to the Dutch. Dutch control of the Riau Archipelago near Singapore was nominal. Because Melaka lay in ruins and was no longer usable, Raffles had to look elsewhere for a center of trade. He decided on Singapore,

KEY EVENTS IN SINGAPORE'S HISTORY

5th century CE   Persians and Indians are trading with people on Singapore.
7th–13th centuries   Singapore is an outpost of the Srivijaya empire.
14th century   Singapore is ruled by Java and Siam.
1823   Singapore comes under British control.
1832   Singapore becomes the headquarters of the British Straits Settlements.
1867–1946   The Straits Settlements are a British Crown Colony.
1869   The opening of the Suez Canal in Egypt increases Singapore's importance as a trading center.
1946   Singapore becomes a separate crown colony.
1942–1946   Singapore is controlled by Japan.
1946   The British regain control of Singapore.
1959   Singapore is granted internal self-government.
1963   British rule ends and Singapore joins the Malaysian Federation.
1965   Singapore becomes an independent nation.
1971   The last of the British troops leave.
1997   Hong Kong reverts to Chinese control, increasing the importance of Singapore as an industrial and commercial center.

but it was by now controlled by the sultan of Riau-Johor, who was friendly with the Dutch. Raffles engineered the removal of the sultan and received facilities at Singapore from the sultan's replacement. The British authorities, although reluctant to approve Raffle's scheme, finally acquiesced. Soon after, Singapore became a successful center of trade.

In 1823, Raffles renewed the lease agreement on Singapore for a lump sum of $60,000 and additional monthly payments of $2,000 in rents. In 1824, England reached an agreement with the Dutch by which the latter agreed to exchange Bengkulu for Melaka and to relinquish all claims to Singapore and Malaya. In return, England agreed not to seek territories in Sumatra and nearby islands. The Dutch were allowed to keep the Riau Archipelago, and the British took control of Johor. Two years later, the British Parliament united Penang, Singapore, and Melaka into a single residency: the Straits Settlements. Later the Straits Settlements were placed under control of the British East India Company headquartered in Bengal, India.

In 1832, Singapore became the headquarters of the Straits Settlements. After the failed Indian revolt of 1857, known as the Sepoy, or Indian, Mutiny, the British government assumed direct control of India from the British East India Company. As a result, Indian control over the Straits Settlements ceased, but the area remained a responsibility of the British sec-

retary of state for India. In 1867 the Straits Settlements became a crown colony and it retained that status until 1946. In that year the Straits Settlements were dissolved, and Singapore was separated from Penang and Melaka. Thereafter, Singapore became a separate crown colony.

After its acquisition by the British, Singapore steadily grew in importance as the volume of trade there multiplied. The opening up of Hong Kong in 1842 did not diminish the importance of Singapore, because all goods going to China had to go through Singapore. The commissioning of the Suez Canal in 1869 greatly facilitated the transit trade through Singapore. During the twentieth century, Singapore grew in importance as the world demand for rubber and tin continually increased.

World War II and Its Aftermath

Nevertheless, the British hold on Singapore was not firm enough to keep it from falling into Japanese hands during World War II. In February 1942, Japan overran Singapore, and it remained under Japan's control until the end of the war. Japanese occupiers dealt harshly with the Singaporeans, especially those of Chinese descent. In 1946, at the end of the war, the British returned to Singapore. By 1957, Malaysia had become independent. In 1959, Singapore was given internal self-government. In the elections held that year, an

Oxford-trained lawyer, Lee Kuan Yew, became prime minister. When Singapore became free of British control in 1963, it joined the Malaysian Federation. Strong anti-Chinese sentiment, among other factors, forced Singapore (whose population is more than 75 percent Chinese) to leave the federation in 1965 and become a republic.

By 1971, the last of the British troops were gone, and Lee continued as prime minister. Under his stewardship, the nation became one of the most prosperous nations in Southeast Asia. Singapore developed close ties with Japan and the West rather than with China, despite the fact that an overwhelming majority of Singaporeans are of Chinese descent. With more than 3 million people, Singapore has a per-capita gross domestic product well above that of some Western European nations. The outlook for continued economic growth is bright. There is, however, a need for more individual freedom.

George Thadathil

Further Reading
Cady, John F. (1964) *Southeast Asia: Its Historical Development.* New York: McGraw-Hill.

Chew, Ernest C. T., and Edwin Lee, eds. (1991) *A History of Singapore.* Singapore: Oxford University Press.

Iriye, Akira, Richard Yang, Edward J. Lazzerini, David Kopf, C. James Bishop, William J. Miller, and John F. Cady. (1979) *The World of Asia.* New York: McGraw-Hill.

Lee, Kuan Yew. (1998) *The Singapore Story: Memoirs of Lee Kuan Yew.* Singapore: Times Edition.

SINGAPORE—POLITICAL SYSTEM The political system of Singapore has given it the reputation of a strong state or an authoritarian and administrative state. Certainly it has been a state with one dominant political party since its independence from British colonial rule in 1959. The birth of the political system in the city-state, which had been a colonial port, involved intense struggle during the establishment of political institutions such as the legislature, civil service, and judiciary, as well as the rules and procedures of political behavior.

Singapore's political system is the product of distinct phases of development by the People's Action Party (PAP), which has been the ruling party since 1965 and has dominated politics in Singapore since the 1960s. The initial phase of the country's political system occurred in the period before Singapore's union with Malaysia in 1963 and its subsequent breakaway in 1965. After Singapore had gained autonomous rule from the British colonial government in 1959, the political institutionalization was fairly basic, with the conventional colonial legislature, civil service, judiciary, and police force.

The People's Action Party
The People's Action Party had its origins in the struggle for independence, when it aimed to mobilize the people against British colonial rule. Formed in 1954, the PAP was an alliance between Fabian socialism and Communism. This combination of ideologies was to have a profound effect on the political conditions that Singapore faced at the time. The PAP also emphasized a multiracial, multilingual, and multicultural strategy for its proposed integration of Singapore's society. Such a political strategy for making a pluralistic society has been described as PAP's "accommodationist political credo of the day, which was one held by all serious political groups of that time" (Chan 1989: 72). This credo was essential for any political party in multiethnic Singapore, with its population mix of Chinese, Malay, and Indian as well as several other groups, including Eurasians and Arabs. Hence, the strategies that allowed the PAP's rise to dominance provided the directions and the policies that have shaped the political system in the nation. In brief, the struggle through which the PAP has come is the process that has structured Singapore's political system.

PAP's 1959 political platform promised its supporters jobs as well as basic urban amenities for the welfare of workers, mass education, emancipation for women, housing for poor people, and a good public-health system. The party's success in delivering these goods and services from the beginning of its tenure in office gave it increasing popular support and subsequently entrenchment in political power for the last four decades or so. PAP's label as a socialist party has been due to its large national programs in housing, transport, education, and health care. Such socialist moorings aside, the PAP government has consistently courted multinational corporations and foreign direct investment and has striven to integrate Singapore's economy ever more closely with that of world markets.

The PAP party stalwarts claim to have learned the skills of political action, party organization, control, and mobilization of society from the Communists who were in the party before the Communists broke away from the democratic socialists in the PAP in 1961. The Communists had been more successful in penetrating and mobilizing student societies, trade unions, farmers' associations, women's associations, and the like.

Prior to the split of the Communists from the PAP's moderate leadership, the latter faced the challenge of a takeover of the party by the Communists, who managed to get moderate party leadership voted out of the PAP's Central Executive Committee, the governing body of the party responsible for major policy making. The day was saved for the moderate party leadership only because the government intervened with police action against subversive action by some of the Communist leaders. This allowed Lee Kuan Yew, leader of the PAP, and other moderates in the party to restructure the membership and party-election system. Since then, only full cadres in the party have been allowed to participate in elections for members of the Central Executive Committee, with the appointment to full cadreship status being determined by a board of selection over which the moderate sector has control. Such restructuring has not gone without challenge—in the late 1950s, members such as the PAP mayor challenged the leadership on the issue of intraparty democracy as well as over the rightist drift of the party's leadership. These members were expelled, and in 1961, there was a historic split when thirteen PAP assemblymen and their supporters left the party to form the Barisan Sosialis, one of several opposition parties registered in Singapore.

The formation of the Barisan Sosialis Party is believed to have removed the mass base of the PAP. Within the PAP, intraparty dissent has been discouraged since then and the formation of factions within the party deemed unacceptable. The presence of a socialist opposition party has also kept the PAP on course in its socialist programs, which combine pragmatism with the overt aims of serving national interest and legitimizing the party's grip on political power.

The Shaping of the Political System, 1959–1965

When the PAP government came into power in 1959, its leaders embarked on the tasks of nation building and managing the democratic mass politics that had begun in the 1950s with the goal of establishing a constitutional government. To make good on its promises to the voters, the PAP government forged an alliance with the civil service that has remained successful and has accounted for the efficiency with which the state has provided housing, employment, and other urban services. In 1959, the Singapore civil service was reorganized into nine ministries. This reorganization allowed the PAP to transfer local government into the hands of the central government. The centralized control of political power has quelled the internal fractiousness of the Communists and other factions within the party, which had previously challenged the leadership of the PAP. Such centralization of power later was extended so that urban and economic develop-

Opposition party leader Chee Soon Juan distributes party literature in downtown Singapore in September 2001.

ment became practically the domain of the state and its planning and development organs.

In 1960, the PAP government established the People's Association to take control of the community centers that were a legacy of the British colonial government. These centers provided the PAP with the basis for meeting the Communists' challenge in their effort at mass mobilization and allowed the prime minister, Lee Kuan Yew, to rebuild grassroots support for the PAP. Mobilization of the civil service allowed the PAP to deliver public goods and services to legitimate its claim to political power, while the grassroots organizations gave it the base to socialize voters into its policies on housing and other social issues.

To quell the work stoppages and labor unrest that had kept foreign investments away in the 1950s, the PAP turned to the labor unions. These were centralized as well, with the National Trade Union Congress developing a framework that controlled the labor force in part through the demobilization and suppression of left-wing elements in the labor movement. This centralization of the unions was achieved partly because joint economic decision making gave employers, unions, and the government a say in issues related to the industrial workforce. The National Wages Council, which includes members from these three sectors, has since 1972 negotiated wage increases for the nation as a whole.

Strengthening the Administrative State, 1965–1980s

Centralization of power and bureaucratization characterized the rise of the PAP government in the early years. These trends were consolidated after the brief union of Malaysia and Singapore between 1963 and 1965. These trends also gave rise to Singapore's label as an authoritarian state. As the bureaucracy and the political leadership have expanded their power into practically every sphere of life in Singapore, the political voice of the citizenry has been largely preempted. Political freedoms were gradually restricted with legislation that disallowed assembly in public to rally support for political or other causes. Between 1961 and 1965, political detention was used against members of the opposition Barisan Sosialis Party. In 1966, this party withdrew from parliamentary politics, leaving the PAP without any political rival that could challenge it in Parliament.

Until the 1980s and the economic recession in 1985, the administrative state in Singapore strengthened its hold on both politics and the economy. The best and the brightest were recruited into the civil service with prestigious government scholarships. Eventually, top civil servants were enlisted to run for election as PAP candidates. The administrative state was viewed as efficient because its practices were aimed at modernizing Singapore society and economy within a few decades.

If rapid economic growth was accompanied by equally rapid growth of incomes, there also was growing dissatisfaction with the PAP, which ultimately led to a decline in voter support for the party in the 1984 elections. Worse still, the opposition won two seats in the seventy-nine-seat Parliament. Already in 1981, a member of the opposition Worker's Party had won a seat, effectively ending the one-party Parliament that had been in place since the 1960s. Opposition party members in Parliament have been on the political scene since 1984.

Reorientation of the Political System since 1984

With the election of opposition party members to Parliament, the PAP began to reconsider the costs of the administrative state in terms of concentration of power with the political leadership and the bureaucracy as well as the disappearance of open politics and citizens' participation in policy making. The Feedback Unit was established in 1984 to encourage citizens to voice their opinions on public policies. Such a chance to be heard had been denied before.

Much of the effort to gain citizens' participation probably has been caused by the change in the PAP party leadership. In 1990, Lee Kuan Yew relinquished his post to a younger leader, Goh Chok Tong, who promised a more participatory approach to governance. The 1985 recession also led to a major restructuring of the planning of Singapore's economy, with the goal of allowing the private sector to participate more in economic de-

velopment. New institutions were brought into place to give the state a more inclusive image, and power became somewhat more decentralized. Town councils were introduced in 1988 to manage the public housing estates in which 86 percent of Singaporeans live. Previously these estates had been run by the government's Housing and Development Board. Parliamentary committees were convened in 1988 as watchdog bodies over key government ministries, although the committees essentially include only PAP members.

Since the 1991 elections, when opposition parties won four seats in Parliament, the political system has been somewhat liberalized. Increasingly, the leadership has been discussing the greater role that ordinary citizens can play in public life. Furthermore, since the early 1990s, members of Parliament have been nominated by the ruling party to represent sectors of society that were underrepresented in Parliament. Candidates are nominated by the public, and nine are selected by a committee of cabinet members. In addition, an opposition party that had not won an election but had secured the most votes among the losing parties could be represented by a nonconstituency member of Parliament. These and other measures appeared to convince the electorate that the PAP was serious about encouraging citizen participation in decision making, particularly in the 1997 elections, when the party won back two of the seats lost to opposition parties in the previous elections.

The Group Representation Constituency (GRC) system was introduced in 1988 by the PAP government. Three adjacent electoral constituencies were combined, and three individual members of Parliament were elected as a team, including at least one member from a minority Malay, Indian, or Eurasian community. The GRC system was further modified before the 1997 election to allow combinations of up to six constituencies. The original justification for this scheme was that because Parliament members would assume additional responsibilities for running town councils, voters would be encouraged to vote more responsibly. The opposition, however, claimed that GRCs were devised solely to "dilute opposition votes by combining constituencies with dominant opposition sympathies with neighbouring constituencies which strongly support the PAP" (Lim 1989: 184). In response, the government's defense of GRCs was that the scheme would ensure minority representation in Parliament, which in turn would curb any tendency to extremism in Singapore that might result from the predominance of Chinese communities.

Kog Yue Choong

Further Reading

Chan, Heng Chee. (1989) "The Structuring of the Political System." In *Management of Success—The Moulding of Modern Singapore*, edited by Kernial Sandhu Singh and Paul Wheatley. Singapore: Institute of Southeast Asian Studies, 70–89.

Drysdale, John. (1984) *Singapore: Struggle for Success*. Singapore: Times Books International.

Lim, Linda Y. C. (1989) "Social Welfare." In *Management of Success—The Moulding of Modern Singapore*, edited by Kernial Sandhu Singh and Paul Wheatley. Singapore: Institute of Southeast Asian Studies, 171–197.

Ooi, Giok-Ling. (1990) "Town Councils in Singapore: Self-Determination for Public Housing Estates." Institute of Policy Studies Occasional Paper no. 4. Singapore: Times Academic Press and Institute of Policy Studies.

Perry, Martin, Lily Kong, and Bronda Yeoh. (1997) *Singapore: A Developmental City State*. Singapore: John Wiley and Sons.

SINGAPORE DEMOCRATIC PARTY

Established in 1980 by Chiam See Tong, the Singapore Democratic Party (SDP) is the leading opposition party in Singapore. Prior to forming the party, Chiam was an independent politician and ran as an independent candidate for elections. In the 1976 and 1979 general elections, Chiam ran against prominent People's Action Party (PAP) candidates but received approximately one-third of the electoral votes. After forming the SDP, Chiam won the Single Member Constituency (SMC) at Potong Pasir in the 1984 and 1988 general elections.

The SDP was viewed as a moderate party under Chiam's leadership. In 1993, there was a split in party leadership. Chiam resigned from the Central Executive Committee and later established the Singapore People's Party (SPP). Chee Soon Juan took over the Singapore Democratic Party leadership and has since taken a more aggressive approach in dealing with the PAP. The government-controlled media, however, have portrayed him as an unreliable and dishonest person. While the SDP has made headway in international media coverage, it has made little progress in political mobilization locally.

Ho Khai Leong

Further Reading

Ho, Khai Leong. (2000) *The Politics of Policy-Making in Singapore*. Singapore: Oxford University Press.

Singh, Bilveer. (1992) *Whither PAP's Dominance? An Analysis of Singapore's 1991 General Elections*. Selangor, Malaysia: Pelanduk.

SINGH, JAI

(d. 1667), military leader for Mughul rulers. Jai Singh rose to prominence during the later part of the reign of the Mughul emperor Shah Jahan (1592–1666). Jai Singh was chief of the heavily fortified city of Amber, near Jaipur in northwestern India. When Shah Jahan became terminally ill, a war of succession broke out among his sons. Jai Singh was then sent on a military expedition against Prince Shuja, whom he pursued all the way to Bengal (now encompassing parts of India and Bangladesh). Then Jai Singh was sent against Prince Dara, whom he defeated at the battle of Deorai and pursued westward into Sind (now in Pakistan).

As Shah Jahan weakened, his third son, Aurangzeb (1618–1707), continued to employ Jai Singh to conduct a campaign in the Deccan (in southern India) against the state of Bijapur. He failed to capture this city, but was more successful against the Maratha warlord Shivaji. The latter was obliged to conclude a treaty with the Mughul emperor in 1665, acknowledging his suzerainty and ceding twenty-three fortresses to him. Jai Singh also persuaded the independent-minded warlord to go to Agra and visit the Mughul court in 1666. Despite all these successes, Jai Singh's failure to capture Bijapur rankled with the future emperor Alamgir, who recalled him from his Deccan campaigns in 1667. On the way back to Delhi, Jai Singh died.

Paul Hockings

Further Reading

Gascoigne, Bamber. (1971) *The Great Moghuls*. New York: Harper & Row.

SINGLE-CHILD PHENOMENON—CHINA

The most important of the twelve major challenges that researcher Y. Wang says China will face in the twenty-first century is the pressure of population growth. It is estimated that by 2030, the population in China will reach 1.6 billion. The situation would be worse except for the rigorous enforcement of a one-child policy. As a countermeasure to the misconceived statement that former leader Mao Zedong (1893–1976) made in the 1960s that "more hands make light work" and as a repudiation of the Confucian ideology that favored many children, China introduced this unique population-control policy in 1971. With the exception of the chaotic period of the Cultural Revolution (1966–1976), the success of this policy is statistically reflected in that today 98 percent of urban children in kindergartens are from one-child families and that nationwide in the upper and lower primary grades (ages six to twelve), more than 70 percent of the students are "only children."

As the one-child family movement has gained momentum in China, people have posed and debated questions regarding the sociological, psychological, and cognitive impact of the policy. Among the questions frequently posed are: Are only children in China intellectually better developed than children with siblings? What are the personality characteristics and social skills of these children?

Although numerous articles have failed to answer these questions satisfactorily, evidence suggests that China's only children demonstrate superior cognitive skills in the earlier years when compared with their peers with siblings. However, these differences become less prominent in later years. It should be stressed that the observed diminishing cognitive variation is based not so much on longitudinal but rather on cross-sectional data. It is likely, therefore, that different aggregates of samples are being dealt with. Within the current limitation, one may conclude that younger only children receive more intensive parental care and greater intellectual stimulation, have more interaction with adults, and are under greater psychological pressure to succeed than their older peers.

A second likely explanation is that schooling works to erase the differences between children of different backgrounds (in this case, the differences between children with siblings and those without siblings'. As Lam (1992) observed, "unique family experiences begin to dissipate (with age) while uniform socialization process in school begins to take root." As for whether or not only children have more social skills (measured in terms of ability to make friends) than children with siblings, available data show few significant differences (Huang 1990). Variation between single children and those with siblings is tempered by such factors as educational attainment, age, and gender.

As for whether the personality of single children will deteriorate over time in a typical family structure of 4:2:1 (four grandparents, two parents, and one child), initial empirical evidence generated from a cross-sectional sample of twelve thousand Chinese children (Lam 1992) provides some useful clues. In essence, in the primary grades, single children were more creative, more focused on achievement, less independent, and more aggressive than children with siblings. In the intermediate grades, the good personality traits persisted, but new negative traits such as self-centeredness appeared, and some negative traits, such as aggressiveness, persisted, although they became less distinct after grade 4. At the junior high level, relative dependence

on others became the only outstanding features segregating single children from their peers with siblings. At the senior high level, the tendency toward greater dependence on others persisted.

The intense socialization process that begins as soon as children enter school seems to have moderating effect on single children's personality development, as schools deliberately limit the number of toys available to encourage sharing, taking turns, and negotiating with others. Chinese educational philosophy is predicated on the conviction that "learning should occur through continual, careful shaping and molding" (Gardner 1989), so that character development will be less influenced by family background.

Less is known about the situation of only children in rural areas, because most of the data analyzed come from urban areas. Researchers have yet to assess the gender imbalance in both urban and rural areas and the accompanying social problems. The question of gender balance is important, however, because male preference is still predominant among the rural and remote districts of China.

Y. L. Jack Lam

See also: **Marriage and Family—China**

Further Reading

Falbo, T., and D. F. Polit. (1986) "A Quantitative Review of the Only-Child Literature: Research Evidence and Theory Development." *Psychological Bulletin* 100: 176–189.

Falbo, T., D. L. Poston, G. Ji, S. Jiao, Q. Jing, S. Wan, Q. Gu, H. Yin, and Y. Liu. (1989) "Physical Achievement and Personality Characteristics of Chinese Children." *Journal of Biosocial Sciences* 21: 483–495.

Freeman, Nancy, K. (1997) "Experiencing Multiculturalism First Hand: Looking at Early Childhood Education in China Teaches Us about Ourselves." Paper presented at the international conference and exhibition of the Association for Childhood Education International, Portland, OR.

Gardner, H. (1989) "Learning Chinese-Style." *Psychology Today* (December): 54–56.

Huang, Gary. (1990) "Family and Friend Relationship of Only Children: A Study of Adult Population in China." Charleston, WV: Appalachia Educational Lab (ERIC Document Reproduction Service ED 319 487).

Jiao, S., G. Ji, and Q. Jing. (1996) "Cognitive Development of Chinese Urban Only Children and Children with Siblings." *Child Development* 67: 387–395.

Lam, Y. L. J. (1992) "Effects of Schooling on Personality and Performance of Single Children in China." *McGill Journal of Education* 27, 2: 113–21.

Wang, Jianjun, and Raymond Brie. (1997) "The Impact of Sibling Composition on Student Science Achievement in

P. R. China." Paper presented at the annual meeting of the American Educational Research Association, Chicago.

Wang, Y. (1999) "The Twelve Challenges Facing China." *Duzhe* 10: 30.

SINHALA
Sinhala is an old Indo-Aryan language spoken by 75 percent of the population of Sri Lanka. Its early history can be traced in Brahmi inscriptions from about 200 BCE. This "Sinhalese Prakrit" is related to north Indian dialects; Sinhalese legends and linguistic evidence suggest that settlers from north India brought their dialects with them before 500 BCE. Its isolation from other Indo-Aryan languages (except Divehi in the Maldive Islands) and long contact with Dravidian languages have given it a unique character.

History

Most early texts have been lost, but the evolution of Sinhala from Prakrit can be traced through numerous cave and rock inscriptions up to the twelfth century CE and Sinhala literature from the tenth century onward. Sinhala evolved by regular sound changes interrupted by periodic reforms and extensive borrowing from other languages. Sinhala eliminated aspirated consonants and the consonant *r*, reduced double consonants to single and diphthongs to vowels, and changed certain consonants (for example, *j* to *d*, *p* to *v*, and *s* to *h*).

Education and scholarship were in the hands of Buddhist monks, whose religious texts remained in Pali. The island had substantial scholarship in the Pali language, which encouraged borrowing. Sanskrit loan words were introduced in particular by Mahayana Buddhists and students of Sanskritic theories of poetics and rhetoric. Many Sanskrit words and idioms were added after the tenth century, and the literature of the twelfth and thirteenth centuries has a high proportion of Sanskrit words.

Tamil influence on Sinhala has always been considerable, in vocabulary, idiom, and grammatical structure. The long interaction through migration and invasion from south India has created many loan words from Tamil, including kinship terms. Tamil probably also influenced the lack of aspirated stops, the contrast between short and long" vowels, and Sinhala's "left-branching" character (a modifier precedes that which it modifies).

Portuguese and Dutch conquest of the coasts led to extensive loan words. Many administrative institutions and domestic innovations, for example, have Portuguese terms; many legal terms are derived from the Dutch, who introduced Roman-Dutch law. The revival of Buddhism in the interior of the island in the eighteenth century was accompanied by a linguistic revival in which Buddhist monks revived classical literary forms and attempted to "purify" Sinhala. This revival persisted in the nineteenth and twentieth centuries under very different circumstances and resulted in today's literary Sinhala.

British colonial domination produced an English-speaking class of people who disparaged Sinhala (and Tamil), a situation that continued well into the postindependence period. In the nineteenth century, this meant that extensive changes in Sinhala took place with little influence from the politically and economically dominant Sinhalese leaders.

The Dutch introduced printing in Sinhala in 1737, but printed materials in Sinhala did not appear regularly until a century later, when British missionaries began publishing religious propaganda. The first Sinhalese-owned press began in about 1835. In the 1860s presses and newspapers published in Sinhala proliferated, and many old texts were reprinted. Writers struggled to decide what idiom of Sinhala to use in their works, torn between a colloquial idiom that would appeal to a wider audience and a literary idiom that would satisfy revivalists.

Education in Sinhala expanded dramatically in the nineteenth century through a system of government grants-in-aid. Most of the grants-in-aid were given to Christian missionary schools, as temple schools did not qualify under the government regulations. In addition, education in Sinhala was intended only to provide a cheap elementary education for the masses, not scholarly training. Thus Buddhist monks lost their traditional role as educators and public support for higher scholarship in Sinhala was lost.

Pamphleteers carried on acrimonious debates over language issues. Writers argued whether to use literary or colloquial forms and which literary forms to use. At one extreme, some wanted to restore Sanskrit and Pali terms used in older texts; at the other, some wanted not only to restore the so-called pure Sinhala (Elu) language from classical texts, but to apply the historical transformations to existing words to coin neologisms in pure Sinhala.

Diglossia

Written literature has diverged widely from colloquial Sinhala, producing the language situation of diglossia, in which the written and spoken languages have very different characteristics. Cornell linguist James W. Gair has argued that there are stable structural differences between literary Sinhala and spoken Sinhala, and within spoken Sinhala between formal and colloquial variants.

Literary Sinhala is characterized by such features as the distinction of masculine and feminine gender in animate nouns; person, number, and (in some tenses) gender distinctions in verbs; the agreement of verbs and subject; and the existence of a passive tense. None of these exists in colloquial Sinhala today and presumably did not in the earlier centuries. Many of these features are redundant, which makes literary Sinhala (except for the lexicon) possible to read without much training but difficult to write.

Colloquial Sinhala is the language of ordinary conversation; formal Sinhala is an intermediate form used on such occasions as public addresses, radio and television news broadcasts, university lectures, and sermons.

M. W. Sugathapala de Silva of the University of York disagreed with Gair's emphasis on the structural differences between these variants and stresses the continuity from one variety to another.

Independent Sri Lanka

English was the language of government, higher education, and the leading sectors of the economy until the Official Language Act of 1956 made Sinhala the official language. Since then there has been a progressive shift of the language of education and government to Sinhala. Many neologisms were coined in the process. These are a combination of new meanings for old words, words with Sanskritic origins, and loan words. The 1978 constitution made Tamil a national language and in 1988 an official language, but at the beginning of the new millennium, government offices increasingly required the public to transact its business in Sinhala.

There is a great deal of variation in the Sinhala one encounters in Sri Lanka today. Much of the vocabulary of literary and colloquial Sinhala is interchangeable, and individuals use varying amounts of literary vocabulary and loan words in their speech. Some words have synonyms that range from very literary to very colloquial; people seem to select their vocabulary according to the situation.

Since the outbreak of civil war in 1983, the replacement of both English-educated and Tamil-educated officials with Sinhala-educated ones has accelerated the use of literary Sinhala in government. At the beginning of the twenty-first century, there continues to be an active attempt to replace Sanskritic terms with new ones derived from Elu, perhaps influenced by the Sinhalese nationalism that has burgeoned during the civil war.

Patrick Peebles

Further Reading

De Silva, M. W. Sugathapala. (1979) *Sinhalese and Other Island Languages of South Asia*. Tubingen, Germany: Gunther Narr.

Dharmadasa, K. N. O. (1993) *Language, Religion, and Ethnic Assertiveness: The Growth of Sinhalese Nationalism in Sri Lanka*. Ann Arbor, MI: University of Michigan Press.

Disanayaka, J. B. (1991) *The Structure of Spoken Sinhala:* Vol. I: *Sounds and Their Patterns*. Maharagama, Sri Lanka: National Institute of Education.

Gair, James W. (1998) *Studies in South Asian Linguistics: Sinhala and Other South Asian Languages*. Edited by Barbara C. Lust. New York: Oxford University Press.

Geiger, Wilhelm. (1938) *A Grammar of the Sinhalese Language*. Colombo, Sri Lanka: Royal Asiatic Society, Ceylon Branch.

SINHALESE The Sinhalese are a predominant ethnic group in the multicultural society of Sri Lanka, an island that is located in the Indian Ocean off the southeast coast of India. The Sinhalese constitute approximately 74 percent of Sri Lanka's 19.4 million people, followed by the Tamils, who make up approximately 18 percent of the population. Taken from a historical perspective, the ethnic structure of Sri Lanka has been largely influenced by colonialists and migrants. The term "Sinhalese" is also used to refer to Sinhala, the dominant Indo-Aryan language of Sri Lanka.

According to an old legend, the Sinhalese are descended from a lion. The literal meaning of the word *sinha* in Hindi is lion. In historical terms, the Sinhalese claim to have descended from the Aryan peoples of northern India. Under King Vijaya, the Sinhalese conquered the aboriginal people known as Vedda as early as 550 BCE. The Tamils arrived from southern India around the first century CE.

Religion

Approximately 93 percent of the entire Sinhalese population are Buddhists. Theravada Buddhism is the predominant sect. Sinhalese Buddhists fall into two categories: low-country Sinhalese and Kandyan Sinhalese. Low-country Sinhalese, constituting 60 percent of all Sinhalese, are modern in outlook and liberal in their approach. In contrast, the Kandyans are known for conservatism and are firmly committed to upholding their historical traditions and cultural values. By and large, all Buddhist Sinhalese are intent on preserving their distinct Buddhist identity.

Historically, the Sinhalese connections with India are traceable to Buddhism, which arrived in Sri Lanka in the third century BCE via India during the great

THE PATH TO SALVATION

"It is important to understand that in Sinhalese Buddhism there is only one way to salvation. All other salvation religions offer devotees several choices—usually between good works and mystical pursuits. Hindus refer to the way of mysticism or meditation (jnana yoga), the way of ritual (karma yoga), and the way of loving devotion (bhakti yoga). But all Sinhalese Buddhists maintain that the only way to obtain redemption is through systematic meditation (bhavanaya), the equivalent of the Hindu jnana yoga. The individual must eradicate mental defilements through a long process of mental self-purification. He must become satpurusa, a self-perfected individual. It is true that Buddhism opened salvation to all regardless of caste or sex. But its actual attainment has always been restricted to a few at any one time; it is the path for the strong in mind."

"This is a radical conception of salvation. It demands extreme virtuosity, individual achievement, and absolute renunciation of the world. The social consequences of these beliefs are therefore equally radical. For the ordinary Buddhist, salvation is considered very difficult because it demands arduous meditation; it is very distant because the necessary practice takes thousands and thousands of rebirths. It is perhaps paradoxical that although nirvanaya is the ultimate goal of the religious life, no Sinhalese is believed to have attained this goal for hundreds of years and few anticipate doing so for many centuries to come. Salvation for the Sinhalese is out of this world in more than one respect."

"The most highly venerated person in Sinhalese society is the one who leaves behind his family and retires to a forest to spend his remaining days in solitary meditation. He is striving for his own salvation, and that is precisely why he is respected."

"The ritual of meditation that hermit monks perform in their secluded forest hermitages directly emulates this world renunciation, the ascetic ideal of the noble sage. The ordinary merit-making rituals, by constantly playing on the same symbolic themes, reaffirm the same ascetic ideal. Even magic rituals, which Sinhalese claim have nothing to do with their Buddhism, refer again and again to the power and glory of Buddha."

Source: Michael M. Ames (1964) "Magical Animism and Buddhism: A Structural Analysis of the Sinhalese Religious System." *Journal of Asian Studies* 23: 25–27.

Maurya empire (c. 324–c. 200 BCE) of King Asoka (273–232 BCE). With the demise of the Maurya empire, Buddhism virtually disappeared from India, but it grew much stronger in Sri Lanka.

The influence of Buddhism on the social and cultural life of Sinhalese people is evident in their observance of such rituals as *bodhi puja*. It is believed that the special devotions that are undertaken in *bodhi puja* will cure patients suffering from incurable diseases as well as grant the devotees peace and happiness. The faithful also perform *baliya* (a kind of traditional dance) in the hope of receiving blessings from Buddha and alleviation of misfortunes and economic sufferings.

Sinhalese literature also shows the primacy of Buddhism as a cultural influence. Buddhist chronicles originally written in Pali were later translated into Sinhala; stanzas from these chronicles are often recited by Sinhalese. Early prose works are filled with Buddhist tales.

Social Structure

At the apex of the Sinhalese social order is the *goigama*, a class of cultivators who consider themselves superior in status to other Sinhalese. Unlike in India, however, the caste system in the Sinhalese community is not institutionalized, and there is not any predominant priestly caste. *Janavamsa* (1848), a famous poem in Sinhala, describes numerous caste divisions among the Sinhalese people.

The Sinhalese Today

Low-country Sinhalese have higher incomes and a higher literacy rate than Kandyan Sinhalese, 90 percent of whom live in rural areas. The 1996–1997 literacy rate among rural people was approximately 87 percent, whereas the literacy rate among urban dwellers was approximately 92 percent. Low-country Sinhalese hold more high-status government jobs than do Kandyan Sinhalese.

There are more low-country Sinhalese than Kandyan Sinhalese in maritime areas, and fishing is one of the main occupations of low-country Sinhalese, who engage in it not at the subsistence level (except perhaps in certain villages in the deep south), but as a lucrative money-earning venture. In the deep south, many low-country Sinhalese are employed in the salt production industry. Coconut-based industries have been key to the financial success of low-country Sinhalese as a whole. The distilling of arrack (an alcoholic beverage distilled from a fermented mash of malted rice) has also led to sizeable capital accumulation and the rise of a Sinhalese bourgeoisie.

The Kandyans, who dwell inland, are largely farmers. Status among Kandyans is determined by the possession of land. During colonial times, the British held large tracts of land as plantations, leading to a shortage of land for the Kandyan peasantry. Those families that did possess large tracts of land followed the lead of the British and cultivated plantation crops.

Sinhalese life today is marred by ethnic conflict with Sri Lankan Tamils, which flared into violence in 1983. Over sixty thousand people have lost their lives in the conflict so far. Its roots lie in the discriminatory policies of the Sri Lankan government against Sri Lankan Tamils in terms of employment, language (Sinhala was made the nation's official language in the 1970s), and appointment to high administrative positions in government. As a consequence, the demand for a separate state by the Liberation Tigers of Eelam (LTTE) has gained momentum within the Tamil community. The situation took the ugliest turn in 1987, when it became virtually impossible for the government to control widespread internal violence. There have been a number of peace initiatives, including one undertaken by the Norwegians in 2000 that was still ongoing in 2002. The lives of both the Sinhalese majority and the Tamil minority will be vastly improved when a lasting peace is attained.

B. M. Jain

Further Reading

Kapferer, B. (1988) *Legends of People, Myths, and State: Violence, Intolerance, and Political Culture in Sri Lanka and Australia*. Bloomington, IN: Indiana University Press.

Manor, J., ed. (1984) *Sri Lanka in Change and Crisis*. London: Croom Helm.

Spencer, J. (1990) *Sri Lanka: History and Roots of Conflict*. London: Routledge.

Tambiah, S. J. (1992) *Buddhism Betrayed: Religion, Politics, and Violence in Sri Lanka*. Chicago: University of Chicago Press.

Wijesinha, Rajiva. (1986) *Current Crisis in Sri Lanka*. New Delhi: Navrang.

Wilson, A. Jeyratnam. (1979) *Politics in Sri Lanka 1947–1979*. London: Macmillan.

SINITIC LANGUAGES Sinitic languages, collectively referred to as Chinese, are spoken by over 1.3 billion people worldwide. The vast majority of Sinitic language speakers (nearly 1.3 billion) are found in the People's Republic of China and Taiwan, but approximately 60 million speakers are located in Southeast Asia, North America, Europe, and elsewhere. Although Sinitic languages are commonly known as "Chinese dialects," many linguists prefer to use the term "languages" because Chinese "dialects" are often not mutually comprehensible. The Sinitic languages have frequently been compared to the Romance languages in terms of their diversity.

Genetic Affiliation

The Sinitic languages are usually classified as belonging to the Sinitic branch of the Sino-Tibetan language family. However, some scholars have proposed that Chinese is genetically related to other language families such as Tai, Hmong-Mien, and Austronesian. Although Chinese clearly shares some vocabulary with neighboring languages, it is not clear whether the earliest strata of this vocabulary are inherited (which would be evidence for genetic relationship) or borrowed.

History

Chinese is first attested in inscriptions from around the fourteenth century BCE onward during the Shang dynasty (1766–1045 BCE). Shang-dynasty Chinese developed into Old Chinese, the language of the Zhou dynasty (1045–256 BCE) and of the poetic anthology *Shijng* (Book of Odes; c. sixth century BCE). The next major stage of Chinese was Middle Chinese, the language of the Sui (581–618 CE) and Tang (618–907 CE) dynasties recorded in Lu Fayan's *Qieyun* rhyme dictionary (601 CE). These early stages of Chinese exerted considerable influence on neighboring languages. Middle Chinese in particular was a source of many loanwords in Japanese, Korean, and Vietnamese. The Min languages apparently split off from the rest of Chinese sometime prior to the Middle Chinese period. All other Sinitic languages with the exception of Min are frequently regarded as descendants of Middle Chinese, though the actual situation may be more complex. The last major premodern stage of Chinese is Old Mandarin, the language recorded in Zhou Deqing's *Zhongyuan yinyun* rhyme dictionary (1324 CE). With the exception of fragmentary evidence, non-Mandarin Sinitic languages have only been attested in written form during the last few centuries, largely due to the efforts of missionaries and linguists.

Languages and Dialects

The Sinitic languages can be divided into three large geographical groups. The first and most important of these is the Mandarin or northern group of dialects spoken natively by the majority of Chinese (885 million first-language speakers north of the Chang (Yangtze) river, in southwestern China, and in Taiwan). The official languages of the People's Republic of China and Taiwan are based on the Beijing dialect of Mandarin. Standard Mandarin is widely spoken as a second language in both countries.

The conservative Jin dialects (45 million speakers in Shanxi and Shaanxi and Henan Provinces) were once considered to be northwestern varieties of Mandarin but are now often classified separately.

The central languages are transitional between the northern and southern groups. Wu dialects (77 million speakers in Zhejiang Province and in Jiangsu Province south of the Chang River) such as Shanghaiese are notable for their extensive tone sandhi (changing the tone of a syllable depending on context). The Xiang (36 million speakers mostly in Hunan province) dialects are heavily influenced by Mandarin. The relatively little known Gan (20 million speakers mostly in Jiangxi Province) dialects were once classified together with Kejia but Gan-Kejia unity has fallen into disfavor among linguists.

The southern languages are often conservative due to their relative isolation from the influence of north-

ern standard languages throughout Chinese history. Yue or Cantonese (66 million speakers mostly in Guangdong and Guangxi Provinces and in Hong Kong) is the best known of these languages. Kejia (34 million speakers) dialects are spoken by the Kejia, or Hakka, a Chinese group of probable northern origin that settled in several southern provinces including Guangdong. The Min dialects (59 million speakers mostly in Fujian, eastern Guangdong, and Taiwan) are highly conservative and heterogenous. The most famous Min dialect is Taiwanese, the native language of 14 million Taiwanese. Taiwanese and other southern Min dialects, like Wu dialects, have complex tone sandhi.

Southern Sinitic languages are widely spoken outside the People's Republic of China and Taiwan. Most of these speakers are in Southeast Asia, though Sinitic speakers can be found almost anywhere in the world. The most important overseas Chinese languages are Cantonese (19 million abroad), Min (particularly the Fujian (Hokkien) and Chaozhou (Teochew) dialects; 5 million abroad), and Hakka (5 million abroad).

Some linguists consider the Bai language (900,000 speakers in Yunnan Province) to be a Sinitic language while others classify it as Tibeto-Burman. Its genetic classification remains controversial though it clearly shares much vocabulary with Chinese.

Orthography and Literacy

Chinese characters (*hanzi*) have been in continuous use since around the fourteenth century BCE. Hanzi are popularly believed to be an "ideographic" writing system comprised of pictures representing ideas. However, *hanzi* actually constitute a "morphosyllabic," rather than an ideographic, writing system. The majority of *hanzi* consist of "phonetics" indicating sounds and "radicals" hinting at meanings. Each *hanzi* represents a morpheme (a minimal unit of meaning: i.e., a root or affix) that is one syllable long. A Chinese word may consist of one or more morphemes and must be written with *hanzi* designating those specific morphemes.

Some Sinitic languages, such as Yue, have *hanzi* for words not in the standard language. Chinese is almost always written with *hanzi*; marginal exceptions utilize pinyin (a system of transliteration into the Roman alphabet) and indigenous *Zhuyin zimu* ("phonetic letters") alphabets. Official People's Republic of China data claim a literacy rate of 93 percent, though other estimates put it much lower. The literacy rate is Taiwan is approximately 92 percent.

Linguistic Sketch

The following description primarily applies to standard Mandarin, though other Sinitic languages share these traits as well.

Most Chinese morphemes are one syllable long and all syllables are pronounced with a distinctive pitch ("tone"). Syllables that differ only tonally may have completely different meanings. Standard Mandarin has four tones: *ma* means "mother" with a high level tone, "hemp" with a high rising tone, "horse" with a low rising tone, and "scold" with a high falling tone. Other Sinitic languages have many more tones, e.g., Cantonese has nine tones. New words are formed via the reduplication of syllables, the addition of suffixes (or, less frequently, prefixes), and the compounding of morphemes.

Unlike most European languages, Chinese has no articles (i.e., equivalents of "the" or "a, an"), no grammatical gender (though a gender distinction in the third person pronoun is made in the written standard language), and no noun declensions or verb conjugations. Number (singular/plural) is only obligatory for pronouns and optional for nouns referring to people. Counted nouns are accompanied by "classifiers": e.g., the classifier *ge* ("piece") in Mandarin *yi ge ren* ("one piece person"). Suffixes mark verbs (which include predicate adjectives) for aspect (completion or non-completion of a situation or action) rather than tense (past, present, or future). "Coverbs" function like prepositions but can be negated like verbs.

The basic word order patterns are topic-comment, subject-verb-object (though Mandarin also has subject-object-verb structures), and modifier-modified. Case is marked by word order and coverbs.

Marc Hideo Miyake

Further Reading

Chao, Yuen Ren. (1968) *A Grammar of Spoken Chinese*. Berkeley and Los Angeles: University of California Press.

Chen, Ping. (1999) *Modern Chinese: History and Sociolinguistics*. Cambridge, U.K.: Cambridge University Press.

DeFrancis, John. (1984) *The Chinese Language: Fact and Fantasy*. Honolulu, HI: University of Hawaii Press.

Grimes, Barbara F., ed. (2000) *Ethnologue*. Retrieved 14 January 2002, from: http://www.sil.org/ethnologue.

Norman, Jerry. (1988) *Chinese*. Cambridge, U.K.: Cambridge University Press.

Ramsey, S. Robert. (1987) *The Languages of China*. Princeton, NJ: Princeton University Press.

SINO-FRENCH WAR

France's victory in its 1884–1885 war with China over Vietnam marked a major expansion of Western imperialism in Asia. The defeat of the Qing dynasty (1644–1912) discredited the dynasty's prevailing strategy of "self-strengthening." The Sino-French War was one of several conflicts in the years from 1839 to 1911 showing the Qing court's indecisiveness in setting policy directions and its inability to enforce traditional tribute relations with surrounding states. The Qing did not take their defeat in the Sino-French War as an opportunity to undertake reform and so found itself in much deeper trouble when a conflict broke out with Japan in 1894 over a similar situation in Korea.

Origins of War

Although Vietnam's Nguyen dynasty (1802–1955) owed its rise in part to French help, once in power, the Nguyen rulers preferred conservative neo-Confucian styles of court life and governance and tried to limit additional French influence and prevent French territorial encroachment. In spite of the Nguyen emperors' increasing reliance on their Qing suzerains for diplomatic and military protection, the French steadily increased their territorial control in Vietnam. Beginning in Cochin China (in the south), the French established a protectorate over Annam (central) and outposts in Tonkin (the northern part of Vietnam) in the years between 1862 and 1880.

In the 1870s and 1880s, the Vietnamese repeatedly sought help from China on the basis of the two countries' long-standing tributary relationship. In China, a debate arose at the Qing court about how best to deal with French adventurism. The self-strengthening school, led by Viceroy Li Hongzhang (1823–1901), championed having the Qing build up its own modern technology and modern military units, but continued to fear battle with French military power. The self-strengtheners counseled a diplomatic settlement with France, while more adventurist officials such as Zhang Zhidong (1837–1909) and Zhang Peilun (1848–1903) advocated military intervention on behalf of the Nguyen dynasty. In fact, since the late 1870s, the Qing had allowed irregular military units called the Black Flags to operate in the Sino-Vietnamese border region. The Black Flag troops, which included remnants from armies of the Taiping Rebellion (1850–1864) along with local brigands, began engaging French units inside Tonkin in 1882 in undeclared guerrilla-style warfare.

When the succession crisis arose in 1883, the Qing court increased its support for the Nguyen cause by permitting regular Qing dynasty troops to join the Black Flags in Vietnam. Still, the two parties at the Qing court continued to debate their respective positions. The self-strengthening advocates advised a diplomatic settlement against what they saw as a strong Western opponent, while the war party wanted vigorous military action against what it saw as hollow threats from a weak France. Still, both parties stopped short of advocating a formal declaration of war.

The Qing court, then dominated by Empress Dowager Cixi (1835–1908), had Li Hongzhang negotiate a settlement with a French diplomat in 1883 that put Vietnam under joint French and Qing protection, but Paris rejected the arrangement. In the field, French units defeated the Black Flags, and a French assault on Qing territory appeared imminent. Hoping again to avoid a formal state of war with France, the empress dowager dismissed Prince Gong (1833–1989), the dynasty's minister of foreign affairs. She then had Li Hongzhang negotiate another settlement with a new French representative, F. E. Fournier, but it was rejected again by Paris and was sharply criticized by the war party in China.

In early 1884 renewed clashes in Tonkin produced modest Qing victories. In July 1884 the French government issued an ultimatum to the Qing. When the Qing failed to respond satisfactorily, the long-burning informal conflict became a state of war. In the first act of formal warfare, on 23 August the French took decisive military action, sinking eleven modern Chinese warships, and destroyed the foreign-built shipyard at Fuzhou on China's southeast coast, hundreds of miles from Vietnam. Thus, the war party's evaluation of French military abilities turned out to be disastrously wrong, while the self-strengtheners saw one of the Qing dynasty's most important military assets destroyed in an afternoon by the French. Hostilities continued along the Chinese-Vietnam border, but the Li-Fournier agreement was revived and accepted by both sides in its final form in June 1885. Under its terms, the Qing dynasty gave up all claims to its interests in Vietnam and French dominance over the Nguyen dynasty was accepted.

French Expansion Assured

The French victory against the Qing dynasty removed the one power that might have checked Western imperialist expansion in Southeast Asia. French dominance over Vietnam was assured. In 1887 France quickly began to establish its grand design for Southeast Asia, the so-called Indochinese Union, a combination of Cochin China, Annam, Tonkin, Cambodia, and Laos controlled from Paris. Through a combination of battlefield and diplomatic victories, the French consolidated their empire in Southeast Asia and held on to this position until 1954. Though defeated, the Vietnamese desire for independence and autonomy

never died out and burst into flame again at the end of World War II in the revolt of the Viet Minh.

David D. Buck

Further Reading
Buttinger, Joseph. (1968) *Vietnam: A Political History.* New York: Praeger.

Eastman, Lloyd E. (1967) *Throne and Mandarins: China's Search for a Policy during the Sino-French Controversy, 1880–1885.* Cambridge, MA: Harvard University Press.

Immanuel, C. Y. Hsu. (2000) *The Rise of Modern China.* 6th ed. New York: Oxford University Press.

Liu, Kwang-ching. (1980) "The Military Challenge: The Northwest and the Coast." In *The Cambridge History of China,* edited by John King Fairbank and Kwang-ching Liu. Cambridge, U.K: Cambridge University Press.

McAleavy, Henry. (1968) *The Black Flags in Vietnam.* New York: Macmillan.

SINO-JAPANESE CONFLICT, SECOND

A minor clash between troops of a Chinese army and Japanese units at the Marco Polo Bridge outside Beijing on 7 July 1937 led quickly to the undeclared 1937–1945 Sino-Japanese war, referred to here as the second Sino-Japanese conflict to avoid confusion with the brief but significant Sino-Japanese War of 1894–1895. Ever since the Japanese victory in this first war, the Japanese government had advanced a variety of schemes to help China emerge from the deep political and social disorder into which it was falling. The Chinese vigorously rejected most of these Japanese schemes. In many ways, by the mid-1930s a second war between Japan and China seemed inevitable because Chinese public opinion was growing increasingly anti-Japanese while the Japanese had used military force to create the puppet state of Manchuko in China's northeast and continued to press their control of other parts of China through military means.

Aggressive Phase, 1937–1939

In the initial aggressive phase of the war from July 1937 through February 1939, the Japanese armies established control over all of north China and the most important parts of east China, including the great port city of Shanghai, along with all the important cities in the Chang (Yangtze) River Valley region and along China's long coastline. In their brutal treatment of both Chinese soldiers and civilians, most infamously during the "Rape of Nanjing," also known as the Nanjing Massacre, in December 1937 through March 1938, the Japanese military acquired a reputation as war criminals that still colors Japanese relations with Chinese, Asians, and many Europeans to this day.

Chiang Kai-shek (1887–1975), leader of the Guomindang (Nationalist Party), lost almost all of his carefully nurtured modern armed forces in this first phase of the war but nonetheless managed to withdraw the remnants of his military and civil government, along with several million supporters, to the fastness of the Sichuan basin, where he made the city of Chongqing his wartime capital.

Attrition Phase, 1939–1944

The attrition phase of the war began in March 1939. The Chinese Nationalists had little industry and few resources other than abundant manpower with which to resist the Japanese. During this phase, the Nationalist government's territorial base was the huge province of Sichuan, most of southwestern China, and some of central Hunan and Hubei Provinces, but for most Nationalist supporters, the war was a long, dispiriting time of deprivation and hardship. The Communist movement led another effort at Chinese resistance against the Japanese from a base in the remote and poverty-stricken area around the city of Yan'an. In theory, since the end of 1936 the Communists and the Nationalists had been cooperating in the struggle against the Japanese, but in reality they operated separately with different approaches to resisting Japan and different goals for the war. The Nationalist approach emphasized building strength with American assistance beyond the reach of the Japanese forces, whereas the Communists felt they needed little or no outside assistance and could count on mobilizing the Chinese people to resist the Japanese through guerrilla warfare.

In March 1940, a disaffected Chinese Nationalist leader, Wang Jingwei (1883–1944), established a collaborationist government under Japanese control at Nanjing that ruled over Japanese-occupied China. Wang died before the end of the war, but he, his close associates, and his wife were all tried for treason following Japan's surrender.

Before 1940, Nationalist China received considerable aid from the Soviet Union, which was looking for ways to check Japanese expansionism on the Asian mainland. But in late 1940, the Japanese and the Soviets signed a nonaggression pact, and Soviet aid to the Nationalists declined quickly. The United States gave little aid to the Nationalists in 1937 when the war broke out, yet by 1940 U.S. support for Nationalist China had grown significantly. The aid involved loans and gifts or low-cost purchases of military goods. Also in 1941 the United States permitted a group of volunteer pilots under Claire Chennault to prepare to go to China. The establishment of this group, which be-

came famous in early 1942 as the Flying Tigers, marks the beginning of several years of cooperation between the United States and the Chinese Nationalists.

The long attrition phase of this war lasted five years, and many important developments occurred during this period that greatly affected both the outcome of the war and the subsequent history of Asia. Throughout this phase, Japan's armies were so thinly spread around Asia that they could not undertake serious offensives in China.

Chiang Kai-shek wanted to hold back his armies from combat and build up their strength so he could defeat the Communists when the inevitable U.S. victory came. Chiang resisted cooperation with his chief U.S. military adviser, General Joseph Stilwell, who was sent to train modern armies for use against Japan. Chiang and Stilwell disliked each other. Chiang distrusted Stilwell's motives and objected to Stilwell's use of Chinese units in Burma. Stilwell was withdrawn in October 1944. Chiang Kai-shek found it much easier to cooperate with the leadership of the U.S. air forces in China, especially General Claire Chennault, and agreed to build new bases from which U.S. bombers could attack Japan.

The small and poorly equipped Communist forces based at Yan'an followed the call of Mao Zedong (1893–1976) for armed struggle against the Japanese. The Communists had developed distinctive approaches in the early 1930s. The keys to their success were lower taxes, fair and simple administration, and programs promoting social and economic justice, all implemented through a small, well-disciplined military force totally controlled by the Communist Party. The Communists worked behind the Japanese lines, especially in northern China. They increased their influence and control by enrolling peasants in part-time militia forces and created a patchwork of small base areas.

In the face of growing Japanese aggression, Mao linked his base-area strategy to the increasingly powerful anti-Japanese nationalism among the hundreds of millions of Chinese living under Japanese occupation. Mao Zedong perfected in these years a historically important concept of protracted guerrilla war against colonialism that had exceptionally wide influence in antiforeign and anti-imperialist struggles in Asia, Latin America, and Africa during the latter half of the twentieth century.

To ensure conformity with their program, the Communist leaders headquartered at Yan'an developed new forms of ideological discipline and methods of working with the common people known as "the mass line." The whole bundle of techniques developed under

Mao's leadership became known as "the Yan'an Way" and became the guiding beacon of Communist rule of China from 1949 until Mao's death in 1976. Thus the war against Japan produced the principles on which China came to be ruled under the Communists.

Japan's Last Offensive, 1944–1945

This long second phase of attrition ended in April 1944 when the Japanese launched their last great offensive of the China war. The Japanese offensive, code-named Ichigo (Number One), aimed to destroy U.S. airbases in the Nationalist-controlled region south and west of the city of Changsha. From these airbases, U.S. long-range bombers were bombing parts of Japan, so Ichigo was defensive in nature. By early 1945, this offensive had stalled because the Japanese armies in China lacked the means to undertake an all-out campaign against the Nationalists and American airpower in Sichuan and southwestern China. In the summer of 1945 the war in China ground to a halt. After the Japanese surrender on 15 August 1945, Japanese troops remained in place all over China, often assisting the arriving Nationalist armies in establishing their authority.

In the summer of 1945, with a U.S. invasion of the Japanese home islands imminent, the Soviet Union, under U.S. urging, broke its nonaggression pact with Japan and invaded Manchuria. This offensive against inferior Japanese forces put the Russians back in control in Manchuria, marking another turn in the fifty-year struggle with Japan for dominance in this region. Once there, the Soviets looted Japanese equipment to rebuild their own war-shattered factories and withdrew by 1947, leaving the battling Nationalist and Communist armies behind.

High Cost of War

The cost of the war in China was enormous. It is estimated that more than one-third of all Japanese wartime expenditures from 1937 to 1945 were swallowed up in the conflict. Japan lost around 400,000 men in China. The Chinese losses were much greater. The Chinese Nationalist armies alone sustained 3.2 million casualties, including 1.3 million killed. No good figures exist for the millions of Communist and civilian casualties. Considerable amounts of the industry and transportation endowment of China survived the war, but the country's economic system lay essentially in tatters as a result of runaway inflation, and disorganization of the money and banking system.

At the end of the war, Chiang Kai-shek raced to establish the authority of his Nationalist government throughout China, even in those extensive areas of the country where the Nationalists had not been in control prior to 1937. The Chinese Communists confident that their "Yan'an Way" could be turned into a nationwide revolutionary movement, prepared to challenge the Chinese Nationalists for control of China. The stage was set for a civil war.

David D. Buck

Further Reading

Boyle, John Hunter. (1972) *China and Japan at War, 1937–1945: The Politics of Collaboration.* Stanford, CA: Stanford University Press.

Chang, Iris. (1997) *The Rape of Nanking: The Forgotten Holocaust of World War II.* New York: Basic Books.

Chi, Hsi-sheng. (1982) *Nationalist China at War: Military Defeat and Political Collapse.* Ann Arbor, MI: University of Michigan Press.

Johnson, Chalmers. (1963) *Peasant Nationalism and Communist Power: The Emergence of Revolutionary China, 1937–1945.* Stanford, CA: Stanford University Press.

Van Slyke, Lyman. (1995) "China." In *The Oxford Companion to World War II*, edited by I. C. B. Dear. New York: Oxford University Press, 210–233.

White, Theodore, and Annalee Jacoby. (1946) *Thunder out of China.* New York: William Sloane.

Wilson, Dick. (1982) *When Tigers Fight: The Story of the Sino-Japanese War.* New York: Viking.

SINO-JAPANESE WAR

The Sino-Japanese War of 1894–1895 reflected several decades of increasing tension between China and Japan over the status of Korea, which China regarded as belonging to its sphere of influence, but which Japan saw as increasingly vital to its own imperialist interests. China continued to believe in a system of tributary relations in which Korea was a vassal state, but Japan had thrown off its feudal past and was rapidly modernizing in the aftermath of the 1868 Meiji Restoration that had returned the Japanese emperor to nominal power.

The stage was set for a clash over Korea as Koreans were caught up in the politics of the moment. Conservatives in Korea wished to continue tributary relations with China, whereas reformers in Korea looked to Japan for modernization and an "opening" of the so-called Hermit Kingdom. Amid increasing political violence, the conservative Korean government called on China for help in suppressing the Tonghak rebellion, a peasant rebellion whose participants were adherents of Tonghak ("Eastern Learning"), a religious movement that opposed both Westernization and the stratification of traditional Korean society. In early June 1894, Chinese troops began arriving.

The Japanese response was immediate and decisive. Within a week of Chinese troop movement into Korea, Japanese military units began crossing the narrow Tsushima and Korea straits to land in Korea. By mid-July, the government in Tokyo demanded that Korea make the sorts of modernizing changes Japan had made in the Meiji Restoration, and Japanese leaders hoped for a pretext for war. Korean leaders hesitated and turned to China for support.

The next step was war. Japanese forces occupied the Korean royal palace and forced the Korean king to ask for Japanese assistance against China. Then the Japanese navy sank a Chinese troop transport, and war was declared on 1 August. Japan was better organized, and its commanders were more willing to take risks. Japanese troops moved quickly up the Korean peninsula and trapped Chinese forces around Pyongyang. Other Japanese troops crossed the Yalu River and seized key positions on the Liaodong Peninsula and then moved into Weihaiwei in northern China. In September 1895, the Japanese navy forced a Chinese fleet to surrender, and the two sides looked to negotiate.

China recognized Korea's independence, ceded the Liaodong Peninsula, Taiwan, and the Pescadores to Japan, and agreed to pay a large indemnity and to extend to Japan all the benefits of the so-called unequal treaties that China had signed with European powers. Russia was concerned about Japan's interest in Korea and southern Manchuria, and with the support of France and Germany (the so-called Triple Intervention) forced Japan to return Liaodong—while demanding an even larger indemnity from China—thus helping to set the stage for the Russo-Japanese War about a decade later.

Charles Dobbs

See also: **Russo-Japanese War; Sino-Japanese Conflict, Second; Tonghak**

Further Reading

Lone, Stewart. (1994) *Japan's First Modern War: Army and Society in the Conflict with China, 1894–1895.* New York: St. Martin's.

Selby, John Millin. (1968) *The Paper Dragon: An Account of the China Wars, 1840–1900.* New York: Praeger.

SINO-TIBETAN LANGUAGES Sino-Tibetan is the largest language family in the world, in terms of the number of people who speak one of its components as their first language. It includes Chinese and its variants; Tibetan; and most of the indigenous languages of the Himalayan region, as well as some of the more important languages of Southeast Asia.

The family is commonly divided into two groups. Whereas the sole constituents of Sinitic are the variants of Chinese (which are mostly, but quite misleadingly, referred to as the "dialects" of Chinese), the Tibeto-Burman branch numbers several hundred often poorly known languages and language groups, the proper linguistic classification of which is still largely a task for future research.

The Bodic languages (*bod*, Tibetan for "Tibet") are further subdivided into Bodish and East Himalayan. The former include Tibetan proper and its variants; Kanauri in northern India; and Newari and the Tamangic languages in Nepal (Tamang, Gurung, and Thakali). East Himalayan is formed by, among others, the Kiranti (or Rai) languages, the Kham-Magar group, and Bahing (Vayu), all spoken in central and eastern Nepal. Baric is a conventional term used for the Kamarupan languages (named after the medieval state of Kamarupa in northeastern India), made up of a large number of lesser language groups, which are further subdivided into the Abor-Miri-Dafla, the Mikir-Meithei, and the Kuki-Chin-Naga groups.

To Burmic belongs the Lolo-Burmese group, the most important language of which is literary Burmese, the state language of Myanmar (Burma); Burmic also contains sizable groups of languages in Thailand, such as Lahu and Lisu.

Karenic, sometimes viewed as a higher-level subgroup of Sino-Tibetan, taxonomically coordinates with Tibeto-Burman, rather than being one of its branches, and consists of the Karen languages Pwo and Sgaw, spoken in Myanmar and Thailand.

Kachinic (e.g., Jinghpo, or Kachin proper, in northern Myanmar) is sometimes classified as a subbranch of Baric, but some researchers group it with Burmic or treat it as a separate Tibeto-Burman branch.

Qiangic, a small family in South China, has been added to Tibeto-Burman recently; it is sometimes viewed as a separate branch of the family, sometimes included in Burmic. Some linguists set up a distinct Rung branch, composed of Qiangic, the Nung languages of northern Myanmar, and Gyarong and Primi/Pumi of Southwest China. The extinct language of the Tangut (the language of the Xi Xia empire, which flourished in Gansu and Shaanxi Provinces between the eleventh and thirteenth centuries), written in a highly unique and complicated script, is mostly viewed as Tibeto-Burman. Its place in the family is still debated, but most researchers opt for its inclusion in either the Rung subgroup or Lolo-Burmese.

The Bai (or Minjia) language of northern Yunnan Province, China, may constitute another, separate Tibeto-Burman group. This, as well as any other, classification of Sino-Tibetan or Tibeto-Burman, can only be viewed as preliminary, and numerous details, as well as some rather drastic revisions, of it are still the subject of current debates.

Another division of the Tibeto-Burman language—into indospheric and sinospheric languages—is based on cultural rather than linguistic criteria. Indospheric languages (the most typical of which are the Bodic and Baric languages) are spoken in the cultural realm of greater India, whereas the sinosphere is dominated by Chinese culture. The millennia-long influences of these dominating cultural areas are reflected in numerous loanwords (from Chinese and Indo-Aryan languages, respectively) found in the languages, as well as in some real linguistic traits. Thus, indospheric languages generally display more complicated morphological systems than languages of the sinosphere (with the Kiranti languages in eastern Nepal being morphologically the most elaborate of the Sino-Tibetan languages), whereas the latter, generally poorer in morphological devices, tend to monosyllabicity of lexemes and display intricate tone systems. However, this division is far from being unequivocal, and it does not imply that direct influence of the eponymous languages is solely responsible for these differences.

Written Sources

Some Sino-Tibetan languages are among those languages of the world with the longest continuous written attestation. First mention is due to Chinese, which has been written in its unique script at least since the fourteenth century BCE.

Tibetan writing begins in the seventh century CE; the script is an offshoot of the Indian family of scripts and continues to be used today. Newari, the language of the original inhabitants of the Kathmandu valley, was written in Devanagari script beginning in the seventeenth century (with at least one manuscript dated as early as the fourteenth century). Lepcha, the state language of Sikkim, had a script of its own, which has been in use from the eighteenth century onward but is little used today. Burmese has been written since the twelfth century in a script that is likewise a development of an Indic predecessor.

A completely different kind of script, which has been called possibly the most complicated writing system humanity has ever used, is the Tangut script, which rendered the language of the Xi Xia empire. Although considerable progress was made in Tangut philology and linguistics during the last decades of the twentieth century, it cannot be regarded as fully deciphered.

The Naxi (or Moso) language of Yunnan Province, China, is well known for a particularly interesting kind of writing system, which mainly consists of iconic, but nevertheless conventionalized, pictographs.

Genetic Relationship

Though the genetic relationship of the Sino-Tibetan languages is no longer in doubt, the details of this relationship are still very far from having been worked out. One of the reasons for this is, quite understandably, the great number of languages in the Tibeto-Burman branch, only a small number of which have been adequately described so far. Moreover, a depressing number of these languages is at present heavily endangered, which renders the collection of reliable data for them the most urgent task of contemporary Sino-Tibetan linguistics. On the Sinitic side, the last decades of the twentieth century saw a great deal of progress in our understanding of the phonological prehistory of Chinese, though too many details are still the subject of controversies to be able to speak of a general consensus on the sound-shape of early Chinese.

Besides subclassification, the most hotly debated topics of Sino-Tibetan linguistics includes such questions as whether the highly complicated verbal concord system of, for example, the Kiranti languages is to be taken as original for Tibeto-Burman or the more isolating typology (the fact that words show only a minimal amount of morphological elements) of the Southeast Asian members of the family—and if a more isolating and tonal parent-language has to be reconstructed, how many distinctive tones should be reconstructed for the parent language, and so on.

Characteristics of Sino-Tibetan Languages

The Sino-Tibetan family shows perhaps more internal typological diversity than any other established group of related languages. Most languages show systematic tonal contrasts, some do not; the basic word order found in most Tibeto-Burman languages is subject-object-verb, but Karenic and Sinitic languages show subject-verb-object syntax (and prepositions as opposed to the postpositions common in the rest of the family). The morphological techniques employed range from mostly isolating (in Southeast Asia and Sinitic), over several degrees of agglutinativity, to high levels of polysynthesis (in Kiranti).

Stefan Georg

Further Reading

Benedict, Paul K. (1972) *Sino-Tibetan: A Conspectus*. Cambridge, U.K.: Cambridge University Press.

Beyer, Stephan V. (1992) *The Classical Tibetan Language*. Albany, NY: State University of New York Press.

Georg, Stefan. (1996) *Marphatan Thakali*. Munich: Lincom-Europa.

Matisoff, James T. (1978) *Variational Semantics in Tibeto-Burman*. Philadelphia, PA: Institute for the Study of Human Issues.

Ramsey, S. Robert. (1987) *The Languages of China*. Princeton, NJ: Princeton University Press.

Van Driem, George. (1987) *A Grammar of Limbu*. Berlin: Mouton de Gruyter.

SINO-VIETNAMESE CULTURE   The term "Sino-Vietnamese culture" designates the part of Vietnamese culture that has been very heavily influenced by China and that uses classical Chinese as its medium of expression. Because Vietnam was part of the Chinese empire from the second century BCE until the tenth century CE, China was able to mold Vietnam in its own cultural image. China introduced methods of cultivating the land, Chinese rituals of life, the Chinese writing system, Buddhism, Taoism, Confucianism, Chinese administrative structures, and so on. Nevertheless, the Vietnamese people continued to speak their own language and retained their sense of national identity. Vietnam rejected Chinese political domination in the tenth century, but Chinese culture continued to exert a powerful influence on Vietnamese institutions as well as on the literature of the scholar-official elite class.

The structures and organization of the Vietnamese government were almost identical to their Chinese models. The monarchical system in Vietnam supported a ruler, called, like the Chinese emperor, the Son of Heaven. Like his Chinese counterpart, he had absolute power and the title of emperor; he was also endowed with a reign name and posthumous glorification. The central government of Vietnam was composed of six ministries. The civil service, or mandarinate, had nine ranks, each divided into two steps, so that it ran from the low 9B to the high 1A. The local administration governed provinces, prefectures, and districts. At the lowest level of government were the villages, also called communes, which had their own hierarchy of notables, selected by the villagers themselves from among the inhabitants of their own locality. These notables were not considered members of the mandarinate; as in China, to become a civil servant one had to pass rigorous examinations that tested appplicants' ability to write official documents, compose poetry in prose and verse, comment on Confucian texts, and analyze critically certain contemporary events. The language of the examinations was classical Chinese. Successful candidates were appointed right away to official positions according to the degrees they had earned. Usually the lowest degree holders would be appointed to ranks 7A–6B and the highest ones to 3A or 3B. The last of these examinations were held in Hue in 1917.

Vietnamese law also followed the example of China. While the code published under the Late Le dynasty (1428–1788) showed some original features appropriate to Vietnamese situations, the Gia Long Code of the Nguyen dynasty (1802–1955) was a close copy of Qing-dynasty legal codes. Even under French colonial rule, the Vietnamese court used the Gia Long Code.

How much of that Confucian influence permeated to the lower levels of Vietnamese society remains a topic of debate to this day. Some scholars maintain that Confucianism stayed within the elite scholar-official class, and that the Vietnamese common people retained their indigenous traditions. This is a difficult position to defend, given that one can find popular songs such as the following, which makes light of Confucian virtues:

> You want to go but I do not let you go
> On your blouse I write three letters
> Loyalty is for our fathers and Filial Piety for our
>   mothers,
> As for us, let us have Love.

In Sino-Vietnamese culture one can list countless Vietnamese works of literature that follow all the techniques and stylistic canons of Chinese literature, down to the plots of novels and the inspirational interior or exterior landscapes of poetry. Ironically, the vast body of Sino-Vietnamese literature includes a large number of anti-Chinese texts, composed to raise the morale of Vietnamese troops in their resistance against Chinese invasion or to celebrate victories over Chinese armies. Classical Chinese was still used in the pamphlets, poems, and letters of anti-French nationalists such as Phan Boi Chau (1867–1940) and Phan Chau Trinh (1872–1926) up to the 1920s.

A writing system that used Chinese characters to transcribe the sounds of Vietnamese words, called *nom*, may have been invented by the eleventh century, but Vietnamese who saw themselves as serious writers never gave it much consideration. *Nom* literature cannot, by any measure, rival Sino-Vietnamese literature as far as works of nonfiction are concerned. As for creative writing, an official 1989 almanac list of the one hundred best books in the entire history of Vietnamese literature included twenty-one written in *nom*, twenty in Sino-Vietnamese, two in French, and fifty-seven in *quoc ngu*, the transliteration system that uses the Roman alphabet. The adoption of *quoc ngu* by the French colonial government, who proclaimed it the official writing system of Vietnam, marked the weaning of Vietnam from Chinese influence.

China was also the route by which Buddhism entered Vietnam. Although Theravada Buddhism could have come to Vietnam from the South, it happened that communication was easier from north to south and thus it was Mahayana Buddhism that came to Vietnam, through China. Buddhism was so eagerly accepted that Buddhist monks became the highest administrators in the first independent governments of Vietnam. The founder of the Ly dynasty was a Buddhist monk of sorts. The Tran dynasty (1225–1400) was also deeply devoted to Buddhism, although the progress of Confucianism pushed Buddhism out of the governing circles and into the hearts of the common people. Practically all Buddhist publications were written in classical Chinese; even certain prayers, which originally were composed in Sanskrit, had their sounds transcribed in Chinese. Vietnamese Buddhism has never actually been cut off from Buddhism in China. Up to the nineteenth century, relations between the two churches could not have been closer: Vietnam purchased incense, books, and other Buddhist necessities regularly from China. Exchanges of monks occurred on a regular basis.

Taoism in Vietnam has never been strongly tied to Taoism in China. It is the least institutionalized religion in Vietnam, with no real worries concerning orthodoxy and no books, sets of prayers, or texts of incantations that need to be exactly reproduced from an original version. In effect, Taoist superstitious beliefs and practices found in Vietnam a favorable enough environment for the faithful to nurture and develop their own conviction without any external props.

In the arts, government, law, religion, indeed, in every aspect of life, Chinese culture has left an enduring imprint on Vietnamese culture. It is a relationship Westerners can understand if they consider the relationship between the cultures of the peoples of Western Europe and ancient Greco-Roman culture.

Truong Buu Lam

See also: **China—Vietnam Relations; Chinese Influence in Southeast Asia**

Further Reading
Dao Duy Anh. (1992) *Viet Nam Van Hoa Su Cuong* (Outlines of Vietnamese Culture). 2d ed. Ho Chi Minh City, Vietnam: School of Teachers Training.

Eckberg, Edgar. Compiler. (1969). *Historical Interaction of China and Vietnam: Institutional and Cultural Themes.* Kansas City: University of Kansas Press.
Woodside, Alexander B. (1971) *Vietnam and the Chinese Model: A Comparative Study of Vietnamese and Chinese Government in the First Half of the Nineteenth Century.* Cambridge, MA: Council on East Asian Studies, Harvard University Press.

SINOP (2002 pop. 31,500). Sinop is a Turkish Black Sea coastal provincial capital. Named for the nymph Sinope and mentioned in the *Argonautica* of Appollonius, the city has two safe harbors and protective inland mountains. Earliest settlements date back to 4500 BCE. Ionians from Miletus founded a city in the eighth century BCE, where Cynic philosopher Diogenes was born in 404 BCE. For centuries the leading Black Sea port, Sinop was in turn Pontic capital, Roman colony, Byzantine port, and Comnene city after the Latin conquest of Constantinople in 1204. After Seljuk conquest in 1214, it was governed by the vizier Parvane and by Gazi Chelebi of the Seljuk dynasty in the name of the Ilkhanid Mongols. Genoese traders were active in the fourteenth century. The Ottomans originally took Sinop from the Isfendiogullari, but lost control during war with Timur (Tamerlane, 1336–1405). The Ottoman sultan Mehmet II incorporated the town in 1458. Sinop, with its mixed Muslim and Christian populations, provided ships for the Ottoman fleet. The port was attacked by Cossacks in 1614, and the Russian naval attack of 1853 started the Crimean War.

Forestry and grain agriculture have been traditional sources of revenue for Sinop, now connected to Samsun by road. In recent years it has been advertised as a tourist destination, with the natural environment and seafood restaurants the major attractions.

Sylvia Wing Önder

Further Reading
Freely, John. (1990) *Classical Turkey*. London: Penguin.
Government of Turkey. (2000) "Turkish Government Institute of Statistics." Retrieved 10 January 2000, from: http://www.die.gov.tr/Turkish/Sonist/Nufus/sinop.gif.

SINUIJU (2002 pop. 377,000). Sinuiju is the capital of North P'yongan Province and one of North Korea's centers of heavy industry. It is located in the northwestern part of the Korean Peninsula at the mouth of the Yalu (Amnok) River.

The Sinuiju railway was constructed by the Japanese in 1904 for the Russo-Japanese War. It was the last stop on the railway line connecting Pusan with northernmost Korea. The city has a cross-border rail link with China. South and North Korea agreed in June 2000 to reconnect the Kyongui rail link—which was severed during the Korean War (1950–1953)—between Seoul and Sinuiju. It will ultimately be linked to the Trans-Siberian Railway and the Trans-China Railway in an attempt to build an "Iron Silk Road" linking Korea to Europe.

Sinuiju once enjoyed a prosperous wood industry (paper, matches), but since the construction of the Sup'ung Power Station on the Yalu River, timber production has decreased and given way to other industries, such as silk and cosmetics production. Major industries include machinery, chemicals, textiles, pharmaceuticals, footwear, clothing, food, and articles for daily use, as well as marine products (anchovies, squid, and oysters). Agriculture (rice, corn, and beans) is also important. The Sinuiju Chemical Fibre Complex produces staple fiber made from the reed grown on nearby Pidan (Silk) Island.

Ariane Perrin

Further Reading
Lee, Ki-baik. (1984) *A New History of Korea*. Trans. by Edward W. Wagner and Edward J. Shultz. Cambridge, MA: Harvard University Press.

SIRAIKI The Siraiki people have historically inhibited the central parts of the classic Indus basin, the area which more or less comprises the modern state of Pakistan. The Siraiki people are considered to be of Indo-Hittite or Indo-European origin, although little is known about the ethnic origins of Siraikis before the invasion of the Indus Valley (c. 326 BCE) by Alexander of Macedon (356–323 BCE). As people of historic Sindhu Desh, the Siraiki people are originally Sindhis. Sindhu Desh gradually disappeared from the world map after the Arab conquest in 611 CE, and its territory was constantly amalgamated into the empires of various Central and West Asian conquerors until the creation of Pakistan in 1947.

The ethnic and sociopolitical fragmentation of traditional Sindhi society, migrations, and invading ethnocultural and religiously oriented influences over centuries have had an impact on Siraiki identity. The historians of Alexander of Macedon referred to Siraiki areas as the country of the Malloi and the Oxydaraiki, two major tribes who were, the historians said, more numerous and warlike than any of the other Indian tribes. They were located near the confluence of the Hydaspes and Akesines (Ravi and Sutlej rivers) and their junction with the Indus. The two tribes spoke the same language and have been referred to as Hydaraiki, Sydracae, and Syrakousi groups. Because the central Indus basin was the common route for invading armies, the Siraiki regions experienced chaos up into the nineteenth century. With the partition of India in 1947, Siraiki and southern Indus areas became a part of Pakistan. Although statistics for the exact Siraiki population are not available, Siraikis are generally considered to number around 40 million. The Pakistani province of Punjab was largely created in Indus regions with an almost two-thirds Siraiki-speaking majority.

The Siraiki language is largely derived from Sanskrit and Prakrit and influenced by Arabic and Persian, as are the other languages of the western Indian subcontinent. Siraiki is the main and central dialect of the eight distinct dialects of Sindhi that are spoken in various parts of the Indus basin. During the British colonial period, the language policy of the British Indian government contributed to serious ethnolinguistic fragmentation. Around 1850, the British decided to provide specialized scripts to some Indus basin dialects, thereby fostering a sense of individual identity for speakers of those dialects. Various dialects of Sindhi were among those standardized with different scripts.

Since the 1960s, a new wave of Siraiki nationalism has aimed at obtaining more cultural and economic autonomy. Some Siraiki nationalists even demanded a separate Siraiki province, albeit without success. Siraiki middle and upper classes however, seem to be well integrated within the political structure and it is unlikely that an anti–status-quo movement can be successful. Members of the Siraiki elite have held some of the most important positions in the federal and provincial government: one president of Pakistan, Farooq Laghari (served from 1993 to 1998), was a Siraiki, and many Siraiki feel very much integrated into Pakistan.

Aftab A. Kazi

Further Reading
Hiranandani, Popati. (1980) *Sindhis: The Scattered Treasure*. New Dehli: Malaah.

Kazi, Aftab. (1987) *Ethnicity and Education in Nation-Building: Case of Pakistan*. Lanham, MD: University Press of America.

McCrindle, J. W. ([1896] 1984) *Ancient India*. Reprint. Patna, India: Eastern Book House.

Wagha, Ahsan. (1990) *The Siraiki Language: Its Development and Growth*. Islamabad, Pakistan: Dderawar.

SISAVANGVONG UNIVERSITY Originally named after a Lao king and later renamed the National University of Laos (NUOL), Sisavangvong University was founded in 1958 as the first university of Laos and was located in the nation's capital, Vientiane. The university merged existing institutions under one administration and was modeled after the French education system. Foreign teachers composed a majority of the staff due to the lack of qualified Lao teachers, but the civil war's instability and shortage of teaching materials hindered the system. After the 1975 revolution, the socialist regime dissolved Sisavangvong University to erase any trace of both the French and the royalist regime, and Lao was reintroduced, replacing French, as the language of scholarship in Laos. The university was demoted to a teacher's college and was used to train new teachers using a Lao curriculum that was heavily imbued with communist values. Many qualified teachers either fled the country or were sent to reeducation camps after 1975. Students were sent to Vietnam, the Soviet Union, or Eastern Bloc countries for higher education.

The National University of Laos was founded in 1995 and consolidated ten existing institutions under the Ministry of Education. The National University consists of the faculties of education, sciences, agriculture and forestry, social sciences and humanities, philology, economics and management, engineering and architecture, medical sciences, and law and public administration. Students devote the first two years to foundation studies and then proceed with three or more years in professional studies to earn a middle diploma, higher diploma, or bachelor's degree.

Linda S. McIntosh

Further Reading
Evans, Grant. (1998) *The Politics of Ritual and Remembrance: Laos since 1975*. Chiang Mai, Thailand: Silkworm.

SISTAN A lowland region lying along the Helmand River, Sistan is made up of the southwestern Afghanistan province of Nimruz (capital, Zaranj) and the Sistan district of the Iranian province of Sistan and Baluchistan (administrative center, Zabol; provincial capital, Zahedan). Spring flooding yields two harvests a year: wheat, barley, millet, and other grains in winter, and cotton and vegetables in summer.

Sistan is the legendary homeland of the hero Rostam from the eleventh-century epic *Shahnameh* of Ferdowsi. Its name is traced back to *Sakastan* or "land of the Scythians," the Scythians having dominated the region toward the end of the first millennium BCE.

Sistan's low terrain allows easy access from Central Asia and the Iranian plateau into the heartland of Afghanistan. Since the time of the Achaemenids (559–331 BCE), it has served as a borderland of successive empires bent on eastward expansion. After the Arab conquest in 652 CE, the distant province became a refuge for rebels against later caliphal authority. From the ninth to the fifteenth centuries, the Saffarids and their successors, known as *maliks* (kings) of Nimruz, ruled the province, acknowledging the suzerainty of Samanids (864–999), Ghaznavids (977–1187), Seljuks (1038–1157), and Ghurids (c. 1000–1215). The region suffered the Mongol invasion of the thirteenth century and the devastating punitive expedition of Timur (1370–1405), who destroyed its irrigation system. In Safavid times (1501–1722/1736), the province served as a base for Persian forays against Mughal India. In 1723 a *malik* of Sistan, Mohammad b. Fath 'Ali Khan, captured Khorasan from the Safavids and claimed royal prerogatives, but his bid for the throne of Persia was foiled by the future Nader Shah Afshar (1736–1747). After Nader Shah's death, the founder of Afghanistan, Ahmad Shah Durrani, established close relations with the *maliks* of Sistan, and in the nineteenth century Persia and Afghanistan came to the brink of war over possession of the region. The border between them was established in 1827 by a British commission and finalized in 1905. The present population is mostly Tajik (East Iranian) and Baluch, engaged in agriculture, pasturing, the food and textile industries, and carpet weaving.

Marta Simidchieva

Further Reading
Barthold, Wilhelm (Vasilii Vladimirovich, Bartol'd). (1984) "Sistan, the Southern Part of Afghanistan, and Baluchistan." In *An Historical Geography of Iran*, translated from the Russian by Svat Soucek, edited with an introduction by Clifford E. Bosworth. Princeton, NJ: Princeton University Press, 64–86.
Bosworth, Clifford Edmund. (1994) *The History of the Saffarids of Sistan and the Maliks of Nimruz (247/861 to 949/1542–1543)*. Costa Mesa, CA, and New York: Mazda Publishers.

SITTANG RIVER Rising in the hills southeast of Mandalay, the Sittang (Sittoung) River flows southward between the Shan Plateau and the Pegu Yoma highland range before entering the flat paddy-field lands of the lower Pegu (Bago) Division. Here it opens out into a wide estuary, famous for its tidal bore, before emptying into the Gulf of Martaban.

Running parallel to the Irrawaddy River, the Sittang Valley is one of the most strategic in Myanmar's history and development. For much of its 320-kilometer course, the river runs close to important road and rail links between central and south Myanmar. The former royal capital at Toungoo is situated on its banks. Other large towns in the valley include Pyu and Nyaunglebin.

Trade and transport are important in local business, but the economy of the valley remains predominantly agricultural. The Sittang Valley is the largest sugar cane-growing region in the country. Rice is also widely grown, but timber from the surrounding hills is the most valuable natural resource.

Martin Smith

Further Reading
Bunge, Frederica M., ed. (1983) *Burma: A Country Study.* Washington, DC: American University Foreign Area Studies, U.S. Government Printing Office.

SIVAS (2002 pop. 259,000). Sivas, capital of the province of Sivas (2002 pop. 779,000), is located northeast of central Turkey, 350 kilometers east of Ankara in the valley of the Kizel Irmak River. Inhabited since Hittite times, the city became historically significant under Emperor Diocletian as the Roman city of Sebaste, capital of Armenia Minor. The Armenian king Sennacherib John of Vaspurakan (Van) ceded his land to Byzantine emperor Basil II in 1021. The city was then lost to the Turkmen Danishmenid dynasty (1155–1192) after the Battle of Manzikert in 1071. In 1174, the city was captured by Rum Seljuk Kilic Arslan II and periodically served as capital of the Seljuk empire along with Konya. Under Seljuk rule, Sivas was an important center of trade and site of a citadel, along with mosques and *madrasah*s (colleges), four of which survive today and one of which houses the Sivas Museum. The city fell to the Ottoman sultan Bayezid I (1389–1402) in 1398, was lost to Timur (Tamerlane; 1336–1405) in 1400, and was recaptured by the Ottomans in 1408. Under the Ottomans, Sivas served as the administrative center of the province of Rum until about the late nineteenth century. Upon the return of Mustafa Kemal Ataturk (1881–1938), the founder of the Turkish Republic, from Amasya, the Congress of Sivas, considered a turning point in the formation of the Turkish Republic, was held in September 1919. It was at this congress that Kemal's position as chair of

the executive committee of the national resistance was confirmed. Sivas is located on an important rail line linking the cities of Kayseri, Samsun, and Erzurum. Its economy is largely based on agriculture.

T. Isikozlu-E.F. Isikozlu

Further Reading
Faroqhi, Suraiya. (1960) "Siwas." In *The Encyclopaedia of Islam.* 2d ed. Leiden, Netherlands: E. J. Brill, 689–691.
(1999). *Statistical Yearbook of Turkey, 1998.* Ankara, Turkey: Devlet Istatistik Enstitusu.

SIXTEEN KINGDOMS The Sixteen Kingdoms is the name given to the period of Chinese history (304–440) when different tribes of non-Han Chinese, including some of nomadic origin, alternated with each other in establishing short-lived kingdoms in northern China. (See Table 1.) Chinese historians list them as the sixteen nations of the five "barbarian" tribes. The period is often called *Wuhu Shiliu Guo,* meaning "*Period of Five Barbarian Tribes and Sixteen Nations.*" The peoples were the Di, Hun, Jiehu, Xianbei, and Qiang, originating from Tibetans, Tangut, Proto-Turkic, Mongol, and Tungus tribes. Eventually the Xianbei people reunified northern China in 440.

TABLE 1

The Sixteen Nations

	Name of the nation	Period	Location in present-day China	Ethnicity
1	Cheng Han	301–347	Sichuan	Di
2	Han (Anterior Zhao)	304–329	Shanxi, and Shaanxi	Hun
3	Anterior Liang	317–376	Gansu	Han
4	Posterior Zhao	319–351	Shandong, Hebei, Shanxi, and Shaanxi	Jiehu
5	Anterior Qin	351–394	Liaoning, Shandong, Hebei, Shanxi, Gansu, Sichuan, and Shaanxi	Di
6	Anterior Yan	337–370	Liaoning, Shandong, Hebei, and Shanxi	Xianbei
7	Posterior Yan	384–409	Liaoning, Shandong, Hebei, and Shanxi	Xianbei
8	Posterior Qin	384–417	Shaanxi	Qiang
9	Western Qin	385–431	Shaanxi	Xianbei
10	Posterior Liang	386–403	Gansu	Di
11	Southern Liang	397–414	Gansu	Xianbei
12	Northern Liang	397–439	Gansu	Hun
13	Southern Yan	398–410	Shandong	Xianbei
14	Western Liang	400–421	Gansu	Han
15	Xia	407–431	Shaanxi	Hun
16	Northern Yan	409–436	Liaoning	Han

During this period, the entire Huang River Valley became a vast battlefield for tribal kingdoms and some remnant Chinese military chieftains. The various nations fought among themselves and blood flowed freely. Although this period is often considered China's Dark Age, due to the chaos and foreign occupation of its territories, the epoch was also a time of great change, as China was transformed by the Indian religion of Buddhism.

Unryu Suganuma

Further Reading
Fairbank, John King, and Merle Goldman. (1998) *China: A New History*. Enlarged ed. Cambridge, MA: Belknap.

Fairbank, John King, Edwin O. Reischauer, and Albert M. Craig. (1989) *East Asia: Tradition and Transformation*. Cambridge, MA: Harvard University Press.

SO CHONGJU

SO CHONGJU (1915–2000), Korean poet. Born in Cholla Province, South Korea, So Chongju, Korea's premier twentieth-century poet, studied the Chinese classics in a village school and subsequently attended normal school in Seoul where he was expelled for nationalist activities. In 1936 he won a poetry award from the *Tonga Ilbo*, a Korean daily newspaper, and helped found the literary magazine *Poets' Village*—two events that launched his literary career. Active in the formation of the Choson Young Writers Association, he was appointed director of arts in the post-Liberation Ministry of Education. In 1954 he was appointed a member of the Academy of Arts. He returned to his alma mater, Tongguk University, in 1959, where he had a distinguished teaching and creative career, during which he won many major Korean poetry awards, including the Asian Freedom Award (1955), the Korean Academy Award (1967), and the May 16 National Award (1987). *Flower Snake* (1941), *Cuckoo* (1948), *Selected Poems* (1956), *Shilla Notes* (1960), *Winter Sky* (1968), *Collected Poems* (1972), *Lessons of Chilmajae* (1975), *Poems of a Wanderer* (1976), and *Poems After the Crane Left* (1982) are among his best-known collections.

For So Chongju, Korea and its people were like celadon, the celebrated green porcelain. In his poems, he sought a return to a greatness as exceptional as celadon's by re-creating the spirit of Shilla, which he thought represented Korea at its best. His poems are earthy, physical, sensuous, but above all they are exquisitely Korean, informed by an all-pervading Zen awareness.

Kevin O'Rourke

Further Reading
Anthony of Taize. (1993) *Brother: The Early Lyrics of So Chongju*. London: Forest.

O'Rourke, Kevin. (1995) *Poems of a Wanderer*. Dublin, Ireland: Dedalus.

Song, Hason. (1991) *Midang So Chongju Yon'gu* (Midang So Chongju Studies). Seoul: Sonil Muhwasa.

SOCIAL ASSOCIATIONS—CHINA

SOCIAL ASSOCIATIONS—CHINA Associations are groups of people who have organized themselves on the basis of common activities or who pursue similar interests. In the People's Republic of China (PRC), there are four different types of associations: state controlled (such as the so-called mass organizations), state supervised (such as professional and entrepreneurs' associations or hobby-based organizations), informal (organizations of fellow townspeople and clans), and illegal (secret societies, underground groups, opposition groups, or criminal organizations). While the state-controlled organizations have existed for almost the entire history of the PRC, the other three types have begun to reemerge only in the course of the reform process. The reason for this reemergence has been the development of new social strata and actors as well as increasing division of labor and specialization in the process of economic reform.

Emerging Special Interest Groups

Since the 1980s, new groups with special interests have been pushing to form efficacious professional organizations and interest associations. Along with formal groups, there are now also informal ones, and to the traditional organization forms have been added modern ones (women's and environmental groups, for example). This development started in rural areas, where it was encouraged by the return to family-based economic structures and the withdrawal of the state from the running of villages. Often, traditional organizations (such as clans, religious and temple organizations, or secret societies) reemerged. In towns, farmers began to form traditional unofficial organizations and interest groups, most often regional groupings, and gangs of beggars also emerged.

Even (illegal) trade unions of migrant workers have developed; these groups organize strikes and demonstrations. As in other developing countries, the sense of alienation felt by farmers in towns led to the spontaneous formation of groups according to local, ethnic, or professional background. In addition, business associations (for example, associations of entrepreneurs, associations of particular branches of an industry, or professional groups), hobby associations, and sport clubs developed in urban areas. Although the nonstate organizations are, to an extent, based on traditional structures, their emergence demonstrates a growing need on the part of the population for autonomous organizations.

Social Organizations as State-Society Mediators

The role of social organizations as mediators between state and society is nothing new in China. Traditional organizations were based on shared occupation (merchants, traders, or craftspeople), intellectual camaraderie, family ties (clans), or shared regional origin (regional groups). Particularly in rural areas, secret societies or farmers' interest groups were important. Most secret organizations promised their members a heavenly state of happiness and tried to establish an egalitarian society built on the principles of morality and higher justice.

Toward the end of the Qing era (1912), numerous "modern" groups were formed in towns. These included professional organizations, groups of intellectuals, chambers of commerce, trade unions, and students', farmers', and women's groups. The weakness of the state in the late Qing era and at the beginning of the republic made these organizations increasingly autonomous. The chambers of commerce were thus able to work actively toward the creation of parliaments and the drafting of a constitution. Students', workers', and professional interest groups played an important part in the May Fourth Movement in 1919.

As central government again took control and became more stabilized after 1927, the ruling Guomindang Party enforced a policy that limited the groups' powers. In 1941 a law was passed that tied associations directly to state institutions and put them under state control. With the foundation of the PRC, most organizations were disbanded or changed into party-controlled or party-supervised institutions.

Role in Cultural History

In terms of cultural history, independent interest groups contradict the Confucian precept of the subordination of all interests to the highest authority. This was also true for the guilds that played such an important role in the European process of development. However, craftspeople and merchants never had a decisive influence on China's fate in history, and guilds hardly ever stood up for people's political and civil rights.

The guilds, which had existed for centuries, were mostly structured like families and stood for particularist interests, but they never had an impact on China's political history. They adapted themselves to the requirements of the government bureaucracy, which controlled towns and markets, and sought to negotiate and petition their way rather than seeking confrontation. They offered their members material advantages, such as supporting them in times of need, and represented their interests in dealings with the authorities. Through a strict codex of rules, the guilds obliged their members to fulfill their duties to the state, especially since the guilds were held responsible by the authorities for their members' behavior. The guilds financed themselves primarily through self-imposed goods taxes. Every guild was headed by a paid state official, who, through his capacity as such, could personally negotiate with senior officials and was officially recognized as a representative of the organization. This corporatist structure, which was easily adaptable to the supervision and control structures of the Communist Party, is in some ways similar to the structure now used by private social organizations in the PRC.

Legalization of Associations

The foundation of academic, professional, social, arts-, sports-, or hobby-based associations has been legal again since the end of the 1980s. Hundreds of thousands of associations and organizations, covering a wide range of social interests, have been created across the country. The 1989 provisional decree offering "Directions for the Registration and Administration of Social Associations" subjected this rapidly growing trend to stronger state regulation, a move that is similar to the policy previously set by the Guomindang. A revised version of this law was passed in 1998. The rules require an official body (authority, state or party institution, or public enterprise) to make a formal application for the association to be recognized and for the official body to take on the formal patronage of the association. As patronage also includes a supervisory function—the heads of the guarantor institution can be made responsible for misconduct by the relevant association—institutions are often prepared to take on this responsibility only in return for (material or immaterial) advantages or because of personal connections.

Association-State Interlinking

It would be wrong to assume that the connection with state or party institutions means that clubs and associations function as merely quasi-state organizations and represent only the interests of party and state. Social pressure that developed following the extension of the market, political liberalization, and growing autonomy in society made the authorization of associations acceptable to the party and the state. The connection with guarantor institutions has, however, resulted in manifold interlinking between associations and the state. Usually associations attempt to articulate and implement their interests through the guarantor institutions. This happens in many different ways, for example, by negotiations or *guanxi* (that is, creating and using connections). This aim can also be achieved by having well-known and respected functionaries as honorary members or "consultants" to gain political protection and recognition. In authoritarian societies, there is hardly any other way to assert one's interests. The close connections with state or party institutions also show that autonomous organizations are not (yet) possible. In present-day China, it is therefore not the pressure group but the *guanxi* group that solves problems and conflicts and does so by means of patronage. A continuation of this trend is the need to seek protection from a powerful guarantor institution precisely because the connection with an authority or public institution functions as protection and enhances the association's status.

In a society in which independent parallel structures are not permitted, interest representation and participation in negotiation processes between the state and interest groups would be impossible without organizations being interlinked in this way. In China today, a social group's interests are not so much asserted as indirectly negotiated, and therefore they require such interconnections. On the one hand, only in this way can social groups attain a certain degree of participation in negotiations. On the other hand, associations can influence politics through the prescribed state guarantor institution. Such half-autonomous organizations can therefore be seen as the forerunners of autonomous economic and political associations. They are two-sided in character, because they have elements of both state dominance and autonomy. The state allows these associations a certain functional autonomy as long as they do not challenge the state.

As economic reforms and social change have moved forward, interest groups have sprung up. The party is attempting, however, to bind the newly developing interest groups into existing formal structures. On the one hand, increasing economic liberalization has meant that the state is no longer able to control all social activities, but on the other hand, it does not see the necessity for this as long as the newly developing interest groups do not evolve into parallel political structures.

Unlike in democratic societies, the corporatist aspect in authoritarian societies pertains purely to the state as the only body with decision-making power; a corporatist structure makes it possible for associations to have a voice in discussion processes. At the same time, however, state supervision prevents the emergence of parallel organizations acting independently of the state. This style of corporatism is also referred to as state or authoritarian corporatism. This kind of corporatist structure was created or strengthened in East Asia (Japan, South and North Korea, Taiwan, PRC) during the course of each nation's development. In the PRC, the historically and culturally developed authoritarian corporatism formed a synthesis with Leninist state corporatism. The continuing reduction of the role of the state in economic matters and further social differentiation will probably ascribe an increasingly important function to social organizations in the social and political processes of change.

Thomas Heberer

See also: **Guanxi**

Further Reading

Gao, Bingzhong. (2001) "The Rise of Associations in China and the Question of Their Legitimacy." *Social Sciences in China* (Spring): 73–87.

Heberer, Thomas. (1996) "Die Rolle von Interessenvereinigungen in autoritäten Systemen: Das Beispiel Volksrepublic China." *Politische Vierteljahresschrift* 2: 227–297.

Pearson, Margaret M. (1994) "The Janus Face of Business Associations in China: Social Corporatism in Foreign Enterprises." *Australian Journal of Chinese Affairs* (January): 25–48.

Saich, Tony. (2000) "Negotiating the State: The Development of Social Organizations in China." *China Quarterly* (March): 124–141.

Shue, Vivienne. "State Power and Social Organization in China." In *State Power and Social Forces: Domination and Transformation in the Third World*, edited by Joel S. Migdal, Atul Kohli, and Vivienne Shue. Cambridge, U.K., New York, and Melbourne, Australia: Cambridge University Press, 65–88.

Unger, Jonathan. (1996) "Bridges: Private Business, the Chinese Government, and the Rise of New Associations." *Chinese Quarterly* (September): 795–819.

White, Gordon. (1993) "Prospects for Civil Society in China: A Case Study of Xiaoshan City." *Australian Journal of Chinese Affairs* 29: 63–88.

SOCIAL REALISM—CHINA

The term "social realism" is used in a Chinese context to describe the trend prevalent in Chinese literature and cinema of the first half of the twentieth century and refers to a realistic, socially reflective, and politically engaged literary and cinematic approach. Realism was introduced into China from the West at the turn of the twentieth century. Since then various terms, including humanitarian realism, critical realism, and social realism, have been used to characterize realism in early twentieth-century Chinese literature. Literary critics, writers, and leading intellectuals have offered various interpretations of this vague concept. Chen Duxiu (1879– 1942), one of the most influential Chinese intellectuals of the period, embraced social realism by calling for a "popular social literature" and a "fresh and sincere literature of realism." The most prominent literary association in the 1920s and 1930s, the Wenxue Yenjiu Hui ("Literary Research Association"), whose literary magazine attracted major fiction writers, proclaimed a realism labeled as "art-for-life's sake." Leftist literary writers and theoreticians such as Zhou Yang (1908–1989) demanded that literature reflect the reality of social life and exercise active critique of social problems.

The embrace of realism by Chinese writers in this period was chiefly motivated by their political and cultural needs: modernizing China and rebuilding Chinese society and culture. This motive is clearly reflected in the literary realism adopted by major writers of the period, including Lu Xun (1881–1936), Mao Dun (1896–1981), Lao She (1899–1966), and Ba Jin (b. 1904). Their works portrayed a critical picture of a sick nation, a hypocritical and stale culture, social injustice and suffering, and the deprivation of human dignity and freedom.

Although strongly influenced by the Western mode of critical realism, the fictional form of Chinese social realism has its own distinct makeup and varieties. Major writers such as Mao Dun, Lao She, and Shen Congwen (1902–1988), for instance, realistically depicted their social concern through, respectively, historical, melodramatic, and lyrical narrative modes and forms of representation. Some writers, however, sacrificed literary forms and artistic integrity by being overly concerned with political content.

Social realism also refers specifically to Chinese leftist and progressive filmmakers during the Chinese civil war (1945–1949), whose "social realist" films documented the social misery of that period. After the establishment of the People's Republic of China in 1949, social realism was replaced by the officially sanctioned socialist realism, which became the dominant theory in literature and arts in Mainland China during the second half of the twentieth century.

Ming Jian

See also: **Ba Jin; Civil War of 1945–1949; Lao She; Lu Xun; Shen Congwen**

Further Reading

Anderson, Marston. (1990) *The Limits of Realism: Chinese Fiction in the Revolutionary Period.* Berkeley and Los Angeles, CA: University of California Press.
Wang, Te-wei. (1992) *Fictional Realism in Twentieth-Century China: Mao Dun, Lao She, Shen Congwen.* New York: Columbia University Press.

SOCIAL RELATIONS—JAPAN Japanese social relations are organized around values of interdependence and reciprocity that guide the creation and expression of human interactions. Often, these values are expressed via the establishment and reproduction of reciprocal obligations through which coworkers, family members, friends, and acquaintances build relationships over time. These interdependencies and obligations are established and expressed both in terms of individual relationships (for example, with friends, family, and coworkers) and in terms of relationships to particular groups or organizations to which one belongs (such as school, company, and community). At the core of Japanese notions about social interaction is the idea that long-term relationships are maintained through a combination of emotional bonds, practical bonds, and symbolic actions, such as gift giving, that mark and represent the continuation of the relationship. Reciprocity and interdependence are involved in both vertical relationships between subordinates and superiors and horizontal relationships among peers.

Obligation and Reciprocity

Obligations in Japan are often organized around concepts that index either an asymmetrical or symmetrical relationship between individuals. Asymmetrical obligations can exist either as a part of the innate character of a relationship, as with the parent-child bond, or from feelings of gratitude and indebtedness that arise out of the benevolent or beneficial actions of another, such as feelings of indebtedness a student has towards his or her mentor. Asymmetric obligation is usually associated with the concept of *on* (literally, "kindness," "favor," or "blessing"), which indexes a feeling of gratitude on the part of the debtor towards the donor for having received some benefit. Although *on* can come to exist in any relationship, as an innate quality it is most closely associated with the debt of gratitude a child owes to his or her parents and, by extension, ancestors for having been brought into the world and raised. The implication with *on* is that the debt incurred is asymmetrical: the debt a child owes to a parent and ancestors, or a student owes to a mentor, can never be satisfactorily repaid, because the feeling of gratitude does not normally lapse. The debtor desires, and may be expected, to express his or her gratitude by continually making efforts to repay at least part of this endless debt. The importance of *on* for understanding social relations in Japan is that rather than being understood as a discrete instance that occurs during the course of a social relationship, *on* operates as a symbolic representation of the relationship itself and the inherent asymmetry of the benefit received.

On is a form of obligation that is closely intertwined with emotional bonds associated with love, friendship, and appreciation, and thus generally carries a positive connotation. Reciprocal obligations, on the other hand, while constituting a basis for securing social relationships, are not always perceived in a positive way. Japanese people live within webs of reciprocal obligations; some of these obligations are incurred without actually desiring to enter into a relationship— for example, through a benefit received by a family member or simply by being related to someone through common membership in family, company, school, or community. It is not unusual for an established relationship, particularly when it is not desired by one or both parties, to be described in terms of being a burden, in that each exchange requires an eventual response, and once engaged in the relationship, it is difficult to break it off without offending the other party. This sort of burdensome obligation is usually expressed as *giri* (literally, "duty," "obligation"), which refers to feelings associated with loss of autonomy that result from being indebted to another. The debtor returns the favor not out of a feeling of gratitude, but out of a desire to be rid of the debt (although, particularly if it involves family or work relationships, this may not be possible) and guilt about possibly not satisfactorily carrying out one's reciprocal obligation.

The concepts of *giri* and *on* are difficult to separate. The character of obligation in a relationship may change over time; a relationship that is initially based upon *on* may become burdensome and, thus, become understood more in terms of *giri* by one or both parties. As noted above, among the most noted areas in which individuals are viewed as having *on* is in the relationship with parents. Simply for having been brought into the world, one owes an enormous debt of gratitude to one's parents. This is responded to through the actions associated with filial piety, including heeding parental wishes and demands, caring for them in old age, and continuing to care for them after they die through rituals associated with ancestor veneration. However, it is not unusual for younger Japanese to describe this debt to one's parents in terms

of *giri* rather than *on*, indicating that the repayment is required, but does not necessarily actually involve gratitude. In many cases, a person's interpretation of the debt owed to parents (or others) involves an ambiguously defined combination of *giri* and *on* and ambivalence about how and when the debt should be repaid. This, of course, allows for considerable room in interpretation and expression by both parties as they manipulate the social and symbolic capital associated with the obligations connected with a relationship.

Interdependence

In Japan, interdependence (sometimes referred to as dependency) has been represented in scholarly literature largely in terms of the concepts of *amae*, *amaeru*, and *amayakasu*. The term *amae*, as it was made famous in the work of Japanese psychologist Takeo Doi, refers to passive dependence (or sometimes love) and is manifested through the desire to be indulged by the individual who is the object of *amae*. Typically, the term is used in describing the behavior of a child toward his or her mother, and normally this form of indulgence relationship is viewed positively (although the term *amae ko* can be used to refer to a spoiled child). Doi argues that the concept of *amae* is not limited to the mother-child bond, but is, in fact, central to how Japanese form social relationships.

Doi paints a very broad and asymmetrical—dependence oriented—picture of the *amae* relationship, one that has been refined by other scholars, such as the anthropologist Takie Lebra. Lebra points out that the seeking of indulgence (*amaeru*) is complementary; it must be enacted along with a reciprocal granting of indulgence (*amayakasu*)—which can involve both the active solicitation and passive acceptance of another's wish to be indulged. *Amaeru* and *amayakasu* thus can be understood in terms of complementary roles that people assume in the process of building and maintaining relationships with each other. As people interact, they engage and manipulate the expression of these roles, usually in terms of self-interest: a person who is good at *amaeru* is able to accept and appropriately respond to the *amayakasu* desire expressed by another, and vice versa. A person may, for example, choose to use the feelings associated with *amae* to get into his or her boss's good graces by reacting to and accepting the desire of the boss to behave in a paternal manner and nurture his or her subordinates (*amayakasu*). The *amaeru-amayakasu* relationship is interdependent and mutually beneficial, but it may be concluded when one or both parties no longer perceive the benefits of the interdependence.

The Limits of Definition

Concepts such as *amae*, *giri*, and *on* are important elements in how Japanese people establish, develop, and maintain emotive and social bonds. However, each of these concepts conveys multiple meanings and interpretations. Rather than being identifiers of Japanese social relations, they are tools that Japanese people use in creating and interpreting those relations. Each of these concepts not only describes elements of social relations in Japan, but also identifies tools that people employ and manipulate as they interact with each other.

John W. Traphagan

Further Reading

Doi, Takeo. (1970) *The Anatomy of Dependence.* Trans. by John Bester. Tokyo: Kodansha.

Hashimoto, Akiko. (1996). *The Gift of Generations: Japanese and American Perspectives on Aging and the Social Contract.* New York: Cambridge University Press.

Kondo, Dorinne. (1990). *Crafting Selves: Power, Gender, and Discourses of Identity in a Japanese Workplace.* Chicago: University of Chicago Press.

Lebra, Takie Sugiyama. (1976) *Japanese Patterns of Behavior.* Honolulu, HI: University of Hawaii Press.

Long, Susan O., ed. (1999) *Lives in Motion: Composing Circles of Self and Community in Japan.* Ithaca, NY: Cornell East Asia Series.

Nakane, Chie. (1970) *Japanese Society.* Berkeley and Los Angeles: University of California Press.

Smith, Robert J. (1974) *Ancestor Worship in Contemporary Japan.* Stanford, CA: Stanford University Press.

———. (1983). *Japanese Society: Tradition, Self, and the Social Order.* New York: Cambridge University Press.

Traphagan, John W. (2000). *Taming Oblivion: Aging Bodies and the Fear of Senility in Japan.* Albany, NY: State University of New York Press.

SOCIAL STRATIFICATION—CHINA

When the socialist government of Mao Zedong (1893–1976) came to power in 1949, one of its major goals was to reduce the stark inequalities of income and wealth that existed at that time. To this end, the government appropriated most private property, expanded public education, abolished labor markets, and instituted wage controls. By the early 1960s, inequalities of income and wealth in rural and urban areas were sharply reduced, and living standards for most Chinese were greatly improved. Ironically, however, socialism introduced new inequalities—among those who did and did not have network ties to government officials and Communist Party members and among those who did and did not work in state-owned firms. Furthermore, one of the most serious inequalities in pre-1949 China—the disparity in income and living conditions between urban and rural areas—was never eradicated under Mao. Just two years after Mao's death in 1976, many of the policies designed to abolish economic inequalities were incrementally dismantled in an effort to marketize the economy. Post-Mao market socialism could reverse many of the equalizing trends of the Maoist era.

Stratification under Mao

In the decades before 1949, China was continuously pummeled by war, acts of imperialism, and domestic turmoil. By the time Mao's government ascended to power, China had become a society in which a small proportion of well-to-do Chinese lived alongside countless impoverished people. In rural areas, where about 80 percent of the population lived, 70 percent of farmers were landless and worked for subsistence wages for a small number of landowners. In cities, unemployment was high, and begging and prostitution were rampant. Thus, the government was faced with the immediate problem of raising living standards for a mostly destitute population.

Reshaping Stratification in Cities The government sought to address economic inequalities in urban areas by appropriating wealth and abolishing labor markets. Privately owned housing was seized and subdivided into much smaller living spaces. Families could rent these apartments but never purchase them, thus eliminating a key means through which inequalities of wealth can be perpetuated from generation to generation.

By 1958, virtually all privately owned urban businesses had been appropriated and socialized as well. Furthermore, in an effort to ensure full employment, market competition for jobs in these firms was eliminated. People leaving school were assigned to jobs bureaucratically. The masses of urban unemployed were either assigned to jobs in factories or businesses or were sent to rural areas to work in agriculture. Once matched to a job, an employee could not quit voluntarily. But employees could not be fired either and thus essentially had a guarantee of lifelong employment.

Urban inequalities were further reduced through salary compression in firms. Differences in the salaries paid for high-skill, high-prestige occupations such as doctors and other professionals, and low-prestige jobs such as unskilled factory work, were much smaller than is typical in capitalist economies. Efforts were also made to increase the social prestige attached to manual labor and to downplay the social importance of white-collar work.

As a result of these economic policies, income inequalities during the Maoist era plummeted. For example, the richest 10 percent of the urban population took in only 21 percent of total urban income, a figure about ten percentage points lower than the average for other developing countries at that time. Living standards for the average urban resident improved substantially.

Furthermore, the determinants of socioeconomic status were different from those in capitalist economies. In capitalist economies, socioeconomic position is largely dictated by income, and therefore by one's educational level. The highest-paying jobs require a long period of education, and there is a big difference in pay between jobs that do and do not require extensive educational training. Mao's government expanded public education a great deal. However, salary compression in urban firms meant that the payoff in income for a lengthy education was not great.

Instead, nonmonetary employment benefits became a much more important source of stratification in urban areas, and these were determined not by what a person did on the job but by the type of work organization in which he or she did it. Though nearly all urban work organizations were government owned, they were not all administered by the same government offices. About three-fourths of urban residents were employed in state-owned work organizations, which were controlled by the central government. The rest worked in collectively owned organizations that were controlled and operated at the municipal level. State-owned firms were allocated bigger budgets and more resources and thus could afford to provide their employees with generous fringe benefits like housing, health insurance, pension plans, and consumer goods. In general, collectively owned firms could not provide such benefits and could pay employees a salary only about three-fourths of what they would have received in state-owned firms. Because housing, health insurance, and pension plans could not be acquired through markets or other government channels, placement in a state-owned firm became the goal among urban Chinese.

Important inequalities also emerged among those who did and did not have personal ties to government officials and Communist Party members. In the absence of markets, government officials and party members had monopoly control over the allocation of economic rewards. Individuals with ties to officials or party members could use these connections to maximize career opportunities or nonwage work benefits.

Maoist Policies in Rural China The socialists also attempted to reduce rural economic inequalities by confiscating resources from the wealthy. In rural China, this wealth consisted primarily of agricultural land. Many well-to-do landlords were killed in retribution for their exploitation of tenant farmers. Starting in 1951, confiscated land was redistributed equally to all rural households, for them to farm privately. However, just a few years later, in 1953, the government began taking this land back, designating it as community property. Families were required to work larger plots of land collectively, in groups of twenty to forty households, and the harvest was split between government and the collective. Individuals were paid for their work in points, which were periodically traded in for money and grain. While average household incomes in rural areas remained low, this collective system of farming raised living standards for poor families and produced communities with much less economic stratification than before.

Gender and Socialism One subjugated social group especially targeted by rural and urban economic policies was women. Prior to 1949, Chinese women had very little social status or political and economic power. Their low social position was underpinned by a patriarchal, patrilineal family structure. Male household heads had near-absolute power in the household and held legal right to all family property. Women—especially new brides joining the family—were marginal, powerless members, who were often treated as servants. Fathers and brothers could provide no protection from abusive treatment by in-laws, since a woman lost most ties to her natal family after marriage.

One key way that Mao's government tried to rupture this family structure was by pulling women into the paid labor force. In urban areas they were incorporated into a growing industrial sector, and in rural areas they were put to work in agriculture. The idea was that women would be able to wield more power within their families if they had an independent income.

Efforts to reduce gender inequalities were somewhat successful. It became routine in both rural and urban areas for women to work, and as a result of being employed their status in the family improved. However, there was—and remains—a great deal of gender segregation in the workforce, with women usually assigned to lower paying jobs and given lowest priority for nonmonetary benefits such as housing. Especially in rural areas, Chinese families remained strongly patriarchal, because the tradition of patrilineal marriage was never challenged by the government.

The Rural-Urban Gap Though Maoist economic policies reduced inequalities within rural and urban communities, there remained a substantial gap in income and living standards between rural and urban areas. As in all developing countries, urban residents in China prior to 1949 enjoyed much higher living standards than rural residents, because of better access to education and good-paying jobs. After both rural and urban economies were socialized, this gap began to get smaller. In 1957, for example, urban residents took in three times the income of rural residents. By 1978, urban incomes were 2.36 times greater than rural incomes. Thus the rural-urban gap was smaller, but still substantial, under Mao. Urban residents continued to have much better access to schools, medical care, and retirement pensions. Generous government investment in urban industries, and low state-set prices for agricultural goods, were factors that kept the rural-urban gap from completely disappearing. Migration laws preventing rural residents from moving to urban areas also kept urban incomes high, by limiting the supply of labor for urban industries.

Stratification after Mao

Just two years after Mao's death in 1976, the new leader, Deng Xiaoping (1904–1997), began to implement economic policies designed to marketize China's economy. In urban areas, private businesses were legalized, and foreign investment was encouraged. A private sector grew quickly, so that by 1999 nearly 35 million urban residents were employed in privately owned firms, according to government estimates. In July 2001, it became legal for private business owners to join the Chinese Communist Party, a further indication of the growing acceptance of private enterprise. Likewise, reforms were instituted in publicly owned firms, requiring them to operate more like private ones. Managers were given greater autonomy in setting wages for workers and also came under greater pressure to operate in the black. Post-Mao economic policies also sought incrementally to institute labor markets in urban areas, in both public and private firms. By the late 1990s, residents of large cities were no longer assigned to jobs by the government and, once employed, could quit or be laid off from their jobs.

Post-Mao economic reforms have reintroduced substantial economic inequalities in urban communities, in part because some residents now earn very high salaries in foreign-invested firms. An equally important contributing factor is the growing unemployment problem. Pressure on public firms to be more profitable after Mao's death gave managers incentives to cut labor costs. Layoffs are becoming more and more common as a result, especially among middle-aged women. Some employers lay employees off to deal with an overstaffing problem. Others wish to replace their urban employees with cheaper recruits from rural ar-

eas, who have been allowed to migrate to urban areas and work in urban firms since 1983. By 1988 about 2 percent of the urban population was unemployed, a figure that is large compared with the Maoist era and increasing every year. Urban unemployment is publicly acknowledged as a serious and growing social problem.

Post-Mao market reforms in rural areas have also been extensive. Beginning in the late 1970s, collective farming groups were disbanded, and rural families were once again assigned land for use at their own discretion. Rural families also became free to allocate household labor to nonagricultural work. Rural families now routinely have one or more members working in industrial jobs, which bring much better pay than agriculture. Encouragement of private enterprise in rural areas has resulted in a mushrooming of industrial work opportunities in rural villages and towns.

Because of these burgeoning industrial job opportunities for rural residents, and because household agricultural production gives rural families greater profit incentives than collective agriculture, rural residents have become much more affluent, on average, than they were during the Maoist era. At the same time, economic inequalities within communities have increased, as some rural residents benefit more than others from these new opportunities.

That post-Mao economic reforms have increased inequalities in both rural and urban communities is not controversial. However, scholars disagree about whether upward economic mobility is still most advantageously pursued through personal ties to political actors. Some sociologists have argued that, as a socialist economy marketizes, political actors such as Communist Party members or government officials lose their monopoly control over economic resources. Opportunities for upward economic mobility open up among individuals who are not political actors or who lack ties to political actors, and the relative economic advantage of those with political capital declines. Individuals with education or work experience start to see greater returns for those attributes. Thus, for example, in a private, profit-driven business, someone with a college education but no political ties will be a more attractive job candidate than someone who has political connections but no college degree.

Others have argued that political actors still maintain privileged access to economic resources or are able to convert their political power into market resources easily. For example, a Communist Party member who wishes to become an entrepreneur can cut through the red tape required to establish a private business much faster than someone who is not a party member.

Changing Social Stratification

Contemporary China is a fascinating case study for social stratification. Since a socialist government was established in 1949, China has undergone an enormous amount of purposive social change in a very short time. Maoist efforts to change the stratification system demonstrate that economic policies can be an effective tool in reducing economic inequalities. In a matter of two decades or so, China went from a country with a large impoverished population in both rural and urban areas to one in which most citizens enjoyed a decent standard of living and in which the distribution of economic rewards was much more equal. Once the post-Mao government began to dismantle these economic policies, however, many of the equalizing trends of the Maoist era began to reverse.

Mao's China has also demonstrated that although reductions in inequalities can be made, it is difficult to eradicate them altogether. The concerted efforts to eliminate gender inequalities were only somewhat successful, and the rural-urban income gap never completely closed. Socialism also introduced new sources of stratification: among those who did and did not have personal ties to political actors and among those assigned to different types of work units.

Rebecca Matthews

Further Reading

(2000) *China Statistical Yearbook.* Beijing: China Statistics Press.

Griffin, Keith, and Renwei Zhao, eds. (1993) *The Distribution of Income in China.* New York: St. Martin's.

Johnson, Kay Ann. (1983) *Women, the Family, and Peasant Revolution in China.* Chicago: University of Chicago Press.

Meisner, Maurice. (1986) *Mao's China and After.* New York: Free Press.

Nee, Victor. (1999) "The Emergence of a Market Society: Changing Mechanisms of Stratification in China." *American Journal of Sociology* 101: 908–949.

Parish, William L., and Martin King Whyte. (1978) *Village and Family in Contemporary China.* Chicago: University of Chicago Press.

Walder, Andrew G. (1986) *Communist Neo-Traditionalism: Work and Authority in Chinese Industry.* Berkeley and Los Angeles: University of California Press.

Whyte, Martin King, and William L. Parish. (1984) *Urban Life in Contemporary China.* Chicago: University of Chicago Press.

Zhou, Xueguang. (2000) "Economic Transformation and Income Inequality in Urban China: Evidence from Panel Data." *American Journal of Sociology* 105: 1135–1174.

SOCIALIST SPIRITUAL CIVILIZATION— CHINA

After the Chinese Communist Party (CCP) adopted economic reform and liberalization policies in the late 1970s, many party members began to worry that if China pursued only the goals of economic development, society might advance in material terms but regress spiritually. The Cultural Revolution (1966– 1976) had done irrevocable damage to the Chinese moral universe. Unbridled pursuit of economic development now could lead to a society whose citizens were materially wealthy but selfish, grasping, and base. They would become psychologically alienated: suspicious and mistrustful of others and unable to cooperate either for the public or their own good. Eventually, material advancement itself would grind to a halt.

Concern mounted as Western films, television programs, and popular music surged into China in the early 1980s. Most of this popular culture would not normally be seen as seriously challenging the Chinese way of life, but older comrades, in particular, feared that in the spiritual vacuum that prevailed following the Cultural Revolution, even otherwise innocuous concepts and products could do great damage. They decided to launch a "campaign against spiritual pollution" in 1983 but had to cut it short after a few months when it started negatively affecting the economy. Clearly, in any contest between material and spiritual civilization, the CCP would favor the material. Nevertheless, the CCP did formally adopt "building a socialist spiritual civilization" as a fundamental government goal at a special CCP meeting in September 1986.

No one believes the CCP achieved this goal or even made significant progress toward it. The problem was twofold. First, there was no clearly articulated image of what a socialist spiritual civilization would look like. What should people think and do to build one? How should they change their behavior? Usually the answers were that people should "have lofty ideals," "proceed from a scientific spirit," "love genuinely beautiful things," and other vague banalities. They should also do the opposite of anything defined as bad in the present. For example, if corruption was defined as bad, they should not be corrupt; if spitting on the sidewalk was defined as bad, they should not spit.

Second, the incentive structures necessary to build material civilization frequently rewarded behaviors opposite to those necessary to build spiritual civilization. Too many "lofty ideals" and too much altruism would lead inexorably to failure in the brutally competitive economy. To get rich was undeniably glorious, but no individual could be assured that today's wealth would not be confiscated in some arbitrary way tomorrow. Self-protection took precedence over concern for the achievement of nebulous public goals. Eventually, a new antimorality took hold that stressed the "virtues" of not being so foolish as to take building a socialist spiritual civilization seriously.

Daniel C. Lynch

Further Reading

Deng Xiaoping. (1987) *Fundamental Issues in Present-Day China.* Beijing: Foreign Languages Press.

Lynch, Daniel C. (1999) *After the Propaganda State: Media, Politics, and "Thought Work" in Reformed China.* Stanford, CA: Stanford University Press.

SOIL LOSS Soil loss threatens Asia's food self-sufficiency, and is listed among the Green Revolution's deleterious effects. (The Green Revolution was a combination of land-tenure reform with research on high-yield varieties and petroleum-based fertilizers and soil additives to augment crop yields in developing countries during the post–World War II period.) The 1977 United Nations Conference on Desertification is credited with bringing attention to soil loss as a threat to sustainable agriculture in Asia. The United Nations Development Program, Food and Agricultural Organization, and Environment Program estimate that half of South Asia's arable soil suffers from degradation. A tripartite study concluded that 43 percent of the region's agricultural land was degraded, affecting Iran most severely, followed by Bangladesh, Pakistan, Sri Lanka, Afghanistan, Nepal, and Bhutan.

The leading cause of soil degradation is erosion; both water and wind detach soil particles and sediment. Hydrological processes, such as sheet and gully erosion, and rilling account for two-thirds of erosion. Soil erosion is expected to seriously compromise food production in the Himalayan foothills, Southeast Asia, and parts of southern China, where government policy prohibits cultivation on slopes steeper than 28 percent. Mass wasting and wind are responsible for the remainder of erosion. In Kazakhstan, the Institute for Soil Management estimates that due to the abandonment of areas degraded by wind erosion, available cropland will be reduced by one-fourth. Rather than representing an extreme case, this is characteristic of the post-Soviet abandonment of marginal, frequently heavily eroded land.

A secondary cause of soil degradation is compaction caused by mechanical tilling. During the Soviet period, agricultural areas of the Newly Independent States (NIS, also known as the Former Soviet Union) experienced expansion of extensive, mechanical cultivation. These areas' soils suffer from compaction due to the use of heavy agricultural machinery. Soil compaction continues to compromise Asian agricultural productivity. Soil depletion is also caused by perennial irrigation practices. Depletion of soil nutrients through repeated plantings during a given agricultural year is an identified cause of soil degradation, leading to abandonment of previously productive acreage in extreme cases. Poor water management, in particular

Soil erosion caused by logging in a rain forest in Borneo. (GALLO IMAGES/CORBIS)

inadequate drainage, is the fourth factor leading to soil degradation. Inadequate drainage leads to waterlogging, or saturation with water, and salinization, excessive saltiness hindering plant growth, which can decrease productivity. In order to mitigate salinity, cultivators in Asia Minor and the Middle East leave 60 percent of rain-fed land fallow each year.

Elizabeth Bishop

Further Reading

Brown, Lester R., and Jennifer D. Mitchell, (1997) "The Agricultural Link: How Environmental Deterioration Could Disrupt Economic Progress." Worldwatch Paper no. 136. Washington, DC: Worldwatch Institute.

Lal, R. (1994) "Soil Erosion by Wind and Water: Problems and Prospects." In *Soil Erosion Research Methods*, edited by R. Lal. Ankeny, IA: Soil and Water Conservation Society, 1–9.

SOL The traditional Korean Lunar New Year's Day (Sol or Sollal) has long been one of the most festive days of the year and is still observed by many Koreans. The lunar calendar year begins on the new moon occurring in the latter part of January or in February. Sol is a family celebration beginning in the predawn hours following the end of Sottal, the last lunar month of the year. For this day, family members gather from far and near at the home of the oldest male member for ancestral rites and entertainment.

The first of two ancestral rites, *charye*, is held before sunrise in the home or sometimes in a family shrine. Tables of foods are offered to the souls of ancestors, followed by full bows. The second memorial rite, *songmyo*, is held at the ancestral tombs or burial mounds, often situated on hillsides near ancestral homes. Here, too, food offerings and solemn ceremonial bows are made.

Early in the morning before breakfast, younger family members, dressed in new or traditional clothes, greet older relatives with a ceremonial bow and wishes of good health and good fortune in the new year. The New Year's meal invariably includes rice cake soup (*ttokguk*). The white slices of rice cake symbolize the solemnity of the occasion and the desire for the new year to be free of misfortune. It is said that after eating a bowl of rice cake soup on this day, one becomes a year older, following the Korean custom of calculating age by the number of calendar years in which one has lived.

The latter part of the day turns festive with the family playing the traditional game of *yut*, a board game with four douse-like sticks that determine how quickly the players may move through the course on the board. Good fortune throughout the new year is believed to be prize for the winning side. The game of the day for young girls and women is bouncing on seesaws consisting of a plank with sheaves of straw or a rolled-up straw mat underneath. Standing on the ends of the

The traditional Korean Confucian New Year's Day celebration includes prayers and food. (NATAHN BENN/CORBIS)

plank, the participants in turn are bounced high into the air. One explanation is that the game derived from the custom of not allowing the womenfolk outside of the walls surrounding the home. By seesawing in the courtyard, young ladies would have the rare opportunity to get a glimpse of any young man who might be passing by outside the walls.

Though both the lunar New Year's Day and the solar (1 January) are official holidays in South Korea, the solar holiday has been reduced to a single day because many people prefer the traditional lunar New Year's Day for the observance of some of Korea's most traditional customs.

David E. Shaffer

See also: **Sottal**

Further Reading
Adams, Edward B. (1995) *Korea Guide.* 8th edition. Seoul: Seoul International Publishing House.
Koo, John H., and Andrew C. Nahm, eds. (1997) *An Introduction to Korean Culture.* Elizabeth, NJ: Hollym.

SOLO (1999 est. pop. 590,000). Solo (Surakarta in Indonesian; Soerakarta in Dutch) is a city on the Solo River in Central Java Province, Java, Indonesia. An important historical and cultural center in Indonesia, Solo was the capital of the powerful Surakarta principality under the Dutch, which in the eighteenth century controlled a significant part of Java.

The area of Central Java was one of the most significant political and cultural centers in the history of Javanese civilization. The history of Solo began when Sunan Paku Buwana II, the king of Mataram, gave orders that a location be found to set up a new capital city of the Mataram kingdom. In 1746, a village on the Solo River was chosen for development. The power of Mataram, however, was weakened by internal political instability and rivalry between traditional rulers. Under the Giyanti Treaty, on 13 February 1755, the Mataram kingdom was divided into two parts, Surakarta and Yogyakarta. The Dutch East India Company established control over both principalities. When in 1949 Indonesia won its independence from the Dutch, the Surakarta principality was incorporated into Central Java Province. It became a commercial center for this region, relying on agriculture and small-scale manufacturing—of goods such as batik cloth, fine metal products, woodcarvings, and traditional musical instruments—as well as tourism.

Rafis Abazov

Further Reading
Florida, Nancy. (2000) *Javanese Literature in Surakarta Manuscripts.* 2 vols. Ithaca, NY: Southeast Asia Program, Cornell University.
Van Groenendael, Victoria M. Clara. (1985) *The Dalang behind the Wayang: The Role of the Surakarta and the Yogyakarta Dalang in Indonesian-Javanese Society.* Dordrecht, Netherlands: Floris.

SONG DYNASTY China's Song dynasty (960–1279) was founded by Zhao Kuangyin (temple name Taizu, reigned 960–976) during a mutiny in 960. The Song achievements are so dynamic and brilliant that some historians claim this dynasty marks the beginning of "modern" China. The Song is divided into two periods. The Northern Song (960–1126) ended when its capital city, Kaifeng, in north China, was captured by the Jurchen Jin dynasty (1125–1234). The Southern Song, whose capital city was located in the south at Linan (present-day Hangzhou), was conquered by the Mongol Yuan dynasty (1279–1368) in 1279.

Political Changes

The Song dynasty was founded when Taizu, the palace army commander-in-chief of the Later Zhou dynasty (951–960), one of the dynasties that ruled part of China during the period of disunity between the Tang and Song dynasties, was supported by his rebellious troops in claiming the imperial throne. To centralize power at the court, Taizu persuaded his military officers to give up their commands in exchange for honorary titles, sinecure offices, and generous pensions. Meanwhile, he stressed the Confucian spirit of humane administration and promoted the civil service examination as the most prestigious means of government recruitment. Under the examination system, candidates for government offices went through a series of tests at three levels: prefecture, Ministry of Rites, and imperial palace. To succeed in the examinations, candidates had to memorize the Confucian classics and be able to answer questions regarding statecraft and imperial policies. Through the examination system, the Song recruited new groups of excellent scholar-officials who, though they lacked previous bureaucratic background, dominated the higher policy-making levels of government. Unlike the old aristocratic families who held power during the Tang dynasty (618–907), this new gentry ruling elite neither enjoyed guaranteed continuity of official status nor was restricted in its upward social mobility. Success in the Song was based on literary learning, examination degree, office holding, and landownership.

Under Emperor Taizong (reigned 976–997), the basic institutions of the new dynasty were adopted. The central government was divided into three major departments: Secretariat-Chancellery, Bureau of Military Affairs, and State Finance Commission, which were independent of one another but were under the emperor's direct supervision. To maintain disciplinary surveillance over officialdom, the court established independent surveillance and remonstrance officials under the offices of the Censorate and the Remonstrance Bureau.

In local areas, the lowest unit of formal government was the district. Districts were in turn grouped in prefectures. The court also established the supervisory units—circuits—to coordinate the relations between prefectures and the central government. Song government was more autocratic than government under previous dynasties had been.

Wang Anshi's Reforms During Emperor Shenzong's reign (1068–1085), growing problems in finance and foreign relations led Chief Counselor Wang Anshi (1021–1086) to launch a multifaceted reform program. He created a fund for low-interest agricultural loans to farmers and small merchants, who were thereby spared the exorbitant demands of moneylenders. He had new land surveys conducted so that property taxes could be assessed more equitably, and he instituted a system that made the government an active agent in trade. Wang also established a village militia system for local policing and for the buildup of army reserves; he replaced corvée labor with a hired service system financed by a graduated tax levied on all families; he emphasized professional courses in law, medicine, and military science in the civil service examinations; and he brought government clerks under stricter supervision and provided incentives for promotion. The reform programs, while achieving some success in certain areas, were largely undermined by determined opposition from the groups that were hurt by the reform measures—large landowners, big merchants, and moneylenders. The opposition vigorously attacked the reformers and forced Wang to resign office.

Wang Anshi's reforms and the conservative opposition to them divided the bureaucracy and weakened the dynasty. During the reign of Emperor Huizong (1101–1125), who is better remembered as an artist and patron of the arts than as an effective ruler, court extravagance weakened the dynasty's finances, the bureaucracy continued to grow, corruption increased, and other signs of dynastic decline—including peasant rebellions—appeared.

CHINA—HISTORICAL PERIODS

Xia dynasty (2100–1766 BCE)
Shang dynasty (1766–1045 BCE)
Zhou dynasty (1045–256 BCE)
    Western Zhou (1045–771 BCE)
    Eastern Zhou (770–221 BCE)
Spring and Autumn period (770–476 BCE)
Warring States period (475–221 BCE)
Qin dynasty (221–206 BCE)
Han dynasty (206 BCE–220 CE)
Three Kingdoms period (220–265 CE)
North and South dynasties (220–589 CE)
Sui dyansty (581–618 CE)
Tang dynasty (618–907 CE)
Five Dynasties period (907–960 CE)
Song dynasty (960–1279)
    Northern Song (960–1126)
    Southern Song (1127–1279)
Jurchen Jin dynasty (1125–1234)
Yuan dynasty (1279–1368)
Ming dynasty (1368–1644)
Qing dynasty (1644–1912)
Republican China (1912–1927)
People's Republic of China (1949–present)
Republic of China (1949–present)
Cultural Revolution (1966–1976)

Threats from the North However, the most serious threat to the dynasty came from the northern nomadic empires. Since the founding of the dynasty, the Song had been harried by raids and invasions from neighboring regimes to the north: the Khitan Liao (907–1125), the Tangut Xi Xia (1032–1227), and the Jurchen Jin. After failed efforts to recover territories lost in northern China, the Song keyed military strategy to defense. The dynasty concluded a peace treaty with the Liao in 1005, in which the Song acknowledged loss of territory and agreed to pay the Liao a handsome annual tribute. The Song signed similar agreements with Xi Xia and the Jurchen Jin as well, all of which severely weakened the Song regime. In the early twelfth century, the Jin attacked the Song capital of Kaifeng and captured the Chinese emperor and the entire imperial house, thus ending the Northern Song.

Establishment of the Southern Song In 1127 Song loyalists put Gaozong (r. 1127–1162) on the throne and established the Southern Song in Hangzhou, south of the Chang (Yangtze) River. In his efforts to restore the ruling house, Gaozong recruited bureaucrats, secured fiscal resources, and extended centralized control. The new ruler, however, did not want to prolong the war with the Jurchens; he valued most the security of his realm. In 1141, on the eve of concluding peace negotiations with the Jurchen Jin dynasty, Gaozong ordered the execution of one of his generals, Yue Fei (1103–1141), who had openly criticized the peace negotiations. Yue Fei later became a symbol of patriotism for refusing to give up on restoring all of China's lost territory. In the treaty of 1142, the Song accepted the Huai River as its northern boundary, agreed to make annual payments to the Jin, and recognized the Jin as its superior. In subsequent years, the Jurchens continued raiding the Southern Song until they were destroyed by the combined attacks of the Mongols and the Southern Song in 1234.

During the Southern Song period, the political system became more centralized. At first, Gaozong delegated power to a team of ministers, who, because of the crisis situation, exercised both civil and military authority. In 1139, however, the ministerial team was dispensed with, and Chief Counselor Qin Gui (1090–1155), the chief minister who was responsible for the execution of Yue Fei, exercised sole power on behalf of the emperor. This institutional change toward absolutism was to continue throughout the Southern Song. Under Emperor Ningzong (reigned 1194–1224), chief counselors Han Tuozhou (1151–1207) and Shi Miyuan (1164–1233) held power successively. The last powerful official of the Southern Song was Jia Sidao (1213–1275), who became chief counselor in 1259 and remained in office until shortly before the dynasty collapsed. Jia tried to strengthen the government by dismissing many incompetents and curbing excessive corruption. By then, however, the Mongols under Khubilai Khan (1215–1294) of the Yuan dynasty (1279–1368) were across the Chang River. Hangzhou was captured without a fight in 1276; and the dynasty ended in 1279 when the last imperial heir died in Guangzhou and the Song fleet was finally destroyed.

Socioeconomic Changes

The Song represents an era of dramatic social and economic changes. The economic focus of the dynasty shifted south. For the first time in Chinese history, more people lived in the rice-growing region of the Chang River valley than in other parts of the country. In agriculture, new types of rice entered China from Champa during the eleventh century; the new varieties shortened the growing season and produced two or three crops a year in the south. Combined with technical improvements in damming methods and water pumps, farmers could grow wet-field rice, the most labor-intensive but also most productive form of agri-

culture, in a much wider range of terrains and climates than before. The increased yields provided food supplies for a population of more than 100 million. Improved tools also raised manpower efficiency.

In manufacturing, Chinese porcelain made in such towns as Jingdezhen gained international fame. Paper making and all the processes involved in book production advanced. Silk products were widely consumed in society, and shipbuilding gained new importance as maritime trade became more important to the economy. Production of gold, silver, lead, and tin also increased, and new techniques and technology made possible the production of more than 100,000 tons of pig iron and steel each year.

A commercial revolution was a remarkable feature of the Song economic transformation. To a great extent, the Song developed a market economy. With different regions specializing in the production of various commodities, a nationwide market was formed in China. Numerous market centers flourished in all cities and major towns, where shops and stalls sold products drawn from all over the country. Commercial organizations became more sophisticated. Brokers provided active services between transaction parties. Some merchants combined brokerage with the operation of storehouses and hostels. An early form of bank, called a deposit shop, was developed in many parts of the empire to facilitate the transactions. Merchants used drafts called *feiquan* ("flying money") and certificates of deposit to reduce the danger of robbery and other inconveniences. During the eleventh century, the Song became the first rulers in the world to issue paper money; its use became widespread. International trade also flourished under the Song. With well-equipped junks, Chinese sailors and merchants moved southward and linked up with merchants from Persia and Arabia.

Commercialization was greatly facilitated by improved communication networks, which made products available even in remote places. Along the government-maintained highways, private hostels and inns served busy traders. Convenient waterways reduced the cost of traveling and shipping. Aided by compasses and other instruments, Song ships navigated the high seas. The market economy had progressed to such a state that the government levied more taxes in commerce than in agriculture or industry. By 1065 the Northern Song government was taking in annual cash tax payments that were twenty times what the Tang had received in 749. The income of the Southern Song consisted of more cash revenues than grain and textile receipts (grain and textiles were also accepted as tax payments at this time).

Economic vitality stimulated the process of urbanization. China had numerous cities with over 100,000 people; the populations of several metropolitan areas approached one million. The Tang city style of strictly regulated and enclosed market blocks was replaced by open trade centers and proliferating stores. The Northern Song capital of Kaifeng, as illustrated in Zhang Zeduan's scroll *Spring Festival on the River* (c. 1186), was filled with stores, stands, restaurants, ships, trade guilds, clinics, and hostels. With a population of perhaps two million and a location near the East China Sea, the Southern Song capital of Hangzhou grew in response to market forces and mercantile necessities, serving as a port for foreign trade. For the first time in China's history, maritime trade became a significant component of the economy, and tariffs substantially contributed to government revenue.

Women were active participants in social life. They bore and reared children, advised husbands and taught sons pursuing official careers, assisted husbands in performing ancestral rites, managed household affairs, and worked by raising silkworms, making clothes, planting grain, pounding rice, selling goods, or keeping books. Women also had the right to own property and were able to inherit their families' property. Despite growing emphasis on the virtue of female chastity, women had the legal right to remarry, and many did. Many women, such as the great poet Li Qingzhao (1084–c. 1151), contributed to the cultural output of the dynasty. Song women suffered a decline in social standing with the spread of foot binding, a custom that was not abandoned until the twentieth century.

Cultural and Intellectual Changes

The most remarkable feature of the Song intellectual world was the advent of Neo-Confucianism. The Neo-Confucian upsurge that had begun in the late Tang embraced many forms, including classical scholarship, historical studies, political reforms, and moral and spiritual cultivation. During the Northern Song, a new Confucian metaphysics emerged, borrowing from Taoism, Buddhism, and classical Confucianism. Confucianists developed ideas such as "Great Ultimate" (*taiji*), "principle" (*li*), "material force" (*qi*), and "mind-and-heart" (*xin*). These ideas were later synthesized by Zhu Xi (1130–1200) into a belief system that was labeled either "Learning of Principle" (*lixue*) or "Learning of the Way" (*daoxue*). To Zhu Xi and his followers, *taiji* was the origin of the universe. Everything that existed was a combination of *li* and *qi*. Education, which consisted of mastering Confucian classics such as the Four Books, meant a deep self-cultivation of moral consciousness and apprehension of universal principles and the true Way. A moral society constituted the only foundation for good government. To propagate his teachings, Zhu Xi developed a curriculum for both educated elite and general audiences and offered lectures at private academies. Although other forms of Neo-Confucianism also flourished at the time, it was Zhu Xi's school of thought that was later declared the state orthodoxy and guided the imperial dynasties through to the early twentieth century.

The Song saw remarkable accomplishments in arts, literature, and historical studies. Landscape painting flourished; artists incorporated cosmological meanings in pictures of natural objects. The Song style of lyric poetry (*ci*) and prose exerted long-lasting influence on later times. By the tenth century, great literary projects were completed, including the *Taiping yulan* (Imperially Reviewed Encyclopedia of the Taiping Era) and *Cefu yuangui* (Outstanding Models from the Storehouse of Literature). Song scholars wrote the first books on ancient bronze bells and tripods and coins, studies that started scientific archaeology in China.

The most famous historical work of the Song was the *Zizhi tongjian* (Comprehensive Mirror for Aid in Government) by Sima Guang (1019–1086). A chronicle that carries the history of China from 403 BCE to 959 CE, this masterpiece marked an important new level for its own genre as well as for general historiography. The *Tonjian jishi benmo* (Comprehensive Mirror, Topically Arranged, c. 1170), in which the chronological entries of the *Zizhi tongjian* were rearranged according to topics, became a model for the third major type of Chinese historical writing (after annals and annal-biographies).

Science and technology also made tremendous progress in the Song. One of the most significant advances was woodblock printing, which was widely used for official documents, classical scholarship, religious texts, medical manuals, calligraphy, and cartography. By the middle of the eleventh century, an artisan named Bi Sheng had invented movable characters, although the invention had little chance to replace woodblock industry at that time. Although explosive powder had been invented in the Tang, it was during the Song that the material was widely applied by the military in a variety of grenades, bombs, and rocket launchers. It was also during the Song that compasses, which had been used by the Chinese for centuries, were first employed in sea navigation. The invention of the abacus, the forerunner of the present-day calculator, facilitated transactions in commercial activities. The world's first treatise on forensic medicine for coroners, the *Xiyuan jilu* (Manual of Forensic Medicine) by Song Ci (1186–1249), was completed in 1247.

Historians tend to characterize the Song as modern because of its breaks with earlier patterns and its new features that approximated later developments. The era saw one of the most sophisticated civilizations of the world in the domains of political institutions, thought systems, science and technology, economic activities, social life, and arts and letters. Even after the Mongol conquest, many of the trends begun under the Song continued their course in Chinese lives.

Jiang Yonglin

Further Reading

Bol, Peter K. (1992) *"This Culture of Ours": Intellectual Transitions in T'ang and Sung China*. Stanford, CA: Stanford University Press.

Ebrey, Patricia. (1993) *The Inner Quarters: Marriage and the Lives of Chinese Women in the Sung Period*. Berkeley and Los Angeles: University of California Press.

Gernet, Jacques. (1962) *Daily Life in China on the Eve of the Mongol Invasion, 1250–1276*. Trans. by H. M. Wright. Stanford, CA: Stanford University Press.

Haeger, John Winthrop, ed. (1975) *Crisis and Prosperity in Sung China*. Tucson, AZ: University of Arizona Press.

SONG ZIWEN

SONG ZIWEN (1894–1971), Chinese Nationalist government official. Better known to Westerners as T. V. Soong, Song Ziwen was an official of the Chinese Nationalist government and a prominent financier. He was born in 1894 and educated at Harvard University, returning to China in 1923 to engage in private business. At the request of brother-in-law Sun Yat-sen (1866–1925), he took over the role of financing the Guomindang (Chinese Nationalist Party) from his father. To this end, he established the Central Bank of China in 1924. The bank became the government treasury in 1928 when Song was appointed minister of finance by another brother-in-law, Chiang Kai-shek (1887–1975). He was devoted to modernizing Chinese financial and fiscal systems during his tenure (1928–1931, 1932–1933). During the second Sino-Japanese conflict (1937–1945), he became minister of foreign affairs in 1942. When the war was over in 1945, he became prime minister (president of the Executive Yuan) and served in this position until 1947. Just prior to the Communist takeover of China in 1949, he moved to the United States, where he remained active in business, banking, and the China Lobby until his death in 1971.

Jody C. Baumgartner

Further Reading

Coble, Parks M., Jr. (1986) *The Shanghai Capitalists and the Nationalist Government, 1927–1937*. Harvard East Asian Monographs, no. 94. 2d ed. Cambridge, MA: Harvard University Press.

Seagrave, Sterling. (1985) *The Soong Dynasty*. New York: Harper & Row.

SONGKET

SONGKET *Songket* is cloth decorated with gold and silver thread and is found in the states of the east coast of western Malaysia. A simple traditional loom with treadle-operated heddles and hand-thrown shuttles is used in weaving *songket*. The Malays of coastal Sarawak also weave *songket* on a frame loom.

Songket is created from a supplementary weft of metallic threads on a background of silk. The word *songket* is related to the word *sungkit*, which means "weft wrapping." *Songket* brocade is composed by the *pilih* technique, with the supplementary weft "floating" over

A woman of the Minangkabau ethnic group in Sumatra, Indonesia, wears a *songket* in the shape of a water buffalo, an important animal in Minangkabau culture. (LINDSAY HEBBERD/ CORBIS)

the wrap. *Pilih* means "to choose or pick." The weaver picks out the wrap threads to be passed over. The introduced weft passes on top of as many as five consecutive warp threads, although it is more common to have three. The introduced supplementary weft form patterns on top of the main weave. Because high-quality gold threads are used, the best *songket* is not stiff. Some examples of *songket* have a combination of cotton wrap and silk weft for a firmer foundation weave. Many types of *songket* are patterned with an interplay of geometric forms and are very ornate pieces of cloth.

Shanthi Thambiah

Further Reading
Fraser-Lu, S. (1988) *Handwoven Textiles of South-East Asia.* Singapore: Oxford University Press.
Gullick, J. M. (1952) "A Survey of Malay Weavers and Silversmiths in Kelantan in 1951." *Journal of the Malayan Branch, Royal Asiatic Society* 25, 1: 134–148.
Maxwell, Robyn J. (1987) *Southeast Asian Textiles: The State of the Art.* Clayton, Australia: Monash University.
Nurwani, Mohd Nawawi. (1989) *Malaysian Songket.* Kuala Lumpur, Malaysia: Dewan Bahasa dan Pustaka.
Selvanayagam, Grace Inpam. (1990) *Songket: Malaysia's Woven Treasure.* Singapore: Oxford University Press.

SOT KURAMAROHIT (1908–1978), Thai writer. Originally from Chantaburi on Thailand's eastern border, Sot Kuramarohit studied at the prestigious Thepsirin School in Bangkok; among his contemporaries were several who were to establish themselves as major writers, including M. C. Akatdamkoeng Raphiphat, Chaem Antarasen, and Sanit Charoenrat. He received a government scholarship to study at Beijing University, and when he returned to Thailand in 1936, he was given responsibility for overseeing Chinese schools in the country at a time when they were regarded as a potential Communist threat. His most acclaimed work is *Pakking: nakhon haeng khwam lang* (Beijing: City of the Past), published in 1941. Set in prerevolutionary China, the novel portrays the life of enforced poverty of a member of the Russian royal family who flees to China and ultimately kills himself rather than become a burden on his daughter. Sot's sympathy for the underdog and political idealism were continuing themes in later works, such as *Khabuankan seri chin* (The Free Chinese Movement) and the long and incomplete *Raya*.

David Smyth

Further Reading
Sodermann, Ute. (1971) "Social Criticism in Modern Thai Narrative Fiction." *Journal of the Siam Society* 59: 25–32.

SOTTAL The twelfth and last month of the lunar calendar is traditionally known as Sottal in Korea. Sottal is a thirty-day period beginning between mid-December and the end of January and ending on the eve of lunar New Year's Day, known as Sol. This month was traditionally a time to tie up loose ends and put things in order. It was especially a time to settle outstanding accounts, as no honorable man would allow a debt of his to be carried over into the new year.

The evening of the last day of the month was by far the most important. It was the time of the year-end night watch, Suse. After the end-of-year house cleaning was finished and darkness began to set in, the house was lit inside and out with lamps and lanterns. This was to keep away evil spirits, who were believed to avoid clean and brightly lit places, so that the house would be filled with good fortune for the new year.

Troupes of musicians with drums and gongs went from house to house dancing and playing loud music to drive out any evil spirits that may have been inside. In the royal court a grand exorcising ceremony was performed by twelve masked dancing guards representing the animal signs of the year and four monsterlike, spear-wielding exorcists. On this new year's eve, all were expected to stay awake keeping the night watch till cockcrow. It was believed that if one slept on this night, their eyebrows would turn white. To avoid this, games and activities of all sorts were played.

Sottal customs were actively observed until the end of the Chosun kingdom at the beginning of the twentieth century. Today, Sottal customs have all but disappeared, but it is still customary to settle one's outstanding debts before the beginning of either the lunar or solar new year.

David E. Shaffer

See also: **Sol**

Further Reading
Adams, Edward B. (1995) *Korea Guide.* 8th ed. Seoul: Seoul International Publishing House.
Choe, Sang-su. (1983) *Annual Customs of Korea.* Seoul: Seomun-dang.
Koo, John H., and Andrew C. Nahm, eds. (1997) *An Introduction to Korean Culture.* Elizabeth, NJ: Hollym.

SOUPHANOUVONG, PRINCE (1901–1995), Lao political leader. Souphanouvong, or the "Red Prince," born in Luang Prabang in 1901, was the leader of the Pathet Lao, or Lao Nation, resistance government. He studied engineering in Paris, where he met his politically active Vietnamese wife, Nguyen Thi Ky Nam, who encouraged Souphanouvong's political aspirations. He was foreign minister in the Lao Issara, or Free Lao, government from 1945 through 1949. As leader of the Lao Issara armed forces, he fought the French and was wounded at Thakhek in 1946. He then strengthened ties with the Viet Minh. He left the Lao Issara in 1949 due to his radical ideology and formed his own resistance government, the Pathet Lao, in 1950. Souphanouvong formed the Lao People's Party in 1956 with Kaysone Phomvihane, and was a lifelong member of its central committee. He also joined all three coalition governments during the Lao civil war (1956–1975). Souphanouvong was opposed by Prime Minister Souvanna Phouma (1901–1984), his half brother, and was arrested after the collapse of the first coalition government in 1959 but escaped in 1960. He became the first president of the Lao People's Democratic Republic on 2 December 1975 in the Pathet Lao's takeover. The "Red Prince" strengthened ties with Vietnam and the Soviet Union as president until his resignation in 1986.

Linda S. McIntosh

Further Reading

Dommen, Arthur J. (1971) *Conflict in Laos: The Politics of Neutralization.* New York: Praeger.

Souphanouvong. (1989) *Autobiography of Prince Souphanouvong.* Kuala Lumpur, Malaysia: Malaysia Mining Corporation Board.

Stuart-Fox, Martin. (1997) *A History of Laos.* Cambridge, U.K.: Cambridge University Press.

SOUTH ASIA—HISTORY

South Asia here refers to the Indian subcontinent and the adjacent mountain fringe separating that region from the rest of Eurasia. It includes the Indo-Gangetic Plain in present-day Pakistan, India, and Bangladesh; the Himalayas and lesser mountain systems to the north, northwest, and northeast of that plain in Pakistan, India, Nepal, Bhutan, and the southern panhandle of Bangladesh; and the assemblage of hills, plateaus, basins, and coastal plains to the south of the plain, mainly in peninsular India, but also including present-day Sri Lanka.

Pre- and Ancient History

When humans first arrived in South Asia is not known. However, hominid artifacts—without accompanying fossil remains—date back several hundred thousand years, and there can be little doubt that *Homo sapiens* established societies of hunters, fishers, and gatherers in the subcontinent tens of thousands of years ago. Pollen samples from Rajasthan in northwest India indicate the presence of grain cultivation in that region almost ten thousand years ago, while some scholars speculate that rice may have been domesticated in the eastern Indian state of Orissa even earlier. Neolithic village-based culture is traceable to the fifth millennium BCE in Kashmir, while settlements marked by Chalcolithic (Copper and Bronze Age) cultures were present over much of Pakistan and adjacent regions of present-day Afghanistan during the subsequent millennium.

By the mid-fourth millennium BCE, the northwestern Chalcolithic cultures had evolved, with apparent rapidity, into the Harappan or Indus Valley culture. This culture was remarkable in numerous respects: it gave rise to large cities, including Mohenjo Daro and Harappa (both thought to have had as many as fifty thousand inhabitants), with baked-brick structures laid out in grid patterns, with citadels, granaries, public baths, drainage systems, and occupationally segregated quarters. Because the city plan varied relatively little over time, the rulers may have been theocratic; weights and measures were standardized over a wide area; there was a simple system of writing that has yet to be deciphered; agriculture employed simple irrigation techniques and included domestic animals; and there is evidence of long-distance maritime and overland trade.

Little is known about the religion of this culture, though figurines and images on clay seals indicate the worship of a mother goddess and various proto-Hindu deities and the exaltation of cattle, especially bulls. The Indus civilization began to decline in its core region on the Indus Plain early in the third millennium BCE, while expanding on its eastern and southern peripheries. Among the reasons hypothesized for the decline are exhaustion of the resource base; climatic desiccation, earthquakes, floods, and other natural disasters; invasions and conquests by Aryans from Central Asia; or a combination of such causes. By the mid-third millennium BCE, the classic form of the civilization had ceased to exist.

Whether the Sanskrit-speaking Aryans were already in South Asia at the time of the Indus civilization—as were Dravidian- and Austroasiatic-speaking peoples—or arrived in a series of wanderings during and after the mid-second millennium BCE is hotly debated. But without a doubt that period witnessed the emergence in the northwestern part of the subcontinent of a distinctive culture known mainly from its rich collections of orally transmitted hymns, the Vedas. These hymns, set to writing many centuries later, prescribed a simple caste-based social system

KEY EVENTS IN SOUTH ASIAN HISTORY

5,000 BCE   People are living in Neolithic villages in Kashmir.

4,000 BCE   Bronze and Copper Age culture is present in Pakistan.

c. 3,500 BCE   The Indus Valley civilization emerges in Pakistan.

c. 2,500 BCE   The Indus Valley Civilization declines.

c. 1,500 BCE   The Aryans enter the region and settle in the northwest region and then spread south and east.

6th century BCE   Magadha state in Bihar emerges as a regional power.

c. 599–527 BCE   Vardhamana, later known as Mahavira, the founder of Jainism lives in Magadha (in present-day Bihar tate).

566–486 BCE   Siddhartha Gautama, the Buddha, lives, and shortly after his death Buddhism emerges as a religion in northern India.

324–200 BCE   The Maurya Empire functions as the first pan-Indian state.

260 BCE   Mauryan ruler Asoka converts to Buddhism.

78–200 CE   The Kushan dynasty in Central Asia rules northeastern India.

c. 320–c. 500 CE   During the Gupta Empire India enjoys it golden age.

510–511   The Huns invade India and end Gupta rule.

710   Muslim Arabs conquer Sind in Pakistan and expand their control over western South Asia.

1186-1192   The Afghanistan-based Muslim Ghurid dynasty extends it rule across northern India.

1192–1526   The Delhi sultanate rules over northern and southern India.

14th–15th centuries   Muslim kingdoms rule in southern and eastern India.

1336–1672   The Hindu Vijayanagara empire is a powerful force in the south.

c. 1500   Guru Nanak founds the Sikh religion is northwest India.

1526–1857   The Mughal empire conquers Delhi and expands it rule over much of the region.

1498   Vasco de Gama sails from Portugal to Calicut, India, opening South Asia to European colonization.

1757   The British defeat the French at the Battle of Plassey, leaving the British free of European rivals in India.

c. 1850–1947   The period of the British rule in South Asia.

1857–1859   The Indian Mutiny is defeated but results in India coming under direct British rule, rather than control through the British East India Company.

1885   The Indian National Congress is founded as a political movement.

1906   The Muslim League is formed as a political movement.

1915   Mohandas K. Gandhi returns to India and leads the independence movement.

1940   The Muslim League sets forth the goal of a Muslim state in Muslim areas of India.

1947   Indian and Pakistan become independent nations.

1948   Burma (Myanmar) and Ceylon (Sri Lanka) become independent nations.

(greatly elaborated over the course of time) and religious practices marked largely by elaborate sacrificial rituals. Originally pastoral nomads, the Aryans rapidly spread across northern India and, in the process, cleared forests and increasingly took to agriculture. By 1000 BCE, they had reached the margins of what is now Bengal and penetrated into the Deccan Plateau. They established numerous small rival states, known as *janapada*s, some of which were monarchical and others republican or oligarchic.

Among these states, that of Magadha, in what is now Bihar, emerged as paramount in the sixth century BCE, possibly due to its access to a wide range of resources, especially iron, which came into widespread use during this period. Several increasingly expansive dynasties succeeded one another in this region, culminating in one founded by Candragupta Maurya in 324 BCE. The Mauryan empire (c. 324–c. 200 BCE), the first pan-Indian state, was a highly centralized, autocratic polity with a well-developed bureaucracy. Its governance was likely influenced by its founders' contacts with the forces led by Alexander of Macedon (356–323 BCE), which had campaigned in the northwest of the Indian subcontinent from 327 to 325 BCE. But the severity of Mauryan rule was tempered by the conversion to Buddhism (c. 260 BCE) of the emperor Asoka (d. c. 238 BCE), who sought to rule through the application of righteous law.

The Mauryan empire survived to 200 BCE; until the establishment of the Gupta dynasty (c. 320–c. 500 CE), most of India was controlled by petty states, though several empires, such as the Deccan-based Satavahanas, did briefly rule over fairly extensive areas. The period witnessed an inexorable advance of Aryan cultural influence into areas of Dravidian culture and of Brahamanical Hinduism into regions of essentially tribal culture, processes that continue to this day. It also saw the establishment of numerous Indo-Greek kingdoms along and beyond the northwestern portals of the subcontinent; movements through the northwest of peoples originating in various parts of inner Asia; and the founding and dramatic expansion of the Kushan dynasty (78–200), which probably extended, at least for a short time, from the Aral Sea to the Arabian Sea and northeastern India.

Far to the south, new centers of civilization sprang up in what are now Tamil Nadu, Kerala, and Sri Lanka. These depended largely on sophisticated systems of irrigation utilizing man-made tanks (reservoirs) and were also the beneficiaries of sea trade in networks that linked them to the Roman and Chinese empires.

Under the Gupta dynasty, whose center of power lay in the eastern Gangetic Plain, Indian culture embarked on its classical or golden age, a period marked by striking achievements in the arts, architecture, letters, philosophy, and other fields. Hinduism, Buddhism, and Jainism all flourished. The Gupta empire was not quite as extensive as that of the Mauryas and was a relatively decentralized confederacy. Its ascendance ended with a defeat by Huns, who invaded India from Central Asia in 510 to 511.

The Medieval and Early Premodern Periods

In the ensuing centuries, numerous small, medium-sized, and occasionally large powers contended for supremacy in their respective regions of India. These powers were centered in a relatively small number of fertile core areas, generally along major corridors of movement, and were often shielded from invasion from several quarters by highlands, deserts, or other terrain barriers. Such areas have been characterized as perennial core regions. Though periodically conquered by rival states, they repeatedly threw off alien rule and gave rise to new, locally based polities. The period also witnessed growing cultural and economic contacts with the increasingly Indianized kingdoms in Southeast Asia, which adopted numerous Hindu and Buddhist religious practices.

The tide of conquest that swept out of Arabia in the wake of the death of the Prophet Muhammad reached the lower Indus Plain as early as 710, with the Arab conquest of Sind. Within the next two centuries, all of South Asia's northwestern borderlands were incorporated within the Islamic caliphate, and raids by land and sea frequently penetrated more deeply into India. Not until well after the passing of the Abbasid dynasty (749/750–1258) did the Ghurid dynasty (mid-twelfth–early thirteenth centuries), based in central Afghanistan, extend Muslim power across the length of the Gangetic Plain, during the period from 1186 to 1192.

But this had no sooner been accomplished than the Ghurid chief, Qutb-ud-Din Aybak (d. 1210), succeeded in splitting the new empire by gaining control of its Indian domains. This marked the establishment of the Delhi sultanate (1192–1526). Under five successive dynasties, the sultanate ruled over northern India and, for long periods, much of the south as well. Among those dynasties, the Khaljis and the Tughluqs achieved, even if only briefly, the status of pan-Indian powers. Recognizing the difficulty of ruling southern India from Delhi, the Tughluqs established a co-capital at Daulatabad, in the north of the Deccan. But the overextended state proved incapable of withstanding internal stress, and the period from the mid-fourteenth to the early fifteenth centuries witnessed the secession of new Muslim kingdoms in southern and eastern India.

Although Hindu power was eclipsed in northern India early in the thirteenth century, a number of significant Hindu states continued to rule over much of the south. Of these, the most important was the Vijayanagara empire, which was locked in a centuries-long struggle with its Muslim neighbors to the north: first with the Bahmani kingdom, established in 1447, and then with the four sultanates into which that kingdom eventually split. Despite a disastrous military defeat in 1565, the Vijayanagara state lingered on until 1672.

Even after the consolidation of Muslim rule in northern India, new waves of warriors, lured by the riches of India, continued to penetrate the subcontinent via the Khyber Pass and other portals in the northwest. Among these were the Persia-based Il-Khans (1256–1353), one of the major successor states of the vast Mongol empire, who repeatedly raided the Punjab in the late fourteenth century, and later, the forces of the fearsome Turkic leader Timur (Tamerlane; 1336–1405). These invaders were precursors of the Mughals (1526–1857), of mixed Mongol and Turkic ancestry, whose leader, Babur (1483–1530), conquered Delhi in 1526 and thereby planted the seed of the mightiest Indian empire prior to that of the British.

The immediate successors of Babur included five more illustrious rulers: Humayun (1508–1556), who was temporarily expelled from India by an Afghan chief, Sher Shah of Sur (1486?–1545); Akbar (1542–1605), renowned for his religious tolerance; Jahangir (1569–1627); Shah Jahan (1592–1666), a remarkable builder; and the stern and orthodox Aurangzeb (1618–1707), under whom, in the late seventeenth century, the empire reached its territorial zenith.

The Colonial Era

The lure of India's wealth—in spices, textiles, jewels, and luxury goods—long predated Mughal rule; but direct European access to that wealth was blocked by the Ottoman Turkish possession of much of the Middle East. To circumvent the Ottoman barrier, the Portuguese, Spanish, and others sought new maritime routes to India. While Christopher Columbus (1451–1506) believed that he had found the way in 1492, it was actually the 1498 voyage of Vasco da Gama (c. 1460–1524) from Portugal around Africa to Calicut in southern India that opened a new age of European penetration of the subcontinent. During the sixteenth century the Portuguese enjoyed an undisputed monopoly on Indian foreign trade, but early in the seventeenth century the Dutch and the British, acting through chartered trading companies, gained a superior position. Somewhat later, the French, Danes, and others came onto the scene.

Initially, the European powers cared little about acquiring territorial possessions in South Asia, though the Dutch did gain control over most of the coast of Sri Lanka (then Ceylon); rather, they sought exclusive trading and warehousing privileges at particular sites known as factories, at many ports along the Indian coast. However, both the British and French became deeply involved in political and military quarrels among Indian states and in intrigues to oust one another from the areas in which they enjoyed privileged positions. This led to a series of wars among the British and French and their respective allies. In 1757, a decisive British victory at the Battle of Plassey in northeastern India resulted in the virtual expulsion of the French from India and in British control over the rich Mughal province of Bengal.

The loss of Bengal, combined with assertions of independence by several provincial governors and rebellions by various Hindu chiefs, greatly weakened Mughal imperial power. Foremost among the rebels were the Marathas, whose chiefs had formed a confederacy that gained control over vast tracts of India during the eighteenth century and reduced the emperor to the status of a puppet. (The precursor of the Maratha confederacy was the Maratha kingdom, carved out by the Hindu king Sivaji, 1627/30–1680, who outwitted the Mughal emperor Alamgir, 1618–1707, the son of Shah Jahan.) Despite these developments, the British East India Company long continued to recognize nominal Mughal overlordship of most of India.

Operating from Calcutta, Madras, and Mumbai (Bombay), the capitals of three major presidencies that the British East India Company established in India, British armies (manned largely by Indians) waged a series of wars against the Marathas and other indigenous Indian powers and steadily expanded the area under their control. Much of the newly acquired territory they chose to rule directly, while other areas became protectorates in which Indian princes were allowed to retain considerable powers while accepting the advice of appointed British residents. Maratha power was extirpated by 1818; by 1849, with the defeat of the Sikh kingdom in the Punjab in the second Anglo-Sikh War, the British gained control of virtually all of India. (The Sikhs, established in the late fifteenth century, were a religious group known for martial skills.) During the remainder of the century, the British rounded out their territories by annexing portions of the northern mountain ramparts of the subcontinent and adjacent regions of modern Myanmar (Burma), whose conquest was effected in three wars over the period from 1824 to 1890.

Spectacular though Britain's rise to ascendance in India was, its supremacy did not go unchallenged. In 1857, a mutiny among Indian troops of the British army in Bengal rapidly spread to army units throughout northern and central India. The rebel cause was soon joined by the nominal Mughal emperor and numerous Indian princes, chiefs, and their followers. Despite initial successes, the rebels could not match the

THE PARTITION OF INDIA

When India gained independence from Great Britain in 1947, the region was divided, creating the nations of India and Pakistan. The plan of division was set forth in the *The Indian Independence Act, 1947.*

An Act to make provision for the setting up in India of two independent Dominions, to substitute other provisions for certain provisions of the Government of India Act, 1935, which apply outside those Dominions, and to provide for other matters consequential on or concerned with the setting up of those Dominions.

Be it enacted by the King's Most Excellent Majesty, by and with the advice and consent of the Lords Spiritual and Temporal, and Commons, in this present Parliament assembled, and by the authority of the same, as follows:

The New Dominions

1. As from August 15, 1947, two independent Dominions shall be set up in India, to be known respectively as India and Pakistan.

2. The said Dominions are hereafter in this Act referred to as 'the new Dominions' and the said 15th of August is hereafter in this Act referred to as 'the appointed day.'

Territories of the New Dominions

1. Subject to the provisions of sub-sections (3) and (4) of this section, the territories of India shall be the territories under the sovereignty of His Majesty which, immediately before the appointed day, were included in British India except the territories which under sub-section (2) of this section are to be the territories of Pakistan.

2. Subject to the provisions of sub-sections (3) and (4) of this section the territories of Pakistan shall be (a) the territories which, on the appointed day, are included in the Provinces of East Bengal and West Punjab as constituted under the two following sections; (b) the territories which, at the date of the passing of this Act, are included in the Province of Sind and the Chief Commissioner's Province of British Baluchistan; and (c) if, whether before or after the passing of this Act but before the appointed day, the Governor-General declares that the majority of the valid votes cast in the referendum which, at the date of the passing of this Act, is being or has recently been held in that behalf under his authority in the North-West Frontier Province are in favour of representatives of that Province taking part in the Constituent Assembly of Pakistan, the territories which, at the date of the passing of this Act, are included in that Province.

3. Nothing in this section shall prevent any area being at any time included in or excluded from either of the new Dominions, so, however, that—(a) no area, not forming part of the territories specified in sub-section (1) or, as the case may be, sub-section (2), of this section shall be included in either Dominion without the consent of that Dominion; and (b) no area which forms part of the territories specified in the said sub-section (1) or, as the case may be, the said sub-section (2), or which has after the appointed day been included in either Dominion, shall be excluded from that Dominion without the consent of that Dominion.

4. Without prejudice to the generality of the provisions of sub-section (3) of this section, nothing in this section, shall be construed as preventing the accession of Indian States to either of the new Dominions.

Source: Maurice Gwyer and A. Appadorai. (1957) *Speeches and Documents on the Indian Constitution, 1921–47.* London: Oxford University Press, 692–693.

superior military organization of the British, and all resistance ceased in 1859.

Predictably, the Indian Mutiny had profound consequences. Among these were the termination of the East India Company's charter, the direct assumption of rule over India by the British crown, the deposition of the Mughal emperor and of those princes who joined in the rebellion, and, in 1877, the proclamation of Queen Victoria as empress of India. Additionally, the mutiny led to an accelerated program of building railroads and telegraph lines for purposes of military security (as well as commerce) and to a profound deepening of the social gulf between the British rulers and their Indian subjects.

Notwithstanding the distrust of Indians to which the mutiny gave rise, as the economy of India and the concerns of government expanded, the British saw no realistic alternative to involving increasing numbers of Indians in administration at various levels and in promoting Indian higher education. The expansion of an indigenous Western-educated elite led, in due course, to political activism and demands for a greater Indian voice in their own governance. Ceylon experienced similar developments.

In 1885, the Indian National Congress was formed, with membership drawn from various religious communities and including sympathetic British as well. As more and more government responsibility was assigned to Indians, the prospect of home rule and even of independence loomed larger. However, fearing that their interests would be compromised in an independent state and in those provinces in which Hindus were in the majority, a group of Muslims formed the Muslim League in 1906. Thereafter, that group and the Congress were principal competing forces, among many, in the struggle for independence and power on the Indian political stage.

In 1915, Mohandas K. Gandhi (1869–1948) returned to India from South Africa and soon became the dominant figure in the Congress Party. His leadership stressed civil disobedience and passive resistance to British rule and was marked by repeated but ultimately abortive efforts at reconciling the political interests of India's Hindu and Muslim communities. In 1940, the Muslim League, under the leadership of Muhammad Ali Jinnah (1876–1948), declared the goal of creating a separate Muslim state or states in the Muslim-majority areas of India. British attempts, during and after World War II, to induce the Congress Party and the Muslim League to agree on constitutional arrangements for a united, federal, independent India proved fruitless. At midnight on 14/15 August 1947, the independence of two dominions, India and Pakistan, the latter with an eastern and western wing, was declared. Burma, which was separated from India in 1937, became independent in January 1948, while Ceylon achieved its freedom the following month.

Joseph E. Schwarzberg

Further Reading

Allchin, Bridget, and Raymond Allchin. (1997) *Origins of a Civilization: The Prehistory and Early Archaeology of South Asia.* New Delhi: Viking.
Allchin, Raymond. (1995) *The Archaeology of Early South Asia: The Emergence of Cities and States.* Cambridge, U.K., and New York: Cambridge University Press.
Basham, Arthur Llewellyn. (1967) *The Wonder That Was India: A Survey of the History and Culture of the Indian Subcontinent before the Coming of the Muslims.* 3d rev. ed. London: Sidgwick & Jackson.
Kulke, Hermann, and Dietmar Rothermund. (1997) *A History of India.* 3d ed. New York: Routledge.
Kumar, Dharma, ed. (1983) *The Cambridge Economic History of India.* Vol. 2: *C. 1757–c. 1970.* Cambridge, U.K.: Cambridge University Press.
Majumdar, Ramesh Chandra, ed. (1951–) *The History and Culture of the Indian People.* 11 vols. Mumbai (Bombay), India: Bharatiya Vidya Bhavan.
Raychaudhuri, Tapan, and Irfan Habib, eds. (1982) *The Cambridge Economic History of India.* Vol. 1: *C. 1200–c. 1750.* Cambridge, U.K.: Cambridge University Press.
Rizvi, Athar Abbas. (1987) *The Wonder That Was India.* Vol. 2: *A Survey of the History and Culture of the Indian Subcontinent from the Coming of the Muslims to the British Conquest.* 3d rev. ed. London: Sidgwick & Jackson.
Schwartzberg, Joseph E., ed. (1992) *A Historical Atlas of South Asia.* 2d printing. New York: Oxford University Press.
Spear, Thomas George Percival. (1995) *The Oxford History of India, 1740–1947.* Oxford: Clarendon Press.
Stein, Burton. (1998) *A History of India.* Oxford and Malden, MA: Blackwell.
Thapar, Romila. (1992) *Interpreting Early India.* Delhi and New York: Oxford University Press.

SOUTH ASIANS IN SOUTHEAST ASIA

The migration of South Asians (migrants from the Indian peninsula as well as their descendants who have consciously retained a distinct ethnic and cultural identity in Southeast Asia) to Southeast Asia dates back to the emergence of regular trade routes connecting China, Southeast Asia, India, West Asia, and Europe in the trade of spices, incense, silk, and other luxury goods. Between the second century BCE and the first century CE, these trade routes were increasingly frequented. Chinese chronicles from the second century BCE reported that merchants were traveling from China across northern India to Bactria (present-day Afghanistan). From different points along this route it was possible to enter Burma and Indochina.

Ptolemy's *Geography*, composed in the second century CE, refers to many geographical names of Indian origin along the sea route connecting India with Southeast Asia. The discovery of isolated Brahmi alphabets on stones in Burma is evidence of Indian influence in this region beginning in the first century CE. Amaravati-style Buddha images (originating in south India, present-day Andhra Pradesh) from the second and third centuries CE have been discovered in Sumatra, Java, Sulawesi, Thailand, and the Annam region of

Vietnam. Yet no Indian record has testified to an early Indian colonization of Southeast Asia.

Nevertheless, there are many references to voyages between Indian ports and Suvarnadvipa (Srivijaya, Sumatra) in ancient Indian folk stories, Buddhist *jataka* tales (tales of the previous lives of the Buddha), and other works. Since most of the heroes are merchants, these stories suggest a peaceful migration of Indian merchants to Southeast Asia. Occasionally, the *jataka*s also mention dispossessed Kshatriya chiefs trying their fortunes in Suvarnadvipa. Accounts of Indian conquest are rare and often circumstantial. Yet there is ample evidence of the influence of various Indian religions (Buddhist, Saiva, and Vaisnava sects) throughout Southeast Asia.

The Rise and Fall of Hindu Kingdoms in Southeast Asia

The Indian influence in Southeast Asia that became manifest from the first century onwards can largely be attributed to intensifying trade relations between India and emerging Southeast Asian polities, whose rulers welcomed Indian merchants and priests at their courts and ports. The earliest of these were Funan in southern Cambodia, first century CE; Kambuja in northern Cambodia, c. 800 CE; Champa in Annam, second century CE; and Lankasuka on the Malay peninsula, second/third century CE. In the seventh century, the Buddhist kingdom of Srivijaya, which had emerged in Sumatra and controlled trade passing through the Malacca and Sunda straits, was praised in Chinese sources as a flourishing center of Buddhist learning. The rulers of Srivijaya maintained close relations with the famous Buddhist university Nalanda (located in the present-day Indian state of Bihar) until the eclipse of both in the twelfth and thirteenth centuries.

In the tenth century, a new Southeast Asian power center emerged in eastern Java under the rule of Airlangga (991?–1049), whose inscriptions testified to trade relations with different South Asian peoples as well as with the Khmer of Angkor and the Chams of Champa. In the eleventh century, the South Indian Cholas succeeded in temporarily conquering Srivijaya. In the thirteenth century, Srivijaya became a vassal of the eastern Javanese kingdom of Singasari and its successor, Majapahit. The latter exerted wide influence in mainland Southeast Asia and entertained trade relations with Jambudvipa (India), Karnataka (South India), and China. The establishment of the Dehli sultanate in the thirteenth century and the contemporaneous eclipse of Srivijaya boosted the advance of Islam to Southeast Asian ports. By the fifteenth century, many Muslim Gujarati and Chulia ships were sailing to Islamic ports along the Straits of Malacca. After the Portuguese conquered Melaka in 1511, the Gujaratis diverted to the Straits of Sunda to enter the northern Javanese ports of Banten, Jepara, and Gresik, which soon became thriving Muslim centers. It was the northern Javanese Muslim polities of Jepara and Demak that eventually destroyed Majapahit, the last Hindu Javanese kingdom, around 1530.

The Arrival of the Europeans

Chulia merchants frequenting the Straits of Malacca were forced to come to terms in the early 1520s with the Portuguese after the latter conquered the South Indian port of Nagapattinam, a center of Chulia shipping, and the ports of Sri Lanka, which had been the preserve of Chulia trade. Muslim Bengalis were mentioned as an important trading group in Portuguese Melaka in the *Suma Oriental*, written by the Portuguese merchant, world traveler, and writer Tome Pires between 1512 and 1515. Gujarati, Chulia, and Bengali trade continued during the initial phase of Dutch hegemony in the Malay archipelago, until the latter consolidated its trade monopoly in the seventeenth century. For twenty years Persian and Indo-Persian merchants rose to preeminence in the Thai kingdom of Ayutthaya under King Narai (reigned 1656–1688).

The Chulias proved to be the most persistent Muslim Indian merchants in Southeast Asia. After the Dutch established themselves in the archipelago, the Chulias concentrated their trade activities on the Malay peninsula, aligning themselves with the British. In 1786, when Fort Cornwallis was founded in Penang, Chulias settled there in large numbers and intermarried with the Malays; in early censuses they were the third largest community, behind the Malays and Chinese. In 1794, the British naval officer responsible for the acquisition of Penang, Francis Light, wrote that each year between 1,500 and 2,000 Chulia men came to Penang to earn a living, eventually returning to India with their savings. These men anticipated the Indian migrations to Southeast Asia that became prevalent in the nineteenth and twentieth centuries.

After the British Parliament abolished slavery in 1834, large numbers of Indians began to migrate as indentured laborers to various parts of the British (and Dutch) colonial empire. In Southeast Asia, it was the teak, rubber, tobacco, and oil-palm plantations of Burma, West Malaya, and North Sumatra that attracted masses of Tamil- and Telugu-speaking migrants, recruited by headmen known as *kangani*. After 1920, the *kangani* system gradually gave way to migration of individual workers. Indian traders, artisans, bankers, contractors, and clerks also turned to Southeast Asia. The Chettiars, a Tamil trading caste group, for example, became prominent money lenders, catering to peasants and workers in Burma, Singapore, and Malaya, providing a link between their illiterate clientele and the modern money economy. Although encouraged by British authorities, they occasionally became targets of indigenous public protest. Other merchant groups included the Gujaratis, who mainly handled textiles and spices, and the Sindhis, who migrated to Southeast Asia after losing their homeland in the partition of India and Pakistan. The latter became successful businessmen in the urban centers of Malaya, Singapore, and West Indonesia. Further Indian migrants included Malayees, Punjabis, Sikhs, Bengalis, and Pashtuns. After World War II, Indian migration continued to Malaya and Singapore, and, to a lesser extent, to Medan in western Indonesia. After the war many migrants adopted new citizenship, while others left Southeast Asia for good, either returning to South Asia or migrating to new regions such as Africa.

The South Indian Population of Southeast Asia Today

In Indonesia, ethnic Indian Hindus and Muslims, a small, heterogeneous minority of several thousand families, have integrated quite well into modern society. They largely work in business; only a minority still work on Sumatran plantations. In Malaysia and Singapore, citizens of Indian origin form the third largest ethnic group, after the Malays and Chinese. A large number still work on Malaysian plantations. At Singapore harbor they work side by side with short-term migrants from India and Bangladesh, the latter also forming the bulk of construction workers in both countries. A much smaller number of ethnic Indians work in business and civil service. In Singapore, citizens of Indian descent enjoy equal civil rights, and economic and educational opportunities, whereas in Malaysia, their status has been threatened by ethnic and religious discrimination. The Malaysian constitution restricts access of non-Malays to education, government, and industrial employment, as well as land, reserving special rights for the Malay majority.

Martin Ramstedt

Further Reading

Arasaratnam, S. (1989) *Islamic Merchant Communities of the Indian Subcontinent in Southeast Asia.* Kuala Lumpur, Malaysia: University of Malaya.

Coedès, Georges. (1962) *Les peuples de la péninsule indochinoise.* Paris: Dunod.

———. (1964) *Les états hindouisés d'Indochine et d'Indonésie.* Paris: E. de Boccard.

Gupta, Anirudha. (1971) *Indians Abroad: Asia and Africa.* New Dehli: Orient Longman.

Jain, Ravindra K. (1970) *South Indians on the Plantation Frontier in Malaya.* New Haven, CT: Yale University Press.

Majumdar, Asis Kumar. (1982) *Southeast Asia in Indian Foreign Policy: A Study of India's Relations with Southeast Asian Countries from 1962–1982.* Calcutta, India: Naya Prokash.

Majumdar, R. C. (1955) *Ancient Indian Colonization in Southeast Asia.* Baroda, India: Maharaja Sayajirao University of Baroda Press.

Pavadarayan, Jayarani. (1986) *The Chettiars of Singapore: A Study of an Indian Minority Community in Southeast Asia.* Bielefeld, West Germany: Dissertation an der Fakultät für Soziologie der Universität Bielefeld.

Ramstedt, Martin, ed. (2002) *Hinduism in Modern Indonesia: Between Local, National, and Global Interests.* London: Curzon.

SOUTH ASIANS, OVERSEAS

Overseas South Asians—people of South Asian descent residing outside South Asia—numbered 20 million in the year 2001, comprising about 2 percent of the population of South Asia. Over 1 million people of South Asian descent reside in just eleven nations, including the United States, Great Britain, South Africa, and Malaysia. More than twenty-two nations have a population of at least 100,000 ethnic Indians.

The Colonial Phase

South Asian emigration can be divided into two distinct phases—the nineteenth-century colonial phase and the twentieth-century postindependence phase. Some scholars also recognize an earlier wave between the seventh and fourteenth centuries, when trade links between India and East Africa and between India and the Far East were established, but the historical literature in this period is somewhat limited. The first large-scale emigration from India took place under British imperial rule and was an attempt to fill the severe labor shortage in the European plantation colonies caused by the abolition of slavery in 1834 and the subsequent emancipation of African slaves. Indians were transported as indentured labor to plantations not only in the British colonies of British Guiana (now Guyana), Trinidad and Tobago, South Africa, and Fiji but also in the former French colonies of Mauritius (ceded to the British in 1814) and Reunion, as well as in the Dutch colony of Netherlands Guiana (now Suriname). Indians were also sent to eastern and southern Africa to build railroads. Between 1834 and 1917 a total of 1.5 million indentured Indians emigrated from the northern, northeastern, and southern provinces of India, recruited by agents based in Calcutta and Madras. The conditions of indenture were abominable, comparable to slavery, and Indians called it *narak* (hell). Although the indenture contracts promised the immigrants free or partly paid return passage to India, basic pay, food, and accommodation, in reality their wages were meager, their living conditions unsanitary, and their movements severely restricted, and they were denied basic services such as education and health care. The indenture system was terminated in 1917 after vehement protests from Indian nationalists brought its ugly practices to light. About two-thirds of the indentured immigrants stayed abroad, however, and their descendants form communities of substantial sizes. Their conditions vary greatly from country to country, though in most countries the majority are rural residents engaged in some form of agricultural production, struggling in economies plagued by overpopulation, underemployment, and racial conflict.

The United Kingdom has large Pakistani and Indian populations. Here, Pakistanis protest Indian occupation of the Kashmir region outside the British Houses of Parliament in London in June 1999. (AFP/CORBIS)

CHAI

Chai—a sweet, milky tea boiled in a saucepan—was once an exotic beverage available in the United States only at ethnic restaurants owned by South Asian immigrants. Of late, however, chai has become popular, so now it is served in most American coffee bars. Still, according to the author of this recipe, chai is best prepared at home.

¾ cup water
½ cup milk
1 full tsp. black tea
1 pod cardamom
2 pea-sized chunks of fresh ginger (mulched)
1–2 whole black peppers
1/8–1/6 cinnamon stick

On a hard piece of paper, crush the tea and spices together. Immediately put this mix in the dish with the water and milk. Keep them on the burner for about 15 minutes, stirring continuously. Add sugar to your taste. Drain in a strainer and serve in a cup.

Source: The Enthusiast's Online Chai Resource. Retrieved 15 March 2002, from: http://www.odie.org/chai/rec/rec101.html.

Indians also emigrated under the British as middle-level functionaries to work the railways, telegraphs, steamships, rice mills, and other manufacturing industries in Burma (present-day Myanmar), Malaya (now part of Malaysia), and East Africa. A more prosperous cohort engaged in trade and commerce in the same countries where its indentured compatriots had already settled. Indian traders *(banias)* kept strictly to themselves, observing caste restrictions, practicing endogamy, and maintaining frequent contact with the homeland. In East Africa their affluence became their undoing in the 1960s, when African leaders of the newly independent countries of Kenya, Uganda, and Tanzania, looking for scapegoats to blame for the economically subordinate position of blacks in their own countries, ordered or encouraged the mass expulsion of Indians, mostly Gujaratis.

The first significant wave of South Asian emigration to the United States and Canada took place in the first two decades of the twentieth century. About seven

CONCERN IN INDIA FOR INDIANS OVERSEAS

A significant number of Indians live in diaspora in many nations around the world. How they are treated in those nations varied and continues to vary widely. The following resolution passed by the Indian National Congress party in 1948 seeks to gain rights for the Indian community in South Africa who lived as second-class citizens, below the whites but above the indigenous Africans.

The Congress has noted with deep regret that the Government of the Union of South Africa continues to treat its Indian citizens in disregard of acknowledged human rights and of the principles laid down in the Charter of the United Nations. That Government has ignored the wishes of the General Assembly of the United Nations and even challenged the fundamental principles on which the United Nations Organization is founded. This repudiation of a vital principle, if persisted in, can only lead to the bitter and far-reaching racial conflicts and may even result in the break-up of the United Nations Organization.

The Congress expresses its full sympathy with all those who have suffered by the policy of racial discrimination of the Government of the Union of South Africa.

Source: Jagdish Saran Sharma. (1965) *India's Struggle for Freedom: Select Documents and Sources.* Vol. 2. Delhi: S. Chand, 254.

thousand Sikhs, mostly farmers from the Punjab, worked as sojourners in the lumber mills and railroad industry of the Pacific Northwest. They faced racist attacks and discriminatory laws directed against all Asians, including the Chinese and Japanese, and many returned to India. Others settled down as farmers in California, marrying Mexican women since antimiscegenation laws prevented them from marrying white women. In 1917 the Barred Zone Act, designed by the U.S. Congress specifically to cut off all immigration from India, successfully stopped any further Indian emigration.

The Postindependence Phase

After World War II, South Asian emigration picked up again, and this time the Western, white-dominated countries of Great Britain, Canada, the United States, and Australia played host. In the 1950s, Britain developed critical labor shortages in its booming industrial market, and largely unskilled workers emigrated from India and Pakistan to fill the gap. Most were Sikhs from the Punjab; entire Punjabi villages were transplanted to specific locales in England in a system of chain migration. Gujaratis also left India in large numbers. The influx of Sikh and Gujarati refugees from East Africa in the late 1960s and 1970s (the "twice mi-

grants," as they are called) added to the growth of the South Asian community in Britain. In the 1980s a hardening of anti-immigrant attitudes and violent racial strife in Britain led to a clampdown on migration from South Asia. The United States, Canada, and Australia offered much more hospitable climates for South Asians at that time, and emigrants turned increasingly to those countries in their search for economic opportunities abroad.

In 1965 major changes to the U.S. immigration law eliminated racial barriers and opened up opportunities for nonwhite peoples from Asia. South Asians from India, Pakistan, and (after 1971) Bangladesh immigrated in unprecedented numbers under an elaborate system of preferences designed to attract highly skilled professionals, such as doctors, engineers, scientists, and teachers, who could fill shortages in the American labor market. The number of Indian immigrants to the United States climbed steadily from 2,458 in 1966 to a peak of 45,064 in 1991. Under the family reunification clause of the 1965 Immigration Reform Act, the skilled immigrants were allowed to bring their lesser-skilled relatives into the United States, so by the 1990s emigration from South Asia crossed all age groups, all socioeconomic levels, and all regions of the subcontinent. The 2000 census counted 1,678,765 people of Asian-Indian origin, who formed one of the fastest-growing subgroups under the Asian-American umbrella.

Both in the United States and in Canada, South Asians have formed vibrant communities and engage in a wide range of occupations, from brain surgeons to cab drivers. They work in information-based, high-technology sectors as well as in low-skilled retail, food, motel, and other service sectors. They tend to concentrate in major metropolitan areas such as New York, Los Angeles, and Chicago, where job opportunities are plentiful, but they do not cluster in ethnic enclaves, preferring instead to scatter and merge into upper-class and middle-class suburbs.

Taking full advantage of the communication and transportation revolutions, South Asian emigrants stay in close touch with their homelands and with other major emigrant South Asian communities all over the world. They have contributed to a paradigm shift, in which emigrants are no longer seen merely as exiles but as world citizens or transnationals who move between different cultures and who participate in the economies of both their home countries and their adopted lands.

Padma Rangaswamy

Further Reading
Clarke, Colin, Ceri Peach, and Steven Vertovec, eds. (1990) *South Asians Overseas: Migration and Ethnicity*. New York: Cambridge University Press.
Motwani, Jagat K., Mahin Gosine, and Jyoti Barot, eds. (1993) *Global Indian Diaspora: Yesterday, Today, and Tomorrow*. New York: Global Organization of People of Indian Origin.
Rangaswamy, Padma. (2000) *Namasté America: Indian Immigrants in an American Metropolis*. University Park: Pennsylvania State University Press.
Tinker, Hugh. (1977) *The Banyan Tree: Overseas Emigrants from India, Pakistan, and Bangladesh*. New York: Oxford University Press.
Veer, Peter van der, ed. (1995) *Nation and Migration: The Politics of Space in the South Asian Diaspora*. Philadelphia: University of Pennsylvania Press.

SOUTH CHINA SEA The South China Sea is bordered by China to the north, Indonesia and Malaysia to the south, Taiwan and the Philippines to the east, and Vietnam and Thailand to the west and has become an increasing flash point in Southeast Asia, because each of those countries lays claim to the Spratley and Paracel Islands. Historically, China has asserted sovereignty over the South China Sea, and with its adoption in 1992 of the Law on the Territorial Wa-ters and Contiguous Areas of the People's Republic of China, it laid claim to the Spratley and Paracel Islands. It built an airstrip and military outpost there and delineated a 12-nautical-mile zone of territorial waters and 200-nautical-mile economic zone, as allowed by international law. China also claims the right accorded to archipelago nations to extend the lines of maritime sovereignty contiguously from the edge of the territory back to the mainland, which encompasses some 800,000 square kilometers of ocean.

Keith A. Leitich

Further Reading
Hull, Richard E. (1996) *The South China Sea: Future Source of Prosperity or Conflict in Southeast Asia*. Washington, D.C.: National Defense University, Institute for National Strategic Studies.
Samuels, Marwyn S. (1982) *Contest for the South China Sea*. New York: Methuen.
Valencia, Mark J. (1995) *China and the South China Sea Disputes: Conflicting Claims and Potential Solution in the South China Sea*. Oxford: Oxford University Press for the International Institute for Strategic Studies.

SOUTH CHOLLA PROVINCE (2000 pop. 2.2 million). Located in the southwestern corner of South Korea, South Cholla Province (Cholla namdo) has an area of 11,964 square kilometers. Kwangju, site of a 1980 civilian uprising, is the provincial capital, but it is an independent and administratively autonomous city. Mokp'o, Naju, Yosu, Yoch'on, Sunch'on, and Kwangyang are other cities in the province, and there are seventeen counties (*kun*).

Only 14 percent of the nearly two thousand islands off the province's coasts are inhabited. Chindo Island, famous for the Chindo breed of dogs native to Korea, is among the best known of these islands. The coastal region accounts for South Cholla's rich marine life and strong fishing industry. The agricultural sector is also vital, with rice, grains and cereals, and potatoes produced in the southwestern and northwestern regions of the province. Mining products include gold, silver, coal, and limestone. South Cholla is in the midst of a renewed industrialization effort, with six new industrial zones planned. Kwangyang has one of the world's largest steel plants.

President Kim Dae Jung (b. 1925) is a native of South Cholla. His election in 1997 marked the end of decades of regional discrimination against the Cholla provinces.

Jennifer Jung-Kim

Further Reading

Cho, Chung-Kyung, Phyllis Haffner, and Fredric M. Kaplan. (1991) *The Korea Guidebook.* 5th ed. Boston: Houghton Mifflin.

Nilsen, Robert (1997) *South Korea Handbook.* Chico, CA: Moon.

SOUTH CH'UNGCH'ONG PROVINCE

(1999 est. pop. 1.9 million). Located in the west central part of South Korea (Republic of Korea), South Ch'ungch'ong Province (Ch'ungch'ong namdo) has an area of 8,585 square kilometers. Present-day Ch'ungch'ong and Cholla Provinces cover the territory once controlled by Paekche (18 BCE–663 CE), one of the original Three Kingdoms subsumed by Shilla (57 BCE–935 CE) and resurrected as Later Paekche (892–936) before its surrender to Koryo (918–1392). Kongju and Puyo, former capitals of Paekche, are located in South Ch'ungch'ong and house many cultural treasures from the early kingdom.

The provincial capital is at Taejon, an autonomous administrative entity that is independent from the province. Taejon continues to grow in importance in the region and nationwide as it supplements Seoul as a second administrative capital. There are six other designated cities—Sosan, Asan, Ch'onan, Nonsan, Poryong, and Kongju—and nine counties (*kun*) in the province.

South Ch'ungch'ong is home to many heavy and light industries producing goods such as electronics, semiconductors, petrochemicals, automobiles, machinery, and apparel. Major agricultural products include rice and other grains, apples, strawberries, tomatoes, ginseng, and tobacco. Despite the province's location on the Yellow Sea, fishery production has been decreasing in recent years due to increased development along the coastline. The forests, which account for 52 percent of the province, are protected diligently through public and private efforts.

Jennifer Jung-Kim

Further Reading

Cho, Chung-Kyung, Phyllis Haffner, and Fredric M. Kaplan. (1991) *The Korea Guidebook.* 5th ed. Boston: Houghton Mifflin.

Nilsen, Robert (1997) *South Korea Handbook.* Chico, CA: Moon.

SOUTH HAMGYONG PROVINCE

(2002 est. pop. 3.3 million). South Hamgyong Province (Hamgyong namdo) is located on the central east coast of North Korea (Democratic People's Republic of Korea, or DPRK) and has a 466-kilometer coastline. The province has an area of 16,745 square kilometers. The province has been geographically restructured seven times since the 1948 establishment of the DPRK. In addition to the provincial capital of Hamhung, there are two other designated cities (Sinp'o and Tanch'on) and fifteen counties (*kun*).

South Hamgyong is mountainous and has an average elevation of 745 meters. The province also has many rivers and tributaries as well as natural lakes. South Hamgyong also claims sixty-four islands just off its coast. Although the region is not particularly agricultural, there are numerous species of indigenous trees, plants, and fruits. Staple crops such as millet, wheat, beans, and potatoes, as well as wild vegetables and fish, make up some of the key ingredients of the traditional foods of South Hamgyong. *Hamhung naengmyon,* a cold noodle dish flavored with spicy pepper sauce, is one of the region's most representative dishes.

Jennifer Jung-Kim

Further Reading

Cho, Chung-Kyung, Phyllis Haffner, and Fredric M. Kaplan. (1991) *The Korea Guidebook.* 5th ed. Boston: Houghton Mifflin.

Storey, Robert, and Alex English. (2001) *Korea.* 5th ed. Berkeley, CA: Lonely Planet.

SOUTH HWANGHAE PROVINCE

(2002 est. pop. 2.5 million). South Hwanghae Province (Hwanghae namdo) lies on the Yellow Sea in the southwest region of North Korea (Democratic People's Republic of Korea). The province has an area of 8,294 square kilometers. Haeju is the provincial capital and the only designated city in the province. There are nineteen counties (*kun*).

The region has yielded many prehistoric artifacts. There are also many relics from the Old Choson (fourth to first century BCE) , Koguryo (37 BCE–668 CE), and Koryo (918–1392) kingdoms.

The province is mostly made up of plains and hills, having an average elevation of 86 meters above sea level. The highest point is Mount Kuwol in the Kuwol mountain range, with an elevation of 954 meters. There are also numerous rivers and streams. The coastline is jagged and irregular, spanning a total of 1,242 kilometers.

South Hwanghae's cuisine features the region's most abundant agricultural products such as grains and vegetables as well as fish and seafood. The province is famous for the Haeju style of *pibimpap* (rice mixed with vegetables), *k'alguksu* (noodle soup), buckwheat noodles, mung bean jelly, and mung bean noodles, as well as sea bream, mullet, seaweed, and vegetables.

Jennifer Jung-Kim

Further Reading
Cho, Chung-Kyung, Phyllis Haffner, and Fredric M. Kaplan. (1991) *The Korea Guidebook.* 5th ed. Boston: Houghton Mifflin.

Storey, Robert, and Alex English. (2001) *Korea.* 5th ed. Berkeley, CA: Lonely Planet.

SOUTH KOREA—PROFILE (2001 est pop. 48 million). Two catastrophic events created the Republic of Korea (South Korea). First, from 1910 until the end of World War II in 1945, Japan ruled Korea as a colony. For the purpose of accepting the surrender of Japanese forces, the Allied forces divided the Korean Peninsula at the thirty-eighth parallel between the Soviets in the north and the United Nations in the south. Originally these were just administrative areas, but soon ideological and political conflicts led to the creation of separate states. With the support of the United States, the southern politician Syngman Rhee (1875–1965) refused a United Nations–supervised election in the entire peninsula. He declared South Korea an independent state on 15 August 1948. The Soviet-backed leader in northern Korea, Kim Il Sung, declared North Korea a state just three weeks later, on 9 September 1948. Second, these conflicts culminated in the Korean War (1950–1953). The creation of two separate hostile states at war with one another has been the greatest tragedy for the Korean people. It is estimated that 20 percent of the population in South Korea has personal ties with people and places in North Korea that have been broken for over fifty years. This situation has created a deep sense of emotional pain in the Korean population.

Geography
South Korea forms the southern half of the Korean Peninsula, which juts out from the northeast rim of Asia. South Korea is surrounded by three seas: the Yellow Sea on the west, the East China Sea on the south, and the East Sea on the east. Its area is 98,480 square kilometers. Its location between China and Japan has placed it in the vortex of political, cultural, and social movements and conflicts. Seoul, just thirty miles south of the border with North Korea, is the capital.

The climate is temperate—dry, cold winters with an average temperature of –6°C and hot, humid summers with an average temperature of 25°C.

South Korea is known for its mountains, plains, and abundant water supplies. The mountains are steep and not well endowed with minerals or ample forests. In 1997, among the more prominent agricultural products, paddy rice was the most bountiful crop, producing 7.3 million metric tons. Barley, the second-largest grain crop, attained barely a quarter of a million metric tons. Considerable harvests of apples (652,000 metric tons), grapes (393,000 metric tons), and other fruits and vegetables provide a healthy domestic diet. The plains also allow considerable livestock husbandry: 3.2 million head of cattle, 7 million pigs, 88 million chickens, and even 1 million beehives. The coastlines allow a thriving fishery industry, totaling more than 3.3 million metric tons of products annually.

Politics
By 1948 the United Nations administration of Korea had been challenged by the threat of Cold War politics in East Asia. In the northern areas, Kim Il Sung was launching a people's revolution: his policies included land reform, purges of religious and pro-Japanese lead-

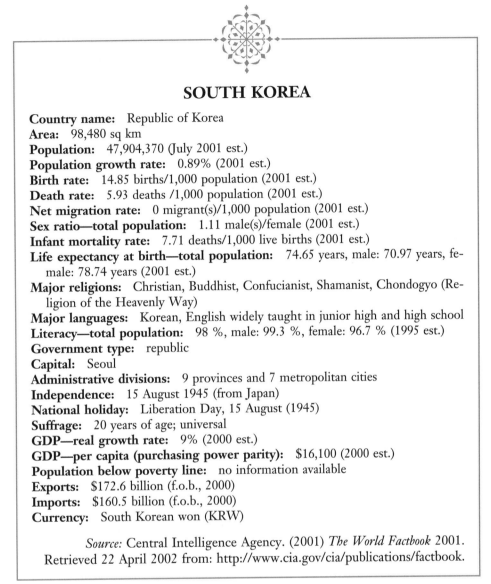

SOUTH KOREA

Country name: Republic of Korea

Area: 98,480 sq km

Population: 47,904,370 (July 2001 est.)

Population growth rate: 0.89% (2001 est.)

Birth rate: 14.85 births/1,000 population (2001 est.)

Death rate: 5.93 deaths /1,000 population (2001 est.)

Net migration rate: 0 migrant(s)/1,000 population (2001 est.)

Sex ratio—total population: 1.11 male(s)/female (2001 est.)

Infant mortality rate: 7.71 deaths/1,000 live births (2001 est.)

Life expectancy at birth—total population: 74.65 years, male: 70.97 years, female: 78.74 years (2001 est.)

Major religions: Christian, Buddhist, Confucianist, Shamanist, Chondogyo (Religion of the Heavenly Way)

Major languages: Korean, English widely taught in junior high and high school

Literacy—total population: 98 %, male: 99.3 %, female: 96.7 % (1995 est.)

Government type: republic

Capital: Seoul

Administrative divisions: 9 provinces and 7 metropolitan cities

Independence: 15 August 1945 (from Japan)

National holiday: Liberation Day, 15 August (1945)

Suffrage: 20 years of age; universal

GDP—real growth rate: 9% (2000 est.)

GDP—per capita (purchasing power parity): $16,100 (2000 est.)

Population below poverty line: no information available

Exports: $172.6 billion (f.o.b., 2000)

Imports: $160.5 billion (f.o.b., 2000)

Currency: South Korean won (KRW)

Source: Central Intelligence Agency. (2001) *The World Factbook* 2001. Retrieved 22 April 2002 from: http://www.cia.gov/cia/publications/factbook.

ers, and socialist economic policies. In the southern areas, Syngman Rhee was empowering Korean military, police, and governmental officials who had worked with the Japanese and strengthening the landlord class. The U.N. could not mediate the conflict.

In the late summer of 1948, the Republic of Korea adopted a constitution. Syngman Rhee, a veteran Korean nationalist and longtime political exile who obtained American support during his residence in the United States, became the first president. His presidency was marked by his counterinsurgency tactics against domestic rivals, his stubborn military strategies against the Communist regime in North Korea, his repressive political policies following the Korean War, and his restructuring of the old economic and political elite. Student protests drove him from office in 1960 and into retirement in Hawaii.

The next three rulers of South Korea were military men. In 1961 General Park Chung Hee (1917–1979) led a military coup against a short-lived civilian government. Over the next eighteen years, the general effectively suspended the constitution and established martial law. His rule was draconian. Students, workers, intellectuals, and political opponents were jailed, tortured, and even murdered or executed. His economic policies reversed the destructive rule of President Rhee by reviving the corporate conglomerates *(chaebol)*, thus creating a rich and powerful business elite. In 1979 student, worker, and middle-class unrest resulted in massive demonstrations. On 26 October

1979, Park was assassinated by the head of the Korean Central Intelligence Agency.

From 1978 to 1981, there was great political unrest. Lieutenant General Chun Doo Hwan (b. 1931), a commander of Korean troops who served the United States in Vietnam during the Vietnam War and was known for his brutality, led a successful military coup on 12 December 1979. Again students protested. General Chun extended martial law and rounded up political demonstrators. He arrested the popular politician Kim Dae Jung (b. 1925) and other leaders. In May 1980, the southern city of Kwangju rose up against Chun's rule. With the support of U.S. military leaders, Chun transferred troops from the border with North Korea and attacked the rebellious city, resulting in the deaths of hundreds, if not thousands, of civilians. Chun's military victory catapulted him into the presidency. His new judiciary sentenced Kim Dae Jung to death for plotting rebellion. Because of international outrage, Kim was instead jailed and later went to the United States for health reasons.

Chun Doo Hwan ruled until 1987, when he supported a military subordinate, Roh Tae Woo (b. 1932), to run for the presidency. Roh won in a plurality with 36 percent of the votes. He opened Korea to the international community by hosting the Olympics, engineering South Korea's entrance into the United Nations, and furthering the shift from an economy based on import-substitution to an economy based on electronic manufacturing and heavy and light industrial exports.

The next two presidents, Young Sam (b. 1927; served 1992–1997) and Kim Dae Jung (served from 1997), were civilian politicians who won open popular elections. These men were elected, in part, because of the democratization movements in East Asia. The Philippines and Taiwan were throwing off martial law and electing civilian reformers to office. President Young Sam brought charges of sedition and corruption against Chun Doo Hwan and Roh Tae Woo. Chun received the death penalty and Roh a long prison term. However, President Kim was involved in issues of corruption, labor unrest, and student protest. His successor was the popular political hero Kim Dae Jung. Kim Dae Jung began his term by pardoning Chun and Roh. During his first year in office, Kim Dae Jung was faced with the Asian economic crisis. He ushered in economic and fiscal policies that reformed the conglomerates, supported some labor reforms, and adhered to the demands of the International Monetary Fund (IMF). His most important policies were in foreign affairs, where he initiated programs to bring

Finance Minister Jin Nyum attends the opening ceremony of the Korea Stock Exchange in Seoul on 2 January 2002. (REUTERS NEWMEDIA INC./CORBIS)

North and South Korea to the negotiating table. Under his presidency, the first large group of Koreans visited each other: one group going to Pyongyang in North Korea, the other to Seoul in South Korea. South Korea began to provide economic aid to North Korea, as well as negotiating some economic investments. President Kim won the Nobel Peace Prize in 2000.

Economic Affairs

Until the Asian financial crisis of 1997, the South Korean economy was considered one of the economic miracles of East Asia. In 1996, the average per capita income was $10,600; the average annual rate of growth in the early 1990s climbed to an impressive 7.2 percent. The crash in 1997 contracted the economy by 5.8 percent. Many banks went bankrupt, the large conglomerates collapsed, unemployment rose more than 7 percent, and many politicians and bureaucrats left their jobs in dishonor. The extent of the crisis can be measured by the International Monetary Fund's rescue program, which provided $57 billion to bail out the government—the largest ever by the IMF. Kim Dae Jung reorganized the conglomerates but also restricted the powers of the labor unions. Despite protests, his government managed to rescue the Korean economy. By 1999 and 2000, South Korea's record achievements in manufacturing outputs and investment had reestablished the economy. Its trade surplus had widened to $2.17 billion in 1999.

Culture

The negative economic effects of colonization and the Korean War prevented South Koreans from investing in cultural and artistic activities until the early

1980s. Many South Koreans are reviving the traditions that had been swept away by the Japanese and destroyed by incessant violence. Korean history has been rewritten to reclaim the glories of its civilization. Traditional music, literature, painting, and ceramics have been studied and revived through the construction of government museums, cultural centers, and artistic endeavors. The private sector has built more than two hundred museums that concentrate on many aspects of Korean creativity. The Sonje Museum of Modern Art in Kyongju reflects the great contributions that Korea has made to contemporary art. South Korean cinema has become a major competitor in international competitions. The democratization of South Korean politics has resulted in an explosion of artistic expression.

Richard C. Kagan

Further Reading

Clark, Donald N., ed. (1988) *The Kwangju Uprising: Shadows over the Regime in South Korea*. Boulder, CO: Westview.

Cumings, Bruce. (1997) *Korea's Place in the Sun: A Modern History*. New York: Norton.

SOUTH KOREA—ECONOMIC SYSTEM

When South Korea gained its independence in 1945, the country had no workable resources or capital except for its unemployed illiterate population. Even before the euphoria at independence had faded away, people found themselves in turmoil, followed by civil war between North and South Korea (1950–1953).

The Separation of North and South Korea

At the start of the transition period, when Korea was being divided (1945–1948), the southern part of Korea was primarily agricultural. It had an area of 98,430 square kilometers, with a population of 9.3 million. Geographically, southern Korea was blessed with relatively rich soil and a mild climate and thus was suited to agricultural activities, particularly rice production. Northern Korea had industrial prerequisites, such as rich mineral resources and a hydroelectric power supply from the Yalu River power-generation station built during the Japanese colonial era (1910–1954).

Before the division, northern Korea had 75 percent of Korea's heavy industry, while southern Korea had almost 75 percent of the light industry. Southern Korea had almost three times as large an area of irrigated rice paddies as the north. The south depended on the chemical fertilizer produced in the north as well as the north's electrical power supply, while the north needed rice from the south. When United Nations–supervised elections were held in the south on 10 May 1948, the north shut off power transmission and other industrial supplies to the south. With the severing of north-south ties, the traditional complementarity between the two parts of Korea was suspended, and the two governments that emerged synchronically in north and south were antagonistic to each other.

North and South Korea have since followed different paths of economic development against a background of a common language, cultural history, and sense of identity. Opposing political ideologies, along with their corresponding economic systems, have created antagonistic relationships and feelings of enmity between the two halves of the country. Particularly since the Korean War (1950–1953), the two Koreas seem to have kept themselves remote from each other across 155 miles of truce line, which remains as a border of military tension between the two rival systems.

South Korea's Capitalist System

South Korea has followed the capitalist road introduced by the United States, which poured in a huge amount of economic aid intended to help the country recover from the complete destruction of its economy during the Korean War. The fundamental elements of the market economic system on which the South Korean economy is based are privately owned means of production (capital, labor, and natural resources), diversification of decision-making processes, and a built-in stabilization mechanism, which operates principally in accordance with market laws.

The general merit of a market-oriented economic system lies in its efficient allocation of resources, advancement of information and technology, and realization of consumer sovereignty and diversification of social power, which accompanies individual freedom and responsibility. However, a capitalist market has its occasional market failures, such as imperfect competition or an insufficient or unbalanced supply of public goods (for example, public education, cooperatives, and free health-care services), and may also generate a growing inequality of income and wealth distribution thanks to the vagaries of the business cycle, in which recession can follow times of economic strength. These problems inevitably necessitate the partial intervention of government into markets by means of macroeconomic planning or adjustment policies. Such policies include progressive income-tax systems and social-welfare programs.

The South Korean economy has been no exception. It has adopted economic-development plans (five-year plans) to speed up economic growth and development since 1962. These plans have been in line with a free-market system and are intended to provide broad guidelines for the macroeconomy. However, government intervention in the markets has sometimes led to corruption when politics becomes too wrapped up in economics. South Korea's economic performance might improve if the government did less and let markets move to allocate resources.

On the positive side, government-led economic planning has increased and improved the information and skills needed to make economic decisions. The government has aided the development of new industries and raised export competitiveness by providing direct assistance and incentives to private entrepreneurs.

The 1980s began to see a decline in the government's oversight of economic activity in South Korea. As the economy has become increasingly complex, and as the country's liberalization and democratization processes demand improved free-market function, the decline in government involvement is natural. It reflects the government's growing understanding of the importance of incentives and markets vis-à-vis the observed inefficiencies of government planning as the economy moves into a more highly developed phase.

The Development of the South Korean Economy

The South Korean economy has grown remarkably over the last four decades. After the civil war, the economy was characterized by cyclical poverty; that is, low incomes led to low savings, which led to low investment, which led to low production, and back to low incomes. To escape from this cycle, the government launched its ambitious First Five-Year Economic Development Plan in 1962.

In the early stage of economic development, the government fostered import-substitution industries, which produced such basic intermediate materials as cement and fertilizers. After that, from the mid-1960s, government emphasis shifted toward labor-intensive industries such as textiles and plywood, which were internationally competitive because of South Korea's low labor costs, and which were capable of absorbing unemployed and underemployed members of the population.

South Korea's greatest resource has always been its people. The South Koreans have demonstrated an awareness of the importance of education as well as a commitment to educate their next generation, even at a substantial financial cost. Thanks to that commit-ment, it has had since the 1950s a highly motivated and educated workforce that has enabled the country to improve under a growth-oriented government. Developing human resources early, despite low per capita incomes, made it possible to lay a solid foundation for subsequent economic development.

Obligatory military service has also produced many highly disciplined and experienced young men who have returned after about three years' active service to civilian industries. Without both the belt-tightening sacrifices of the once-poor Korean parents for their children's education and the hard training in the military service, the foundations for subsequent high growth in the 1960s and 1970s would never have been laid.

The government at that time also focused on efficient mobilization and allocation of investment resources. Several specialized banks were established to finance such underdeveloped strategic sectors as small- and medium-sized enterprises and housing construction. To encourage foreign-capital inflow, the Foreign Capital Inducement Act was passed in 1966, and foreign banks were allowed to open branches from 1967. In the course of growth-oriented industrialization, the country had to encourage the investment of a large amount of foreign capital, since domestic savings were insufficient to finance the enormous investment demand.

Economic Development in the 1970s and 1980s

In the early 1970s, South Korea experienced dramatic changes and challenges both at home and abroad. Internationally, there was a new climate of protectionism, along with the worldwide stagflation caused by the first oil crisis in 1972. South Korea's labor-intensive light industries, whose competitiveness was gradually weakening as a result of rapid wage increases, faced fierce competition from other developing countries. These circumstances forced the Korean economy to modify its economic structure toward heavy and chemical industries such as shipbuilding, iron and steel, automobiles, machinery, and petrochemicals. Investments in these newly favored sectors were encouraged by tax and financial incentives. As a result, the share of heavy and chemical products in exports expanded from 13 percent in 1970 to 39 percent in 1979.

In parallel with industrial restructuring, South Korea expanded its construction and manufacturing exports to the oil-producing countries of the Middle East, whose import demand had increased due to abundant oil revenues. The construction boom in the Middle East contributed to an improvement in the Korean domestic-employment situation and served as an important source of foreign exchange.

FIVE LARGEST COMPANIES IN SOUTH KOREA

According to *Asia Week*, the five largest companies in South Korea are as follows:

Company	Sector	Sales ($ in millions)	Rank in Asia
Samsung Electronics	Technology, Appliances	38,487.5	22
Hyundai	Trading, Investment	36,032.7	25
Samsung	Trading, Construction	35,935.5	26
Hyundai Motor	Automobiles	28,752.6	30
LG Electronics	Consumer Electronics	20,085.2	47

Source: "The Asia Week 1000." (2001) *Asia Week* (9 November): 115.

By virtue of the successful economic development plans and timely industrial structure transformation, South Korea was able to retain a strong pace of growth in the 1970s. Exports expanded rapidly at the rate of approximately 40 percent per year. The value of exports, which was below $55 million in 1962, crossed $658 million in 1969 and reached $15 billion in 1979. The economy grew at a high average rate verging on 9 percent a year, and per capita gross national income (GNI) rose from $210 in 1969 to $1,636 in 1979. This remarkable progress allowed South Korea to emerge as one of the newly industrializing Asian economies, along with Taiwan, Singapore, and Hong Kong.

However, in carrying out ambitious economic-development plans, the economy was handicapped by a conspicuously insufficient rate of domestic savings. This gap between investment and savings—known as the deficit current account—was typically bridged by inducing an inflow of foreign capital or by expanding the money supply, despite recognition of the importance of prudent monetary management in avoiding inflationary pressures in the process of economic development. In consequence, foreign debt kept piling up, and chronic inflation lingered on.

The second oil crisis (1979) and domestic political instability also took a heavy toll. By 1980, the nation faced many difficulties throughout the entire economy, including its first negative growth since 1962 and a huge current account deficit (–$3.5 billion). These caused a shift in the government's policy stance to a stability-oriented growth strategy. Along with structural adjustment measures to enhance economic efficiency, the government strongly pursued the opening up of the economy, through trade and capital market liberalization, and deregulation on a stage-by-stage basis as part of the move to encourage private initiative in economic management. Efforts at both deregulation and opening up the economy at that time unfortunately did not make great progress, owing to the immaturity of the political and economic environment. However, tight monetary and fiscal policies greatly contributed to the construction of a stable foundation for the South Korean economy, as did the renewed stability of international oil prices. The inflation rate was brought down to single-digit level in the 1980s, and the current account significantly improved to a record $5.4 billion surplus in 1989. Annual real gross domestic product (GDP) growth rate was 12.2 percent in the decade, raising the per capita GNI to $5,185 in 1989.

The Economy in the 1990s

As South Korea moved into the 1990s, however, the structural fault lines of its high-cost, low-efficiency industrial structure grew more pronounced amid a sharp increase in competitive pressure. High costs had become endemic, and there were large wage increases as a result of the emergence of a strong labor movement amid the democratic reform of Korean politics and society, following the Seoul Olympic games in 1988. Land was expensive and interest rates were also high, mostly due to repeated waves of price instability and inflexible adherence to management strategies of both external expansion and duplicated investment on the part of firms, such as competitive investment into semi-conductor production facilities and automobile production plants. The financial and real sectors (manufacturing, labor, capital, trade, and so forth) became markedly less efficient because market principles could not operate properly in a socioeconomic environment characterized by previous overregulation and government meddling in the financial and corporate sectors. By the mid-1990s, the Korean economy was 99 percent free of government intervention.

Efforts to improve productivity, such as introducing new technologies, were likewise inadequate. Moreover, South Korean companies faced intense competition from foreign companies in both domestic and international markets, owing to the rapid growth of recently developing countries, the launch of the World Trade Organization, and the accelerated opening of South Korea's markets in order to meet Organization For Economic Cooperation and Development (OECD) criteria, such as free trade of goods and capital.

GDP grew at 7.5 percent per year on average during the period from 1990 to 1996. The current account balance, which had continued in surplus since the mid-1980s, slid into a deficit that reached $23 billion by 1996, amounting to 4.4 percent of 1996 GDP. Total foreign debt also widened sharply from $29.4 billion as of the end of 1989 to $104.7 billion at the end of 1996.

From early 1997, foreign-currency liquidity conditions continued to worsen, and by November South Korea was on the brink of defaulting on its external debts. One important external signal came from the collapse of the market for semiconductors, a major South Korean export, in 1996, which caused the current account deficit to jump from 1.7 percent of GDP in 1995 to 4.4 percent in 1996. But the South Korean government did not take this drop seriously, for by mid-1997 the deficit was already back to a 2.5 percent annual rate and heading lower. Nor did the government believe that the currency could possibly be threatened, because the economic fundamentals (growth, trade, foreign exchange, and so on) were thought robust.

However, from early 1997, foreign investors began to keep a close eye on the South Korean economy, in light of the increasing weakening of its financial systems, which had accumulated huge nonperforming loans due to a string of large corporate bankruptcies. The Southeast Asian currency crisis that started in Thailand in July 1997 unsettled foreign creditors and encouraged them to withdraw their investments from South Korea as well. Leading international credit-rating agencies such as Standard and Poor's and Moody's downgraded South Korea's sovereign rating sharply in October. Then South Korea was suddenly refused a rollover for its short-term debts by foreign banks, Japanese banks in particular. Japan, which was suffering from large nonperforming loans in its domestic markets due to the collapse of equity and land prices in 1990–1991, began to collect maturing debts from Asian countries and refused to roll over South Korea's short-term debts. Furthermore, the depreciation of the Japanese yen in 1995–1996 aggravated the trade positions of Southeast Asian countries and South Korea as well. The rising expectation of a massive depreciation of the Korean currency (the won), due mainly to the large current account deficit, also played a substantial part in the worsening of the foreign-exchange situation.

Consequently, the South Korean government turned to the International Monetary Fund (IMF) for a bailout and signed up for an IMF rescue plan amounting to $55 billion on 3 December 1997. In exchange for these rescue funds, the IMF demanded a fundamental overhaul of the South Korean economy and a contractional macroeconomic policy of higher taxes, reduced spending, and high interest rates (with tight monetary policy). In accordance with these agreements, South Korea has been pressing ahead with structural reforms in the financial and corporate sectors and in the labor market, while accelerating liberalization of trade and capital accounts.

South Korea's Economy Today

After the currency crisis, the real economy was deeply depressed by the credit crunch and the sharp contraction of consumer and business confidence. But since early 1999, the economy has recovered and has continued to exhibit strong growth. The GDP grew at a rate of 9 percent in 2000, and consumer price inflation rose by only 1.8 percent in that year. Per capita GNI bounced back to $9,700 in 2000, just a little short of the pre-crisis level of $10,307 in 1997.

South Korea, though still having many problems to overcome, is now heading toward a constant reshaping of its economic systems and practices on the basis of market principles. The country pursues dynamic economic growth, converting the industrial structure into one led by high value-added industries, and accelerating both product development and quality improvement through technological innovations. The economic system is actively creating a new engine of growth by converting to knowledge-intensive industries and the information and communication sector in the twenty-first century.

Hwang Eui-Gak

Further Reading
Bank of Korea. (2000) *Monthly Bulletin.*

Feldstein, Martin. (1998) "Refocusing the IMF." *Foreign Affairs* 77, 2: 20–23.

Hwang, Eui-Gak. (1993) *The Korean Economies: A Comparison of North and South.* Oxford: Clarendon Press.

———. (1999) "The East Asian Financial Crises: Cause, Consequence, and Lessons." *South African Journal of Economics* 67, 2 (June): 173–194.

Organization for Economic Cooperation and Development. (1999) *Economic Surveys 1999–2000: Korea.* Paris: OECD.

SOUTH KOREA—EDUCATION SYSTEM

Confucianism dominated education in Korea until the end of the nineteenth century, when a modern schooling system was introduced. During the Koryo dynasty (918–1392) and the Choson dynasty (1392–1910), civil officials were selected through the state examination system, which tested mainly an applicant's knowledge of Confucianism. This system made the learning of Confucian classics an educational tradition of the elite class.

In 1895, a royal decree mandating education reform established a modern education system. King Kojong (d. 1907) started to build public primary, secondary, vocational, and normal schools in the capital and in the provinces. Many private schools were also founded around the country. The modernizing of education under the Choson dynasty was interrupted, however, by the Japanese invasion of Korea in 1905. Korean education was restored in 1945, when the country was liberated from Japanese colonial rule.

Structure of the Education System

The South Korean education system consists of five parts: preschool, primary, secondary, higher, and continuing education.

Preschool education is carried out by nursery schools and kindergartens. Nursery schools and kindergartens are mostly private institutes, some of which get financial support from the government. Two-thirds of students are enrolled in private kindergartens. Fifty percent of children three to five years of age receive preschool education. Generally, parents pay substantial amounts for preschool education.

Primary education is compulsory and free from the age of six for six years. The enrollment rate for primary schooling reached 100 percent in the early 1960s. Almost all primary schools are public, enrolling 90 percent of all students.

Secondary education lasts for six years: three years in middle school and three years in high school. Students enter middle school generally at the age of twelve. Middle school education is compulsory and

Children at the Son Shin Elementary School in Seoul, South Korea, in 1989 practice the violin. (STEPHANIE MAZE/CORBIS)

free. The enrollment rate is 100 percent for children twelve to fourteen years; 23 percent are enrolled in private middle schools. Almost all graduates from middle schools advance to high school.

High schools provide two tracks: general academic and vocational. General high schools enroll 61 percent of the total number of high school students, while vocational high schools enroll 39 percent. Most high school students pay a tuition fee.

About 67 percent of high school graduates advance to higher education. Higher education includes junior colleges, four-year colleges, universities, and other institutions of higher learning, such as the Open University (which teaches via the Internet, broadcasting, and correspondence courses rather than classroom lectures), colleges in workplaces, and cyber colleges. Junior colleges provide two to three years of postsecondary education, with mostly vocational and technical programs. Colleges offer four years of courses at the undergraduate level. Universities provide graduate programs for masters' and doctors' degrees, as well as undergraduate programs for bachelors' degrees.

Higher education in South Korea depends heavily on private institutions, which enroll 81 percent of the total number of students. Students in higher education generally bear the substantial part of their educational costs, though students at the Open University and teachers' colleges pay only nominal tuition fees.

For all schools and universities, an academic year consists of two semesters. The first semester begins on 1 March and ends on 31 August. The second semester runs from 1 September through the end of February. The minimum number of school days for an academic year is established by law. Primary through high schools must provide instruction for more than

220 days. Colleges and universities must give lectures for more than thirty-two weeks per academic year. There are two vacations every year: summer vacation from mid-July through August and winter vacation from late December through February.

Administration and Curriculum Policy

The structure of educational administration includes three layers of administrative authorities: the Ministry of Education and Human Resources, the boards of education at the municipal and provincial levels, and district offices of education at the local level.

The Ministry of Education and Human Resources (the former Ministry of Education, renamed in 2001) is the central authority responsible for executing the constitutional mandates for national education. The Ministry formulates and implements national policies and plans related to education and human-resource developments. The Ministry is also authorized to control the school curriculum and textbooks.

There are sixteen boards of education at municipal and provincial levels. Members of the board are elected by the electoral college, consisting of representatives of parents, teachers, and residents. The top executive officer of the board is the superintendent of education, who is elected every four years by the school council members. At the local level, 180 district offices of education take charge of supervising primary and middle schools as well as kindergartens in a city or county, under the direction of the provincial board of education. The head of the district education office is appointed by the provincial superintendent.

Curriculum regulation prescribes the national curriculum and the criteria for textbooks for each school level. The government determines and monitors almost every detail of curriculum, so that the curriculum contents and time allocations are uniform at each school level around the nation, with only a few variations by province. The national curriculum is subject to regular revisions every five years or so. The seventh, and current, national curriculum was implemented in the year 2000.

Education Reform

The government has pursued education reform since the early 1990s. The Presidential Commission on Education Reform presented an overall reform plan to the president in May 1995. The plan stressed the following points: all education must be student oriented; school and curriculum must be diversified to provide more choices in learning experience; there must be accountability in school management; equal opportunity and new technology must be adopted to facilitate continuing education; and the quality of education must be improved.

Currently the government emphasizes developing human resources to cope with the knowledge-based society. Every level and type of schooling has been reformed to meet the new challenges. At the same time, the government has proposed constructing an open system for lifelong learning, which provides everyone with learning opportunities at any time and place. An overall scheme for building a lifelong learning society was enacted in the Lifelong Education Act in March 2000.

Kim Shinil

Further Reading

Adams, Don, and Esther Gottlieb. (1993) *Education and Social Change in Korea.* New York: Garland.

Kim Shinil. (April 1987) "Korean Education Past and Present." *Korea Journal* 27, 4: 4–20.

Ministry of Education. (2000) *Education in Korea: 1999–2000.* Seoul: Ministry of Education.

———. (1996) *The Korean Education System: Background Report to the OECD.* Seoul: Korean Educational Development Institute.

Presidential Commission on Education Reform. (1996) *Education Reform for New Education System.* Seoul: Presidential Commission on Education Reform.

Shin, Se-ho. (1995) "Korea, Republic of." In *International Encyclopedia of National Systems of Education*, edited by T. Neville Postlethwaite. 2d ed. Oxford, U.K.: Elsevier Science, 515–524.

SOUTH KOREA—HUMAN RIGHTS Korea's political tradition (especially during the Choson dynasty, 1392–1910) legitimized an authoritarian regime based on a rigid class-based hierarchy of ruler and ruled, male power and female subordination, and a system of harsh penalties for crimes against the state and uncompromising demands for loyalty to social and political superiors. The state instituted a rigid system of lineage rules and village contracts that enforced social control and indoctrination. The official state ideology, Neo-Confucianism, instructed the ruler to win the affections of the people for fear that their grievances would reach to Heaven and thus invite natural disasters of flood and famine and man-made disasters of private suffering and public rebellion. Policies that promoted compassion, sympathy, or humaneness were utilized with an eye toward protecting the state. The individual did not have rights—one had duties and responsibilities to the social group and the polity.

By the end of the nineteenth century, domestic economic crisis and foreign pressures created vital changes in the perception of rights. Korean intellectuals, such as Yu Kil-chun (1856–1914), who traveled to America and Europe from 1883 to1884, advocated for political reforms based on egalitarianism and respect for the rights to life, liberty, and property. During the twentieth century, the influence of Christianity was felt in ideas of cosmopolitanism and natural rights. Despite the harshness of Japan's colonial rule (1910–1945), many reformers argued for "Western" rights for women, labor, religion, and conscience.

Constitutional and Political Evolution

Japan's surrender of its Korean colony in August 1945 created a legal vacuum. The "peace" created a division between the north and south. American advisers, working with the United Nations command, supervised the surrender and political rebuilding of the south. However, the U.S. representatives in Korea had no knowledge of Japanese or Korean law. Furthermore, the Americans brought Syngman Rhee (1875–1965) from thirty years of exile to head the government in Seoul. He had no sympathy at all for the reformers who had fought for human rights. The new government in Seoul inherited more than 95 percent of its legal system from Japan. The 1948 Korean constitution included references to several standard political and socioeconomic rights—equality before the law; personal liberty; freedom of domicile; freedom from unlawful search; freedom of speech, press, assembly, and association; equality of men and women; and the right to elect public officials and to hold public office. However, these rights were qualified by the statement that they could be denied if they threatened the public order or the welfare of the community.

The constitution reflected Japanese and German influences in establishing a strong president, a weak assembly, and a dependent judiciary with limited jurisdiction. From 1947 to 1993, Seoul was ruled dictatorially by four presidents. The first president, Syngman Rhee, was placed in office in 1945 by the U.S. government. He authored the National Security Law (which was based on Japanese colonial laws), which made any criticism of the state illegal. The punishment for such crimes against the state included imprisonment, the death penalty, and even government-sanctioned assassination. Under President Rhee's rule, more than 250,000 Koreans lost their lives in police raids or military operations that targeted Communists or fellow travelers (Communist sympathizers). The Korean War allowed Rhee to use the army to arrest and execute his opposition. Student and popular unrest in 1960 forced his resignation and exile to Hawaii.

On 20 August 1960, President-elect Yun Po Sun (1897–1990), a graduate of the University of Edinburgh, established the Second Republic. He crafted a new constitution that provided for greater freedoms of speech and the press. According to author Andrew Nahm, within the next year newspapers and journals increased from 600 to 1,600, and journalists numbered 160,000. There were 2,000 demonstrations totaling more than 900,000 protesters. In May 1961, General Park Chung Hee (1917–1979) reacted to the political and economic unrest by leading a military coup that put him into office for more than eighteen years.

During this time, Park created the extraconstitutional Supreme Council for National Reconstruction. This council centralized all executive, legislative, and judicial power in Park and his clique. This group manipulated state agencies to control the populace, organize economic gain for the elite, and suppress all dissent. Arrests and executions reached major proportions. Torture of political opponents became so widespread that former president Yun Po Sun categorized President Park's regime as a "government by torture" (Cohen and Baker 1999: 178). Civilian unrest grew so strong in the early 1970s that Park declared martial law in 1972. Finally, in an effort to give himself even more power, he established the Yushin (Revitalizing Reform) Constitution, which assured him of nearly total control of the economy and society. Park's rule was so onerous that his own Korean Central Intelligence Agency director, Kim Jae Kyu, shot Park during a state dinner on 26 October 1979.

Within three weeks, on 12 December 1979, Major General Chun Doo Hwan (b. 1931) seized the presidential Blue House (so-called because of its blue roof tiles) and occupied key governmental offices in central Seoul. General Chun, who was known as ruthless and uncompromising, had acquired his power by leading a division of Korean troops in Vietnam. On 17 May 1980, Chun declared extraordinary martial law to consolidate his power and to destroy the growing power of his civilian competitors, the so-called three Kims—Young sam (b. 1927), Kim Dae Jung (b. 1925), and Kim Jong Pil (b. 1926).

One day after Chun's declaration, 18 May, a prodemocracy student demonstration erupted in the historically radical city of Kwangju. General Chun, with the alleged support of U.S. military authorities, declared the protest an insurrection and moved crack troops from the border with North Korea to Kwangju. Here the troops slaughtered 400 to 2,000 protesters

Protestors in central Seoul agitate for the release of 400 political prisoners on 10 December 1998.

among a crowd of 300,000. General Chun claimed that North Korean agents had infiltrated the group of students. Because of this perceived threat, he gave himself emergency powers to suspend the freedom and rights of the people as defined by the constitution and began a national campaign to weed out all dissidents, traitors, and critics. He arrested the three Kims; in September 1980, the criminal court found Kim Dae Jung guilty of sedition and condemned him to death. After U.S. pressure, he went into exile in the United States for health treatments.

General Chun remained in office until 1987, when nationwide demonstrations broke the government's will to prevent constitutional and human-rights reform. On 16 December 1987, Roh Tae Woo (b. 1931), the prime minister and Chun's designated successor, won the election for president. His regime was marked by rapid reforms and concluded in 1993 with the first popular elections for the presidency. The next president, Young Sam, moved from military to civilian rule. In 1998, Kim Dae Jung became president and proceeded to democratize South Korea by repealing the national security laws, releasing political prisoners from incarceration, and traveling to Pyongyang to discuss measures for reconciliation with North Korea. In 2000, he received the Nobel Peace Prize in recognition of his lifelong commitment to, and sacrifice for, human rights.

Protest

Japan's postwar democracy was, in part, supported and created through the institutions and collaboration of the Allied Occupation. The U.S. role in South Korea did not promote any liberalism or democracy. The Korean War (1950–1953) and its aftermath trapped Seoul in the role of a proxy in the Cold War between the United States and its Communist rivals in Moscow, Beijing, and Pyongyang. Although many American politicians, military leaders, and even scholars argue that Korea was not disposed to promoting and sustaining a democratic and human-rights tradition, the evidence of a strong, self-sacrificing, and intelligent prodemocratic movement in Korea belies such negative testimonials.

The strength of the human-rights movement can be expressed in terms of the attempts the Korean government made to extinguish it. To establish their rule, the military governments in Seoul were forced to create a repressive police state that attempted to control the activities and expression of all its citizens. Anyone who seemed to support human rights was faced with possible arrest, torture, and even execution. Hundreds of thousands of people, including liberal nationalists, socialists, labor organizers, women's representatives, and even satirical writers, faced daily harassment and threats. Some daring writers, like the popular and many-times-arrested iconoclast Kim Chi-ha, criticized the bureaucracy, military, and foreign policy in scathing short stories and poetry. Hwang Suk-young's *The Shadow of Arms* harshly described the cruel and venal role of the South Korean military in the Vietnam War. His writings, coupled with his illegal trip to North Korea, resulted in a trial and jail sentence upon his return to Seoul. Others, like Ahn Jung-hyo, hid their writings until the demise of military rule and then published novels that were critical of the Korean and Vietnam Wars.

In the late 1990s, Kwangju became the site of the launch of the Asian Charter for Human Rights. Under the presidencies of Kim Young-sam and Kim Dae Jung, the Republic of Korea has been engaged, both officially and through many nongovernmental organizations, in human-rights activities domestically and abroad. In addition to democratizing the government, President Kim Dae Jung is initiating and extending human rights to cover women, children, and patients. Internationally, the Republic of Korea has appointed a human-rights ambassador to the United Nations and has been actively engaged in the Commission on Human Rights.

Richard C. Kagan

Further Reading

Ahn Jung-hyo. (1990) *The Silver Stallion*. New York: Soho.

———. (1989) *White Badge*. New York: Soho Press.

Cohen, Jerome A., and Edward J. Baker. (1999) "U.S. Foreign Policy and Human Rights in South Korea." In *Human Rights in Korea: Historical and Policy Perspectives*, edited by William Shaw. Cambridge, MA: Harvard University Press, 171–220.

Hwang Suk-young. (1994) *The Shadow of Arms*. Ithaca, NY: Cornell University Press.

Nahm, Andrew C. (1996) *Korea: A History of the Korean People: Tradition and Transformation*. 2d ed. Elizabeth, NJ, and Seoul: Hollym.

Neary, Ian. (2001) *Human Rights, Children's Rights, and Patients' Rights in Japan, South Korea, and Taiwan*. London: Routledge.

Shaw, William, ed. (1999) *Human Rights in Korea: Historical and Policy Perspectives*. Cambridge, MA: Harvard University Press.

Sung, Suh. (2000) *Nineteen Years in South Korea's Gulag*. Boulder, CO: Rowman and Littlefield.

SOUTH KOREA—POLITICAL SYSTEM

South Korea has a democratic form of government based on the separation of powers and checks and balances. But it took a long time until the realization of the ideal of democracy. Authoritarian rule began with South Korea's autocratic first president, Syngman Rhee (1875–1965), and his successors and the military continued the practice, infringing on human rights and delaying the development of democratic procedures. Democratization processes began in the late 1980s.

The Creation of South Korea's Modern Political System

As soon as Japan surrendered on 15 August 1945, two groups competed to initiate the creation of a new nation-state in Korea. On the one hand, the Committee for the Preparation of an Independent State, led by Yo Un-hyong (1886–1947) and Ann Chae-hong (1881–1965), was established. The committee held a nationwide assembly in Seoul and declared the creation of the People's Republic of Korea on 6 September 1945. On the other hand, the Committee for the National Congress, composed of supporters of the exiled provisional government in Shanghai, China, refused to join the People's Republic of Korea and attempted to set up a provisional government and organize a political party in the tradition of the independence movement. On 8 September 1945, however, the U.S. armed forces proclaimed General Order No. 1, which refused to recognize both the legitimacy of the provisional government and the existence of the republic; instead, the order maintained that the U.S. military government was the only authoritative polity in Korea. The military government ruled South Korea for three years.

Under the military government, various political groups competed: Syngman Rhee and his associates, provisional government leaders, and Communists. As the military government restructured the institutional arrangement and succeeded in controlling the left-oriented social forces in Korean society, the competition among right-wing groups intensified. While Rhee and his associates favored the establishment of a separate state in the south alone, Kim Ku (1876–1949) and provisional-government leaders made desperate efforts to build a unified Korean state. The U.S. military government favored Rhee, because Kim Ku's group attempted to make an alliance with political leaders leaning toward the left. Accordingly, the emergence of two independent political systems in Korea can be attributed not only to the dissonance between the United States and the Soviet Union on the Korean problem but also to the internal dynamics of the relationship between the U.S. military government and the political groups in South Korea.

The formal launch of the Republic of Korea took place with the support of the United Nations in 1948. The general election for a National Assembly was held on 10 May 1948, under the supervision of the U.N. Temporary Commission on Korea. After the National Assembly adopted a constitution, it elected Syngman Rhee president. The Republic of Korea was inaugurated on 15 August 1948, and U.S. military rule ended.

Syngman Rhee's Autocratic Rule

From the beginning, the political system under President Rhee's leadership drifted. Not only did his alliance with the right-wing political party collapse, he also proved to be a leader with an authoritarian management style. Moreover, the Korean War (1950–1953) brought about a national crisis that threatened South Korea's existence. The political situation deteriorated further because of Rhee's desire to prolong his presidency during wartime.

In 1952, he consolidated his power base by adopting the direct presidential election, and two years later he illicitly passed a constitutional amendment permitting lifelong presidency. Based on this amended constitution, he won his third term as president in May 1956. However, when student demonstrations and civil violence followed election fraud connected with his campaign for a fourth term in 1960, he resigned and fled to Hawaii, where he lived in exile.

The fall of Rhee's rule was immediately accompanied by a constitutional revision from the presidential system to the parliamentary. Under the new constitution, Chang Myon (1899–1966) took power. To some extent, Chang's rule was seen as a democratic transition not only because of his moderate personality but because of his policies liberalizing a Korean society that had become increasingly restricted under his precursor's authoritarian rule. However, he could neither manage the exploding and massive popular demand for reforms, nor find a way to give the ruling party unity and solidarity. After nine months, he was overthrown by a military coup led by General Park Chung Hee (1917–1979) on 16 May 1961.

Park Chung Hee's Rule and After

During the period of military government between 1961 and 1963, Park consolidated his political and economic power by the introduction of a law banning the political activities of politicians and by the establishment of the Korean Intelligence Agency and the Economic Planning Board. After two and half years of military government, Park was elected president in December 1963 under the new constitution, which allowed presidents to serve two four-year terms. Even though he became president through direct popular election, his government lacked legitimacy because his

political career was rooted in a military coup. Therefore, he introduced new goals of modernization and economic development and led an industrialization drive to strengthen the weak legitimacy of his government. Although the industrial drive during the 1960s brought many social problems, it also contributed to the unprecedentedly rapid economic growth of modern South Korea. Gaining some popularity, Park was elected to his second term in 1967.

At the end of the 1960s and 1970s, however, Park had to confront a growing opposition. In 1969, he pushed to pass a constitutional amendment that gave the incumbent president the chance to run for three consecutive four-year terms. Then he became president for a third term after the 1971 election, defeating his opponent Kim Dae Jung (b. 1925). Park's ambition did not end here. He declared a state of national emergency in December 1971; in October 1972, he suspended the constitution and dissolved the National Assembly. Finally, Park introduced the notorious Yushin system (literally "revitalization"), departing far from democratic values, norms, and procedures. Unlike the official promulgation statements, the Yushin system not only seriously weakened the balancing power of the legislative body but also legalized oppressive measures like press censorship.

The Yushin system has been seen as the most authoritarian regime in modern Korean history, even though under it the country continued to achieve a high rate of economic development. The Yushin system allowed Park to rule without any restriction on the duration of his powers. The rights of opposition leaders were infringed on, and intelligence agencies and legal mechanisms were used to repress working people. Park successfully controlled the ruling camp in particular and the National Assembly in general by introducing a constitutional amendment whereby he himself chose members of the Yujonghoe (political circle of revitalization), the group loyal to him, which held one-third of the seats in the legislature.

The Yushin system collapsed after an aide assassinated Park in October 1979, following civil violence that erupted in the cities of Pusan and Masan when people denounced the Yushin system. Nevertheless, the old regime was not automatically transformed. The opposition party and political society in general were divided, and there was no alternative force to lead a democratic transition. Given this situation, the existing military rule continued, until General Chun Doo Hwan (b. 1931) staged a coup in December 1979.

Chun then masterminded the bloody repression of an uprising in Kwangju, where in May 1980 people

PREAMBLE OF THE PROVISIONAL REPUBLIC OF KOREA GOVERNMENT (SOUTH KOREA)

Adopted 17 July 1948

We the people of Korea, proud of a resplendent history and traditions dating from time immemorial, upholding the cause of the Provisional Republic of Korea Government born of the Independence Movement of 1 March 1919 and the democratic ideals of the uprising on 19 April 1960 against injustice, having assumed the mission of democratic reform and peaceful unification of our homeland and having determined to consolidate national unity with Justice, humanitarianism and brotherly love, and to destroy all social vices and injustice, and to afford equal opportunities to every person and provide for the fullest development of individual capabilities in all fields, including political, economic, social and cultural life by further strengthening the basic free and democratic order conducive to private initiative and public harmony, and to help each person discharge those duties and responsibilities concomitant to freedoms and rights, and to elevate the quality of life for all citizens and contribute to lasting world peace and the common prosperity of mankind and thereby to ensure security, liberty and happiness for ourselves and our posterity forever, do hereby amend, through national referendum following a resolution by the National Assembly, the Constitution, ordained and established on 12 July 1948, and amended eight times subsequently.

Source: International Court Network. Retrieved 8 March 2002, from: http://www.uni-wuerzburg.de/law/ks00000_.html.

---

had called for the end of military intervention in politics. Chun was elected president through the rubber-stamp approval of the electoral college, under a new constitution that allowed him one seven-year term of office. But throughout his presidency, Chun confronted strong opposition not only from students but also from the middle class, because of his lack of legitimacy.

Transition to Democratic Rule

Chun handed over power to his military-academy colleague Roh Tae Woo (b. 1932). In 1987, Roh presented the June 29th Declaration, which was the beginning of a gradual democratic transition in South Korea. Roh introduced a constitutional amendment that allowed the direct election of the president, who could serve for one five-year term.

Owing to differences between the opposition leaders, Young Sam (b. 1927) and Kim Dae Jung, Roh won the 1987 presidential election with only 35.9 percent of the vote. Although he was criticized for indecisive leadership, Roh introduced the policy of *Nordpolitik*, whereby he attempted to develop relationships with the Soviet Union and China and to circumscribe North Korea. Along with the breakdown of the socialist bloc in Eastern Europe, Roh's *Nordpolitik* succeeded in normalizing relations with the Soviet Union (1990) and China (1992) and led to the Agreement between South and North Koreas on Reconciliation, Nonaggression, Exchange, and Cooperation in December 1991. According to this agreement, South and North Koreas were to recognize each other's systems; make efforts to transform the state of armistice into a solid state of peace; not use force; and enhance economic, cultural, and other exchanges.

The inauguration of President Young Sam in 1993 marked a peaceful transition from military to civilian rule and the end of three decades of mili-

DAUGHTER OF PARK CHUNG HEE ENTERS PRESIDENTIAL POLITICS

"In December 2001, Park Geun Hye, the daughter of former South Korean President Park Chung Hee who was assassinated in 1979 after eighteen years in office, announced that she would seek the nomination for president of the conservative Grand National Party. She currently represents the city of Taegu in the National Assembly. She mentioned her experience in assisting her father from 1974 to 1979 after her mother was killed by an assassin's bullet meant for her father. Her agenda includes promoting economic growth, increasing women's participation in Korean society, and moving more cautiously on reunification."

Source: Don Kirk (2001) "Candidate for President Invokes Korea of Her Father." *The New York Times* (19 December): A13.

tary rule. Kim enjoyed unprecedented popularity in the early stages of his presidency, when he attacked the corruption of previous governments and of private associations in the military and proposed reform policies. Kim was determined to send the two former presidents, Chun and Roh, to prison on charges of instituting a military coup and corruption. But he lost popularity when the drifting economy was faced with a financial crisis in 1997, which was solved with the help of the International Monetary Fund. Kim's declining performance finally brought about a power shift from the ruling party to the opposition party for the first time in fifty years of modern political history. The lifelong opposition leader Kim Dae Jung was elected president in 1997.

The Constitutional Prescriptions for the Political System

With the exception of Chang Myun's government between 1960 and 1961, South Korea has always been governed by a president. The present constitution prescribes a single five-year term for the president, with the intent of achieving strong and stable leadership.

The presidential system was adopted in South Korea because Koreans favor strong political leadership, particularly in the situation of national division and confrontation between south and north.

At the top of the executive branch of government, the president functions not only as head of state in domestic affairs but also represents the state in foreign relations. The president must carry out his constitutional duty to safeguard the nation's independence and work for peaceful reunification of North and South Korea. The president is the chairman of the State Council, that is, the cabinet, and has the power to appoint and dismiss the prime minister and the cabinet ministers as well as other senior officials, including heads of government agencies and ambassadors, although the National Assembly must approve his choices. The president also serves as commander-in-chief of the armed forces.

The president performs executive functions through the State Council, which is made up of the president, prime minister, and heads of executive ministries. As the principal executive assistant to the president, the prime minister supervises the executive ministers under the direction of the president. Several organizations aid the president: the National Security Council, the Advisory Council on Democratic and Peaceful Unification, the Presidential Council on Science and Technology, and so on. The National Intelligence Service is authorized to collect strategic intelligence and to plan and coordinate intelligence and security activities.

Because of the presidential system, which gives the chief executive so much power, and the long history of military rule, the legislature has not always fully performed its constitutional functions. Nevertheless, legislative power is vested in the National Assembly, a unicameral body. Major functions of the National Assembly include the power to propose, deliberate on, and approve or reject legislative bills; finalize and inspect closing accounts of the national budget; consent to the conclusion and ratification of treaties; and concur in the declaration of war or the conclusion of peace. It also has the right to impeach the president and to approve his emergency orders, thereby theoretically enabling it to check any abuse of presidential prerogatives. In addition, it has the right to inspect government operations and may recommend the removal of the prime minister and executive ministers from office. The National Assembly may also review the qualifications of its members and take disciplinary actions against them.

Of the National Assembly's 273 members, 227 are elected by popular vote for a term of four years, and the remaining 46 legislators are distributed proportionately among the political parties. This proportional representation system is aimed at encouraging legislative participation by leading experts through the political parties. Members are not held responsible outside the National Assembly for any opinions expressed or votes cast within the legislative body.

The Supreme Court, as the highest judiciary body, examines the decisions of the appellate courts in civil and criminal cases and makes final decisions on appeals from these courts. Its decisions are final and indisputable, forming judicial precedents. The chief justice is appointed by the president to a single six-year term with the consent of the National Assembly, and the justices of the Supreme Court are appointed by the president, based on the recommendations of the chief justice. Judges in all lower courts are appointed by the chief justice, with the consent of the Supreme Court Justices Council.

Five appellate courts hear appeals of verdicts by district courts in civil and criminal cases. They hold trials and make decisions for or against lower-court verdicts. They may also decide administrative litigation filed by individuals or organizations against government decisions, orders, and actions. District courts are established in major cities and exercise jurisdiction over all civil and criminal cases filed at a lower level.

Even though the South Korean political system has accomplished significant progress toward procedural democracy, there exist some hurdles impeding its maturity of democratic culture. Not only does regionalism still prevail in elections, boss-oriented politics also sometimes stimulates severe strife in political circles. However, it seems likely that the rapidly extended freedom of press and nongovernmental organizations will play the role of balancing and checking in the process of building a healthy and sound political system in the future.

Sung Chull Kim

Further Reading
Cumings, Bruce. (1997) *Korea's Place in the Sun: A Modern History*. New York: Norton.

Kim, Byoung-Lo Philo. (1992) *Two Koreas in Development*. New Brunswick, NJ: Transaction.

Koo, Hagen, ed. (1993) *State and Society in Contemporary Korea*. Ithaca, NY: Cornell University Press.

SOUTH KOREA–EUROPEAN UNION RELATIONS

Although diplomatic relations between the Republic of Korea (ROK, or South Korea) and the European Union (EU) were established in July 1963, it was not until the end of the 1980s that significant ties began to be formed. Even as European leaders were preoccupied with the challenge of implementing the Single Market (to remove physical, tax, and technical barriers to ensure the freedom of movement of people, capital, and goods among member states) by 1992, South Korea's transition to democracy, along with its increasing importance in the global economy, led EU policy makers to realize the necessity of improving relations with East Asia's third-largest economy. This aim was part of a general change of EU policy toward Asia, which sought to promote European business interests in a region perceived to be the engine of world growth. From the Korean perspective, the integration of the European market to form the world's largest single trading bloc was an opportunity to sustain South Korea's outward-oriented development strategy and reduce its excessive dependence on the U.S. market.

Economic issues, especially trade policy and market-access negotiations, have dominated bilateral relations. The export success that fueled the transformation of the ROK into a major trading country led to frequent trade frictions with the EU and the establishment of import restrictions—notably antidumping duties—on Korean products, raising the specter of "Fortress Europe," the fear that European integration would secure benefits only for member countries and that outsiders would face protectionism. South Korea responded with a surge of direct investment in European manufacturing, starting in the early 1990s. From the European standpoint, one major source of conflict has been the existence of structural barriers in the ROK, such as lax enforcement of intellectual property rights, negative sentiment against imported cars, and restrictive regulations on pharmaceuticals, which hinder access to the Korean market.

The Framework Agreement on Trade and Cooperation was signed in October 1996, was ratified by all EU member states and the ROK, and entered into force in April 2001. This agreement was a clear indication that the EU and the ROK recognized the importance of institutionalizing and deepening their relations by committing all parties to work toward improved market access and cooperation on a wide range of issues such as maritime transport, intellectual property, and standards. These trends were impacted by the Asian financial crisis of 1997, in which currency speculation in Thailand spread rapidly to other Asian economies. The contagion reached South Korea, leading to sharp declines in the value of the Korean currency (won), the stock market, and other asset prices. In the aftermath of the crisis, the opening of the Korean market accelerated—chiefly to alleviate the capital-shortage constraint—and the EU emerged as the largest source of foreign direct investment, showing European firms' strong commitment to South Korea's potential for expansion.

Despite the continued importance accorded to economic relations, the EU has also realized the need to broaden its bilateral agenda with South Korea and support international efforts to secure stability in Northeast Asia. Political dialogue, focusing mainly on the Korean peninsula, has gradually increased since the mid-1990s. In 1997, the EU joined the Korean Peninsula Energy Development Organization, a consortium founded by the United States, Japan, and the ROK to replace North Korea's nuclear facilities with more proliferation-resistant light-water reactors; since 1995 the EU has been a consistent donor of assistance including humanitarian aid (40 million euros of medicines, water and sanitation proects, and winter clothes), food assistance (188 million euros of food, fertilizers, and farm cooperative projects), and contributions to the KEDO project (75 million euros). As a long-standing advocate of direct dialogue between the two Koreas, the EU has been a strong supporter of the policy of the South Korean president Kim Dae-jung to seek engagement with the north, and the decision by most EU member states to establish diplomatic ties with Pyongyang (North Korea), ahead of the United States, was encouraged by Seoul to help invigorate the peace process. This European foray into intra-Korean affairs should be perceived as a complement to—not a substitute for—the leading U.S. role on the peninsula and may be a significant initiative to heighten Europe's diplomatic profile in the region.

Serge Perrin and Hong Sik Cho

Further Reading

Dent, Christopher M. (1999) *The European Union and East Asia: An Economic Relationship.* London and New York: Routledge.
European Commission. (2001) "Europa: The European Union On-Line." Retrieved 30 April 2001, from http://europe.eu.int/comm/external_relations/south_korea/intro/index.htm.
Maull, Hanns, Gerald Segal, and Jusuf Wanandi, eds. (1998) *Europe and the Asia Pacific.* London and New York: Routledge.

SOUTH KOREA–UNITED STATES RELATIONS

In 1882 the United States became the first Western power to sign a treaty (the Treaty of Amity and Commerce) with Korea. At that time, U.S. policy toward Korea was one of nonintervention. The treaty was signed to increase trade and improve the circumstances of Americans who were shipwrecked on the Korean coast on their way to and from China. The Koreans signed the treaty with the hope of enlisting the United States in Korea's efforts to offset growing Japanese power in the region. However, such a relationship did not develop, and Japan annexed Korea in 1910.

American involvement became prominent again at the end of the Japanese occupation of Korea, when Japan surrendered to the Allied forces after its World War II defeat in 1945. The United States established a military government south of the thirty-eighth parallel on the Korean Peninsula. In an attempt to establish a democratic Korea and to contain Communist expansion in Asia, the United States initiated United Nations–sponsored elections, which gave birth to the Republic of Korea (ROK) on 15 August 1948.

Security Relations

The U.S.-ROK relationship was cemented when North Korea invaded South Korea in June 1950. The Korean War (1950–1953) saw U.S. and U.N. troops together with ROK forces fighting to a stalemate with the North Koreans. The signing of the 1954 U.S.-ROK Mutual Defense Treaty created a new security alliance that committed the United States to defending the ROK against external aggression. Since then, South Korea has depended on the presence of U.S. troops located in various bases around the peninsula to deter any attempted North Korean invasion.

Due to domestic difficulties in the late 1960s, the administration of President Richard Nixon (1913–1994) decided to reduce its military presence in the Asia-Pacific region. The United States removed twenty-four thousand troops from South Korea but declared it would still defend the ROK in the event of attack from North Korea. With U.S. assistance totaling $1.5 billion, South Korea increased its defense capabilities to match those of North Korean forces by the 1970s.

In 2002, regular joint ROK-U.S. military exercises and thirty-seven thousand U.S. troops stationed in South Korea reflected America's strong commitment to the security of South Korea. To reciprocate for American support over the years, South Korea sent 300,000 ROK soldiers to fight in the Vietnam War (1954–1975) and offered assistance totaling $500 million during the Persian Gulf War (1990–1991).

The 1990s saw the United States playing a mediating role in inter-Korean relations. South Korea and

South Korea and the United States have strong military and economic relations. Here, U.S. Defense Secretary William Cohen reviews a South Korean honor guard on his arrival in Seoul on 28 July 1999. (REUTERS NEWMEDIA INC./CORBIS)

the United States consistently coordinated efforts to resolve threats arising from nuclear and missile issues on the Korean Peninsula. In 1993, North Korea refused to allow the International Atomic Agency (IAEA) to inspect its nuclear reactors. This triggered speculations about North Korea's capacity to produce nuclear weapons, which, if such capabilities existed, could have a tremendous impact on the security of the Korean Peninsula.

A settlement was reached with North Korea through the 1994 Agreed Framework. The United States and its allies, namely South Korea and Japan, agreed to finance and provide the Democratic People's Republic of Korea (DPRK) with a pair of light-water nuclear reactors through the Korean Peninsula Energy Development Organization. In return, North Korea agreed to freeze its nuclear activities and to allow inspections by the IAEA to determine whether it had violated the Nonproliferation Treaty by using spent nuclear fuel to reprocess plutonium in order to manufacture nuclear weapons.

Subsequently, in 1997, the South Korean president Young Sam (b. 1927) and U.S. president Bill Clinton (b. 1946) jointly initiated four-party peace talks between the United States, the ROK, the DPRK, and the People's Republic of China, North Korea's ally to the north. The talks were held to build confidence, promote inter-Korean dialogue, and establish a per-manent south-north agreement ending hostilities in the Korean Peninsula. Although these goals have not been realized, the four-party talks have provided the best opportunity to date for the United States and South Korea to discuss broader security issues with North Korea.

Economic Relations

In the aftermath of the Korean War, to reconstruct and stabilize its war-torn economy, South Korea depended heavily on U.S. aid and economic assistance. By 1973, the United States had provided a total of $3.5 billion to rebuild South Korea's economy. The economic relationship between the two countries changed from one of client-patron to that of a mutually interdependent association when the Korean economy began to show remarkable growth in the early 1980s. For the last thirty years, the United States has figured prominently as an important source of investment, technology transfer, and foreign capital for South Korea. South Korea's dependence on exports for growth made the United States (the world's largest market) its most important trading partner. Moreover, the United States also became the principal supplier of raw materials and machinery to resource-poor South Korea.

In the late 1980s, Washington began to take exception to South Korea's trade surpluses, which became a source of friction between the two countries.

Correcting this trade imbalance became a priority. The Koreans agreed to give up their status as a "priority foreign country" in terms of trade practices with the United States and to work for appreciation of the Korean won and liberalization of Korea's import market.

The two-way trade volume between South Korea and the United States expanded from $300 million in 1963 to $67 billion in 2000. The United States has become the largest trading partner and investor country in South Korea. South Korea in turn is the United States's seventh-largest trading partner, sixth-largest export market, and fourth-largest market for agricultural goods.

Tensions in ROK-U.S. Relations

Although U.S.-ROK relations are strong, they are multifaceted. In recent years, anti-Americanism has begun to emerge within South Korean nationalism. The Kwangju uprising (1980) was a turning point in the Korean public's view of U.S. involvement in its internal affairs. Following the killings of demonstrators by government troops in the Kwangju uprising, many student activists blamed the United States for supporting the oppressive regime of President Chun Doo Hwan and for causing the division of the Korean Peninsula. Student demonstrations in 1980s led to the burning of the American Cultural Center in Pusan (1982), the seizure of the United States Information Service building in Seoul (1985), and attempted arson at the American Cultural Center in Kwangju (1989).

These days, public criticism of the stationing of American troops in South Korea is on the rise, due to civil and criminal incidents involving U.S. soldiers and locals, use of Korean land and facilities, and mistreatment of Korean employees by the U.S. military. Many agree that contentious issues cannot be dealt with until the one-sided Status of Forces Agreement, which gives preferential treatment to American troops in South Korea, is altered to take into account the demands of the host country. However, these bilateral frictions are outweighed by the mutual security concerns of the peninsula, which remain the cornerstone of South Korea's relations with the United States.

Geetha Govindasamy

Further Reading

Curtis, Gerald, and Sung-joo Han. (1983) *The U.S.–South Korea Alliance: Evolving Patterns of Security Relations.* Lexington, MA: Lexington Books.

Dong, Wonmo, ed. (2000) *The Two Koreas and the United States.* Armonk, NY: M. E. Sharpe.

Khoo, Youngnok, and Sung-joo Han, eds. (1985) *The Foreign Policy of the Republic of Korea.* New York: Columbia University Press.

Kwak Tae-Hwan, ed. (1982) *U.S.-Korean Relations: 1882–1982.* Seoul: Institute for Far Eastern Studies, Kyungnam University.

SOUTH KYONGSANG PROVINCE

(1998 pop. 3 million). South Kyongsang Province (Kyongsang namdo) is located in South Korea in the southeastern portion of the Korean peninsula. It contains the major metropolitan center and port of Pusan. The region is characterized by the vast basin of the Naktong River, which descends from the north, and is bounded by Mount Chiri to the west, Mount Kaya and North Kyongsang Province to the north, and the Sea of Japan (East Sea) to the south and east. Due to the rugged topography of the surrounding mountains, subareas within the region share cultural traits, such as a dialect and customs, that are quite different from those of outlying regions.

South Kyongsang Province has a large industrial agglomeration, due mainly to heavy investments in the region by the South Korean government since the 1960s. Automobile and petrochemical factories are largely concentrated along the southeast stretch of cities beginning in North Kyongsang Province and extending from Ulsan through Pusan, Ch'angwon, and Chinju. A thriving import-export zone was established in Masan Bay in the vicinity of the cities of Masan, Ch'angwon, and Chinhae.

South Kyongsang Province conserves the eighty thousand woodblocks that constitute the Korean Buddhist canon (Tripitaka Koreana) at Haein Monastery, which has been named a World Heritage Cultural Treasure by UNESCO. The blocks were carved under royal patronage during Mongolian invasions of Korea between 1236 and 1251 and are the oldest complete Buddhist canon in Chinese characters. The province also boasts several mask dance traditions, which were customarily performed on the fifteenth day of the first moon according to the lunar calendar.

Richard D. McBride II

Further Reading

Eckert, Carter J., Ki-baik Lee, Young Ick Lew, Michael Robinson, and Edward W. Wagner. (1990) *Korea Old and New: A History.* Seoul: Ilchokak.

Korean Overseas Culture and Information Service. (1999) *A Handbook of Korea.* 10th ed. Seoul: Korean Overseas Culture and Information Service.

Lee, Ki-baik. (1984) *A New History of Korea.* Trans. by Edward W. Wagner. Cambridge, MA: Harvard University Press.

SOUTH MANCHURIA RAILWAY   As the southern branch of the Chinese Eastern Railway, the South Manchuria Railway originally connected the central Manchurian city of Changchun to the harbors of Lushun (Port Arthur) and Dalian (Dairen) on the Liaodong Peninsula. It was built and controlled by czarist Russia under terms of the 1898 Pavlov, or Sino-Russian, Treaty of Beijing. The railway and the Guandong (Kwantung) Leased Territory in southern Manchuria were transferred to Japanese control in 1905 under terms of the Treaty of Portsmouth at the conclusion of the Russo-Japanese War. Over the next four decades, the South Manchuria Railway played a central role in Japan's exploitation of the region's natural, agricultural, and industrial resources.

To manage the railway, a unique company was established in June 1906—the South Manchuria Railway Company (Minami Manshu Tetsudo Kabushiki-gaisha, often referred to by its abbreviation, Mantetsu). The company quickly assumed the role of an auxiliary colonial government in the region, supervising not only the railway and harbors but also the great coal mine at Fushun, the steel works at Anshan, dozens of research facilities and laboratories, hospitals, schools, electrical generating plants, water facilities, and the police forces in many of the towns through which the railway ran. Under dynamic leadership, such as that of its first president, the former governor of the colony of Taiwan, Goto Shimpei, the Mantetsu hydra became a driving force in the development of the Japanese presence in Manchuria. Although it often found itself at odds with the local military establishment, the Guandong Army, the South Manchuria Railway Company was not merely a passive commercial enterprise; it was an agent that actively promoted Japanese colonial rule.

After creation of the puppet state of Manzhouguo (Manchukuo) in the early 1930s and the Japanese invasion of China in 1937, the roles played by the South Manchuria Railway Company in the governing and managing of Manchuria and its economy were diminished. A new entity, the Manchuria Heavy Industry Company, came to assume many of the administrative responsibilities and industrial assets formerly managed by Mantetsu. The South Manchuria Railway Company, however, continued to supervise the transportation network in the region, which now involved the movement of thousands of Japanese settlers to central and northern Manchuria as well as constant demands from the military for logistical support. Overall, the company's fortunes declined during World War II as inflation took a toll on its assets and financial structure.

Following Japan's surrender at the end of World War II in the Pacific, management of the original 1,128-kilometer railway was transferred to the Soviet Union and China, per terms of both the Yalta Conference and the Sino-Soviet Treaty of 14 August 1945. After the Chinese Communist Party came to power in 1949, the railway line was transferred to sole Chinese control. During the late twentieth century, the railway lines first laid down by Russian and later Japanese colonial rulers continued to play an important role in the region's transportation infrastructure, allowing for the movement of coal, steel, and manufactured heavy machinery to the commercial port of Dalian for shipment to Chinese cities to the south as well as for export abroad.

Robert John Perrins

Further Reading
Ito, Takeo. (1988) *Life along the South Manchuria Railway: The Memoirs of Ito Takeo*. Trans. by Joshua Fogel. Armonk, NY: M. E. Sharpe.
Matsusaka, Yoshihisa Tak. (2001) *The Making of Japanese Manchuria, 1904–1932*. Cambridge, MA: Harvard University Press.
Myers, Ramon H. (1989) "Japanese Imperialism in Manchuria: The South Manchuria Railway Company, 1906–1933." In *The Japanese Informal Empire in China, 1895–1937*, edited by Peter Duus, Ramon H. Myers, and Mark R. Peattie. Princeton, NJ: Princeton University Press, 101–132.

SOUTH P'YONGAN PROVINCE   (2002 est. pop. 3.4 million). South P'yongan Province (P'yongan namdo), in North Korea (Democratic People's Republic of Korea), surrounds the capital city of P'yongyang and the city of Namp'o. Both P'yongyang and Namp'o, however, are independent administrative entities and are autonomous from the surrounding province. This province is the political, economic, and social center of North Korea. It also has historical significance as the seat of Korean civilization because the first confederacy of tribes arose in this region.

The province has an area of 12,383 square kilometers and a population of 2,853,737 (excluding the populations of P'yongyang and Namp'o). South P'yongan's five cities are P'yongsong (which is also the provincial capital), Sunch'on, Anju, Kaech'on, and Tokch'on. There are also fifteen counties (*kun*).

South P'yongan is highly industrialized, but it also has a significant agricultural sector. Heavy manufacturing sectors include coal, electricity, construction materials, machinery, automobiles, chemicals, and mining. Foodstuffs, textiles, leather, paper, and household items are the top light manufacturing products. Wheat and corn are the key agricultural products. Livestock include cattle, sheep, and goats. The region's orchards yield apples and chestnuts. Because of the province's 400-kilometer coastline along the Yellow Sea, croakers, anchovies, and oysters are among the key seafoods produced.

Jennifer Jung-Kim

Further Reading

Cho, Chung-Kyung, Phyllis Haffner, and Fredric M. Kaplan. (1991) *The Korea Guidebook*. 5th ed. Boston: Houghton Mifflin.

Storey, Robert, and Alex English. (2001) *Korea*. 5th ed. Berkeley, CA: Lonely Planet.

SOUTHEAST ASIA—HUMAN RIGHTS

Notions of human rights are controversial in Southeast Asia, as elsewhere, because they embrace basic values reaching to the core of personal, social, and national identity, and encompass complex moral, philosophical, and cultural issues played out simultaneously at global and local levels. The search for common values is nevertheless essential to a peaceful and stable world, as communication and cooperation will otherwise remain very difficult.

Context of Human Rights in Southeast Asia

The realization of universal human rights confronts two major obstacles. The first is the idea that culture is relative to each society. Consequently, attempts to impose universal human-rights concepts are seen as Western cultural imperialism by many non-Western countries. The second asserts national sovereignty as superior to international human-rights law. Sovereignty is precious to all countries, but especially to those that have achieved it more recently, as in postcolonial Southeast Asia.

United Nations human-rights covenants and conventions provide a primary frame of reference for this article, representing the highest level of international agreement so far achieved. These texts should not be seen as fixed or infallible "tablets of stone," but as evolving in relation to changes in technology, society, and notions of human dignity. The United Nations, based on nation-states and upholding national sovereignty, yet bound by its charter to promote human rights, appears to be the only institution capable of providing an acceptable and comprehensive framework for pursuing dialogue and dispute resolution in

this complex field. This is evidenced by increasing accession to U.N. human-rights treaties during the past decade by the ten countries of Southeast Asia constituting the Association of Southeast Asian Nations (ASEAN): Singapore, Indonesia, Malaysia, Thailand, the Philippines, Brunei, Myanmar (Burma), Cambodia, Laos, and Vietnam.

Human Rights: General Features

Universal understandings of human rights are held together across diverse cultural and religious contexts by a common thread of respect for human dignity, based on ideals of how human beings ought to treat each other. But controversy centers on notions of rights as inalienable entitlements to be enjoyed by all persons. Also, some rights, for example, freedom of religion, may contradict others, as when religious interpretations oppose freedom of expression or the rights of women. Protecting cultures and minority groups can allow imposition of uniform practices on all members.

It is widely agreed that rights and responsibilities go together. But whereas a liberal view would recognize responsibilities to uphold others' rights, authoritarian or totalitarian states, as well as many traditional societies, assume the right to define citizens' responsibilities and make rights conditional on their performance. The U.N. General Assembly's Declaration on the Right and Responsibility of Individuals, Groups, and Organs of Society to Promote and Protect Universally Recognized Human Rights and Fundamental Freedoms in March 1999 upheld the liberal position.

Two major streams of human rights are commonly identified: (1) civil and political; and (2) economic, social, and cultural. The former includes freedom of expression in all forms, freedom of association and organization, free and fair elections, and legal due process. The latter includes rights to food, shelter, health, education, employment, and cultural and religious expression. These rights intersect at many points, most obviously in relation to the rights of workers, women, ethnic groupings, and religious minorities. Principles of universality, indivisibility, and interdependence of all human rights are central to U.N. human-rights doctrine. In practice, each state and society accords higher priorities to some rights over others. The Cold War and rival outlooks between "developed" and "developing" countries have created many artificial divisions between the two major human rights streams.

Application of the indivisibility principle requires convergence between ideas of democracy, development, and human rights. Failure to achieve this lies at the heart of conflicts between Western and Southeast Asian countries. Automatic equation of human rights with liberal understandings of democracy is misleading. While principles of democratic participation are upheld in all major human-rights treaties as essential to many other rights, democratic rights do not constitute the sum total of human rights. Even in Western countries, the will of democratic majorities can override the rights of minorities unless these are constitutionally and in other ways protected. Similarly, rights to minimum health, nutrition, shelter, education and literacy, equal opportunities for men and women, and sustainable and equitable management of the environment are not guaranteed by civil and political rights. Rather, they constitute necessary, if not sufficient conditions for their fulfillment.

U.N. Human Rights System

U.N. covenants and conventions constitute treaties between all participating states. Ratification of or accession to them requires states to harmonize their domestic law and practice with treaty obligations. Sovereignty is preserved through the right to declare reservations or understandings. States that invoke their domestic constitution and practices as the determinants of their treaty obligations breach Article 27 of the Vienna Convention on the Law of Treaties.

The 1948 Universal Declaration of Human Rights (UDHR) represents the core statement of U.N. human-rights principles. These were spelled out in two major covenants adopted in 1966—the International Covenant on Civil and Political Rights (ICCPR) and the International Covenant on Economic, Social, and Cultural Rights (ICESCR)—supplemented by spe-

cialized conventions, notably the Convention on the Elimination of All Forms of Racial Discrimination (CERD); the Convention against Torture and other Cruel, Inhuman, or Degrading Treatments or Punishments (CAT); the Convention on the Elimination of All Forms of Discrimination against Women (CEDAW); the Convention on the Rights of the Child (CROC); the Convention relating to the Status of Refugees and the Convention on the Prevention and Punishment of the Crime of Genocide.

Table 1 indicates the extent of ASEAN states' ratification of the above eight United Nations human-rights treaties. The United States and China, as key members of the U.N. Security Council, are included for purposes of comparison.

Ratification does not guarantee that states will implement human-rights treaties, as shown by forced child labor and alleged genocide towards toward minorities in Myanmar (Burma). By contrast, Singapore is meticulous in only ratifying treaties to the extent it is prepared to support them with domestic laws and policies. Regime changes, timing, and context help explain apparent inconsistencies in states' treaty participation. Reservations and qualifications also offer useful insights into their policies and practice. Ratification nevertheless gives opportunity and legitimacy to both domestic and international groups in advocating human-rights improvements.

Brunei participates only in the children's rights convention. All the ASEAN states except Brunei support the convention to eliminate discrimination against women. The United States accedes to neither treaty. Together with the antigenocide convention, these two treaties generate greatest support from

TABLE 1

Accession to/Ratification of U.N. Human Rights Treaties by ASEAN States, U.S., and China

(Date Entered into Force)

	ICCPR	ICESCR	CAT	CROC	CEDAW	CERD	Refugees	Genocide
Brunei	—	—	—	26/1/96	—	—	—	—
Cambodia	26/8/92	26/8/92	14/11/92	14/11/92	14/11/92	28/12/86	5/10/92	14/10/50
Indonesia	—	—	27/11/98	5/10/90	13/10/84	25/7/99	—	—
Laos	—	—	—	7/6/91	13/9/81	24/3/74	—	8/10/50
Malaysia	—	—	—	19/3/95	4/8/95	—	—	20/12/94
Myanmar	—	—	—	14/8/91	21/8/97	—	—	14/3/56
Philippines	23/1/87	3/1/76	26/6/87	20/9/90	4/9/81	4/1/69	22/7/81	7/7/50
Singapore	—	—	—	4/11/95	5/11/95	—	—	18/8/95
Thailand	29/1/97	5/12/99	—	26/4/92	8/9/85	—	—	—
Vietnam	24/12/82	24/12/82	—	2/9/90	19/3/82	9/7/82	—	9/6/81
China	—	—	3/11/88	1/4/92	3/9/81	28/1/82	24/9/82	18/4/83
U.S.	8/9/92	—	20/11/94	—	—	20/11/94	—	25/11/88

SOURCE: UNCHR treaty website, http://www.unhchr.ch/tbs/doc.nsf.

ASEAN states. But most have entered reservations based on domestic social and religious concerns. Several, including the USA and China, insist on their prior consent being sought each time torture and genocide allegations are referred to international tribunals. Together with the refugees' convention, the antitorture convention is least supported by ASEAN states.

Only five ASEAN states support the convention to eliminate racial discrimination. Vietnam, Laos, Myanmar, and Thailand discriminate against or are in active conflict with ethnic minorities in varying degrees. Singapore and Malaysia have developed policies aimed at protecting interethnic and religious harmony. While these policies have achieved a fair measure of success, they would not conform to the requirements of the anti-racial discrimination (CERD) convention. Indonesia ratified this convention in May 1999, indicating its intention to overcome historically strained relations with Chinese and other ethnic minorities.

The Philippines and Cambodia participate in all eight treaties. Despite authoritarian rule under President Ferdinand Marcos, the Philippines has a historically deep-rooted democratic culture, with extensive capacity for popular mobilization in both political and nongovernment spheres. By contrast, Cambodia ratified all but one of the treaties in a rush at the end of 1992 while still in a state of political, legal, and economic chaos following many years of civil war in the wake of the overthrow of the Khmer Rouge in 1979. Its actions were probably aimed at gaining international approval and assistance. Even so, rudimentary frameworks of democracy and human rights are emerging there. Vietnam has ratified six of the eight treaties, all except one in the early 1980s. But lack of freedom of association and rights to practice religion alleged by Amnesty International, Human Rights Watch, and others undermine its human rights credentials.

Overall, Southeast Asian states remain cautious in acceding to either the ICCPR or ICESCR. Cambodia, the Philippines, Thailand, and Vietnam participate in both. Other ASEAN states participate in neither. Indonesia, which has drawn up a five-year human-rights national action plan, aims to ratify at least the ICCPR before 2003. Thailand, which instituted a new democratic constitution in 1997, ratified the ICCPR in that year and the ICESCR in December 1999. Although former Philippines President Marcos ratified the latter but not the former, other ASEAN states have shown little inclination to favor the economic and social over the civil and political rights convention, despite assertions that development must precede democracy. This is probably because the ICESCR contains many civil- and political-rights aspects, and

because it lacks a specific developing country focus. This latter aspect was addressed in the U.N. Declaration on the Right to Development (Resolution 41/128, 4 December 1986). The United States continues to oppose both this declaration and the ICESCR and heavily qualified its eventual acceptance of the ICCPR.

Asian Values

Asian values were put forward to counter intensifying pressures for democratization placed on non-Western countries following the end of the Cold War. A U.N. global and regional human-rights consultation in 1993 lent urgency to finding a common position. In their Bangkok Declaration, Asian governments asserted that while human rights are universal in nature, they must be contextualized in relation to history, institutions, culture, religions, and stage of economic development of individual states. While there are several variants, core themes affirm values of harmony, cooperation, order, respect for authority, and family over those of individualism, competition, freedom, and separation of powers. Freedom of expression, even in asserting the truth, should be tempered by consideration of the potential social impact of what is said. Hence, the Indonesian government, under President Suharto, laid down the principle of the media as "free and responsible."

One variant promotes "Asian democracy." This acknowledges the principle that sovereignty derives from the people as a whole, such that governments must ultimately rule for their benefit and be judged on the basis of performance. This entails an active government role, usually in partnership with the private sector, in promoting economic development. Alleged "gridlock" and "opposition for its own sake" associated with liberal democracy are rejected in favor of "strong government" by Confucian-style wise rulers. A more liberal version emphasizes "Asian renaissance" based on inter-civilizational dialogue between equals. While emphasis on family and community remain strong, human rights are claimed as the common heritage of mankind. Asian values rhetoric should not be used as a smokescreen for corruption or to protect repressive governments.

Emphasis on culture in Asian values discourse raises questions as to who defines and interprets it. Culture is best understood as not fixed, but evolving and contested, with increasing exchange and adaptation of ideas and practices in an interconnected global world. Universality need not imply uniformity in application. Indeed, repression of cultural variety would constitute a denial of basic human-rights principles.

Asian values rhetoric concerning "community" disguises the extent to which states shape and control communities. The Asian Forum of Non-Government Organizations strongly opposed their governments on these issues during the 1993 U.N. consultation process, affirming principles of universality and indivisibility.

While most regional countries have been content to defend their systems as appropriate to their situation, Malaysia and, at an earlier stage, Singapore have vigorously counterattacked Western systems and values as leading to economic stagnation, social disorder, and decline, with Asian values widely proposed as the key to the region's success. The East Asian economic crisis beginning in mid-1997 proved an embarrassment in this context.

The financial crisis and its aftermath represent a fundamental and continuing threat to Southeast Asia's economic and social human rights. While inflation, exchange rates, balance of payments, consumer spending, and, more gradually, employment appear to be recovering, the human costs are likely to persist into the longer term. Examples include 435 Malaysian small businesses declared bankrupt in 1997–1998; an additional 40 million Indonesians falling into poverty, plus 12 percent similarly affected in Thailand; rising unemployment, with severest impact on women and migrant workers; withdrawal of children from school; and reduced public services affecting levels of health and nutrition. The indirect costs in terms of family tensions, crime, and social disorder are less easily quantified but are already widely evident (UNDP 1999: 40).

The economic crisis has further intensified pressures for democratization. In Indonesia, it set off a chain of events that led in May 1998 to the overthrow of President Suharto, who had ruled since 1966. Indonesia's democratic transition thus coincided with major tasks of economic restructuring. Democratic elections were successfully held in June 1999, with forty-eight parties competing. The newly elected Parliament replaced President Bacharuddin Jusuf Habibie in October 1999 with a well-respected liberal reformist Muslim scholar, Abdurrachman Wahid. Habibie can nevertheless be credited with liberalization of political structures and of media and public life generally, and with beginning processes of judicial and constitutional reform. Wahid has continued the process, also taking steps to curb the powers of the military. However, economic recovery remains slow, with institutional weakness, mismanagement, and corruption deep-rooted.

New laws granting autonomy (devolution) to provinces and districts will be crucial to democratization. However, opinion is divided on whether devolution will protect or destroy national unity. Destructive

ethnic and religious conflict has escalated, partly encouraged by elements seeking to restore the former regime. Long-standing movements for secession have experienced vigorous revival in Aceh and Irian Jaya provinces. The separation of East Timor, following massive violence and destruction by Indonesia's military and supporting militias, has created a huge rebuilding task for the East Timorese and United Nations Temporary Administration for East Timor (U.N. TAET) before full independence in 2002 or 2003.

The Philippines and Thailand have moved strongly in a democratic direction since replacing authoritarian cum military rulers in 1986 and 1992. While the Philippines has long-established democratic institutions and culture, Thailand had only experienced a brief and turbulent period of democracy from 1972 to 1975. Consolidating democracy will entail greater respect for and commitment to constitutional processes at all levels of government, among politicians and parties, and throughout civil society. This process is more advanced

A Filipino human rights demonstrator sits inside a barbed-wire cage in Manila in 1984 to protest human rights abuses during the period of Marcos rule. (BETTMANN/CORBIS)

In Kuala Lumpur, Malaysia, in August 2001, three women appeal the detentions of their husbands under the Internal Security Act. They are seated before the Human Rights Commission. (AFP/CORBIS)

in urban relative to rural areas, where patronage and corruption is deep-rooted. This gap is reflected in economic disparities, particularly in chronically poor areas of northeast Thailand. However, the 1997 Constitution established a Counter Corruption Commission with strong powers. Corruption, including criminalization, is also endemic in the Philippines' political processes, despite high levels of popular awareness and participation. The country also faces problems in reconciling demands for regional autonomy in Muslim areas of Mindanao with maintaining national unity.

In Singapore, which adopted the British (Westminster) democratic model of parliamentary and cabinet government from the outset, one-party rule has been consolidated by combining restrictive controls on political and other popular mobilization with widely shared economic growth, health, and educational benefits. The government is exploring new approaches to participation but shows no signs of shifting to open forms of liberal democracy.

Malaysia has built on a similar system. Its constitution affirms basic political and personal freedoms, with due legal process. However, citizens' rights are constrained by extensive security legislation linked to major checks on judicial independence. Governments frequently use their parliamentary dominance to amend the Constitution.

Malaysian politics are dominated by issues of race and religion. The ruling coalition National Front is based on acceptance of dominance by the United Malays National Organisation (UMNO). Although the Malay vote is strongly contested by the Islamic Party (PAS), which remains outside the ruling coalition, both regard the preeminence of the Malay race, as original "sons of the soil," as a nonnegotiable fundamental of Malaysian politics. UMNO controls key cabinet positions and determines allocation of party nominations at elections. Non-Malays accept Malay constitutional privileges and seek concessions within that framework. Fear of Islamic rule, combined with relative economic prosperity, keeps most non-Malays in the government camp.

The New Economic Policy (NEP) was set in place after 1970 to promote Malays in business and education, with the reasoning that national unity would be endangered unless the nexus between ethnic, urban-rural, and occupational divisions inherited from British rule was overcome. Critics assert that affirmative action policies should be refocused toward a determined attack on poverty regardless of race.

The 1971 Sedition Amendment Act removed major areas from public discussion relating to Malay rights, the citizenship rights of other races, the status of the national language and the Islamic religion, and the rights and privileges of the king *(Yang de-Pertuan Agong)* and sultans, who act as state rulers. The uncertain and arbitrary nature of these restrictions inhibits in-depth debate concerning education, civil-service recruitment and employment practices, rights of women, and family. Rights of Moslem women are subject to Islamic law.

Apparent evolution toward political openness was reversed by the dismissal and jailing of Deputy Prime Minister Anwar Ibrahim in September 1998, against a background of differences with Prime Minister Datuk Seri Mahathir bin Mohamad over economic management and political reform. Ibrahim also strongly attacked governmental use of Asian values to legitimize avoidance of accountability. Trial processes and sentencing on grounds of corruption and sodomy have been widely condemned in both international and Malaysian human-rights circles.

A continuing obstacle to institutionalizing human rights in Southeast Asia is the lack of a U.N. regional arm. This has been partly offset by the establishment of national human-rights institutions (NHRIs). These institutions assist their governments in developing national human-rights plans, aimed at strengthening links with the U.N. system, while also monitoring national laws and practices. They network via the Asia-Pacific Forum of National Human Rights Institutions (APFNHRI), which in May 2000 included Australia, Fiji, India, Indonesia, New Zealand, the Philippines, and Sri Lanka. Malaysia, and Thailand have also established NHRIs. Definitions of human-rights goals by some states only partly conform to U.N. instruments.

The "Paris Principles," established in 1991, require independence in terms of resources, initiation and conduct of inquiries, reporting, recommendations to government, and public education. Legal autonomy of institutions is best protected, as in Thailand and the Philippines, when their establishment is incorporated in the national constitution. The NHRIs' recommendations are only advisory, and while the NHRIs' informal access and networks can often prove influential, ultimately the implementation depends on the effectiveness and integrity of political, administrative, and judicial processes.

Future Trends

Both ends and means will continue to be disputed in realizing goals of universal human rights. A priority aim at this stage should be to involve both governments and civil society groups in strengthening frameworks for dialogue, for which acceptance of the indivisibility principle is an essential prerequisite. Recent political and economic upheavals in East Asia show the urgency of integrating all streams of human rights. Adherence to U.N. human-rights treaties can provide a global framework for cooperation between Western and Asian countries, on a basis of equality

and mutual accountability, in enlarging the human rights of their diverse peoples.

Philip J. Eldridge

Further Reading
Crouch, H. (1996) *Government and Society in Malaysia.* Ithaca, NY: Cornell University Press.

Diamond, L. (1999) *Developing Democracy: Towards Consolidation.* Baltimore, MD: John Hopkins University Press.

Eldridge, P. (2002) *The Politics of Human Rights in Southeast Asia.* New York: Routledge.

Falk, R. (1995) *On Humane Governance: Towards a New Global Politics.* Cambridge, MA: Polity Press.

Held, D. (1995) *Democracy and the Global Order: From the Modern State to Cosmopolitan Governance.* Cambridge, U.K.: Polity Press.

Ibrahim, A. (1996) *The Asian Renaissance.* Singapore: Times Books International.

Milner A., ed. (1996) *Australia in Asia: Comparing Cultures.* Melbourne, Australia: Oxford University Press.

Muzzaffar, C., ed. (1995) *Dominance of the West over the Rest.* Penang, Malaysia: Just World Trust.

Schwarz, A. (1999) *A Nation in Waiting: Indonesia in the 1990s.* 2nd ed. St. Leonards, Australia: Allen and Unwin.

Tang, J., ed. (1995) *Human Rights and International Relations in the Asia-Pacific Region.* New York: Pinter.

UNDP (United Nations Development Program). (1999) *Human Development Report,* New York: Oxford University Press.

Vincent, R. (1986) *Human Rights and International Relations.* Cambridge, U.K.: Cambridge University Press.

SOUTHEAST ASIA TREATY ORGANIZATION
The Southeast Asia Treaty Organization (SEATO) was an alliance of Southeast Asian and Western nations. It was established on 8 September 1954, less than two months after agreements reached at the Geneva Conference had paved the way for the French withdrawal from Indochina, to provide defense and economic cooperation in Southeast Asia and the South Pacific. The founding nations were Australia, France, Great Britain, New Zealand, Pakistan, the Philippines, Thailand, and the United States. Like the North Atlantic Treaty Organization (NATO), the Southeast Asian alliance was intended to prevent the spread of Communism; but, unlike the NATO pact, the SEATO agreement did not obligate one member to assist another against a military threat. Although SEATO sanctioned the U.S. military effort in Vietnam, and although several SEATO members sent troops to fight there, SEATO itself played no direct role in the war. The organization weakened in the late 1960s with France ending active participation in 1967, followed by Pakistan's withdrawal in 1972. SEATO was unable to

intervene in the civil wars in Laos or Vietnam due to its rule requiring unanimity and the role of the organization in regional affairs was seriously questioned by 1973. With the U.S. withdrawal from Vietnam and the Communist victories throughout the region in 1975, SEATO became an anachronism and was disbanded on 30 June 1977.

James Chin

Further Reading

Cohen, Warren I., and Akira Iriye, eds. (1990) *The Great Powers in East Asia, 1953–1960.* New York: Columbia University Press.

Buszynski, Leszek. (1983) *SEATO: The Failure of an Alliance Strategy.* Singapore: Singapore University Press.

SOUVANNA PHOUMA, PRINCE (1901–1984), Lao political leader.

Born in Luang Prabang, Prince Souvanna Phouma was the moderate leader of Laos from the time of its struggle for independence until the Pathet Lao takeover in 1975. Souvanna Phouma was the nephew of King Sisavangvong and half brother of Prince Souphanouvong, his political adversary. He studied engineering in Hanoi and France and worked for the public works administration of Indochina. The restoration of Haw Pra Keo, once a Buddhist shrine but now the Museum of Art and Antiquities, was one of his achievements in the civil service. Souvanna Phouma joined the Lao Issara, or Free Lao, resistance government led by his brother Prince Phetsarat as minister of public works. He fled

Prime Minister Souvanna Phouma in 1969. (BETTMAN/CORBIS)

to Thailand with other members of the Lao Issara when the French regained control in 1946, but he returned to Laos when the Lao Issara disbanded in 1949. In 1951 Souvanna formed the Progressive Party and was elected prime minister of Laos in the same year. During his first administration, he negotiated Laos's independence from France at the Geneva conference in 1953. The political instability of the civil war caused the removal and reinstatement of Souvanna as premier seven additional times, including in three coalition governments. After the proclamation of the Lao People's Democratic Republic, Souvanna Phouma served the government as a political adviser until his death in 1984.

Linda S. McIntosh

Further Reading

Dommen, Arthur J. (1971) *Conflict in Laos: The Politics of Neutralization.* New York: Praeger.

Stuart-Fox, Martin. (1997) *A History of Laos.* Cambridge, U.K.: Cambridge University Press.

SOVIET-VIETNAMESE TFOC

The relationship between Vietnam and the Soviet Union took a dramatic turn with the signing of a treaty of friendship and cooperation between the two countries. Since the 1930s, relations between the two have passed through several phases. It was only after the Sino-Soviet split of the late 1950s that the Soviet Union grudgingly helped its fellow Communist government.

Until the unification of Vietnam in the mid-1970s, Hanoi judiciously maintained a balanced relationship with China and the Soviet Union. After that, the steady deterioration of relations with China turned Hanoi toward Moscow. The United States was eager for a rapprochement with China and remained cool toward Vietnamese overtures. Vietnam moved closer to the Soviet Union and became a full-fledged member of the Moscow-dominated COMECON (Council for Mutual Economic Assistance) in June 1978. China then suspended its $300 million assistance to Vietnam. Existing economic assistance from the Soviet Union was not sufficient for Hanoi's needs, and Vietnam also wanted more support for its Cambodian policy. Strategic assistance was necessary, and Vietnamese-Soviet military cooperation could help provide it.

On 3 November 1978, Vietnam signed a twenty-five-year Treaty of Friendship and Cooperation (TOFC) with the Soviet Union. The military clause obliged both to consult each other " if one was threatened by aggression for eliminating that threat." Vietnam also allowed the Soviet Union to use naval facilities at the Da Nang and Cam Ranh Bay bases. Armed with the TOFC, Vietnam intervened in Cambodia the following month. The treaty provided more of a psychological advantage for the Vietnamese than a strategic one. However, China was not deterred from helping the Khmer Rouge, and a strong supposition existed at the time, never disproved, that the Chinese quite clearly understood that the bogging down of Vietnamese forces in Cambodia would work to China's advantage. The Soviets did not take any direct military action at the time of the Chinese invasion of Vietnam in February 1979. Apart from economic and military aid, Vietnam received primarily rhetorical support. The Vietnamese seemed satisfied with the material and diplomatic support from the Soviets. Hanoi's relations with Beijing remained strained, and it became increasingly dependent on Moscow to sustain its military support for the Cambodian government in Phnom Penh against the ousted Khmer Rouge forces. Vietnam received about $800 million in 1978 from Moscow, which increased to $1.4 billion the following year. National interest rather than ideological solidarity was shown to be the most important factor in relations between Communist countries, and Southeast Asia was drawn further into great-power rivalry. Vietnam also could not normalize its relations with the United States, because its troops were stationed in Cambodia. It therefore moved closer to the Soviet Union.

The Soviet Union also made an important contribution to Vietnam by providing fellowships for Vietnamese to pursue advanced studies in the USSR. Training in medicine, science, and math was often of high quality. This is perhaps one reason why currently Vietnam does well in the scientific olympics.

It was only after the disintegration of the Soviet Union that Vietnam's relations with both China and the United States improved considerably. However, Vietnam's historical ties with the successor state, the Russian Federation, continued, and there is currently Russian-Vietnamese collaboration in offshore oil exploration and production.

Patit Paban Mishra

Further Reading
Pike, Douglas. (1987) *Vietnam and the Soviet Union: Anatomy of an Alliance.* Boulder, CO: Westview.
Karnow, Stanley. (1983) *Vietnam: A History.* New York: Viking.

SPECIAL ECONOMIC ZONES—CHINA
China's late-twentieth-century process of economic transition essentially began with the establishment of what are known as special economic zones (SEZs). SEZs are geographically insulated areas with economic openness to the outside world that are regulated by the government in a discriminatory manner in their favor, so that special and flexible economic policies and measures are adopted primarily to promote foreign investment, technology transfer, and exports. In 1979, China designated the first four SEZs—Shenzhen, Zhuhai, Shantou, and Xiamen—as part of its domestic economic reform. By limiting its experiment to those four SEZs, China sought to minimize the unnecessary economic, social, and political costs that are often associated with a drastic policy switch and to gain necessary experience in carrying out the transition.

Serving both as windows to the outside world and as laboratories to formulate various reform policies, the SEZs played a pivotal role in China's overall economic transition during the last two decades of the twentieth century. Numerous measures aimed at reforming the existing economic system and reaching a higher degree of economic openness were developed and tested in the SEZs. In many regards, the effect of the SEZs has far exceeded their limited geographical boundaries. It is safe to say that without the successful operation of the SEZs, China's reforms would not have gone so far and the transitional process would not have been so smooth.

China's Approach to SEZs
At the outset of the economic reform and open-door policy, the Chinese central government realized that development could not happen in all places at once (that would have been too costly) and that certain policies needed to be tested within limited areas before being implemented nationwide. It planned to take advantage of the global trend of industrial relocation to attract foreign investment to its capital-starved economy. Foreign investment would allow China to make full use of its large reserve of inexpensive surplus labor to produce labor-intensive goods for export and, ultimately, to create foreign-exchange earnings. The government also recognized the importance of advanced foreign technology for stimulating growth and for making possible technology transfer. It was hoped that inland enterprises could later learn from the experience of the SEZs.

Supported by growing local enthusiasm for such policies, particularly from Guangdong province, the SEZs functioned as a laboratory where various methods aimed at overcoming the drawbacks associated with a central-planning system could be developed.

Fourteen more cities were designated as coastal open cities in 1984; here, the entire city began to adopt policies similar to those implemented in the SEZs, such as promoting foreign investment. The following year saw the declaration of the Chang (Yangtze) River, Pearl River, and southern Fujian deltas as open economic zones. In April 1988, a fifth SEZ was established, in Hainan, after Hainan was newly designated as a province, so that the entire province functioned as a zone. In the same year, a coastal development strategy, officially called the weixiang xing fazhan zhanlue (Outward-Oriented Development Strategy), was launched in the coastal areas. This policy had a much larger scale and wider range, embracing twelve provinces and cities under the direct control of the central government. In April 1990, the Pudong New Area was formally established, with policies favorable for inducing rapid construction, large investments, and so on, for building a center of finance, commerce, and high technology. In the eighth five-year plan (1991–1995), the focus was placed more on the development of particular industries than of regions.

Economic Incentives and Political Considerations

In the Chinese SEZs, flexible and innovative packages were assembled that offered incentives for foreign investors. These included preferential tax rates, concessions, and exemptions from certain taxes, administrative fees, and need for high or mid-level approval. Most exported and imported items were exempted from custom duties and the industrial and commercial consolidated tax. The SEZs also introduced reform measures dealing with labor-related issues. Employment contracts with specified term limits and dismissal of unqualified employees were permitted for the first time.

There were certain political considerations in establishing the early SEZs. The zones were not selected on the basis of whether there was a strong industrial base, an adequate urban infrastructure, or a technologically innovative capacity. The SEZs had to be easily separated from the vast inland areas, because drastically different policies were to be tested in the zones, and no one could be certain that the policies would succeed. At an early stage, fences were built around them, and checkpoints were stationed to inspect traffic. Administrative procedures also were used to control population inflows to the zones. Furthermore, the SEZs were not built into major industrial centers at first, so as to avoid significant losses if the experiment should fail. Moreover, the central government intended to use these zones as intermediary or buffer zones for the future reunification of Hong Kong, Macao, and Taiwan with the mainland, and so they were chosen partially for their proximity to those places. Finally, the overseas Chinese community was targeted as a potential source for productive capital: the SEZs were set up along the southeast coast in Guangdong and Fujian, which were the places of origin of many overseas Chinese.

As an integral and critical component of China's gradualist approach toward economic reform and opening up, the SEZs have developed over the past two decades into self-contained mini-economies along the lines of "one country, two systems." In these SEZs, nonsocialist measures could be adopted. The SEZs have moved China much further down the path to economic transition than would have been possible with export-processing zones, because the latter may not reform the traditional socialist system but mainly process products for export. The measures that proved to be effective and successful in the SEZs have been extended, whenever feasible, to the rest of the country. This, in turn, has helped the entire economy to become more open and efficient in a step-by-step manner.

Assessment

Judged by most social and economic indicators, the performance of the SEZs has, for the most part, been extraordinary. Despite the unfavorable initial conditions, such as a lack of industrial, infrastructure, and technological support, the pace of development of the zones has not only exceeded the national average so far, but it has also narrowed the gap with some major industrial centers, such as Shanghai, that have long been considered to be the backbone of growth and trade in the Chinese economy. This happened within a short time.

Xiaobo Hu

See also: **Shanghai Pudong New Area; Shenzhen Special Economic Zone**

Further Reading

Fewsmith, Joseph. (1986) "Special Economic Zones of the PRC." *Problems of Communism* 35, 6: 78–85.
Gao Shangquan, and Chi Fulin, eds. (1997) *New Progress in China's Special Economic Zones*. Beijing: Foreign Languages Press.
Ge Wei. (1999) *Special Economic Zones and the Economic Transition in China*. Singapore: World Scientific.

SPEELMAN, CORNELIS (1628–1684), governor-general of the Dutch East India Company. Born in Rotterdam, the Netherlands, Speelman came to the

Dutch East Indies (modern-day Indonesia) in 1645 at the age of seventeen. He rose through the ranks of the Dutch East India Company, serving as governor of Coromandel, a territory on the east coast of South India, from 1663 to1665. He learned several local languages and wrote widely on political, social, and cultural topics. In 1668, allied with Arung Palakka (1634–1696), prince of Boni, a kingdom in southern Sulawesi, he led Dutch military forces to defeat Makassar, then the most powerful state in the eastern archipelago of the Dutch East Indies and a trading center for the company's European rivals. The Treaty of Bungaya (18 November 1668) that followed granted the company a monopoly of trade in Makassar and hegemony over its former empire. As member of the Council of the Indies from 1671, Speelman argued vigorously for extending the company's territorial control in the Indies, rather than focusing simply on trade, and he led Dutch military forces in eastern Java in 1676. As governor-general (1681–1684) he ordered the conquest of Banten in the west of the island. His rule was marred by his corruption and abuse of power, and the Dutch East India Company confiscated his estate after his death.

Robert Cribb

Further Reading

Andaya, Leonard Y. (1981) *The Heritage of Arung Palakka: A History of South Sulawesi (Celebes) in the Seventeenth Century.* The Hague, Netherlands: Martinus Nijhoff.

Vlekke, Bernard H. M. (1943) *Nusantara: A History of the East Indian Archipelago.* Cambridge, MA: Harvard University Press.

SPICE TRADE   Spices such as salt, saffron, pepper, ginger, cardamom, nutmeg, clove, and cinnamon have, since time immemorial, been highly valued as medicine, ointment, aphrodisiacs, stimulants, antiseptics, and preservatives. Their use as seasonings for various dishes or ingredients for incenses and oils predates recorded history. The ancient recognition of the therapeutic value of salt, for instance, resonates through the etymology of the Latin words *salus* ("bliss") and *salubritas* ("health"), which are derived from the Latin word *sal* ("salt"). In the European Middle Ages, pepper and salt were widely used as preservatives for meat. The healing and stimulating capacities of spices like ginger, nutmeg, and cardamom contributed to the fact that in various ancient cultures, such as those of early China and India, cooking was regarded as a sacred act.

Most spices are native to the tropical and subtropical regions of South and Southeast Asia. The Moluc-cas were the spice islands par excellence because they were the home of the "holy trinity" of nutmeg, clove, and pepper. Nutmeg and clove were, in fact, native to the Moluccas and had not been transplanted to other tropical regions before the arrival of the Europeans in Southeast Asia. Pepper, on the other hand, is said to be indigenous to the Malabar Coast of India, but it had long been cultivated throughout Southeast Asia. Sumatra, for instance, became a favorite destination of European East India merchants for its wealth in pepper. Ginger is probably native to Southeast Asia, but it was already widely known in ancient India and China. Cinnamon, also already widely used in Asian antiquity, originates from Sri Lanka. Cardamom is native to the rain forests of South India. South India and Sri Lanka were the exclusive areas of its cultivation when Europeans arrived in the Indian Ocean. Saffron, for which India, especially Kashmir, and Northern China have been famous, probably originates in the Mediterranean, the Near East, and Iran. The demand for spices such as pepper, cinnamon, cardamom, ginger, turmeric, saffron, nutmeg, and clove, which were domesticated in South and Southeast Asia, was an important factor in the evolution of long-distance trade.

By 2000 BCE, different spice routes had reached the Middle East. Many references to the early Arabian trade in spices are to be found in the Bible (for example, Joseph was sold to a group of Ishmaelite spice merchants on their way to Egypt). In the fourth century BCE, the Greek historian Herodotus wrote that wild animals and steep cliffs render the spice gardens, lying somewhere in the distant East, inaccessible. His account was inspired by the stories of Arab traders, who tried to withhold the true origins of their highly prized goods.

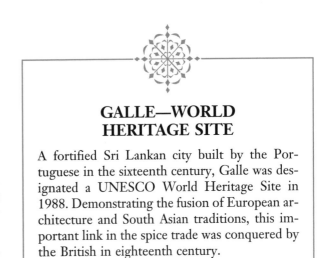

GALLE—WORLD HERITAGE SITE

A fortified Sri Lankan city built by the Portuguese in the sixteenth century, Galle was designated a UNESCO World Heritage Site in 1988. Demonstrating the fusion of European architecture and South Asian traditions, this important link in the spice trade was conquered by the British in eighteenth century.

The Romans then succeeded in breaking the Arabian monopoly on the trade with India for more than three centuries. Yet, after the fall of Rome in the sixth century, the Arab monopoly was quickly restored. The spice routes to the East soon also functioned as conduits for the new Arab religion, Islam, propagated in the seventh century by Muhammad (c. 570–632), who had married a widow of a wealthy Arabian spice merchant.

The threshold to the European market, however, was guarded by Christian Byzantium. In 1204 it was sacked by its economic rival, Venice, which then became the Western trade center for spices until the sixteenth century. By 1500, European discoverers, seeking to evade the heavy taxes imposed by the Ottomans in the Levant and the Marmadukes in Egypt, had found the sea passage to the spice regions of India, Ceylon, Sumatra, and the Moluccas. In the following centuries, several European East India companies competed with each other in monopolizing larger or smaller segments of the spice trade in the Indian Ocean and the South China Sea. From 1600 onward, the most successful merchant associations were the British East India Company and its Dutch equivalent, the Vereenigde Oostindische Compagnie. By the late eighteenth century, however, their spice monopolies were broken due to the successful transplantation of South and Southeast Asian spice plants to other parts of the world.

Martin Ramstedt

See also: **British in Southeast Asia; Dutch East Indies; Dutch in Southeast Asia**

Further Reading
Bruijn, Jaap R.,and Femme S. Gaastra. (1993) *Ships, Sailors, and Spices: East India Companies and Their Shipping in the 16th, 17th and 18th Centuries.* Amsterdam: NEHA.
Corn, Charles. (1998) *The Scents of Eden: A Narrative of the Spice Trade.* New York, Tokyo, and London: Kodansha.
Schivelbusch, Wolfgang. (1992) *Das Paradies, der Geschmack, und die Vernunft: Eine Geschichte der Genußmittel.* Frankfurt am Main, Germany: Fischer.

SPIRIT CULTS
Spirit worship is one of the oldest practices in Myanmar (Burma), preceding in many cases the practice of Buddhism. Many ethnic groups in Myanmar continue to practice in various forms what is broadly referred to as animism. The Burman spirit cults, however, are highly organized cults associated with a hierarchy of the Thirty-Seven Spirits (*nats*). These cults are unusual in the Southeast Asian region for their elaborate systematic organization. Also un-usual is their close association with royal roles and symbolism, both in terms of historical provenance (they were often associated with royalty before meeting a violent death) and ritual roles (the mediums often adopt royal dress and language when performing and do so in "palaces"). A similar elaborate system is found among the Mon peoples.

The Thirty-Seven Nats were supposedly instituted by Anawratha (1044–1077), one of the most prominent kings of the Pagan dynasty, at the base of the Shwezigon Pagoda in the then capital Pagan in 1059. There are supposedly thirty-seven "inner" and thirty-seven "outer" spirits. Chief among them is Mahagiri, who is venerated at the center of most Burman households and is symbolized by a coconut. Anawratha, who converted to Buddhism, placed Sakka, the king of the gods in Buddhist cosmology, over and above the powerful Mahagiri *nat*, and thereby Buddhicized the pantheon. According to oral history, Anawratha is supposed to have said, "Man will not come for the sake of the new religion. Let them come for their old gods and gradually they will be won over." Thus, around the same time the kingdom was declared Buddhist, influential figures who died a violent death were placed and commemorated close to relics of the Buddha.

Anthropologists have long argued over the relative placing of the spirit cults vis-à-vis Buddhism. Are the spirit cults the fundamental religion of the Burmese, with Buddhism only a veneer? Are they in conflict at the psychological level, or do they form a continuum? What is certain is that there are fundamental differences between Buddhism and the spirit cults. Whereas the spirit cults are mostly interpreted as dealing with the mundane world, with wealth and success within it, Buddhism takes primary aim at the supramundane world. In Myanmar, attitudes to spirits vary. At one extreme are the professional preoccupations of the mediums (*natkadaw*, "wives of *nats*"), the propitiation and offering of the *nats* by their clients, and the preoccupation with *nats* by heads of state, ministers, and civil servants. Many Burmese, however, merely give their respects so that the spirits are peaceful and do no harm. Few, however, will ignore *nats* altogether in Myanmar.

Gustaaf Houtman

Further Reading
Rodrigues, Yves. (1992) *Nat-Pwe: Burma's Supernatural Sub-Culture.* Gartmore, U.K.: Kiscadale.
Spiro, M. E. (1967) *Burmese Supernaturalism: A Study in the Explanation and Reduction of Suffering.* Englewood Cliffs, NJ: Prentice Hall.

Temple, Sir Richard Carnac. (1906) *The Thirty-Seven Nats: A Phase of Spirit-Worship Prevailing in Burma.* London: W. Griggs.

SPORTS.

See **Asia Games; Baseball—Japan; Buh; Buzkashi; Cockfighting; Cricket; Fish Fighting; Judo; Karate; Kendo; Kites and Kite Flying; Longboat Racing; Nu Shooting; Olympics; Sepak Takraw; Tai Chi.**

SPORTS—CHINA

Chinese physical culture has always oscillated between two poles: at one extreme, violent competition; at the other, the peaceful quest for physical and spiritual harmony. Boxers, wrestlers, and other athletes embody the first extreme; devotees of tai chi, a kind of graceful gymnastic exercise, represent the second. Chinese sports, which fall by definition into the first category, have often been modified by influences from the second. For millennia, Chinese culture has had gentle sports as well as rough ones. Good form has often been prized above competitive success.

Traditional China

In ancient China, as in European antiquity, most sports were rough. Extant references to sports frequently refer to them in conjunction with military preparation. In the Zhou period (1045–256 BCE), for instance, soldiers ran, jumped, threw objects of various sorts, wrestled, and practiced their skills as archers, swordsmen, and charioteers. They seem also to have demonstrated their prowess as weight lifters. *Kangding* (tripod lifting) was popular as early as the Qin dynasty (221–206 BCE).

By the time of the Han dynasty (206 BCE–220 CE), foot soldiers and mounted knights had replaced charioteers as the mainstay of the army, and the practice of *wushu* (military skills) was highly developed. Although the unarmed techniques of *wushu* were especially prized, archery too had numerous devotees, and the sport was immensely popular during the Song dynasty (960–1279). An eleventh-century district survey found 588 archery societies enrolling 31,411 members, nearly 15 percent of the local population. During the Qing dynasty (1644–1912), China's Manchu rulers preferred that their subjects not practice the martial arts. *Wushu* nonetheless experienced a surge in popularity during the nationalistic reaction to Chinese defeat in the Opium War of 1842.

Ball games, played with carefully sewn stuffed skins, with animal bladders, or with found objects as simple as gourds, chunks of wood, or rounded stones, are uni-

versal. Ball games of all sorts were quite popular among the Chinese. When they began, no one knows, but stone balls have been dated to the sixth millennium BCE. *Cuju,* which resembled modern soccer football, is mentioned in the *Shiji,* one of the oldest extant Chinese texts. The famed Han-dynasty poet Li Yu (50–130 CE) also wrote of football. Games similar to modern badminton and shuttlecock were played in the first century CE.

Through most of China's recorded history, racket games were popular among women. A Ming-dynasty (1368–1644) scroll painting, "Grove of Violets," depicts elegantly attired ladies playing *chuiwan,* a game combining elements of modern billiards and golf. According to the *Wanjing* (1282), the players took turns striking a wooden ball and sending it into holes marked with colored flags. The ethos of the game stressed fairness and harmony among the players.

Harmony seems not to have been foremost among the values of China's Mongol rulers. The martial arts flourished, and mounted archers were the backbone of the army. If Marco Polo (1254–1324) can be believed, the Mongol dynasty produced a royal heroine comparable to the Greek girl Atalanta, who raced against and defeated a number of suitors. Princess Aiyaruk was said to have owned more than ten thousand horses, winning one hundred at a time as she outwrestled a long line of doomed suitors.

Mongol emperors like Khubilai Khan (1215–1294) were passionate about the hunt, but the golden age for that sport seems to have been during the Manchu dynasty. Kangxii (1654–1722) was said to have hunted with a retinue of seventy thousand horsemen and three thousand archers, which suggests that his prey had very little chance of survival.

Throughout Chinese history, aristocrats obsessed with the quest for harmony tended to disdain sports, a tendency strengthened by the arrival of Buddhism during the Han dynasty. In the moralistic eyes of Confucian sages, playing ball games was little better than drinking, gambling, and womanizing. Yet even Confucian scholars succumbed to the seduction of archery and granted the sport a half-hearted endorsement. "There is no contention among gentlemen," wrote Confucius (551–479 BCE). "The nearest to it is perhaps archery." It was not, however, the warrior's grimly competitive archery. "Even the way they [the archers] contend is gentlemanly" (Riordan/Jones 1999: 28).

Archery was also a sport for women. It was practiced by a number of court ladies, including the Dowager Empress Chonga. For men and women who found archery too bellicose a pastime, there was *touhou,* which required the player to toss an arrow into a vase. In time, the game was refined to the point where nine officials were required for a two-person match.

Adults as well as children flew kites, some of which were fanciful works of art in paper and wood. This form of amusement was known as early as the Warring States period (475 –221 BCE) but became a national obsession during the Tang dynasty (618–907 CE). In its competitive version, contestants sought to maneuver their kites so that they cut the strings of their opponents' kites. A much older sport, dragon-boat racing, elicited the same aesthetic impulse. This sport evolved from impromptu races among boats decorated with images of dragons that protected the crews from storms. Eventually, races were held to commemorate the drowned. The most famous of these races was in memory of the poet Qu Yuan, who perished in 278 BCE. By the Tang dynasty, there were fixed dates and strict rules for the races, which had become major events. Some of the boats were "manned" by female crews.

Polo, which probably had its origins on the plains of Central Asia, reached China in 627 CE. It became a passion among those wealthy enough to own horses. All sixteen emperors of the Tang Dynasty were polo players. One of them, Xizong (reigned 874–888), remarked that he would take top honors if civil-service examinations were based on polo. The army used the attractions of the game as a way to improve its men's equestrian skills. This may not have been a good idea. When the Mongols invaded, several Chinese generals were said to have been more competent at polo than at warfare. If numerous terra-cotta figures can be trusted as evidence, polo was also played by aristocratic Chinese women. The sport lost favor during the Song dynasty.

Introduction of Western Sports

Western sports came to China toward the end of the Qing dynasty. Europeans resident in China established the Canton Regatta Club in 1837. The first modern track meet was held at St. John's University, a Christian school, in 1890. Six years later, American missionaries introduced basketball at the Tianjin YMCA. YMCA workers were responsible for the first national sports festival, held in Nanjing in 1910, and for the quadrennial Far Eastern Games (1913–1934), at which Chinese athletes competed against those from Japan and the Philippines. Other Americans founded and directed educational institutions such as the Chinese Physical Training School (Shanghai, 1914).

As the Confucian scholar's disdain for the merely physical waned, Western sports increasingly influ-

enced the behavior of Chinese men, especially those of the urban middle and upper classes. In time, modern sports revolutionized the lives of middle-class and upper-class women. In the course of the twentieth century, images of the ideal female gradually changed from the delicately immobile court lady barely able to hobble on her deformed feet to the robustly active young girl racing up and down a basketball court. Female athletes became "icons of desirable sexuality" (Hong 1997: 275). From a feminist perspective, modern sports have been emancipatory.

From 1912 to 1949, modern sports were mainly an urban phenomenon. Although national sports festivals were an increasingly salient aspect of Chinese culture, the nation's athletic elite did poorly in international competition. China's National Olympic Committee was not officially recognized until 1931. At the 1932 Olympic Games, where Japanese swimmers astonished the world by winning eleven of the sixteen medals in the men's competition, sprinter Li Zhangzhun was the lone Chinese representative. He was eliminated in the heats.

The low level of elite sports (and the generally unhappy state of Chinese physical education) from the 1920s to the 1950s can be explained by the trauma of civil war and foreign invasion. Communist victory in 1949 heralded the transformation of Chinese sports as well as the rest of Chinese culture. Mao Zedong (1893–1976) had written in 1917 that physical education is "more important than intellectual and moral education" (Hong 1997: 131), but resources were scarce in 1949, and progress was slow. In 1951, the government inaugurated an inexpensive way to enhance the nation's fitness. China's masses began to perform early-morning out-of-doors gymnastic exercises in accordance with commands broadcast by state radio. The sequence of national sports festivals was resumed in 1959.

In this first decade of Communist rule, the emphasis was on national defense. The government's physical culture program included not only tai chi and conventional sports like track and field but also paramilitary training with bayonets, hand grenades, and other weapons.

Although the regime's avowed aim was to promote fitness and sports for the masses, the state-run All-China Athletic Federation recognized that athletes who broke world records and won international championships contributed to their country's prestige. Limited government support for elite sports bore early fruit in the 1950s. Chen Jingkai set a world's record in bantamweight weight lifting; Zeng Fengrong and

Rong Guotuan won world championships in high jumping and table tennis. Quarrels with the International Olympic Committee over the status of Taiwan culminated in 1958 with Chinese resignation from the committee. At the same time and for the same reason, the People's Republic of China (PRC) withdrew from the international federations for soccer and other sports. The PRC did not make its debut at the Olympic Games until 1984.

The Republic of China (Taiwan) continued to send teams to the Olympics. In the 1960 games, held in Rome, Yang Chuan-kwang barely lost the decathlon to his close friend, the American Rafer Johnson.

Unfortunately for those who dreamed of international supremacy, the "Great Cultural Revolution" (1966–1976) drastically altered the regime's approach to sports. Mao's motto was "Friendship first, competition second." Sports contacts were, however, limited to friendly nations like the People's Republic of Korea. Athletes and coaches who had had international experience were suspect. Were they truly committed to Maoism? Some of them, like Zhuang Zedong, the world champion in table tennis (1961–1966), were sent to prison. Others, like table tennis stars Rong Guotuan and Fu Jifang, committed suicide. At the elite level, Chinese sports were devastated.

During the PRC's ten years of turmoil, athletes representing the Republic of China (Taiwan) continued to compete internationally. One of the island's most successful sprinters, Chi Cheng, was third in the eighty-meter hurdles at the 1968 Olympics in Mexico City. Two years later, competing in the United States, she set world records in the 100-yard and 200-yard sprints (10.0 and 22.7 seconds) and in the 100-meter hurdles (13.2 seconds).

The policy of the PRC veered again in the 1980s. The new motto was "Break out of Asia and advance on the world." To achieve this goal, the government invested heavily in sports infrastructure. Although physical education was required in all schools, gifted athletes received special attention. Borrowing from the model developed by the Soviet Union, the government established a network of special schools to train an athletic elite. By 1990 there were 150 such schools (while the Soviet Union had a mere 46). Large sums went to build sports facilities. Research into sports physiology and sports psychology was strongly supported at Beijing University. To maximize performance in Olympic sports, the government decided in 1997 to eliminate all traditional Chinese sports (except *wushu*) from the annual national sports festival.

Current Emphasis on International Sports

The system worked. The achievements of Chinese athletes have been spectacular. Thanks in part to substantial government investment in sports infrastructure and relatively generous subsidies to athletes, the

The Shanghai Shenhua Football Club and the A. C. Milan Club in Shanghai in May 1996. (STEPHEN G. DONALDSON PHOTOGRAPHY)

Chinese began to win international championships. At the 1982 Asian Games in New Delhi, Chinese athletes won sixty-one events and ended thirty-one years of Japanese domination. Two years later, Chinese Olympians returned from Los Angeles with fifteen gold, eight silver, and nine bronze medals.

To ensure Olympic success at Seoul in 1988, the PRC spent over a quarter of a billion dollars, more than fifty million dollars for each gold medal earned. Generous rewards for individual athletes were a part of the regime's program; diver Fu Mingxia's victory brought her a bonus that was three hundred times a teacher's annual salary.

In the 1990s, female runners like Wang Junxia set new world records by astonishing margins. Wang Junxia's time over 3,000 meters was 8:06.11 minutes, an unprecedented improvement of 3.28 percent over the old record. (No previous track record had ever been lowered by more than 2.51 percent.) At the 1994 world swimming championships, Chinese women won twelve of a possible sixteen gold medals. In response to the suspicion that such performances were drug enhanced, Chinese coaches referred to hard training and the ability of peasant women to "eat bitterness." It was true that Chinese athletes trained harder than their Western counterparts, but it was also true that Chinese men had failed to achieve such stellar performances and that a large number of female athletes tested positive for anabolic steroids. Between 1972 and 1994, ten of the world's elite swimmers had failed drug tests; in 1994 alone, eleven Chinese swimmers failed.

In 1993, the desire to "break out of Asia and advance on the world" motivated the government to modify its ban on openly professional sports and launch a twenty-four-team soccer league (followed by leagues for basketball and volleyball). In keeping with the regime's new openness to capitalist development, soccer teams pay their players ten times the salary of the average Chinese worker. Transfer payments are allowed and foreign players are lured with bonuses. The money comes not only from ticket sales but also from corporate sponsors such as Hyundai, Samsung, Panasonic, and Pepsi-Cola. The sports of the People's Republic seem more and more like the sports of Europe and North America, a tendency that will doubtless be accelerated in 2008, when Beijing hosts the summer Olympic Games.

Allen Guttmann

Further Reading

Brownell, Susan. (1995) *Training the Body for China*. Chicago: University of Chicago Press.

Hong, Fan. (1997) *Footbinding, Feminism, and Freedom: The Liberation of Women's Bodies in Modern China*. London: Frank Cass.

Knuttgen, Howard G., Ma Qiwei, and Wu Zhongyuan, eds. (1990) *Sport in China*. Champaign, IL: Human Kinetics.

Kolatch, Jonathan. (1972) *Sports, Politics, and Ideology in China*. Middle Village, NY: Jonathan David.

Riordan, James, and Robin Jones, eds. (1999) *Sport and Physical Education in China*. London: E. & F. N. Spon.

Wagner, Eric, ed. (1989) *Sport in Asia and Africa*. Westport, CT: Greenwood.

SPORTS—INDIA The warriors of India's Vedic age (2000–1400 BCE) hunted with bows and arrows and with spears. To perfect their skills as swordsmen, they fenced. Like the warriors of other cultures, they hardened their bodies and tested their skills as runners, jumpers, and wrestlers. If the *Mahabharata* (composed 400 BCE–400 CE) and the *Ramayana* (composed 500–300 BCE) can be taken as guides, swimming, weight lifting, wrestling, archery, and sword fighting were hallmarks of the Epic age (1400–1000 BCE). In the *Mahabharata*, epic hero Arjuna successfully relies on meditation to enhance his skills in archery. Instructed by Lord Krishna, Arjuna has a commitment to ethics that sets him apart from his brother Bhima, who is merely an athlete.

Meditation and yogalike techniques to control and even to deny the reality of the body gained in importance after the Epic age. This ascetic tendency was intensified in the fifth century BCE when the spread of Buddhism challenged Hindu religious dominance of the subcontinent. For devout Buddhists, the quest for enlightenment took priority over physical fitness and military prowess. Although boxing and wrestling were popular at Nalanda, the ancient Buddhist university, the pull of contemplative pursuits was also strong. Among the students' other "sports" were hopping over diagrams marked on the ground and guessing other people's thoughts. During Muslim rule of northwestern India (1526–1857), there was renewed concern for things of this world, including horse races, polo, and archery.

Bharatiya kushti and kalarippayattu

Adherence to Hinduism or Islam was quite compatible with a passion for wrestling and the martial arts. In fact, these activities were and still are perceived by Indians as forms of the religious life. *Bharatiya kushti* (Indian wrestling) and *kalarippayattu* (exercises in an open pit) are representative examples of the Indian melding of sports and religion.

Bharatiya kushti is practiced in the north. Indians who are devoted to this sport commit themselves wholeheartedly to the quest for a holy life. The wrestler's exercises, which include swinging eighty-kilogram "Indian clubs," are supervised by a guru whose word is law. He instructs his disciples in *pranayama* (controlled breathing) as well as in exercises familiar to Western athletes. These exercises are, however, done with a difference. When the wrestlers do their knee-bends and push-ups, they recite mantras. In accordance with the devout Hindu's unremitting struggle against pollution, the wrestlers must strictly control their diet, their sexual habits, the way they breathe, and even their urination and defecation.

Within the wrestler's world, there are, however, surprising departures from orthodox belief and behavior. Caste, which is otherwise a basic fact of Hindu life, is ignored. Some acts normally perceived as polluting are acceptable. Brahmins who have just been initiated into the practice of *bharatiya kushti* might, for instance, massage the feet of an experienced lower-caste wrestler. When wrestlers meet in actual competition, they seem to enact an unconscious inversion of "normal" Hindu life. "In a world of strict rules of body purity, wrestlers enact a ritual of physical contact saturated in sweat, mucus, and occasionally blood" (Alter 1992: 196–197).

Kalarippayattu, which has been practiced in Kerala since at least the twelfth century, is unique to the southwestern coastal region. Less obsessed with purity and pollution than *bharatiya kushti*, the sport has attracted Muslims and Christians as well as Hindus. In their search for physical health and spiritual enlightenment, the practitioners of *kalarippayattu* combine exercises reminiscent of karate with yogalike positions. As students master these exercises and positions, they are allowed to practice with weapons, advancing as they become increasingly proficient from long staves to short sticks and then to the curved *otta* (which resembles an elephant's tusk) and to daggers, swords, maces, and spears. Competition plays a more important role in *kalarippayattu* than in *bharatiya kushti*.

Western Sports

British rule introduced India to Western sports, the most important of which was certainly cricket. Seamen employed by the British East India Company played the game at Cambay (Khambhat) in 1721 and the Calcutta Cricket Club was in existence by 1792. The first cricket club for natives, the Orient, was not founded until 1848. The founders were Parsis, and for decades this religious minority produced the most ardent and successful Indian cricketers. Although traditional princely pastimes (such as pig sticking) continued to be popular, many native rulers became world-class cricketers. Among the Indian princes who played and promoted cricket were Rajendra Singh (1872–1900), ruler of the state of Patiala, and his son, Bhupinder Singh (1891–1938). Bhupinder's son, Yadavendra Singh (1913–1974), combined an active career as a cricket player with involvement in politics. He chaired the All-India Council of Sports and founded the Asian Games Federation; he also worked with Mohandas (Mahatma) Gandhi (1869–1948) and Jawaharlal Nehru (1889–1964) for the cause of Indian independence.

The most famous of India's innumerable world-class cricketers was K. S. Ranjitsinhji (1872–1933). "When he batted," wrote Neville Cardus, "a strange light was seen for the first time on English fields" (Cashman 1980: 35). Like the English language, cricket is today one of the few nongovernmental institutions uniting India's religiously and linguistically diverse population.

Cricket flourished at Mayo College and other schools for the sons of the Indian elite, but British educators such as C. E. Tyndale-Biscoe had only limited success when they attempted to force soccer and rugby football on their native pupils. One problem was that the leather balls used for these games were *jutha* (unclean). Efforts to popularize rowing and track-and-field sports were an almost total failure. The sons of the Indian elite saw no point in exhausting themselves in work that they thought was more properly done by members of the lower castes.

The example of British soldiers was apparently more persuasive than the commands of British teachers. The first Indian football clubs were for Europeans only, but the Indian Football Association (1893) decided in 1909 to allow native clubs into its annual tournament. When the Bengali team Mohan Began reached the finals in 1911, *The Englishman* announced in its 19 July 1911 issue, "Bengali Calcutta has gone football mad." In the final match, Mohan Began defeated the East Yorkshire Regiment. Soccer has been eclipsed by cricket, but Mohan Bagan continues to play the game.

Young Men's Christian Association (YMCA) workers such as Henry Gray and Harry Crowe Buch were responsible for the introduction and diffusion of basketball, volleyball, and softball. Buch founded the National YMCA School of Physical Education in Madras in 1920; it was an immensely influential institution. Missionary efforts to involve Indian girls in sports were mostly in vain. After independence in 1947, the government began a series of national sports festivals for girls and women, but female athletes are still drastically underrepresented in Indian sports.

Among the more unusual governmental efforts to promote physical education and sports was the establishment of the Himalayan Mountaineering Institute of Darjeeling (1954). It was inspired by the ascent of Everest on 29 May 1953 by Edmund Hillary (b. 1919) and Tenzing Norgay (1914–1986).

Darabji Jamshedji Tata and A. G. Neohren officially inaugurated the Indian Olympic Association in 1927, a full seven years after Indian athletes made their debut at the Antwerp games. Olympic success has come mostly in the form of gold medals for field hockey. Thanks largely to the efforts of G. D. Sondhi, who served on the International Olympic Committee from 1932 to 1966, New Delhi was chosen to host the first Asian Games, which took place in 1951.

Allen Guttmann

Further Reading

Alter, Joseph S. (1992) *The Wrestler's Body: Identity and Ideology in North India.* Berkeley and Los Angeles: University of California Press.

Bose, Mihir. (1990) *A History of Indian Cricket.* London: André Deutsch.

Cashman, Richard. (1980) *Patrons, Players, and the Crowd: The Phenomenon of Indian Cricket.* New Delhi: Orient Longman.

Wagner, Eric, ed. (1989) *Sport in Asia and Africa.* Westport, CT: Greenwood.

SPORTS—ISLAMIC ASIA

The sports of the Islamic peoples of Asia are a varied mix of traditional sports, many of which were played centuries before the birth of Islam, and modern sports, nearly all of which were imported from Europe and North America.

Traditional Sports

Throughout the Islamic regions from Turkey to Iran and Pakistan, hunting was "the sport of kings." Innumerable references to hunting in Persian poetry link Persian sportsmen to their distant pre-Islamic ancestors, whose passion for the hunt was chronicled by the Greek historian Xenophon (c. 431–c. 352 BCE). Hunting scenes, crowded by depictions of rulers, courtiers, attendants, and an assortment of panicky prey, are among the most common topics of sixteenth- and seventeenth-century Mughal art.

Closely associated with the hunt was the sport of archery. The mounted hunters who brought down their quarry with bows and arrows honed their skills at target archery, shooting not at abstract targets but at natural objects like gourds or sacks of sand. Accuracy was not the only mark of a good archer. Among the Turks, "flight shooting" (for distance) was a favorite sport. Muhammad II (1431–1481) constructed an *Ok Meydan* (arrow field) north of Istanbul. Stones were placed on the field to mark the record. Composite bows made of wood and horn enabled Turkish archers to outperform their European contemporaries.

Equestrian games were also dear to the hunter's heart. Varieties of polo were popular throughout Asia. In all probability, polo evolved from *buzkashi* and other rough games played by the nomadic peoples of Central Asia. In the Afghan form that has survived into the present, *buzkashi* was characterized by a dusty melee in which hundreds of mounted tribesmen fought over the headless carcass of a goat. The winner was the hardy rider who managed to grab the animal by a leg and drag it clear of the pack.

Polo was played throughout present-day Kurdistan and as far west as Constantinople (today's Istanbul), where French crusaders came upon the game in 1204, but the game's center of gravity was in Persia and northwestern India. In the Islamic era, the game was painted by innumerable miniaturists and celebrated by poets such as Firdawsi (c. 935–c. 1020) and Hafez (1325/26–1389/90).

After the Islamic conquest of what is now Pakistan and northwest India, Mughal art frequently depicted polo players. Akbar (1542–1605), the most famous of the Mughal emperors, was renowned for his polo skills. We know that Mughal women sometimes played the game; three miniature paintings commemorate a match played by Queen Humay. In today's Pakistan, Islamic fundamentalists decry polo as an affront to the Prophet, but the Shandur Tournament is an important national event endorsed by the government, visited by throngs of tourists, and broadcast live by state-run television.

Archery was the Turkish sultans' favorite sport, but their subjects wrestled. The most skillful *pahlavan* (wrestlers) were summoned to the court in Constantinople. In villages throughout the Ottoman realm, men formed wrestling guilds and frequented "houses of strength," where Allah was invoked to secure a wrestler's victory and poets were enlisted to celebrate it. Similar "houses of strength" (*zurkhaneh*) are still an important part of Iranian culture. Open only to Muslims, the *zurkhaneh* is a place of worship as well as a sports site. While the wrestlers prepare for their match, a *morshed* or ritual chanter chants and drums and reminds them of the deeds of the greatest *pahlavan* of all, the fourteenth-century poet Mahmud Kharazmi.

Introduction of Western Sports

Throughout the Islamic Near East, traditional sports have been marginalized if not wholly replaced by modern sports introduced from Europe and the United States, but the process was neither swift nor easy. The government of Ottoman Turkey strongly resisted the introduction of modern sports. In 1896, when the wrestler Koc Mehmet applied to the sultan for permission to participate in the first Olympic Games of the modern era, he was sent to prison as punishment for his audacity. When a Turkish group organized a soccer team in Constantinople in 1899, nine years after British seamen and diplomats had begun to play the game at Izmir, the sultan ordered the team dissolved. Turkish citizens were allowed to watch while British residents in Constantinople played soccer, but the Turks were warned by the police not to mingle with foreign spectators. In 1905, the sultan gave reluctant permission for his subjects to form what became Turkey's most famous soccer club—Galatasary. In 1910, two years after a revolution restricted the sultan's authority, the League of Football Clubs of Constantinople was established. In the 1920s, the secular government of Mustafa Kemal Ataturk (1881–1938) was far more positive about Western ways. By the time of Ataturk's death, soccer had become a major sport. It remains immensely popular. In 1986, nearly half of all Turkish sports-club members played the game.

Iranian soccer began with the British officers of the South Persia Rifles. In the years from 1916 to 1921, they taught the game to native troops. A national soccer federation was established in 1919, and soccer players were soon as numerous as wrestlers.

Until the Islamic Revolution of 1978, modern sports of all sorts were promoted by the shah, Muhammad Reza Shah Pahlavi (1919–1980), and his brother Gholam Reza, head of Iran's National Olympic Committee. Throughout the shah's reign, however, there was considerable resistance to modern sports on the part of clerical leaders, who felt such activities to be an affront to Islam. Islamic fundamentalists found women's sports to be especially objectionable. The fact that state-run television broadcast sports on Friday (and showed the shah's wife as a swimmer and a water skier) contributed to the monarchy's downfall. Once the Islamic Revolution had taken place, however, the Ayatollah Khomeini (c. 1900–1989) was ready to accept most modern sports for men and even for women—if the women were properly dressed and carefully protected from the gaze of male spectators. In 1993, the First Islamic Women's Games were held in Tehran (without male coaches or male spectators).

In Olympic and other international competition, Turks and Iranians have been especially successful in weightlifting and wrestling, two sports traditionally associated with the "houses of strength."

Although Islamic fundamentalism is a force in Pakistan, modern sports have met with less resistance there than in Iran. Since its independence in 1949, Pakistan has produced some of the world's best field-hockey teams, but the nation's greatest successes have been in squash rackets. Since its recognition by the International Cricket Conference in 1952, Pakistan has also become a major power in that sport.

Relations with the International Olympic Committee

Although Turkey's Selim Sirry Bey (d. 1930) was the first Asian to join the International Olympic Committee (IOC), in 1908, the Islamic nations of Asia have had uneasy relations with that organization. For decades after the establishment of Israel, Islamic states refused to compete against what they termed the "Zionist entity." Israel was not invited to the Mediterranean Games when they were held in Beirut (1959) or to the Asian Games when they took place in Jakarta (1962). The latter exclusion had major consequences. The IOC, protesting not only the exclusion of Israel (and Taiwan) but also the rough treatment given to an IOC member, suspended Indonesia from the Olympic movement. The response of Indonesia's President Sukarno (1901–1970) was to launch the Games of the New Emerging Forces (GANEFO). (Forty-eight nations, mostly Asian and African, sent teams to GANEFO I in 1963, after which the organization quietly disappeared.)

Indonesia was not the only Islamic state to clash with the IOC. A number of states boycotted the 1956, 1980, and 1984 games. There has also been tension over the reluctance of most Islamic nations to send female athletes to the Olympic Games.

Differences in Approach by Islamic Regions

In general, the Islamic nations of Southeast Asia have been less receptive to Western sports than their co-religionists in the Near East and South Asia.

Cricket was played in Singapore as early as 1837. The whole palette of modern sports followed. They spread rapidly among the native elites in Singapore and Penang. (An international golf tournament was held in Penang in 1888.) Missionary teachers such as Mabel Marsh and Josephine Foss saw badminton, tennis, net ball, and basketball as instruments to emancipate Asian women, but they were more successful with the peninsula's Chinese and Indian girls than with ethnic Malay girls.

The first prime minister of the independent state of Malaysia, Tunku Abdul Rahman (1903–1990), was a soccer enthusiast who had played the game at Cambridge University. Under his leadership, the government invested in a splendid new stadium, and soccer flourished, but other modern sports have had a precarious postcolonial existence.

Dutch colonists in what is now Indonesia made an effort to promote *korfball*, a Dutch version of basketball, but they failed. They had more success with *voetball* (Dutch for football, the sport known to Americans as soccer), and several soccer leagues were organized on Sumatra and Java. Basketball, volleyball, and other modern games followed. Internationally, Malaysian and Indonesian athletes have been dominant in badminton, a modern sport that probably has its origins in the ancient Chinese game of shuttlecock.

Western sports have not, however, eliminated traditional games. In Indonesia and Malaysia, traditional sports may be an endangered species, but they have managed to survive. Among them are *sepak raga* and *sepak takraw*. *Sepak raga*, the Malay version, is similar to Japanese *kemari* in that the players, using any part of the body except the forearm and the hand, strive to keep the ball in the air. This is also the goal of *sipa*, which is played by the Muslim minority in the Philippine Islands. Like many traditional Asian games, *Sepak raga* emphasizes harmony of movement, abetted by flute, gong, and drum music. Indonesian *sepak takraw*, which is one version of a game played throughout Southeast Asia, is closer to volleyball. Instead of using their hands, however, the players use their feet or their heads to propel the hollow rattan ball over the net. Competition is keen.

One reason for *sepak takraw*'s survival is that it has become, in many ways, a modern sport. To save the game from extinction, players from throughout the region organized the Asian Sepak Takraw Federation, agreed upon a common set of rules, and campaigned for the acceptance of the sport in the Asian Games, a goal achieved when the eleventh Asian Games took place in Beijing in 1990.

Allen Guttmann

Further Reading
Klopsteg, Paul. E. (1934) *Turkish Archery and the Composite Bow*. Evanston, IL: Paul E. Klopsteg.
Titley, Norah M. (1979) *Sports and Pastimes: Scenes from Turkish, Persian, and Mughal Paintings*. London: British Library.
Wagner, Eric, ed. (1989) *Sport in Asia and Africa*. Westport, CT: Greenwood.

SPORTS—JAPAN

Japanese sports may be classified either as traditional (those sports played in Japan for centuries, before contact with the West) or modern (those sports that Japan has adopted enthusiastically from the West in the late nineteenth century and after).

Sumo

Of all Japanese sports, sumo wrestling is probably the most distinctive. According to one interpretation of the legends collected in the *Nihongi* (720 CE), the first sumo match between two mortals occurred in 23 BCE when a certain Nomi no Sukune was asked by Emperor Suinin to deal with Taima no Keyaha, a notorious bully who had boasted that he was the strongest man on earth. Nomi no Sukune engaged his boastful opponent and crushed his ribs with one kick and broke his back with another.

Better informed historians trace the origins of sumo to the annual matches performed at the imperial court in Nara. These matches, which took place on the seventh day of the seventh month of the lunar calendar, began in 734 CE. A garden adjacent to the Shishinden ("Hall for State Ceremonies") was strewn with white sand for the ceremony. Announced by drums and gongs, thirty-four wrestlers entered the garden. They were followed by officials, musicians, and dancers. One team wore paper hollyhocks in their hair; the other wore paper calabash blossoms. After each match, musicians beat their drums, struck their gongs, and performed a ritual dance. The annual event, which served as a demonstration of imperial authority, continued after the court's removal to Heian-kyo (modern Kyoto) in 794 CE.

The court had no monopoly on the sport. Sumo was performed as part of festival celebrations at temples and shrines. The most famous example is proba-

Students practice at a sumo wrestling school in Tokyo in 1995. (TEMPSPORT/CORBIS)

bly karasu-zumo ("crow wrestling"), which still takes place at Kyoto's Kamo Shrine. Boys representing the god Takemikazuchi wrestle against other boys representing the earthly sphere.

After the end of the Heian period in 1185, political power shifted to Kamakura and sumo was rarely performed at court. During the Tokugawa period (1600/1603–1868), sumo became an urban phenomenon. Woodblock prints of street-corner sumo show not only the massively muscled wrestlers but also the citizens of Osaka and Edo (modern Toyko) jostling one another for a glimpse of their heroes. In the Meiji (1868–1912) and Taisho (1912–1926) periods, in the midst of Japanese modernization, sumo was "retraditionalized" in order to underline its position as a symbol of Japanese culture. Among the innovations were the referee's new clothes; he is now anachronistically attired in Heian-period kimono and headgear.

Kemari

The kimono-clad courtiers of Heian-kyo did attend sumo matches, but for exercise they chose *kemari*, a ball game they borrowed, like their written language, from China. The game was played outdoors on a square earthen court with sides about six or seven meters in length. At each of the corners was a pine, willow, cherry, or maple tree. The eight players were stationed two to a tree. The object of the game was to keep a deerskin ball aloft. Since the clogs that were normal footwear were inappropriate, players wore leather shoes. The number of times a player kicked the ball before he passed it on was not fixed, but three was considered most appropriate—one kick to receive the ball and bring it under control, one to send it high above the player's head, and one to pass it to another player. Players were not judged by the number of successful kicks but rather by the "three virtues of the ball," which were proper posture, swiftness and skill, and mastery of strategy. From the twelfth century to the nineteenth, *kemari* was a popular aristocratic pastime. It is still played by the members of the Kemari Preservation Society.

Archery

Toughened warriors of the samurai class were no more likely to spend their time at *kemari* than they were to compete in bouts of sumo against nearly naked peasants. Warriors preferred to demonstrate their physical prowess as archers and fencers. Archeologists have found obsidian arrowheads from the Stone Age, and "heavenly feathered arrows" were a token of the mythical emperor Jimmu's right to rule the Japanese

islands, but the earliest historical documents relating to archery as a sport date from late in the seventh century CE. Although the Japanese gripped the bow in the Mongolian fashion, with the thumb wrapped over the bowstring, they used the long bow derived from southeastern Asia rather than the much shorter Mongol bow. The long bow, which measures over two meters, is still used and is still gripped as it was in the Heian period, with two-thirds of the bow's length above the archer's hand.

Archey, like sumo, became incorporated into the annual calendar of ceremonies performed at the imperial court. In the *Dairishiki*, which chronicles court ceremonies from 646 to 930, archery matches far outnumbered all other ceremonies. The light bows used at court were probably more effective as symbols of authority than as weapons of war.

Jarai was typical of the many kinds of target archery performed over the centuries at the imperial court. *Jarai* matches were held at the Burakuin ("Court of Abundant Pleasures") in the middle of the first lunar month. Twenty noblemen, including imperial princes, were selected to participate. A second team was chosen from the palace guards. Standing on mats made of calfskin, aiming at deerskin targets, the nobles shot first, followed by the guards. A gong rang once to indicate that an arrow had hit the target's outer ring. The gong rang twice if the arrow lodged in the middle ring, three times if the innermost ring was struck. Heralds announced the results along with the contestant's name, rank, and office. The archer's rank influenced the prize he received. Members of the imperial family aimed their arrows at a target 20 percent larger than the one provided for the nobility.

A courtier's performance at the rather gentle sport of *jarai* was no predictor of his battlefield prowess. *Yabusame*, which required equestrian as well as archery skills, was more like the real thing. In *yabusame*, the contestants drew their bows and loosed their arrows while galloping down a straight track some 220 to 270 meters long. The archers were required to shoot in quick succession at three small targets (about 55 centimeters square) placed on meter-high poles 7 to 11 meters from the track and spaced at intervals of 72 to 90 meters.

During the relatively pacific Tokugawa era, the importance of archery as a battlefield skill declined. The samurai continued to practice with bow and arrow, but the motivation for their practice was not what it had been when the accuracy of one's aim made a life-or-death difference. Archery was simultaneously a recreation, a sport, and a form of spiritual training. Throughout the Tokugawa period, schools of archery

FUJIWARA MICHINAGA (966—1027) COMPETES AT ARCHERY

"He appeared at the Southern Palace one day while his nephew Korechika was holding an archery contest in the presence of Regent Michikane. Surprised by the visit, which he considered suspicious, Michinaga's brother Michitaka nevertheless welcomed him warmly and let him shoot before Korechika, even though his rank was inferior. Korechika lost by two hits, whereupon Michitaka and some others proposed an extension of the match. 'Shoot twice more,' they said."

" 'All right, extend it,' Michinaga said, somewhat annoyed. As he prepared to shoot again, he said, 'If Emperors and Empresses are to issue from my house, let this arrow hit the mark.' And didn't his arrow strike the heart of the target? Next Korechika prepared to shoot. He was extremely nervous, and it may be that his hands trembled. At any rate, his arrow flew off into the sky without coming near the target. Michitaka turned pale."

"Michinaga got ready again. 'If I am to serve as Regent, let this arrow find the mark,' he said. The arrow hit the very center, striking with such force that the target almost broke. Regent Michikane's cordiality vanished, and he showed his displeasure by ending the match."

Source: Adapted from *Ôkagami.* (1980) Princeton, NJ: Princeton University Press, 197.

proliferated as *kyujutsu* (techniques of the bow) became *kyudo* (the way of the bow). When the spokesmen of the various schools codified the rules and techniques of their particular styles, they tended to express their thoughts in the religious terminology—Shinto, Buddhist, or Confucianist—that was the common currency of learned men. Zen Buddhism contributed to the idea of archery as a spiritual activity, but it was only one of several influences.

Fencing

Fencers trod the same path as archers, as *kenjutsu* (techniques of the sword) became kendo (the way of the sword). The difference was that archers had no need to transform weaponry into sports equipment. Fencers, however, had to modify their equipment to avoid the deadly damage inflicted by the Japanese sword (a much sharper instrument than its European counterpart). The wooden sports swords that had been in use since before the sixteenth century were lethal weapons in the hands of a skilled and determined swordsman. Bamboo swords, which dated from the sixteenth century, were not as dangerous, but they still caused serious pain and injury. In response to the chal-

lenge, kendo enthusiasts developed protective gear to make their sport safer: *kote* (gloves for the hands and lower arm), the *men* (a cotton helmet with a metal protector for the face), the *do* (a chest protector), and the *tare* (armor for the waist and groin). This equipment was not devised all at once but evolved over time. By the beginning of the eighteenth century, the mask, gloves, and trunk padding had achieved something like their present form and were widely used for simulated combat. (The predictable lament of the traditionalists was that all these innovations distanced the sport too far from the conditions of manly combat.)

While many swordsmen proclaimed *kenzen ichinyo* ("the sword and Zen are one"), others saw their sport as a way to perfect Confucianist or Shinto discipline. Still others—a growing number in modern times—are indifferent to the religious aspects of the sport. In periods of intense nationalism, kendo has been promoted as a paramilitary discipline. During World War II, Japan's military government glorified the sport (even as it denigrated baseball). In 1945, the new Ministry of Education, under the direction of the supreme commander for the allied powers, banned all martial arts from the school curriculum, forbade them as a student club activity, and even prohibited kendo practice on school properties. The Allied Occupation ended in 1952, and kendo returned to the schools a year later. In the kendo clubs that have proliferated in secondary schools, 40 percent of the membership is now female, a remarkable deviation from the stereotype of the frail and subservient Japanese woman.

Western Sports

During the Meiji period (1868–1912), when Japan was opened to Western influences, the whole range of modern sports was introduced to Japan. Government attempts to modernize the military led to the introduction of gymnastics. French officers taught Japanese soldiers to fence in the European way, and Austrian officers taught them to ski. British and American residents in the trading communities of Kobe and Yokohama founded clubs for their favorite sports, including cricket, soccer football, baseball, tennis, and golf. Although these Westerners established sports clubs for their own enjoyment, the Japanese with whom they interacted were quick to emulate them.

The Meiji government invited European and American educators to teach in the newly established system of secondary schools and colleges. These educators introduced Japanese students to baseball, soccer football, rowing, and track-and-field sports. Foreign missionaries, especially those associated with the YMCA, promoted basketball, volleyball, field hockey, and badminton. Japanese who had lived abroad brought back with them table tennis, handball, basketball, and volleyball. Participation in the Olympics and other international sports events introduced wrestling, weightlifting, and canoeing, and voluntary sports clubs took up activities such as yachting and mountain climbing.

Frederick W. Strange (d. 1889), an English educator, arrived in Tokyo in 1875 imbued with the Victorian conviction that sports are the proper antidote for an excess of intellectual endeavor. He summoned his students "to come out and play games." The track-and-field meet he organized on 16 June 1883 was probably Japan's first. The following year, Strange founded a boat club modeled on those at Oxford and Cambridge. In 1885, the club's team raced against the foreigners of the Yokohama Athletic Club. In 1887, the club organized intercollegiate races on the Sumida River, which flows through Tokyo.

Horace Wilson, an American teacher at what later became Tokyo University, introduced baseball in 1873. The diffusion of the game throughout the educational system was accelerated in 1896 when a team of schoolboys defeated the Yokohama Athletic Club in a widely publicized four-game series. At the college level, Waseda, Keio, and Meiji universities formed a three-team baseball league in 1914. A year later, the Asahi newspaper started a national tournament for middle schools. Newspaper entrepreneurship was also responsible for professional baseball in Japan. In 1936 Shoriki Matsutaro, publisher of the *Yomiuri* newspaper, launched a highly successful seven-team league. The league expired during World War II, but the professional game was revived in 1950 and flourishes in the Central and the Pacific Leagues.

A professional soccer league, begun in 1993, failed to replace baseball as the nation's favorite team sport, but another sport of British origins emerged in the late twentieth century as the trademark pastime of the *sarariman* ("salary man" or white-collar employee). Although scarcity of land makes golf an extremely expensive sport, corporate executives are willing to spend a million dollars or more for membership in exclusive golf clubs.

While their fathers are at the golf club (or at one of Japan's many indoor driving ranges), Japan's adolescents head for their own sports venues. They have been quicker than young people in other parts of Asia to take up skateboarding, in-line skating, rock-climbing, hang gliding, windsurfing, and other "postmodern" sports.

Japan's participation in the Olympic Games began in 1912 when two runners were sent to Stockholm. They were accompanied by Kano Jigoro (1860–1938), who had become Japan's representative on the International Olympic Committee three years earlier. (Kano's contribution to Japanese sports included the invention of judo in 1882, a martial art that Kano envisioned as a compromise between tradition and modernity.) Except for Hitomi Kinue (1907–1931), a spectacular runner who earned a silver medal in 1928 in the first women's 800-meter race, Japanese track-and-field athletes have rarely done well at the Olympics. High points in Japan's Olympic history occurred in Los Angeles in 1932, when the men's swimming team overwhelmed its rivals, winning eleven of a possible sixteen medals; in Tokyo in 1964, when the women's volleyball team upset the favored Russians; and in Nagano in 1998, when Harada Masahiko's flawless flight secured gold for the Japanese ski-jump team. His feat was a personal vindication because he had jumped poorly at the Lillehammer games in 1994 and cost his team the gold medal. No wonder he became known as "Happy Harada."

Allen Guttmann

Further Reading

Cuyler, Patricia. (1980) *Sumo: From Rite to Sport*. New York: Weatherhill.

Friday, Karl F., and Seki Humitake. (1997) *Legacies of the Sword*. Honolulu, HI: University of Hawaii Press.

Guttmann, Allen, and Lee Thompson. (2001) *Japanese Sports*. Honolulu, HI: University of Hawaii Press.

Hurst, G. Cameron, III. (1998) *Armed Martial Arts in Japan*. New Haven, CT: Yale University Press.

Kano Jigoro. (1986). *Kodokan Judo*. Tokyo: Kodansha.

Whiting, Robert. (1977) *The Chrysanthemum and the Bat*. New York: Dodd, Mead.

———. (1989) *You Gotta Have Wa*. New York: Macmillan.

SPORTS—KOREA

Throughout most of its history, Korea has been strongly influenced by Chinese (and to a much lesser degree) Japanese culture. Before the Koryo period (918–1392), the states of Paekche (18 BCE–663 CE), Shilla (57 BCE–935 CE), and Koguryo (37 BCE–668 CE) were engaged in nearly constant wars with China, with Japan, and with each other. Like the sports of other Asian cultures, the earliest Korean sports tended to be closely related to warfare. Mounted archery was known in prehistoric times and skill with swords and spears was highly prized. *Ssirum*, a popular traditional wrestling game, dates back to the early Koguryo kingdom. The origins of the Korean variant of the unarmed martial arts, *t'aekwondo* (or tae kwon do, as it is spelled in English), "the way of the foot and the hand," are unknown. The sport, which is now closely associated with modern Korea, may have originated in the kingdom of Shilla or, like many of Korea's sports, it may have had Chinese or Japanese origins.

During the Koryo period, Buddhism flourished and the interest in sports, especially military sports, slackened. It is likely that Korea's gentler sports—such as kite flying and see-sawing, often part of seasonal festivals—flourished in this era. Notable among sports for women was a kind of swinging competition in which the contestants stood on a plank suspended from ropes. The Choson period, which lasted from 1392 until Japanese annexation in 1910, saw a renewed interest in sports, especially military sports.

Advent of Western Sports

Late in the nineteenth century, Western sports came to Korea. In 1898, a year after observing British sailors playing the game in the port of Inchon, Koreans organized their first soccer team. Missionaries from the Young Men's Christian Association (YMCA), mostly Americans, played a leading role in the introduction of modern sports. P. L. Gilllette taught the fundamentals of baseball in 1905 and basketball in 1907. Volleyball followed in 1916. The YMCA, which had its headquarters at the royal capital of Seoul, was also behind the organization of the Choson Sports Association in 1920.

The Olympic baseball stadium in Seoul, Korea. Although not a traditional Korean sport, baseball has become a major amateur and professional sport in Korea. In the 1990s, several Korean players played in American professional baseball leagues. (JANET WISHNETSKY/CORBIS)

By that time, Japanese military men and government officials were actively promoting kendo, judo, and—less predictably—table tennis. Koreans began to participate in the Olympic Games in 1932—as members of the Japanese team. Patriotic athletes resented their role as representatives of Japan. Sohn Kee-Chung, winner of the 1936 Olympic marathon, saw himself listed as "Kitei Son" (a Japanized version of his name), and vowed never again to compete under the Japanese flag. His country honored him at the 1988 Olympics in Seoul. He lit the Olympic flame.

Sports in Divided Korea

The post-1945 division of the Korean peninsula between the Communist north and the non-Communist south led to the creation of two very different sports systems. While tae kwon do is practiced north and south (and internationally as well), the Republic of Korea (South Korea) opted for commercialized sports on the American and Japanese model. Professional baseball is the nation's most popular spectator sport. The level of play is high enough for a few Korean players, such as Pak Ch'an-ho (Chan Ho Park), to play professionally in the United States. Baseball is also popular as a recreational sport.

In recent years, South Korea has had a boom in golf. Pak Se-ri (Se Ri Pak) and Kim Mi-hyon (Mit Hyun Kim) are among the world's most successful golf professionals. Winter sports have also become popular, stimulated in part by Korean successes at the Winter Olympics.

The People's Republic (North Korea) imitated the Soviet Union's state-run system (with an emphasis on paramilitary sports). Despite its relative poverty, the north has invested heavily in its sports infrastructure. Kim Il Sung Stadium, for instance, seats 100,000 spectators. In international competition, Koreans from both sides of the thirty-eighth parallel have done well in weightlifting, boxing, wrestling, and—not surprisingly—tae kwon do.

When the International Olympic Committee (IOC) selected Seoul to host the 1988 summer games, the Pyongyang government demanded that half the events occur in the north. The IOC offered them the opportunity to host all the competitions in archery and table tennis and some of the contests in cycling and soccer football. The offer greatly displeased the Republic of Korea and failed to satisfy the People's Republic, which stayed away from Seoul, as it had from Los Angeles in 1984. The north's boycott did little to diminish the south's pride in its team, which harvested twelve gold, ten silver, and eleven bronze medals.

Allen Guttmann

Further Reading

Culin, Stewart. (1958) *Games of the Orient.* Rutland, VT: Tuttle.
Wagner, Eric, ed. (1989) *Sport in Asia and Africa.* Westport, CT: Greenwood.

SPRATLY ISLANDS DISPUTE

The Spratly Islands group, whose ownership is disputed by the People's Republic of China (PRC), Vietnam, the Philippines, Malaysia, Brunei, and Taiwan, is located in the middle of the South China Sea, the geostrategic heart of Southeast Asia. The island group includes hundreds of uninhabitable small islands, coral atolls, reefs, and shoals scattered across the South China Sea and covering an area of approximately 180,000 square kilometers. With the possibility of abundant oil and natural gas reserves and marine life resources around the islands, the economic stakes make resolving this territorial dispute challenging.

Basis of Claims

Although the PRC claims the Spratlies have belonged to China since ancient time, all of the claimants, including Taiwan, occupied islands in the Spratly archipelago before the PRC gained a foothold. In March 1988, following a skirmish with Vietnamese forces, China wrested control of six islands in the Spratly group from Vietnam.

North Vietnam initially recognized the islands as Chinese territory, but after the unification of Vietnam in 1975, the Vietnamese government began to claim the Spratly chain and occupied several islands. In 1977, Vietnam established a 320-kilometer (200-mile) exclusive economic zone over part of the South China Sea that included the Spratly Islands.

In 1947, the Philippines claimed some of the islands that lay off its coast. This claim was based on the argument that Japan occupied these islands during World War II but abandoned the islands after the war, leaving them up for grabs. The Philippines undertook various measures, such as naval inspections, tours, and diplomatic notes, to assert its ownership. In 1974, the Philippine navy actually took control of five islands, and in 1978 a presidential decree claimed the Kalayaan Islands, as it terms the islands, as an integral part of the Philippines.

Malaysia asserted a claim to the continental shelf in 1979 and then established an exclusive economic zone adjacent to Borneo in 1980. As a result of those claims, Malaysia claims several islands in the Spratly group and occupies three atolls. Brunei claims the continental shelf off its coast, which includes the Louisa Reef;

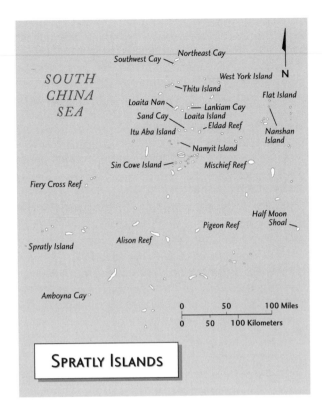

SOUTH CHINA SEA

Southwest Cay — Northeast Cay
West York Island
Thitu Island
Flat Island
Loaita Nan — Lankiam Cay
Sand Cay — Loaita Island
Itu Aba Island — Eldad Reef
Nanshan Island
Namyit Island
Sin Cowe Island — Mischief Reef
Fiery Cross Reef
Half Moon Shoal
Pigeon Reef
Alison Reef
Spratly Island
Amboyna Cay

0   50   100 Miles
0   50   100 Kilometers

SPRATLY ISLANDS

it too bases its claims to Spratly islands on its claim to the continental shelf. In contrast, other countries base their claims upon prior occupation or discovery.

Reasons for Recent Interest

The Spratly Islands dispute has received more attention in recent years because it is a likely flash point for conflict in the region. At present, no country in the region possesses the military capacity to impose its claims. A negotiated settlement of the dispute is important in the post–Cold War era when economic cooperation is crucial for regional development. The South China Sea is a major sea lane and is important to world trade. Two hundred oil tankers pass by the Spratly Islands every day, and any disruption of trade would have a significant negative impact on the region. The necessity of regional economic cooperation has opened the door to the possibility of a negotiated settlement.

Prospects for Settlement

All claimants express a willingness to find a peaceful and mutually beneficial solution to the dispute. After maintaining a defiant position regarding its claims to the South China Sea throughout the 1970s and 1980s, the PRC signaled a new flexibility in 1990, with Beijing stating that it was willing to shelve the sovereignty question and move ahead with joint develop-

ment. This was in contrast with earlier statements asserting that China would take control of the islands by force, if necessary. Indonesia stepped forward as an honest broker and since 1990 has held several workshops on managing potential conflict in the South China Sea. The PRC has participated in the Indonesian-sponsored sessions, but the meetings have achieved no real progress toward any significant joint development efforts. China, in fact, favors bilateral negotiations because the basis for the various national claims is different and Beijing holds that dealing with these claims in a multilateral setting only complicates negotiations. Because of the many nations involved, any settlement will likely require difficult multilateral negotiations and mutual accommodation. At the second workshop, which was held in 1991, all claimants agreed to halt independent development and made a pledge to not use force to settle the disputes.

Nevertheless, Beijing's subsequent actions made clear its willingness to move unilaterally and to use force if necessary to defend its claims. In 1992, before the third workshop, China's National People's Congress promulgated a law on territorial waters that asserted China's claims of undisputed sovereignty over the islands of the South China Sea and authorized the use of military force to prevent other states from occupying the islands. China used military force to occupy three more islands in 1992, and in 1994 it dispatched two warships to the South China Sea to blockade a Vietnamese oil rig, demanding that Vietnam stop encroaching upon China's sovereignty.

China is strengthening its foothold on the islands and enhancing its ability to use force if necessary to protect its strategic interests and ensure its stake in the development of the region's resources. The PRC can now more directly challenge the claims of the other parties to the dispute and can do so more confidently. Other parties to the dispute are also being more assertive. Despite Chinese objections, the Southeast Asian states issued an official Spratly Declaration in 1992 calling for military restraint and joint development while leaving open the question of sovereignty. However, none of the Southeast Asian states show any inclination to compromise with each other on the issue of sovereignty. In 1993, the Philippines expanded its military facilities in their five Kalayaan Islands to enable civilian and military planes to use the runway.

Incentives for Settlement

It is in every country's interest to settle the territorial dispute to facilitate closer relations among the economically dynamic states in the region. The potential resources of the South China Sea would contribute to China's ambitious economic development. Under the circumstances, Beijing is more likely to cooperatively pursue joint development while leaving the conundrum of sovereignty to a later date.

While historical and legal questions complicate any resolution of the Spratly Islands dispute, all parties remain interested in finding a peaceful solution. The natural resources of the Spratly Islands call for joint development, and all parties will only achieve optimum advantage through pragmatic cooperation. This requires that states in the region compromise on the sovereignty question to facilitate further cooperation on more fundamental economic and security issues.

Eric Hyer

Further Reading

Catley, Bob, and Makmur Keliat. (1997) *Spratlies: The Dispute in the South China Sea.* Brookfield, VT: Dartmouth Publishing Co.
Lo, Chi-kin. (1989) *China's Policy toward Territorial Disputes: The Case of the South China Sea.* London: Routledge.
Samuels, Marwyn S. (1982) *Contest for the South China Sea.* New York: Methuen.
Valencia, Mark J., Jon M. Van Dyke, and Noel A. Ludwig. (1997) *Sharing the Resources of the South China Sea.* The Hague, Netherlands: Martinus Nijhoff.

SPRING FESTIVAL—CHINA The Spring Festival is the most important seasonal festival in China, marking the end of an old year and the beginning of a new one. Among the most joyous and colorful Chinese seasonal festivals, it is also the longest, extending from the sixteenth day of the twelfth month to the fifteen day of the first month, affecting every aspect of life in society. On New Year's Eve, entire families are expected to gather together for an evening meal; the event is comparable in significance to the family meals held on Christmas Eve in the West.

The premodern (pre–twentieth century) Chinese calendar year followed the lunar year, and the Spring Festival was connected with this calendar. The Nationalist revolution in 1912 and the Communist revolution in 1949 not only brought about fundamental changes in political institutions, but also introduced the Western calendar as a way to "modernize" China. The official New Year's Day was moved to 1 January, and the Lunar New Year was renamed the "Spring Festival."

Businesses large and small celebrate this occasion with a year-end banquet. Bonuses of cash in red envelopes are given to employees so that they can travel home for the holiday. In China, Taiwan, Hong Kong,

and Singapore, the new lunar year also signals the beginning of the monthlong Lunar New Year holiday. Most businesses close or curtail operations throughout the festival. The twenty-fourth day of the twelfth month marks the second major ritual that involves individual families. This is the day when each family sends its residential kitchen god back to heaven; it is customary for the family to prepare sweet foods or foods made from glutinous rice as sacrifices to the kitchen god.

On New Year's Eve, all family members gather for the evening meal. By lighting incense before the meal, the head of the family symbolically invites the departed ancestors and deities to join the occasion. After the meal, children pay their respects to their parents by bowing (in China) or kowtowing (in Taiwan and Hong Kong) to them. In return, parents give their children money in red envelopes. On New Year's Day, people wearing new clothes visit their kin, friends, and neighbors. The celebration lasts until the fifteenth day of the first month, the Lantern Festival, after which all businesses resume normal operations and employees return to work.

Huang Shu-min

Further Reading

Bodde, Derk. (1975) *Festivals in Classical China: New Year and Other Annual Observances during the Han Dynasty, 206 B.D.–A.D. 220.* Princeton, NJ: Princeton University Press.
Eberhard, Wolfram. (1958) *Chinese Festivals.* New York: Abelard-Schuman.

SRI LANKA—PROFILE (2001 est. pop. 19.4 million). A small island nation located at the southernmost tip of the Indian subcontinent and measuring only 65,610 square kilometers, Sri Lanka has a diversified geography that includes harmoniously associated landscapes of lowlands and highlands (reaching a lofty elevation of 2,524 meters). It is richly blessed by natural beauty, and greatly benefits from its location and climatic conditions.

Climate and Agriculture

Its tropical location and the monsoons have given Sri Lanka a good environment for cultivating tropical crops, of which tea, rubber, and coconut palms are the most important. A wide variety of tropical vegetables and fruits are also grown, mostly on family farms; common crops are bananas, mangos, pineapples, avocados, and melons, as well as cashew nuts and many spices, including chili peppers, black pepper, cardamom, cinnamon, and nutmeg, which altogether flavor the traditional hot, spicy local curries. In the cold tropical

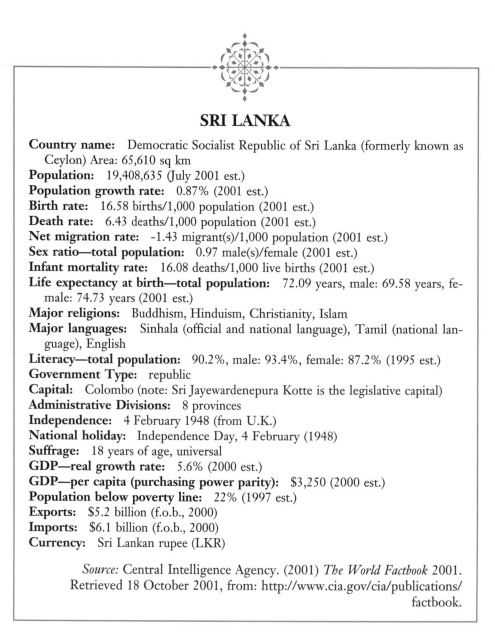

SRI LANKA

Country name: Democratic Socialist Republic of Sri Lanka (formerly known as Ceylon) Area: 65,610 sq km

Population: 19,408,635 (July 2001 est.)

Population growth rate: 0.87% (2001 est.)

Birth rate: 16.58 births/1,000 population (2001 est.)

Death rate: 6.43 deaths/1,000 population (2001 est.)

Net migration rate: -1.43 migrant(s)/1,000 population (2001 est.)

Sex ratio—total population: 0.97 male(s)/female (2001 est.)

Infant mortality rate: 16.08 deaths/1,000 live births (2001 est.)

Life expectancy at birth—total population: 72.09 years, male: 69.58 years, female: 74.73 years (2001 est.)

Major religions: Buddhism, Hinduism, Christianity, Islam

Major languages: Sinhala (official and national language), Tamil (national language), English

Literacy—total population: 90.2%, male: 93.4%, female: 87.2% (1995 est.)

Government Type: republic

Capital: Colombo (note: Sri Jayewardenepura Kotte is the legislative capital)

Administrative Divisions: 8 provinces

Independence: 4 February 1948 (from U.K.)

National holiday: Independence Day, 4 February (1948)

Suffrage: 18 years of age, universal

GDP—real growth rate: 5.6% (2000 est.)

GDP—per capita (purchasing power parity): $3,250 (2000 est.)

Population below poverty line: 22% (1997 est.)

Exports: $5.2 billion (f.o.b., 2000)

Imports: $6.1 billion (f.o.b., 2000)

Currency: Sri Lankan rupee (LKR)

Source: Central Intelligence Agency. (2001) *The World Factbook* 2001. Retrieved 18 October 2001, from: http://www.cia.gov/cia/publications/factbook.

environment of the highlands, even a large variety of so-called British vegetables from the middle latitudes are grown.

Sri Lanka is divided into a wet zone that occupies the southwestern quarter and the highlands, and a dry zone that covers all others quarters. The wet zone is defined by perennial rainfalls and the dry zone is characterized by a striking dry period, ranging from four to six months(from April/May until August/September).

People

The two ethnic groups that account for 92 percent of the Sri Lankan people—the Sinhalese (74 percent) and the Tamils (18 percent)—originated in India. The Sinhalese, who are thought to be of Indo-Aryan origin, probably entered around the fifth century BCE. The larger part of the Tamils, from southern India, entered Sri Lanka at the start of the Christian era, while a smaller part came only during the British colonial period in the nineteenth century and early twentieth century for employment in the plantation industries. Subsequently, both groups established their own culture and civilization in Sri Lanka. Today, the Sinhalese community is Buddhist, whereas the Tamil community is Hindu. (Small numbers of Sri Lankans—7 percent in all—from both ethnic groups are Christians, as a result of the influence of colonial powers in Sri Lanka, particularly the Portuguese in the sixteenth and seventeenth centuries. The 7 percent of the population who

INDIA

Palk
Strait

Jaffna
Peninsula

Jaffna

Elephant Pass

Bay of
Bengal

Palk Bay

Mannar
Island

NORTHERN

Mannar

Gulf of
Mannar

Kalpitiya

Anuradhapura

NORTH
CENTRAL

Trincomalee

Puttalam

NORTH
WESTERN

Matale

CENTRAL

Batticaloa

EASTERN

Kandy

Victoria
Falls
Reservoir

Badulla

UVA

Colombo

Mount Lavinia

SABARAGAMUWA

WESTERN

Laccadive
Sea

SOUTHERN

Galle

Hambantota

SRI LANKA

INDIAN OCEAN

0   25   50 Miles
0   25   50 Kilometers

N

The Portuguese were the first Europeans to colonize Sri Lanka; they gained control of the coastal regions by the beginning of the seventeenth century. The Dutch, called in by the Sinhalese kingdom of Kandy to help drive out the Portuguese Dutch, stayed and colonized the island themselves from the mid-seventeenth century until the British took over in 1796. The British called the island Ceylon, the name by which it was known until 1972. While the Portuguese and Dutch were interested in the island's many spices, including the endemic cinnamon (*Cinnamomum ceylanicum*), British interests centered on the cultivation of tea and rubber after coffee and cinchona failed. Agricultural exploitation on a large scale was concentrated on the southwestern quarter, including the dense evergreen tropical forests of the highlands, which were cleared and converted into plantations. The colonists also exploited the island's wealth of gemstones (such as blue sapphire, ruby, and moonstone) and ivory.

Economy

The economic development of Sri Lanka following independence resulted in diversification of agriculture and industry, with light industry (particularly the manufacturing of garments) becoming the backbone of a liberalized and privatized economy. Sri Lanka's economic growth was also due in part to generous international aid. Sri Lanka's fishing industry is organized and practiced in traditional ways. Fishing boats are only partly mechanized and fishing occurs mostly in the coastal areas, while deep-sea fishery resources have been exploited only slightly, due to the lack of fishing vessels. Fishing catch is commonly low, though Sri Lanka has an important export trade in prawns and lobsters. Animal husbandry is not widely practiced, which leads to deficits in milk and meat. Sri Lanka offers a wide variety of traditional (called "antique") and modern handicrafts, including woodcarving, silversmithing, jewelry making, and batik textile manufacture. While the rate of unemployment is officially 10 percent, the lack of jobs that pay well has led hundreds of thousands of young Sri Lankans (mostly women) to seek work in the Middle East, commonly as housemaids.

Sri Lanka has a flourishing tourism industry, mostly for vacationers from Western Europe (in 1999, there were 450,000 arrivals). Although tourism is concentrated in sun and beach resorts along the western and southern coasts (for example, in Negombo, Kalutara, Beruwala, Bentota, and Hikkaduwa), ecotourism and health tourism have also become popular. The latter is an interesting development. As Europeans have become familiar with traditional ayurvedic medicine (the medicine of ancient India), they have traveled to Sri

are Muslim are descended from early Arab traders, who came mostly during the ninth and tenth centuries.) Both the Sinhalese and the Tamils speak their own languages (Sinhala and Tamil, respectively). English is also widely spoken, particularly by members of the upper and middle class. Since 1983, a civil war has been fought in north and northeastern Sri Lanka; Tamil rebels desire an independent Tamil homeland, Eelam, which is strongly opposed by the Sinhalese-dominated Sri Lankan government.

History

The early Sinhalese invaders settled in the semi-dry north-central, northern, and eastern lowlands, and introduced an effective system of paddy rice cultivation based on irrigation water stored in large natural reservoirs. The important Anuradhapura kingdom flourished from the fourth century BCE until the eleventh century, followed by the Polonnaruwa kingdom until the thirteenth century, when Tamil incursions from south India forced the Sinhalese reign to withdraw to a safer interior part of Sri Lanka. In the thirteenth century, with the weakening Sinhalese reign and an ascendent Tamil power over the north of Sri Lanka, the country was no longer unified, instead breaking into the three independent kingdoms of Kandy and Kotte (both Sinhalese) and Jaffna (Tamil) until the colonial period started in the early sixteenth century.

Lanka to seek treatment according to this practice in ayurvedic clinics and in hotels that offer this service.

Manfred Domroes

Further Reading

Johnson, B. L. C., and M. Le Scrivenor. (1981) *Sri Lanka: Land, People, and Economy.* London: Heinemann.

Farmer, B. H., ed. (1977) *Green Revolution? Technology and Change in Rice-Growing Areas of Tamil Nadu and Sri Lanka.* London: English Language Book Society and Macmillan.

Domroes, M. (1976) *Sri Lanka: Die Tropeninsel Ceylon.* Darmstadt, Germany: Wissenschaftliche Buchgesellschaft.

Domroes, M., and H. Roth, eds. (1998) *Sri Lanka—Past and Present: Archaeology, Geography, Economics.* Weikersheim, Germany: Margraf.

Peiris, G. H. (1996) *Development and Change in Sri Lanka: Geographical Perspectives.* New Delhi: Macmillan.

SRI LANKA—ECONOMIC SYSTEM   Sri

Lanka is a relatively poor country, although a per capita income of $3,250 (2000 est.) makes it a lower-middle-income nation. Some 22 percent of the population lives in poverty, fewer than earlier (1985–1986: 40.6 percent). Earnings from traditional export crops (tea, rubber, coconut) accounted for about 19 percent of total export earnings (1998). Their importance sharply declined during the last three decades of the twentieth century relative to garments, textiles, and other industrial products. Creation of sufficient job opportunities for a rapidly increasing labor force and reduction of poverty are two pressing socioeconomic problems.

Sri Lanka is a famous example of a poor country with a remarkable performance in improving quality of life. On the Human Development Index of the United Nations Development Programme (UNDP), Sri Lanka ranked 90th of 174 countries in 1997, twenty-two places above its ranking for per capita gross national product (GNP). This impressive performance can be attributed to the high adult literacy rate (almost 91 percent), high school enrollment ratio of both sexes, and high life expectancy (over 72 years).

Economic Policy

From its independence in 1948 until 1989, government development policy stressed making large capital-intensive investments to expand food production at the expense of plantation-based export crops; promoting industrial growth by establishing public enterprises and protecting the domestic market against foreign competition; and increasing government use of price controls, private investment licensing, and trade restrictions.

This approach failed to generate growth (the average annual per capita rate was 2 percent between 1960 and 1977) and employment commensurate with the large fiscal resources it required. In 1977 Sri Lanka responded to the dismal economic outcome of the closed-economy era by embarking on an extensive economic liberalization program, becoming the first South Asian country to do so. The leading role in the economy was transferred to the private sector, and export-led growth was fostered, with significant trade reform and removal of restrictions on foreign investment. Financial reforms included adjusting interest rates to levels above the rate of inflation, opening the bank sector to foreign banks, and freeing credit markets to determine interest rates. New incentives for export-oriented investment were provided under an attractive free-trade zone (FTZ) scheme. The reform process lost momentum in the early 1980s, first because of a shift toward politically appealing investment projects and subsequently as a result of the onset of ethnic conflict. In a decisive move to infuse momentum into the unfinished reform process, a significant second-wave liberalization package was implemented in 1990, with a view to attaining the status of newly industrialized country (NIC) by the year 2000. The package included a sharp reduction in the budget deficit (from 12.5 percent of GDP in 1989 to 10 percent in 1990 and 8.1 percent in 1993), elimination of import licensing for most nonagricultural products, reduction of tariff rates and introduction of four tariff bands, elimination of export duties, devaluation of the Sri Lankan rupee, and reduction of income and corporate taxes (to 40 and 35 percent, respectively) to stimulate the capital market. There was a shift in investment policy away from the enclave strategy of attracting foreign private investment in export promotion zones toward a more neutral environment for all investments. As a result Sri Lanka today is one of the most open economies in the developing world.

Economic Performance

Private investors have generally been bullish in their response to market-oriented reforms (while hesitant during periods of macroeconomic instability and escalation of civil war). After the initiation of reforms in 1977, net foreign direct investment rose from a negligible level in 1978 to average over 4 percent of gross domestic investment during 1979–1982. Economic growth catapulted to 6 percent yearly, led by export growth of 13 percent. After the onset of the civil war, however, acceleration of investment halted. After the new round of reforms and de-escalation in the civil war, private investment increased again from 11 percent of GDP (1988) to 18 percent (1993). During the 1990s macroeconomic performance in Sri Lanka remained fairly good despite internal and external problems and grew at an annual average of about 5.4 percent.

Agriculture remains the primary source of income for Sri Lanka's predominantly rural population, although its share in GDP had fallen to 21.5 percent by 1998; 38.2 percent of the labor force is employed in that sector. Agriculturally the country can traditionally be divided into an export-oriented plantation sector and a subsistence-oriented peasant sector growing food crops. About 33 percent of the total land area is cultivated, 19 percent under tea and rubber, the remainder under food crops. A growing share of export crops is produced by small holders, whereas the food-crop sector has become fully commercialized.

Government interventions in agricultural markets ever after independence included protection of domestic rice production, the staple crop; taxation of plantation crops (tea, rubber, and, to a lesser extent, coconut); food subsidies to consumers, both in the form of rice rations sold in government shops (up to 1977) and in the form of subsidies for wheat and sugar; large subsidies for rice production, primarily in the form of large public irrigation schemes; and subsidies to and rationing of agricultural inputs, such as fertilizer.

The big agricultural estates were left intact after independence; the level of direct (export, income) and indirect taxes (effects of import protection system) did however increase until owners neglected investments (or shifted them to other countries) and maintenance. Production of rubber and tea began to stagnate in the 1960s, and quality deteriorated. After losing market shares globally in 1972 through 1975, many estates owned by foreign or local individuals and companies (above 20 hectares) were nationalized and brought under the umbrella of two state corporations. Their disappointing performance slowly led to a policy reversal: in 1992 the management of state-owned estates was given to twenty-two private companies on a profit-sharing formula, and export taxes were eliminated. In 1995 the government initiated a program to privatize the estates completely.

Hectare productivity in rice production is fairly low by Asian standards, but it is higher in the dry zone, provided that adequate irrigation is provided. Ninety-four percent of the nation's paddy fields are less than five acres in size. The government tried to bring more land under cultivation with a program in which several hundred thousand acres were distributed in small holdings to landless peasants to be operated as family farms. The biggest scheme was the Accelerated Mahaweli Development Programme (1969), implemented during the Jayawardene administration (1977) with the help of massive foreign assistance. Huge costs absorbed about 10 percent of gross national investment between 1978 and 1994. As a result of both the expansion of area under cultivation and the rise in productivity under the impact of the "green revolution," paddy cultivation has grown from 603,000 metric tons in 1952 to over 1.6 million metric tons in 1970 and to 2.69 million metric tons in 1999.

Today the country is more or less self-sufficient as regards staple food, but this result was achieved at considerable cost. Sri Lanka traditionally restricted rice imports, and local prices are therefore considerably above import parity level. This noncompetitive output is maintained not only by import restrictions, but also by massive public transfers (irrigation water without cost recovery, fertilizer, subsidized credit), amounting to nearly 5 percent of GDP.

The desire to achieve self-sufficiency also discouraged diversification and development of a functioning land market. The area under other food crops has not grown, despite higher return per acre, because widespread availability of off-farm labor in villages makes it difficult to attract laborers, which in turn makes the low labor requirements of paddy more appealing. The Land Reform Laws limited private holdings in paddy to ten hectares; in public irrigation schemes the maximum is two hectares. Government policies have also imposed restrictions on land use. Legal restraints preventing reallocation of paddy land to other crops were in force until 1991.

Industry

Sri Lanka inherited an extremely small manufacturing sector at independence, accounting for only 4 percent of GDP in 1950, two years after independence. Manufacturing was developed with the help of a heavily protected local market; state interventions in industry, trade, and finance; and the running of over one hundred state industrial corporations, newly established or taken over from private companies. Hence by 1977, the public sector accounted for 24 percent of GNP, over one-third of the nation's investment, 40 percent of employment in the formal sector (that is, in "modern" companies with more than twenty workers), and 60 percent of value-added in manufacturing. Many domestic firms developed poor management practices, hampered by heavy government interference and protection against outside competition. Privatization did not become government policy until 1987, when a Presidential Commission on Privatization was created. After a slow start the privatization program was the most vigorously pursued area of structural reforms. Despite an unfavorable environment, the government succeeded in selling all its tea and rubber estates and its equity stake in the National Development Bank and Air Lanka, the national carrier. Private participation in infrastructure also expanded.

Manufacturing in 1998 accounted for 16.5 percent of GDP and 15.2 percent of employment. The growth of the manufacturing sector has been fairly rapid after the second round of reforms (8.4 percent per year between 1988 and 1998), especially in the textile sector; in chemicals, petroleum, rubber, and plastic products; and in food, beverage, and tobacco products. These three sectors account for 40, 20, and 22 percent of industrial output, respectively. The garment sector, which until 1977 played a very small role in the economy, profited most from liberalization. In 1998 gross garment exports exceeded U.S. $2.4 billion and accounted for 52 percent of overall exports. Despite this remarkable growth record, 65 percent of fabrics and accessories needed as inputs are imported. Garment exports are governed by the Multifiber Arrangement, which has attracted East Asian investors to Sri Lanka.

Financial Sector

The most prominent problem in the financial sector is the high cost of finance. Real interest rates are high by international standards (since 1986 between 5 and 8 percent), impeding expansion and business diversification. High fiscal deficits, caused by domestic borrowing, an accommodating monetary policy, and inefficiencies in the financial system contributed to high real rates. The banking sector suffers from the dominance of the two state-owned banks (Bank of Ceylon and People's Bank). These banks, despite two asset clean-up operations in 1993 and 1996, continue to hold fragile portfolios. Recently the management of monetary policies has improved, and greater operational autonomy of the Central Bank is under consideration. The public banks will be placed under performance contracts, but privatization is impossible under current political circumstances.

The Central Bank of Sri Lanka, the sole bank of issue, also acts as a financial adviser to the government and administers monetary policy. In 1979 foreign banks were allowed to open branches in Sri Lanka with a view to attracting foreign investment. By the end of 1994 seventeen foreign banks had branch offices in Colombo. In the same year Foreign Currency Banking Units were established in commercial banks, as a prelude to the development of an offshore banking center in Sri Lanka.

Public Finance

Sri Lanka has a long history of budget deficits, fueled by generous public subsidies and services, massive transfers to state enterprises, massive recruitment into the public sector, and—more recently—escalating security expenses and generous wage increases in the public sector. In 1998 Sri Lanka spent about 30 percent of its total current expenditure on interest payments, 25 percent on defense, and 10.6 percent on pensions to former civil servants. Revenue shortfalls also contributed to the budget deficit: the newly introduced goods and services tax led to smaller collections, and divestiture income suffered from the slowing down of the privatization program with the onset of the Asian financial crisis. Tax revenue amounted to 14.5 percent of GDP in 1998.

Employment is politically one of the most salient problems, with the traditionally high unemployment rate (usually around 15 percent, today under 10 percent) and the concentration of jobless among the youth and, perhaps surprisingly, those with high educational attainment. Factors contributing to high unemployment include the relatively slow rate of (capital-intensive) growth under import substitution, excessively restrictive labor legislation, poor quality of education acquired compared with labor market aspirations, and the government's tendency to hire large numbers of unemployed graduates, thus increasing incentives to stay unemployed for a while.

Human Development

Sri Lanka's early achievements in human development can be attributed to its early investments in education, to healthcare provided free of cost, and also to its extensive outreach capacity for civil administration and its well-defined delivery network of schools and hospitals. As a result Sri Lanka catapulted to developed country standards on several social indicators and even today preserves its edge over other developing countries in basic social indicators. The status of women is also generally higher than in similar countries (female enrollment at universities is 50 percent). However the performance record in health, education, and poverty reduction during the last three decades of the twentieth century did not improve in consonance with earlier achievements, especially taking into account the quality of services provided.

Estimated adult literacy is 90 percent, and gross enrollment ratios in primary and secondary schools are

105 and 74 percent, respectively (a percentage over 100 is possible because of late enrollments; enrollments are computed as a percentage of an age cohort). Despite successes of the past, today the education sector faces many problems: an unsatisfied demand for university education, low quality and relevance of education to labor market (high unemployment rates among the educated and significant underemployment of university graduates) and social needs, insufficient financing, and poor management practices. Public expenditure on education is comparatively very low, and per pupil expenditures heavily skewed toward tertiary education.

Sri Lanka has an array of programs to assist poor people. Food subsidies were once the main program, consisting of rice rations, but by the late 1970s costs of food subsidies became unsustainable (5 percent of GDP); in 1978 rice rations were restricted to the poorest half of the population. Despite retargeting of the program in 1991, leakages to nonpoor households are massive. Today the main poverty program is the Samurdhi, which provides direct income support in the form of food coupons for over 50 percent of the population and aims to promote self-reliance and rural entrepreneurship through training, credit, and savings schemes.

External Sector

One major reform area since 1989 has been the trade regime. The pace of trade reforms has been fast, including elimination of most nontariff barriers, lowering of tariffs (the maximum rate falling from 100 percent in 1989 to 35 percent in 1995), reduction of the number of tariff bands to three (35, 20, and 10 percent), and reducing discretion in the implementation of tariff rules. Despite these reforms the average tariff rate is still higher than in East Asia (20 percent as opposed to 8.5 percent). In 1977 the share of manufactures in total merchandise exports was only 5 percent. Since then manufactured exports grew rapidly (from 7 percent in the 1980s, to 9 percent from 1988 to 1998), making Sri Lanka one of the low-income countries with the fastest export growth. Today Sri Lanka exports primarily to the United States (40 percent of exports), the United Kingdom, and Germany, and imports primarily from Japan, India, South Korea, and Hong Kong.

The promotion of foreign investment has been a pivotal element of Sri Lanka's market-oriented reforms. The most important aspect of the new policy was setting up the Greater Colombo Economic Commission in 1978 with wide-ranging powers to establish and operate export-processing zones (EPZs). The first zone opened at Katunayka airport (1978), followed by two other zones in 1982 and 1991. The investment-promotion policy package included a tax holiday of up to ten years, duty exemption for the import of inputs, and industrial services at subsidized rates. A new Investment Policy Statement in 1990 abolished restrictions on the ownership structure of projects outside the EPZs and provided ETZ status to export-oriented foreign ventures in all parts of the country. Foreign direct investment played a pivotal role in expanding export of manufactured goods. The share of foreign firms in total exports of manufactured goods increased from 24 percent in 1977 to almost 80 percent in the mid-1990s.

Outlook for the Twenty-First Century

With strong social indicators and natural endowments, Sri Lanka could have achieved substantially higher growth and poverty reduction had it not been for a history of ethnic conflict and the excessive role of government in the economy until the 1980s. Since the transformation from an inward-looking socialist system to a market economy, GDP has grown at a satisfactory rate, albeit below the country's potential. The most obvious reason is the eighteen-year-long war, which has led to political stalemate (regarding a federal resolution to the conflict) and the deceleration of reforms since the late 1990s. The country remains vulnerable on the external front (still running a high current-account deficit) and fiscally (running a high budget deficit on account of military spending). The most important challenge is to resolve the ethnic conflict and launch a second wave of economic reforms, which should include further privatization and reform of public-sector institutions.

Joachim Betz

Further Reading

Athukorala, Prema-chandra, and Sarath Rajapatirana. (2000) "Liberalization and Industrial Transformation: Lessons from the Sri Lanka Experience." *Economic Development and Cultural Change* 48, 2: 543–572.

De Silva, S. B. D. (1982) *The Political Economy of Underdevelopment.* Boston: Routledge and Keagan.

Karunatilake, H. N .S. (1987) *The Economy of Sri Lanka.* Dehiwala, Sri Lanka: Center for Demographic and Socio-Economic Studies.

Kelegama, Saman. (2000) "Development in Independent Sri Lanka: What Went Wrong?" *Economic and Political Weekly* (22 April): 1477–1490.

Snodgrass, David R. (1967) *Ceylon: An Export Economy in Transition.* Homewood, IL: Richard D. Irwin.

World Bank. (1998) *Social Services: A Review of Recent Trends and Issues.* Washington, DC: World Bank.

———. (1999) *Sri Lanka: A Fresh Look at Unemployment.* Washington, DC: World Bank.

SRI LANKA—EDUCATION SYSTEM
Education in the sense of a state's obligation to provide for a tax-financed general system of primary, secondary and "high"-schools did not exist in Sri Lanka's Buddhist medieval society. Buddhist monasteries imparted sacred knowledge, the basic tenets of the Buddhist faith, and the techniques for the monks' salvation. When in Sinhalese villages there existed a local school, set up by a resident monk—which was not generally the case— then access to this school was restricted to the main cultivating caste, the Goyigamas. It was only under colonial rule—first by the Portuguese in the seventeenth century, later by the Dutch and the British—that a much more broadly based system of education was established.

The religious orders, especially the Jesuits, set up a network of missionary schools in the Sinhalese-dominated southwest and on the Jaffna peninsula in the north, settled by Tamils. These mission schools left a lasting imprint. On the Jaffna peninsula the main cultivating caste, the Vellalas, now embraced at least in outward appearance the Christian faith, monopolized access to these schools, and used this access as a means for social and economic advancement. A comparable development could be observed in the Sinhalese lowland, where besides Goyigama-caste elites, lower but ambitious elites among the fisher and cinnamon-peeler castes now increasingly embraced the Catholic faith to gain access to modern education. Under Dutch colonial rule these elites, by now embracing the Dutch Reformed faith, continued to visit and patronize the Dutch missionary schools, for which the notoriously parsimonious Dutch East India Company provided meager funds.

Education under the British
It was only with the advent of the British that a really modern and widespread system of schools and colleges was established. Three factors contributed to the emergence of a system of colonial education that was in substance secular and in quality exemplary: the competition among different Protestant denominations, the funding mechanism of "grant in aid," and the enlightened self-interest of the colonial government. Different Christian denominations were allowed to establish schools and colleges. These groups, including the Wesleyans and the American Baptists, penetrated into peripheral regions untouched by any Buddhist village schools; in their colleges these missions imparted technical skills as well as classic Western education. Members of the newly emerging "liberal professions"—lawyers, doctors, engineers, and surveyors—were trained in these schools.

The mechanism of grant in aid contributed to the spread and diversification of new schools: under grant in aid not only missionary organizations but local communities, de facto caste associations, and Hindu, Muslim, or Buddhist elites could establish their own schools and receive government funds, as long as their curricula and quality control conformed to British standards. It was due to grant in aid that the indigenous elites could avoid the farce of embracing the Protestant faith to secure a modern education. It was finally the enlightened self-interest of the British government—its perception that it was in need of well-qualified yet poorly paid (that is, native) officers—that resulted in generous funding of and the continuing interest in a decentralized and self-propagating school system, which was increasingly controlled by indigenous elites.

Education since Independence
The gentleman politicians who monopolized politics in Ceylon (as Sri Lanka was called until 1972) immediately before and after independence in 1948 were the result of this education system. It was finally the richest and the most ambitious among them, Solomon West Ridgeway Diaz Bandaranaike (1899–1959), who transformed this system for the training of civil servants into a system of primary mass education and into a medium for the propagation of Sinhalese nationalism. When Bandaranaike's party, the Sri Lanka Freedom Party (SLFP), came to power in 1956, it initiated a massively funded program for the extension of primary and, to lesser degree, secondary education.

Already at the beginning of the 1960s more than 90 percent of primary school–age children were enrolled in schools, and some thirty years later, as a result of continuing mass enrollment in primary education, Sri Lanka attained a literacy rate of 87 percent. This was the highest literacy rate in South and Southeast Asia; neighboring India achieved only 43 percent, Pakistan 30 percent, and Singapore 86 percent. Sixty percent of the population had been in school for a minimum of five years, and 35 percent for a minimum of ten years. Yet, this spread of primary mass education coincided with the politicization, or "Sinhalization," of the school system and a deterioration of quality.

Education and "Sinhalization"
Establishing mass literacy in Sri Lanka constituted a major element in Bandaranaike's program of ethnic Sinhalese nation building. The SLFP had won the 1956 elections with the promise of establishing "Sinhalese only," the ethnic majority language as the only official and administrative language on the island, to the detri-

ment of the elites' English and the Tamil language of the minority Tamils. School enrollment served the twofold purpose of bringing literacy in the Sinhalese language to the Sinhalese majority and propagating the nationalist formula of "the unified land, the Sinhalese race, and the Buddhist faith." Children were taught in their mother languages, Tamils in Tamil and Sinhalese in Sinhalese. There was no sustained interest in providing Tamils with the capability to speak Sinhalese or in teaching English. This process of vernacularization, a de facto Sinhalization of the island's schools, administration, and politics, was paralleled by the nationalization of Sri Lanka's private schools and elite colleges. Christian and Hindu elite colleges were strictly supervised by the state, while Buddhist village and monastery schools were controlled and instrumentalized by the emerging Sinhalese state.

This not only led to a deterioration of standards (the percentage of teachers without certificates rose from 13 percent in 1950 to 30 percent in 1961) but also prepared the way for the Tamil-Sinhalese conflict and civil war, which has engulfed the island since 1983. As the island's sluggish economy was unable to provide jobs for ever more ambitious Sinhalese primary and secondary school graduates, there emerged a Maoist as well as chauvinist youth organization, the Tamil Youth League, which in 1973 threatened the government with a first major insurrection.

This radicalization of the primary school–educated Sinhalese youth was paralleled by the growing alienation and militancy of Tamil youth, who could not find employment in a Sinhalese-language-speaking and Sinhalese-dominated state administration and state economy. While the two Sinhalese mass parties attempted to satisfy the demands of the young Sinhalese for state patronage, jobs, and unrestricted access to the universities at the expense of the Tamils, young Tamils discriminated against by the employment practices of the Sinhalese state or denied access to higher education now demanded their own state. The mass education system of Sri Lanka thus contributed to an ethnic civil war, which by now has led to the decay of its institutions and a further decline of its standards. In 1998 the World Bank assisted the government of Sri Lanka in initiating reforms of the education system to improve its efficiency, to redesign its curricula, and to correct its pro-Sinhalese bias.

Jakob Rösel

Further Reading

Manor, James. (1989) *The Expedient Utopian: Bandaranaike and Ceylon.* Cambridge, U.K.: Cambridge University Press.

Obeyesekere, Gananath. (1974) "Some Comments on the Social Backgrounds of the April 1971 Insurgency in Sri Lanka (Ceylon)." *The Journal of Asian Studies* 33, 3: 367–384.

Sumathipala, K. H. M. (1968) *History of Education in Ceylon, 1796–1965.* Colombo, Sri Lanka: Tisara Prakasakayo.

SRI LANKA—HISTORY Sri Lanka is an island nation just north of the equator and southeast of India. The country's ancient civilization flourished in the north-central plains of the island, but as this civilization declined during the first millennium CE, the island's location on the sea routes of the Indian Ocean made Sri Lanka vulnerable to European colonization, which lasted from 1517 to 1948. In 1972 the country officially changed its name from Ceylon to Sri Lanka. Since 1983 Sri Lanka has been engulfed in civil war.

Sinhala, an Indo-European language spoken only on the island, is the mother tongue of three-quarters of the population. About 12 percent of the population is Sri Lankan Tamils, who speak Tamil (the dominant language on the adjacent coast of India) and, like the Sinhalese, claim descent from the island's earliest settlers. Another 6 percent of the population is Tamils descended from immigrant laborers who came from southern India in the nineteenth and early twentieth centuries. Muslims form 7 percent of the population. The Sinhalese are mostly Buddhist, and the Tamils are primarily Hindu, although there is a sizable Christian population of both Sinhalese and Tamils dating back to the Portuguese colonization of the island in the early 1500s.

The modern economic and political center of Sri Lanka has been in the central highlands, of which the southwest is in the wet zone watered by two monsoon seasons and convectional rain throughout the year. Until the thirteenth century, however, most of the population lived in the remaining two-thirds of the island, which receives between 76 and 178 centimeters of rainfall a year, but is called the dry zone because most rain falls during only a three-month monsoon season.

Ancient Civilization

The island underwent a relatively rapid transition from a late Stone Age hunter-gatherer society to Iron Age farming by the sixth century BCE, followed by the emergence of a kingdom with its capital at Anuradhapura in the north central plains in the third century BCE. The appearance of writing in Brahmi script in around 500 BCE—the earliest appearance of the script anywhere in South Asia—throughout the island suggests that the inhabitants shared a common culture.

KEY EVENTS IN SRI LANKA HISTORY

6th century BCE   Peoples in Sri Lanka shift from hunting/gathering to agriculture.

3rd century BCE   A kingdom emerges with its capital at Anuradhapura in the north central plains.

c. 500 BCE   Writing in the Brahmi script is in use.

400s CE   The *Mahavamsa* or Great Chronicle, a history of the island compiled by Buddhist monks, is written.

1017–1075   Anuradhapura declines and the island is ruled by the Tamil Chola empire.

1100s–1466   The Sinhalese kingdom revives, with its capital now at Polonnaruwa, but fades with Parakramabahu VI of Kotte, the last Sinhalese ruler of the entire island.

1619   The Portuguese take control of the coastal regions.

1658   The Dutch displace the Portuguese with the aid of local allies.

1796   The British East India Company replaces the Dutch.

1802   The British parliament makes the island the Crown Colony of Ceylon.

1840s   The British develop profitable coffee and later tea and rubber plantations.

1915   Riots and British repression create a climate leading to political reform.

1919   The Ceylon Nation Congress is founded.

1931   The Donoughmore Reforms create a State Council with substantial power in the hands of a Board of Ministers.

1948   On 4 February Ceylon becomes an independent nation.

1970s   Tamil politicians advocate separatism and violent confrontations between the Sinhalese and Tamils increase.

1972   The nation's name is changed from Ceylon to Sri Lanka.

1977–1989   Economic reforms supporting a market-oriented economy lead to income growth but do not create economic stability.

1983   Tamil terrorist attacks lead to massive attacks by the Sinhalese and a civil war that continues in 2002.

1987–1990   Some 60,000 Indian troops are on the island to help control the civil war.

1990s   Efforts to end the civil war fail and central government stability is hampered by a series of assassinations.

The earliest settlements were along rivers, but people soon began building reservoirs to store the monsoon rains for year-round agricultural use. The reservoirs were elaborated over the centuries into an extraordinary system of hydrological engineering and irrigated agriculture. Long, gently sloping canals extending back to the rain-drenched highlands fed massive reservoirs. Anuradhapura may not have asserted sovereignty over the entire island as it claimed, but it was the largest and most powerful city-state on the island.

Sinhalese kings sponsored the Theravada Buddhist religion, and Buddhist monastic orders in turn supported the rulers. The island became a world center of Buddhist scholarship and remained Theravada Buddhist even when Mahayana Buddhism and then Hinduism displaced it on the mainland gradually over a long stretch from the first century BCE to the twelfth century CE (Bengal). The *Mahavamsa* or Great Chronicle, a history of the island compiled by Buddhist monks, was written in the fifth century CE when Buddhism was waning among their Tamil neighbors; the chronicle emphasizes the unity of state and religion and the Tamil threat from southern India. Its fears appeared to be justified as Anuradhapura declined and the Tamil-ruled Chola empire gained mastery over the island for about seventy-five years (1017–1075).

The Sinhalese kingdom revived for two centuries, with its capital now at Polonnaruwa, but further invasions and the appearance of malaria in the dry zone put a final end to the ancient civilization. The depopulated dry zone separated the Sinhalese regions to the south and west from the Tamil-speaking areas to the north and east. Muslim trading communities arose along the coasts from the eleventh century onwards. The strongest Sinhalese kingdom flourished at Kotte near the present site of Colombo, where the island's gems and cinnamon were attractions in the growing Indian Ocean trade. Parakramabahu VI of Kotte (reigned 1411–1466) was the last Sinhalese king to claim sovereignty over the entire island.

Colonialism

In the course of the sixteenth century the Portuguese empire extended its control of the coasts, driving the remaining Sinhalese into Kandy in the central highlands and conquering the last Tamil kingdom in 1619. From 1638 to 1658 the Dutch defeated the Portuguese with the aid of local allies. Coastal inhabitants allied themselves with the colonial rulers through language, religion, and economic interest. They served in the colonial administration and produced crops for export. Cultural differences eventually arose between the Sinhalese of the coast and the interior, and these persist today. In the Kandyan interior, for example, the Govigama caste remained dominant in relation to other castes, while along the coast intercaste relations weakened and other castes challenged Govigama predominance.

The British East India Company replaced the Dutch in 1796, and parliament made the island the Crown Colony of Ceylon in 1802. The central kingdom of Kandy was occupied in 1803 and annexed in 1815, uniting the entire island under a single government. The British created an export economy in the 1840s by developing coffee plantations cleared from highland forests; these were British owned but cultivated by laborers of Indian origin. The plantations, particularly after tea succeeded coffee and rubber was added, gave the colony a measure of prosperity unknown elsewhere in South Asia. Land taxes were abolished in 1892, and the colony had some of the best schools, health care, roads, railways, harbors, and other public services in Asia.

Prosperity came at a price as the economic and social gap between the affluent elites and the peasants and laborers increased. English missionaries provided much of the education. The elites became English-educated, Anglicized, and often Christian, monopolizing em-

POLONNARUWA—WORLD HERITAGE SITE

Designated a World Heritage Site in 1982, Polonnaruwa became the second capital of Sri Lanka when Anuradhapura was destroyed in 993 CE. The historic ruins are also home to many Brahman monuments and the ruins of a thirteenth century garden-city.

ployment in government service and the professions. The Sinhalese Buddhist majority in particular felt dispossessed.

The colony had its first legislative council in 1833, but it was a weak body of officials and representatives of economic and ethnic interests. British repression of Sinhalese leaders following riots in 1915 convinced the elite of the need for political organization. The Ceylon Nation Congress was founded in 1919 with Sinhalese and Tamil cooperation. Reforms in 1920 and 1924 allowed greater participation under a restricted franchise. The results satisfied no one, and Britain sent a commission led by Lord Donoughmore to propose reforms.

In 1931 the Donoughmore Reforms created a State Council (approved by the Legislative Council over the objections of minority members) with substantial power in the hands of a Board of Ministers. As it was elected on universal adult franchise (except for people of Indian origin, whose votes were restricted), control went to whoever could win the support of the Sinhalese Buddhist majority. The State Council improved health services, education, and the extension of cultivation, but did little to change the colonial plantation economy that provided the resources for these programs.

As independence neared, tensions between ethnic groups increased. The civil rights of Tamils of Indian origin were further restricted, and Sinhalese representatives created a de facto Sinhalese government. Don Stephen Senanayake (1884–1952), a wealthy planter, and Solomon West Ridgeway Dias Bandaranaike (1899–1959), son of the Maha Mudaliyar (the highest-ranking Sinhalese official) competed for leadership. The British ignored minorities who feared Sinhalese domination and placed their support behind Senanayake, the more conservative of the two. He became prime minister upon independence on 4 February 1948, under a constitution prepared by the Board of Ministers with British assistance.

Independent Sri Lanka

Senanayake created the United National Party (UNP), drawing leading politicians of all ethnic groups. After his death in 1952, his son Dudley Stephen (1911–1973) and kinsman Sir John Kotelawala (1897–1980) succeeded him, in place of Bandaranaike, who founded the Sri Lanka Freedom Party (SLFP). Bandaranaike, appealing to Sinhalese Buddhist nationalists, won a landslide victory in April 1956 in a coalition with minor parties called the People's United Front (Mahajana Eksat Peramuna or MEP).

The 1956 election set a pattern in which the parties alternated in power on the strength of the opposition's appeal to the majority community. The opposition tended to raise expectations of the Sinhalese Buddhists that governments were unable to satisfy. The MEP promised, for example, to make Sinhalese the official language, which to the Sinhala-

For the last quarter century, Sri Lanka has been involved in an internal ethnic conflict pitting the minority Tamils against the Sinhalese-controlled government. This sign outside the Pesalai office of the U.N. High Commissioner for Refugees prohibits weapons. (HOWARD DAVIES/CORBIS)

educated population meant that they would inherit the jobs and status of the English-educated elites, something the latter could never allow. A Buddhist monk assassinated Bandaranaike in September 1959. Bandaranaike's widow, Sirimavo (b. 1916), took the leadership of the SLFP after his assassination and served as prime minister from 1960 to 1965 and from 1970 to 1977 (heading a United Front coalition). Dudley Senanayake was prime minister briefly in 1960 and 1965–1970.

Sri Lanka's leaders have been unable to transform the colonial economy into a successful independent one. The first UNP governments squandered foreign exchange reserves on luxury consumption and politically motivated social services with no clear strategy for growth. The SLFP introduced a wide range of inefficient state corporations that swelled budget and balance-of-payment deficits. As a result, there were not many industrial or service-sector jobs to absorb the rapidly growing population. High unemployment, declining balances of trade, and inflation followed. Over half the population depends on agriculture, primarily rice cultivation, for their livelihood. By the 1960s exports of tea, rubber, and coconuts no longer provided enough foreign exchange to pay for necessary imports, and the nation depended increasingly on foreign aid for survival.

Economics was at the heart of a Sinhalese insurrection in March 1971. The Marxist-oriented People's Liberation Front (Jatika Vimukti Peramuna or JVP) was suppressed in a few months. Sirimavo Bandaranaike then nationalized plantations and industrial enterprises while creating a vast array of state corporations, which brought the economy to a virtual halt by 1975. Under the regime of President Junius Richard Jayewardene (1906–1996) from 1977 to 1989, the UNP implemented market-oriented reforms that continue today with the daughter of the Bandaranaikes, Chandrika Bandaranaike Kumaratunga (b. 1945) as president. The economy grows at a modest 5 percent a year, but depends largely on the uncertain markets for textile and tea exports, tourism, and remissions of Sri Lankans working abroad. In the last two decades of the twentieth century economic problems were dwarfed by civil war.

The United Front passed a new constitution in 1972, which changed the nation's name from Ceylon to Sri Lanka and increased the authority of the government to act without constitutional restraints. It abolished commissions that limited patronage powers, placed public policy before civil rights, and gave a constitutional foundation to the preeminent position of the Sinhala language and Buddhist religion. The UNP

326

produced its own constitution after its landslide victory in 1977. It created a directly elected president as head of state and established proportional representation, in part as a means of avoiding the landslides that made constitution writing possible. Jayewardene was succeeded in January 1989 by his prime minister, Ranasinghe Premadasa (1924–1993).

Civil War

Policies enforced to redress what Sinhalese nationalists considered centuries of decline at the hands of colonial rulers provoked a reaction from minority communities, particularly the Sri Lankan Tamils. Sinhala was made the only official language of the country, and the nation's Buddhist heritage was emphasized in public affairs. The majority community had preference in colonization of land developed at public expense, university admissions, and government employment.

In the 1970s Tamil politicians advocated separatism, and violent confrontations between the Sinhalese and Tamils increased. Tamil terrorist groups increased their activities. After one such attack in July 1983, massive attacks by Sinhalese on Tamils throughout the island led to a civil war in which an estimated 75,000 people were killed by the end of the century.

Violence escalated throughout the 1980s, exacerbated by the presence of over 60,000 Indian troops from 1987 to 1990. When Indian troops fought on the island, a JVP attempt to overthrow the government was subdued only after brutal tactics on both sides led to a estimated 60,000 deaths. In the north the Liberation Tigers of Tamil Eelam (LTTE) under the leadership of Velupillai Prabhakaran (b. 1954) crushed other separatist groups and seized control of the movement by 1986. The last years of UNP government were marked by a spate of assassinations. Premadasa was killed on 1 May 1993 by a suicide bomber and succeeded by Dingiri Banda Wijetunga (b. 1922), who appointed Ranil Wickramasinghe (b. 1951) as prime minister.

Kumaratunga's campaign promise to end the civil war helped her win a landslide victory. After efforts to call a truce with the LTTE failed, she used military superiority to force the separatists to negotiate. The military succeeded in capturing the Jaffna Peninsula in December 1995, but repeated efforts to open the road between Colombo and Jaffna were beaten back, and the struggle continues. Throughout Kumaratunga's first term the LTTE launched attacks on military bases in the north and east. The April 2000 loss of Elephant Pass, which protected the Jaffna Peninsula from the LTTE, was the largest government setback of the war.

Kumaratunga's peace proposals included constitutional changes that would grant greater autonomy to the provinces, including a Tamil province in the north and east. The proposal was supported by over one hundred organizations that joined in a National Peace Alliance, but was opposed by Sinhalese nationalists and many Buddhist monks. The UNP opposed the plan until Kumaratunga's reelection in December 1999 (during which she was injured by another suicide bomber); in the first half of 2000 the UNP's Wickramasinghe, the leader of the opposition, met to discuss a consensus that both parties could support. The government of Norway offered its services as mediators with the LTTE, who rejected the proposals.

The appalling death and destruction of the civil war continues as a war of attrition. In recent years Sri Lanka's army of 120,000 troops made slow and costly gains, which were thwarted by LTTE attacks. The losses reduced military morale and resulted in large-scale desertions. Campaigns to enlist more soldiers and grant amnesty to deserters did not meet with much success. Hundreds of thousands of Sri Lankans sought asylum abroad, and many people in the northern and eastern island survive in refugee camps.

Patrick Peebles

See also: **Buddhism—Sri Lanka; Ethnic Conflict—South Asia**

Further Reading
Bartholomeusz, Tessa J., and Chandra Richard de Silva, eds. (1998) *Buddhist Fundamentalism and Minority Identities in Sri Lanka*. Albany, NY: State University of New York Press.

De Silva, Kingsley Muthumuni. (1998) *Reaping the Whirlwind: Ethnic Conflict, Ethnic Politics in Sri Lanka*. New Delhi: Penguin India.

Kemper, Steven. (1991) *The Presence of the Past: Chronicles, Politics, and Culture in Sinhala Life*. Ithaca, NY: Cornell University Press.

McGowan, William. (1992) *Only Man Is Vile: The Tragedy of Sri Lanka*. New York: Farrar, Straus, & Giroux.

Seneviratne, H. L. (1999) *The Work of Kings: The New Buddhism in Sri Lanka*. Chicago: University of Chicago Press.

Spencer, Jonathan, ed. (1990) *Sri Lanka: History and the Roots of Conflict*. New York: Routledge.

SRI LANKA—HUMAN RIGHTS
Sri Lanka is a democratic island-state with a multiparty system. After attaining independence from the British empire in 1948, Sri Lankan ruling elites retained the colonial constitution while from time to time incorporating legislative acts. A new constitution adopted in 1972

provided for a parliamentary democracy, but leaders favored the Sinhalese majority in matters of employment, official language, and recruitment criteria in educational institutions.

As a result, the Tamils felt discriminated against and in 1983 launched a movement demanding a separate homeland in the northeastern provinces for Tamil speakers. Since then, millions of Tamils have become refugees in India, and many civilians have suffered heavy casualties. Increased fighting between government security forces and the Liberation Tigers of Tamil Eelam (LTTE) resulted in extrajudicial killings and displacement of more than 150,000 persons all over the country.

Torture, rape, and harassment by the police and security forces have become common. Emergency powers have been in force since 1983. Under the emergency regulations, state authorities have the power to arrest people, restrict their movements, and ban activities of unions. During 1999 and 2000, the media were censored, and coverage of the ongoing civil war, including arbitrary detention of journalists and closing of printing presses, was banned. In June 2000, because of international pressure, the government removed restrictions on foreign media. Such violations of human rights by state agencies contributed to the erosion of democratic institutions and undermined people's faith in democracy and the rule of law.

The LTTE bombed civilian public places in the north and east of the peninsula, killing more than a hundred civilians in suicide bombings in 2000. The LTTE also recruited children younger than fifteen years of age to serve in combat operations. The National Human Rights Commission in Colombo, including nongovernment officials and international human-rights organizations, investigated cases of abuse of civil liberties by state agencies and the LTTE with little result, because of apathy, noncooperation of state agencies, and the unabated civil war. Unless an amicable political solution is found to end the ethnic war, there is little hope for improvement in the human-rights situation in Sri Lanka.

B. M. Jain

Further Reading
Amnesty International. (2000) *Amnesty International Annual Report, 2000.* London: Amnesty International Publications.

Human Rights Watch. (2000) *Human Rights Watch World Report, 2000.* New York: Human Rights Watch.

SRI LANKA—POLITICAL SYSTEM   Sri

Lanka (called Ceylon until 1972) is unique among Britain's former colonial territories in that already in 1931 the island was granted a democratic constitution, which was based on full franchise, the universal and secret ballot, and de facto political control and parliamentary government by Sri Lankan political figures and parties. Unrestricted political control was eagerly embraced by the Sinhalese and Tamil political elites, who attempted without success to forestall the introduction of universal and secret voting rights. While the Tamil minority and Tamil politicians saw themselves threatened by Sinhalese majority rule, the Sinhalese politicians had to learn the idiom of democratic mass politics practically overnight and had to control the mass of Sinhalese voters. To secure this control, weaken demands for land distribution, and marginalize socialist parties, these plantation-owning politicians embraced a virulent anti-Tamil and pro-Sinhalese ethnic nationalism. This strategy, combined with the fears of the indigenous and the Indian Tamil minorities, led to the development of an ethnic party system. The Ceylon National Congress (CNC) in 1946 transformed into the United National Party (UNP) and mobilized Sinhalese voters. The Tamil Congress (TC), dominated by educated upper-caste Tamils from Jaffna, articulated the demands of the Sri Lankan Tamils. The Ceylon Indian Congress (CIC), a trade union turned into a political party, organized the Indian laborers working in the up-country "tea gardens." Based on the two-thirds Sinhalese Buddhist majority, the CNC/UNP would monopolize political control until independence.

The Soulbury Constitution of 1946

Sri Lanka entered independence in 1948 on the basis of a Westminster-type (that is, British-style) political system as set out in the Soulbury Constitution of 1946 and remained in the Commonwealth. Although the ethnic party system and the preponderance of a Sinhalese and Buddhist majority combined with a majority voting system tended to marginalize the influence of the Tamil minority—the Indian Tamils, mostly estate laborers, lost their voting rights in 1949—the Soulbury Constitution contained several safeguards for the protection of minorities. In multiethnic election districts, for instance in Colombo and Kandy, there existed, since 1931, so-called multiple-member constituencies. To these districts two or three parliamentary seats were allocated, and voters controlled two or three votes. Well-organized Tamil or Muslim groups in such districts were thus able to secure parliamentary representation. In cases of discrimination on ethnic or religious grounds, spokesmen for the minorities could address the Privy Council in London, a special advisory committee of the British government. An ethnically balanced public employment commission also existed to ensure that employment in the expanding public administration and state economy was based on open and fair examinations and on merit.

Nonetheless, the twenty-five years of the Soulbury Constitution saw a constant deterioration of interethnic relations. A second Tamil party, the Federal Party, emerged in 1949. With the Tamil minority vote split in two, Tamils lost any hope of influencing the island's ethnic pro-Sinhalese party politics. Still more threatening was the founding of the Sri Lanka Freedom Party (SLFP) in 1951. This second, vastly more chauvinistic pro-Sinhalese mass party competed with the UNP for the Sinhalese electorate. After its election victory in 1956, the SLFP government not only introduced Sinhala as the sole state language, it embarked on a vast program of "Sinhalization" of the education system, public services, and state-controlled economy. In 1960 the UNP and the SLFP began to outbid each other in pro-Sinhalese "nation-building" promises, chauvinistic slogans, and government politics, which further marginalized the political and economic influence of the minorities.

The Republican Constitution of 1972

In 1951 the SLFP rejected the Soulbury Constitution as an outdated relic of colonialism. In 1970, after its third election victory, SLFP prepared a new constitution, enacted in 1972, which, according to Article 16.2, transformed Sri Lanka (Ceylon) into "a free, sovereign and independent republic," which was "pledged . . . [to] the progressive advancement towards . . . a socialist democracy."

In reality, an ethnic democracy was established. Article 2 of the constitution declared that "Sri Lanka is a unitary state." Demands for a devolution of power, as expressed by the Federal Party, were perceived as a threat to the constitution. In addition, Article 6 stated that "Sri Lanka shall give Buddhism the foremost place and accordingly it shall be the duty of the state to protect and foster Buddhism." Furthermore, according to Article 8.2 "any regulation for the (enhanced) use of the Tamil language . . . shall not in any manner be interpreted as being an provision of the constitution, but shall be deemed to be subordinate legislation."

During the seven years of the SLFP-dominated United Front government, interethnic relations deteriorated further, as did economic conditions. With Sri

Lanka near bankruptcy, in 1977 the UNP returned in triumph to power with a four-fifths majority in parliament and a promise of constitutional reform. The SLFP's election defeat was so severe that the Tamil United Liberation Front—the reunited TC and FP—for the next decade would form the main opposition. Secure in his parliamentary majority, UNP leader Junius Richard Jayewardene (1906–1996) decided to prepare a new constitution and establish a de facto one-party authoritarian regime.

The Semipresidential Constitution 1978

The constitution enacted in 1978 represented a profound break with the island's fifty-year-old parliamentary tradition, transforming it into a semipresidential system along French lines. Jayewardene, the president of the new Democratic Socialist Republic of Sri Lanka, as the island was renamed, not only functioned as commander in chief and influenced foreign policy, he controlled five to seven additional ministries and had complete control over the UNP's members of parliament and ministers. Thanks to his four-fifths majority in parliament, he could amend his constitution at will—and did so more than sixteen times until his resignation in 1988. With the help of such amendments, in 1982 he engineered a referendum through which he postponed parliamentary elections until 1989 and thus secured his power base.

The new constitution implemented a new voting system of proportional representation, which was supposed to avoid the distortions resulting from the "first past the post" majority voting system introduced in 1931. In 1970, for instance, the SLFP won ninety-one seats with 37 percent of the vote, while the UNP, with 38 percent, won only seventeen seats and thus lost the election. Under the new system of proportional representation, the 160 single-member constituencies were replaced by 22 electoral districts. Candidates were elected on the basis of party lists. In addition to these 196 members, 29 additional seats were apportioned as "bonus seats" in the same proportion as the proportion of the number of votes polled by each party. Through this bonus system, the two pro-Sinhalese UNP and SLFP parties (which together controlled more than two-thirds of the vote) regularly received twelve to fifteen additional seats.

It is ironic that a new semipresidential political system intended to bring stability to the island's increasingly polarized ethnic and ideological politics would provide the basis for an authoritarian UNP regime. At the same time it constituted the framework in which ethnic civil war between the Tamil Tigers (a Tamil

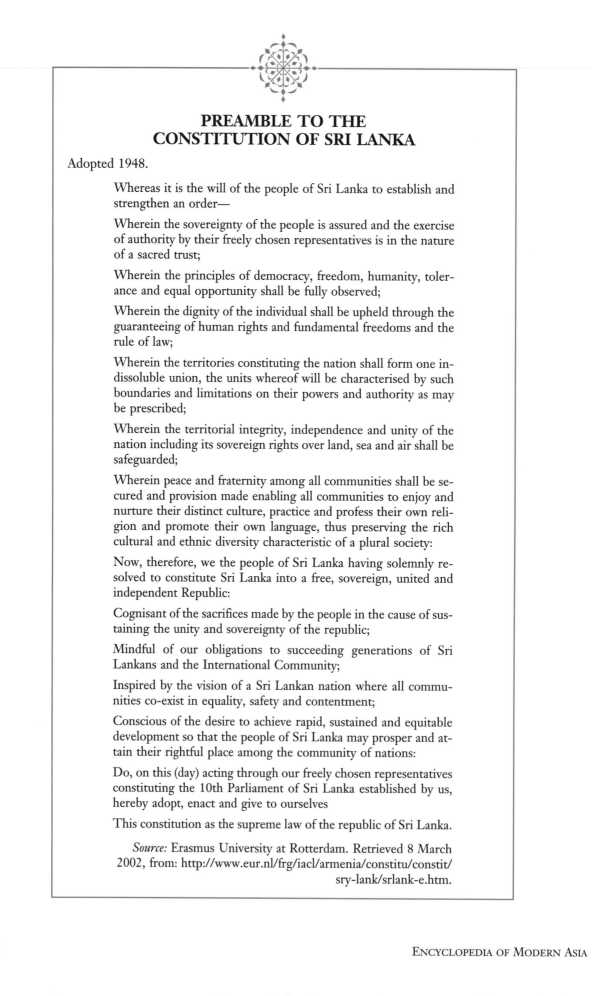

PREAMBLE TO THE
CONSTITUTION OF SRI LANKA

Adopted 1948.

Whereas it is the will of the people of Sri Lanka to establish and strengthen an order—

Wherein the sovereignty of the people is assured and the exercise of authority by their freely chosen representatives is in the nature of a sacred trust;

Wherein the principles of democracy, freedom, humanity, tolerance and equal opportunity shall be fully observed;

Wherein the dignity of the individual shall be upheld through the guaranteeing of human rights and fundamental freedoms and the rule of law;

Wherein the territories constituting the nation shall form one indissoluble union, the units whereof will be characterised by such boundaries and limitations on their powers and authority as may be prescribed;

Wherein the territorial integrity, independence and unity of the nation including its sovereign rights over land, sea and air shall be safeguarded;

Wherein peace and fraternity among all communities shall be secured and provision made enabling all communities to enjoy and nurture their distinct culture, practice and profess their own religion and promote their own language, thus preserving the rich cultural and ethnic diversity characteristic of a plural society:

Now, therefore, we the people of Sri Lanka having solemnly resolved to constitute Sri Lanka into a free, sovereign, united and independent Republic:

Cognisant of the sacrifices made by the people in the cause of sustaining the unity and sovereignty of the republic;

Mindful of our obligations to succeeding generations of Sri Lankans and the International Community;

Inspired by the vision of a Sri Lankan nation where all communities co-exist in equality, safety and contentment;

Conscious of the desire to achieve rapid, sustained and equitable development so that the people of Sri Lanka may prosper and attain their rightful place among the community of nations:

Do, on this (day) acting through our freely chosen representatives constituting the 10th Parliament of Sri Lanka established by us, hereby adopt, enact and give to ourselves

This constitution as the supreme law of the republic of Sri Lanka.

Source: Erasmus University at Rotterdam. Retrieved 8 March 2002, from: http://www.eur.nl/frg/iacl/armenia/constitu/constit/sry-lank/srlank-e.htm.

independence movement) and the government and a Sinhalese terrorist insurrection against the UNP emerged. The UNP regime suffered for its failure to control the escalating civil war and its success in destroying an insurrection in 1989 led by the Janata Vimukti Peramuna (JVP; People's Liberation Front).

Facing Civil Unrest

In order to combat the Tamil Tigers, the UNP enacted dozens of antiterrorist laws, introduced martial law in the northern and eastern provinces, and transformed itself into a counterinsurgency regime that systematically abrogated constitutional safeguards. The JVP-led insurrection (1987–1990) was destroyed with the help of death squads and vigilante groups recruited in the constituencies of the beleaguered UNP politicians. These death squads systematically hunted, abducted, tortured, and killed suspected JVP members. After some 40,000 Sinhalese youth "disappeared" or were killed in this fashion, the insurrection collapsed in early 1990, but judicial safeguards and the rule of law also disappeared.

Against this background of massive violations of human rights and the constitution, in 1994 parliamentary and presidential elections had to be organized. A reorganized SLFP led by Chandrika Kumaratunga (b. 1945), the daughter of Sirimavo Bandaranaike (b. 1916; prime minister from 1960 to 1965 and from 1970 to 1977), confronted a fragmented and insecure UNP, which had not recovered from the assassination of its new leader, Ranasinghe Premadasa, who succeeded Jayewardene in 1989. The SLFP was aligned with two traditional leftist parties and the newly established Sri Lanka Muslim Congress in a so-called Peoples Alliance (PA). The PA promised a return to the rule of law, the eventual reversion to a parliamentary constitution, the establishment of a more benign form of capitalism, and new initiatives to end the civil war. But in a highly radicalized election campaign, the PA succeeded in winning the parliamentary (and later presidential) elections but failed to establish a strong parliamentary majority and thus government. It lacked the two-thirds majority to change the constitution and also lacked the political will to offer a genuine devolution of power to the Tamil minority and thereby bring the civil war to an end.

A political and military stalemate emerged, which continues to the present. In the 2000 parliamentary and presidential elections, a victorious PA again failed to establish a clear majority in parliament. In 2001, the PA lost its parliamentary support, and the UNP returned to power. But the UNP's return to government only strengthened the parliamentary, political, and

Sri Lankan soldiers perform on 4 February 2000 at a ceremony in Colombo to mark the 52nd anniversary of Sri Lanka's independence from Britain. (AFP/CORBIS)

military stalemate. Lacking a decisive majority in parliament, the UNP is set to govern until 2004 in "cohabitation" with a strong PA president, Mrs. Kumaratunga. It is doubtful that the UNP will jeopardize its political support among Sinhalese voters by making concessions to the Tamil minority.

Jakob Rösel

Further Reading

Manor, James. (1990). *The Expedient Utopian: Bandaranaike and Ceylon.* Cambridge, U.K.: Cambridge University Press.

———, ed. (1984) *Sri Lanka in Change and Crisis.* New York: St. Martin's.

Kearney, Robert N. (1973) *The Politics of Ceylon (Sri Lanka).* Ithaca, NY: Cornell University Press.

Wriggins, W. Howard. (1960) *Ceylon: Dilemmas of a New Nation.* Princeton, NJ: Princeton University Press.

SRINAGAR (2000 pop. 606,000). The summer capital of the Indian state of Jammu and Kashmir, Srinagar lies between two hills, the Hari Parbat and the Shankar Acharya (also known as Takht-i-Suleiman). The original town of Srinagar was founded in the third century BCE by Emperor Ashoka (reigned 273–232 BCE) of the Maurya dynasty (c. 324–c. 200 BCE) on the site that now is occupied by the village of Pandrathan. The area now known as Srinagar was settled by King

Pravarasena in the sixth century CE. Through the ages, Srinagar developed as a center of art, culture, and learning.

The city had experienced several natural disasters. Before the nineteenth century, Srinagar had been destroyed and rebuilt six times. Two major fires, in 1892 and 1899, devastated large portions of the city. There have been eleven major earthquakes in the city since the fifteenth century.

Modern Srinagar runs for nearly two miles along the Jhelum River, which divides the city into two parts. There are several historic sites within the city, including the Hari Parbat Fort (constructed in the eighteenth century by Atta Mohammed Khan), the Shah Hamdan Mosque (one of the oldest Islamic religious structures in the city), and the Jama Masjid. Srinagar is also a city of gardens, mostly landscaped under Mughal rule.

Sanjukta Das Gupta

Further Reading

Rushbrook Williams, L. F., ed. (1975) *A Handbook for Travellers in India, Nepal, Kashmir, Bangladesh, and Sri Lanka.* London: Murray.

SRIVIJAYA   The maritime Buddhist empire of Srivijaya emerged in the seventh century CE as the first sea power to dominate the Strait of Malacca and the Sunda Strait, the key positions along the spice route connecting China, the Malay archipelago, India, and the West. The scarcity of sources—inscriptions, Buddhist statues, temple ruins, and other archaeological remains, as well as Chinese, Arab, and European reports—has caused difficulties in determining the different centers and the varying boundaries that constituted Srivijaya from the seventh to the fourteenth century. The earliest centers were probably Palembang and Jambi in Suvarnadvipa, the "gold land" in central South Sumatra.

Already in the seventh century, Srivijaya reached out to Java and the Malay peninsula, where Kedah and Perak along Malaysia's west coast, and Perlis guarding Srivijaya's trade interests on the Kra isthmus, became its most important vassals. In 686, the Chinese Buddhist pilgrim I-Ching recommended Srivijaya as a flourishing center of Buddhist learning. In 671, he had spent six months there, "in a walled city inhabited by a thousand monks," studying Sanskrit grammar while waiting for the monsoon winds that would carry his vessel to India. Having spent another, longer stint in Srivijaya on his way back to China, I-Ching also wrote

that Mahayana Buddhism was new in Srivijaya, whereas the Mulasarvastivadanikaya, the Hinayana canon in Sanskrit, was widely followed. In the first half of the eighth century, Srivijaya was visited by Vajrabodi, abbot of the famous Mahayana Buddhist cloister of Nalanda in Bihar, India, and first guru of the Yogacara sect.

Several years later the Sailendras, a Mahayana Buddhist dynasty best known for building the famous Borobudur temple, came to power in Central Java. Between 1011 and 1023, another famous Buddhist teacher, Atisa (982–1054), the reformer of Tibetan Buddhism, studied in Srivijaya. At that time the growing trade and shipping between India and China, controlled by Srivijaya, had already attracted the rivalry of both East Java and the Cholas of south India. In 1025, the Cholas attacked Srivijaya, captured its maharaja, and devastated the country. As a result Srivijaya's power waned. In 1286, its decreasing realm was temporarily conquered by Kertanagara (reigned 1268–1292), king of East-Javanese Singosari. Singosari's successor, Majapahit, regarded Srivijaya as its principal vassal. The major trade points along the Strait, however, were already held by the Muslim states of Samudra-Pasai in North Sumatra and Malacca on the Malay Peninsula.

Martin Ramstedt

Further Reading

Coedès, Georges, and Louis-Charles Damais. (1992) *Sriwijaya: History, Religion, and Language of an Early Malay Polity.* Collected Studies by Georges Coedès and Louis-Charles Damais. Kuala Lumpur, Malaysia: Malaysian Branch of the Royal Asiatic Society.

Subhadradis Diskul, M. C., ed. (1980) *The Art of Srivijaya.* Kuala Lumpur, Malaysia: Oxford University Press.

Suleiman, Satyawati, Rumbi Mulia, R. P. Soejono, Soejatami Satari, and Hasan M. Ambary, eds. (1981) *Studies on Srivijaya.* Jakarta, Indonesia: National Research Centre of Archaeology.

Wolters, O. W. (1967) *Early Indonesian Commerce: A Study of the Origins of Srivijaya.* Ithaca, NY: Cornell University Press.

———. (1970) *The Fall of Srivijaya in Malay History.* London: Lund Humphries (Asia Major Library).

SSIRUM   *Ssirum* is one of the most popular traditional games in Korea, dating back to the early Koguryo kingdom (37 BCE–668 CE). *Ssirum* is a wrestling game in which one wrestler tries to make the opponent fall to the ground. The rules of *ssirum* are that (1) the two opponents, standing in a *ssirumpan* (a circle of sand nine meters in diameter), bind their right thighs and waists with a *satba* (a two-foot-long sash); (2) each opponent kneels facing the other, with the right hand grasping the *satba* bound around the waist and right thigh of the other; and (3) at the signal of a referee, the two opponents rise and begin to pull and push until one opponent falls to the ground. There are three basic skills: hand skill, leg skill, and lifting skill.

Ssirum matches are held not only during national holidays, including the Tano Festival day (5 May), but also during the leisure seasons. The game was handed down from the Koguryo kingdom through the Koryo kingdom (918–1392 CE) and the Choson dynasty (1392–1910 CE), becoming the most popular game among men, from the king to the common man. Today there are many professional and amateur *ssirum* wrestlers, and even women and children play the game.

Young-Il Na

Further Reading

Institute of Korean Culture. (1982) *Survey of Korean Folk Culture*. Seoul: Korea University.

STATE LAW AND ORDER RESTORATION COUNCIL—MYANMAR

After the 1988 uprising and protests sparked by ineffective socialist economic policies, the armed forces of Burma (Myanmar) on 18 September 1988 took control of the notional civilian government of Maung Maung, which had succeeded that of Ne Win, and created the State Law and Order Restoration Council (SLORC). Each of the fourteen administrative areas (seven states and seven divisions) that make up Burma are further subdivided into districts, townships, and then village tracts (in rural areas) or wards (in urban areas). Law and Order Councils (LORC) operate at every level. After the takeover, all state organs, including the People's Assembly, the Council of State, and the Council of Ministers were abolished, and their duties were assumed by the SLORC. The Burma Socialist Programme Party collapsed. A Supreme Court was established as the supreme judicial authority, its members appointed by the SLORC.

The SLORC, which included army chiefs but not ministers, functioned as the highest authority in Burma and oversaw the cabinet. It embarked on "Myanmafication" when it hastily instituted the Adaptation of Expressions Law on 18 June 1989. This involved a comprehensive Burmanization of place-names. Burma was renamed Myanmar, and Rangoon became Yangon. General Saw Maung was chairman at the foundation of the SLORC, but this office was handed over on 23 April 1992 to General Than Shwe, who was also declared prime minister.

Though the SLORC held elections in May 1990, as had been promised by Ne Win in his resignation speech, in the process of electioneering in the first half

A public notice posted by the SLORC in Yangon in September 1996. (STEPHEN G. DONALDSON PHOTOGRAPHY)

of 1989, the diverse ethnic groups began to meet with the National League for Democracy (NLD) to work out a national framework for sharing power. In response, the SLORC restricted the movements of politicians. After the National League for Democracy won with a landslide majority and the SLORC's favored National Unity Party failed to get a substantial vote, it reinterpreted the elections retrospectively as electing a body to draft a constitution.

Seeking to clean up its image with the international community, on 15 November 1997 the SLORC renamed itself the State Peace and Development Council (SPDC) but introduced no democratic elections and no major political reforms. Though accompanied by a few changes in personnel, there was no major change in government policy, and the net effect was one of little or no difference between the SPDC and its predecessor. Like the SLORC, the SPDC includes army chiefs but not ministers and functions as the highest authority in Myanmar. Though dominated by military personnel, SPDC officials are not formally linked to the army. The chairman is Than Shwe, and the first secretary is Khin Nyunt.

Gustaaf Houtman

Further Reading

Carey, Peter, ed. (1997) *Burma: The Challenge of Change in a Divided Society*. New York: St. Martin's.

Fink, Christina. (2001) *Living Silence: Burma under the Military Rule*. London: Zed.

Maung Maung, U. (1999) *1988 Uprising in Burma*. Edited by Franklin Mark Osanka. New Haven, CT: Yale University Press.

Rotberg, Robert I., ed. (1998) *Burma: Prospects for a Democratic Future*. Washington, DC: Brookings Institution Press.

Steinberg, David I. (2001) *Burma: The State of Myanmar*. Washington, DC: Georgetown University Press.

Taylor, R. H. (2001) *Burma: Political Economy under Military Rule*. New York: St Martin's.

STATE PEACE AND DEVELOPMENT COUNCIL. See **State Law and Order Restoration Council—Myanmar.**

STATUS OF FORCES AGREEMENT—JAPAN The Status of Forces Agreement (SOFA) between Japan and the United States provides guidelines for the activities of U.S. armed forces assigned to facilities in Japan. It is typical of the more than eighty such SOFAs that have been negotiated with other allies of the United States, such as NATO na-

tions and the Republic of Korea. A separate United Nations–Japan SOFA addresses issues regarding the deployment of forces from the United Nations Command, which was formed during the Korean War.

The U.S.–Japan SOFA was negotiated in 1960 to replace earlier agreements such as the Administrative Agreement (Article III of the 1952 Security Treaty between the U.S. and Japan) and the 1954 Status of Forces Agreement. In 1960 the Treaty of Mutual Cooperation and Security was signed, giving the United States use of land, air, and naval facilities in Japan "for the purpose of contributing to the security of Japan and the maintenance of international peace and security in the Far East" (Green and Cronin 1999: 330–332). Concurrently with the signing of this treaty, the revised U.S.-Japan SOFA was agreed upon.

1960 SOFA Provisions

The 1960 SOFA sets the conditions under which U.S. military forces may operate in Japan. It also dictates how U.S. military personnel and U.S. civilian employees of the U.S. government (and their dependents) assigned to support American armed forces in Japan will be treated under Japanese law. It exempts U.S. aircraft and ships from paying tolls or operating fees to which commercial vessels would be subject, as well as exempting vehicles from toll charges and permitting travel between military facilities. The SOFA also provides U.S. military personnel use of public utilities and services that are available to Japanese ministries and agencies, and provides for acquisition of land for military facilities. In addition, it provides for local workers to be hired indirectly: local Japanese workers are actually employed by the Japanese government and work on the U.S. installations. In contrast, on U.S.-controlled facilities in the Republic of Korea local workers are hired directly by the U.S.

By mutual agreement, offensive military operations may be prohibited by the government of Japan. Because Japan's constitution renounces war, American use of military facilities to launch offensive strikes on other countries would be construed as unconstitutional. For this reason, Japanese bases were not used for direct operations during the U.S. conflict in Vietnam. This does place constraints on the U.S. military forces assigned to Japan; for example, a U.S. naval vessel or Air Force aircraft leaving from Japan cannot proceed directly to an area of conflict without violating this limitation.

The U.S.-Japan SOFA is unique in that the ministry involved is not the Japan Defense Agency (JDA), but the Ministry of Foreign Affairs (MOFA). The facilities provided for U.S. military forces are thus not supported by their Japanese counterparts, but by the diplomatic arm of Japan's government. This has led to conflicts within the Japanese government, because while the MOFA is concerned with the international aspects of U.S.-Japan relations, other ministries are more concerned with domestic matters. This involvement with the MOFA permits greater cooperation between U.S. armed forces and the Japanese government than might be possible with other agencies, which would likely be more supportive of domestic interests. For example, when exercise areas are needed for naval training, the MOFA is able to exert more pressure for restricting fishing operations than the JDA could.

While the U.S.-Japan SOFA frees U.S. personnel from certain obligations, such as various forms of taxation and most customs fees, it restricts them from taking part in any political activity in Japan. The legal jurisdiction for offenses considered to be security violations against Japan is retained by Japan, even if the offense is not covered by U.S. law.

One of the more controversial aspects of the U.S.-Japan SOFA is contained in Article XVII, which deals with criminal jurisdiction over U.S. personnel in Japan. For those Americans who are covered by this SOFA, the American government retains authority to prosecute violations of U.S. law, while Japan may prosecute violations of Japanese law. However, if an American covered by this SOFA is apprehended and detained by U.S. forces, that person may be kept in U.S. custody until he or she is formally charged by Japanese authorities. This is seen by many Japanese as a special protection for foreigners, similar to the practice of extraterritoriality which Western nations forced upon China and Japan under the unequal treaties of the mid-nineteenth century. However, extraterritoriality protected foreigners from Japanese legal prosecution, whereas the U.S.-Japan SOFA actually subjects those U.S. citizens (military stationed in Japan, their family members present in Japan, and civilians working for the military) to both U.S. and Japanese law. The SOFA does specify that anyone covered by the SOFA is entitled to the same protections of due process (the rights to prompt and speedy trial, to be informed of the specific charges, to confront witnesses, to have legal representation) guaranteed under the U.S. constitution.

The Situation in Okinawa

The U.S.-Japan SOFA is a particularly difficult issue on the island of Okinawa, where the highest concentration of U.S. military forces exists. Because of the large number of U.S. facilities on Okinawa and the large military populations of those bases, movement of units between facilities has the appearance of a continued U.S. occupation of the island. The large military presence also increases the likelihood of conflicts with residents. Since 1972, when the United States returned control of the Ryukyu Islands to Japan, more than 4,500 military-related crimes—including twelve murders—have occurred on Okinawa. Japan's Foreign Ministry has appeared reluctant to apply the SOFA as effectively in Okinawa as it might on the main island of Honshu, leading to criticism against that ministry as well as against the United States.

One subsequent development that affects the SOFA is the establishment of the Special Action Committee on Okinawa (SACO). Following widespread popular demonstrations against the U.S. presence in Okinawa in 1995, in order to preclude further demands to revise the SOFA, the Japanese and American governments agreed to establish a special committee to deal specifically with Okinawan issues. At the time the U.S. military facilities occupied approximately one-fifth of Okinawa, and one purpose of the SACO was to reduce and consolidate those facilities.

One difficulty in consolidating facilities both on Okinawa and the main islands of Japan is that in addition to the U.S.-Japan SOFA, a separate agreement exists between Japan and the United Nations for access to military facilities. Negotiated during the Korean War and based on an agreement between Japanese Prime Minister Yoshida and U.S. Secretary of State Acheson, this U.N.-Japan SOFA gives the military forces of the United Nations Command permission to use certain mainland facilities (Yokota Air Base, Camp Zama, Yokosuka Naval Base, and Sasebo Naval Base), as well as Okinawa's Kadena Air Base, Futenma Marine Corps Air Station, and White Beach Naval facility. Nations in the United Nations Command include France, Australia, Belgium, Canada, Colombia, Ethiopia, Greece, Luxembourg, the Netherlands, the Philippines, New Zealand, Turkey, Thailand, and the United States. Although the Korean War is long past, the United Nations Command still exists and if necessary could base military operations from the facilities named above without prior approval from the government of Japan. The U.N.-Japan SOFA is based largely on the original U.S.-Japan SOFA, even including the legal protections of the U.S. constitution.

Thomas P. Dolan

Further Reading

Funabashi, Yoichi. (1999) *Alliance Adrift*. New York: Council on Foreign Relations.

Green, Michael J., and Patrick M. Cronin. (1999) *The U.S.-Japan Alliance: Past, Present, and Future.* New York: Council on Foreign Relations.

Paterson, Thomas, J. Garry Clifford, and Kenneth Hogan. (2000) *American Foreign Relations: A History to 1920.* Boston: Houghton Mifflin.

STEEL INDUSTRY—KOREA The steel industry has been the backbone of economic development in much of the world. Both North and South Korea, since their independence in 1945 from Japan, have pursued an economic development strategy centered on heavy industrialization, including steel. There are two distinct steelmaking technologies: the larger, more expensive, integrated blast furnace–based units that use iron ore and coal and the smaller electric furnaces that melt and purify scrap to extract steel. Both technologies are found in both countries.

North Korea adopted a self-reliant *(juche)* socialist approach with central planning and a high rate of investment. The Five Year Plan of 1957–1961 radically altered the structure of the economy in favor of heavy industry. Endowed with iron ore and coal, North Korea adopted blast furnace technologies (such as the Bessemer and Open Hearth); provided by China and the Soviet Union, these were small-scale and already obsolete. North Korea's steel production was estimated to be under 7 million tons in 1995, approximately 300 kilograms per capita.

Devoid of raw materials and an industrial foundation, capitalist South Korea pursued a more open, albeit selective economic development strategy. It first pushed light industry exports, such as textiles, garments, and footwear and then pursued a strategy of heavy industrialization beginning in 1973. The government established the Pohang Iron and Steel Company (POSCO) in 1968, constructing two world-class integrated plants at Pohang (1970–1983) and Kwangyang (1982–1992). The former received Japanese technological and financial assistance, while the latter relied principally on European technologies. By the late 1990s, POSCO had become the world's largest steel company, displacing long-established Nippon Steel of Japan. Privately-owned electric furnaces contributed roughly 40 percent of South Korea's total output of 41 million tons in 1999.

While both Korean governments violated free market principles in fostering their respective industry, South Korean steel became internationally competitive. It imported inexpensive, high quality raw materials and modern technologies. Low wages, sound industrial training, and government subsidies contributed to competitiveness and a per capita output of nearly 912 kilograms by 2000. Exports defrayed import costs and created the basis for technological learning in a virtuous cycle. North Korea, however, with its isolationist policy, was already stagnating in the late 1970s. It failed to take advantage of expanding global markets and modern technologies. The collapse of the Soviet Union, its ally and coal source, cut off supplies of vital raw materials.

The South Korean economy and its steel industry expanded without interruption, except during the 1970s oil crisis. Along with POSCO, private firms such as Hanbo Steel invested heavily in new technologies. However, the cozy relationship between *chaebol* (highly diversified, family-owned conglomerates) and government in South Korea had created a vast network of indebtedness. The Asian financial crisis of 1997 pushed many *chaebols*, including Hanbo, into bankruptcy. As globalization pushes national firms to become more competitive, many South Korean firms will witness reorganization, perhaps privatization, and some foreign ownership. The thawing of relations in the post–Cold War era and the economic maturity of South Korea suggests the possibility of complementing the North's market and raw materials with the South's capital and superior technologies. The proposed unification could usher in a new regional dynamic with an even more powerful, united Korean steel industry.

Anthony P. D'Costa

Further Reading
Amsden, Alice H. (1990) *Asia's Next Giant: South Korea and Late Industrialization.* New York: Oxford University Press.

Chung, Joseph Sang-hoon. (1974) *The North Korean Economy: Structure and Development.* Stanford, CA: Hoover Institution Press, Stanford University.

D'Costa, Anthony P. (1999) *The Global Restructuring of the Steel Industry: Innovations, Institutions, and Industrial Change.* London: Routledge.

Eberstadt, Nicolas. (1999) *The End of North Korea.* Washington, DC: American Enterprise Institute Press.

Lee, Hyong-Seog. (1997) "A Comparative Cost Analysis for an Integrated Steel Works for North Korea by Economic Cooperation between South and North Korea in Iron and Steel Industry." Ph.D. diss., Cornell University.

STORYTELLING Stories are passed on in families, libraries, schools, and elsewhere in the United States today by parents, grandparents, teachers, and several hundred professional storytellers. Storytelling in the United States encompasses a range of traditions, from the oldest Native American tellings to more recent tellings in immigrant communities. In other areas, too, of the non-Asian world, storytelling continues with a similar mix of folk and professional styles. But the widest range and the richest diversity of techniques and stories are surely found today in Asia.

Storytelling remains a part of life in much of modern Asia. Storytellers of various backgrounds help to pass on values and morals, influence voters, keep history alive, and promote rural development. Stories are told by grandparents at home, by learned tellers in South Asian temples, and by East Asian librarians and teachers. Indeed, this age-old medium remains vital today in much of Asia.

Settings and Audience

The teller and audience in various settings are mutually responsive. Older tellers often share with family members in homes during meals or at bedtime. Groups of ten to a hundred may gather to listen in Chinese tea houses, while more than a hundred might hear tellers in Japanese *yose* theaters. Although outdoor village audiences in India can be large, much telling there also occurs in smaller temples and halls. In earlier times, storytelling in Malaysia often took place in friendly, close-knit *kampong* communities.

Technology today increases the reach of Asian storytellers: their stories are now sold on cassette or videotapes, broadcast on radio or television, and found on the Internet. But the art of the live Asian storyteller depends on a close connection to the audience. One reason given for the fading of *lum pun* storytelling in Thailand is the tellers' move to the newer raised stages, farther from the audiences.

Storytelling Materials

The Asian storytelling repertoire ranges from folk tales and romances to famous epics or classics like China's *Romance of the Three Kingdoms*. Religious stories remain important: those of the Prophet and his followers are favored in Muslim Asia, while tales of Hindu gods, the Buddha, and of the land's many spirits are heard elsewhere.

True stories of wars and freedom struggles are also popular in this region, with its painful history of colonialism. Hero tales, past and present, are passed on as well, from those of the valiant Trung sisters of long-ago Vietnam to accounts of the more modern, multitalented Filipino, Jose Rizal.

Tales of tricksters and fools are favorites: clever Judge Rabbit of Cambodia, the foolish Pak Pandir in Malaysia, the quick-witted Andare of Sri Lanka, and the comical Indonesian Si Kabayan are just a few of many. Problem stories and riddle tales help to sharpen wits, while ghost tales and stories with a range of strange creatures from the Japanese *oni* to the Nepalese *yeti* are greatly enjoyed.

Some storytellers update their traditional repertoires to adapt to changing tastes or a sponsor's interests. New themes of the Indian *patua* storytellers include stories of court cases, accidents, and political change, as well as moral tales about dowry and family planning. In the 1950s and 1960s, Lao tellers were hired by United States Information Agency to urge support for American aid projects and the royal Lao government.

Storytelling Language and Gesture

Buddhist monks in Southeast Asia use the power of chanting and recitation to share stories of the Buddha's life, including the popular *Jataka* tale (Buddhist birth story) of Prince Vessantara. The Korean *p'ansori* teller excels in verbal repetition: in "The Song of Silk," the teller rapidly lists forty-five types of silks and ninety-seven pieces of furniture as they flow from a gourd.

Japanese librarian tellers favor a very quiet telling style, with few gestures but rich language, as do a number of Asian folk tellers. Indian *ottan thullal* tellers from Kerala State, however, use an elaborate *mudra* (hand sign) language to tell their stories. Japanese *rakugo* tellers, while kneeling on the stage, create a cast of characters using largely their voices and facial expressions.

Music

Music is an integral part of many Asian telling techniques. Some stories are told entirely in ballad form. At times, the chanted voice, perhaps accompanied by a steady beat, tells a tale—a technique that was favored by tellers of the Ainu minority in Japan in the past. Korean *p'ansori* tellers train their voices for long years, sometimes even shouting under waterfalls to produce voices of incredible range and texture.

> A clear floating voice is like the whooping of a
>   crane in blue sky,
> A sudden bouncing voice seems to be a peal of
>   thunder.
> A rapid changing voice is like a desolate cold wind
>   among the bare trees.
>
> (Bang-song 1976: 26)

Asian storytellers often use instruments: drums, bells, clay pots, and similar percussion instruments are the most popular, followed by lutes and other stringed instruments. A musical bow provides unusual interest in the South Indian *villapattu* style, while the *xingmu*, a wood block used in China, can imitate thunder, a far-off noise, the sadness of farewell, or a sword raised in battle.

Humor

Several Asian storytelling styles are famed for their use of humor. *Xiangsheng*, a popular Chinese style performed solo or in pairs, features comic tales and characterizations satirizing human foibles and social abuses.

Japanese *rakugo* tellers, who are seen on television, in college clubs, and in *yose* (vaudeville-type theaters), are known for superb timing and clever wordplay and characterization. Many of their humorous tales are based on characters from Japan's Edo period (1600/1603–1868), although modern stories poke fun at today's world of baseball, jet travel, and noisy robots.

Improvisation

In a number of traditions, improvisation keeps classic Asian stories fresh and contemporary. Since the audience knows the story, the teller has greater scope to embroider it and to improvise. Weaving in side stories or comments—sometimes combining old and new—is a popular improvisational technique. Such material may be traditional or modern—about politics, history and legend, daily life, almost anything. This technique, skillfully used in the Indian *harikatha* style, keeps the well-known *Ramayana* relevant. One such teller, describing Sita's wedding a thousand years ago, juxtaposed past and present when he said: "Everybody prepared for the great event, but it was hard to get materials since the department stores were empty after their big discount sales."

Props

Visual storytelling props have been used for over two thousand years in busy Asian marketplaces, temples, festivals, and courtyards. Painted sets of story scenes migrated from old India to early twentieth-century Japan. There, a roving *kamishibai* (paper theater) storyteller carried large cards on his bicycle, selling food snacks before telling tales of samurai, science fiction, and comic characters. Although the traveling tellers are rare today, librarian and teachers tell stories from both published and handmade sets in Japan, Vietnam, Singapore, and Korea.

Scrolls of various sizes—both vertical, like the *pata*s in northeast India, or horizontal, like the *phad* of West India—are unrolled by wandering tellers to share long tales. Traveling Tibetan tellers of old shared epics of the hero Gesar or Buddhist tales with the aid of *tanka*s, ornate painted silk hangings.

One of the simplest props is the folding fan used in Korean *p'ansori* for dramatic emphasis, and in Japanese *rakugo* to portray a sword, a pipe, a pole, a writing brush, a bowl of noodles, and more. Elaborate costumes and makeup are less common. Although several singing styles, like the Indian *ottan thullal*, include use of colorful makeup and costume, many professional tellers favor simpler traditional robes, dresses, or wrapped cloth.

Asian storytelling is indeed varied, communicating messages both religious and secular, through amateurs and professionals of both sexes. The techniques that the Asian teller has evolved show an amazing range of complexity, appealing to audiences young and old. Asian storytelling forms may change; some will fade away since they no longer answer the needs of modern Asia. Yet other forms will survive and thrive, for the storyteller speaks from the heart with words worth hearing.

Cathy Spagnoli

Further Reading

Blackburn, Stuart. (1988) *Singing of Birth and Death: Texts in Performance*. Philadelphia: University of Pennsylvania Press.

Gurumurthy, Preemila. (1994) *Kathakalaksepa*. Madras, India: International Society for the Investigation of Ancient Civilizations.

Mair, Victor. (1988) *Painting and Performance*. Honolulu, HI: University of Hawaii Press.

Morioka, Heinz, and Miyoko Sasaki. (1990) *Rakugo, the Popular Narrative Art of Japan*. Cambridge, MA: Council on East Asian Studies at Harvard.

Phil, Marshall. (1994) *The Korean Singer of Tales*. Cambridge, MA: Harvard University Press.

Richman, Paula, ed. (1991) *Many Ramayanas: The Diversity of a Narrative Tradition in South Asia*. Berkeley and Los Angeles: University of California Press.

Sen Gupta, Sankar. (1973) *The Patas and the Patuas of Bengal*. Calcutta, India: Indian Publications.

Song, Bang-Song, (1976) "Kwangdae Ka: A Source Material for the P'ansori Tradition." *Korea Journal* (August).

Spagnoli, Cathy. (1998) *Asian Tales and Tellers*. Little Rock, AR: August House.

Stevens, Catherine. (1972) "Peking Drumsinging." Ph.D. diss., Harvard University.

Sweeney, Amin. (1994) *Malay Word Music: A Celebration of Oral Creativity*. Kuala Lumpur, Malaysia: Dewan Bahasa dan Pustaka Kementerian Pendidikan Malaysia.

Yanagita, Kunio. (1986) *The Yanagita Kunio Guide to the Japanese Folk Tale*. Trans. by Fanny Hagin Mayer. Bloomington, IN: Indiana University Press.

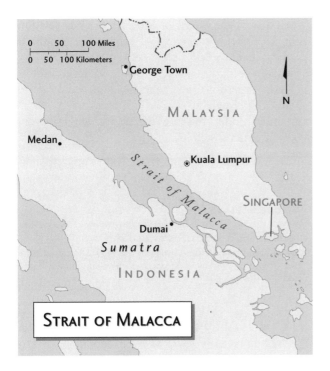

0 50 100 Miles
0 50 100 Kilometers

•George Town

MALAYSIA

N

Medan.

⊗ Kuala Lumpur

Strait of Malacca

SINGAPORE

Dumai•

Sumatra

INDONESIA

STRAIT OF MALACCA

STRAIT OF MALACCA

The funnel-shaped Strait of Malacca stretches 600 nautical miles between the west coast of peninsular Malaysia and the east coast of Sumatra. Named after the ancient city of Malacca (Melaka, in Malay), it is one of the busiest and most economically important straits in the world.

Geologically, the strait is part of the extensive shallow Sunda Shelf that extends seaward from mainland Southeast Asia to a depth of 200 meters. Although largely sheltered, its waters are influenced by the monsoons. Mangroves dominate the coast, especially on the Sumatran side. Coral reefs are limited.

Historically, the strait acted as a conduit for Europeans coming east and the region's commodities moving west. Today it is an important sea route for local and international trade and shipping traffic, and for the tankers that supply three-quarters of Japan's oil imports—making it highly vulnerable to pollution from oil spills and other sources. The strait is vital to the surrounding countries, which share common interests in its use and management, and in issues concerning legal boundaries, navigation rights, traffic separation, pollution, and piracy.

The Strait of Malacca's economic significance is enhanced by two growth triangles strategically located to boost future economic cooperation and development: the Indonesia-Malaysia-Thailand growth triangle in the north and the Singapore-Johor-Riau growth triangle in the south.

Wong Poh Poh

Further Reading

Chua Thia-Eng, S. Adrian Ross, and Huming Yu, eds. (1997) *Malacca Straits Environmental Profile.* Quezon City, Philippines: MPP-EAS Technical Report 10.

Cleary, Mark, and Goh Kim Chuan. (2000) *Environment and Development in the Straits of Malacca.* London: Routledge.

STRAITS SETTLEMENTS

From 1826 to 1946, the term "Straits Settlements" was the collective name for the British colonies of Penang (former Prince of Wales Island), Singapore, and Melaka (former Malacca), today all part of Malaysia. The British East India Company had acquired these territories, situated at the strategic Straits of Malacca, at various times in the eighteenth and nineteenth centuries, for protection of the trade route that led to China from the Indian subcontinent.

In 1786, the sultan of Kedah ceded Penang to the East India Company, and this became the first territory of the Straits Settlements. When the permanent occupation of Penang was assured, the East India Company expanded its territorial claim to Melaka, which became part of the Straits Settlements in 1826, the same year as Singapore. Sir Thomas Stamford Raffles had acquired Singapore from the sultan of Johor for the British East India Company in 1819. The sultan of Brunei transferred the island of Labuan to Britain in 1846; the island was governed by British North Borneo from 1889 to 1905 and was incorporated into the Straits Settlements in 1912. The Cocos Islands, in the Indian Ocean southwest of Java, Indonesia, were acquired by Britain in 1857 and became part of the Straits Settlements in 1886. Britain acquired Christmas Island, off western Java, in 1888, and it merged with the Straits Settlements in 1889.

In 1826, the administrative headquarters of the Straits Settlements was at George Town (now Penang city), and the Settlements were ruled by the Indian government. A governor, an advisory council, and a number of civil servants were based in Penang city. Each territory had a resident, whose responsibility was to assist the governor. In 1836, the headquarters was moved to Singapore, and in 1867, responsibility for the Straits Settlements was taken from India and the territories were made a crown colony controlled by the British.

The British shrewdly used these territories to establish their influence in the Malay Peninsula. Between 1832 and 1946, the Straits Settlements were major ports of call for ships plying between Europe and East Asia. With the opening of the Suez Canal in 1869, these ports became even more important for the British empire, as they formed the main sorting and export centers of rubber. Immigrant populations of Europeans, Chinese, Malays, and Indians in the Settlements also grew substantially, attracted by the prosperity in these regions. In 1942, the Japanese invaded Singapore, and British administration of the Straits Settlements was temporarily suspended.

The Straits Settlements crown colony was dissolved in 1946. Singapore became a separate crown colony, then part of the Federation of Malaysia in 1963–1965, and finally an independent republic in 1965. Penang and Melaka were incorporated into the Federation of Malaya in 1948 and became states in Malaysia in 1963. Labuan joined North Borneo in 1946, then Malaysia in 1963, and became a federal territory of Malaysia in 1984. Christmas Island was given to Australia in 1958. The Cocos Islands were placed under Australian rule in 1955, were purchased by Australia in 1978, and became part of Australia in 1984.

Khai Leong Ho

Further Reading
Hall, David George Edward. (1981) *A History of South-East Asia*. 4th ed. Basingstoke, U.K.: Macmillan.
Ryan, N. J. (1969) *The Making of Modern Malaysia and Singapore*. Kuala Lumpur, Malaysia: Oxford University Press.

STRAITS TIMES, THE The Straits Times is Singapore's oldest and longest-running English-language newspaper. It was started in 1845 by Catchick Moses, a prominent Armenian merchant, and Robert Carl Woods, the newspaper's first editor. It began as an eight-page weekly, and expanded to twenty-four pages in 1928. In December 1931, *The Sunday Times* made its debut and was a great success as the newspaper made efforts to be striking in style as well as content. It was fine-tuned to include popular features as well as light-hearted articles. The newspaper ceased publication during the Japanese occupation, but it quickly reestablished itself and became the best-selling newspaper in the country. In 1956 the newspaper began to print a separate edition in Kuala Lumpur, Malaysia.

In 1984 Singapore Press Holdings (SPH) was formed with the merger of three publicly listed publishing companies: the Straits Times Press (1975) Limited, Times Publishing Berhad, and Singapore News and Publications Limited. In October 1988, Times Publishing Berhad was separated from the group.

Singapore Press Holdings has a monopolistic grip on newspapers published in the Republic of Singapore.

The chair of the board of SPH has a close relationship with the ruling party of Singapore, giving the public the impression that the newspaper is being "guided" or "controlled." The newspaper editors, however, regard the newspaper's major mission as "responsible journalism"—in which press freedoms are subsumed under the broader and more important goals of societal stability.

Khai Leong Ho

Further Reading
Seow, Francis. (1998). *The Media Enthralled: Singapore Revisited*. Boulder, CO: Lynne Reiner.
Tan Yew Soon and Soh Yew Peng. (1994) *The Development of Singapore's Modern Media Industry*. Singapore: Times Academic Press.

STUDENT UPRISING OF 1973—THAILAND The early 1970s saw the beginnings of Thai student political activism, with the growth in power and influence of the National Student Center of Thailand (NSTC). The concentration of many of Thailand's leading universities in one city, Bangkok, facilitated the mobilization efforts of the NSTC.

The spark that ignited the October 1973 student uprising was the arrest on 6 October of student leader Thirayudh Boonme and ten other activists for distributing leaflets urging early promulgation of a permanent constitution. The students were accused of being engaged in a plot to overthrow the government. Three days later, approximately two thousand students gathered at Thammasat University for a peaceful rally to protest the government's actions. The government in response offered to grant bail to the arrested students, but the NSTC and student demonstrators demanded the unconditional release of the students. By 13 October, the demonstrations had dramatically escalated, with approximately eighty thousand protesters completely packing Rajdamnoen Avenue (literally meaning "royal road," the major road of old Bangkok running from the old parliament building to the large park across from Thammasat University) from end to end. Much in evidence among protestors were the Thai flag and pictures of the king and queen.

Historical Background
Though Thailand was ostensibly a constitutional monarchy from 1932 to 1973, in fact the Thai military dominated in a frequently authoritarian manner for much of this period. Civilian leaders were frequently deposed in military coups. The three major

Thai political leaders during this period were Field Marshall Pibul Songgram, who served as prime minister from 1938 to 1944 and from 1948 to 1957; Field Marshall Sarit Thanarat, who served as prime minister from 1959 to 1963; and Field Marshall Thanom Kittikachorn, who served as prime minister in 1958 and from 1963 to 1973. During Thanom's rule, gatherings of more than five individuals for discussions of politics were prohibited, an edict reflective of his government's repressiveness.

In the early 1970s, perhaps as a reflection of what was happening in many parts of the world, Thai student activism emerged, stimulated by Thai intellectuals, many of whom had been educated overseas. Beginning in 1972, the NSTC became a major source of student activism, taking their issues to the general public. The government's abrogation of the constitution in November 1971 certainly contributed to the growth of student activism.

Violence Erupts

At 5:30 A.M. on Sunday, 14 October, the government announced that the student detainees were being unconditionally released and that a new constitution would be promulgated within a year. By 6:30 A.M., for reasons that are unclear, a series of tear gas explosions sparked an escalation of violent confrontation between the demonstrators and the Thai police and military, with hundreds of innocent people and demonstrators being killed. Many buses were hijacked and key buildings such as the National Lottery and the Revenue Department were burned down. This was the biggest demonstration in Thai history and the violence involved was unprecedented. The students were joined in their protests by thousands of ordinary citizens from all walks of life. Prior to this critical incident, Thailand had been famous for peaceful coups.

After a meeting with the king (who has no real political power but has great influence in granting legitimacy or withdrawing legitimacy from political leaders, as a result of his great popularity and prestige), the three military leaders (popularly known as the "three tyrants"), Field Marshall Thanom Kittikachorn, Field Marshall Praphat Charusanthien (Deputy Prime Minister and Minister of Interior), and Thanom's son Colonel Narong Kittikachorn (a high-ranking military officer and head of the Board of Inspection and Follow-up of Government Operations, which gave him considerable power to eliminate political rivals) agreed to tender the resignation of their government. The king announced that Professor Sanya Thammasakdi would be the new prime minister of an interim government in a transition to genuine democracy. On the next day, 15 October, it was announced that the three military leaders had gone into exile. With their departure the mood dramatically changed. People from all sectors of society volunteered to help clear away the debris left over from the uprising.

The Meaning and Implications of the October Uprising

This critical incident in October 1973 and the transition from an absolute to a constitutional monarchy in 1932 are the two most pivotal incidents in twentieth-century Thai political history. There is debate as to whether the 1973 incident should be called a student revolution. Did it fundamentally change the course of Thai politics? Certainly the immediate changes in the period 1973–1976 were dramatic in moving Thailand toward genuine democracy. These changes, however, were abruptly terminated with a successful right-wing military coup against the democratic government in October 1976. This extremely repressive regime, however, lasted for only a year and was overthrown by a popular coup on 20 October 1977.

The student leaders and those who sacrificed their lives for Thai democracy were considered to be heroes. Four special commemorative stamps were issued on 25 January 1975 by the interim government of Judge Sanya Dharmasakti to honor them and a monument was erected in Bangkok in their memory. October 14 was given the name, Wan Maha Wippasok (the Most Tragic Day). That Thailand has been significantly more democratic after 1973 than before is a tribute to the impact of the uprising.

As of the beginning of 2001, the 1973 uprising was still an issue. The Thai Ministry of Education commissioned one of Thailand's leading poets, Naowarat Pongpaiboon, to write an account of the students' revolution and its aftermath to be titled "The October 14, 1973, Incident" so that Thai students will have a chance to study this important part of their modern political history. Ironically, one of the editors for the publication turned out to be Suvit Yodmani, son-in-law of Field Marshall Thanom, who strongly objected to alleged inaccuracies and distortions in the draft of the book, delaying publication.

In reflecting on the October demonstrations there is also considerable debate as to what ignited the violence. Certainly the students were committed to nonviolence in their demonstrations and Thanom claims to have ordered his generals to refrain from opening fire (a copy of his order exists). Thus there is the distinct possibility that what the Chinese call a "black hand" or the Thais call a "third hand"—a third party who seeks political power to replace an existing regime and attempts to discredit that regime—might have played a key role in causing the violence to erupt. In a January 2001 article in the *Siam Post*, Major-General Witoon Yasawat, then 74 and ailing, admitted he acted on behalf of a third party, but did not identify it.

Despite the controversies surrounding it, the 14 October incident was a critical turning point in the maturation of modern Thai politics, and its heroes and heroines will never be forgotten.

Gerald W. Fry

Further Reading
Fineman, Daniel. (1997) *A Special Relationship: The United States and Military Governments in Thailand, 1947–1958.* Honolulu, HI: University of Hawaii Press.

Heize, Ruth-Inge. (1974) "Ten Days in October—Students versus the Military, an Account of the Student Uprising in Thailand." *Asian Survey* 14, 6 (June): 491–508.

Prizzia, Ross, and Narong Sinsawasdi. (1974) *Thailand: Student Activism and Political Change.* Bangkok, Thailand: Duang Kamol.

Singh, Ajary, and Julian Gearing. (2000) "The Murky Events of October 1973: A Book Proposal Reopens Thailand's Wounds." *Asiaweek* 26, 3 (January 28).

Zimmerman, Robert F. (1974) "Student Revolution in Thailand: The End of the Thai Bureaucratic Polity?" *Asian Survey* 14, 6: 509–529.

SUFISM—SOUTH ASIA Sufism (Arabic *tasawwuf*; from *sufi*, "man of wool") refers to the practices of religious mystics who differentiated themselves by wearing garments of coarse wool or *suf*. Arising from Islam in the seventh century and spreading throughout South Asia, adherents of Sufism were perhaps once inspired by the desire to escape earthly dilemmas and difficulties; today Sufism finds widespread expression in most Middle Eastern and South Asian nations.

By the ninth century the mystical movement emphasized the *tariqh* (the Sufi "road of life," or "path") as a way to communicate with Allah through love and devotion. A religious disciple (*murid*) might travel the *tariqh* through the teaching of a *shaikh* or *pir* (preceptor), ultimately achieving a mystical union with God.

The *khanqah*, or abode of Sufi saints, became centers of activities like religious discourse and *sama* (musical gatherings). The saints' *dargah* (tombs) became places of pilgrimage for both Muslims and Hindus. Sufism offered a common meeting point of spirituality for both religions and provided a basis for mutual understanding between Muslims and non-Muslims.

From the fifteenth century onward, Sufism expanded. Mir (1550–1635), a noteworthy Sufi saint, propounded the doctrine of *wahadat-ul-wujud* (unity of being or "monoism"). His disciple, Mullah Shah Badakhshi, was the preceptor of Dara Shikoh (1615–1659), the son of the Turkmen ruler and Mughal emperor Shah Jahan (1592–1666). The teachings of the Sufi saints also reached the common people because preceptors taught in vernacular languages. Certain trends in Sufism, however, led to orthodoxy. Saikh Ahmed Sarhindi (1564–1624), disciple of Baqi Billah (1563–1603), opposed the doctrine of monoism and called for strict adherence to the *shari'a* (Islamic law).

It was in South Asia that Islam met Hinduism. It was not the Muslim iconoclasts but the peaceful missionaries of Sufism who converted Hindus. Sufism endeavored for Hindu-Muslim unity. It also bridged the gulf between the Muslims of foreign origin and local converts. The liberal atmosphere created by Sufism still lingers in South Asia.

The Sufis formed various orders, and today there are about one hundred, many in Iran. The Persian poet Jalal ad-Din ar-Rumi (c. 1207–1273) established an order in which dances, such as those of the whirling dervishes (still in existence, with headquarters in Turkey), were practiced. The *naqshbandi* order is popular in the Atroshi region of Bangladesh, and the former president, Hossain Mohammad Ershad (b. 1930), was a patron of this order, which formed a political party (Bangladesh Zaker Sangathan) in 1990.

Patit Paban Mishra

Further Reading
Islam, Riazul. (1999) *Sufism and Its Impact on Muslim Society in South Asia.* Karachi, Pakistan: Oxford University Press.

Mujeeb, M. (1967) *The Indian Muslims.* London: George Allen and Unwin.

Shah, Idries. (1984) *The Sufis.* London: Octagon.

SUFISM—SOUTHWEST ASIA Sufism, or Islamic mysticism, has for centuries been integral to the religious lives of Muslims in Southwest Asia (modern Afghanistan and Pakistan). Sufism flourished in the region since its introduction from Persia and the Arab world in the eleventh century, and it remains popular today, with perhaps a majority of the people having some association with the tradition. It seems likely that its popularity even facilitated the spread of Islam there

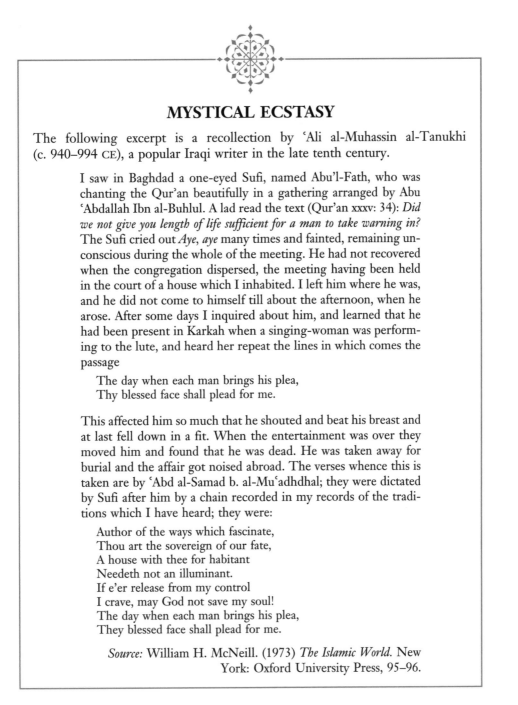

MYSTICAL ECSTASY

The following excerpt is a recollection by 'Ali al-Muhassin al-Tanukhi (c. 940–994 CE), a popular Iraqi writer in the late tenth century.

I saw in Baghdad a one-eyed Sufi, named Abu'l-Fath, who was chanting the Qur'an beautifully in a gathering arranged by Abu 'Abdallah Ibn al-Buhlul. A lad read the text (Qur'an xxxv: 34): *Did we not give you length of life sufficient for a man to take warning in?* The Sufi cried out *Aye, aye* many times and fainted, remaining unconscious during the whole of the meeting. He had not recovered when the congregation dispersed, the meeting having been held in the court of a house which I inhabited. I left him where he was, and he did not come to himself till about the afternoon, when he arose. After some days I inquired about him, and learned that he had been present in Karkah when a singing-woman was performing to the lute, and heard her repeat the lines in which comes the passage

The day when each man brings his plea,
Thy blessed face shall plead for me.

This affected him so much that he shouted and beat his breast and at last fell down in a fit. When the entertainment was over they moved him and found that he was dead. He was taken away for burial and the affair got noised abroad. The verses whence this is taken are by 'Abd al-Samad b. al-Mu'adhdhal; they were dictated by Sufi after him by a chain recorded in my records of the traditions which I have heard; they were:

Author of the ways which fascinate,
Thou art the sovereign of our fate,
A house with thee for habitant
Needeth not an illuminant.
If e'er release from my control
I crave, may God not save my soul!
The day when each man brings his plea,
They blessed face shall plead for me.

Source: William H. McNeill. (1973) *The Islamic World.* New York: Oxford University Press, 95–96.

because significant conversions to the new faith coincided with the spread of Sufism.

In general terms there are two distinct, yet frequently overlapping, forms of the Sufi tradition in Southwest Asia. The first of these has been termed "orthodox" because its followers adhere closely to the form of Sufism originally introduced by the great *pir*s (Sufi masters). This form is based upon initiation of individual disciples (singular: *murid*) into a *tariqat* (Sufi order). Members of each *tariqat* meet in small groups with their *pir* at a *khanaqah* (Sufi lodge) to be instructed and to engage in often intensely emotional spiritual practices such as *dhikr* (reciting the names of God). Like Sufis elsewhere in the Islamic world, they seek mystical experience of God, with the ultimate aim of achieving unity with the divine power.

Many of the *tariqat*s were introduced from outside the region, with the greatest flowering occurring during the twelfth and thirteenth centuries. Four *tariqat*s became especially prominent. First, and most influential,

A devotee of Sufi saint Bari Iman attends the ceremony marking the saint's anniversary in Islamabad, Pakistan, on 9 June 2000. He wears some 115 kg of chains to show his devotion. (REUTERS NEWMEDIA INC./CORBIS)

is the Nakshbandiya, which was founded in Bukhara in present-day Uzbekistan by Baha'uddin Naqshband (1318–1389). This *tariqat* is found throughout the region. Second is the Qadiriya *tariqat*. It was founded in Baghdad by 'Abd al-Qadit al-Jilani (1077/1078–1166) but became established in India during the thirteenth century and from there attracted a particularly loyal following among the Pashtun tribes of eastern Afghanistan. Third, and also originating in Baghdad, is the Suhrawardiyya *tariqat*, which was founded by Abu Najib al-Suhrawardi (c. 1155–1191) and introduced to Southwest Asia during the thirteenth century. It has a strong following in Pakistan, especially in the areas of Sind and southern Punjab, but a much weaker presence in Afghanistan. Fourth is the Chishtiya, which is the only one of the major *tariqat*s to have actually originated in this region. Founded in the city of Chishtiya (Herat Province) by Abu Ishaq but introduced to India by Maudud Chishti (1142–1236), this *tariqat* is now more popular in Pakistan than in Afghanistan, although many inhabitants of the area surrounding Chishtiya remain followers. The *tariqat*s have traditionally found very strong support among the urban middle classes, with large cities such as Herat and Kabul becoming important spiritual centers and home to renowned Sufis, including the celebrated poets Abu Ismail Abdullah Ansari of Herat

(1005–1089) and Nur od-Din 'Abd or-Rahman ebn Ahmad Jami (1414–1492), who was born in Jam, Khorasan, but died in Herat.

Sufi Practices

Sufis are generally viewed as unorthodox or even heretical in the Muslim world in part because of their aim of achieving oneness with God, but also because they often reject orthodox practices and observance of the *shari'a* (sacred law of Islam), viewing these as obstacles to spiritual development. In contrast, members of the major *tariqat*s in this region are notable for their integration with orthodox Muslim life. Members of the Chishtiya *tariqat*, for example, engage in unorthodox practices such as the use of music during worship, yet many view obedience to the *shari'a* as an essential step toward spiritual development. Also of note is the historically close relationship between Sufi *pir*s and other Muslim leaders, primarily the ulama (orthodox religious scholars, singular: *'alim*) and mullahs (clerics). Their roles, in fact, sometimes overlap, it being acceptable for a *pir* to also be an *'alim*, allowing him to fulfill the role of spiritual guide as well as instructor in the Qur'an, *shari'a*, and *fiqh* (Islamic jurisprudence). Similarly, the close association of many ulama with the Sufi tradition is reflected in the emphasis they place on spiritual matters (as opposed to purely theological and legal matters) in their teachings. Instead of being in conflict or competition with one another, orthodox Islam and mystical Sufism came to be viewed as complementary, with the former addressing outward or worldly concerns and the latter addressing the inward or spiritual concerns that orthodox Islam tends to neglect.

Sufism in Rural Areas

The form of Sufism just described—based on the *tariqat*s and individual mystical practices—is predominant in the cities and towns. In rural areas, however, Muslims practice a popular form of Sufism that incorporates elements of pre-Islamic and Hindu traditions and that is based upon veneration of *pir*s and hereditary saints. *Barakat* (divine grace) is believed to emanate from both living *pir*s and the shrines (usually called *ziyarat*) dedicated to deceased *pir*s, giving them magical powers. *Barakat* is also thought to emanate from hereditary saints—descendents of the *pir*s, known in Pakistan as *sajjada-nishin* and in Afghanistan as *ruhsni*. For this reason they, too, are venerated despite the fact that they are usually uneducated, with no formal religious training.

Like the more orthodox *pir*s associated with the *tariqat*s, the *pir*s and saints of popular Sufism have traditionally coexisted peacefully with the rural ulama and mullahs. Unlike orthodox Sufism, however, popular Sufism places emphasis on collective as well as individual aspects of religious experience. Whole families, clans, and even entire tribes promise allegiance to a local *pir* or saint, who in return assumes responsibility for the people's spiritual well-being and gives sanction to local political leaders. His tasks include maintaining the shrine with which he is entrusted, carrying out rituals, and performing supposedly miraculous deeds such as pronouncing blessings and healing the sick. Followers (singular: *mukhlis*) visit the shrines in order to give offerings of food or money, to make vows, and to seek advice, cures, and charms. However, the *pir* or saint effectively assumes the role of intermediary between his followers and God, carrying out spiritual practices such as *dhikr* on behalf of the whole community. Initiation into a *tariqat* and performance of individual spiritual practices are therefore regarded as unnecessary. Spiritual development, conformity to orthodox Islam, and consideration of theological issues are effectively less important than the alliances that sustain traditional ethnic or tribal power structures.

The belief among Sufis of this region in the importance of attending to both spiritual and worldly concerns gave rise in the nineteenth and twentieth centuries to a tradition of political activism by Sufi *pirs* and saints. During this period, *pirs* in Afghanistan, often working in alliance with tribal leaders, helped lead numerous political uprisings against Afghan rulers and foreign imperialists. Farther east, Sufi leaders in the Punjab actively opposed British colonial rule and agitated for the creation of Pakistan. Certain Sufi factions also became politically influential during this time, a noteworthy example being the Mujaddidi family, whose members are descended from the Nakshbandiya reformer Ahmad Sirhindi (1564–1624). Such activity places these leaders in pronounced contrast to the world-renouncing Sufis known elsewhere in the Islamic world.

Opposition to Sufism

Since the nineteenth century, Muslim intellectuals and fundamentalists have been vocal in their opposition to Sufism, arguing it to be a corruption of the faith. Some, notably the Indian poet and nationalist philosopher Muhammad Iqbal (1877–1938), have made popular saint veneration the main target of their criticisms, viewing it as an idolatrous practice. The influence of the *pirs* and saints has also been gradually undermined as a result of repressive government policies and the incorporation of religious leadership into the modern state system. In Afghanistan, *pirs* were officially replaced by state-sponsored ulama in the 1930s.

Sufism there has also been weakened by decades of political instability. The Soviet invasion of 1979 and the rise of radical Islamic fundamentalism have been particularly damaging, forcing the *tariqat*s to operate in a clandestine way. In Pakistan, official repression has been much less severe, yet still significant. In 1959 and 1961, the Pakistani government assumed administrative control over the shrines and began to actively discourage popular saint veneration, undermining the authority of the hereditary saints.

The status of Sufism as an integral part of Muslim life in this region is no longer as assured as it once was. It is difficult to predict how permanent the impact of decades of sociopolitical upheavals and government repression will be. Sufism is for now, officially at least, a less visible element of religious life. The Sufi tradition does nevertheless continue to function, and popular practices remain widespread.

Diane Rixon

See also: **Islam—Southwest Asia**

Further Reading

Ewing, Katherine. (1983) "The Politics of Sufism: Redefining the Saints of Pakistan." *Journal of Asian Studies* 42, 2 (February): 251–268.

Gilmartin, David. (1988) *Empire and Islam: Punjab and the Making of Pakistan.* London: I. B. Tauris.

Olesen, Asta. (1995) *Islam and Politics in Afghanistan.* Nordic Institute of Asian Studies Monograph Series, no. 67. Richmond, U.K.: Curzon.

Roy, Olivier. (1986) *Islam and Resistance in Afghanistan.* Cambridge, U.K.: Cambridge University Press.

Schimmel, Annemarie. (1975) *Mystical Dimensions of Islam.* Chapel Hill, NC: University of North Carolina Press.

SUHARTO (b. 1921), Indonesia's second president. Born 8 June 1921, Suharto, like many Javanese, was given only one name. At age nineteen he joined the Dutch colonial army (KNIL). During the Japanese occupation (1942–1945), he first worked in the Keibuho militia in Yogyakarta, later joining the Volunteer Army of the Defenders of the Fatherland (PETA). After Japanese capitulation he fought for independence from the Dutch; after independence he joined the Indonesian army.

Suharto first acquired prominence in 1961 when, as a major-general, President Sukarno appointed him operational commander under the Supreme Command for the Liberation of West New Guinea (KOTI). Suharto's ascent continued when, as commander of the army's strategic reserve (KOSTRAD),

Former president Suharto in October 1998. (AFP/CORBIS)

he crushed the supposedly Communist rebellion of 30 September 1965. Assuming command over the army—the preeminent political force in the ensuing turmoil—he led a purge of alleged Communists. By 11 March 1966, Suharto had effectively deposed Sukarno and set out to establish his New Order regime. This was implemented via the nonpartisan, nonideological system of Pancasila Democracy, which professed to foster social harmony and economic development. In March 1967 the Consultative Congress appointed Suharto acting president, and a year later, on 27 March 1968, it made him president.

In 1971 Suharto permitted general elections to confirm his rule. He achieved long-lasting stability because of his successes as "Father of Development." Encouraging oil production and Western investment, he received international awards recognizing Indonesia's successes in food production and family planning. By the late 1980s, however, Indonesia's business community was exasperated at the Suharto family's increasing control of the most lucrative areas of the economy. Moreover, liberal intellectuals were calling for more democracy, and senior military figures had begun working for Suharto's removal. With the military no longer automatically behind him, Suharto diversified his power base by courting the Muslim community. In 1990 he made his first pilgrimage to

Mecca. With the Asian economic crisis, his legitimacy collapsed, leading to his resignation on 21 May 1998.

Martin Ramstedt

Further Reading

Cribb, Robert, and Colin Brown. (1995) *Modern Indonesia: A History since 1945*. New York: Longman.

Emmerson, Donald K., ed. (1999) *Indonesia beyond Suharto: Polity, Economy, Society, Transition*. New York: M. E. Sharpe.

Hill, Hal, ed. (1994) *Indonesia's New Order: The Dynamics of Socio-Economic Transformation*. St. Leonards, Australia: Allen & Unwin.

Ramage, Douglas E. (1997) *Politics in Indonesia: Democracy, Islam, and the Ideology of Tolerance*. New York: Routledge.

Vatikiotis, Michael R. J. (1993) *Indonesian Politics under Suharto: The Rise and Fall of the New Order*. New York: Routledge.

SUI DYNASTY   The Sui (581–618 CE), a short-lived dynasty in Chinese history, was founded by Yang Jian (514–604) and ended when Yang Guang (569–618), a son of Yang Jian and the second emperor of the dynasty, was murdered by one of his generals. The dynasty reunified China after the country had experienced three centuries of division (280–581), and it initiated or completed several important institutions adopted by later dynasties.

The personal failings of Yang Guang, the harsh conscriptions of peasants for large engineering projects and military services by the state, and the continuing rivalries within aristocratic clans eventually led to rising peasant rebellions, internal struggles between political groups, and the collapse of the dynasty.

The Reign of the Emperor Wendi, 581–604

In 581, Yang Jian (541–604), a general of the Northern Zhou dynasty (557–581), deposed the last emperor of the dynasty and founded the Sui dynasty. Yang Jian had been born into an aristocratic family and was trained in horsemanship and the arts of war at an early age. He rose to prominence as a military commander, and his marriage to a daughter of another powerful aristocratic clan also helped to establish him as a leading general and politician. In 580, he was appointed the regent for the eight-year-old Northern Zhou emperor, but, within one year, Yang Jian and his supporters had weakened the power of the imperial family and were able to establish a new dynasty. In 581, Yang Jian named himself "Wendi" ("emperor of culture") of the Sui dynasty that controlled most of northern China.

Claiming to be the legitimate heir of the great Han dynasty (206 BCE–220 CE), Emperor Wendi had the ambition to rule all of China. In 581–583, he constructed a new capital city near Xi'an in east central China. In 582–584, Wendi sent forces north to Shanxi and Gansu, to attack Turkish nomads whose raids on the northern frontiers threatened China's security and stability. Having defeated these invaders and gained control of northern China, Wendi turned to southern China, which had long remained separated from the north. With careful planning, in 587 his military expeditions extinguished the puppet state of Later Liang (555–587) and controlled the central Chang (Yangtze) River area; in 589, his armies destroyed the corrupt state of Chen (557–589), and he incorporated the lower Chang area into the territory of the Sui. He had now reunified China.

In the following year, he crushed revolts on the lower Chang led by the former local aristocratic clans of the Chen state and consolidated the dynasty's control of the area. His armies also invaded the region of today's northern Vietnam in 602 and brought it briefly under the reign of the Sui dynasty.

During his reign, Emperor Wendi introduced a series of significant institutional arrangements to ensure stability. In 581, he reformed the government system that he had inherited from the previous dynasty. The power at the political center was restructured around three central ministries: the Department of State Affairs, the Chancellery, and the Secretariat, which supervised six boards: Civil Office, Finance, Rites, Army, Justice, and Public Works. By removing the office of prime minister, the emperor became the chief executive who exerted direct control of daily political and administrative affairs.

At the local level, the reform reduced the previous three-level system of administration—prefecture (*zhou*), district (*jun*), and county (*xian*)—to the two levels of prefecture and county. He also decided that only the Board of Civil Office had the authority to make appointments of local governors and magistrates, in contrast to the previous system in which local governors could appoint officials. These changes allowed the emperor to keep tight control over local areas and introduced a new era of centralization, undermining the influence of the powerful aristocratic clans who had previously often dominated through the appointments of local officials.

To improve the new political system, Wendi introduced a state examination system aimed at recruiting talented commoners into the administration. Nevertheless, aristocrats still provided a large number

CHINA—HISTORICAL PERIODS

Xia dynasty (2100–1766 BCE)
Shang dynasty (1766–1045 BCE)
Zhou dynasty (1045–256 BCE)
    Western Zhou (1045–771 BCE)
    Eastern Zhou (770–221 BCE)
Spring and Autumn period (770–476 BCE)
Warring States period (475–221 BCE)
Qin dynasty (221–206 BCE)
Han dynasty (206 BCE–220 CE)
Three Kingdoms period (220–265 CE)
North and South dynasties (220–589 CE)
Sui dyansty (581–618 CE)
Tang dynasty (618–907 CE)
Five Dynasties period (907–960 CE)
Song dynasty (960–1279)
    Northern Song (960–1126)
    Southern Song (1127–1279)
Jurchen Jin dynasty (1125–1234)
Yuan dynasty (1279–1368)
Ming dynasty (1368–1644)
Qing dynasty (1644–1912)
Republican China (1912–1927)
People's Republic of China (1949–present)
Republic of China (1949–present)
Cultural Revolution (1966–1976)

of officials to the central government because of their hereditary rights to such offices.

Wendi also reformed China's military system. In the sixth century, a military system termed *fubing* (garrison soldier) had been created in north China. To defend their territories from the nomads on the northern borders, previous rulers had established garrisons in frontier regions and had appointed a dozen generals each to control a number of garrisons. The families that provided soldiers to garrisons were registered as the inherited, professional military households and were exempted from taxation and corvée (forced-labor) obligations. Most military households were non-Han minorities. A general often maneuvered the soldiers for his political gain because he controlled them and their families for life and thus had their loyalty.

In 590, Wendi, a former *fubing* general himself, decided that all military households should be registered and administered under local prefectures and counties. This reform initiated a gradual process of demilitarization, which brought military households under the control of civil officials, dissolved the concentration of military professionals in the north, and prevented generals from contriving revolts. A by-product of this reform was a significant integration of minorities into Han Chinese society.

In economic affairs, in 582 Wendi redefined the *juntianzhi* (equal-field system) that the previous northern dynasties had created. According to his new system, at the age of twenty-one years a man was entitled to eighty *mu* (1 acre equals 6.07 *mu*) of cultivated land from the state, and a woman received half of that amount. A peasant, even if he or she did not actually own the property, had the right to pass it to his or her children and the freedom to sell it. Having received land for use, a peasant family had to pay rent *(zu)*, the de facto land tax, fulfill corvée labor for twenty days per year, and pay two bolts of cotton or silk cloth. By redistributing land to farmers and collecting tax in kind, the new dynasty intended to improve agricultural production and to establish a stable revenue resource. Although the taxation depended on whether the dynasty had effective control of the rural population, the equal-field system succeeded in fulfilling its objectives. Agricultural production recovered from the wartime disruptions of the previous era, and state granaries were filled with grain and cloth, an exception in Chinese history.

Although Wendi was sometimes cruel and hotheaded, his law, the *Kaihuang* Code (emperor's new law), which was issued in 581 and amended in 583, reduced many cruel punishments in previous Chinese laws, such as the exposure of the severed head of a criminal and the dismemberment of the body. The Code's original 1,735 clauses were reduced to 500 in 583. It retained four main types of punishments, the death penalty, deportation, forced labor, and the bastinado (beating the soles of the feet with a stick). Officials who committed crimes could pay the fines from their salaries or could commute their sentence into official demotion. The succeeding Tang dynasty followed this Code as it was revised during the Sui dynasty.

The Reign of the Emperor Yangdi, 604–618

In 604, Yang Guang, the second son of Yang Jian, succeeded to the throne after his father's death and declared himself "Yangdi" ("emperor of flaming"). Before being crowned, he had helped his father with administrative affairs and thus gained experience in ruling the country. However, in Chinese history he is known as a tyrant and a corrupt ruler whose reign was extravagant, megalomaniac, and licentious.

During his reign, Yangdi continued the institutions his father had established. He introduced more categories in the state examination, to allow more officials to be drawn from nonaristocratic classes. In 609, a census to establish the tax basis showed a total of 8.9 million registered households and a population of 46 million people.

In 605, Yangdi began to build the second Sui capital in Luoyang, several hundred kilometers to the east of Xi'an, in order to consolidate the dynasty's control of east and south China. His most important accomplishment, however, was the construction of the Grand Canal. His father had already started several canal projects, and between 605 and 610 Yangdi completed the Grand Canal that ran for two thousand kilometers between Hangzhou, an important resort city in east China, and Luoyang in the north, connecting the Chang River and the Huang (Yellow) River. Until modern railroads were laid in China, the Grand Canal was the main communication system between north and south China.

Yangdi continued employing labor forces for other projects by enforced corvée conscription. While the building of the second capital had employed 2 million laborers for ten months and the construction of the Grand Canal had required 10 million laborers working for ten years, Wendi forced 3.5 million laborers to construct roads between 607 and 608, made a quarter of a million laborers repair the Great Wall several times, and forced many workers to build traveling palaces along the Grand Canal for his use. For the fourteen years of his reign, Yangdi lived in Luoyang because it was close to south China. Nearly every year Yangdi traveled to the lower Chang, each time using thousands of boats and forcing tens of thousands of people to serve him and the local areas to pay his expenditures. One of the purposes of his travel was to collect concubines. His exhaustion of the workforce caused numerous deaths and provoked peasant resistance, but Yangdi often executed rebellious peasants when they were caught.

His worst use of military force came during his invasions of Koguryo (in modern Korea). In 598, Koguryo, a tributary kingdom of China's, had a military conflict with the Sui dynasty over the issue of south Manchuria. Using this conflict as the excuse and probably fearing a threat to China because of an alliance between the Turks and Koreans, in 612 Yangdi sent a large military force of 1.13 million to invade Koguryo. However, the expedition was not only poorly organized but also confronted strong Korean resistance; the Sui army suffered a humiliating defeat, and only 2,700 solders returned. Yet Yangdi seemed to have become obsessed with Koguryo and territorial expansion. In 613 and 614, he organized two more costly invasions. The first met defeat. Because many peasant rebellions had sprung up in China, Yangdi had to withdraw the forces from Koguryo when the Koreans asked for a peaceful surrender.

By 614, a peasant rebellion in north China, which had started in 611, had grown to 100,000 people and became a powerful challenge to the Sui dynasty. In 616 and 617, two more large peasant rebellions broke out in north and central China. Although some took place in the aftermath of floods or natural catastrophes, Yangdi's endless conscription of labor forces was probably the major provocation of these revolts. While the peasants were forced to work under harsh conditions and often died of exhaustion, Yangdi lived luxuriously and avoided hearing bad news; thus he was little informed about the true extent of the resentment in the country. His officials lied to him, and one official who spoke the truth was beaten to death. Eventually, some of his high-ranking officials also organized a rebellion, and the power struggle among the aristocratic clans intensified. In 618, Yangdi was murdered in his bathhouse by a general, a descendant of the imperial family of the dynasty from whom Yangdi's father had seized power.

Impact of the Sui Dynasty

By reunifying China, the Sui dynasty accomplished a great deal. The creative imagination of Wendi and his advisers redefined China and established a series of institutions that had lasting influence. The creation of the state examination system was particularly important for building a stable, elite bureaucracy based on education and talent, which not only changed the structure and composition of the ruling class but also changed China into a society governed by civilian officials rather than by the military aristocracy.

However, the Sui rulers tried to complete too many tasks in too short a time and exhausted the country. The rule of Yangdi triggered the collapse the dynasty. Despite its short existence, the Sui dynasty's reunification of China and its institutional accomplishments paved the way for the ascendance of the Tang dynasty during which China reached a glorious moment in its imperial history.

Yixin Chen

Further Reading
Roberts, J. A. G. (1999) *A Concise History of China*. Cambridge, MA: Harvard University Press.
Twitchett, Denis, ed. (1979) *The Cambridge History of China*. Vol. 3: *Sui and T'ang China, 589–906, Part 1*. Cambridge, U.K.: Cambridge University Press.

Wright, Arthur F. (1960) *The Confucian Persuasion*. Stanford, CA: Stanford University Press.

SUKARNO (1901–1970), nationalist leader and Indonesia's first president. Sukarno emerged as a major figure in the nationalist movement in the second half of the 1920s, both for his spellbinding oratory and for his eclectic political philosophy, which emphasized unity amongst nationalists to counter Dutch power. After studying engineering in Bandung, Sukarno founded the Partai Nasional Indonesia (Indonesian National Party) in 1927, and was jailed for sedition in 1929. He was released in 1932, but in 1933 he was exiled to Flores and from 1938 to Bengkulu. He was the most prominent nationalist figure to work with the Japanese occupation authorities after 1942, and he

A choir performs beneath a huge portrait of Sukarno in Blitar on 20 June 2001 to mark the 31st anniversary of his death. (AFP/CORBIS)

applied his oratory both to supporting the Japanese war effort and to spreading covert nationalist messages. As a member of the independence preparatory body Badan Penyelidik Usaha Persiapan Kemerdekaan Indonesia, he formulated the Pancasila in June 1945 as a statement of the moral and philosophical principles that united the otherwise disparate nationalist movement.

As the nationalist figure with broadest national standing, he was chosen president after the declaration of independence in August 1945, but his past collaboration with the Japanese was a liability in international negotiations and he was largely excluded from executive power. During the parliamentary period (1950–1957), his role remained ceremonial but he became increasingly vocal in criticizing the parliamentary system as divisive and ineffective. From 1957 he made cabinets answer to him, rather than to Parliament, and in 1959 he restored the short-lived 1945 constitution, which gave him enormous executive power. He called his political system "Guided Democracy," and emphasized its alleged roots in traditional Indonesian practice. He particularly praised *musyawarah* (thorough consultation) and *mufakat* (consensus as expressed by community leaders) as a system preferable to majority rule. In 1963 he was declared president-for-life.

As executive president, he paid little attention to administration but focused instead on nation-building, developing a unifying national ideology (NASAKOM, nationalism-religion-communism), recovering West Irian (West New Guinea), which remained under Dutch rule, and generally combatting Western imperialism. Infrastructure and administration crumbled during the early 1960s, leading to great hardship. Tension between the army and the Communist Party over the likely successor to Sukarno became enormous by 1965, culminating in an ambiguous abortive leftist coup in October 1965, which enabled General Suharto to begin pushing Sukarno from power. Sukarno ceded his executive powers to Suharto in March 1966 and was stripped of the presidency in March 1967. He died in 1970 under house arrest.

Robert Cribb

Further Reading
Dahm, Bernhard. (1969) *Sukarno and the Struggle for Indonesian Independence.* Ithaca, NY: Cornell University Press
Legge, J. D. (1984) *Sukarno: A Political Bibliography.* 2nd ed. Sydney: Allen & Unwin.

SUKHBAATAR, DAMDINY   (1893–1923), Mongolian communist leader. Damdiny Sukhbaatar was Mongolia's official national hero during the Communist era (1921–1991). Born into a serf family in Yost Beysiyn *hosuu*, in what is now Sukh-Batar Aimig, he began his military career in the Mongolian army during Mongolia's Autonomous Period (1911–1921), fighting on the eastern border with China. Later he worked as a typesetter and became involved in a revolutionary circle formed in response to Mongolia's helplessness in the face of Chinese and White Russian intervention. In August 1920, Sukhbaatar was among the members of a group sent to establish political contact with Soviet Russia. He remained at Irkutsk while others in the group went to Moscow. After returning to Mongolia in early 1921, Sukhbaatar helped organize partisan detachments to fight against the White Russian general Ungern-Sternberg (1885–1921), then occupying Mongolia.

Sukhbaatar subsequently became a member of the Central Committee of the Mongolian People's Revolutionary Party and minister of war. After the liberation of the city of Urga (now Ulaanbaatar) from the army of Ungern-Sternberg, he continued to serve as minister of war in the new Mongolian People's Republic established in October 1921, the same year of the establishment of the Mongolian People's Army. Shortly before his death, Sukhbaatar visited Soviet leader Vladimir Lenin (1870–1924) in Moscow and received the Order of the Red Banner for his contributions to the Mongolian Revolution. After his death, Sukhbaatar became the national hero of the new Mongolia. Today his remains lie in a mausoleum on Ulaanbaatar's central square, named in his honor and dominated by his equestrian statue.

Paul D. Buell

Further Reading
Bawden, C. R. (1989) *The Modern History of Mongolia.* London: Kegan Paul.
Sanders, Alan J. K. (1996) *Historical Dictionary of Mongolia.* Lanham, MD, and London: Scarecrow.

SUKHOTHAI   Meaning "Dawn of Happiness," Sukhothai is one of Thailand's most important cultural and historical centers. Roughly 430 kilometers (270 miles) north of Bangkok, Sukhothai was originally an outpost of the Khmer empire, before rival Thai princes united to overthrow the foreign rulers and establish their own kingdom. Founded in 1238, Sukhothai was the capital of the first Thai kingdom for over 125 years. Under King Ramkhamhaeng (reigned 1278–1318), Sukhothai expanded into a powerful empire, occupying parts of what is today Laos and Cambodia, and es-

SUKHOTHAI—WORLD HERITAGE SITE

Designated a UNESCO World Heritage Site in 1991, Sukhothai was the capital of the first kingdom of Siam in the thirteenth and fourteenth centuries. Many historically significant monuments can still be found among the ruins.

tablishing diplomatic relations with several other states. As a political center, Sukhothai was eventually eclipsed by other Thai kingdoms. It fell under the domination of Ayutthaya in 1365, and then, by the late eighteenth century, came under the control of the new capital of Siam at Bangkok. However, Sukhothai remained the center of a uniquely Thai culture, language, and religion. Artworks, particularly sculptures, from the Sukhothai era are national treasures in Thailand and represent some of the finest Buddhist artifacts in the world. Much of the modern Thai language, including its written script, was developed during the Sukhothai period, taken in part from Khmer, Mon, and other regional language systems. Similarly, Thai reverence for the monarchy—a system that still dominates Thailand—stems from the Sukhothai era, with its establishment of centralized rule by a benevolent monarch.

Today, Sukhothai remains a focus of Thai culture. It is renowned for its many temples, ancient ruins, and the enormous Buddhist statutes that stand guard around the city and local countryside. Far removed from the hustle of bigger cities, Sukhothai offers the experience of a more traditional Thailand, steeped in a rich history.

Arne Kislenko

Further Reading
Gosling, Betty. (1991) *Sukhothai: Its History, Culture, and Art.* Singapore: Oxford University Press.

Klausner, William J. (1987) *Thai Culture in Transition.* Bangkok, Thailand: Siam Society.

Moore, Elizabeth, Philip Stott, and Suriyavudh Sukhasvasti. (1996) *Ancient Capitals of Thailand.* Bangkok, Thailand: Asia Books.

Wyatt, David K. (1994) *Studies in Thai History.* Chiang Mai, Thailand: Silkworm.

SUKI In various Philippine languages such as Tagalog and Bisaya, the term *suki* refers not only to a regular and familiar customer but also to a preferred seller of fish, vegetables, or grocery. *Suki* is a relationship that exists between, for example, fishers and vendors who sell the fish at the market, between farmers and market vendors, and between vendors and their clients in the marketplace. These personal trade relationships are embedded in the Philippine value system.

The *suki* relationship is commonly understood in economic terms, but it has also far-reaching integrative social functions. In the Philippines, relationships with strangers are in general thought of as dangerous. Sorcery is only one possible danger. If people are forced to interact with others they do not know, they feel insecure. Therefore, everybody tries either to avoid such interactions or to transform the relationship into a personal, more secure bond. In the rural Philippines, the *suki* relationship is one possibility to establish relations to nonkin, to people from other islands, the hinterland, or the city. These relationships are based on mutual trust and obligation.

The sellers offer credit and discounts or special treatment concerning the quality (e.g., size, freshness) of their products to their *suki*. The buyers have the advantage of buying on credit, but they are also obliged to buy again from the same seller in the future. Both sides share a feeling of *utang na loob*, a debt of gratitude. For a client who has received credit from a seller, it would cause shame (*hiya*) to buy from another vendor who offers better or cheaper products. In the long run, *suki* is a reciprocally advantageous security system for people living in poor, unstable, and therefore risky circumstances.

The mutually beneficial and personal character of the *suki* relationship should not be seen as a completely harmonious, stable system without conflicts. Conflict does occur, and alliances can change through time. The *suki* relationship does not always guarantee both sides an equality of positions in bargaining. Fish vendors, for example, are in a better position than are small-scale fishermen because the latter have no real option but to accept the price asked by the vendors.

Bettina Beer

Further Reading
Hollnsteiner, Mary Racelis. (1968) *Reciprocity in the Lowland Philippines.* In *Four Readings on Philippine Values*, edited by Frank Lynch. Quezon City, Philippines: Ateneo de Manila University Press, 22–49.

Jocano, F. Landa. (1997) *Filipino Value System: A Cultural Definition.* Metro Manila, Philippines: Punlad Research House.

Kawada, Makito. (1994) "Public Market in Bantayan: Social Ties in Local Economic Activities." In *Fishers of the*

Visayas, edited by Iwao Ushijima and Cynthia Neri Zayas. Visayas Maritime Anthropological Studies, 1. Diliman, Quezon City, Philippines: CSSP Publications, University of the Philippines, 203–231.

SULAK SIVARAKSA

SULAK SIVARAKSA (b. 1933), Thai intellectual and social activist. Sulak Sivaraksa is perhaps Thailand's best-known intellectual committed to social activism and criticism. He was educated in England. Upon returning to Thailand he taught at both Chulalongkorn and Thammasat Universities. From 1963 to 1969, he was editor of the influential *Social Science Review.* He is credited by many (from both the left and right) for playing a major role in persuading Thai students to abandon their political passivity fostered by military dictatorships and to become much more politically conscious and active. These students subsequently mobilized in a massive demonstration to overthrow Thailand's military dictatorship on 14 October 1973.

Sulak's thinking has been strongly influenced by the prominent Thai politician/philosopher Pridi Banomyong; the professor/technocrat Dr. Puey Ungphakorn; Gandhi; Buddhadasa Bhikku, a prominent Thai Buddhist thinker; Thich Nhat Hanh, a prominent overseas Vietnamese Buddhist thinker; E. F. Schumacher, British author of *Small Is Beautiful;* and the Quakers. He has done extensive grassroots organizing in Thailand, founding many key nongovernmental organizations oriented toward an alternative, more humanistic, sustainable form of development. He is highly critical of Thailand's modern consumer society and prefers the traditional term "Siam" to Thailand.

Because of his radical thinking, he has on several occasions been arrested by the government for lèse-majesté and for expressing provocative views and has spent time in exile (1976–1978, 1991–1992). Ultimately, he has been acquitted of charges against him or granted amnesty. In both 1993 and 1994 Sulak was nominated for the Nobel Peace Prize, and he is a recipient of the Right Livelihood Award. Sulak is a prolific writer, and several of his many publications are listed in the references below. Sulak has been a major figure over five decades in fostering Thai civil society.

Gerald W. Fry

Further Reading
Sulak Sivaraksa. (1980) *Siam in Crisis: Collected Articles by S. Sivaraksa.* Bangkok, Thailand: Komol Keemthong Foundation.
———. (1985) *Siamese Resurgence: A Thai Buddhist Voice on Asia and a World of Change.* Bangkok, Thailand: Asian Cultural Forum on Development.
———. (1988) *A Socially Engaged Buddhism.* Bangkok, Thailand: Inter-Religious Commission for Development.
———. (1992) *Seeds of Peace: A Buddhist Vision for Renewing Society.* Berkeley, CA: Parallax.
———. (1993) *When Loyalty Demands Dissent: Sulak Sivaraksa and the Charge of Lese Majeste in Siam 1991–1993.* Bangkok, Thailand: Santi Pracha Dhamma Institute.
———. (1998) *Loyalty Demands Dissent: Autobiography of an Engaged Buddhist.* Berkeley, CA: Parallax Press.

SULAWESI

SULAWESI (2002 pop. 14.4 million). Sulawesi, formerly known as Celebes, is a large island in the Malay Archipelago in eastern Indonesia. It is divided into four provinces: Sulawesi Utara (North Celebes), Sulawesi Tengah (Central Celebes), Sulawesi Tenggara (Southeast Celebes), and Sulawesi Selatan (South Celebes). Manado in the north and Ujung Pandang (formerly Macassar) in the south are the largest cities. Mountainous, volcanic, and unusual in shape, Sulawesi consists of four large peninsulas covering 227,654 square kilometers.

Sulawesi lies in the transition zone between Asiatic and Australian flora and fauna and has a tropical climate with distinct rainy and dry seasons. There are extensive teak forests and many kinds of orchids; fauna include unique animals such as the *anoa* (dwarf buffalo) and babirusa (large wild swine) as well as tapirs and *maleo* birds. The economy is based on subsistence agriculture, especially rice, and on the export of such products as timber, spices, cacao, coconuts, fish, and minerals. Predominant indigenous groups include the Toraja, Buginese, Makassarese, and Minahasa.

Ruled by Buddhist and Hindu empires prior to the rise of Islamic states in the sixteenth century, the island was later colonized by the Dutch, who arrived in 1609. In recent times, there has been conflict between the large Christian minority and the Muslim majority in the city of Poso in central Sulawesi.

Michael Pretes

Further Reading
Ricklefs, Merle Calvin. (2001) *A History of Modern Indonesia since c. 1200.* Basingstoke, U.K.: Palgrave.
Whitten, Anthony, Muslimin Mustafa, and Gregory S. Henderson. (2001) *The Ecology of Sulawesi.* Boston: Tuttle.

SULAYMANIYA

SULAYMANIYA (2002 est. region pop. 1.5 million; 2002 est. city pop. 643,000). The region of Sulaymaniya, a *muhafaza* (governorate) in northeast Iraq and southeast Kurdistan, and the ancient city of the same name, are rich in history. Sulaymaniya is 90 kilometers east of the city of Kirkuk and has an altitude of 838 meters. It is west of the natural mountainous frontier of Iraq and Iran and north of the Diyala River and its tributaries, the Tandjaru and Sirwan, and the Little Zab River.

Nearby is Mount Nisir, where the ship of Utnapishtim (the prototype for the biblical Noah) came to rest after a great deluge, as told in the epic of Gilgamesh, an ancient Mesopotamian hero. In 745 BCE, the Assyrian ruler Tiglath-pileser III (745–727 BCE) captured Arameans in Mazamua, near present-day Sulaymaniya. Part of the Syrian Church's diocese of Beth Garmai was located in the region around 4 BCE.

Sulaymaniya, like much of Kurdistan during the medieval Islamic period (661–1514), enjoyed virtual autonomy, although all of the major Islamic dynasties—from the Umayyad on—nominally ruled over the area. During the Ottoman empire (1453–1922), the strongest local dynasty was the Baban (1500–1850), ruled by emirs and *pir*s (chiefs). In 1850, however, the Ottomans crushed these local rulers, and political authority passed to religious sheikhs led by the Barzinja family, whose ancestor, Hadji Kaka Ahmad, is buried in Sulaymaniya city.

After a prolonged dispute between Turkey and Britain from 1923 to 1926, the region of Sulaymaniya became an official part of Iraq in June 1925. Britain controlled Sulaymaniya as part of the Mandate of Iraq until 1958. However, from 1919 to 1927, Sheikh Mahmud, a Kurdish leader demanding greater autonomy for the Kurds, controlled much of Sulaymaniya; at one time he proclaimed himself the king of Kurdistan.

From the end of British control in 1958 to the end of the twentieth century, the Sulaymaniya region was in constant conflict with the Iraq government and was the center of contention for the Kurdish nationalist movement in Iraq. The discord began in 1965, when Jalal Talabani (b. 1933) broke from the dominating Kurdistan Democratic Party (KDP), led by the legendary Kurdish leader Molla Mustafa Barzani (1903–1979). In 1975, Talabani created the Patriotic Union of Kurdistan (PUK), which was based in Sulaymaniya. The accord following the Persian Gulf War of 1991 provided a Kurdish safe haven—and air protection by the United States and Great Britain—for the region above the thirty-sixth parallel, but conflict between the KDP and PUK increased from 1992 to 2000. By 2000, the PUK was drawing closer to Iran and the KDP to Turkey and the United States; these alignments impeded the development of unity in this region of northern Iraq and southern Kurdistan, which is controlled by the Kurds.

By 2000, nearly all of the population of the city was Kurdish. Under the control of the PUK, Salaymaniya was becoming the cultural, medical, and educational center of Kurdistan Iraq, while sharing political power with the Kurdish Regional Government in Arbil, which was under the control of the KDP.

Robert Olson

Further Reading
Edmonds, Cecil J. (1957) *Kurds, Turks, and Arabs: Politics, Travel, and Research in North-Eastern Iraq, 1919*. London: Oxford University Press.

Hassanpour, Amir. (1992) *Nationalism and Language in Kurdistan, 1918–1945*. San Francisco: Mellen Research University Press.

Van Bruinessen, Martin. (1992) *Agha, Shaikh, and State: The Social and Political Structure of Kurdistan*. London: Zed.

SULEIMENOV, OLZHAS OMAROVICH
(b. 1936), Kazakh writer and politician. Olzhas Omarovich Suleimenov contributed to the rise of Kazakh nationalism during the Soviet era by publishing his controversial book *Az i Ia* (1975), which was a historical-philosophical essay on Turkic historical destiny, the history of interaction between nomads (Turks) and settlers (Slavs), and the place of the Kazakhs in the historical development of Eurasia. Born in Almaty, Suleimenov worked as a journalist and editor before his book won him nationwide recognition and a reputation as the "opener of the difficult issues in national history." The book was condemned by Moscow policymakers as nationalistic and was banned until 1989.

With the introduction of Gorbachev's policy of glasnost, Suleimenov became increasingly active in Kazakh political life, sharply criticizing Moscow policymakers' mistakes in Kazakhstan. In February 1989, Olzhas Suleimenov, on the wave of the growing criticism of nuclear testing in Semipalatinsk, founded one of the first political movements in Kazakhstan—*Nevada-Semipalatinsk*. This movement became a prominent and influential nongovernmental organization from 1989 to 1991, preceding the rise of national parties and organizations. In 1991 he founded the People's Congress of Kazakhstan.

Suleimenov remains one of the most popular writers and politicians in post-Soviet Kazakhstan. He supports moderate nationalism, liberal reforms, and a balanced approach to the Law on Languages. He and his supporters have contributed to moderating mainstream Kazakh nationalism by making it more liberal and compromising.

Rafis Abazov

Further Reading
Harsha, Ram. (2001) "Imagining Eurasia: The Poetics and Ideology of Olzhas Suleimenov's Az i Ia." *Slavic Review* 60, 2: 289–311.
Suleimenov, Olzhas. ([1989] 1992) *Az i Ia* Almaty, Kazakhstan: Kazakhstan Publishing House.

SULU ARCHIPELAGO Stretching northeast to southwest from Basilan Island, south of Mindanao's Zamboanga peninsula, to Sabah, Malaysia, the Sulu archipelago exceeds 320 kilometers (200 miles) in length, consists of over 500 islands, and occupies an area of 2,813 square kilometers (1,086 square miles). It is surrounded on the north and west by the Sulu and Mindanao seas and on the south and west by the Celebes Sea.

Islam was first introduced to the Philippines in the Sulu archipelago in the late thirteenth century. A majority of the population (97 percent) is Muslim. Politically the archipelago is comprised of two provinces: Sulu and Tawi-Tawi, with a combined population in 1995 of 787,000. In a 1989 plebiscite Sulu and Tawi-Tawi joined the Autonomous Region of Muslim Mindanao. Most of the inhabitants of the archipelago belong to one of three ethnic groups: Tausug, Samal, and Bajau. Commercially, numerically, and politically, the Tausug is the dominant group.

Dating back to the Spanish and American colonial periods, the Muslims of the Sulu archipelago have a long history of resistance. In the early 1970s, Nur Misuari, a Tausug, formed the Moro National Liberation Front seeking the secession of Mindanao and Sulu from the Philippines. The ensuing guerrilla war against the Philippine army resulted in 50,000 casualties.

Robert L. Youngblood

Further Reading
Majul, Cesar Adib. (1985) *The Contemporary Muslim Movement in the Philippines.* Berkeley, CA: Mizan.
Nimmo, Harry A. (1994) *The Songs of Salanda and Other Stories of Sulu.* Seattle, WA: University of Washington Press.
Sleeby, Najeeb M. (1908) *The History of Sulu.* Manila, Philippines: Bureau of Printing.

SUMATRA (2000 pop. 42.7 million). Sumatra, Indonesia's second-largest and westernmost island, is populated by a number of distinct peoples, including the Acehnese, Minangkabau, Batak, and Malay. Its earliest major states were coastal trading kingdoms; these were often situated on river mouths, where they could control the flow of goods up and down stream. From the late seventh century onwards, the state of Srivijaya was the most powerful Sumatran empire, until it was eclipsed in the fourteenth century. The first evidence of the arrival of Islam in Sumatra comes from Marco Polo, who visited the island c. 1292. The nineteenth

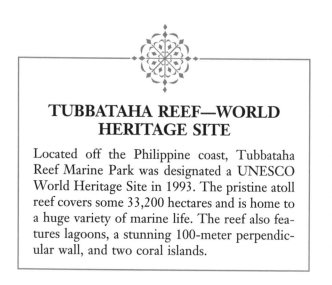

TUBBATAHA REEF—WORLD HERITAGE SITE

Located off the Philippine coast, Tubbataha Reef Marine Park was designated a UNESCO World Heritage Site in 1993. The pristine atoll reef covers some 33,200 hectares and is home to a huge variety of marine life. The reef also features lagoons, a stunning 100-meter perpendicular wall, and two coral islands.

century witnessed profound changes: politically, Dutch colonial rule was gradually imposed throughout the entire island; and since the 1860s the introduction of plantation crops, especially tobacco and rubber, and the exploitation of oil have turned Sumatra into the archipelago's richest export area. Under the Japanese occupation (1942–1945), the island was administratively united with Malaysia, but in 1945 local nationalist leaders supported the pro-Republican cause, bringing Sumatra under Indonesian control. In 1958 a rebel government, the PRRI (Revolutionary Government of the Indonesian Republic), was announced in Sumatra. This rebellion was crushed in 1961, consolidating the hegemony of Java over the outer islands, and the heavily Javanese army over other political forces. Since Suharto stepped down in 1998, decentralization, regional autonomy, federalism, and separatism have once again become hotly debated issues throughout Indonesia, especially in the Sumatran provinces Aceh and Riau.

Edwin Wieringa

Further Reading

Carle, Rainer, C. E. Cunningham, and B. Dahm, eds. (1987) *Cultures and Societies of North Sumatra*. Berlin: Reimer.

Marsden, William. (1975) *The History of Sumatra*. Kuala Lumpur, Malaysia: Oxford University Press.

Ricklefs, Merle C. (1981) *A History of Modern Indonesia*. London: Macmillan.

SUMMER PALACE Thanks to its well-documented and tragic history, the Summer Palace of Beijing is one of the most famous imperial parks worldwide. It became known in the West when Father Attiret in 1743 mailed a report on its garden that helped change the history of landscape design. The ruins of Yuanming Yuan (Garden of Perfect Brightness) and the placid waters of Yihe Yuan (Garden of Concord and Peace) form a Chinese tourist attraction that is second only to the Forbidden City. Improperly so called because the Qing (1644–1912) court used to spend summers away from Beijing in the cooler hills of Chengde, the Summer Palace is a vast complex of gardens, lakes, pavilions, temples, and hills located only 10 kilometers from the walls of Beijing. It encompasses the Yuanming Yuan residence of the Kangxi emperor (1654–1722) and the Qianlong emperor (1711–1799) and the Yihe Yuan residence that the Cixi dowager empress (1835–1908) built in 1888. A French-British military expedition destroyed the Summer Palace in 1860; only the western section was restored. Within its present limits, the Yihe Yuan

SUMMER PALACE—WORLD HERITAGE SITE

The Summer Palace in Beijing was designated a UNESCO World Heritage Site in 1998 for its superb landscape architecture that incorporates the disparate elements of temples, gardens, pavilions, temples, and palaces.

Summer Palace consists of Kunming Lake and Wanshou Hill, whose Buddhist temples dominate the site.

Philippe Foret

Further Reading

Wong, Young-tsu. (2001) *A Paradise Lost: The Imperial Garden Yuanming Yuan*. Honolulu, HI: University of Hawaii Press.

SUMO. See **Sports—Japan.**

SUN BEAR An endangered species, the sun bear *(Helarctos malayanus)* has a short, sleek coat with a whitish or orange U-shaped crescent mark on its chest

The Malayan sun bear. (YOGI, INC./CORBIS)

and muzzle, which gives the animal its name. It is also known as the honey bear due to its habit of ripping into bees' nests for honey. The sun bear is the smallest member of the bear family. Its coat is a deep brown to black color. Perfectly equipped for an omnivore diet, with large jaws for cracking open hard fruits, long curved claws, naked soles, and an extraordinarily long tongue, the bear can easily tear apart trees and eat the insects found inside; it also eats small birds. A Malayan sun bear adult male can grow to be about 122 centimeters when standing on its hind legs and can weigh up to 308 kilograms. A female usually weighs about 132 kilograms. Skillful climbers, the bears spend most of their time in the trees; they are primarily nocturnal and nap and sunbathe during the day. Due to the tropical climates of the bears' habitat in Southeast Asia—Bangladesh, Borneo, Burma, Cambodia, Laos, Vietnam, Malaysia, Thailand, and Sumatra—the bears are not known to hibernate.

Stacey Fox

Further Reading
Craighead, Lance. (2000) *Bears of the World*. Stillwater, MN: Voyageur.

SUN YAT-SEN (1866–1925), Chinese revolutionary. Sun Yat-sen was born near Guangzhou (Canton) to a farming family. His personal name was Wen, his style or secondary name was Yat-sen, and his revolutionary name, by which he is better known in China, was Zhongshan (Chung-shan). Sun first attended a village school, then went to Honolulu at age thirteen with his elder brother for his secondary education, and later received a medical degree from the College for Medicine for Chinese in Hong Kong. Disgusted with the ineffectiveness of the Qing (Manchu) dynasty (1644–1912), he became a revolutionary. Travels to Hawaii, Hong Kong, and later in Britain and the United States had a profound influence on the young Sun.

In 1894, he formed the Review China Society among overseas Chinese with the goal of expelling the Manchus and forming a republic. He later formulated a set of ideals for the republic called the Three People's Principles: nationalism, democracy, and livelihood, which are roughly analogous to Abraham Lincoln's "of the people, by the people, and for the people." Sun also envisioned the amalgamation of the best Western concepts of government with those of traditional China in a five-power constitution consisting of the executive, legislative, and judiciary plus a censorate (to check abuses by officials) and an examination system for the recruitment of a bureaucracy. In

1905, the Revive China Society was subsumed by the Tungmeng Hui (United League), with membership among Chinese students abroad, military officers of the Qing army, and overseas Chinese.

After ten abortive uprisings between 1895 and 1911, the eleventh, the Wuchang Uprising of 10 October 1911, spread like wildfire. It resulted in Sun's election as provisional president of the Republic of China and the abdication of the Manchu emperor on 12 February 1912. Sun resigned as president in favor of General Yuan Shikai on condition that the latter supported the republic.

Yuan, however, betrayed the republic by abrogating the elected parliament, which was dominated by the Nationalist Party (the Tungmeng Hui became the Nationalist Party or Guomindang in 1912), culminating in his failed attempt to become emperor. After Yuan's usurpation attempt, politics in China degenerated into civil wars between rival warlords.

Frustrated in his attempts to obtain help from Western democracies, Sun turned to the newly established Communist government in Russia for military and organizational help in 1922 and agreed to the Russian stipulation that the Nationalists accept members of the infant Chinese Communist Party into their ranks. Sun then reorganized the Nationalist Party and commissioned his lieutenant, Chiang Kai-shek (1887–1975), to build up an army committed to his ideology. Sun died in 1925 in Beijing during a last attempt to negotiate a peaceful unification of China.

Sun is honored as the father of the republic. The Three People's Principles are the guiding ideology of the Republic of China on Taiwan, where the people have achieved democracy and where the principle of livelihood has been realized in the high standard of living and largely equitable distribution of income among all citizens.

Jiu-Hwa Lo Upshur

Further Reading
Bergere, M. C. (1998) *Sun Yat-Sen*. Stanford, CA: Stanford University Press.
Schiffrin, Harold. (1968) *Sun Yat-sen and the Origins of the Chinese Revolution*. Berkeley and Los Angeles: University of California Press.
———. (1980) *Sun Yat-sen: Reluctant Revolutionary*. Boston: Little, Brown.
Sharman, Lyon. ([1934] 1968) *Sun Yat-sen: His Life and Its Meaning*. Reprint ed. Stanford, CA: Stanford University Press.
Wilbur, C. Martin. (1976) *Sun Yat-sen: Frustrated Patriot*. New York: Columbia University Press.

SUN YIXIAN. See **Sun Yat-sen.**

SUNDANESE   The Sundanese are one of Indonesia's main ethnic groups, inhabiting the Sunda area of the western part of Java. This area stretches from the Bogor and Sukabumi Regencies in the west, to the Kuningan and Banjar Regencies in the east, which border the Cirebon Regency of Central Java province. The area comprises mostly rugged mountains in its south and center, with a flat fertile lowland in the north that serves as Indonesia's largest rice production area.

The Sundanese form the majority in the province of West Java (population 35.5 million) and are Indonesia's second-largest ethnic group after the Javanese who inhabit the central and eastern parts of Java. While related culturally to the Javanese, they maintain a distinct culture, apparent from different language, costumes, and traditions.

Historically, the largest Sundanese kingdom was Padjadjaran, a Hindu kingdom whose seat was in the eastern part of the Sunda lands. Even at the height of the Majapahit, a Javanese kingdom whose sway encompassed much of present-day Indonesia, Padjadjaran enjoyed freedom until finally subdued in the Bubat War of 1357 CE. Because of this war, many Sundanese still remain uneasy about their relationship with the Javanese.

Unlike the Javanese kingdoms, whose historical monuments (*candi*, "temples") are scattered around their heartland, Sundanese kingdoms left few monuments. It is believed that the Sundanese did not use stone in building palaces or places of worship, instead using the wood that was abundant in their land. During the struggle for Indonesian independence, the Sundanese created their own state, Negara Pasundan, in 1947, which eventually became one of the states within the federal Republic of the United States of Indonesia. When federalism was abandoned in 1950, Pasundan disbanded, becoming the province of West Java in the unitary Republic of Indonesia. Many Sundanese have occupied important positions in the Indonesian government. The most prominent of these were Djuanda Kartawidjaja (prime minister, 1959; first minister 1959–1963) and Umar Wirahadikusumah (vice president, 1983–1988).

Irman G. Lanti

Further Reading
Pincus, Jonathan. (1996) *Class Power and Agrarian Change: Land and Labor in Rural West Java*. New York: St. Martin's.

Rosidi, Ajip, et al., eds. (2000) *Ensiklopedi Sunda: Alam, Manusia dan Budaya: Termasuk Budaya Cirebon dan Betawi* (Sunda Encyclopedia: Nature, Man, and Culture: Including Cirebon and Betawi Cultures). Jakarta, Indonesia: Pustaka Jaya.

Williams, Sean. (2001) *The Sound of the Ancestral Ship: Highland Music of West Java*. Oxford: Oxford University Press.

SUNDARBHANS   The Sundarbhans (or Sunderbans) are the densely forested wetlands of the sea-face delta of the combined Ganges and Brahmaputra River, as they empty into the Bay of Bengal. Two-thirds of the area falls within Bangladesh, and the western third in West Bengal State, India. This area is about 200 kilometers from east to west and 50 kilometers from north to south, the much indented coast forming its southern boundary. The western boundary is the Hooghly River and the eastern the Meghna. Despite the relative closeness of Calcutta to the north, the Sundarbhans were once generally inaccessible and desolate; but since 1990 the West Bengal government has been promoting the area for tourism. The Sundharbans are today the world's largest remaining tropical mangrove forest, a national park where there is a great variety of wildlife, including Bengal tigers, deer, boar, monkeys, and crocodiles. The human population is reportedly very sparse.

Paul Hockings

Further Reading
Greenough, Paul. (1998) "Hunter's Drowned Land: An Environmental Fantasy of the Victorian Sunderbans." In *Nature and the Orient: The Environmental History of South and Southeast Asia*, edited by Richard H. Grove, Vinita Damodaran, and Satpal Sangwan. Delhi: Oxford University Press, 237–272.

SUNG DYNASTY.   See **Song Dynasty.**

SURABAYA   (2000 pop. 8 million). Surabaya, Indonesia's second largest city and capital of East Java, is situated at the mouth of the Brantas River opposite Madura island. Legend has it that Surabaya derived its name from a ferocious fight between a shark (*sura*) and a crocodile (*baya*) in the Mas River. According to official accounts, Surabaya was founded on 31 May 1293. Sunan Ngampel-Denta, one of the nine saints who Islamized Java, is said to have lived in Surabaya in the second half of the fifteenth century. In the sixteenth century the kingdom of Surabaya was the leading power in East Java, being a center of culture, but in

1625 it was forced to surrender to Mataram. It was seized by the Dutch East India Company in 1743. Since the second half of the nineteenth century, Surabaya has been transformed into the metropolis it is today. The area of Greater Surabaya, known as Gerbangkertosusila, "Gate to Prosperity and Decency" (an acronym: Gresik-Bangkalan-Majakerta-Surabaya-Sidoarjo-Lamongan), taking up 12 percent of the province of East Java, is nowadays inhabited by more than 8 million people. The tenth of November 1945, when Surabaya was the scene of heavy fighting between Indonesian nationalist forces and British troops, is commemorated as Heroes' Day.

Edwin Wieringa

Further Reading

Broeshart, A. C., J. R. van Diessen, R. G. Gill, and J. P. Zeydner. (1997) *Soerabaja: Beeld van een stad*. Purmerend, Netherlands: Asia Maior.

Frederick, William Hayward. (1978) "Indonesian Urban Society in Transition: Surabaya, 1926–1946." Ph.D. diss., University of Hawaii.

McCutcheon, L. (1977) "Migrant Adjustment in Surabaya, Indonesia." Ph.D. diss., Brown University.

Silas, J. (1980) "Villages in Transition: A Case Study of Rural to Urban Transformation in Surabaya." *Prisma* 9, 17: 36–45.

SURKHOB RIVER A major Central Asian river also known as the Kunduz in its lower course, the Surkhob is one of the major tributaries of the Amu Dar'ya (Oxus). The river rises in Afghanistan in the Baba Range of the Hindu Kush and flows for 420 kilometers, draining a basin of some 31,300 square kilometers. Like many other rivers in the region, its flow is heavily dependent on meltwater, with the greatest flow occurring in spring and early summer. The river's mean annual flow is 120 cubic meters per second, though this varies according to season. Within Afghanistan, the river's waters are used for electricity generation at the Pul-i Khrumri plant, supplying power to the north of the country.

The name "Surkhob" is also given to the western end of the river Vakhsh at the confluence of the Kyzylsu and the Muksu in Tajikistan; all three rivers form a single tributary of the Amu Dar'ya. Fed by meltwater and experiencing its greatest flow in July (3,120 cubic meters per second), and with an average of 660 cubic meters per second, this river of 524 kilometers and a catchment of 39,100 square kilometers has been heavily used for irrigation (the irrigation system is controlled

from the town of Vakhsh) and hydroelectric power, resulting in heavy soil salinization in the lower reaches, although these remain navigable. Qurghonteppa (Kurgan-Tyube or Kuragn-Teppe) is the main town on this river, with a railway link to the capital, Dushanbe.

Will Myer

Further Reading

Great Soviet Encyclopaedia. (1978) London and New York: Macmillan.

Shul'ts, V. L. (1965) *Reki Srednei Azii* (Rivers of Central Asia). Leningrad, USSR: Nauk.

SUSTAINABILITY Sustainability has been variously defined, but for Asia it means not only long-term growth prospects but also the ability of the natural environment to sustain the large population and economic expansion in the region. Development, reflected in varying degrees of industrialization, urbanization, and integration with the global economy, is progressing at different rates and in different directions. Given that some 60 percent of the world's population is living in Asia, there are major challenges to development and its long-term sustainability. Among the countries that make up Asia are some with the largest populations in the world—China, India, and Indonesia.

Until the financial crisis and resultant economic downturn in Asia in 1997, countries in Southeast Asia and East Asia were experiencing among the world's fastest rates of economic growth. These rapidly industrializing economies had secured an estimated 10 percent share of the world's markets. Rapid economic growth and industrialization can be attributed to the region's relatively open policy toward foreign investment. Indeed, the Asian countries, particularly those in East and Southeast Asia, were actively competing for foreign direct investment.

The rapid pace of industrialization in Asia, particularly East and Southeast Asia, is not surprising because the region can be considered one of the richest in natural resources in the world. Raw materials range from West Asia's and Southeast Asia's oil resources to fisheries in Southeast Asia and the rain forests of Indonesia. Indeed, the region's natural resources made it the target of colonizing powers in the past. Now, not only does Asia provide most of the energy needed in the rest of the world, but it also has large shares of the world's market for shrimp and other food resources. In addition, it has a huge population base, which implies not only large markets but also a large and relatively inexpensive labor pool.

Rapid Industrialization and Economic Growth

Indicators of growth in industry and, particularly, manufacturing in the rapidly industrializing regions of Asia provide some idea of how fast development has occurred. Whereas in 1990 energy consumption in the rapidly industrializing regions of Asia, such as East and Southeast Asia, was estimated at about 1 billion metric tons, consumption had increased to 1.5 billion metric tons in 2000. Trade as a percentage of gross domestic product (GDP) for East Asia increased from 17 percent in 1990 to 58 percent in 1996, the year before the onset of what is now known as the Asian economic crisis. Overall the growth in gross national product (GNP) per capita between 1965 and 1996 was 5.5 percent for East Asia and 6.7 percent for China alone. South Asia lagged to some extent and registered a growth figure in GNP per capita between 1965 and 1996 of 2.2 percent.

In the economies of most Asian countries, agriculture remains important in spite of the more rapid growth of the manufacturing and services sectors. The primary industries that are focused on the processing of natural resources, such as the oil or timber industries, remain important for the revenues of Asian countries, particularly those in West Asia and some of the Southeast Asian states, such as Brunei and Indonesia. There has also been much attention paid to the tourism sector, which has been exploiting the natural environment, such as the beaches and warm water of the coastal areas, as well as heritage areas. The latter are widely distributed throughout Asia, given that some of the world's oldest civilizations—the Chinese, Indian, and Arabian—and some of the world's major religions, such as Buddhism, Hinduism, and Islam, originated there. In small Southeast Asian countries like the city-state of Singapore, the tourism sector has contributed 16 percent to the GDP.

Urbanization

With industrialization has come rapid urbanization, because cities have been the foci of foreign investment in both industrial and service sectors. Many of the cities have expanded to become metropolitan regions through the extension of transport infrastructure and built-up areas. These so-called mega-urban regions have doubled in population every fifteen to twenty years, and some have population densities of more than thirty thousand people per square kilometer.

The wealth of Asia's cities has been a strong magnet for international and local labor migration, both skilled and unskilled. On intraregional and international levels, low-skilled workers have gravitated to rich countries from poorer countries in search of higher wages, usually in domestic and blue-collar work eschewed by locals. The intraregional and international flows of workers only add to the burgeoning populations, which had already been increasing rapidly due to internal rural-urban flows of people looking for work as well as higher wages.

Environmental Impact and Sustainable Growth

Rapid economic growth based on natural resources as well as rapid industrialization has had an enormous impact on the natural environment in Asia. The fast pace of urbanization has further exacerbated the burden on the environment, so that the pollution and degradation that are evident can be described as just short of disastrous. The flip side to the rising consumption of energy is the rising volume of carbon emissions.

Environmental conditions in Asia, compared with other regions in the rest of the world and with world averages, are poor: intense pollution levels have been registered there between 1991 and 1995. For air pollution, indicators such as particulates (milligrams per cubic meter) put the level at 248, compared with 40 for Latin America, 49 for the Organization for Economic Cooperation and Development (OECD) countries, and 29 for Africa. The pollution level was twice the world average, which was 126. For sulfur dioxide, a toxic gas (milligrams per cubic liter), the level for Asia was 0.023, higher than Africa's 0.015 and Latin America's 0.014. The level was higher only in the OECD countries, at 0.068, and the world average, at 0.059, was only slightly higher than in Asia. Water pollution appeared equally intense, judging from the suspended solids (milligrams per liter), at a level of 638, compared with 224 in Africa and 97 in Latin America. Levels in the OECD countries and overall world average were 20 and 151, respectively. Other indicators, such as the biochemical oxygen demand (BOD) levels (milligrams per liter), were also substantially above the world average, which was 3.5. Asia's level was 4.8, higher than Africa's 4.3, Latin America's 1.6, and the OECD countries' 3.2.

A combination of rapid urban and industrial growth together with the widespread environmental strategy of growing first and cleaning up later has contributed to the environmental problems now seen in Asia. There has, therefore, been low energy efficiency within industry, natural-resource depletion, materials-intensive production, pollution of rivers and groundwater supplies, as well as unhealthy air, particularly in cities. Enforcement of environmental laws has been difficult because of limited resources, the sizes of the countries, and the prevalence of small- and medium-sized industries in most of developing Asia. The new wealth from rapid economic growth has also led to a boom in private transportation, resulting in massive traffic congestion in many Asian cities.

The result has been poor living and working conditions for workers and their families, including slum formation and the intensive environmental degradation associated with it; air pollution from increased traffic between residences and workplaces, schools and shops; appropriation and depletion of environmental resources for urban use, such as rural reservoirs for urban water supplies; multiple-source water and land pollution; noise from traffic and construction; and loss of prime agricultural land, coastal ecologies, regional forests, and upland vegetation around (larger) cities targeted for resource extraction, industrial location, and infrastructure and housing development.

Several examples of the environmental impact of rapid industrialization and urbanization serve to illustrate the slim balance in which sustainability hangs in Asia. One instance has been the regional haze arising from forest fires in Indonesia, which were started in order to clear land for conversion of forests to plantations of oil palm. Forest fires had burned huge areas in Indonesia's old-growth tropical forests long before the major 1997–1998 fires that wiped out nearly 10 million hectares. During the dry season that is experienced in the region, the fires have become uncontrollable, and a haze has been caused because of the fires as well as the continued burning of the underground peat long after the forests have been destroyed. This haze has enveloped neighboring areas in Malaysia and Singapore as well as southern Thailand. Its regular occurrence has considerably affected tourism in the region and caused widespread health problems for people living in the affected areas.

Across Asia, per capita availability of water declined by about 50 percent between 1955 and 1990. Asia has the lowest per capita availability of freshwater in the world, with Central Asia and parts of Southeast Asia already well above the threshold of "high water-stress" conditions (when the ratio of use to availability exceeds 40 percent). Indeed, some countries in Central Asia are already using 90 percent of their available freshwater resources. Use of available freshwater resources is 25 percent in the northern portions of China and Mongolia. Many other parts of Asia will suffer the same fate during the next twenty-five years. China and India, with projected populations of 1.5 and 1.4 billion, respectively, by 2025, will encounter serious water shortage.

Future Sustainability

Not surprisingly, most countries in Asia are not rated very high in indexes of sustainability. Countries such as Japan and Singapore generally fare unfavorably in terms of sustainability compared with Scandinavia and other developed countries. Given the environmental sustainability problems, there is much cause for concern about the long-term economic development prospects of Asia. Already the Southeast Asian region and some of the East Asian economies have experienced a major financial and economic crisis in 1997. This has seen new flows of foreign direct investment go largely to China, which is undergoing a major economic boom. Yet China, too, faces the myriad economic, social, and environmental sustainability issues of other regions within Asia. Only careful and effective management of both growth and its environmental impact can help Asia maintain its course of high growth on a sustainable and long-term basis.

Ooi Giok Ling

Further Reading

Dauvergne, P. (2000) "Globalisation and Environmental Change: Asia's 1997 Financial Crisis." *Current History* (November): 389–395.

Douglass, Mike. (1998) "East Asian Urbanization: Patterns, Problems, and Prospects," Project Discussion Paper. Stanford, CA: Asia/Pacific Research Center, Institute for International Studies, Stanford University.

Douglass, Mike, and Ooi Giok Ling. (2000) "Industrialising Cities and the Environment." In *Asia's Clean Revolution: Industry, Growth, and the Environment*, edited by David P. Angel and Michael T. Rock. London: Greenleaf, 104–127.

Kog, Yue-Choong. (2000) "Natural Resource Management and Environmental Security in Southeast Asia: Case Study of Clean Water Supplies to Singapore." Institute of Defence and Strategic Studies Working Paper, no. 15. Singapore: Nanyang Technological University.

Lohani, B. (1998) *Environmental Challenges in Asia in the 21st Century*. Manila, Philippines: Asian Development Bank.

McGee, Terry G. (1997) "Five Decades of Urbanization in Southeast Asia—A Personal Encounter." Occasional Paper, no. 60. Shatin, Hong Kong: Hong Kong Institute of Asia-Pacific Studies, Chinese University of Hong Kong, 43.

World Bank. (1998) *East Asia: The Road to Recovery*. Washington, DC: World Bank.

SUTLEJ RIVER Sutlej (or Satlaj) River is the easternmost and longest of the "five rivers" that give Punjab its name. It rises near the Manasarowar Lakes in Tibet at an elevation of about 4,630 meters. Here its Chinese name is Xiangquan He. The Sutlej River flows west through deep Himalayan valleys, entering

India in the Kinnaur district, and passing through the plains of the Indian Punjab near Rupar, it joins with the Beas River near the Harike Barrage. The Sutlej's confluence with the Chenab River, some 480 kilometers further downstream (west of Bahawalpur in Pakistan), forms the Panjnad River (literally, "five rivers," since it carries the waters of the Beas, Sutlej, Ravi, Chenab, and Jhelum Rivers). The river joins with the Indus River near the town of Chachran, and from Kasur to its junction with the Indus, the Sutlej flows in a south-west direction through Pakistan. The division of the Sutlej waters has long been a source of tension between India and Pakistan, and still is as of 2002.

The Sutlej is altogether 1370 kilometers long. In the early nineteenth century, it formed the boundary between the Sikh states and British territory. In the twentieth century, the Sutlej was diverted to feed two irrigation systems in the Punjab, creating much new fertile land. In the late twentieth century, a huge Pakistani dam, the Sutlej Barrage (also referred to as the Islam Barrage), was constructed somewhere north of Bahawalpur. Above this point navigation is limited. Powerhouses at Bhakra, Dehar, Pong, Ganguwal, and Kotla generate electricity, which is divided between the Indian states of Punjab, Haryana, Rajasthan, and Himachal Pradesh, according to an agreement between the states.

Paul Hockings

Further Reading
Spate, O. H. K. (1972) *India and Pakistan: A General and Regional Geography.* 3d ed. New York: Dutton.

SUZHOU (2002 est. pop. 763,000). Suzhou (sometimes referred to in older publications as Soochow) is one of the most beautiful cities in China, with many canals, spectacular architecture, arching bridges, and elegant classical gardens. These gardens are popular tourist destinations, along with Lake Taihu west of the city. Much of Suzhou is surrounded by the Outer Moat, and the Grand Canal (the world's longest man-made waterway) passes through the city. The city is located in southern Jiangsu Province and was founded in the fifth century BCE. Marco Polo, according to legends, called it the "Venice of the East."

Suzhou was the capital of the kingdom of Emperor Wu (140–86 BCE), although it was not named Suzhou until the Sui dynasty (581–618 CE). The city was destroyed in the fourteenth century and again during the Taiping Rebellion (1850–1864). In 1896, it became a treaty port and was opened to the West.

SUZHOU—WORLD HERITAGE SITE

As the classic example of Chinese landscape architecture, the Suzhou gardens were designated a UNESCO World Heritage Site in 1997 and 2000. This sixteenth-century masterpiece is considered by many to be unsurpassed in its design.

Silk has historically been the most famous of Suzhou's exports, and it is also noted today for its beautiful embroidery. It is located in the subtropical zone and has a mild climate and enough rain and sunshine for excellent yields in the surrounding rice paddies. The economy is diversified today with chemicals, paper, ceramics, metallurgy, cotton textiles, machine tools, and electronics.

Carole Schroeder

Further Reading
"Suzhou." (1996) ChinaPages. Retrieved 22 April 2002, from: http://www.chinapages.com/jiangsu/suzhou/suzhou_int.htm.
Young, Margaret Walsh, and Susan Stetler, eds. (1987) *Cities of the World: Asia, the Pacific, and the Asiatic Middle East.* Vol. 4. 3d ed. Detroit, MI: Gale Research Company.

SUZUKI DAISETZU TEITARO (1870–1966), Japanese Buddhist philosopher. D. T. Suzuki (called Suzuki Daisetsu in Japan) played a key role in introducing Zen Buddhism to the West. Born Suzuki Teitaro in Kanazawa, Ishikawa Prefecture, he taught English before attending university and studying Zen at Engakuji Temple in Kamakura. In 1897, he moved to La Salle, Illinois, where he worked as an editor for the Open Court Publishing Company, which published a number of his early English-language works on Buddhism. Twelve years later, he returned to Japan where he later taught at Tokyo Imperial University, Gakushuin, and Otani University.

Suzuki's English-language works, including the three-volume *Essays in Zen Buddhism* (1927–1934) and *An Introduction to Zen Buddhism* (1934), were among the first studies to introduce Zen to the West and were studied by figures as diverse as psychoanalyst Carl Jung and composer John Cage. *Zen Buddhism and Its Influence on Japanese Culture* (1938, later renamed *Zen and Japanese Culture*) was influential in promoting the view of Zen as a cornerstone of the Japanese arts. Suzuki's English works have been reprinted countless times and have been translated into numerous languages, including Japanese. The 1999 Japanese edition of his complete works contains fourteen volumes.

Jeffrey Angles

Further Reading

Abe Masao, ed. (1986) *A Zen Life: D. T. Suzuki Remembered.* New York: Weatherhill.
Suzuki, Daisetz Teitaro. (1927) *Essays in Zen Buddhism.* Series no. 1. London: Luzac.
———. (1933) *Essays in Zen Buddhism.* Series no. 2. London: Luzac.
———. (1934) *Essays in Zen Buddhism.* Series no. 3. London: Luzac.
———. (1934) *An Introduction to Zen Buddhism.* Kyoto, Japan: Eastern Buddhist Society.
———. (1956) *Zen Buddhism: Selected Writings.* Edited by William Barrett. New York: Doubleday.
———. (1959) *Zen and Japanese Culture.* Princeton, NJ: Princeton University Press.
———. (1999) *Suzuki Daisetsu zenshu* (Complete Works of Suzuki Daisetzu). Rev. ed. Tokyo: Iwanami Shoten.

SWETTENHAM, FRANK (1850–1946), British administrator in the Malay States. Born outside Belper in Derbyshire, England, Frank Athelstane Swettenham was one of the most outstanding British colonial administrators of the Malay States and was instrumental in creating the political entity of British Malaya. Armed with a fluency in the Malay language and culture, diplomatic skills, and personal charm, Swettenham helped shape the destiny of the Malay Peninsula.

At age twenty-four, Swettenham participated in the drafting of the historic Pangkor Treaty and witnessed its signing in 1874, which introduced British colonial rule in the peninsular Malay States through the British Residential System. Theoretically the resident was appointed as an adviser to the Malay sultan; in practice the resident wielded executive power except on issues relating to Malay traditions and the Islamic faith. Shortly after, he became assistant British resident to the court of Sultan Abdul Samad of the western peninsular Malay State of Selangor, and then became assistant colonial secretary (Native Affairs, 1876–1882), resident to Selangor (1882–1889), and resident to the western peninsula state of Perak (1889–1895). He brought much economic progress, particularly in railway, mining, and commercial agriculture.

Swettenham was a prime initiator of a federated scheme aimed at centralizing the disparate political entities of the Malay Peninsula to hasten economic development. In 1895, he persuaded the Malay rulers to sign a treaty that created the Federated Malay States, with himself as resident-general (1896–1900).

Swettenham retired in 1904 and assumed the chairmanship of several rubber companies. In 1909–1910, he was chairman of the Royal Commission on Mauritius. He was a prolific writer and remained concerned in Malayan affairs, publicly airing his views during the decentralization debate of the 1920s and the Malay Union controversy of 1946.

Ooi Keat Gin

Further Reading

Allen, J. de V. (1964) "Two Imperialists: A Study of Sir Frank Swettenham and Sir Hugh Clifford." *Journal of the Malaysian Branch of the Royal Asiatic Society* 37 (Part 1): 41–73.
Barlow, Henry Sackville. (1995) *Swettenham.* Kuala Lumpur, Malaysia: Southdene.
Gullick, John Michael. (1992) *Rulers and Residents: Influence and Power in the Malay States, 1870–1920.* Kuala Lumpur, Malaysia: Oxford University Press.

SYR DAR'YA At approximately 2,200 kilometers in length, the Syr Dar'ya (Jaxartes and Sayhun) is Central Asia's second-longest river after the Amu Dar'ya. It derives most of its waters from the melting snows and glaciers of the Tian Shan Mountains. On the modern political map, from the system's headwaters in Kyrgyzstan, the river flows through Uzbekistan, Tajikistan, Kazakhstan, and into the Aral Sea. Settlements existed near the river's delta during the Bronze Age, and evidence suggests that associated ecologies

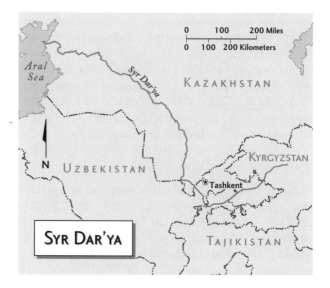

were more pastoral than those along the Amu Dar'ya until the Iron Age. By the time of Alexander of Macedon's fourth-century-BCE incursions into the river's territories, settlements and associated irrigation systems were on the rise. The river's upper portions in the Ferghana Valley were especially supportive of irrigated urban centers, and the valley and the river's lower portions thus emerged as key routes of the more northern caravans traveling the Silk Road.

Russian plans to use the Syr Dar'ya as a steamboat route did not endure long in the late nineteenth century, but initial Soviet goals of adding to the river's natural wetlands to support rice cultivation began to materialize rapidly by the 1960s. Prior to this time, most canals were in the Ferghana Valley and Golodnaya Steppe. Under development schemes, however, widespread paddies were created on the lower portions of the river. As with the Amu Dar'ya, ecological ramifications of the river's diversions have been tremendous and continue to contribute to the crisis of the wider Aral region.

Kyle Evered

Further Reading

Bosworth, Clifford Edmund. (1973) *The Ghaznavids*. 2d ed. Edinburgh: Edinburgh University Press.

Glantz, Michael H., ed. (1999) *Creeping Environmental Problems and Sustainable Development in the Aral Sea Basin*. Cambridge, U.K.: Cambridge University Press.

Litvinskii, Boris A. (1989) "The Ecology of the Ancient Nomads of Soviet Central Asia and Kazakhstan." In *Ecology and Empire: Nomads in the Cultural Evolution of the Old World*, edited by Gary Seaman. Los Angeles: Ethnographic Press, 61–72.

TABRIZ (2002 pop. 1.2 million). Located in a valley amid the foothills of the Sahand Mountains in Iran, Tabriz, the capital of the province of East Azerbaijan, is a city just east of Lake Orumiyeh. Hot springs in and around the city were inducements for early settlement and subsequent development. Tabriz's location has made it vulnerable to earthquakes, however, and the city has experienced some of the most destructive quakes in recorded history as measured by fatalities: the 1727 quake caused 77,000 deaths, and the 1780 quake caused 100,000. Other major quakes occurred in 858, 1042, and 1641, and slight tremors are commonplace in the daily lives of Tabriz's residents.

Tabriz owes much of its development to its central position along overland trade routes in the region over the centuries. Many sources throughout history referred to the city's ideal position for travel between the Iranian Plateau and either the Caucasus or Anatolia. Therefore, even though most sources trace the origins of the city to the Sasanid dynasty (224/228–651 CE), it is often speculated that Tabriz is only the most recent settlement on roughly the same site, an earlier manifestation possibly being the ancient Armenian city Tauris of the third century CE.

The city's accessibility for trade, however, has also made Tabriz prone to conquest, and control of the city has shifted often throughout history. In the thirteenth century, the city avoided destruction during the Mongol-Turkic invasions of Southwest Asia by surrendering; it was designated as a political capital by the invaders and thereafter began to thrive economically even more than it had previously. Between the thirteenth and fifteenth centuries, Tabriz thus became an important seat of power and administration for groups like the Il Khan Mongols, the Kara Koyunlu and Ak Koyunlu Turks, and the Timurids. In 1500, Tabriz then passed to Persians under the emergent Safavid dynasty (1501–1722/1736) when it was conquered by Ismail I prior to his conquests of the rest of Persia (Iran). The city became and remained the Safavid capital until the seventeenth century, when the Ottoman Turks posed too great a risk to that location and the capital shifted to Esfahan. In 1827, Russia captured Tabriz for the first time. Although the Russians retreated when a peace was reached in 1828, this opened up Persia for increasing trade with Russia and Britain—much of it being conducted through the foreign missions thereafter established in Tabriz. Russian (and later Soviet) troops returned to Tabriz in the early twentieth century and were stationed there often, even through much of World War I, the Russian Revolution, and World War II. Although the Soviet Union attempted to establish a secessionist republic based out of Tabriz, the Soviets withdrew in 1946 because of international pressures, thus enabling Persia to reclaim the city.

Tabriz has long been a center of arts and handicrafts (especially ceramics, pottery, and tile work, Tabriz-style miniature paintings, and jewelry and silverwork), with exchange networks throughout the eastern Mediterranean and southwestern Asia. Indeed, Tabriz's Blue Mosque of 1465 is Iran's greatest example of glazed tile work, although it has been severely damaged over the years by earthquakes. However, the main handicraft and related trade of Tabriz has historically been carpet weaving. The great covered bazaar of Tabriz was built in the fifteenth century, and the city functioned as Persia's commercial capital into the twentieth century. As such, it was a nexus for globalizing trade relations

The ruins of the Blue Mosque in Tabriz, built in 1465 and later damaged by an earthquake. (ROGER WOOD/CORBIS)

between the empire and commercial centers closer to the Black, Mediterranean, and Caspian Seas. Tabriz's economic connections with the West—and especially with Russia—were further enhanced by construction of a road from Tabriz to the Russian frontier outpost of Julfa in 1906. Persia's first railway was opened along the same route in 1916. With the Russian Revolution and later with the Soviet withdrawal from Tabriz, however, the city was essentially relegated to a peripheral city in Iran. But overland trade with Turkey did continue and, in addition to Tabriz's large population, prevented the city from being entirely marginalized. Nonetheless, the city—and its Azeri Turk majority—remained highly suspect to Iranian government officials because of its Soviet connection.

As the urban center of an ethnolinguistic minority that makes up between 20 and 30 percent of the Iranian population, Tabriz is also a focal point for political issues that extend into the Caucasus and beyond. Such issues were well reflected amid discussions over the Republic of Azerbaijan's requests to open a consulate in Tabriz in the mid-1990s. Although ethnolinguistically distinct, Tabriz is like other Iranian cities in terms of its rapid population growth over the past decades.

Kyle T. Evered

Further Reading

Issawi, Charles. (1970) "The Tabriz-Trabzon Trade, 1830–1900: Rise and Decline of a Route." *International Journal of Middle East Studies* 1, 1: 18–27.

Melville, Charles Peter. (1981) "Historical Monuments and Earthquakes in Tabriz." *Iran* 19: 159–177.
Tagizadek, Seyyed Hassan. (1960) "The Background of the Constitutional Movement in Azerbaijan." *Middle East Journal* 14, 4: 456–465.

TAE KWON DO Tae kwon do is a Korean martial art that since the 1950s has become popular around the world. It is estimated that over 20 million people in 140 nations participate in the sport. The origins are unclear, and different scholars suggest Korean, Chinese, and Japanese origins. The history of tae kwon do as a modern sport begins in the twentieth century, when the Japanese banned the sport upon annexing Korea in 1910. The ban produced greater interest in the sport and caused it to be linked in the Korean mind with Korean nationalism and independence. The Korean War (1950–1953) introduced the sport to U.S. soldiers, who brought it back to the United States, initiating its emergence as a worldwide sport. In 1973 South Korea afforded the World Tae Kwon Do Federation recognition as the international governing body of the sport.

Like other Asian marital arts, tae kwon do involves offensive and defensive postures and movements classified as kicks, strikes, stances, and blocks. Advancing up through the ranks of the sport requires rigorous training that emphasizes body control, agility, balance, timing, and technique. Tae kwon do especially stresses kicking, including powerful flying kicks. This has made the sport more popular than other martial arts with women and children, who have less upper body strength than men. There are now various schools of tae kwon do, with the basic division being between those that stress competition and those that stress training and personal development.

David Levinson

Further Reading

Park, Yeon Hee. (1993) *Fighting Back: Taekowndo for Women.* East Meadow, NY: Y. H. Park.

T'AEBAEK MOUNTAINS The T'aebaek Mountain range in the eastern part of the Korean peninsula is part of the geological "backbone" of the region. This range runs parallel to the coast from Kangwon Province in the north and through North Kyongsang Province to the south. Two of Korea's major rivers originate in the region of the T'aebaek Mountains: the Han River, which flows southwest through Seoul before emptying into the Yellow Sea, and the Naktong River, which flows south to the Korea Strait. In addition, the Kum and Somjin Rivers begin in these mountains.

The T'aebaek Mountains were formed by tectonic interactions; geologically it is located on the Yongnam Massif. This region is still subject to earthquakes. This tectonic activity has given the range its steep slopes and heights exceeding 1,900 meters (6,233 feet).

The range is named for T'aebaek, one of three mountains considered sacred by Koreans. The association between T'aebaek and Korea's legendary founder, Tangun, as well as the historic sites around the mountain, make it a special place for Koreans, and it is a popular tourist site. According to legend, Korea's divine founder Hwanung descended to T'aebaek and eventually began the Korean race.

Thomas P. Dolan

Further Reading
Korean Overseas Information Service. (1993) *A Handook of Korea*. Seoul: Samhwa.

TAEDONG RIVER The Taedong River is located in the Democratic People's Republic of Korea (North Korea) and flows southwest from the Nangnim mountain range in the northeast region of South P'yongan Province out to the Yellow Sea. With a length of 438 kilometers, it is the fifth longest river on the Korean peninsula and the second longest in North Korea.

The Taedong River, with the Samgak River as its estuary, is generally deep and carries a large volume of water, enabling substantial transportation between the river ports of Namp'o, Songnim, and Pyongyang. The Taedong is believed to have been an important seat of civilization since prehistoric times, and it has also been called Yolsu, P'aesu, P'ae[gang], and Wangsong[gang] throughout history. The river was the site of the General Sherman Incident of 1866, in which an American trading ship was destroyed by Koreans as it tried to sail up the Taedong River to Pyongyang.

Jennifer Jung-Kim

Further Reading
Cho, Chung-Kyung, Phyllis Haffner, and Fredric M. Kaplan. (1991) *The Korea Guidebook*. 5th ed. Boston: Houghton Mifflin.
Storey, Robert, and Alex English. (2001) *Korea*. 5th ed. Berkeley, CA: Lonely Planet.

TAEGU (2000 est. pop. 2.5 million). Taegu is the third most populous city in South Korea (Republic of Korea). The city's origins date back to the Shilla kingdom (57 BCE–935 CE), when it was called Talguhwahyon or Talbulsong. It has been called Taegu since 757 and has been classified as a city since 1949.

Taegu is located in North Kyongsang Province about 80 kilometers inland from the eastern coastline. The city, however, is designated a metropolitan city (*kwangyokshi*) and is administratively independent of the province, although Taegu also functions as the provincial capital. Taegu has seven districts (*ku*) and one county (*kun*).

Taegu is mostly urban; its primary manufacturing industries are textiles, machinery and metals, automobile parts, and electronics. The textile industry accounts for the largest portion of the region's manufacturing, with more than 2,100 companies involved in all aspects of spinning, weaving, dyeing, and sewing.

Taegu lies in a basin, surrounded by mountains to the north and south, with the Shinch'on Stream running westward into the Kumho River, which in turn flows into the Naktong River. Recent efforts have focused on environmental and beautification issues to improve the quality of life and to increase tourism.

Jennifer Jung-Kim

Further Reading
Nilsen, Robert. (1997) *South Korea Handbook*. Chico, CA: Moon.
Storey, Robert, and Alex English. (2001) *Korea*. 5th ed. Berkeley, CA: Lonely Planet.

TAEJON (2000 pop. 1.4 million). Taejon, a city of 540 square kilometers, is located in South Ch'ungch'ong Province in South Korea (Republic of Korea). Taejon has been administratively autonomous since its 1995 designation as a "metropolitan city" (*chikhalsi*). It functions as a second administrative capital, housing many federal government organizations.

The city of Taejon has had many names, but its current name, meaning "big field," shows its agricultural roots. Taejon became commercialized after it became a stop on the Seoul-Pusan Railway in 1905. The Taejon-Mokp'o Railway, built in 1914, connects the city to South Cholla Province in the southwest. The city has become a hub for the nation's railroads and highways.

Taejon is growing rapidly because of its ideal location only 153 kilometers from Seoul. Taejon hosted the 1993 World Expo, bringing much attention to the city. The city is also a center for science and technology, with its Korea Institute of Science and Technology at the forefront of scientific development.

Jennifer Jung-Kim

Further Reading
Cho, Chung-Kyung, Phyllis Haffner, and Fredric M. Kaplan. (1991) *The Korea Guidebook.* 5th ed. Boston: Houghton Mifflin.
Nilsen, Robert (1997) *South Korea Handbook.* Chico, CA: Moon.

TAEJONGGYO Taejonggyo (the Religion of the Divine Progenitor; sometimes spelled Daejonggyo) was founded by Na Ch'ol (1863–1916) in 1901, a time when Christian missionaries were challenging the traditional religious beliefs and practices of Korea, and Japan was threatening Korea's existence as an independent nation. Taejonggyo arose as a nationalistic response to this political and spiritual crisis. The central tenet of Taejonggyo is that Koreans need not worship any foreign gods such as Jesus or Buddha. They have a god of their own, the same god who, as the legendary ruler Tangun, ruled over a vast and powerful Korean kingdom five thousand years ago. Na taught that the worship of this Divine Progenitor had been the primary religion of the Korean people until the Mongols invaded the Korean peninsula in the thirteenth century and allowed foreign ideas and religions to penetrate and weaken indigenous Korean culture.

Taejonggyo scriptures include texts that are said to have been composed five millennia ago, when Tangun ruled Korea. Unfortunately, those texts were lost for centuries and were recovered only early in the twentieth century. They include the *Ch'onbugyong* (The Heavenly Amulet Classic), which explains the origin of the universe in only eighty-one Chinese characters. Another, the *Samil sin'go* (The Teachings of the Trinitarian God), only 360 characters long, describes the terrestrial and celestial realms and their inhabitants. According to Taejonggyo doctrine, ancient Koreans worshiped three persons in one God: God the Creator (Hanim), God the Teacher (Hanung), and God the Ruler (Tangun Hanbaegom).

Taejonggyo claims to have half a million followers. A government survey in 1995, however, found less than 10,000 Koreans who listed Taejonggyo as their religious affiliation. Nevertheless, Taejonggyo has helped shape the contours of Korean history in the twentieth century. During the thirty-five years of Japanese colonial rule, from 1910 until 1945, it encouraged nationalists, such as the anti-Japanese writer and activist Sin Ch'aeho (1880–1936), to assert pride in their country by claiming that Korea was once a powerful empire ruled by a divine being. After liberation from the Japanese, the Republic of Korea designated 3 October, the date on which Taejonggyo celebrates God's appearance among men as the ruler Tangun, a national holiday. The sacred texts of Taejonggyo are increasingly becoming accepted as authentic ancient historical documents even by those who do not believe Tangun is a god. Though it is a religion with relatively few adherents, Taejonggyo is nonetheless influential.

Don Baker

Further Reading
An Hosang. (1963) "Dae-Jong-Gyo: Religion of God-Human Being." *Korea Journal* 2, 5: 9–13.
Ministry of Culture and Sports, Republic of Korea, ed. (1996) *Religious Culture in Korea.* Elizabeth, NJ: Hollym.

TAEWON'GUN. See **Yi Ha-ung.**

TAGALOG. See **Philippine Languages.**

TAGORE, RABINDRANATH (1861–1941), Indian poet. One of the foremost literary figures of modern India, Tagore was born 7 May 1861 into an affluent and cultured family in north Calcutta, in Bengal, and died there on 7 August 1941. He had an aversion to formal education and never attended university. Nevertheless, his precocious talent was evident at eight, and in sheer volume and diversity his creative career is unparalleled, consisting of numerous works of poetry, plays, short stories, novels, paintings, and sketches. He set his songs (of which more than 2,500 were published) to music, and *Rabindrasangeet* (Rabindra's Music) achieved immense popularity.

He was greatly influenced by Western liberal and humanist traditions, as well as indigenous traditions and folk culture, and acknowledged Hindu, Muslim, and British influences on his creativity. Though widely traveled, he achieved international fame only after a collection of his poems, *Gitanjali* (Song Offerings), was translated into English. On the basis of this work alone he was awarded the Nobel Prize in literature in 1913, the first Indian to be so honored. However, in 1919 he renounced both the prize and a knighthood bestowed by the British (King George V) in protest over

Rabindranath Tagore in 1929. (BETTMANN/CORBIS)

the massacre of Indian civilians in Amritsar, Punjab. His pride in Indian nationalism was tempered initially by his favorable response to aspects of the British connection. His perceptions of imperial rule changed, however, and during the interwar years he condemned it as inhuman and uncreative. One of his poems was adopted as the national anthem of independent India, and Mohandas K. Gandhi bestowed on him the title *gurudev* (great teacher).

Tagore's diverse works reveal the mainsprings of his thought: he divided his songs into five categories—*puja* (devotional), *prem* (love lyrics), *prakriti* (on nature), *swadeshi* (patriotic), and *bibhidha* (miscellaneous). He was a worshipper of truth and beauty (as in *Chitra, Urbasi, Gitanjali, Gitali, Naibedya*), a spiritualist with a mystical frame of reference (as in *Jiban Devata*, or Lord of Life, *Raktakarabi*, or Red Oleanders). He was a humanist and thought in terms of world peace and internationalism, giving these ideals practical form by setting up a university in Calcutta at Shantineketan (Abode of Peace) called Vishva Bharathi (World University). Yet he was aware of the social and economic problems of the common person—poverty, oppression, ignorance—and wrote against social ills such

as untouchability (as in *Chandalika*). He was also concerned with social uplift (as in *Desher Unnati*, or Prosperity of the Country, and in *Katha O Kahani*, or Tales and Stories).

Chandrika Kaul

Further Reading

Dutta, Krishna, and Andrew Robinson. (1995) *Rabindranath Tagore: The Myriad-Minded Man*. London: Bloomsbury.
Kripalani, Krishna. (1961) *Tagore: A Life, 1861–1941*. New Delhi: Malancha.
Lago, Mary M., and Ronald Warwick, eds. (1989) *Rabindranath Tagore: Perspectives in Time*. Basingstoke, U.K.: Macmillan.
Tagore, Rabindranath. (1983) *Reminiscences*. New Delhi: Macmillan.
Thompson, Edward J. ([1948] 1991) *Rabindranath Tagore: Poet and Dramatist*. Reprint. Oxford: Oxford University Press.

TAI CHI Tai chi chuan (taijiquan), sometimes referred to in English as Chinese shadow boxing, is a centuries-old martial arts system. Legend holds that tai chi chuan ("supreme ultimate boxing") was first developed by Zhang Sanfeng, a Taoist monk said to live on Wudang Mountain toward the end of the Song dynasty (960–1279). Other accounts credit Chen Wanting (1597–1664), of Wen County, Henan Province, with originating tai chi chuan in a variety now known as the Chen style. Over time, four additional varieties developed: the Yang, Sun, and two Wu styles. The 1980s also saw the emergence of a radically simplified People's Republic of China twenty-four-movement form, which exists solely for the purpose of exercise.

Theory and Practice

The essence of all tai chi chuan practice is in the principles governing the forms rather than in the forms themselves. These principles are drawn from traditional Chinese medicine, to regulate the *Qi*, or vital energy; from Yin-Yang theory, to provide balance; from the Confucian "Doctrine of the Mean," the "Book of Changes"; and from Taoist philosophy, all of which guide movement and strategy. These and other principles combine with the techniques of Chinese pugilism to form a self-defense system that promotes good health and longevity.

Forms and Styles

The most fundamental of tai chi chuan practices is the solo form, consisting of a lengthy series of conjoined postures, performed individually, at a slow and usually constant tempo. Synchronized group practice of the solo form is commonplace as well. Some styles also practice an advanced, mixed-tempo solo form, and all styles maintain fixed-step and free-form varieties of two-person forms, as well as sword and other weapons forms.

The primary differences among the five major styles of tai chi chuan exist more in terms of the number of movements in a given form; the height and length of one's stances, or postures; and the pace or tempo of movement. However, virtually no differences exist in the basic principles governing the varied forms for any of the five major styles.

Contemporary Tai Chi Chuan

In the early 1900s, Yang Chengfu, a famous Yang-style master, began teaching the formerly secret tai chi chuan to the public. Eventually, other styles followed his lead. This esteemed martial art has since become popular worldwide as a practice that rejuvenates and promotes good health and longevity.

Charles Ettner

Further Reading

Chen, Wei-ming. (1986) *T'ai Chi Ch'uan Ta Wen: Questions and Answers on T'ai Chi Ch'uan.* Trans. by Benjamin Pang Jeng Lo and Robert W. Smith. Berkeley, CA: North Atlantic Books.

Cheng, Man-ching. (1981) *Tai Chi Chuan: A Simplified Method of Calisthenics for Health and Self Defense.* Richmond, CA: North Atlantic Books.

———. (1985) *Cheng Tzu's Thirteen Treatises on T'ai Chi Ch'uan.* Trans. by Benjamin Pang Jeng Lo and Martin Inn. Berkeley, CA: North Atlantic Books.

Lo, Benjamin Pang Jeng, Martin Inn, and Robert Amacker. (1986) *Essence of Tai Chi Chuan: The Literary Tradition.* Berkeley, CA: North Atlantic Books.

Lowenthal, Wolfe. (1991) *There Are No Secrets: Professor Cheng Man-ch'ing and His Tai Chi Chuan.* Berkeley, CA: North Atlantic Books.

TAI SHAN Tai Shan (Mount Tai) is located in central Shandong Province, China, to the north of the town of Tai'an. The main peak, Jade Emperor, is 1,545 meters (5,069 feet) above sea level. Mount Tai is a tilted fault-block mountain with extremely complex geology. Mount Tai, the most important and the most easterly of the Five Sacred Mountains of Taoism, is associated with the rising sun and birth. Its other name, Dongyue, means "Eastern Peak." Mount Tai's importance in Chinese culture, as a site of imperial pilgrimage, was solidified by the Qin emperor Shi Huangdi. More than 250 Taoist, Buddhist, and Confucian temples were built on the mountain, of which 22 remain in use. To-

TAI SHAN—WORLD HERITAGE SITE

Tai Shan was designated as a UNESCO World Heritage Site in 1987 because of the two-thousand-year-old art stored within it. A site of imperial pilgrimage and artistic inspiration since the Han dynasty, it has immense historical value.

day, 97 ruins, 819 stone tablets, and 1,018 stone inscriptions are preserved on Mount Tai. The summit, with the temple dedicated to the Jade Emperor, the highest deity in Taoism, is reached by nearly 7,000 stone steps. On Mount Tai's slopes are many ancient trees, including the Han dynasty cypresses, planted by the Han emperor Wu Di. Mount Tai was added to UNESCO's World Heritage List in 1987.

Michael Pretes

Further Reading

Munakata, Kiyohiko. (1991) *Sacred Mountains in Chinese Art.* Urbana and Chicago: University of Illinois Press.

Perkins, Dorothy, ed. (1999) *Encyclopedia of China.* New York: Facts On File and Roundtable Press.

TAIJIQUAN. See **Tai Chi.**

TAI-KADAI LANGUAGES Tai-Kadai languages are used by more than 85 million speakers in Southeast Asia and southern China. Depending on criteria used, between forty and a hundred spoken languages can be recognized. All of these are tonal, with over two hundred different tone systems distinguished.

The two national languages of the group, Thai and Lao, sometimes called Laotian, account for well over half the total of Tai-Kadai speakers. The spelling "Thai" is used for the national language of Thailand and for some regional varieties in that country. "Tai" is used for the wider Tai subfamily of Tai-Kadai and also in the names of some specific varieties.

Branches and Subfamilies of Tai-Kadai

Thai and Lao belong to the relatively well-known Southwestern branch of the Tai subfamily. This branch is also represented in Assam in India (for example, by the Khamti language), in Yunnan in China (by Lue and Tai-Dehong), in Myanmar (by Shan and

Dehong), and in Vietnam mainly south of the Red river (by Black Tai and White Tai).

The remainder of the Tai-Kadai family extends from Vietnam mainly north of the Red River (where the Nung and Tay languages are found), into the Chinese provinces of Guangxi (the Zhuang language), Guizhou (the Bouyei, Sui, and Gelao languages), and Hunan (the Kam language), to the island of Hainan (the Hlai and Be languages). Most authorities recognize a high-level Kam-Tai subfamily including the Kam-Sui languages along with the three main branches of Tai (Northern, Central, and Southwestern).

Speculation about how the rest of the family fits together includes a so-called Kadai branch, hence the family name Tai-Kadai. This branch would comprise Gelao, Laha, and other varieties in China and Vietnam still being investigated. The exact relationship of the languages on Hainan Island to the rest of the family is also under investigation.

Sound and Writing Systems

Much basic vocabulary in Tai-Kadai languages is monosyllabic, although compounding is common. More initial consonants are distinguished than finals, usually limited to nasals, semivowels, and final stops (*p*, *t*, *k*, and glottal stop). Unlike most languages in the family, Thai and Lao distinguish pairs of short and long vowels, represented here as *i*, *ī*.

Tonal systems have been reported, from languages with three tones (Aiton, in India) to nine (Kam, in China), or even more if stopped syllables are counted separately. Some idea of tonal shapes can be given through pairs of digits on a one-to-five scale, with the first suggesting the approximate beginning pitch level and the second digit, the ending level. Many vocabulary items in Tai-Kadai languages differ only in tone. Thus *sip* means "ten" in languages of the Kam-Tai subgrouping, but with low tone (11) in Thai, mid-high (44) in Lao, low-rising (24) in Dehong, high-rising (45) in White Tai, and mid-level (33) in the Lungming dialect of Zhuang.

Tai-Kadai languages in the southern and western areas, with long cultural connections to India, have been using alphabetic Indic-based writing systems for over seven hundred years. Eight such scripts are currently in use. To the north and east, varieties in contact with Chinese once used modified character-based writing but romanizations have been recently introduced.

For Thai and Lao, some vowels are written above consonants; for example, the *i* vowel sign in *sip* (ten) is written above the *s* letter. Other vowels are written

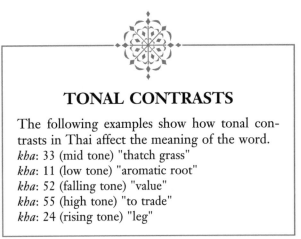

TONAL CONTRASTS

The following examples show how tonal contrasts in Thai affect the meaning of the word.
kha: 33 (mid tone) "thatch grass"
kha: 11 (low tone) "aromatic root"
kha: 52 (falling tone) "value"
kha: 55 (high tone) "to trade"
kha: 24 (rising tone) "leg"

under, after, and even before their initial consonants. Tone is shown through superscript marks. Also, consonant letters are arranged in three classes affecting tonal representation differently.

Written Thai and Lao differ somewhat. Thai spelling is etymological with proliferation of consonant letters. Modern Lao is more directly phonetic.

Syntax and Semantics

Like languages nearby, Tai-Kadai varieties do not use inflectional morphology; that is, they do not use endings to show tense or number. Such distinctions are assumed from context or are optionally indicated through special words or constructions. The most basic Tai-Kadai sentence orders are subject-verb and subject-verb-object, so the Thai sentence *chan* 24 *rak* 55 *thoe*: 33 and Lao equivalent *kho':i* 31 *hak* 33 *caw* 31 both mean "I love you" and here show the same basic word order as English. On the other hand, modifiers usually follow modified nouns; hence Thai *ba:n* 52 + *yay* 11 "house + big," or "a big house."

For counting and specifying objects, classifier constructions are used. (An example of a classifier in English is "head" in the sentence "three head of cattle.") Thus Thai *man* 33 *sa:m* 24 *hua* 24 "yam three head," or "three yams"; Lao *mu*: 13 *ha*: 31 *to*: 11 "pig five body," or "five pigs."

Ultimate Connections

It used to be assumed that Tai-Kadai languages, being tonal, were directly related to Chinese and indeed much Chinese-derived vocabulary is present. However, basic Tai-Kadai noun-modifier order is not Chinese and there is evidence for deep relationships with the Austronesian and Austroasiatic families as well. The ultimate connections of Tai-Kadai remain a controversial topic and will be an important area for future research.

Anthony Diller

Further Reading

Benedict, Paul K. (1990) *Japanese/Austro-Tai: Linguistica Extranea, Studia 20.* Ann Arbor, MI: Karoma.

Diller, Anthony. (1996) "Thai and Lao Writing." In *The World's Writing Systems*, edited by Peter T. Daniels and William Bright. New York: Oxford University Press, 457–466.

Edmondson, Jerold A., and David B. Solnit, eds. (1988) *Comparative Kadai: Linguistic Studies beyond Tai.* Dallas, TX: Summer Institute of Linguistics.

Luo, Yongxian. (1997) *The Subgroup Structure of the Tai Languages: A Historical-Comparative Study.* Journal of Chinese Linguistics Monograph Series, no. 12. Berkeley and Los Angeles: University of California Press.

Matisoff, James. (1990) "On Megalocomparison." *Language* 66, 1: 106–120.

Preecha Juntanamalaga. (1988) "Social Issues in Thai Classifier Usage." *Language Sciences* 10, 2: 313–330.

Smalley, William A. (1994) *Linguistic Diversity and National Unity: Language Ecology in Thailand.* Chicago: University of Chicago Press.

TAIMANOV, ISATAI

TAIMANOV, ISATAI (1791–1838), Kazakh rebel leader. In 1812 Isatai Taimanov became one of the elders of a *bersh* (more than 3,500 families) community migrating within the southern areas of Kazakhstan adjacent to the Caspian Sea. In 1814 his position as elder was confirmed by the governor of Orenburg. Some time later Taimanov became the governor of the whole *bersh* community. He was arrested several times (1817, 1823, 1824) by the colonial governors for resisting the khan's rule.

Taimanov protested against the oppression of the peasantry in the Bukeev Horde and became a popular hero. In February 1836, supported by Makhambet Utemisov, he was one of the instigators of a mass uprising, largely of Kazakh peasants, which included about two thousand men under arms by 1837. In October 1837 Taimanov and his supporters laid siege to the Khan Djaghir's quarters, but they were routed in a battle at Tas-Tyube later that year. This unsuccessful result is considered a decisive event in the rebellion. Taimanov then led the survivors to the Minor Zhuz (Mladshii zhuz) on the left bank of the Ural River, strengthened his forces, and joined Sultan Kaip-Galii Ishimov, who under the support of Khiva's khan was trying to wrest the Minor Zhuz from the Russian empire. In July 1838 Taimanov died at the river Ak-Bulak in battle against czarist military forces sent to suppress the rebellion, which died with him.

Islamov Bakhitor

TAINAN

TAINAN (1999 pop. 760,000). Located on the coastal edge of the fertile Jianan Plateau, Tainan is the oldest Chinese settlement on Taiwan and the island's fourth largest city. Until the late nineteenth century, Tainan served as the political, cultural, and economic center of Taiwan. Tainan was a Dutch settlement and trading post from 1624 to 1662. In 1661 the Chinese rebel leader Zheng Chenggong (1624–1662), better known under the English name Koxinga, failed in an attempt to restore the Chinese Ming dynasty (1368–1644) and fled to Taiwan. His army quickly overcame the Dutch, and he established his government in Tainan. In 1684 the Manchurian Qing dynasty (1644–1912) conquered Taiwan and incorporated Taiwan as part of Fujian Province of China.

This history has left Tainan with a wealth of historic sites, including two forts built by the Dutch and a number of important temples. Tainan's more than two hundred temples, ranging from the Tainan Confucius Temple (1662) to the elaborate new Temple of Matzu (Goddess of the Sea) at Luermen, provide some of the best remaining examples of southern Chinese architecture in Taiwan.

Tainan is an important center of industry, education, culture, and tourism. Historically, the area has been important for sugar and rice cultivation, fisheries, oyster raising, and salt production. Tainan is now home to some of Taiwan's largest private industrial enterprises, including petrochemical and food processing plants. It is slated to become a high-tech center upon completion of the Tainan Science-Based Industrial Park in 2002.

Scott Simon

Further Reading

Croizier, Ralph. (1977) *Koxinga and Chinese Nationalism: History, Myth, and the Hero.* Cambridge, MA: East Asian Research Center, Harvard University.

Rubenstein, Murray, ed. (1999) *Taiwan: A New History.* Armonk, NY: M. E. Sharpe.

TAIPEI

TAIPEI (1998 pop. 2.6 million). Taipei is the largest city on Taiwan and, since 1949, has been the capital of the Republic of China (the Chinese state that does not recognize Beijing's sovereignty). Located at the far north of Taiwan island, in the basin of the Tamshui, Keelung, and Takokan rivers, it is a major commercial and political center, with a wide range of businesses, cultural institutions, and temples.

In 1885, the ruling Chinese Qing dynasty (1644–1912) declared Taiwan a separate province, and Taipei, a city formed from earlier Chinese and aboriginal set-

The monumental gate at the Chiang Memorial in Taipei. (MACDUFF EVERTON/CORBIS)

tlements, became its capital. During the Japanese colonial rule over Taiwan (1895–1945), Japanese relationships with Taipei's Chinese population varied between repression of nationalism and accommodation to some political aspirations of the emergent middle-class elites. When Taiwan reverted to Chinese rule in 1945, tensions with the new Chinese Nationalist governor, Chen Yi, led Taipei to become a major center of the February 28th Incident of 1947, during which the city-dwellers' mass protests against the Nationalist government were put down with some brutality. After 1949, Taipei became the "temporary" capital of the administration of Chiang Kai-shek (1887–1975). During this period, Taipei benefited from the economic boom in East Asia, and became a prosperous city. After Chiang's death, Taiwan democratized, and Taipei's mayoralty was held for the first time by an opposition politician, Chen Shui-bian, in 1994–1998.

Taipei's architecture reflects the city's stages of development. Little is left from the pre-1895 era, but the Japanese period has bequeathed many colonial baroque buildings, including National Taiwan University and the Presidential Office Building. From the 1950s, many undistinguished concrete buildings were hastily erected, a process aided by Taipei's lack of planning laws, but since the 1980s, greater care has been taken to build more sympathetically, with many new buildings, such as the Central Rail Station and the Chiang Kai-shek Memorial, incorporating traditional Chinese architectural themes.

Taipei's environment is marked by heavy pollution. Until the early 1980s, highly polluting soft coal was burned without effective restrictions, and Taipei's position in a basin exacerbated the resulting smog. Taipei's relative decline as a manufacturing center reduced emissions (between 1954 and 1986, the proportion of Taiwan's industrial workers based in Taipei fell by half to under 8 percent), and the city authorities have attempted to cut motor vehicle traffic by building a mass transit rail system.

Rana Mitter

Further Reading

Chen Chiang-siang. (1956) *The City of Taipei*. Taipei, Taiwan: Fu-min Geographical Institute of Economic Development.

Helms, Bernd Hans-Gerd, and Linda Chih-ling Hou, eds. (1996) *Insight Guides: Taiwan*. Hong Kong: APA Publications.

Lai Tse-han, Ramon H. Myers, and Wei Wou. (1991) *A Tragic Beginning: The Taiwan Uprising of February 28, 1947*. Stanford, CA: Stanford University Press.

Selya, Roger Mark. (1995) *Taipei*. Chichester, U.K., and New York: John Wiley.

TAIPING REBELLION Led by Hong Xiuquan (1814–1864), a frustrated candidate in the civil-service examinations and a self-proclaimed Christian, the Taiping Rebellion (1851–1864) seriously challenged

China's Qing dynasty (1644–1912) and was the largest rebellion in Chinese history.

The Taiping Rebellion occurred in a period of unprecedented crisis, when the Qing dynasty was plagued by an exploding population (the population tripled in two centuries to exceed 430 million by the 1850s) and challenges from Western powers that it could not meet, as evidenced in its defeat in the Opium War (1840–1842).

The Origins

From a peasant family of the Hakka group in a village close to Guangzhou (Canton), Hong Xiuquan was raised to pursue a career as a scholar-official. Having repeatedly failed to pass the provincial-level civil-service examinations, Hong was hit with a hallucinatory episode in 1837. A few years later, upon reading a set of Christian tracts, *Quanshi Liangyan* (Good Words for Exhorting the Age), which was compiled by a Chinese Christian, Hong made connections between Christian theology and his visions and was convinced that he was actually God's second son, Jesus' younger brother, and that he was sent to earth to expel devils, namely the Manchus (who ruled China during the Qing dynasty), from China.

Having baptized himself and a few friends and relatives, Hong began his evangelical mission in his hometown. Later, along with one of his converts, Feng Yunshan (1822–1852), Hong went to Guangxi Province after having lost his teaching post at the village school due to his Christian convictions. In the poverty-stricken Zijing Mountain area, Hong and Feng found enthusiastic adherents among poor peasants and charcoal burners. A religious community was formed, which began secretly preparing for an armed uprising.

The Early Stage (1851–1856)

In late 1850, Hong called for a rebellion against the Qing dynasty. He proclaimed the establishment of Taiping Tianguo (the Heavenly Kingdom of Great Peace) in January 1851 and declared himself the Heavenly King shortly after. The Taipings, as they become known in English, set up an elaborate military system in which men and women were segregated and submitted all their properties to a public treasury. They began to march north to the Chang (Yangtze) River valley in 1852. The Qing armies, which had not encountered such a fierce enemy for decades, failed to stop the advances of the spirited Taipings. In the spring of 1853 the Taipings, totaling 1 million or more, took Nanjing, a political and economic center

in southeastern China. Hong made Nanjing his capital and renamed it Tianjing (Heavenly Capital).

After taking Nanjing, the Taipings moved quickly to expand their military victories. A northern expedition was dispatched to take Beijing, the capital of the Qing dynasty, and a western expedition was sent to take control of the middle Chang River valley and the areas surrounding Nanjing. Although the northern expedition failed, the Taipings were successful in expanding their territories in the middle and lower Chang River valleys. Administrative apparatuses that combined military and civil functions were set up in the conquered territories. A utopian land program blueprinting equal distribution of land was promulgated. Many social and cultural reforms, such as banning opium smoking, foot binding, prostitution, and so forth, were carried out. Repudiating Confucianism as the devil's teaching, the Taipings adopted Hong's version of Christianity as their official religion and used it as the basis for their civil-service examinations, in which both men and women were encouraged to participate.

Intrigued by the Christian dimensions of the Taiping Rebellion, Britain, France, and the United States sent envoys to Nanjing to investigate the new regime. Although the Westerners were deeply disappointed by the Taiping religion, which they thought was a great distortion of Christianity, and by the rebels' lack of commitment to order and construction, the Western powers decided not to act against the Taipings immediately because they had not settled their conflicts with the Qing government. As a result, they adopted neutrality toward the rebellion for the moment.

When the Taiping Rebellion reached its apogee in 1856, fatal infighting occurred. Threatened by the swelling power of Yang Xiuqing (1820?–1856), the prime minister of the Taiping regime, Hong had him killed by another leader, Wei Changhui (1823–1856). Later, Hong also had Wei killed. Tens of thousands of Taiping followers were slain in the incident. Feeling that he was no longer trusted, Shi Dakai (1831–1863), a talented general, led his army out of Nanjing and carried on an independent campaign against the Qing.

The Late Stage (1856–1864)

The Taiping Rebellion was greatly weakened by the events of 1856 and lost much territory to the Qing armies in the wake of the incident. Meanwhile, the Qing dynasty found a powerful force in suppressing the rebellion, the Xiang (Hunan) army led by Zeng Guofan (1811–1872), a high official and famed Confucian scholar. Zeng commanded strong support among the gentry class by upholding Confucian values in countering the Taipings' form of Christianity. Recruited exclusively from Zeng's hometown in Hunan Province and highly paid and well trained, the soldiers of the Xiang Army began to push the Taipings into a defensive position. Two new leaders and outstanding generals of the Taipings, Li Xiucheng (1823–1864) and Chen Yucheng (1837–1862), orchestrated a series of successful campaigns to break the impasse, advanced to eastern Jiangnan, and approached Shanghai, an important treaty port since the Opium War. Hong Xiuquan's cousin, Hong Ren'gan (1822–1864), arrived in Nanjing after having stayed in Hong Kong for years, breathing new life into the waning regime by attempting to reform the Taiping political and economic systems using Western models.

During 1856–1860, the Qing dynasty was engaged in the Arrow War with Britain and France. The conclusion of the war coincided with a change of the rulership of the Qing dynasty. The new leaders, the Empress Dowager Cixi (1853–1908) and Prince Gong Yixin (1833–1898), effected a radical turn in foreign policy, becoming cooperative with the West, which encouraged the Western powers to side with the Qing dynasty in China's civil war. In early 1862 Li Xiucheng attacked Shanghai again, triggering Western intervention. A foreign mercenary army, the "Ever-Victorious Army," headed first by Frederick Townsend Wade (1831–1862) of the United States and then by Charles George Gordon (1833–1885) of Britain, became the major agent of the Western intervention. After 1862, the Taipings retreated city by city under the joint attack of the Xiang Army and the Ever-Victorious Army. In June 1864 Hong Xiuquan died of illness. One month later, the Xiang Army captured Nanjing, which effectively ended the Taiping Rebellion, even though the remaining Taiping forces continued to fight until 1868.

About 20 million lives were lost in the extensive warfare associated with the Taiping Rebellion and other rebellions of the period. One consequence of the rebellion was that the Qing government lost much of its power to the provincial authorities. Although Taiping Christianity failed to leave any lasting impact on Chinese society, its anti-Manchu nationalism was inherited by the anti-Qing revolutionaries, and its utopian egalitarianism was echoed in the Chinese Communist revolution in the twentieth century.

Yingcong Dai

See also: **Zeng Guofan**

Further Reading
Gregory, J. S. (1969) *Great Britain and the Taipings*. London: Routledge and Kegan Paul.

Jen Yu-wen. (1973) *The Taiping Revolutionary Movement*. New Haven, CT: Yale University Press.

Michael, Franz, and Chang Chung-li. (1966–1971) *The Taiping Rebellion: History and Documents*. 3 vols. Seattle, WA: University of Washington Press.

Shih, Vincent. (1967) *The Taiping Ideology: Its Sources, Interpretations, and Influences*. Seattle, WA: University of Washington Press.

Spence, Jonathan. (1996) *God's Chinese Son: The Taiping Heavenly Kingdom of Hong Xiuquan*. New York: Norton.

Wagner, Rudolf. (1982) *Reenacting the Heavenly Vision: The Role of Religion in the Taiping Rebellion*. Berkeley and Los Angeles: University of California Press.

TAISHO PERIOD
Japan's Taisho period (1912–1926) was the period of the reign of the Taisho emperor, the son and successor of the Meiji emperor, during whose reign Japan had ended its long isolation from most of the rest of the world and began its quick modernization. The Taisho period started on a liberal note, with so-called Taisho Democracy, a national movement to protect constitutional government and to democratize not only politics but also the economy, education, and other areas of culture. The Taisho period can be divided into the pre–World War I period and the postwar period.

Prewar and Wartime Japanese Politics and Diplomacy
In 1912 the Japanese army, eager to expand the interests of Japan after the Republican Revolution in China, demanded that the cabinet establish two army divisions in Korea. When the cabinet turned down the demand because of budget restraints, the army minister resigned, an act which, due to the rules set out by the Japanese constitution of the time, forced the resignation of the rest of the cabinet. The public criticized this tyrannical behavior of the army, and there were cries for an end to the influence of the *genro* (elder statesmen who, though their role was not laid out in the constitution, manipulated politics behind the scenes) and protection of constitutional government. The movement spread over the nation quickly, and successive cabinets could not but concede to the public's criticism of the *genro* and military authorities. The *genro* stabilized the political situation by nominating Okuma Shigenobu (1838–1922), who was popular among the public, as prime minister.

Using the Anglo-Japanese Alliance as an excuse, the second Okuma cabinet declared war on Germany and

JAPAN—HISTORICAL PERIODS

Jomon period (14,500–300 BCE)
Yayoi culture (300 BCE–300 CE)
Yamato state (300–552 CE)
Kofun period (300–710 CE)
Nara period (710–794 CE)
Heian period (794–1185)
Kamakura period (Kamakura shogunate) (1185–1333)
Muromachi period (1333–1573)
Momoyama period (1573–1600)
Tokugawa or Edo period (Tokugawa shogunate) (1600/1603–1868)
Meiji period (1868–1912)
Taisho period (1912–1926)
Showa period (1926–1989)
Allied Occupation (1945–1952)
Heisei period (1989–present)

entered World War I in 1914. As a result, upon Germany's defeat, Japan gained Qingdao city of Shandong province, a Chinese naval base that had been leased to Germany in 1898. The Okuma cabinet also issued the Twenty-one Demands to China (demands that China recognize Japan's territorial gains in Manchuria, which China assented to, and demands that China give Japan special rights in China proper, which China successfully resisted). This action caused anti-Japanese sentiment among the Chinese. The Lansing-Ishii Agreement, signed by the United States and Japan in 1917, constituted a U.S. acknowledgment of Japan's special interest in China and Japan's rights in South Manchuria. To further Japanese interests in China, the Japanese government made significant loans to the Chinese government.

Japan was involved in a military action in Siberia in 1918, along with the United States, England, and France, but sent many more troops than the Western powers and kept them there much longer. The action was very expensive and very unpopular at home; furthermore, the continued presence of Japanese troops in Siberia after troops from the other powers had withdrawn caused friction with the United States.

The Socioeconomic Impact of World War I on Japan

World War I was a boon to the Japanese economy. Increasing overseas demand enabled Japan to export much more than before the war, greatly improving its balance of payments. During the Russo-Japanese War (1904–1905), Japan had been a debtor country (1.1 billion yen). Economic good times that started in 1905 led to Japan's becoming a creditor country (2.8 billion yen) by 1920. With an increase in exports and a decrease in imports, however, the imbalance between supply and demand grew, and inflation intensified. Prices more than doubled during the same period, but wages continued to fall until 1918, causing workers economic hardship.

The wartime business expansion also increased urbanization. More people worked in nonagricultural and nonforestry industries than in agricultural and forestry industries. Population decreased in cities of fewer than 10,000 residents but increased in cities of more than 100,000. Such urbanization brought about expansion of local public financing, especially in big cities. Roads, water and sewage systems, schools, and parks were improved, and private investment in such areas as railroad and housing construction expanded greatly.

Because rice was in short supply due to speculative holding back of rice by landowners and merchants during the Siberian intervention, and because there was larger demand for rice in rapidly growing urban areas, its price increased. In July 1918, housewives of a fishing village in Toyama Prefecture rioted over the price of rice, and the riot eventually expanded nationally.

Intellectuals in the First Half of the Taisho Period

Minobe Tatsukichi (1873–1948), a law professor at Tokyo Imperial University, and Yoshino Sakuzo (1878–1933), also a professor at Tokyo Imperial University, promoted theories that supported the democratic movement. Minobe believed that supreme power belonged not to the emperor but rather to national common purpose and that the emperor's power should be limited; he described the emperor as one organ of the state. Minobe supported party politics and the appointment of party members to the cabinet in a period when many still thought the cabinet should be above the political wrangling party politics brought with it. Yoshino, for his part, believed that the public's participation in government should be through a representational system instead of leaving a politics to a small elite. He did not assert the sovereignty of the people but rather democratization of politics within the limits of the Meiji constitution.

In literature, various schools emerged that advocated self-fulfillment based on individualism; they grew out of and in opposition to schools of literary naturalism, which advocated factual or realistic representation and which had been popular at the beginning of the twentieth century. The new schools included the Shirakaba ha, or White Birch school, whose most famous authors included Mushanokoji Saneatsu (1885–1976) and Shiga Naoya (1883–1971); the Shin-Shichou (New Trend of Thoughts) school, with which the famous writer Akutagawa Ryunosuke (1892–1927) was at one time connected; and the Tanbi-Ha (Aestheticism School) of the sensual Nagai Kafu (1879–1959) and Tanizaki Jun'ichiro (1886–1965). Western-style theater, especially that which went under the name of "New Theater," became popular.

Postwar Politics and Diplomacy

The rice riots brought down the government of Terauchi Masatake (1852–1919), a military man, making it possible for Hara Takashi (1856–1921), the head of Japan's largest political party, the Seiyukai (Friends of Government Party), to become the first prime minister to have risen to power from within a political party (as opposed to through the military or by virtue of having been involved in crafting the Meiji government).

By the terms of the Treaty of Versailles, which ended World War I, Japan acquired a mandate to the islands in the South Pacific north of the equator and expanded its influence in East Asia as well. Chinese students in Beijing protested Japan's continuing presence on the peninsula of Shandong; China did not sign the Treaty of Versailles.

Amid external pressures, such as the Russian Revolution and formation of the League of Nations, Taisho Democracy reached its zenith in Japan. There was agitation for universal male suffrage (not attained until 1925), and labor unions quickly increased their memberships. Ichikawa Fusae (1893–1981), a feminist and politician who led the women's suffrage movement, and other women activists formed the Shin Fujin Kyokai, a women's association, and won the right of women to organize and attend political meetings. The public made gains in the freedoms of speech and association, and the socialist influence became strong. The Shakaishugi Doumei (Japanese Socialist League) was founded in 1920, and the Nihon Shakaito (Japan Communist Party) was founded in 1922.

In 1921, the Taisho emperor was declared mentally incompetent, and his son, the crown prince Hirohito, was made regent. Amid corruption in the government, Prime Minister Hara was assassinated in November 1921.

The new international order in Asia—the so-called Washington System—was formed by the Washington Conference (1921–1922), which was held to discuss limitations on naval armament, the rules of naval war, and so on. The conference stipulated that the Anglo-Japanese Alliance and the Lansing-Ishii Agreement be rejected and that China's Shangdong peninsula be returned to China. Furthermore, Japan was to pull its forces out of Siberia at the beginning of 1922. Kato Tomosaburo (1861–1923), an admiral and naval chief of staff, formed the cabinet in 1922. Kato cut down on the number of warships in accordance with the provisions of the Washington Conference. In 1924, the establishment of an "aristocratic cabinet" under Kiyoura Keigo (1850–1942) caused the second movement for constitutional government by the Goken San Pa (Three Coalition Parties for Constitutional Government), a coalition that included the Seiyukai, the Kenseikai (Constitution Party), and Kakushin Kurabu (Reform Club). Goken San Pa won a great victory in the general election in 1924. As a result, the Kenseikai became the majority party, and Goken San Pa dominated the House of Representatives and forced the resignation of Kiyoura. After the resignation, the Goken San Pa administration was formed, with Kato Takaaki (1860–1926) as prime minister. Henceforth, the party cabinet system, in which the president of the majority party of the House of Representatives became the prime minister, became the rule.

The first national movement to protect constitutional government and the movement to obtain universal male suffrage developed to reflect the public's will in politics. The second movement to protect constitutional government developed to allow political parties to lead public opinion. During Kato's administration the Universal Manhood Suffrage Law was passed, swelling the ranks of eligible voters to 20 percent (from only 2 percent at the time of the Russo-Japanese war). The proletariat made advances in representation in Parliament, and the Rodo Nomin To (Workers' and Farmers' Party), a party organized for laborers and farmers, was formed in 1926. The Kato cabinet opened diplomatic relations with the Soviet Union and decided to reduce armaments to the level of the Russo-Japanese War. On the negative side, Kato also enacted the Peace Preservation Law, which restricted freedoms of the press and of association.

Postwar Depression and the Kanto Earthquake

After World War I, Japan suffered a postwar depression. Initially, businesses had continued to grow even after the war, and people became absorbed in speculation in stocks and commodities. With the recovery of European and American exports, however, the Japanese started importing more. Production capacity, which had increased during the war, fell because of decreased demand. Furthermore, exports grew slowly because of competition in the Asia-Africa market from the economies of Europe and the United States. The wartime boom's strong demand for capital had made the financial market tighten quickly. With the fall of the stock market in March 1920, the boom ended. The four major exchanges dealing in stocks, cotton yarn, raw silk, and rice were closed, and many banks and companies declared bankruptcy. Laborers also suffered from production cutbacks and wage cuts. The Japanese economy experienced severe recession and deflation. This deflationary environment saw the establishment of an oligopolistic economy largely controlled by four major financial conglomerates—Mitsui, Mitsubishi, Sumitomo, and Yasuda—often referred to as *zaibatsu*s. With their abundant funds, those four companies established new industries, with such products as chemical fertilizer, electrical equipment, and rayon.

To make matters worse, the Kanto earthquake hit the industrial area of Tokyo and Yokohama in September 1923. The second Yamamoto cabinet declared a moratorium on the collection of loans to prevent economic turmoil. Furthermore, the government issued special notes, the so-called Earthquake Disaster Notes, to make up for the loss within the limit of the 100 million yen by which the Bank of Japan discounted the notes issued by commercial banks. The discounted notes, however, amounted to 430 million yen, and half of them fell insolvent, inducing concern over the credibility of the banks. This unsuccessful settlement of the notes resulted in severe financial disaster in the Japanese economy.

Intellectuals in the Second Half of the Taisho Period

Kawabata Yasunari (1899–1972), who in 1968 would become the first Japanese Nobel Prize winner for literature, became a leader of the school of Japanese writers that in the 1920s propounded a lyrical and impressionistic style, in opposition to the then-popular proletarian style, which portrayed the bleakness of proletarian existence in a rough, direct manner. The Tsukiji Shogekijo, a small theater in Tokyo formed by writer and director Osanai Kaoru in 1924, was influential in the further development of New Theater. The Free Educational Movement, which advocated education that respected a child's spontaneity and individuality, emerged in opposition to the uniform and controlled public education sponsored by the Ministry of Education.

From Taisho to Showa

Crown Prince Hirohito had been his father's regent from 1921; in 1926, with the death of the Taisho emperor, he became emperor, and the Showa period began. Although the Taisho period had seen the growth of a labor movement, universal male suffrage attained, and the development of party politics, the unstable economic climate and the power of the military set the stage for Japan's increasing militarism during the 1930s.

Akihiro Kawakami

See also: **Meiji Period; Russo-Japanese War; Showa Period; Sino-Japanese War**

Further Reading

Imai Seiichi, ed. (1990) *Nihon kindaishi no kyozo to jitsuzo* (False and Real Images of Modern Japanese History). Tokyo: Otsuki Shoten.
Inoguchi Takashi, and Daniel I. Okimoto. (1988) *The Political Economy of Japan*. Stanford, CA: Stanford University Press.
Kinbara Samon, ed. (1994) *Taisho Democracy*. Tokyo: Yoshikawa Kobunkan.
Minami Ryoshin. (1970) *Nihon keizai no tenkanten* (The Turning Point of the Japanese Economy) Tokyo: Sobunsha.
Namamura Takahusa. (1986) *Nihon keizai* (The Japanese Economy). Tokyo: Tokyo University Press.
Okawa Kazushi. (1974) *Choki keizai tokei* (Long-Term Economic Statistics). Tokyo: Toyokeizai Shinposha.
Yui Masaomi, ed. (1977) *Taisho Democracy*. Vol. 12. Tokyo: Seiyudo.

TAIWAN—PROFILE (2001 est. pop.22.4 million). Taiwan, officially known as the Republic of China (ROC), is an island about 100 miles (161 kilometers) off the southeast coast of China. It is roughly shaped like a tobacco leaf. The origin of the Chinese name Taiwan is unknown, but some scholars suggest it may be a phonetic rendering of an aboriginal name for the island. It is also known in the West as Formosa, or "beautiful island," a name given it by Portuguese explorers. Taiwan is approximately 36,000 square kilometers in size. Taipei, in the north of the island, is its largest city and capital. Taiwan is bounded to the north by the East China Sea, which separates it from Japan; to the east by the Pacific Ocean; to the south by the Bashi Channel, which separates it from the Philippines; and to the west by the Taiwan Strait, which separates it from China. In addition to the main island of Taiwan, the ROC government also has jurisdiction over Lanyu, Green Island, the Pescadores, Kinmen, Matsu, and a number of smaller, uninhabited islands.

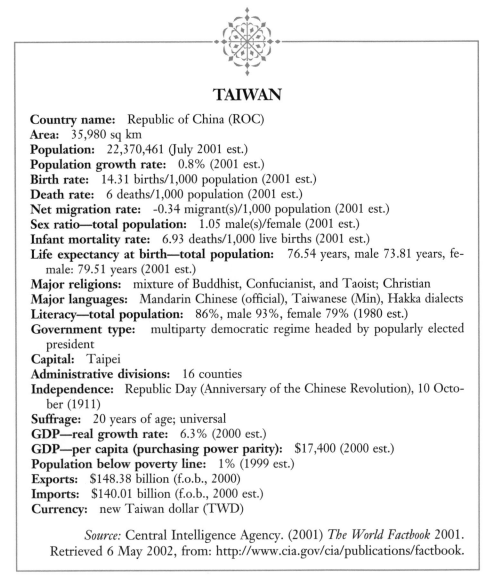

TAIWAN

Country name: Republic of China (ROC)
Area: 35,980 sq km
Population: 22,370,461 (July 2001 est.)
Population growth rate: 0.8% (2001 est.)
Birth rate: 14.31 births/1,000 population (2001 est.)
Death rate: 6 deaths/1,000 population (2001 est.)
Net migration rate: -0.34 migrant(s)/1,000 population (2001 est.)
Sex ratio—total population: 1.05 male(s)/female (2001 est.)
Infant mortality rate: 6.93 deaths/1,000 live births (2001 est.)
Life expectancy at birth—total population: 76.54 years, male 73.81 years, female: 79.51 years (2001 est.)
Major religions: mixture of Buddhist, Confucianist, and Taoist; Christian
Major languages: Mandarin Chinese (official), Taiwanese (Min), Hakka dialects
Literacy—total population: 86%, male 93%, female 79% (1980 est.)
Government type: multiparty democratic regime headed by popularly elected president
Capital: Taipei
Administrative divisions: 16 counties
Independence: Republic Day (Anniversary of the Chinese Revolution), 10 October (1911)
Suffrage: 20 years of age; universal
GDP—real growth rate: 6.3% (2000 est.)
GDP—per capita (purchasing power parity): $17,400 (2000 est.)
Population below poverty line: 1% (1999 est.)
Exports: $148.38 billion (f.o.b., 2000)
Imports: $140.01 billion (f.o.b., 2000 est.)
Currency: new Taiwan dollar (TWD)

Source: Central Intelligence Agency. (2001) *The World Factbook* 2001. Retrieved 6 May 2002, from: http://www.cia.gov/cia/publications/factbook.

History

Until the seventeenth century, Taiwan was inhabited almost exclusively by a number of aboriginal groups of Austronesian origin, although it was also visited by Chinese fishers and used as a haven for Japanese and Chinese pirates. Interested in using the island as an intermediate port between Japan and their colony in the Philippines, the Spanish established a settlement in the north of the island in 1626, which they held until evicted by the Dutch in 1642. In 1624, the Dutch established a trading post and settlement on the Southwest coast of Taiwan, near what is today the city of Tainan. The presence of Spanish and Dutch colonies on the island, and the prospect of work on new sugar plantations, brought an influx of Chinese immigrants to Taiwan.

In 1662 the Chinese rebel Zheng Chenggong (1624–1662; known in the West as Koxinga), who had hoped to restore the defunct Ming Dynasty in China, was driven out of China and fled with his armies to Taiwan. Zheng quickly defeated the Dutch and set up his own government on the island. He brought with him a new influx of Chinese immigrants. The Manchurian Qing Dynasty (1644–1912) took control of Taiwan in 1683, and it remained a part of Fujian Province until 1883, after which it was administered as a separate province. During Qing rule, Chinese colonizers took over the entire western part of the island. The original aboriginal inhabitants of the western plains largely intermarried with the Chinese. The aboriginal populations of the central mountains and east coast remained free from Chinese administrative control during the Qing period.

TAIWAN

As a result of the Sino-Japanese War (1894–1895) and the Treaty of Shimonoseki, Taiwan became a Japanese colony in 1895 and was administered for the first time in history as a single political unit. At the conclusion of World War II, Japan was forced to relinquish its colonies in Asia, and Taiwan was placed under ROC control. In 1949, the Chinese Communist Party established the People's Republic of China. The Chinese Nationalist Party (Guomintang, GMT), then led by General Chiang Kai-shek (1887–1975), retreated to Taiwan and has governed the island ever since. Following anti-GMT riots and violent government reprisals in 1947, the island was under martial law until 1987. The GMT has continued to claim jurisdiction over the Chinese mainland, and the Communist government of the PRC also claims sovereignty over Taiwan.

Geography

Taiwan is a largely mountainous island, formed geographically by the collision zone of the Philippine Sea plate, pushing up from the southeast, and the Eurasian plate, pushing down from the northwest. The alluvial plains and terraced tablelands of the western coast constitute the principle population areas and major cities. The major ports are Keelung, on the northern tip of the island, and Kaohsiung, on the southwestern coast. The Central Mountain Range runs down the center of the island from north to south, the tallest peak being Yu Shan at 3,997 meters. The east coast of the is-

land, with the exception of a major rift valley extending from Hualian to Taidong, is largely unsuitable for agriculture and sparsely settled.

Taiwan straddles the Tropic of Cancer, giving it long, hot summers and cool winters. The tropical south remains free of frost all year, but it does snow in the higher mountain areas of the north. The mean annual precipitation is 102 inches. Rainfall is heavier in the north, where winters are cold and rainy, than in the south, which generally remains warm and sunny. Typhoon season lasts from July to September, and can bring violent storms to Taiwan.

Politics

Taiwan was under martial law from 1947 until 1987. Beginning in 1986, in response to a growing opposition movement, the GMT began to liberalize the government and martial law was abolished in 1987. When Chiang Kai-shek's son and successor Chiang Ching-kuo (1910–1988) died, he was replaced by his hand-picked successor, Vice President Lee Teng-hui (b. 1923). In 1996, Lee Teng-hui returned to office as the first democratically elected president in the history of the ROC, and in 2000 Chen Shui-bian (b. 1951) became the first non-GMT candidate to be elected president of Taiwan.

Since the lifting of martial law in 1987, Taiwan has evolved into a multiparty democracy. Although the GMT still advocates eventually reunification with mainland China, some factions have been perceived as pro-independence, especially after Lee Teng-hui declared in 1999 that China and Taiwan are de facto two independent countries. The Democratic Progressive Party (DPP), the party of Chen Shui-bian, grew out of the opposition movement in the 1980s and controls most of the local and municipal governments. The DPP is split among pragmatic factions that focus on local governance and fundamentalist factions that advocate a formal declaration of independence from China. In 1993, the New Party emerged from among the right-wing ranks of the GMT to become the strongest advocates for unification with China. Taiwan also has a number of small parties, including a Green Party and the Taiwan Independence Party.

Economy

In 1997 Taiwan's gross national product yielded $284.8 billion, making it the world's twentieth-largest economy. In 1997 the industrial sector accounted for 34.9 percent of gross domestic product, agriculture accounted for 2.7 percent, and the growing service sector 62.4 percent. Foreign trade has played a vital role in Taiwan's economic development, enabling it to amass the third-largest foreign-exchange reserves in the world.

From 1945 to about 1975, government initiatives led Taiwan from import substitution to export promotion policies. Although some state industries have since undergone privatization, the government has historically run key industries such as electricity, steel, and petroleum. The state constructs basic infrastructure (highways, railways, and waterways), oversees the financial system (including banks and the stock market), and helps develop new sectors through technology transfers and dissemination of market information.

Taiwan is best known for its dynamic private sector. Entry costs for entrepreneurs are among the lowest in the world, a fact that accounts for the proliferation of small, often short-lived, stores and enterprises around the island. In the 1970s and 1980s, Taiwanese people often preferred to go into business for themselves, saying it is better to "be the head of a chicken than the tail of an ox." Flexible, often family-run manufacturers took the lead in producing consumer goods for the export market.

With a rise in the value of the new Taiwan dollar (Taiwan's currency) and the correspondingly high cost of Taiwanese labor, Taiwan has undergone industrial restructuring, with a shift from labor-intensive to capital-intensive production. Labor-intensive manufacturing processes, such as shoes and electric goods, have shifted production to mainland China and southeast Asia, with domestic production shifting to high-tech, capital-intensive industries. The Taiwanese economy is becoming increasingly dependent on the computer and related industries. In 1997 the hardware information technology industry yielded a total production value of US$30 billion, making it Taiwan's most important foreign exchange earner. Since 1995 Taiwan has been the world's third largest computer hardware supplier, trailing only behind the United States and Japan.

Peoples

At 601 persons per square kilometer, Taiwan is second only to Bangladesh for population density. Taiwan has an ethnically heterogeneous population. The original Austronesian aborigines, now divided into several diverse ethnic groups, live primarily in the central mountains or on the east coast, although young people often migrate to the major cities in search of work. Together, Taiwanese aborigines constitute about 2 percent of the population. In recent years, there has been a renaissance of aboriginal culture, their rights to cultural survival being enshrined in the 1997 revisions to the constitution.

The majority of the Taiwanese population are descendents from immigrants who arrived from China's Fujian and Guangdong provinces. The largest ethnic group are the Hokkien Chinese from southern Fujian Province. They speak Taiwanese, a dialect originating in the Xiamen area of Fujian Province that has evolved largely through the addition of loan words from Japanese, and is now considered on Taiwan to be a language distinct from Chinese. The Hakka, originally from Guangdong Province, also speak a distinct dialect. They live mostly in the foothills on the west coast.

The arrival of the GMT on Taiwan in the 1940s also brought with it an influx of predominantly Mandarin-speaking immigrants. These late arrivals, who come from all parts of China, are known as "mainlanders" in popular discourse, and now comprise about 15 percent of the total population. For the decades immediately following GMT takeover of Taiwan, they controlled the government and key industries, leaving the so-called "native Taiwanese" in charge of small-scale industry and petty commerce. In recent years, this ethnic division of labor has been challenged by the rise of an indigenous middle class and the increasing importance of class divisions. Due to the political dominance of the mainlanders and prohibitions against speaking Taiwanese in school or public discourse, Mandarin has become the lingua franca of Taiwan. In recent years, however, there has been a revival of interest in both the Taiwanese and Hakka languages, now frequently used in the media and in public transportation announcements.

Culture

Taiwan is home to most of the world's major religions, including Buddhism, Taoism, Protestant Christianity, Roman Catholicism, and Islam. Confucianism, with its emphasis on morality, family ethics, and academic thinking, has deeply influenced the Chinese people of Taiwan. Religion is not a divisive issue on Taiwan, however, as most Taiwanese people are eclectic in belief, practicing a combination of different faiths. In recent years, there has been a rise in so-called new religions, such as new sects of Buddhism with largely urban congregations and Yi-Guan-Dao, which combines Christianity, Islam, Buddhism, Taoism, and Confucianism into one religion.

The family is the most important theme in Taiwanese culture. Based on the Confucian concepts of filial piety and ancestor worship, the patrilineal family has long been the foundation of Taiwanese society. In the past, the family was the main economic institution in society, providing members with savings, investment, and production functions, as well as with social services. Those material dimensions of the family have been increasingly taken over by the state and private market in recent years, transforming the family into unit based primarily on emotional ties. Nationalist ideologies on Taiwan, however, still stress the importance of the family as a key cultural institution, which they perceive to be fundamentally different from families in other societies.

Taiwan is a rich fusion of Chinese, Japanese, aboriginal, and Western cultures. The National Palace Museum in Taipei is the repository of perhaps the world's best collection of traditional Chinese paintings, pottery, porcelain, curios, and sculptures. In addition to the visual arts, Taiwan also has a rich musical and theatrical culture that includes Chinese opera, Taiwanese opera and puppet theater, and aboriginal folk music. Performances at state-sponsored cultural centers, as well as in private venues, are frequent across the island. Architecture on the island is an eclectic mix of Qing-dynasty Chinese architecture, Japanese architecture, and the glass-and-steel architecture of pan-Asian modernity. Western influences are playfully integrated into the Meiji architecture of the Japanese period and the postmodern apartment complexes and skyscrapers of the 1990s.

The Question of National Sovereignty

The major issue currently facing Taiwan is the question of national sovereignty. The People's Republic of China sees Taiwan as a renegade province and would like to unify Taiwan into China in the next century. They have offered Taiwan high level autonomy in the context of "one country, two systems." China has increasingly isolated Taiwan diplomatically, preventing the ROC government from entering international organizations such as the World Health Organization and the United Nations. The Chinese military has also indicated preparedness to use military means to unify Taiwan and China if other strategies prove unworkable. On the Taiwanese side, President Chen Shui-bian has said that Taiwan and China are separate, sovereign states. With inflexibility on both sides, there is little hope that the issue will be resolved in the near future.

Scott Simon

Further Reading

Ahern, Emily, and Hill Gates. (1981) *The Anthropology of Taiwanese Society.* Stanford, CA: Stanford University Press.

Fei, John C. H., Gustav Ranis, and Shirley W. Y. Kuo. (1979) *Growth with Equity: The Taiwan Case.* New York: Oxford University Press.

Galenson, Walter. (1979) *Economic Growth and Structural Change in Taiwan : The Postwar Experience of the Republic of China.* Ithaca, NY: Cornell University Press.

Gold, Thomas. (1986) *State and Society in the Taiwan Miracle.* Armonk, NY: M. E. Sharpe.

Ho, Samuel P. S. (1978) *The Economic Development of Taiwan, 1860–1970.* New Haven, CT: Yale University Press.

Murray, Stephen, and Keelung Hong. (1994) *Taiwanese Culture, Taiwanese Society: A Critical Review of Social Science Research Done on Taiwan.* Lanham, MD: University Press of America.

Rubinstein, Murray. (1999) *Taiwan: A New History.* Armonk, NY: M.E. Sharpe.

Simon, Denis Fred, and Michael Y. M. Kau. (1992) *Taiwan: Beyond the Economic Miracle.* Armonk, NY: M. E. Sharpe.

Taiwan Government Information Office. (1999) *ROC Yearbook.* Taipei, Taiwan: Government Information Office.

Wade, Robert. (1990) *Governing the Market: Economic Theory and the Role of Government in East Asian Industrialization.* Princeton, NJ: Princeton University Press.

TAIWAN—EDUCATION SYSTEM Throughout Chinese history, education has been valued highly. The affirmation of this tradition is written into the law of the land. The 1946 Constitution of the Republic of China (Taiwan) establishes minimum spending thresholds for educational expenditures: not less than 15 percent of the total national budget, not less than 25 percent of the provincial budget, and not less than 35 percent of the municipal budget. The writers of the constitution displayed great foresight when they also took on the responsibility to "safeguard the livelihood of those who work in the fields of education . . . [and] increase their remuneration from time to time" (Article 165). The result of this legal affirmation is that Taiwan has developed one of the best systems of education in the world.

Total Expenditures and Enrollments

According to official government records, Taiwan's total government spending in 1999 for education, science, and culture exceeded $17.33 billion, or about 6.5 percent of the gross national product or 15.6 percent of government expenditures, and roughly $619 per citizen. When the Republic of China established control over Taiwan in 1945, the island's population was under 10 million people. Today the government exerts its authority over a population of 22 million.

In 1950, 17,111 students were enrolled in Taiwan's twenty-eight kindergartens. Preschooling was uncommon. In 1981 laws were passed to set basic standards. In 1998, 238,787 children attended 2,874 registered preschools, including both public (37 percent) and private (67 percent). The total preschool enrollment, including crèches and nursery schools, is 40 percent of the age group. This is lower than the 80 to 90 percent enrolled in many developed nations.

In the 1998 school year, 2.9 million elementary and junior high school students were enrolled in Taiwan's nine-year compulsory education system, and 916,000 students were enrolled in higher education. The elementary grades contain 97.8 percent of all school-age children between the ages of six and eleven. The total enrollment rate of the population between age six and twenty-one is 80 percent, and more than one-fifth of Taiwan's total population is attending an educational institution of some type. The effect of these educational opportunities has been to drop the national illiteracy rate to 5.3 percent.

There are 137 institutions of higher education, with an undergraduate class of 916,000 and a graduate class of 54,000. In terms of percentage of the population, these totals rank the Republic of China comparatively high in the world.

Educational Policies before the 1990s

The first forty years of Taiwan's education policy were designed to accomplish academic and political purposes: the academic goals stressed science, math, engineering, and history. To achieve a productive workforce, students were channeled into academic and vocational paths early. Several difficult examinations detered more than 70 percent of the students from entering higher educational programs. The pedagogical approach used rote learning, uniform examinations, continuous testing, and an authoritarian learning environment.

The political goals were to sinicize the Taiwanese. Mandarin Chinese was compulsory and was the only form of Chinese taught. Students and citizens were forbidden from and punished for using local Taiwanese dialects or languages in the classrooms or in public offices. An unswerving loyalty to the goals of the Republic of China was demanded. The students were required to study the biography and writings of Sun Yat-sen (1866–1925), the founder of the Republic of China, and to prepare for the return to China by studying Chinese history, geography, literature, and the tenets of Confucianism. While the government of Taiwan was under martial law (1947–1987), all educational institutions were staffed with political or military officers who maintained ideological discipline. These officers had the authority to keep files on students and to have them arrested. School officials openly practiced discrimination against Taiwanese natives because of their ethnic background and culture.

In 1949, 2 million refugees from the mainland entered Taiwan, adding to the 9 million Taiwanese. These Chinese mainlanders formed about 8 percent of the total population but controlled the political, military, and educational institutions.

Reforms in the 1990s

Academically, following the 1987 abrogation of martial law, Taiwan's authorities recognized the need to develop more paths to educational fulfillment. These have included alternative educational opportunities for gifted children; for special-needs students such as the blind, deaf, and handicapped; and for non-Mandarin speakers. Educational programs have been extended to adults and now incorporate support for social and cultural centers.

Educators recognize that though Taiwanese students excel in science, they are not good problem solvers and lack a sense of curiosity and initiative. Consequently, the educators have realized that they must provide greater flexibility in course requirements and teaching approaches. Instead of separating academic and vocational education, there is now a tendency to integrate the two types of learning. Due to the economic and technological environment created by the Information Age, students who enter comprehensive high schools can participate in designing their own curriculum and can prepare independently for their career choices. Reforms in program flexibility, length of the learning time line, and the grading system reflect an awareness of the individual student's needs. These reforms have called for more compensation to teachers who have to retool and who have to spend more time in individualized teaching preparations.

The abrogation of martial law in 1987 has resulted in the liberalization of Taiwan's educational system. The most significant change has been in the teaching of Taiwan's history. Local and regional history have entered the curriculum, and the general history of China and the role of the Nationalist Party, the Guomindang (or Kuomintang, the ruling party), has been reduced. In 1998 an unsuccessful attempt to quash a standardized textbook on Taiwan's historical identity resulted in an upsurge of locally focused writings, including classes on minority languages, music, culture, and history. Newspapers, radio, television, and other media promote Taiwan's peculiar multiculturalism. The current political challenge is how to combine a local, national, and international curriculum without explosive conflict between the groups that support independence for Taiwan and those who support reunification with the mainland. Of course, Beijing's ire will increase as Taiwan's education becomes more independent from the history of China as understood by the nationalist ideology on the mainland.

Richard C. Kagan

Further Reading

Smith, Douglas C. (1997) *Middle Education in the Middle Kingdom.* Westport, CT: Praeger.

The Republic of China Yearbook. (2000) Taipei, Taiwan: Government Information Office.

Wilson, Richard W. (1970) *Learning to Be Chinese: The Political Socialization of Children in Taiwan.* Cambridge, MA: MIT Press.

Yee, Herbert S. (1999) *The Political Culture of China's University Students: A Comparative Study of University Students in Mainland China, Hong Kong, Macau, and Taiwan.* Commack, NY: Nova Science Publishers.

TAIWAN—HUMAN RIGHTS   Following Japan's defeat in World War II, Taiwan once again became part of China. The Nationalists' rule in Taiwan was so oppressive, however, that the Taiwanese rose up against them on 28 February 1947. In response, the government imposed martial law in Taiwan, which remained in place until 1987. Political opponents were kept imprisoned on Green Island. These prisoners consisted of Mainlanders—Chinese who fled the mainland at the time of the Communist victory—who criticized Chiang Kai-shek's Nationalist government, and Taiwanese who suffered from Taipei's repressive and brutal attacks on their demands for political representation and calls for independence. Martial law *(jie-yen-fa)* placed enforcement and punishment of alleged crimes against state security in the hands of the Garrison Military Command. Secret trials and torture were extensively practiced by the military, and disappearances and unexplained deaths were commonplace.

The first major public breakthrough for opponents of martial law was the trial, on charges of treason, of the Gaoxiung (Kaohsiung) Eight. In order to coincide with United Nations Human Rights Day on 10 December 1979, the defendants organized an antigovernment protest march, which resulted in violence and destruction. The trial was made public as a result of international pressure. For the first time, the mechanics of martial law were made visible to the public. The defendants received sentences ranging from twelve years to life in prison. Eventually all were released early, and several, along with their lawyers, became active in Taiwan's human rights movement. Lu Xiu-lien (b. 1944) suffered in jail but later recovered and became a leading women's rights activist and in 2000 became the vice president of the Republic of China. Chen Shui-bian (b. 1951), a young commercial lawyer who represented the Gaoxiung Eight, turned to opposition politics and eventually became the mayor of Taipei (1994) and the president of the Republic of China in 2000. He appointed human rights professionals to high government offices: Lin Feng-ching, a proponent of social activism, ecology, anti-nuclear issues, and human rights, became Taipei's director of the Bureau of Reconstruction; Chen Chu, director of the Taiwan Human Rights Association, became director of Social Affairs for Taipei City. He also activated human rights policies in all areas of life.

The end of martial law on 15 July 1987 resulted in a dramatic propagation of human rights organizations and campaigns. Green Island prison was closed. Taiwanese nationalists successfully obtained greater political representation. The indigenous people and ethnic groups such as the Hakka established newspapers, radio, and television programs. Women, environmentalists, gays, laborers, fishermen, migrant workers, artists, health providers, social workers, and even criminals joined the chorus for a culture of human dignity based on human rights laws.

Richard C. Kagan

Further Reading

Neary, Ian. (2002) *Human Rights, Children's Rights, and Patients' Rights in Japan, South Korea, and Taiwan.* London: Routledge.

TAIWAN—POLITICAL SYSTEM   In the last decade of the twentieth century, the Republic of China on Taiwan became the first full-fledged multiparty democracy in Chinese history. The ongoing process of democratization has been accompanied by a growing feeling of Taiwanese identity vis-à-vis Chinese identity and has led to increasing tensions with the People's Republic of China, which considers Taiwan to be a renegade province. Both developments—democratization and Taiwanization—have greatly influenced the process of constitutional reforms and the balance of power between different political parties. They cannot be understood correctly without knowing the historical background, that is, the constitution of 1947, that was reformed in 1989.

Constitution of 1947 Structure

The Constitution of 1947 permitted democracy, guaranteed civil liberties, and promoted political participation. It was an eclectic mixture of Chinese and

Western elements. It outlined a political system consisting not of three, but of five powers, called the councils *(yuan)*. Two councils derived from the traditional Chinese institutions of the examination system and the censorate. The Examination Yuan fulfills the functions of a civil-service commission, while the Control Yuan (equivalent to the censorate) oversees government administration. The three other councils—the Executive, the Legislative, and the Judicial Yuan—can be compared with the three powers in Western parliamentarism, in which the chief of the cabinet (Executive Yuan) is the head of government and is responsible to the parliament (Legislative Yuan).

However, the constitution also had elements from a presidential system: the National Assembly and the president. The National Assembly elected the president and had, for example, the right to change the constitution. The president acted as the head of state and was the supreme commander of the armed forces. He also had the right to rule in times of unrest with the help of emergency powers. Although his powers exceeded those of a president in parliamentary systems, this presidency was not really an executive institution.

As a consequence of this amalgam, the 1947 constitution was neither presidential nor purely parliamentary. It was complicated by severe legal problems: not only was it marred by two competing legislative and executive blocs (the Legislative Yuan and the premier versus the National Assembly and the president), but also the relationship between those blocs was not clear. There were no functional boundaries, nor did any feasible system of checks and balances exist. No regulation, for example, existed for the instance in which the president and the premier, who is responsible to the Legislative Yuan but has to be nominated by the president, come from competing political parties.

Constitutional Practice until 1990

In practice, the constitution of 1947 was in effect only for six months. From 1948 on, and especially after the defeat of the Nationalists in the civil war and their withdrawal to Taiwan in 1949, the president of the republic and chairman of the Nationalist Party (Guomindang, GMD), Chiang Kai-shek (1887–1975), ruled with the help of emergency decrees and martial law. As a consequence, the bifurcated but predominantly parliamentary system of 1947 was replaced by a dictatorship dominated by the president.

Constitutional Reforms since 1990

Starting in 1986, the GMD allowed some liberalization of the Nationalist government on Taiwan. It

PREAMBLE TO THE CONSTITUTION OF THE REPUBLIC OF CHINA (TAIWAN)

Adopted on 25 Dec 1946.

The National Constituent Assembly of the Republic of China, by virtue of the mandate received from the whole body of citizens, in accordance with the teachings bequeathed by Dr. Sun Yat-sen in founding the Republic of China, and in order to consolidate the authority of the State, safeguard the rights of the people, ensure social tranquility, and promote the welfare of the people, do hereby adopt this Constitution to be promulgated throughout the land for faithful and perpetual observance by one and all.

Source: International Court Network. Retrieved 8 March 2002, from: http://www.uni-wuerzburg.de/law/tw00000_.html

abolished martial law, legalized the formation of political parties, and removed restrictions on civil rights. In 1990, the GMD decided to reelect all representative institutions and to reform the constitution. In 1991 Lee Teng-hui, who succeeded Chiang Kai-shek's son Chiang Ching-kuo as president, rescinded the emergency laws. In the following years, the political system on Taiwan has been readjusted toward a presidential system of government.

The National Assembly was stripped of most of its powers and is no longer directly elected; it is now mainly responsible for constitutional changes. The president, who since 1996 has been elected directly, has gained in power. The premier has become a kind of executive agent of the president, who, albeit still with only a few clearly defined executive powers of his own, is now able to dominate the Executive Yuan. The Legislative Yuan now can propose a no-confidence vote against the premier. However, it runs the risk of being dissolved by the president if it does so. Whereas these changes are a step in the direction of a system with more checks and balances, the problem of a bifurcated political system remains unsolved. If a political party different from that of the president should dominate the Legislative Yuan, the president would have to nominate a premier from that party. Because the president and the premier are not urged to cooperate in a state council and because the legal executive powers of the president are still very limited, a constitutional crisis could well be the consequence.

Electoral Competition between Political Parties

Parallel to the constitutional reforms, since 1990 the party system has undergone far-reaching changes, which in the end led to the landslide defeat of the GMD in the presidential elections of March 2000. In 1986, the GMD tolerated the establishment of the Democratic Progressive Party (DPP), which united major forces of the previous opposition against the GMD. Since the early 1970s, this opposition had fought for democratization and Taiwanization of the polity. In the years after 1986, the GMD managed to incorporate many of the opposition's demands and therefore was able to maintain the upper hand in most of the central elections. The changes of GMD policy meant that the party was increasingly troubled by inner-party struggles between Lee Teng-hui's policy of further Taiwanization and those who leaned toward the long-term goal of reunification with the mainland.

In August 1993, the first split resulted in the establishment of the New China Party, which was not able to garner more than 10 percent of the votes in the elections. In 1999, the GMD split a second time, with James Soong, the previous governor of Taiwan Province and the GMD secretary general, declaring that he would run as an independent candidate in the presidential elections. In these elections, the GMD candidate, Lien Chan, got 23.1 percent of the vote; James Soong received 36.8 percent; and the DPP candidate, Chen Shui-bian, got 39.3 percent. The conflicts within the GMD hence enabled the DPP to score a historic victory and, at the same time, led to the situation of a president who has to cope with a Legislative Yuan dominated by another party.

Results of Ten Years of Reform

After more than a decade of constant reforms and tremendous changes, the political system of the Republic of China on Taiwan today is fully democratized and is by and large characterized by a consensus that Taiwan has its own identity. A vibrant and still-changing party system has developed that makes it hard to predict future developments. As a result of the GMD split that followed the presidential elections of March 2000, James Soong established a new political party, the Peoples First Party. This party's performance will have at least as great an influence on the future political development of Taiwan as the outcome of the GMD party reforms triggered by the defeat of March 2000 and the performance of the DPP as a quasi-government party.

The constitutional situation has improved, but it still needs further adjustments in order to clarify the power relation between the president, the premier, the Legislative Yuan, and the National Assembly, so as to ensure a stable political system with a government that will be able to react quickly and with a unified voice when dealing with future internal and external challenges.

Axel Schneider

See also: **Chen Shui-bian; Chiang Kai-shek; Lee Teng-hui**

Further Reading

Chang, Charles Chi-hsiang, and Tien Hung-mao, eds. (1996) *Taiwan's Electoral Politics and Democratic Transition: Riding the Third Wave.* Armonk, NY: M. E. Sharpe.

Chao, Linda, and Ramon H. Myers. (1998) *The First Chinese Democracy: Political Life in the Republic of China on Taiwan.* Baltimore: Johns Hopkins University Press.

Chu Yun-han. (1992) *Crafting Democracy in Taiwan.* Taipei, Taiwan: Institute for National Policy Research.

Rigger, Shelley. (1999) *Politics in Taiwan: Voting for Democracy.* New York: Routledge.

Rubinstein, Murray A. (1999) *Taiwan: A New History.* Armonk, NY: M. E. Sharpe.

Schneider, Axel. (2000) "Constitutional Reforms in the ROC on T'ai-wan: Internal and External Parameters of Regime Change." *Harvard Studies on Taiwan: Papers of the Taiwan Studies Workshop* 3: 171–202.

Tien Hung-mao. (1989) *The Great Transition: Political and Social Change in the Republic of China.* Stanford, CA: Hoover Institution Press.

TAIWAN ECONOMIC MIRACLE

Taiwanese economic growth in the past forty years has been phenomenal. In 1962 Taiwan had a per capita gross national product (GNP) of $170, placing the island's economy squarely between Zaire and Congo. By 1997 Taiwan's per capita GNP, adjusted for purchasing power parity (PPP), had soared to $19,197, contributing to a Human Development Index similar to that of European countries such as Spain, Portugal, and Greece. This economic feat has been well recognized in business and scholarly communities, with Taiwan often touted as the prime example of growth with equity. In popular discourse in both Taiwan and abroad, this rapid economic growth has been called the "Taiwan economic miracle." In Taiwan this ideology is usually associated with the ruling Guomindang (Kuomintang, GMD) party and its adherents.

Most economic scholars have attributed Taiwan's economic growth to the successful implementation of neoliberal free market economic principles. Others have emphasized the role of GMD policy as leading

FIVE LARGEST COMPANIES IN TAIWAN

According to *Asia Week*, the five largest companies in Taiwan are the following:

Company	Sector	Sales ($ millions)	Rank in Asia
Chinese Petroleum	Oil Refining	14,975.2	75
Taiwan Power	Energy	9,811.4	139
Chunghwa Telecom	Telecommunications	5,893.7	216
Taiwan Semiconductor	Technology	5,416.8	232
Mitac International	Computers	5,257.6	238

Source: "The Asia Week 1000." (2001) *Asia Week* (9 November): 116.

to a developmentalist state. Some scholars have claimed that Taiwan's economic miracle is the result of a Chinese Confucian culture that emphasizes education, family values, and an industrious work ethic. In all of its variations, the ideology of the Taiwan economic miracle has justified GMD rule of Taiwan through depiction of the island as the embodiment of capitalist productivity, bureaucratic efficiency, and Chinese tradition. This ideology links capitalistic development to nationalist sentiment, making opposition to capitalism seem non-Chinese and unpatriotic.

Ever since martial law was lifted in 1987, the ideology of the Taiwan economic miracle has come under question by both Taiwanese and Western scholars. Some scholars note that Taiwan's phenomenal economic growth actually began under Japanese occupation of the island. Some point out the influence of U.S. aid on the island, which contributed greatly to Taiwan's gross domestic product during the Cold War decades of the 1950s and 1960s and also opened up the U.S. market to Taiwanese products. These historical arguments are usually identified in Taiwan with the DPP (Democratic Progressive Party).

Some scholars look beyond the "miracle" at problems such as ethnic divisions in Taiwanese society, the evolution of economic classes, and the environmental destruction wrought by rapid industrialization. Within Taiwan, the nationalist implications of the ideology have been criticized most vocally by the labor and feminist movements. If many people believe that hard work is a Taiwanese national characteristic and a reason for the economic miracle, for example, it is difficult for unions to advocate a forty-hour workweek. The ideology, therefore, has had largely a conservative influence on society, creating greater adherence to the GMD and restraining the growth of progressive political movements on the island.

Scott Simon

Further Reading

Fei, John C. H., Gustav Ranis, and Shirley W. Y. Kuo. (1979) *Growth with Equity: The Taiwan Case.* New York: Oxford University Press.

Galenson, Walter. (1979) *Economic Growth and Structural Change in Taiwan : The Postwar Experience of the Republic of China.* Ithaca, NY: Cornell University Press.

Gold, Thomas. (1986) *State and Society in the Taiwan Miracle.* Armonk, NY: M. E. Sharpe.

Simon, Denis Fred, and Michael Y. M. Kau. (1992) *Taiwan: Beyond the Economic Miracle.* Armonk, NY: M. E. Sharpe.

Wade, Robert. (1990) *Governing the Market: Economic Theory and the Role of Government in East Asian Industrialization.* Princeton, NJ: Princeton University Press.

TAIWAN—INVESTMENT IN ASIA

After three decades of economic development—which included phases of import substitution, export expansion, and industrial upgrading—Taiwan fostered a special economic environment, characterized by small- and medium-sized enterprises (SMEs) and specialized industrial networks. Following rises in wages and land prices, coupled with an appreciating currency at home, Taiwanese firms embarked on a major stream of outward foreign direct investment (FDI) in the mid-1980s.

Taiwanese Investment in China

According to official records of the People's Republic of China (PRC), Taiwanese investment on the mainland first took place in 1983. The volume of investment projects, however, did not significantly increase until 1988. In 1991, the Taiwanese government eventually legalized indirect investment in the mainland, via a third country, but the surge in the stream of FDI into the PRC took place between 1993 and 1996.

Taiwan's investment in China showed a strong trend toward certain locations. Before 1992, Guangdong and Fujian (two southeast coastal provinces of China) had accounted for 67.3 percent of the total investment amount, and 88 percent of cases. In 1999, Guangdong province continued to attract the largest percentage of Taiwan's investment dollars (29 percent), Jiangsu and Fujian attracted about 10 percent each, and the more northern reaches of Beijing and Liaoning attracted 5 percent and 2 percent of funding, respectively. It is well known that Taiwan's FDI in China has always played a pioneering role for both Western and Japanese FDI, with the adventurous SMEs playing a crucial role in these pioneering endeavors.

As to industrial distribution, in 1991, the labor-intensive industries (including electrical and electronics components, vehicles, shoemaking, plastic products, clothing, and so on) were the leading outgoing industries for Taiwanese investment in China. With the upgrading of Taiwan's industries, however, technology-and capital-intensive industries have gradually assumed a leading role in outward FDI to mainland China. In the last three years of the twentieth century, the electronics industry (including home appliances and personal computers) accounted for almost 40 percent of the total annual investment in China. The petrochemicals, basic metals, and textiles industries accounted for a further 6 to 7 percent, respectively.

Taiwanese Investment in Southeast Asia

Taiwan's investment in Southeast Asia has, however, demonstrated quite a different pattern from its investment in China. By the end of 1999, Taiwan's FDI in Southeast Asia was about equal to that in China (around 40 billion New Taiwan dollars in contracts, respectively). In terms of the number of FDI firms, however, there are only around 5,500 firms in Southeast Asia as compared to 40,000 in China. This means that the average scale of Taiwanese investment in Southeast Asia is much larger than in China. Taiwan is now the second-largest investor in both China and Vietnam, the third-largest in Malaysia and Cambodia, the fourth-largest in Thailand, and the fifth-largest in the Philippines and Indonesia. As a trading partner, Taiwan ranks between fifth and ninth in each of these countries.

Distinctive Features of Taiwan's Investment in Asia

Through FDI, Taiwanese firms are constructing a regional production network to supply a broad range of differentiated and competitive products. Among the various industries, electronics and personal computers take the leading roles in international manufacturing division of labor. There are sixteen products currently achieving the highest market share in the global market in computers and peripherals, among which switching power suppliers, keyboards, mouses, desktop personal computers, sound cards, cases, and monitors all have a 70 percent or higher proportion of their products produced abroad.

Previously established national industrial networks provide the Taiwanese SMEs with their competitive edge in overseas production. Such export-oriented, subcontracting-based FDI exhibits two distinctive characteristics. First, Taiwan's FDI is trade-creating rather than trade-substituting; in order to maintain their core strength in export competition, Taiwanese firms have to rely on an intrafirm and interfirm division of labor and on network resources at home to support their offshore production operations. Second, Taiwanese FDI firms are small by international standards, typically lacking managerial and financial resources. Their subsidiaries are therefore given a high degree of autonomy in managerial decisions. This results in the rapid pace of localization.

These two distinctive characteristics of Taiwanese firms represent a unique approach to internationalization. Taiwanese firms combine domestic resources with those of Southeast Asia and China to strengthen global competitiveness. Unlike Western multinational firms, which generally undertake FDI either to explore local markets or to create export enclaves in a labor haven, Taiwanese FDI is aimed at network linkages that provide access to local resources that promote growth and technology upgrading. Taiwanese firms specialize in small niche markets, in which they strive for a leadership position. Through FDI, they construct a regional production network to supply a broad range of differentiated and competitive products. With the support of a regional production network, they can more readily respond to shifting demands from all sides.

Last but not least, at the beginning of the twenty-first century a unique phenomena emerged. Through the efforts of some domestic or international charity associations (for example, the Tzu-chi Buddhist Compassion Relief Foundation and World Vision Taiwan), Taiwanese FDI firms transformed their international industrial networks into networks of compassion and relief for disaster-hit, poor, or needy areas. Therefore, Taiwanese overseas investment networks may lead to a diverse wave of "entrepreneurs of loving kindness" in Asia in the twenty-first century.

Lee-in Chen Chiu

Further Reading

Chen, Tain-Jy. (1998) *Taiwanese Firms in Southeast Asia: Networking across Borders.* Cheltenham, U.K.: Edward Elgar.

Chen, Tain-Jy, and Ku Ying-Yua. (1999) "The Characteristics and Effects of Taiwan's Direct Investment in Southeast Asia." In *Southeast Asian Trade and Investment: Post-Crisis Reforms and International Cooperation,* edited by Manuel F. Montes and Godwin C. Chu. Honolulu, HI: East-West Center, 169–190.

Chiu Chen, Lee-in. (2001) "Taiwan's Economic and NGO Social Services Network in the Asia-Pacific Region." In *Taiwan, East Asia, and Copenhagen Commitment,* edited by Lee-in Chiu Chen. Taipei, Taiwan: CIER, 233–256.

———. (2000) "Taiwan's Economic Influence: Implications for Resolving Political Tensions." In *Taiwan Strait Dilemmas: China–Taiwan–U.S. Policies in The New Century,* edited by Gerrit W. Gong. Washington, DC: CSIS Press, 127–146.

Chiu Chen, Lee-in, and Chin Chung. (1993) "An Assessment of Taiwan's Indirect Investment toward Mainland China." *Asian Economic Journal* 7, 1: 41–70.

Kao, Charng. (1994) "Economic Interaction between the Two Sides of the Taiwan Strait." In *Globalization, Regionalization, and Taiwan's Economy,* edited by Chien-nan Wang. Taipei, Taiwan: CIER, 141–169.

La Croix, Sumner J., Michael Plummer, and Keun Lee, eds. (1995) *Emerging Patterns of East Asian Investment in China: From Korea, Taiwan, and Hong Kong,* New York: M. E. Sharpe.

TAIWAN, MODERN

(2002 est. pop. 23.3 million). Taiwan is an island situated approximately 176 kilometers east of the Chinese mainland. Han Chinese (China's dominant ethnic group) account for 98 percent of Taiwan's population; the other 2 percent are indigenous peoples whose ancestral origins lie in neolithic southern China and Austronesia. Regionally and historically, the population originated in two great migrations from the mainland: those Chinese who came to Taiwan before 1895, who originated in Fujian and Guangdong provinces, and the nearly two million who came with the Nationalist Chinese following the Communists' 1949 victory in China's civil war.

The Establishment of the Republic of China on Taiwan

When Chiang Kai-shek's Nationalist Party (the Guomindang, GMD) arrived in Taiwan, it began a campaign against the Taiwanese and their culture. On 28 February 1947 the Chinese military escalated a dispute into an islandwide repression that left thousands of Taiwanese dead and instituted years of "White Terror," in which many Taiwanese patriots were arrested, punished, and even executed. The Taiwanese language was banned from educational institutions and government offices, and Taiwanese membership in professional, governmental, civic, and social organizations was greatly restricted. Chiang Kai-shek established the Republic of China (ROC) on Taiwan and asserted that it was the legitimate government of all China.

When the Korean War broke out in June 1950, President Truman sent troops to Korea and simultaneously blocked off the Taiwan Straits from a possible Communist Chinese invasion of the Republic of China. This decision established the policy that there was just one China, and that the Republic of China was its legitimate government. In addition, the decision confirmed the belief that the Nationalist Chinese were using Taiwan only as a springboard to return to China. Officially, the national capital was still Nanjing, with Taipei the temporary capital of the exiled regime. For over thirty years, the ROC did not engage in any large infrastructure construction projects, even refraining from building public parks or recreational areas, because of that attitude.

The GMD extended its powers into the all areas of society: the military, schools, banks, industry, and secret police. Because the newly arrived mainlanders were a minority of the population, they had to make alliances with local groups. Beginning in 1950, chief executives and representative bodies under the provincial level were directly elected by the citizenry. However, these elections were carefully monitored and managed. Buying votes was common. The local leadership working in harmony with the GMD became powerful and wealthy through government contracts, real estate manipulation, and protection rackets. Because Taipei was the seat of the central government of Taiwan, it was somewhat spared the worst evils of this system.

In 1971, the Republic of China withdrew from the United Nations, and its seat was transferred to the People's Republic of China. In March 1979, the United States embassy in Taipei was formally closed, replaced by the American Institute in Taiwan. This procedure was a way to mask the reality that the United States had recognized the Communist government in Beijing as the sole government of China. The shock of these diplomatic crises spurred domestic criticism of the GMD regime.

Rebellion against the GMD

The diplomatic failures, combined with growing strength and tolerance of local elections, led to increasing calls for political reform. In 1979 the *Formosa Journal* initiated a Taiwanese reform movement that threatened the mainlanders' rule and culminated in the Kaoshiung Incident of 10 December 1979. A police attack on the Taiwanese opposition resulted in multiple injuries and the beginning of the arrests, detentions, beatings, and forced exile of thousands of Taiwanese activists. The trial of the leadership for sedition was the first internationally attended political tribunal in the history of the Republic of China. The publicity and disclosure of the government's repression consolidated and energized local and international support for a democratic and open system of government. It was not until March 1996, however, that the people of Taiwan elected a president—Lee Teng-hui (b. 1923)—by direct popular vote. He received 54 percent of the vote.

Taiwan Moves toward Independence

In terms of diplomatic affairs, Lee's tenure was challenging. Under Lee, the term "one China" was redefined as "one country and two areas separately ruled by two political entities," a definition maintained by his successor, Chen Shui-bian (b. 1951).

On 18 March 2000 Chen Shui-bian, the Democratic Progressive Party (DPP) candidate, and a leader in the movement for Taiwan's independence, was elected president of the Republic of China. The GMD suffered when its vote-buying practices were revealed, and many members of the industrial Taiwanese elite feared that a GMD victory would result in further escalation of the corruption and the destruction of the Taiwanese economy. Beijing's leadership threatened Taiwan with dire consequences if Chen Shui-bian won, but those threats only increased Chen Shui-bian's support. Chen had also been respected during his tenure as mayor of Taipei (1994–1998) and was highly regarded for his leadership in Taiwan's human-rights movement.

Recent Cultural Developments

As long as the Republic of China defined itself by its anti-Communist stance, the cultural emphasis was on preserving Chinese tradition. When the claim to represent all of China was shattered, there was a dramatic growth in new cultural forms. Hakka (a Chinese minority people with a population on Taiwan), Taiwanese, and indigenous tribal music grew in popularity. At first modern art was influenced by foreign mentors in the United States, Japan, and Europe, but gradually a Taiwanese modern art emerged with its own unique emphasis on feminism, localism, and cosmopolitanism. Art was no longer sandwiched between the slices of tradition and ideological purity. The Taipei Museum of Modern Art has become one of the key venues for new artists. Taiwanese artists appear more frequently at international art shows. In the 1990s Taiwanese films won international awards: among them *The Wedding Banquet* and *Such a Life*. Modern Taiwan can also take pride in significant accomplishments in the areas of economic development and human rights. Its national security, economic progress, social justice, and cultural creativity have become an integral part of Asia and of the world.

Richard C. Kagan

Further Reading

Copper, John F. (1997) *The Taiwan Political Miracle: Essays on Political Development, Elections, and Foreign Relations.* Lanham, MD: University Press of America.

Rigger, Shelly. (1999) *Politics in Taiwan.* New York. Routledge.

Rubinstein, Murray A., ed. *Taiwan: A New History.* Armonk, NY: M. E. Sharpe. 1999.

TAIWAN STRAIT The Taiwan Strait, also known by its Portuguese name, the Formosa Strait, is the 190-kilometer-wide body of water that separates the west coast of the Republic of China (Taiwan) and Fujian Province of the People's Republic of China. It also links the East Sea and the South China Sea. The Taiwan Strait is home to the Pescadores (Penghu) Archipelago, a group of sixty-four small islands covering an area of approximately 80 square kilometers off the west coast of Taiwan. The largest islands of the Pescadores Archipelago are Penghu, Yuweng (Yuneng), and Baisha (Paisha), whereas the best known are the Taiwanese-controlled islands of Jinmen (Quemoy) and Mazu (Matsu).

Keith Leitich

Further Reading

Gurtow, Melvin, and Hwangm Byong-Moo. (1980) *China under Threat: The Politics of Strategy.* Baltimore: Johns Hopkins University Press.

Lilly, James R., and Chuck Downs, eds. (1997) *Crisis in the Taiwan Strait.* Washington, DC: National Defense University Press.

Zhao, Suisheng, ed. (1999) *Across the Taiwan Strait: Mainland China, Taiwan, and the 1995–1996 Crisis.* New York: Routledge.

TAIWAN–UNITED STATES RELATIONS

The relations between the Republic of China (Taiwan) and the United States can be divided into three historical stages. The first was the period of the civil war between China's Communists and the Nationalists; the second was the period during which the United States recognized the Nationalist government in Taipei as the legitimate government of all China; and the third, which continues today, is period that began when the United States recognized the Communist government in Beijing as the legitimate government of China.

Stage 1: The Chinese Civil War, 1945–1950

During World War II, the Nationalist Republic of China, still had control of a good portion of mainland China. It was with the Nationalists that the United States allied itself against Japan. At the Cairo Conference of December 1943, the Allies agreed that P'eng Hu (the Pescadores) and Taiwan (which had been ceded to Japan in 1895) would be returned to China following Japan's defeat. The establishment of Mao Zedong's government in Beijing and the exile of Chiang Kaishek's government to Taipei, Taiwan, created a crisis in U.S. diplomacy. The American government was still debating whether to support Beijing's or Taipei's claims to Taiwan when the Korean War broke out in June 1950. On 27 June 1950, President Harry S. Truman ordered the U.S. Seventh Fleet to prevent a Communist attack on Taiwan and asked the Republic of China to cease air and sea operations against the mainland.

Stage 2: Diplomatic Recognition of Taiwan, 1950–1978

On 3 October 1949, the United States issued a statement reaffirming its support of the Nationalist Government. That same year, on 7 December, the Nationalist Government established itself on in Taipei. On 27 June 1950, in reaction to the hostilities in Korea, the United States moved the Seventh Fleet into the Straits of Taiwan to protect the island. In May 1951, the United States and Taiwan established the Military Advisory and Assistance Group (MAAG) to aid in securing Taiwan's boarders from hostile assaults. This relationship provided Taiwan's government with American military, economic, and political support. Taiwan became an important base for American military and diplomatic interests. President Chiang Kaishek sent "advisors" to Korea; rice to Vietnam; and allowed his territory to be an operations center for U.S. Navy SEAL raids on China and electronic listening stations on communications in mainland China. The so-called China Lobby organized citizens in Taiwan and

America not only to support Taipei but also to criticize Americans suspected of being pro-Communist or anti-Chiang Kai-shek.

The alliance between Americans and Chinese on Taiwan, based on anti-Communism, laid the foundation for nearly unquestioning support of Chiang's island nation. However, between 1970 and 1972 President Nixon and his secretary of state Henry Kissinger sought relations with Beijing in order to weaken the Soviet Union, pressure the North Vietnamese to the peace table, and develop trade. Beijing demanded that the United States recognize the claim of China to the island of Taiwan. This meant that America must sever diplomatic relations with Taiwan, support China's accession to Taiwan's seat in the United Nations, and agree to withdraw American military from the island.

The Joint U.S.-China Communique (subsequently known as the Shanghai Communique), signed on 28 February 1972 between President Richard Nixon and Premier Zhou Enlai, precipitated a crisis over the Taiwan Strait. Since the United States and the People's Republic of China could not reach an agreement on the status of Taiwan, each side stated its position. The Chinese side unequivocally declared that "Taiwan is a province of China . . . the liberation of Taiwan is China's internal affair in which no other country has the right to interfere . . . . The Chinese Government firmly opposes any activities which aim at the creation of 'one China, one Taiwan,' 'one China, two governments,' 'two Chinas,' an 'independent Taiwan' or advocate that 'the status of Taiwan remains to be determined.'" Furthermore, the Chinese maintained the right to use military force against Taiwan.

The United States acknowledged that "all Chinese on either side of the Taiwan Strait maintain there is but one China and Taiwan is a part of China. The United States does not challenge that position. It reaffirms its interest in a peaceful settlement of the Taiwan question by the Chinese themselves."

The public communique appeared to support a peaceful process for the resolution of the Taiwan crisis. In fact, secret discussions assured the Chinese that Taiwan was just an "irritant" and that the United States was unwilling to support Taiwan's autonomy. Nixon's own State Department officials tried ineffectually to change the wording from "all" Chinese to "some" Chinese in order to acknowledge the voice and rights of the millions of Taiwanese who did not share the view that Beijing should rule them.

Chiang Kai-shek's death in 1975, and President Jimmy Carter's normalization of relations with Beijing eroded the Nationalist's commitment to reconquer the Chinese mainland. Taiwanese domestic reaction reflected a belief that an independent Taiwan was a possibility. A tug of war began, with Taiwanese calling for independence and China calling for the return of the island to Beijing's jurisdiction. The Taiwan Strait once again became the focus for a military crisis.

Stage 3: Looking for a Peaceful Resolution, 1978–Present

In December 1978, in accordance with the promises of the Shanghai Communique, President Jimmy Carter severed formal diplomatic relations with Taiwan and normalized relations with the People's Republic of China. When formal diplomatic relations with the Republic of China were severed, the U.S. Congress reacted angrily. From January to April 1979, Congress crafted the Taiwan Relations Act (TRA), and passed it with a sizable majority. This act established a shadow embassy in Taiwan (called the American Institute in Taiwan), and promised Taipei that the United States would provide military support and assistance as long as China threatened the island militarily. The TRA allowed Taiwan to establish fictive diplomatic agencies in the United States, which later became known as the Taipei Economic and Cultural Office. The Congress declared that the TRA trumped the communique because it was a legislative act and thus law, not just a statement of policy or a diplomatic document agreed upon secretly and between a few individuals. Beijing clearly resented this interference in its jurisdiction and has sought to have the TRA revoked.

In 1982, the governments of China and the United States issued a second Shanghai Communique that created much controversy. President Ronald Reagan encouraged Taiwan to unify with China but linked the reduction of U.S. arms sales to Taipei with a commitment by Beijing to seek only a peaceful settlement regarding unification. Once again, the new communique conflicted with the protections provided by the Taiwan Relations Act. The last major declaration on the Taiwan issue occurred in 1999 during President Bill Clinton's visit to Beijing and Shanghai. He reiterated the U.S. policy of neither recognizing two Chinas nor an independent Taiwan. He gave added support to Beijing's position by declaring that the United States would not support Taiwan's representatives in any international organization that gives membership to an established independent state. This meant that Clinton would prevent Taiwan from joining the United Nations.

Meanwhile, relations between Taiwan and Beijing were developing their own momentum. In the late 1980s, the Republic of China established a legal and organizational mechanism to develop relations with China. In 1991, President Lee Teng-hui terminated Taiwan's goal of reuniting with China by means of force. During the 1990s, both sides established organizations to deal with issues of trade, communication, investment, and travel. China has insisted that practical issues be discussed only after the political issue of unification is agreed upon. Taiwan's strategy is to place the goal of unification into the far future when China has democratized and has risen to the economic and political standards and levels of Taiwan.

The danger of armed conflict still remains, however. China's military exercises in 1995 and its blatant brandishing of weapons and warlike rhetoric prior to the Taiwan presidential election of 2000 alarmed Taiwan and its supporters. The election in 2000 of pro-independence presidential candidate Chen Shui-bian exacerbated the crisis in the Taiwan Strait: China's military leaders stated that Taiwan must show good faith to begin talks concerning unification or face military consequences. Some American military experts believe that China will forcefully incorporate the "renegade" province before 2010. Others believe that there is still time to negotiate and find a peaceful solution. Washington, D.C., is sill undecided on what type of military support should be given to Taiwan. Is a Theater Missile Defense shield necessary? What types of defensive weapons will defend Taiwan and not create an arms race? American diplomacy has so far prevented outright war in the region. Yet, any unilateral dramatic change in the unstable cross-Strait situation will surely result in major, and perhaps dire, consequences for East Asia.

Richard C. Kagan

Further Reading

Cooper, John F. (1997) *The Taiwan Political Miracle: Essays on Political Development, Elections and Foreign Relations.* Lanham, MD: University Press of America.

Koen, Ross Y. (1974) *The China Lobby in American Politics*, edited with an introduction by Richard C. Kagan. New York: Harper and Row.

Mann, James. (1999) *About Face: A History of America's Curious Relationship with China, from Nixon to Clinton.* New York: Knopf.

TAJ MAHAL The Taj Mahal at Agra in the state of Uttar Pradesh, India, is a mausoleum built by Mughal emperor Shah Jahan (reigned 1628–1658) in memory of his favorite wife, Arjumand Banu Begum, and its name is believed to be an etymological distortion of her title Mumtaz Mahal (Chosen One of the Palace). The

The Taj Mahal in July 1996. (STEPHEN G. DONALDSON PHOTOGRAPHY)

Taj Mahal took more than a decade to complete (1632–1643), and it reflects mausoleum or sepulchral architecture of the Mughal period in India, combining Central Asian architectural practices, mainly of the Timurid dynasty (flourished fifteenth–sixteenth centuries), and Mughal influences within its planning, layout, architectural style, and decoration.

An isolated structure today, the mausoleum once formed part of a larger ensemble of buildings fronting the Yamuna River that included surrounding gardens, a ceremonial tennis court, subsidiary tomb enclosures, and a commercial complex divided by two bazaar streets intersecting to form four caravansaries (inns).

TAJ MAHAL—WORLD HERITAGE SITE

Considered one of the eight wonders of the world, there can be no doubt as to why the Taj Mahal was designated a UNESCO World Heritage Site in 1983. Despite the best efforts of UNESCO, the beautiful white marble tomb is threatened by pollution from local industry and excessive tourism.

By the tomb's completion, the surrounding area had developed into a township called Mumtazabad (known today as Tajganj), and an imperial command decreed that the bazaars and the caravansaries, together with thirty villages from the district of Agra, provide income toward the upkeep of the mausoleum.

While the Taj Mahal is bilaterally symmetrical, its central axis, beginning at the gatehouse and culminating at the tomb, is also emphasized. The tomb, with its four minarets, clad in white marble and flanked symmetrically by a mosque and an assembly hall, sets the main accent to the palace complex. In variation, radial symmetry dominates the layout of the gatehouse and the tomb proper, both of which follow the ninefold plan, creating distinct points of punctuation in an ordered landscape. The Taj Mahal garden is an elaborated version of a typical Mughal riverfront garden, with a raised terrace (the plinth for the main buildings) combined with a lower *char bagh* (quadripartite garden). The Taj Mahal was designated a World Heritage Site by the United Nations Educational, Scientific and Cultural Organization (UNESCO) in 1983 and is one of the primary tourist attractions in India and a symbol of India around the world.

Manu P. Sobti

Further Reading
Bagley, W. E., and Z. A. Desai. (1989) *Taj Mahal: The Illumined Tomb*. Seattle, WA: Aga Khan Program for Islamic Architecture and University of Washington Press.

Koch, Ebba. (1991) *Mughal Architecture*. Munich: Prestal-Verlag.

TAJIKISTAN—PROFILE

(2001 est. pop. 6.6 million). The Republic of Tajikistan emerged as an independent county after the 1991 collapse of the Soviet Union, the poorest of the post-Soviet republics. It entered the twentieth century ranking 108 out of 174 countries in the Human Development Index, and with a per capita gross domestic product of only $215.4. These low figures contrast with high adult literacy rate of 95–99 percent. Tajikistan has a total area of 143,100 square kilometers. Most of its population lives in valleys, which constitute only 7 percent of country's territory. The capital of Tajikistan is Dushanbe.

Geography

Tajikistan lies in the heart of Central Asia and is bordered on the east by China, on the north and west by Kyrgyzstan and Uzbekistan, and in the south by Afghanistan. Far from seas and oceans, Tajikistan is an alpine country, with more than half the country above 3,000 meters. Geographically, Tajikistan can be divided roughly into four parts: north, east, center, and southwest. The northern part includes the Zeravshan and Syr Dar'ya River basins and consists of semidesert land and foothills. The east is alpine country, with the highest mountain ranges in Central Asia, the Pamirs and Tian Shan. This is the biggest yet least populated region of the country. Two main mountain passes leading north and east are closed by snow for several months of the year and separate the northern and eastern regions from Dushanbe, which is located in the central part of the country. Central Tajikistan stretches from the alpine border with Kyrgyzstan and the Pamir foothills in the east to the fertile Hisor valley and the border with Uzbekistan in the west. The fourth, southwestern region includes the Vakhsh and Panj River basins, and is crossed by relatively low mountain ranges.

Like other Central Asian countries, Tajikistan has a dry climate with little rainfall, so it depends on irrigation. The climate of Tajikistan is sharply continental, ranging from a low of –20°C in January to a high of 30°C in July, depending on altitude. Thanks to its snow, ice, and glaciers, Tajikistan has more then 60 percent of Central Asia's water resources.

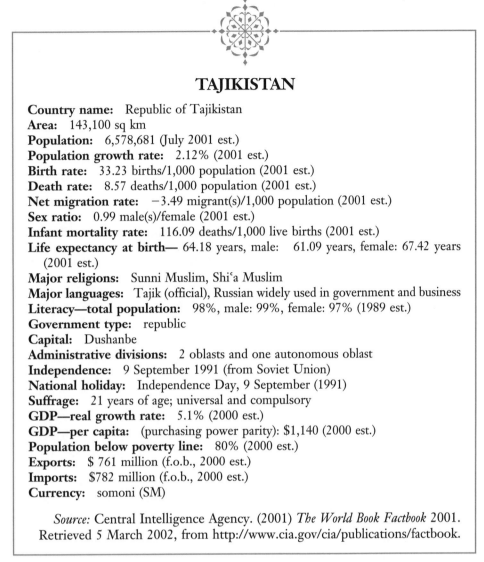

TAJIKISTAN

Country name: Republic of Tajikistan

Area: 143,100 sq km

Population: 6,578,681 (July 2001 est.)

Population growth rate: 2.12% (2001 est.)

Birth rate: 33.23 births/1,000 population (2001 est.)

Death rate: 8.57 deaths/1,000 population (2001 est.)

Net migration rate: −3.49 migrant(s)/1,000 population (2001 est.)

Sex ratio: 0.99 male(s)/female (2001 est.)

Infant mortality rate: 116.09 deaths/1,000 live births (2001 est.)

Life expectancy at birth— 64.18 years, male: 61.09 years, female: 67.42 years (2001 est.)

Major religions: Sunni Muslim, Shi'a Muslim

Major languages: Tajik (official), Russian widely used in government and business

Literacy—total population: 98%, male: 99%, female: 97% (1989 est.)

Government type: republic

Capital: Dushanbe

Administrative divisions: 2 oblasts and one autonomous oblast

Independence: 9 September 1991 (from Soviet Union)

National holiday: Independence Day, 9 September (1991)

Suffrage: 21 years of age; universal and compulsory

GDP—real growth rate: 5.1% (2000 est.)

GDP—per capita: (purchasing power parity): $1,140 (2000 est.)

Population below poverty line: 80% (2000 est.)

Exports: $ 761 million (f.o.b., 2000 est.)

Imports: $782 million (f.o.b., 2000 est.)

Currency: somoni (SM)

Source: Central Intelligence Agency. (2001) *The World Book Factbook* 2001. Retrieved 5 March 2002, from http://www.cia.gov/cia/publications/factbook.

The People and Languages

Tajiks, an Aryan people, were the first to settle in Central Asia. Tajiks are Muslims, predominantly Sunnis of the Hanafi school. They speak Tajiki, a western Iranian language very close to Farsi and Dari of Iran and Afghanistan, respectively. Some 200,000 Shi'a Imami Ismaili Tajiks of Badakhshan speak eastern Iranian. There are also few thousand Yaghnobi speakers living in the central part of the country. Since independence, Tajiki (written in Cyrillic script) has been the state language, while Russian is used for international communication.

History

The first urban settlements in what is now Tajikistan appeared 2,500 years ago, founded by peoples of Iranian origin. In the sixth to fourth centuries BCE the region was a part of the Achaemenian (Persian) empire. It was conquered by Alexander of Macedon at the end of the fourth century BCE. An amalgam of local and Hellenic cultures flourished in southern Central Asia in the fourth to the third centuries BCE. In the third century CE Central Asia fell under the control of Iranian Sasanid dynasty (224/28–651 CE). During the seventh and eighth centuries Arab troops brought Islam to the urban Tajik centers of Central Asia. Modern Tajiks trace the origins of their statehood to the Samanid dynasty (864–999), the first Muslim state in Central Asia to be independent of the Arabs. In the eleventh century, dynasties of Turco-Mongolian stock were established, pushing Tajiks to the political periphery.

The profile of today's Tajikistan was defined by Anglo-Russian competition at the end of the nineteenth century. In the 1860s, Russia had conquered the Central Asian Kokand khanate. Another Tajik-populated state, the Bukharan emirate, became a Russian vassal in 1869. The British, meanwhile, controlled what are now Pakistan and India. Afghanistan, as a buffer state with its northern edge along the Amu Dar'ya, served as a natural defensive line between the Russian and British empires.

Soviet power was established in what is now Tajikistan in 1917–1921. In 1924, central and southern Tajikistan became an autonomous republic within the Uzbek Soviet Socialist Republic. In 1929 Khujand (current Sogdian) province was transferred from Uzbekistan to Tajikistan and the country given the status of a separate Tajik Soviet Socialist Republic.

Tajikistan declared its independence in September 1991. Immediately, a political struggle between a coalition of Islamic groups and newborn secular democratic movements who opposed the old Soviet elite erupted. In the brutal civil war of 1992–1993, 50,000 people lost their lives and more than 650,000—a tenth of the population—fled in terror. More than 35,000 homes were destroyed, and the total damage of the war reached $7 billion.

Politics

Talks sponsored by the United Nations in 1994–1997 led to peace and the incorporation of the United Tajik Opposition into the government. Tajikistan's constitution, adopted in 1994, declared the country to be independent, democratic, unified, and secular with separated executive, legislative, and judicial powers. Tajikistan is the only state of post-Soviet Central Asia in which an Islamic movement has opted to officially participate in the political process. The supreme legislative body is the bicameral Majlisi Oli (Supreme Council). In the November 1999 presidential elections, Emomali Rakhmonov, the leader of the People's Democratic Party of Tajikistan, won 96.91 percent of votes. His opponent from the Islamic Renaissance Party got only 2.1 percent.

Economy

After Tajikistan gained independence in 1991, its economy declined, with the gross domestic product (GDP) dropping by more than 50 percent between 1991 and 1997. In 1998, the country provided just 0.3 percent of the total GDP of the Commonwealth of Independent States (CIS), the association of former Soviet republics, putting it in last place among the former USSR states. Average monthly salary stood at $11 in 1999. According to World Bank estimates, 85 percent of Tajikistan's population live below the poverty line.

The national economy is structured as it was in Soviet times. Agriculture, represented mostly by the cotton production, is the most important sector and employs about a half the population. It is joined by some non-ferrous metallurgy, electricity generation, and light industry. In finance, a two-level bank system was created, headed by an independent national bank. In 1997, a new tax code was adopted. Privatization began in 1992 with selling of household and small enterprises, but a lack of capital and foreign investment seriously limits economic growth.

Kamoludin Abdullaev

Further Reading
Djalili, Mohammad Reza, Frederic Grare, and Shirin Akiner, eds. (1998) *Tajikistan: The Trials of Independence*. London: Curzon Press.
United Nations Development Program (UNDP). (1998) *Tajikistan. Human Development Report 1998*. Dushanbe, Tajikistan: United Nations Development Program (UNDP).
———. (1999) *Tajikistan. Human Development Report 1999*. Dushanbe, Tajikistan: UNDP.
———. (2000) *Tajikistan. Human Development Report 2000*. Dushanbe, Tajikistan: UNDP.

TAJIKISTAN—ECONOMIC SYSTEM
Tajikistan's economy is affected by its topography. It is a mountainous country, situated from 300 to 7,495 meters above sea level. The territory is seismic, but without volcanic phenomena. Its location deep in the heart of Asia, far from any sea, gives it a sharply continental climate. It is dry, with a plenty of solar days (250 per year) and harsh daily and seasonal temperature fluctuations. Nine-tenths of Tajikistan is mountainous, and the mountains have a large effect on the climate, which ranges from subtropical in valleys to arctic in the East Pamirs.

Agriculture

Tajikistan is severely limited in agricultural land as 65 percent is not used for any form of agriculture, and plowed fields account for only 0.6 percent of Tajikistan's total area. Nonetheless, under the Soviet Union, agriculture was emphasized and accounted for almost one-quarter of Tajikistan's internal gross output and one-third of all its exports (in the form of cotton fiber); almost half the able-bodied population was involved in agriculture. The main product was cotton.

Other forms of agriculture—stock-raising and production of cereal crops—were limited by the lack of arable land to producing only for internal needs, and in fact were unable to supply those needs. Today, arable lands are used for cotton growing, and irrigated fields are the basis of agricultural production. Of the new land that is suitable for bringing under cultivation, the overwhelming proportion is on hillsides and is only suitable for fruit trees.

Water Resources

The total flow of water through Tajikistan is 52.2 cubic kilometers annually, or 44 percent of the total annual average flow of all Central Asian rivers. Almost all rivers are fed by glaciers, which occupy approximately 8,000 square kilometers, or 6 percent of the country.

Tajikistan has, therefore, significant potential hydroelectric resources. The potential stocks make about 300 billion kilowatt-hours per year. Turkmenistan is second among former Soviet republics (after Russia) in hydropower resources, and is first in terms of density of hydropower resources.

During the Soviet period, the Soviet Union supported the accelerated development of hydroengineering in Tajikistan. Five hydropower stations were constructed; they produced 90 percent of the electricity generated in Tajikistan. Construction of three more stations began, but they were left uncompleted at the time of the Soviet Union's collapse.

Fossil Fuels and Mineral Resources

Coal is Tajikistan's most abundant fossil fuel. There are fifteen coal-rich areas in the country, with the estimated reserve of four billion metric tons. However, almost all the deposits are difficult to exploit because of the complicated mountainous geological structure and the remoteness of the sites (far from railroads). Of the fifteen coal deposits, only one, the Shourab brown coal layer, has been exploited and an insignificant amount of coal was also extracted from the Fan-Yagnob deposit. In spite of its reserves, Tajikistan imports 85 percent of its coal needs. Tajikistan's reserves of oil and gas are insignificant and not of high quality. Domestic output of gas covered only 13 percent of demand and gas and oil were imported.

Tajikistan is fortunate in its many mineral resources: non-ferrous, rare and precious metals, raw materials for the chemical industry, and building materials. The most plentiful mineral deposits are salt, antimony, and strontium. Tajikistan is also the leading Central Asian nation for deposits of lead, zinc, bismuth, and fluorspar; its iron ore is practically the only iron in the region with industrial value. Tajik-istan also is home to the world's second-largest silver deposits.

Under the Soviets, Tajikistan's mining industry included enterprises for extraction of ores and manufacture of concentrates of antimony, mercury, lead, zinc, gold, silver, and a number of other nonferrous and rare metals. The manufacture of aluminum accounted for 50 percent of all industrial output. However, difficulties gaining access to these minerals and the absence of modern technologies for extraction in mountainous conditions constrained development of the listed stocks. Of four hundred mineral deposits, only a hundred have been exploited. Today, Tajikistan's largest nonferrous metallurgical enterprises are Adrasman and Anzob Mining Ore Combines, Tajik Aluminum Plant, and Isfara Hydrometallurgical Combine.

Manufacturing

While part of the Soviet Union, Tajikistan manufactured cable products, household refrigerators, power transformers, chemicals, store equipment, parts for automobiles and agricultural and textile machines, and other items. Most of the enterprises had small capacities and were not very productive. The chemical industry boasted two large plants (Yavan Chemical and Vakhsh Nitrogen Plants).

Issues Since Independence

Under the Soviet Union, the Tajik economy was not allowed to develop independently. Furthermore, economic decisions were made based on short-term needs without taking into account the economic costs of the probable environmental harm. As a result, significant damage was done to the environment. Inappropriate irrigation and intensive use of pesticides have led to salination and degradation of the soil. At present, 200,000 hectares of Tajikistan's arable lands, or 30 percent of its irrigated lands, are saline and 50,000 hectares have suffered double salination and are lost from cultivation. Major damage was also done to the country's water resources as overuse of fertilizers and pesticides means that contaminated water flows in the rivers after irrigation.

With the declaration of independence in 1991, Tajikistan began to conduct its own economic policy, stressing a gradual transition to a market economy. A program of large-scale reform was developed to correct the problems caused by the Soviet-managed economy. However, transition from a centralized planned economy to a market economy has proven to be very difficult. An economic crisis, civil war, and natural disasters have all conspired against success. The civil war alone is estimated to have cost $7 billion in damages. As a consequence of all these unfortunate events, there was a steady downward trend in all branches of the economy until 1996. Only in 1997 did the gross national product (GNP) finally rise—by 1.7 percent in comparison with the previous year. However, the GNP has yet to reach even 40 percent of its 1990 level.

The investment industry has suffered greatly. The physical volume of domestic investments has increased by 3.8 percent since 1991. The government is the only investor but it is severely constrained by its budget; specifically, it is burdened by its external debt. Annually, 13–14 percent of export expenditure goes to service the external debt, with serious negative consequences for economic growth.

With the signing of a peace agreement (1997) ending Tajikistan's civil war (1991–1997), attempts were made to revive the economic reform program. Privatization of state-owned enterprises and property has proceeded, promoting growth of the private sector. The private sector generates 44 percent of the GNP and by 1998, Tajikistan was relatively economically stable.

The Prospects for Sustainable Growth

Investment, a driving factor of progress, is necessary for rehabilitation of the economy and its steady development. The Tajik government is looking for external sources of investment, although the economy has simultaneously both attractive and negative features.

The appeal consists of large stocks of natural resources, cheap labor, and an investment-friendly government. However, as a whole, the investment climate in Tajikistan is seen as adverse. It is seen as politically and socially unstable, and its economic policies are also seen as being subject to change. The absence of property-rights guarantees also make foreign investors wary. So far, foreign companies have been interested only in those industries that offer short-term profits, namely, mining. Thirty-three joint ventures registered in 1998; with investors coming from Russia, Uzbekistan, Switzerland, the United States, and other nations.

Tajikistan, for its part, is interested in moving from being an exporter of raw materials to being an exporter of value-added goods; it also wishes to solve its unemployment problem and increase its revenues so that it can expand its social programs. Therefore, the government is interested in the long-term direct investments for development of such priority sectors as hydro engineering, deep processing of cotton, fuel and heating, and mining.

Development of hydropower is seen as most promising. The construction of hydropower stations in mountainous surroundings does not remove lands from agricultural use, which is a powerful factor in support of development of this sector. Cheap and ecologically pure energy can be exported to countries as far away as northern China and Pakistan.

In the absence of foreign investors, it is necessary to cultivate domestic private investors. One possibility has been to develop production of fruits and vegetables, with an eye toward marketing the produce in Siberia. Tajikistan's population is largely rural and has a propensity for agricultural work; small volumes of manufacture and the presence of the state programs to attract private entrepreneurs are expected to promote growth in the sector.

Another strategy is to use tax receipts from private enterprises and farms for long-term investment in the capital-hungry hydroengineering sector. Eventually priorities will be shifted toward the fuel and heating industry, cotton processing enterprises, and others. The country has a vast variety of energy sources—solar, geothermal, and hydroelectric, not to mention its coal deposits. If sufficient investments are directed towards this sector, Tajikistan should have the potential to meet not only internal, but also external demands. Future development of the fuel and heating industry might focus on developing nonconventional energy sources, such as solar and geothermal energy.

Finally, some consideration is being given to developing Tajikistan's tourist potential. The major potential is Tajikistan's mineral springs, including two hundred mineral springs, a third of which are also hot springs.

Munavvara Mukhidinovna Nuridinova

Further Reading

Akhrorova, Alfiya. (1988) *Problems of Tajik Energetic Complex Effectiveness.* Dushanbe, Tajikistan: Donish.

Komilov, Sirodjiddin, Nuridin Kayumov, and Mirmakhmad Nurmakhmadov. (1998) *Strategy to Market Economy.* Dushanbe, Tajikistan: Tajik Department of International Economic and Social Reforms.

Ministry of Nature Protection. (1996) *The State of Environment in 1992–1994: National Report.* Dushanbe, Tajikistan: Ministry of Nature Protection.

Rakhimov, Rashid. (1988) *Tajikistan in the Common National Economy of the USSR.* Dushanbe, Tajikistan: Donish.

Republic of Tajikistan. (1999) *Annual Statistics, 1998.* Dushanbe, Tajikistan: State Statistical Agency.

Saidmuradov, Khabibullo, and Kirill Stanyukovich, eds. (1982) *Tajikistan: Nature and Resources.* Dushanbe, Tajikistan: Tajik Academy of Sciences.

TAJIKISTAN—EDUCATIONAL SYSTEM

The educational system in Tajikistan has a strong Soviet/Russian influence. During the Soviet era (1918–1991) a comprehensive educational infrastructure and modern educational system provided free education emphasizing sciences, mathematics, and practical skills. By the 1930s the government eradicated mass illiteracy. According to official statistics, in 1989 more than 1.3 million students or approximately 23 percent of the population attended 3,100 schools. In addition, 41,700 students attended forty-two specialized secondary schools, and there were ten institutes of tertiary education. However, knowledge of Russian, which was a medium of instruction at most tertiary institutions, was poor; only 27 percent of Tajiks stated that they were fluent in Russian.

After independence in 1991, the educational system in Tajikistan underwent two major changes. First, there was a greater emphasis on the use of the Tajik language as the medium of instruction. Second, there was a considerable withdrawal of state funding of the educational system as a consequence of the 1992–1997 civil war (in 1998, Tajikistan spent only 2.2 percent of the GDP on education).

The constitution of Tajikistan (1994) stipulates that general education is compulsory and free and that the state guarantees access to free general, vocational, specialized, and higher education in state-controlled educational establishments. Tajik, Uzbek, and Russian are the major languages of instruction. The constitution also guarantees that all ethnic groups may use their mother tongue.

At the age of seven, children begin an eleven-year compulsory education program, composed of four years of primary school and a seven years of secondary school. According to official statistics, in 1998 more than 1.4 million students, or approximately 20 percent of the population, attended 3,522 primary and secondary schools. In addition, there were fifty specialized secondary schools and seventy-four vocational and technical schools. According to official statistics, approximately 94 percent of all those between the ages of seven and sixteen were enrolled in some kind of educational institution, although the dropout rate is high.

After completing a secondary school, students may enter a tertiary educational institution (university or institute), which usually offers a five-year program. According to official statistics, in 1999, 75,400 students attended twenty-four tertiary educational institutions. Students may complete postgraduate studies at a three-year *aspirantura* program, which combines coursework and dissertation writing. Upon completion of *aspirantura* students receive a degree of *kandidat nauk* (equivalent to a Ph.D.).

Throughout the 1990s the quality and accessibility of the educational system in Tajikistan declined due to the civil war, severe economic recession, and chronic shortage of textbooks. According to the United Nations Development Program, fewer female students entered the educational system. The government of Tajikistan is trying to reform its educational system by attracting private investment and international assistance to the educational sector.

Rafis Abazov

Further Reading
Asimov, M. (1984) *Encyclopedia: Tadzhikskaia Sovetskaia Sotsialisticheskaia Respublika* (Encyclopedia: Tajik Soviet Socialist Republic). Dushanbe, Tajikistan, USSR: Glavnaya Nauchnaia Redaktsia Tadzhikskoi Sovetskoi Entsiklopedii.

Landau, Jacob, and Barbara Kellner-Heinkele. (2001) *Politics of Language in the Ex-Soviet Muslim States: Azerbaijan, Uzbekistan, Kazakhstan, Kyrgyzstan, Turkmenistan, Tajikistan.* Ann Arbor, MI: University of Michigan Press.

United Nations Development Program. (1999) *Tajikistan: Human Development Report, 1999.* Dushanbe, Tajikistan: United Nations Development Program.

TAJIKISTAN—HISTORY

Tajikistan, formerly known as the Tajik Soviet Socialist Republic, was one of the Central Asian republics of the Soviet Union from 1929 to 1991. The independent Republic of Tajikistan emerged in 1991. The Tajiks are Iranian-speaking peoples, descendants of the group known as Aryans, who were mentioned in the Avesta, the Zoroastrian scripture (third to seventh century). The Iranians settled in the transriver region of Central Asia 2,500 years ago or even earlier, and it was probably here that the Zoroastrian religion came into being.

The Ancient and Medieval Periods

The Iranian ancestors of the Tajiks constituted the core of the populations of Khorezm, Bactria, and Sogdiana—ancient states of Central Asia lying between the Amu Dar'ya and Syr Dar'ya Rivers. The area of present-day Tajikistan has always been attractive to foreign powers because of its strategic location and its resources. Cyrus the Great (c. 585–529? BCE), ruler of the Achaemenid Persians, subjugated this region in the sixth century BCE and incorporated it into the Persian empire; Alexander of Macedon conquered it around 328 BCE. The Seleucids, heirs to Alexander's empire, continued to rule here, but the Saka, nomadic invaders

KEY EVENTS IN TAJIKISTAN HISTORY

6th century BCE   The region is ruled by the Persians.

328 BCE   Alexander of Macedon conquers the region and it comes under Seleucid rule.

130 BCE   The Saka displace the Seleucids.

c. 50 BCE   The Kushans displace the Saka.

6th–7th centuries CE   Arabs bring Islam to the cities of Central Asia.

9th century   The Samanid dynasty displaces the Arab rulers.

13th century   The region comes under Mongol control.

16th century   Ties are cut with Persia and Uzbeks establish the khanate of Bukhara.

1869   The Russians take control of the khanate of Bukhara.

1876   Most Tajik regions are under Russian control.

1921   Under Soviet control, Tajik areas are placed within the Turkistan Autonomous Soviet Socialist Republic.

1924   Southern Tajikistan is placed within the Uzbek Soviet Socialist Republic.

1991   The Republic of Tajikistan is founded.

1992–1993   The period of most intense fighting during the Tajik Civil War.

1997   United Nations peace talks end the civil war.

2002   Tajikistan provides some assistance to the United States during its invasion of Afghanistan.

from the eastern steppes, overran the region around 130 BCE, followed by the Kushans, also from the eastern steppes, in the mid-first century BCE.

During the seventh and eighth centuries CE, Arab armies brought Islam to the Tajik-populated urban centers of Central Asia, and the Iranians became one of the major contributors to Muslim culture. At the end of the ninth century, Arab rule began to disintegrate, and the Samanid dynasty (864–999), with its capital in the city of Bukhara, replaced it. Eventually the Mongols absorbed the Tajik lands into their empire in the thirteenth century.

Modern Tajik historiography traces the origins of Tajik statehood to the Samanid state, when Tajik culture was home to some of the finest scholars and poets of the Muslim world. Despite the various Turkic and Mongol rulers whose dynasties dominated the lands inhabited by the Tajiks, the Tajik element prevailed in the administration and culture in Mawarannahr, the Arabic name for Central Asia.

The sixteenth century marked important changes in Tajik history. First, the Safavid dynasty in present-day Iran (1501–1722/1736) declared Shi'ism its state religion and thereby cut all ties with the Tajiks, who remained Sunni Muslims. Second, Turkic Uzbek nomads led by Shaybani Khan overran Central Asia, establishing the khanate of Bukhara in the region inhabited by Tajiks.

The Colonial Period

The geographic and political profile of today's Central Asian states, including Tajikistan, was defined by superpowers at the end of the nineteenth century. Great Britain, after having subdued the Indian subcontinent, stopped near the Hindu Kush Mountains, a few kilometers from the Amu Dar'ya River. Russia occupied the right bank of the Amu Dar'ya and made the emirate of Bukhara a Russian protectorate in 1869. During the next several years, the other Central Asian states, the khanates of Khiva and Quqon, fell to Russia and most Tajik regions were under Russian rule by 1876.. Present-day Afghanistan served as a buffer state, and the Amu Dar'ya along this country's northern edge formed a natural defensive line between the British and Russian empires.

Thus from this time onward, Tajiks have lived in different sociopolitical and economic settings, because their original lands were divided into different polities. Some Tajiks, in the Bukharan emirate (a vassal of Russia), continued to live as they had for centuries. In the Pamir Mountains, as well, notwithstanding the establishment of Russian rule, there was almost no change. By contrast, northern Tajikistan, having been annexed by Russia to constitute part of the Turkistan Government-Generalship, with the capital in Tashkent, experienced rapid modernization.

The Soviet Period

After the Russian Revolution of 1917, Soviet power was established in northern Tajikistan at the end of 1917 and in the south in 1921, when the area of present-day Tajikistan became part of the Turkistan Autonomous Soviet Socialist Republic. In 1924, national delimitation of Central Asia granted central and southern Tajikistan the status of autonomous republic in the Uzbek Soviet Socialist Republic. Again as in 1895, the Tajiks had lost, as Stalin's mapmakers handed over major centers of Tajik culture—Samarqand, Bukhara, Khojend—to Uzbekistan. Khojend (since 1936 Leninabad) province was transferred to Tajikistan in 1929, and the country was given the rank of a separate Tajik Soviet Socialist Republic.

Notwithstanding many disadvantages and hardships associated with the Soviet imposition of power—civil war and emigration, unfair national delimitation (which created a republic whose population was less than 60 percent Tajik), Stalin's purges of the 1930s, the Soviet struggle against religion, forcible resettlement of various ethnic groups in the 1950s and later, experiments with the Tajik language—there were also great achievements in education, health care, culture, and arts. During this time, examples of unique national literature, media, and historiography were formed and preserved. A basis for the national economy was established, collectivization of primitive private farming was carried out, and relatively stable transport links between the different regions of Tajikistan and with the neighboring Soviet republics were constructed. Authority at the nation level was developed that covered the whole territory of the Tajik SSR. A modern literary language was developed, common to this day for all Tajiks. The capital city, Dushanbe, emerged as a shared administrative and cultural center. The Tajiks, cut off from their southern Muslim neighbors, communicated mostly with other peoples of the Soviet Union and with Slavs. All these factors shaped the outlines of Tajik national identity and of their state.

Soviet rule was also destructive, however. Most important was the obvious disharmony in terms of distribution of power and resources between regions, enhanced by the inequality of regional economies. In addition, Tajikistan was the poorest republic with the lowest per capita gross domestic product.

Postindependence

Tajikistan, following the examples of the other republics of the Soviet Union, adopted a declaration of state independence in September 1991. In 1990–1992, this political awakening took the form of a struggle of the Islamic opposition allied with the newborn secular nationalistic and democratic movements versus the old Soviet elites who had remained in power. This conflict was gradually overtaken by the region-based group discord that soon led to civil war.

The opposition's initial aim was to take power from the pro-Communist, northern, Leninabad (current Sogd) province that had been the center of the dominant political elite during Soviet times. Fighting broke out intermittently in Dushanbe and in central and southern Tajikistan in 1992. Paradoxically, the regions opposing the north finally achieved their aim through bloody struggle among themselves. The Kulabis (south), initially clients of the north, were supported by the Hisoris (center), and proclaiming slogans of struggle against "Islamic fundamentalism," entered into conflict with their closest neighbors, the Gharmis and Qarateginis (both center) and the Pamiris (east). In fall 1992, the Kulabis and Hisoris received the help of external powers, mostly countries of the former Soviet Union, and reestablished central control of the country. The November 1992 session of the Tajikistan parliament appointed a Kulabi, Imamali Rakhmonov, as chairman, thus putting the end to the Leninabadis' domination. Nevertheless, in south and central Tajikistan, the struggle lasted into 1993 and later, causing a massive flow of refugees into neighboring Afghanistan. During this brutal civil war of 1992–1993, as many as 50,000 people lost their lives, and more than 650,000 people—one-tenth of the population—fled in terror. More than 35,000 homes were destroyed, and the costs of damage and destruction reached $7 billion, one of the bloodiest and costliest wars in the former Soviet Union.

United Nations-sponsored peace talks led to the General Agreement on the Establishment of Peace and National Accord in June 1997, followed by the incorporation of the United Tajik Opposition into the government. Nevertheless, today's Tajikistan remains a country with an ailing political regime, a weak national identity, and a fragile economy. Although open warfare has ended, the Tajiki national solidarity is still undermined by subnational contests between rival, regionally based entrepreneurs for political and military dominance. Quasi-military groups formally incorporated into the national army are beyond civilian control. In spite the efforts of Russian border guards, the Tajik-Afghan border is unreliable, and there is constant narcotic trafficking. In 2002, because of its strategic importance as a neighbor of Afghanistan, Tajikistan drew more attention from the United States, which sought and to some extent gained its cooperation in the military against the Taliban in Afghanistan.

Kamoludin Abdullaev

Further Reading

Allworth, Edward, ed. (1967) *Central Asia: A Century of Russian Rule.* New York: Columbia University Press.

Atkin, Muriel. (1989) *The Subtlest Battle: Islam in Soviet Tajikistan.* Philadelphia: Foreign Policy Research Institute.

Djalili, Mohammad Reza, Frederic Grare, and Shirin Akiner, eds. (1998) *Tajikistan: The Trials of Independence.* London: Curzon Press.

Ghafurov, Bobojon. (1998) *Tojikon: Ta'rikhi qadimtarin, qadim, asri miyona va davrai nav* (The Tajiks: Early Ancient, Ancient, Medieval, and Modern History). Vols. 1 and 2. Dushanbe, Tajikistan: Irfon.

Rakovska-Harmstone, Teresa. (1970) *Russia and Nationalism in Central Asia: The Case of Tajikistan.* Baltimore: John Hopkins University Press.

TAJIKISTAN—POLITICAL SYSTEM The emergence of the Republic of Tajikistan after the dissolution of the Soviet Union in 1991 is one of the most painful state-building attempts in modern Central Asian history. During the last years of the twentieth century and into the twenty-first century, this country has experienced civil war, the subsequent return of opposition and Islamic fighters, and a redistribution of power as a consequence of the conflict. Born in crisis and chaos, the current political system is a product of deep-seated traditional political loyalties, Soviet-style norms and practices, and recent rationalization of the old system.

Traditional Institutions of Power

The basic unit of traditionally sedentary Tajik society and the dominant institution of power was the *avlod*—a patriarchal extended family that sometimes took the form of a patrilineal clan. The *avlod* was loyal to regional groupings and, ultimately, to the local ruler. For generations this system gave its members survival, autonomy, and adaptability, serving tradition and sustaining society, despite the fact that *avlod* loyalties sometimes challenged a monarch's power and authority. Representative government and the concept of popular sovereignty were only weakly rooted in Tajik political culture. In the Soviet era (1918–1991) the *avlod* system was considerably eroded, yet it persisted as a parallel system of power in the quasi-national government. This community-oriented identity

and clan network determined political loyalty during the civil war in 1992–1993 and after.

System of Power in Transition

Tajikistan, following the example of other Soviet republics, in September 1991 declared independence and proclaimed a presidential system of government. The presidential election of November 1991 led to a struggle of an opposition coalition of Islamic groups and newborn secular democratic movements against old Soviet elites. The struggle turned into open armed confrontation in 1992, with the antagonism to communism that had united the opposition coalition gradually eclipsed by discord among regional groups. In November 1992 a government led by Emomali Rakhmonov gained control of the state with the backing of Russia and Uzbekistan. In November 1994 Rakhmonov (by this time a chairperson of the parliament) was elected president of Tajikistan.

The current constitution of the Republic of Tajikistan was adopted on 6 November 1994 after a nationwide referendum. It replaced the Soviet constitution that had been in effect since 1978 and that had been amended after independence. According to the constitution, Tajikistan is an independent, democratic, unified, and secular state with separate executive, legislative, and judicial powers. The supreme legislative body, a parliament, is the Majlisi Oli (Supreme Council). Amendments to the constitution, adopted in a general referendum on 26 September 1999, authorized direct presidential elections for one seven-year term (instead of a maximum of two five-year terms). In the November 1999 presidential elections, Emomali Rakhmonov won 96.91 percent of the votes, while his opponent, Davlat Usmon (representing the Islamic Revival Party), received only 2.1 percent. The amendments also replaced the national unicameral parliament with a bicameral one. In March 2000, the Majlisi Oli consisted of two chambers: the Majlisi Namoyandagon (Assembly of Representatives, or lower chamber) and Majlisi Melli (National Assembly, which acts as the upper chamber, or senate). The Majlisi Namoyandagon has sixty-three members directly elected on a half-mixed basis (65 percent as single-member district candidates and 35 percent according to party lists) for a five-year term. Members of the upper house—the Majlisi Melli— are indirectly elected for a five-year term; thirty-three members are elected by local *majlise*s (legislative bodies), and the remaining eight deputies of the Majlisi Melli are appointed by the president. The new election laws simultaneously guarantee pluralism and proportional representation. The lawmakers' aim was to undermine traditional patron-client networks and to provide for a presidential system balanced by a strong legislature. However the autonomy of the legislature vis-à-vis executive power is challenged by a growing presidential authority. According to the constitution the prime minister's post is nominal, because the president is the head of both state and government. As high administrator the president has exclusive authority to appoint heads (chairpersons) of *veloyat*s (provinces), *nohiya*s (regions), and cities, thus providing a strong vertical chain for the exercise of executive power. The president controls religious affairs as well, because heads of regions appoint local religious administrators. Through the Council of Justice, the president enjoys exclusive power to nominate judges and control the courts. Finally, as leader of the most powerful of the regional groupings in the country, the Kulabis, the president enjoys considerable support from the regional elite and Kulabi-dominated military forces.

Multiparty Developments

In the 1990s eleven parties (in addition to the previously existing Communist Party of Tajikistan, or CPT) were formed in the country, but by 1999 only six remained. The biggest of the current Tajik political parties is the People's Democratic Party of Tajikistan (PDPT).

The PDPT was formed in December 1994, one year after the current government came to power. In March 1998 President Rakhmonov joined the PDPT and assumed its leadership. Second place is occupied by the Communist Party of Tajikistan (formed in December 1924). The Communists inherited a relatively well-developed administrative infrastructure throughout the country, as well as considerable assets, and they enjoy the support of that part of the Tajik citizenry that longs for the restoration of the USSR. From another perspective, the CPT, lacking the protection of outside patrons and the effective support of regional elites and armed forces, has all but lost mass-elite linkages and therefore any real influence on politics.

The opposition forces are represented by the Islamic Renaissance Party of Tajikistan (IRPT) and the Democratic Party of Tajikistan. These parties formed the Demo-Islamic bloc in 1990 to operate within the legal-framework of a secular legal and political system. The failure of this anticommunist initiative, leading to open warfare in 1992 and the cessation of the activity of these parties in June 1993, did not prevent the formation of another alliance of the same elements, the United Tajik Opposition (UTO), on the eve of the inter-Tajik peace talks in 1994. In 1994–1999 the UTO took part in these peace talks, which culminated in June 1997 in the signing of the General Agreement on the Establishment of Peace and National Accord.

After some debates and United Nations involvement, in November 1998 the Majlisi Oli legalized the IRPT. Thus Tajikistan is so far the only state of Central Asia where an Islamic movement, after a long period of confrontation with the government, has been permitted to participate in the political process.

All Tajik political parties generally lack institutionalized ties connecting voters, leaders, candidates, and activists. They have an elitist character, lack a mass base, and have an amorphous infrastructure. Both progovernment and opposition parties poorly articulate issue-based programs in their agendas.

Future Problems

Tajikistan's political structure has proved politically unstable in the long term. The facade of the Western-patterned legal system in Tajikistan hides a remarkable blend of secular and traditional features that can only poorly connect civil and political society or promote the interests of individuals and different solidarity groups. Quasi-democratic rule is being built on a highly fragmented society in which protection of civil liberties is promised but not practiced.

This situation has led to increasing violence and corruption in both society and government. The instability of the political system has been worsened by a severe economic crisis that has discredited the present regime. The noninclusive character of the government and the absence of free competition for leadership positions, with a resultant disproportionate distribution of power among regions, enable *avlod* loyalties to continue to hamper nation-building efforts. The position of the central government is uncertain, and its authority is disregarded in many areas. As a result, sectarian militias and foreign governments exert great influence.

The current political system of Tajikistan prevents effective political mobilization and impedes the development of a coherent party system, opening the way to the consolidation of strong authoritarian rule, but there are some grounds for positive developments in the future. During the 1990s the Tajiks gained a far richer experience in political struggle than did other Central Asian nations. It is to be hoped that this political education will yield promising strategies for the future and will indicate a way to escape from the present impasse and conflicts.

Kamoludin Abdullaev

Further Reading

Akiner, Shirin. (1994) "Post-Soviet Central Asia: Past Is Prologue." In *The New States of Central Asia and Their Neighbors*, edited by Peter Ferdinand. New York: Council on Foreign Relations Press.

United Nations Development Programme. (1999) *Tajikistan: Human Development Report 1999*. Dushanbe, Tajikistan: United Nations Development Programme.

Wagner, Steven. (1997) *Public Opinion in Tajikistan, 1996*. Washington, DC: International Foundation for Electoral Systems.

TAJIKISTAN CIVIL WAR A civil war erupted in Tajikistan in May 1992 and lasted until December 1997, when the winning faction, called the Kulabis, succeeded, after bloody clashes, in expelling the bulk of the opposition forces, known as Gharmis, along with tens of thousands of civilians, who took refuge in Afghanistan.

When the Soviet Union collapsed at the end of August 1991, Tajikistan was the only former Soviet Muslim republic in which the Communist Party immediately lost power, although during the presidential elections of November 1991, the former head of the Communist Party, Rahman Nabiev, was elected president. His victory, however, exacerbated political factionalism. Two coalitions fought each other, with different regional identities and ideological alignments. The conservative or neo-Communist faction was composed of two regional groups: the Leninabadis, originating in the northern province of Leninabad, which had provided all the first secretaries of the Communist Party since 1949, including Nabiev; and the Kulabis, from the province of Kulab in southern Tajikistan. The opposition coalition brought together four groups: the Democratic Party, headed by Shadman Youssof; the Rastakhiz (Resurrection) Movement; the Pamiris (Ismaeli people, from the Gorno-Badakhshan autonomous region; Ismaili is a heterodox branch of Shiʿa Islam); and the Islamic Renaissance Party, headed by Mohammed Sharif Himmatzade; the latter is an Islamic fundamentalist party whose constituency is almost exclusively people originating from the Gharm Valley in southern Tajikistan.

Fighting erupted in Dushambe, the capital, in early May, due to a clash between Kenjaiev, the chairman of the parliament, who was supported by the Kulabis, and Naujavanov, the minister of the interior, a Pamiri who was supported by the Gharmis. The conflict extended throughout the south of the country, with the opposing forces mainly Kulabis and Gharmis, who provided the leadership and the bulk of the fighters on each side. In May 1992, the Gharmis succeeded in expelling the Kulabis from Dushambe. They established a coalition government, but kept Nabiev as president until his forced resignation in September. The Kulabis, entrenched in their province, undertook an offensive toward Dushambe beginning in September 1992, with the covert support of Russian troops. After months of fighting and massacres of civilians, the opposition coalition was driven out of Dushambe in December and fled to Afghanistan.

The victorious Kulabis chose Imamali Rahmanov as president. His government included some Leninabadis, but clearly expressed the Kulabi monopoly in the state. Nevertheless in 1993, a process of negotiation brought together the Kulabis, supported by Moscow, and the Gharmis, supported by Tehran, under United Nations auspices. In June 1997, a peace settlement established a coalition government, headed by Rahmanov, with one-third of cabinet appointments allocated to the Gharmis. The settlement ended the civil war and ensured the supremacy of southern Tajikistan. The civil war in Tajikistan indicates the prevailing role of regional identities in ideological commitments in the former Soviet Central Asia.

Olivier Roy

Further Reading

Djalil, Mohammed Reza, Frédéric Grare, and Shirin Akiner, eds. (1998) *Tajikistan, the Trials of Independence*. Richmond, U.K.: Curzon.

Roy, Olivier. (2000) *The New Central Asia, the Creation of Nations*. London: I. B. Tauris.

TAJIKS Tajiks (or Tadzhiks) are the original Iranian population of Central Asia, the present-day inhabitants of the nation of Tajikistan. Various groups of Tajiks, in Tajikistan, parts of central and southern Uzbekistan, northern Afghanistan, the Uighur Autonomous Region of Xinjiang in northwestern China, northern Pakistan, as well other parts of the Central Asia, sprang from various sources at various times and places; yet they all represent disparate branches of the common Iranian world. Tajiks were the first to settle in Central Asia, in the region that was later overwhelmed by peoples of Turko-Mongolian stock.

Origin and Cultural Traits

The origin of the word "Tajik" is disputed. Most scholars of the Tajik language currently believe that the word "Tajik" is derived from *toj* (crown). Some other scholars have suggested that the word was originally the name of an Arab tribe (Taj or Tazik) that invaded Central Asia, bringing Islam to the region in the seventh and eighth centuries. In medieval Tajiki-Farsi literature and historical chronicles the word "Tajik" was used in the general sense of "Persian," as the opposite of "Turk." In Russian usage of the sixteenth century and later, "Tajik" was applied to the urban populace of Central Asia, distinct from the ruling Uzbek nomads. Currently the term "Tajik" applies to the people of the Central Asian Trans-river, who are Europeans of Pamiro-Ferghanian type.

The Tajiks are Muslims, predominantly Sunnis of the Khanafi school; there are also 300,000 Shi'a Imami Ismailis. Tajiks today speak different Iranian languages. In addition to Western Iranian (Tajiki and Dari), Tajiks in Tajikistan, Afghanistan, and China speak Eastern Iranian (Permian and Yaghnobi languages), using Tajiki, an Iranian tongue, as a common language.

Tajiks lived in houses constructed of mud and stones in urban centers and oases of Central Asia. They were famous gardeners, merchants, poets, and scholars. Tajik arts reached high levels, and the towns along the caravan routes linking the Near East, China, and India were centers of trade. The tenth through sixteenth centuries were a golden age for Tajiks. Their language served as a lingua franca in Central Asia and was the mother tongue of famous poets such as Rudaki (c. 859–940 or 941), Sa'di (c. 1213–1294), Hafez (c. 1325–c. 1389), Omar Khayyam (1048?–1131), and Firdawsi (c. 935–c. 1020). The celebrated medieval doctor Avicenna (Abuali Ibn Sina; 980–1037) also spoke the Tajik language.

Turko-Mongol tribes constantly migrated westward into the area inhabited by the Tajiks, pushing them to the periphery. By the early twentieth century the term "Tajik" was used to label so-called mountainous Tajiks (the population of Qarategin, Mastchah, Darvaz, and Badakhshan in modern Tajikistan), while Tajiki-speakers on the plains were called Sart.

Dispersion

As an ethnic group the Tajiks never formed a stable political unit. Until the 1920s there was no official Tajik territorial-administrative unit. In Tajikistan there are four historical areas of the Tajik population: the valleys of the northern part of the country (Fergana Valley); the foothills and mountains of central Tajikistan (Zarafshon River basin); the foothills, mountains, and narrow valleys of southern Tajikistan (Qarategin, Khatlon); and the vast alpine country of Pamir. Each of these subgroups of Tajiks is marked by distinct political and material culture, physical appearance, dialect, customs, music, and folklore.

A Tajik herdswoman in traditional dress. (DEAN CONGER/ CORBIS)

The valley dwellers of the north are descendants of the Sogdian culture, representatives of the rich urban civilization of Samarqand, Bukhara, Khujand, and Fergana. After Russian dominance was established in the area and according to the national delimitations drawn by the Soviets in 1924, the Tajik descendants of these cultural centers live in different states. The Tajiks of Sogd (former Leninabad) Province, known as Leninabadis, live almost exclusively in Tajikistan, while most of the Bukharan and Samarqandi Tajiks dwell in Uzbekistan. This part of the Tajik-populated area joined Russia in the second half of the nineteenth century, and these Tajiks experienced the political, cultural, and economic transformations of Communism.

The Tajiks of the central and southern regions, living in narrow valleys, foothills, and mountains, in contrast to the northern Tajiks, were almost completely independent and free of outside influence until the twentieth century. The most important of these groups were the Kulabi, Gharmi, Qarategini, and Hisari Tajiks. Their traditional communities were strongly attached to their places of origin. Both northern and southern Tajiks speak the Tajik language, albeit with dialectical peculiarities, and are Sunni Muslims.

In Tajikistan's Gorno-Badakhshan region live other Iranian peoples known as Pamiris. Officially identified as Tajiks, they are ethnically and linguistically distinct from the previously mentioned groups of Tajiks. Pamiris are almost all Shi'a Ismailis, speaking a language unconnected to Tajik and to other nonwritten Pamirian languages. In addition to 200,000 Tajikistan Pamiris in Gorno-Badakhshan, almost 100,000 Pamiris live in the adjacent mountain regions of Afghanistan, China, and Pakistan. The number of Tajiks in Tajikistan has risen from approximately 738,000 in 1926 (approximately 72 percent of the total population) to approximately 4.2 million in 2000 (69 percent of the population).

Like the Tajiks of Tajikistan, the Tajiks of the left bank of the Amu Dar'ya River, being autochthonous and the oldest inhabitants of today's Afghanistan, have no known common place of origin, nor is it known when they appeared here. Currently compact masses of Tajik population live in central Afghanistan—in Kabul Province, areas of Charikar, Istalif, Panjsher, Gurband, Salang, and the southern and northern slopes of the Hindu Kush. Another large group of Tajiks lives in western Afghanistan—in Herat, Ghor, and partly in Nimroz and Farakh Provinces. Tajiks constitute the main population of northeastern Baghlan, Takhor, Qunduz, and Badakhshan Provinces in Afghanistan. In the northern provinces of Balkh, Juzjan, Samangan, Fariab, and Badgis, Tajiks live together with Uzbeks and Turkmen.

Estimates of the number of Tajiks in Afghanistan vary widely from 25 to 50 percent or even more of the total population of the country. According to official data, Afghanistan's total population in 1987 reached 16.1 million. Thus, on the eve of the 1989 Soviet invasion, the number of Afghani Tajiks varied between 4 and 8 million. This number equals or even exceeds the number of Tajiks in Tajikistan. In addition to the Tajiks of Tajikistan and Afghanistan, more than 1 million Tajiks live in Uzbekistan, predominantly in Samarqand, Bukhara, and Surkhandarya Provinces. This disassociation of various groups of Tajiks has always been a principal obstacle to the creation of a unified Tajik state.

Kamoludin Abdullaev

Further Reading

Dupree, Louis. (1980) *Afghanistan.* Princeton, NJ: Princeton University Press.

Ghafurov, Bobojon. (1998) *Tojikon: Ta'rikhi qadimtarin, qadim, asri miyona va davrai nav* (The Tajiks: Early Ancient, Ancient, Medieval, and Modern History). 2 vols. Dushanbe, Tajikistan: Irfon.

Karmysheva, Belkis. (1976) *Ocherki etnicheskoi istorii iuzhykh raionov Tadzhikistana i Uzbekistana* (On the Ethnic History of the Southern Regions of Tajikistan and Uzbekistan). Moscow: Nauka.

Kisliakov, Nikolai. (1954) *Ocherki po istorii Karategina: K istorii Tadzhikistana* (Essays on the History of Qarategin: On the History of Tajikistan). Stalinabad, Tajikistan.

Kushkeki, Burhanuddin Khan. (1926) *Kattagan i Badakhshan* (Qataghan and Badakhshan). Tashkent, Uzbekistan.

Masov, Mrahim. (1996) *The History of a National Catastrophe.* Minneapolis, MN: Sorayya Publishers.

Monogarova, Ludmila. (1992) *Tadzhiki* (The Tajiks). Moscow: RAN.

TAKLIMAKAN DESERT   The Taklimakan Desert, the world's second largest sand desert, is located in the southern part of the Xinjiang Uygur Autonomous Region in northwestern China and covers an area of 338,000 square kilometers. About 85 percent of the desert consists of shifting sand dunes, averaging 100 to 150 meters in height, while dunes in the western parts only average 5 to 25 meters in height. The desert has a temperate climate and very low precipitation of under 50 millimeters annually. It constitutes the central part of the Tarim Basin, which in the western part rises to 1,560 meters above sea level. The basin is partly surrounded by mountains reaching more than 6,000 meters in height. In the north, the desert borders on the Tian Shan and in the west and the south, it borders on the Kunlun and the Altun Mountains. Glacial streams from the mountains run far into the desert, where they disappear, and there is some growth of poplar and

tamarisk trees along the riverbeds. There are a few oasis towns along the Hotan River bed, which also constitutes the main route across the desert from south to north. Since the 1980s, large oil fields have been exploited, and in the 1990s more than 500 kilometers of roads have been constructed for the oil industry.

Bent Nielsen

Further Reading

Blackmore, Charles. (1996) *The Worst Desert on Earth: Crossing the Taklamakan.* Reprint ed. London: John Murray.

Chinese Academy of Sciences, Team of Integrated Scientific Investigation of the Taklimakan Desert. (1993) *Wondrous Taklimakan: Integrated Scientific Investigation of theTaklimakan Desert.* Beijing: Lubrecht & Cramer and Science Press.

Zhu, Zhenda, and Dieter Jäkel. (1991) *Reports on the 1986 Sino-German Kunlun Shan Taklimakan Expedition.* Berlin: Gesellschaft für Erdkunde zu Berlin.

TALIBAN The Taliban (plural of *talib*, which is Arabic/Persian for "student of Islamic religious law") regime ruled Afghanistan from November 1994 to November 2001 under the leadership of mullah Muhammad Omar (b. 1959). After the terrorist attacks on the United States on 11 September 2001, when more than three thousand people were killed in New York and Washington, DC, the United States believed that the Taliban regime was sheltering the al-Qaeda terrorists of Osama bin Laden, a Saudi dissident and millionaire who was suspected of having masterminded the attacks. Earlier, the United States had also accused Osama bin Laden of masterminding the bombings of American embassies in Kenya and Tanzania on 7 August 1998, which killed more than two hundred people, including nineteen Americans.

In spite of repeated calls from the United States and other nations, including some Muslim nations, the Taliban did not hand over Osama bin Laden to the United States for interrogation and trial. The administration of President George W. Bush (b. 1946) starting bombing Afghanistan on 7 October 2001, leading to the collapse of the Taliban regime in Kabul. The U.S.-led international community installed an interim regime, composed of anti-Taliban forces of the Northern Alliance, under the leadership of a Pashtun tribal elder, Hamid Karzai (b. 1957), who took the oath of office in Kabul on 22 December 2001.

Although most of the Taliban foot soldiers disbanded and rejoined their communities, Taliban pockets of resistance continued in eastern parts of Afghanistan, especially in Kandahar Province.

Four former Taliban soldiers on a street in Kandahar in January 2002, after general amnesty was given to Taliban fighters. (AFP/CORBIS)

The Taliban came to power in November 1994 at the end of a civil war (1992–1994) that raged between different mujahideen (holy warrior) factions. Once in power, the Taliban imposed a strictly puritanical and literal interpretation of the *shari'a* (Islamic law). The Taliban closed female educational institutions and banned women from working outside of their homes. Women could not venture out of their homes unless a male relative accompanied them. Women were forced to wear the Afghan traditional veil *(burqa)*.

Taliban authorities also banned music, television, theater, cinema, kites, cards, and other activities as useless and time wasting. They also required men to grow beards and to strictly observe Islamic rituals, including the daily five prayers. The Taliban carried out the Hadood (Islamic punishments) in public: stoning to death for adultery, fornication, or any sexual, even consensual, relations outside wedlock. They amputated hands of thieves and flogged gamblers and alcohol users.

When the Taliban regime collapsed in November 2001 as a result of the U.S. bombing of its strongholds in Afghanistan, some women in Kabul threw away their *burqa*s, and some men shaved off their beards to demonstrate freedom from the Taliban.

Abdul Karim Khan

Further Reading
Matinuddin, Kamal. (1999) *The Taliban Phenomenon: Afghanistan, 1994–1997.* Karachi, Pakistan: Oxford University Press.
Rashid, Ahmed. (2001) *Taliban: Militant Islam, Oil, and Fundamentalism in Central Asia.* New Haven, CT: Yale University Press.

TAMAN SISWA The Taman Siswa, or "Garden of Students," was an anticolonial educational movement in the Dutch East Indies founded by the Javanese nobleman Raden Mas Soewardi Soerjaningrat, also known as Ki Hadjar Dewantoro (1889–1959), in July 1922. Dutch-educated, Dewantoro was an active member of the nationalist movement, the founder of the Indies Party, and a member of the Sarekat Islam (Islamic Association), the first political party in the Netherlands East Indies with Indonesian nationalist leanings. He propagated a course of action that would use Western methods to fight the Dutch. During his exile in the Netherlands (1913–1918), he became convinced that strengthening the cultural roots of his people through "nationalist" education would effectively counter the impact of colonialism. Influenced by the educational theories of Maria Montessori and Ra-

bindranath Tagore, Dewantoro established the Taman Siswa school system, enlisting the support of many fellow nationalists. The curriculum included lessons in Javanese ethics, traditional handicraft, dance, and music, as well as Western subjects. In the late 1930s, Taman Siswa operated 207 schools in Java, Sumatra, and Kalimantan. Following independence, Taman Siswa survived as an appendage of the state school system. Dewantoro retained leadership until his death in 1959. As minister of education, he helped to shape the educational policy of the modern Indonesian state.

Martin Ramstedt

Further Reading
Meijers, C. H. (1973) *De Taman Siswa en het regeringsonderwijs: Ontwikkelingen in het Indonesische onderwijs vanaf 1945.* Amsterdam: Doctoraalscriptie.
Reksohadiprodjo, Mohammad Said. (1976) *Taman Siswa's Gedachten Wereld.* Jakarta, Indonesia: Yayasan Idayu.
Tsuchiya, Kenji. (1988) *Democracy and Leadership: The Rise of the Taman Siswa Movement in Indonesia.* Honolulu, HI: University of Hawaii Press.

TAMERLANE. See **Timur.**

TAMIL LANGUAGE Tamil belongs to the South Dravidian subgroup of the Dravidian family of languages and has been spoken from prehistoric times in southern India and northeastern Sri Lanka. There are about 60 million speakers of Tamil in these two areas today; outside India and Sri Lanka, Tamil speakers are reported from Malaysia, South Africa, Singapore, Fiji, Thailand, and Mauritius. During its more than two-thousand-year uninterrupted history, three distinct stages in its development may be distinguished: Old Tamil (c. 300 BCE–ce 700), Middle Tamil (700–1600), and Modern Tamil (1600 to the present). Apart from distinct historical variations, Tamil exhibits three other dimensions: geographic (regional and local dialects), social (primarily Brahman versus non-Brahman speech), and diglossic (i.e., "high" formal variety against "low" informal varieties). The central dialect spoken by educated non-Brahmans around the cities of Tanjore, Trichy, and Madurai is considered to represent the standard.

The modern Tamil sound system has a native core and a borrowed periphery. The core inventory contains twelve vowels, the native *a, i, u, e, o,* both short and long; there are two peripheral diphthongs. There is a core of sixteen consonants in three groups: stops *k, c, ṭ, t, p;* nasals *ñ, ṇ, n, m;* and liquids *y, r, l, v, ṛ, ẓ, ḷ.* The consonantal periphery, borrowed mostly from Indo-Aryan, Perso-Arabic (Persian and Arabic), and English sources, includes *b, d, ḍ, j, g, s, f, h.* The specific sounds of Tamil are primarily the retroflexes *ṭ, ṇ, ḷ, ẓ*—consonants articulated with the reversed tongue-tip against the palate—and the alveolar flap *r*— a consonant articulated like a "flap" with the tongue-tip behind upper teeth.

Like other South Asian languages, Tamil is written in alphasyllabic script descended from the southern variety of Asokan Brahmi (the script used in India from around 250 BCE for Buddhist inscriptions carved at the order of Emperor Asoka).

Morphology

Tamil morphology is agglutinating (words change meaning through the addition of lexical elements to a base) and suffixal (these additional elements are added on at the ends of base words rather than at the beginning or in the middle), inflections (changes in tense, number, person, and so on) are marked by suffixes attached to a lexical base (root), which may be enlarged by derivational suffixes so as to form a stem. There are two main parts of speech, nouns and verbs. So-called indeclinables indicate such categories as adjectives, adverbs, and postpositions, and these may originally have been nouns and verbs. Nouns mark grammatically gender (two basic genders, rational and nonrational, corresponding roughly to human, nonhuman; human classified further as masculine and feminine), number, and case. Tamil nouns distinguish singular and plural in eight cases: nominative, accusative, dative, sociative, genitive, instrumental, locative, and ablative. Personal pronouns in the plural distinguish between first person inclusive and exclusive.

Tamil verbs consist of a lexical stem and a set of bound suffixes. The stem consists of a base and, optionally, a set of stem-forming suffixes. Inflected verbs are finite and nonfinite. Finite verbs mark both tense and subject-verb agreement, nonfinite verbs do not. Finite verbs typically mark the end of a sentence; all other verbs must be nonfinite. For example, the sentence, "When I came home and saw him, I said, 'How are you?' and then I went to eat," would be translated into Tamil as, "Having-come home after, him having-seen, 'You-how' having-said, then I to-eat went." There are basically three tenses: past, nonpast (including future), and present (which is a later independent development). The basic order of constituents in a Tamil clause is Subject-Object-Verb. Hence the sentence structure may be described as head-final and left-branching. Head-final means that the main part of a

word or a sentence is always placed at the end (final); for example, "He came fast" would be "fast came-he" in Tamil. Left-branching indicates that the finite verb stands at the right end of a sentence, which runs from left to right. Each sentence has one finite predicate; all other predicates are nonfinite.

The lexicon of Tamil consists of a native Dravidian core and borrowings from Sanskrit (and other Indo-Aryan languages), Perso-Arabic, Portuguese, and English. At the beginning of the twentieth century a movement to remove Sanskritic elements from the Tamil vocabulary and replace them with Tamil ones was initiated and is still vigorous.

K. V. Zvelebik

Further Reading
Asher, R. E. (1985) *Tamil.* Croom Helm Descriptive Grammars. London: Routledge.

Lehmann, Thomas. (1989) *A Grammar of Modern Tamil.* Pondicherry, India: Pondicherry Institute of Linguistics and Culture.

Schiffman, Harold. (1979) *A Grammar of Spoken Tamil.* Madras, India: Christian Literature Society.

TAMIL NADU (2001 est. pop. 62.1 million). Spread over an area of 130,058 square kilometers, the state of Tamil Nadu is located on the southeastern side of the Indian peninsula. Bounded by the Bay of Bengal and the Indian Ocean in the east and the south respectively, the state has more than 1,000 kilometers of coastline. To its north and west lie the southern states of Karnataka, Kerala, and Andhra Pradesh. Apart from the coastal plain in the east, the state contains the range of Western Ghats, a mass of hilly regions in the north and the west averaging 1,220 meters above sea level. All the rivers in the state are rain-fed and flow eastward from the Western Ghats. The most prominent river, Kaveri (Cauvery), is 760 kilometers long.

Tamil Nadu has a 6,000-year history, predating the Aryan entry into India. The Dravidian culture associated with the state was concentrated in the south after the Aryans settled in north India in the third millennium BCE. Tamil Nadu was formerly a part of the Dravida country ruled by three significant dynasties, Chola, Pandya, and Chera from the fourth century BCE. The end of this rule in the thirteenth century saw these territories annexed by the rising Vijayanagar empire in the south. Later, the area was divided into a number of small kingdoms. The English arrived in Madras in 1639 as representatives of the East India Company. Most of south India, including Tamil

Nadu, came under British rule. After Indian independence and under the States Reorganisation Act of 1956, the erstwhile Madras province was divided into the states of Madras, Andhra Pradesh, and Kerala on the basis of language. Tamil-speaking Madras state changed its name to Tamil Nadu on 14 January 1969. The state capital changed its name from Madras to Chennai in 1996. The state legislature has one house—the Legislative Assembly—with 235 seats. Fifty-seven members from the state are elected to the national parliament—18 for the upper house (Rajya Sabha) and 29 for the lower house (Lok Sabha). The state is divided into twenty-nine administrative districts.

The backbone of Tamil Nadu's economy is agriculture. Rice and sugarcane are major crops, giving highest yields nationally. Tea and coffee plantations are a major source of revenue. The state government encourages small, medium, and large-scale industries through corporations set up for the purpose. In recent years, the state has seen a spurt in industrial investment growth, particularly in key sectors such as power and information technology. The state excels in the production of cotton, sugar, leather, and petrochemicals.

The cultural life of Tamil Nadu is a repository of rich forms and traditions. The dance style of Bharatanatyam and the practice of Carnatic music, important elements of Indian cultural ensemble, trace their origins to this state. Tamilians are great lovers of food, music, and films. Pongal, celebrated in the month of January to mark the time of harvest, is the major festival of the state.

Ram Shankar Nanda

Further Reading
Krishna, Nanditha, and V. K. Rajamani. (1992) *Arts and Crafts of Tamil Nadu*. Ahmedabad, India: Mapin International.

TAMILS The name "Tamil" denotes native speakers of the Tamil language, mainly residing since antiquity in the southernmost region of India and in northern and eastern Sri Lanka, but found today also as immigrants in Southeast Asia, Africa, Guyana and the Caribbean, the United States, Canada, and England.

The Tamil language, of the Dravidian family, appears in third-century BCE inscriptions, and Dravidian influences noted in Sanskrit suggest that an ancestor of Tamil was widely spoken in India as early as 1000 BCE. Today it is the official language of the state of Tamil Nadu in India and one of the national

languages of Sri Lanka; related languages are spoken in neighboring states.

Tamils were prominent in sea trade, and there is evidence of Tamil commerce with Greece and Rome and with Southeast Asia from around the first century BCE. Areas of the Tamil region were ruled from about the early third century BCE to the fifth century CE by the Chera, Chola, and Pandya dynasties and from about the sixth to the ninth centuries CE by the Pallava dynasty. These and other dynasties were displaced by the Vijayanagara empire at its peak (fourteenth century) and then by the Telugu-speaking Nayaka rulers (sixteenth to early eighteenth centuries CE).

The Tamil region has figured prominently in India's cultural history. Tamil literature dates from as early as around the second century BCE; it includes the Sangam (Acadamy) poetry and the *Tolkappiyam* (Ancient Poem), a grammar. Even in these works, there are signs of the influence of Sanskrit from the north. The gradual process of Sanskritization was driven by Brahman priests and scholars, whom local rulers settled on donated lands. Nevertheless, Tamil poetry retained a personal voice and a vivid immediacy that contrasted with the impersonal and stylized character of Sanskrit works.

From around the sixth century CE, a new Tamil literature of devotional poems began to be composed by traveling bards, who applied the conventions of the Sangam poetry to poems praising the gods of famous temples. During this period, local deities were assimilated to pan-Indian deities of the Brahmanical Sanskrit sources. This sparked a wave of vernacular religious expression throughout India over the next several centuries. Jainism and Buddhism vied with devotion to the gods Vishnu and Siva for royal patronage in the region. Meanwhile, Brahmans integrated Tamil devotional texts with their Sanskrit liturgies, creating the distinctive Saiva Siddhanta and Shrivaishnava traditions, Tamil religious movements teaching devotion to the deities Siva and Vishnu, respectively.

In postcolonial India, the linguistic and ethnic rivalry between south and north has continued. In South India, Tamil was touted as the original language and culture of India, with the carriers of Old Indo-Aryan (Sanskrit) represented as the first imperialist invaders, warlike barbarians who drove the peace-loving Tamils toward the south. An analogous situation was perceived in the dominance of North Indians in national politics and the adoption of Hindi (the language of a broad swath of North India) as the principal national language. Hence, South Indians (and Tamils in particular) have fiercely resisted using Hindi.

In Sri Lanka, where Tamils have often been treated as foreigners by the Sinhalese-speaking majority, Tamil nationalist guerrillas called the Liberation Tigers of Tamil Eelam (Nation) (LTTE) seek an independent Tamil homeland in the Jaffna Peninsula in the north and along the northeast coast. Many Indian Tamils have provided support to this insurgency, and the Indian prime minister Rajiv Gandhi (1944–1991) was assassinated by an LTTE suicide bomber protesting India's intervention in Sri Lanka.

Meanwhile, regional parties claiming to represent the interests of Dravidian culture have long dominated the politics of the state of Tamil Nadu, often promoting Tamil chauvinism. During British rule and immediately after independence, Tamil-speaking regions were subsumed within Madras state, but in the 1950s Telegu-, Kannada-, and Malayalam-speaking regions were hived off as separate states, and in 1969 the Madras state's name was officially changed to Tamil Nadu (Tamil Country). Under chief minister Jayalalitha (b. 1948), Tamil Nadu in 1996 discarded the British colonial name of the capital (Madras) to adopt the older Tamil name Chennai. Yet opposition to Hindi has receded somewhat as English gets entrenched as the language of national affairs.

Timothy Lubin

Further Reading
Nilakanta Sastri, K. A. (1964) *The Culture and History of the Tamils.* Calcutta, India: K. L. Mukhopadhyay.
Vira Raghavan, C. (1973) *Tamil Nadu.* New Delhi: Ministry of Information and Broadcasting.
Zvelebil, Kamil Veith. (1974) *Tamil Literature.* Wiesbaden, Germany: Otto Harrassowitz.

TAN SIEW SIN (1916–1988), Malaysian political figure. Tan Siew Sin was born in Malacca, Malaysia, on 21 May 1916, the only son of Tan Cheng Lock, a prominent businessman and founding member of the Malaysian Chinese Association. He was educated in Malacca and also attended Raffles College in Singapore as well as Middle Temple in London. Tan was a *baba*, a descendent of Chinese families that had migrated to Malaya before British colonization; these families adopted the local Malay customs, cultural practices, and language.

Tan Siew Sin was a major political figure in Malaya after it gained independence from the British and after the formation of Malaysia. He was elected a member of parliament in 1955. Between 1957 and 1959 he was minister of commerce and industry and in 1959 became the first minister of finance, a position he held until 1969, when he became minister with special functions (finance). In 1970 he resumed his duties as finance minister, a position he held until his retirement in 1974.

Tan Siew Sin knew the Malays well and spoke the language fluently. However, although president of the Malaysian Chinese Association—part of the Barisan Nasional coalition, the ruling political party in Malaysia since its independence from British rule—he spoke no Chinese. He, together with Malaysia's first prime minister, Tunku Abdul Rahman, who was a close friend, oversaw the imposition of Malay as the national language and the withdrawal of government assistance for schools providing Chinese-language education. The perception among the Chinese community that he had neglected their cultural interests led to the erosion of support for the Malaysian Chinese Association during his tenure as president.

Kog Yue Choong

Further Reading
Morais, J. Victor. (1981) *Tun Tan: Portrait of a Statesman.* Singapore: Quins Private Ltd.

TANAKA GIICHI (1863–1929), Japanese politician. Tanaka Giichi was a soldier and politician from the former feudal domain of Choshu (modern Yamaguchi Prefecture). He started his career in the Imperial Army, later becoming president of Japan's largest party, the Rikken Seiyukai, and prime minister in 1927.

Tanaka was born in 1863, the son of a samurai retainer. He attended the Army Academy and the Army War College. During the Russo-Japanese War (1904–1905) he served as an aide to General Kodama Gentaro (1852–1906), chief of staff of the Manchurian army. In 1906, Tanaka drafted the infamous Imperial Defense Guideline (Teikoku Kokubo Hoshin), a basic document for Japan's foreign and military policy until 1945.

In 1910, Tanaka played a leading part in founding the reservists' association (Teikoku Zaigo Gunjin-kai). He also served as army minister from 1918 until 1921, and again in 1923. Two years later, Tanaka was asked to become president of the Seiyukai party. He accepted, thus starting a new career as a party politician. As the leader of the largest party in the lower house, he was named prime minister in 1927, serving concurrently as foreign minister and minister of colonization. Unable to deal with urgent budgetary problems or to settle Japan's China policy, the cabinet had to resign in July 1929. Tanaka died shortly afterward.

Sven Saaler

Further Reading
Bamba, Nobuya. (1972) *Japanese Diplomacy in a Dilemma.* Kyoto, Japan: Minerva Press.
Duus, Peter. (1968) *Party Rivalry and Political Change in Taisho Japan.* Cambridge, MA: Harvard University Press.
Morton, William F. (1980) *Tanaka Giichi and Japan's China Policy.* New York: St. Martin's Press.
Smethurst, Richard J. (1974) *A Social Basis for Prewar Japanese Militarism: The Army and the Rural Community.* Berkeley and Los Angeles: University of California Press.

TANCH'ONG *Tanch'ong* is the Korean technique of decorating wooden buildings. Although *tanch'ong* work dates back to at least the Three Kingdoms period (57 BCE–668 CE), the earliest extant examples date to the Koryo dynasty (918–1392). In *tanch'ong*, the eaves, ceilings, and upper column supports of buildings were painted in bright primary colors for beauty, as well as to protect the wood, hide imperfections, and emphasize the building's function. These techniques continued to be developed throughout the Choson dynasty (1392–1910).

Specially trained artisans were required for the exacting work. The ends of supporting beams or eaves of ceilings often featured a dominant motif of flowers or pomegranates. The space between the ends or eaves might depict a narrative featuring auspicious symbols such as dragons and cranes, or scenes from Buddhist sutras. Elegant designs and geometric patterns might be used elsewhere on the building, or a single flower or animal could contrast the more elaborate decorations.

The use of contrasts in design and colors was very important in *tanch'ong*. Reds were used on sun-exposed areas and provided a sharp contrast to the green-blue tones used on unexposed areas. The natural paints were composed of clay, iron, copper, or malachite pigments for their vivid colors and resistance to the elements.

Jennifer Jung-Kim

Further Reading
Korean Overseas Information Service. (1995) *Tanch'ong.* Korean Heritage Series no. 4. Seoul: Korean Overseas Information Service.

TANG DYNASTY China's Tang dynasty (618–907 CE), which was founded by Liu Yuan (also known by his temple name Gaozu, reigned 618–626), marked one of the most glorious periods in the history of China. After the short-lived Sui dynasty (581–618 CE), the Tang ruled China for nearly three centuries, governing one of the most successful empires of the time in the world. Its government institutions, legal establishments, economic developments, cultural achievements, and territorial expansions all exerted significant impact on later Chinese dynasties and defined the identity of Chinese civilization.

Political Changes

Li Yuan, who inherited the title of the dynastic duke of Tang during the Sui dynasty, was a member of a northern aristocratic family who had intermarried with the ethnic minority Xianbei tribal aristocracy. When the Sui collapsed in 617, he seized the Sui capital Chang'an, and ascended the throne in 618, thus founding the Tang dynasty.

During Gaozu's reign, the Tang undertook the enterprises of expanding and consolidating the empire and establishing various institutions. The Gauzu's armies defeated several major rivals and completed the pacification of the country in 624. Gaozu basically continued the administrative institutions of the previous Sui dynasty. In the central government, three agencies reporting to the emperor (the Secretariat, the Chancellery, and the Department of State Affairs, which were collectively known as the Three Departments) served as the administrative core. Local administration consisted of two tiers: the inferior district and the superior prefecture. The military system of garrison militia *(fubing)* combined agricultural and military duties. Gaozu revived the civil-service examination system to recruit government officials on the basis of merit, although aristocrats continued to be influential in dynastic politics.

Like the Sui, the Tang legal system consisted of four major components: the *Code, Statutes, Regulations,* and *Ordinances,* which not only laid the foundation for later dynasties of imperial China, but also influenced the legal systems of Japan, Korea, and Vietnam.

Gaozu's second son Li Shimin (temple name Taizong, reigned 626–649) took the throne in a military coup. Taizong's reign, traditionally known as the "era of good government," was one of close personal interaction between the ruler and his Confucian advisers. Generally, Taizong developed and refined the policies of his father's reign, including revision of the law codes and expansion of the civil-service examination system. He made particular efforts to balance the political influence of the regional aristocratic groups and uphold the pr-eminent position of his own clan, the Li. In foreign affairs, Taizong subdued the eastern Turks and began to expand Chinese power in Central Asia.

Empress Wu   Taizong's ninth son, Li Zhi (temple name Gaozong, reigned 649–683) ascended the throne at the age of twenty-one. In the early years of his reign, Gaozong relied on advice from the statesmen of his father's court and continued some reform programs. Gradually, however, Gaozu's court came to be dominated by Wu Zhao (627–710, reigned 690–705), one of the most remarkable women in Chinese history. Born into a merchant family, Wu Zhao had been a low-ranking concubine of Taizong's who managed to become Gaozong's legitimate empress in 655. In 660, when Gaozong suffered a stroke, the empress took charge of the central government. Over the next twenty years, while Empress Wu continued many of the policies of the former Tang rulers, she initiated some practices to consolidate her position. For instance, she designated Luoyang as a second capital in 657 and took up permanent residence there in 683, thus removing the political center from the base area of the northwestern aristocracy. Empress Wu also encouraged lower ranks of bureaucracy by creating new posts, providing more opportunities for advancement, and increasing their salaries. In order to promote the legitimacy of the dynasty, Empress Wu revived the ancient *feng* and *shan* sacrifices on Mount Tai (Taishan), the eastern holy peak in present-day Shandong Province, and patronized Buddhism.

Under Gaozong and Empress Wu, the Chinese continued their efforts to extend and consolidate the empire. By 661, they had defeated the western Turks and established a Chinese protectorate in the western regions. But they faced serious threat from Tibet. By the early seventh century, Tibet had emerged as a unified state. Although Tibet became China's tributary state under Song-tsen Gampo (reigned 620-649), the Tibetans exerted constant pressure on present-day Qinghai and Sichuan. After Gaozong died in 683, Empress Wu, now the empress dowager, took control of the imperial succession and purged her opponents at court by means of terror and a secret police force. In 690, she ascended the throne and proclaimed a new dynasty: the Zhou. Empress Wu then formally became an "emperor," the only woman sovereign in China's history. Some senior officials at court forced her to abdicate in 705 and restored the Tang dynasty.

Li Longji (temple name Xuanzong, reigned 712–756) took the throne by means of series of political in-

CHINA—HISTORICAL PERIODS

Xia dynasty (2100–1766 BCE)
Shang dynasty (1766–1045 BCE)
Zhou dynasty (1045–256 BCE)
  Western Zhou (1045–771 BCE)
  Eastern Zhou (770–221 BCE)
Spring and Autumn period (770–476 BCE)
Warring States period (475–221 BCE)
Qin dynasty (221–206 BCE)
Han dynasty (206 BCE–220 CE)
Three Kingdoms period (220–265 CE)
North and South Dynasties (220–589 CE)
Sui dyansty (581–618 CE)
Tang dynasty (618–907 CE)
Five Dynasties period (907–960 CE)
Song dynasty (960–1279)
  Northern Song (960–1126)
  Southern Song (1127–1279)
Jurchen Jin dynasty (1125–1234)
Yuan dynasty (1279–1368)
Ming dynasty (1368–1644)
Qing dynasty (1644–1912)
Republican China (1912–1927)
People's Republic of China (1949–present)
Republic of China (1949–present)
Cultural Revolution (1966–1976)

trigues. The early years of his reign saw the heyday of the Tang, a time of institutional progress, economic prosperity, and cultural flowering. The most important change occurred in the military. In the early Tang, troops were organized through the *fubing* militia system, under which men of agricultural households served in the army on a rotation basis. Such a system proved inadequate to defend the empire against threats from the highly mobile nomadic horsemen of the frontiers. Xuanzong's reign saw the development of professional soldiers who settled permanently in military colonies and a consequent growth of the military commanders' power. In the 740s, some non-Chinese governors were appointed to take charge of certain strategic military domains, among whom An Lushan, a professional soldier of Sogdian and Turkish ethnic background, rose to prominence. He was later to lead a rebellion.

Under Xuanzong, the aristocracy reasserted its political dominance. Although under Empress Wu and in the early years of Xuanzong's government many chief ministers obtained their positions by passing the civil-service examinations, after 720 men of aristocratic origins increasingly received appointments. What complicated court politics more was that from the 740s, the emperor refused to take active interest in government affairs, being taken up by the charms of his concubine Yang Guifei, one of the most famous beauties in Chinese history. Those close to the emperor strove to become the power behind the throne; among them was An Lushan, who rebelled against the Tang in 755.

The An Lushan Rebellion The An Lushan rebellion (755–763) marked a turning point in the history of the Tang and nearly destroyed the dynasty. The rebel troops seized the Tang capitals Luoyang and Chang'an and controlled most of north China. Xuanzong fled to Sichuan. Although An Lushan was assassinated by a subordinate in 757, the rebellion continued for six more years.

Influence of Eunuchs Although the rebellion was put down, the Chinese lost their grip on many frontier areas, including the western regions. Within the Tang empire, the political authority of the central government declined. Some northern regions became virtually autonomous, and other areas fell under the control of military governors, who enjoyed enormous power in both military and civil matters. Under Xianzong (reigned 805–820), the Tang court regained a great deal of control over the powerful provinces and put down several major rebellions in Sichuan, the Chang (Yangtze) delta, Hebei, and Shandong. Xianzong's success, however, to a great extent was based on the loyalty of his eunuchs, who controlled the dynasty's elite palace armies and supervised the provincial administrations. Eunuchs began to play an increasing part in Tang politics under Daizong (reigned 762–779). They murdered Xianzong and determined the succession of most subsequent young emperors. Although Wuzong (reigned 841–846) temporarily revived the fortunes of the dynasty by imposing some restrictions on the eunuchs' power, Yizong's reign (859–873) saw a resurgence of their influence at court.

During its last several decades, the dynasty suffered serious floods and drought as well as political chaos and foreign threats. In 874, a wave of peasant rebellions broke out; their leader Huang Chao (d. 884) took Luoyang in 880 and Chang'an in 881. Although the rebel forces were finally suppressed and the Tang court returned to Chang'an, the dynasty was left powerless. Most parts of the empire was either occupied by non-Chinese forces or controlled by rival military leaders. In 907, the warlord Zhu Wen ended the Tang and established his own Liang dynasty.

Socioeconomic Changes

The Tang era witnessed economic prosperity. Under Gaozu, the government undertook a land distribution policy known as the equal-field system. This system had been used during the northern dynasties and under the Sui; it granted peasants a certain amount of land, in return for which they paid taxes in grain, cloth, and labor on public-works projects. This land and tax system remained in force until An Lushan's rebellion. Gaozu also established mints and issued a new currency that remained standard throughout the T'ang dynasty. The Grand Canal, an extensive system of waterways that were constructed during the Sui dynasty to link wealthy south China with the Yellow (Huang) River valley, facilitated the Tang economic transactions as well as political stability.

The Tang was cosmopolitan and open to foreign influences. About two million people lived in the capital Chang'an, the most populous city in the world at that time. A variety of foreign goods were displayed in the marketplaces of the major cities, where Chinese mingled with people from various Asian countries, including Japan, Korea, and India. Foreigners not only came to trade and study, but also served as grooms, entertainers, dancers, and musicians. Some foreign customs, such as playing polo, became fashionable.

The social structure in the Tang changed significantly after An Lushan's rebellion. With the decline of the aristocracy, the ruling class obtained their political power more from education and possession of landed property than from birth alone. When the equal-field land distribution system collapsed, many peasants disposed of their lands and became tenants or hired laborers of the rich based on formal contracts. Local elites seized opportunities to establish large, landed estates that were managed by bailiffs and cultivated by tenants, hired workers, or slaves.

After mid-750s, the old taxation system ceased to function. During Dezong's reign (779–805), the chief minister, Yang Yan, applied a new two-tax system generally to the empire. This system combined various taxes into one single tax, which was to be paid, in the summer and autumn, on the basis of the value of property instead of number of household members. This taxation method generated revenues for the Tang, and remained China's basic tax structure until the sixteenth century.

The late Tang also saw important demographic changes. By 742, according to an official population survey, there were about 9 million households or more than 50 million registered individuals in the empire. Due to factors such as warfare and natural disasters, the population in the north fell dramatically, and more and more people migrated to the lower Chang valley and into Zhejiang.

Despite political instability, the economy continued to grow in the late Tang. The population movements to the south promoted the agricultural expansion in the more fertile and productive lands of the country. New crops such as tea, sugar, and new varieties of grain were developed, and the double-cropping of land with rice and winter wheat produced greater quantities of foods. Silk production also increased rapidly in the Chang delta region. With regard to commerce, the merchant class enjoyed legal freedom to engage in business, and became prosperous dealing in salt, tea, banking, and overseas trade. In addition to the two great markets in Chang'an and Luoyang, large markets appeared in local areas, and the local markets facilitated the development of new urban centers. The increased volume of trade brought an increasing use of money, particularly the privately circulated silver, and various credit and banking institutions began to emerge. To facilitate commercial transactions, money drafts were invented in 811.

Cultural and Intellectual Changes

One of the most dramatic cultural achievements in the Tang was the development of Buddhism. Although the Tang court gave their preference to Taoism due to the claim that they were descended from Laozi, the legendary founder of the belief system, they also recognized the strength of Buddhism and provided it with great favor and lavish patronage through most of the period. The famous pilgrim Xuanzang (c. 596–664) went to India in 629 and returned in 645 with a large number of Buddhist sutras. It was during the Tang that Buddhist doctrine became sinicized and Chinese indigenous Buddhist schools emerged. Three were most prominent. The Celestial Terrace (Tiantai) school, named after a famous monastery, emphasized synthesis and harmony of all Buddhist teachings. The Pure Land (Jingtu) school believed that salvation, or rebirth in the Pure Land, could be attained by chanting the Buddha's name. The Meditation (Chan) school stressed intuitive enlightenment through meditation. Buddhist monasteries, free of all obligations to the state, acquired tremendous wealth by accepting gifts and conducting business. These communities, however, often encountered criticism from Confucianists and Taoists, both out of intellectual rivalry and because all these belief systems competed for economic resources from the government. In 843–845, the pro-Taoist emperor Wuzong persecuted Buddhism; during that period some 4,600 monasteries and 40,000 shrines and temples were destroyed, 260,000 monks and nuns were returned to lay status, and much monastic lands were confiscated and sold. This suppression marked the beginning of Buddhism's decline in China.

Other intellectual currents also developed in the Tang. Since Confucianism offered political theories and institutional rules to build the centralized empire, the court promoted its spread, particularly through the civil-service examinations. In the late Tang, the prominent writer Han Yu (768–824), while attacking Buddhism, emphasized the revival of the orthodox Confucianism, which influenced the development of the Neo-Confucianism during the Song dynasty (960–1279). Zoroastrianism, Islam, and Nestorian Christianity also entered China.

During the Tang, many fields of art flourished. Poetry reached its golden age. About three thousand poets are known to us today, among whom Li Bo (701–762) and Du Fu (712–770) are perhaps the most prominent. The essayists Han Yu (768–824) and Liu Zongyuan (773–819) promoted the "ancient style of prose" (guwen) movement to reform literature. The Tang also saw the first serious attempts to write short stories. Both Buddhist and secular sculpture flourished. Artisans created large monumental sculptures in Buddhist rock cave temples and small metal images of the Buddha and bodhisattvas. The six relief sculptures of Taizong's battle horses that guarded his tomb represented the masterpieces of the secular sculpture of the age. The frescoes at the caves of Dunhuang synthesized the cultural themes and artistic styles of China, India, and Central Asian countries. Under the Tang, woodblock printing also developed.

Legacy of the Tang

The Tang represented the golden age of China's imperial times. The early Tang epitomized the Chinese civilization achieved by then; and the late Tang initiated reforms that left long-lasting effects on later dynasties. The extensive and unified empire strengthened a political ideology of "great unity." Their achievements in political institutions and religion attracted a great number of foreign students to study, and had far reaching influences on neighboring countries. Japan, for example, learned from the Tang the imperial institutions, bureaucracy, law codes, written language, Confucianism, Buddhism, literature, art, and architecture. The economic prosperity in the Tang promoted international trade, which in turn facilitated cultural exchange between Chinese and other peoples. The technology of making paper, for instance, was transmitted to the West during the Tang. The Tang dynasty was so influential to Chinese culture that present-day overseas Chinese call Chinatowns *Tangren jie*—the "streets of the Tang people."

Jiang Yonglin

Further Reading
Hartman, Charles. (1986) *Han Yu and the T'ang Search for Unity.* Princeton: NJ: Princeton University Press.
Johnson, David. (1977) *The Medieval Chinese Oligarchy.* Boulder, CO: Westview Press..
McMullen, David. (1988) *State and Scholars in T'ang China.* Cambridge, U.K.: Cambridge University Press.
Twitchett, Denis C. (1970) *Financial Administration under the T'ang Dynasty.* Cambridge, U.K.: Cambridge University Press.
Wechsler, Howard J. (1974) *Mirror to the Son of Heaven: Wei Cheng at the Court of Tang T'ai-tsung.* New Haven, CT: Yale University Press.

TANGE KENZO (b. 1913), Japanese architect. Kenzo Tange was Japan's leading postwar architect and the first Japanese architect to win the prestigious Pritzker Prize. Beginning in 1938, Tange spent four years in the office of Kunio Maekawa (1905–1986), a pioneer of modern architecture and disciple of French architect Le Corbusier (1887–1965). Upon leaving Maekawa's employ, Tange returned to his alma mater, the University of Tokyo, to further study modernist architecture's spatial organization and urban scale.

Kenzo Tenge with his first sculpture, "Theme Tower," in New York City in April 1966. (BETTMANN/CORBIS)

Following World War II, Tange's competition-winning proposal for the Hiroshima Peace Park brought his first commission and immediately established him in international architectural circles; he was the first of Japan's architects to receive such recognition.

Several of his subsequent works accommodated the international community, most notably his 1964 designs for the Olympics, as well as St. Mary's Cathedral (1964). Moreover, Tange established a vocabulary for postwar democracy in local government offices (Tokyo City Hall, 1957; Kagawa Prefectural Offices, 1959; and Kurashiki City Hall, 1960). Many of these buildings were unusual for their large public spaces, intended for gatherings of an unprecedented scale.

Several of Tange's most important designs, including his 1961 plan for Tokyo Bay and his 1964 proposal for the Tsukiji district, were never built, and in the 1970s, he turned his attention abroad. In the 1980s, however, Tange returned to Japan and produced a number of works that fulfilled his earlier intentions, including the New Tokyo City Hall (1991) and the United Nations University Building (1992). Tange's early work was a remarkable blending of bold, sculpted concrete forms and delicate detailing he ascribed to Yayoi traditions. In his later buildings, however, his work lost its delicacy and focused on monumentality.

Dana Buntrock

Further Reading
Bettinotti, Massimo, ed. (1996) *Kenzo Tange Architecture And Urban Design, 1946–1996.* Milan, Italy: Electa.
Boyd, Robin. (1962) *Kenzo Tange.* New York: George Braziller.
Gropius, Walter, and Kenzo Tange, with photographs by Yasuhiro Ishimoto. (1960) *Katsura: Tradition and Creation in Japanese Architecture.* New Haven, CT: Yale University Press.
Kawazoe, Noboru, and Kenzo Tange. (1965) *Ise: Prototype of Japanese Architecture.* Cambridge, MA: MIT Press.

TAN'GUN MYTH The oldest extant versions of the myth of Tan'gun, an ancient Korean myth, date to the thirteenth century, when the inhabitants of the Korean Peninsula, united by resistance to the Mongol invasions, began envisioning themselves as one people with a shared history. According to one version of this myth, in the *Samguk yusa* (Legends and History of the Three Kingdoms of Ancient Korea), Tan'gun was the product of a union between a bear-turned-woman and the son of the ruler of heaven. Tan'gun founded a state called Choson in 2333 BCE, shortly after the legendary emperor Yao assumed the throne in China. Tan'gun ruled over much of Northeast Asia for 1,500 years. He then retired and became a mountain god.

The Tan'gun myth probably began as a foundation myth of one of the various ethnic groups that later merged to form the people known today as Koreans. However, when a national Korean cultural identity was forged during the Koryo dynasty (918–1392), the Tan'gun myth was transformed into an assertion of ancient political unity. In the early twentieth century, when ethnic identity began to be defined biologically as well as culturally, the Tan'gun myth was reinterpreted to show that Tan'gun was also the first Korean, the ancestor of all Koreans alive today.

Don Baker

Further Reading

Grayson, James Huntley. (2000) *Myths and Legends from Korea: An Annotated Compendium of Ancient and Modern Materials.* Richmond, Surrey, U.K.: Curzon Press.

Jorgensen, John. (1998) "Who Was the Author of the Tan'gun Myth?" In *Perspectives on Korea,* edited by Sang-Oak Lee and Duk-Soo Park. Sydney, Australia: Wild Peony Press, 222–255.

TANIZAKI JUN'ICHIRO (1886–1965), Japanese novelist. Tanizaki Jun'ichiro was born in Tokyo and moved to Osaka after the Great Tokyo Earthquake of 1923. He is one of the most widely translated of modern Japanese novelists, and his fiction is marked by urbanity, attention to style, and themes of obsessive love, the femme fatale, and masochism. His debut short story, "Shisei" (Tattoo, 1910), set the tone for later work with its emphasis on sensual romanticism, taste for the grotesque, and admiration of beautiful, sadistic women. *Tade Kuu Mushi* (1928–1929; trans. as *Some Prefer Nettles,* 1955) is a semiautobiographical novel of a failing marriage. In it, the protagonist, Kaname, discovers his preference not for his Eurasian mistress Louise but for the old-fashioned O-Hisa, and all the traditional culture associated with her. Tanizaki's move to Osaka turned his interests to the classical literature of Japan. He spent the years 1935–1941 rendering *The Tale of Genji* into modern Japanese. In *Sasameyuki* (Thin Snow, 1943–1948; trans. as *The Makioka Sisters,* 1957), his longest work, the free-form structure, like that of *Genji,* relies on in-depth characterization and evocation of a complete world. In his fiction he preferred the sensual and sensuous over the intellectual and political. A master of historical fiction, Tanizaki continued his stylistic experimentation in the diary format of *Kagi* (The Key, 1956), a psychological study of sex and old age. His last novel, *Futen ryojin nikki* (Di-

ary of a Mad Old Man, 1961–1962), pursues this theme, ending not in death but hope. Tanizaki was frequently nominated for the Nobel Prize for Literature, but he was never awarded it.

William Ridgeway

Further Reading

Ito, Ken. (1991) *Visions of Desire: Tanizaki's Fictional Worlds.* Stanford, CA: Stanford University Press.

McCarthy, Paul Francis. *The Early Life and Works of Tanizaki Jun'ichiro.* Cambridge, MA: Harvard University Press, 1975.

TANO For centuries Tano was one of the four major holidays celebrated on the Korean Peninsula. Observed on the fifth day of the fifth lunar month, which usually falls in the first half of June, Tano was also celebrated in China and Japan. Tano, an auspicious day due to the double fives associated with its date, was marked by ceremonies and offerings of cartwheel-shaped rice cakes to honor the village spirits. The day was first designated a royal holiday in the Shilla kingdom (57 BCE–935 CE) and celebrated by all classes.

During the Choson dynasty (1392–1910), presents of Tano fans were made to the king and to friends and relatives. Tano became the day for women to wash their hair and bathe in sweet flag (*Acorus calamus* or, in Korean, *ch'angp'o*) water to ward off disease and guard against misfortune. Large hairpins carved from the sweet flag root and colored red were worn in the hair as an amulet to ward off evil. Swinging was also popular among women. Long ropes were strung from the tallest trees for this purpose, and stand-up swinging contests from specially constructed six- to ten-meter-high swings were held. For men, *ssirum* wrestling competitions were held as well as other contests of strength. Evening entertainment in both the king's court and the village square consisted of mask dances and theatrical presentations. The Tano tradition is marked today by televised *ssirum* matches, art exhibitions, and musical and theatrical performances.

David E. Shaffer

See also: **Ssirum**

Further Reading

Adams, Edward B. (1995) *Korea Guide.* 8th ed. Seoul: Seoul International Publishing House.

Choe, Sang-su. (1983) *Annual Customs of Korea.* Seoul: Seomun-dang Publishing Co.

Koo, John H., and Andrew C. Nahm, eds. (1997) *An Introduction to Korean Culture.* Elizabeth, NJ: Hollym.

TANZIMAT *Tanzimat* is a Turkish word meaning "regulation" or "reorganization" that refers to a period of reforms in the Ottoman Empire between 1839 and 1876 under sultans Abdulmejid and Abdulaziz. The brilliance of the Ottoman Empire began to fade in the eighteenth century, when the imperial armies suffered a series of defeats in Europe and the gap in economic and social conditions between the Ottomans and the West widened. Starting with the Tulip Era (1718–1730) Ottoman statesmen and intellectuals started to question the situation of the empire and think of ways to revive it. Initial reform movements concentrated on military institutions, but under Selim III (1789–1807), a comprehensive reform project, including reorganization of both military and civil institutions, was implemented. A corps of regular infantry was established; the first permanent Ottoman diplomatic missions were opened in the main capitals of Europe; and modern military high schools were founded. But strong opposition, especially from the Janissaries (classical infantry troops) and conservative religious circles, stopped Selim's reforms.

Mahmud II (1808–1839) restarted his uncle Selim's reform program, but in a more determined way, and eliminated all opposition, both civil and military. With the abolishment of the Janissary troops in 1826, no serious obstacle to the reforms remained. Besides military and educational reforms, Mahmud II reorganized the Ottoman government. The Grand Vizier became Prime Minister; ministerial offices were founded, and a Council of Ministers was formed. In addition, some advisory councils such as the Supreme Council of Judicial Ordinances and the Deliberative Council of the Army were established in 1836; they became the forerunners of Turkey's modern parliament.

Mahmud II's son Abdulmejid gave further impetus to the reforms. His Noble Decree of the Rose Chamber on 3 November 1839 opened a new era of multidimensional transformation in the empire that is called the Tanzimat Period. Under the decree, the sultan yielded some of his authority to a Supreme Council of the Judicial Ordinances, which had the power to make laws, subject to the sultan's approval. It guaranteed to the sultan's subjects the security of their lives, honor, and goods; an equal length of military service for all; open and equitable legal processes; and equality of subjects whatever their religion.

During the Tanzimat Period, three prime ministers—Mustafa Reshid, Ali Pasha, and Fuad Pasha—undertook substantial reforms in the political, social, and economic fields, mostly modeled on the French experience. In 1840 the first secular penal code was adopted and secular courts were established. In the same year the Ottoman Bank was established and the first Ottoman banknote was printed.

In 1856 an imperial decree assured equality in taxation and in certain other levies, where previously there had been discrimination between Christians and Muslims. Nor was modernization during the Tanzimat Period limited to administration. Ottoman literature, music, theater, and sports were also transformed from classical Islamic to Western forms.

The Tanzimat reforms came to a halt in the mid-1870s, during the last years of Abdulaziz's reign. When the ideas for a Turkish constitution and a parliament were rejected by Sultan Abdulhamid II, the Tanzimat Period ended.

Mustafa Aydin

Further Reading
Davison, Roderic H. (1963) *Reform in the Ottoman Empire, 1856–1876.* New York: Gordian Press.
Findley, Carter. (1980) *Bureaucratic Reform in the Ottoman Empire: The Sublime Porte 1789–1922.* Princeton, NJ: Princeton University Press.
Kadioglu, Ayse. (1996) "The Paradox of Turkish Nationalism and Construction of Official Identity." *Middle Eastern Studies* 32, 2.

TAOISM The term *Taoism* (or, in pinyin romanization, *Daoism*) has been used to denote different philosophies, a variety of religious practices, numerous procedures of alchemy, and various approaches to traditional Chinese medicine. It is also used to connote things profound, mysterious, and sublime.

Although many Taoists believe that the teachings of Taoism were manifested by the cosmic Way (Tao) itself, its historical origins are obscure. Shamanistic practices of South China and Southeast Asia may be the source of Taoist ideas of nature and mystical union with nature. Some historians attribute the birth of Taoism to hermits such as Yang Zhu (c. late fourth century BCE), who is noted for advocating a type of individualism. Tradition usually credits its inception to Laozi (the "old master," said to have flourished in the sixth century BCE), who may or may not have been a historical person. Legend has it that Confucius met Laozi but did not understand him. A careful study of Confucian and Taoist teachings reveal a number of common values, such as humility, frugality, admitting ignorance, caution in speech, and ruling without coercion. Though Confucianism and Taoism may have sprung from a common ground, they parted company to form complementary but opposing belief systems. An old saying has it that the Chinese were "Confucian by day and Taoist by night."

Early Taoism

The seminal text, called *Laozi* (after Laozi) or *Daodejing*, is attributed to Laozi. Its teaching of "acting by nonaction" makes the most sense in the political arena where the ruler "administers the empire by engaging in no activity" (Chan 1963: 166) while ministers handle the affairs of state. The *Laozi* advocates a type of limited anarchy or laissez-faire approach to government that is echoed in the *Analects* of Confucius. The Legalists (philosophers who took a generally negative view on human nature), especially Hanfeizi (d. 232 BCE), were attracted to passages in the *Laozi* advocating that the masses be kept ignorant and left to lead a simple existence. Some of the poems in the *Laozi* give guidance on self-cultivation and descriptive cosmology. These aspects of the text gave it a lasting quality, inspiring further philosophical speculation, meditative techniques, and religious ideals. By the time of Emperor Wu (156–87 BCE) of the Han dynasty (206 BCE–220 CE) the *Laozi* was being chanted at court.

Zhuang Zhou (c. fourth to third centuries BCE) is the second major figure in Taoism, and the text that bears his name, the *Zhuangzi*, has left its mark on Taoist philosophy and religion. We know very little about his life. He may have held a minor post; he probably declined being prime minister. Based on the first seven, or inner, chapters of the *Zhuangzi*, which are attributed to Zhuang Zhou, we can surmise that he was a man of letters and a very creative thinker and writer.

Because things are constantly changing, Zhuangzi advocated a type of contextual understanding in which things abide according to the circumstances of their existence. Part of his contextualism led to the realization that one's understanding is always limited to one's restricted perspective. Zhuangzi celebrates the world of change and transformation with the expectation that humans can transform and return to the serene unity of nature. The *Zhuangzi* is replete with meditative images and practices—being as clear as the dawn, being like dead ashes or a withered tree, fasting the heart-mind, losing the self—images that were used later in Zen Buddhism to describe meditation.

The *Zhuangzi* also contains many fanciful figures, gods, spiritual beings, and immortals. It is easy to see how some later readers understood the text to be proposing that in the process of entering the serene unity of nature one becomes an immortal. Zhuangzi's imaginative images were later taken to be literal descriptions of the immortals; hence it was thought that immortals do not eat the five grains, that they live off of the mountain wind and dew, that they fly in the clouds or air and drive dragons, and so on. The outer chapters of the *Zhuangzi* discuss *shen* (spirit), *jing* (vital essence), and *qi* (vital breath, or energy), which became important concepts in later Taoist meditation, alchemy, medicine, and liturgy.

Yellow Emperor and Huanglao Taoism

Many innovations in philosophy, especially political philosophy, alchemy, and medicine from the third to the first centuries BCE were attributed to the mythical Yellow Emperor (Huangdi), who, according to legend, ruled China in the third millennium BCE. For example, the afterword of the classic *Lushi chunqiu* (Master Lu's Spring and Autumn Annals, c. 241 BCE) claims that the cosmic harmony teachings of that text were derived from his doctrines. Certainly *Huangdi neijing* (The Yellow Emperor's Classic of Internal Medicine) is the *locus classicus* of Chinese medicine.

The political philosophy of the Yellow Emperor and Laozi became closely associated during the Warring States Period (403–221 BCE), and the contraction Huanglao (Huang + Lao) was commonly used in the early Han dynasty. The Huanglao teachings entailed longevity practices, renouncing wealth, and governing without interference. The Huanglao political philosophy sought to make Taoism practicable.

While some read and interpreted the *Laozi* and *Zhuangzi* as philosophical guides in rulership, cosmology, and self-cultivation, others interpreted those texts in a spiritual manner as companions to the *Chuci* (Songs of Chu), which depict ecstatic journeys of shamans *(wu)*. Out of shamanic, alchemical, and longevity techniques developed the magical and medical arts of the *fangshi*, the men of methods. The *fangshi* were also called *daoren* (people of *dao*) or *daoshi* (scholars of *dao*); in this context *dao* means "methods" or "arts" while also connoting the cosmic Way. The practice of acting by not acting and the quest for longevity and thus immortality, which were advocated independently in different sections of the *Zhuangzi*, became fused during the Han dynasty.

Later Taoism

During the latter portion of the Han dynasty, known as the Later, or Eastern, Han dynasty (25–220 CE), the country was weakened by flood and famine, and rebellion became inevitable. Two different revolutionary Taoist movements developed. In eastern and central China, a rebel group known as the Yellow Turbans,

THE TAO OF TEA

Tea is more than just a beverage as far as the Chinese are concerned. The Taoist philosophy views tea as a harmonization of earth, metal, water, wood, and fire—as the following extract demonstrates:

EARTH

WATER

rain and mist

and

FIRE

Sunshine

combine to make the tea leaves

EARTH is the source of colorful ceramics, tea's adornment.

METAL is the resource from which kettles are fashioned.

WATER, in its purest form, is 'the friend of tea'.

WOOD is the substance from which tea is born.

FIRE is the 'teacher of tea' in that it moulds tea's character during processing and again during its brewing.

Water and fire interact to release the hidden potentialities of the leaf.

Source: John Blofeld (1985) *The Chinese Art of Tea*. Boston, MA: Shambhala. (144)

who worshiped Huanglao, rose up, but they were vanquished by the Han army. Despite their demise, many of their practices persisted, especially among women and peasants. Those practices probably influenced the development in Sichuan of the Way of the Five Baskets of Rice (Wudoumi Dao), a Taoist movement of the same period that later evolved into the Way of the Celestial Masters (Tianshi Dao). Both the Yellow Turbans and the Celestial Masters advocated that the ideal Taoist sage-ruler is also a religious leader; both followed the *Taipingjing* (Classic of Great Peace), which advocated a utopian philosophy and was written before 140 CE by an unknown author, both effected cures through the written confession of one's faults and meditation retreats in solitude, reciting sacred texts, and an ecclesiastical hierarchy based on the triad of Heaven (executive administrators who communicated with the gods and received revealed texts), Earth (mid-level managers who administered the lower level), and Man (lower level managers who organized and instructed laypeople).

By the third century, the Celestial Masters had infiltrated the aristocracy. Kou Qianzhi (d. 448 CE) brought the Celestial Masters into prominence between 424 and 448 at the court of Wei, one of the small kingdoms that flourished between the collapse of the Han dynasty and China's reunification under the Sui dynasty in 581. This was the first time Taoism was officially instituted as a state religion. Although various sects developed later, the original system of organization and the hereditary descent of the Celestial Master as the head of the Taoist Church continue to this day.

Profound Studies

After the Han, while liturgical Taoism was gaining momentum, there was a renewed interest in philosophical Taoism, which is associated with the Seven Worthies of the Bamboo Grove and so-called Profound Studies (*xuanxue*). The Seven Worthies were noted for defying social conventions, drunkenness, and engaging in pure conversations. Two of the Seven Worthies wrote important commentaries on the *Laozi* and *Zhuangzi*. The commentary of Wang Bi (226–249) on the *Laozi* and the commentary of Guo Xiang (d. 312) on the *Zhuangzi* are the most noteworthy of this period. Wang and Guo advocated Taoist cosmology, but remained Confucians in their social and political thought. Wang Bi strengthened the understanding of imperceivable existence (*wu*, often rendered as "nonbeing") and vacuity (*xu*); he was also the first to outline the relationship between substance and function that would dominate later philosophical thought. Guo Xiang developed the concept of natural spontaneity (*ziran*), proposing an intriguing philosophy of spontaneous order.

Other Sects of Religious Taoism

Before the Celestial Masters movement had gained prominence in the south, Ge Hong (c. 280–343 CE), a Taoist alchemist, wrote *Baopuzi* (The Master Who Embraces Simplicity). Inspired by the descriptions of immortals in the *Zhuangzi*, *Songs of Chu*, and the *Biographies of Immortals*, Ge Hong sought immortality for himself. Some of his basic practices included physical and mental fasting and purification, aligning mediation and alchemy techniques with auspicious days of the calendar, ingesting vegetable and mineral drugs, increasing vital essence (*jing*, semen) symbolically in meditation or literally by sexual hygiene techniques, avoiding cereals, and using sacred texts and talismans that give the practitioner the divine assistance needed to effectively summon spirits, align macro- and microcosmic correlations, and attain immortality. Shortly after Ge Hong's death, the Highest Purity (Shangqing) sect developed.

Highest Purity

Founded at Mount Mao, the Highest Purity sect was the first school to be demarcated within, and subsequently to seek separation from, the Celestial Masters tradition. Between 364 and 370, Yang Xi (c. 330–386) received revealed texts at night from gods and spirits; these formed the foundation upon which the Highest Purity developed. The multitalented historian, biographer, herbalist, and Taoist theoretician Tao Hongjing (456–563) complied and codified the texts, making an early Taoist canon. The Highest Purity teachings downplayed the physiological exercises, drug use, and legal aspects of the Celestial Masters and greatly modified their alchemical practices. The Highest Purity movement emphasized interiorization, placing special emphasis on visualization techniques in meditation.

Spiritual Treasure Liturgy

The Highest Purity school had reached its climax by the end of the fourth century. Drawing from the Highest Purity texts, Confucian moral virtues, and the rituals of Buddhism and the Celestial Masters, the Spiritual Treasure (Lingbao) liturgy took shape. Influenced by Buddhism, the Spiritual Treasure school advocated that one's personal liberation could only be had with the universal liberation of countless humans. Other influences led to the chanting of Spiritual Treasure texts, the use of mantra chants, and mudras (hand gestures).

The Spiritual Treasure liturgy developed in complexity over the next 1,600 years. The rites basically have three parts. First, the altar must be prepared with the announcement of vespers. The core of the ritual enacts the mystical union of the high priest with the Tao. The priest undertakes a symbolic cosmic journey to ascend into the heavens, seeking audience with the gods and Tao. He dances the "step of Yu," brandishing his sword to ward off demons while his thumb traces his footsteps on the joints of his fingers. This is accompanied by acolytes chanting texts; playing instruments, and burning incense. Finally, the master returns from the heavens to make the proclamation of merits. By uniting the forces of the cosmos within himself and the spirits that inhabit his body, the priest has increased his personal power and brought benefit to the community. Taoist rites came to play political and social therapeutic functions in that they were believed to restore political harmony or cure society and individuals of physical and spiritual problems.

Taoism continued to grow and transform. During the Tang dynasty (618–907) it became a state religion again. Tang dynasty Taoism was noted for its development of interiorization; the macrocosm was contained within the adept's body. In the Song dynasty (960–1279), Wang Zhe (1123–1170) established a monastic movement called the Complete Reality or Fundamental Truth (Quanzhen) school which still exists today.

After Buddhism entered China, Buddhist translators used Taoist terms to translate Buddhist concepts. Antinomian tendencies in Buddhism wedded Taoism to produce Chan (in Japanese, Zen) Buddhism in China. As noted above, religious Taoism borrowed ritual practices and philosophical ideas from Buddhism; these included funeral rites and the concepts of reincarnation and universal liberation. Zen Buddhism left a lasting impression in Korea and Japan, and Taoism's love of nature and the quest for immortality influenced Korean and Japanese arts and religious beliefs.

Taoist philosophy and religion are alive and well in China today. The 1982 constitution of the People's Republic of China reinstated freedom of religion, and Taoist monks and priests returned to the temples and monasteries. Taoist religion and philosophy are taking root in North America too, among Chinese immigrants and non-Chinese alike. Philosophical ideas and religious and meditative practices labeled "Taoism" continue to inspire and liberate the human imagination.

James D. Sellmann

Further Reading

Addiss, Stephen, and Stanley Lombardo. (1993) *Tao Te Ching (Lao Tzu)*. Indianapolis, IN: Hackett Publishing.

Benn, Charles D. (1991) *The Cavern-Mystery Transmission: A Taoist Ordination Rite of a.d. 711.* Honolulu, HI: University of Hawaii Press.

Bokenkamp, Stephen R. (1997) *Early Taoist Scriptures*. Berkeley and Los Angeles: University of California Press.

Chan, Wing-tsit. (1963) *A Source Book in Chinese Philosophy*. Princeton, NJ: Princeton University Press.

Cooper, J. C. (1990) *Chinese Alchemy: The Taoist Quest for Immortality*. New York: Sterling Publishing.

Dean, Kenneth. (1993) *Taoist Ritual and Popular Cults of Southeast China*. Princeton, NJ: Princeton University Press.

Girardot, N. J. (1983) *Myth and Meaning in Early Taoism: The Theme of Chaos (hun-tun)*. Berkeley and Los Angeles: University of California Press.

Graham, Angus C. (1981) *Chuang-Tzu: The Inner Chapters*. Channel Islands, U.K.: Guernsey Press.

———, trans. (1960) *The Book of Lieh-tzu*. London: John Murray.

Huang, J., and M. Wurmbrand. (1987) *The Primordial Breath: An Ancient Chinese Way of Prolonging Life Through Breath Control*. Torrance, CA: Original Books.

Kohn, Livia. (1993) *The Taoist Experience: An Anthology.* Albany, NY: State University of New York Press.

Kwok, Man Ho, and Joanne O'Brien. (1990) *The Eight Immortals of Taoism: Legends and Fables of Popular Taoism.* New York: Penguin Books USA.

Lau, D. C., and Roger T. Ames. (1998) *Yuan Tao: Tracing Tao to Its Source.* New York: Ballantine Books.

Ni, Maoshing, trans. (1995) *The Yellow Emperor's Classic of Medicine.* Boston, MA: Shambhala Publications.

Robinet, Isabelle. (1997) *Taoism: Growth of a Religion.* Stanford, CA: Stanford University Press.

———. (1993) *Taoist Meditation: The Mao-Shan Tradition of Great Purity.* Albany, NY: State University of New York Press.

Saso, Michael R. (1972) *Taoism and the Rite of Cosmic Renewal.* Pullman, WA: Washington State University Press.

———. (1978) *Taoist Master Chuang.* New Haven, CT: Yale University Press.

Watson, Burton. (1968) *The Complete Works of Chuang Tzu.* New York: Columbia University Press.

Welch, Holmes, and Anna Seidel. (1979) *Facets of Taoism.* New Haven, CT: Yale University Press.

TAOISM—KOREA Taoism, along with Buddhism and Confucianism, first entered Korea during the Three Kingdoms period (c. 300–668). Unlike Buddhism and Confucianism, however, Taoism never established a significant institutional presence outside the capital. The only Taoist temples in Korea were government-sponsored temples, and the few Taoist priests performed rituals for the king and the central government only. There were no Taoist temples available to the general population.

State support of Taoist temples was sporadic. In 650 the Koguryo kingdom (37 BCE–668 CE) erected two Taoist temples in the short-lived hope of gaining a spiritual advantage over its rival Korean kingdoms. The Koryo dynasty (918–1392) funded several Taoist temples to supplement its network of Buddhist temples. One of those official Taoist temples survived into the Choson dynasty (1392–1910), and its priests continued to perform rituals on behalf of the royal family until that temple was destroyed in the Japanese invasion of the 1590s. When the last official temple disappeared, Taoism in Korea lost its separate institutional identity.

Taoism nevertheless survived in Choson Korea as a part of popular religion and as the source of longevity-enhancing practices among the neo-Confucian ruling elite. Publication of two Taoist works from China, the *Yushujing* (Classic of the Jade Pivot) and the *Qixingjing* (Classic of the Big Dipper), and their popularity among commoners in the second half of the dynasty, is evidence of the Taoist penetration of Korea's popular religion, as is the publication after 1700 of Korean vernacular translations of Taoist manuals of life-span calculation. The inclusion of such Taoist deities as the Jade Emperor among the gods shamans worshiped is further evidence of the assimilation of elements of Taoism into popular religion.

Internal alchemy, on the other hand, was assimilated into the neo-Confucian culture of the ruling elite. Starting in the fifteenth century, scholars began reading and writing commentaries on such alchemical texts as *Hwangdingjing* (The Yellow Court Classic) and the *Cantong qi* (Triplex Unity). Renowed neo-Confucian scholars such as Yi Hwang (1501–1570) practiced Taoist breath-control techniques and physical exercises. Interest in internal alchemy techniques subsided after the seventeeth century, only to revive again in the 1970s. In the final decades of the twentieth century, there was an internal alchemy boom as centers for studying "cinnabar field breathing" and pursuing the "way of mountain immortals" began opening throughout South Korea.

Don Baker

Further Reading
Yi Nunghwa. (1977) *Choson Togyo-sa* (The History of Korean Daoism). Trans. by Yi Chongun (in Chinese and Korean). Seoul: Posong munhwasa.

TARAI The Tarai is an important geographical subregion in the north of India and the south of Nepal that is home to several national parks and the site of a regional Green Revolution in agriculture. The Tarai is a narrow strip of land running along the base of the foothills of the Himalaya Mountains. It varies from about two to fifteen miles in width and extends from the Indo-Pakistan border through Nepal and the Indian states of Uttar Pradesh, Bihar, and West Bengal.

In the first half of the twentieth century the Tarai consisted of a series of swamps and forests famous for abundant wildlife, including elephants, tigers, and leopards. The Tarai had a small human population that included *adivasi*, or indigenous groups, such as the Tharus, Buxas, Gujjars, and Gaddis. The size of the human population was limited by the impact of the virulent malaria endemic to the area.

Beginning after 1950, the Tarai in both India and Nepal was subject to a substantial process of economic development. The swamps and forests were cleared and new agricultural technologies were introduced, which led to the initiation of the Green Revolution. As part of this process, India's first land-grant university, G. B. Pant University, was located in the Tarai region of Uttar Pradesh. The Tarai is also home to some of the premier national parks and Project Tiger reserves in South Asia, including Corbett National Park and Dudhwa National Park in India and Royal Chitwan National Park in Nepal.

Eric Strahorn

Further Reading
Singh, L. R. (1965) *The Tarai Region of U.P.: A Study in Human Geography.* Allahabad, India: Ram Marain Lal Beni Prasad.

TARIAN ASYIK *Tarian Asyik*, which means "the dance of a lover," is a classical Malay court dance that was popular in Kelantan (a state on the east coast of West Malaysia) and Patani (a state south of Thailand that was part of the Patani Malay Sultanate in the fifteenth century). *Hikayat Patani* (The Story of Patani, 1730) mentions that during the reign of Raja Kuning (a queen who ruled Patani in 1644), there were twelve *asyik* dancers at her court who gave performances during official ceremonies as well as at festivals and court marriages. The dancers were maids of the palace.

The dance was created on the instructions of a king who mourned for his favorite pet, a beautiful bird that had escaped its cage. The king went on a long search to find the bird, but he came back empty-handed. Brokenhearted, he asked that a dance be created that imitated the movements of the lost bird. Initially ten dancers enter the stage and sit gracefully. Then Puteri Asyik (Princess of Love) enters and the dance begins. The gracious and delicate movements of the dancers create a romantic atmosphere. The dancers wear long dresses made of silk and display jewelry on their bodies and waistbands. The musical instruments that accompany the dance include eleven types of *gedombak asyik* (a small drum), *gambang* (a xylophone-like instrument, usually made of slabs of wood or bronze), and rebab (a bowed lute). Dancers wear local flowers in their hair. Today, the dance would be performed by young girls, and it has become a dance for the common people and is usually performed at festival and cultural shows, obviously no longer a court entity.

Nor Faridah Abdul Manaf

Further Reading
Brandon, James R. (1993*) The Cambridge Guide to Asian Theatre.* Cambridge, U.K.: Cambridge University Press.
(1999) *Ensiklopedia Sejarah dan Kebudayaan Melayu.* Kuala Lumpur, Malaysia: Dewan Bahasa dan Pustaka/Kementerian Pendidikan Malaysia.

Harris, Mark. (1990) *National Museum Kuala Lumpur: History and Culture of Malaysia.* Kuala Lumpur, Malaysia: Syarikat S.Abdul Majeed.Ismail, Yahaya. (1989) *The Cultural Heritage of Malaysia.* Kuala Lumpur, Malaysia: Dinamika Kreatif Sdn. Bhd.

TARIAN PORTUGIS *Tarian Portugis*, or "Portuguese dance," is a term given to an eclectic performance repertoire associated with the Malaysian-Portuguese community. The dances are performed, often for tourists audiences, by troupes from the Portuguese Settlement in Malacca.

The *Tarian Portugis* tradition was "invented" in 1952, when a small group of upper-class Eurasians from Malacca who were preparing to entertain a visiting Portuguese dignitary learned a few dances from a book on Portuguese folk dances. The dance group remained popular after its initial performance and new dances were slowly added to the repertoire. The upper-class community faded away after Malaysian independence, and the dance group was taken over by youngsters from the lower-class fishing community who lived in Malacca's Portuguese Settlement (a reservation-like village established in 1926 by the British colonial government).

Since these performers were not able to learn new repertoire from printed sources, they composed and choreographed new dances in a similar style, using Kristang (the local Portuguese creole language) instead of Portuguese (which no one fully understood) for texts. In the mid-1970s, there was a new injection of repertoire from Portugal, though this time the dances were more "folkloric," with faster music and more complex choreography.

The only dance that can properly be described as indigenous to the community is the *branyo*, a flirtatious social dance in which couples advance and retreat without touching each other. Characterized by an alternating 3-2 rhythmic pattern, the *branyo* is similar to (and perhaps a precursor of) the national Malaysian social dance, *joget*. The most famous *branyo* tune, "Jinkly Nona," has become a national Malaysian folk song. Verses from this song are found in Portuguese communities from Sri Lanka to Macao, linking the Malacca community to a wider historical Portuguese diaspora.

Margaret Sarkissian

Further Reading
Sarkissian, Margaret. (2000) *D'Albuquerque's Children: Performing Tradition in Malaysia's Portuguese Community.* Chicago: University of Chicago Press.

TARIM BASIN The Tarim Basin encompasses the interior drainage in northwest China located between the Tian Shan and Kunlun Shan of Central Asia. The region comprises 906,500 square kilometers (530,000 square miles) of mostly shifting sands, dry lake beds, and undulating expanses of arid terrain. The Taklimakan Desert occupies the lower basin. The Tarim appellation appropriately describes a river that either flows into a lake or that meanders amid desert sands. Temperature extremes of minus 20° to plus 50°C (minus 4° to 120°F) and annual precipitation of just 50–100 millimeters (2–4 inches) define this desert climate. Vegetation is very sparse except for riparian stands of poplar and wormwood, willows, sea buckthorn, Ural licorice, and Indian hemps.

Oasis agriculture in small and far-flung settlements produces grains, cotton, fruits, wool, and silk. Khotan jades, and tourism are growing in importance. Recent oil discoveries will make this a significant source of China's energy supplies in the next century. Since the 1980s, archaeologists have unearthed well-preserved remains of bodies dating back at least 4,000 years. Nuclear tests have also been conducted here.

Stephen F. Cunha

Further Reading

Mallory, J. P., and Victor H. Mair. (2000) *The Tarim Mummies: Ancient China and the Mystery of the Earliest Peoples from the West.* New York: Thomas and Hudson.

Rudelson, Justin Jon. (1997) *Oasis Identities: Uyghur Nationalism along China's Silk Road.* New York: Columbia University Press.

TARSUS (2002 est. pop.212,000). The town of Tarsus is located in southern Turkey on the Cilician Plain, just twenty kilometers from the Mediterranean Sea. Tarsus was the capital of a minor kingdom as far back as the Bronze Age (2500 BCE) and lies on a navigable river, the Tarsus Cayi, at the junction of the main coastal road and the link to the interior through the Cilician Gates.

Its strategic location made Tarsus a target of various powers' expansions; the Assyrians campaigned there around 700 BCE, and Rome absorbed the city in 67 BCE. The city was especially important during the Roman and early Byzantine empires. The Arabs conquered it in the seventh century, and other invaders—Byzantines, Crusaders, Mamluks—successively took the city until it fell to the Ottomans in the early sixteenth century.

Tarsus is famous as the meeting place of Cleopatra (69–30 BCE, who arrived by barge) and Mark Antony after his triumph at the battle of Philippi; a Roman gate in the city is named after the Egyptian queen. Tarsus was also the birthplace of Saint Paul, who described it as no mean city.

Partly excavated ruins abound in the back streets; the town's current prosperity is based on cotton and light industry. With Tarsus American College and a university, it has remained an educational center.

Kate Clow

Further Reading

Cahen, Claude. (2001) *The Formation of Turkey.* Trans. by P. M. Holt. Harlow, U.K.: Longman.

Wilson, A. N. (1997) *Paul: The Mind of the Apostle.* New York: Norton.

TASHKENT (1997 pop. 2.5 million). The capital of Uzbekistan, Tashkent is the largest city in Central Asia. Located 440 to 480 meters above sea level, Tashkent occupies an advantageous position on the frontier between the Eurasian steppe and the oases of Transoxiana. The earliest archeological remains date from the beginning of the Common Era, and the city officially celebrated its two-thousandth anniversary in 1983. Known as Shash or Chach, the city lay astride the trade routes connecting East Asia with the Middle East and Europe. The first mention of the name "Tashkent" dates from the eleventh century.

Although always a substantial trading center, Tashkent was never politically prominent until the nineteenth century, when Russian armies conquered it in 1865 and made it the capital, in 1867, of Russian Turkestan. The consolidation of Russian rule catapulted Tashkent into preeminence in Central Asia. The Russians built a separate European quarter next to the old city, its planned layout a self-conscious advertisement for the new imperial order. Although this "new city" was not ethnically segregated, its spirit was very much that of a Russian city. It was here that revolution took place in 1917, accomplished mostly by Russian workers. The legal division between "old" and "new" Tashkent ended only in the mid-1920s, while in social fact its traces still remain.

In the Soviet period the city grew dramatically. The industrialization drive of the 1930s swelled the city's population, and substantial industrialization took place during World War II. Elements of urban planning transformed the old city, while parts of it were entirely redeveloped. From the 1950s on, Tashkent became a showpiece to the Third World of the Soviet path to development and industrialization. Thousands of stu-

The Daviat Muzieyi Museum and Mosque in Tashkent in 1997. (DAVID SAMUEL ROBBINS/CORBIS)

dents from Africa, Asia, and the Middle East attended its universities and institutes.

A massive earthquake leveled Tashkent in 1966; only the adobe houses in the old city survived intact. As a result of extensive rebuilding, Tashkent is an excellent example of Soviet city planning, but with few traces left of its antiquity. A new wave of construction in the 1990s produced several public buildings in a "neo-Timurid" style expressing the identity the post-Soviet regime has sought to forge for Uzbekistan.

Today Tashkent forms the core of the most industrialized zone in Central Asia, with light industry and agricultural machinery predominating. Tashkent boasts the busiest airport in Central Asia, four universities, the Uzbekistan Academy of Sciences, and numerous vocational institutes.

Adeeb Khalid

Further Reading

Istoriia Tashkenta s drevneishikh vremen do pobedy fevral'skoi burzhuaznoi-demokraticheskoi revoliutsii (History of Tashkent from Earliest Times to the February Bourgeois-Democratic Revolution). (1988) Tashkent, Uzbekistan: Fan.

Khalid, Adeeb. (1996) "Tashkent 1917: Muslim Politics in Revolutionary Turkestan." *Slavic Review* 55: 270–;en296.

Pougatchenkova, Galina, T. Abdouchoukourov, and Kh. Toursounov. (1983) *Tachkent à deux mille ans* (Tashkent at the Year 2000). Paris: United Nations Educational, Scientific and Cultural Organization.

TATA FAMILY The Tata family, a Bombay-based family of Parsi industrialists, philanthropists, and businessmen, rose to prominence in the nineteenth century. Most prominent was Jamsetji Nasarwanji Tata (1839–1904), who had entered his father's office in 1858 after an education at Elphinstone College, Bombay, and so begun a brilliant commercial career. First he worked in establishing cotton mills in Bombay and Nagpur, and invested heavily in property, plowing the profits back into numerous educational and social welfare concerns for the benefit of the general public. Then he formed a company to exploit the iron ores of Orissa, since his elder son Dorabji Tata (1859–1932) had found the iron reserves there. A younger son, Ratanji Tata (1871–1918) helped his father form the Iron & Steel Company and its heavy engineering facilities. This enterprise culminated early in the twentieth century in the development of a new and modern industrial city, Jamshedpur, which is still the center of the Indian steel industry, located near iron ore, coal, and ready tribal labor.

Among J. N. Tata's other achievements were the introduction of a silk industry near Bangalore, on Japanese principles, and the building of the great Taj Mahal Hotel in Bombay. Among his many benefactions was the founding of a research institute at Bangalore which in time became the Indian Institute of Technology.

A grandson, Jehangir R. D. Tata (1904–1993), worked for much of his life in the Tata Iron & Steel

Company. In 1929 he became the first aircraft pilot to qualify in India, and in 1932 he started the Tata Sons Aviation Department, to provide airmail services in South Asia (initially Karachi-Bombay and Bombay-Delhi). This private airline grew to become Air India eventually. In 1938 he became the director of all the Tata companies.

Paul Hockings

Further Reading
Harris, Frank R. (1925) *Jamsetji Nusserwanji Tata: A Chronicle of His Life.* London: Oxford University Press.
Kulke, Eckehard. (1974) *The Parsees in India: A Minority as Agent of Social Change.* Munich: Weltforum Verlag.

TATARS   The name Tatars (also spelled Tartars) refers to several Turkic peoples and ethnic groups living in Asia and Europe, among them the Astrakhan Tatars, Budjak Tatars, Crimean Tatars, Dobrudja Tatars, Siberian Tatars, and Volga-Ural Tatars. The most populous group, the Volga-Ural Tatars, numbered approximately 6.7 million people in1989. They are the Russian Federation's second-largest nation, and together with the Astrakhan and Siberian Tatars are usually called just Tatars.

Subgroups of the Volga-Ural Tatars include the Kasimov Tatars, Kazan Tatars, Mishars, and Kryashens. In turn, the Kazan Tatars include Central, Teptyar-Bashkir, Southeastern, Perm, Chepets, and Ichkin groups. The Mishars are further subdivided into Northern, Southern, Lyambir, and Ural groups; the Kasimov Tatars comprise the White Aimak, Black Aimak, Black Zipun, and Bastan groups; and the Kryashens include Kazan-Tatar Kryashens, Yelabuga, Nagaibek, Molki, and Chistopol groups.

The Crimean Tatars consist of three main groups: the Nogais, Tats, and Yaliboylus. All Crimean Tatars were exiled from Crimea (then part of Russia; now in Ukraine) to Uzbekistan and Kazakhstan in 1944 for alleged collaboration with the Germans during World War II. They regained their civil rights in 1956 and have been permitted to return to Crimea since the late 1980s. They live mostly in Crimea (250,000), Turkey (possibly 5 million, though most are assimilated) and Uzbekistan (250,000).

The Budjak Tatars live in Romania, mostly around Medgidia, Mangalia and Kostence. They number about 25,000 people. The Dobrudja Tatars live mostly in Bulgaria. According to a 1992 census, only 4,515 Bulgarians identified themselves as Tatars. These Bulgarian Tatars are scattered throughout northeastern

TATARS—THE EARLY WESTERN VIEW

The following text written by two French missionaries in the mid-nineteenth century provides a less than positive view of Muslim Mongols.

With the exception of their equestrian exercises, the Mongol Tartars pass their time in an absolute *far niente*, sleeping all day, and squatting all day in their tents, dosing, drinking tea or smoking. At intervals, however, the Tartar conceives a fancy to take a lounge abroad; and his lounge is somewhat different from that of the Parisian idler; he needs neither cane nor quizzing glass; but when fancy occurs, he takes down his whip from its place above the door, mounts his horse, always ready saddled outside the door, and dashes off into the desert no matter wither. When he sees another horseman in the distance, he rides up to him; when he sees the smoke of a tent, he rides up to that; the only object in either case being to have a chat with the new person.

Source: Huc Evariste-Regis and Joseph Gabet.([1851] 1987) *Travels in Tartary, Thibet and China, 1844–1846.* New York: Dover Publications, 54.

Bulgaria, especially around Dobrich. Dohric, Vetovo, Rousse, Varna and Shoumen are the towns with the largest Tatar communities. The only remaining Tatar village is Onogour (in Dohrich district).

All Tatars speak related dialects, except for Polish, Lithuanian, and Belorussian Tatars, who have lost their Tatar language and speak, respectively, Polish, Lithuanian, and Belorussian.

History
The ancestors of Tatars created numerous states, such as the Hun kingdoms in Central Asia (204 BCE–216 CE) and central Europe (376–454 CE), Avarian khaganate, or kingdom (562–803), Great Bulgaria (603;en640), and Volga Bulgaria (910–1236) in Europe; and the first and second Turkic khaganates (551–742) and Khazarian khaganate (560–969) in Europe and Asia.

The term Tatar was first mentioned in the epitaph of the Turkic *khagan* (king) Bilge and his brother Kul-Tegin in the eighth century CE. Together with the

Mongols, the Tatars conquered vast territories in Asia and Europe in the thirteenth century under Genghis Khan and set up the largest land empire the world has ever known, the Mongol empire. The western part of this Empire later became known as the Golden Horde, which flourished in the fourteenth century. At that time, several Tatar cities were larger than any contemporaneous European city. Both nomadic and settled Turkic and non-Turkic peoples of the Golden Horde contributed to the melting pot known as Tatars. Kipchak, a Turkic language, became the common language for the Tatars.

In the fifteenth century, after the Golden Horde had broken up into several Tatar states, the languages and cultures of the population of those states continued developing. Different territories had different proportions of the same components (Turkic peoples of Europe and Asia) and numerous non-Turkic elements, including Finno-Ugrians (Mordva, Udmurts, Maris), Slavs (Russians, Ukranians), Jews, and so forth. In addition, the Tatars captured many people from neighboring countries, including Latvians and Poles, and incorporated them into the Tatar states, which led to the development of particularities in the dialects and cultures of the descendants of Golden Horde Tatars.

Later all the Tatar states were subjugated by the growing Russian state. The majority of the Tatars continued to identify themselves as such, but with modifying words (for example, Crimean Tatars); others, such as the Balkars, Bashkirs, Karachays, Kazakhs, and so forth, took one of numerous tribal names. Furthermore, the presence of "Tatar" in an ethnym does not mean that the group in question is particularly close to other groups that use the word. For example, the language and culture of the Kazan Tatars are much closer to those of the Bashkirs than they are to those of Crimean Tatars.

Though many Russian noble families were of Tatar origin and Tatars had a great positive influence on Russian history, the rulers of Russia divided the Tatars into a variety of ethnic and territorial groups, declaring them separate nations and giving separate language status to their dialects. This Russian policy continues today.

The Tatars Today

Most Tatars are Sunni Muslims, though the Kryashens are Orthodox Christians. Tatars are not very devout Muslims; they never were very devout, even when they lived in their own independent states. Most Tatars go to the mosque only twice a year, during two biggest Muslim feasts. Usually during these feast days, after visiting the mosque, Tatars go home or visit one another and drink vodka. Drinking alcohol is not compatible with being a Muslim and Arab Muslims bitterly condemn Tatars for this habit. There are also certain Tatar groups, descended from Golden Horde Tatars and now known as Karaims and Krymchaks, who are of the Jewish faith. The contemporary Tatar lifestyle does not differ significantly from that of surrounding peoples, although Tatars do have a greater inclination toward trading and entrepreneurship than do Russians and other neighboring peoples. Being Tatar is still something of which young people are proud, even if they no longer speak Tatar.

With the foundation of the Soviet Union in the 1920s, the Volga-Ural and Crimean Tatars were established in the Tatar and Crimean Autonomous Soviet Socialist Republics, respectively, in 1920 and 1921. The Crimean Republic was dissolved in 1945, and now Tatars have only one state in the Russian Federation: the Republic of Tatarstan. It is situated in the Volga and Kama river basin, with the City of Kazan as the capital.

Irek Bikkinin

Further Reading
Rorlich, Azade-Ayse. (1986) *The Volga Tatars: A profile in national resilience*. Stanford, CA: Hoover Institution Press, Stanford University.
Schamiloglu, Uli. (2002, in press) *The Golden Horde: Economy, Society, and Civilization in Western Eurasia, Thirteenth-Fourteenth Centuries*. Madison, WI: Turko-Tatar Press.
Urazmanova, Raufa, and Sergei Cheshko, eds. (2001) *Tatary (Tatars)*. Moscow: Nauka.

TATSUNO KINGO (1854–1919), first modern Japanese architect. Tatsuno Kingo was born the son of a low-ranking samurai of the Karatsu domain, in what is today Saga Prefecture. He left the province to go to Tokyo to study at the Imperial College of Engineering (forerunner of the Department of Engineering at Tokyo University) under Josiah Condor (1852–1920), a British architect who came to Japan in 1877. After Tatsuno graduated in 1879 at the top of this class, he went to London and trained under the Gothic-revival architect William Burges (1827–1881). In 1883, he returned to Japan and became a professor and dean of the School of Engineering at Tokyo Imperial University. He worked to found an architectural academy and promoted the introduction of modern architectural construction methods and materials.

His career can be divided into an early period during which he employed and introduced classic design and a later period in which he developed his free classic style. Tatsuno helped to introduce Western-style architecture to Japan, first with the Bank of Japan Building (1896) built in Italian Renaissance style; then with the Tokyo Station Building (1914), a brick-built structure based on Amsterdam Central Station, which was the last great Meiji period (1868–1912) construction project.

Nathalie Cavasin

Further Reading
East Japan Railway Company. (1990) *Tokyo eki to tatsuno kingo: ekisha no naritatchi to Tokyo eki no dekiru made* (The Tokyo Station and Tatsuno Kingo: The Formation of the Station Building and the Station Itself). Tokyo: East Japan Railway Culture Foundation.

TAURUS MOUNTAINS   The Taurus (*Toros*) Mountains are a folded limestone range lying between the Dalaman and Seyhan Rivers in southern Turkey. The range forms a horizontal S-shape, lying parallel to the Mediterranean coast, bordered on the south by an irregular level coastal strip and on the north by the central plateau, at an altitude of 1000 meters. The Taurus range is up to 150 kilometers wide from north to south and encompasses Turkey's lake district, including the freshwater lakes of Beysehir and Egirdir and the salt lakes of Burdur, Aci, and Salda. The main subsidiary ranges are (from west to east) the jagged Beydaglar (maximum height 3,070 meters), the Sultan Daglari (maximum height 2,610 meters), the Dedegol Daglari (maximum height 2,998 meters), the Bolkarlar (maximum height 3,585 meters), and the rose-pink Aladaglar (maximum height 3,756 meters).

In Greek and Roman times the southern plain was extensively cultivated and linked to the interior by roads running north from Antalya, Perge, and Tarsus. Control of the Cilician Gates, the major pass through the Taurus, was always of vital importance to local rulers. The Seljuks made Alanya their major port, and a network of caravan roads, some still in use, with inns (*kervansaray*), linked the capital at Konya to the south coast. Present-day main roads cut the range north from Antalya, Aksu, Manavgat, Silifke, and Adana.

The sparse population inhabiting the Taurus is mainly Yoruk, an original Turkish ethnic group with a distinctive highland culture. They practice transhumance, moving in spring with their flocks of goats and sheep from the coastal strip to high summer pastures. Many have settled permanently in the lowlands, where tomatoes, cotton, and cut flowers under glass are grown, or around the lakes, where apples are grown;

mountain villages are being abandoned. The Forestry Ministry (Orman Bakanligi) owns over 50 percent of the land in the Taurus and provides employment by cultivating pines. Mineral deposits of chrome, with some iron and lead, are either worked out or uneconomic. The southern coast is a popular tourist destination; not many venture into the mountains, but the Koprulu and Goksu Rivers are seasonally used for white-water rafting; trekking is important in the Beydaglari and Aladaglari.

Kate Clow

Further Reading
Dubin, Marc, and Enver Lucas. (1989) *Trekking in Turkey*. Victoria, Australia: Lonely Planet.

TAXILA   Taxila was the capital of Gandhara, an ancient kingdom in northwest India east of the Khyber Pass, which flourished from the sixth century BCE to the fifth century CE. Today Taxila lies in ruins near the modern city of Islamabad in Pakistan, but in its heyday the city was a center of culture and learning. Its location on the main route through the mountains into India ensured Taxila's importance in the commerce linking India, West Asia, and the rest of the world, and its vulnerability to foreign invaders.

Enfolded into the Persian empire in the sixth century BCE by Cyrus the Great (c. 585–c. 529 BCE), Gandhara became one of the wealthiest satrapies in the empire, and Taxila absorbed Persian culture along with its Vedic traditions. Alexander of Macedon (356–323 BCE) visited the city in 326 BCE during his conquest of Gandhara, but after Alexander's death, the Maurya dynasty (c. 324–c. 200 BCE) emerged to rule India.

Taxila became a center of Buddhism after the conversion of the Mauryan ruler Asoka (d. 238 or 232 BCE) around 261 BCE. During the succeeding Kushan dynasty (78–200 CE), established by Buddhist nomadic invaders from Central Asia, Taxila maintained its importance as a Buddhist center. The Gandharan style of Buddhist art emerged in Kushan times. Mirroring the blend of foreign, particularly Hellenistic Greek, and Indian elements in the society of Taxila, Gandharan art introduced the first representations of Buddha as a human being, depicted in elegant Greek style. Through the second century CE, Gandharan art had an immense impact on Buddhist art in Central Asia, China, and Japan, as well as India.

From the second century on, however, Taxila began to decline. The city was ravaged by the armies of

TAXILA—WORLD HERITAGE SITE

Designated a UNESCO World Heritage Site since 1980, Taxila vividly displays the varied cultural influences, from Mongolian to Greek, that were incorporated into Indus architecture between the fifth century BCE to the second century CE.

the Persian Sasanid dynasty (224/228–651) in the second century and was finally destroyed by the Huns in the fifth century.

Archaeologically, the city is represented by three successive sites. The Bhir Mound (Taxila I), the earliest site, is thought to have existed for three centuries until the second century BCE. Sirkap (Taxila II) was perhaps the most important city in the early historical period in northwestern India and remained in existence until the second century CE, when the Kushan rulers shifted the capital to the nearby site called Sirsukh (Taxila III).

Sima Roy Chowdhury

Further Reading

Basham, Arthur Llewellyn. (1967) *The Wonder That Was India: A Survey of the History and Culture of the Indian Subcontinent before the Coming of the Muslims.* London: Sidgwick & Jackson.

Chandra, Moti. (1977) *Trade and Trade Routes in Ancient India.* New Delhi: Abhinav Publications.

Foucher, Alfred. ([1917] 1972) *The Beginnings of Buddhist Art and Other Essays in Indian and Central Asian Archaeology.* Reprint. Varanasi, India: Indological Book House.

Nehru, Lolita. (1989) *Origins of the Gandharan Style: A Study of Contributory Influences.* New Delhi : Oxford University Press.

Ray Chaudhari, Hem Chandra. (1996) *Political History of Ancient India: From the Accession of Parikshit to the Extinction of the Gupta Dynasty; With a Commentary by B. N. Mukherjee.* New Delhi : Oxford University Press.

TAY HOOI KEAT

(1910–1989), Malaysian painter. Active in Penang in British Malaya, Tay Hooi Keat became well-known during the 1930s for watercolor paintings depicting Malayan life and scenery. His style combined traditional Chinese brushwork with European techniques. Tay was a leader of the Nanyang Art movement of colonial Malaya, which was characterized by a diffusion of studio techniques and ideas about painting brought to Penang and Singapore by teachers trained in modern-oriented schools in coastal China.

Chinese by descent, Tay was educated in English in Christian schools in Penang, where he also later taught. During the late 1940s, he studied painting in London on a British Council grant. In 1957, the year of Malaya's establishment as an independent nation, Tay founded the Thursday Art Group in Penang, a group of artists committed to promoting modern Malayan forms of artistic expression. In the later stages of his career, Tay painted mainly in oils.

Tay Hooi Keat is the best-known early proponent of modern Malayan artistic consciousness, and examples of his work may be seen in major galleries in Malaysia and Singapore.

Emily Hill

Further Reading

Hsu, Marco. (1999) *A Brief History of Malayan Art.* Trans. and expanded by Lai Chee Kien. Singapore: Millennium Books.

TAY SON REBELLION

The Tay Son Rebellion (1771–1802) was a major peasant uprising in Vietnam that united the country for a short time under one popular ruler. The rebellion, which ended the Le and Trinh dynasties, was led by three brothers from the village of Tay Son in Binh Dinh Province, Nguyen Nhac, Nguyen Lu, and Nguyen Hue. The ruling Nguyen family's taxation policy and internal corruption led to increased financial exactions from the population in the south. Besides the peasant support, the Tay Son brothers also attracted support from powerful Chinese merchants who opposed restrictive trade practices. The brothers' main slogan was to seize the property of the rich and distribute it to the poor. In 1771, they began to build an army of disaffected peasants and minorities in the An Khe Highlands near Binh Dinh. By 1773, the army of some ten thousand men attacked and seized the Nguyen fort at Qui Nhon and later took control of the provinces of Quang Ngai and Quang Nam. In each liberated village, the Tay Son forces punished oppressive landlords and scholar-officials and redistributed their property. The Tay Son forces also distributed the food from storehouses to the hungry, abolished taxes, burned the tax and land registers, and freed prisoners from local jails. Army deserters, merchants, scholars, local officials, and monks supported the rebellion as it moved forward.

In 1776, the Tay Son killed all of the Nguyen family in Gia Dinh (later Saigon), except one sixteen-year old nephew, Nguyen Anh, who escaped to the swamps of the Mekong Delta. The Trinh, who ruled northern Vietnam, had taken advantage of the Tay Son rebellion to invade Nguyen territory after a century-long truce in their civil war. The Trinh armies in southern Vietnam eventually reached accommodation with the Tay Son and withdrew from the south, giving the Tay Son effective control over the southern part of the country by 1778. The youngest brother, Nguyen Hue, a military genius, was able to defend the Tay Son south from a counterattack by Nguyen Anh (1783), and from a massive assault by the Siamese armies (1785). By 1786, the Tay Son had captured the north from the Trinh, who were embroiled in a succession struggle and whose land had been hit by typhoons and plagued by poor harvests. The three brothers had united Vietnam, with each brother ruling a part of the country. Nguyen Hue, who had proclaimed himself king and changed his name to Quang Trung in 1788, was able to defend the northern area of the country and the principle city of Thang Long (later Ha Noi) from the Chinese (especially at the Battle of Ngoc Hoi-Dong Da in 1789). As king, Quang Trung carried out effective fiscal and military reforms, redistributed land, promoted crafts and trade, and actively sought education reform. He was also eventually able to establish friendly relations with China. Quang Trung died of unknown causes in 1792, and his ten-year-old son took the throne, only to be easily ousted in 1802 by the surviving Nguyen lord, Nguyen Anh, who took power and established the Nguyen dynasty as Emperor Gia Long.

Richard B. Verrone

Further Reading

Buttinger, Joseph. (1958) *The Smaller Dragon: A Political History of Vietnam.* New York: Praeger Publishers.

Hodgkin, Thomas. (1981) *Vietnam: The Revolutionary Path.* London: Macmillan.

Li, Tana. (1998) *Nguyen Cochinchina: Southern Vietnam in the Seventeenth and Eighteenth Centuries.* Ithaca, NY: Cornell SEAP.

Nguyen, Khac Vien. (1987) *Vietnam: A Long History.* Hanoi, Vietnam: Foreign Languages Publishing House.

Nguyen, Van Thai, and Nguyen Van Mung. (1958) *A Short History of Viet Nam.* Saigon, South Vietnam: The Times Publishing Company.

Truong, Buu Lam. (1968) "Intervention versus Tribute in Sino-Vietnamese Relations, 1788–1790." In *The Chinese World Order,* edited by John K. Fairbank. Cambridge, MA: Harvard University Press.

TEA—CHINA The English word "tea" is derived from the southeastern Chinese pronunciation of *cha,* the name by which the beverage is known in north China and areas in contact with the north. The drink is an infusion of the leaves of the shrub *Camellia sinensis.* Before the Song dynasty (960–1279), powdered tea was preferred, but more recently tea has been consumed as dried (green tea) and often as dried and fired (sometimes fermented) leaves (black or "red" tea). Tea is accorded health-promoting qualities in China, and recent research has largely confirmed claims at least for green tea, but in categories different from those of traditional Chinese medicine.

Knowledge of the tea plant goes back as far as three thousand years ago in China. Valued at first as a medicine and a stimulant for meditation, it had by late Tang dynasty (618–907 CE) times come into more general

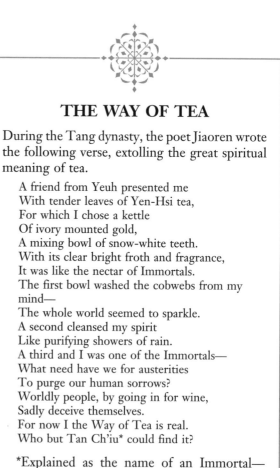

THE WAY OF TEA

During the Tang dynasty, the poet Jiaoren wrote the following verse, extolling the great spiritual meaning of tea.

> A friend from Yeuh presented me
> With tender leaves of Yen-Hsi tea,
> For which I chose a kettle
> Of ivory mounted gold,
> A mixing bowl of snow-white teeth.
> With its clear bright froth and fragrance,
> It was like the nectar of Immortals.
> The first bowl washed the cobwebs from my mind—
> The whole world seemed to sparkle.
> A second cleansed my spirit
> Like purifying showers of rain.
> A third and I was one of the Immortals—
> What need have we for austerities
> To purge our human sorrows?
> Worldly people, by going in for wine,
> Sadly deceive themselves.
> For now I the Way of Tea is real.
> Who but Tan Ch'iu* could find it?

*Explained as the name of an Immortal—which carries the implication that one must come to that state in order to "know" the Way of Tea.

Source: John Blofeld (1985) *The Chinese Art of Tea.* Boston, MA: Shambala, 139.

use. Its mass popularity as a beverage dates from Song dynasty (960–1279) times, when tea cultivation in the mountainous south, particularly the Fujian highlands, became one foundation for the rapid economic expansion of the period. Once well established in Chinese cultivation, tea quickly spread to China's neighbors, including various Central Asian peoples, who took to it avidly, and to Europeans. Ultimately, it became the world's most popular drink. Although tea was not originally a primary commodity of the large-scale Chinese trade with the West that developed after the sixteenth century, it soon became one, and by the eighteenth century the Chinese tea trade was one of the driving forces of the world economy and an object of intense competition among the mercantile powers.

Today tea is found in many forms, from the mundane to teas costing small fortunes per ounce. By and large, the different forms are marked by regional variants, but cultivation, harvesting, and processing technology are also important in arriving at different varieties. China has also been known for its blended medicinal teas in which tea is combined with numerous other ingredients carefully chosen for their medicinal properties. Among the varieties, legend has it that the fermented "red" teas so preferred by the Europeans were first invented by accident when a whole shipment spoiled, only to have the tea eagerly purchased by European go-betweens. In fact, such teas were already being made in China, but it is also true that China tailored its tea production for European tastes just as it prepared special forms of porcelains and textiles for European customers.

Paul D. Buell

Further Reading

Anderson, E. N. (1988) *The Food of China*. New Haven, CT: Yale University Press.

Dermigny, Louis. (1964) *La Chine et l'Occident, le Commerce à Canton au XVIIIᵉ Siècle, 1719–1833.* 4 vols. Paris: Éditions Jan Touzot.

Huang, H. T. (2000) *Biology and Biological Technology*: Science and Civilization in China series. Cambridge, U.K.: Cambridge University Press.

———. *Fermentations and Food Science*. Science and Civilization in China series. Cambridge, U.K.: Cambridge University Press.

TEA—SOUTH ASIA Although tea (*Camellia sinensis)* is native to China, tea production shifted from there to South Asia in the first half of the nineteenth century. Today South Asia is the most important producer and exporter of tea (in 1998 accounting for 30.3 percent and 38.8 percent, respectively). A massive workforce, about 1.5 million people, is engaged in tea production in South Asia, and tea is responsible for a considerable, though declining, share of export earnings for the producing countries. Tea is produced in about twenty-five countries, the most important (outside South Asia) being China, Kenya, Turkey, and Indonesia. The main consumers are (in descending order of consumption) Russia, the United Kingdom, the United States, and Egypt. Tea is produced in three main varieties: as orthodox tea (main producer is Sri Lanka), as CTC-tea (where the leaf is cut, teared and curled before firing/heating; main producers are India and Kenya) and as green tea (manufacture without firing; main producer is China). In South Asia a large and growing proportion of tea is consumed internally (in India more than two-thirds of production) as a popular and extremely cheap soft drink (often prepared on the road in "tea stalls") and sold most often in packets, very rarely in bags or as iced tea.

India

India is by far the most important tea producer in the world. In India tea production began in 1838 and slowly spread from Assam (still the most important tea-growing area) to other parts of north India and later to south India (Nilgiri Hills). First planted by individual farmers, tea quickly became a company business owned by British firms, which withdrew from the subcontinent (especially in the 1950s and 1960s) only because of declining tea prices, growing labor unrest, strict (government-imposed) social obligations (to provide employees with free housing, schooling, health care and so on), and narrow ceilings on foreign ownership.

Most Indian tea is produced on big plantations; small landholders play a role only in south India. Although India is responsible for nearly 30 percent of world tea production, it accounts for only 16 percent of world exports, as an increasing proportion is consumed locally. The government has often intervened in tea exportation by setting export quotas to protect local consumers (tea is treated as an essential commodity), by restricting plantations' land acquisition and use through land reform acts, and by imposing heavy taxes on tea companies. The Indian tea industry is in a healthy condition, apart from a few "sick gardens" taken over by the government, and productivity per hectare is very high. Nonetheless in 2001 south Indian wholesale prices of five rupees per kilogram made tea production unprofitable for small producers.

Sri Lanka and Bangladesh

In Sri Lanka tea production began in 1867. Individual planters were soon replaced by British companies, which managed their estates by means of local agency houses. Fieldwork and picking were carried out by an immigrant workforce that arrived in large numbers from south India until the Indian colonial government called a halt to the emigrations in the 1930s. The state has supported the expansion of the plantation system by taking over land to which nobody could provide a legal title, providing infrastructure, and ensuring generous tax treatment.

Independence in 1948 led to almost immediate revolt against the plantation system, escalating export taxes, government interference, and finally (in 1972 and 1975) nationalization of the tea estates, which were brought under two state corporations. Their unsatisfactory performance slowly paved the way for privatization of management in 1992 and for full privatization after 1996. Sri Lanka has lost export market shares (1998: 21 percent) and reputation for tea quality until recently; since privatization, performance is improving.

Bangladesh is responsible for only 1.9 percent of world tea production and consumes 60 percent of its own production.

The Future

Tea was once the pillar of India's and Sri Lanka's export economy and as such an easy target of anticolonial agitation. Since independence, tea has lost much of its former economic importance in these countries. The falling relevance of tea exports (but not consumption) for South Asia could not have been avoided, because world consumption is increasing very slowly, causing tea prices (in real terms) to stagnate or decline.

Joachim Betz

Further Reading

Betz, Joachim. (1993) *Agrarische Rohstoffe und Entwicklung: Teewirtschaft und Teeproduktion in Sri Lanka, Indien, und Kenia* (Agricultural Raw Materials and Development: Tea Business and Tea Production in Sri Lanka, India, and Kenya). Hamburg, Germany: German Overseas Institute.
De Silva, S. B. D. (1982) *The Political Economy of Underdevelopment*. London: Routledge and Keagan.
Forrest, Denys. (1985) *The World Tea Trade*. Cambridge, U.K.: Woodhead-Faulkner.
Rote, Ron. (1986) *A Taste of Bitterness: The Political Economy of Tea Plantations in Sri Lanka*. Amsterdam.

TEA CEREMONY The Japanese tea ceremony *(chanoyu)* is a ritualized form of preparing and serving tea, usually in a carefully designed and controlled setting known as the tea room *(chashitsu)*. A distinctive feature of the ceremony is its containment entirely within this single room. The host, using a kettle and other implements, prepares tea and serves it in bowls to his guests. All participants in the ceremony, host and guests, are seated on tatami (rush mats), the traditional floor covering for Japanese rooms. The host serves his guests sweets and, depending on the formality of the ceremony, a meal, consisting of perhaps a few vegetables and a piece of fish. The host himself does not partake of either tea or food.

The tea ceremony evolved during the fifteenth and sixteenth centuries and reached its high point in the time of Sen no Rikyu (1521–1590), who is universally recognized as the greatest of the tea masters. In Rikyu's day, the leading tea masters stood at the apex of Japanese cultural life. They were respected not only as skilled performers of the ceremony itself, but also as men of taste in the various arts associated with the ceremony, including ceramics and lacquerware, room construction and decoration (the masters designed and decorated their own tea rooms), painting, calligraphy, and flower arrangement. Whereas the tea ceremony was performed almost exclusively by men in premodern times, from the late nineteenth century it became predominately a female pursuit.

Tea Enters Japan

Tea entered China from Southeast Asia, and by the seventh century CE it had become a popular drink throughout the country. Tea was esteemed by the Chinese for its medicinal value; it contains tannic acid, which is good for the health. In addition, it was treasured by the elite of society for its supposed spiritual quality. It was thought that by drinking tea one would be transported to a spiritual realm transcending everyday, mundane life.

Tea was transmitted to Japan in the early ninth century. The emperor and his courtiers in the capital city of Heian-kyo (Kyoto), enamored of China's higher civilization, drank and appreciated tea as an elegant beverage. At Buddhist temples, priests and monks consumed it primarily for their health. Tea drinking largely died out, however, in the late ninth and tenth centuries as the Japanese ended what had been approximately three centuries of cultural borrowing from China. The beverage was reintroduced to Japan in the late twelfth century by the Zen Buddhist priest Eisai (1141–1215), who praised tea as a medicine beneficial to the heart. Eisai also strongly recommended tea as an aid in the Buddhist practice of seated meditation. By the fourteenth century, tea had spread throughout Japan and had become a national drink.

There are three kinds of tea: black (fully fermented), oolong (partially fermented), and green (unfermented). Tea can be prepared in two ways—through infusion (dipping tea leaves into hot water) or by dissolving the leaves, after they have been ground into a powder, in the hot water. The tea ceremony uses green tea in powdered form. After placing powdered tea into a bowl several times larger than the Western tea cup, the host ladles in water and stirs tea and water into a frothy mixture with a split-bamboo whisk.

The Four Features of the Tea Ceremony

The tea ceremony, as it evolved in the fifteenth and sixteenth centuries, consists of four principal features: rules, setting (the tea room), personal relations (between and among host and guests), and taste (the aesthetic values governing the ceremony, its setting, and the articles used and displayed in it). Rules transform the commonplace function of drinking tea into a ceremony, which today is quite complex, with elaborate and detailed procedures governing every ritualistic aspect. The principal burden rests on the host, who must conduct himself in a highly formal manner, creating a proper and hospitable atmosphere. He or she must handle every implement in a carefully prescribed way. Whereas one can learn the rules for being a guest in a relatively short time, acquiring the true art of being a host takes years.

The tea room is a variation of a style of room that took form in the fifteenth century and became what we know today as the standard Japanese room. The room has sliding doors, either *shoji*, which consist of lattice-work frames covered with translucent rice paper, or *fusuma*, opaque cardboard-covered panels. There is an alcove, asymmetrical hanging shelves, and a low, installed desk that can be used by someone seated on the floor. The floor is covered with tatami. As a variant of the standard room, the tea room may lack features such as the asymmetrical shelves and the installed desk. Some tea rooms, however, have a unique feature of their own—the "crawling-in entrance" (*nijiriguchi*). This is a square or rectangular entryway, 45 centimeters in height from the floor, cut into one of the room's walls that obliges a person to enter by crawling on the hands and knees. The willingness to use this special entrance signifies humility and the acceptance of social equality among all the participants in a ceremony, at least for the duration of the ceremony. The *nijiriguchi* also gives guests the feeling that they are entering a unique microcosmic world.

The personal relations among the participants in a tea ceremony are traditionally imbued with the spirit of Buddhism, although the non-Japanese participant who may not be a Buddhist is unlikely to feel that there is anything particularly religious about a tea ceremony. Among the values that people of tea emphasize are harmony *(wa)* and respect *(kei)*, which presumably can be accepted by all people, whatever their religion or cultural background.

The aesthetics of the tea ceremony are many; indeed, they embrace the classical aesthetics of Japanese art and culture in general as they evolved over many centuries. Of particular importance to devotees of tea, however, is the aesthetic of *wabi*, a preference for the quiet, simple, and austere. Although not all tea ceremonies embody the aesthetic of *wabi* (some are more colorful and elaborate than others), the *wabi*-style is universally recognized as the ideal.

The Tea Ceremony in the Early 2000s

The tea ceremony is one of Japan's most enduring arts, and to learn how to handle oneself correctly at a tea ceremony is to acquire the essential features of traditional Japanese etiquette and manners. This is particularly so for young women, the principal students of the tea ceremony in modern times. Through study of the tea ceremony, young women learn how to wear kimonos correctly, how to walk and sit in a kimono, how to serve tea and food properly to guests, and how to conduct themselves with elegance and style.

Paul Varley

See also: **Tea Houses**

Further Reading

Anderson, Jennifer L. (1991) *An Introduction to Japanese Tea Ritual.* Albany, NY: State University of New York Press.

Hirota, Dennis, ed. (1995) *Wind in the Pines.* Fremont, CA: Asian Humanities Press.

Sadler, A. L. (1962) *Cha-no-yu, the Japanese Tea Ceremony.* Tokyo: Tuttle.

Sen Soshitsu. (1998) *The Japanese Way of Tea.* Honolulu, HI: University of Hawaii Press.

Varley, Paul, and Isao Kumakura, eds. (1989) *Tea in Japan, Essays on the History of Chanoyu.* Honolulu, HI: University of Hawaii Press.

TEAHOUSES Conceived as a place for aesthetic and intellectual fulfillment, the Japanese teahouse (*chashitsu*) is known for the simplicity of its design. Tea was a part of Zen monastic practice as early as the twelfth century, but it was not until the fifteenth century that the Zen priest Murata Shuko (c. 1422–1502) founded the formal tea ceremony. Shuko created the first tearoom, within the Togu-do, for the shogun

A woman performs the Japanese tea ceremony at the Yabunochi Tea School in Kyoto. (MICHAEL S. YAMASHITA/CORBIS)

The teahouse is reached by a path *(roji)* of stones placed in a seemingly random pattern. This path symbolizes the initiation into the tea ceremony where the guest breaks ties with the outside world and achieves tranquility with each step along the approach. The teahouse thus serves as a haven from worldly cares; once inside, the guest is encouraged to cultivate a mood of meditative calm. The interior is small and the decor is simple: a painting and a flower arrangement set within an alcove *(tokonoma)* are typical adornments. Each item is selected so that no color or design is repeated, and asymmetry prevails. The beauty of the teahouse is appreciated only by those who are able visually to complete that which is incomplete. In the sixteenth century, the teahouse offered a refuge from politics and warfare. The tranquility and refinement of the teahouse continue to offer a refuge from the outside world.

Catherine Pagani

See also: **Tea Ceremony**

Further Reading
Hayashiya Tatsusaburo, et al. (1980) *Japanese Arts and the Tea Ceremony.* New York: Weatherhill.
Okakura Kakuzo. ([1906)] 1964) *The Book of Tea.* Reprint ed. New York: Dover Publications.

Yoshimasa (1435–1490). The teahouse as a separate structure came into being in the late sixteenth century when the tea master Sen no Rikyu (1520–1591) designed a building specifically for preparing and drinking tea. The teahouse provides space not only for guests to enjoy tea but also for cleaning and storing tea utensils, along with a small anteroom for the waiting guests. While the teahouse is characterized by its restraint, this was not always the case: the shogun Hideyoshi (1536–1598) took this to the opposite extreme and used his gold-covered teahouse as a gaudy display of his power.

The teahouse itself was designed to embody a style of contrived poverty, with little interior or exterior ornamentation. Raw wood, thatched roofs, and straw tatami mats are typical of the natural materials used. This minimalism, however, is the result of careful consideration in which every detail contributes to the impression of refined simplicity. Care is reflected in both the design and construction of the teahouse: the precision and expert workmanship required here far exceed that of much more elaborate buildings, and those involved in its construction are considered to be artisans of the highest order. As important as the building itself is its garden setting. One type, the dry landscape garden, is a microcosm of the natural world in which raked sand suggests water, rocks are islands, and moss and shrubs are forests. Such gardens were designed for contemplation; strolling would disrupt the patterns in the carefully raked sand.

TEDZHEN RIVER Rising in Afghanistan at an elevation of 3,000 meters, the Tedzhen (Tejen) is one of the main suppliers of water to northern Afghanistan, northeast Iran, and southern Turkmenistan. Within Afghanistan and Iran the river is known as the Hari Rud, taking the name Tedzhen only within Turkmenistan, where it waters the city and oasis of the same name.

The river is 1,150 kilometers in length and drains an area of 70,600 square kilometers. Fed by meltwater, the river's main flow is between the months of March and May, with a maximum flow of 990 cubic meters per second. The mean flow is just 30 cubic meters per second, and between the months of August and November the riverbed is usually dry. The river does not freeze.

In its upper reaches the river is no more than a mountain stream, but further downstream it provides the main source of water to the important Herat oasis in Afghanistan, where large volumes of water are diverted for irrigated agriculture. Below Herat, the Tedzhen forms the border between Afghanistan and Iran before becoming the boundary between Iran and Turkmenistan. Within Turkmenistan it flows via two reservoirs, the Tedzhen (142 million cubic meters) and the Second Tedzhen (180 million cubic meters) into a broad valley where it splits into several channels before drying in the Kara Kum Desert. The entirety of the river's flow is here used for irrigation and the lower course has to be fed via the Kara Kum Canal.

Will Myer

Further Reading
Prokhorov, A. M., ed. (1973–1983) *Great Soviet Encyclopedia.* Translation of *Bol'shaia sovetskaia entsiklopediia.* New York: Macmillan.
Murzaev, E. (1957) *Srednyaya Aziya: Fiziko-geograficheskiy ocherk.* Moscow: Gosuderstvennoe Izdatel'stvo Geograsficheskoi Literatury.

TEHRAN (2002 est. pop. 11 million). The city of Tehran, capital of Iran, is located in the north-central part of the country at the foothills of the Elburz Mountains. It is the second largest city in the Middle East, after Cairo, with a population of more than 10 million. According to the historical records, Tehran was first cited by a twelfth-century traveler named Yaqut. Since then, Tehran has been mentioned more regularly in the literature, demonstrating its growing importance.

During the sixteenth and seventeenth centuries, the Safavid monarchs chose Tehran as a temporary residence. In 1796, Agha Mohammad Shah Qajar made Tehran his capital due to its ideal geographic location. However, city conditions were not modernized much during the reigns of Agha Mohammad or his two successors. In fact, it was not until Naser od-Din Shah's reign (1848–1896) that structural changes to the city were undertaken due to the influences of what the Qajar monarch had seen in his travels to Europe.

More substantial improvements to the city were not made again until Reza Shah Pahlavi's reign (1925–1941). During this time, the architectural landscape shifted to the neoclassical style, and many of the older buildings and features of the city were torn down, including ornate gates that were considered symbols of the "old Tehran." Moreover, summer resorts were built in the foothills of the Elburz Mountains, which became a popular retreat for the city's residents. The city underwent another architectural facelift in the early 1950s that was influenced by Iranians who had studied abroad, particularly in the United States. The 1960s and 1970s witnessed a tremendous expansion of the population of Tehran and of construction in the city, mainly because of the influx of capital from ample oil revenues. This growth brought with it the usual negative externalities associated with rapid development, such as pollution, housing shortages, crime, and even traffic jams. In the 1980s, the war with Iraq caused severe structural and economic damage to Tehran, which the government worked to restore in the 1990s.

A view of the interior of the Golestan Palace in Tehran. (BRIAN A. VIKANDER/CORBIS)

Currently, Tehran is home to several universities, including the famous University of Tehran, as well as museums such as the Archaeological and Ethnological Museums and the Golestan Palace. An international airport is located within the city's periphery to the west. Buses and taxis comprise the main public transportation system in Tehran, but a light rail system is under construction. The government is a major employer of the city's residents, and several industries are based in Tehran, including construction, financial, manufacturing, and petroleum processing. For these reasons, Tehran is considered Iran's cultural, social, political, and economic center.

Houman A. Sadri

Further Reading
Adelkhah, Fariba. (2000) *Being Modern in Iran.* New York: Columbia University Press and Centre d'Études et de Recherches Internationales.
Barthold, W. (1984) *An Historical Geography of Iran.* Trans. by Svat Soucek. Princeton, NJ: Princeton University Press.

TELUGU Telugu are speakers of the Telugu language, a part of the Dravidian language family, which also includes Tamil, Kannada, and Malayalam. Also known as Andhras, these people mainly live in the Indian state of Andhra Pradesh (population estimated at 74.0 million in 1998), but many Telugu live in adjoining states, and a significant number are found throughout the southeastern Indian state of Tamil Nadu. Smaller migrant communities are located in the United States, the United Kingdom, Singapore, and South Africa. The Telugu are predominantly Hindus.

The Telugu region of India has undergone a long history of changes. Over two millennia ago, the Andhra kingdom, with its capital, Paithan, lying in the current state of Maharashtra, was a Buddhist stronghold. Successor kingdoms included the dynasties of the Pallavas, eastern Chalukyas, Kalingas, Kakatiyas, and Cholas. The Hindu Vijayanagar empire in Karnataka and the southern part of Telugu land were the last Hindu kingdoms that ruled the Telugu. The Bahmani and Golkonda kingdoms that followed much later reflected Muslim domination in central India. During the sixteenth century European traders began to arrive at the seaport city of Machilipatnam, and by the eighteenth century the British had control of much of southern India, which they governed from Madras. The British also controlled the sultanate of Golkonda, based at the city of Hyderabad, which in turn dominated much of the central regions. Following Indian independence from the U.K. in 1947, most of the Telugu territory became the newly established state of Andhra Pradesh.

Shanti Raju

Further Reading
Robinson, Marguerite S. (1988) *Local Politics: The Law of the Fishes: Development through Political Change in Medak District, Andhra Pradesh (South India).* New Delhi: Oxford University Press.

TEMENGGONG *Temenggong* (also spelled *temenggung*) was the title of a high-ranking official, the commander of the troops and police, in the premodern Malay states. The term is undoubtedly related to the Javanese *tumenggung.* In the kingdom of Majapahit in the second half of the fourteenth century, this title was given to the commander in chief who belonged to the five top officials of the realm. In the Malay world there is general agreement that a ruler was supported by four senior officers, but there is no unanimity as to who these four were. Depicting the world of Melaka in the fifteenth and early sixteenth centuries, the *Sejarah Melayu* (Malay Annals) mentions the *bendahara* (prime minister), *penghulu bendahari* (treasurer), and *laksamana* (admiral), along with the *temenggong.* The *temenggong's* principal concern was Melaka's security, and he was therefore in charge of the police and acted as chief magistrate. Later he became more important than the *penghulu bendahari* and was considered to be the *bendahara*-designate, equivalent to deputy prime minister in charge of internal affairs. According to the *Undang-Undang Melaka* (Laws of Melaka, i.e., the Melaka Digest), which dates from the fifteenth century, the *temenggong* was given jurisdiction over crimes committed in the country and matters such as the investigation of crime and the apprehension of criminals in the land, and was allowed to execute people he arrested without waiting for a royal order. The *Syair Sultan Maulana* (Poem of Sultan Maulana), dealing with events in the sultanate of Kedah in the beginning of the nineteenth century, shows us the *laksamana* of Kedah acting as commander of the fleet and its *temenggong* as commander of the troops.

Concerning the expressions *adat parpatih* and *adat tumenggung,* British colonial writers have erroneously translated *adat perpatih* as "law of ministers" and *adat tumenggung* as "law of the minister for war and police," which obscures the real character of the two systems. In the first place, the term *adat* has a much wider meaning than "law"; it also means "custom" and "etiquette" and extends to the legal system. Second, Parpatih and

Tumenggung were the names (or titles) of two legendary Minangkabau ancestors, Parapatih nan Sabatang and Kyai Katimanggungan, after whom the two varying *adat* were called. So *adat perpatih* designates the custom of the Minangkabau state of Negri Sembilan, and *adat temenggung* denotes "the customs instituted by our ancestor Kyai Katumanggungan"—the custom of the surrounding Malay territories.

Edwin Wieringa

See also: **Adat**

Further Reading

Andaya, Barbara, and Leonard Andaya. (1982) *A History of Malaysia*. London: Macmillan Education.

Josselin de Jong, P. E. (1951, 1980) *Minangkabau and Negri Sembilan; Socio-political Structure in Indonesia*. The Hague: Netherlands: Nijhoff.

Liaw Yock Fang. (1976) *Undang-Undang Melaka: The Laws of Melaka*. The Hague, Netherlands: Nijhoff.

Skinner, C. (1985) *The Battle for Junk Ceylon; The Syair Sultan Maulana, Text, Translation and Notes*. Dordrecht, Netherlands, and Cinnaminson, NJ: Foris Publications.

TEMPLE OF HEAVEN Built between 1406 and 1420, the Temple of Heaven served as the prayer site for the emperors of the Ming (1368–1644) and Qing (1644–1912) dynasties in China. Every year, on the fifteenth day of the first lunar month, the emperor would come to the Hall of Prayer for Good Harvest (Qi Nian Dian) to pay homage to Heaven and pray for a good harvest. He would pay homage to his ancestors as well, because he was also regarded as the Son of Heaven. In early winter, the emperor would come again to thank Heaven for the good harvest. If a drought plagued China during the summer, the emperor would also come to the temple to pray for rain.

The Hall of Prayer for Good Harvest was built with much symbolism. Of the twenty-eight pillars that support the domed structure, the four large ones represent the four seasons, the twelve inner pillars represent the months in the lunar calendar, and the twelve outer pillars represent the twelve two-hour time periods of a day. The hall, 32 meters high and 24.2 meters in diameter, is also a masterpiece of traditional Chinese architecture. The Taiji Stone—on the Circular Mound Altar—and Echo Wall are sites where Chinese architects demonstrated their mastery of acoustics. The Temple of Heaven became a UNESCO World Heritage Site in 1998.

Jian-Zhong Lin

Further Reading

Yu Chen, ed. (1999) *Great Sites of Beijing*. Beijing: Beijing Arts and Crafts Publishing House.

The Hall of Prayer for Good Harvests at the Temple of Heaven in Tiantan Park, Beijing. (DEAN CONGER/CORBIS)

TEMPLER, GERALD (1898–1979), High Commissioner of Malaya. Gerald Templer was born in the year 1898 and was trained at the Royal Military College in England. He replaced Henry Gurney (who was assassinated during an ambush) as the High Commissioner of Malaya in 1951. He took on this post at the time Malaya was at the height of the Malayan Emergency (1948–1960), a full-scale war between the Malayan Communist Party (MCP) and the Malayan government. It was an armed revolution by the Communists, who wanted to set up a Communist state. However, the British succeeded in crushing the rebellion. Templer held both the civil and military offices, but as he himself was a soldier, he concentrated more on the military front, leaving the civil office to the deputy high commissioner, Donald MacGilivray.

During his tenure, Templer expanded the Malay Regiment by bringing in troops from Britain, Fiji, East Africa, Australia, and New Zealand, making it a Commonwealth effort to bring the Emergency to an end.

He showed great enthusiasm in his work. He was usually associated with tough military policies. He also introduced the so-called white areas, which were also known as the New Villages. These were areas that were tested and found clear of Communist insurgencies. Templer traveled throughout Malaya investigating the black areas—areas under Communist control or in which people supported the insurgents and punished those found guilty of working with the Communists.

Templer left Malaya in 1954, after considerably improving the military situation there. His policies and actions undoubtedly reduced the activities of the Communists in Malaya.

Mala Selvaraju

Further Reading

Cloake, John. (1985) *Templer: Tiger of Malaya: The Life of Field Marshal Sir Gerald Templer*. London: Harrap.
Ryan, N. J. (1974) *The Making of Modern Malaysia and Singapore*. Kuala Lumpur, Malaysia: Oxford University Press.

TEMPO *Tempo* is Indonesia's largest-circulation weekly newsmagazine. Founded in 1971 by Gunawan Mohamad, the magazine was best known for hard-hitting reportage that often got its editors in trouble with President Suharto's authoritarian New Order regime. *Tempo* was respected for standing up to censorship and to the draconian regulations that regulated Indonesia's quiescent media. *Tempo* was banned in June 1994 for a report on Indonesia's purchase of thirty-nine East German warships and the corruption surrounding the deal. *Tempo*, along with two other magazines, was arbitrarily closed under a 1984 decree that allowed the government to revoke the license of any media organ whose coverage was not "responsible." The closure and the government's two attempts to have loyal allies of Suharto purchase the magazine, which is 60 percent owned by the workers, provoked violent demonstrations among its 400 staff, trade unions, and other supporters of press freedom. On 3 May 1995, in a surprising display of judicial independence, a court overruled the ban, stating that under Indonesia's press law, censorship and press bans were illegal. Although the court ordered the government to renew *Tempo*'s license, the government refused and the Supreme Court eventually overturned the lower court's decision, effectively banning *Tempo*. Undeterred, the editors began publishing *Tempo* on the Internet. *Tempo* resumed publication following Suharto's resignation in May 1998. In 1990 it became the first publicly traded print media company in Indonesia, and it expanded rapidly. In addition to *Tempo* magazine, there is now an English edition, a daily newspaper, *Tempo Koran*, and an online edition, *Tempo Interactive* (www.tempointeractive.com). *Tempo* remains the most widely read and respected newsmagazine in the country.

Zachary Abuza

TENASSERIM DIVISION (2002 est pop. 1.3 million). Tenasserim (Tanintharyi) is a town (founded in 1373) and division of southeastern Myanmar (Burma). The name *Tenasserim* is a Western corruption of the indigenous name for the town (pronounced Ta-nin-tha-ree) and, since 1989, Tanintharyi has officially replaced the colonial version. The division of Tenasserim is located between Mon State (to the northeast), the Andaman Sea (to the west), and Thailand (to the east). The division's population is chiefly Burman, Karen, and Mon. The capital of the division is Tavoy (Dawei).

Tenasserim's premodern importance was as a portage for the carrying trade of maritime merchandise across the narrow Kra Isthmus separating the Indian Ocean from the South China Sea. The opening of British ports at Penang in the late eighteenth century and Singapore in the 1820s, however, ushered in the decline of Tenasserim's maritime economy. After the British acquired the province of Tenasserim as a result of the First Anglo-Burmese War (1824–1826), they seriously considered giving it back to the Burmese because of its poor economic outlook. The British were able to build a moderately prosperous colonial economy, however, through the exploitation of teak wood reserves, shipbuilding, and tin mining, largely with immigrant labor from China and India.

Michael W. Charney

Further Reading
Cady, John F. (1958) *A History of Modern Burma.* Ithaca, NY: Cornell University Press.
Harvey, G. E. ([1925] 1967) *History of Burma: From the Earliest Times to 10 March 1824 The Beginning of the English Conquest.* Reprint ed. London: Frank Cass.

TERESA, MOTHER (1910–1997), Catholic missionary in India and winner of the Nobel Peace Prize. Mother Teresa of Calcutta was born Agnes Gonxha Bojaxhiu in Skopje, Serbia (now Macedonia). In 1928 she left for India as a Catholic missionary, taking the name Teresa. At first she taught in a convent school in Calcutta, and in 1937, when she took her final vows, she became principal of the school. In 1948, however, she left this position to begin work in the vast slums of Calcutta, where she opened a school for destitute children. In 1950 she founded a sisterhood, the Missionaries of Charity, in many ways reminiscent of the much earlier Sisterhood of Charity founded by Saint Vincent de Paul in 1633. Gradually other nuns joined her, and in 1952 Mother Teresa opened the House for the Dying, an early hospice for the poor. In 1957 Mother Teresa began working with lepers, and her sisterhood ministered in many disaster areas around the world. Universally revered for her humility, Mother

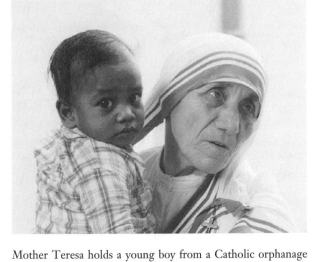

Mother Teresa holds a young boy from a Catholic orphanage in Calcutta in December 1979. (BETTMANN/CORBIS)

Teresa was awarded the Nobel Peace Prize for her relief work with the poor in 1979. Soon after her death in 1997, the Vatican began taking steps toward eventually conferring sainthood on Mother Teresa.

Paul Hockings

Further Reading
Williams, Paul. (2002) *The Life and Work of Mother Teresa.* Indianapolis, IN: Alpha.

TERMEZ (2002 pop. 128,000). Termez is a port city on the Amu Dar'ya River in southern Uzbekistan, near the border with Afghanistan. It serves as the administrative center of Uzbekistan's Surkhandarya oblast (province).

The ancient town of Termez, slightly north of the current city, flourished in the first century BCE and was destroyed late in the seventeenth century CE. The present city originated as a Russian fort built in 1897. The city and nearby area is home to the remains of a Buddhist monastery, ruined forts, and medieval mausoleums. Termez celebrated its 2500th anniversary in 2001.

Termez entered the international spotlight in 1991 because of its proximity to northern Afghanistan. The Friendship Bridge, built across the Amu Dar'ya River during the Soviet-Afghan war (1979–1989), is the only bridge connecting Central Asia and Afghanistan. It was closed by Uzbekistan in 1998 when Taliban forces took control of the northern Afghan city of Mazar-e Sharif. Beginning in late 2001, the United Nations and international aid agencies used the bridge and port to deliver food, blankets, and other humanitarian aid into Afghanistan, after the collapse of the Taliban government. The presence of American and other forces is controversial and the city is largely closed to visitors.

Rebecca M. Bichel

TERRACE IRRIGATION In much of Asia, a shortage of natural lowland areas suitable for food cultivation has led to extensive terracing along the edges of the uplands. This was done in order to increase the acreage of flooded fields, which are required for wet rice cultivation. From India and China, where terracing first originated, to many parts of Java and Bali in Indonesia, in North Vietnam, and in Luzon in the Philippines, terraced irrigation works extend like huge flights of steps far up along mountainsides. These terraced fields have been built since antiquity and maintained at a prodigious cost in human labor and toil.

One of the major tourist attractions of the Philippines are the stone-walled terraces in northern Luzon. (STEPHEN G. DONALDSON PHOTOGRAPHY)

The rice terraces provide the most spectacular agricultural landscapes in Asia. Here, permanent irrigation has allowed the conversion of slopes along uplands into rice fields and fields of other crops with which the rice crop is alternated. While much of irrigation technology on terraced land is somewhat crude, dependent on mud and brush dams and short distribution canals, some groups of farmers, such as the Balinese and the northern Vietnamese, have created complex hydraulic systems. These societies have, since an early time, developed elaborate systems for carrying as well as regularizing the water supply to fields used for crop cultivation. The famous Ifugao rice terraces of northern Luzon are one example, although they contribute a relatively small proportion of the national total of rice production and are not representative of typical Filipino rice culture.

How Terraces Are Built

Terrace building and water control, reputedly the "eighth wonder of the world," is a distinctive cultural phenomenon of Asia. Terracing, as done in many parts of Asia, consists of building stone walls, often without mortar, along the slope and contours of uplands being converted into cultivated land. The walls might be given a slight batter (receding upward slope) or inward lean at the top. These walls often exceeded six meters in height and were topped with sluices for water drainage. Earth materials would then be used to fill each unit to a level just below the top of the wall. By then staggering the field units in overlapping manner at different levels, a whole mountain slope might be terraced toward the top such that it resembled a sculptured system of fields covered with rice and other types of crops. The field units may be as narrow as 2.5 meters but as long as 90 meters on steep slopes. They are, however, commonly much wider and not so long. For irrigation, water is usually introduced at the top of a terrace series or sometimes as a complementary supply at an intermediate point. The water that is sup-

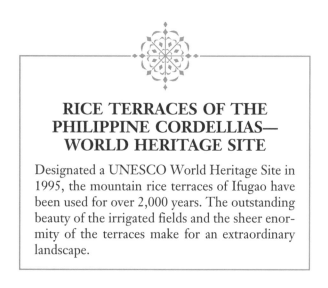

RICE TERRACES OF THE PHILIPPINE CORDELLIAS— WORLD HERITAGE SITE

Designated a UNESCO World Heritage Site in 1995, the mountain rice terraces of Ifugao have been used for over 2,000 years. The outstanding beauty of the irrigated fields and the sheer enormity of the terraces make for an extraordinary landscape.

TERRACING IN THE PHILIPPINES

Terraced fields snaking up hillsides are a spectacular sights and major tourist attraction in Southeast Asian nations such as the Philippines and Indonesia. The following extract describing the types of terraces built by the Ifugao ethnic group of the northern Philippines indicates that terracing is more complex than it appears from a distance and a technology vital to the local economy.

> *Habal* "swidden" (slope field, camote field, kaingin). Slopeland, cultivated and often contour-ridged (and especially for sweet potatoes). Other highland dry-field crops (including taro, yams, manioc, corn, millet, mongo beans, and pigeon peas, but excluding rice except at elevations below 600–700 meters (2,000 feet) above sea level) are also cultivated in small stands or in moderately intercropped swiddens. Boundaries remain discrete during a normal cultivation cycle of several years. When fallow, succession us usually to a canegrass association. . . .
>
> *lattan* "house terrace" (settlement, hamlet terrace, residential site). Leveled terrace land, the surface of which is packed smooth or paved but not tilled; serving primarily as house and granary yards, work space for grain drying, and so forth; discrete, often fenced or walled, and named. . . .
>
> *qilid* "drained field" (drained terrace, ridged terrace). Leveled terrace land, the surface of which is tilled and ditch mounded (usually in cross-contour fashion) for cultivation and drainage of dry crops, such as sweet potatoes and legumes. Drained fields, though privately owned, are kept in this temporary state for only a minimum number of annual cycles before shifting (back) to a more permanent form of terrace use. . . .
>
> *payo* "pond field" (bunded terrace, rice terrace, rice field). Leveled farmland, bunded to retain irrigation water for shallow inundation of artificial soil, and carefully worked for the cultivation of wet-field rice, taro, and other crops; privately owned discrete units with permanent stone markers; the most valued of all land forms.
>
> *Source:* Harold C. Conklin. (1967–68) "Some Aspects of Ethnographic Research in Ifugao." *New York Academy of Sciences, Transactions,* ser. 2, 30: 107–108.

plied then moves through sluices in each field by gravity downward across each level of the terrace. Finally, the water empties into a stream channel at the bottom of the valley.

Water control, which is crucial in the use of terraces, consists of careful adjustment of the volume of water in the beginning and, hence, its distribution throughout the system of field units making up the terraced series. The system must therefore be able to

bring in the required volume of water at any time during the growing season. The system must also be able to divert excess water at any point at any time.

Types of Terracing

The types of terrace walls built and the materials used vary across Asia. While the Ifugao in northern Luzon build terrace walls of stone with a slight batter, the Bontoc people in the same region build stone walls with almost no batter. By contrast, the Kallnga, also in northern Luzon, use a stone base wall and upper walls of earth with a high batter. Some groups build a few high-quality terrace walls with only a few levels, while others are known for terracing that is relatively sophisticated.

In Bali, both terracing and irrigation practices are elaborately organized through a remarkable system of aqueducts, and in some cases water is carried via tunnels through hillsides in order to distribute it from reservoirs to the cultivated fields.

Tremendous amounts of labor and toil go into the construction of the terrace walls, from the gathering of the earth fill for each field unit to the maintenance and repair that ensures the soundness of the terrace walls. Skilled water control, however, is the most important factor in maintaining good soil as well and high productivity of the field units.

With the possible exception of Java in Indonesia, all the main rice-growing areas of Southeast Asia acquired the basic method of wet-rice cultivation by cultural borrowing from India or China. The skills of some Southeast Asian wet-rice cultivators have declined rather than improved within recent times. The Thai farmers who had first learned of irrigated cultivation from the Chinese farmers of Yunnan, and who would have been familiar with the art of hillside terracing for irrigation, apparently lost this art in the course of migrating to the Menam lowlands. Similarly, in peninsular Malaysia, the Malays, who it is assumed learned their wet-farming techniques from the upland peoples of Sumatra in Indonesia—where, again, terracing was in widespread use for irrigated cultivation—also show no knowledge of the practice.

Terracing and Soil Fertility

Terracing of the fields not only served irrigation purposes but also provided a high degree of protection against the ever-present threat of soil erosion as well as loss of soil fertility. In many areas of rice and other crop cultivation using terraced irrigation and such traditional methods of farming, cultivation has continued for hundreds and even thousands of years without any serious erosion or loss of soil fertility. This has been the case particularly in areas where irrigation or floodwaters bring abundant mineral matter and where there is deposited a seasonal layer of fertile silt.

The existing area of wet-field terrace systems has grown probably because of population pressures on land as well as land scarcity in areas such as mountainous parts of Asia. Other crops apart from rice that are cultivated in terraced fields include corn, cabbages, potatoes, beans, bananas, and even coffee trees.

Yue Choong Kog

Further Reading
Dutt, Ashok K. (1996) *Southeast Asia: A Ten-Nation Region.* Dordrecht, Netherlands: Kluwer Academic Publishers.
Fischer, Charles A. (1964) *Southeast Asia.* London: Methuen and Co.
Wernstedt, Frederick L., and J. E. Spencer. (1967) *The Philippine Island World.* Berkeley and Los Angeles: The University of California Press.

TET Tet marks the Vietnamese New Year, considered the most important holiday and festival of the Vietnamese lunar calendar. Falling between 19 January and 20 February, the festival is celebrated during the first week of the first month of the lunar calendar. The first night of the new moon is considered the most important. Vietnamese view the holiday as a time of renewal and integration that solidifies the family. Tet is essential to Vietnamese cultural identity. During a week of leisure and celebration, people engage in such activities as various as painting and decorating homes, feasting, buying new clothes, visiting pagodas with the family, setting off fireworks, and making offerings and paying reverence to deceased family members. The playing of drums, bells, and gongs marks Tet festivities. Tet is celebrated by Vietnamese around the world.

Richard B. Verrone

Further Reading
Hu'u Ngoc. (1997) *Tet: The Vietnamese Lunar New Year.* Hanoi, Vietnam: The Gio'i Publishers.

TEXTBOOK SCANDAL (1902–1903). Thirty years after the Meiji government promulgated Japan's first compulsory education law, which called for a national school system under its authority, a protracted political and ideological debate over local versus centralized control of curriculum and textbooks would be brought to a dramatic conclusion in 1902–1903, with the so-called Textbook Scandal. The Ministry of Education, established in 1871, initially granted local governments considerable discretion over the selection of textbooks, and there was a variety to choose from. While the Ministry sponsored some publications, including translations of Western textbooks, most were produced by the private sector with little government oversight.

Beginning in the 1880s, the Ministry of Education moved to expand the central government's control over textbooks. In 1880, the post of "investigator" was created to scrutinize teaching materials used in the schools. Translations of Western works were ordered replaced, together with some works judged too liberal. The following year, the Ministry ordered schools to report which textbooks they were using, in order to weed out those banned by the Ministry. The Textbook Authorization Ordinance of 1887 required publishers who wished to sell textbooks to schools to submit them first to the Ministry for inspection and authorization. According to the Ministry, this measure was necessary to insure uniform coverage, quality, and price. However, it also heightened the specter of bureaucratic interference in local school affairs and served to expand the debate over control from the local to the national level.

One problem that the new authorization system failed to address was graft in the publishing industry. The magnitude of this problem was revealed in 1901, when newspapers began reporting on a government investigation that eventually discovered that more than twenty publishers had distributed bribes, gifts, and entertainment to local education officials, government school inspectors, and others in an effort to market their textbooks. By the end of 1902, the government had brought charges against 152 individuals, including principals, other school officials, bureaucrats, and the publishers. Eventually, 112 people were convicted in what became known as the Textbook Scandal (*kyokasho gigoku jiken*).

This incident was the principal catalyst for parliamentary action that would consolidate government control over textbooks. After first amending the laws to discourage graft, the parliament in 1903 gave the Ministry of Education exclusive authority to commission and publish all elementary school textbooks. This system remained in effect through the end of World War II.

Mark Lincicome

Further Reading

Karasawa Tomitaro. (1956) *Kyokasho no rekishi* (A History of Textbooks). Tokyo: Sobunsha.
Marshall, Byron K. (1994) *Learning to be Modern: Japanese Political Discourse on Education*. Boulder, CO: Westview Press.

TEXTILE AND CLOTHING INDUSTRY—EAST ASIA

Textile production has played a key role in the initial stages of industrialization of the East Asian economies by generating manufacturing output, employment, and exports, often with government support. As labor-intensive industries, textile and garment making are suited to developing economies with comparative advantages in low-cost labor. With experience acquired in mechanization and foreign exchange earned in textile exports, a developing economy gains in manufacturing sophistication and moves on to higher value-added and more capital-intensive industries as its labor costs rise. This strategy of industrialization was established by Japan in the late nineteenth century and was followed by other East Asian economies in their successful drives to economic modernization in the post–World War II period.

Japanese Industrialization Model

The Japanese model follows four phases in the product cycle: importation; import substitution; exportation; and reimportation. In the mid-nineteenth century, imports of Western textiles generated a new demand and created opportunities for technology transfer. An indigenous textile industry developed to meet domestic demand and to substitute for imports, with 1879 being the year when domestic production first surpassed imports, and 1910 when exports first eclipsed imports. Cotton textiles became Japan's most important export industry from the 1920s through the 1930s, when Japanese colonial domination over Taiwan, Korea, and Manchuria helped to spur markets abroad.

The Textile Industry in Postwar Japan

Postwar revival restored the textiles industry as the leading export industry in the 1950s, but production and exports declined steadily from the early 1950s, as percentages of gross domestic product and total exports, respectively. Textiles and clothing's share of exports fell from 36 percent for 1950–1959 to 19 percent in 1960–1969 to 6 percent in 1970–1979. Within the sector, there was a shift to synthetic fibers and yarns, a segment that is more capital-intensive and dependent on research and development. The Japanese economy increasingly focused on other more technologically sophisticated sectors.

A turning point for Japanese competitiveness in textiles came with the Plaza Accord of 1985, an agreement between the United States, Japan, France, Germany, and the United Kingdom to drive down the price of the overpriced dollar. The result was a rising yen, making Japanese exports more expensive. Production of fabrics and spun yarns declined precipitously in the 1990s, while man-made fibers maintained output until 1997, when it began to drop. From a large exporter of textiles and clothing before the 1970s, Japan has become a net importer of clothing and a small exporter of textiles. Japan now has the world's second-largest textiles and clothing deficit in the world after the United States.

The Textile Industry in the Newly Industrializing Economies

From the 1960s, Hong Kong, Taiwan, and South Korea took up the production of textiles, successfully penetrated export markets formerly dominated by Japan, and became world leaders in textiles and clothing. Their successful transition to industrialism prompted their collective label as the newly industrializing economies (NIEs). Hong Kong became the world's leading clothing exporter from 1973 to 1985, overtaken by Italy only in 1978–1979.

Comparative advantage in the more labor-intensive clothing segment was lost more rapidly than in textile production. The NIEs' textile exports accompanied by a shift to synthetic fibers have remained at around a

A textile worker making wool rugs in Shanghai, China, in 1996. (STEPHEN G. DONALDSON PHOTOGRAPHY)

quarter of total world trade in the 1990s, while share of clothing exports fell from around a quarter in the 1980s and early 1990s steadily to 16 percent by 1999.

China became a major player in the world textile market with the launching of market reforms from the 1980s. Output value of the textile and clothing industry grew at an annual rate of 15.6 percent from 1986 to 1995, while exports increased from $8.5 billion to $38 billion. China overtook Italy as the economy with the biggest trade surplus in textiles and clothing in 1991, and since surpassing Hong Kong as the world's leading clothing exporter, its lead has widened over time. In 1999, after a decade of 13 percent growth per year, China's clothing sector snared 16.2 percent of world trade, while Hong Kong had only 12 percent. In 1997 and again in 1999, China passed Germany as the world's number-one textile exporter.

The East Asian textile exporters confronted several problems that necessitated structural reform. First, world textile trade was characterized by considerable trade barriers. From 1974 to 1986, this trade was governed by four Multi-Fibre Arrangements (MFA), which allowed industrialized economies to protect their domestic industries through quotas on textile and clothing imports by bilateral agreements or unilateral action. In 1986, the MFA was to be phased out by the World Trade Organization's Agreement on Textiles and Clothing, which would remove export quotas over a ten-year period. Meanwhile China and other East Asian exporters confronted not only export quotas in the advanced economies (except Japan) but also periodic charges of dumping or illegal shipments and imposition of sanctions.

Second, as the economies of the East Asian exporters expanded, labor and production costs rose, making their textile industries vulnerable to competition by lower-cost producers. Third, the spread of preferential agreements and the formation of regional trade blocs such as the North American Free Trade Agreement in 1994 and the European Union in 1993 threatened market shares in Europe and North America. Hong Kong was hit especially hard by the erosion of its American market share by Mexican and Canadian producers.

A common response is to move up the quality and technology gradient. The NIEs have shifted from being net importers to being significant exporters of synthetic fibers. Production was upgraded by automation, mechanization, and computer-aided design. More emphasis was placed on the production of upmarket and high-fashion clothing merchandise. Taiwan and Korea increasingly moved away from textiles and clothing to such value-added production as electronics and semiconductors. In addition, the outsourcing of labor-intensive manufacturing (clothing) by the NIEs (and Japan as well) to China, Southeast Asia, and other low-cost producers released resources for higher value-added activities and also helped to sustain demand for the textile exports of NIEs. Hong Kong especially has relocated factories to China on a large scale since the 1980s, bringing the benefits of massive investments and training efforts.

As a socialist economy undergoing market reforms, China has suffered from the problem of money-losing state-owned enterprises (SOEs), which dominated the textile industry but were plagued by labor redundancy, high pension and benefit costs, and outdated equipment. Reform of these SOEs took precedence in government efforts to reform the state-owned sector in 1998: money-losing factories were closed by the hundreds, 1.16 million workers were laid off, and 9.6 million antiquated cotton spindles were taken out of production by 1999, when the state sector realized a profit of $97 million after having sustained staggering losses over the previous six years.

Future Prospects for the East Asian Textile Industry

Despite their increasing shift to high value-added industries and recent uncertainties in the global economy, the East Asian economies will probably retain significant positions in the world textile and clothing trade. Collectively their exports were responsible for 36.9 percent of total world trade in textiles and 32.6 percent of total world trade in clothing in 1999. Japan remains a key supplier of manufacturing technology to its Asian neighbors, and recent Japanese innovations such as clothing with built-in protection against bacteria and microwave radiation, intelligent or smart textiles that respond to the environment through the embedding of microprocessors or nanotechnology (for example, to keep people warm in cold climates and cool in hot weather), and washable suits may differentiate its manufacturers from competitors and allow them to charge high prices for such unique products.

Among economies with a surplus in textile and clothing trade, South Korea may soon overtake Italy for the number-two spot, while Taiwan and Hong Kong retain respectively the number-four and -five positions. As for number-one China, even as machinery exports replaced textiles and clothing as its top export sector in the late 1990s, its competitive position in the world textile marketplace is likely to be enhanced by its entry into the World Trade Organization.

Robert Y. Eng

Further Reading

Meyanathan, Saha Dhevan, ed. (1994) *Managing Restructuring in the Textile and Garment Subsector: Examples from Asia*. Edi Seminar Series. Washington, DC: World Bank.

Textiles Intelligence. (2001) "Trends in World Textile and Clothing Trade." *Textile Outlook International* (January): 46–88.

Textiles Intelligence. (1997) "World Textile Trade and Production Trends." *Textile Outlook International* (July): 9–37.

TEXTILES—BHUTAN The weaving culture of the landlocked Himalayan kingdom of Bhutan is centuries old. Silk, wool, acrylic, metallic threads, and cotton, intricately and deftly woven on hand-hewn backstrap and treadle or shaft looms, meet a wide range of daily clothing needs, as well as religious and decorative requirements of the Bhutanese.

The rugged mountain conditions and clustered-village structure, social customs, and daily life of the Bhutanese all contribute to the need for each family to weave fabrics in their own home. The country is unique in that it is dependent on hand-weaving skills for the provision of everyday apparel. The traditional practice, which continues today, is for mothers to teach their daughters to weave. Most women over twelve years of age possess high-quality weaving skills. Men often assist with shearing, washing, carding, combing, and spinning the various local yarns.

Although past written records on weaving are sparse, the tradition of hand weaving spans several centuries, and traditional and classical motifs and designs from the past continue to be woven on a daily basis. Thus, a motif in use today may have originated several centuries ago.

Regional and cultural variations produce a vast array of unique and delightful fabric ornamentation. Although a tradition of weaving is evident among Bhutan's neighbors, weaving holds a considerably elevated position in the Bhutanese national culture.

The range of weaving output includes clothing, blankets, bedcovers, scarves, carryalls, floor and seat coverings, napkins, table covers, and decorative items for both daily use and special religious and ceremonial occasions. The indigenous resources of wool from goats, sheep, and yaks and some natural silk are supplemented by the additional use of cotton and other yarns imported through trade with neighboring countries. The limited use of silk is due to the fact that the Bhutanese are highly dependent on silk imports, as the process of destroying cocoons is contrary to Buddhist precepts adhered to by the majority of Bhutanese.

The national dress, worn daily by the inhabitants, creates a constant demand for high-quality weaving. The dress for women includes the *kira* (a wraparound garment), the *kera* (sash/belt), *wangde* (inside or underblouse) and *teku* (outer blouse or short jacket), *koma* (clip), and *japtha* (chain jewelery). For men, the *gho* (robe or large outer coat) is the principal item of clothing and is worn with a belt and shoulder scarf. The *gho* is also known in rural areas as a *kho* or *baku*.

Composition of the *Kira, Kera,* and *Goh*

The *kira* highlights Bhutanese weaving ability, imagination, sense of proportion, intricate design, and color balancing. Each *kira* is designed and woven according to size and decorative requirements and reflects family pride in their weaving and design skill. The *kira* is tightly wound around the body and belted with a woven *kera*. Two *koma* at the shoulder hold the *kira* in place, while a joining *japtha* forms a decorative link between the *koma* and hangs at the front. This unique piece of jewelry is usually made of silver with a gold finish and is embellished with turquoise and coral.

The *kira* is composed of three loom widths of approximately 50 centimeters and is 250 centimeters in length. A complete *kira* measures about 150 by 250 centimeters, with a fringe 2.5–10 centimeters at each end. Although the *kira* is one flat piece of fabric, each differs in size both in width and length, so that it can comfortably fit the particular child or adult who will wear it. Each of the three individual loom widths consists of a continuously woven main section, two end-border panels and one central panel. The end borders contain design strips that range in number from six to fourteen and are woven according to a special and traditional sequence and always in pairs. The two strips in each pair are of similar width; however, the widths of the various pairs may vary from one to another. Designs utilized within the paired strips may be grouped as meanders, continuously repeated designs or motifs. The *kira* contains a wide range of design patterns, and may number 1,500 individual motifs on one piece. The patterns and motifs used have been strongly influenced by the Buddhist and Bonpo religions, as well as by the personal and individual expression and interpretation of craftspeople. Their inspiration is doubtless drawn from the physical structure of the country—mountains, rivers, waterfalls, clouds, mists, cascades, hills and valleys—and from the abundance of flora and fauna as well as the natural phenomena of lightning and earthquakes. The final creation is a visually pleasant and colorful garment.

During recent times the *kera* has been reduced in width. Earlier, the belt was 30–45 centimeters in width and folded lengthwise into three sections. Currently, the width is approximately 7.5–10 centimeters and is not folded when worn. Complex and intricate embellishments were featured extensively in the past, with designs set into complex design strips across the fabric. As many as eighty design strips have been known to be incorporated into one belt.

For males, the *gho* is made from three to four generous lengths of fabric, which allows for comfortable wrapping around the body, oversized sleeves, placement of the *kera*, and an ample front pouch to carry personal items such as food, documents, and knives. It is woven in a striped or check design from cotton, wool, or silk or a combination of two yarns. When worn, the stripes are in a vertical position. A specially tailored white undershirt, usually of white cotton, is turned over at the cuff to form a 13-centimeter band of white. The most lavish *gho* is of silk-on-silk (raw or refined), in gold and burgundy-red stripes embellished with elaborate and ornate designs.

Other Woven Goods

Special cloths are also woven for use when dining. These are usually 208 by 90 centimeters in size. One example is the *chagsi pangkheb* (wall hanging, laptop napkin, or cloth) formed from three loom widths of woven fabric, two narrow side lengths, and one central length. The background is of white cotton with embellishments in red, dark blue, and black. The finest are of silk-on-silk, with several vibrant colors being utilized. A range of special designs is usually reserved for these pieces.

Heavy wool items such as blankets, small carpet pieces, seat and bedcovers, and outerwear for inclement weather, are also woven, generally in the central region of Bhutan. Such pieces are usually of natural and earth tones and subdued hues and adorned with bold geometric designs. A number of textiles found in the *dzong*s (monastic and administrative centers) and temples also underline the strong textile base of Bhutan's material culture. Monks' cushions, altarpieces, and covers for religious relics are among those items where weaving skills are evident. Merit is earned when a weaver prepares a fabric as a gift to a monastery or religious person or event.

The tradition of weaving high-quality fabrics in the home continues throughout Bhutan. New designs, colors, and yarns have gradually been introduced during the past thirty to forty years. The quotidian donning of national dress and religious and other special needs ensures the continuation of traditional hand weaving in the kingdom.

David Barker

Further Reading

Adams, Barbara. (1984) *Traditional Textiles of Bhutan.* Bangkok, Thailand: White Orchid.

Barker, David. (1985) *Designs of Bhutan.* Bangkok, Thailand: White Lotus.

———. (1985) "Bhutanese Handwoven Textiles." *Arts of Asia* 15, 4 (July–August): 103–111.

Bartholomew, Mark. (1985) *Thunder Dragon: Textiles from Bhutan.* Tokyo: Shikosha Publishing.

Bean, S., and D. Myers, eds. (1994) *From the Land of the Thunder Dragon: Textile Arts of Bhutan.* London: Serindia Publications.

Grieder, Susanne. (1995) *Gesponnen Gewoben Getragen: Textilien aus Bhutan.* Zurich: Volkerkundemuseum der Universitat Zurich.

Kapma, Alet, and Wouter Ton. (1993) *Bhutanese Weaving: A Source of Inspiration.* Thimphu, Bhutan: National Women's Association of Bhutan.

Myers, Diana. (1998) *Glimpses of the Past, Visions of the Present: Costume and Ceremonial Textiles of Bhutan.* Washington, DC: Textile Museum Journal.

———. (1995) "The Kushung and Shingka of Bhutan." *Hali,* 78 (December/January): 73–81.

———. (1995) "The Social Life of Cloth in Bhutan." *Fiberarts,* 21, 5 (March/April): 25–31.

———. (1994) "Textiles in Bhutan: Cloth, Gender and Society." In *Bhutan: Aspects of Culture and Development,* edited by Michael Aris and Michael Hutt. Gartmore, Scotland: Kiscadale.

Pommaret, Francoise. (1994) "Textiles in Bhutan: Way of Life and Identity Symbol." In *Bhutan: Aspects of Culture and Development,* edited Michael Aris and Michael Hutt. Gartmore, U.K.: Kiscadale, 173–190.

Yablonsky, Gabrielle. (1997) "Textiles, Religion and Gender in Bhutan: A Dialogical Approach." In *Tibetan Studies: Proceedings of the 7th Seminar of the International Association for Tibetan Studies,* edited Ernst Steinkellner, H. Krasser, and M. Much. Vienna: Osterreichische Akademie der Wissenschaften, 1081–1102.

TEXTILES—LAOS Historically, Lao women of most ethnic groups weave. The resulting textiles were woven for personal use and were a representation of daily life and cultural traditions. Intricate and complex designs performed such supernatural functions as warding off evil spirits and bringing good fortune and fertility to a newly wedded couple. Textiles were produced both for wear and for ceremonial ornamentation, as well as for such domestic uses as mats and wall cloths for welcoming guests to the home for special ceremonies. Textiles used for clothing could denote a person's age and social status, or both, often through the use of color. Textile motifs may be geometric, such as the diamond or lozenge shape, or mythological, such as the *siho* or *kosasing,* a half-elephant, half-lion figure; the *nak,* a serpent prominent in the Lao Buddhist tradition; and the *mom,* a mythical bird.

Looms and Weaving Techniques

A variety of weaving technologies is used in Laos, including both frame and body-tensioned looms. The most commonly used method is the traditional Lao floor loom with a vertical heddle. This loom consists of a wooden frame loom with a horizontal warp, the threads that are stretched to form the base and width of the woven fabric. Each thread, or warp end, is passed through a primary heddle, the mechanism that raises and lowers alternating warp threads through the use of foot peddles, or treadles, to form an opening called a shed. A secondary set of long-eyed heddles is used to create and store a supplementary design. The design is preserved with a series of pattern rods that correspond to a design the weaver wants to weave. This patterning and storage method is unique to Laos and allows for the diversity and complexity of Lao weaving.

Depending on the type of weave and patterning that is in use, the weaver passes the weft threads in between the shed with either a shuttle or manually. The warp is tensioned over a back beam and then looped back above the weaver. The warp is then tied on a beam above the weaver's head. The weaver can adjust the tension of the warp as the fabric progressed by reaching overhead and adjusting the knotted warp ends.

As the weaver weaves one row of weft, a beater, or reed, is pulled forward to beat the newly woven row into the body of the textile. The reed or comb is suspended overhead and is composed of tightly spaced bamboo teeth. Two warp ends are passed through an individual tooth of the reed that in turn keep the warp ends evenly spaced. The spacing of the teeth also determines the density, or thread count, of the fabric. Lao language has a specific term to indicate the number of threads in a warp. This measurement is known as a *lope,* a unit of 40 dents in the comb. The number of *lope* identifies the density of traditional fabrics.

Most Lao weavings are decorated using a supplementary weft, and in some cases a supplementary warp, patterning. The brocade, or pattern, is inlaid into the background of the fabric by alternating the background weave with the supplemental design. A continuous supplementary weft design is one in which the pattern and color extend across the width of the fabric. Discontinuous supplementary weft design is one in which the design and color are inlaid at various intervals across the weft line. This allows the weaver to create a wide range of complex patterns and designs in various colors.

Two other traditional methods of creating design in Lao fabrics are *mat mi,* known universally as ikat, and tapestry. With *mat mi,* the weft yarns are first dyed a base color and then wrapped onto a rectangular frame that is sized to coordinate with the width of the fabric. The yarns are wrapped in bunches depending on the length/width of the textile. These groups of weft threads are then measured and tied to form a specific design. The bundle is then dyed a second color, the wrapping removed, and the skein placed on a skein winder. The weaver winds the dyed thread onto a bobbin that is then placed into a shuttle. As the shuttle is passed back and forth between the warp threads, the design evolves as it has been dyed into the thread. An even more complex style of weaving that is used by some Lao ethnic groups, especially the Tai Daeng and Tai Kao in the north, is *sin muk*. With *sin muk*, narrow vertical bands of *mat mi* and supplementary weft are patterned with intersecting bands of supplementary warp threads, creating an intricate checkerboard patterning.

Regional Weaving Styles

Approximately sixty-eight diverse ethnic groups live within the borders of Laos, each with its own unique style of weaving. The lowland Lao today represent an amalgamation of many of these groups. Traditionally, lowland silk skirts are tightly woven with a glossy, lightweight, and stiff texture. Skirts are often accented with gold and silver threads and employ Western dressmaking elements such as darts and metal fasteners. In southern Laos, designs are more influenced by Khmer culture, employing narrow vertical bands of alternating motifs, often in *mat mi*. Elephants, humans, and tiered structures figure prominently in their designs. The Phuan are located in the central mountains of Laos. These people tend to use a more orderly design, with horizontal bands and blocks of motifs. Color is heavily used to distinguish members within their group and to separate their designs from those of other ethnic groups.

The wild and mountainous northern terrain has isolated small bands of people, resulting in an extremely diverse region of intricate weaving styles. Various Tai groups each have their own style of patterning. The Tai Daeng of the northeast are well known for weaving intricate patterns within the body of the fabric. The Tai Lue people combine various weaving techniques with the use of tapestry weave. Many of their designs use bright colors and bold motifs. Waistbands are woven into the body of the skirt rather than attached as a separate piece. Head cloths are the most distinctive design of the Tai Dam people. Black cotton rectangles are patterned with thin lines of color and a bright rectangle. Decorative patches are woven on either end. Other northern groups, especially the Hmong and Yao, use other patterning techniques, such as batik and embroidery.

Lao Textiles Today

Following the end of civil war in 1975, large migrations of people from the north came down to the Mekong River plain. As a result, traditions from the diverse ethnic groups intermingled. Simultaneously, heirloom textiles were sold off to raise money to survive. The combination of this mingling of styles, the exodus of old textiles, and the simplification of designs threatened the loss of ancient motifs and traditions. Synthetics and Western styles also became more and more integrated into Lao weavings. Today, silk production is growing popular in rural Laos, with farmers producing high-quality, hand-reeled silk.

Traditional Lao weaving continues to be widespread and is recognized as a unique and exquisite art. The complex designs and techniques still practiced by Lao weavers make them among the most skilled in the world. Ancient Lao weaving traditions continue to be passed on from mother to daughter, which ensures the preservation of their unique textile heritage.

Carol Cassidy

Further Reading

Connors, Mary F. (1998) *Lao Textiles and Traditions.* Kuala Lumpur, Malaysia: Oxford University Press.

The Museum at the Fashion Institute of Technology. (1995) *Beyond Tradition: Lao Textiles Revisited.* Hong Kong: Pearl River Printing Company.

THAI The Thai people of Thailand (*Khon Thai*), numbering more than 46.4 million, form part of a much larger population of speakers of Tai languages dispersed through the neighboring countries of Laos, Vietnam, China, Myanmar (Burma), and Malaysia. With disputed origins in southwestern China, Tai peoples began migrating into northern mainland Southeast Asia well before the eleventh century, establishing chiefdoms from the twelfth century onwards. The characteristic political organization was a *muang*, or petty state, consisting of a royal class and king, free peasants, and slaves, which was established in river valleys based on the cultivation of paddy rice. However, smaller populations of tribal Tai people inhabited the mountains surrounding these valley states and practiced shifting upland agriculture. In southwestern China and Southeast Asia, Tai rulers adopted Theravada Buddhism, which became a constituent part of their social systems, while minority Tai populations practiced animism and ancestral worship.

THERAVADA BUDDHISM IN THAI LIFE

A strong adherence to Theravada Buddhism is one of the basic elements of Thai culture. The following extract of text describes the importance of the Buddhist priest and the reverence for life in the village of Bang Chan in Central Thailand.

One of those most serious concerns for a priest is that of killing any form of life. Association in any way with the taking of a human life removes the priest from the order and from the possibility of ever becoming a priest again. A priest is further committed to avoiding the killing of any form of life around him. Thai villagers consider all forms of life to be ranged roughly across a continuum of value. Taking the life of one's parents or of a priest is the most serious offense one could commit. Ranked below this would be taking the life of other human beings and then proceeding down through the animal kingdom. The head-priest said that killing a chicken would be much less serious than killing a buffalo, and that killing a snake would be less serious than killing a chicken. According to the seriousness of each moral offense, an individual receives moral punishment in the form of de-merit, or negative karma (baab).

Most Thais would expect to receive more baab from a more serious offense. It is particularly serious (therefore the source of much baab) for a priest to take any form of life. One informant explained that a priest gets the same amount of baab from killing any form of life. I did not check this point, but it is clear that priests and laymen alike consider it very serious for priests to take any visible form of life. The seriousness of this normative concern is manifest every day around the temple. I have described under daily role activities the cloth strainers on the bamboo water dippers which the priests use in order not to snuff out tiny insects as they water the temple garden or take their showers. Equally indicative is the fact that priests do not dig in the earth, because they might inadvertently kill some small creature.

When the village was rushing to complete a new residence hall in the temple before the celebration of the elevation in title of the head-priest and his assistant, large working parties frequently came and supplemented the regular workers. The priests and novices worked tirelessly into the night on the heavy construction work, but only the novices could dig the old pillars out of the ground and dig holes to set the new pillars. Priests could mix concrete, because the building sand was not thought to harbor any life, but they could not dig the soil. A priest must be attentive to the foliage when he spits or urinates.

The temple is associated in most people's minds with compassion for all living creatures. A number of stray cats, dogs, and chickens normally live at rural temples, cared for by the surplus food contributions which the priests cannot eat. Sometimes a farmer, unwilling to kill off a senile ox, asks to have him allowed to stay at the temple and graze. The farmer makes some offering the temple, and the aged draft animal ends his days grazing within earshot of the auspicious chants of the priests.

The priests do not, however, welcome pests such as mosquitoes. In the evening I often noticed smoke curling up from a little incense stick which people burn to drive away mosquitoes. The headpriest surprised me when a village asked if we had many mosquitoes in our house. Vigorously moving his arms in a spraying motion, the headpriest said that spraying was quite good. He seemed to be making a technical judgment rather than a moral one, and he was talking about our house. I never saw any priest spray around the temple. The priests in Thailand generally raise no objection to the World Health Organization spray campaigns. They probably did not actively support or oppose the campaigns.

Source: Jaspar C. Ingersoll. (1969) The Priest and the Path: An Analysis of the Priest Role in a Central Thai Village. Ann Arbor, MI: University Microfilms, 158–160.

The Thai and Tai

Today the major areas of dense concentrations of Tai-speaking peoples are the Xishuangbanna and Dehong regions of Yunnan province of China; parts of northern Vietnam and adjacent Laos, which are inhabited by tribal White, Black and Red Tai; the Shan (Tai Yai or Tai Long) State in Myanmar; Laos proper, in which the majority population, the Lao, are Tai speakers closely related to the Thai; and Thailand, which was itself formed out of a number of smaller Tai kingdoms: Ayutthaya and Sukhothai, Chiang Mai and Chiang Rai. There is also a small Thai population in northern Malaysia.

While the great majority of the citizens of Thailand follow Theravada Buddhism, those in the southern Thai states, whose borders were negotiated between Thailand (then Siam) and British Malaysia, are Islamic. The majority population of Thailand's impoverished and dry northeast (Isan) are ethnically Lao. In Nan province, in Thailand's north, there is a population of Tai Lu who are the same as the Tai Lu of Xishuangbanna in China. The ancient kingdom of Chiang Mai and other *muang* in north Thailand have been firmly integrated into the Thai polity, and their populations of Khon Muang (people of the *muang*) and Khoen, Lue, Nong, and Yong practically assimilated into the general Thai identity radiating from the Central Thai of the Chao Phraya (Menam) River basin. There are also populations of Tai Yai (Shan) in northern Thailand.

Thai Society and Culture

The Thai people, like other lowland Tai groups, adapted culturally to a hot monsoon climate. Cultural characteristics include a particular style of teak or bamboo stilted architecture, the wearing of the sarong, a love of boats and rivers and markets in or along the waterways, the cultivation of rice in paddies combined with fishing, and the practice of Theravada Buddhism. Traditionally every village had its *wat*, or temple, and the relation between monks assigned to the local temple and village men who would become ordained as monks for a time before marriage was particularly close. Monks were invited to officiate at most major life events, including weddings, house-building, and funerals (although they did not always officiate at weddings, and they might be replaced by Taoist monks at funerals). Art forms include traditional Thai music, temple murals and wooden carvings, the dancing of the *ramwong* (traditional Thai dance), and the survival of Hindu theater epics such as the *Ramayana* (*Ramakien* in Thai) in puppet form. Monastic Buddhism has combined with traditional beliefs in the power of spirits (*phi*), astrology, and the magic of charms, amulets and tattoos conferring invincibility into what has appeared to many to be a seamless whole. The tying of wrists with threads is still performed to "recall the soul" (*sukhwan*) at sickness or after long journeys.

Despite this appearance of homogeneity, important differences still remain between different local Tai traditions in what is today modern Thailand, such as those of the Yuan and the Lue in the north, the Phu Tai and Lao Phuan of the northeast, and the Khon Pak Tai of the south. The northern Thai (Yuan or Khon Muang), for instance, traditionally had a form of matrilineal descent associated with spirit cults in which mediums communicated with the spirits of long-dead ancestors for the purpose of curing sickness, or with the spirits of royal princes. A period of uxorilocal residence before marriage was common for many of the Tai peoples, and women customarily inherited land and the house, the youngest daughter remaining in the house, where her husband joined her, to take care of her aged parents. Over the past sixty years such practices have inevitably been modified by the impact of modernization, but they are still maintained in some areas.

Gender

Gender relations are particularly marked in Thai society. Women have traditionally enjoyed great freedom in the realms of marketing and business, though they have been restricted in access to important public domains such as the monkhood and politics. Except among the noble classes, which for some time had already shown a tendency to reckon descent patrilineally, descent was bilaterally reckoned until King Chulalongkorn (1853–1910) introduced patrilineal surnames in 1901. A man could take more than one wife, and concubinage or the taking of a "minor wife" or mistress is still quite common today.

External Influences and Social Change

The Thai society of Thailand has been marked by both Indian and Chinese influences. Hindu and Buddhist beliefs have deeply permeated Thai society and culture, and are reflected in the many terms in the Thai language derived from Pali and in the continued presence of Brahmin priests at court. More recently, the influence of Chinese settlers who have extensively intermarried with Thai has been strong. Sino-Thai families have been dominant in both business and politics, although Chinese in-marriers often lose their Chinese identities and become assimilated as Thai within two to three generations.

Modern economic relations and the end of the absolute monarchy in 1932 have transformed Thai society. The feudal *sakdina* system, in which social ranks were differentiated by entitlement to labor, has given way to a modern agricultural peasant society with a significant degree of industrialization, in which relations of patrons with clienteles continue to be important. The hiring of agricultural labor and the advent of cash crops have transformed the traditional agricultural cycle centered on transplanting the rice and harvesting it at the end of the rainy season. Traditional forms of labor exchange have been largely destroyed as landless and impoverished migrants increasingly flock to urban centers, particularly Bangkok, where slums, industrial and vehicular pollution, and the prevalence of child labor and prostitution are causes of major international concern.

Looking Ahead

Faced with the tensions and difficulties of modern life and continuing efforts to reform the political system, the younger generation has embraced new forms of Buddhism. Meditation, never a common feature of traditional Theravada Buddhism, is increasingly popular, and charismatic monks appeal to huge audiences via video and television. In urban centers and even rural areas, the tradition of making donations to the monks and temples has eroded even as young people are showing increasing interest in nontraditional forms of Buddhism. Thai society has often been seen as uniquely flexible and adaptable to external influences. The tensions and conflicts this has brought in its wake are rarely recognized.

Nicholas Tapp

Further Reading

Chunyang, An, and Liu Bohua, eds. (1985) *Where the Dai People Live.* Beijing: Foreign Languages Press.

Davies, Richard. (1984) *Muang Metaphysics: A Study of Northern Thai Myth and Ritual.* Bangkok, Thailand: Pandora Press.

Embree, John F., ed. (1969) *Loosely Structured Social Systems: Thailand in Comparative Systems.* New Haven, CT: Yale University Press.

Keyes, Charles. (1987) *Thailand: Buddhist Kingdom as Modern Nation State.* Boulder, CO: Westview Press.

Lufan, Chen. (1990) *Whence Came the Thai Race? An Inquiry.* Kunming, China: Institute for Southeast Asian Studies, Yunnan Academy of Social Sciences.

Tambiah, Stanley J. (1970) *Buddhism and the Spirit Cults in North-East Thailand.* Cambridge, U.K.: Cambridge University Press.

Terwiel, Berend J. (1975) *Monks and Magic: An Analysis of Religious Ceremonies in Central Thailand.* Lund: Studentlitteratur; Richmond, U.K.: Curzon Press.

Turton, Andrew, ed. (2000) *Civility and Savagery: Social Identities in Tai States.* Richmond, U.K.: Curzon Press.

Yin Ma, ed. (1989) *China's Minority Nationalities.* Beijing: Foreign Language Press.

THAI REVOLUTION OF 1932 On 24 June 1932, troops commanded by General Phya Bahol Balabayuha took control of Bangkok in a bloodless revolution, arresting some forty top officials and inviting King Rama VII (1893–1941), also known as Prajadhipok, the last born of King Chulalongkorn's sons, to rule under a constitution that stripped him of all authority except for the right of pardon.

Prior to the revolution, Thailand was officially an absolute monarchy, with the prime minister appointed by the king. The revolution resulted from the growing discontent felt by the populous toward the king's brothers, who dominated many positions in the government despite their incompetence, thus preventing the new educated middle class from rising to positions of responsibility. In addition, the Great Depression caused the bottom to fall out of the rice market, by 1931 resulting in an enormous budget deficit. With the king away in Europe for medical treatment, members of the cabinet clashed, and the government was in gridlock. Military officers and civil servants, whose salaries were cut, were equally discontented and unable to articulate their grievances through the channels of an absolute monarchy.

After the revolution, a constitution drafted by Chulalongkorn University law professor Dr. Pridi Panomyong came into effect on 10 December 1932. The coup leaders, many of whom adopted democratic ideals after the king sent them to study in Europe, selected members of the senate, who in turn appointed an executive council as provisional cabinet to promulgate laws and control ministers. To appease conservative opinion, the coup's military leaders did not take over the government. Phya Manopakam, respected president of the Court of the Appeal, was chosen president of the provisional executive council, though he continued policies of the past and even cracked down on dissent. The new constitution, though backpedaling somewhat on democratic reforms to gain the support of the king, nevertheless launched the country as a constitutional democratic monarchy. King Rama VII even accepted the apologies of the coup leaders for their illegal actions, recognizing that the princes, not the monarchy, were resented.

In October 1933, Prince Bovaradej led an armed counterrevolution, which failed when the king did not lend it support. However, in 1935, when the assembly tried to remove the king's power to veto cases of capital punishment, he abdicated. In the end, the bureaucracy and the military gained power at the expense of royal prerogatives, not the people.

Michael Haas

Further Reading

Landon, Kenneth Perry. (1939) *Siam in Transition*. Chicago: University of Chicago Press.

Mokarapong, T. (1972) *History of the Thai Revolution: A Study in Political Behavior*. Bangkok, Thailand: Chalermnit.

Vella, Walter F. (1955) *The Impact of the West on Government in Thailand*. Berkeley and Los Angeles: University of California Press.

THAILAND—PROFILE

THAILAND—PROFILE (2001 pop. 61.8 million). Thailand lies in the heart of Southeast Asia, stretching from the Mekong River in the north to the Andaman Sea and Gulf of Thailand in the south. Known as Siam until 1939, Thailand has an ancient history and a rich, unique culture.

Geography

With an area covering 514,000 square kilometers, Thailand is the third largest country in Southeast Asia. It is slightly smaller than the state of Texas and roughly the size of France. Its population is the fourth largest in Southeast Asia, with approximately 8 million residing in the capital, Bangkok. There are four fairly distinct regions in Thailand: the north, marked by mountains and valleys; the rugged, sparsely forested northeast, which suffers from poor soil, seasonal droughts, and flooding; the fertile central region, dominated by the Chao Phraya River; and the tropical southern peninsula, extending down to the Malaysian border. Climate is dependent on monsoons, but it basically provides three seasons: hot (March–June); rainy (July–October); and cool or dry (November–February). Temperatures in the hot season often reach 40°C in many parts of Thailand, while during the cool season they drop as low as 10°C in the north. Rains are hardest and longest in the south and central regions, often causing serious flooding, while the northeast frequently suffers from drought.

Economy

Approximately 70 percent of Thailand's people work in agriculture. Major farming exports include rice, sugar, and fruit. Traditionally, fishing, textiles, rubber, mining, forestry, and tourism have also been important. Over the past two decades, multinational corporations have contributed to diversifying the Thai economy, and the presence of these corporations encourages more industry. Thailand now produces an increasing quantity of manufactured goods such as vehicles, electronics, and computers. In recent years, Thailand has endured significant economic problems as a result of the Asian recession, a reduction in foreign investment, and weaknesses in Thai industrial and business practices. However, with the assistance of international agencies such as the International Monetary Fund (IMF), Thailand's economy shows signs of recovery. For the year 2000, the gross national product of $2,130 was again one of Southeast Asia's highest. Substantial reform in areas such as banking and the improvement of the transportation and communications infrastructure are essential for further progress.

Politics

Thailand is the only country in Southeast Asia never to have been colonized. As Siam, it was ruled solely by kings until a revolution in 1932 introduced a constitutional monarchy. Attempts to establish a parliamentary democracy failed, and Siam fell under the rule of military dictators. In 1939 Siam was renamed Thailand, and a period of anti-Western nationalism

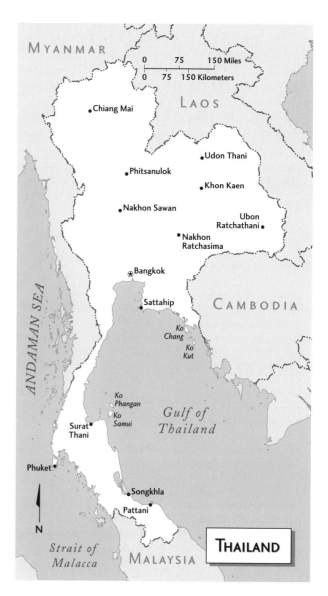

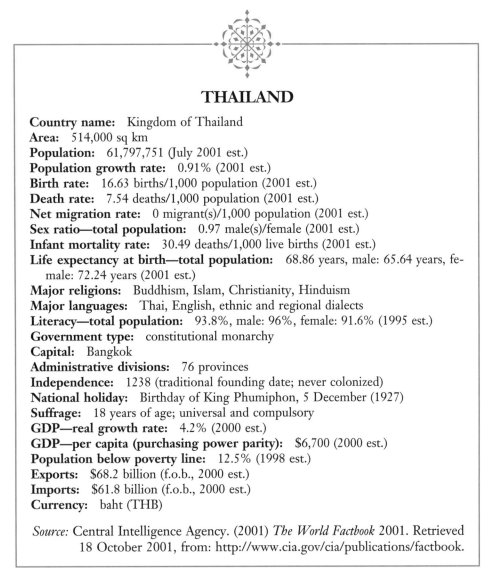

THAILAND

Country name: Kingdom of Thailand

Area: 514,000 sq km

Population: 61,797,751 (July 2001 est.)

Population growth rate: 0.91% (2001 est.)

Birth rate: 16.63 births/1,000 population (2001 est.)

Death rate: 7.54 deaths/1,000 population (2001 est.)

Net migration rate: 0 migrant(s)/1,000 population (2001 est.)

Sex ratio—total population: 0.97 male(s)/female (2001 est.)

Infant mortality rate: 30.49 deaths/1,000 live births (2001 est.)

Life expectancy at birth—total population: 68.86 years, male: 65.64 years, female: 72.24 years (2001 est.)

Major religions: Buddhism, Islam, Christianity, Hinduism

Major languages: Thai, English, ethnic and regional dialects

Literacy—total population: 93.8%, male: 96%, female: 91.6% (1995 est.)

Government type: constitutional monarchy

Capital: Bangkok

Administrative divisions: 76 provinces

Independence: 1238 (traditional founding date; never colonized)

National holiday: Birthday of King Phumiphon, 5 December (1927)

Suffrage: 18 years of age; universal and compulsory

GDP—real growth rate: 4.2% (2000 est.)

GDP—per capita (purchasing power parity): $6,700 (2000 est.)

Population below poverty line: 12.5% (1998 est.)

Exports: $68.2 billion (f.o.b., 2000 est.)

Imports: $61.8 billion (f.o.b., 2000 est.)

Currency: baht (THB)

Source: Central Intelligence Agency. (2001) *The World Factbook* 2001. Retrieved 18 October 2001, from: http://www.cia.gov/cia/publications/factbook.

---

swept the country until after World War II. The military dominated Thailand until 1973, when a bloody revolt finally brought about a civilian government. However, military leaders continued to influence politics from behind the scenes, manipulating governments into the 1990s. Another popular uprising in 1992 again forced the military from power and led to the return of civilian authority.

Since that time, Thai politics have been marked by coalition governments and scandals that have undermined both the development of democracy and international confidence in Thailand. Vote buying, patronage, and strong-arm tactics are common problems in elections. Attempts in the late 1990s to reform the system, including the adoption of a new constitution (1997) and the establishment of an elections commission (1999), have yet to be effective. Moreover, although curtailed in recent years, the involvement of the Thai military in government remains a significant issue, especially given recent economic problems. On the other hand, Thai politics has an important stabilizing force in the king, Bhumipol Adulyadej (b. 1927), who has ruled since 1946—the longest-reigning living monarch in the world. Although his powers are largely ceremonial, his political skill and the popularity he commands with the people give him considerable positive influence. Similarly, Thailand's economic dependence on the international community puts emphasis on the need to reform and democratize the political system.

Religion

About 95 percent of the Thai people are Buddhists. Early Theravada Buddhism came from India in the thirteenth century CE, although most Thai themselves refer to their faith as Lankavamsa Buddhism, which came from Sri Lanka during the fourteenth century CE. Thailand has retained the most traditional practices of Buddhism. The Theravada sect is one of the oldest, and followers consider their Buddhism to be less "corrupted" than that found in the Himalayan mountains or East Asia. Every Thai male is expected to join the Buddhist brotherhood (or *sangha*), usually between finishing school and joining the workforce. Most spend several months learning scripture, discipline, and meditation as a monk, and this time is considered one of the most important in any man's life. There are more than twenty thousand Buddhist monasteries in Thailand, and approximately 200,000 monks, many of whom are ordained.

The other 5 percent of the Thai people are predominately Muslim and live mainly on the southern peninsula. About 1 percent of the Thai are Christians, Hindus, Confucianists, Taoists, or animistic. Thailand has traditionally enjoyed religious tolerance, with little conflict between minority faiths and the majority Buddhists. In fact, various religious festivals and holidays are celebrated openly throughout the country and are a significant dimension of life in Thailand. Many Thai homes and businesses have places of worship, and most have a "spirit house," a structure (like a temple) mounted on a pedestal, where spirits of the building can live. Often spirit houses are large and ornate, reflecting Thai concerns about spirituality and the afterlife.

Peoples

Nearly 80 percent of those living in Thailand are ethnic Thai. About 15 percent are Chinese, while the remainder includes Malays, Cambodians, Lao, Burmese, Vietnamese, and various hill tribes. Although there have been periods of violent suppression of these groups (particularly the Chinese), the relationship ethnic minorities have with the majority population generally has been better in Thailand than in other Southeast Asian countries. This is partly because many minorities have been absorbed into the Thai majority over time. For example, many Chinese have adopted Thai names and customs, while retaining their culture and language at home. The Lao are ethnically and linguistically related to the Thai and blend easily into the mainstream. The hill tribes inhabit the isolated north, and many Cambodian, Vietnamese, and Burmese are refugees from war in their countries and live in camps or controlled areas of Thailand.

Culture and Customs

Thailand is a culturally rich and diverse nation. Its art, architecture, literature, and dance are world renowned. Thai cuisine, noted for its range of flavors and spices, is extremely popular in the West. Although the country is progressively influenced by Western culture, traditional Thai values remain important to everyday life. Religion, a profound reverence for the monarchy, and deep respect for family elders and ancestors are key in this regard. Thai society is male dominated, but women play a crucial role in maintaining family structure, in addition to contributing to the workforce and economy. The Thai are known for their friendliness as well as their interest in foreigner travelers. Many speak English, particularly those in business and the service industries. With everything from jungles to deserted beaches, and ancient temples to modern cities, Thailand offers tourists a great deal. All of this helps to make Thailand the most-visited country in Southeast Asia (8.7 million arrivals in 2000).

Current Issues

Although Thailand's relative stability remains a model for other Southeast Asian nations, it nevertheless confronts major issues. Extreme poverty and other social ills such as prostitution and the drug trade are significant problems. Widespread corruption and graft continue to undermine the development of democracy. Further political reform and more stable economic growth will help better Thailand's future.

Arne Kislenko

Further Reading
Girling, J. S. (1981) *Thailand: Society and Politics.* Ithaca, NY: Cornell University Press.

Hewison, Kevin, ed. (1997) *Political Change in Thailand: Democracy and Participation.* London: Routledge.

Keyes, Charles F. (1987) *Thailand, Buddhist Kingdom as Modern Nation-State.* Boulder, CO: Westview Press.

Pasuk Phongpaichit, and Chris Baker. (1995) *Thailand, Economy And Politics.* New York: Oxford University Press.

Somsakdi Xuto, ed. (1987) *Government and Politics of Thailand.* Oxford, U.K.: Oxford University Press.

Thongchai Winichakul. (1994) *Siam Mapped: A History of the Geo-Body of a Nation.* Honolulu, HI: University of Hawaii Press.

Wyatt, David K. (1982) *Thailand: A Short History.* New Haven, CT: Yale University Press.

THAILAND—ECONOMIC SYSTEM Although Thailand is the only Southeast Asian country never to have been colonized, it has had a long history of international dealings and trade with other countries that have influenced its economy. Thailand has been fortunate to have a rich supply and diversity of natural resources, as well as large stretches of fertile land and

FIVE LARGEST COMPANIES IN THAILAND

According to *Asia Week*, the five largest companies in Thailand are as follows.

Company	Sector	Sales ($ in millions)	Rank in Asia
Petroleum Authority	Oil Refining	9,211.6	151
Electric Generating Authority	Energy	4,013.6	327
Siam Cement	Cement	3,196.0	420
Thai Airways International	Air Transport	3,034.3	449
Esso Standard Thailand	Oil Refining	2,220.3	616

Source: "The Asia Week 1000." (2001) *Asia Week* (9 November): 116.

favorable growing conditions. This base of natural resources and cultivatable soil gave Thailand a strong agrarian foundation on which it has built a complex, multifaceted economy, which is now well established in the industrial and high technology sectors.

Chinese Migration

Between the early nineteenth century and 1940, there was an in-migration of Chinese. The Thai kings encouraged this migration so long as these immigrants assimilated, that is, adopted Thai names, spoke the Thai language, and so on. Many remained in Thailand, where they excelled in business ventures. Although they became Thai, they used personal connections within families and between other Chinese families both in Thailand and in China to foster a strong business community. Through the 1940s, Thailand's business was distinctly small scale. Some families did well, but the most of the population was still dependent on agriculture, with only 2 percent of the labor force working in industry. The change in Thailand's economic climate began to occur after the Japanese occupation of World War II. Several Chinese families established banks, with the Bangkok Bank dominating trade, financing, and remittance back to China. For the next two decades, a third of the nation's savings flowed into the Bangkok Bank, while three other banks accounted for most of the remaining funds accrual.

Growth Led by Agricultural Exports

Between 1950 and 1970, the Thai government developed a strategy of growth led by agricultural exports. Agribusiness grew and thrived through a government policy using both public and private initiatives. The government expanded the irrigation and road systems and encouraged leading banks to channel funds to agribusiness. This growth in agriculture resulted in a significant increase in exports, making Thailand the world's leader in rice exports. Thai politicians and government officials also encouraged expansion through import substitution (a push to produce domestic substitutes for imported essentials). Although the government was heavily dependent on revenue from trade tariffs, the rates were lower on capital goods and industrial inputs. As a result, a relatively small percentage of the manufactured growth was attributed to import substitution.

Business leaders in the Asian countries of the Four Tigers, (South Korea, Taiwan, Hong Kong, and Singapore) were being pushed (and coerced) by government officials into export-led industrialization. Thai bureaucrats, on the other hand, let business leaders take the lead. The government stayed out of the way or supported policies and strategies suggested by business leaders. This freedom for development led to a rapid rise in industrialization, but sometimes with environmental and social ramifications, as companies wholeheartedly exploited natural resources.

Modern Thai Economy

In the early 1960s, agriculture's share of the national income was about 40 percent, while manufacturing accounted for only about 13 percent. Indeed, until the 1990s, the agrarian portion of the economy continued to dominate, supporting the rest of the nation during economic slowdowns. As the economy shrank, farmers took up the economic slack by purchasing less and receiving less money for their rice and other agricultural products.

During the 1960s, the Thai industrial and service sectors slowly began to contribute a greater share of the gross domestic product (GDP). In 1989 manufacturing commanded over 28 percent of the GDP (and nearly 60 percent of the exports), while agriculture had fallen to nearly 14 percent. These ratios continued to magnify during the 1990s. (See Table 1.)

During the late 1980s and early 1990s, Thailand's economy grew at the fastest rate of any member of the Association of Southeast Asian Nations (ASEAN). Of its ASEAN trade neighbors, Thailand had the greatest growth for the period through 1995.

Thailand's Economic Crisis

The economic boom carried with it greater consumer and legislative confidence than ever before. In the mid 1980s, the baht was again attached to the U.S. dollar. As the dollar value slipped against the yen, the baht grew cheaper for the Japanese, encouraging greater investment and trade with Thailand. This gave

TABLE 1

Thai Exports

(in billion of baht)

Export structure	1990	1996	1997	1998	1999
Agriculture	130.0	231.0	258.0	304.4	266.6
% of total exports	22.1	16.4	14.3	13.5	12.0
Agro-industries	71.0	142.0	170.0	202.6	204.6
% of total exports	12.1	10.1	9.4	9.0	9.2
Principal mfg.	359.0	994.0	1280.0	1624.7	1631.7
% of total exports	61.0	70.4	70.8	72.3	73.7
Mining and fuel	7.0	28.0	51.0	44.3	47.9
% of total exports	1.2	2.0	2.8	2.0	2.2
Others	22.0	16.0	48.0	72.1	63.4
% of total exports	3.7	1.1	2.7	3.2	2.9
Total exports	589.0	1411.0	1807.0	2248.1	2214.2

Thailand a distinct export advantage, which strongly supported its manufacturing industries. Increased trade with Japan and a general increase in its exports resulted in greater amounts of foreign investments being made in Thailand. This gave Thailand's leaders the confidence needed to liberalize its economic structure.

Although finance companies, which followed different rules from banks, came close to collapse in a 1983–1985 economic slowdown, they flourished in the late 1980s and beyond. Similarly, the Securities Exchange of Thailand (SET) had an historic high of 1753.73 in January 1994. Numerous companies floated their stock at this time.

Between 1990 and 1993, Thailand liberalized its financial market. Foreign funds flowed into Thailand as investors saw great opportunities. With so much money, financial institutions and banks approved loans for projects that only a few years earlier would have been rejected, not the least of which were property development projects. Then exports began to decline drastically. Japan's purchasing power faltered as the yen weakened due to Japan's economic recession. Furthermore, Japanese investments in Thailand also fell. Thailand no longer could boast of being the lowest-cost labor market in Asia, as other developing countries began to compete in the labor-intensive markets. Thailand's finance companies were approaching dire straits. They had escalated their asset values through leveraging, a successful strategy so long as money continued to flow inward. In June 1997 sixteen finance companies were instructed by the central bank to cease operation. In the next month, forty-two more were closed. By the end of 1997, fifty-six finance companies had been closed.

Property opportunities abounded during the early 1990s. Major landholders began a construction boom

FLOWERS IN THAI CULTURE

Before the flower industry was commercialized in rural Thailand and most flowers were grown for export, flowers were grown mainly for display in the home and sold by vendors. The following is the opening of a flower-buying repartee played as a game by children in villages in Central Thailand.

> *Nag*: Ta-log-tog-terg
> Villagers: What can I do for you?
> *Nag*: I'd like to buy some flowers.
> Villagers: What kind of flowers?
> *Nag*: *Campii* flowers
> Villagers: They haven't bloomed yet.
> *Nag*: How about *Campaa* flowers?
> Villagers: They haven't bloomed yet.
> *Nag*: How about going to a movie with me?
> Villagers: Which one?

> *Source:* Wanni W. Anderson. (1983)
> *Children's Play and Games in Rural Thailand:*
> *A Study in Enculturation and Socialization.*
> Ann Arbor, MI: University Microfilms, 170.

unheard of in other parts of the world. A large amount of money had been borrowed abroad at interest rates lower than those obtainable in Thailand. Consequently, when the economy slowed, foreign loans had to be repaid in devalued baht currency as the baht floated from about twenty-five baht to the dollar to well over forty baht to the dollar. Few people had anticipated the risk of monetary devaluation when they considered borrowing money abroad.

Many of these financial problems exacerbated one another, leading to a financial crisis for Thailand in July 1997. Finance companies were closed. The major banks held billions of baht of nonperforming loans—those that are not being repaid in a timely manner—and numerous people were either unemployed or underemployed. In Thailand in general and in Bangkok specifically, thousands of square meters of office space, homes, and warehouses sat unoccupied and often unfinished. The SET, having hit a high in 1994, was at its lowest point on 1999, with an index of 481.92. The tentacles of the financial crisis reached every person in the Kingdom of Thailand in one way or another. Although an economic recovery was in process, the economic crisis continued to be real and evident in 2001.

Looking Forward

Thailand's economic development has differed from that of the Asian Tigers. The government encouraged business leaders to shift the nation's agrarian economy to an advanced industrial economy. This was successful until Thailand's economic and financial liberalization during the boom period of the late 1980s and early 1990s. When hit by the economic crisis in mid-1997, Thailand, together with many other Asian countries, was not capable of correcting its economic system quickly enough.

Although Thailand has corrected some of its problems, the crisis left the financial system with a large number of nonperforming loans. New bankruptcy laws have been implemented, but the bankruptcy process needs to be accelerated to resolve disputes between creditors and debtors more quickly. Growth rates will undoubtedly continue to be slower than they were before the crisis, but export levels have increased somewhat, lending a longer-term optimism.

Kenneth D. Ramsing

Further Reading

Keyes, Charles F. (1989) *Thailand: Buddhist Kingdom as Modern Nation-State.* Bangkok, Thailand: Editions Duang Kamol.

Kulick, Elliott, and Dick Wilson. (1992) *Thailand's Turn: Profile of a New Dragon.* London: Macmillan Press.

Jomo, K. S. (1998) *Tigers in Trouble: Financial Governance, Liberalization and Crisis in East Asia.* London: Zed Books.

Pasuk Phongpaichit, and Chris Baker. (1998) *Thailand's Boom and Bust.* Chiang Mai, Thailand: Silkworm Books.

World Bank Policy Research Report. (1993) *The East Asian Miracle; Economic Growth and Public Policy.* New York: Oxford University Press.

THAILAND—EDUCATION SYSTEM Known as Siam until 1939 and between 1945 and 1948, Thailand has been ruled by absolute monarchs from the founding of the nation in 1238. In 1932, it became a constitutional monarchy, and it remains so today. The current ruler, H. Bhumipol Adulyadej (King Rama IX) (b. 1927), who has shown a great commitment to education, is the longest-reigning monarch in the world. The fact that Thailand was never colonized has had important implications for the evolution of its educational system, which for the most part uses the Thai language and script.

Traditional and Missionary Education

Traditionally, Thai education took place in Buddhist temples *(wat)*, and monks were the learned members of the community and teachers. Even today, so-called temple schools located on temple grounds account for 20 percent of the nation's schools. Temple schools were the dominant source of organized education from the thirteenth to the mid-nineteenth century. Buddhist priests provided both moral training and the basics of a literary culture. But since only men can be ordained as monks, the system discriminated against women.

Siam generally had an open attitude toward missionaries, and they were free to establish churches, schools, and medical facilities. A few Catholic missionaries arrived in the seventeenth century, but it was not until the early nineteenth century that missionaries were allowed to enter in substantial numbers. The missionary with the most enduring influence on Siamese education was Dan Beach Bradley, who served from 1835 to 1873 and introduced a printing press to produce materials in the Siamese alphabet. Missionary schools such as Mater Dei and Wattana are among Thailand's most prestigious.

Modernization and Reform

King Chulalongkorn (1868–1910) is Thailand's most beloved monarch and was Siam's great modernizer and visionary. He was deeply committed to improving education in Siam, and also introduced fellowships to allow Siamese to study in Europe. Under his successor,

A teacher and students at a village school in rural Thailand in c. 1994. (ROBERT HOLMES/CORBIS)

King Wachirawut (Rama VI), (1911–1925), a compulsory education act was passed in 1921. By the time of the fall of the absolute monarchy in 1932, approximately 80 percent of the country had access to primary school facilities.

During the four decades that followed the establishment of a constitutional monarchy, Thai politics were dominated by the military, primarily under the leadership of the field marshals Pibul Songgram (1897–1964), Sarit Thanarat (1909–1963), and Thanom Kittikachorn (b. 1911). During this period there was a great quantitative expansion in Thai education, with the goal of providing every village with a school. Also, there was a significant expansion in secondary and higher education. Despite such expansion, the most common level of education for most Thais remained only the completion of four years of primary schooling, hardly adequate for sustaining literacy in a complex written language such as Thai. During the first part of this period, Thailand had a 4-3-3-2 structure of education, with four years of lower primary schooling, three years of upper primary, three years of lower secondary, and two years of upper secondary. The 1960 National Scheme of Education brought in a 7-3-2 system, with seven years of primary schooling, three years of lower secondary education, and two years of upper secondary.

Also during this period, there was a serious lack of unity in education. The powerful Ministry of the Interior, responsible for local government, was in control of most primary schools, while the Ministry of Education was responsible for most secondary schools, and the University Bureau (later to become the Ministry of University Affairs) was responsible for higher education. Largely as the result of a close Cold War alliance with the United States, Thailand received substantial foreign aid, which enabled many Thais, particularly in the civil service, to receive fellowships for graduate study in the United States.

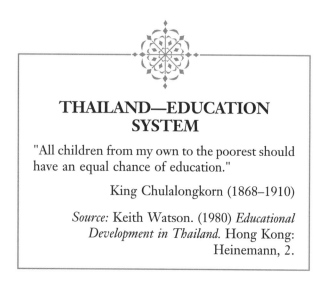

THAILAND—EDUCATION SYSTEM

"All children from my own to the poorest should have an equal chance of education."

King Chulalongkorn (1868–1910)

Source: Keith Watson. (1980) *Educational Development in Thailand.* Hong Kong: Heinemann, 2.

The Democratic Period

Since 1973, democratic rule has mostly prevailed, with only two successful military coups (October 1976 and February 1991). A student revolution on 6 October 1973 led to the overthrow of the military dictatorship of Thanom and ushered in a number of political and educational reforms. Curricula were liberalized to include a diversity of ideological material, particularly from the left, that previously had been banned. There were deep concerns about excessive educational disparities, inequalities, and administrative inefficiencies resulting from a lack of unity in education.

Two major changes emerging from this period were a new National Scheme of Education (approved in 1977), which established a 6-3-3 education structure. With six instead of seven years of primary education, universal primary education was more attainable. Under the previous seven-year primary system, many rural youth were completing only four years of education. The second change, approved in 1980, was the return of the control of primary education to the Ministry of Education from the Ministry of Interior. This period saw the continued expansion of education at all levels. By 1980, Thailand had more than three hundred colleges.

The 1980s and early 1990s saw Thailand achieve rapid macroeconomic growth led by rapid export expansion and industrialization. With an abundant supply of cheap labor, Thailand became an attractive site for offshore manufacturing, particularly from Japan. However, as wages rose in the mid-1990s, Thailand's international competitiveness declined. With its workforce's relatively low average level of education, Thailand's ability to raise its productivity was limited.

The Asian Economic Crisis and Renewed Efforts at Educational Reform

Thailand's economic crisis became globally known on 2 July 1997, when the government allowed the Thai baht to devalue. Thailand subsequently went into its worst economic recession since the end of World War II. However, as an important part of the response to the crisis, major political and economic reforms have been introduced. In the education area, a new National Education Law, mandated by the new 1997 constitution and promulgated in August 1999, makes nine years of education compulsory and requires that all Thai citizens be guaranteed twelve years of free education. The law also mandates the implementation of key education reforms. Two key elements of the reform are decentralization of education to Local Education Areas and school-based management and the reform of learning to a participative learner-center approach. To the extent that these reforms can become reality, Thailand's opportunities to be internationally

---

EQUAL RIGHTS IN EDUCATION

"In the provision of education, all individuals shall have equal rights and opportunities to receive basic education provided by the State for the duration of at least 12 years. Such education, provided on a nationwide basis, shall be of quality and free of charge."

Source: National Education Act. (1999) Chapter 2, Section 10: 5.

---

competitive and improve its standard of living will be dramatically enhanced.

Gerald Fry

Further Reading

Amnuay Tapingkae and Louis J. Setti, eds. (1973) *Education in Thailand: Some Thai Perspectives.* Washington, DC: U.S. Office of Education, Institute of International Studies.

Bennett, Nicolas. (1975) *Problems of Financing: The Thai Educational System during the 1960s and 1970s.* Paris: UNESCO Press.

Buchmann, Claudia, and Dan Brakewood. (2000) "Labor Structures and School Enrollments in Developing Societies: Thailand and Kenya Compared." *Comparative Education Review* 44, 2: 175–204.

Fry, Gerald W., and Ken Kempner. (1996) "A Subnational Paradigm for Comparative Research: Education and Development in Northeast Brazil and Northeast Thailand." *Comparative Education* 32, 3: 333–360.

Knodel, John. (1997) "The Closing of the Gender Gap in Schooling: The Case of Thailand." *Comparative Education* 33, 1: 61–86.

Office of the National Education Commission (ONEC). (1999) *National Education Act of B. E. 2542 (1999).* Bangkok, Thailand: ONEC, Office of the Prime Minister.

———. (2001) *Education in Thailand: 2001/2002.* Bangkok, Thailand: ONEC, Office of the Prime Minister.

Sobsan Utakrit. (1999) "The Technical-Vocational Education and Training System in Thailand." *International Journal of Sociology* 29, 1: 42–65.

Suwanwela, C. (1996) "Academic Freedom and University Autonomy in Thailand." *Higher Education Policy* 9, 4: 277

Varaporn Bovornsiri, Pornlert Uampuang, and Gerald W. Fry. (1996) "Cultural Influences on Higher Education in Thailand." In *Comparative Perspectives on the Social Role of Higher Education.* New York: Garland, 55–77.

Watson, Keith. (1980) *Educational Development in Thailand.* Hong Kong: Heinemann Asia.

Witte, Joanna. (2000) "Education in Thailand after the Crisis: A Balancing Act between Globalization and National Self-contemplation." *International Journal of Educational Development* 20, 3: 223–246.

Wyatt, David. (1969) *The Politics of Reform in Thailand: Education in the Reign of King Chulalongkorn.* New Haven, CT: Yale University Press.

THAILAND—HISTORY

Scholars debate the origins of the Thai people and the beginning of their civilization. Modern Thai history also provokes controversy. Thailand's role in World War II and the Vietnam War remain contentious issues. Thai history is unique and important in understanding Southeast Asia.

Early History

Permanent settlements in Southeast Asia appeared roughly 40,000 years ago, with distinct ethnic and language groups developing about 10,000 years ago. Some anthropologists believe that the Tai people migrated from southern China, while others believe they evolved from earlier settlers in the region. During the first millennium CE, the Tai population increased, though their settlements were often absorbed by powerful empires of the Chinese, Vietnamese, Khmer, and Burmese. In the eighth century, the Tai peoples fragmented into five language subgroups: the northern Tai (Chuang) in southern China; the upland Tai in present-day Vietnam; the Lao; the western Tai (including such groups as the Shan and Lahu); and the central Tai (or Siamese), who settled in modern-day Thailand. Although scattered, most Tai-descended peoples retained a separate identity, language, and religion, which enabled the development of a unique culture.

Ancient Empires

During the thirteenth century, the balance of power in Southeast Asia changed dramatically. Mongol conquests weakened regional empires, making possible the rise of small Tai kingdoms. One, Sukhothai, was particularly successful in promoting Tai independence from Khmer and Burmese rule, dramatically expanding its influence as the larger empires declined. Sukhothai kings introduced a writing system, which subsequently became the basis for the modern Thai language. They also helped further the establishment of Theravada Buddhism throughout Tai lands. In this light, Sukhothai is widely regarded as the first truly Thai kingdom and represents a "golden age" in Thai history and culture.

Despite such achievements, Sukhothai was not without its rivals. After decades of warfare between several Tai kingdoms, one, Ayutthaya, came to dominate, forcibly annexing Sukhothai in 1376. Almost a century of violent struggles with the Burmese and Khmer eventually led to Ayutthaya's collapse in 1569. However, a resurgence of Ayutthaya occurred in 1583, when King Naresuan (1555–1605) organized a revolt and repulsed the Burmese. Naresuan developed important trade and political links between Ayutthaya and China, which his successors expanded to include European powers new to the region. Tai influence increased in another new Asian order.

Siam Emerges

In the early sixteenth century, the Portuguese became the first Europeans to deal with the Tai, but it was not until a century later that the Dutch, and then the British and French, made real inroads. Trade was the primary motivation in any relationship between the Tai and Europeans, but other dimensions evolved. Tai rulers tried to balance independence with the economic and political benefits of European alliances. Meanwhile, in 1760, war with the Burmese erupted again. For years the Burmese advanced, gradually seizing Ayutthaya's provinces. Then, in 1767, the Burmese sacked Ayutthaya itself. Warlords took over most Tai lands. However, within a year, several old Tai kingdoms reasserted themselves. The most important was based at Thonburi, near the present-day capital of Bangkok. Led by Taksin (1747?–1782), Thonburi's armies recaptured most of Ayutthaya's lands and extended Tai control into Laos. Taksin's successor, Chaophraya Chakri, or Rama I (1737–1809), moved the capital to Bangkok, which quickly grew into a vibrant, cosmopolitan city. Rama I also reformed Tai laws, politics, and trade, establishing for the first time a unified Siamese empire and beginning the Chakri dynasty, which still rules Thailand today.

Throughout the early nineteenth century, Bangkok solidified its power. However, during the reign of Phra Nangklao, or Rama III (reigned 1824–1851), the threat from Europeans was renewed. British conquest of present-day Myanmar (Burma) eliminated Siam's mortal enemy, but new pressures emerged. Some Europeans demanded preferential trading privileges and challenged Bangkok's rule in remote provinces. Skillful negotiation by the Siamese avoided war. Siam became the largest empire in the region by outlasting its old foes and accommodating potential new ones. In this, Rama III is often seen as the champion of traditional Siamese culture in a region increasingly dominated by Westerners.

The Era of Colonization

During the nineteenth century, European powers colonized Southeast Asia. Siam's independence was

KEY EVENTS IN THAILAND'S HISTORY

c. 40,000 BCE   Permanent settlements appear in Southeast Asia.

c. 10,000 BCE   Distinct ethnic groups emerge in Southeast Asia.

13ᵗʰ century   Tai kingdoms emerge, including Sukhothai..

1376   Ayutthaya kingdom achieves dominance.

1569   Ayutthaya kingdom collapses under Burmese and Khmer assault.

1583   Ayutthaya kingdom revives and expels the Burmese.

1760–1767   The Burmese capture much of the Ayutthaya kingdom.

18ᵗʰ century   Late in the century and into the nineteenth, The Burmese are expelled and a Tai kingdom established at Bangkok.

19ᵗʰ century   Contact with Western nations (Britain, France, United States) intensifies and Thailand modernizes.

1910   Thailand has lost land to Britain and France but remains independent.

1917   Thailand joins World War I as an ally of the United States.

1932   A coup ends the absolute monarchy.

1939   Thailand becomes the official name.

1941   Japan invades Thailand.

1942   Thailand declares war on Britain and the United States.

1950s–1960s   Thailand and the United States develop a strong relationship.

1973   Political unrest sweeps the nation leading to to more freedom and then a return to military rule into the 1980s.

1990s   Politics remain unstable with conflict over military versus civilian rule.

1997   Thailand suffers from the Asian financial crisis.

1997   A more democratic constitution is enacted.

2001   The general election is undermined by widespread fraud.

---

seriously threatened, but strong leadership and artful diplomacy kept it intact. Two of Thailand's most revered kings, Mongkut, or Rama IV (1804–1868), and his son Chulalongkorn, or Rama V (1853–1910), were instrumental in this process. King Mongkut introduced political, bureaucratic, and cultural reforms designed to "civilize" and modernize Siam. He also successfully played rival Europeans off against one another. In courting the United States, Mongkut gained an important friend outside Europe and broadened Siam's international relationships. King Chulalongkorn furthered the reforms, as well as Siam's ties with the United States. However, tensions between the British and French late in the century began a period of territorial readjustment for Siam, as both impinged on its frontiers. By 1910, Siam had been forced to surrender much of Malaya and Burma to the British and Siamese Cambodia and its Lao territories to the French, losing nearly half of the territory it controlled at the height of Rama III's reign.

Nationalism and Revolution

Vajiravudh, or Rama VI (1881–1925), attempted to strengthen his kingdom by promoting the "Thai nation": a Siamese nationalism based on love of the country, the religion, and the monarchy. Although this had antiforeign overtones, in international affairs Siam remained aligned with Western powers. When World War I broke out in 1914, Siam declared neutrality, but after the United States intervened in 1917, Siam quickly followed suit. By joining the Allies, the Siamese earned a place at the Paris Peace Conference, where, with U.S. help, they negotiated an end to the special privileges that the British and French had in the kingdom.

After the war, Siam confronted a serious financial crisis, which was worsened by the worldwide Great Depression beginning in 1929. Moreover, Siam's King Prajadhipok, or Rama VII (1893–1935), was challenged by Western-educated Siamese intellectuals who demanded further reforms to modernize the kingdom. Amid these problems, a small group staged a daring coup in 1932. Prajadhipok cooperated to avoid a bloody civil war. In doing so, he became the last absolute king of Siam.

The Military Rises

The military's participation in the coup represents a dramatic turning point in Thai history. Ideological differences between the plotters led to political instability, which worsened when Prajadhipok abdicated the throne in 1935. The new king, Ananda Mahidol (1925–1946), was just ten years old, leaving Siam effectively without a monarch. Throughout the 1930s, Siamese politics were marked by tremendous infighting. The military's influence grew considerably with the appointment of Prime Minister Plaek Khittasangkha (Luang Pibul Songgram, or Pibul; 1897–1964). He wanted to create a "new nation," renaming the country Thailand in 1939. Pibul believed the more nationalistic name would help modernize the country, rejecting Siam as an archaic "colonial" and foreign term. He also adopted a stringent economic nationalism and cultural "reforms," which banned speaking languages other than Thai and enforced traditional dress codes.

Pibul's nationalism translated into a very controversial foreign policy. He admired Japanese militarists and European dictators. Encouraged by their success and the outbreak of World War II in 1939, Pibul tried to retake the lost "provinces" of Laos and Cambodia. In a brief war with the French in 1940, Thailand regained its former territory with support from the Japanese. However, most Thais did not like the anti-Western nationalism that Japan and Pibul represented. In 1941, after being denied access en route to Malaya, the Japanese invaded Thailand. Pibul eventually allowed the Japanese transit in exchange for guarantees of Thai independence. Then, following Japanese advances against the Western powers, Pibul joined an alliance with Japan. One month later, in January 1942, Thailand declared war on Britain and the United States.

War and an Uneasy Peace

Many Thais did not support war with the West. Some formed resistance groups, most led by Pridi Banomyong, Pibul's former minister of foreign affairs and then regent, and Seni Pramoj, the Thai ambassador to the United States and leader of the so-called "Free Thai" government in exile. Others saw cooperation with Japan as in keeping with the traditional flexibility of Thai foreign policy and the only way to protect their country from what otherwise would have been a harsh Japanese occupation. Still others welcomed the Japanese over Western domination. They saw the war as an opportunity to regain territory that had been lost to the French and British over the centuries. In fact, during World War II, Thai forces fought the British in Burma and Malaya in efforts to reestablish the old provinces.

Officially, Thailand was the only independent ally of Japan. However, Thai resistance movements worked closely with Western forces operating throughout Southeast Asia, and during the war Thai opposition to the Japanese grew. In 1944, Pibul was deposed as prime minister. A civilian government returned to power, facing the difficult task of explaining Thailand's role to the Allies. The United States was convinced that the Thai people were not truly behind Pibul and disregarded Thailand's declaration of war. Thai leaders then successfully lobbied the United States for help in negotiating with the British and French, reducing many of their reparations claims. Still, Thailand did have to pay. In addition to money and goods, the Thais surrendered to the British and French all territories temporarily gained during the war in Burma, Malaya, and Laos.

Unstable civilian governments led Thailand between 1944 and 1947. A key figure during this time was Pridi Banomyong, who became a champion of the left in Thai politics. In March 1946, he became prime minister, but rumors about his ties to Communists weakened him. In June 1946, King Ananda was mysteriously killed, and Thai conservatives linked Pridi to the incident, forcing him to resign. The military retook control. Although another civilian became prime minister, the armed forces were behind the scenes. Eliciting minimal opposition within the country and little response from the international community, the military restored Pibul to power in April 1948.

Thailand and the Cold War

Pibul's personal history was a concern, but his strong leadership was an asset during the late 1940s, when revolutions throughout Asia were gaining strength. There was concern that Thailand would be next to endure such conflict. In this context, the United States saw Pibul as an ally in containing the spread of Communism. Throughout the 1950s, the U.S.-Thai relationship flourished. U.S. economic, technical, and military assistance poured into Thailand, developing a stronger economy, but also legitimizing military rule. Many Thais were uneasy about such a strong connection to a foreign power and worried about American influence on their country. Thus, from 1955 to 1957, Pibul developed his friendship with the United States while secretly pursuing relations with China. This strategy, however, undermined confidence in Pibul. In

The historic Bridge on the River Kwai in 1998. (JOSEPH SOHM; CHROMOSOHM INC./CORBIS)

September 1957, another military coup toppled the government. Pibul fled the country, and Field Marshal Sarit Thanarat (1908–1963) took over.

Sarit considered himself the defender of traditional Thai institutions and introduced harsh reforms to preserve Thai culture. Sarit was also notoriously corrupt, amassing a huge fortune while in office. Nonetheless, Thailand's economic progress made Sarit popular with the people. He also gained support for restoring the prestige of the monarchy. The king, Bhumipol Adulyadej (b. 1927), was at the center of Sarit's nationalism and symbolized Thai unity. In foreign policy, Sarit cooperated closely with the United States. Thailand was a principal member of the U.S.-led Southeast Asian Treaty Organization (SEATO), and became a base for U.S covert operations in Cambodia, Laos, and Vietnam. Thailand was one of only two Southeast Asian nations to join SEATO. However, Sarit often doubted U.S. resolve to fight Communism and its commitment to his country (Bamrungsuk 1988: 118–125, 156).

The War in Vietnam

Sarit's successor, Field Marshal Thanom Kittikachorn (reigned 1963–1973), did not share such reservations and built an even closer relationship with Washington. Thailand played a crucial role in supporting the war in Vietnam. Over 11,000 Thai soldiers served there, one of the largest contingents from a U.S. ally. Fully 80 percent of the ordnance dropped on Vietnam came from planes based in Thailand. Thai support for the war also lent credibility to U.S. claims that it was defending Asian allies from Communism. Although the Thais were well compensated for their contributions, they were not simply mercenaries. They had legitimate security concerns related to Laos, Cambodia, and Vietnam. From Laos, the northeast was a potential route of Communist expansion into Thailand. Most Thais therefore supported U.S. efforts to combat Communism elsewhere in Southeast Asia, rather than wait for it to overrun their country.

There were, however, considerable problems with the U.S.-Thai relationship. Some Thais warned that their culture was threatened by such a large U.S. presence. By 1968, some 45,000 U.S. service people were stationed in Thailand, and thousands more in Vietnam rolled in on leave. Cities like Bangkok were dramatically transformed by neon lights, massage parlors, and wild bars. Many Thais thought that Americans were crude and that they did not show respect for Thai culture. They also feared that the United States was not winning the Vietnam War and that one day Thailand would be surrounded by Communist countries that would remember and resent its role in the war.

Reaction and Revolution

This scenario appeared to unfold in the early 1970s when the United States withdrew from Vietnam.

Divisions in the Thai government emerged over the direction of foreign and economic policies. There was also pressure from a new generation that wanted more democracy and an end to military rule. In 1973, growing discontent with the government led to a series of protests, culminating in mid-October with massive demonstrations by students and the population in Bangkok. When the military responded with brutal force, only personal intervention by the king prevented further widespread violence. Thanom and his associates fled the country, and major political changes swept Thailand.

Civilian governments that followed were weak, but there was an expansion of political and social freedoms. There were also changes in Thailand's foreign policy. Establishing better relations with China became a priority, especially as the United States disengaged from Southeast Asia and Communist governments came to power in Cambodia, Laos, and Vietnam. By 1976, however, many Thais worried that the country was too radical and favored a return to military rule. Clashes between students and conservative extremists often turned violent. Once again the Thai military and police intervened, with the storming of Thammasat University and the 6 October coup, this time supporting a new but harsh civilian government. Censorship, arrests, and strict laws marked the return of repressive authoritarianism to Thailand. Although another coup toppled the government within a year and restored many freedoms, the military remained the most powerful force in Thai politics. However, conscious of past events and concerned about international opinion, the soldiers remained in the shadows. Governments into the 1980s were heavily influenced by the armed forces and were led by former Thai army generals, acting as "civilian" politicians. Nonetheless, some democratic reforms did take hold. Regular elections were held without the military's direct intervention, allowing for a relatively peaceful transition of power. Moreover, fairly diverse and viable political parties began to emerge, slowly changing the landscape of the Thai polity and paving the way for more reform.

Boom and Bust

By the late 1970s, it was clear that Thailand had avoided the revolutions that engulfed its neighbors. Despite periodic rumblings, it was also clear that many Thais favored stability and traditional institutions over democratization. Still, economic development and external relations remained problematic. In December 1978, Vietnam invaded Cambodia, driving thousands of refugees into Thailand and placing the Vietnamese military near the Thai border. Bangkok secured an impor-

tant, if fairly superficial, alliance with China while supporting Cambodian resistance against the Vietnamese—even the notorious Communist Khmer Rouge. In return, the Chinese stopped their support for the Communist Party of Thailand and its insurgent movement. As part of this complex foreign policy, Thailand pursued close economic relations with Japan and Southeast Asian nations, stimulating growth during much of the decade.

In the 1990s, the question of political reform resurfaced. Following a string of corrupt governments, many Thais again demanded change. The military openly seized power in February 1991, with the promise of fair elections. However, in March 1992 voting was marred by fraud, which provoked more protests. Violence exploded in May when another general, Suchinda Kraprayoon, became prime minister. Just as he had in 1973, the king intervened, criticizing the military and calling for peace. Since then, coalition governments have struggled with reforming Thailand's political structure and economy. For much of the 1990s, the country enjoyed a financial boom, joining the economic "tigers" of Asia. However, in response to a severe debt and foreign-exchange crisis in July 1997, the Thai government elected to float its currency—the baht—precipitating a disastrous economic contagion that spread to many Asian markets and eventually to Russia and Brazil. Thailand's fortunes were clearly reversed, and doubts about its long-term economic future quickly resurfaced.

Thailand Today and Tomorrow

Thailand's recovery from the crisis has been slow. So too has the process of political restructuring. Despite a new, more democratic constitution in 1997 and changes to business, finance, and electoral practices, Thailand's reform problems continue. Corruption remains a major issue affecting both the economy and government. The most recent election, in January 2001, was undermined by widespread tampering. There are serious reservations about the new government's connections to big business and the Thai military and about its commitment to genuine reform.

Notwithstanding these difficulties, Thailand remains a relatively stable nation. Reverence for the monarchy and great respect for King Bhumipol himself continue to be stabilizing factors. So do a well-defined sense of nationhood and Thailand's good foreign relations. In fact, traditional institutions and ideas have served Thailand well during some very tumultuous times in its history. The question remains how well the country will adapt to a rapidly changing future.

Arne Kislenko

Further Reading

Alagappa, Muthiah, ed. (1995). *Political Legitimacy in Southeast Asia: The Quest for Moral Authority.* Stanford, CA: Stanford University Press.

Fineman, Daniel Mark. (1997) *A Special Relationship: The United States and Military Government in Thailand, 1947–1958.* Honolulu, HI: University of Hawaii Press.

Klein, James R. (1998) "The Constitution of the Kingdom of Thailand, 1997: A Blueprint for Participatory Democracy." Asia Foundation, Working Paper 8, March.

Muscat, Robert J. (1990) *Thailand and the United States: Development, Security, and Foreign Aid.* New York: Columbia University Press.

Neher, Clark D., and Wiwat Mungkandi, eds. (1990) *U.S.-Thailand Relations in a New International Era.* Berkeley, CA: Institute of East Asian Studies, University of California, Berkeley.

Pasuk Phongpaichit, and Chris Baker. (1998) *Thailand's Boom and Bust.* Chiang Mai, Thailand: Silkworm Books.

Randolph, R. Sean. (1986)*The United States and Thailand: Alliance Dynamics, 1950–85.* Berkeley, CA: Institute of East Asian Studies, University of California, Berkeley.

Reynolds, Craig J., ed. (1991) *National Identity and Its Defenders (Thailand, 1939–1989).* Clayton, Australia: Centre for Southeast Asian Studies, Monash University.

Reynolds, E. Bruce. (1994) *Thailand and Japan's Southern Advance, 1940–1945.* New York: St. Martin's Press.

Sukhumbhand Paribatra. (1987) *From Enmity to Alignment: Thailand's Evolving Relations with China.* Bangkok, Thailand: Institute of Security and International Studies, Chulalongkorn University.

Surachart Bamrungsuk. (1988) *United States Foreign Policy and Thai Military Rule, 1947–1977.* Bangkok, Thailand: Editions Duangkamol.

Wijeyewardene, Gehan, and E. C. Chapman, eds. (1993) *Patterns and Illusions: Thai History and Thought.* Canberra, Australia: Richard Davis Fund and Australian National University.

Wyatt, David K. (1994) *Studies in Thai History: Collected Articles.* Chiang Mai, Thailand: Silkworm Books.

———. (1982) *Thailand: A Short History.* New Haven, CT: Yale University Press.

Zimmerman, Robert F. (1985) *Reflections on the Collapse of Democracy in Thailand.* Singapore: Institute of Southeast Asian Studies.

THAILAND—POLITICAL PARTIES Political parties first emerged in Thailand with the end of the absolute monarchy in 1932, when the new ruling clique established the People's Party. Nevertheless, the history of Thai political parties is not a happy one. During the first four decades following 1932, political parties were banned completely for two lengthy periods: from 1933 to 1945, and from 1958 to 1968. When parties were able to function, the great majority were established by rival factions of the political elite; forming a party was typically the response of a defeated faction following a coup d'état. In other words, party politics was often a secondary form of politics; real power lay mainly in the hands of the military and the bureaucracy. Nor was party politics about mass politics. The People's Party has aptly been described as an "oligarchy," and few Thai parties have ever had substantial numbers of members.

Thai parties have been criticized for being unprincipled, lacking clear policies, being dominated by personalities, being undisciplined, being unstable, lacking real public support, clashing with government officials, being too numerous, being dominated by financiers, and misunderstanding their own roles. Many commentators have wanted to transform the existing parties into "real" parties, based on mass membership organizations with a more ideological basis. Legislation has been introduced in an attempt to accomplish this. The 1981 Political Parties Act, for example, set minimum numbers of members for political parties and required that parties contest a quarter of all parliamentary seats. Some political parties, such as the United Thai Peoples' Party (established by the Thanom Kittikachorn government in 1968) were established specifically as "mass" parties, designed to mobilize large memberships.

The Political Economy of Parties

In practice, such attempts have been doomed to failure. Most Thai parties are actually driven by financial rather than ideological considerations. A typical Thai party is composed of a number of factions, or cliques. Each clique is led by a boss figure, who assumes the role of patron. Often, these cliques correspond roughly to geographical areas, as politicians tend to work together in regional groupings. Faction bosses cultivate close relationships with business interests in particular regions or economic sectors. It is common for these faction leaders to work closely with local crime bosses, commonly known as *chaopho* (godfathers). Sometimes the politicians are themselves *chaopho*. Godfathers typically engage in such illegal business activities as logging, smuggling, drug dealing, gambling, and prostitution rings To operate these businesses with impunity, they require political protection; hence their willingness to fund politicians, cliques, and parties that will cooperate, passively or actively, with their businesses.

At the same time, political economy explanations of Thai political parties are not sufficient to account fully for their activities. Thai parties seek to present a respectable image to the media and to the voting public, especially the more sophisticated Bangkok electorate. While most major parties are managed by a secretary-general, who serves as principal fund raiser and trouble shooter, they often chose a well-educated and presentable individual to act as party leader. The party leader is the public face of the party, while the secretary-general controls the purse-strings. From 1988 to 2000, Thailand had four prime ministers who were also leaders of political parties: Chatichai Choonavan (Chart Thai), Chuan Leekpai (Democrat), Banharn Silp-archa (Chart Thai), and Chavalit Yongchaiyudh (New Aspiration). With the exception of Banharn, these men were all well-respected public figures: Chatichai was a former general and ambassador from an elite family; Chavalit was a former army commander and career military man; and Chuan was a well-educated, silver-tongued lawyer. Banharn, a provincial businessman of Chinese descent, had serious problems during his short term as prime minister. He was the former secretary-general of the Chart Thai Party, a brilliant behind-the-scenes fixer who did not gain broad public acceptance as a national leader. Thai political parties could not survive on the basis of fund raising and wheeling and dealing alone: they needed to present a serious and somewhat plausible face to the wider world. Chatichai, Chavalit, and especially Chuan were able to place an apparent distance between their own leadership, and the backstairs deal making that had put them into office.

Stasis and Change

Thai parties are constantly changing. In part, this reflects movements of politicians from one party to another, as faction leaders routinely switch parties in the run-up to elections. Yet it also reflects an eternal optimism among politicians, commentators, and the wider voting public that a new party can emerge and break the existing mold of Thai party politics. Recent examples of "new style" parties have included Palang Dharma (Moral Force), founded by Buddhist ascetic and former Bangkok governor Chamlong Srimuang in 1988; New Aspiration, set up by former army chief Chavalit Yongchaiyudh in 1990; and Thai Rak Thai (Thai loves Thai), created by telecommunications magnate Thaksin Shinawatra in 1999. New parties tend to promise higher levels of integrity, greater technocratic competence, and more substantive popular support than existing parties. They are typically led by a high-profile public figure, and initially recruit some prominent individuals to bolster the party's image. Over time, however, they demonstrate a tendency toward greater pragmatism, and gradually begin to embrace many of the features of other Thai parties that they initially disdained.

Thai governments are coalitions, generally bringing together as many as five or six parties. A typical coalition is built around one lead party, working with a couple of medium-sized parties and a couple of rather smaller partners. Because of factional defections, a large party at one election may shrink to nothing by the next. The Samakkhi Tham Party was the single largest party in the March 1992 election, but it did not contest the September 1992 election at all. Palang Dharma was the leading party in Bangkok in July 1995, winning sixteen seats; yet in November 1996, it gained only one. During the 1995 general election, Chart Thai and the Democrats were the two main rivals. By 1996, the rivals were the New Aspiration and the Democrats. And by 2000, the key contest was between Thai Rak Thai and the Democrats. These parties present slightly different images and appeal more strongly in different parts of the country. Chart Thai is a somewhat conservative, pro-business party, with its core support in central Thailand. New Aspiration uses populist rhetoric to appeal especially to government officials and farmers, especially in the Northeast. The Democrats (Thailand's oldest party, dating back to 1946) have a slightly more liberal platform and internationalist image, with their main support in Bangkok and the South. Thai Rak Thai combines a very modern image with the use of nationalist and pro-poor rhetoric.

The 1997 constitution, widely considered one of Thailand's most liberal, included provisions intended to strengthen the party system and measures designed to prevent politicians from switching parties. The effectiveness of these changes remains to be seen. However, the January 2001 general elections—the first to be held under the new rules—did see the Thai Rak Thai Party gain an unprecedently large electoral mandate. The campaign was characterized by a much greater emphasis on policy issues than had previously been the case. In the aftermath of the elections, there were signs that Thai Rak Thai might absorb some of its coalition partners, with the aim of establishing a one-party-dominant system.

Coalition politics can make for unlikely bedfellows. Because his Chart Thai Party had a poor image with the residents of Bangkok, Banharn Silpa-archa's 1995–1996 administration formed an alliance with the more respectable Palang Dharma. When clean-living Chuan Leekpai began his second spell as prime minister in 1997, his coalition was based on support from the Prachakorn Thai Party's "cobra" faction, led by Vattana Assavahame, a controversial figure accused of having strong connections with *chaopho*. Any coalition requires the collaboration of respectable figures and power brokers of questionable integrity. However, these collaborations are characterized by serious tensions, and consequently are unstable. Thailand's current lineup of political parties is certain to continue waxing and waning, provoking alternating moods of optimism and despair among both political analysts and ordinary voters.

Duncan McCargo

Further Reading

Girling, John L. S. (1981) *Thailand: Society and Politics.* Ithaca, NY: Cornell University Press.

Lithit Dhiravegin. (1985) *Thai Politics: Selected Aspects of Development and Change.* Bangkok, Thailand: Tri-Sciences Publishing House.

McCargo, Duncan. (1997) *Chamlong Srimuang and the New Thai Politics.* London: Hurst.

———. (1997) "Thailand's Political Parties: Real, Authentic and Actual." In *Political Change in Thailand: Democracy and Participation*, edited by Kevin Hewison. London: Routledge.

Ockey, James. (1994) "Political Parties, Factions and Corruption in Thailand." *Modern Asian Studies* 28, 2: 251–277.

Pasuk Phongpaichit and Sungsidh Piriyarangsan. (1994) *Corruption and Democracy in Thailand.* Bangkok, Thailand: Political Economy Centre, Faculty of Economics, Chulalongkorn University.

THAILAND—POLITICAL SYSTEM

Thailand's political system has been in a state of near-constant flux since the end of the absolute monarchy in 1932. The 1997 constitution ushered in a series of reforms designed to strengthen the integrity of the political order and to promote greater stability. The reforms reflected anxieties about a surge in vote buying and electoral abuses during the 1980s and 1990s. The political system is a difficult one to classify, because it contains both democratic and nondemocratic elements. The formal structures of representative democracy coexist with a powerful bureaucracy.

On 24 June 1932 a clique calling itself the "Peoples Party" seized power from the then king, Rama VII (Prajadhipok), in a bloodless coup. This clique was composed of members of the civilian bureaucracy and of the military, some of whom had been educated in France. The new regime abolished the absolute monarchy while retaining the monarch, calling for a democratic order. Nevertheless, the ruling clique was divided from the outset over the nature of the political system it envisaged for Siam, as Thailand was then known. While elections were held at various junctures (nine in all from 1932 to 1973) and political parties emerged, for the next forty years, the country's politics were characterized by bureaucratic dominance,

elite infighting, and strong military influence. Periods of civilian rule alternated with spells of military government, with the military frequently in the ascendant from 1947 to 1973.

Instability is a hallmark of Thai politics. Between 1932 and 2000, Thailand had sixteen constitutions, sixteen successful coups, fifty-three different cabinet administrations, and twenty-two different prime ministers. Yet, despite this near-constant change, there was considerable continuity in government policy, largely because much of the day-to-day decision making remained in the hands of civil servants. The scholar Fred Riggs famously characterized the Thai political system after 1932 as a "bureaucratic polity," in which the government officials (both civilian and uniformed) ran Thailand according to technocratic and military priorities, with little reference to the needs of either the private sector or the wider public. However, the bureaucratic polity model has been criticized by other scholars, who see it as a static, conservative interpretation that underplays the extent of political opposition and conflict.

Controversies and Conflicts

The year 1973 was a turning point for politics in Thailand. In this year, student-led mass protests in Bangkok culminated in the ouster of military-backed Prime Minister Thanom Kittikachorn (b.1911), who was obliged to leave the country. A period of relatively open politics followed, which was characterized by growing ideological polarization. However, on 6 October 1976 the military and rightist forces initiated a bloody showdown with the students, beginning with a dawn massacre of student activists at Thammasat University.

Protestors outside Bangkok's government building in November 1999 wear masks of senior government officials who the protestors believe are not adequately handling the national bank scandal. (REUTERS NEWMEDIA INC./CORBIS)

PREAMBLE TO THE CONSTITUTION OF THAILAND

Enacted on the 11th Day of October B.E. 2540.

Being the 52nd Year of the Present Reign.

May there be virtue. Today is the tenth day of the waxing moon in the eleventh month of the year of the Ox under the lunar calendar, being Saturday, the eleventh day of October under the solar calendar, in the 2540th year of the Buddhist Era.

Phrabat Somdet Phra Paramintharamaha Bhumibol Adulyadej Mahitalathibet Ramathibodi Chakkri Narubodin Sayammintharathirat Borommanatthabophit is graciously pleased to proclaim that whereas Constitutions have been promulgated as the principle of the democratic regime of government with the King as Head of the State in Thailand for more than sixty-five years, and there had been annulment and amendment to the Constitutions on several occasions, it is manifest that the Constitution is changeable depending upon the situation in the country. In addition, the Constitution must clearly lay down fundamental rules as the principle of the administration of the State and the guideline for the preparation of the organic laws and other laws in conformity therewith; and whereas the Constitution of the Kingdom of Thailand, B.E. 2534 as amended by the Constitution Amendment (No. 6), B.E. 2539 established the Constituent Assembly, consisting of ninety-nine members elected by the National Assembly, charged with the duty to prepare a draft of a new Constitution as the fundamental of political reform and His Majesty the King graciously granted an audience to members of the Constituent Assembly for taking His Royal speeches and receiving blessings in carrying out this task, and, thereafter, the Constituent Assembly prepared the draft Constitution with the essential substance lying in additionally promoting and

protecting rights and liberties of the people, providing for public participation in the governance and inspecting the exercise of State power as well as improving a political structure to achieve more efficiency and stability, having particular regard to public opinions and observing procedures provided in the Constitution of the Kingdom of Thailand, B.E. 2534 as amended by the Constitution Amendment (No. 6), B.E. 2539 (1996) in every respect;

Having carefully considered the Draft Constitution prepared by the Constituent Assembly in the light of the situation of the country, the National Assembly passed a resolution approving the presentation of the draft Constitution to the King for His Royal signature to promulgate it as the Constitution of the Kingdom of Thailand;

Having thoroughly examined the draft Constitution, the King deemed it expedient to grant His Royal assent in accordance with the resolution of the National Assembly;

Be it, therefore, commanded by the King that the Constitution of the Kingdom of Thailand be promulgated to replace, as from the date of its promulgation, the Constitution of the Kingdom of Thailand, B.E. 2534 promulgated on 9th December B.E. 2534.

May the Thai people unite in observing, protecting and upholding the Constitution of the Kingdom of Thailand in order to maintain the democratic regime of government and the sovereign power derived from the Thai people, and to bring about happiness, prosperity, and dignity to His Majesty's subjects throughout the Kingdom according to the will of His Majesty in every respect.

Source: International Constitutional Law. Retrieved 11 April 2002, from: http://www.uni-wuerzburg.de/law.

Yet, after a brief authoritarian interlude from 1976 to 1977, Thailand embarked on a "semidemocratic" path. Elections were reinstituted in 1979, and for the next twelve years, electoral politics gained increasing significance. Bureaucratic power gradually waned as professional politicians became more and more influential. During the 1980s, a wide range of interest groups and civil-society organizations gained in strength and influence, including the print media, nongovernmental associations, heterodox Buddhist sects, and environmental movements. This expanded public sphere also challenged state power and undermined the bureaucracy.

Conflicts again emerged during the troubled period from February 1991 to May 1992, which saw the first successful military coup in fourteen years; a period of technocratic, military-backed government; the promulgation of a new constitution; and a controversial general election. Street protests against the premiership of former coup leader Suchinda Kraprayoon (b. 1933) in May 1992 culminated in the shooting of dozens of unarmed protestors by the military. The "May events" effectively destroyed the credibility of the military as a political force, leaving civilian-elected politicians firmly in the ascendant.

However, disquiet over the way in which many elected politicians abused the electoral system—and then sought to exploit ministerial office to advance their own financial and business interests—led to growing demands for reform of the political order. These demands culminated in the promulgation of the 1997 constitution, which followed an extensive process of public consultation. For all its shortcomings, this constitution was popularly hailed as one of Thailand's most liberal and democratic.

Components of the Political System

The Thai Parliament has two chambers: the House of Representatives and the Senate. The lower house, which is the more important of the two, is composed of four hundred members elected from single-seat constituencies, and one hundred elected by proportional representation using a "party list" system. MPs elected by constituencies are not entitled to become ministers (unless they resign their seats), whereas those elected on a party-list basis are free to assume ministerial positions. Politicians have been purposely divided into two groups: local representatives chosen for their electability and more respected senior figures of ministerial caliber. Members of the Senate may not be members of political parties: the Senate is supposed be a council of elders, a nonpartisan body that stands above the fray of day-to-day politicking. In practice, however, some of those elected to the Senate are far from politically neutral. Elections are held every four years for the lower house and every six years for the Senate.

Elected Thai governments are coalitions, typically combining the strengths of five or six political parties. Thai prime ministers therefore find their power constrained by the need to mediate the demands of competing coalition partners. An unruly form of cabinet government is generally the order of the day. Historically, Parliament has been rather weak, and relatively little legislation has been passed. Most government decisions are issued in the form of cabinet decrees. Parliamentary debates have been largely a forum for the opposition to criticize government policy, notably in the form of set-piece, knockabout, no-confidence debates that are a regular feature of the Thai political calendar.

Several new bodies were also established after 1997 to oversee and to police the political system: an independent election commission, a national anticorruption commission, a constitutional court (to resolve legal anomalies and disputes relating to the constitution), a national human-rights commission, and an administrative court (to resolve disputes between citizens and government officials). Given well-established problems of vote buying and electoral fraud, and the persistence of political corruption, these bodies face considerable challenges in performing their functions effectively.

While the monarchy has no formal role in politics, there have been explicit royal interventions at critical junctures, most recently in May 1992. King Bhumibol (b. 1927) has emerged as the ultimate arbiter in times of political crisis. Although he has performed this role with great skill, he has done so on the basis of enormous public esteem and legitimacy built up over more than half a century. It is very doubtful whether any successor could hope to emulate this feature of his rule.

Local government remains extremely weak. With the exception of the Bangkok Metropolitan Authority—which has an elected governor—Thailand's seventy-six provinces are largely administered by appointed governors dispatched from the interior ministry in Bangkok. These governors are rotated regularly. Elections take place for provincial, municipal, and subdistrict councils, but so far these bodies have gained little autonomy from the central Thai state. The result is an excessively centralized political order, where most important decisions are made in Bangkok.

Thailand has a muddled and troubled political history, yet it has emerged as one of the most open and pluralistic societies in Southeast Asia. While the political reform process of the late 1990s has brought about a variety of changes, the Thai political system still contains numerous structural problems and weaknesses, which form the subject of intense public debate.

Duncan McCargo

See also: **Chart Thai; Ekaphap; Manhattan Incident; National Peacekeeping Council—Thailand; Phalang Dharma Party; Student Uprising of 1973; Thai Revolution of 1932; Thailand—Political Parties; Thammasat University Riots (1976)**

Further Reading

Callahan, William A. (1998) *Imagining Democracy: Reading "The Events of May" in Thailand.* Singapore: Institute of Southeast Asian Studies.

Connors, Michael Kelly. (1999) "Political Reform and the State in Thailand." *Journal of Contemporary Asia* 29, 2: 202–226.

Girling, John L. S. (1981) *Thailand: Society and Politics.* Ithaca, NY: Cornell University Press.

Hewison, Kevin. (1996) "Political Oppositions and Regime Change in Thailand." In *Political Oppositions in Industrializing Asia*, Garry Rodan, ed. London: Routledge.

Maisrikrod, Surin, and Duncan McCargo. (1997) "Electoral Politics: Commercialisation and Exclusion." In *Political Change in Thailand: Democracy and Participation*, Keven Hewison, ed. London: Routledge.

McCargo, Duncan, ed. *Reforming Thai Politics.* Copenhagen, Denmark: Nordic Institute of Asian Studies, forthcoming (2000 or 2001).

Riggs, Fred W. (1966) *Thailand: the Modernization of a Bureaucratic Polity.* Honolulu, HI: East-West Center.

THAIPUSAM Thaipusam is one of three festivals celebrating aspects of the Hindu deity Lord Murugan, the others being Pankuni Uttiram (March–April) and Vaikasi Visakam (May–June). It falls on the first month of the Tamil year, Thai, on the day closest to the full moon when the constellation Pusam is in the ascendant. In one founding charter, it marks the occasion when Lord Murugan received his lance (*vel*), which symbolizes knowledge and wisdom. The mythological attributes of Lord Murugan are complex; he is variously depicted as a god-king, a warrior, an ascetic youth, a teacher, a divine lover, and a personal savior.

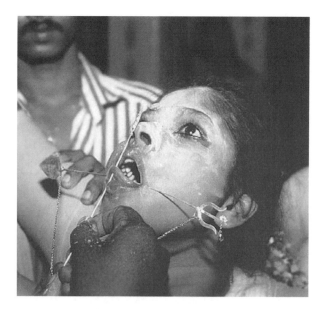

An attendant attaches skewers to the face and tongue of a Hindu woman celebrating Thaipusam in Singapore. (EARL & NAZIMA KOWALL/CORBIS)

In Southeast Asian countries where diaspora southern Indian communities are sizeable, Thaipusam is the most visible and spectacularly celebrated Hindu festival, attracting massive crowds of pilgrims and curious spectators alike. In Malaysia, the Batu Caves shrine complex, situated some seven miles from the Kuala Lumpur city center, is the largest and most well-known pilgrimage destination for both locals and foreigners. The celebration begins, before dawn, with a procession of a brightly decorated chariot bearing the deity through the city streets and then onward to the Batu Caves shrine. During this time, pilgrims make supplications or perform various devotional acts in fulfillment of vows or as penance. Heads are shaved, and free food and drink are distributed without discrimination. Some pilgrims carry *kavadi* ("ritual burden") for a distance, after a stipulated period of ritual preparation (e.g., fasting, abstinence, and chanting of hymns). There are various kinds of *kavadi*. Pots of milk are common with women and children; for men the typical *kavadi* consists of a metal or wooden frame decorated with an assortment of peacock feathers, flowers, colored paper, styrofoam, and other paraphernalia, which is borne on the shoulders. Additionally, many young men pierce their bodies with numerous hooks and skewers after entering a trance state.

As a complex public religious event, Thaipusam has many facets and meanings, including individual self-fulfilment, different emphases of Hindu spirituality, and as an expression of ethnic Tamil group identity in the context of religious and ethnic pluralism in countries like Malaysia and Singapore.

Yeoh, Seng-Guan

Further Reading

Babb, Lawrence. (1976) *Thaipusam in Singapore: Religious Individualism in a Hierarchical Culture.* Singapore: National University of Singapore.

Clothey, Fred W. (1978) *The Many Faces of Murukan: The History and Meaning of a South Indian God.* The Hague, Netherlands: Mouton.

Collins, Elizabeth Fuller. (1997) *Pierced by Murugan's Lance. Ritual, Power, and Moral Redemption among Malaysian Hindus.* DeKalb, IL: Northern Illinois University Press.

Lee, Raymond L. M., and Susan E. Ackerman. (1997) *Sacred Tensions. Modernity and Religious Transformation in Malaysia.* Columbia, SC: University of South Carolina.

Sinha, Vineeta. (1993) "Hinduism in Contemporary Singapore." In *Indian Communities in Southeast Asia*, edited by Kernial Sandhu Sandhu and A. Mani. Singapore: Times Academic Press and Institute of Southeast Asian Studies.

THAKINS Members of the Dobama Asiayone Movement, also known as the Thakin Party, were commonly referred to in the 1930s as Thakins, by the designation they put in front of their names. During the colonial times, when addressing the British, the Burmese were generally required to use the designation *thakin* ("lord" or "master"), much as "sahib" was used in India. Young Burmese began to use this designation for themselves to make a point about their own mastery over their country. The Dobama Asiayone (variously translated as "We Burmans," "We Burmese," or "Our Burma"), founded by Ba Thoung in May 1930, managed to bring together traditionalist Buddhist nationalist elements with modern political ideals. Its song became Burma's national anthem. In the early 1940s and 1950s its members—including Aung San and U Nu—were later to become extremely influential in the national independence movement and in the post-independence Anti-Fascist People's Freedom League (AFPFL) governments. During the Japanese occupation it was conjoined in 1942 with Ba Maw's Sinyetha Party to be known as Do Bama Sinyetha Asi Ayon. It lost support after its reorganization by Ba Maw into the Maha Bama Asi Ayon in 1944, when the AFPFL took over in importance.

Gustaaf Houtman

Further Reading
Khin, Yi. (1988) *The Dobama Movement in Burma (1930–1938)*. Ithaca, NY: Cornell University.

THAKSIN SHINAWATRA (b. 1949), Thai prime minister. On 9 February 2001, Dr. Thaksin Shinawatra (pronounced "Shin-a-wat") became Thailand's twenty-third prime minister. In general elections held in January, the new political party, Thai Rak Thai (Thais Love Thais), which he founded in 1998, won a landslide victory, the first in modern Thai political history in which a single party won a near majority (248 of 500) of all parliamentary seats. A native of Chiang Mai, Dr. Thaksin is particularly strong politically in Thailand's north.

From 1973 to 1987, Dr. Thaksin served in the Royal Thai Police Department. After resigning from the government, he went on to became a dynamic telecommunications business entrepreneur and one of the wealthiest individuals in the world. In 1994, Dr. Thaksin decided to enter Thai politics and held several different cabinet posts during the period 1994–1997. As prime minister Dr. Thaksin has advocated policies that defy typical International Monetary Fund dictates. He has, for example, implemented populist policies of providing a three-year debt relief for farmers, a million-baht credit scheme for every village, universal health care with a minimal charge per hospital visit, higher interest rates to strengthen the baht, and avoidance of international loans with policy strings attached. He is deeply committed to strengthening Thailand's capabilities in information technology.

The Constitutional Court of Thailand reviewed charges that Dr. Thaksin failed to report accurately his financial assets when he became involved in Thai politics in 1997. On 3 August 2001, by a narrow vote of 8 to 7, Dr. Thaksin was found not guilty. Had he been found guilty, he would have been banned from Thai politics for five years.

At present it is somewhat premature to assess Dr. Thaksin's leadership. The key question is whether he is an old-style politician in a new guise or a genuine reformer. His alleged attempt to infringe on press freedom and his image of representing "dictatorial money politics" has certainly reduced his popularity, particularly among intellectuals, journalists, activists, and urban citizens. On a more positive note, he seems open to meet with diverse social groups with grievances. Also as of March 2002, the Thai stock market was the third best performing (in U.S. dollar terms) in the world in 2002, perhaps reflective of domestic and international investors' confidence in his leadership of the country.

Gerald W. Fry

Further Reading
"Familiar Faces Joining Thaksin's Camp." (2001) *Far Eastern Economic Review* 164, 2: 16–20.
Sarakon Adunyaanon. (1995) *Thaksin Shinawatra: Asawin Kluun Luuk Thi Saam* (Thaksin Shinawatra: Knight of the Third Wave). Bangkok, Thailand: Matichon.
"Thai Landslide—Thaksin Shinawatra Sweeps to Power on the Votes of Poor Villagers, but His Government Will More Likely Represent Big Business." (2001) *Far Eastern Economic Review* 164, 2: 16–20.
Vatikiotis, Michael, and Rodney Tasker. "Thaksin, in His Own Defense." (2002) *Far Eastern Economic Review* 165, 14: 14–18. Retrieved 10 April 2002, from: http://www.feer.com/articles/2002/0204_11/p014region.html.

THAN SHWE (b. 1933), military head of state in Myanmar. Than Shwe became the first chairman of the ruling State Peace and Development Council (SPDC) in Myanmar (Burma) in 1997, having succeeded General Saw Maung as chairman of the ruling State Law and Order Restoration Committee (SLORC) in April 1992. He is generally seen as holding the balance between opposite factions in the army for and against political reform. He is also simultaneously army commander-in-chief, head of state, prime minister, and defense minister.

Than Shwe joined the army in 1953 and in 1958 was attached to the Psychological Warfare Department. He was lecturer at the Central University of Political Science in Rangoon between 1963 and 1967. In 1981 he became central committee member of the Burma Socialist Programme Party and in July 1988 he was appointed to the central executive committee and was made deputy minister of defense. Promoted to commander of the southwest region in 1983, he became vice chief of staff in 1985. He was promoted to lieutenant general in 1987 and full general in 1990. At the time of the 1988 uprising he was chairman of the Irrawaddy Division under the Burma Socialist Programme Party. He has been the patron of the Union Solidarity and Development Association (USDA) since its foundation.

Gustaaf Houtman

Further Reading

Kanbawza,Win. (1994) *A Burmese Perspective: Comparative Study of the Two Military Juntas, Thailand and Burma.* Bangkok, Thailand: CPDSK Publications.

THANJAVUR (2002 est. pop. 220,000). Thanjavur (or Tanjore) is an important city in the south of Tamil Nadu, India, and one of the most ancient. Located on the Vedavar River near the head of the agriculturally rich Kaveri Delta, the city first gained prominence in the tenth through twelfth centuries under the Chola dynasty.

In about 1010, the famed Brihadishvara Temple was erected, and it is still the main attraction in the city. The pyramidal stone tower rises to a height of 66 meters and is capped by a massive stone and a gold pot finial that was donated by the royal founder, Rajaraja I (reigned 985–1014). The centerpiece inside is a massive stone lingam (phallic symbol), and facing the east entrance to the shrine is a huge bull (Nandi) in black granite, which is said to have been brought from a place some 650 kilometers away. The art gallery in the former raja's palace is also worth a visit for its fine collection of Tanjore bronzes of the Chola age. Tamil University has recently been built on the outskirts of the city.

Paul Hockings

Further Reading

Heitzman, James. (1997) *Gifts of Power: Lordship in an Early Indian State.* New Delhi: Oxford University Press.

Michell, George, and Philip Davies. (1989) "Thanjavur." In *The Penguin Guide to the Monuments of India*, edited by George Michell and Philip Davies. New York: Viking Press, vol. 1, 473–75; vol. 2, 574–75.

THANOM KITTIKACHORN (b. 1911), Thai prime minister. Born August 11, 1911, Thanom Kittikachorn graduated from the royal military academy of Chula Chom Klao in 1931. He was involved in the overthrow of Pibul Songkram's government in 1957. After the inconclusive elections of December 1957, he became the caretaker prime minister until October, when Sarit Thanarat assumed power. As Sarit's deputy, Thanom became the prime minister after Sarit's death in December 1963 and became field marshal in 1964.

Thanom ruled with Field Marshal Praphat Charusathien and General Kris and continued the policies of Sarit, but without the same degree of control. The main problem was the increasing Communist insurgency. Thailand was closely aligned with the United States in the war in Vietnam. International investment and U.S. military expenditure in Thailand resulted in considerable economic growth for the country. In the February 1969 elections, Thanom's United Thai People's Party secured 75 seats out of 219 in the lower house, giving them the largest representation among the thirteen parties. However, military rule was imposed in 1971. Student unrest and mass demonstrations led to the end of Thanom's

Prime Minister Thanom Kittakachorn in Washington, D.C., in 1968. (BETTMANN/CORBIS)

regime in October 1973, shortly after which Thanom and his family fled to the United States. The end of authoritarian rule by student unrest and demonstrations has remained a symbol of the democratic aspirations of the Thai people, and the government's decision to honor Thanom in 1999 for his service to the Royal Guard was dropped due to protests.

Patit Paban Mishra

Further Reading

Sardesai, D. R. (1997) *Southeast Asia: Past and Present.* 4th ed. New Delhi: Vikas.

Tarling, Nicholas, ed. (1992) *The Cambridge History of Southeast Asia*, 11. Cambridge, U.K.: Cambridge University Press.

THANT, U (1909–1974), Burmese official and secretary-general of the United Nations. Educator and third secretary general of the United Nations (1961–1971), U Thant was one of the few Burmese to have held high-level international office. Educated at National High School, Pantanaw, and at the University of Rangoon, he served mostly as headmaster of National High School, Pantanaw, until 1947. He was also briefly secretary to the educational reorganization committee of the government of Japanese-occupied Burma. U Nu recruited him in various capacities, including as press director in 1947, as director of broadcasting in 1948, as secretary of the Ministry of Information in 1949 and, briefly, as Secretary to the Prime Minister in 1954.

U Thant is best remembered, however, for his services to the U.N., where he embarked on a rapid career. He began serving as Burmese delegate to the U.N. in 1952, and became permanent U.N. representative in 1957. He was appointed vice president of the U.N. General Assembly in 1959. In November 1961, after the death of U.N. Secretary-General Dag Hammarskjöld, the United States and the Soviet Union disagreed on the successor, and U Thant was appointed in a compromise. He was elected permanent secretary-general in November 1962, and extended by a further five years in December 1966.

U Thant was a devout Buddhist and meditator, and he brought valuable qualities to the resolution of international problems. During his first term as secretary general he resolved some major international tensions, including the removal of Soviet missiles from Cuba (1962). He had less success in his second term, when the U.N. moved from peacekeeping to questions of economic and social development.

Secretary-General U Thant in his United Nations office in New York on 24 November 1961. (BETTMANN/CORBIS)

When he retired from the U.N., he was succeeded by Kurt Waldheim in 1971, by which time Burma had been under military rule for almost a decade. After his death from cancer in New York on 25 November 1974, his body was returned to Burma, only to became the focus for demands for democratic reforms. His remains were briefly seized by students on 5 December 1974 and buried in a makeshift mausoleum on the grounds of the Arts and Science University in Rangoon.

Gustaaf Houtman

Further Reading

Baal-Teshuwa, Jacob, ed. (1964) *U Thant: Toward World-Peace.* New York: Thomas Yoseloff.

Bingham, June. (1966) *U Thant: The Search for Peace.* New York: Knopf.

Manton, Thomas Brewster. (1968) *U Thant: A Political Biography—An Enquiry into the Background and the Major Political Actions of the Third Secretary-General of the United Nations.* Washington D.C.: The American University.

Nassif, Ramses. (1988) *U Thant in New York, 1961–1971: A Portrait of the Third UN Secretary-General.* New York: St. Martin's Press.

Selth, Andrew. (1989) *Death of a Hero: The U Thant Disturbances in Burma, December 1974.* Nathan, Australia: Griffith University, Division of Asian and International Studies, Centre for the Study of Australian-Asian Relations.

Thant, U. (1958) "A Burmese View of World Tensions." *Burma* VIII (July): 14–21.

———. (1978) *View from the UN.* Garden City, NY: Doubleday.

THAR DESERT The Thar Desert, or Great Indian Desert, is an arid region of 208,000 square kilometers in northwestern India and eastern Pakistan; it is the largest desert in South Asia. Located between the Indus and Sutlej River valleys, much of the Thar Desert consists of shifting sand dunes and stony plains, along with smaller areas of grassland. Rainfall is highly erratic, ranging between 100 and 500 millimeters per year. About 90 percent of rain falls between July and September. Mean average temperatures range between 24° and 26°C in summer and between 4° and 10°C in winter. Summer temperatures may reach 50°C, especially in May and June, the hottest months. Despite its dryness, the Thar Desert supports a diverse flora and fauna, including twenty-three species of lizards and twenty-five species of snakes. The Great Indian bustard, Indian gazelle, black buck, and caracal (wild cat) are also found. Much of the region's economy is based on pastoralism, especially sheep and goats, and on a limited amount of irrigated agriculture. The largest cities are Jodhpur and Bikaner, India. India tested its first nuclear device in the area in 1974.

Michael Pretes

Further Reading
Sharma, R. C. (1998) *Thar: The Great Indian Desert*. London: Tiger Books.
Spate, Oskar Hermann Khristian. (1954) *India and Pakistan: A General and Regional Geography*. New York: Dutton.

THAT LUANG The That Luang, or Phathat Luang (Great Sacred Stupa), is a Buddhist site in Laos that is said to enshrine a relic, or bone, of Buddha. Legend states that the original shrine was built in 307 BCE. King Setthathirat (reigned 1534–1571) erected the stupa in 1566 on the grounds of the shrine after he moved the capital from Luang Prabang to Vientiane. The stupa consists of three levels: a base of 41 square meters (135 square feet), a first level containing thirty miniature replicas of the central spire, and a second level consisting of the central spire on a base of blooming lotus petals. The That Luang is 45 meters (148 feet) high. King Anouvong (1767–1829) added the cloister around the That Luang during his reign. The That Luang survived the razing of Vientiane in 1828 when the Siamese attacked in retaliation for King Anouvong's unsuccessful attempt to win independence from Siam. The French restored the stupa in 1900 in a Western style after it was abandoned following the Siamese invasion. Between 1931 and 1935, using an indigenous style, the Lao renovated the That Luang to its present state. The That Luang is an excellent example of classical Lao Buddhist architecture and a symbol of the Lao nation and appears on the Lao currency. During the twelfth lunar month, the That Luang's importance is celebrated at an annual festival held on its grounds.

Linda S. McIntosh

Further Reading
Evans, Grant. (1998) *The Politics of Ritual and Remembrance: Laos since 1975*. Chiang Mai, Thailand: Silkworm Books.
Phouvong Phimmasone. (1953) "The That Luang of Vieng Chan: An Historical and Biographical Study." *Asia* 3, 9: 91–101.

THAT LUANG FESTIVAL The That Luang Festival is an important Theravada Buddhist holiday for the Lao nation. The festival is held during the full moon of the twelfth lunar month, usually November, at That Luang (Phathat Luang) or the Great Sacred

An elephant marches in the White Elephant Procession during the That Luang Festival in Vientiane, Laos. (NIK WHEELER/ CORBIS)

Stupa in Vientiane (pronounced Viangchan). The site of Phathat Luang is sacred, since the Lao believe the stupa enshrines a relic of Buddha. Both monks and laypeople from the various provinces of Laos congregate in the capital to celebrate the auspicious occasion with three days of religious ceremony followed by a week of festivities occurring twenty-four hours a day.

A procession of laypeople begins at Wat Si Muang in the city center to Phathat Luang to make offerings to the monks in order to accumulate merit for rebirth into a better life. The religious part concludes as laypeople, carrying incense and candles as offerings, circumambulate Phathat Luang three times in honor of Buddha, *Dhamma* (the Teachings of Buddha), and the *Sangha* (organization of Buddhist monks). Folk and popular music troupes and drama performances provide entertainment at the festival. Merrymakers can also buy goods and food at the fair.

Linda McIntosh

Further Reading
Evans, Grant. (1998) *The Politics of Ritual and Remembrance: Laos since 1975.* Honolulu, HI: University of Hawaii Press.

THICH NHAT HANH (b. 1926),Vietnamese Buddhist master. Known to followers as Thay (spiritual teacher), Thich Nhat Hanh is a peace activist, scholar, and writer. During the Vietnam War, he lobbied in the United States and Europe against the war and advocated a negotiated settlement. Martin Luther King, Jr. nominated him for the 1967 Nobel Peace Prize. He led the Buddhist delegation to the Paris peace talks. He was exiled for his pacifist views and now lives in France.

In the early 1960s, he studied and taught in U.S. universities. In Vietnam he organized wartime relief through the School of Youth for Social Service (established 1964). He also established the Buddhist University in Saigon and a publishing house. In France he founded the Unified Buddhist Church (1969) and Plum Village as a retreat center (1982). Similar centers were established in the United States. He lectures across the globe on mindful living. He conceives of religion as action-oriented and makes religion accessible to the public by projecting it as something joyful, not solemn. His teachings are practical and not aimed exclusively at followers of a particular faith. He has written many books, including *Being Peace* (1988), *Our Appointment with Life* (1990), *The Art of Mindful Living* (1992), *Peace Is Every Step* (1992), *Living Bud-*

dha Living Christ (1995), and *The Long Road Turns to Joy* (1996).

Udai Bhanu Singh

Further Reading
Thich Nhat Hanh. (1999) *The Blooming of a Lotus.* Delhi: Full Circle.
———. (1997) *Transformation and Healing.* Delhi: Full Circle.

THIMPHU (2002 est. pop. 58,000). Thimphu has been the capital of Bhutan since 1962, when it replaced Paro. It is a small town, which was founded in 1581. A road now links the town with northern India. Thimphu is located on the Raidak River. It contains a major fortified monastery, Tashichho Dzong. It also has a small hydroelectric plant, a small airfield, and a secondary school. After considerable remodeling, the Tashichho Dzong now houses some central government offices, although the older section is still the home of the abbot and his monks. Thimphu is also the name of the surrounding district (2002 est. pop. 95,000). Here rice, wheat, maize, and timber are produced.

Paul Hockings

THIRTEEN MING TOMBS The thirteen tombs of Ming emperors are collectively known in China as the Thirteen Ming Tombs. In these mausoleums, located about fifty kilometers northwest of Beijing, rest thirteen emperors, twenty-three empresses, and many concubines of the Ming dynasty (1368–1644). The construction of the mausoleums started with Changling (Perpetuity Mausoleum) in 1409 and ended with Siling (Remembrance Mausoleum) in 1644, covering an area of more than forty square kilometers.

Changling is the centerpiece of the Ming Tombs, with a ten-kilometer-long Divine Path flanked by eighteen pairs of stone sculptures and the magnificent Ling'en Hall, where living emperors came to pay respect to the deceased ones. Stone Archway, the entrance to the mausoleums, stands as part of Changling.

Excavation of Dingling (Stability Mausoleum) in 1956, the mausoleum of Emperor Wanli, who ruled from 1573 to 1620, unveiled the mystery that had shrouded the mausoleums. An all-stone underground palace lies 17 meters below the ground. It is 87.34 meters long and 47.28 meters wide, divided into five halls with a total area of 1,195 square meters. Among the more than three thousand unearthed artifacts are the emperor's gold crown, which is woven with extremely fine gold thread, and the empress's phoenix crown, adorned with 3,500 pearls and 150 precious stones. The tomb complex was listed as a UNESCO World Heritage Site in 2000.

Jian-Zhong Lin

Further Reading
Paludan, Ann. (1981) *The Imperial Ming Tombs.* New Haven, CT: Yale University Press.
———. (1991) *The Ming Tombs.* New York: Oxford University Press.
Yu Chen, ed. (1999) *Great Sites of Beijing.* Beijing: Beijing Arts and Crafts Publishing House.

THOMPSON, JIM (1906–1967?), developer of the Thai silk industry. Jim Thompson (James Harrison Wilson Thompson) is best known for developing the Thai silk industry, a major success story of post–World War II Asia, and making it world famous. He was the grandson of General James Harrison Wilson, who wrote *Travels in the Middle Kingdom* about his experiences in China and who was a friend of the Siamese crown prince Vajiravudh, the son of King Chulalongkorn.

While serving in the Office of Strategic Services (OSS) at the end of World War II, Thompson developed a deep love for Thailand and subsequently decided to remain there. He lived in a specially constructed teak home that represented the best of traditional Thai architecture and housed a magnificent collection of Buddhist and Asian art. On Easter Sunday afternoon in 1967, while on a holiday in the Cameron Highlands of Malaysia, Thompson disappeared. His death remains a mystery, with many conflicting explanations, including political intrigue. In a bizarre turn of events, Thompson's elder sister, Katherine, was found brutally murdered in her Pennsylvania home a few months later. Today the Jim Thompson Thai Silk Company continues to thrive under the direction of former employees, and Thompson's magnificent home is now a museum.

Gerald W. Fry

Further Reading
De Souza, Edward Roy. (1996) *Solved! The Mysterious Disappearance of Jim Thompson, The Legendary Thai Silk King.* London: Minerva Press.
Warren, William. (1993). *Jim Thompson: The Legendary American of Thailand, The Remarkable Career and Strange Disappearance of Jim Thompson.* Bangkok, Thailand: Jim Thompson Thai Silk.
———. (1998) *Jim Thompson: The Unsolved Mystery.* Singapore: Archipelago Press.
Warren, William, Jean Michel Beurdeley, and Luca Invernizzi. (1999) *Jim Thompson: The House on the Klong.* Singapore: Archipelago Press.

JIM THOMPSON'S LEGACY

In the quote below, Jim Thompson explains his desire to leave Thailand with a legacy of great art:

I have elected to make Thailand my permanent home, and as I live here and am very interested in the artistic heritage of the country, I have tried to build up as fine a collection as I can to leave to this country. I know that the museum does not have funds to buy many of the fine pieces that turn up, and rather than see them leave the country, I have tried to buy the really exceptional ones to keep them here . . . this house and its contents will belong to the Siamese people since I have already willed it to them by way of the Siam Society.

Source: William Warren. (1993) *Jim Thompson: The Legendary American of Thailand, The Remarkable Career and Strange Disappearance of Jim Thompson.* Bangkok, Thailand: Jim Thompson Thai Silk, 118.

THOUGHT WORK—CHINA The government of the People's Republic of China (PRC) relies to an unusually high degree on what its ruling Chinese Communist Party (CCP) calls "thought work." In practical terms, thought work refers to the management of communication flows, the "environment of symbols" from which people derive their understandings of the world, their values, and their action strategies to pursue interests. Crucial to managing thought work is control over the mass media and telecommunications systems. Although domination of these systems cannot lead directly to government control over the entire environment of symbols, and certainly not to control over the content of all thought, domination of the media and telecommunications is the most critical component of the thought work enterprise. If the government does not dominate these systems, other groups will. That will give these groups a strategic bastion from which to challenge the government's leadership over society.

There was never any question of other groups challenging the government for control over thought work under Mao Zedong (1893–1976). Mao certainly worried about "rightists," "counterrevolutionaries," and "revisionists" influencing thought work, and sometimes his opponents did use the media to publish veiled criticisms of his rule. But these disagreements were among people who were essentially components of the government. They were not disagreements between people inside government and outside. Moreover, the disagreements never lasted long. They would soon be eliminated, and government control would be increased. By the decade of the Cultural Revolution (1966–1976), the government had reduced the number of media performances to which people could be exposed to eight sanitized plays, eight songs, and three film clips. There was utterly no competition for the government's own political messages, which were propagated endlessly in the CCP's newspapers and through a vast radio network that included a loudspeaker in almost every village.

After Mao died in 1976, a new generation of Chinese leaders decided that excessive control over thought work had acted as a hindrance to China's social and economic development. They began relaxing controls in the late 1970s as part of a sea change in government policy that included an opening to the outside world and transformative economic reforms. The development of a market economy fundamentally changed the incentive structures facing the managers of newspaper publishing houses, television stations, and other media units. They became much less interested in serving the government and much more interested in serving readers and audiences so that they could sell advertising. Inevitably, media content changed as a result. At the same time, technological developments such as the spread of television, telephones, and eventually the Internet also made it increasingly difficult for the government to control thought work. By the close of the twentieth century, it faced a crisis. It could still prevent the open circulation of blatantly unacceptable political messages but little else. It could not set the agenda for what people would discuss and think.

It did retain the impulse to control thought work, though—a problematic contradiction that frequently produced tensions in Chinese society. Periodically the government would launch crackdowns on undesired public communication—arresting writers and publishers, banning the sale of satellite television receivers, and closing down Internet cafes. In this way, the government would try at least to eliminate from the thought work market such extremely pernicious items as hard-core pornography and radical social commentary. Very soon, however, people would again start producing and exchanging communications that the government did not like. They would effectively take back control of the thought work market.

The Chinese case suggests that in an era of open-market economies and expanding networks of global communication no government can control thought work. The impulse to control it lingers but should probably be seen as a legacy of centuries past that cannot survive contemporary global transformations.

Daniel C. Lynch

Further Reading

Deng Xiaoping. (1987) *Fundamental Issues in Present-Day China*. Beijing: Foreign Languages Press.

Fitzgerald, John. (1996) *Awakening China: Politics, Culture, and Class in the Nationalist Revolution*. Stanford, CA: Stanford University Press.

Johnson, David, Andrew J. Nathan, and Evelyn S. Rawski, eds. (1985) *Popular Culture in Late Imperial China*. Berkeley and Los Angeles: University of California Press.

Lynch, Daniel C. (1999) *After the Propaganda State: Media, Politics, and "Thought Work" in Reformed China*. Stanford, CA: Stanford University Press.

Mao Zedong. (1967) *Selected Readings from the Works of Mao Tse-tung*. Beijing: Foreign Languages Press.

Meisner, Maurice. (1986) *Mao's China and After: A History of the People's Republic*. New York: The Free Press.

THREE AND FIVE ANTIS CAMPAIGNS

In the early years after the founding of the People's Republic of China in 1949, the Chinese Communist Party (CCP) launched two political campaigns, with the purpose of reinforcing party control over rural and urban China. Both campaigns targeted mainly urban dwellers and people working in the modern business sector.

First, the CCP initiated the Three Antis Campaign against corruption, waste, and bureaucratism. The campaign targeted cadres in government and industry, especially those who had become acquainted with China's capitalists. Second, the party launched the Five Antis Campaign against bribery, tax evasion, theft of state assets (that is, state property and economic information), cheating on government contracts, and stealing capital. This campaign targeted the Chinese capitalists themselves. Some of the blacklisted capitalists were left to function as government employees; many were simply eliminated and disappeared from the business circle.

The Five Antis Campaign also had a hidden agenda. It seized factories and capital from the blacklisted capitalists and placed them under government control. Through these efforts, the CCP expanded its influence over China's modern economic sectors. At the same time, the campaign helped the party to identify potential supporters who could be recruited into the CCP, thereby consolidating the party's grip over every aspect of Chinese society. From 1947 to 1953, the membership of the CCP increased from 2.7 million to 6.1 million.

Stephanie Chung

Further Reading
Goldman, Merle. (1981) *China's Intellectuals: Advise and Dissent.* Cambridge, MA: Harvard University Press.

THREE GORGES DAM PROJECT
The three gorges dam project, located at the middle reaches of the Chang (Yangtze) River at Yichang in China's Hubei Province, is one of the largest dam projects in the world. It will be 175 meters high and 2,335 meters long. The volume of embankment will be 26.43 million cubic meters, which is twice that of what is currently the world's largest dam, in Brazil. The capacity of the spillway will be 98,800 cubic meters. It is projected to have a hydroelectricity capacity of 18.2 gigawatts and an annual generation capacity of electricity of 84.7 billion kilowatt hours.

A passage will be built in the dam to allow ships of up to 3,000 tons to pass through. The dam reservoir, at a water level of 175 meters above the sea level, can be 662.9 kilometers long and can have a water area of 1,054 square kilometers and a capacity of 39.3 billion cubic meters. Some 17.2 billion cubic meters are allocated to dead storage and 22.1 billion cubic meters to flood control. The project was started in 1993 and is expected to be completed by 2009 and will require a total investment of about $12 billion in 1993 currency. The actual investment will be more than $25 billion by 2009.

The three gorges dam project faces very difficult challenges. The project affects nineteen counties and cities with an area of 54,000 square kilometers and a population of 14.4 million. It will result in the submersion of 632 square kilometers of land, including 245 square kilometers of arable land, and the largest single dam-related displacement of people ever. About 1.1 million people need to be relocated. The dam may also cause other problems such as ecological changes, water pollution, and, in particular, mud deposits. In the upper reaches of the Chang River, the estimated land degradation area will amount to 355,000 square kilometers, and it is estimated that its annual land erosion may deposit 0.48 billion metric tons of sediment in the reservoir.

Xing Quan Zhang

Further Reading
China Academy of Science. (1996) *Report on Environmental Impacts of the Three Gorges Project.* Beijing: Science Press.
Tao J L. (1996) *The Three Gorges Project—66 Questions.* Beijing: The Three Gorges Press.

THREE IMPERIAL REGALIA—JAPAN
Symbols of the emperor's right to rule, Japan's imperial regalia *(sanshu-no-shinki)*, take the form of three sacred treasures—the mirror, the sword, and the jewel, all of which are believed to have been handed down from emperor to emperor throughout Japanese history. The initial stage of imperial enthronement ceremonies occurs when the regalia are passed into the possession of the new emperor, legitimizing his claim to the throne.

The regalia are thought to have been divinely bestowed and have been venerated throughout history. Their origins are described in accounts of the mythological creation of Japan. The curved jewel of increasing prosperity *(yasakani-no-magatama)* and the mirror of illuminating brightness *(yata-no-kagami)* were used to lure Amaterasu Omikami, the sun goddess, out of a cave, where she had hidden herself after a quarrel with her brother, Susanoo no Mikoto, the storm god. The sword is said to have been cut from the tail of an eight-headed serpent slain by Susanoo no Mikoto. He named it the "sword of the gathering clouds of heaven" *(ame-no-murakumo-no-tsurugi)* before presenting it to Amaterasu. She then passed the three treasures to her grandson Ninigo-no Mikoto as symbols of his authority when he descended from heaven to rule over Japan. Later the sword is said to have been used by the imperial prince Yamato-take to cut an escape route when surrounded by fire on a grassy plain, and from then on it has been known as the grass-cutter sword *(kusanagi-no-tsurugi)*.

Throughout Japanese history, the regalia have been the cause of disputes and political intrigues, and copies and counterfeits have been made. The epic *Tale of the Heike* recounts how the grass-cutter sword, or perhaps a copy, was lost in the decisive twelfth-century naval battle at Dannoura, where the infant emperor Antoku perished. During the fourteenth century, the regalia played an important role in the power struggles between the Northern and Southern imperial courts, which arose because the princes of the two imperial lines fought for the right to rule as emperor.

The mirror is now believed to be enshrined in the inner sanctum of the Grand Shrine at Ise and the sword in Nagoya's Atsuta Shrine. The jewel and replicas of the mirror and sword are in the possession of the current emperor and are enshrined in the Kashiko-dokoro Shrine on the grounds of the Tokyo Imperial Palace. Wrapped in layer on layer of silk and enclosed in boxes, the regalia have long been kept hidden from view, and their exact appearance is uncertain. They have never been exhibited or displayed, and their use in the imperial accession ceremony takes place behind closed doors. They played a crucial role, however, in the 1989 enthronement of the present emperor Akihito and continue to legitimize the Japanese imperial line.

Lucy D. Moss

Further Reading

Holtom, Daniel Clarence. (1996) *The Japanese Enthronement Ceremonies: With an Account of the Imperial Regalia.* London: Kegan Paul Japan Library.

Martin, Peter. (1997) *The Chrysanthemum Throne: A History of the Emperors of Japan.* Honolulu, HI: University of Hawaii Press.

McCullough, Helen C., trans. (1988) *The Tale of the Heike.* Stanford, CA: Stanford University Press.

THREE KINGDOMS PERIOD Korea's Three Kingdoms period is generally considered to have lasted seven centuries—from the first century BCE into the seventh century CE. State institutions and autonomy, however, did not appear until the early fourth century. The three kingdoms developed out of the tribal leagues, which progressed to a stage of state-building and overpowered the Han Chinese commanderies situated on the Korean Peninsula. The combined territory of the Koguryo (37 BCE–668 CE), Paekche (18 BCE–663 CE), and Shilla (57 BCE–935 CE) kingdoms covered the entire peninsula and an even larger area to the north.

The Koguryo kingdom, by far the largest, occupied the mountainous north, including a large part of Manchuria, whereas the Paekche and Shilla kingdoms divided the southern coastal plains. In addition, a tribal league known as Kaya occupied a wedge of territory in the south but was gradually absorbed by neighboring Paekche and Shilla. The three kingdoms were fiercely competitive, and each maintained close ties with China in hopes of gaining an advantage over the other kingdoms.

CHINA—HISTORICAL PERIODS

Xia dynasty (2100–1766 BCE)
Shang dynasty (1766–1045 BCE)
Zhou dynasty (1045–256 BCE)
    Western Zhou (1045–771 BCE)
    Eastern Zhou (770–221 BCE)
Spring and Autumn period (770–476 BCE)
Warring States period (475–221 BCE)
Qin dynasty (221–206 BCE)
Han dynasty (206 BCE–220 CE)
Three Kingdoms period (220–265 CE)
North and South Dynasties (220–589 CE)
Sui dyansty (581–618 CE)
Tang dynasty (618–907 CE)
Five Dynasties period (907–960 CE)
Song dynasty (960–1279)
    Northern Song (960–1126)
    Southern Song (1127–1279)
Jurchen Jin dynasty (1125–1234)
Yuan dynasty (1279–1368)
Ming dynasty (1368–1644)
Qing dynasty (1644–1912)
Republican China (1912–1927)
People's Republic of China (1949–present)
Republic of China (1949–present)
Cultural Revolution (1966–1976)

The warring kingdom of Koguryo was the first to firmly establish itself by overpowering China and Puyo and the nomadic tribes of Northeast Asia. Led by a strong military aristocracy, it expanded to include all the lands north of Seoul and reached deep into Manchuria. Koguryo established a Confucian academy to educate the nobility and compiled a state history consisting of one hundred volumes before it adopted Buddhism as the royal creed in 372 CE. The Koguryo kingdom reached the height of its expansion in the fifth century during the reign of King Kwanggaet'o (reigned 391–413) and his successor, King Changsu (reigned 413–491).

The Paekche kingdom developed out of the confederated Mahan states of the southwestern part of the peninsula. Due to fighting with both Koguryo and China, many people of Puyo fled to the southwest. Being more advanced than the indigenous population, they gained control, and the kingdom evolved. Paekche also developed a highly sophisticated state organization and adopted Confucian and Buddhist hierarchical structures. Constantly bothered by Koguryo incursions into its northern territory and by Shilla in

THREE PAGODAS PASS

the east, Paekche allied itself with the Japanese and the North and South dynasties of China. Through these alliances, Paekche served as a conduit of culture from China to Japan. Paekche had significant influence on the culture of the Asuka period by sending diplomats, scholars, artists, and craftsmen to Japan from the middle of the fourth century.

Growing out of a confederation of Chinhan states in the southeastern portion of the peninsula, Shilla was the last of the three kingdoms to develop. It was centered around the walled city-state of Saro, later known as Kumsong and now as Kyongju. Because its territory was situated farthest from China, it was less influenced by China and did not accept Confucianism and Buddhism until the sixth century. Because of constant pressure and attacks from the Japanese as well as Koguryo and Paekche, Shilla strengthened its military. This buildup featured the Hwarang (Flower of Youth Corps), elite young soldiers with a chivalric code of leadership, unquestioned service to the kingdom, and religious and ethical zeal. Shilla absorbed the neighboring Kaya federation in the mid-sixth century and skillfully allied itself with Tang China, Koguryo's fierce enemy. Tang aid first helped Shilla defeat Paekche and then Koguryo to unify the Korean Peninsula under Shilla rule in 668.

David E. Shaffer

Further Reading
Eckert, Carter J., Ki-baik Lee, Young Ick Lew, Michael Robinson, and Edward W. Wagner. (1990) *Korea: Old and New*. Seoul: Ilchokak Publishers.
Han, Woo-keun. (1970) *The History of Korea*. Trans. by Lee Kyung-shik. Seoul: Eul-yoo Publishing.
Henthorn, William E. (1971) *A History of Korea*. New York: Free Press.
Lee, Ki-baik. (1984) *A New History of Korea*. Trans. by Edward W. Wagner. Seoul: Ilchokak Publishers.
Nahm, Andrew C. (1988) *Korea: Tradition & Transformation*. Elizabeth, NJ: Hollym.

THREE PAGODAS PASS Three Pagodas Pass or Phra Chedi Sam Ong is located in Thailand's Kanchanaburi Province on the Thai-Myanmar (Burma) border. It is the name of a settlement as well as the mountain pass. The name is derived from three miniature Buddhist shrines, memorials to the invasions of Thailand by the Burmese. This was the favorite Burmese invasion route during the Ayutthaya period (1350–1767). The shrines were constructed in the eighteenth century.

The area was used by the Japanese army in World War II as its point for invading Burma. It was a stop on the infamous "Death Railway," a railroad route designed by the Japanese to link Bangkok, Thailand, and Moulmein, Burma. The "Bridge over the River Kwai" spanning the Khwae Noi River was part of this railway, which was constructed by Allied prisoners of war and "liberated" Asians. Most of this railway was destroyed after the war.

Today, area residents are Thai, Karen, and Mon. The Myanmar government has been trying to attract tourism, touting it as a hub for regional day trips. Many of those trips are to war-related sites. Journalist Micool Brooke described the area in 1999 as "more like a demilitarized zone than a link between friendly countries."

Linda Dailey Paulson

Further Reading
Gooden, Christian. (1996) *Three Pagodas: A Journey Down the Thai-Burmese Border*. Halesworth, Suffolk, U.K.: Jungle Books.
Kinvig, Clifford. (1998) *River Kwai Railway: The Story of the Burma-Siam Railroad*. London: Brassey/B.T. Batsford.

THREE REVOLUTIONS MOVEMENT
The Three Revolutions movement (*Samdae hyongmyong undong*; refers to the ideological, technical, and cultural revolutions of the Communist Party) was a campaign that took place in North Korea in the mid-1970s. The purpose of the movement was to boost the sagging North Korean economy by sending young students to factories and cooperative farms to stimulate economic activity. Their task was to encourage and guide factory workers and farmers to meet their production quotas. More important than classroom learning, North Korean leader Kim Il Sung (1912–1994) emphasized, was the hands-on education that the students would receive through their experiences at the actual work site. This part of the movement naturally caused friction between students and farmers, who felt it inappropriate that they be made to accept guidance from someone who knew little or nothing about the job.

A second part of the movement was efforts by Kim Il Sung to replace the old with the young in factories as a way of promoting new ideas. Many festivals were arranged to promote the value of North Korean youth. At a broader dimension, the young were to take over the revolution and pass it on to later generations. In the higher echelons of government, the movement provided the setting for Kim Il Sung to designate his son, Kim Jong Il (b. 1941), to carry out future Worker Party (the political organ of the North Korean Communist Party) operations. According to University of Hawaii professor Dae-Sook Suh, the succession issue was one that few outside of Kim Il Sung's inner circle knew of. However, by placing his son at the head of the Three Revolutions movement, Kim Il Sung sought to prepare others to accept the important role that his son would play in the party, especially after the Dear Leader had passed away.

In addition to the designation of Kim Jong Il to head the Three Revolutions movement, there were other signs that suggest that this period was an important one for the younger Kim's rise to eventually succeed his father. Kim Chong-suk (1919–1949; Kim Il Sung's first wife and mother of Kim Jong Il), a figure previously not rendered important by the Communist regime, was honored as "one who served Kim Il Sung close to her body." A museum was built in her memory, as well, at this time. In Kim Il Sung's relatively early push to establish his successor can be seen the caution that he took to ensure that his regime was not usurped by reformers, as it was in the Soviet Union following the death of Joseph Stalin (1879–1953).

According to Dae-Sook Suh, in 2000 the Three Revolutions Movement was known as the Three-Revolution Work Team Movement and defined as ideology, arms, and science and technology (Suh 2001: 76).

Mark E. Caprio

See also: **Kim Il Sung**

Further Reading
Dae-Sook Suh. (1988) *Kim Il Sung: The North Korean Leader.* New York: Columbia University Press.
———. (2001) "New Political Leadership." In *The North Korean System in the Post-Cold War Era,* edited by Samuel S. Kim. New York: Palgrave.

TIAN HAN (1898–1968), modern Chinese playwright. Tian Han, one of the founders of modern Chinese drama, was born in Hunan Province and studied science in Japan from 1916 to 1922, but his interest was in literature, drama, and movies. Beginning in the 1920s, he wrote a number of plays and became one of the most important modern Chinese playwrights.

Tian Han was a romantic dramatist. All his works were rich in poetic flavor, and his early works showed a style of both sentimentalism and aestheticism, especially *Return to the South* and *Sound of the Deep Pool.* His favorite themes were art and love. In 1929, his style changed, and he wrote his representative work, *The Noted Actor's Death,* with realism. This drama showed the conflict between art and money and between good and evil and portrayed an actor with dignity. It has become a classic in Chinese literature. During the second Sino-Japanese conflict (1937–1945), Tian Han devoted himself to the anti-Japanese drama movement. He wrote the drama *Lugou Bridge* to reflect the war. After the war, he wrote his famous work *The Beauties.* Besides dramas, Tian Han wrote many scenarios and many song lyrics. The Chinese national anthem "March of the Warriors" was written by Tian in the 1930s.

She Xiaojie

Further Reading
Pan Xulan. (1993) *Dictionary of New China's Literature.* Nanjing, China: Jiangsu Literary Publishing House.

TIAN SHAN This great sickle-shaped arc of mountain ranges and intervening valleys stretches 2,414 kilometers (1,500 miles) east/west along the frontier between Kyrgyzstan, southeastern Kazakhstan, and the Xinjiang Uygur Autonomous Region of southwestern China. The complex is 320 to 480 kilometers (200–300 miles) wide and covers 1,036,000 square kilometers (400,000 square miles). A central knot of high peaks reaches 7,439 meters (24,406 feet) on Pobeda Peak. The Pamir ranges are to the southwest, the Dzungarian and southern Kazakhstan plains fall below to the north, and the Tarim Basin lies southeast.

To early Silk Road travelers, these "Heavenly Mountains" (*tian* is Chinese for "sky" or "heaven") offered an alpine respite of steppe, forest, and glacial lakes. The interior continental location produces short, cold winters followed by long, hot summers. Winds of Mediterranean and Gulf of Arabia origin

bring moisture to the windward western and north-western slopes (up to 800 millimeters, or 32 inches, annually), while leaving the eastern and interior regions in an arid rain shadow (less than 100 millimeters, or 4 inches). Common fauna include the wolf, fox, wild boars, bears, snow leopard, mountain goat, Manchurian roe, and mountain sheep.

Kyrgyz predominate in the western Tian Shan; Uighurs form a majority on the eastern side. Ethnic Russians, Chinese, Kazakhs, Tajiks, and Tatars also settle the periphery. The economy revolves around irrigated agriculture (lowlands) and livestock herding (uplands). Oil and gas extraction, mining of nonferrous metals, and tourism are also important throughout this region.

Stephen F. Cunha

Further Reading

Howard-Bury, Charles. (1990) *Mountains of Heaven: Travel in the Tian Shan Mountains, 1913.* London: Hodder & Stoughton.

Poole, Robert M., and Thomas Nebbia. (1988) "Tian Shan & Pamir." In *Mountain Worlds.* Washington, DC: National Geographic Society.

TIANANMEN SQUARE Tiananmen Square is located in the center of Beijing, the capital city of the People's Republic of China (PRC) and is listed first among the city's sixteen scenic spots. Originally designed and built in 1651, the square was enlarged fourfold in 1958 to cover 100 acres, making it the biggest public square in the world. It is best known in the West for the "Tiananmen Incident" of 1989.

The square is actually named for the Tiananmen Gate (Gate of Heavenly Peace), which is on the northern side of the square. Outside the gate are two marble pillars called the *huabiao*. The *huabiao* are said to date back to the sage kings of Yao and Shun in China's mythical times. Originally wooden, they served as notice boards, or "wood of direct speech" *(feibang zhi mu)*, which stood just outside the court for the purpose of soliciting public criticism. They were replaced during the Han dynasty (206 BCE–220 CE) by stone pillars, eventually becoming elaborately sculpted columns in traditional Chinese architectural style and a common sight on the grounds of imperial palaces. However, they still symbolize people's right to speak up against official injustice.

The Presence of Mao

The posthumous presence of Mao Zedong (1893–1976) is visually and physically prominent at the

Chinese students protesting in Tiananmen Square beneath a poster of Mao Zedong in the spring of 1989. (DAVID & PETER TURNLEY/CORBIS)

square. The official portrait of the former chairman of the Chinese Communist Party (CCP) has hung on Tiananmen Gate since 1949. It is flanked by two slogans: "Long Live The Unity of the Peoples of the World!" and "Long Live The People's Republic of China!" Mao is also the only permanent resident of the square: in a mausoleum on the south side, the body of Mao lies in a crypt covered in a crystalline sarcophagus surrounding by flowers. The body is retired after public viewing hours to an earthquake-proof chamber deep in the bowels of the square. An Ancestral Hall of the Revolution contains relics of other first-generation revolutionary leaders like Liu Shaoqi (1898–1974), Zhu De (1886–1976), and Zhou Enlai (1898–1976).

In the center of the square, a marble obelisk known as *Monument to the People's Heroes* commemorates those who died for change and revolution in China from 1840. Every morning at daybreak a ceremonial guard facing it hoists the five-star red flag of the PRC. To the east, the Museum of History and the Revolution has more often than not been "closed to the public" due to the constant vacillation of party policy and the rewriting of Chinese history. Instead, it has been used for exhibiting official and avant-garde artwork, contemporary fashion shows, and so forth. To its west is the Great Hall of the People, which, with its ten thousand seats, is the annual meeting site of the National People's Congress. All major plenums of the CCP and government are held there as well.

The Tiananmen Incident

On 15 April 1989, students gathered in Tiananmen Square to mourn the death of reformist CCP general secretary Hu Yaobang. When government officials refused their petitions at the Great Hall of the People, the students clashed with police. The party mouthpiece, *People's Daily*, published an editorial on 26 April accusing a "handful of plotters" of creating "turmoil" with the object of overthrowing the regime. The next day, 200,000 students from over forty universities marched to the square in protest. Hundreds, then thousands, of Beijing University students began a hunger strike on 13 May around the *Monument to the People's Heroes*. Premier Li Peng (b. 1928) and moderate officials affiliated with General Secretary Zhao Ziyang (b. 1919), who was later dismissed, failed to defuse the situation before the arrival of Soviet leader Mikhail Gorbachev (b. 1931) for a summit with Deng Xiaoping (1904–1997), China's paramount leader. The welcoming ceremony at the square for Gorbachev was abandoned: Chinese president Yang Shangkun (b. 1907) later gave Beijing's loss of face and international prestige as one reason for the crackdown. On 20 May, martial law was declared, but for two weeks the students, now joined by workers, reporters, army personnel, and civil servants—numbering at one point over 2 million—blocked the advance of 150,000 troops toward the city. On 3–4 June, army tanks rolled in, clearing the square and killing an undisclosed number of civilians.

The term "prodemocracy" would oversimplify description of a student-led movement that made a complex set of demands, which included dialogue with the government, crackdown on official corruption, vague political reforms, greater funding for education, a freer press, and so forth. The students used the word "democracy," but they were short on specifics. They stressed the need to improve the existing system, not to overthrow it. Many acknowledged party leadership and believed that an American-type democracy was unsuitable for China. It may also be argued that they were not sufficiently versed in liberal democratic traditions to represent their interests and aspirations.

They did, however, think that by playing to the international news media (over one thousand foreign journalists had converged in Beijing for the Deng-Gorbachev summit), they could gain Western sympathy and thereby advance their cause. This partly explains why on 30 May, students unveiled the ten-meter-high *Goddess of Democracy* statue in the square. Ironically, Deng himself had been misled by Premier Li to believe that the demonstrators wanted to overthrow the party government.

Officially orchestrated mass demonstrations were common in Tiananmen Square after 1949. Mao reviewed gatherings of Red Guards there during the Cultural Revolution (1966–1976). In the aftermath of the 1989 incident, the CCP organized Young Pioneers parades to show that the "revolutionary successors to the Communist enterprise" had taken back the square from protestors. Tens of thousands celebrate Labor Day (1 May) and National Day (1 October) with fireworks and floats. However, traditional group calisthenics like tai chi chuan, practiced daily in the square, have to an extent replaced the mass movements today.

Anthony Alexander Loh

Further Reading
Fewsmith, Joseph. (2001) *China since Tiananmen: The Politics of Transition.* Cambridge, U.K.: Cambridge University Press.

Liu, Melinda. (1989) "Beijing Spring: Loss of the Mandate of Heaven." In *Beijing Spring*, edited by David C. Turnley. New York: Stewart, Tabori & Chang, 25–43.

Ming Pao News reporters and photographers. (1989) *June Four: A Chronicle of the Chinese Democratic Uprising.* Trans. by Zi Jin and Qin Zhou. Fayetteville, AR: University of Arkansas Press.

Nathan, Andrew J. (1989) "Chinese Democracy in 1989: Continuity and Change." *Problems of Communism* 38 (September–October): 16–29.

Nathan, Andrew J., and Perry Link, eds. (2001) *The Tiananmen Papers.* New York: Public Affairs.

Spence, Jonathan D. (1990) "The Gate and the Square." In *Children of the Dragon*, edited by Human Rights in China. New York: Collier, 16–37.

Unger, Jonathan, ed. (1991) *The Pro-Democracy Protests in China: Reports from the Provinces.* Armonk, NY: M. E. Sharpe.

Wu, Hung. (1991) "Tiananmen Square: A Political History of Monuments." *Representations* 35 (Summer): 84–117.

TIANJIN (1997 est. pop. 5.15 million). Located near the mouth of the Hai River 137 kilometers southeast of Beijing, Tianjin (Tientsin) is one of three centrally administered cities in the People's Republic of China. In 1997, the metropolitan population of Tianjin was

9 million, while the city proper had 5.15 million residents. Aside from its importance as a major port in northeast China, Tianjin is also a major industrial center, producing textiles, light and heavy machinery, automobiles, and cement.

During the Ming (1368–1644) and Qing (1644–1912) dynasties, Tianjin was the northern terminus of the Grand Canal and an important transfer site for the shipment of grain northward to the imperial capital at Beijing. Under the terms of the 1858 Treaty of Tianjin that concluded the Second Opium War, the city was opened to foreign trade. Over the remainder of the nineteenth century, it grew to become the second busiest port in China after Shanghai. Nine foreign nations were granted concessions in Tianjin: France, Britain, Germany, the United States, Russia, Japan, Italy, Austria-Hungary, and Belgium. During the turmoil of the Boxer Uprising (1899–1900), Tianjin sustained heavy damage at the hands of the international army that was sent to rescue the besieged foreign community in Beijing. By the early twentieth century, the Japanese community in Tianjin had emerged as one of the largest foreign communities in the port. Observers in the 1920s and 1930s noted that many of the Japanese businesses and traders in Tianjin were involved in the booming opium and narcotics trade. When the Japanese army invaded China in 1937, the city was seized and remained under occupation until the end of the Pacific War in 1945. During this conflict, Tianjin played an important role in the regional transportation and communications networks, as it was not only a port, but also a key railway town with access to the Grand Canal and Huang (Yellow) River.

During the Chinese Civil War (1947–1949), the Communists targeted Tianjin as an important urban center in the revolution. After the victory of the Chinese Communist Party in 1949, Tianjin's industrial base was enhanced under the new government's state-planned economy, and hundreds of new factories and manufacturing plants were established. With the move to a market economy in the 1980s, Tianjin became one of the first Special Economic Zones to be opened to foreign investment and trade along the Chinese coast. The development of the Bohai oil fields in the Yellow Sea during the 1990s resulted in a corresponding development of the petrochemical plants and refineries.

Robert John Perrins

Further Reading
Hook, Brian, ed. (1998) *Beijing and Tianjin: Towards a Millennial Megalopolis*. New York: Oxford University Press.

Kwan, Man Bun. (2001) *The Salt Merchants of Tianjin: State-Making and Civil Society in Late Imperial China*. Honolulu, HI: University of Hawaii Press.

TIBET (2002 est. pop. 2.7 million). Traditionally, Tibet comprises the central Asian landmass between the Himalayas in the south, the Kunlun range to the north and the Karakorams to the west, while in the east it is bounded by the region of the great rivers, the Chang (Yangtze), Mekong, and Salween. With most of its territory situated above 4,500 meters and its capital city, Lhasa, located at 3,607 meters, Tibet has been popularly termed "The Roof of the World."

While the extent to which Tibet was part of China in earlier periods is in dispute, Tibet has certainly been part of China since the Communist invasion in 1950, and exists today only in the much-reduced area of the Tibetan Autonomous Region (TAR) of China. A Tibetan Government-in-exile headed by the Dalai Lama (the spiritual and temporal leader of the Tibetan peoples), has been established in India, and there are also Tibetan exile communities in Switzerland and the United States. The Tibetan government continues to campaign for Tibetan self-determination and the ongoing Sino-Tibetan dispute invests facts and figures in regard to Tibet with important political implications. Historically, however, there has been a distinction between "political" Tibet, the area ruled by the Lhasa government prior to 1950, and "ethnic" or "cultural" Tibet, that area inhabited by mainly Buddhist peoples of Tibetan origin.

Geography
"Political" Tibet had an estimated population of between 1.8 and 3 million peoples, of whom around half

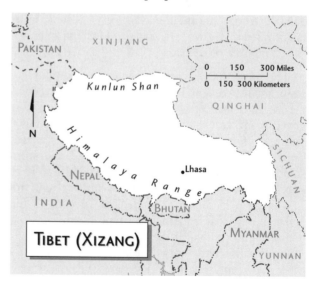

TIBET–CHINA RELATIONS IN THE 1840s

Although written over 150 years ago by two French missionaries, this account of relations between the Tibetans and Chinese could in major ways characterize relations in 2002.

The Chinese you find at Lha-Ssa are for the most part soldiers or officers of the tribunal; those who fix their residence in this town are very few in number. At all times the Chinese and the Thibetans have had relations more or less important: they frequently have waged war against each other, and have tried to encroach on one another's rights. The Tartar-Mantchou dynasty, as we have already remarked upon elsewhere, saw from the commencement of their elevation the great importance of conciliating the friendship of the Tale-Lama, whose influence is all powerful over the Mongol tribes; consequently they have never failed to retain at the court of Lha-Ssa two Grand Mandarins invested with the title of *Kin-Tchai [Ch'in-ch'ai]*, which signifies ambassador, or envoy-extraordinary. The ostensible mission of these individuals is to present, under certain fixed circumstances, the homage of the Chinese Emperor to the Tale-Lama, and to lend him the aid of China in any difficulties he may have had with his neighbours. Such, to all appearance, is the purport of this permanent embassy; but in reality they are only in attendance to flatter the religious belief of the Mongols, and to bind them to the reigning dynasty, by making them believe that the government of Peking has great veneration for the divinity of the Buddha-La.

Source: Huc Evariste-Regis and Joseph Gabet. ([1851] 1987)
Travels in Tartary, Thibet and China, 1844–1846. New York:
Dover Publications, 185.

were semi-nomadic yak herders. (Today's TAR population includes a large number of Han Chinese immigrants, who may now constitute a majority of the population in the Tibetan capital of Lhasa.) The settled urban and agricultural populations were concentrated in the river valleys, particularly in the triangle formed by the major settlements of Lhasa, Shigatse (Xigaze) and Gyantse.

While situated at a latitude similar to Algeria, the altitude and location of the Tibetan plateau produces a cold and generally dry climate, although southeastern Tibet includes areas of tropical jungle. The western Tibetan area around the Gangdise (Kailas) mountain range and Lake Mapam Yumco (Manasarowar) is the source of four great rivers: the Indus, Ganges, Brahmaputra, and the Sutlej, while Mount Everest, which is situated on the Nepal-Tibet border, is, at 8,848 meters the world's highest mountain.

Sedentary agriculture is limited by the climate. Barley is the major crop and in its roasted form as *tsampa* comprises, with yak meat and tea (imported from China), the staple diet of the majority of the population.

History

The origins of the Tibetan peoples appear to be linked to Central Asian nomadic tribes such as the Qiang and Yue Zhi (Tokharians). The first unified Tibetan state was a tribal confederacy formed in the seventh century under the rule of King Songtsen Gampo (or Srong-brtsan Sgam-po; c. 608–650 CE), who established his capital at Lhasa. The introduction of a Tibetan script and Buddhist teachings are among the innovations attributed to his reign. The dynasty he founded lasted until the assassination of King Langdharma, around the year 842.

Tibet was a formidable military power during this period, constantly engaged in warfare with neighboring powers and strong enough to sack the Chinese capital of Xi'an in 763. At its height the Tibetan empire reached as far west as Samarqand. Buddhism became increasingly important, particularly in the court, and the first Tibetan monastery was established at Samye around 779. But there was considerable opposition to the new faith among aristocratic factions associated with followers of the indigenous Tibetan belief system (later identified with the Bon faith but probably at that time an unsystematized tradition that included elements of divine kingship and sacrificial practice).

Buddhism became firmly established during the eleventh and twelfth centuries, when Indian Buddhist texts were systematically translated into the Tibetan language. Of the four major sects of Tibetan Buddhism that developed on the basis of these teachings, the Gelugpa sect eventually emerged as preeminent, and from the sixteenth century onwards, Tibet was ruled by a line of incarnate Gelugpa monks with the title of dalai lama. Religious factions in Tibet tended to seek Mongol or Chinese patronage, and China became increasingly involved in events in Tibet in the eighteenth century. Thus, from 1793 until 1911–1912, China was able to exert at least nominal suzerainty over Lhasa.

In 1903–1904, the British imperial Government of India dispatched a mission to Lhasa that forced the Tibetans to accept British representatives and effectively opened the country to Western ideas and influences. But despite some modernization in the next couple of decades, Tibet remained an essentially conservative religious society, strongly resistant to change. The thirteenth Dalai Lama (1876–1933), a strong nationalist leader, lead Tibet to independence after the Chinese revolution in 1911, and Tibet survived as a de facto independent state until the Communist Chinese invasion in 1950. Her independence, however, was not officially recognized by any major powers, with China continuing to claim Tibet as part of her territory.

Since 1950, the Tibetans have suffered a continuous assault on their cultural identity, with tens or even hundreds of thousands of Tibetans killed, imprisoned, and tortured as a result of Chinese colonialist policies.

Culture

Despite the continuing existence of the Bon faith and its many cultural manifestations, the outstanding feature of Tibetan culture is generally considered to be its unique form of Buddhism, a synthesis of the Mahayana and Tantric forms of the faith. Buddhist influence permeated virtually all aspects of traditional society. An estimated 20 percent of the male population were monks, and more than six thousand monasteries were distributed throughout the Tibetan cultural world. These were important political and economic centers as well as the guardians of Tibetan cultural and artistic expression. Outside of the monasteries, pilgrimage to sacred cities and mountains was a particularly significant religious expression for all classes of people.

A small aristocratic class enjoyed considerable privilege, although in comparison to their contemporaries in neighboring states, the Tibetan peasantry were tolerably well treated. Women too, enjoyed greater than average freedom, particularly in the social and economic spheres, although they were almost entirely excluded from religious power.

There were cultural influences from both China and India, but Tibetan culture was strikingly distinct from that of its neighbors. This was particularly marked in such areas as literary traditions (in particular the lengthy *Gesar of Ling* epic), language, and art and architecture, with buildings such as Lhasa's Potala Palace and Jokhang temple, as well as the regional monasteries, being of striking originality. Much of this culture has been destroyed in the TAR, but much has been remembered or preserved in exile.

Alex McKay

Further Reading

Coleman, Graham. (ed.) (1993) *A Handbook of Tibetan Culture. A Guide to Tibetan Centres and Resources throughout the World.* London: Rider.

McKay, Alex. (ed.) (2002) *The History of Tibet.* 3 vols. Richmond, U.K: Curzon Press.

Richardson, Hugh. (1984) *Tibet and its History.* Boston: Shambhala Publications.

———. (1998) *High Peaks, Pure Earth: Collected Writings on Tibetan History and Culture*, edited by Michael Aris, London: Serindia Publications.

Samuel, Geoffrey. (1993) *Civilized Shamans: Buddhism in Tibetan Societies.* Washington DC: Smithsonian Institution Press.

Snellgrove, David, and Hugh Richardson. (1968) *A Cultural History of Tibet.* London: Weidenfeld and Nicolson.

Stein, Rolf, A. (1972) *Tibetan Civilization.* Stanford, CA: Stanford University Press.

Tarthang, Tulku (ed.) (1986) *Ancient Tibet: Research Materials from The Yeshe De Project.* Berkeley, CA: Dharma Publishing.

Tucci, Giuseppe. (1980) *The Religions of Tibet.* London: Routledge & Kegan Paul Ltd.

TIBET—IMAGE IN THE MODERN WEST

Tibet occupies a unique place in the Western imagination. Since Marco Polo (1254–1324) and other thirteenth-century Western travelers provided the first European accounts of Tibetan exotic practices such as necromancy (sorcery), the West has imagined Tibet as a mythical place of magic and mystery, a peaceful land preserving esoteric spiritual wisdom. It is commonly described by such colorful allusions as the "roof of the world," the "forbidden land," the "land of the lamas," or Shangri-La, as if the country were otherworldly, beyond ordinary description.

The reality behind the image of mythical Tibet remains partly obscured today, because of a combination of historical circumstances and human and commercial needs. But many Tibetans consider the mythical image of their country to be detrimental to their prospects of political self-determination.

Origins of the Tibetan Image

During the nineteenth century, the British empire in India spread northward to the borders of Tibet, but the Tibetan government, fearing a threat to the Buddhist religious system, refused to allow Europeans to enter. Tibet refused even to enter into diplomatic correspondence with the British, who resorted to the use of spies to obtain information about their northern neighbor.

Tibet's policy of isolation from European influences was assisted by its forbidding mountainous geography. Ironically this remoteness only succeeded in making the country more attractive to Westerners, many of whom made clandestine journeys into "forbidden" Tibet. The nineteenth-century Western romantic landscape aesthetic furthered the perception of Tibet as a pristine and beautiful land. Travelers such the botanist Sir Joseph Dalton Hooker (1785–1865) promoted this image to the reading public in his 1855 *Himalayan Journals*, with their descriptions of the "deep dark blue of the heavens . . . the perfect and dazzling whiteness of the earthly scene." While the more prosaic observations of British intelligence agents were restricted to official circulation, these images flourished alongside more exotic depictions of customs such as the use of skulls for drinking cups.

Because the public knew so little about Tibet, it became the repository for numerous fantasies. One image was promoted by the esoteric writings of Helena Petrovna Blavatsky (1831–1891), the founder of the Theosophical movement, which was concerned with occult practices and spiritism. Blavatsky claimed that the Mahatmas (Sanskrit "great souls"), a race of spiritual masters dwelling in Tibet, were the source of psychic revelations that led to the development of Theosophy.

The Western discovery of Tibet's unique form of Buddhism, a blend of Indian Mahayana and Tantric beliefs with indigenous Tibetan elements, did little to dispel Blavatsky's fantasies. Tibetan religious systems were then poorly understood, and Western observers tended to focus on the colorful and esoteric aspects of Tibetan religion. Tibetan Buddhism was even termed Lamaism (which is not a Tibetan noun), a title ideologically framed to represent a faith that had degenerated from what Western scholarship classified as pure, original Buddhism and that was infused with demonic elements.

Contemporary Western perceptions of Tibet were affected by political factors, particularly at the beginning of the twentieth century, when fears of Russian influence in Lhasa led to the invasion of Tibet by British Indian forces. The imperial media at that time sought to portray the Tibetan system as a form of Oriental despotism, with the Tibetan people oppressed by a parasitic and corrupt clergy. These images coalesced with those promoted by Christian missionaries, who were forbidden to enter Tibet and who naturally produced negative images of Tibetan religion.

After the British forces reached Lhasa in 1904, the mystical heart of Tibet in the Western imagination was relocated to more remote places, eventually to hidden valleys (a concept known to the Tibetans themselves). The image of a timeless and tranquil hidden valley in the Himalayas was featured in James Hilton's best-selling 1933 novel *Lost Horizon*. Its depictions of a Himalayan paradise known as Shangri-La were imagined as Tibet, firmly fixing the otherworldly image in the Western mind.

The writings of the French traveler Alexandra David-Neel (1868–1969) and the translation of the *Tibetan Book of the Dead* in the 1920s were other significant elements in the construction of a mythical Tibet. This trend culminated in the works of Lobsang Rampa, which first appeared in the 1950s. Rampa's tales of his fantastic life in Tibet remain best-sellers, even though Rampa was soon revealed to be an Englishman, Cyril Hoskings (1910–1981), who had never been to Tibet.

Commercial and Political Factors

Commercial factors have also encouraged the production of colorful images of Tibet, with publishers responding to the continuing demand for accounts of the esoteric aspects of Tibetan culture. That demand seems to spring from a human need for fantasies of

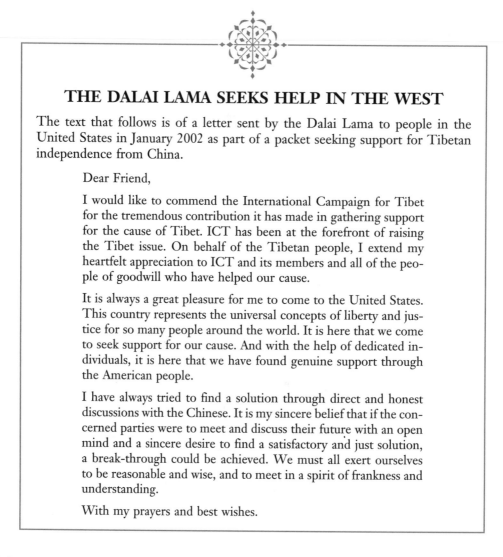

THE DALAI LAMA SEEKS HELP IN THE WEST

The text that follows is of a letter sent by the Dalai Lama to people in the United States in January 2002 as part of a packet seeking support for Tibetan independence from China.

Dear Friend,

I would like to commend the International Campaign for Tibet for the tremendous contribution it has made in gathering support for the cause of Tibet. ICT has been at the forefront of raising the Tibet issue. On behalf of the Tibetan people, I extend my heartfelt appreciation to ICT and its members and all of the people of goodwill who have helped our cause.

It is always a great pleasure for me to come to the United States. This country represents the universal concepts of liberty and justice for so many people around the world. It is here that we come to seek support for our cause. And with the help of dedicated individuals, it is here that we have found genuine support through the American people.

I have always tried to find a solution through direct and honest discussions with the Chinese. It is my sincere belief that if the concerned parties were to meet and discuss their future with an open mind and a sincere desire to find a satisfactory and just solution, a break-through could be achieved. We must all exert ourselves to be reasonable and wise, and to meet in a spirit of frankness and understanding.

With my prayers and best wishes.

place and from the sense that this imagined Tibet might possess the cure for the perceived ills of Western society.

There are also political aspects to the selection and continuing vitality of Tibet as the repository of fantasies. One scholar has noted that Tibet was fascinating because it was unknown; after Europeans had colonized a faraway land, it always became uninteresting.

But during the first half of the twentieth century, there was also a political purpose behind these images. After the Tibetans had expelled the last Chinese officials in 1912, British India became Tibet's main patron. In contrast to the images they had promoted earlier when Tibet was deemed hostile, the British now sought to promote the idea of a strong, unified Tibetan state with a distinct identity separate from that of China. Tibet's popular image helped to promote its separate and unique status and to strengthen the country, and while the British now provided more realistic

information on Tibet to the informed public, they made no attempt to counter the politically valuable mythical image.

The Consequences of the Image

There are many "Tibets" in the Western imagination today, the reality blending with the layers of romantic images. New images have emerged in recent years, with constructions of an environmentally conscious, feminist, nonviolent Tibet becoming increasingly widespread. These images are promoted by both the Tibetan refugee community and their Westerner supporters.

Today Tibet enjoys widespread recognition largely as a result of its many colorful associations, with much of its culture now within the realm of popular Western culture. But while the mythical image of Tibet helps the country retain the moral high ground in its struggle with China, the stereotypes not only deny the historical realities of Tibet, they deny Tibetan agency and obscure the very real Tibetan struggle for political self-determination.

Alex McKay

Further Reading

Bishop, Peter. (1989) *The Myth of Shangri-La: Tibet, Travel Writing, and the Western Creation of Sacred Landscape.* London: Athlone Press.

Dodin, T., and H. Rather, eds. (2001) *Imagining Tibet: Perceptions, Projections, and Fantasies.* Boston: Wisdom Publications.

Hilton, James. (1933) *Lost Horizon.* London: Macmillan.

Korom, Frank J., ed. (1997) *Constructing Tibetan Culture: Contemporary Perspectives.* Quebec, Canada: World Heritage Press.

Lopez, Donald, S. (1998) *Prisoners of Shangri-La: Tibetan Buddhism and the West.* Chicago: University of Chicago Press.

McKay, Alex. (1997) *Tibet and the British Raj: The Frontier Cadre, 1904–1947.* Richmond, U.K.: Curzon Press.

Shakya, Tsering. (1992) "Of Real and Imaginary Tibet." *Tibetan Review* 27, 1: 13–16.

TIBETAN UPRISING Tibet, currently an autonomous region in southwestern China whose status has long been disputed, enjoyed de facto, if not legally recognized, independence during the 1913–1950 period. The Chinese, however, claimed Tibet as a part of their territory, and the Communist takeover in China in October 1949 was an obvious threat to Tibetan self-determination, as the Communists were openly prepared to use military force to take over Tibet. After failed attempts to arrange negotiations on neutral territory, Chinese military forces invaded Tibet in October 1950 and quickly succeeded in conquering the largely demilitarized Tibetan state.

During the 1950s, Chinese policies designed to transform traditional Tibetan society and to integrate Tibet into the Communist system were applied with increasing force. As a consequence, Tibetan resistance to the assault on their religion and culture rapidly increased, culminating in the nationalist revolt of 1959. But the Tibetans were vastly outnumbered and ill equipped for an armed struggle. Their resistance was crushed, and the fourteenth Dalai Lama (b. 1935), the spiritual and temporal leader of Tibet, was forced to flee into exile in India. Since that time, China has continued to rule Tibet through military force, while the Dalai Lama remains the head of the Tibetan government-in-exile in India.

Events in 1950–1958

In January 1950, when the Indian government formally recognized the new Communist government in Beijing, the Chinese informed India of their intention to peacefully "liberate" Tibet. To the Communists, the Tibetans were an oppressed people at the mercy of a feudal elite, and they expected to be welcomed as liberators. When Sino-Tibetan negotiations failed, the Chinese forces launched their full-scale military invasion of Tibet on 7 October 1950. An appeal to the United Nations went unanswered due to Tibet's ambiguous status under international law. The Tibetan state maintained only a small army of around eight thousand men, and within days, Chamdo, the main Tibetan administrative center in Kham (eastern Tibet), fell to the invaders.

The province of Kham was home to the Tibetan-speaking Khampa peoples, who, while loyal to the Dalai Lama as head of their Tibetan Buddhist faith, enjoyed considerable autonomy and did not necessarily view themselves as subjects of either Lhasa or Beijing. The Khampas had a strong martial tradition, and the Kham region became the center of armed opposition to China.

After the Chinese invasion, the Tibetan National Assembly requested that the young Dalai Lama assume full secular power in Tibet, several years earlier than planned. The Chinese, meanwhile, forced a Tibetan delegation to sign the Sino-Tibetan Agreement of 1951 (known as the "Seventeen Point Agreement") by which Beijing absorbed Tibet into its empire. Guarantees of Tibetan autonomy and religious freedoms in that agreement were soon breached as China began to absorb the Tibetan administration and usurp the functions of the Tibetan government. Increasing numbers of Chinese soldiers and settlers moved into Tibet, particularly after the completion in 1954 of a drivable road to Lhasa through eastern Tibet. Many of the Chinese Communists had genuinely expected to be greeted as liberators by the people they saw as feudal masses; they were surprised by Tibetan opposition to their presence.

In 1954 the Dalai Lama traveled to Beijing, where he met the Chinese leader, Mao Zedong (1893–1976), and in 1956 he was permitted to travel to India for the 2,500th anniversary of the enlightenment of the Buddha celebrations. While there, he was advised by the Indian government to accept Chinese control of Tibet, and, with the Chinese hinting at compromise, the Dalai Lama returned to Tibet in the hope of reaching a solution through discussion with the Communist leadership.

The years 1955 and 1956 saw a rapid acceleration of the transition to communism throughout China, culminating in the disastrous "Great Leap Forward" policy in 1958. Within Tibet, there was an accelerated

Tibetans living in Darjeeling, India, mark the Tibetan Uprising in a march in 1989. They display banners calling for the re-establishment of Tibetan rule in Tibet. (ALISON WRIGHT/CORBIS)

program of collectivization, the widespread institution of "class struggle," particularly against monastic authorities, and attempts made to make the large Tibetan nomadic population sedentary.

These policies brought a strong Tibetan reaction. By 1956 an organized guerrilla movement, the Chushi Gandruk ("Four Rivers, Six Ranges") was active throughout eastern Tibet. The Dalai Lama's policy of nonviolence meant that he was unable to offer his personal support to the guerrillas, and he continued to attempt to mediate a peaceful solution to the crisis until his departure from Tibet. But many elements of the Tibetan government supported the guerrillas in their struggle, which was then primarily defending Tibetan Buddhism and the Tibetan social system rather than explicitly trying to build a nationalist movement.

Tibetan resistance to the Chinese Communists attracted the intention of the intelligence services of various countries, including the U.S. Central Intelligence Agency (CIA). By 1958 significant amounts of CIA aid began to reach the guerrillas.

Uprising of 1959

By 1959 the disturbed conditions throughout eastern Tibet had led to a large influx of refugees entering Lhasa, which exacerbated food shortages caused by the large numbers of Chinese troops stationed there. By early March of that year, the population of

Lhasa was further swelled by the large crowds who gathered for the Monlam Chenmo (Tibetan New Year) celebrations; traditionally an unruly period in which the monastic powers dominated the secular structures of state.

Greatly adding to the unstable situation in the Tibetan capital was the invitation to attend a theatrical performance issued by the Chinese military commander in Lhasa to the Dalai Lama. On 9 March the Tibetan leader was instructed by the Chinese to come to the military barracks the following day without his usual armed escort. This invitation was interpreted by the Tibetan public as a Chinese attempt to seize the Dalai Lama.

A large crowd, estimated at around thirty thousand people (Lhasa's population in 1950 was around twenty thousand), gathered around the Norbu Lingka, the summer palace of the Dalai Lama. Their primary aim was to prevent their leader from taking up the Chinese invitation, but the apparently spontaneous demonstrations took on a nationalist character because the crowds also began to protest against the Chinese presence in Lhasa and to demand Tibetan independence. A showdown became inevitable.

On 17 March Chinese troops fired several artillery shells into the grounds of the Norbu Lingka, apparently in an attempt to frighten the Tibetans into submission. That night, a prearranged plan was put into operation whereby the Dalai Lama, disguised as an ordinary Tibetan soldier, was smuggled out of the palace. His escape was kept secret for several days, and with a small group of his supporters he succeeded in making his way south through the mountains to India. An estimated eighty to a hundred thousand Tibetans joined him in India, and a Tibetan government-in-exile was established at Dharmsala in north India.

Meanwhile, in Lhasa the Chinese commenced a full-scale military crackdown. Exact figures are difficult to ascertain, but thousands of Tibetans were killed or executed in the ensuing days, with Chinese army intelligence reports admitting that their forces had "eliminated" 87,000 of their opponents in Lhasa and surrounding areas in March–October 1959 alone.

Coalescence of Resistance

A sense of Tibetan national identity was greatly stimulated by the Communist invasion of Tibet and in the eyes of the Tibetans and much of the world, the events of March 1959 were a nationalist uprising against the rule of a foreign power. Tibetan resistance subsequently coalesced around the figure of the Dalai Lama, whose insistence on nonviolent resistance has meant that the history of Tibetan armed resistance to China has been largely forgotten. But the events of 1959 remain a historical division between traditional and modern Tibet.

Alex McKay

Further Reading

Ali, S. Mahmud. (1999) *Cold War in the High Himalayas: The USA, China and South Asia in the 1950s.* Richmond, U.K.: Curzon.

Barnett, Robbie, and Shirin Akiner, eds. (1994) *Resistance and Reform in Tibet.* London: C. Hurst.

Goldstein, Melvyn, William Siebenschuh, and Tashi Tsering. (1997) *The Struggle for Modern Tibet: The Autobiography of Tashi Tsering.* Armonk, NY: M. E. Sharpe.

Richardson, Hugh. (1984) *Tibet & its History.* Boston: Shambhala.

Shakya, Tsering. (1999) *The Dragon in the Land of Snows: A History of Modern Tibet since 1947.* Washington, DC: Columbia University Press.

Smith, Warren. (1996) *Tibetan Nation: A History of Tibetan Nationalism and Sino-Tibetan Relations.* Boulder, CO: Westview.

TIBETANS The people of Tibet inhabit the Tibetan Plateau, the highest continuous landmass in the world, which averages over 3,500 meters in height, including the Himalayas in the south, the Zangbo (or Brahmaputra) River Valley, and the northern Chang-

THE TIBETAN CAMPAIGN FOR INDEPENDENCE

The following is a statement prepared by the Dalai Lama and sent to individuals in the United States with a request that they sign it and send it to Secretary of State Colin Powell.

Affirmation of Religious Freedom to Secretary of State Colin Powell

WHEREAS . . . The people of Tibet, led by the Dalai Lama, are struggling to maintain a magnificent and ancient spiritual culture on Earth; and,

"WHEREAS . . . The Tyranny that has driven more that one hundred thousand Tibetans from their homeland and threatened the existence of Tibetan culture is an affront to all humankind; and,

"WHEREAS . . . Confronting the issue of Tibet is a basic issue of morality, a defining action for the human community.

"THEREFORE . . . I Affirm my deep commitment to religious and spiritual liberty by calling on you to take immediate and strategic action to save Tibet's religious and cultural heritage.

Signed _____

thang Desert. There are between 4 and 6 million Tibetans, of whom some 2.4 million live in the area of the present Tibet Autonomous Region of the People's Republic of China. There are also substantial populations in the Chinese provinces of Yunnan, Gansu, and Sichuan and in Qinghai, formerly the Tibetan province of Amdo. Since 1959, there have also been some 100,000 Tibetan exiles in India and the southern Himalayas and small refugee populations in Western countries.

The Tibetans are basically of East Asian type, with considerable variations. The nomads of the east, the Khampas, are tall and aquiline featured, while the people of the central provinces of U and Tsang are smaller and have high cheekbones. Several dialects of one language family, the Tibeto-Burman, are spoken, with the Lhasa dialect providing the cultivated norm and classical Tibetan being used for scriptures.

The Tibetan way of life has been based on the harsh realities of geography, with nomadic animal husbandry, particularly the yak; agriculture, with barley as a staple; and trade, frequently mixed with pilgrimage, being important. Tibetans tend to be instantly recognizable, with a traditional coat, or *chuba*, for the men and an apron in three vertical sections of colorful horizontal stripes for the women.

The consciousness of the Tibetans as a single people is based on the unity of their civilization, linked inseparably to the Buddhist religion, which pervades every aspect of everyday life. Tibetan homes have a prayer room with a scroll painting of a guardian deity with which the family is linked and statues of Buddhist saints. Tibetans are great pilgrimage goers and constantly utter sacred formulas, such as *om mani padme hum*, an invocation of Tibet's protective Buddha, Chenrezi, at their daily tasks, as well as inscribing them on prayer flags, walls, or stones.

Since Tibet's incorporation into the People' Republic of China (1951), the status of Tibetans has become controversial. China claims that Tibet has been part of China since the thirteenth century. It has attempted to control Buddhism and has launched ideological campaigns against Tibetan claims of separate nationhood, insisting that Tibetans are one of fifty-five minority nationalities in China. Tibetans in exile, led by the fourteenth Dalai Lama (b. 1935) from Dharamsala in India, affirm a distinct national identity based on separate history, ethnicity, and culture and claim that China has systematically abused the human rights of the Tibetans.

Michael Kowalewski

Further Reading

Bell, Charles. (1928) *The People of Tibet.* New Delhi: Motilal Banarsidass.

Dalai Lama. (1988) *My Land and My People.* London: Times Warner International.

Norbu, T. J. (1987) *Tibet Is My Country.* London and Boston: Wisdom Publications.

Snellgrove, David, and Hugh Richardson. (1968) *A Cultural History of Tibet.* London: Weidenfeld & Nicholson.

TIBETO-BURMAN LANGUAGES Tibeto-Burman languages constitute one of the two branches of the large Sino-Tibetan family of languages (the other branch, the Sinitic languages, make up the dialects and varieties of Chinese languages). Languages of this family are spoken over a vast area of South and Southeast Asia, from the Karakoram mountains in the northwest to the isthmus of Malakka in the southeast. Speakers of various Tibeto-Burman languages are found in the Himalayan regions of Pakistan and India

(Jammu and Kashmir, Himachal Pradesh, Sikkim), the Indian northeast (Arunachal Pradesh, Assam, Mizoram, Tripura, Manipur, Meghalaya) and adjacent regions of Bangladesh, in Nepal, Bhutan, Myanmar (Burma), Thailand, Laos, Vietnam, and China (Tibet, Qinghai, Gansu, Yunnan, Sichuan).

In terms of the number of single languages belonging to the family, the Tibeto-Burman stock is, in Asia, second only to Austronesian. Though the principal subgroups of Tibeto-Burman are largely established, a comprehensive and uncontroversial subgrouping cannot yet be elaborated, mainly because we do not possess linguistically adequate descriptions for the better part of the several hundred single languages that make up the Tibeto-Burman stock.

Overview

The following classificatory overview assumes Tibeto-Burman to consist of six primary subgroups: Bodic, Baric, Burmic, Karenic, Qiangic, and possibly Rungic. Given that the linguistic classification of Tibeto-Burman is, at the time of writing, still a matter of considerable debate and controversy, it should be borne in mind that different classifications exist, and the one adopted here does not claim to be the only scientifically adequate one. (Most controversies surround the Southeast Asian branches of Tibeto-Burman.)

Bodic Languages One way of classifying Tibeto-Burman languages is to divide them into those spoken in the indospheric area (that is, the area under the cultural influence of India) and those spoken in the sinosphere (that is, the area under the cultural influence of China). This division is independent of purely linguistically based subdivisions of the stock and does not necessarily coincide with linguistic subdivisions. Using this division, we can say that Bodic (from Tibetan *bod* = "Tibet") languages are spoken in the indospheric part of the Tibeto-Burman area. Bodic may be further subdivided into the variants of Tibetan proper, Kanauri, Tamangic, Newari (these four are often taken together as the Bodish subgroup), Kiranti (Rai), Kham-Magar, and Bahing or Vayu (the latter three are often grouped together as the East Himalayish branch of Bodic).

Tibetan dialects, the first of the subgroupings of Bodic languages, are often classified according to their respective behavior regarding the preservation or simplification of the often very complicated consonant clusters found at the beginning of words in the old written language. Thus, archaic dialects (with some or most of these clusters intact) are opposed to innovative dialects where the onset of words has been simplified, mostly to the degree of allowing not more than one word-initial consonant. This feature corresponds largely to that of tonality, with innovative dialects showing more tonal contrasts than archaic ones, which may be marginally tonal or even completely atonal. Since archaic dialects are found mostly on the fringes of the Tibetan-speaking area, in the far west and far northeast, respectively, and archaisms generally do not allow classifying the dialects of a language (or the members of a family) in a historically meaningful way, the following enumeration of the most important Tibetan dialects—some of which would certainly justify treatment as independent languages—is mainly geographically based (the numbers of speakers are, where stated, approximate only): The Northeastern and Eastern groups of dialects are mostly referred to as Amdo (in Qinghai, and parts of Gansu) and Kham (Qinghai, Yunnan, Sichuan, eastern Tibet), respectively. Both include a large number of subdialects, which are mostly, but not invariably, rich in clusters and nontonal (i.e. "archaic"). Western Tibetan (mostly "archaic") is made up mainly of Balti (400,000 speakers in Northeastern Pakistan and Jammu and Kashmir, India), Purik (120,000 speakers in Kashmir), and Ladakhi (50,000 speakers in Ladakh and Jammu and Kashmir). The dialects of Lahul and Spiti (Himachal Pradesh) are described as "transitional" with respect to the archaic-innovative dichotomy. Central Tibetan dialects include the prestige variety and lingua franca for all of Tibet, Uke, (dBus-skad) or Tibetan proper, the best-known variety of which is the dialect of Lhasa. Tibetan dialects in Nepal are mostly innovative but sometimes transitional, the most important ones being the varieties of Dolpo and Mustang (gLo-skad) in the west, and Sherpa, Jirel, and Kagate in the east. Southern Tibetan includes the dialects spoken in Sikkim and Bhutan, mostly innovative, with Dzongkha being the national lingua franca of the Kingdom of Bhutan.

Tibetan has a long tradition as a literary language, beginning in the seventh century CE. Today, it continues to be the written medium of the Tibetan community in the Tibetan Autonomous Region of the People's Republic of China, as well as of the Tibetan diaspora. In Bhutan, Dzongkha is an officially written language; Ladakhi and Balti, too, are occasionally written, Ladakhi in Tibetan script, sometimes with reformed spellings. For Balti, a special script, based on the Perso-Arabic alphabet, was designed in the early twentieth century.

Kanauri (often grouped together with Tibetan into a Tibeto-Kanauri group) languages include Kanauri (25,000 speakers), Kanashi (1,000 speakers), and Bunan (2,000 speakers), spoken in Himachal Pradesh and Uttar Pradesh, India.

Almoran languages are Byangsi, Chaudangsi, Darmiya, and others, all of which are spoken in western Nepal and across the border in India, by about 2,000 speakers each.

Tamangic languages are all spoken within the boundaries of Nepal: Tamang (500,000 speakers), scattered over almost all of Nepal, but centered around the Kathmandu valley; Thakali (5,000 speakers), in the valley of the river Kali-Gandaki, Chantyal, western Nepal (Myagdi district); Gurung (150,000 speakers), in western Nepal (Gorkha and Kaski districts); and the languages of the villages of Manang, Nar, and Tsuk in the Mustang district.

Newari (500,000 speakers) is spoken in the Kathmandu valley (Kathmandu, Bhaktapur, Patan), where it continues to be the most common spoken language, despite the fact that Indo-Aryan Nepali is the state language of Nepal. Newari has been written at least since the seventeenth century.

The Kiranti (or Rai) languages are located in the eastern hills of Nepal, up to the Sikkimese border. The best known languages are Bantawa, Lohorung (10,000 speakers), Limbu (200,000 speakers), Thulung (20,000 speakers), and Chamling. Some investigators include the Kham-Magar languages (Kham, 25,000 speakers in western Nepal; Magar, 500,000 speakers to the south of Thakali) and Bahing or Vayu (3,000 speakers in eastern Nepal) in Kiranti. The theory of a closer relationship between Kiranti and Newari ("Mahakiranti") is also advocated.

Baric Languages The geographic center of the Baric branch of Tibeto-Burman (also called the Kamarupan branch; not all investigators agree that the languages subsumed under either term constitute a valid first-level branch of Tibeto-Burman) is northeastern India, Myanmar, and parts of southern China. The Konyak-Bodo-Garo subgroup includes the Konyak languages (for example, Ao, 80,000 speakers in Nagaland; Konyak proper, 95,000 speakers in Assam and Nagaland; and many more languages) and the Bodo-Garo languages (Bodo, 1,000,000 speakers in Assam and West Bengal; Garo, 500,000 speakers in western Assam and 90,000 speakers in northern Bangladesh; Dimasa, 70,000 speakers in the Cachar hills, Assam). The Kuki-Chin-Naga subgroup is further subdivided into Kuki-Chin (with 700,000 speakers of a great number of Chin dialects in Myanmar, as well as in Assam, Manipur, and Nagaland), and Kuki languages such as Anal, Lushei, and possibly Lepcha, together totaling about 412,000 speakers). Of the Naga languages, which are centered in Nagaland (Konyak languages are sometimes, erroneously, also referred to as "Naga," obviously for purely ethnographic reasons), the better-known languages are Sema (65,000 speakers in Nagaland and Assam), Mao (60,000 speakers in Manipur and Nagaland), and Angami (40,000 speakers in Manipur and Nagaland). The Mikir-Meithei group consists of Mikir and Meithei (Mikir with more than 1,000 000 speakers in northeastern India, Bangladesh, and Myanmar; Meithei with 200,000 speakers in Assam). Abor-Miri-Dafla or Mirish languages include, among others, Adi or Miri (400,000 speakers in Assam), Lhoba (200,000 speakers in Arunachal Pradesh), and Nisi (30,000 speakers in Assam and Arunachal Pradesh). Mru (60,000 speakers in Myanmar's Arakan hills) may constitute an independent subbranch of Baric, as may Jinghpo or Kachin (600,000 speakers in Kachin State, Myanmar, and adjacent regions of China). Kachin has alternatively been classified as Burmic or as an independent first-level branch of Tibeto-Burman, Kachinic.

Burmic Languages Burmic, or Burmese-Lolo, languages are widespread in Southeast Asia, namely in Myanmar, parts of Thailand, Laos, Vietnam, and south China (Yunnan). They can be clearly subdivided into a Burmish and a Lolo subbranch. Burmish languages may be further grouped into Northern Burmish (Achang, 20,000 speakers in western Yunnan; Atsi, 80,000 speakers in Yunnan who are officially part of the Jinghpo nationality; Maru, 100,000 speakers in Kachin state, Myanmar) and Southern Burmish, which consists mainly of Burmese and its varieties. Burmese is the national language of Myanmar, spoken by more than 20,000,000 speakers, and has been a literary language since the twelfth century. The written standard is focused on the dialect of the Irrawaddy valley. The Lolo subbranch consists of Northern Lolo and Southern Lolo. Northern Lolo in turn includes Lisu (more than 600,000 speakers in Yunnan, Sichuan, and Northern Thailand), Yi (more than 3,000,000 speakers in Sichuan, Yunnan, and southeastern Tibet; this language is also referred to as Lolo, but the term is nowadays regarded as derogatory), and Naxi or Moso (250,000 speakers in Yunnan and Sichuan). Southern Lolo includes Akha (350,000 speakers in Yunnan, Thailand, Laos, and Vietnam), Hani (more than 500,000 speakers in Yunnan), and Lahu (more than 500,000 speakers in Yunnan, Myanmar, Thailand, and Laos). There are also a number of clearly Loloish languages that could not be assigned to either group. One example is Tujia, spoken by 200,000 speakers in Hunan and Hubei, China.

Karenic Languages Karenic languages, sometimes viewed not as a part of Tibeto-Burman but as a higher-level grouping, coordinate with Tibeto-Burman within Sino-Tibetan and are spoken on both sides of the Thailand-Myanmar frontier (notably in Myanmar's Karen state); the two most important varieties are Pwo Karen (1,300,000 speakers in both countries but mostly in Myanmar) and Sgaw Karen (2,000,000 speakers, of whom 300,000 live in Thailand).

Qiangic, Rungic, and Other Languages The remaining languages and small groups have not been assigned to any of the above-mentioned groups so far, and their ultimate place in the family remains open. These are Qiang(ic), with 130,000 speakers in western Sichuan; Nungish (including Rawang, with 100,000 speakers in Kachin state, Myanmar, Tibet, and Yunnan; and Nung, with 6,000 speakers in Yunnan); Primi ,or Pumi, with 25,000 speakers in northwest Yunnan; and Gyarong (sometimes viewed as another Bodish language), with 100,000 speakers in Sichuan. The latter three groups have been tentatively united into a Rungish branch of Tibeto-Burman.

The Bai or Minjia language, spoken by more than 1,000,000 speakers in northern Yunnan, has resisted most attempts to classify it linguistically; it is sometimes viewed as a language isolate or as another Sinitic language, but the view that it forms an independent first-level branch of Tibeto-Burman ("Baic") is gaining ground.

Typology, Tone, and Morphology

Though the genetic unity of the family is clearly established, the different branches of Tibeto-Burman show a considerable degree of typological diversity. In terms of word order, most Tibeto-Burman languages are verb-final, with the notable exception of Karenic, where the basic order is subject-verb-object, as in Chinese.

The mainly culturally motivated division of Tibeto-Burman languages into sinospheric and indospheric languages has some linguistic corollaries, in that the former languages conform more to the linguistic type of Southeast Asian languages, or, for that matter, Chinese, in possessing few if any morphological markers attached to lexical roots (the so-called isolating typology widespread in the area), whereas some languages of the Kiranti group (in the indosphere) rank among the morphologically most complex languages of Asia.

Lexical tone is widespread in the family (a system of two register tones may be reconstructible for the protolanguage), but actual tone systems differ widely, and some of them, especially the systems found in the more central varieties of Tibetan, represent late and secondary developments from a nontonal stage. The general pattern to be observed is that tonal systems tend to replace earlier contrasts of voicing of root-initial consonants (with initial voiceless consonants yielding high tone, and voiced consonants leading low tone, a phenomenon particularly observable in Bodish languages), but numerous details remain to be worked out. In Southeast Asia, some Tibeto-Burman languages are particularly rich in tonal contrasts, such as Nasu (Loloish), which has seven tones, but nontonal languages occur as well, such as Northern Qiang (the closely related Southern Qiang, by contrast, has six phonemic tones).

An important typological parameter in Tibeto-Burman morphological systems is that of person agreement of verbs. The range of possibilities exploited in Tibeto-Burman languages reaches from completely apersonal verbs, over verbal systems with subject agreement only, to systems that signal both subject and object person in the morphological verb complex.

A language like Thakali (Tamangic), for example, shows no person agreement at all, as in *nga tru-si mu* "I am sitting," *ki tru-si mu* "you are sitting," *the tru-si mu* "s/he is sitting" (*nga, ki, the* are the personal pronouns, *tru* the verbal root "to sit," *-si mu* a nonfinite, participle-like verbal form called a "converb," made final by the copula *mu*), where only the different personal pronouns serve to distinguish between subject persons. Byangsi, a language of the Almoran group, has a person-agreement system in verbs that shows, as in many European languages, the person of the subject in the verb. Thus *zage-ye* "I eat," *zage-no* "you eat," *zage-n* "she/he eats." In some Kiranti languages, transitive verbs encode the person of the object as well. For example, Chamling: *ta-tyok-u* "you saw him/her," *ta-tyok-a* "she/he saw you," *tyok-u-m-ka* "we saw him/her" (where *tyok-* is the verbal root "to see," *ta-* the marker of the second person, *-u* the third-person object, and *-m-ka* the first-person exclusive; note that third person is marked only when in object function). The actual verbal agreement paradigms of Kiranti languages are much more complicated than this fragment can illustrate and pose considerable problems of synchronic and diachronic interpretation. Opinions are still divided on whether the complex agreement patterns of the Kiranti type represent the original state of proto-Tibeto-Burman or, rather, are secondary developments of these languages, possibly under the influence of Munda (Austroasiatic) languages, which are spoken further south in India.

Stefan Georg

Further Reading

Beyer, Stephan V. (1992) *The Classical Tibetan Language.* New York: State University of New York Press.

DeLancey, Scott. (1987) "Sino-Tibetan Languages." In *The World's Major Languages*, edited by Bernard Comrie. London: Routledge, 797–810.

Denwood, Philip. (1999) *Tibetan.* Amsterdam and Philadelphia: Routledge.

Ebert, Karen H. (1994) *The Structure of Kiranti Languages: Comparative Grammar and Texts.* Zurich: Universität Zurich.

Georg, Stefan. (1996) *Marphatan Thakali.* Munich, Germany; Newcastle, U.K.: Lincom-Europa.

Hale, A. (1974) *Research on Tibeto-Burman Languages.* The Hague, Netherlands: Mouton.

Ramsey, S. Robert. (1987) *The Languages of China.* Princeton, NJ: Princeton University Press.

TIGER   The tiger (*Panthera tigris*) is one of the world's strongest and most endangered creatures. The largest member of the cat family, it inhabits the swamps, forests, and grasslands of Asia. The tiger's coat of thick fur can vary from yellow to dark orange-brown. Tigers are the only striped cats and the pattern of each tiger's dark vertical stripes is unique (like a human fingerprint), providing excellent camouflage. White tigers, with brown stripes and blue eyes, are very rare in the wild. Tigers have sharp teeth and extremely powerful jaws, neck, and limbs. They can run very fast for short periods of time and leap huge distances. They are also strong swimmers and can cross wide rivers. Tigers are generally about three meters long, including tail. An adult male tiger weighs 180 to 250 kilograms.

All tigers belong to the same species, but there are several subspecies. The best known are the Siberian (Amur) tiger (*Panthera tigris altaica*), which lives in the forests of the Russian Far East; the Bengal tiger (*Panthera tigris tigris*), which lives in the grasslands and forests of India, Myanmar (Burma), and the Himalayas;

A pair of Bengal tigers photographed in c. 1994. (DAVID A. NORTHCOTT/CORBIS)

MANAS WILDLIFE PRESERVE— WORLD HERITAGE SITE

Designated by UNESCO as both a World Heritage Site (1985) and a World Heritage Site in Danger (1992), the Manas Wildlife Preserve is still a vitally important refuge for many animals including the majestic Bengal tiger.

and the Sumatran tiger (*Panthera tigris sumatrae*), which inhabits the Indonesian island of Sumatra.

The tiger is a carnivore that usually hunts alone and at night. Its prey ranges from large mammals, such as deer and wild pigs, to monkeys, frogs, and fish. Prey is usually killed with a strong bite to the neck. Occasionally young elephants and rhinoceroses are attacked. The killing of cattle and other livestock sometimes brings tigers into conflict with people. Rarely do tigers attack and kill people.

Tigers are solitary animals and each tiger has its own territory. Male territories often overlap with female territories. Cubs are usually born in litters of two or three and stay with their mother for two years. A tiger's life span is about twenty years.

Tigers are critically endangered. Very few tigers remain in the wild, and several subspecies, such as the Javanese tiger (*Panthera tigris sondaica*), are believed to already be extinct. Tigers are illegally killed for their bones, which are used in traditional Chinese medicines, and for their coats. They also suffer from the effects of deforestation and habitat destruction. Many zoos have set up breeding programs, and India and Nepal have designated special tiger reserves.

Lucy D. Moss

Further Reading

Alderton, David, and Bruce Tanner. (1998) *Wild Cats of the World.* New York: Sterling.

IUCN–World Conservation Union. (2000) "The 2000 IUCN Red List of Threatened Species." Retrieved 13 March 2002, from: http://www.redlist.org.

Thapar, Valmik. (1992) *The Tiger's Destiny.* London: Kyle Cathie Ltd.

TIGRIS RIVER The Tigris (biblical name, Hiddekel; in Arabic, Dijlah; in Turkish, Dicle) is one of the two great rivers of Mesopotamia (present-day Iraq). Approximately 1,900 kilometers long, it rises in southeastern Turkey at Lake Hazar in the Taurus Mountains and flows southeast for about 450 kilometers toward the city of Cizre, to form a 32-kilometer border between Turkey and Syria before entering Iraq. Unlike its twin the Euphrates River, the Tigris flows directly toward the Mesopotamian plain to join the Euphrates at the town of al-Qurnah, in southeast Iraq, whence it forms the Shatt al-Arab, 193 kilometers long, before it discharges into the Persian Gulf.

Along its upper course, the Tigris flows swiftly in well-defined channels through the gorges of east Anatolia and the Syrian and Iraqi plateaus. Numerous left-bank tributaries augment its water during its passage through Iraq. Downstream from the city of Mosul, the Tigris is joined by its two main tributaries, the Greater Zab and the Lesser Zab, originating in the eastern Zagros Mountains. Close to Samarra, the river enters the head of the Mesopotamian alluvial plain and begins to meander slowly toward the gulf. Here the Tigris receives water from other tributaries, which together with the two Zab streams provide more than 50 percent of its discharge. The flow of the Tigris, however, varies considerably, and its flow decreases rapidly along its lower course through seepage, evaporation, and intensive water use.

Losing velocity, the river deposits its silt and raises its bed level above the surrounding alluvial plain. It becomes prone to its renowned seasonal overflows and to historically altering its course. To avert the danger of inundations, in addition to expanding irrigation schemes and generating power, Iraq has constructed a system of dams and barrages on the river. Over its remaining course toward the gulf, the main stream of the river is divided into several channels 320 kilometers south of Baghdad, which irrigate the rice-growing areas and feed into the extensive marshes formed along the southern part of the plain.

Along the Tigris emerged the earliest centers of urban civilizations sustained by ancient waterworks. On its banks stood some of the great Mesopotamian cities, including the Assyrian capitals of Nineveh, Calah, and Ashur; the Hellenistic city of Seleucia; the capital of the Sasanids, Ctesiphon; and the Abbasid capitals of Baghdad and Samarra.

Manat H. Al-Shawi

Further Reading

Biswas, Asit K., ed. (1994) *International Waters of the Middle East: From Euphrates-Tigris to Nile.* Oxford, U.K.: Oxford University Press.

Hillel, Daniel. (1994) *Rivers of Eden: The Struggle for Water and the Quest for Peace in the Middle East.* New York: Oxford University Press.

Soffer, Arnon. (1999) *Rivers of Fire: The Conflict over Water in the Middle East.* Lanham, MD: Rowman & Littlefield.

TILE WORK—CENTRAL ASIA

Glazed bricks with painted or painted-and-molded designs had been used as early as the thirteenth century BCE, as architectural decorations in the Elamite kingdom in modern Iran; Assyrian royal architecture also made use of such glazed brick decorations, although the most elaborate known examples are undoubtedly Nebuchadnezzar's (604–562 BCE) vast constructions in Babylon and the palace at Susa, the capital of the Achaemenid Persian dynasty (559–358 BCE).

Tile work became a decorative element in the architecture of Central Asia with the establishment of Islamic culture in that region, particularly on buildings of brick. The use of embellishment incorporating geometric and vegetal patterns, harmoniously balanced colors, and elaborate script decoration is an architectural achievement unique to the Islamic tradition.

In the tenth century, the Abbasid dynasty (749/750–1258) commissioned scientists to develop a white glaze that imitated the appearance of Chinese porcelain over the local brown clays. The result was tin glaze, considered very precious and used on royal dishes. This lead-based glaze was combined with the following metal oxides to produce colors: tin for white, copper for turquoise and green, cobalt for deep blue, iron for brown and yellow, manganese for purple mauve, and combined oxides for black. Tiles were incorporated into architecture in the late medieval period. In Central Asia under the Selljuks, Mongols, Timurids, and Khanates, buildings were decorated with precious glazed tiles to provide both body and soul with a soothing environment. Designs evolved from individual colored shapes as in mosaics; textured clay tiles were carved and glazed; eventually, square tiles with patterns extending beyond the individual squares were produced. Under the Abbasids, when Persian domination extended to Central Asia, tile decoration was again introduced to this area.

In Islamic architecture in Central Asia, tile decoration adorned public buildings, mausoleums, and royal residences. At first, turquoise-colored tiles were used as contrast with the terra-cotta color of the bricks; in eastern Islamic tradition, turquoise represents good luck and heaven. In time, *eyvan*s (open halls around mosque courtyards), minarets (prayer towers), *minbar*s (pulpits), domes, and complete walls of mausoleums, *madrasa*s (religious schools), and mosques were decorated with tile work. Patterns could be created by using individual mosaic pieces of different colors to form

Detail of an Islamic tile work geometric motif from Samarqand, Uzbekistan. (GERARD DEGEORGE/CORBIS)

extremely complex geometric or floral designs that were intertwined to magnify a text or floral, astrological, or geometric themes.

Colored patterns were achieved by various methods. Mosaics were glazed pieces cut after firing; a colored pattern was arranged face down and covered with plaster, with reinforced sticks embedded into the mixture. Such panels could be lifted and attached to a façade. *Cuerda seca* (Spanish, "dry line") technique allowed the separation of color on a tile in chambers segregated by a grease line. Another method of coloring tiles was to use thick tin glaze with color additions painted on the unfired surface. Tin glaze is highly viscous, and colors stay fixed. Golds and red luster (a metallic glaze developed in Seljuk pottery) painted onto the tin-glazed fired surfaces required an additional firing to achieve a brilliant gold color. Designs could also be painted onto small tiles of various shapes. Textured patterns sometimes formed elaborate sections of columnar structures bordering doorways and accentuating the colored themes of a building.

The building process *banna'i*, developed under Timur (1336–1405) and his successors, created patterns of glazed brick ends in blue, white, or black, contrasting with the unglazed terra-cotta building material. Further color was added by using light blue, white, purple, black, green, and amber on a field of dark blue. *Thuluth* and *kufic* scripts decorated vertical and horizontal borders. The scripts often quoted from the Qur'an, sometimes passages related to the function of the particular building, or they acknowledged a donor of the building. When whole surfaces were adorned with geometric patterns that grew in algebraic complexity but had no central focus or theme, this technique reflected a philosophical aspect of Islamic design; such decoration was conducive to meditation or expressed a spiritual concept. Patterns were sometimes based on the cycles of the moon and were amplified with subdivisions and large areas of visual unity by using color.

The best place to study architectural tiles as they were used up to the fifteenth century is at the city of Samarqand in Uzbekistan. Here one can observe every technique used in tile making: glazed terra-cotta, polychrome glazed carved tiles, *cuerda seca*, mosaic, overglaze, underglaze, and luster. During Timur's rule, when this city was his capital, large areas of architectural surfaces received decorative tile treatment with a restricted number of motifs, according to his mandates. In the mausoleum complex of the Timurid dynasty, the Sha-i Zinda, one tomb may exhibit examples of carved brick or flat tiles decorated in underglaze, glaze, overglaze, and luster techniques. On the façade of the tomb of Shirin Bika Agha (Timur's sister), every inch of surface is covered with blue, turquoise, and white patterns, creating a dazzling visual effect that encourages meditation. In contrast, stunning examples of *banna'i* on the portal and minaret of the *masjid-i jami* of Timur use bold contrast between raw terracotta and glazed brick ends to define the huge forms capped with a brilliant sky-blue dome. Timur's tomb retains the brilliant lustered niches that make up the interior of the dome.

Marcia Selsor

Further Reading

Hillenbrand, Robert. (1994) *Islamic Architecture*. New York: Columbia University Press.

Hoag, John D. (1977) *Islamic Architecture*. New York: Abrams.

Lentz, Thomas W., and Glenn D. Lowry. (1989) *Timur and the Princely Vision*. Los Angeles and Washington, DC: Los Angeles County Museum of Art and Arthur M. Sackler Gallery, Smithsonian Institution.

Pulatov, T., and L. Y. Mankovskaia. (1991) *Bukhara: A Museum in the Open*. Tashkent, Uzbekistan: Gafur Gulyam Art and Literature Publisher.

TIMBER INDUSTRY—MALAYSIA

Timber as an export commodity began contributing to the Malaysian economy only toward the end of the nineteenth century. The timber industry started in today's East Malaysian state of Sabah (formerly British North Borneo) in the 1880s. Despite attempts in neighboring Sarawak (ruled by the Brooke Raj and then a British colony from 1946), it was only after World War II (1941–1945) that the industry became significant there and even overtook Sabah in both production and exports. Likewise the industry became important in peninsular Malaysia (formerly British Malaya) after

1945. In 1963, Sabah and Sarawak joined the independent Federation of Malaya (1957), which in 1963 became the Federation of Malaysia.

The timber industry of Sabah began with a chance sale of felled timber from a clearance of land near the seaport town of Sandakan for sugar planting. In February 1885, the first shipment of felled timber headed for Australia. Other shipments followed, and by the 1930s Sandakan had become one of the major timber ports of the world.

The leading market for the tropical hardwood known as *billian* was Hong Kong, where it was used for sleepers in the expanding railway network then being undertaken in China. Timber companies at that time were in European hands, namely the British North Borneo Trading and Planting Company and the British Borneo Timber Company. Timber was Sabah's major export from the 1910s onward; exports, mainly in logs, reached their peak in 1937. Before 1941, Sabah was the third-largest timber exporter in the British empire, with markets in Hong Kong, Japan, Britain, and Australia.

In Sarawak, the Borneo Company exported small quantities of *billian* to Hong Kong and Calcutta. But inexperience, difficult terrain, and fluctuating timber prices hampered large-scale operations during the pre-1941 period. A few Chinese logging companies also served the overseas market, and the European-owned VAMCO Timber Company pioneered the export of sawn timber and plywood in the 1930s.

Timber Production in Independent Malaysia

Timber production and exports from peninsular Malaysia became significant only from the late 1960s. Together with production from Sabah and Sarawak, timber became the third leading export of Malaysia after rubber and tin. The 1980s and 1990s witnessed Malaysia's becoming one of the world's largest exporters of tropical hardwood, accounting for 37 percent of world production (1998). Timber-based industries produced a wide assortment of wood products, from sawn timber, plywood, and veneer to prefabricated houses and furniture, including rattan furniture for domestic and overseas markets.

The two major organizations related to the timber industry are the Forest Research Institute of Malaysia (FRIM) and the Malaysian Timber Industry Board (MTIB). FRIM undertakes research in forest development aimed at sustainable growth and conservation of the resource base. MTIB regulates and controls the timber trade, including marketing and distribution, and promotes effective utilization of Malaysian-produced timber.

Conservation Issues

Conservation and regulation of the timber industry began in Sabah in the early 1910s, with the establishment of the Forestry Department. Forest reserves were designated, and silviculture and research were undertaken to ensure that the forest remained a sustainable resource asset. In the post-1945 period, measures to arrest the adverse consequences of logging activities and to ensure sustainable management of forest resources included the creation of the Permanent Forest Estate (PFE) and the rehabilitation of logged-over forest through different types of silvicultural treatments. The National Forestry Policy implemented since 1978 was revised in 1992 to include the conservation of biological diversity, sustainable utilization of genetic resources, and the role of local communities in forest development.

The adverse effects of logging activities on the environment have been overstated, as has the negative impact of logging on forest dwellers. Measures have been undertaken to ensure that the nomadic livelihood of the Penans in Sarawak and of some Orang Asli communities in peninsular Malaysia is not overlooked or compromised vis-à-vis the timber industry. Prudent steps adopted by the Malaysian government include setting aside vast areas (44 percent of total land area) as PFE, as well as the designation of some 2.12 million hectares as national parks and wildlife and bird sanctuaries. Malaysia has actively supported organizations such as the International Tropical Timber Organization (ITTO) with its ITTO Year 2000 Objective, and the United Nations Conference on Environment and Development (UNCED). Malaysia wholly subscribed to the Statement of Principles on Forest under Agenda 21 of UNCED. Furthermore, Malaysia is undertaking bilateral-cooperation forest projects with Denmark, Germany, and Japan to enhance sustainable forest development further.

The Malaysian timber industry contributed 5.3 percent of total export earnings of some RM 17.1 billion in 1999 and steadily increasing to RM 17.7 billion in 2000.

Ooi Keat Gin

Further Reading

Amarjit, Kaur. (1998) *Economic Change in East Malaysia: Sabah and Sarawak since 1850.* Basingstoke, U.K., and London: Macmillan; New York: St Martin's Press.

Kumar, Raj. (1986) *The Forest Resources of Malaysia: Their Economics and Development.* Singapore: Oxford University Press.

Ooi Keat Gin. (1997) *Of Free Trade and Native Interests: The Brookes and the Economic Development of Sarawak, 1841–1941.* Kuala Lumpur, Malaysia: Oxford University Press.

TIMOR SEA The Timor Sea is a small stretch of water between the island of Timor and northern Australia. As a result of the colonial division of Timor between the Netherlands (west) and Portugal (east), the western half of the island is now part of Indonesia's East Nusa Tenggara Province, while East Timor, under effective Indonesian rule from 1975 to 1999, is now an independent entity. Under the provisions of the Law of the Sea, the Timor Sea had to be demarcated, but, controversially, Australia negotiated with Indonesia to divide the sea between itself and East Timor, despite Indonesia's illegal acquisition of the former Portuguese territory.

In 1989 an agreement entitled the Treaty Between Australia and the Republic of Indonesia on the Zone of Cooperation in an Area Between the Indonesian Province and Northern Australia, also known as the Timor Gap Treaty, was signed (and implemented in 1991). The treaty established a zone of cooperation of 61 thousand square kilometers to facilitate the exploitation of petroleum resources. The central area of the zone, known as zone A (or ZOCA), consists of 34,970 square kilometers of seabed estimated to be able to yield 7 billion barrels of oil and 50 trillion cubic feet of natural gas. The Timor Gap Treaty allowed Australia to divide future revenues equally with Indonesia; both countries also were to provide to each other 10 percent of revenues derived from the zones nearest their respective shores (zones B and C). On 10 February 2000, by the Exchange of Notes between Australia and the United Nations Transitional Administration in East Timor, the parties agreed to roll over the Timor Gap Treaty, but with revenues now going to East Timor. In 2001 the United Nations renegotiated the treaty in favor of East Timor (ZOCA revenues of 90 percent), and this is expected to generate between $150 million and $200 million a year by around 2005.

Anthony L. Smith

TIMUR (1336–1405), emperor of the Mongol empire. Born in what is now Uzbekistan, Timur, known as Temur-i-Lenk ("Timur the Lame," or in English, Tamerlane) because his right arm and leg were paralyzed from arrow wounds, was the last of the great nomadic Mongol emperors. He carved an empire from the remnants of the Mongol territories in Central Asia and spent his life campaigning throughout the Middle East, India, and Russia. He defeated the Golden Horde (a separate wing of the Mongol empire, which flourished in Russia in the latter half of the thirteenth century) in 1387 and 1391, sacked Delhi in 1398, and

SHAKHRISYABZ—WORLD HERITAGE SITE

Designated a UNESCO World Heritage Site in 2000, Shakhrisyabz (in Uzbekistan) is a collection of monuments from the medieval empire of Timur. The important historical site, which dates back to the fifteenth century, represents the zenith of Timurid craftsmanship.

defeated Bayezid I (c.1360–1403), sultan of the Ottoman empire, in 1402. During his reign he was known as Emir (Amir) Timur.

Timur is remembered most for his conquests and cruelty. He orchestrated many massacres and left numerous towers of skulls as reminders to the conquered of his authority. Although today we remember him for his brutality, he was also noted for being very intelligent, an expert chess player, fluent in several languages—despite being illiterate—and well-versed in debate. Playwrights such as Christopher Marlowe (1564–1593) penned plays about him, inspired by his larger-than-life character. Timur died in 1404 while undertaking the conquest of Ming-dynasty China. Although his empire disintegrated after his death, his descendents established the Mughal empire in India.

Timothy May

Further Reading
Arabshah, Ahmed ibn. (1936) *Tamerlane or Timur the Great Amir.* Lahore, India: Progressive Books.
Gonzalez, Clavijo. (1928) *Embassy to Tamerlane.* London: George Routledge and Sons.
Hookham, Hilda. (1962) *Tamburlaine the Conqueror.* London: Hodder and Stoughton.
Manz, Beatrice Forbes. (1991) *The Rise and Rule of Tamerlane.* New York: Cambridge University Press.

TIN INDUSTRY The only tin-bearing mineral of any significance is cassiterite, SnO_2. It is comparatively rare, and the bulk of the world's deposits are located in a belt running from southern China to Indonesia. The deposits are of two kinds, primary deposits in lodes underground and secondary or alluvial deposits formed through erosion. Since the alluvium is close to the surface, it is easily extracted, and the heavier particles of cassiterite are separated by washing. Asia is particularly fortunate since the bulk of its deposits are alluvial.

The low melting point of tin makes it easy to reduce the cassiterite to metal through smelting and contributes to its utility in a wide variety of products. Around 3000 BCE the inhabitants of Southwest Asia recognized the metallurgical properties of tin and added a small proportion of tin to transform copper into the much more versatile bronze. Bronze made sharper weapons and better tools than did stone, and it became an essential element in the emergence of civilization. As civilization developed, especially in China, tin was consumed in large quantities for functional objects, such as mirrors, plates, and wine cups, as well as ceremonial objects, such as bells and candlesticks for ancestral altars. Religion provided a particular stimulus, and by the eighth century CE tin was beaten into thin strips to form backing for joss paper, a sacrificial paper inscribed with prayers and burned. With the industrial revolution in Europe, entirely new uses emerged, including coating for steel in tin cans, tinfoil for wrapping food, collapsible tubes for paints and pastes, solder, and bearing metals.

The combination of utility and scarcity made tin a particularly valuable commodity, and it therefore played an important role in the development of trading networks. At first these connected Southeast Asia to China, India, and the Near East. By 1850 a global market had emerged, and Southeast Asia supplied well over half of the world demand, a position the region maintained until the 1980s. The history of the industry can be divided into phases.

The Emergence of the Chinese
From earliest times the main centers of tin production were the Ko-chiu district in Yunnan, southwest China, and the Tavoy region in Myanmar (Burma). In the sixteenth century the earliest European traders, the Portuguese, found that the main centers had moved to Phuket, Thailand, and Melaka, in present-day Malaysia. By the eighteenth century the Dutch had turned the island of Bangka, Indonesia, into the largest producer. For the following two hundred years immigrant Chinese displaced local Burmese, Malay, and Thai miners, and a few became wealthy mine owners and merchants. Mines were an important source of wealth not simply because of the richness of their deposits but also because of the opportunities for exploitation of the immigrant labor force through gambling and opium. Collapsing political authority in Malaya (now Malaysia) led to open warfare from 1862 to 1872 as rival sultans and Chinese gangs vied for control over the tin trade, forcing British intervention and the creation of the Federated Malay States in 1874. Siam (now Thailand) avoided a similar fate thanks to the role played by the

Khaw family. The founder of this extended Sino-Thai family had arrived in the tin district in the 1820s and was largely responsible for its overall economic development throughout the nineteenth century. Chinese rioting in 1876 was curbed by the Khaws and the family then became the dominant economic force in the region, with extensive mining, shipping, general commerce, and tax farming. It also became a dominant political force thanks to support from the central government in Bangkok. In the Dutch East Indies (DEI) Chinese mining was subject to direct European control, on Bangka by the Dutch government and on Belitung and Singkep by private Dutch companies.

Displacement of the Chinese

Europeans had a technical advantage in smelting tin concentrates, producing a high-quality metal better suited to the needs of American and European industry. In 1886 the Singapore smelter of the Straits Trading Company (STC) opened and began to eliminate the small, local Chinese smelters. In response the Khaw family built a modern smelter in Penang (an island in present-day Malaysia) in 1907, but the family sold out to British capitalists in 1910. The whole region then had just three important smelting complexes, Bangka, Penang, and Singapore, which treated ores from Alaska to South Africa.

Traditional Chinese mining techniques became obsolete as the quality of the deposits declined, and beginning in 1900 European technologies predominated. The gravel pump, which broke down the tin-bearing alluvium under a high-pressure jet of water, was widely adopted by Chinese miners, but the most important technical innovation was the bucket dredge, which could work low-grade and hitherto inaccessible deposits at a low cost. Dredges worked on the seabeds off Thailand and the DEI, but they also reworked deposits the Chinese considered exhausted. Dredging transformed the industry, significantly increasing production in the 1920s and drawing on fresh sources of capital, mainly from Britain and Australia. Both the capital and technical requirements of dredging led to a consolidation of the tin industry into a few corporate groups, of which the most important was the London Tin Corporation (LTC).

The LTC originated in an Anglo-German jute-trading firm in Calcutta, India, that first developed dredging in Burma in the early 1920s. The company then extended its reach throughout the world, becoming the largest producer in Malaya, Siam, and Japan. Good prices and expanded production in the 1920s generated large revenues for local governments.

The tin industry avoided the worst of the depression of the 1930s thanks to the cooperation of most of the important tin producers, members of the International Tin Committee formed through the efforts of the LTC, including Malaya, the DEI and Siam, but not including China or Burma.

China remained largely insulated from these processes of modernization. The close link between Chinese miners and local smelters blocked the sale of ores to foreign interests and perpetuated obsolete technologies. However, by 1935 the Yunnan provincial government developed a smelter that produced a metal of international standards and opened a modern mine.

Displacement of the Europeans

Much mining capacity was destroyed during the Japanese conquest of Southeast Asia in 1942, which changed the balance of power in the tin industry. The United States entered the post;enWorld War II period determined to build a stockpile to protect against any repetition of the interruption of tin supplies, a policy confirmed by the 1949 revolution in China and the Communist insurgency in Malaya (1948–1960). By 1954 the stockpile was completed, and the world again faced the problem of chronic excess productive capacity, requiring regulation through a new form of international commodity control, the International Tin Council.

In the DEI, the industry was quickly rehabilitated thanks to good contracts for the U.S. stockpile. However, these contracts coincidentally expired as Indonesia became fully independent in 1954, and it then proceeded to take over all Dutch mining interests, which the government eventually consolidated into a fully nationalized company, PT Timah. At first the lack of fresh investment, managerial inefficiency, and attacks on the Chinese miners combined to reduce production, but investments in seagoing dredges stimulated recovery during the1970s. Political uncertainty in Malaysia, which was established as a federated country in 1963, meant that rehabilitation drew more on local Chinese capital, which also acquired control over the STC. The New Economic Policy of the Malaysian government accelerated these trends, and in 1978 Malaysia Mining Corporation was formed, which acquired London Tin and other European dredging companies. In 1981 Malaysia Mining forged close links with the remaining STC smelter in Malaysia.

The Thais restructured their interests in LTC and other foreign dredging companies to permit majority Thai ownership. In 1965 Thailand realized its goal of establishing an important domestic smelter, though it remained under foreign control. In both Malaysia and Thailand the balance shifted away from bucket dredging back toward small-scale techniques, such as gravel pumps on land and suction boats offshore. The LTC rebuilt its Burmese dredges, which were nationalized in the 1960s. As the new state corporation shifted production toward gravel pumps, overall output declined. Government control over all the mines of Ko-chiu, China, allowed modernization and considerable expansion in production there.

China's limited cooperation with other tin-producing countries in their attempts to control output contributed to the collapse of the International Tin Council in 1985 and to a large drop in price. Indonesia and China managed to survive the tin crisis, but production fell off sharply in both Thailand and Malaysia, bringing to an end the strategic role tin played in their economies.

John Hillman

Further Reading

Cushman, Jennifer. (1991) *Family and State: The Formation of a Sino-Thai Tin-Mining Dynasty, 1797–1932.* Singapore: Oxford University Press.

Golas, Peter. (1991) "Tin Mining in Nineteenth-and-Twentieth-Century China: High Production, Low Technology." In *Science and Technology in Modern China*, edited by Yang Tsui-hua and Huang Yi-lung. Taipei, Taiwan: Academia Sinica, 261–294.

Hedges, Ernest. (1964) *Tin in Social and Economic History.* London: Edward Arnold.

Hillman, John. (1988) "Malaya and the International Tin Cartel." *Modern Asian Studies* 22, 2: 365–389.

Somers Heidhues, Mary. (1992) *Bangka Tin and Mentok Pepper: Chinese Settlement on an Indonesian Island.* Singapore: Institute of Southeast Asian Studies.

Thoburn, John. (1994) *Tin in the World Economy.* Edinburgh: Edinburgh University Press.

Wong Lin Ken. (1965) *The Malayan Tin Industry to 1914.* Tucson, AZ: University of Arizona Press.

Yip Yat Hoong. (1969) *The Development of the Tin Mining Industry of Malaya.* Kuala Lumpur, Malaysia: University of Malaya Press.

TIPU SULTAN

TIPU SULTAN (1749–1799), ruler of Mysore, a kingdom located on the southwest coast of the Indian subcontinent. Tipu Sultan is remembered for his relentless struggle against British colonial rule during his reign. The son of Hyder Ali, he was born at Devanhalli in the modern Indian state of Karnataka. Tipu joined his father in the First Mysore War (1767–1769), the first of four battles fought between the British and the rulers of Mysore, in which the British were defeated.

Gumbaz, the mausoleum of Tipu Sultan in Seringapatam, India. (SHELDAN COLLINS/CORBIS)

When he became king following the death of Hyder in 1782, Tipu inherited a powerful kingdom. The peace treaty of 1784, signed between the British and Tipu, was a temporary phenomenon that became the main obstacle to British domination in south India. Tipu had sought the help of the French and the Turks in building an alliance against the British but with little success. In the third Mysore war, Tipu was defeated by the British and ceded half of his territories to the British empire in 1792. The subsidiary alliance system (the surrender of territory by Indian rulers for the upkeep of British subsidiary troops) implemented by Richard Colley Wellesley, the new governor-general of Bengal (1797–1805), was a clever ploy to bring Indian rulers under the suzerainty of the British empire, and Tipu fiercely opposed it. His capital, Seringapatam, fell to the British army on 4 May 1799; in this final Mysore battle, Tipu died.

A Muslim himself, Tipu adopted a tolerant policy of rule; he treated Hindus well and gave grants to their religious institutions. He showed great concern for the welfare of all of his subjects. Trade and commerce greatly improved, and he built a modern navy. Tipu's passion was driving the British out of India, and he became a martyr for that cause.

Patit Paban Mishra

Further Reading
Ali, Sheikh B. (1992) *Tipu Sultan*. 2d ed.. New Delhi: NBT.
Goel, Sita Ram. (1995) *Tipu Sultan: Villain or Hero?* New Delhi: Voice of India.

TNI. See **Military, Indonesia.**

TOBOL RIVER A tributary of the Irtysh, the Tobol River rises in the southern Urals of northwest Kazakhstan not far from the Russian border and flows in a roughly northerly direction first across the Turgay Plateau and then, after crossing the border into Russia, across the West Siberian lowland. The river joins the Irtysh not far from the city and port of Tobol'sk.

With a basin of 426,000 square kilometers, the Tobol is some 1,591 kilometers long. Of this the lower 437 kilometers are navigable, the river being used among other things to float timber to the main waterway of the Irtysh. The waters are also regulated to supply industry in the cities of Rudny, Qostanay, Kurgan, and Yalutorovsk.

The river's length and the two distinct geographical areas (the high-altitude dry steppe of the Turgay Plateau and the temperate rain forest of the Siberian taiga) through which it flows give it distinct characteristics. Like other Central Asian rivers, it is fed mainly by snow. This is supplemented in Siberia by rainfall. Its upper (Kazakhstan) course freezes in November, with the melt occurring at the end of April. In this region, the river's greatest flow occurs during May and June. The lower (Siberian) course freezes in October, with the melt at the end of May. Here the greatest flow is in August. In common with other rivers of the region, the Tobol's flow is highly variable. Its average flow at the confluence with the Irtysh is 805 cubic meters per second, but the maximum August flow is 6,350 cubic meters per second.

Will Myer

Further Reading
Allworth, E. (1989) *Central Asia: 120 Years of Russian Rule*. Durham, NC: Duke University Press.
Bolshaia Sovetskaia Entsiklopediia. (1978) English ed. New York: Macmillan.

TOCHIGI (2002 est. pop. 2 million). Tochigi Prefecture is situated in the central region of Japan's island of Honshu, where it occupies an area of 6,414 square kilometers. Tochigi's primary geographical features are the Yamizo, Taishaku, and Ashio mountains which fringe a central plain irrigated by the Nakagawa and other rivers. It is bordered by Gumma, Fukushima, Ibaraki, and Saitama prefectures. Once known as Shimotsuke Province, it assumed its present name and borders in 1873.

The prefecture's capital city is Utsunomiya, base during the Kamakura (1185–1333) and Muromachi (1333–1573) periods to the Utsunomiya family, the region's military governors. In the Edo period (1600/1603–1868), it was a castle town and post station. In the early 2000s, it manufactures aircraft, farm machinery, and television sets. The prefecture's other important cities are Ashikaga, Tochigi, Sano, Kanuma, and Oyama.

Tochigi's main economic activity is agriculture: It grows rice, grains, and vegetables. Also productive are the forestry and woodworking industries, and at one time copper mining was important. Current industries include textiles, metals processing, and machine fabrication. The former post-station town of Tochigi is noted for its traditional sake brewing, wooden clogs, and lime production.

Visitors and pilgrims are drawn to Nikko National Park, site of the Tokugawa family tomb. The famed pottery town of Mashiko features the studio of Hamada Shoji (1894–1978), a leader of the folk art revival movement. Other scenic destinations are the Nasu Highland, Kegon Falls, and Lake Chuzenji.

E. L. S. Weber

Further Reading
"Tochigi Prefecture." *Japan: An Illustrated Encyclopedia*. Tokyo: Kodansha.

TOFU One of the great breakthroughs in human nutrition was the discovery of how to process difficult-to-digest soybeans into nutritious tofu, or *doufu*. Tofu is made by soaking soybeans overnight, grinding them finely with water, and boiling them into a slurry, filtered to produce soy milk. This can then be precipitated using various settlers, commonly magnesium salts, Japanese *okara*, and pressed into slabs. It is uncertain when tofu was first made, but the technology was well known in China by early medieval times and possibly as early as the Han dynasty (206 BCE–220 CE).

Imitation of cheese making as practiced in the Altaic region has been cited as one possible source of the idea.

In recent times, tofu has become a mainstay of Chinese cooking and is a cheap and easily accessible source of protein. It is less well represented in early recipe books, but this may be due to its plebeian origins. Other tofu products include the "skin," *doufupi*, skimmed off and dried, and *choudoufu*, "stinking bean curd," a fermented product that is an acquired taste.

Paul D. Buell

Further Reading

Anderson, E. N. (1988) *The Food of China*. New Haven, CT: Yale University Press.

Huang, H. T. (2000) *Biology and Biological Technology*: Science and Civilization in China series. Cambridge, U.K.: Cambridge University Press.

———. *Fermentations and Food Science*. Science and Civilization in China series. Cambridge, U.K.: Cambridge University Press.

Shurtleff, William, and Akiko Aoyagi. (1975) *The Book of Tofu*. Berkeley, CA: Ten Speed Press.

TOHOKU REGION

Japan's Tohoku region is its northeast; the word "Tohoku" means "Northeast." Tohoku consists of the prefectures of Aomori, Iwate, Akita, Yamagata, Miyagi, and Fukushima on the main island of Honshu. The region is bordered by the Sea of Japan on the west, the Tsugaru Straits to the north and the Pacific Ocean on the east. Major cities are Sendai, Aomori and Akita, located along the coasts.

Winters are long and there is considerable snowfall along the coast of the Sea of Japan and in the central mountains, making Tohoku a favorite destination for skiers. Summers are hot, but less humid than in the southern part of Honshu.

Historically Tohoku remained out of the national political and cultural spotlight. During the eleventh and twelfth centuries a branch of the powerful Fujiwara family had their seat at Hiraizumi (in present-day Iwate Prefecture), and in the sixteenth century the warrior Date Masamune (1567–1636) established the Sendai domain and extended control over almost all of Tohoku.

Primarily an agricultural area, Tohoku's serves as Japan's rice bowl. Its long winter restricts other products to such crops as apples (in Aomori), rape (Yamagata), cherries (Yamagata), and timber (throughout the region). Tohoku is characterized by low population-density, a large number of members per household, and a high number of households with members 65 years or older. This demography reflects a lack of lo-cal economic opportunity due to the high dependence on agriculture. With the exception of Miyagi Prefecture, which had a population increase of 1.6 percent in the period from 1995 to 2000, the prefectures of the Tohoku region saw a drop in population ranging from 0.3 percent to 2 percent.

The conservative nature of the people and remoteness from the metropolises of Tokyo and Osaka allow Tohoku to retain local traditions more than other rural areas of the country. Those traditions include the large-scale early August festivals of Kanto at Akita, Nebuta at Aomori, and Tanabata at Sendai.

James M. Vardaman, Jr.

TOJO HIDEKI

(1884–1948), prime minister of Japan. Tojo Hideki was the prime minister of Japan throughout most of World War II (1941–1945). A

Former premier Tojo testifying at the War Crimes Tribunal in Tokyo on 26 December 1947. (BETTMANN/CORBIS)

Tokyo-born career army officer, Tojo served as an attaché in Europe in the early 1920s and later joined the Control Faction, an influential clique within the Japanese military. In the mid-1930s, Tojo's star rose with the ascendance of the Control Faction over rival army cliques. In 1935 he was transferred to Manchuria, where he served on the staff of the Guandong (Kwantung) Army. Recalled to Tokyo in 1938, Tojo was appointed a vice-minister of the army, followed by promotion to army minister in the cabinet of Konoe Fumimaro (1891–1945) in 1940.

An ardent militarist, Tojo was a keen supporter of the alliance with Nazi Germany and the expansion of the war with China. Following the collapse of the Konoe cabinet in October 1941, Tojo was appointed prime minister in an atmosphere of escalating tensions with the United States. As Japan's material inferiority became increasingly apparent despite an earlier string of victories in the Pacific, Tojo attempted to centralize and coordinate the war effort by taking personal control of key posts in the cabinet and the army. However, this attempt aroused powerful opposition in civil and military circles, and Tojo resigned under pressure following the loss of Saipan, an island in the northern Marianas, in July 1944. After the war, he was convicted of war crimes and was hanged in Tokyo on 23 December 1948.

John M. Jennings

Further Reading
Browne, Courtney. (1967) *Tojo: The Last Banzai*. New York: Holt, Rinehart & Winston.
Butow, Robert. (1961) *Tojo and the Coming of the War*. Princeton, NJ: Princeton University Press.
Hoyt, Edwin P. (1993) *Warlord: Tojo against the World*. Lanham, MD: Scarborough House.

TOKAIMURA NUCLEAR DISASTER
Japan's latest and largest nuclear disaster—the world's worst since Chernobyl—happened in September 1999 at a nuclear fuel processing service firm in the small village of Tokaimura, 125 kilometers northeast of Tokyo in Ibaraki Prefecture. This disaster occurred when JCO Corporation workers were handling uranium and provoking the release of high levels of radiation from the plant. It was level 4 on the International Nuclear Event Scale of 0 to 7, but according to many experts it could have been rated level 5. Previously, the worst nuclear disaster in Japan was a level 3 and took place in 1997 at a nuclear fuel reprocessing plant, also in Tokaimura. The 1979 Three Mile Island accident in the United States was a level 5, and the 1986 Chernobyl accident reached level 7.

The Tokaimura disaster has raised questions about the failure of the nuclear accident system and problems in countermeasures and crisis management to deal with disasters. In June 2000, Japan's Special Measures Law for Nuclear Accidents took effect, which requires the government to conduct a comprehensive drill every year. As Japan depends more and more on nuclear power for electricity, reforms of the nuclear safety policy are being considered.

Nathalie Cavasin

Further Reading
Masuzoe Yoichi. (2000) "Japan's Nuclear Disaster," *Look Japan* 2: 16–18.
Mukaidani Susumu. (2000) "The Terror of Tokaimura," *Look Japan* 2: 19–24.
Yoshida Yasuhiko. (2000) "Nuclear Safety Issue Jars Japan to Reconsider its Policy Program," *Japan Quarterly* 47, 1 (January–March): 56–64.

TOKUGAWA PERIOD
The Tokugawa period, also referred to as the Edo period, is typically dated from 1600, the year of the military victory of Tokugawa Ieyasu (1543–1616) at Sekigahara, to the Meiji Restoration in 1868. This period saw Japan move from a country divided by civil war to a unified, stable, and mature state. Ieyasu established central authority over the country through the Tokugawa *bakufu* (shogunate) in Edo (present-day Tokyo). Regional authority was maintained by more than 250 daimyo (military chieftains) who governed their *han* (domains) with considerable autonomy. Society was divided into four distinct classes: warriors, peasants, artisans, and merchants, and the government maintained tight restrictions on all of them. Urbanization spread rapidly in the period, creating profound economic, cultural, and social changes.

Tokugawa Political and Social Control
The Tokugawa *bakufu* grew out of Tokugawa Ieyasu's experience with clan government during his time as daimyo, before his victory at Sekigahara. In 1603, after being appointed shogun by the emperor, Ieyasu began staffing the *bakufu* with his loyal retainers.

Ieyasu maintained firm control over the daimyo by redistributing land confiscated because of his victory at Sekigahara. Domains totaling about one-fourth of all land came to be ruled directly by the Tokugawa family and its vassals; the remaining territory was divided among the daimyo. The daimyo were categorized as *fudai*, longtime loyal vassals who were given strategically important lands; *shimpan*, collateral daimyo from lineages related to the Tokugawa; and

JAPAN—HISTORICAL PERIODS

Jomon period (14,500–300 BCE)
Yayoi culture (300 BCE–300 CE)
Yamato State (300–552 CE)
Kofun period (300–710 CE)
Nara period (710–794 CE)
Heian period (794–1185)
Kamakura period (Kamakura Shogunate) (1185–1333)
Muromachi period (1333–1573)
Momoyama period (1573–1600)
Tokugawa or Edo period (Tokugawa Shogunate) (1600/1603–1868)
Meiji period (1868–1912)
Taisho period (1912–1926)
Showa period (1926–1989)
Allied Occupation (1945–1952)
Heisei period (1989–present)

tozama, outside lords who joined Ieyasu either shortly before or after Sekigahara and who remained potential rivals.

The *bakuhan* (a combination of the *bakufu* and *han*) system of government begun by Ieyasu was, for all practical purposes, completed by the time of the third shogun, Tokugawa Iemitsu (1604–1651). In the 1630s and 1640s, in order to provide an increased sense of legitimacy and bureaucratic professionalism among samurai office holders, *bakufu* offices such as the *roju* (senior councilors), *wakadoshiyori* (junior councilors), *hyojosho* (judicial council), *sojaban* (master of shogunal ceremony), *tairo* (great councilor), *ometsuke* (inspector general), *jisha bugyo* (temple and shrine commissioner), *kanjo bugyo* (finance commissioner), and *machi bugyo* (town commissioners) were established.

Bakufu control over the daimyo was also securely in place by Iemitsu's reign. While in theory the daimyo remained autonomous rulers of their domains, in practice the *bakufu* dictated general rules of conduct and placed restrictions on personal freedom of action. For example, daimyo were not allowed to marry or repair castles in their domains without shogunal permission. They could also be shifted from one domain to another or deprived of their domains entirely. The most important control measure was the *sankin kotai* (alternate attendance) system, which required that the daimyo spend alternate years in attendance at the shogunal court in Edo and leave their wives and children behind whenever they returned to their domains.

Tokugawa control over the peasantry was also strengthened under the first three shoguns. Villages inhabited primarily by *hyakusho* (small taxpaying farmers) served as the basic unit of control in the countryside. Although villagers, led by a *nanushi* or *shoya* (headman), administered their own affairs, they were required to form *gonin-gumi* (neighborhood associations) to foster mutual assistance and responsibility regarding issues such as taxation and law enforcement. Villagers were also prohibited from changing occupations or selling their land, and restrictions were placed on what they could wear and eat.

Using neo-Confucian principles borrowed from China, Tokugawa leaders saw Japanese society as divided into four classes, with the samurai on top, followed by the peasants, artisans, and merchants. In practice, there was little distinction between the last two groups, who were generally collectively referred to as townspeople. Living outside this hierarchical scheme were outcasts called *eta* and *hinin*.

The samurai lived primarily in Edo and other castle towns and were restricted to military and government service. The peasants, who made up 80 percent of the population, lived in villages at night and cultivated their fields by day. The townspeople usually resided in designated sections of urban areas and served the needs of the samurai. Over time, these social divisions became blurred, as some townspeople and rural landlords became extremely wealthy, and certain lower-level samurai and tenant farmers faced poverty, but the legal boundaries between the classes never disappeared.

Tokugawa Policies on Trade and Christianity

As the Tokugawa political and social structures were becoming formalized, the *bakufu* also developed strict control measures regarding foreign trade and Christianity, culminating in the national-seclusion policies of the 1630s. From the earliest days, Ieyasu had attempted to control the foreign trade of the Portuguese and Spanish at Nagasaki through the *shuinsen* (vermilion seal) ship policy, which officially sanctioned vessels to trade abroad, and the *itowappu* (raw-silk monopoly) system, which granted designated Japanese merchants the exclusive right to purchase, distribute, and negotiate the price of raw silk brought into Japan by Portuguese ships.

The 1600 shipwreck at Kyushu of a Dutch ship with an English pilot aboard afforded Ieyasu another opportunity to wrest control away from the Portuguese and Spanish, who had monopolized trade and tied it to the proselytizing efforts of Catholic missionaries.

Ieyasu offered both the Dutch and English an opportunity to trade in Japan. The Dutch accepted his invitation in 1609, and the English followed four years later. Both traded out of the island of Hirado, while the Portuguese and Spanish remained at Nagasaki. The nonproselytizing Dutch and English Protestant traders gave Ieyasu exactly what he desired—foreign trade without a Christian missionary presence.

With alternatives to Portuguese and Spanish foreign trade now available, Ieyasu issued a nationwide ban on Christianity in 1614. Soon thereafter, prominent Japanese and Western Christians were deported; those Western missionaries who did stay went underground with their beliefs. The second and third shoguns stepped up efforts to eradicate Christianity in Japan, first through a series of executions and later through torture-induced recantations.

In 1622, the Spanish were expelled for continued proselytizing. The following year the English departed of their own accord after a series of financial losses. This left the Dutch at Hirado and the Portuguese in Nagasaki as the only remaining Western traders in Japan.

In the 1630s, the *bakufu* promulgated a series of edicts that became the basis for what is known as Japan's *sakoku* (national seclusion) policy regarding foreign trade and Christianity. By these edicts, the *bakufu* prohibited all ships and Japanese subjects from leaving Japan for a foreign country; those Japanese already abroad could not return. In addition, the Japanese wives and children of foreigners were deported. Other measures called for payments to Japanese who turned in Christians to the government and strict inspection of foreign ships in search of Christians and Christian materials. In 1639, in the aftermath of the Shimabara Rebellion, another edict was issued banning the Portuguese from Japan.

A statue of Tokugawa Ieyasu, the first Tokugawa shogun, at Nikko National Park. (RIC ERGENBRIGHT/CORBIS)

SHRINES OF NIKKO— WORLD HERITAGE SITE

Designated as a World Heritage Site in 1999, the Nikko shrines are a vivid reminder of the incredible craftsmanship of the Tokugawa period in Japan. The shrines are perfectly blended with the breathtaking natural beauty of the area.

Over the next few years, the *bakufu* implemented additional Christian control measures, including the establishment of religious census registers, temple registration, oaths of apostasy, *fumi-e* (requiring suspects to trample on Christian images to prove they were not Christians), and the office of religious investigation. While failing to eradicate Christian beliefs completely among the Japanese populace, the *bakufu* did manage to drive the religion so far underground that it would not reappear publicly until the mid-nineteenth century.

In 1641, the Dutch were transferred from Hirado to the man-made island of Dejima in Nagasaki Harbor. From this time on, Japanese foreign trade was conducted only with the Chinese and Dutch at Nagasaki and with the Chinese and Koreans through the Ryukyus and Tsushima.

Economic and Cultural Developments

An unexpected development in the transformation of the samurai from rural warriors to civil bureaucrats living in castle towns was the rapid urbanization of Tokugawa Japan. Edo grew to a population of 1 million people, while Kyoto and Osaka had about 300,000, and even domain castle towns recorded more than 50,000 residents. Trade in silk, cotton, paper, porcelain, and sake made some merchants rich, and they, in turn, came to support a vibrant urban culture of artists and entertainers.

Urban culture flourished in the forms of literature, theater, and painting. Ihara Saikaku (1642–1693) wrote popular prose fiction about love and money among the townspeople, and the traveling poet, Matsuo Basho (1644–1694), adopted haiku as his principal medium of expression. Chikamatsu Monzaemon (1653–1724) wrote plays about townspeople and their conflicts between duty and human emotion for both the *jorui* (puppet) and Kabuki theaters. While a number of painting schools flourished in the Tokugawa period, the one that best represented the new urban culture was ukiyo-e (literally, "pictures of the floating world"). This school of woodblock printmaking was begun by Hishikawa Moronobu (1618–c. 1694) in the seventeenth century, and it peaked in the eighteenth and nineteenth centuries under Kitagawa Utamaro (1753–1806), Katsuhika Hokusai (1760–1849), and Ando Hiroshige (1797–1858).

Although the samurai enjoyed the cultural prosperity of the cities, many were unable to keep pace with the expanding urban economy, since their primary source of income was a fixed stipend tied to rural production. The *bakufu* made a number of unsuccessful attempts at neo-Confucian–inspired fiscal reform in the eighteenth and nineteenth centuries (the Kyoho, Kansei, and Tempo reforms), but the economic status of the samurai continued to deteriorate.

Urbanization affected the life of people in the countryside as well. The needs of urban markets turned traditionally subsistence peasants into commercial farmers, a few of whom became large landowners, while the majority fell to the status of landless laborers. Tax evasion and peasant rebellions became more and more common as the Tokugawa period evolved.

Intellectual Trends

In the Tokugawa period, the orthodox school of thought was *shushigaku* (Zhu Xi neo-Confucianism), which stressed loyalty, hierarchy, and stability. The official *bakufu*-sponsored school of neo-Confucianism was begun by Hayashi Razan (1583–1657), a trusted adviser of Tokugawa Ieyasu. A contending school of neo-Confucianism was *oyomei* (Wang Yangming), which was founded by Nakae Toju (1608–1648).

Outside neo-Confucianism were schools such as *kogaku* (Ancient Learning), which advocated returning to the original works of Confucius and his immediate disciples. Famous members of this school included Yamaga Soko (1622–1685), Ito Jinsai (1627–1705), and Ogyu Sorai (1666–1728). *Kokugaku* (National Learning) rejected Confucian ethics and searched for meaning in traditional Shinto texts. Its leading advocates were Motoori Norinaga (1730–1801) and Hirata Atsutane (1776–1843). *Rangaku* (Western Learning) explored Western science and mathematics after the shogun lifted the ban on the importation of Western books in 1720. Honda Toshiaki (1744–1821) was a leading scholar of this school.

The Downfall of the *Bakufu*

By the mid-nineteenth century, rising prices, peasant uprisings, samurai unrest, natural disasters, and famine provided formidable obstacles to effective *bakufu* rule. Exacerbating the situation was poor *bakufu*

leadership, which by this time had come to be dominated by senior councilors. Added to these troubling domestic developments was the growing threat of encroachment from the West.

In 1853 and 1854, Commodore Matthew Perry led American naval expeditions to Japan and demanded that the *bakufu* grant the United States trading and diplomatic rights in the country. The weakened bureaucracy had no choice but to agree, a fact that greatly angered some of the samurai, especially those from southern and western Japan. When *bakufu* leaders signed commercial treaties with the West in 1858, and foreign merchants, missionaries, sailors, and government officials began to pour into designated Japanese ports, the situation worsened. By the 1860s, many in Japan were demanding the dissolution of the *bakufu* and the restoration of imperial rule to unify the country and resolve the crisis. With forces from the powerful *tozama* domains of Satsuma and Choshu leading the way, the last Tokugawa shogun was overthrown in late 1867, and early the following year, in what is known as the Meiji Restoration, a new government was established.

Lane Earns

Further Reading
Hall, John W., ed. (1991) *The Cambridge History of Japan*, 4: *Early Modern Japan*. Cambridge, U.K.: Cambridge University Press.

Jansen, Marius B. (1992) *China in the Tokugawa World*. Cambridge, MA: Harvard University Press.

Toby, Ronald P. (1984) *State and Diplomacy in Early Modern Japan: Asia in the Development of the Tokugawa Bakufu*. Princeton, NJ: Princeton University Press.

Totman, Conrad. (1993) *Early Modern Japan*. Berkeley and Los Angeles: University of California Press.

Wakabayashi, Bob Tadashi. (1986) *Anti-Foreignism and Western Learning in Early Modern Japan*. Cambridge, MA: Harvard University Press.

TOKUSHIMA (2002 est. pop. 823,000). Tokushima Prefecture is situated in the eastern region of Japan's island of Shikoku, where it occupies an area of 4,146 square kilometers. Tokushima's primary geographic character is a generally mountainous terrain intersected by plains along the rivers Yoshinogawa and Nakagawa. The prefecture is bordered by the Inland Sea, the Kii Channel and the Pacific Ocean, and by Kawaga, Kochi, and Ehime prefectures. Once known as Awa Province, Tokushima assumed its present name and borders in 1880.

The prefecture's capital is Tokushima city, situated along the island's longest river, Yoshinogawa. During the Edo period (1600/1603–1868), it was the castle town of the Hachisuka family, who completed their fortress in 1586. Under their rule, the town flourished as a port for the export of indigo dye. Following legislation enacted to promote industry in remote regions, Tokushima was declared a New Industrial City in 1964. In the early 2000s, it is the site of chemical, textile, lumber, furniture, paper, and foodstuff processing industries. The prefecture's other important cities are Naruto and Anan.

Tokushima Prefecture remains primarily a rural region. Indigo plants are still grown, and tobacco and salt are produced. The leading crops are rice, fruits, vegetables, and mulberry trees. Fishing and forestry remain important activities in the south. Visitors are drawn to Tokushima city's August dance festival (Awa Odori) and to the Naruto whirlpools and coastal scenery in the Inland Sea National Park.

E. L. S. Weber

Further Reading
"Tokushima Prefecture." (1993) *Japan: An Illustrated Encyclopedia*. Tokyo: Kodansha.

TOKYO (2002 est. city pop. 8.2 million). Tokyo is the capital of Japan, and the nation's commercial and industrial center. Situated on Tokyo Bay along the Pacific coast of central Honshu Island, the city proper comprises twenty-three urban wards. The wider metropolitan area (consolidated in 1943 as Tokyo-to, or Tokyo Metropolitan Prefecture) includes twenty-seven smaller cities, one county, and four island administrative units with numerous towns and villages, all occupying an area of 2,168 square kilometers. The metropolitan prefecture has an estimated population of 11.8 million (2002 estimate).

Its site has a long history of habitation, as proven by excavated artifacts from the Jomon (10,000 BCE–300 BCE), Yayoi (300 BCE–300 CE), and Kofun (300–700) periods. In the seventh century, the area was made part of Musashi Province. Its official founding date is 1457, when warlord Ota Dokan erected a castle overlooking the centuries-old fishing village of Edo (the name means "river gate"), located near the mouth of the Sumida River and bordering the fertile Kanto Plain.

In 1590, national unifier Toyotomi Hideyoshi (1537–1598) sent his ally and rival Tokugawa Ieyasu (1543–1616) off to rule Edo. After Hideyoshi's death, Ieyasu completed Japan's unification and in 1603 founded the Tokugawa shogunate in Edo. On the ruins of the first castle, he constructed his own fortress;

Tokyo is known for its dense population and crowded streets, such as this street filled with shoppers in August 1991. (CATHERINE KARNOW/CORBIS)

it burned in 1647. Edo suffered more than ninety serious fires over the next centuries. The town which grew up around the castle consisted of the so-called High City (Yamanote) of samurai residences and the Low City (Shitamachi) of workshops, markets, theaters, bathhouses, and commoners's homes on the northwestern marshlands. Artisans, merchants, and peasants flooded into Shitamachi to work in an Edo swelled by the 1635 directive that the nation's some 300 feudal lords establish residences there. A city of canals and the terminus of five great highways, Edo in 1720 had a population of over a million, making it the world's most populous city at that time.

The unexpected 1853 arrival of American ships, followed by the devastating 1855 Ansei earthquake, helped to destabilize the shogunate. In 1868 Edo was renamed Tokyo (the name means "eastern capital") and the Emperor Meiji arrived from Kyoto to take up residence in Edo Castle, rebuilt as the Imperial Palace. Over the following decades Tokyo underwent rapid modernization and intense growth. The 1923 earthquake almost completely destroyed it; by 1930 it had risen again.

The World War II bombing raids once again leveled the city; the war was followed by some seven years of Allied occupation, administered from Tokyo. The economic recovery of the 1950s and 1960s paved the way for the city to host the 1964 Olympic Games and led to a new spurt of construction. The ever-increasing land prices and housing shortages were addressed by a program to create a series of urban subcenters, contributing to the labyrinthine conglomeration of self-contained neighborhoods, retail hubs, and satellite towns that Tokyo is today. Increasing pollution forced large manufacturers to relocate to outlying districts and onto land reclaimed from Tokyo Bay.

Today Tokyo is the nation's center for air and rail travel, government offices, financial institutions, corporate headquarters, mass media, the arts, and higher education (with some 185 colleges and universities). Chief among its numerous attractions are the historic Imperial Palace grounds, Ueno Park with its zoo and many museums, and the Meiji and Yasukuni shrine complexes.

E. L. S. Weber

Further Reading

Bestor, Theodore C. (1989) *Neighborhood Tokyo*. Stanford, CA: Stanford University Press.

Cybriwsky, Roman. (1996) *Historical Dictionary of Tokyo*. Nethuchen, NJ: Scarecrow Press.

Fowler, Edward. (1997) *San'Ya Blues: Laboring Life in Contemporary Tokyo*. Ithaca, NY: Cornell University Press.

Hastings, Sally Ann. (1995) *Neighborhood and Nation in Tokyo, 1905–1937*. Pittsburgh, PA: University of Pittsburgh Press.

Jinnai, Hidenobu. (1995) *Tokyo: A Spatial Anthropology*. Translated by Kimiko Nishimura. Berkeley and Los Angeles: CA: University of California Press.

TONGHAK Tonghak (Eastern Learning) is the oldest indigenous organized religion in Korea. Founded in 1860 by Ch'oe Che-u (1824–1864), by the end of the nineteenth century it had attracted enough followers to pose a serious threat to the Choson dynasty (1392–1910), which had ruled Korea since the late fourteenth century. In the first half of the twentieth century, under the name Ch'ondogyo (the Religion of the Heavenly Way), it was a major contributor to nationalistic resistance against Japanese colonial rule. In recent decades in South Korea, it has retreated from political activism, returning to its purely religious roots. In North Korea, however, a Ch'ondogyo-centered political party is a nominal junior partner to the ruling Communist Workers' Party.

The Origins of Tonghak

As its name reveals, Eastern Learning appeared in Korea in response to the penetration of Western Learning, a premodern Korean term for Catholicism. Though there were only about 20,000 Catholics in Korea in the mid-nineteenth century, Ch'oe knew that China had recently suffered its second major military defeat in three decades at the hands of Europeans, whom he identified with Catholicism. This frightened him, since China was for him, as it was for most Koreans at that time, the font of those values and moral principles that defined civilized society. He therefore began preaching Eastern Learning to counter the destabilizing and immoral effects of Western Learning.

In his attempt to defend traditional beliefs and values, Ch'oe created a new form of Korean religion. Drawing on Confucianism for his ethical principles and on Korea's folk religion for his rituals, Ch'oe added two elements borrowed from the Catholicism he was fighting against: a focus on one God, and the notion that those who shared belief in that one God constituted a separate and distinct community within Korean society.

Ch'oe's monotheism alarmed the Korean government, especially since one of the terms he used for God, the Lord of Heaven, was the same term the outlawed Catholics used for God. Since Korea's small Catholic community had insisted that loyalty to their God superseded loyalty to the king, Ch'oe's use of Catholic theological terminology made him appear subversive, as did the formation, without government authorization or oversight, of a community of Tonghak believers.

That subversive potential seemed to be realized in 1862 when there were outbreaks of antigovernment violence across the southern third of the Korean peninsula. These antigovernment protests were fueled by anger at government corruption and excessive taxation and had no connection with the infant Tonghak religion. Nevertheless, the government assumed the attacks on its authority were the result of peasants becoming emboldened by Ch'oe's claim that his Lord of Heaven was superior to any king. Ch'oe was arrested and hanged in 1864 for spreading doctrines that undermined the authority of the state.

Ch'oe's death did not end the faith in his teachings. Instead, after his death, a distant relative who was also one of his earliest converts, Ch'oe Shi-hyong (1827–

1898), succeeded him as head of the Tonghak community. The second patriarch systematized Tonghak thought by collecting Ch'oe Che-u's essays and poems and publishing them as Tonghak scripture. He also organized the Tonghak community into a nationwide underground hierarchical network, linking individual believers in their villages through their district head to regional and national leaders.

As the Tonghak community grew not only larger but also more organized and more conscious of its identity as a distinct community within Korean society, it began demanding that the government recognize it as a legitimate organization, starting with a retraction of the 1864 condemnation of Ch'oe and his ideas. Tonghak demands for an end to government persecution grew louder after a treaty between Korea and France in 1886 gave Catholics, but not Tonghak followers, the freedom to practice their religion openly. Starting in November 1892, large groups of Tonghak believers began gathering near government offices in the countryside to call for the exoneration of their founder and an end to attacks by government officials on their community.

The Tonghak Peasant Rebellion

This religious protest was overshadowed by a peasant rebellion that broke out in 1894. It was led by a local Tonghak leader, Chon Pong-jun (1854–1895), who used the Tonghak underground network to mobilize peasants throughout southern Korea for attacks on local government offices. That network helped the peasant rebellion spread rapidly and become the largest peasant uprising Korea had ever seen, strong enough to seize control of Chonju, the capital of the southwestern province of Cholla, less than two months after the rebellion began.

Chon's rebellion had not been organized or even authorized by the second patriarch. In fact, Ch'oe Shi-hyong was at first opposed to the use of the Tonghat name and organization in armed rebellion. Tonghak doctrine, however, included the assertion that Korea was on the verge of a revolutionary transformation into a utopian community. This millenarian strain in Tonghak thought made many followers receptive to rebellion. Not only had Chon utilized the underground organization Tonghak had built, some Tonghak doctrines, such as Ch'oe Che-u's proclamation that humanity was on the verge of a Great Transformation, appeared on banners carried by the rebels. Thus this rebellion is often called the Tonghak Revolution.

That appellation, however inaccurate it may have been in the early stages, gained credibility in October 1894 when the second patriarch declared that the rebellion was just and that Tonghak believers should participate in it. Ch'oe Shi-hyong's decision to join forces with Chon Pong-jun was a tactical error. Chon's rebel army was annihilated by a joint Japanese-Korean force before the year was out. Chon was quickly captured and executed. Ch'oe went into hiding, but within four years he too was captured and executed.

The defeat of the Tonghak Revolution and the execution of the second patriarch did not mean the end of the Tonghak religion. Before Ch'oe was captured, he passed the torch of Tonghak leadership to Son Pyong-hui (1861–1921), revered today as the third patriarch.

From Tonghak to Ch'ondogyo

In 1905, Son, who had fled from Korea in 1901, returned when he discovered that the government had grown too preoccupied with Japanese threats to Korean sovereignty to pay much attention to him and his followers. In a successful effort to distance his followers in 1905 from the rebels of 1894, he dropped the name Tonghak and proclaimed himself leader of a new religious organization he called Ch'ondogyo. It is as the Religion of the Heavenly Way that Tonghak has survived into the twenty-first century. Under Son's guidance, the Religion of the Heavenly Way began to operate openly as a mainstream religious organization, opening worship halls and holding regular worship services. Nevertheless, it retained a revolutionary potential because of the challenge its doctrines posed to inequality in society. Ch'oe Che-u had called for men and women to serve God. Ch'oe Shi-hyong added that just as people should respect God, they should also respect their fellow human beings. Son Pyong-hui further amplified that statement with the phrase "God dwells within each and every human being," which has become a core tenet of Ch'ondogyo doctrine.

Because of their belief that all human beings deserve respect, followers of Ch'ondogyo resisted Japanese colonial rule over Korea. Son Pyong-hui was one of the chief architects of the 1 March 1919 declaration of independence from Japanese rule, which resulted in nationwide protests.

After liberation from Japanese rule in 1945, Korea was divided into a Communist zone in the north and a non-Communist zone in the south. Political activists among Ch'ondogyo members gravitated toward the north, where the Ch'ondogyo Young Friends Party was officially recognized as a junior partner within a united front dominated by the Workers' Party.

Perhaps because of the taint of collaboration with Communists in the North, Ch'ondogyo has not been able to play any significant political role in South Korea. It survives in the Republic of Korea today as a small religious organization claiming around 1 million members and slightly less than 300 worship halls.

Don Baker

Further Reading
Beirne, Paul. (1999) "The Eclectic Mysticism of Ch'oe Cheu." *Review of Korean Studies* 2: 159–182.

Kim, Yong Choon. (1989) *The Ch'ondogyo Concept of Man: An Essence of Korean Thought.* Seoul: Pan Korea Book Corporation.

Lew, Young-Ick. (1990) "The Conservative Character of the 1894 Tonghak Peasant Uprising: A Reappraisal with Emphasis on Chon Bong-jun's Background and Motivation." *Journal of Korean Studies* 7: 149–180.

"The Peasant War of 1894." (1994) *Korea Journal* 34: 4 (special issue).

Weems, Benjamin B. (1964) *Reform, Rebellion, and the Heavenly Way.* Tucson, AZ: University of Arizona Press.

TONGIL-KYO. See **Unification Church**

TONKIN GULF The Tonkin Gulf is connected to the Pacific Ocean at the northwest arm of the South China Sea. The gulf is 500 kilometers long, 250 kilometers wide, and 70 meters deep at its deepest point. It borders northern Vietnam to the west, Hainan Island to the east, and China to the north and east, and receives the Red River out of northern Vietnam. The main ports on the gulf include Ben Thuy and Haiphong in northern Vietnam and Pei-hai (Pakhoi) in China. The gulf's main shipping route is through the Hainan Strait, between China and Hainan Island.

The Gulf of Tonkin is probably best known in recent history as the site of the so-called Gulf of Tonkin Incidents, when in August 1964, torpedo boats of the Democratic Republic of Vietnam (DRV) fired on U.S. naval forces that were in the area in an intelligence-gathering operation. The incidents resulted in the U.S. Congress's adopting the Gulf of Tonkin Resolution on 7 August 1964; this resolution supported an increase in American involvement in the Vietnam War. Naval activity in the gulf was heavy during the war; Soviet ships ferried supplies to the DRV, and the United States sought to interdict the activity, particularly in 1972, when the U.S. Navy mined the entrances to North Vietnamese ports.

Richard B. Verrone

Sanpans crossing the Vietnam–China border in the Tonkin Gulf off the coast of Mong Cai, Vietnam, in 1993. (ROBERT MAASS/ CORBIS)

Further Reading
Cima, Ronald J., ed. (1989) *Vietnam: A Country Study.* Washington, DC: U.S. Government Printing Office.

Dutt, Ashok J., ed. (1985) *Southeast Asia: Realm of Contrasts.* 3d rev. ed. Boulder, CO: Westview Press.

Moise, Edwin E. (1996) *Tonkin Gulf and the Escalation of the Vietnam War.* Chapel Hill, NC: University of North Carolina Press.

TONLE SAP Cambodia's Tonle Sap, or "Great Lake," is one of the unique geographical wonders of the world. Southeast Asia's largest freshwater lake, Tonle Sap is located in the center of the Cambodian Basin, a low-lying area of land only 30 to 100 meters above sea level. Bounded by the Dangrek Mountains, a steep escarpment on the edge of the Khorat Plateau to the north, and the Chuor Phnom Kravanh (Cardamon range) to the south, the Tonle Sap Basin extends west to the border with Thailand.

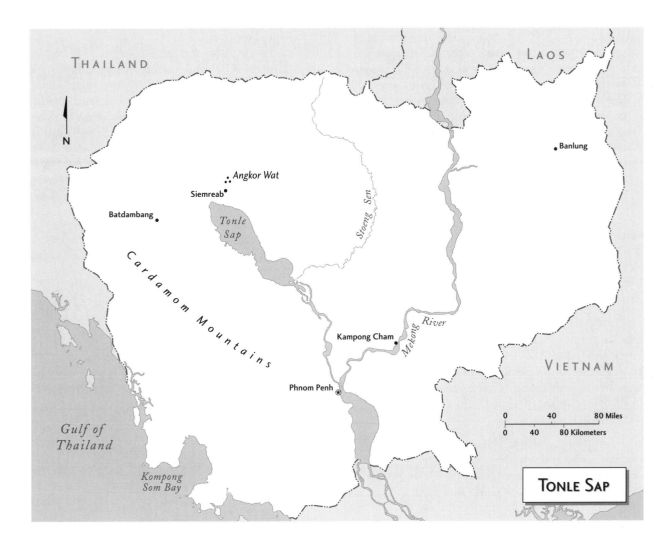

TONLE SAP

Connected to the Mekong River by the Tonle Sap River, the lake is part of a unique hydrological phenomenon unknown in any other part of the world: during the monsoon, or rainy season, the enormous amount of rain causes the Mekong to rise so much that the Tonle Sap River can no longer empty into it. Instead, the two rivers reverse course, and the Tonle Sap River then flows north into the lake, causing it to triple in size from 27,000 hectares during the dry season to more than 150,000 hectares during the rainy season. Flooding almost one-seventh of Cambodia, the rise in water levels provides irrigation for crops and an abundance of freshwater fish (the largest source of protein for the Khmer people), while the deposition of silt created by the river's reversal enriches the agricultural soils surrounding the lake. As a result, an estimated 75 percent of the total land area surrounding Tonle Sap— approximately 100,000 hectares—is fertile lowland.

However, there are critical concerns over the increasing environmental degradation caused mainly by human activities. Further economic development, in addition to the lack of effective policies to manage and protect the watershed, poses significant threats to the Tonle Sap ecosystem in the future. The Tonle Sap Biosphere Reserve, officially recognized by the United Nations Educational, Scientific, and Cultural Organization (UNESCO) on 28 October 1997, is the first step in addressing these issues at local, national, and international levels.

Greg Ringer

Further Reading

Boner, Neou. (1998) *The Creation of Tonle Sap Biosphere Reserve.* Bangkok, Thailand: Mekong River Commission.

Ringer, Greg. (2000) "Tourism in Cambodia, Laos, and Myanmar: From Terrorism to Tourism?" In *Tourism in South and Southeast Asia: Issues and Cases*, edited by C. Michael Hall and Stephen Page. Oxford, U.K.: Butterworth-Heinemann, 178–194.

Stensholt, Bob, ed. (1997) *Developing the Mekong Subregion.* Clayton, Victoria, Australia: Monash Asia Institute.

TOTTORI

TOTTORI (2002 est. pop. 611,000). Tottori Prefecture, situated in the western region of Japan's island of Honshu, occupies an area of 3,494 square kilometers. Its primary geographical features are the Chugoku Mountains, south of a coastal plain. Tottori is bordered by the Sea of Japan and by Hyogo, Okayama, Hiroshima, and Shimane prefectures. Once divided into Inaba and Hoki provinces, it assumed its present name and borders in 1881.

The prefecture's capital is Tottori city, which grew up as a castle town around the seventeenth-century Ikeda family fortress. Devastated by a 1943 earthquake and a 1952 fire, the city has been totally reconstructed. Today it is home to food processing, woodworking, electrical appliance, and machinery plants, as well as Tottori University. The prefecture's other important cities are Kurayoshi and Yonago.

The prefecture is archaeologically rich, with artifacts excavated from the Jomon (10,000–300 BCE) and Yayoi (300 BCE–300 CE) periods and has numerous tomb mounds from the Kofun period (300–710) scattered across the Tottori Plain. The region was controlled by a series of feudal lords through the Edo period (1600/1603–1868).

Today the region remains primarily rural, raising rice, tobacco, vegetables, livestock, and fruit, especially pears. Also important are forestry and fishing. Visitors are drawn to the Tottori Sand Dunes and to Daisen-Oki National Park.

E. L. S. Weber

Further Reading
"Tottori Prefecture." (1993) *Japan: An Illustrated Encyclopedia*. Tokyo: Kodansha.

TOURISM

TOURISM Asia is one of the major destination areas for today's international tourists; as home to the majority of human beings alive today, Asia accommodates the largest flows of domestic or internal tourism. East and Southeast Asia, with more than 97 million international tourists in 1999, received 14.6 percent of the world's international tourists (11.1 percent more than 1998). South Asia, with almost 6 million international tourists in 1999, received about 1 percent (and 8.3 percent more than 1998). These gross figures mask regional differences and annual fluctuations. Even the definitions are problematic: various authorities subdivide the continent differently. For instance, if Iran is included in South Asia, tourism figures are much higher than if it is omitted.

Domestic Tourism

In the largest Asian countries domestic tourism outstrips international tourism. For instance Japan has over 300 million annual tourist (overnight) trips, whereas fewer than 4.5 million international tourists visit Japan yearly. Domestic tourism in the major Asian nations has long been based on pilgrimages, most of which continue today, along with conventional Western-style cultural and environmental tourism. As in Europe, it is difficult to differentiate between pilgrims and religious tourists converging on a historical site.

South Asia In India Hindus were expected to visit sacred sites, including some now in Pakistan, Bangladesh, and Nepal. There are also Buddhist, Sikh, and Muslim sites in the same region; for all Muslims the international pilgrimage to Mecca (the hajj) is a lifetime goal. Many local shrines once operated syncretistically, as foci of worship for Hindus as well as Muslims; this is rarely the case today.

During the Raj, the period of British rule over the Indian subcontinent, nontraditional appreciation for historical, cultural, and natural sites of India was encouraged by institutions such as the Archaeological Survey and the Monuments Commission, and by the development of transportation in the country. The British not only visited historical sites such as the Taj Mahal; they established seasonal resorts in cool mountainous areas such as Simla, Darjeeling, and Pune (Poona). These resorts also attracted wealthy Indians and are still favored destinations.

After independence in 1947, Indians adopted the secular tourism of British and other foreigners. Under the Raj the Indian government provided employees and their families with the LTC (Leave Travel Concession), which covered second-class train fare for internal travel every three years. Many people used the LTC to visit relatives or tourist sites, often combining the two. After 1947 the internal travel promoted by the LTC continued, and some destinations previously exclusively religious (like the Himalayan shrines of Badrinath and Kedarnath) assumed a secular dimension. Increasingly, young, well-educated Indians (and to a lesser extent natives of Pakistan, Bangladesh, and Nepal) share the secular tourist experiences of international visitors. These include not only cultural and historical tourism but also ecotourism (travel focused on environmental concerns) and trekking as well as recreational tourism to beach and mountain resorts, major cities, and theme parks.

Southeast Asia The nations of Southeast Asia exhibit the same patterns of modern domestic tourism, interest in historical and national sites, recreational and

TOUR GUIDES IN CHINA

The Importance of Living—by Li Yutang, a popular author in pre–World War II China—aimed to give American readers a cosmopolitan glimpse at life in the Far East in the 1930s. In the extract below, Li Yutang explains the peculiar charms of Chinese tour guides.

> Chinese tourists suffer like American tourists at Radio City, with the difference that Chinese guides are not professional, but are fruit-sellers, donkey drivers and peasant boys, whose information is less correct, if their personalities more lively. Visiting Huch'iu Hill at Soochow one day, I came back with a terrible confusion of historical dates and sequence, for the awe-inspiring bridge suspended fifty feet over the Sword Pond, with two round holes in the slabs of the bridge through which a sword had flown up as a dragon, and became, according to my orange-selling boy, the place where the ancient beauty Hsishih attended to her morning toilet! (Hsishih's "dressing table" was actually about ten miles away from the place.) All he wanted was to sell me some oranges. But then I had a chance at seeing how folklore was changed and modified and "metamorphosed."

Source: Lin Yutang. (1938) *The Importance of Living: A Personal Guide to Enjoyment.* New York: Reynal & Hitchcock, Inc., 329.

amusement-park tourism, and, increasingly, eco-tourism, as does India. Before the dominance of Islam in Java, thousands of pilgrims from as far away as mainland Asia visited great Buddhist centers such as the thousand-year-old Borobudur. These sites fell into disuse but re-emerged in the nineteenth century as targets of secular tourism for Dutch colonists and visiting Europeans. These Javanese sites were incorporated into the international panoply of UNESCO's World Heritage Sites, and Indonesians now visit them in the same secular spirit as foreigners. All over Southeast Asia modern tourism has emerged, originating in imitation of former colonists or (in the case of Thailand) other foreigners. In Vietnam, Cambodia, and Laos, old patterns of internal travel are combined with or superseded by secular visits to places like Angkor Wat, where pre–Vietnam War colonizers visited, and where modern Cambodian tourists are joined by the ever-increasing numbers of postwar foreign tourists. In Indonesia religious tourism is now dominated by the Islamic hajj to Mecca; most domestic travel is secular. The same is true of Malaysia; its more than 25 million domestic tourist trips a year focus on hill resorts such as Cameron Highlands, beach areas such as Penang Island, and natural and historical sites, combined in the instance of the Batu caves near Kuala Lumpur.

East Asia Because of the strong shared cultural and, in part, political background between the nations of East Asia, tourism here differs somewhat tourism in the rest of the world, and especially from the Euro-American tourist system.

Japan Contemporary Japanese domestic tourism still includes traditional group pilgrimages, for instance, around Shikoku Island or to centers such as the Eheiji Zen temple complex, the Ise Shinto grand shrine, and the many sect headquarters in Kyoto. For decades such group tourism, using public transportation, also swamped famous cultural and historical sites, especially in big cities such as Kyoto, Tokyo, and Osaka, but also in outlying places such as Kamakura, Himeji Castle, and the ancient capital of Nara. Even in the premodern period, Japanese tourists, on foot, ostensibly for health or religious purposes, numbered in the tens of millions a year.

The last two decades of the twentieth century saw a transformation of Japanese domestic tourism, partly because of the rise in ownership of personal automobiles and a a massive road-building program of intercity expressways, tunnels, and bridges, with other roads extending to the 70 percent of Japan that is mountainous. Increased vacation time promoted the nuclear family as the unit of recreation.

Peer-group tourism, starting as day trips for preschool students and then in the form of school, club, and sports groups, continues in the adult world of work-party, union, or farmer-group tourism. These groups visit local attractions such as hot springs, travel to Hong Kong for shopping and almost anywhere for golf, and visit other Asian destinations for disguised sex tourism.

New forms of rural recreation, such as fishing, boating, camping, golf, and skiing, attract millions from crowded cities in all seasons. The government has encouraged nostalgia for the countryside, natural hot springs, organic foods, and village life to counter the flow of urbanization. The national railways and major travel companies cooperated in a (Re-)Discover Japan campaign in the 1970s and an Exotic Japan campaign of the 1980s, signaling that many urbanites were unfamiliar with hinterland Japan and were ignorant of unique regional festivals and customs.

China Domestic tourism in China was traditionally the province of priests and literati, or educated people; most ordinary Chinese could visit only local natural or historical sites. After 1949 travel was restricted except for military and party members, and many local tourist attractions were destroyed as signs of superstition. Indeed one motivation to become a Red Guard in the 1960s was the freedom to commandeer trains and travel all over China in the name of Mao's Cultural Revolution.

The overthrow of the Gang of Four in 1978 gave Chinese people more leisure time to spend in recreation and travel. Most recreation, however, is still local, limited to short holidays and concentrated in activities and areas that rarely compete for the spaces and infrastructure required by foreign tourists.

Nevertheless powerful forces impel Chinese people to travel further. Centripetal travel, until recently opposed and controlled by the central government, is symbolically equated with power and wealth in post-Mao China. These movements flow from the hinterlands to the metropolitan centers, for both tourism (where they compete with foreign tourists) and for work. They combine business with pleasure, a feature long characteristic of Chinese (and Japanese) tourism, even for Red Guards in the Cultural Revolution.

A centrifugal motivation for modern internal tourism is not spatial but temporal, the nostalgic desire to escape the here and now for the historical, cultural, and natural past. Though Westerners may be motivated to see the traditional China of *The Last Em-*

Chinese tourists taking photographs in Leshan, Sichuan, China, in May 1996. (STEPEHEN G. DONALDSON PHOTOGRAPHY)

WHY DO THEY CLIMB?

It is often not apparent to people who live in tourist destinations why tourists like to come there. This certainly seems to be the case with the Sherpas of Nepal in the Himalayas.

> Sherpas are generally mystified that Westerners come to Khumbu at such great expense and in such great numbers, whether to trek or to climb. Even the most experienced *sardars* admit they cannot fathom why Europeans climb, although they make guesses. One hunch is that they climb for fame, since the books they write always include plenty of pictures of themselves. But Sherpas also know that books are bought, so a second hypothesis is that people climb to make money. One *sardar*, for example, thought this was the case with the British mountaineer Chris Bonnington since he has written (and presumably sold) so many books; but the same *sardar* believed that fame drives Reinhold Messner (the first climber to ascend all fourteen 8,000-meter peaks) to the summits. Another *sardar* wondered whether science was not the prime motivation, while still another held that climbers climb to clear their minds from the worries of office work. If he were an office worker, he said, he might well need to clear his mind too, but if so he would do it by going on a weekend picnic rather than by climbing.

> *Source:* James F. Fisher. (1990) *Sherpas: Reflections on Change on Himalayan Nepal.* Berkeley and Los Angeles, CA: University of California Press, 129.

peror, the Chinese populace feels nostalgic, not for a return to a past way of life, but for experiences of the past that lend rootedness and stability to their present lives. This nostalgia encompasses local attractions in the countryside, old neighborhoods in cities, "lineage tourism," in which city dwellers visit ancestral home communities, and "heritage tourism," in which, for example, affluent urbanites of Hong Kong who could not visit their own home villages adopted the nearby Ping Shan walled community.

Urban Chinese seek out proximity to or images of nature. Of China's 1.2 billion citizens, 70 million are members of one of fifty-five minority nationalities, many of whom are concentrated in the southern province of Yunnan. The *minzu*, the people of nature, have inhabited the consciousness of the Han-Chinese majority for centuries. In some Chinese regions, the minorities are represented, as in Korea and Japan, by newly created folk culture villages, which bring together typical artifacts and crafts and demonstrate peasant performances for expectant Han tourists.

Nostalgia for Maoist socialism is another complex motivation for contemporary Chinese to travel. There are tearful reunions between rural villagers and bands of urbanites who were sent to live with them in the days of the Cultural Revolution. During Mao's lifetime Red Guards and other Mao devotees made pilgrimages to Shaoshan, Mao's home village, where a lucrative tourist trade came to flourish in later years.

International Tourism
International tourism is generally considered an economic phenomenon, planned since colonial times as an export industry to bring foreign exchange into relatively poor countries. Asian nations have put forth schemes to encourage inbound tourism. At the same time, many of them have in the past strictly controlled the outflow of tourists to save precious foreign currency. Many countries reap great economic benefits from incoming tourism, especially China, Hong Kong, Macao, Malaysia, Thailand, and Myanmar (Burma). For Nepal and the Maldives tourism is the most important

export industry. As hard currency is desired, the countries targeted by advertising are European, North American, and Australasian, and, within Asia, Singapore and East Asia. Major extravaganzas, such as Olympic Games, world's fairs, and trade shows, are planned to put a country or city "on the map."

In much of Asia, regional tourism from adjacent countries generally outstrips other forms of international tourism. International travel within Asia is sometimes almost domestic, as it is between Canada and the United States. Bhutan, India, and Nepal are a close-knit group, though none receives the majority of tourists from within the region. Singapore, Malaysia, and Indonesia form another near-domestic set. The ethnically related set of China, Hong Kong, and Macao exhibits levels of mutual tourism that, even with unreliable figures, surpasses any other international flows.

Generally the poorer Asian countries are recipients of tourists, and the wealthier countries are the donors. Bangladesh, India, and Pakistan all "export" less than 1 percent of their population a year; the Maldives, with a small but wealthy population, sends one in three of its population abroad. Laos and Vietnam export few travelers, whereas Singapore's affluent citizens average 1.5 overseas trips per capita. East Asia is generally more affluent than the rest of Asia. Though China (so far) allows less than 1 percent of people (still over 7 million) to travel abroad annually, nearby Hong Kong and Macao enjoy seven and twenty visits per capita, respectively. Japan, Taiwan, and, increasingly, Korea

all send 7 to 25 percent abroad annually, which allows for considerable growth by European standards.

Most international tourists to Asia travel from Europe, East Asia (mainly Japan), and North America (mainly the United States). Europeans dominate in Bhutan, India, Sri Lanka, and the Maldives, both in cultural and beach-tourism destinations. East Asian tourists dominate in Myanmar, a country whose dictatorial politics may well put off many Europeans and Americans. Southeast Asia is more evenly split, though Europe is nowhere ascendant over East Asia. Local Southeast Asian tourists are dominant in Laos and Indonesia, and East Asian tourists in most of the other countries. In East Asia every country is dominated by tourists from other East Asian countries. North America leads Europe in Japan, Hong Kong, Taiwan, and slightly in Korea, but not in Macao and China.

South Asia International tourism to South Asia is dominated by India with 2.4 million visitors and followed surprisingly closely by Myanmar and Iran with over 1 million each. India, Pakistan, Bangladesh, and Myanmar are all ex-British colonies. Their attractions are mostly cultural and historical and, for some, religious; India has more UNESCO Cultural World Heritage sites than any other country in the world. South Asia also attracts some of Europe's beach tourists, especially Sri Lanka, parts of India (Goa), and the Maldives.

The palaces that used to house Indian princes have increasingly become important destinations for both

TABLE 1

Tourism Flows within South Asia, 1998

(in thousands)

Tourism to:	Bangladesh	Bhutan	India	Myanmar	Nepal	Pakistan	Sri Lanka	Iran	Maldives
From:									
Bangladesh	Dom.	0	340	0	6	7	10	2	0
Bhutan	0	Dom.	3	0	1	0	few	few	0
India	58	1.3	Dom.	4	130	67	44	13	12
Myanmar	0	0	0	Dom.	0	few	few	0	0
Nepal	5	0	38	0	Dom.	few	few	0	0
Pakistan	12	0	44	0.6	4	Dom.	10	115	1
Sri Lanka	2	0	118	0	11	2	Dom.	1	0
Iran	1	0	10	0	0	8	0	Dom.	0
S.E. Asia	12	0.1	133	256	40	9	17	4	5
E. Asia	20	1.1	129	914	11	7	22	11	47
Europe	37	3.1	925	361	165	43	248	631	305
N. America	16	1.6	328	88	44	14	18	2	5
Total inbound	172	6.3	2,482	1,381	464	429	381	1,174	396
% from S. Asia	45%	0.39%	24%	5.5%	35.6%	25%	13.4%	25%	5%
Total outbound	623	0	2396	99	118	708	381	965	11
Proportion of population outbound (per year)	1/215	0	1/423	1/425	1/185	1/200	1/50	1/42	1/3

(Dom. = Domestic)

SOURCE: Compiled from data in World Tourism Organization (2000).

TABLE 2

Tourism Flows within Southeast Asia, 1998

(in thousands)

Tourism to:	Laos	Indonesia	Malaysia	Philippines	Singapore	Vietnam	Thailand
From:							
Laos	Dom.	0	0	0	1	5	50
Indonesia	0	Dom.	353	15	875	4	69
Malaysia	2	515	Dom.	49	415*	20	918
Philippines	2	95	0	Dom.	151	10	78
Singapore	2	1,414	2,937*	48	Dom.	32	586
Vietnam	78	0	0	4	17	Dom.	51
Thailand	273	45	256	16	161	18	Dom.
N. America	25	197	417	537	458	51	428
N.E. Asia	32	952	3,236	816	1,834	749	2,735
S. Asia	10	62	84	31	395	6	259
Europe	53	701	1,620	311	1,162	186	1,460
Total inbound	500	4,606	9,892	2,149	6,342	1,716	7,842
% from S.E. Asia	73%	45%	27%	.3%	27%	1%	2.5%
Total outbound	56	1,710	3,870	1,670	6,547	262	6,129
Proportion of population outbound (per year)	1/250	1/126	1/6	1/47	1.5 per cap.	1/315	1/9.8

*The traffic between Singapore and Malaysia may be considered short-term, local day tripping (for example, for shopping), as between the U.S. and Canada or China and Hong Kong.

(Dom. = Domestic)

SOURCE: Compiled from data in World Tourism Organization (2000).

domestic and foreign tourists. Many impoverished royal families strike deals with multinational hotel chains to turn their palaces into luxury tourist residences. Here tourists' main motivation is a colonial nostalgia for Europeans and local Indian allies. Another form of tourism is youth drifter tourism, characterized by low-cost and low-tech travel such as trekking.

Nepal and other Himalayan regions have benefited from mountaineering. Nepal also developed "nature tourism" in its national parks in the lowland Terai,

TABLE 3

Tourism Flows within East Asia, 1998

(in thousands)

Tourism to:	Japan	China	Hong Kong	Taiwan	South Korea	Macau
From:						
Japan	Dom.	1,600	945 (2,380 in 1996)	2,200	1,900	167
China	267	Dom,	2,300	few	210	1,317
Hong Kong	365	47,000*	Dom.	54	229	4,012
Taiwan	843	2,174	1,812	Dom.	108	822
South Korea	742	632	179	60	Dom.	23
Macau	few	7,100	441	few	few	Dom.
N. America	784	879	1,020	336	455	102
Europe	577	2,100	960	160	401	262
Total inbound	4,106	75,000	11,000(?)	3,298	3,600	7,100
% from East Asia	64%	95%	77%	65%	70%	94%
Total outbound	16,000	7,400	50,000*	6,100	3,100	8,000*
Proportion of population outbound (per year)	1/8	1/162	7 per cap.*	1/3.6	1/15	20 per cap.

*Figures for travel between Hong Kong, Macau, and China include many trips just across the border for shopping and tourism, comparable to Canadians visiting the United States.

(Dom. = Domestic)

SOURCE: Compiled from data in World Tourism Organization (2000).

where tourists follow yesterday's big game hunters in safari-like treks. Though encouraged by the Chinese for economic purposes, Tibetan tourism is a paradox; after the Chinese takeover in 1951, the Chinese suppressed the main attractions, Buddhist monks and their ancient establishments, and religious leaders and many other Tibetans fled abroad. While South Asian tourism is growing steadily, the cessation of hostilities in such areas as Kashmir, Assam, Myanmar, Afghanistan, and Sri Lanka would give travel a major boost.

Southeast Asia Most of Southeast Asia, like South Asia, emerged from a period of European colonization (Dutch, British, French, and Japanese) after World War II, and countries made tourism a major development goal. Though Thailand was never a colony, its near-colonial status as a rest-and-recuperation destination for allied troops in the Vietnam War in the 1960s contributed to its rise as a tourist destination.

Southeast Asia has perhaps the greatest range of tourist attractions in Asia. Singapore, Saigon, and Bangkok are modern urban destinations for shopping and entertainment. Yogyakarta, Hue, and Phra Nakhon Si Ayutthaya (or Ayutthaya) are ancient former capitals with famous architectural remains; Angkor Wat and Borobudur are World Heritage sites and ancient pilgrimage and temple complexes, once lost to the jungle, rediscovered and "museumized" by European interests, and now proudly reclaimed by local peoples. Beach tourism is popular on many coasts, especially in Bali, Penang, the Philippines, and both shores of central Thailand. Gambling is promoted in the Cameron Highlands of Malaysia, and there are also golf and horse racing. Southeast Asia is notorious for sex tourism. Though rare in the Islamic parts of Malaysia and Indonesia, it is infamous in Bangkok, parts of the Philippines, Vietnam, and Cambodia. Though much of the blame has fallen on locally based American troops, the traditionally patriarchal and stratified nature of these cultures also encouraged a flourishing domestic sex industry, which attracts foreign tourists.

East Asia The countries of East Asia have followed similar strategies in encouraging foreign tourists to visit, though China's pattern is somewhat divergent.

Japan After encouraging inbound tourism as part of its successful development strategies in the 1950s, Japan capped its efforts with the Olympic Games in Tokyo 1964 and the World's Fair in Osaka 1970. Both events produced massive infrastructure investment—the Bullet Train joined the cities in 1964—and attracted huge, mainly domestic, crowds. As Japan grew wealthy, her citizens traveled abroad and enriched their Asian destinations: Hong Kong and Singapore

for shopping, Okinawa (which reverted to Japan in 1972), Guam, and later Hawaii for recreational tourism. Japanese travelers are a major force in tourism to China and important visitors to Taiwan and South Korea. In the last decade of the twentieth century, the flow became two-way. While Japanese now increasingly visit mainland North America and Europe, their young people have taken up drifter tourism in Asia and the Mediterranean region.

China During the Maoist era's "state tourism," political allies were housed in friendship hotels and shown industrial and agricultural successes; routes were restricted, and services were not widespread. After 1978, overseas tourists were encouraged. So-called compatriots came from Macao, Hong Kong (and later Taiwan), Singapore, and Malaysia, along with some Westerners and Japanese. Travel and accommodations were separated, with lower rates for Chinese. Part of the strategy was to encourage Chinese overseas to visit "home." Much of the growth of tourism (and other developments) resulted from joint ventures combining overseas Chinese capital and mainland Chinese permission and labor.

Travels from world centers to China and more interestingly from Chinese metropolises outward are equally important aspects of modern tourism. From 1978 China developed a massive foreign tourist industry. The China National Tourism Administration spent over $50 billion on tourism in 2000, and China has opened most areas to foreign tourists, particularly in the hinterlands, where visitors can see such attractions as the archaeological army in Xi'an, colorful minorities in the south, and the Silk Road through Xingjiang Uygur to the west.

Taiwan and Korea Both Taiwan and Korea followed Japan in attracting overseas tourists while developing industries and restricting outflows for economic or military reasons. Many of their tourists have been nearby Japanese and former colonists, and sex tourism disguised as *kasaeng* (geisha) tourism in Korea flourished with official tolerance until the 1980s. Both countries increased their overseas tourism; they constitute the largest numbers of tourists to Japan. Taiwanese, understandably, send even larger numbers to Hong Kong and Macao; at the end of the twentieth century their major destination became China.

Hong Kong and Macao Hong Kong and Macao, like Singapore in Southeast Asia, are highly urbanized former colonies with many attractions for shoppers, gourmets, and gamblers. Along with Chinese visitors, they enjoy a large clientele from North America and Europe and, for Hong Kong, from Japan. The coun-

POST-9/11 TOURIST SECURITY CONCERNS IN PAKISTAN

This notice posted by the Travel and Cultural Services of Pakistan indicates the concern for tourist safety following the September 11th attack on the United States in 2001 and the U.S.-led invasion of Afghanistan.

SECURITY SITUATION IN PAKISTAN

Security & safety has always been questioned and people have always had wrong ideas about the situation in Pakistan. We do believe and wish to assure all tourist in Pakistan of the following things.

1. There is no threat to lives or goods of any foreign tourist in any area of Pakistan. There are no purse snatchers as in South America or Africa. Nor there are any kind of hatreds or dis-likeness to foreign tourist in Pakistan

2. Pakistan being a Muslim country has a liberal atmosphere for women. They are free to roam any where they want but as it is demand of the Muslim society we do recommend modest dress for both men & Women. A T shirt and full pants or Skirt is fine. T shirt with half sleeves is perfect.

3. There had been some troubles lately in Karachi but all that is in a part of Karachi where there is no interest of tourist nor some one ever needs to go or pass bye. Mind Karachi is spread in the area of 2200 Sq. Kms, Secondly Government is taking very strict measures to cut this problem.

4. The Interior of Sind is culturally very rich province and has no Problems as such . When you are there in Moen Jo Daro or any other place you are well taken care of by the friendly locals and our staff.

5. Khyber pass & other tribal areas have a system of tribal jury and sometimes there are clashes among the tribes but they can not be witnessed on the main road where Tourist travel. Yet we provide proper security guards for the tours in these tribal areas.

6. The Mountainous areas of Hunza, Gilgit, Chitral, Swat, Karakorum Highway & Skardu are very safe and there is no violence or any major trouble in these areas.

Travel & Culture Services Pakistan

36 National Square Khayaban-e-Jami Clifton Karachi Tel; 579289 - Fax: 92-21-5832632 Email : culture@tours.hypermart.net

Source: Travel and Cultural Service Pakistan. Retrieved 3 March 2002, from: http://ctours.freeyellow.com/

tries became SARs (Special Administrative Regions) of China in 1997 and 1999, respectively, with little interruption in their tourist flows.

Implications

International tourism is a fragile phenomenon. In Asia as elsewhere, tourism depends on absence of conflict. Diseases, civil strife, and physical disasters depress flows. During the past forty years of decolonization and tourist growth, events in Asia have stemmed the rising tides of tourism. Internal conflicts, civil wars, rioting, and unrest cause mass travel cancellations. Most dramatic was the televised clash between student demonstrators and the military in Tiananmen Square in Beijing in 1989, which reduced foreign visits to China for several years. Japanese and Western tourists reduced their numbers by nearly one million for a year or so, and the number of Chinese compatriots visiting China dropped by seven million in one year. Hong Kong lost 38 percent of the Taiwanese tourists who normally stopped there on their way to China. Civil unrest in Sri Lanka, breaking into civil war since 1984, drastically reduced its attractiveness as a tourist destination. Interethnic clashes in Malaysia and later in Indonesia halted tourist visits for significant periods.

However, enmity and a state of war may not entirely prevent organized tourism. The South Korean Hyundai Company, which operates passenger ships, built a port in North Korea to allow nearly half a million South Koreans annually to visit Kumgang Mountain, sacred to all Koreans.

International conflicts can also bring a halt to local or national tourism, as did conflicts between India and Pakistan in Kashmir, an otherwise prime tourist destination; between India and China at their Himalayan border; between Vietnam and Cambodia; between Thailand and Myanmar spilling over from Myanmar's civil wars; and even between China and Taiwan. Tensions in Afghanistan and Iran have sometimes halted tourism to or in these areas. China's suppression of nationalist and religious elements in Tibet at times broke into civil strife in which tourists were involved. In the last decade of the twentieth century, economic reversals in East and Southeast Asia caused a falling off in intraregional tourism. The diminished number of Japanese tourists, leaders in the region has considerably affected Hong Kong and China.

The future of outbound tourism in East Asia has growing global significance. Outbound tourism from China is expected to rise from 10 million in the year 2000 to 50 million by 2010 and 100 million by 2020, perhaps making China the leading source of tourists globally. In January 2001 China's leaders outlined a policy to encourage inbound tourism to reach 120 million by 2020 (putting China ahead of France) and to increase domestic tourism, already at 750 million annually.

At present, however, China limits outgoing tourism to fifteen approved countries, adding Taiwan in 2001; Europe and North America are not included. Only 2 percent of Chinese have passports, and there is a chronic shortage of airplanes even at present tourism levels. European analysts predict that in 2020 the countries foremost in tourism will be Germany, Japan, the United States, and China.

Nelson H. H. Graburn

Further Reading

Cheung, Sidney C. H. (1999) "The Meanings of a Heritage Trail in Hong Kong." *Annals of Tourism Research* 26, 3: 570–588.

Crick, Malcolm. (1994) *Resplendent Sites, Discordant Voices: Sri Lankans and International Tourism.* Chur, Switzerland: Harwood Academic Publishers.

Ecumenical Council for Third World Tourism. (1984) *Third World Peoples and Tourism: Approaches to a Dialogue.* Bangkok, Thailand: Ecumenical Council for Third World Tourism.

Forshee, Jill, Christina Fink, and Sandra Cate, eds. (1999) *Converging Interests: Traders, Travelers, and Tourists in Southeast Asia.* Berkeley, CA: Center for Southeast Asian Studies.

Graburn, Nelson H. H. (1983) *To Pray, Pay, and Play: The Cultural Structure of Japanese Domestic Tourism.* Aix-en-Provence, France: Centre des Hautes Études Touristiques ser. B, no. 26.

———. (1983) "Tourism and Prostitution." *Annals of Tourism Research* 10, 3: 437–456.

———. (1995) "The Past in the Present in Japan: Nostalgia and Neo-Traditionalism in Contemporary Japanese Domestic Tourism." In *Change in Tourism: People, Places, Processes,* edited by Richard Butler and Douglas Pearce. London: Routledge, 47–70.

———. (1997) "Tourism and Cultural Development in East Asia and Oceania." In *Tourism and Cultural Development in East Asia and Oceania,* edited by Shinji Yamashita, Kadir Din, and J. S. Eades. Bangi, Malaysia: University of Malaysia Press, 194–212.

Hall, C. M., and S. Page, eds. (1998) *Tourism in South and Southeast Asia: Issues and Cases.* Oxford: Butterworth-Heineman.

Hatton, Michael. (1999) *Community-Based Tourism in the Asia-Pacific.* Toronto: Asia-Pacific Economic Cooperation.

Hitchcock, Michael, Victor King, and Michael Parwell, eds. (1993) *Tourism in South-East Asia.* London: Routledge.

Ishimori, Shuzo, Umesao Tadao, and Harumi Befu, eds. (1995) *Japanese Civilization in the Modern World 9: Tourism.* Osaka, Japan: National Museum of Ethnology, Senri Ethnological Studies no. 38.

Ivy, Marilyn. (1995) *Discourses of the Vanishing.* Chicago: University of Chicago Press.

Iyer, Pico. (1988) *Video Night in Kathmandu, and Other Reports of the Not-So-Far East.* New York: Vintage Departures.

Lew, Alan A., and Lawrence Yu, eds.(1995) *Tourism in China: Geographic, Political, and Economic Perspectives.* Boulder, CO: Westview Press.

Linhart, Sepp, and Sabine Frustuck, eds. (1996) *The Culture of Japan as Seen through Its Leisure.* Albany, NY: State University of New York Press.

Mosher, Maggie. (1988) "A Case Study of Tourism in Chinese Peasant Society." *Kroeber Anthropological Society Papers* 67/68: 55–61.

Oakes, Tim. (1998) *Tourism and Modernity in China.* London: Routledge.

Opperman, Martin. (1997) *Pacific Rim Tourism.* Wallingford, U.K.: CAB International. Picard, Michel. (1989) *Bali: Cultural Tourism and Touristic Culture.* Singapore: Archipelago Press.

Richter, Linda. (1989) *The Politics of Tourism in Asia.* Honolulu, HI: University of Hawaii Press.

Schein, Louisa. (2001) *Minority Rules: The Miao and the Feminine in China's Cultural Politics.* Durham, NC: Duke University Press.

Scofield, Trevor, and Li, Fung Mei. (1998) "Tourism Development and Cultural Policies in China." *Annals of Tourism Research* 25, 2: 362–392.

Wang, Yue, and P. J. Sheldon. (1995) "The Sleeping Dragon: Outbound Chinese Travel Market." *Journal of Travel and Tourism Management* 4, 4: 41–54.

World Tourism Organization. (2000) *Tourism Highlights 2000.* 2d ed. Madrid, Spain: World Tourism Organization.

Xiao Hong Gen. (1997) "Tourism and Leisure in China: A Tale of Two Cities." *Annals of Tourism Research* 24, 2: 357–370.

Xu Gang. (1999) *Tourism and Local Development in China: Case Studies of Guilin, Suzhou, and Baidaihe.* London: Curzon.

Yamashita, Shinji, Kadir Din, and J. S. Eades, eds. (1997) *Tourism and Cultural Development in East Asia and Oceania.* Bangi, Malaysia: University of Malaysia Press.

TOXIC-WASTE DISPOSAL   The adoption of the Basel Convention on the Control of Transboundary Movements of Hazardous Wastes and their Disposal in Basel, Switzerland, on 22 March 1989 made it illegal to export toxic wastes to Antarctica. In 1994, the Basel Convention was strengthened by the "Basel ban," which made it illegal to export toxic waste from the world's richest twenty-nine countries to the world's developing nations. The Basel ban has only managed to hide and obscure toxic waste exports, however, as the demand for cheap and discreet waste disposal has exploded. Most of the 30–50 million tons of toxic waste that is shipped internationally every year is simply subcontracted out to the lowest bidder, with no questions asked about its final destination. Some 80 percent of this waste is exported from industrialized nations in East Asia, Europe, and the Americas to developing countries in Africa and Asia. Lax enforcement of local environmental law and an uneducated populace create easy dumping grounds for multinational corporations faced with rising disposal costs in their own nations.

Mislabeling or misrepresenting toxic waste is by no means an isolated incident: In March 1992 close to 1,000 metric tons of cadmium and lead-laced dust from Gaston Copper Recycling Corporation in South Carolina was sold to Stoller Chemical Company, who mixed it with fertilizer and sold to Bangladeshi farmers. The deception wasn't discovered until nearly all of the deadly mixture of carcinogenic and neurotoxic chemicals had already been used to fertilize fields.

Shipbreaking

A dramatic and very visible example of the toxic-waste trade is shipbreaking. Massive container ships from all over the world are sent to for dismantling to Gujarat, India, and to Guangzhou, China. Some rudimentary equipment and safety measures are used in China, but in India, when a decommissioned oil tanker or aged freighter is towed up onto the beach, thousands of people scramble onto the ships and rip them apart with their bare hands, with and no thought given to the deadly polyvinyl chlorides (PVCs), asbestos, and toxic marine effluents. According to Greenpeace, the incidence of cancer amongst the shipbreakers in nearly 25 percent.

In the slightly more restrained shipbreaking yards in China, analysis of sediment in the waters around the area demonstrated extremely high levels of heavy metals, hormone disrupters, dioxin-producing polychlorinated biphenyls (PCBs), and fuel oil. Chinese workers for the most part use adequate protective gear, but China's share of the world's shipbreaking is going down.

India handles nearly 70 percent of the world's shipbreaking at present, and Bangladesh and Vietnam are entering the fray in preparation for the scheduled doubling of shipping tonnage for scrap in 2005. Shipbreakers can take some comfort in that ships have been getting much safer in the past thirty years (about the average lifespan of commercial ship), so that future shipbreaking will be marginally safer. Growing awareness of the problem is also likely to initiate eventual reform, although it may take some time in India, which gets approximately 15 percent of its steel from scrapping ships.

Electronic Waste

One of the most serious toxic-waste disposal problems facing Asia is that of electronic waste—the deadly by-products of computer manufacturing and obsolescence. Some 315 million computers in the United States alone are expected to become obsolete by the year 2004, and most will end up in Asia. Computer manufacture was once considered an environmentally friendly operation, but it is gradually emerging from organizations such as California's Silicon Valley Toxic Coalition (SVTC) just how big the problem of computer waste really is.

According to the SVTC, a single cathode-ray-type monitor (the sort that looks like a television screen) is loaded with harmful elements or chemicals, including brain-damaging lead, PVCs, and brominated flame retardants that have been linked to birth defects and cancer. Unfortunately, according to the U.S. Environmental Protection Agency, it is ten times cheaper to send a computer monitor to China than it is to recycle it.

The computer itself also contains mercury, cadmium, and chromium—all poisonous. Regrettably, computers are also made with valuable metals, such as copper, that make them irresistible to uninformed and ill-prepared "dirty recycling" operations willing to accept them. The Computer Recyclers Association of the Philippines (CRAP) imports dioxin-laden Australian computer waste because of the copper it contained, without being aware of the hazards. Unfortunately, without effective international enforcement of the prohibitions against exporting toxic waste, toxic-waste trafficking is not likely to disappear.

James B. McGirk

Further Reading

American University. (2002) *TED Case Studies: U.S.-Bangladesh Waste Trade*. Retrieved 12 April 2002, from: http://www.american.edu/TED/BENGALI/htm.

Basel Action Network. (2002) *Toxic Trade News*. Retrieved 12 April 2002, from: http://www.ban.org.

Greenpeace. (2002) *Ships for Scrap IV: Steel and Toxic Wastes for Asia*. Retrieved 19 March 2002, from: www.greenpeace.org

Silicon Valley Toxics Coalition. (2000) *SVTC Clean Computer Campaign*. Retrieved 12 April 2002, from: http://www.svtc.org/cleancc/pubs/technotrash.htm

TOY INDUSTRY—CHINA The world toy industry was a $69.5 billion business in 2000. U.S. toy imports alone totaled $15.1 billion, of which China supplied $10.7 billion, or 71 percent. Back in the early 1980s, Hong Kong was the world's largest toy exporter. But labor and land became more expensive with Hong Kong's development. In 1984 the nearby special economic zone of Shenzhen, China, offering a tariff-free foreign investment zone with low-cost labor and factory space, was opened. Hong Kong toy manufacturers moved more and more production across the border. By the early 1990s, Hong Kong, Taiwan, and other Asian corporations, having obtained exclusive rights to produce toys according to the specifications established by the giant toy makers of the West and Japan, manufactured brand-name toys as well as toys under their own labels in joint ventures in China, concentrated in the southern province of Guangdong near Hong Kong. China become the world's largest toy manufacturer and leading exporter, reaching an export volume of $8 billion in 1993.

But low wages; appalling safety, health, and working conditions; and prohibition on labor organizing prompted the international labor movement to call for a boycott of Chinese toys until working conditions were improved. Fatal industrial disasters in the industry were cited by American human rights and labor activists to support their call for eliminating most-favored-nation (MFN) status for China. American toy makers, with growing investment in China and dependency on Chinese exports, argued against such demands, which they claimed would lead to higher prices for American consumers and loss of jobs for American workers who packaged Chinese goods or completed the assembly of toys partially assembled in China.

Economic forces, not politics, brought about an improvement of safety standards and the increasing replacement of hazardous sweatshops by well-lit, well-ventilated modern factories employing adult workers. The product trend was swinging toward more complex, sophisticated, and interactive toys in the late 1990s. Big buyers preferred to outsource to bigger Chinese manufacturers that could meet the volume demands, handle more complex toys, and also comply with their codes of conduct regulating working conditions. The Chinese industry was consolidated; many small toy factories closed shop even as the industry as a whole grew.

In the late 1990s, some six thousand toy manufacturers existed in China, more than 80 percent of which were funded by overseas capital. China and Hong Kong together accounted for some 60 percent of the world toy trade.

Robert Y. Eng

Further Reading

"Chinese Toy Making: Where the Furbies Come From." (1998) *The Economist* (19 December).

"Chinese Toy Making: The Worker." (1998) *The Economist* (19 December).

TOYAMA (2002 est. pop. 1.1 million). Toyama Prefecture is situated in the central region of Japan's island of Honshu. It occupies an area of 4,252 square kilometers. Its geography features mountains encircling a central plain. Toyama is bordered by Toyama Bay and the Sea of Japan, and by Niigata, Nagano, Gifu, and Ishikawa prefectures. Once known as Etchu Province, it assumed its present name in 1871 and its present borders in 1883.

The prefecture's capital is the city of Toyama, growing up as a castle town around the fortress built in 1532 by the Maeda family. Today it is home to Toyama University and is the heart of the Hokuriku Industrial Region, with shipbuilding and aluminum refining as its main industries.

During the Edo period (1600/1603–1868), the region was ruled by the Maeda family as Japan's wealthiest domain. Today rice remains the primary crop, followed by pears, tea, and vegetables. Tulip bulbs are grown for export. The fisheries are active, with Toyama Bay noted for its firefly squid. Plentiful hydroelectric power fuels the machinery, chemical, metals processing, lumber, and textile industries. Visitors are drawn to the Himi coast, the Kurobe Gorge in Chubu Sangaku National Park, and the rustic steeproofed farmhouses of the Gokayama district.

E. L. S. Weber

Further Reading

"Toyama Prefecture." *Japan: An Illustrated Encyclopedia*. (1993) Tokyo: Kodansha Ltd.

TRABZON (1998 est. pop. of city 144,000). Trabzon (Trebizond), capital of Trabzon province (1998 est. pop. 850,000) in a mountainous region of north-

The Hagia Sopjia Byzantine Church in Trabzon in 1990. (DAVID SAMUEL ROBBINS/CORBIS)

eastern Turkey on the Black Sea, took its name from the table-shaped plateau on which the city is located. Known as Trapezus in antiquity, the city was colonized by Greeks from Sinope, also on the southern shore of the Black Sea, west of Trabzon.

The city was occupied by the Seljuks at the end of the eleventh century and became the capital of the Greek empire of Trebizond from 1204 to 1461. Captured by the Mongols in 1240, it remained under their rule until conquered by the Ottoman sultan Mehmed II (1432–1481) in 1461. The Ottomans ordered the city's churches converted to mosques; one of these, the Aya Sofya, became a museum in 1964. Sultan Selim the Grim (1467–1520) served as governor (1490–1512) until his accession to the throne in 1512. His son Suleyman the Magnificent (1494 or 1495–1566) was born in Trabzon and raised there until he took the throne in 1520.

Trabzon's historical importance derives from its location on one of the most important routes between Europe and Central Asia and its use as a seaport. Venetian and Genoese merchants frequently visited Trabzon before the Ottoman conquest, and for centuries exports from Asia, such as silk, cotton fabrics, and wine, passed through its port.

During World War I Trabzon was attacked by the Russians in 1915 and was occupied by them in 1916. The Turks recaptured the city on 24 February 1918. The town's population consists mainly of boatmen and fishermen. Trabzon continues to be known for its tobacco, hazelnuts, and tea.

Tipi Isikozlu-E. F. Isikozlu

Further Reading
Faroqhi, Suraiya. (1960) "Tarabzun." In *The Encyclopaedia of Islam.* 2d ed. Leiden, Netherlands: E. J. Brill, 216–219.
Statistical Yearbook of Turkey. (1999) Ankara, Turkey: Devlet İstatistík Enstitüsü.

TRAILOK (reigned 1448–1488), reformer of Ayutthaya (Thailand). The eldest son of King Boromaraja II (reigned 1424–1448) of Ayutthaya, Prince Ramesuen (Trailok) was appointed governor of Pistanuloke Province in 1438. He succeeded his father in 1448. He attempted to subjugate the Lan Na kingdom of King Tilokracha, but his efforts were in vain. Trailok then turned his attention toward the administrative problems faced by the expanding nation because the existing structure was not adequate.

Trailok divided Ayutthaya into provinces instead of principalities, and a prince was put in charge of each province. There was to be one royal army. Army and civilian branches of civil administration were separated. Each branch was divided into departments. In view of growing maritime commerce, a separate department was created for foreign affairs and trade. The Kot Montien Ban (Palace Law) of 1458 created a hierarchy for royalty, each rank having separate laws. For smooth succession to the throne, the position of heir apparent was created for the eldest son or full brother of the king. The grades that determined the social status of a person were set in accordance with the person's land holdings. Some of the reforms of the king violated the principle of equality before law, but they gave stability to Ayutthaya. Trailok also did much to encourage the arts and literature.

Patit Paban Mishra

See also: **Thailand—History**

Further Reading
Tarling, Nicholas, ed. (1992) *The Cambridge History of Southeast Asia.* Vol. 1. Cambridge, UK: Cambridge University Press.
Wyatt, David K (1986) *Thailand: A Short History.* New Haven, CT: Yale University Press.

TRAN DO (b. 1922), Vietnamese general. Born 1922 in Thai Binh Province, Do joined the Indochina Communist Party in 1940. A career military officer, he rose quickly through the ranks, serving in the battle of Dien Bien Phu before being sent to South Vietnam in 1963. He served as Deputy Party Secretary of the Southern Liberation Armies, the top political officer in the Central Office for South Vietnam, the office through which Hanoi directed the National Liberation Front and its guerrilla army, the People's Liberation Armed Force. A top military commander, he helped plan the 1968 Tet Offensive. Do was responsible for infiltrating more northern troops into the south in order to maintain Hanoi's control over the southern rebellion.

In addition to his military positions, Major General Do served on the Vietnamese Communist Party's Central Committee from 1960 to 1991, as vice-chairman of the National Assembly, and head of the Central Committee's Culture and Arts Department. In that post, Do became a staunch advocate of intellectual freedom and the abolition of ideological controls on arts and letters. He drafted key documents for the party in the mid-1980s that liberalized intellectual life, but ideological conservatives forced his retirement in October 1988. Do became a vociferous critic of the regime in the 1990s and began a letter-writing campaign attacking corruption, the lack of a free press, and the lack of political and economic reform. He was expelled from the Vietnamese Communist Party in January 1999 and remains the most prominent dissident in the country.

Zachary Abuza

TRAN VAN GIAU (b. 1911), Vietnamese revolutionary and historian. Tran Van Giau was born in Tan An, south of Ho Chi Minh City (Saigon) in 1911. He received his secondary education in France and reportedly obtained a doctorate in history from the University of Toulouse. While in France he became involved in the Vietnamese revolutionary movement and joined the Indochinese Communist Party (ICP). In 1931 he was recruited, with several others, to study at the Oriental School in Moscow (the Stalin School). He returned to Saigon in 1933 and headed the ICP's executive committee. He was arrested briefly on a number of occasions (1933, 1935, and 1939) and was sent to Poulo Condore prison on Con Dao Island, but he was nonetheless able to play an active role in the war against France in 1945. In 1946 the ICP removed him from his position, allegedly for his brutal repression of potential rivals. He then was sent to Thailand as a representative of the Vietminh. By 1954 Tran Van Giau was no longer an influential political figure, but he rose to prominence once again as a leading historian of Vietnam and Vietnam's communist movement. As such, he has produced a considerable body of work on contemporary Vietnamese history.

Micheline R. Lessard

Further Reading
Duiker, William. (1981) *The Communist Road to Power in Vietnam.* Boulder, CO: Westview Press.
Hue Tam Ho Tai. (1992) *Radicalism and the Origins of the Vietnamese Revolution.* Cambridge, MA: Harvard University Press.
Marr, David G. (1981) *Vietnamese Tradition on Trial 1920–1945.* Berkeley and Los Angeles: University of California Press.
Trinh Van Thao. (1990) *Vietnam du Confucianisme au Communisme.* Paris: l'Harmattan.

TRANS ALAI The most northerly section of the massive Pamir Mountains, the Trans Alai Range stretches east to west for 240 kilometers along the frontier between Kyrgyzstan and Tajikistan. The unbroken and somewhat rounded summits rise abruptly from all directions with only minor foothills. The fertile Alai valley of Kyrgyzstan lies north, and Tajikistan's Muksu and Markansu valleys lie south. Lenin Peak (7,134 meters, originally Mount Kaufmann) is the second highest peak in the Pamirs and was the second highest point in the former Soviet Union. In contrast to other Central Asian summits, the gentle southern slopes and ordinarily reliable summer weather attract throngs of mountaineers.

The snowbound upper elevations give way to deep canyons that shade 12,170 square kilometers (776 square miles) of "Turkestan type" glaciers, where overburden from moraines and rock falls insulates the ice from summer heat. Winter snow and spring rains nourish lush steppes and alpine pastures that Kyrgyz and Tajik herders utilize for goats, sheep, horses, and yaks from June to August. The Pamirs Highway between Osh, Kyrgyzstan, and Khorog, Tajikistan, crosses the range at Kyzalart Pass (4,280 meters). Winter snows frequently close this lone vehicle route, leaving the Gorno-Badakhshan Autonomous Oblast of Tajikistan isolated from the outside world. Saline Kara Kul Lake nestles south of the pass and is an important stop for migratory waterfowl.

Stephen F. Cunha

Further Reading
Craig, Robert. (1980) *Storm and Sorrow in the High Pamir.* Rev. ed.. New York: Simon & Schuster.
Maier, Frith. (1994) "A Women's Climbing Tragedy Remembered: Peak Lenin, 20 Years Ago." *Climbing* 146, 30: 32–33.

TRANS-MONGOLIAN RAILWAY The Trans-Mongolian Railway, a prominent offshoot of the Trans-Siberian Railway, connects Mongolia with the border of China and via the Trans-Siberian Railway with Moscow. Starting at Ulaan Ude in Russia, the rail line extends approximately 530 kilometers to Ulaanbaatar, Mongolia, and a further 730 kilometers through the Gobi Desert to the border with China at Dzamiin Uud. At this point the trains must change tracks, owing to the fact that Soviets built their railways a gauge wider to prevent foreign invasions by rail. From the Chinese border, the train travels another 800 kilometers past the Great Wall to Beijing.

The rail from Ulaan Ude to Ulaanbaatar was finished in 1949 by a Mongolian-Soviet joint-stock company. Soon after, the rail extended to the border with China. The Trans-Mongolian Railway quickly became the primary mode of transportation between Mongolia and Russia and consequently increased economic and cultural relations between the two countries. In addition to providing transportation between Moscow, Ulaanbaatar, and sometimes Beijing, the line served as a main line for spurs to several important mining sites. Rail lines now run from the Trans-Mongolian Railway to mines in Choir, Erdenet, Bor Ondor, and Baganuur.

Daniel Hruschka

Further Reading
The Academy of Sciences of the Mongolian People's Republic. (1990) *Information Mongolia*. Oxford: Pergamon Press.

TRANSPORTATION SYSTEM—CHINA

China, with its enormous and increasingly urbanized population, faces unprecedented challenges and opportunities in the way in which it transports its citizens and goods. The country's recent rapid period of economic growth is set to continue for the foreseeable future, placing increased pressure on its political leaders and urban designers to move toward more efficient and environmentally benign transportation systems for its people and products.

Roads

The main focus for upgraded transportation systems has been on China's road and vehicle network. China's light industry and agricultural sectors rely heavily on road-based transportation. Although China has more than 100 people per motor vehicle, compared with 1.3 people per motor vehicle in the United States, the number of motor vehicles in China more than tripled in the 1985–2000 period. There are more than 11 million vehicles: 6 million trucks and buses, 3.6 million cars, and 1.4 million other vehicles (mainly motorcycles).

More foreign automobile companies are entering China to meet the demand for new vehicles. Volkswagen commenced manufacturing automobiles in Shanghai in 1985. Other major companies have also commenced manufacturing for the Chinese market, including Daihatsu, Citroen, Peugeot, General Motors, and Daimler-Chrysler. Most vehicles are built in the Shanghai region and near Dalian in the northeastern province of Liaoning.

China has increased its road system such that now all towns can be reached via the highway system. Approximately 1.3 million kilometers of roads stretch across the country. In 1998 alone, 37,000 kilometers of highways were built; of those, 1,487 kilometers were expressways.

A consequence of China's growth in motor vehicles is increased use of energy (mostly oil). If China achieved U.S. levels of vehicle ownership, it would have more than 900 million vehicles—nearly 50 percent more than the total number of vehicles in the world in 2001. China would need to consume more oil than is currently produced throughout the world.

Rail

China has an extensive rail network, with Beijing being the hub for the north-south line to Shanghai and Guangzhou. Rail lines also extend to the west and connect China to Europe. New lines are being built, particularly in southern China and other industrial areas. There are nearly 60,000 kilometers of railway lines, most of which were built since 1949.

China's first subway was constructed in Beijing in 1969. Many of the densely populated cities have developed or plan to develop commuter rail transportation systems involving subways and light rail. These include the cities of Shenyang, Changchun, and Harbin in the northeast and other major cities, including Shanghai, Guangzhou, Nanjing, Shenzhen, and Chongqing.

In 2001 the length of China's light rail system was approximately 120 kilometers. By 2005 it is expected that more than 400 kilometers of rail transit systems will have been built, reflecting a construction cost of more than 130 billion yuan ($15.7 billion) between 2001 and 2005.

Air

In the period since 1970, China has constructed and expanded numerous airports, mainly to handle increasing tourist traffic and to link remote areas. By 1999 more than 140 airports were open to civil airplanes.

Beijing is the hub of domestic air travel from which airlines reach all provinces, autonomous regions, and municipalities. The other two international gateway airports are in Guangzhou and Shanghai. Around thirty Chinese airlines serve the domestic market. China has a fast-growing fleet of Western aircraft and is one of Boeing's top three customers.

Water

As China has a coastline of over 18,000 kilometers and 110,000 kilometers of navigable inland waterways, it is easy to understand why water transport has a long history in the country. Countless boats transport goods along rivers and the coast. The major inland navigable rivers are the Chang (Yangtze) (known as the "golden waterway" of China's inland river transport), Huang (Yellow), Pearl, Heilongjiang, Huai, Qiantang, Minjiang, and Huangpu, as well as the Grand Canal between Beijing and Hangzhou. The volume of passenger transportation is approximately 12 billion trips per year. There are more than five thousand berths at around seventy major inland river ports. There are twenty large ports for international shipping in China, with Shanghai Harbor being one of the largest in the world.

Transport Options

China is presented with enormous dilemmas concerning the most appropriate mode of development as the country seeks to continue its economic growth. The path it chooses will significantly affect numerous countries. China's transportation policies will increasingly influence the world energy market and transboundary environmental deterioration, particularly a reduction in regional air quality and an increase in greenhouse gases if there are increased emissions of gasoline-driven vehicles. China's transportation policies will also affect the health of its citizens, because the emissions from gasoline-driven vehicles are detrimental to people's health. However, China can focus on less environmentally harmful alternatives, such as vehicles powered by natural gas or batteries, as well as electric hybrids and fuel-cell vehicles powered by nonpolluting and renewable hydrogen. China is relatively unhindered in developing these options because the country is not heavily dependent on oil. It has little existing petroleum vehicle-related investments, such as is common in many Western countries, and it can base its transport infrastructure on cleaner fuels. China is particularly interested in vehicles powered by natural gas because natural gas is abundant in several provinces.

China is investigating cleaner fuel technologies through institutions such as the Institute of Natural Gas Vehicles in Beijing. Currently, China's transportation policy is focused both on the development of "cleaner" vehicles and on increasing investment in mass transportation systems in the cities. China's latest five-year plan (2001–2005) focuses on coordinating economic development among different regions and between urban and rural areas. The plan increases the priority given to environmental protection and indicates that China will attempt to pursue less environmentally harmful transportation systems than were favored by many Western countries at a similar stage of economic development.

Warwick Gullett

Further Reading

Cannon, James S. (1998) *China at the Crossroads: Energy, Transportation, and the 21st Century.* New York: Inform.
MacArthur, Peter, and John Low. (1994) *Tapping into China's Transport Infrastructure Market.* Canberra, Australia: Australian Government Publishing Service.
World Bank. (1985) *China: The Transport Sector.* Washington, DC: International Bank for Reconstruction and Development, World Bank.

TREATY OF AMITY AND CO-OPERATION OF 1976

The Treaty of Amity and Co-operation (TAC) was signed in the first Association of Southeast Asian Nations (ASEAN) summit on 24 February 1976, in Bali, Indonesia, by the five ASEAN founding members—Indonesia, Malaysia, the Philippines, Singapore, and Thailand. The TAC fundamentally mirrors the ASEAN mode of interaction among members. The TAC signifies the group's commitment to the principles of respecting each nation's independence, national identity, the right to be free from external interference, and the noninterference in internal affairs of member countries.

In the 1992 ASEAN summit in Manila, Philippines, the decision was made to allow other Southeast Asian states to join the TAC, gaining observer status and establishing links with the ASEAN group. It paved the way for other nations to join the ASEAN family: Brunei Darussalam (1984), Vietnam (1995), Laos (1997), Cambodia (1999), and Myanmar (1999). Today the ASEAN region has a total population of about 500 million with a roughly combined gross national product of $600 billion. Against this backdrop, the TAC embodies the collective will and aspirations of all Southeast Asians.

As a political commitment, the TAC reflects one of the most important ASEAN initiatives for implementing regional order and cooperation among member countries. With the endorsement of the United Nations General Assembly in 1992, the TAC became an important instrument in enhancing regional peace and stability. In accordance with the Charter of the United Nations, the TAC is recognized as a mechanism for promoting regional relations on a broad consensual basis and settling intra-ASEAN disputes through the rule of law.

Against all odds and despite internal rivalries and territorial disputes among highly diverse member countries, the deep-seated principles of the TAC have been inspirational in the realization of ASEAN-10, which has successfully incorporated all Southeast Asian countries to be a part of ASEAN; in developing more cohesive and effective political, economic, and social relations; as well as sustaining regional peace and stability. There has been no interstate conflict or military confrontation among ASEAN members since the founding of the group. More importantly, through an agreed code of conduct, ASEAN has played a constructive role in integrating Southeast Asia into the international economy through the Asia-Pacific Economic Cooperation Forum (APEC). The association has also enhanced regional and international security by promoting multilateral security dialogue with non-ASEAN members via the ASEAN Regional Forum (ARF), which consists of twenty-two member countries.

Geetha Govindasamy

Further Reading

ASEAN: The First Twenty Years. (1987) Singapore: ASEAN Secretariat.

Flores, Jamil Maidan. (2000) *ASEAN Functional Cooperation: Toward a Caring Community.* Jakarta, Indonesia: ASEAN Secretariat.

Ganesan, Narayanan. (1999) *Bilateral Tensions in Post-Cold War ASEAN.* Singapore: Institute of Southeast Asian Studies.

Hourn, Kao Kim, and Jeffrey A. Kaplan. (2000) *ASEAN's Non Interference Policy: Principles under Pressure?* London: ASEAN Academic Press.

Muhammad Ghazali Shafie, Tan Sri. (2000) *Malaysia, ASEAN, and the New World Order.* Bangi, Malaysia: Universiti Kebangsaan Malaysia.

Severino, Rodolfo. (1999) *ASEAN Rises to the Challenge.* Jakarta, Indonesia: ASEAN Secretariat.

TREATY OF GANDOMAK

The Treaty of Gandomak was signed in May of 1879 between Afghanistan and Britain. The Afghan leader, Yaqub, came to power with the death of his father, Sher Ali, in February of 1879 and soon faced a crisis: Britain, enraged by Afghanistan's refusal to allow a British mis-

sion in Kabul after witnessing an unwanted Russian mission in Kabul, had sent troops into Afghanistan at the end of 1878. Before his death, Sher Ali had tried to enlist the assistance of Russia to counteract these troops but to no avail. Because the British had already occupied a large portion of the nation, Yaqub agreed to the terms of the Treaty of Gandomak in order to stop Britain from invading the rest of Afghanistan.

For all practical purposes, the Treaty of Gandomak turned Afghanistan into a British protectorate. It provided Afghanistan with British financial support and military support if Afghanistan faced foreign aggressors. In exchange, Afghanistan relinquished control of its foreign affairs to London and allowed the establishment of British missions in the capital and other major regions of the country. Moreover, London was given control over the strategic Khyber and Michni passes as well as several Afghan frontier areas. The Treaty of Gandomak, which clearly favored London, was signed by Yaqub only because of British military superiority. Following a failed Afghan military campaign against the British in October of 1879, Yaqub was forced to resign for fear of his life after having signed a treaty so disadvantageous to Afghanistan.

Houman A. Sadri

Further Reading

Adamec, Ludwig W. (1996) *Dictionary of Afghan Wars, Revolution, and Insurgencies.* Lanham, MD: Scarecrow Press.

Nyrop, Richard F. (1986) *Afghanistan: A Country Study.* Washington, DC: American University.

TREATY OF GIYANTI

The Treaty of Giyanti (1751) largely concluded the Third Javanese War of Succession, placed further parts of Java under Dutch control, and partitioned the Javanese kingdom of Mataram (1570s–1751) into the principalities of Surakarta and Yogyakarta. In 1746, Prince Mangkubumi of Mataram (1715?–1792) rebelled against King Pakubuwono II of Mataram (1710–1749) over the latter's extensive concessions to the Vereenigde Oostindische Compagnie (VOC; United East Indies Company or Dutch East India Company) on the north coast of Java. On Pakubuwono's death in 1749, Mangkubumi declared himself king, while the VOC supported Pakubuwono's son, Pakubuwono III (?–1788).

Neither side could prevail in the costly civil war, which is known as the Third Javanese War of Succession (1746–1751). In February 1755, Mangkubumi and the VOC signed a treaty, confirming the VOC's control of the north coast of Java and recognizing

Mangkubumi as ruler of approximately one-half of Mataram. He took the regal name Sultan Hamengkubuwono I and established his court at Yogyakarta, while Pakubuwono III continued to rule in Surakarta. The territories of the two principalities stretched from Cilacap in the west to Blitar in the east and were a complicated patchwork of allegiances. Only at the beginning of the nineteenth century were the two states further reduced in size and a relatively simple border drawn between them.

Robert Cribb

See also: **Dutch East India Company; Dutch in Southeast Asia**

Further Reading
Ricklefs, M. C. (1974) *Jogjakarta under Sultan Mangkubumi, 1749–1792: A History of the Division of Java*. London: Oxford University Press.

TRENGGANU (2002 est. pop. 927,000). The state of Trengganu lies along the eastern shore of peninsular Malaysia. It has an elongated coastline of about 250 kilometers facing the South China Sea. Until offshore oil and gas were discovered in 1978, Trengganu was one of the least developed states in the country in terms of conventional economic indicators. Mainstay activities continue to revolve around fishing and smallholding agriculture, although tourism—the state's picturesque beaches and marine life are the main attractions—and the oil boon are now bringing significant social and economic changes.

Trade links between Trengganu and China existed by the twelfth century, if not earlier, as evidenced by Chinese literary sources. The town of Kuala Berang was noted as an important trading center, and Trengganu was known by various names like Chau Chu-fei and Teng Ya-nu. An inscription dated 1303 CE uncovered in Kuala Berang indicates that an Islamic polity was also in place, predating by a century the founding of the Melaka Sultanate. However, in terms of empire building Trengganu has not been a major player. At different periods, it was a vassal state of its more powerful neighbors Melaka, Johore, and Siam before coming under British control in 1909 and subsequently becoming a constituent state of independent Malaysia in 1957.

Yeoh Seng-Guan

Further Reading
Shaharil, Talib. (1984) *After Its Own Image: The Trengganu Experience, 1881–1941*. Kuala Lumpur, Malaysia: Oxford University Press.

Sutherland, Heather. (1978). "The Taming of the Trengganu Elite." In *Southeast Asian Transitions: Approaches through Social History*, edited by Ruth McVey. New Haven, CT: Yale University Press.
Zawawi, Ibrahim. (1998). *The Malay Labourer: By the Window of Capitalism*. Singapore: Institute of Southeast Asian Studies.

TRIBES AND TRIBAL FEDERATIONS—CENTRAL ASIA In Central and Inner Asia before modern states emerged, tribes and tribal federations were the dominant forms of political and social organization. When states arose in the region—whether imposed by an external power or emerging from the tribal organization itself—these new states bore the imprint of tribal relationships. Even today critical aspects of political and social life are rooted in earlier forms of organizations.

Varieties of Tribes and Federations

Many anthropologists no longer use the term "tribe," first, because it has become value laden; for example, expressions like "tribal warfare" imply that tribes are inherently warlike. Second, it is difficult to define "tribe" in terms of anthropological evidence, especially in relation to the once-favored evolutionary theory of human groups.

Nonetheless, there is something distinctive about social and political organizations in prestate Central and Inner Asia, and the term "tribe" serves to describe this distinctiveness. Some scholars have thought of tribes as "rural groups that have a name and distinguish between members and nonmembers, which occupy a territory, and which within that territory assume either all responsibility, or at least a significant proportion of the responsibility, for the maintenance of order" (Ahmed and Hart 1984: 1). Key to this view of a tribe is a relative political decentralization; power is normally exercised at the local level and is more diffuse than that experienced under state structures.

Traditionally, in Central and Inner Asia tribes were either sedentary or nomadic. Sedentary tribes practiced agriculture and sometimes engaged in commerce. They had a close relationship to the territory they inhabited; place-names often coincided with group identification. In the long-sedentary areas of Uzbekistan, for example, group identification with place remains common. Among sedentary populations, differences in dialect, customary practices, and mode of economy can become pronounced.

Tribal organization was different among nomads (those who migrated less predictably) and transhumants (those who migrated seasonally). First, genealogy played a much stronger role in organizing nonsedentary tribes. Because they had a looser relationship to any given place, something other than physical location was needed to distinguish the members of a nomadic tribe from the nonmembers. Central and Inner Asian nomads were expected to commit to memory at least seven generations of ancestors and often more, to locate themselves in one or another tribal group.

A second distinguishing feature of nomadic tribal organization was a pattern of fissure and fusion. Groups cohered and dissolved, depending on outside threats and prevailing environmental conditions. A population, for example, that faced an outside threat might cohere as a single entity to address the threat, but after the threat diminished, the entity would probably disintegrate into smaller groups. Such fissure and fusion were understood to occur along genealogical lines; kin ties defined group boundaries, and ties of even closer kinship defined subunits.

Both sedentary and nomadic or transhumant tribes could cohere into federations. These typically began as political alliances but often evolved into something more stable. In Kazakhstan, for example, these federations (*zhuz* in Kazakh) came to be described in the genealogical terms usually limited to closer kin-based units. Each federation commanded a degree of bargaining authority with outsiders and could issue calls to arms against external foes. Especially in sedentary areas, what began as alliances or federations of different tribes evolved into stable quasi-state structures with centralized authority and mobilizable troops, if not a standing army.

Tribes and Statehood

Since it is decentralized and local, tribal organization stands in contrast to the organization of states, which typically centralize power and project it over a wide territory. Tribes may have standing political and social elites, but they lack the durable bureaucratic structures of a modern state. In Central and Inner Asia tribal organizations in many ways represented an alternative to state structures.

Tribal organization generated an alternative ideology that emphasized egalitarian values. In reality there was considerable social stratification, with aristocratic lineages enjoying positions of privilege and commercial strata enjoying the prospect of greater accumulation of wealth. Compared with nontribal contexts, however, egalitarian values were much more pervasive. The granting of hospitality to guests, widespread gift giving, and attention to the social and economic standing of kin were all expressions of such egalitarian norms.

The tribally organized societies of Central and Inner Asia often resisted the imposition of state structures, especially in geographically remote regions where resistance could be more effective than in more accessible regions. For example, long after the Soviet Union had forcibly sedentarized the nomadic Kazakhs and had imposed bureaucratic structures on them, a spirit of resistance remained strong among the relatively remote populations on the Mangyshlak Peninsula. In parts of Soviet Central Asia, state authorities allowed local tribal elites to govern populations much as they always had, because patterns of tribal authority were difficult to undermine.

If states could be imposed on tribally organized populations, as in the Soviet Union from 1917 to 1991, tribes could also generate state structures from within. Prominent examples were the statelike structures created by Genghis Khan, which dominated much of Eurasia in the thirteenth and fourteenth centuries and had numerous features usually associated with states (for example, tax systems, recruitment of administrators). By creating state structures from within, Genghis Khan allowed a tribally organized core to project its power across a vast territory more effectively than had he relied on coercion alone.

Recent Transformations

What happens when states and tribally organized societies have come into contact? In Central and Inner Asia, state structures have often proved effective at governing certain populations but not others. Populations at the margins of state control have a far different relationship to the state than do populations under direct state control. Tribal populations at the margins may question the legitimacy of the ruling state elite. In Afghanistan, for example, many non-Pashtuns have felt that the ruling Taliban elite privileged Pashtuns to the detriment of non-Pashtuns. In Kyrgyzstan southern groups commonly perceive that northern elites exercise dominance illegitimately.

If urbanization and the spread of literacy accompany the imposition of state structures, a process of "detribalization" may occur in urban areas. Given the mixing of populations and the wide array of opportunities available in cities, tribal links may weaken or even disappear. In the former Soviet Central Asia sizable populations in urban areas may know little about their tribal heritage. Any detribalization that does occur, however, is mitigated by strong ties that many retain to the countryside, where tribal background continues to be important. In addition, in a city, many urban dwellers use networks based on kinship or ties to place to find employment and housing. Scholars continue to debate why detribalization sometimes occurs quickly, sometimes slowly, and sometimes not at all.

Even if state structures come to govern tribes as physical entities, tribal identities continue to be vibrant and important as mental constructs with social and political significance. Thus the tribes and tribal federations of Central and Inner Asia are not merely a matter of historical or anthropological curiosity; in critical ways they remain important to the peoples themselves. Among elites, competition over scarce resources is in critical part a contest of groups based on tribal background. Moreover, much of this contest takes place behind the scenes, since elites claim to represent broad populations, not single tribal groups; they therefore often disallow public discussion of tribal backgrounds. By making such discourse difficult or even illegal, elites lend it an aura of secrecy that makes tribal background a potentially explosive issue. Not surprisingly, in genuinely democratic contexts, such as in Mongolia in 2001, tribal background and heritage are less explosive issues than in more repressive societies, but even in Mongolia they remain politically sensitive.

Edward Schatz

Further Reading
Ahmed, Akbar S., and David M. Hart. (1984) *Islam in Tribal Societies: From the Atlas to the Indus.* London: Routledge and Kegan Paul.
Bacon, Elizabeth E. (1966) *Central Asians under Russian Rule: A Study in Culture Change.* Ithaca, NY: Cornell University Press.
Evans-Pritchard, E. E. (1940) *The Nuer: A Description of the Modes of Livelihood and Political Institutions of a Nilotic People.* Oxford: Oxford University Press
Khazanov, Anatoly M. (1994) *Nomads and the Outside World.* 2d ed. Madison, WI: University of Wisconsin Press.

TRINCOMALEE (2002 est. district pop. 356,000; est. city pop. 82,600). Since the British seized the island of Sri Lanka in 1796, Trincomalee has been the main city and center of the district of the same name. It is located in the north of the Batticaloa District of Eastern Province and to the south of the Mullaitivu District of Northern Province. From the time of the medieval South Indian Chola dynasty that ruled over northern Sri Lanka in the eleventh century, the district was overwhelmingly populated by Hindu Tamils. The city of Trincomalee was established at an extensive and nearly circular natural harbor, which the British considered the best and most beautiful in Asia. From medieval times, the city was therefore well suited to attract long-distance trade. The Cholas established a Siva temple dedicated to Trikoneshvara on the promontory of the bay. It is from this temple, which was destroyed by the Portuguese in 1624 in order to build fortifications, that the city and district derive its name. When the Vereenigte Ostindsche Companie (Dutch East India Company) drove the Portuguese from the island, the Dutch erected commanding fortifications at the site, and since British times the city prospered as the island's second and most important harbor and as a trade center dominated by local Hindu Tamils and Muslim merchants. Since the 1950s, however, because of Sinhalese colonization, the nationalization of the harbor, and the establishment of industrial plants, the ethnic balance has shifted in favor of Sinhalese farmers and workers. In the early 2000s, the district population consists of 34 percent Sinhalese, 37 percent Tamils, and 29 percent Muslims.

Jakob Roesel

Further Reading
Ballou, Maturin M. (1894) *The Pearl of India.* Boston: Houghton Mifflin.

TRIPURA (2001 pop. est. 3.1 million). Tripura (formerly Tipperah) is a small state in northeast India. Its area is 10,486 square kilometers. Indian territory lies to the northeast, and Tripura is bordered on all other sides by Bangladesh. The region is mostly wooded and hilly; approximately 50 percent is forested, and shifting cultivation has been a traditional practice. The highest range of hills (up to 1,000 meters) is Jampui Kang. The chief rivers—the Meghara, Titas, Gumti, and Dakatia—are navigable throughout the year.

For approximately thirteen hundred years before its accession to the Indian Union, Tripura was a Hindu princely state ("Hill Tipperah," to the British). It became a state of India in 1949, then a centrally administered Union Territory in 1957, and reverted to a state in 1972. The capital is Agartala, which is the location of Tripura University. Tripura is divided into three districts, and is governed by a sixty-member legislative assembly. The main languages spoken by the people are Bengali, Kakbarak, and Manipuri. About 24 percent of the land is cultivated. Rice, wheat, tea, oilseeds, cotton, jute, mulberry, and sugarcane are grown. The largest industries are tea cultivation and handloom production, and there are small steel and food processing plants. Sericulture is also developing in the state.

Paul Hockings

TRIVANDRUM (2001 est. pop. 745,000). Trivandrum, or Thiruvananthapuram as it is now officially called, is the capital of the state of Kerala, India. *Thiru-Anantha-puram* means the "abode of the sacred thousand-headed serpent Anantha," who forms the couch on which reclines Lord Vishnu, the preserver. Built on seven hills, Trivandrum has grown as a major tourist destination in recent times, as it is close to many fine beaches. The city covers an area of 74 square kilometers and is located in the extreme south of Kerala on the Arabian Sea.

Historically, Trivandrum was part of the territory ruled by the Ay kings up to the tenth century CE. The rulers of Venad concentrated their power in the southern part of Kerala and by the eighteenth century their control extended over the region between Trivandrum and Cape Comorin. The name also reflects the city's best-known temple, Sri Padmanabhaswamy Temple, dedicated to Padmanabha, or Lord Vishnu. In 1750 Marthanda Varma, the ruler of Travancore, dedicated the entire state to the deity of the temple.

The modern city is known for the high literacy rate of its population, as a regional center for music and the arts, and as the locale of India's first space center, now a tourist attraction.

R. Gopinath

TRUNG SISTERS In 39 CE, a Vietnamese nobleman named Thi Sach and his wife Trung Trac led the first revolt against the Chinese who had ruled Nam Viet ("southern country of the Viet") since 111 BCE. The successful military campaign enabled the Vietnamese to free themselves from Chinese rule. Trung Trac, along with her sister Trung Nhi, established a court northwest of Hanoi at Me-linh. Vietnamese tradition states that the execution of Thi Sach by the Chinese had ignited the rebellion, while Chinese sources indicate that Thi Sach simply followed his wife's authority. The Vietnamese recognized Trung Trac as queen until the Chinese, under General Ma Yuan, invaded with an army numbering around 20,000 and eventually defeated the Vietnamese forces. At the battle of Lang Bac, some 10,000 Vietnamese surrendered, and thousands more were executed. Vietnamese tradition holds that the Trung sisters escaped the Chinese and committed suicide by leaping into the Day Hat River. Chinese sources, however, claim that Trung Trac and Trung Nhi were captured and beheaded, and their heads were sent to the Han court. By late 43, Ma Yuan had regained control over the Red River Delta area, and the Chinese thus secured their rule over the Vietnamese.

The Trung Sisters (Hai Ba Trung, "the two ladies Trung"; also known as Truong Vuong or Trung Nu Vuong, "the queens Trung") are today revered by many Vietnamese as the most important heroines in Vietnamese history. The anniversary of their deaths is Vietnamese Women's Day, and the Vietnamese hold annual ceremonies honoring them on the sixth day of the seventh month of the lunar calendar. In practically every Vietnamese city, there is a street named "Hai Ba Trung" in honor of the two Vietnamese revolutionaries.

Richard B. Verrone

Further Reading
Taylor, Keith. (1983) *The Birth of Vietnam*. Berkeley and Los Angeles: University of California Press.
Tucker, Spencer. (1999) *Vietnam*. Lexington, KY: University Press of Kentucky.

TRUONG VINH KY (1837–1898), Vietnamese linguist, collaborator with the early French regime. Truong Vinh Ky (Petrus Jean-Baptiste Vinh Ky) was a Catholic-educated Vietnamese scholar who collaborated with the early French colonial regime in southern Vietnam. Ky was also a brilliant linguist who spoke more than twenty-five Asian and European languages and was a pioneer in early efforts to popularize *quoc ngu* (the romanized form of Vietnamese). Born in the Mekong Delta region of Ben Tre, Ky was educated by Catholic priests in his home village and later at missionary schools in Cambodia and Penang, Malaysia. In 1858 he returned home to become a village teacher, only to leave again in 1863 to serve as an interpreter for a Vietnamese imperial delegation to France. While there, he met Victor Hugo and Ernest Renan among other European intellectuals and became convinced of the value of European civilization and culture and the potential benefits of French colonial tutelage for his own country.

On his return from Europe, Ky resumed his role as an educator, now serving the French colonial regime. He taught at the College des Interprètes in Saigon, where he trained many early colonial officials and later gave French lessons to a future Nguyen emperor, Dong Khanh (reigned 1886–1888). Truong Vinh Ky was also a prolific researcher and writer, producing more than one hundred books on topics ranging from grammar and linguistics to history and geography. He wrote and published the first work in romanized Vietnamese in 1866, and between 1869 and 1872 he served as editor of the earliest romanized Vietnamese newspaper, *Gia Dinh Bao*. Ky's *Cours D'histoire Annamite* (1875) was the first French-language survey of Vietnamese history, and he also produced the first French-Vietnamese dictionary.

George Dutton

Further Reading
Bang Giang. (1993) *Suong Mu Tren Tac Pham Truong Vinh Ky* (Haze over the Works of Truong Vinh Ky). Ho Chi Minh City, Vietnam: Nha Xuat Ban Van Hoc.
Durand, Maurice, and Tran Huan Nguyen. (1985) *An Introduction to Vietnamese Literature*. Trans. by D. M. Hawke. New York: Columbia University Press.
Osborne, Milton. (1969) *The French Presence in Cochinchina and Cambodia: Rule and Response (1859–1905)*. Ithaca, NY: Cornell University Press.
Truong Vinh Ky (1875) *Cours D'histoire Annamite*. Ho Chi Minh City, Vietnam: Imprimerie du Gouvernement.
Xuan Thu Khong. (1958) *Truong Vinh Ky, 1837–1898*. Ho Chi Minh City, Vietnam: Tan Viet.

TSEDENBEL, YUMJAAGIYN
(1916–1991), Mongolian premier and president. Yumjaagiyn Tsedenbel was born in the Uvs province of Mongolia and ruled Mongolia as its premier from 1952 to 1974 and then as its president from 1974 to 1984.

In 1931, he had joined the Mongolian Youth League and in 1939 the Mongolian People's Revolutionary Party (MPRP). From then on, his life was dedicated to politics.

In 1940, Tsedenbel became the general secretary of the MPRP and forced the introduction of the Cyrillic alphabet into Mongolia, replacing the vertical classical Mongolian script introduced by the great Mongol leader Genghis Khan (c. 1162–1227). In the 1940s and early 1950s, he served in numerous positions in the government and the MPRP, until the death of Choybalsan (1895–1952), Mongolia's prime minister at the time. In 1952, Tsedenbel became the premier of Mongolia.

In many Mongols' eyes, Tsedenbel was merely a Soviet puppet who followed the example of Leonid Brezhnev (1906–1982), the Soviet leader and general secretary of the Communist Party. Furthermore, people believed his Russian wife possessed too much influence. His detractors had reason for criticism. Tsedenbel developed a cult of personality and in 1962

purged many of Mongolia's leading academics and politicians. Although few were actually executed, many suffered in exile. Tsendenbel's rule came to an end in 1984, when Batmonkh (b. 1926) took over the post of prime minister while Tsendenbel was in Moscow. Although Tsedenbel stayed in Moscow and died there in 1991, he was buried in Ulaanbataar, the capital of Mongolia.

Timothy M. May

Further Reading
Bawden, Charles R. (1968) *The Modern History of Mongolia*. New York: Frederick A. Praeger.
Dashpurev, D., and S. K. Soni. (1992) *Reign of Terror in Mongolia, 1920–1990*. New Delhi: South Asian Publishers.
Rupen, Robert. (1979) *How Mongolia Is Really Ruled*. Standford, CA: Hoover Institution Press.
Sanders, Alan. (1996) *Historical Dictionary of Mongolia*. Lanham, MD: Scarecrow Press.

TSENG KUO-FAN. See Zeng Guofan.

TSUENBAL. See Tsedenbel.

TSUSHIMA ISLAND
(1996 pop. 44,000). Tsushima Island, which is actually two main islands totaling 694 square kilometers and more than one hundred smaller ones in the strait between Japan and South Korea, belongs to Nagasaki Prefecture. Its principal industries are fishing and forestry. The island's largest city is Izuhara.

As Japan's closest landmass to the Asian continent, Tsushima traditionally served as an integral link in Japan's relations with China and Korea. The island was devastated by the Mongols during their two invasions of Japan in 1274 and 1281. In the following centuries, Tsushima became a base for Japanese pirate *(wako)* activity in the area. In an effort to halt the pirate menace, Korea sent punitive expeditions against the island in 1389 and 1419. From the fifteenth through the mid-nineteenth centuries, Korean-Japanese trade was supervised by the So daimyo family of Tsushima and restricted to walled compounds *(wakan)* in Korea.

After American commodore Matthew Perry opened Japan to the outside world in the 1850s, Tsushima also played a key role in the country's new relationship with the West. In 1861, Russia failed in an attempt to take the island. Then, in 1905, the decisive naval battle of the Russo-Japanese War was fought in the waters off

Tsushima, assuring Japan of victory over the European power.

Lane R. Earns

Further Reading
Toby, Ronald. (1984) *State and Diplomacy in Early Modern Japan.* Princeton, NJ: Princeton University Press.

TU LUC VAN DOAN Tu Luc Van Doan (Independent Literary Group) was a literary club founded in Vietnam by a group of well-known writers, following the lead of Nguyen Tuong Tam, also known as Nhat Linh. Its goal was to use literature as a means of bringing about profound literary and social changes in colonial Vietnam. Among the "Ten Commandments" of the organization were resolutions to write original works, not to translate foreign authors, and to write simply, using pure Vietnamese language while at the same time applying Western methodologies to Vietnamese literature. Other commandments expressed the group's commitment to improve society and respect individual freedom, to encourage patriotism by emphasizing the beauty and distinctive character of Vietnam in literature, and to denounce Confucianism as anachronistic.

The club published two magazines, *Phong Hoa* (Customs) and *Ngay Nay* (Today), which attracted a wide readership. It also managed a publishing house named Doi Nay (Modern Life), which produced, from 1933 to 1936, close to sixty thousand copies of novels or poetry collections. Tu Luc Van Doan exerted a tremendous influence on Vietnamese literature. It published the first modern novels in Vietnam and initiated the new poetry movement shaped by nationalist and anticolonial sentiments.

Lam Truong Buu

Further Reading
Phan Cu De. (1990) *Tu Luc Van Doan: con Nguoi va van Chuong.* Hanoi, Vietnam.

TUJIA The Tujia are the eighth-largest ethnic group in China; numbering 5.7 million, they are more numerous than the better-known Mongols and Tibetans. Settlements of the Tujia are distributed over western Hunan and western Hubei provinces, as well as in several autonomous counties under the jurisdiction of Chongqing municipality.

Origins of Tujia Language and Present-Day Usage
Some linguists consider the Tujia language to be part of the Yi language branch of the Sino-Tibetan language family. According to others, however, although the Tujia language shares some characteristics with the Yi languages, those characteristics are not enough to make the Tujia a member of that branch. Nonetheless, it is beyond question that the language, like those in the Yi branch and some others, belongs to the Tibeto-Burman subfamily of the Sino-Tibetan family. The language has no written form.

Chinese is the dominant language used by the Tujia; many Tujia speak nothing but Chinese. Some are bilingual, speaking both Chinese and Tujia. A number also speak the language of the Miao (known outside of China as the Hmong), one of their immediate neighbors. Less than 200,000 Tujia still rely on the Tujia language as their major means of communication.

Tujia Names
In their own language, the Tujia call themselves *Bidzih-ka.* In history, they were called various names by their neighbors, based on perceived ethnic markers or distinguishing signs, such as their totem (the white tiger, at one time the totem of their chief), or names of rivers or places where they lived. The name "Tujia" came into being in the late seventeenth century when a large number of Han Chinese (the Chinese ethnic majority people) migrated into the Tujia area. The term, which means "aboriginal families" in Chinese, was coined to distinguish the natives from the immigrants. This name did not become official until October 1956, when the Tujia were granted the status of "unitary ethnic group" *(danyi minzu)* by the Chinese government.

Tujia History
The early history of the Tujia is a matter of dispute. Based on clues in Chinese historical literature, some scholars believe that the Tujia are descendents of the Ba, a tribe extinguished by the Qin Dynasty (221–206 BCE). Based on linguistic characteristics and some customs that are close to the Yi in Yunnan, on the other hand, some scholars think that the ancestors of the Tujia are the *wuman* or "black barbarians," who lived in southwestern China. The fact that in the 1970s two significant Neolithic sites were found in Tujia area suggests that those regions were inhabited as early as the prehistoric period.

The picture since the Later Han dynasty (25–220 CE) is much less uncertain. Located close to the great historical powers, the Tujia have a longer history of involvement in China's national politics than many other Chinese minorities. As early as the tenth century, so-called bridled and tethered prefectures *(jimi fuzhou)*, or native tributary administrations, were established in the area. The establishments were converted into a system of native chieftains *(tusi zhidu)* in the thirteenth century. Under this system, minority areas in the Chinese empire were ruled by families of native chieftains instead of officials appointed by the central government. This system lasted in the Tujia area until 1723.

Conflict was the keynote of the recorded early history of interactions between the ancestors of the Tujia and Chinese society. With the establishment of the tributary system and the subsequent system of native chieftains, the Tujia became increasingly sinicized. During the Ming (1368–1644) and Qing (1644–1912) dynasties, a considerable number of Tujia soldiers, called different names at different times, were sent to coastal areas to fight against the Japanese and British invaders.

In the meantime, many upper-class Tujia received a Confucian education and entered the gentry-scholar rank. Some accomplished poets and scholars of the Tujia gained national reputations. When the native-chieftain system was abolished in the eighteenth century, some Tujia customs and conventions were condemned as "corrupted" or "ugly" and were reformed by force. As a result, the Tujia were further assimilated, and many of their ethnic characteristics were lost.

Tujia Culture

Love-based marriage was a tradition among the Tujia. In recent centuries until the early 1950s, however, parental approval had become a norm, and wealth and social status became decisive factors. Cross-cousin marriage (a preferential rule requiring marriage between cross-cousins—mother's father's brother or father's sister's daughter if such a person is available) and levirate (the custom whereby a man marries the widow of his deceased brother) are commonly practiced among the Tujia. In some areas, maternal parallel-cousin marriage (a convention in which one marries an opposite-sex child of one's mother's sister) is also practiced.

Seniority of age is highly venerated by the Tujia. Elderly men and women are respected and treated well while alive, and elaborate funerals are held at their death. Mortuary ritual is also held for people who die

at a younger age, but with less care and expense. No ceremony is held for the death of a child.

There is no organized religion among the Tujia. Their faith, a mixture of animism, ancester worship, and worship of deified deceased chiefs and heroes, has apparently been influenced by the folk religion of the neighboring Han Chinese.

The Tujia have a long tradition of sophisticated folk arts. Over seventy prescribed movements are available for dancers of the popular *bai shou wu* ("hand waving dance") to depict such things as hunting, agricultural activities, battling, and feasting. Legends tell about the genesis and migration of their ancestors as well as their aspirations for and fantasies about the ideal life. Almost every Tujia is an accomplished singer of improvised or traditional ballads, which cover all aspects of daily life and feeling.

The traditional Tujia economy is diversified. Agriculture in narrow strips of terraced fields is complemented by logging, hunting, fishing, and growing or working on cash crops. The Tujia are also known for their traditional weaving, knitting, and embroidery. A variety of light and heavy industries have been developed in the Tujia area, and Jishou University was established there in 1958. In the past two decades, over 95 percent of Tujia children received at least primary education.

Chuan-kang Shih

Further Reading

Zhou, Minglang. (1998) "Majority Language Spread versus Minority Language Loss in China—A Case Study of Tujia." In *Sociolinguistic and Psycholinguistic Perspectives on Maintenance and Loss of Minority Languages*, edited by Tom Ammerlaan, et al. Münster, Germany: Waxman.

Wu Yongzhang. (1988) *Zhongguo tusi zhidu yuanyuan yu fazhan shi* (History of the Origin and Development of the Chinese Native Chieftain System). Chengdu, China: Sichuan minzu chubanshe.

TUMEN RIVER   The Tumen River (Tumangang) is the second-longest river on the Korean Peninsula. In all, it extends 520 kilometers, first flowing northeast from the slopes of Mount Paektu and then southeast through narrow gorges to the East Sea or Sea of Japan. The river is rather shallow due to the dry climate of its drainage basin, which has an area of 24,296 square kilometers. However, in its lower reaches, the Tumen is as wide as 300 meters and is navigable for 80 kilometers. The river is frozen for three to four months of the year.

The Tumen River became the permanent northern-frontier border of Korea when six garrison forts were established there during the reigns of the Choson monarchs T'aejo (1392–1398) and Sejong (1418–1450). In 1909, the river was officially recognized as the international border between China and Korea. A Sino-Russian agreement in 1860 gave Korea and Russia a 16.5-kilometer border demarcated by the Tumen River. Korea and Russia have not signed any treaty to verify this border, but it is undisputed.

The Tumen River and its tributaries have been developed into a valuable source of hydroelectric energy. Efforts are being made to transform the Tumen River area into a free-trade zone.

Brandon Palmer

TUNGABHADRA RIVER

TUNGABHADRA RIVER The Tungabhadra (or Tumbudra) River is a major tributary of the Kistna River, which flows eastward across peninsular India. The Tungra and the Bhadra rivers rise in the Western Ghats, join in Shimoga District, and the Tungabhadra flows 640 kilometers eastward across northern Karnataka and Andhra Pradesh states. The river falls into the Kistna River in Raichur District, becoming its chief tributary before it continues eastwards to the Bay of Bengal. The river was of great economic importance to the Hoysala and Vijayanagar kingdoms (c. 1110–1327 and 1336–1565, respectively), and the Vijayanagar capital at Hampi lay on its right bank. Here and elsewhere its waters have been used for irrigation, but because of its rapid flow and rocky channel, most reaches are only navigable by small boats. The huge Tungabhadra reservoir was constructed at Hospet in the mid-twentieth century (1945–1953). Its power generator is located at Mallapuram.

Paul Hockings

Further Reading

Fujiwara Kenzo (1982). "Development of the Irrigation under the Tungabhadra Project." In *Geographical Field Research in South India, 1980*, edited by Fujiwara Kenzo. Hiroshima, Japan: University of Hiroshima, Research and Sources Unit for Regional Geography.

TUNGUS LANGUAGES

TUNGUS LANGUAGES The Tungus (or Tungusic) languages are a group of genetically related languages spoken in eastern Siberia and northeastern China, mostly in the provinces of Heilongjiang and Liaoning, and the Inner Mongolian Autonomous Region. Smaller Tungus-speaking groups are also found in Xinjiang and Mongolia. Traditionally, the family is subdivided into a Northern and a Southern branch, though this classification has occasionally been called into question.

The North Tungus languages are Evenki (formally often called simply Tungus), spoken by around 10,000 speakers in central and eastern Siberia, between the Yenisey and Amur rivers. In China, the language of the Evenki nationality, usually called Solon, has 20,000 speakers in Heilongjiang. The Oroqen (in Chinese, *Elunchun*) language, with about 4,000 speakers in Inner Mongolia, is also close to Evenki, as is Negidal, on the lower Amur (about 200 speakers). Even, formally known as Lamut and spoken exclusively in Siberia by 5,000 people, is officially written in Cyrillic script.

The South Tungus languages include Nanai (formally known as Gold), with about 5,000 speakers on the lower Amur. The 1,500 members of the Hezhen nationality in Heilongjiang, China, also speak a language close to Nanai. Ul'cha (c. 1,000 speakers) and Orok (fewer than 100 speakers on Sakhalin island) are vanishing languages of the Nanai group. Udi (or Udihe) and Oroch, both with fewer than 500 speakers in the Amur region, form a close-knit subgroup, which is generally considered South Tungusic.

Manchu has one of the longest written traditions of the Tungus languages. The first Manchu documents, written in Mongolian script, date from the beginning of the sixteenth century. Manchu was the official language of Qing dynasty China (1644–1912). Today, very few speakers remain; most of them living in Heilongjiang. The Sibe nationality, originally a Manchu tribe relocated to Xinjiang in 1764, numbers 80,000 speakers. An early predecessor, though some scholars view it as a mere dialect, of Manchu is the Jurchen language, recorded in a unique script from the Jin dynasty (1115–1234). Some Jurchen texts were compiled in Ming times as well.

Stefan Georg

Further Reading

Benzing, Johannes. (1956) *Die tungusischen Sprachen. Versuch einer vergleichenden Grammatik*. Wiesbaden, Germany: Steiner.

Menges, Karl Heinrich. (1968) "Die tungusischen Sprachen." In *Handbuch der Orientalistik, Erste Abteilung, Fünfter Band, Dritter Abschnitt: Tungusologie*, edited by Spuler, Berthold et al. Leiden, Netherlands: Brill, 21–256

Janhunen, Juha. (1996) *Manchuria: An Ethnic History*. Helsinki, Finland: Finno-Ugrian Society.

TURA LOWLAND The Tura (or Turanian) Lowland (in Kazakh *Turan Opyty*, in Uzbek *Turon Pasttekisligi*, in Turkmen *Turan Pesligi*) is a vast plain area located east of the Ustyurt Plateau, and extending from the Kopet-Dag Mountains along the Turkmenistan-Iranian border in the southwest, to the western Siberian Plain in the north along the Russian-Kazak border. Portions of it are occupied by the republics of Turkmenistan in the south, Uzbekistan in the middle, and Kazakhstan in the north. The middle of the lowland is an internal drainage basin occupied by the Aral Sea. Once the world's fourth largest lake, the Aral Sea has been shrinking due to extensive upstream river water withdrawals from its two main water suppliers: the Amu Dar'ya and Syr Dar'ya Rivers. Beginning in the 1960s, a drastic increase in the amount of water withdrawn from the two river systems was used to irrigate more and more land to cotton. Much of the water did not reach the Aral Sea; it either drained away into lower depressions in surrounding areas or evaporated.

The Tura Lowland also contains the Kyzyl Kum (Qyzylkum) and Kara-Kum (Qorakum) deserts separated by the Amu Dar'ya River. Lying between 43° and 60° N latitude, and sitting in the rain shadow of the Tian Shan and Pamir Mountains to the south, they are the highest midlatitude deserts in the world.

David R. Smith

Further Reading
Lydolph, Paul. (1977) *Geography of the USSR*. New York: John Wiley and Sons.
National Imagery and Mapping Agency (NIMA). (2000) "GEOnet Names Server." Accessed 20 October 2000 from http://gnpswww.nima.mil/geonames/GNS/.

TURGAY PLATEAU The Turgay Plateau is a major geographical feature of northwest Kazakhstan, extending 630 kilometers north to south and 300 kilometers east to west at an elevation of between 200 and 300 meters. Formed mostly of clay and sand and characterized by low hills, ridges, and shallow (often salt) lakes, the plateau holds deposits of magnetite, iron ore, bauxite, and coal. The plateau has a sharply continental climate. The northern region, which forms part of the steppe belt, is used for the dry farming of cereals and was incorporated into the Virgin Lands scheme initiated by Nikita Khrushchev (1894–1971) in 1954, Kazakhstan being a part of the Soviet Union until the Soviet Union dissolved in 1991. It now has a predominantly Russian and Ukrainian population.

The arid south, which is semidesert, is used for pastoralism, traditionally the preserve of the ethnic Kazakhs. This southern region is characterized by tablelands divided by deep depressions and ravines left by dried-up rivers.

The Turgay Plateau is crossed by the Turgay Ravine, which stretches north-south for a distance of some 800 kilometers, linking the West Siberian Lowland with the north Tura Lowland and connecting Siberia with Central Asia. With a flat bottom and heavily eroded sides, the width of the ravine varies from 20 to 75 kilometers. The Turgay River flows north and the Ubagan River south through the ravine. The groundwater is heavily mineralized and the ravine contains many salt lakes. Agriculturally, the region is used for pasture.

Will Myer

TURKEY—PROFILE (2001 est. pop. 66.5 million). Turkey, officially known as the Republic of Turkey (in Turkish, Turkiye Cumhuriyeti), is the European gateway to Asia, one reason that the region has been home to so many cultures and civilizations since at least 6500 BCE. The country is situated in southeastern Europe and in the peninsula of Asia Minor in western Asia. The European part of Turkey is known as Thrace (Trakya), and the Asian part as Anatolia (Anadolu). Rectangular in shape, Turkey covers 780,580 square kilometers, with almost all of the land (approximately 97 percent) located in Asia. Turkey is 1,660 kilometers long from east to west and 550 kilometers wide from north to south. It is bordered by Georgia and Armenia in the northeast, the Nakhitchevan Autonomous Region of Azerbaijan and Iran in the east, Iraq and Syria in the southeast, and Greece and Bulgaria in the northwest.

Three-fourths of Turkey's boundaries are maritime, with a coastline totaling 8,372 kilometers. The Black Sea coastline is 1,695 kilometers in length; the Aegean, 2,805; and the Mediterranean, 1,577. The Marmara coastline, which links the Black Sea to the Aegean Sea, is 927 kilometers long and includes two straits: the Bosporus, between the Black Sea and the Sea of Marmara, and the Dardanelles, between the Sea of Marmara and the Aegean Sea.

Hittites, Urartians, Lydians, Ionians, Romans, and Byzantines are some of the many peoples who in ancient days conquered and populated the area of modern Turkey. The Seljuk Turks settled there in the eleventh century, establishing the first Turkish empire

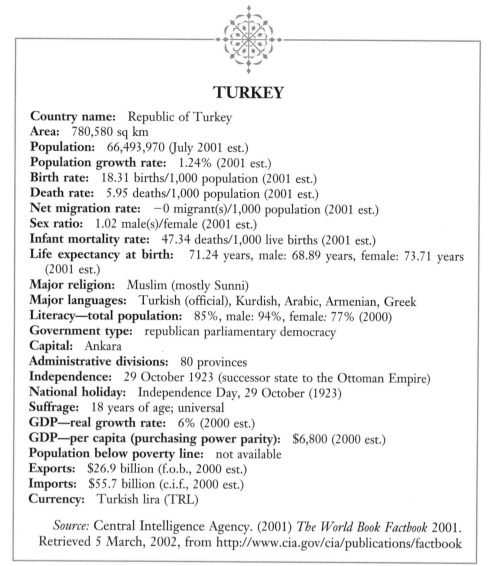

TURKEY

Country name: Republic of Turkey

Area: 780,580 sq km

Population: 66,493,970 (July 2001 est.)

Population growth rate: 1.24% (2001 est.)

Birth rate: 18.31 births/1,000 population (2001 est.)

Death rate: 5.95 deaths/1,000 population (2001 est.)

Net migration rate: −0 migrant(s)/1,000 population (2001 est.)

Sex ratio: 1.02 male(s)/female (2001 est.)

Infant mortality rate: 47.34 deaths/1,000 live births (2001 est.)

Life expectancy at birth: 71.24 years, male: 68.89 years, female: 73.71 years (2001 est.)

Major religion: Muslim (mostly Sunni)

Major languages: Turkish (official), Kurdish, Arabic, Armenian, Greek

Literacy—total population: 85%, male: 94%, female: 77% (2000)

Government type: republican parliamentary democracy

Capital: Ankara

Administrative divisions: 80 provinces

Independence: 29 October 1923 (successor state to the Ottoman Empire)

National holiday: Independence Day, 29 October (1923)

Suffrage: 18 years of age; universal

GDP—real growth rate: 6% (2000 est.)

GDP—per capita (purchasing power parity): $6,800 (2000 est.)

Population below poverty line: not available

Exports: $26.9 billion (f.o.b., 2000 est.)

Imports: $55.7 billion (c.i.f., 2000 est.)

Currency: Turkish lira (TRL)

Source: Central Intelligence Agency. (2001) *The World Book Factbook* 2001. Retrieved 5 March, 2002, from http://www.cia.gov/cia/publications/factbook

in Asia Minor. The Ottoman Turks founded their empire in the fourteenth century.

Geography

Turkey has a rich topography, with broad plateaus in the central region, low mountain ranges in the north and south, and mountainous highlands in the east. There are three main climates with subvariations. On the western coast, from the Marmara region down to the south, the climate is mild and wet in winter and hot and dry in summer. The Mediterranean coast enjoys warmer weather. The Black Sea region is temperate and rainy year round. The interior has a semi-continental climate with hot, dry summers and cold, snowy winters. The climate is coldest in eastern Anatolia, where temperatures can fall as low as −23° to −40°C. The hottest summers occur in southeast Anatolia, where the temperature reaches as high as 40°C.

Turkey is divided into seven geographical regions: Mediterranean, Aegean Sea, Marmara, Black Sea, central Anatolia, eastern Anatolia, and southeast Anatolia. The highest mountain is the biblical Mount Ararat, with an altitude of 5,165 meters. Kackar (altitude 3,923 meters), and Erciyes (3,917 meters) are other notable mountains. The Euphrates, Kizilirmak, Sakarya, and Tigris are the country's longest rivers.

People

Turkey's population is relatively young, with a dependency ratio of 64.68 percent. In 2001 the population growth rate was estimated at 1.24 percent. Population density per square kilometer was 79. Most

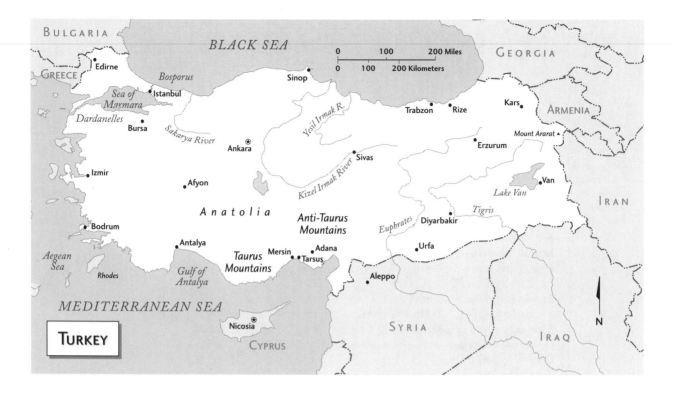

of the population is concentrated in the western part of the country, with two-thirds of the population living in cities. Istanbul, with a population of more than 9 million, is one of the largest cities in the world.

The rights of non-Muslim minorities, namely, Greeks, Armenians, and Jews, were regulated by the Treaty of Lausanne in 1923. Officially there are no ethnic minorities in the Muslim population of Turkey. While the ethnic origins of the Turks vary, they are united by their shared Turkish identity. The Kurds, the second-largest ethnic group in Turkey, were long denied an independent ethnic identity and were labeled "mountain Turks." Although the exact number of Kurds in Turkey is not known, there are estimated to be between 10 and 20 million. Other minorities include Arabs, the Laz, Tatars, Circassians, and Syriacs.

Turkey is a secular state without an official religion, but more than 98 percent of the population is Muslim. Most follow the Hanafi school of Sunni Islam. There is a substantial minority of Alevi (a subdivision of the Shi'a sect). Although the exact number is not known, the Alevi population is estimated at around 10 to 15 percent of the Muslim population in Turkey. Non-Muslims, including Armenian Orthodox Christians, Greek Orthodox Christians, Roman Catholics, and Jews, constitute the remaining 2 percent of the population. The official language of the country is Turkish. Various dialects of Kurdish, Arabic, and Armenian are some of the other languages spoken in the country. Although a ban on the use of the Kurdish language was lifted in 1991, there are still some restrictions on education and public broadcasting in Kurdish.

Political History

The Republic of Turkey was established in 29 October 1923 as a unitary state and was ruled by the single-party regime of the Republican People's Party for more than two decades. The first president of the republic was Mustafa Kemal Ataturk, who held the post between 1923 and 1938, followed by President Ismet Iononu (served 1938–1950). Since 1946 the country has been a multiparty parliamentary democracy, but Turkey's experiment in democracy suffered major setbacks because of interventions by Turkey's military in 1960, 1971, and 1980. The army's role in politics was institutionalized in the 1961 constitution, with the creation of the National Security Council (NSC). The NSC's role was expanded under the 1982 constitution.

The Turkish government structure is based on the principle of the separation of powers, although this principle is not always realized in practice. The executive body consists of the president, the prime minister, and the Council of Ministers. (Ahmet Necdet Sezer was elected president in 2000, the tenth president in the history of the Turkish republic.) The president is the head of state and is elected by the Turkish Grand National Assembly (TGNA) for seven years; the president in turn appoints the prime minister, who is the head of the government, and, on the recommendation of the prime minister, the Council of Ministers, or cabinet. The post of prime minister is usually offered to the leader of the majority party in parliament. According to the 1982 constitution, the legislative body, the TGNA, is unicameral and consists of 550 deputies elected for five years in a general election. The election system is based on proportional representation (that is, the number of seats a party has in parliament is proportional to the percentage of the popular vote that the party received), with a 10 percent national threshold. The voting age is 18.

The judicial system is composed of civilian courts, the constitutional court, and state security courts. Civilian courts include peace courts, criminal courts, and commercial courts. State security courts deal with crimes against the state, whereas the constitutional court decides the constitutionality of legislation. An independent court system is guaranteed under the constitution.

After the 1999 general elections political parties represented in the TGNA were the Motherland Party (ANAP), the Republican People's Party (CHP), the True Path Party, the Virtue Party, the Democratic Leftist Party (DSP), and the Nationalist Action Party (MHP). Bulent Ecevit, the leader of the DSP, is the prime minister of the fifty-seventh cabinet, formed on 4 June 1999.

Administratively, Turkey is divided into eighty provinces, each under a provincial governor appointed by the Council of Ministers. The provinces are headed by appointed junior governors. Provinces are also organized as municipalities, of which there were 3,126 in 2000.

The Turkish army is responsible for defending the republic against internal and external enemies. According to the internal service code of the armed forces, the army is the guardian of the Kemalist state. The Turkish military is one of the largest in the world, with total active personnel of 639,000 in 1998. In 1998, 11 percent of the budget was allocated for defense expenditure. Military service is obligatory for male Turkish citizens over the age of twenty; Turkey does not recognize conscientious objection.

Economy

Turkey is a free-market economy with a large public sector. The country is a customs union partner with the European Union and a member of the World Trade Organization. Although the annual growth rate is relatively high (3.9 percent in 1998), the Turkish economy is far from stable. In the 1990s it suffered from high in-flation (99.1 percent in 1997), soaring unemployment, an expanding budgetary deficit, and an inefficient public sector, whose large deficits hamper the economy. The Turkish privatization board continues to make evaluations about privatizing the telecommunications, iron and steel, and banking sectors.

Turkey's gross domestic product (GDP), based on purchasing power parity calculations, was estimated at $444 billion in 2000, with a GDP per capita of $6,800. The official unemployment rate for 5.6% percent in 2000, but the unofficial estimates in the late 1990s indicated a rate as high as 30 percent, especially among urban youth. Turkey's budget deficit in 1998 was $18.9 million, and the foreign debt at the end of 1998 reached $79.8 million.

Although agriculture forms the largest sector of the Turkish economy, employing 46 percent of the economically active population in 1998, its contribution to the GNP was only 17.6 percent. In 1998 only 34 percent of arable land was used for agriculture. Wheat, sugar beets, barley, potatoes, fruits, corn, cotton, tea, tobacco, hazelnuts, and olives are the main agricultural products. Turkey's mineral natural resources include coal, iron ore, copper, chrome, manganese, borax, and bauxite. In 1998 the mining sector employed 0.8 percent of the economically active population and represented 1 percent of GDP.

Major industries in Turkey include textiles, food processing, iron and steel, and cement production. The industrial sector accounted for 22 percent of employment and 26 percent of GDP in 1998. The service sector made the biggest contribution to GDP, at 57 percent. The fastest-growing sector is tourism: in 1998, 9.5 million visitors came to Turkey and produced a revenue of $7.2 million.

Turkey's principal exports include clothing and textiles, iron, steel, metals, vegetables, and fruits. In 2000 exports totaled $26.9 million. Principal imports, including machinery, minerals, metals, and petroleum products, totaled an estimated $55.7 million in 2000. Turkey's main trade partners are Germany, the United States, Italy, the United Kingdom, Saudi Arabia, Libya, and Iran.

Turkey's total energy production is insufficient to meet anticipated requirements, which are growing by approximately 10 percent a year. The electrical energy demand for 2000 was projected at 130 billion kilowatt hours (kWh), whereas current hydroelectric potential was only 120 billion kWh. The government plans to fill the gap by encouraging private-sector investments in the power-generation and distribution sectors through a build-operate-transfer system, by which

Turks wave flags as they climb the steps of the Ataturk mausoleum in Ankara on 29 October 1998 in celebration of the 75th anniversary of the proclamation of the Turkish Republic. (AFP/CORBIS)

public services and infrastructures are financed and managed privately for a set period of time, at the end of which they are transferred to the government. Currently, energy is derived from thermal power plants using lignite, coal, and hydroelectric power.

The transportation network consists of 320,600 kilometers of provincial roads and highways (only 59,842 kilometers of which are highways). Railroads, long neglected, are operated by the State Railways, a state economic enterprise. Turkey has thirty-eight airports: the largest is Istanbul Ataturk Airport. Istanbul, Izmir, Trabzon, Mersin, and Iskenderun are major seaports.

Culture

Turkey is a land of contrasts. The country's rich historical heritage and its location as a bridge between East and West produce a unique cultural mosaic. The old and the new, secular and Islamic, modern and traditional live side-by-side and influence architecture, music, and lifestyles. Although modern Turkey is a secular, Western-oriented state, Islamic values play a significant role in people's lives. The relative strength of Islamic and secular values in daily life varies between rural and urban populations and between regions and social classes.

During the last few decades Turkey has experienced rapid social change. Population growth and migration to the big cities accompanied high inflation, unem-

ployment, and uneven distribution of wealth. As a result, social tensions have increased. Urbanization and economic necessities have changed traditionally defined gender roles and family life: large patrilineal families have been replaced by nuclear families with an average household size of four persons. Nevertheless, the family is still an important institution in Turkey. The country has one of the lowest divorce rates in the world: 0.5 percent per 1,000 population. Although serious steps have been taken to improve women's rights (polygamy was abolished in 1925; laws were amended to offer women equal rights of divorce and inheritance; women's suffrage was granted in 1934) and to promote gender equality, the emancipation of women depends on their level of education and their social class. There have been women politicians and members of parliament, cabinet members, as well as a female prime minister (Tansu Ciller, served 1993–1996). There is no gender discrimination in legal and educational systems.

Traditional cultural expressions, which had been ignored by the early republican regimes, have been revived during the last few decades, including folk dancing and singing. Turkish folk music is sung by *asiklar* (troubadours), playing traditional instruments such as the stringed *saz*. The mystical music of the whirling dervishes is another traditional music form.

Efforts to Westernize Turkish society are evident in the nation's flourishing arts, drama, and classical and contemporary music. State-supported cultural activities encompass a national network of theaters, orchestras, opera and ballet companies, and various conservatories.

After a massive literacy program in the 1980s, the literacy rate rose to 85 percent by 2000. In 1998 elementary school enrollment was 9,581,180. Compulsory elementary education was increased to eight years to weaken the importance of religious high schools.

Turkey has colorful media: major newspapers include *Cumhurriyet, Hurriyet, Sabah, Milliyet, Star, Yeni Yuzyil, Zaman, Turkiye, Radikal,* and *Turkish Daily News.* Newspaper circulation is constantly supported by promotions. Aside from national papers, there are more than 700 local newspapers. The circulation of each national magazine varies between 10,000 and 50,000. The state monopoly on broadcasting was ended in the early 1990s, and, in addition to the TRT (Turkish Radio and Television Corporation), there are privately owned national stations such as ATV, Show TV, KanalD, Star TV, Bayrak TV, and more than one thousand private radio stations.

Current Issues

At the end of the second millennium Turkey faced serious economic, social, and political problems. Democratization and human rights abuses are among the most important issues, as are the Kurdish problem and Islamic fundamentalism. Corruption, uneven distribution of wealth, and chronic inflation plague the country's economy.

Ayla H. Kilic

Further Reading

The Europa World Year Book. (1998). London: Europa Publications.
Republic of Turkey. Retrieved 22 September 2000, from: http://www.turkey.org.
Turkish Republic, Undersecretariat of Treasury. Retrieved 22 September 2000, from: http://www.treasury.gov.tr.
United Nations Statistical Department. Retrieved 22 September 2000, from: http://www.un.org.
World Bank. (1998) *World Development Report.* Oxford: Oxford University Press.

TURKEY—ECONOMIC SYSTEM

The Republic of Turkey was founded in 1923 as the last nation-state that emerged when the Ottoman empire disintegrated after World War I (1914–1918). World War I and the War of Independence (1919–1922) against foreign occupation of the Anatolian Peninsula had a devastating impact on the new nation's economy. Following independence, the nationalist elites founded a single-party system (1924–1946) in which the Republican People's Party (RPP) undertook modernization of Turkey's social, political, and economic structure.

The Izmir Economic Congress of 1923 formally recognized private enterprise as an essential economic actor but gave the state the means to protect private enterprise because it was too weak to undertake massive infrastructure investments alone. In desperate need of capital, the state adopted policies to support private enterprise and encourage foreign investments. The economic environment for foreign capital investments was favorable because the 1923 Lausanne Treaty, by which Turkey was recognized as an independent state, precluded the new regime from imposing a protective customs regime until 1929.

To create the capital necessary for financing its ambitious modernization project, the state prioritized agriculture. Its policies contributed to an 87 percent increase in agricultural output between 1923 and 1926. After passage of the Law for the Encouragement of Industry in 1927, the state introduced policies to provide indirect support, such as subsidies and trade concessions to local infant industries. State banks and credit institutions were also used to raise financial support for local industries.

Although the state was partially successful in creating infant industries that accounted for 14 percent of the national product in 1929, agriculture remained the basis of the economy. Thus, the decline in agricultural product prices after the Great Depression of 1929 hurt Turkish exports and foreign currency earnings. Turkey began to experience a mounting economic crisis with the depreciation both of its lira currency and its balance of trade position. Also in 1929, the restrictive customs terms of the Treaty of Lausanne expired, and the Turkish state had the opportunity to take comprehensive protectionist measures. A new era began.

Etatism

To legitimize state intervention in the economy the RPP devised the approach known as etatism, which it interpreted as an instrumental policy to initiate a state-led industrialization effort. The etatist policies further involved the state in the economy, giving it a new role as a protector, producer, and planner. In its role as protector, the state first erected a protectionist customs regime and used the specialized state banks, such as the Agricultural Bank and the People's Bank, to generate direct credits for agriculture and commerce. As a producer, the state founded state economic enterprises (SEEs). These giant companies, owned or controlled by the state, produced intermediate and consumer goods in sectors such as textiles, mining and extraction works, paper, chemicals, and pottery. As a planner, the state began to draw up five-year industrial plans to coordinate public and private efforts for development. The first plan was launched in 1934, but the second one (launched in 1938) became obsolete with the outbreak of World War II. Further state expansion in the economy was accelerated by the nationalization of foreign firms between 1931 and 1939. The state-led industrialization model not only restored the state as a principal actor but also instigated an increase in the private sector's contribution to the national product from 14 percent in 1929 to 19 percent in 1939 by placing the private sector under pervasive state protection. Protectionism was expanded in agriculture after 1938, when the Soil Products Office was founded to determine subsidy levels for wheat. This subsidization policy was later broadened to include other agricultural products. The legacy of the 1930s was the fact that state intervention in the economy created a mixed economy in which the public and private sectors operated as adversaries governed by different rules.

Although Turkey remained neutral when World War II broke out in 1939, wartime developments halted its industrialization attempts. The National Protection Law of 1940 tightened state control over the economy by giving the government absolute power in determining general price and production levels. The government also devised new fiscal policies to mobilize public and private resources for military objectives, causing a 5.6 percent decrease in industrial output. Agricultural output declined by 7.2 percent, causing food shortages. Deterioration of the living standards was coupled with growing income inequalities. In the prewar period (1933–1939), the share of industry and agriculture in national income had increased steadily. Wartime developments (1939–1945), however, caused a temporary stagnation in these sectors but a boom in the service sector, whose contribution to national income reached almost 50 percent. The wartime economy also generated a new problem—inflation—and the increase in the general price level posed a threat to the nation's balance-of-trade position.

From 1945 to the 1970s

The first priority of the postwar Turkish governments was to improve the competitiveness of Turkish exports, whose prices had risen above the world average. To this end, the Turkish lira (TL) was devalu-

ated by almost 54 percent in 1946. The RPP government in 1947 also launched the Economic Development Plan, which loosened etatist policies. It was trying to cope with the liberal challenge posed by the new opposition party, the Democratic Party (DP), founded in 1946.

Reacting to wartime economic constraints and the deterioration of living conditions, urban and rural classes realigned their political loyalties, and the DP won the 1950 elections. The party promised to liberalize the economy and broaden the scope of the state's support to the private sector. In conjunction with new trends in the Cold War period, Turkey began to integrate more with the Western alliance system against the Soviet Union and began to receive more foreign aid. The new DP government was able to allocate more public funds to support industry and agriculture.

The mechanization of agriculture, elimination of some taxes, and massive public investments in infrastructure coincided with favorable weather conditions and caused an annual growth rate of 11.5 percent in agriculture between 1950 and 1953. Turkey experienced an economic boom in the first half of the 1950s with an annual growth rate exceeding 10 percent. Industrial expansion was achieved mostly in the subsectors producing consumer goods and intermediate industrial goods such as cement, chemicals, construction material, and rubber and plastics.

Economic policies between 1954 and 1957 were designed on an as-needed basis to reverse inflation and solve the balance-of-payments difficulties by relying more on foreign debt. The National Protection Law was, however, reenacted to restore government control over price increases. These measures helped reduce the foreign trade deficit but failed to restore price stability and could not prevent a shortage of goods and the emergence of a black market. In 1958, the government introduced the nation's first comprehensive austerity program, which included standard stabilization measures such as devaluation, reduction of budget spending, price increases on SEE products, restraints on public spending, and rescheduling of foreign debt. The adverse effects of the deterioration of price stability and the restrictive economic program enforced by the DP since 1957—felt most severely by those groups with fixed incomes, such as the civil and military bureaucracies—paved the way for the first military takeover on 27 May 1960.

With the return to civilian rule in 1961 and a new constitution, the state introduced the policy of inward-looking, import-substitution industrialization (ISI). The aim was to create a capital-intensive industrial base in a mixed economy through centrally planned five-year development plans. ISI was followed until 1980 with the goal of stimulating domestic-capital accumulation by protecting private or public infant industries through restrictive customs tariffs. In the first phase of ISI, which lasted through the 1960s, primary industries requiring low technologies, such as textiles, developed rapidly. In this phase, infant private and public industries took advantage of state protection in the form of incentives, import permits, and subsidies, and industry's share of GDP was 22.6 percent by the end of the decade.

During this time, economic development could be sustained as long as intermediate industrial goods and raw materials used by domestic industry could be imported. Some 95 percent of all imports were used by domestic industry. Yet, the by-product of the protectionist policies was an overvalued currency that hurt exports. By the end of the 1960s, Turkey began to reexperience the balance-of-payments difficulties that had dogged the economy since the mid-1950s. As an immediate remedy, the TL was devalued by 66 percent in 1970.

From 1971 to the Twenty-First Century

When the military intervened on 12 March 1971, the nation was trapped in the vicious cycle of growing imbalances of payments, mounting foreign debts, and public deficits. The interim civilian governments between 1971 and 1973 imposed stabilization policies and temporarily achieved their goal by taking advantage of the stimulating impact of the 1970 devaluation on exports. Moreover, emigrant workers' remittances had become a major source for restoring the balance of payments. Turkey had exported labor to Europe, especially Germany, in the 1960s, and these workers' remittances, which amounted to only 2 percent of export earnings in the 1960s, soared to 50 percent in 1970–1971 and 90 percent in 1973. The stabilization measures and workers' remittances combined to provide a temporary solution to the balance-of-payments problems and created a surplus in current accounts in 1971 and 1972.

In the first half of the 1970s, Turkey entered the second phase of the ISI model, characterized by growth in those industrial sectors that required use of semiadvanced technology, such as chemicals, automobiles, electrics and electronics, and consumer durables. An increase in the volume of foreign investments was partially responsible for the dynamism in these sectors. The decline of the share of agriculture in national income from 36 percent in 1936 to 24 percent in 1973

Cranes at work in the Golden Horn shipyard in Istanbul in c. 1997. (DAVE BARTRUFF/CORBIS)

was an indicator of the economy's shift from agriculture to industry, a process that intensified after 1980. In 1983, agriculture accounted for only 17 percent of the national income.

With the first oil crisis in 1973–1974 the economy began to deteriorate because policymakers responded by subsidizing the rising world oil prices rather than restructuring Turkey's energy production and consumption policies. Moreover, the economic slowdown in Europe resulted in a decline in export earnings; thus, the nation's balance-of-trade position worsened, experiencing an average growth rate of 0.3 between 1977 and 1980. Declining emigrant workers' remittances complicated the economic crisis. Coupled with accelerated public deficits that boosted inflation to triple-digit levels by the end of the 1970s, declining remittances caused the economy to overheat. Public-sector deficits were financed by short-term external borrowing, which amounted to 66 percent of the nation's total foreign debts in 1977—debts on which Turkey could not repay even the interest in 1978. Then came the second oil crisis, in 1979.

On 24 January 1980, one of the most comprehensive structural adjustment programs toward the institutionalization of a market-oriented growth strategy was announced by the minority government of the Justice Party, which had been founded in 1961 as an heir to the DP. This program had four basic objectives: reduction of the external deficit and inflation, deregulation of the financial system, liberalization of the trade regime, and institutionalization of a market-oriented growth model. Like previous austerity programs, this program included standard stabilization measures such as devaluating the TL, abandoning the fixed exchange rate policy, eliminating most subsidies, freeing the prices of SEE products, reorganizing the taxation system, and encouraging foreign investments.

A girl in Izmir, Turkey, weaving a carpet c. 1997. (RICHARD T. NOWITZ/CORBIS)

On 12 September 1980, the military intervened. A new constitution was submitted to popular approval in 1982. Between 1980 and 1983, civilian-technician governments uncompromisingly imposed the stabilization program. In 1983, elections were held for the transition to civilian rule. The first civilian government was formed by the Motherland Party (MP), founded in 1983, and it further developed the export-oriented growth strategy between 1983 and 1987. These measures increased the share of manufactured goods in exports while decreasing the share of agricultural products, a trend that continued throughout the 1990s. Gradual abandonment of quantitative restrictions in the customs regime, continuous devaluations, export credits, export tax rebates, and sectoral incentives, as in the case of tourism, aimed to increase Turkey's export earnings to overcome the chronic balance-of-payments problem. The post-1983 governments also launched build-operate-transfer (BOT) schemes in the energy and infrastructure construction sectors. Under the BOT system, the government contracts out major infrastructure projects to private companies that build and operate a project for a fixed term prior to the transfer of the project to the public sector. Moreover, a program for privatization was initiated in 1986 to serve both as an alternative and a complement to the government's plan for stimulating foreign capital inflow.

The MP governments focused on deregulation of the financial sector, and the new Banking Law of 1985 transformed it into one of the most dynamically developed sectors. The opening of the Istanbul Stock Exchange Market in 1986 was another critical step for the integration of the Turkish economy with the international financial system, and it began to serve as a gateway for the inflow of international capital. Finan-

cial liberalization transformed the dynamics of the Turkish economy completely. Prior to 1980, Turkey's economic crises emerged due to foreign debt problems; after 1983, economic crises emerged due to the deflation policies that aimed to protect the competitiveness of Turkey's export sector.

In 1987, a referendum was held, and the exclusion of some political leaders, imposed after the 1980 military intervention, was ended. This was bad news for the Turkish economy because stiff political competition drove the ruling MP to adopt monetary expansion to finance growing public spending, which boosted inflation. Growing public spending on massive investments in infrastructure, transportation, and public construction works contributed to inflation rising to 55 percent in 1987 from 48.3 percent in 1984. By the end of the 1980s, economic growth had slowed, and Turkey entered a new period of recession. Restrictive monetary policies that the government tried to impose to contract domestic demand in the short run could not control inflation, which reached 70 percent in 1988. Inflationary pressure posed a real threat to the stability of an economy experiencing chronic budget deficits and suffering from foreign and domestic debt problems. To stimulate free exchange of TL for other currencies and to encourage the inflow of foreign capital, convertibility was adopted in August 1989.

The 1991 Gulf War hit the stagnant economy hard because Turkey abided by the U.N. blockade of Iraq, thereby cutting all its trade ties with that nation. In domestic politics, the adverse effects of the export-oriented growth strategy, which relied on the reallocation of national income in favor of the export sector, and the monetary policies of the MP governments, which hit fixed-income groups the hardest, worsened income distribution inequalities. Consequently, the MP lost the 1991 elections, and Turkey entered a new decade of government by coalitions. The post-1991 governments loosened the restrictive monetary policies by reactivating subsidies and price support policies in agriculture and by boosting public deficits.

These policies were designed to stimulate domestic demand but resulted in weakening the current account balance, causing a financial crisis in 1994. In response, that same year the government launched a new austerity program, the goal of which was to bring short-term stability to the financial sector. It also included standard austerity measures promising reductions in inflation and public deficits and improvements in balance payments. To these ends, the TL was devalued by 56.2 percent in April 1994, at the peak of the crisis. The austerity program required strict monetary policies that political considerations made the government reluctant to impose. Still, at least temporarily, the government achieved its goals of suppressing domestic demand and reducing public expenditures at the cost of slowing down the economy. Although the program was unsuccessful in solving chronic inflation, the economy began to recover in 1995–1996, and Turkey's entrance into the Customs Union with the European Union in 1996 brought a new dynamism in some sectors—industry, trade, and communications—although its effects on the whole economy remain ambiguous.

The financial sector benefited most from the liberalization attempts in the post-1980 period. Yet, the lack of complex legal-administrative regulations further limited government control over the financial sector. The difficulties of the free-for-all game in the financial sector surfaced when the government, in cooperation with the International Monetary Fund (IMF), introduced a fixed exchange rate policy within the framework of a general deflationary economic program in 1999 to control inflation and restore the balance of payments. The financial sector found it increasingly difficult to adapt to the changing rules of the game because since 1994 it had made most of its profits from the government's policy of financing public deficits from short-term loans and by manipulating the nation's high inflation and foreign exchange rate policy. The widening gap between the inflation rate and the foreign currency exchange rate and the overvalued TL made the government's policies obsolete. In November 2000 and February 2001, Turkey experienced one of its worst financial crises, losing almost one-third of its foreign currency reserve in a week when a dispute between the prime minister and the president triggered a crisis of confidence that resulted in the outflow of foreign capital. In response, the government adopted a new restructuring program. It revised its foreign currency regime and abandoned the fixed exchange rate policy (the pillar of the IMF's antiinflationary program) in favor of a fluctuating exchange rate policy. It also received a massive amount of foreign aid from the IMF and adopted a new structural reform program requiring wide-ranging privatization in the banking, telecommunications, and energy sectors as well as a series of austerity measures for curbing government spending and reducing inflation.

Nazim Irem

Further Reading

Aksoy, S. (1971) *Turkiye'de Toprak Meselesi* (The Land Question in Turkey). Istanbul, Turkey: Gercek Yayinevi.

Balim-Harding, Cigdem. (1995) *Turkey—Political, Social and Economic Challenges in the 1990s.* New York: Leiden.

Bulutay, Tuncer, Yahya S. Tezel, and Nuri Yildirim. (1974) *Turkiye'de Milli Geliri 1923–1948* (National Income of Turkey, 1923–1948). Ankara, Turkey: Siyasal Bilgiler Fakultesi.

Kepenek, Yakup. (1996) *Turkiye Ekonomisi* (Turkish Economy). 8th ed. Istanbul, Turkey: Remzi Kitabevi.

Kuruc, Biray, Tuncay Artun, et al. (1987) *Birakiniz Yapsinlar Birakiniz Gecsinler, Turkiye Ekonomisi 1980–1985* (Laissez Faire Laissez Passez, Turkish Economy 1980–1985). 3d ed. Istanbul, Turkey: Bilgi Yayinevi.

Lovatt, Debbie, ed. (2001) *Turkey since 1970: Politics, Economics, and Society.* New York: Palgrave Publishers.

Onis, Ziya. (1999) *State and Market: The Political Economy of Turkey in Comparative Perspective.* Istanbul, Turkey: Bogazici University.

Rittenberg, Libby. (1998) *The Political Economy of Turkey in the Post-Soviet Era.* Westport CT: Praeger.

Sonmez, Atilla. (1999) "Turkiye'de 1950 Sonrasi Sanayilesme Politikasi Uzerine Gozlemler" (Observations on the Industrialization Policy in Turkey in the Post-1950 Period). *International Conference on "History of Turkish Republic: A Reassessment."* Vol. 2. Istanbul, Turkey: Tarih Vakfi Yayinlari.

TURKEY—EDUCATION SYSTEM

Education has been a consistent barometer of political and social trends in the late Ottoman empire and the Turkish Republic. Due to its importance for successive Ottoman and Republican governments, education has come to symbolize the direction in which society is intended to move. Together with the military, education has obtained an emblematic quality that ensures its central role in Turkish society. Due to this centrality, the ways in which the history of education in Turkey has been written reflect an ongoing debate about the desired blend of the secular and the religious.

Like most premodern societies, the Ottoman empire had a tradition of restricted state involvement in education. The government's provision of education extended only to training soldiers or the small number of scribes who ran the empire. In the absence of major state initiative, most education was religious: It was largely scriptural in content, usually imparted in or close to a place of worship, and taught by men of religious learning. Those who received education, always a small minority of the population and well under 10 percent until the empire's last decades, did so at the hands of the ulama (the learned men of Islam), priests, or rabbis, depending on their faith.

With the advent of Western-style military reform in the late eighteenth century, the Ottoman state embarked on a radical process of enlargement that had direct consequences for education. Fielding a standing army based on drill and centralized command required schools for officers as well as specialized branches, such as artillery and medical units. Creating a modern army was extremely expensive and therefore necessitated finding new ways of extracting revenues from the land and its people. In short, this meant expanding the bureaucracy on a massive scale. Whereas once an estimated two thousand scribes ran the empire, over the course of the nineteenth century this number ballooned to over thirty-five thousand. Because all of these bureaucrats had to be able to read and write, educating them properly became a priority.

Tanzimat Reforms

In 1839, the first year of the Tanzimat period of reforms (1839–1876) under Sultan Mahmud II, the Ottoman government issued the first in a long series of memoranda dedicated to education reform. The thrust of these early attempts was to incorporate the existing schools, mostly the Qur'an schools, and to use them as the basis for an imperial system. The overriding objective was to train loyal and capable bureaucrats, it being understood that adopting the religious and moral approach of the Muslim schools was the only possible way forward. This piecemeal approach continued until 1869, when, under strong, centralizing French influence the empire adopted the Education Regulation, which would guide education developments for the rest of the empire's life and for many of its successor states, including the Turkish Republic.

Although decreed in the final years of the Tanzimat period, the Education Regulation was largely implemented only from the 1880s onward, during the reign of Sultan Abdulhamid II (reigned 1876–1909), who strongly believed in the necessity of a modern education system that would combine the latest in European content, such as chemistry and French, with the religious and historical material suitable to Ottoman and Islamic tradition. Expanding both horizontally among the provinces and vertically from primary to higher levels, including a university in Istanbul from 1900, the new system would be altered by successive regimes, acting as a vehicle for an increasingly Turkist political agenda, first haltingly during the Young Turk period (1908–1918) and then much more forcefully in the smaller Turkish Republic (1923–present).

Atakurk's Reforms

The earlier years of the Republic demonstrated that the new government of Mustafa Kemal (1881–1938, later Ataturk, or Father of the Turks), although inheriting the core of the Ottoman system, was bent on a radical reorientation of society, toward the West and

away from its Islamic past. Among the many ruptures was the abolition of the *medrese* (Islamic seminary) system run by the ulama. But in many ways Republican education only intensified existing trends in education. Freed from the pressure of the Great Powers and with a much more homogeneous and smaller population to educate, the young Republic pursued its twin themes of tightening the restrictions on foreign schooling and making its own schools more nationalist in orientation. The Unity of Education Law of 1924 set the tone by insisting that all education institutions be regulated by the Ministry of National Education. Two years later, a regulation demanded that all teachers of such sensitive subjects as history, geography, and language be approved by the new capital in Ankara and had to be supportive of the concept of the Turkish nation. Schools were now obliged to display prominently portraits of Mustafa Kemal.

Meanwhile, Kemal was devising two highly symbolic policies that would literally reshape education in Turkey: changing the alphabet and engineering a radical reform of the Ottoman Turkish language, a rich combination of Arabic, Persian, and Turkish. The forced adoption of the Latin alphabet, and of Western numerals, in 1928 was backed by some sound linguistic arguments—the Arabic script was not well suited to render Turkish words—but was ultimately intended to sever ties with Turkey's Islamic heritage. The movement was spearheaded by Kemal himself, who now appeared around the nation, chalk in hand, as a sort of teacher in chief. The language reform, summarized by one scholar as a "catastrophic success," ensured that students in the Republic would learn a language that was increasingly unintelligible to their grandparents and, perhaps more to the point, would be cut off from the language of their elders.

The Resurgence in Religious Education

During the Single Party period (1923–1945), the government pressed ahead with its nationalist agenda in the schools while reaching out to the rural population. In order to combat high rates of illiteracy, it launched the Village Institute scheme designed to provide rural areas with teachers who would energize the literacy drive. A largely successful initiative, it was disbanded when the Democrat Party came to power in the watershed elections of 1950. In the run-up to the election, as the major parties began to court the conservative vote, the government began to offer more in the way of religious education, such as elective religious education, special training for preachers in the schools (1947), and the creation of a theological faculty at Ankara University (1949). After winning the elections of 1950, the Democrat Party expanded religious education dramatically, thereby undermining the secularist principles of the Kemalist state. The return of the Republican People's Party, the party founded by Ataturk, to power after the military coup of 1960 produced only an increase in the attention paid to religious schools, indicating their broad support in Anatolia.

Education from the 1970s into the Twenty-First Century

During the 1970s, when Turkey entered a period of political turmoil, education was once again at the center of activity. Strikes, protest, and violence between the right and the left were often played out on university campuses, and numerous academics were fired for their views or resigned in protest of the government's policies. After the military coup of 1980, the government established the Higher Education Council, which has run university-level education in a strong-handed capacity ever since.

In recent years, the salient features of Turkish education have included the ongoing controversy over whether or not women are to be permitted to attend courses while wearing the headscarf, the question of overcrowding in schools, truancy due to child labor, and the mushrooming of private universities across the nation. Continuing a trend begun in late Ottoman times, the solutions that will emerge will doubtless reflect a struggle as much over ideology as resources.

Benjamin C. Fortna

Further Reading
Fortna, Benjamin C. (2002) *Imperial Classroom: Islam, the State, and Education in the Late Ottoman Empire.* Oxford: Oxford University Press.
Somel, Aksin Selcuk. (2001) *The Modernization of Public Education in the Ottoman Empire, 1839–1908.* Leiden, Netherlands: Brill.

TURKEY—HUMAN RIGHTS
Turkey is the only democratic state with a predominately Muslim population. Its political leaders have created a constitutional republic with a democratically elected Parliament and an independent judiciary. Turkey has ratified a number of international human-rights conventions, including the European Convention for the Protection of Human Rights and Fundamental Freedoms (which includes the right of individual petition and the compulsory jurisdiction of the European Court of Human Rights). As part of its efforts to promote human rights, the government established the Parliamentary Human Rights Commission in 1990 and the Human Rights Ministry in 1991.

Despite these achievements, domestic and international critics have faulted Turkey's human-rights practices. Critics have alleged: (1) torture and the suspicious deaths of prisoners while in detention; (2) disappearances and extrajudicial killings of opposition politicians, human-rights activists, journalists, and Kurdish nationalists; (3) government infringements on the freedoms of speech, press, and association; (4) denial of due process to persons under the jurisdiction of state security courts and in the state-of-emergency region; (5) the destruction of Kurdish villages in the southeast by the Turkish military; and (6) suppression of Kurdish cultural expression.

Some members of the nation's political elite, bureaucracy, and military claim that Turkey is threatened from within by "reactionaries" (Islamists) and "separatists" (Kurdish nationalists) and that they are willing to curb human rights to meet these threats.

Religious and Ethnic Minorities

Turkey's 1924 constitution establishes Turkey as a secular state and provides for freedom of worship. In accordance with the 1923 Lausanne Treaty, Greeks, Armenians, and Jews are permitted to maintain their own schools and to teach their religion and language. These small minorities report little discrimination in daily life.

Turkey has many other ethnic minorities who are not officially recognized as such. These include Laz, Circassians, Georgians, Kurds, and Arabs. Human-rights violations have been especially inflicted on the Kurds—the largest ethnic and linguistic minority, who may now represent one-fourth of the population (roughly 15 million people). There are no legal barriers to Kurds' participation in political and economic affairs, and many members of Parliament and senior officials and professionals are Kurds. However, the government has long denied the Kurds basic cultural and linguistic rights. Kurds who publicly assert their Kurdish identity or espouse speaking Kurdish in the public domain risk harassment or prosecution. Since 1991 private spoken and printed communications in Kurdish have been legal; however, the use of minority languages in television and radio broadcasts, by political parties, and in schools is restricted by a series of laws and constitutional articles that prosecutors invoke arbitrarily.

For over fifteen years, the military has fought the Kurdistan Workers Party (PKK), whose goal originally was the formation of a separate state of Kurdistan in southeastern Turkey. A state of emergency, declared in 1987, has continued in those southeastern provinces that face substantial PKK terrorism. The state-of-emergency region's governor has exercised quasi martial-law powers, imposing restrictions on the press, removing from the region persons whose activities are deemed detrimental to public order, and ordering village evacuations.

Approximately 560,000 villagers were forcibly evacuated from their homes between 1987 and 1999. A parliamentary committee concluded in 1998 that the state was partly responsible for the displacements and that it had failed to adequately compensate villagers who had lost their homes and lands. The European Court of Human Rights has ruled in favor of villagers who sued over forcible evacuations and has ordered Turkey to pay damages.

Although the constitution provides for freedom of speech and press, the government has limited these freedoms on the basis of national security. The criminal code provides penalties for those who "insult the president, the parliament, and the army." Prosecutors also rely on other provisions in various laws restricting freedom of expression.

The state-of-emergency governor, courts, police, and the body overseeing state broadcasting have denied the Kurdish population in the southeast use of their language in election campaigning, education, broadcasting, and in some cultural activities, such as weddings. Printed material in Kurdish is legal; however, the police have commonly interfered with the distribution of Kurdish newspapers. Kurdish music recordings are widely available, but bans on certain songs and singers exist. Radio and television broadcasts in Kurdish are illegal.

A total of 114 intellectuals and human-rights activists were sentenced in April 1999 to a year in prison each, on charges of "separatist propaganda," for signing a 1993 declaration calling for a peaceful solution to the Kurdish conflict. In July 1999, the European Court of Human Rights ruled on thirteen Turkish cases involving freedom of expression in which the plaintiffs were jailed or fined for books, articles, or statements that they wrote or published on Kurdish issues. These plaintiffs were convicted either of "inciting ethnic hatred" or "disseminating propaganda against the indivisibility of the state" or for "revealing the identity of officials responsible for combating terrorism." The European court found that the Turkish government violated the plaintiffs' right to freedom of expression in eleven of these thirteen cases, denied plaintiffs in nine cases the right to have their cases

heard by an independent and impartial tribunal because of the presence of military judges on the state security courts, and in one case violated the prohibition against no punishment without law. But despite government restrictions, the media criticize government leaders and policies daily. Lively debates on human rights also occur.

Torture and Other Cruel Punishment

Security forces and police have tortured, beaten, and abused persons regularly. The lack of universal and immediate access to an attorney and long detention periods for those held for political crimes are major factors in torture. Despite the government's cooperation with unscheduled foreign inspection teams and public pledges by successive governments to end the practice, torture continues to be a serious human-rights problem. The Turkish Human Rights Foundation (HRF) estimated the number of credible reports of torture at its five national treatment centers at 700 in 1999, compared with 673 in 1998. But the HRF believed that these figures underrepresented the actual number of persons tortured while in detention or prison.

Human-rights monitors say that security officials increasingly use methods that do not leave physical traces, such as beating with weighted bags instead of clubs or fists. Commonly employed methods of torture reported by the HRF's treatment centers include administering electric shocks and systematic beatings; stripping and blindfolding; exposing to extreme cold or high-pressure cold water hoses; beating the soles of the feet (falaka) and genitalia; hanging by the arms; depriving of food and sleep; hanging heavy weights on the body; dripping water onto the head; burning; hanging sandbags on the neck; nearly suffocating by placing bags over the head; raping with truncheons and gun barrels; squeezing and twisting testicles; and other forms of sexual abuse. Female detainees often face sexual humiliation and, less often, more severe forms of sexual torture.

Government officials admit that torture occurs but deny that it is systematic. The U.N. special reporter for torture conducted investigations at the invitation of the government in late 1998. He reported that although torture was practiced systematically and on a large scale through the mid-1990s, there had been "notable improvements" since 1997.

Human-rights monitors have reported that government forces use excessive force, sometimes resulting in deaths, during raids on criminals or alleged terrorist and militant safe houses. Police and prison guards have also been accused of extrajudicial killings, often resulting from torture. In 1999, at least thirty trials were under way because of such charges.

Right to a Fair Public Trial

The judicial system is composed of general law courts, military courts, state security courts (SSCs), and the Constitutional Court. The High Court of Appeals hears appeals for criminal cases, including from SSCs. Military courts, with their own appeals system, hear cases involving military law, members of the armed forces, and civilians who are accused of impugning the honor of the armed forces or undermining compliance with the draft.

SSCs have posed the main problem for due-process rights. These courts sit in eight cities and try defendants accused of crimes such as committing terrorism, committing gang-related crimes, smuggling drugs, belonging to illegal organizations, and espousing or disseminating ideas that are "damaging the indivisible unity of the state." These courts may hold closed hearings and may admit testimony obtained during police interrogation in the absence of counsel. Until mid-1999, the SSCs were composed of panels of five members: two civilian judges, one military judge, and two prosecutors. A 1998 ruling by the European Court of Human Rights found that the presence of a military justice on the SSCs was inconsistent with relevant European conventions. In June 1999 the government amended the Constitution and passed legislation replacing the military judge with a civilian judge.

Attorneys defending controversial clients have been subject to spurious legal charges, such as accusations that they are couriers for clients who are alleged terrorists. The government charged twenty-five lawyers in 1993 and 1994 with aiding and abetting the PKK or belonging to a terrorist organization. Sixteen of these defendants complained of torture and mistreatment while held incommunicado after their arrests.

Human Rights for Women

Women enjoy all political and educational rights. They work in all professions. Trafficking in women and girls to Turkey from eastern Europe for the purpose of forced prostitution has been a problem since the 1990s. The government in late 1998 issued a regulation prohibiting the traditional practice of "virginity testing" of women about to be married unless requested by the women themselves.

Government Attitude toward Human Rights

Security forces and prosecutors have commonly harassed, intimidated, indicted, and imprisoned human-rights monitors, journalists, and lawyers for ideas that they expressed in public forums. The government has closed branches of human-rights organizations in the southeast. In 1999, prosecutors had former Human Rights Association president Akin Birdal jailed on charges of inciting hatred and enmity in nonviolent statements he made about the Kurdish problem and torture.

However, the government is publicly committed to improving human-rights practices. The state minister for human rights and the minister of justice have led government efforts to implement legislative and administrative reforms. The armed forces have instituted human-rights training for officers and noncommissioned officers. Human-rights education is mandatory in primary schools and elective in high schools.

In August 1999, Parliament passed legislation increasing sentences for persons convicted of torture from a maximum of five to eight years. Government officials have been in regular dialogue with the Council of Europe's Committee for the Prevention of Torture (CPT) and allow unannounced prison visits by the CPT.

Paul J. Magnarella

Further Reading

Amnesty International. (2001) *Amnesty International Annual Reports*. Retrieved 13 March 2002, from: http://www.amnesty.org.

Bureau of Democracy, Human Rights, and Labor. (2000) *Turkey Country Report on Human Rights Practices*. Washington, DC: U.S. Department of State.

Human Rights Watch. (2001) *Human Rights Watch Annual Reports*. Retrieved 13 March 2002, from: http://www.hrw.org.

Magnarella, Paul J. (1994) "The Legal, Political and Cultural Structures of Human Rights Protections and Abuses in Turkey." *Journal of International Law and Practice* 3, 4: 39–67.

TURKEY—POLITICAL SYSTEM
The political life of the Republic of Turkey began with the first meeting of the Turkish Grand National Assembly (TGNA) in 1920. The TGNA sprang from the conventions of the Association for the Defense of the Rights of Anatolia and Rumelia, held in Erzurum and Sivas in 1919.

The TGNA was a *régime d'assemblée* where all authority was vested in the assembly itself; there was no head of state. The government, known as the government of the Grand National Assembly, had no control over the assembly. The assembly elected cabinet members by direct vote from among its members. The first assembly had two groups of representatives: 92 deputies of the last Ottoman Parliament, which had terminated its last session in protest of the Allied occupation of Istanbul in 1920, and 349 members elected from each district under an indirect two-tier system (voters elected electors, who voted for assembly members) according to procedures defined by Mustafa Kemal (later Ataturk, 1881–1938).

The assembly was the result of a loose alliance of the urban middle class, the intelligentsia, army commanders, and bureaucrats, with local notables and landowners. Although the immediate aims of these groups were the same, there was an underlying conflict of interests when it came to the form and structure of the new state. One group, the supporters of Kemal, wanted to establish a secular state. Another group, created by the defenders of a constitutional monarchy, wanted to save the sultanate through reform.

To overcome the obstacles created by the assembly government system, Kemal proposed an amendment to the constitution. Under the new constitution Turkey would become a republic; the TGNA would elect the president from among its members; the president would appoint the prime minister, who would form the cabinet; and the cabinet would start work after the confidence vote of the assembly. Approval of this draft marked the victory of the first group and initiated the republican era.

The 1924 constitution established a unicameral legislature. Deputies were elected under the indirect two-tier election system. Because the candidates were defined by the party caucus; the election process was a symbolic approval of the Kemalist elite by the electorate. To be elected a deputy, candidates had to be literate and over thirty years of age. Once elected, deputies would become representatives of the nation, not of a specific district. Election districts were defined according to a ratio of one deputy to forty thousand voters. During the early years of the republic, the right to vote was limited to males over eighteen years. In 1934 the age limit was changed to twenty-two, and women were given the right to vote.

The One-Party Era

In 1923 Mustafa Kemal was elected the first president of the republic. He remained in that post until his death in 1938. Under his rule the Republican People's Part (RPP) became the official party of the country. He was not only the president of the republic but also leader of the RPP, chairperson of the party's Assembly Group Executive Committee, and chairperson

of the General Executive Committee of the party. In 1935 the RPP passed a resolution officially uniting party and state. The secretary-general of the party assumed the post of minister of interior affairs in the cabinet. Chairpersons of provincial organizations became governors of their provinces. In 1937 the six arrows of the RPP's party emblem (representing the six principles of Kemalism— republicanism, nationalism, populism, etatism, secularism, and reformism—were included in the constitution, which laid the basis for the ideological unification of the party and the state.

The death of Kemal and the election of Ismet Inonu (1884–1973) to the presidency did not change the political climate. At the party congress of 26 December 1938, Inonu was elected permanent chairperson of the party and given the title of national chief. The slogan "One party, one nation, one leader" was adopted. Although Inonu tried to create a broader consensus in the country, the policies of the World War II era increased discontent among various segments of society. Internal and external developments forced the RPP government to liberalize political life. In his speech on the opening day of the assembly in November 1945, Inonu announced the need for opposition parties for the well-being of the country and promised to achieve the necessary adjustments in the election system.

Transition to the Multiparty Period

In January 1946 a number of dissidents from the RPP formed the Democrat Party (DP). Although the programs of the two parties scarcely differed, popular discontent with the RPP provided support for the new party. The leaders of the DP emphasized the arbitrary character of a one-party state, an idea that attracted not only the bourgeoisie but the urban intelligentsia and the masses as well. As a measure against the unavoidable rise of the DP, the RPP decided to hold an early election in 1946 so that the Democrats would have little time to organize. The DP refused to take part in an election until the laws became more democratic. Consequently, the government amended the election law, replacing indirect election with direct elections. The election law went through further amendment before the 1950 election.

The new election system was a simple majority system. Ballots were cast secretly, and results were counted openly. Each province was organized as an electoral district. Under the winner-takes-all principle, the party receiving the majority of votes in a given province won all the seats in that province. The new election law made it possible for the DP to gain 83 percent of the seats (408 out of 487) with only 47 percent of the votes in the 1950 election.

THE PREAMBLE TO THE CONSTITUTION OF THE REPUBLIC OF TURKEY

Adopted 7 November 1982

Following the operation carried out on 12 September 1980 by the Turkish Armed Forces in response to a call from the Turkish Nation, of which they form an inseparable part, at a time when the approach of a separatist, destructive and bloody civil war unprecedented in the Republican era threatened the integrity of the eternal Turkish Nation and motherland and the existence of the sacred Turkish State.

This Constitution was prepared by the Consultative Assembly, given final form by the Council of National Security, which are the legitimate representatives of the Turkish Nation, and adopted, approved and directly enacted by the Turkish Nation,

And is entrusted for safekeeping by the Turkish Nation to the patriotism of its democracy-loving sons and daughters, in order that it may be understood to embody the ideas, beliefs and resolutions set forth below and be interpreted and implemented accordingly, commanding respect for, and absolute loyalty to, its letter and spirit:

- The direction of the concept of nationalism as outlined by Ataturk, the founder of the Republic of Turkey, its immortal leader and unrivalled hero; and in line with the reforms and principles introduced by him;

- The determination to safeguard the everlasting existence, prosperity and material and spiritual well-being of the Republic of Turkey, and to ensure that it attains the standards of contemporary civilisation, as a full and honourable member of the world family of nations;

- Recognition of the absolute supremacy of the will of the nation, and of the fact that sovereignty is vested fully and unconditionally in the Turkish Nation and that no individual or body empowered to exercise it on behalf of the nation shall deviate from democracy based on freedom, as set forth in the Constitution and the rule of law instituted according to its requirements;

- The understanding that separation of powers does not imply an order of precedence among the organs of State, but reflects a civilised division of labour and mode of cooperation restricted to the exercise of specific State powers, and that supremacy is vested solely in the Constitution and the laws;

- The determination that no protection shall be afforded to thoughts or opinions contrary to Turkish National interests, the principle of the existence of Turkey as an indivisible entity with its State and territory, Turkish historical and moral values, or the nationalism, principles, reforms and modernism of Ataturk, and that as required by the principle of secularism, there shall be no interference whatsoever of sacred religious feelings in State affairs and politics;

- The understanding that it is the birthright of every Turkish citizen to lead an honourable life and develop his material and spiritual resources under the aegis of national culture, civilisation and the rule of law, through the exercise of the fundamental rights and freedoms set forth in this Constitution, in conformity with the requirements of equality and social justice;

- The recognition that all Turkish citizens are united in national honour and pride, in national joy and grief, in their rights and duties towards their existence as a nation, in blessings and in burdens, and in every manifestation of national life, and that they have the right to demand a peaceful life based on absolute respect for one another's rights and freedoms, mutual love and fellowship, and the desire for, and belief, in "Peace at home, peace in the world."

Source: Turkish Embassy at Washington, D.C. Retrieved 8 March 2002, from: http://www.turkey.org/politics/p_consti.htm.

Kemal Ataturk, the founder of modern Turkey after World War I, remains of considerable symbolic importance in contemporary Turkey. Here, a wall of the Constitutional Court is adorned with a mask depicting Ataturk. (AFP/CORBIS)

The 1950 election was critical. Voter turnout was very high: more than 90 percent of registered voters voted in the election. The election also marked the beginning of new political alignments. The DP was supported by the relatively developed western regions, whereas the RPP relied on the traditional eastern provinces for support. The 1950 election marked the beginning of the era of machine politics in Turkey, with government services being provided in return for votes.

Multiparty politics in Turkey could not function with the institutions inherited from the one-party system. In the constitutional structure of the 1950s the only effective check on the government was the assembly, but the assembly was under the control of the DP, which saw itself as the representative of the national will and tolerated no opposition. The lack of effective checks and balances paved the way for the arbitrary rule of the DP and limitation of individual rights and freedoms. In an effort to limit opposition,

the DP government amended the election law so that pre-election coalitions between opposition parties were prohibited, and election campaigns were limited to forty-five days.

The Era of Military Interventions

The arbitrary rule of the DP and its antidemocratic measures led the army to attempt to overthrow the government. The 1960 military coup was in reaction to the DP's oppression and its violation of the constitution. Following this intervention, the military junta, calling itself the Committee of National Unity (CNU), dissolved the TGNA and banned the DP. Party leaders, including the prime minister and the president, were arrested; the prime minister and two of his cabinet ministers were executed. Within the first year of the intervention, a constitutional assembly was created to prepare a new constitution and election laws. In July 1961 a referendum was held to approve the new constitution, which was accepted by 60.4 percent of the voters.

The constitution was designed to prevent the hegemony of the governing party over the assembly. The general framework of the new system was a strong bicameral legislature, a weak executive, and an autonomous judiciary. The lower chamber of the TGNA was the National Assembly, which consisted of 450 members elected every four years. Deputies were elected under a proportional system known as the d'Hondt system. According to this system, the votes cast in each constituency were divided by the number of the seats. The quotient was then used to divide the vote cast for each party list or independent candidate.

The second chamber, the Senate, consisted of 150 members elected for a term of six years by straight majority vote, with one-third retiring every two years. The senators were required to have an advanced degree and to be over forty years of age. All the members of National Security Council (NSC), the body overseeing the military were made lifetime senators, and fifteen "contingent senators" were appointed by the president. Presidents would also become senators once their terms ended. The president was elected by a two-thirds majority from among the TGNA's members and served for seven years.

Before the 1961 election, the CNU made party leaders sign a declaration promising not to discuss or criticize the military intervention and its consequences. In a further compromise, the political parties accepted a protocol to elect as president General Gemal Gursel, head of the CNU, and not to seek amnesty for imprisoned Democrats.

In 1965 an amendment of the election law gave small parties, which represented newly mobilized social and economic forces, access to the political process. The new system was called the national reminder system (NRS). Under this system, votes for parties that had failed to meet the constituency quotas would be transferred to a national pool and later used to acquire available seats on the provincial level. The 1968 amendment of the election law by the ruling Justice Party (JP) abolished the NRS to prevent small parties from gaining weight in the assembly. The Turkish Workers Party challenged that amendment in the constitutional court; that action led to the abolishment of the quota system. The simple d'Hondt system was in effect between 1969 and 1980.

During the 1960s Turkey went through a socioeconomic transformation. Adoption of an import-substitution policy accelerated the expansion of a capitalist economy and made it difficult for small merchants and artisans to compete. As a reaction, these groups withdrew their support from the JP and inclined toward small parties on the right, which promised more nationalist economic policies and protection of moral values. The Nationalist Action Party and the National Order Party (NOP) were two such parties founded to attract lower-middle-class votes.

By 1971 Turkey was in a state of turmoil. Student protests turned violent; workers' demonstrations and strikes paralyzed industry. Bombings, kidnappings, and bank robberies became daily occurrences. The Justice Party government was unable to control the situation. On 12 March 1971 the Turkish army demanded the resignation of the cabinet. During a two-year interim, Turkey was ruled by party cabinets composed mostly of civilian technocrats. Individual rights and freedoms were curtailed, and leftist organizations were suppressed.

The 1973 election ended the interim period and brought new actors into the political arena. This election was another important milestone in Turkish political life. It reflected a new realignment in the political arena. The RPP, which had adjusted its policies in the late 1960s to the left of center, now moved further to the left under the leadership of Bulent Ecevit. The support base of the RPP moved from the tradition-oriented eastern provinces to the more developed and industrialized west. The Islamist National Salvation Party, which replaced the NOP, and the Nationalist Action Party, representing small business-people, merchants, artisans, and newly urbanized social groups, became key parties in the assembly.

In the 1970s the fragmentation and polarization of Turkish politics reached their peak. Since no single party received sufficient votes to form a government, a series of unsuccessful coalitions, headed by either Ecevit or Suleyman Demirel, of the JP, ruled the country. Increasing anarchy and chaos brought Turkey to the brink of a civil war. Partisan attitudes and ideological polarization affected every institution. Labor strikes, inflation, and shortages caused a deteriorating economic situation. The lack of compromise between political parties created parliamentary deadlocks. Deputies switching parties for political gain led to cabinet crises and weakened the government. Finally, the assembly's failure to elect a new president led the army to intervene into politics once more.

Post-1980 Developments

Following the 1980 military coup, the NSC dissolved the parliament, banned political parties, detained their leaders, and declared martial law throughout the country. In 1981 a consultative assembly, handpicked by the NSC, was ordered to draft a new constitution, new political-party laws, and election laws. The new constitution, which was approved by referendum in November 1982, aimed to reinstate a strong executive. Excessive powers were given to the president. Because the NSC was given the role of a consultative assembly in which to express opinions and advise governments on issues related to national security, the army was guaranteed a permanent role in the political process. Political parties were forced to cut their ties with trade unions and other civilian organizations. Civil servants and students were forbidden to join political parties.

The 1983 election law is also based on the d'Hondt system. It provides a single-chamber national assembly of 550 deputies. The members are elected through a weighted party-list system of proportional representation for a five-year term. Parties must obtain 10 percent of the popular vote before they can win representation in the assembly. The party receiving a majority of the vote wins an extra bonus of seats. The system does not favor small parties, which were held responsible for the weak governments of the 1970s. The president of the republic is elected by the assembly for a seven-year term.

A new multiparty system began in 1983 with the participation of three political parties approved by the NSC. In the general election of 1983, Turgut Ozal's Motherland Party gained a surprise victory. In 1989 Ozal was elected the eighth president of the republic. He increased the powers of the president, making the presidential office an important decision-making center. Turkey's policies during the Persian Gulf War, for example, were largely defined by the president himself, which led to the resignation of a chief army commander.

The new constitution and the election law, however, did not solve the country's problems. In 2000, the country was still ruled by coalition governments. Economic and social problems loomed larger than ever. Interparty rivalry, corruption, and the rise of Islamic forces led to the NSC issuing an army memorandum, which resulted in the resignation of the Islamist-led Welfare Party and the True Path Party cabinet in 1997. Turkey is now ruled by a three-party coalition of the Democratic Left Party, the Motherland Party, and the extreme-rightist National Action Party. Although some steps have been taken to improve personal rights and freedoms, democratization is still an important goal to reach.

Ayla H. Kilic

Further Reading
Dodd, C. H. (1983) *The Crises of Turkish Democracy.* Walkington, U.K.: Eothen Press.
Heper, Metin, and Jacob Landou, eds. (1991) *Political Parties and Democracy in Turkey.* London: I. B. Tauris.
Schick, Irvin C., and Ertugrul Ahmet Tonak, eds. (1987) *Turkey in Transition: New Perspectives.* Trans. by Rezan Benatar and Irvin C. Schich. New York: Oxford University Press.

TURKEY, REPUBLIC OF The territory that is Turkey is at the crossroads of East and West, North and South, and its history up to the twentieth century is one of regional control by a succession of major empires.

Turkey is the location of Catal Huyuk, one of the world's oldest Neolithic settlements, dated to 7500 BCE. From 1900 to 1300 BCE the region was under the rule of the Hittites, and from the about 1200 to 700 BCE the Greeks established several kingdoms along the coast. In 546 BCE the Persians moved in, to be defeated in 334 by Alexander of Macedon. In 130 BCE the Romans made Anatolia (the Asian portion of present-day Turkey) a province and from 42 to 57 CE St. Paul spread Christianity across the region. With the establishment of Constantinople in the fourth century, the region became the center of the Byzantine empire. Under pressure from the Seljuk Turks in the east and the Crusaders from Europe, the Byzantine empire declined and was finally displaced by the Ottomans with the fall of Constantinople and in 1453. Following the reign (from 1520) of Suley-

man I (1494–1566), which marked its high point, the Ottoman empire declined over the centuries until what was left was dispatched in World War I.

During the twentieth century, Turkey was transformed from a pro-Islamic autocratic empire with a diverse population, inadequate defenses, and rebellious provinces in Europe into a compact, secular, and constitutional republic with a homogeneous population, massive armed forces, and a policy of integration with Europe. However, a civil society has been slow to develop. In general, the military, civil service, and politicians still do not respect or trust the common people; this is exemplified by the oppressive army, police, and bureaucracy, weak civil rights, political corruption, and inequitable wealth distribution.

End of Ottoman Turkey
In the nineteenth century, Turkey, the "sick man of Europe" (to quote Czar Nicholas I), blocked Russia's southern expansion into the Balkans and controlled its sea exit through the Bosporus and Dardanelles Straits to the Mediterranean. Ottoman Egypt, with its new Suez Canal, controlled the link between Britain and her colony of India. Russia invaded Turkey three times, and Britain, while providing protection, occupied Egypt and Cyprus in 1882. Following Russia's incursion to the walls of Istanbul, in 1878 Britain and France, the Great Powers, insisted that Bulgaria, Serbia, and Romania become semi-independent rather than Russian satellites. So, after fifty years of Balkan and Black Sea wars, the rebellious Christian provinces of Turkey in Europe were abandoned in favor of an Asian Islamic state.

In 1900, the Ottoman empire consisted of Anatolian Turkey, Thrace, Albania, Macedonia, Syria, Palestine, Iraq, Arabia, Yemen, and Libya, ruled through a

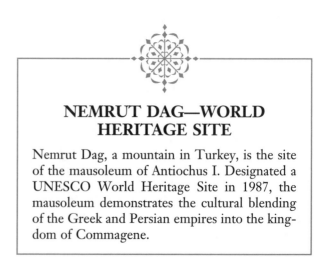

NEMRUT DAG—WORLD HERITAGE SITE

Nemrut Dag, a mountain in Turkey, is the site of the mausoleum of Antiochus I. Designated a UNESCO World Heritage Site in 1987, the mausoleum demonstrates the cultural blending of the Greek and Persian empires into the kingdom of Commagene.

KEY EVENTS IN THE REPUBLIC OF TURKEY HISTORY

1908 Parliament meets and deposes the Ottoman ruler and establishes a constitutional government.

1913 Turkey's boundary in Europe is redrawn to the present-day line.

1918 The end of World War II leaves much former Ottoman territory in the hands of the British, Greeks, and French.

1920 Anatolia is portioned among Greece, France and Italy and Turkey reduced in size.

1920–1923 The period of the war of independence ends which ends with the Treaty of Lausanne and the establishment of the Republic of Turkey.

1924–1928 Ataturk is Turkey's first leader and institutes reforms toward secularization and ties with Europe.

1938 Ataturk dies.

1939–1945 Turkey remains officially neutral in World War II but joins the Allies in 1945.

1952 Turkey joins NATO.

1955 Most Greek residents of Istanbul flee the country.

1960 The military comes to power through a coup, leading to several decades of political instability and repression.

1978 The Kurd Partiya Karkaren Kurdistan is founded.

1980 The army establishes the National Security Council.

1982 Turgut Ozal is elected president.

1983 Turkey establishes an independent state in northern Cyprus.

1988–1999 Period of separatist conflict involving the Kurds.

1990–1991 Turkey supports the United States in the Persian Gulf War.

1995 The Islamic party does well in national elections

1996 The Susurluk scandal reveals political corruption

1997 The military intervenes to "safeguard secularism."

1999 Turkey is placed on the European Union candidate list.

2001 Turkey experiences a serious economic crisis.

network of governors and spies by the autocratic sultan Abdulhamid II (1842–1918). In reaction to Russian aggression and the self-seeking proselytizing of the Great Powers, the sultan had persecuted and then massacred thousands of his Armenian Christian subjects. Rebellious army officers in Macedonia, linked with political reformists of the Committee of Union and Progress (CUP) in Salonika (Thessalonica) and supported by the Islamic hierarchy (ulama), demanded restoration of the 1876 constitution, which only had been implemented for a few months before Sultan Abdulhamid used the new conflict with Russia as an excuse to suspend it. After a hiatus of thirty-two years, the parliament met in December 1908; the Third Army provided support to enable the parliament and the ulama to depose Abdulhamid II on charges of tyranny.

The Ottoman empire ended in a declaration of constitutional government under a titular head of state; the three young leaders of the CUP— Ismail Enver (1881–1922), Mehmet Talat (1874–1921), and Ahmed Cemal (1872–1922)—with the army chief of staff, Sevket Pasa, wielded real power, advocating a policy of Turkish nationalism, modernization, and social reform.

The CUP triumvirate could protect the empire no better than could the sultan. Italy occupied Libya in 1911; the Balkan states used the moment to embark on a liberation crusade, their blitzkrieg tactics soon forcing an armistice. Enver, returning from Libya, rejected peace; the province of Edirne (Adrianople) was soon lost, but victorious Bulgaria turned on its allies, and in the peace, Turkey's boundary in Europe was redrawn at the present line in 1913.

When Britain refused an alliance, Enver, as minister of war, secretly signed with Germany. Winston Churchill, as first lord of the British admiralty, confiscated two battleships ordered from British shipyards by the Turks; Enver, in retaliation, opened the Straits to two German battleships, which sailed northward under Turkish flags to attack Russian ports just before the start of World War I. Enver attacked Russia overland, losing 78,000 troops from cold and disease in the Caucasus. Turkish-Armenian rebels seized the eastern city of Van and handed it to the advancing Russians, but as the Turkish army reversed the tide and the Russians retreated, the rebels faced massive deportations; between 300,000 and 1 million people, up to half the Armenian population of Anatolia, perished during forced marches to Syria.

British destroyers attempted to force open the Straits for Britain's Russian allies; a predominately Australian expeditionary force was landed at Gallipoli in 1915 to extinguish the Turkish guns; General Mustafa Kemal (later Ataturk; 1881–1938) saved Istanbul at a loss of seventy thousand men. In 1917, the conquering Allies advanced from Egypt into Arabia, Palestine, and Syria, pushing back the Turkish Fourth Army until, as it reached Aleppo, the armistice of Mudros was signed in 1918. The triumvirate of Enver, the civilian Cevdet, and Talat fled, leaving the British in occupation of Istanbul and thus in control of the sultan, the Greeks in Izmir, and the French in Syria.

Independence War

In May 1919, Mustafa Kemal reached Samsun on the Black Sea and rallied war-weary nationalist groups into a fresh Turkish resistance. Linking with the Twentieth and Fifteenth Army Corps under Ali Fuat and Kazim Karabekir, he summoned local representatives to the councils of Erzurum and Sivas, where he formed a new nationalist parliament. In Istanbul, the British suppressed a newly elected assembly of the parliament and obtained the sultan's signature on the Treaty of Sèvres in 1920. That treaty partitioned Anatolia between Greece, France, and Italy; created an independent Armenia and Kurdistan; and allocated Turkey only part of the central Anatolian plateau, with no Mediterranean coastline and no capital. The Treaty of Sèvres, which still colors Turkish views of Europe, united opposition behind the nationalist government in Ankara in 1920. Nationalist forces repelled an Armenian offensive, dislodged the French from around Adana, and forced British withdrawal from Istanbul. In 1923, the Allies were forced to renegotiate terms in the Treaty of Lausanne, when Turkey, represented by Ismet Inonu (1884–1973), argued for the frontiers

as they are today, except for Hatay (returned in 1939) and the Dardanelles (which reverted to Turkish sovereignty in 1936).

Turkish forces finally drove the Greek army toward Izmir, where an Allied fleet rescued survivors of a terrible fire in 1922. The remaining Christian Greeks outside Istanbul were hastily exchanged with the Muslim population (both Greek and Turkish) of Thrace, thus aligning Turkish nationalism permanently with Islam. Since 1914, Turkey had lost 600,000 soldiers and 20 to 25 percent of its population, proportionately more than any other participant in World War I.

Ataturk's Reforms

Kemal immediately initiated reforms, including secularization of the state and abolition of the caliphate (1924), the change to Western attire (1925), a new European-style civil and penal code (1926), the change to a Latin alphabet and elimination of Arabic (1928), and a literacy campaign. Perpetuating Ottoman authoritarianism, he used a growing bureaucracy to impose these programs on conservative peasants. Trade, once the prerogative of Greeks and Armenians, had collapsed; state monopolies on basic foodstuffs (sugar, tobacco, animal feeds, and so forth)—plus nationalization of mines and shipping, intended to regenerate agricultural marketing and industry—faltered in the 1930s depression.

Mustafa Kemal, now known as Ataturk, died in 1938; his colleague, Inonu, who had become prime minister in 1923 and who was elected president upon Ataturk's death, continued with authoritarian but peaceful policies, making nonaggression treaties with Russia (1925), France and Britain (1939), and Germany (1941), accepting arms from Britain, then dealing in chrome for arms with Germany, all the time determined to remain neutral during World War II. Turkey accepted Jews fleeing Nazism but imposed a harsh, discriminatory wealth tax on Christians and small businesses in 1942. As World War II ended in 1945, Turkey joined the Allies, sent a contingent to Korea in 1952, and joined NATO's strategic southern flank also in 1952. American bases and political influence were the price of financial support and arms.

Postwar Coups

Adnan Menderes (1899–1961), a charismatic landowner, led the first opposition party, the Democratic Party, to a landslide victory in 1950. He revived Islam, borrowed abroad to invest in agriculture, and muzzled press opposition until a discontented military clique under Colonel Alp Aslan Turkes (1917–1997) took power and imposed a liberal constitution in 1960. Menderes was tried and hanged. Unused to democracy, unstable coalitions under Suleyman Demirel (b. 1924), a goatherd turned civil engineer, and urban socialist Bulent Ecevit (b. 1925) attempted to rule, while nationalist extremists (led by Turkes) and revolutionary youth groups fought on the campuses. In 1971, the army, forcing Demirel to resign, temporarily imposed a nonpolitical technocrat government, martial law, and press restrictions, but Ecevit and Demirel resumed government alternately, spending irresponsibly in a time of rapid oil price rises. Crises with Greece over the status of the island of Cyprus and with Armenian nationalist movements in Soviet Armenia and in the diaspora over the assassination of several Turkish diplomats resulted in intercommunal violence, including fighting between Sunni and Alevi (Shi'ite) Muslims and factional street murders.

The army, with tacit American support, again intervened in 1980 and formed the National Security Council, which arrested politicians, closed trades unions, and placed universities under direct control.

A former World Bank economist, the charismatic Turgut Ozal (1927–1923), headed the center-right Motherland Party and won in the general elections in 1982, held under a new, restrictive constitution. He forced through liberalization of the economy with infrastructure development, attraction of foreign investment, convertibility of the lira, creation of a stock exchange, and international trade agreements. In contrast, education was repressively restructured, and the National Security Council maintained military control over politics. Gradually a few civil-rights restrictions were lifted; journalists tested the limits of the law but were often prosecuted.

Ozal gave asylum to 300,000 refugees fleeing repression in Bulgaria in 1989, a contrast to the poor treatment of Kurdish refugees from the Iraq-Iran War. In 1989, forcing through his own election to the presidency, which as prime minister he was able to accomplish by bending the election rules, he continued a pro-American policy, granting the Allies use of Turkish bases and airspace against Iraq's Saddam Hussein during the Persian Gulf War (1990–1991). President George H. W. Bush, visiting in 1991, failed to deliver the promised benefits to offset the cost of sanctions, loss of tourism, and refugee support.

After early elections in 1991, Demirel formed a coalition with the socialists; the Islamic Party under Necmettin Erbakan (b. 1925) also obtained record votes (17 percent). Ozal, as president, meddled in government until his death in 1993; he was succeeded by Demirel, leaving American-sponsored Tansu Ciller (b. 1944) as Turkey's first woman prime minister. Initial optimism degenerated as corruption, inflation, and civil unrest were unchecked. In the town of Sivas, an Alevi group in conference was attacked by a fundamentalist Sunni mob; thirty-seven died. The major municipalities, now run by the Islamists, appeared progressive and graft-free, enabling Erbakan's party to obtain more votes in the 1995 elections. Ciller and Mesut Yilmaz (b. 1947, of Ozal's party) formed a minority coalition until Ciller, accused of corruption, allied with Erbakan to save herself. In 1996, an accident involving a car containing a Ciller politician, a police chief, a wanted assassin, a drug dealer, many weapons, and incriminating papers revealed political corruption and became known as the Susurluk scandal, named for the small town where the fatal accident occurred.

Controversially, the army, more worried by Islamism than corruption, demanded Erbakan's resignation and immediate implementation of eighteen measures to "safeguard secularism" in February 1997. Banned from politics, Erbakan delegated the re-formed party to Recai Kutan (b. 1928) but remained influential among Islamists. This "coup by proxy" delayed much necessary legislation and thus short-circuited Turkey's application for European Union membership.

A right-left minority coalition between Yilmaz and Ecevit was soon tainted by the Susurluk investigations and a tape recording of Yilmaz allegedly interfering in a privatization bid; government was handed to Ecevit alone. In the euphoria following the capture of Kurdish guerrilla leader Ocalan, elections in April 1999 gave Ecevit 22 percent, followed by the Nationalists at 18 percent and Islamists at 15 percent; Ciller and Yilmaz were sidelined.

Prospects for Europeanization

A coalition between Ecevit, Devlet Bahceli (b. 1944), and Yilmaz rushed through an ambitious legislative program to deal with tax evasion, privatization, and social security, thus enabling Turkey to be added to the European Union candidate list. Economic revival was prevented by a downturn in tourism caused by threats from Kurdish nationalist guerrillas and a catastrophic earthquake, 7.0 on the Richter scale, which struck just south of Istanbul, killing eighteen thousand and damaging the industrial heartland in August 1999.

At the end of 1999, Turkey was placed on the European Union candidate list, albeit in last place. Entry depends on improvements in human rights, not just fulfillment of economic criteria. The Turkish parliament, with much internal resistance, is implementing a program of constitutional amendments demanded by the Union as a price for membership.

Relations with Greece

During the 1950s, the Greek population of Istanbul became hostages in disputes between Turkey and Greece over the island of Cyprus, which was self-governing under the protection of Britain and which had large populations of both Greeks and Turks. Mobs in Istanbul were provoked to destroy Greek property, causing a rapid Greek exodus from that city in 1955; after incidents on Cyprus, a U.N. peacekeeping force was installed. In 1960, the island became independent. Several thousand Greek permanent residents of Turkey were summarily deported in 1963 as a result of renewed violence in Cyprus. Following a Greek attempt to annex the island in 1974, Turkey rapidly invaded and occupied the northern half, declaring it an independent republic in 1983.

Northern Cyprus remains a drain on mainland Turkish finances. Mutually threatening military maneuvers have been phased out as Greek-Turkish relations have entered a period of détente following sympathy engendered by earthquakes in Istanbul and Athens in 1999. Currently, leaders of the two communities on Cyprus are negotiating directly and urgently, as the European Union is likely to unilaterally admit Greek Cyprus if an agreement is not reached shortly.

The Kurdish Question and the Army

The Kurdish populations of Turkey, Iraq, and Iran almost achieved independence under the Treaty of Sèvres, but Ataturk subsequently denied their separate identity and culture. A Kurdish-language ban and the abolition of the caliphate led to Sheikh Said's Kurdish revolt in 1925, followed by revolts at Ararat in 1930 and Dersim (now Tunceli) in 1939; despite repression, the Kurdish tribal structure remained. In 1978, Abdullah Ocalan (b. 1953) formed the guerrilla group Partiya Karkaren Kurdistan (PKK, Kurdistan Workers' Party), based in and funded by Syria, and commenced a violent independence campaign in 1984. The Turkish army countered with cross-border attacks on Syria, imposition of martial law in twelve provinces, and news blackouts. Between 1988 and 1999, the army and PKK depopulated villages and killed thirty thousand, forcing mass migration to Istanbul and Europe. Ozal attempted an economic solution; electricity generated at huge dams on the Euphrates River revived agriculture and industry along the border. In 1999, Syria, threatened with water shortages and invasion, expelled Ocalan and closed PKK camps; violence was confined to the extreme east and funding to drug-smuggling operations. Ocalan was kidnapped in Kenya and returned to Turkey for trial; his death sentence was appealed to the European Court in 2000. The army now insists that politicians should implement a nonmilitary solution, but moderate Kurds are still not represented in parliament.

The end of the war in the southeast, rapprochement with Greece, the cowing of Syria, the American occupation of northern Iraq, and the end of the Cold War mean that the Turkish army is almost without opponents (real or imagined). Turkish military spending is officially 9 percent of Turkey's gross national product (without defense industries); the real figure is unknown, and the treasury in 2000 attempted to restrain new equipment purchases.

The twenty-first century started in an optimistic mood, with a united government pursuing a vigorous economic program, an apparently bureaucratic but clear route to Europe, a deescalation of tension with Greece, and a new president, Ahmet Sezer (b. 1941). Of the "old guard"—Erbakan, Demirel, Turkes, and Ecevit—only the latter retained power; Yilmaz and Ciller, defiled by corruption, commanded a rump of followers, leaving a deficit in talented leaders for the new millennium.

However, in February 2001 a dispute over the constitution between Sezer and Ecevit (leading the coalition government) resulted in a complete loss of confidence in the World Bank–devised economic program that had pegged the Turkish lira against a currency basket. Private speculation and public panic forced the government to allow the lira to float; it lost half its value overnight. Unable to meet foreign-denominated debts, twenty-three collapsing banks were taken over by the treasury, and the government borrowed heavily from the World Bank as part of a drastic restructuring program. Civil unrest was, amazingly, avoided, and Turkey has now set out on a gradual path to economic recovery. The bitter effects of this crisis may not be forgotten at the next election; a new religious party as well as HADEP, the Kurdish socialist party, wait in the wings.

Dependence on the World Bank has been one factor in Turkish cooperation with U.S. "antiterrorist" aggressive action against their coreligionists; the Turkish people worry as their troops are sent to Afghanistan and the United States plots action against their neighbor Iraq.

Kate Clow

See also: **Archaeology-Turkey; Cyprus; Kurds; Ottoman Empire**

Further Reading

Fromkin, David. (1989) *A Peace to End All Peace—Creating the Modern Middle East 1914–1922.* London: Andre Deutsch.

Pope, Nicole, and Hugh Pope. (1997) *Turkey Unveiled: Ataturk and After.* London: John Murray.

Poulton, Hugh. (1997) *Top Hat, Grey Wolf and Crescent: Turkish Nationalism and the Turkish Republic.* London: Hurst & Co.

TURKEY–RUSSIA RELATIONS

In 1453, when the Ottoman Turkish sultan Mehmet (Muhammad) II (1432–1481) conquered Byzantium (Constantinople), the historic capital of the Eastern Roman empire, the Russian grand duke Ivan, whose wife was a niece of the last Byzantine emperor, laid claim to the symbolic imperial legacy by declaring Moscow to be the third Rome (Constantinople having been the second). In ensuing years, there was constant tension and rivalry between Russia and Ottoman Turkey. This rivalry was at once ideological, symbolic, and strategic.

Nineteenth-Century Relations

Ideologically and symbolically, Russia hoisted the banner of the Christian churches against the Muslim Turks, who were perceived as infidels in a continuing holy war. In the late eighteenth century, Russia annexed the Crimea and came to dominate the Black Sea from the Caucasus on the east to the mouth of the Danube River in the west. The next goal for expanding Russian power was the imperial city of Istanbul (the Turkish name for Constantinople) and the straits of the Bosporus and the Dardanelles, connecting the Black Sea with the Aegean and Mediterranean Seas. Russian attempts to achieve this goal by military conquest and diplomatic maneuvering were one of the main issues in nineteenth-century European diplomacy. Russia sought access from the Black Sea to the Aegean and Mediterranean Seas for commercial purposes and to prevent foreign navies from entering the Black Sea and attacking its southern shore.

The expansion of Russian power in Eastern and Southeastern Europe alarmed the other European powers, especially Great Britain. Among other things, the British were worried about their lines of communication and trade with their Asian colonies, especially India. These lines ran through the Mediterranean Sea and Ottoman territories to the east and south, such as Egypt. Russian expansion into this region was seen as a great danger to British interests. Consequently, throughout the nineteenth century, the British supported Ottoman Turkish resistance against Russia.

Relations in the First Part of the Twentieth Century

By the time of World War I (1914–1918), the Ottoman empire was so weak that Russia was on the verge of achieving its historic goal of controlling the Black Sea straits and the imperial city of Istanbul. The war drastically changed this situation, however. As Russia suffered major military setbacks at the hands of Germany, the Bolshevik Revolution overthrew the czarist monarchy and effectively ended the war in that part of the world. The Bolsheviks renounced traditional Russian imperialist policies, including those pertaining to the Ottoman empire and the Black Sea straits.

The Ottoman Turks, who were aligned with Germany and Austria-Hungary, also suffered major military defeats in World War I. By the end of the war, the once mighty Ottoman empire had been reduced to the territory of Asia Minor (Anatolia) and eastern Thrace. The victorious western Allies (particularly Britain and France) planned to divide those territories among themselves and to internationalize the straits and Istanbul. However, a nationalist uprising among the Turks and other Muslims of Anatolia thwarted these plans and led to the establishment of the nationalist and secularist Republic of Turkey.

The period between the two world wars saw an unusual friendship between Turkey and Russia (by then

This undated political cartoon shows Russia as a bear and Britain as a lion—both threatening Turkey. (BETTMANN/CORBIS)

the Soviet Union), as both sought to maintain independence from the West. Border disputes in the Caucasus region were resolved, and the Soviets supported Turkish control of the straits as a means of preventing foreign navies from entering the Black Sea and threatening the USSR. This newborn good will was formalized in a Treaty of Friendship.

But this amity was not to last. At the end of World War II in 1945, the Soviets, flush with victory, denounced the Friendship Treaty and reasserted the old Russian claims. At Yalta in February 1945, Joseph Stalin (1879–1953), the Soviet leader, indicated that he no longer trusted the Turks to defend Soviet interests in the Black Sea and the straits, declaring that Turkey held Russia by the throat.

A vigorous Soviet campaign of pressure and threats against Turkey followed. This was designed to force the Turks to agree to a Soviet naval base in the straits and to cede territory in the Caucasus region. The Turks feared that acquiescence would turn their country into a Soviet satellite and so sought the support of the West, particularly the United States. The United States and its allies responded positively. In 1947, President Harry S. Truman (1884–1972) proposed and Congress approved a massive program of aid to Greece and Turkey to bolster their resistance against Soviet threats; this came to be known as the Truman Doctrine.

Turkey thus became a frontline outpost in the Cold War and a close U.S. ally. In 1952, Turkey became a member of the North Atlantic Treaty Organization (NATO), the major anti-Soviet alliance. The United States helped to modernize and strengthen Turkish armed forces. Turkey was one of the few countries to send combat troops to support the U.S.-led campaign against the Communist North Korean regime during the Korean War (1950–1953).

A chain of electronic observation posts was established along Turkey's Black Sea coast, by means of which the United States monitored missile launchings from Soviet bases in Central Asia. Nuclear-armed Jupiter missiles aimed at the Soviet Union were deployed on Turkish soil, as were manned U.S. fighters, bombers, and reconnaissance planes, including high-attitude U-2 spy planes, one of which the Soviets shot down in 1960.

Throughout the Cold War, Russian-Turkish relations were a mirror image of Turkey's relations with the United States: when problems arose in the Turkish-U.S. relationship, relations with Russia tended to warm up. Thus, after President Lyndon Baines Johnson (1908–1973) warned the Turkish government in June 1964 that the United States might not defend

Turkey if it was attacked by the Soviet Union, the Turkish prime minister visited Moscow, and the Soviet prime minister visited Ankara, the Turkish capital, both unprecedented events. The two governments concluded economic and cultural-exchange agreements.

Later Twentieth-Century Relations

With the collapse of the Soviet Union and the end of the Cold War in 1991, relations between Turkey and Russia were altered once more. First, the two countries shared no common border for the first time in several centuries. The Caucasus republics of Georgia, Armenia, and Azerbaijan, which do have common borders with Turkey, became independent. Second, other former Soviet republics in Central Asia also became independent, and Turkey faced the temptation to revive dormant pan-Turkist sentiment to form a new block of Turkic states that could become a political platform.

Thus, rivalry for political influence and power in the Caucasus and Central Asia emerged between Turkey and Russia. Russia enjoyed inherent advantages as the result of strong infrastructural ties built up during the Soviet era, but was greatly weakened by the severe economic problems that accompanied the collapse of the Soviet Union and hence was no longer a direct threat to Turkey's security.

Russia-Turkey Relations in the Twenty-First Century

As a result of these profound political changes, the relationship between Russia and Turkey at the beginning of the twenty-first century was a complex web. Trade between the two countries expanded greatly. Russia supplied natural gas to Turkey, and Turkish firms landed extensive contracts in Russia, particularly in large construction projects. Competition between Russia and Turkey developed in other areas, particularly in the planning of pipelines to carry oil from new Caspian Sea sources to world markets via Turkish ports on the Mediterranean Sea, bypassing existing pipelines through Russia.

These Russian pipelines pass near Chechnya in the Caucasus, the scene of bloody uprisings against Russian rule. The Chechens are a Muslim people, and a significant minority of ethnic Chechens live in Turkey. Thus, Turkey opposed Russian campaigns in Chechnya. However, Turkey's ability to act on its sympathy for the Chechens was hamstrung by the danger that Russia could retaliate by more actively supporting the rebellious Kurdish minority in eastern Turkey. Russia had already disconcerted Turkey by signing a deal with the Greek Cypriot regime for the supply of modern intermediate-range ballistic missiles (known as the S-300), which could reach deep into Turkish territory from bases in Cyprus, upsetting the military balance between Turkey and Greece. In the end, the missiles were to be based on the island of Crete, far removed from Turkey. But the potential for increased tension between Russia and Turkey clearly remains and could flare up anew at any time.

Turkey and Russia found themselves on the same side of the anti-terror campaign led by the United States after the attacks on American soil on 11 September 2001. Turkey volunteered to send troops to Afghanistan to assist in the fighting against Osama bin Laden and his supporters and showed a strong interest in assisting in the formation of a new government in Afghanistan after the apparent defeat of its Taliban government. Russia was also in a cooperative mode, as were the former Soviet republics in Central Asia that border on Afghanistan and whose cooperation was important for the United States–led campaign.

Franck Tachau

Further Reading

Fuller, Graham E. (1992) *Turkey Faces East: New Orientations toward the Middle East and the Old Soviet Union.* Santa Monica, CA: RAND.

Gokay, Bulent. (1997) *A Clash of Empires: Turkey between Russian Bolshevism and British Imperialism.* London: Tauris Academic Studies.

Hale, William. (2000) *Turkish Foreign Policy, 1774–2000.* London: Frank Cass.

Kuniholm, Bruce R. (1980) *The Origins of the Cold War in the Middle East.* Princeton, NJ: Princeton University Press.

Makovsky, Alan, and Sabri Sayari, eds. (2000) *Changing Dynamics in Turkish Foreign Policy.* Washington, DC: Washington Institute for Near East Policy.

Mango, Andrew. (1994) *Turkey: The Challenge of a New Role.* Westport, CT: Praeger (published with the Center for Strategic and International Studies).

Mastny, Vojtech, and R. Craig Nation, eds. (1996) *Turkey between East and West: New Challenges for a Rising Regional Power,* Boulder, CO: Westview Press.

Rubin, Barry, and Kemal Kirisci, eds. (2001) *Turkey in World Politics: An Emerging Multiregional Power.* Boulder, CO: Lynne Rienner.

Tachau, Frank. (1984) *Turkey: The Politics of Authority, Democracy, and Development.* New York: Praeger.

TURKEY–UNITED STATES RELATIONS

Government-to-government relations between the United States and Turkey did not assume serious proportions until World War I. Before then, the major symbols of Turkish-American relations had been a series of schools established by American Protestant missionaries during the nineteenth century. Their main goal had been to proselytize, a fact that discouraged Muslim children from enrolling. The most prominent of these schools was Robert College, built on a commanding height overlooking the narrowest point in the Bosporus, adjacent to the Rumeli Hisar fortress built by the Turks in 1453 to besiege the city of Byzantium. Today, this institution is known as Bosporus University, one of the leading institutions of higher education in Turkey and now controlled by the Turkish government.

Relations after World War I

At the Versailles Peace Conference of 1919, which ended World War I, President Woodrow Wilson (1856–1924) set forth his Fourteen Points, including the right of self-determination for all nations and peoples. This principle was opposed to the plans of the other Allies, who wanted to divide the remaining Ottoman territories among themselves.

Despite American sentiment against Turks, which was fanned by U.S. citizens of Greek and Armenian extraction, some Turkish nationalists were tempted by the idea of an American mandate. This would frustrate Allied plans and prevent such ethnic communities as the Kurds and Armenians from creating states that could displace the Turkish population and foreclose hopes of retaining a Turkish state. American failure to ratify the Versailles Treaty and refusal to join the League of Nations sabotaged this proposal. The successful campaign of the Turkish nationalists under the leadership of Mustafa Kemal (Ataturk, 1881–1938) blocked the Allied plans for division of the remainder of the Ottoman empire and snuffed out Kurdish and Armenian hopes for statehood. The reformist nationalist and secular Republic of Turkey established in 1923 forced the American schools in that country to reconsider their missions. The minority populations that had formed most of their enrollments were much reduced in size. Religious proselytism was outlawed under the republic. Those schools that remained open thus began enrolling more Turkish Muslims and secularized their curricula, giving up their original proselytizing mission. Several of them, particularly Robert College, the Tarsus Boys' School, and schools in Izmir and Uskudar (a residential suburb of Istanbul) for girls, became highly prized institutions that trained members of the new political elite, including future members of parliament and at least one prime minister.

Relations after World War II

In general, however, Turkish-American relations remained minimal until the end of World War II. During that war, Turkey again proved its strategic

Presidents Bill Clinton of the United States and Suleyman Demirel of Turkey review an honor guard during Clinton's visit to Turkey in November 1999. (REUTERS NEWMEDIA INC./CORBIS)

importance by remaining neutral and allowing neither Nazi Germany nor the Western Allies and the Soviet Union the advantage of running supply lines through its territory, including the Black Sea straits. The Turks also steadfastly resisted pressure from the West to declare war on Nazi Germany until February 1945, when the outcome of the conflict was certain and the danger of Turkish territory becoming a battlefield had waned.

With the end of the war, Turkish-American relations were transformed. The United States responded positively to Turkish requests for support against aggressive Soviet demands for territorial and other concessions, which would have reduced the country to the status of a Soviet satellite. In 1946, the USS *Missouri*, then the largest battleship in the world, paid a courtesy call at Istanbul; in 1947, President Harry S. Truman (1884–1972) proposed the Truman Doctrine, a massive program of economic and military aid to Greece and Turkey, meant to bolster their resistance against Soviet expansionism. In 1950, Turkey's active participation in the Korean War helped cement the relationship with the United States; two years later, Turkey became a member of the North Atlantic Treaty Organization (NATO).

Turkey, by now a close U.S. ally, was a frontline state in the Cold War. A chain of electronic observation posts was established along the Black Sea coast to enable the United States to monitor Soviet missile launchings in Central Asia. Nuclear-armed Jupiter missiles aimed at the Soviet Union were deployed on Turkish soil, as were manned U.S. fighters, bombers, and reconnaissance planes, including high-attitude U-2 spy planes, one of which the Soviets shot down in 1960. Turkish policy supported America in international politics, going so far as to allow the United States to use Turkish territory as a staging area for troops bound for Lebanon during the crisis in that country in 1958.

In the 1960s, the U.S.-Turkish relationship suffered several serious setbacks. The Soviet-American crisis of 1962, provoked by the Russians placing nuclear missiles in Cuba, was the first blow. Because the Soviets demanded the removal of Jupiter missiles from Turkey as a quid pro quo, it became evident that the United States could sacrifice Turkish interests without warning. In any event, the Jupiters were removed later on grounds of obsolescence, but the point hit home nonetheless.

A second and more serious problem erupted in 1964, when Turkey prepared to invade Cyprus to defend the Turkish minority on the island against the Greek majority. U.S. president Lyndon Baines Johnson (1908–1973) warned Turkey that he would not come to that country's aid if the Soviets supported Greece militarily. This letter undermined Turkish confidence in the United States and led to a major rethinking of Turkey's relations with the USSR, its neighbors, and the Third World in general. The Johnson letter also had an explosive effect on Turkish public opinion, opening the way for widespread acceptance of leftist suspicions about the United States and turning the large-scale American military and diplomatic presence in the country into a public-relations liability. Relations hit a new low when the U.S. Congress (provoked, in Turkish eyes, by American Greek and Armenian ethnic lobbies) imposed an arms embargo in response to the Turkish occupation of northern Cyprus in 1974. Use of Turkish military bases for the staging of U.S. troops in a Middle Eastern crisis, as had occurred in 1958, could no longer be taken for granted.

During the 1990–1991 Persian Gulf War, for example, the chief of the Turkish general staff resigned in protest against the decision by President Turgut Ozal (1926–1993) to cooperate fully with the U.S.-led anti-Iraqi military coalition. Ozal sought to prove Turkey's continuing strategic value to the United States and the West—in the face of the collapse of the Soviet Union and the end of the Cold War—by shutting down the Iraqi oil pipeline that crossed Turkish territory, strictly observing the UN-imposed sanctions on Iraq, and allowing heavy use of air bases on Turkish soil for bombing sorties against Iraq.

The United States was more understanding than was the European Union, which Turkey aspired to join, with regard to alleged human-rights violations against the Kurds. The Turkish government had treated the Kurdish insurrection that broke out in 1984 with harsh military repression. On the other hand, Turkey was apprehensive about U.S.-sponsored material and political support for the Kurds of Iraq, just across the border from Turkey; these Kurds had established limited autonomy from the Iraqi government of Saddam Hussein (b. 1937) in the wake of the Persian Gulf War. Despite concern over Iraqi Kurdish support for the insurrection in Turkey, and despite Turkey's desire to resume trade relations with Iraq, Turkey allowed the continued use of bases on its soil for this operation, as well as for flights designed to prevent the Iraqi air force from entering the no-fly zone in northern Iraq.

Relations in the New Millennium

At the start of the twenty-first century, the United States supported Turkish efforts to finance the so-called Ceyhan project, which called for a pipeline connecting the newly developed Caspian Sea oil fields with world markets via a Turkish port on the Mediterranean. The common interest of the two governments stemmed from the political realm—the desire to by-

pass Russian pipelines. The oil industry was reluctant because of excessive costs and political instability in the Caucasus region through which the projected line would pass.

Finally, the late 1990s witnessed a change in Turkish foreign relations—a burgeoning informal alliance between Turkey and Israel, favored by the Turkish military. The initial trade-off involved access to Turkish air space for the Israeli air force (allowing Israeli planes to approach Iranian territory) in exchange for large-scale contracts with Israeli industry to modernize various Turkish weapons systems. Joint naval maneuvers were also conducted, and the military aspects of the new relationship spilled over into trade and academic exchanges. Since Turkey and Israel were major American allies in the Middle East, this development was strongly encouraged by the United States.

Frank Tachau

Further Reading

Abramowitz, Morton, ed. (2000) *Turkey's Transformation and America Policy.* New York: Century Foundation Press.

Hale, William. (2000) *Turkish Foreign Policy, 1774–2000.* London: Frank Cass.

Harris, George S. (1972) *Troubled Alliance: Turkish-American Problems in Historical Perspective, 1945–1971.* Washington, DC: American Enterprise Institute.

Khalilzad, Zalmay, Ian O. Lesser, and F. Stephen Larrabee. (2000) *The Future of Turkish-Western Relations: Toward a Strategic Plan.* Santa Monica, CA: RAND.

Kuniholm, Bruce R. (1980) *The Origins of the Cold War in the Middle East.* Princeton, NJ: Princeton University Press.

Makovsky, Alan, and Sabri Sayari, eds. (2000) *Changing Dynamics in Turkish Foreign Policy.* Washington, DC: Washington Institute for Near East Policy.

Mango, Andrew. (1994) *Turkey: The Challenge of a New Role.* Westport, CT: Praeger (published with the Center for Strategic and International Studies).

Mastny, Vojtech, and R. Craig Nation, eds. (1996) *Turkey between East and West: New Challenges for a Rising Regional Power.* Boulder, CO: Westview Press.

Rubin, Barry, and Kemal Kirisci, eds. (2001) *Turkey in World Politics: An Emerging Multiregional Power.* Boulder, CO: Lynne Rienner.

Rustow, Dankwart A. (1987) *Turkey: America's Forgotten Ally.* New York: Council on Foreign Relations Press.

Spain, James W. (1984) *American Diplomacy in Turkey: Memoirs of an Ambassador Extraordinary and Plenipotentiary.* New York: Praeger.

Stearns, Monteagle. (1991) *Entangled Allies: US Policy toward Greece, Turkey, and Cyprus.* New York: Council on Foreign Relations Press.

Tachau, Frank. (1984) *Turkey: The Politics of Authority, Democracy, and Development.* New York: Praeger.

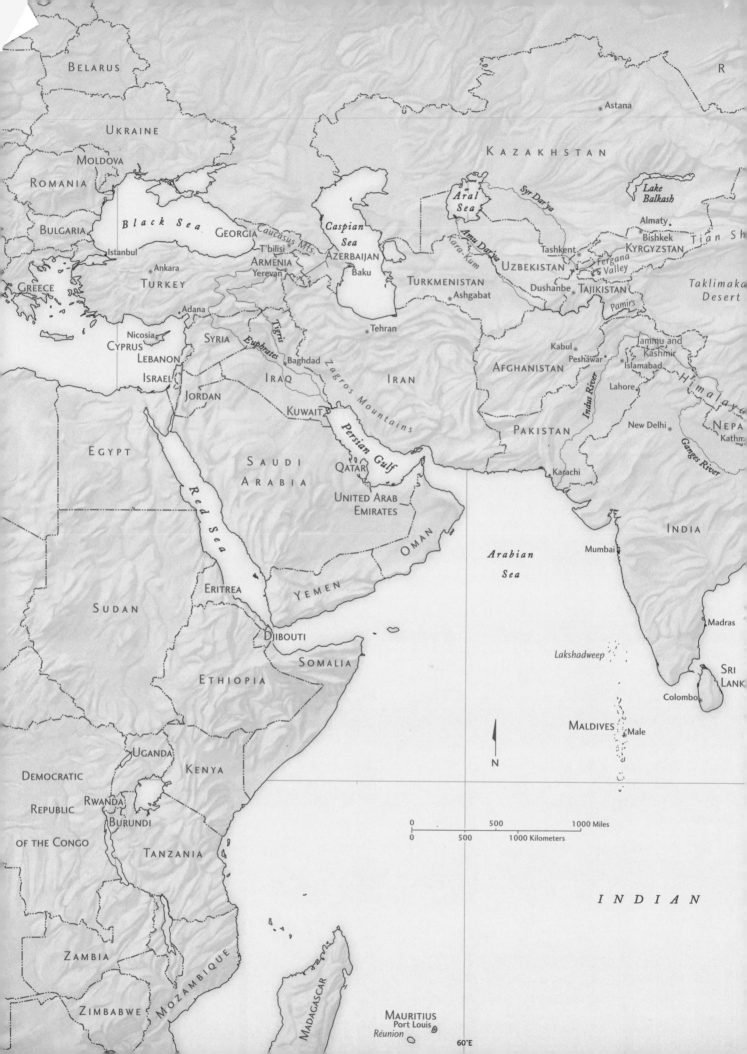

BELARUS

UKRAINE

MOLDOVA

ROMANIA

BULGARIA

GREECE

Black Sea

Istanbul

Ankara

TURKEY

NICOSIA

CYPRUS

LEBANON

ISRAEL

JORDAN

EGYPT

Red Sea

SUDAN

ERITREA

DJIBOUTI

ETHIOPIA

SOMALIA

UGANDA

KENYA

RWANDA

BURUNDI

DEMOCRATIC

REPUBLIC

OF THE CONGO

TANZANIA

ZAMBIA

ZIMBABWE

MOZAMBIQUE

MADAGASCAR

GEORGIA

Caucasus Mts.

T'bilisi

ARMENIA

Yerevan

AZERBAIJAN

Baku

Adana

SYRIA

Euphrates

Tigris

Baghdad

IRAQ

KUWAIT

Zagros Mountains

Persian Gulf

QATAR

UNITED ARAB
EMIRATES

SAUDI
ARABIA

OMAN

YEMEN

*Caspian
Sea*

TURKMENISTAN

Ashgabat

Tehran

IRAN

Kara Kum

*Arabian
Sea*

Amu Dar'ya

*Aral
Sea*

KAZAKHSTAN

Astana

R

Syr Dar'ya

Tashkent

UZBEKISTAN

Dushanbe

*Lake
Balkash*

Almaty

Bishkek

KYRGYZSTAN

*Fergana
Valley*

TAJIKISTAN

Pamirs

Tian Sh

*Taklimaka
Desert*

Kabul

AFGHANISTAN

Peshāwar

Islamabad

Lahore

PAKISTAN

New Delhi

*Jammu and
Kashmir*

Himalaya

NEPA

Kathm

Indus River

Karachi

Mumbai

INDIA

Ganges River

Madras

SRI
LANK

Colombo

Lakshadweep

MALDIVES

Male

N

0   500   1000 Miles

0   500   1000 Kilometers

MAURITIUS
Port Louis
Réunion

60°E

INDIAN